Intervention and Reflection

Intervention and Reflection

BASIC ISSUES IN BIOETHICS

TENTH EDITION

Ronald Munson
University of Missouri–St. Louis

Ian Lague

CENGAGE
Learning

Australia • Brazil • Mexico • Singapore • United Kingdom • United States

CENGAGE
Learning®

Intervention and Reflection: Basic Issues in Bioethics, Tenth Edition
Ronald Munson, Ian Lague

Product Director: Paul Banks

Product Manager: Debra Matteson

Senior Content Developer: Florence Kilgo

Product Assistant: Michelle Forbes

Marketing Manager: Sean Ketchem

Senior Content Project Manager: Jill Quinn

Senior Art Director: Marissa Falco

Manufacturing Planner: Julio Esperas

IP Analyst: Alex Ricciardi

IP Project Manager: Betsy Hathaway

Production Service/Compositor:
MPS Limited

Cover Designer: John Walker Design

Cover Image: SILVIA RICCIARDI/Science
Photo Library/Getty Images

Library of Congress Control Number: 2015944287

Student Edition:

ISBN: 978-1-305-50840-8

Loose-leaf Edition:

ISBN: 978-1-305-94941-6

Cengage Learning
20 Channel Center Street
Boston, MA 02210
USA

Cengage Learning is a leading provider of customized learning solutions with employees residing in nearly 40 different countries and sales in more than 125 countries around the world. Find your local representative at **www.cengage.com**.

Cengage Learning products are represented in Canada by Nelson Education, Ltd.

To learn more about Cengage Learning Solutions, visit **www.cengage.com**.

Purchase any of our products at your local college store or at our preferred online store **www.cengagebrain.com**.

Printed in the United States of America
Print Number: 01   Print Year: 2016

To Miriam
"Giver of bright rings"
—R.M.

To Karen and Rich
Who taught and mended
—I.L.

Ronald Munson Ronald Munson is Emeritus Professor of Philosophy of Science and Medicine at the University of Missouri–St. Louis and a nationally acclaimed bioethicist. After receiving his Ph.D. from Columbia University, he was a Postdoctoral Fellow in Biology at Harvard University and a Visiting Fellow at the Harvard Medical School.

Munson has served as a bioethicist for the National Eye Institute and the National Cancer Institute, as an editor for the *American Journal of Surgery*, and as a member of the Washington University Human Studies Committee. Munson's other books include *Raising the Dead: Organ Transplants, Ethics, and Society; The Woman Who Decided to Die: Changes and Choices at the Edges of Medicine; Reasoning in Medicine; and Elements of Reasoning*, 7e (with Andrew Black). He is also the author of the novels *Nothing Human, Fan Mail, Night Vision*, and *The Harvard Game*.

Ian Lague Ian Lague is a journalist and editor based in Portland, Oregon. He received his M.A. from Columbia University's Graduate School of Journalism, with a special focus on health reporting, and holds a philosophy degree from Swarthmore College. A former Managing Editor of *Boston Review*, he has edited and written articles on such topics as the prescription drug wholesale industry, distributive justice in caregiving, and the role of public funding in private health care enterprises. He is a co-editor, with Joshua Cohen, of *The Place of Tolerance in Islam* (Beacon Press, 2002) and has served as a developmental editor for college textbooks in applied ethics, bioethics, and critical thinking.

Brief Contents

Contents

PART II Controls 233

3 *Genetic Control* 234

4   *Reproductive Control* 349

9   *Distributing Health Care* 680

Preface

In shaping the tenth edition of *Intervention and Reflection*, we have tried to capture both the intellectual excitement and the moral seriousness of contemporary bioethical debate. We hope, in particular, to make that debate accessible and engaging for those who are new to the field or who are reading this book in non-academic contexts. By emphasizing individual cases and presenting the relevant medical, scientific, and social background, we seek to make readers active participants in the ethical deliberations that surround clinical practice and biomedical research.

Topics

This edition addresses a set of topics that we consider some of the most challenging and urgent in contemporary bioethics. Some will be familiar from media reports and political controversies while others will be new to many readers. All involve problems of sufficient depth and complexity to benefit from sustained philosophical analysis. It is our conviction that such analysis can help clarify ethical positions and elevate the quality of public discourse, even though it may not definitively answer all the questions raised in the process. Topics and questions addressed in this text include:

- Autism and vaccinations: Is there a duty to vaccinate?
- Placebos and paternalism: Must patients always be told the truth?
- Withholding treatment from children: Can it be justified in the name of religion or culture?
- Torture and medicine: May health professionals assist "enhanced interrogations"?

- Randomized clinical trials: Do they violate standards of clinical practice?
- Conflicts of interest: Do research sponsors suppress negative results?
- Embryo selection: Is screening for disability a form of discrimination?
- Precision medicine: Will society benefit from an era of personalized care?
- Surrogate motherhood: Does assisted reproduction exploit disadvantaged women?
- State abortion laws: Do they impose an "undue burden" on reproductive autonomy?
- Severely impaired infants: Is there such a thing as "wrongful life"?
- Euthanasia: Is there is difference between killing and letting die?
- Scarce medical resources: Should they be distributed on the basis of "social worth"?
- Transplant organs: Should they be sold on a regulated market?
- The Affordable Care Act: Has it achieved genuine health care reform?
- Maternal–fetal conflict: Do pregnant women lose a right to refuse treatment?
- African American health disparities: How does race impact the provision of care?
- Disabilities: Are they medically objective or socially constructed?
- The *DSM* and sexual minorities: Do diagnoses reflect social prejudices?
- Clinical trials in rich and poor countries: Should the same standards apply?
- Female genital cutting: Is there hypocrisy in Western condemnations?

Readings

The text contains a selection of articles that we believe demonstrate the value of serious reflection on biomedical topics. All are accessible and nontechnical, and many exemplify the practice of bioethics at its best. Although philosophers are strongly represented, the authors also include jurists, scientists, clinical researchers, social critics, activists, and practicing physicians. The moral problems of medicine always have scientific, social, legal, and economic aspects, and to deal with them sensibly and thoroughly, we need the knowledge and perceptions of thinkers from a variety of disciplines.

We have also made an effort to include thinkers with sharply divergent perspectives on the issues at hand. Bioethics remains an intellectually exciting discipline, in part, because of the vigorous debates it generates, and to ignore these conflicts would be misleading. Worse, it would deny readers the opportunity to engage with opinions and arguments radically different from their own. Reasoned inquiry depends, in part, upon exchanges across serious moral disagreements. Without them, it is far too easy for power or prejudice to narrow our opinions and, ultimately, undermine the quality of our public discourse.

How to Use This Book

Intervention and Reflection has been developed with a modular structure, to give instructors, students, and nonacademic readers maximum flexibility in how they approach the material. The chapters may be read in any order and we expect that most instructors will want to teach only a selection of them in a one-semester or one-quarter course. In addition, professors who emphasize theoretical issues in their courses may wish to start by assigning Part VI: Foundations of Bioethics, which provides a basic introduction to a range of ethical theories and principles. Although major topics and themes in the text are interconnected and cross-referenced, we have also provided key definitions and arguments in multiple locations, in keeping with the modular approach.

In the first five parts of this book, each chapter contains several different components. Each opens with Case Presentation and Social Context features, which are followed by the chapter's Briefing Session. The Readings appear next, and after them the Decision Scenarios.

Case Presentations

In the Case Presentations, we include a narrative account of events and individuals with lasting bioethical significance. Cases have been selected not only because they have generated controversy, but also because they raise pivotal issues in clinical practice and medical and biological research.

Some of the people at the focus of the cases will be familiar, such as Steve Jobs, Henrietta Lacks, Angelina Jolie, Karen Quinlan, Jack Kevorkian, Brittany Maynard, Sherri Finkbine, and Dax Cowart. Other figures will be new to most readers. One important aspect of the Case Presentations is that they remind us that, in dealing with bioethical questions, we are not engaged in an abstract intellectual game. Real lives are often at stake and real people may suffer or die.

Social Contexts

The Social Context features provide information relevant to understanding the current social, political, or biomedical circumstances under which issues are being debated. They offer a broader and deeper view of problems such as distributing health care under the Affordable Care Act, racial disparities in health care outcomes, and the development of personalized "precision" medicine. Bioethics has the potential to improve the quality of public discourse on such topics, but it must also be grounded in a thorough understanding of the social situations in which they arise.

Briefing Sessions

In each chapter's Briefing Session, we discuss specific moral problems that occur in medical and biological practice, research, and policymaking. In addition, we present relevant factual information to help readers understand how such problems arise. Finally, we suggest some ways that moral theories or principles might be used to address some of the issues that have been raised. Given limitations of space, however, such suggestions are offered only as starting points in the pursuit of satisfactory answers.

Readings

The Readings make up the next, and perhaps most important, component of each chapter. They provide a range of nontechnical arguments and viewpoints relevant to the problems addressed by the chapter. Although each selection stands alone, we have tried to present opposing positions together to offer readers a fair and evenhanded view of the questions involved. The multiplicity of topics addressed in the book means, however, that we cannot always represent the full range of substantive positions on a given issue. We hope readers will delve deeper into topics of particular interest, using the text as a starting point to weigh competing arguments and to develop a general point of view. The arguments are offered to prompt inquiry, not to make it unnecessary.

Decision Scenarios

The Decision Scenarios constitute the final component of each chapter. These are brief, dramatic accounts of situations that require moral reasoning or in which ethical or social policy decisions have to be made. Each scenario is followed by questions that prompt the reader to identify the moral issues at stake and to advance arguments about how they should be addressed. Thus, the Decision Scenarios are exercises in bioethics designed to prompt structured reflection and discussion.

Foundations of Bioethics

For some readers, the most important feature of this book will be Part VI: Foundations of Bioethics. In the first section of Chapter 12, we sketch the basic structure of five major ethical theories and indicate how they might be used to answer pressing moral questions in medicine and research. In the second section, we present and illustrate several major moral principles. These principles are endorsed (or at least expressed in practice) by most of the theories discussed in the first section. Even so, we do not try to demonstrate how the principles follow from particular theories, but instead present them as independent precepts that can be used to guide moral decision-making. In the third section, we provide a brief introduction to four important ethical theories that are not easily reduced to a set of principles: capability ethics, virtue ethics, care ethics, and identity-based ethical theories.

The main purpose of Part VI is to give those without a background in ethics the information they need to frame and evaluate moral arguments about basic issues in bioethics. In classroom settings, it may be assigned first, to give students a theoretical basis for analyzing the topics and arguments presented in earlier chapters. In keeping with the modular design of the text, we have also made it possible to assign individual sections of Part VI (e.g., "Major Moral Principles") for use with particular biomedical topics.

Notes and References

The Notes and References section provides a detailed account of the source material used in the Case Presentations, Briefing Sessions, Social Contexts, and Decision Scenarios. For space reasons, however, these Notes and References are not included in the printed book. They are instead available on the book's website, which can be found at www.cengagebrain.com.

Online Resources

This edition's Instructor Companion Site includes the following materials:

- PowerPoints, which provide a condensed summary of the main topics and arguments in each chapter
- Multiple-choice quizzes
- True-false quizzes
- A final exam quiz
- Notes and References

Additional Resources

Websites for the National Library of Medicine, the National Institutes of Health, and the Centers for Disease Control all provide access to Medline, the National Library of Medicine's bibliographic database, making it possible to carry out extensive research on almost any bioethical, clinical, or biomedical topic. Medline indexes not only medical journals, but also journals in bioethics.

Those interested in specific conditions such as diabetes, Huntington's, or breast cancer, or specific interventions such as stem-cell therapies or heart transplants, can readily acquire a great deal of up-to-the-minute information by consulting relevant and reputable online resources. Those maintained by research institutions (e.g., Johns Hopkins and the Mayo Clinic) and advocacy groups (e.g., the American Cancer Society and the March of Dimes Foundation) are generally the most up-to-date and trustworthy.

Content Changes in the Tenth Edition

This edition of *Intervention and Reflection* has been thoroughly revised and updated to reflect key developments in clinical practice, biomedical science, law, and public policy, as well as broader shifts in society and culture. Major changes include:

- New chapters on Medicine in a Pluralistic Society and the Challenge of Global Bioethics.
- Expanded coverage throughout of changes related to the Affordable Care Act, with specific features on health care pricing, inflation, and uncompensated care.
- Expanded coverage of issues related to gender, race, and LGBT identities.
- Expanded coverage of mental health issues throughout.
- Nineteen new Case Presentations explore emerging issues in bioethics through their impact on individual lives. New cases include those of Brittany Maynard and physician-assisted death, Henrietta Lacks and the HeLa cell line, Kim Horbas and the ASR hip implant, Angelina Jolie and genetic testing, Domenico Dolce and "synthetic children," and Lee Larson and cochlear implants. New cases also address specific controversies surrounding health professionals' involvement in torture, the Seattle "God Committee," and the Guatemala syphilis experiments of the 1940s.
- Ten new Social Context features report on highly charged debates over such topics as precision medicine, gender-based medical research, the *DSM* and sexual minorities, CRISPR gene-editing technologies, state abortion laws, America's obesity epidemic, the Affordable Care Act, racial health disparities, and male and female genital cutting.
- Twenty-two new Readings extend the scope of the previous edition, but continue to present arguments relevant to key bioethical debates. New selections include those from Gerald Dworkin,

Michelle Gold, Marcia Angell, Emma D'Arcy, Michael Sandel, Bonnie Steinbock, Patrick Lee, Robert George, David DeGrazia, Mark Hall, Richard Lord, Avik Roy, John Geyman, Hilde Lindemann, Dorothy Roberts, Tia Powell, Edward Stein, Alice Dreger, Susan Wendell, Thomas Szasz, David Resnik, A. J. McMichael, Angela Wasunna, and Sirkku Hellsten.

- All eleven Briefing Sessions have been revised to reflect changes in law, policy, statistics, biology, and medicine.
- Eighteen new Decision Scenarios have been added, each prompting students to make decisions or support policies by appealing to relevant facts and moral principles.

Envoi

This book, with its Case Presentations, Briefing Sessions, Social Context features, Decision Scenarios, and Foundations of Bioethics discussion, is more ambitious than many other bioethics texts. We have been pleased by past responses from academic colleagues and independent readers. Even their criticisms have been tempered by a sympathetic understanding of the difficulty of producing a book of this scope that attempts to do so many things.

We are under no illusions that the book has achieved perfection, and would still appreciate comments or suggestions from those who use the book and discover ways it needs to be corrected or can be improved. Communications may be e-mailed to munson@umsl.edu, ian@inwiteditorial.com, or mailed to Ronald Munson's university address (Department of Philosophy, University of Missouri–St. Louis, St. Louis, MO 63121).

Books, like people, continue to acquire intellectual debts throughout their lives. This means that many who contributed to this project over the years have to settle for an acknowledgment that is less than what they are rightly owed.

Our most enduring debt is to those authors who have allowed their work to be printed here. We hope they will find no grounds for objecting to our presentation of their arguments and ideas. We are also grateful to the following reviewers for their criticisms and recommendations: Matthew Gifford, University of Massachusetts, Amherst; Sheila Hollander, University of Memphis; Denise Kearney, Southwestern Community College; Jeanne Kusina, University of Toledo; David Paul, Western Michigan University; Kenneth Richman, MCPHS University; and Andrew Swift, St. Ambrose University.

At Cengage and its affiliates, we are grateful to Debra Matteson, Florence Kilgo, Sharon Tripp, Sylvie Pittet, Jill Quinn, Ruchika Abrol, Charu Khanna, and many others for their patience, good judgment, and hard work. Outside the world of publishing, Ian Lague would like to thank, in particular, Karen Heintz, Rich Lague, Karen Lee, Katie McShane, Alice Dreger, Sam Grobe-Heintz, Rollie Wolfe, and Heather Schwartz for their substantive suggestions, criticisms, and insights. Ronald Munson adds: Miriam Munson's name deserves to appear on the title page as an indication of how grateful I am to her for her hard work and keen judgment. Her quick eye and sharp intelligence kept me from making many errors, large and small. The book is better because of her.

In spite of expert advice, we have not always listened to those who have taken the trouble to warn and educate us, and this is reason enough for us to claim the errors here as our own.

Ronald Munson

Ronald Munson
University of Missouri–St. Louis
munson@umsl.edu

Ian Lague

Ian Lague
ian@inwiteditorial.com

—September 2015

Part I

Rights

Chapter 1

Physicians, Patients, and Others: Roles and Responsibilities

CHAPTER CONTENTS

CASES AND CONTEXTS

CASE PRESENTATION

Donald (Dax) Cowart Rejects Treatment—and Is Ignored

The man stretched out on the steel platform is thin to the point of emaciation. The skin of his face and body has been severely burned, leaving a patchwork of raw and blistered flesh. A pad covers one eye socket, and the eyelid of the other eye is sewn shut. His fingers are charred down to the knuckle and disfiguring burns have partially destroyed his nose, lips, and ears. Bandages wrapped around his legs and torso give him the look of a mummy in a low-budget horror movie.

In obvious pain, the man writhes on the platform as white-uniformed attendants in gauze masks raise him up with a motorized lift. With casual efficiency, they lower him into a tank of clear liquid and take up brushes to scrape away the dead tissue that covers his body. As they begin their work, the man screams in pain and continues screaming until he passes out hours later. When he wakes up, he knows he has only a few hours before the same procedure will begin all over again—day after day, for months, possibly years, to come. . . .

The real-life horror story that brought Donald Cowart to this moment began in July of 1973. Earlier that year, he had left active duty in the Air Force after three years of service (including a tour of duty in Vietnam), and returned to his family home in east Texas, to wait there for an opening as a commercial airline pilot. He was twenty-five years old, a college graduate, and in

excellent health. A high school athlete who had played football and basketball and run track, Cowart had kept himself in top physical condition. He played golf, surfed, skydived, and rode horses. While waiting for an airline job, he decided to join his father's business as a real estate broker. The two had recently grown closer, so working together was a pleasure for both of them.

And then everything changed forever.

One hot Wednesday afternoon in July, Don and his father, Ray, drove out to the country to take a look at a piece of land they thought might be a good buy. They parked the car next to a dip in the road, a cool shady spot beside a dry creek bed. They took a walking tour of the land, but when they returned to the car, it wouldn't start.

Ray Cowart got out, raised the hood, and tinkered with the carburetor. Don, in the driver's seat, turned the key repeatedly, grinding the engine so much that he worried he would run down the battery. After three or four minutes of cranking the key, a blue flame suddenly shot from the carburetor and Ray Cowart jumped back. On the next turn of the ignition, a tremendous explosion rocked the car, shattered the windshield, and threw Don sideways onto the passenger seat. A huge ball of live fire engulfed not just the car but much of the surrounding countryside.

In the moments after the explosion, Don managed to get the car door open and ran through the flames toward the woods. But after encountering thick underbrush already crackling with flames, he turned away and ran straight down the road. He hurtled through three thick walls of fire, throwing himself to the ground as he cleared each one in an effort to smother the flames.

Getting to his feet after the last wall of flames, Don ran again, shouting for help. He noticed his vision was blurred, as if he were underwater, and he realized his eyes had been seared by the fire. *This can't be happening*, he thought as he ran. But the pain assured him that it was. He heard a voice shouting, "I'm coming!" and only then did he stop running and lie down in the road.

In the immediate aftermath of the accident, Don assumed that his car's gas tank had exploded, and only after he had been in a hospital for several days did he learn that the blast and fire were caused by a leak in a propane gas transmission line from a nearby oil refinery. Seeping from the line, a huge pool of gas had collected in the dry creek bed, saturating the air to such an extent that the car wouldn't start because the engine couldn't get enough oxygen. The spark from the Cowarts' car had finally ignited the gas.

When the farmer who had heard Don's shouts arrived on the scene, his first words were "Oh, my God!" It was Don's first confirmation of how severe his burns were.

"Get me a gun," he told the farmer, after the man had dragged him to the side of the road.

"What do you want with a gun?" the farmer asked.

"Can't you see I'm a dead man?" Don told him. "I'm going to die anyway."

"I can't do that," the farmer said gently.

When the first ambulance arrived, Don sent it to pick up his father. When the second came, he told them he didn't want to go to the hospital. "All I wanted to do was die and to die as quickly as possible," he recalled nine years later. Over his protest, the attendants put him in the ambulance. Cowart asked them to pick him up by his belt, because his burns were so excruciating he couldn't bear to be touched.

Don and his father were taken to a small nearby hospital, but because of the extent of their injuries, it was soon decided that they should be transported together to the burn unit of Parkland Hospital in Dallas, 140 miles away. "I'm sorry, Donny boy," his father told him after

they were placed in the ambulance. Ray Cowart died on the way to Parkland. Upon arrival, Don continued to insist that he be allowed to die.

Don's mother had heard about an accidental explosion on the radio, but she learned her husband and son were involved only when the police called her out of an evening church service. After rushing to Dallas to be with Don, she was approached by his physicians to sign consent forms for surgery and treatment. Knowing nothing about burn therapies, she took the advice offered to her by the physicians. She was told about Don's protest against being treated, but she expected his wish to be allowed to die to pass as soon as he began to recover. Nevertheless, it became clear that Don would be severely disfigured and disabled as a result of the accident.

Charles Baxter, Don's attending physician at Parkland, estimated that Don had extremely deep burns over about 65 percent of his body. His face, upper arms, torso, and legs had suffered severe third-degree burns, and both ears were virtually destroyed. His eyes were so damaged that his left eye had to be surgically removed, and he eventually lost the vision in his right eye. His fingers were burned off down to the second joint, making it impossible for him to pick up anything. The pain was tremendous, and even though he was given substantial doses of narcotics, it remained unbearable for more than a year.

To control the many infected areas on his body, Don had to be submerged daily in a tank of highly chlorinated water to destroy the microorganisms breeding on the surface of his wounds. As described at the start of this case, his wounds were then brushed and scraped to remove dead tissue. The experience was excruciatingly painful, and Don described it as akin to being "skinned alive."

Despite Don's protests and refusals, these "tankings" were continued throughout his hospital stay. "It was like pouring alcohol on an open wound," Don remembered. Being lifted out of the tank was also excruciating, because the room was freezing, and every nerve in the damaged parts of his body produced agony. "All I could do was scream at the top of my lungs until I would finally pass out with exhaustion. The tankings took place seven days a week—week after week after week."

Rex Houston, the family's attorney and close friend, filed a lawsuit against Exxon, the owner of the leaking propane transmission line, for damages resulting from the explosion. He was concerned that the case go to trial as soon as possible. Don was unmarried and had no dependents, so if he died before the case was heard, the lawsuit would be unlikely to produce much money. But with Don as a living plaintiff, a young man who had lost the use of both hands and both eyes, the suit had considerably more potential.

Nonetheless, Don continued to express his wish to die. He asked a nurse with whom he had developed a rapport to give him a drug that would kill him or at least to help him do something to take his own life. As sympathetic as she was, she refused his request. Don also asked a family friend to get a gun for him, but quickly noted that such a request was pointless, because he had no fingers to pull the trigger.

Dr. Baxter's initial response to Don's request to die was dismissive: "Oh, you don't want to do that," he would say. He was convinced that Don talked about wanting to die only because of his previously charmed life. He felt Don's persistence was rooted in an effort to gain control over his environment and manipulate his caregivers. Don would later reject this interpretation of his motives.

Don's mother considered her son's medical condition too serious to allow him to make decisions about his own treatment. "Everything was discussed with her in detail," Dr. Baxter recalled. "She was most cooperative and most helpful. We approached the problem of his desire to die very openly. . . . Even the possibility that it could be allowed was discussed with her. She was never in favor of it, because basically she thought he did not have this desire." A woman of deep religious conviction, Mrs. Cowart also believed that Don should be kept alive until he had time to become reconciled to God. (Don had rebelled against his parents' religious views as a teenager.)

When his burns had healed enough so that they were no longer immediately life-threatening, Don was moved to the Texas Institute of Rehabilitation in Houston. He agreed to give their burn-care program a try, but after three weeks he began to refuse treatment again. He had discovered how many years of pain and suffering his treatment would likely entail. The doctors at the institute honored his request that his bandages not be changed, and in a few days, the burns on his legs became infected again and the grafted skin

peeled away. His condition once again became imminently life-threatening.

Dr. Robert Meier, a rehabilitation specialist responsible for Don's care, called a meeting with Don's mother and attorney. They decided that because Don's burns had become infected, he should be rehospitalized in an acute care center. Don was transferred to the University of Texas Medical Branch at Galveston in April of 1974. Once there, he again refused treatment. Psychiatrist Robert B. White was called in by the surgeons in charge of Don's case, because they thought Don's refusal might be the result of clinical depression or some form of mental illness. If he were found incompetent, a legal guardian could be appointed to give permission for the additional surgery they recommended. After examining Don and with the concurrence of a second psychiatrist, Dr. White concluded that Don was fully competent and not suffering from any kind of mental illness. He was, moreover, intelligent, self-aware, and highly articulate.

Don wanted to leave the hospital so he could go home and die. But he couldn't leave without help, and neither his physicians nor his mother would agree to assist him. His mother wanted him taken care of, and moving him home to die of massive infection was more than she could accept. Don accused her of being responsible for prolonging his hopeless condition. He refused to give his permission for surgery on what was left of his hands, which had become even less usable due to scarring and contracture. Eventually, he consented, but only with his surgeon's assurance that he would give Don enough drugs to control the pain.

Surgeon Duane Larson was puzzled by Don's ongoing insistence that he wanted to die. Don was no longer on the verge of death and would, in his view, recover some degree of normalcy. He would find new ways to enjoy life. "In essence he was asking people to participate in his death," Dr. Larson said.

One alternative Dr. Larson suggested to Don was for him to be treated until he was well enough to leave the hospital; then he could kill himself, if he still wanted to. Another alternative was to get Don to see how different strategies could be employed to lessen his pain and make him more comfortable. But Dr. Larson also thought Don might be brought to see that some of his outbursts were merely angry "little boy feelings" anyone would experience after going through such a terrible ordeal.

"Don't ask us to let you die," Dr. Meier had told Don at the rehabilitation center, "because in a sense what that means is we're killing you. If you want to die, then let me fix your hands, operate on them and open them up so at least you can do something with them, and if you want to commit suicide then, you can. But don't ask us to stand here and literally kill you."

Years later, Cowart still rejects Meier's perspective. "The argument that not treating a patient is the same as killing borders on the ridiculous," he said. "If letting the patient die is characterized as playing God, then treating the patient to save his life has to be as well. In the final analysis, I was nothing but a hostage to the current state of medical technology." Just a few years earlier, Cowart would have died from his injuries, but the management of burns had advanced sufficiently to keep him alive. He was, he said, "forced to receive treatment," because he was "too weak to resist and unable to walk out on my own." Ironically, Cowart's treatment took place during the mid-1970s, a period of time when U.S. culture was placing new emphasis on the importance of individual liberties and freedom of choice.

Don Cowart was treated for ten months. He was left completely blind, he lost all his fingers except the stump of his left thumb, and only retained remnants of his ears, nose, lips, and eyelids. One of the powerful antibiotics he was treated with severely damaged his hearing and he also lost full use of his right arm. He had to have help with everything and was unable to take care of even his most basic bodily needs. His pain was still constant and he had trouble walking on his own.

Discharged from the hospital, he took up residence in his mother's house. At first he was relieved to be out of the hospital, but after a few weeks he fell into a deep depression. Frustration built up as he experienced his loss of independence, lost the ability to sleep, and worried about what he was going to do with the rest of his life. His career prospects seemed dim and romantic relationships seemed at best a remote possibility. One night he disappeared from his mother's house and was found crouched beside the highway, waiting to throw himself in front of a truck.

Because of his disfigurement, he was reluctant to go out in public, but eventually he began to go to stores and restaurants, protected by his blindness from the stares and reactions of others. Money from an out-of-court settlement with Exxon gave him a measure of financial independence.

In 1976, Cowart enrolled in Baylor Law School, moved in with a married couple, and learned to do some things for himself. But in the spring of that year, beset by severe sleep disturbance and upset by the breakdown of a personal relationship, he tried to kill himself with an overdose of sleeping pills and tranquilizers. He was found in time for him to be taken to the hospital and have his stomach pumped. Despite what Dr. Larson and others had told him while his burns were being treated, it seemed that he wasn't going to be allowed to kill himself. Don was rehospitalized for depression, insomnia, and dependence on sleeping pills, and eventually returned to law school.

Despite years of frustration and setbacks, Cowart graduated from law school in 1986. He changed his name to "Dax," to make it easier for him to identify his own name in spite of his hearing loss, and it seemed to mark a new chapter in his life. He passed the bar, married a high school classmate, and set up a law practice. He also began speaking about his experiences before audiences and became an advocate for patient autonomy. In the past three decades, Dax's life has been filled with the usual share of complications and challenges. He has been twice divorced and remarried, and has struggled, at times, to keep his law practice afloat. But he now expresses broad satisfaction with his life and takes pleasure in his ability to advocate for patients like himself.

His mother is sure she made the right decision in signing the consent forms for treatment, particularly now that her son's life is filled with the satisfactions of marriage and a rewarding career. She does wish she had asked the doctors to give him more pain medication, however. They hadn't told her that more medication was an option—reflecting fears common to the era about painkiller addiction that many contemporary physicians now view as excessive.

Dax doesn't blame his mother for her decisions. He blames his doctors for putting her in the position of having to make them. *He* should have been the one asked, Dax insists. "The individual freedom of a competent adult should never be restricted," he says, "except when it conflicts with the freedom of some other individual." For Cowart, the individual should be able to decide what minimum quality of life is acceptable to him or her. This is not a decision that should be made by physicians or anyone else on behalf of a competent person.

Now that Dax Cowart is living a satisfactory life, is he glad his physicians and his mother continued his treatment against his wishes? "I'm enjoying life now, and I'm glad to be alive," Cowart says. "But I still think it was wrong to force me to undergo what I had to, to be alive." He frames this argument as one in which laudable ends don't justify the horrible means. "If you had to do something as deeply painful as skinning someone alive or boiling them in oil in order to keep them alive, would you think it was worth it?"

Nor would the assurance of pulling through be enough to make him change his mind. "If the same thing were to occur tomorrow, knowing I could reach this same point, I still would not want to undergo the pain and agony that I had to undergo to be alive now. I should want that choice to lie entirely with myself and not others."

SOCIAL CONTEXT
Autism and Vaccination

Autism spectrum disorders (ASDs) are a group of developmental disabilities. The disorders involve difficulties (often severe) in learning language and in communicating and interacting with others. The spectrum of autism disorders is wide, and the behaviors of people who fall within it can range from mildly awkward or withdrawn to highly agitated, compulsively repetitive, or violently self-destructive. ASDs are often accompanied by abnormalities in cognitive ability, learning, attention, and sensory processing.

The behavioral symptoms of autism typically appear before a child turns three. Parents may watch their baby develop in expected ways for a period of months or even years, then notice that the child stops making eye contact and seems to lose interest in them and in the surrounding world. These changes in behavior may be signs that the child is no longer following the path of normal development and needs to be evaluated.

The term *spectrum* indicates that a range and variety of behaviors can be considered autistic. Disorders within the spectrum are given specific diagnoses by experts who test the child, observe the child's behavior, and compare it with what might be expected given the child's age. Included in the spectrum are autistic disorder (autism), Asperger's syndrome, childhood disintegrative disorder, and pervasive developmental disorder, not otherwise specified (PDD-NOS).

People with Asperger's syndrome or PDD-NOS have fewer symptoms compared with people with autism, and in terms of language ability, intelligence, and social skills, they are usually only mildly impaired. In the discussion that follows, however, we will frequently use autism to refer to the entire autistic disorders spectrum, unless there is a reason to be more specific.

Numbers and Facts

The Centers for Disease Control now estimates that an average of one out of every sixty-eight children has an autism spectrum disorder. Given that nearly four million children are born every year in the United States, about 58,800 a year will be diagnosed with the disorder. If the prevalence has been the same over the last twenty years, this means that over a million people ages twenty-one or younger have some form of autism.

Generally accepted facts about autism also include the following:

- Males are nearly five times more likely than females to be autistic.

- Autism occurs in all races and in all parts of the world.

- A sibling of someone with autism is significantly more likely to be autistic than someone in the general population (as much as twenty-five times more likely according to some studies).
- Parents who have a child with autism have a 2 to 18 percent chance of having a second child with autism.
- Families with an autistic child are more likely to have a family member with a neurological disorder or a chromosomal disorder than families in the general population.
- Older parents are at a higher risk of having a child with an ASD.
- About 10 percent of children with autism also have an identifiable genetic or chromosomal disorder such as Down syndrome, fragile X syndrome, or tuberous sclerosis, and autism is also associated with a range of other neurological and metabolic conditions.
- About 38 percent of children with autistic spectrum disorders have an intellectual disability (defined as an IQ of 70 or lower).
- About 25 percent of children with ASD are nonverbal and do not talk at all.
- Autism is a lifelong condition that cannot be "cured."
- The estimated costs of caring for children with ASD are over $9 billion a year in the United States.

Causes

The causes of autism are unknown. The disorder almost certainly has a genetic component, but it is not a genetic disease in the way that sickle-cell anemia or cystic fibrosis are genetic diseases. Autism, instead of being produced by a single inherited gene, may result from the interaction of a group of genes. However, some genetically predisposed infants may not develop the disorder because they don't encounter some unknown environmental factor that acts as a trigger. It may also be possible that there is not "a cause" of autism, but that different sets of conditions may result in the symptoms that fall within the autism spectrum.

The elusive nature of autism's causes has over the years generated a number of theories that have been thoroughly discredited. During the 1950s and 1960s, a favorite theory was that autism is the result of psychodynamic processes in the individual. Mothers who are cold and rejecting were held to be responsible for producing children who lacked language and empathy and withdrew from the world. No one accepts such a view today.

Increase in Autism?

Before the 1980s, the term *autism* was used to diagnose symptoms now considered limited to the *autistic disorder* portion of the ASD spectrum. The disorder was a rare diagnosis, and only 0.5 percent of children (10 in 2,000) received it.

Autism disorder is now viewed as only one of several diagnoses in a spectrum of disorders. Applying the diagnostic criteria that reflect this view, CDC researchers now estimate that 1.47 percent, or 14.7 per 1,000 children, have an autism spectrum disorder. These estimates are dramatically higher than those using the old diagnostic criteria. Similar studies in Asia and Europe have found an average prevalence of ASDs of roughly 1 percent, while a study in South Korea found a prevalence as high as 2.6 percent. What's more, ASD prevalence estimates using the new criteria have continued to rise each year (from 6.7 per 1,000 in the year 2000 to 14.7 per 1,000 in 2010).

Nevertheless, many scientists don't think the increase in the number of *reported cases* of autism represents an equivalent increase in the number of *actual cases*. Rather, the change in diagnostic criteria and a number of social factors may account for most of the dramatic increase in the number of reported cases. For example, (1) greater awareness of ASDs means that many children who in the past would have been considered merely somewhat awkward or atypical are now being diagnosed as autistic; (2) the old criteria classified only "low-functioning" children as autistic, but now "high-functioning" children are also included in the category; (3) more physicians are sensitive to the need to look for early signs of autism, which results in more diagnoses and even some charges of "overdiagnosis"; (4) parents today are often more medically sophisticated and more attentive to their children's behavior, and so pediatricians seek to satisfy them by diagnosing autism in borderline cases; (5) the funding associated with special-education programs may give parents and school districts an incentive to seek out a diagnosis of autism (or another well-recognized disorder), even when a child's difficulties may be more ambiguous.

All of these factors may be responsible for some of the increase in the number of reported autism cases. Researchers are not questioning the fact that autism is a real disorder or the value of identifying many cases of autism that once would have been missed. Nor does anyone doubt the urgent need to find ways to reduce the incidence of severe autism. But the statistical impression of a rapidly growing autism "epidemic" is probably a distortion of the actual situation. A 2014 study from the University of Queensland in Australia, which attempted to control for some of the factors discussed above, actually found that the rate of autism had been constant between 1990 and 2010.

Vaccines and Autism: First Shot

The question of whether the number of autism cases is on the rise is of pivotal importance for those who hold the controversial view that vaccinations are a cause of the disorder. A crucial assumption for such a view is that the number of reported cases represents a rise in actual cases. One version of the argument is that an increase in the use of vaccines has been paralleled by an increase in cases of autism, and that therefore vaccines cause autism.

The debate over vaccines and autism can be traced back to 1998, when a British pediatrician named Andrew Wakefield described what he saw as autistic symptoms in patients who had adverse reactions to the MMR injection—a combination of vaccines designed to protect children against the viral diseases measles, mumps, and rubella.

Wakefield and his collaborators published a paper that year in *The Lancet* medical journal, in which they reported that a dozen children in London's Royal Free Hospital who had intestinal symptoms (pain, bloating, and inflammation) also displayed autism-like symptoms. Furthermore, the paper claimed that eight of the twelve had started displaying autistic symptoms within days of being injected with the MMR vaccine.

The paper did not claim that the MMR vaccine was the cause of autism. The authors suggested, however, that the exposure to the measles virus in the vaccine might have been a contributing factor. Later, Wakefield, speaking only for himself, expressed the view that the virus in the vaccine might cause inflammation in the gut and the inflammation might affect brain development. Thus, the MMR vaccine would be the initiating event in the causal chain leading to autism.

Thimerosal

Even before the *Lancet* paper, parents of autistic children had already been primed to suspect vaccines might cause autism, as the medical journalist Alice Park has pointed out. Beginning in the 1930s, an organic mercury-based compound called thimerosal was used in vaccines as a pre-servative to keep molds and bacteria from growing in them. Although thimerosal only exposes patients to *ethylmercury*—which is a different compound from the *methylmercury* pollution that causes nervous system harm—some critics objected to its use. That methylmercury and other heavy metals can cause brain damage was already a familiar fact. It was also understood that children are particularly susceptible to damage from heavy metals because their brains are still undergoing development.

It thus made intuitive sense to many people that thimerosal was responsible for autism. Not only was mercury known to de-stroy brain tissue, but the timing was right. Children in the United States and many other countries are given several vaccines by their second year, and it is around this time that the first symptoms of autism typically appear. Based on this association, many people assumed that childhood vaccination caused brain damage, which then produced the symptoms of autism.

As intuitively convincing as this train of thought may seem, it is a clear example of fallacious post hoc reasoning that con-fuses correlation and causation. That the symptoms of autism appear after vaccina-tions does not prove that vaccines cause the symptoms. (After you start wearing your winter coat, the geese fly south, but putting on your coat doesn't cause them to fly south.) Evidence of a different kind is needed.

This evidence seemed to be at hand in 2001, when the FDA released the results of a study showing that six-month-old children who received all five of their recommended vaccinations were being given twice the amount of mercury the Environmental Pro-tection Agency considered safe for people who eat fish as a regular part of their diet. These included the common DPT (diphtheria, pertussis, and tetanus), hepatitis-B, and Hib

(*Haemophilus influenzae* type B) vaccinations. Prompted by this startling finding, the FDA and vaccine makers went into overdrive, and by the end of 2001, they had introduced versions of all five vaccines that eliminated thimerosal or reduced it to trace amounts. The drug-makers also removed thimerosal from almost all the other recommended vaccinations for U.S. children under six years old. (The only recommended vaccinations that still contained higher levels of thimerosal were certain influenza vaccines for children over two, and thimerosal-free versions of these have subsequently been made avail-able.) As a result, from 2002 onward Ameri-can children under six have had virtually no exposure to thimerosal from vaccinations.

Proponents of what had become known as the "vaccine hypothesis" expected the rates of autism to drop dramatically after the removal of thimerosal from vaccines: no thimerosal, no autism. But the opposite happened. As we have seen, the reported rate of autism has *increased* since 2001, when thimerosal-free vaccines entered the system, so that its occurrence among eight-year-olds is now one in sixty-eight.

In 2001, the Centers for Disease Con-trol and the National Institutes of Health helped set up an independent panel to re-view and evaluate the scientific literature concerning the alleged connection between thimerosal and autistic symptoms, among other issues. Based on a three-year review of epidemiological and other studies, the panel concluded that there was no evidence to support a such a connection. They also found no evidence for a biological mecha-nism by which thimerosal could cause autism. The panel went on to conclude that further funding to investigate the possibility of such a link was not a sound use of re-sources. Instead, the panel held, the money should be spent on investigating the genet-ics and developmental biology of the disease and how to treat it.

In subsequent years, there have been dozens of rigorous studies on the thimerosal–autism connection, some with hundreds of thousands of subjects, as well as literature reviews by bodies such as the American Medical Association, the World Health Organization, and the American Academy of Pediatrics. None have found a causal connection between thimerosal and ASDs.

MMR Vaccine

What about the claim made by Wakefield and his collaborators that active virus in the MMR vaccine may be responsible for triggering inflammatory processes in the gut that result in autism? In 2004, ten of Wakefield's thirteen collaborators published a retraction of their paper in *The Lancet*, stating that their data were not adequate to support such a claim, and subsequent investigations have found that the study's authors actually committed deliberate fraud, picking and choosing data and falsifying their findings.

It was revealed that Wakefield himself had financial and other conflicts of interest connected with his plans to market another measles vaccine, something he could not do with much hope of success so long as the MMR vaccine was standard. He was also on the payroll of a lawyer suing vaccine manufacturers. In 2010, after years of investigation, the British General Medical Council concluded that in gathering data used in the original 1998 *Lancet* paper, Wakefield had violated ethical principles. In addition to "dishonest" presentation of his data, he had subjected children in the study to invasive tests such as lumbar punctures and colonoscopies that were irrelevant to their treatment, and he performed these tests without informed consent. Wakefield had shown, the panel said, a "callous disregard" for the suffering of the children involved in his research. After the release of the panel's report, *The Lancet* itself completely retracted

the 1998 paper that had connected vaccines with autism. Wakefield was later barred from practicing medicine in the U.K.

Since the initial suggestion was made in the 1998 Wakefield paper, more than thirty rigorous studies have been published that explore the connection between MMR and the development of autism. None of the studies, all published in peer-reviewed scientific journals, has found such a link. (The very few studies that have suggested correlations between vaccines and autism have used highly questionable methodologies that have not held up under scientific scrutiny.) The scientific community has rejected the MMR vaccine as a causal factor responsible for autism just as decisively as it has rejected the link between thimerosal and autism.

Court Rulings

The scientific findings have formed the basis for court decisions involving vaccines and claims of harm. In 2002, the U.S. Court of Federal Claims combined the cases of 5,000 families with autistic children seeking compensation from the federal Vaccine Injury Compensation Trust Fund. (The fund is part of a larger "Vaccine Court" set up in 1986 to handle legal cases arising from the tens of millions of vaccines administered each year and to help ensure a consistent supply of vaccines in the U.S. health care system.) Families with children who can establish they developed certain injuries or conditions likely caused by vaccination are often automatically compensated from the fund, in exchange for surrendering their right to sue the vaccine manufacturers.

The Omnibus Autism Proceedings began in 2002 with a court composed of three judges acting as special masters. (Special masters are civil court officers appointed because of their expertise in areas relevant to issues about which the courts must decide.)

The court heard nine cases based on three different theories about the causes of autism.

In three separate cases decided in March 2010, the masters all ruled that thimerosal did not cause autism in the children whose families made claims for compensation. One master found it "extremely unlikely" that vaccines caused autism in the cases under consideration, and another expressed the view that many parents "relied upon practitioners and researchers who peddled hope, not opinions grounded in science and medicine." In three earlier cases decided in February 2009, the special masters had made the same rulings, and their decisions had been upheld on appeal.

Antivaccine groups often point to a handful of cases in which parents of children diagnosed with autism have been awarded compensation by the fund. In all of these cases, however, the compensation was awarded not based on the child's autism, but for other injuries that may have been associated with vaccination, usually due to rare allergic reactions to which the children were genetically predisposed. In no case did the court rule in favor of any connection between vaccination and autism.

"Vaccines Weaken the Immune System"

Perhaps because the rise in the number of reported cases of autism has been paralleled by an increase in the number of vaccinations children receive, some parents find it hard to believe vaccines are not in some way responsible for the disorder.

The idea behind any vaccine is that injected antigens (proteins) will trigger an immune response. The immune system will turn out antibodies against the antigen, and should the immune system encounter the antigen again (be exposed to a virus, for example), the preexisting antibodies will respond immediately. Vaccines build up the body's immunity to the antigens and are designed to produce the same natural immunity developed by survivors of infectious diseases such as measles and chicken pox.

A more recent variation on the vaccine–autism hypothesis depends upon the idea that the proteins in vaccines damage or overwhelm the immune system, triggering interactions with the nervous system that produce autistic symptoms. Current recommendations in the United States are that babies be inoculated against as many as fifteen diseases and get twenty-eight vaccinations before they are six months old. Thus, vaccine critics claim, the number of antigens in the vaccines overwhelm the child's immune system or generate an autoimmune response, and this results in whatever brain changes may be responsible for autism.

Despite a number of studies on the vaccine overload hypothesis, there is still no solid evidence to support it, apart from the fact that the number of vaccines given to infants has increased. This is, again, an instance of post hoc reasoning. In addition, there is still no scientific evidence that the proposed phenomenon of immune-system overload actually exists. Indeed, its very meaning is unclear.

Perhaps the more important flaw in the overload hypothesis is that it rests on the mistaken assumption that the increase in the number of vaccines has meant an increase in the number of antigens to which infants are exposed. The smallpox vaccine given to people until the early 1970s (when it was determined that the disease had been eradicated) contained 200 different antigens, and was never associated with any increase in autism cases. By contrast, the total number of antigens in all fifteen of the standard vaccines is only 150, which is many times lower than the antigen load in the seven vaccines children received in 1980. This reduction reflects the fact that scientists are now able to identify and isolate just those proteins (antigens) that trigger the immune response and provide immunity from the disease.

Critics of the protein-overload hypothesis also point out that infants are exposed to thousands of new proteins every day. They eat new foods, breathe in dust, and are exposed to pollen, dirt, and animal dander. Not to mention the fact that the average child is infected with four to six viruses a year. There is no obvious reason why exposing children to additional antigens should trigger a process that leads to autism, and no evidence that immunized children have weaker immune systems than nonimmunized children.

Finally, autism does not appear to be an autoimmune disorder. It involves none of the inflammatory or immune activation responses found in diseases such as multiple sclerosis or lupus. Thus, it is difficult to find a biological mechanism that would support the vaccine-overload hypothesis, and at this point many researchers suggest that resources would be better spent on more promising avenues of inquiry.

Vaccines Can Harm

Human biology is amazingly complex, and individuals vary widely in multiple subtle ways. Some infants are born with a rare genetic predisposition to react badly to gluten in their diet, while other genetic factors can dramatically change the way different individuals react to the same drugs. It should be no surprise, therefore, that some infants have a genetic predisposition for adverse reactions to some of the substances in vaccines.

In 2008, a Georgia girl with a preexisting cellular disease developed a severe allergic reaction to the vaccines she received as an infant and later developed autism-like symptoms. She is the first, and so far the only, reported case in which it is plausible to say that a vaccine caused autism.

This and other types of adverse reactions show that in rare instances vaccines can cause harm of the sort that defenders of the vaccine hypothesis fear. Rare cases are important for prompting additional scientific inquiry, but they don't prove that all or even a significant number of cases of autism can be ascribed to vaccines. Rare cases should certainly not become the basis for rewriting public health policies, especially when the harms caused by the diseases that vaccines protect against are well established and all too common.

Protection

The traditional childhood diseases of diphtheria, whooping cough (pertussis), polio, measles, rubella, and mumps are now rare in developed countries. Yet, hardly more than a generation ago these diseases, which now seem as exotic to most people as the bubonic plague, were common in almost every American household. All are serious diseases that cause not only suffering, but also brain damage and death, among infants and children.

To get a sense of how dangerous the diseases still are, consider that in 2013, an estimated 145,700 people died—sixteen every hour—from measles alone. Nearly all these deaths were of children under five in countries where vaccinations are not routine. But while measles is still one of the leading causes of death for young children, it no longer causes 2.6 million deaths a year, as it did in 1980, before widespread vaccination for the disease globally.

Indeed, before national adoption of the measles vaccine in the 1960s, the United States saw three to four million cases each year, causing five hundred deaths annually, and many more cases of permanent brain damage and deafness. To take an even more striking example, more than 15,000 Americans died from diphtheria in 1921, a death toll that prompted a widespread vaccination effort later that decade. As a result, the infection rate plummeted and only one case of diphtheria has been reported in the United States since 2004. In more recent history, an epidemic of rubella (German measles) killed 2,000 babies and caused 11,000 miscarriages in 1964–1965. As a result of another vaccination effort, the number of annual rubella cases had dropped to nine by 2012.

The importance of immunization to individuals is obvious, but having a high percentage of the population vaccinated has a general benefit as well. Newborn infants, as well as children and adults who have compromised immune systems because of certain illnesses (e.g., HIV infection) or treatments (e.g., chemotherapy), cannot be vaccinated because their bodies may not be able to respond by developing the proper immunity. They depend on the immunity of those around them to protect them.

The greater the percentage of people in a population who are immunized against a given disease, the less likely it is that an infectious agent will establish itself within the population and threaten the lives of those who are most vulnerable. This phenomenon is known to immunologists as *herd immunity*.

Herd Immunity

Herd immunity serves as a barrier to protect a population from the ravages of infectious diseases. The higher the percentage of people inoculated, the stronger the barrier. When the percentage starts to decline, the barrier grows weaker and more porous. Those who are most susceptible to the disease have a greater likelihood of becoming its victims.

The story of what happened with pertussis (whooping cough) in Japan in the 1970s is a prime example of what occurs when the barrier weakens. By 1974, Japan had nearly eliminated pertussis through a vaccination

program. That year, an estimated 80 percent of Japanese children received the pertussis vaccine, and there were only 393 cases of pertussis reported in the entire country, with no associated deaths. During the next two years, however, fears spread about adverse reactions to the vaccine and rumors emerged that it was no longer necessary. By 1976 only 10 percent of Japanese infants were being vaccinated for pertussis, and in 1979 the country suffered a major outbreak of the disease. There were more than 13,000 cases of pertussis that year, and 41 deaths. When Japanese doctors began using a different type of vaccine (with potentially fewer side effects), vaccination rates rose again, and by the mid-1980s pertussis cases had dropped back to their pre-epidemic levels. A similar epidemic of polio broke out in Nigeria in the mid-2000s after vaccination rates dropped below the herd-immunity threshold. The disease spread to other countries, and led to a significant loss of life and permanent disability for thousands of people.

Public health officials in the United States have long recognized the importance of herd immunity to the well-being of the country, and it has not been left to voluntary decisions by individuals. All states have laws requiring that children be vaccinated before they are enrolled in school, and more than 77 percent of children are immunized by their first day. The rewards are obvious. The CDC estimates that vaccinating all U.S. children born in a given year from birth to adolescence saves 33,000 lives, prevents fourteen million infections, and saves $10 billion in medical costs. (On a global scale, the World Health Organization reports that vaccines prevent an estimated six million deaths every year.)

The laws requiring vaccination are not ironclad, however. In the United States, physicians can issue waivers for children with compromised immune systems, and forty-eight states grant parents waivers to childhood vaccinations when they object on religious grounds. (Seventeen states permit parents to seek waivers on personal philosophical grounds.) In all, it has been estimated that about 6 percent of U.S. children enter school unvaccinated on a waiver of some sort: 1 percent medical and 5 percent religious or "philosophical." Getting a "personal belief" waiver often requires little or no effort or evidence beyond signing a form, although some states, such as California and Oregon, have recently made them more difficult to obtain.

Parents who believe that vaccines are likely to cause harm to their children have caused a sharp decline in the inoculation rate during recent years. Quite often, their fear is based on the belief that vaccines are responsible for the reported increase in autism. Hence, they believe their children should not be vaccinated and that other parents should not be required to vaccinate their children either.

Parents who decide not to vaccinate their child must depend on herd immunity for their child's protection. Sometimes, however, this defense fails disastrously. Take for instance the case of Kelly Lacek, as discussed in *Time* magazine in 2008. Lacek decided to stop vaccinating her two-month-old son Matthew when her chiropractor expressed doubts about the safety of thimerosal vaccines.

All was well until Matthew turned three. Lacek returned home to find him suffering from a high fever and struggling to breathe. Physicians at the ER were puzzled, until one experienced physician asked Lacek if Matthew had been fully vaccinated.

It turned out that Matthew had been infected with *Haemophilus-b*, a bacterium that produces fever and a swelling of the tissues of the throat, which makes breathing difficult. Hib also causes meningitis, a brain infection that, untreated, can lead to death. Indeed, before the widespread adoption of the Hib

vaccine, about 20,000 American children got the disease each year and between 600 and 1,200 of those died of it. Fortunately, Matthew survived, and his mother made sure that he and his siblings received all recommended immunizations.

Parents' Perception of Best Interest

Parents, with rare exceptions, want to do what is in the best interest of their children. There is no reason to believe that parents who refuse to vaccinate their children on the basis of their beliefs about the risk posed by vaccines or their religious beliefs are acting in bad faith. They believe they are entitled to make decisions about the welfare of their children and some feel that it is a violation of their rights for the state to order them to take measures they believe are wrong.

This is a view ordinarily supported by society. We leave it up to parents to decide how much time their children spend online, whether they get the shoes they want, and whether they have to eat their spinach. We expect parents to follow the "best interest" principle in making decisions about children, and we usually allow parents to exercise their judgment about what counts as their child's best interest.

The view becomes problematic, however, when the beliefs of the parents conflict with standards generally accepted within the society. If parents believe, for example, that their child will not die if they recite a certain incantation while plunging a knife into his chest, we try to prevent that from happening. The parents may not be mentally ill, but their beliefs cannot be justified in terms of accepted standards of evidence, and society has an obligation to protect the child.

The situation becomes especially problematic when the religious beliefs of the parents are shared by a significant number of people, yet those beliefs are at odds with what society believes to be in the best interest of the child. These conflicts occur, for the most part, with respect to not seeking medical treatment for an ailing child. Although our society generally supports religious freedom, it also supports the view that a child's best interest should be served according to society's accepted standards. Hence, such conflicts will continue to arise, unless we decide that one should always take precedence over the other.

Another sort of problem arises when the decisions of parents affect the welfare of society. This is what happens when parents refuse to have their children immunized. The drop in the rate of immunizations, as in the examples of Japan and Nigeria, weakens herd immunity and, as a consequence, the barrier between infectious diseases and the most vulnerable population in the society—the youngest, the oldest, and many of the sickest. Not having one's child immunized thus has a consequence for others, as well as for the child.

Major outbreaks of infectious diseases in the United States in recent years have been traced to the antivaccination movement. In December 2014, a major measles outbreak originated with a single visitor to Disneyland in southern California, then raced through seven states and to two foreign countries, infecting 147 people. Research published in *JAMA Pediatrics* later determined that the outbreak was made possible only by vaccination rates between 86 and 50 percent in the relevant communities. In 2014, the number of measles cases hit a twenty-year high, with 85 percent of the cases occurring in people who were unvaccinated for religious, personal, or philosophical reasons. In 2010, a massive whooping cough outbreak occurred in California that killed 10 children and involved 9,000 cases (the most since 1947). Subsequent epidemiological research revealed that most cases were clustered around families who had sought legal exemptions from vaccinating their children,

and spread from there across the state and, indeed, to the rest of the country. There is even evidence that fears about vaccines have started to impact standard childhood injections that are not even vaccines.

In 2014, physicians in Tennessee reported an unusually high number of cases of "vitamin K deficiency bleeding," a rare but highly dangerous condition that can cause brain damage or death from bleeding in the brain. It occurs due to a deficiency of the blood coagulant vitamin K, which can occur in infants who are exclusively breast-fed. Since 1961, most infants have received nearly 100-percent effective protection from this problem with one standard injection of vitamin K after birth. But many websites that warn parents against the dangers of vaccines have also started to attack vitamin K injections, often because of the trauma supposedly caused to a newborn by receiving any injection. Many of these sites have even suggested that the injection also causes autism, although it is unclear what substance in the vitamin K shot would be responsible for this. Initial research from the CDC has found significant numbers of parents leaving hospitals and birthing centers after refusing vitamin K injections for their newborns.

It seems clear that the more parents refuse vaccinations and other standard childhood public health measures, the more likely it is that there will be an increase in the number of cases of infectious diseases and other childhood medical problems. This means more death, suffering, and disability that could have been avoided.

Whose Choice?

Should parents always be free to simply decide whether vaccinations are in the best interest of their children, as they are in many states? As we saw above, it may be reasonable to conclude that parents who reject vaccination are not acting in their children's best interest, as judged by the accepted standards (scientific and medical) of society. Further, there is substantial evidence that such parents do not only put their own children at risk; they also put the broader society at risk, particularly its most vulnerable members.

In 1905, the U.S. Supreme Court, in *Jacobson v. Massachusetts*, addressed the issue of whether the state's requirement that everyone be vaccinated for smallpox violated a person's "inherent right" to "care for his own body and health in such way as seems to him best." (The plaintiff, a minister living in Cambridge, Massachusetts, had refused to pay a five-dollar fine for refusing to be vaccinated against smallpox.) The Court pointed out that, in general, the state has the right to impose burdens and restraints on citizens for the good of all. Jacobson, the Court ruled, could not expect to enjoy the benefits of living in a community in which people have been vaccinated without accepting the risks of vaccination himself. What's more, even if some scientists questioned the efficacy of vaccination, the legislature had the right to adopt and enforce one of the competing scientific views.

With respect to beliefs about vaccination and autism, we are in a situation similar to that in the *Jacobson* case: If we prize the right of parents to make decisions about their child on the basis of their beliefs about the child's best interest, then we must pay a double price. We must accept that, on the basis of the knowledge we have, the child will run a serious risk of dying from an infectious disease that could have been prevented. We must also accept that the herd immunity protecting us from a number of deadly diseases will be reduced, and may reach a critical tipping point.

Envoi

On March 1, 2010, the journal *Pediatrics* reported the results of a survey of 1,500 parents of children ages 17 or younger. Despite all evidence to the contrary, one out of four parents say they think some vaccines cause autism in healthy children. Nearly one in eight have refused at least one recommended vaccination. A similar study conducted in 2014 found that 33 percent of parents with children under 18 believed that "vaccines cause autism." This trend runs counter to the fact that the scientific evidence has overwhelmingly supported the opposite conclusion.

The controversy over vaccination will continue, but the debate will not be over science. The hundreds of studies that have found no causal link between autism and vaccinations make it one of the most thoroughly examined questions in contemporary medicine. The debate that bioethicists and public health officials now face is about how our society should approach parents who continue to believe that the causal link is real and refuse to vaccinate their children.

CASE PRESENTATION
Faith and Medicine: Suffer the Little Children?

In March 2008, eleven-year-old Kara Neumann began to feel tired and sick, then became progressively weaker. She lost her ability to walk, and eventually she could no longer speak. "Kara laid down and was unable to move her mouth," the police report later said. She was so ill that she "merely made moaning sounds and moved her eyes back and forth."

Kara's parents, Lelani and Dale Neumann, were worried about their daughter and prayed for her recovery.

They did not, however, call a doctor or take Kara to a hospital ER for treatment. The Neumanns adhered to the doctrines of an online Christian fellowship called Unleavened Bread Ministries. The group's website presents stories of healing through faith and prayer alone. According to these testimonies, all diseases, whether of people or animals, can be cured by prayer and divine intervention. "Jesus never sent anyone to a doctor or hospital," reads an essay by Pastor Bob, one of the site's regular contributors. "Jesus offered healing by one means only! Healing was by faith."

Kara's aunt in California did not share the Neumanns' belief that faith and prayer could cure their daughter. When she learned from them how sick Kara was and that they intended to do no more than pray for her, she phoned the sheriff's department in the Neumanns' hometown of Wenton, Wisconsin, and implored them to intervene to save Kara's life. The department dispatched an ambulance to the Neumanns' house and Kara was rushed to the nearest hospital, where she was pronounced dead on arrival.

The medical examiner later determined that Kara died from ketoacidosis, the result of undiagnosed and untreated type 1 (juvenile-onset) diabetes. The islet cells in her pancreas had failed to produce the hormone insulin in sufficient quantities, and as a result, glucose couldn't enter muscle cells to be converted into energy. Needing energy, her body then began to break down fats, producing toxic fatty acids known as ketones. Ketoacidosis is characterized by severe dehydration and nausea, followed by the impairment of muscle, lung, and heart function. The last stage is irreversible coma and death.

Thousands of children each year are diagnosed with type 1 diabetes, and the overwhelming majority are successfully treated with diet, exercise, and insulin injections. Kara was examined by a doctor when she was three, but that had been her last visit. Her death could almost certainly have been prevented by appropriate medical care.

Number of Cases

Rita Swan, the director of an organization called Children's Health Care Is a Legal Duty, estimates that in the last twenty-five years about three hundred children have died because their parents failed to obtain medical treatment for them for religious reasons. (Swan's own sixteen-month-old son died after she failed to take him to be treated for what turned out to be meningitis. This led her to renounce her Christian Science upbringing and become an advocate for children's health care.) A majority of U.S. states have laws that exempt parents from child abuse and neglect laws if they withhold medical treatment from their children due to their belief in healing by faith or in the unreality of disease.

Hardly a year passes without a case in which a child dies or is seriously injured because parents reject standard medical treatments for religious reasons. Since 2011, over twelve children in Idaho whose parents belong to a faith-healing church called Followers of Christ have died from medically untreated (but highly treatable) illnesses such as sepsis, pneumonia, and complications from food poisoning. (Later, a local television station launched an investigation after discovering that more than a quarter of the recent graves in the nearby cemetery belonged to children under 18.) In 2012–2013, two Oregon children whose parents belonged to a similar faith-healing group called Church of the First Born died of treatable illnesses: type 1 diabetes in one case and an infected burst appendix in the other. Similar deaths of children have been caused in recent years by such conditions as untreated urinary tract infections and bronchial pneumonia. In a famous case in 2009, Colleen Hauser fled her home in Minnesota with her son Daniel so that he wouldn't have to submit to court-ordered chemotherapy for Hodgkin's lymphoma. Daniel had a cancerous tumor in his chest that was likely to be fatal without standard treatment, but Colleen Hauser and her husband wanted Daniel to have natural healing treatments based on American Indian traditions. A warrant was issued for Colleen Hauser's arrest, but she eventually returned home and allowed Daniel to be treated at a Minneapolis hospital.

The American Academy of Pediatrics is one of several groups that have campaigned to eliminate religious exceptions from child-protection laws. Some states, such as Oregon, have eliminated spiritual treatment as a defense against homicide charges. Others, such as Idaho, still have broad religious exemption laws that protect parents in groups such as the Followers of Christ from being prosecuted for manslaughter, negligent homicide, capital murder, or child abuse in the preventable deaths of their children. Most of these laws were enacted in the 1970s, partly as a result of lobbying efforts by the Church of

Christ, Scientist, one of the oldest and most influential groups that advocate healing through prayer. The Christian Science church and its offshoots have also generated some of the most controversial and high-profile cases in which children have died or suffered severe medical consequences after their parents failed to provide them with medical care.

The Death of Robyn Twitchell

The case of Robyn Twitchell began in Boston in April of 1986. One night after eating dinner, two-year-old Robyn began crying, which soon escalated to hours of vomiting and screaming. Because both Robyn's parents, David and Ginger Twitchell, were devout Christian Scientists, their approach to these alarming symptoms differed from that of many other religious Americans. The tenets of Christian Science hold that disease has no physical reality but is instead an illusory "error" caused by a materialist view of the world. Because God is a complete being and the ultimate reality, disease is an indication of distance in one's relationship with God. To restore this relationship, healing must be mental and spiritual. It seeks to break down the fears, misperceptions, and disordered thinking that lead to illness. The role of a Christian Science practitioner is to employ teaching, discussion, and prayer to assist someone suffering from an illness to discover its spiritual source. While Christian Scientists are not forbidden from seeking medical attention in emergencies, doing so is seen to undermine the process of spiritual healing and is often regarded as a failure of faith.

Acting on the basis of these beliefs, the Twitchells responded to their son's symptoms by calling in Nancy Calkins, a Christian Science practitioner. Calkins prayed for Robyn and sang hymns, but although she visited him three times during the next five days, he showed little sign of getting better. A Christian Scientist nurse was brought in to help feed and bathe Robyn, and on her chart she noted that he was still vomiting and described him as "listless at times, rejecting all food, and moaning in pain." On April 8, 1986, Robyn began to have spasms and his eyes rolled up into his head. He finally lost consciousness and died later that evening.

Doctors later found that Robyn had died of a bowel obstruction that could have been easily treated by medicine

and surgery. Medical experts determined that Robyn would not have died had his parents sought medical attention for him.

The Twitchell Trial

After Robyn's death, David and Ginger Twitchell were charged with involuntary manslaughter. In a trial lasting two months, the prosecution and defense both claimed that important rights had been violated. The Twitchells' attorneys appealed, in particular, to the First Amendment guarantee of the free exercise of religion and claimed that the state was attempting to deny them this right.

Prosecutors responded by pointing out that courts have repeatedly held that not all religious practices are protected. Laws against polygamy and laws requiring vaccinations or blood transfusions for minors, for example, have all been held to be constitutional.

The prosecutors also claimed that Robyn's rights had been violated by his parents' failure to seek care for him as required by law. They cited the 1923 Supreme Court ruling in *Prince v. Massachusetts*, which held that "Parents may be free to become martyrs of themselves, but it does not follow they are free to make martyrs of their children."

The jury found the Twitchells guilty of manslaughter, and the judge sentenced them to ten years' probation. John Kiernan, the prosecutor, had not asked for a jail sentence. "The intent of our recommendation was to protect the other Twitchell children," Kiernan said in an interview. As a condition of their probation, Judge Sandra Hamlin instructed the Twitchells that they must seek appropriate medical care for their three children if they showed signs of needing it, and that they must take them to a physician for regular checkups.

While the Twitchells were spared the twenty years in prison that could have followed their manslaughter conviction, they still rejected the state's right to prosecute them. "This has been a prosecution against our faith," David Twitchell said. (On another occasion, however, David Twitchell said of his son Robyn that "if medicine could have saved him, I wish I had turned to it.") The Christian Science church also criticized the decision, and a spokesman said it was not possible to combine spiritual and medical healing as the ruling required. "They're trying to prosecute out of existence this method of treatment," he concluded.

The Twitchell case directly challenged the Christian Science church in the city where it is based, and it was first thought to represent a kind of watershed in the prosecution of parents who withhold medical care from their children. "The message has been sent," John Kiernan said after the Twitchells were sentenced. "Every parent of whatever religious belief or persuasion is obligated to include medical care in taking care of his child." In recent decades, cases similar to the Twitchells' have come to light across the country, and Christian Science parents have been convicted of involuntary manslaughter, felony child abuse, or child endangerment in states such as California, Arizona, and Florida. Nevertheless, none of these parents have served jail time, and even the Twitchells' conviction was later overturned on technical legal grounds.

At the same time, parents belonging to smaller religious groups such as the Church of the First Born, Faith Assembly, and True Followers of Christ have been convicted and imprisoned for failing to provide their children with medical care. Critics claim Christian Scientists have been treated more leniently than members of these fundamentalist groups because a high proportion of Christian Scientists are middle to upper-middle class and occupy influential positions in business, government, and the law. They also point to the influence of the Christian Science church in the language and passage of numerous spiritual healing exemptions to state laws.

Envoi

The case of Lelani and Dale Neumann (discussed above) seems to conform to the pattern by which members of smaller fundamentalist faith-healing organizations fare worse in the legal system than Christian Scientists. In August of 2009, they were each convicted of second-degree reckless homicide. They were sentenced to serve thirty days in jail each year for the next six years and were placed on ten years' probation. In July of 2013, the Wisconsin Supreme Court upheld their convictions.

Nevertheless, the Neumanns could have received a maximum prison term of twenty-five years for their actions. The prosecutor in their case only asked for a three-year sentence. Since 1982, more than fifty convictions have been handed down by courts in cases in which children have died because medical care was withheld for religious reasons, but most are still overturned on appeal or result in probation rather than jail time. This contrasts with the tough sentences that are regularly handed out to parents convicted of causing their children's deaths for nonreligious reasons. As critics point out, many of these parents are similarly "well-intentioned," in that they sincerely believe that withholding medical care or food, or enacting severe corporal punishments, are in their children's long-term best interests. The differential outcomes between these cases of parental abuse or neglect and those involving religiously motivated parents reflects the central—and often unresolved—role that religion still plays in contemporary American society.

SOCIAL CONTEXT
For Their Own Good: Placebos and Paternalism

Jane Hunter (as we will call her) had been exhausted for eight months. She was constantly fatigued, and she felt so tired most mornings that it was all she could do to get out of bed. Standing up, she often felt lightheaded and dazed, and the exertion of cooking breakfast would leave her worn out for hours. Her throat was sore much of the time and her lymph nodes were swollen—but apart from a nasty virus last year, she didn't seem to have caught anything. Before the onset of her illness, Jane had been a physically active young professional, but now she was unable to complete the most basic exercise routine. She was considering taking a leave of absence from her job because each day at work left her exhausted, with debilitating pain in her muscles.

Jane had always been stoic about her health and rarely complained about problems, but she had been to see Jerrold Chang, her primary care physician, three times during the past six months. He had examined her and ordered a variety of tests to rule out diabetes, lupus, lung cancer, kidney disease, leukemia, and other sorts of blood disorders. All the tests came back negative.

"I can't find anything wrong with you using standard measurements," Chang said. "But I am still concerned about your symptoms. I think you might have something called systematic exertion intolerance disease, or SEID."

"I've never heard of that." Jane felt alarmed. "How serious is it?"

"It's also known as chronic fatigue syndrome," Dr. Chang said. "Research has shown it to be a serious disease that afflicts as many as 2.5 million Americans. The most common symptoms are extreme fatigue after even minor exertion, unrefreshing sleep, headaches, muscle aches, and faintness or weakness when standing up. Your case seems pretty classic."

"I've heard of chronic fatigue syndrome," Jane said. "Is there anything you can do to treat it?"

"To be honest, SEID is still poorly understood and there is no FDA-approved treatment for it. But I'd like you to see a colleague of mine for a second opinion. Her name is Ellen Deutch and she's a rheumatologist, which means she focuses on inflammatory diseases."

Jane's symptoms didn't improve during the four weeks she had to wait before she was able to see Dr. Deutch. When she was finally able to tell her story, Deutch gave her another physical exam. She explained to Jane that she was checking in particular to see if Jane's thyroid had any nodules. Deutch then looked at the laboratory results from the numerous tests Dr. Chang had ordered.

"I agree with Dr. Chang that you most likely have SEID," Deutch told her. "I don't see a reason to perform any more tests at the moment, but I would like you to make an appointment to return in a month so I can check on your progress."

"You aren't going to give me any drugs or anything?" Jane was surprised and disappointed. She had hoped that her new doctor would be able to help her escape from the prison of fatigue and pain her life had become.

Dr. Deutch thought for a moment. "We can try something that might help. I'm going to give you some tablets that are a combination of dextrose and a small amount of sodium chloride. Some people with your condition have found them helpful." Deutch began writing on a prescription pad. "I want you to take two tablets three times a day, then let me know next time if you think they are helping."

Traditional Practice

Scenes similar to the one just described are played out in the consulting rooms of physicians every day. Patients with intractable conditions or mysterious symptoms go to their doctors and ask them for help. Their doctors examine them thoroughly, order a battery of tests, but find no treatable condition. Yet hoping to help their patients feel better, the doctors prescribe something anyway.

The tablets Dr. Deutch prescribed for Jane are nothing but sugar mixed with a trace of table salt. They cannot be categorized as an active drug and are completely harmless. Jane would probably get a similar dose of the contents of the tablets by eating a small candy bar. In other words, Deutsch has prescribed a *placebo*, with the hope that it may ameliorate Jane's symptoms.

The word *placebo* is Latin for "I shall please." The use of placebos in medicine dates back at least to the eighteenth-century and can be seen to evolve out of patients' (not unreasonable) expectation that their doctors do something or prescribe something to improve their conditions. Before the modern era, this might have meant prescribing a particular diet, bleeding the patient, or administering enemas. These procedures were part of legitimate medical practice based on accepted theory. (The theory dominant in the West for about two thousand years was that disease results from an imbalance in four humors—blood, phlegm, black bile, and yellow bile—and the aim of treatment was to restore the balance.)

But even if a doctor did not know how to treat a mysterious illness or believed nothing was actually wrong, many patients still expected to be treated. Thus, the doctor might prescribe an emetic, such as *nux vomica*, or a laxative, such as syrup of figs, just to satisfy the patient. Such substances have definite and often unpleasant effects, however, so many physicians preferred to give their patients a box of pills made from sugar or bread dough. These pills would be harmless, produce no side effects, and assure the patient that the doctor was taking the medical complaint seriously.

Perhaps most strikingly, the pills and other placebo treatments would also often work. As many later studies would verify, placebos can have a dramatic effect on a broad range of conditions, sometimes with majorities of patients experiencing significant symptom relief. Most traditional physicians learned during apprenticeship that this "placebo effect" was often successful in treating patients with a wide range of illnesses. Hence, prescribing placebos became a standard part of medical practice, both because of its effectiveness and also because it helped doctors deal with challenging cases.

Tradition Challenged

Starting in the 1960s and the 1970s, many of the customary practices of physicians were called into question. In particular, critics challenged the prevalence in medicine of *paternalism*—policies or practices by which a person's autonomy or liberty is constrained by those in authority, supposedly for the person's own good. Until the 1960s, for example, it was common for a doctor not to tell a patient that she had cancer, based on the assumption that such knowledge would be harmful. Critics asked what gave the doctor the right to withhold such information. Shouldn't a patient have the right to make informed decisions about what is going on in her body? For that matter, why should the doctor decide whether or how a patient should be treated? Shouldn't those decisions be left up to the patient? Such questions reflected the growth of the doctrine of *informed consent*, or the idea that physicians must get patients' uncoerced permission for proposed medical interventions and inform them about possible consequences and alternative options, including no medical intervention at all.

Informed consent was not a new idea in medical practice, but most often it was sought in a merely formal fashion and used as a means to protect surgeons from lawsuits. During the 1960s and 1970s, however, in response to pressure from patient advocates and ethicists, the medical community began to acknowledge the importance of patient autonomy. This meant recognizing that informed consent is essential to protecting autonomy in cases in which a patient's best interest is concerned. On this model, the doctor informs and advises, but it is the patient who makes the final decision about whether to accept a treatment.

One consequence of incorporating informed consent and patient autonomy into medical practice was that physicians had to change many of their traditional patterns of behavior. Patients could no longer be kept in ignorance "for their own good." They had to be provided with information so that they could participate in making decisions directly affecting them.

Doctor and patient are increasingly seen as partners working together in the best interest of the patient. This situation requires *transparency* on the part of both patient and doctor. The patient shouldn't hide anything from his doctor, because the doctor needs reliable information to make a diagnosis and decide what to recommend as the best course of treatment. The doctor shouldn't hide anything from her patient, because the patient needs reliable information to exercise his autonomy and make a decision about what treatments he is willing to accept. Both effective medical practice and informed consent require trust and openness.

The transparency required by the doctor–patient relationship seems prima facie incompatible with the use of placebos. It is easy to see why prescribing placebos is typically seen as a deceptive practice. In such cases, a doctor who tells her patient, "You have a medical problem and this drug can be effective in treating it," is asserting something she believes to be fully or partially untrue. If the patient doesn't have a problem that fits into a recognized diagnostic category, doesn't the patient have a right to know this? And if the patient, like Jane, has a poorly understood illness for which there is no established treatment, doesn't he or she have a right to know that, rather than being manipulated with a sugar pill?

Placebos, in the view of many, are also relics of a time when medicine employed few genuinely effective drugs. This era extended well into the twentieth century, when thousands of drugs and compounds that had not been tested for effectiveness or safety were still listed in the pharmacopoeia and prescribed by doctors. The FDA has been charged since 1938 with ensuring the safety and effectiveness of drugs before they are allowed on the market, although many drugs in use have still not been thoroughly tested. For many critics, placebos are a

remnant of the days when a doctor might give his patients an alcohol- or turpentine-based "snake oil" rather than an effective and reliable medication. On this view, placebos undercut our commitment to a scientific and evidence-based medicine that is accessible to patients and physicians alike. They evoke the paternalism of an era in which physicians would dismiss patients with acronyms such as "LOL-NAD" ("a little old lady in no apparent distress") and send them away with a prescription for a two-week course of sugar pills.

Placebos in Practice

Despite the new emphasis on transparency in the doctor–patient relationship, a 2008 survey of U.S. physicians in the specialties of internal medicine and rheumatology showed that about half (46%–58%, depending on the phrasing of the question) regularly prescribe placebo treatments and most (62%) believe that the practice is ethically permissible.

Contemporary physicians are less likely to prescribe such traditional placebos as sugar pills or saline (saltwater) solutions, however. (Jane's rheumatologist would have to contend with the fact that most pharmacies no longer compound drugs to order.) Rather, most (41%) give their patients analgesics (aspirin or acetaminophen, for example) or vitamins (38%) as placebo treatments. A few (13%) prescribe antibiotics or sedatives. Whatever placebo they prescribe, most physicians (68%) accompany it with a statement such as "This is a potentially beneficial medicine not typically used for your condition." Only rarely (5%) do doctors disclose to patients that the treatment they are prescribing is a placebo.

The practice of using placebos isn't confined to U.S. physicians. Another survey showed that 86 percent of general practitioners in Denmark use placebos, and surveys in

Sweden, Israel, New Zealand, and the United Kingdom produced similar results.

As we noted above, one of the primary reasons that physicians use placebos is because they can be surprisingly effective. Various studies have shown that a significant number of patients (perhaps as many as 12%–20%) gain medical benefit from whatever treatment they receive, and in some studies large majorities of patients have experienced symptom relief as a result of placebos. (It is for this reason that double-blind clinical trials with a large number of patients have become the standard for determining the effectiveness of a drug.) Thus, when a doctor gives a placebo to a patient with a vague or mysterious complaint and no clear evidence of a specific, treatable disease, the placebo has a reasonable chance of benefiting the patient.

One common misperception of the placebo effect is that it indicates that patients who benefit from it were merely "imagining" their original symptoms, which were then dispelled by the psychological effect of the placebo. This hypothesis was discredited by several studies that demonstrated that the pain-relieving effect of placebos could be effectively blocked by the administration of naxolone, an opiate antagonist. This result indicated both that the original pain was real and that in these cases the "placebo effect" involved the production of the body's natural painkillers.

There can be no doubt that a doctor who prescribes a placebo is not honoring the presumed commitment to transparency. However, the doctor may be benefiting the patient. If the primary duty of the physician is to provide such benefit and to relieve the patient's suffering, then the case can be made that the physician is sometimes justified in setting aside or violating the implicit commitment to transparency. Paternalism may be justified in these situations.

It is harder, however, to make the case for physicians who prescribe so-called "active" placebos—that is, drugs given as placebos that have significant pharmacological consequences. Sugar pills are harmless, but people may have serious and potentially fatal allergic reactions to antibiotics. Similarly, sedatives may produce disturbed sleep, arrhythmias, or life-threatening respiratory distress. Physicians who prescribe active placebos may be hard-pressed to justify putting their patients at risk when the drugs they prescribe have, by definition, no medically established connection to their patients' symptoms.

Accepting the Limits of Medicine

The routine use of placebos in medical practice always raises ethical questions. Prescribing a placebo can be a physician's way of getting rid of a troublesome patient whose problem she can't solve. In the worst case, it can be a physician's way of shirking responsibility for a difficult diagnosis or helping a patient understand that what is bothering him is probably not the symptom of a disease. In the best case, prescribing a placebo can be the physician's way of relieving a patient's distress and providing real medical benefit without causing harm.

Physicians prescribe placebos, in part, because they wish to meet their patients' expectations that they do something to help. Despite our society's rejection of paternalistic authority in medicine, both patients and physicians often consider it unacceptable for a doctor to admit that he can't diagnose a patient's symptoms or do something about them. (Traditionally and even today, "doing something" has often been construed to mean prescribing a drug. This is one reason antibiotics have been widely overprescribed in many industrialized countries.)

But what patients should most appropriately expect from their physicians is an informed judgment about their complaint and symptoms—and an honest acknowledgement that those judgments are limited and fallible. If both patients and physicians were able to accept the reality that sometimes medicine has nothing to offer to treat difficult and intractable conditions, then physicians would likely be less inclined to prescribe placebos.

SOCIAL CONTEXT

The Obesity Epidemic: Autonomy versus Public Health

There is broad consensus among medical researchers and clinicians that obesity is one of the most serious threats to public health in the United States and across the globe. Obesity is causally associated with the following disorders: type 2 diabetes, hypertension, heart disease, cancer, stroke, kidney failure, and blindness, not to mention slow-to-heal wounds that can lead to foot and leg amputations. Someone with a body mass index (BMI) of 30 or more is, by definition, obese. (BMI is the ratio of height to weight. Thus, someone who is six feet tall is obese when he reaches 221 pounds; someone five feet, six inches tall is obese when she reaches 186 pounds.) As the number of obese people in the population rises, the number of diseases caused by obesity also rises, and each disease is associated with high medical costs, disability, and death.

A Heavy Toll

The human cost of obesity is particularly dramatic in the United States and other industrialized nations. A 2005 *New England Journal of Medicine* study identified obesity as the primary cause of a trend by which, for the first time in America's history, life expectancy is growing shorter rather than longer. A 2009 study of nearly 900,000 individuals from North America and Western Europe found that obesity takes two to four years off of the average life span and that being severely obese (a BMI above 40) reduces

life span by eight to ten years. A 2014 analysis of twenty health studies found that obesity costs individuals as much as fourteen years of life.

Researchers from Columbia University's Mailman School of Public Health estimate that obesity is responsible for 18 percent of the deaths of Americans aged 40 to 85, and many experts think obesity will soon overtake or already has overtaken tobacco as the leading cause of preventable death in the United States. (Obesity already accounts for more deaths than high cholesterol and alcohol abuse, not to mention suicide and homicide.) The number of cases of disability and sickness associated with obesity is estimated to be several times greater than the hundreds of thousands of deaths in America that are caused by obesity each year.

As disheartening as these statistics are, many experts think that the situation is likely to get worse before it gets better, mostly due to high levels of childhood obesity. "A 5-year-old growing up today is living in an environment where obesity is much more the norm than was the case for a 5-year-old a generation or two ago," said Bruce Link, one of the Columbia researchers. "Drink sizes are bigger, clothes are bigger, and greater numbers of a child's peers are obese. . . . And once someone is obese, it is very difficult to undo. So it stands to reason that we won't see the worst of the epidemic until the current generation of children grows old."

Good News and Bad News

The past decade has produced one piece of good news with regard to obesity in the United States: the average rate of obesity in the United States appears to have remained more or less constant since 2005. This obesity "plateau" initially gave public health experts hope that increased nutritional awareness had actually restrained Americans' consumption of high-fat, high-calorie foods. Nevertheless, Americans' waistlines continued to expand during the same period and the overall obesity rate remains extremely high, especially compared to that of previous generations. More than 34 percent of adults are now obese—a percentage that has doubled since 1980. During the same period, the percentage of obese children tripled, to reach 17 percent.

While the average rate of obesity may have leveled off in the United States, the numbers remain starkly different for different segments of the population. For example, children whose adult head of household didn't complete high school were twice as likely to be obese as those whose adult head of household completed college. In addition, African Americans and Hispanic Americans have significantly higher rates of obesity (47.8 and 42.5 percent, respectively), compared with European Americans (32.6 percent) and Asian Americans (10.8 percent). Perhaps the most striking differences with regard to obesity are geographic, with southern and midwestern states reporting obesity rates well over 30 percent, while coastal and mountain states reporting significantly lower obesity rates. Projections by the Trust for America's Health indicate that many states will have majority-obese populations by 2030.

Soaring Costs

The costs of caring for America's obese population are steep, with as much as $147 billion estimated for 2008 alone, representing almost 10 percent of all medical spending. Other estimates have placed the cost of American obesity even higher. The American Diabetes Association estimates that diabetes costs Americans $245 billion a year, the vast majority of it for the type 2 diabetes commonly triggered by obesity and inactivity.

Diabetes is one of the most visible manifestations of the obesity epidemic. Almost 30 million adults and children (9 percent of the population) have diabetes, and 1.7 million new cases are diagnosed each year. Every twenty-four hours, the disease causes 48 people go blind, 120 to develop end-stage kidney disease, and 238 to lose limbs to diabetes-related amputations. The disease kills about 70,000 Americans a year, more than the combined death toll from AIDS and breast cancer. About 95 percent of diagnosed cases of diabetes are type 2. Although genetic factors clearly dispose some people toward developing diabetes, the immediate triggers for the disease are obesity and inactivity—and 85 percent of people with type 2 diabetes are overweight or obese. Researchers hope that the discovery, in 2006, of a variant gene that increases the risk of developing diabetes will eventually allow those who have it to get tested and make lifestyle changes long before they develop the disease.

One of the challenges of diabetes care is that people can suffer from prediabetic conditions for seven to ten years before the disease is finally diagnosed, and by that time, significant damage may already be occurring in the patient's body. Numbness and tingling in the hands and feet may signal damage to the nervous system, bleeding in the retina can cause significant vision loss, poor circulation can produce lingering wounds that are prone to infection and tissue death. (About 70 percent of limb amputations are due to diabetes.) High blood pressure caused by the disease can damage the kidneys, requiring dialysis or a transplant.

Given that twenty-one million people are now being treated for diabetes, it is not surprising that the annual medical costs add up to $245 billion. Common per-patient charges include such items as the following: stroke care, $100,000; limb amputation, $45,000; end-stage kidney disease, $87,000. With high obesity rates causing an increase in the number of type 2 diabetics, the annual cost of care for this group of patients can be expected to soar.

Public Health or Private Choice

Public health advocates have long argued that if we could keep people from becoming obese, the costs of health care would decrease and people would live longer and healthier lives. But what would we have to do to reduce the incidence of obesity? And how far are we as a society prepared to go in regulating the weight of our citizens?

Many medical ethicists regard obesity as an urgent public health issue that should be addressed by government policy. One of their core arguments is that the diseases caused by obesity—not unlike the diseases caused by smoking—impose significant costs on society as a whole. The resources we spend coping with type 2 diabetes and other obesity-related illnesses might be better spent on prenatal care, on providing health care for the poor or uninsured, or on education or scientific research. By preventing obesity-related illnesses before they develop, we could reduce the need for urgent (and often uncompensated) care at hospitals and emergency rooms—care that currently drives up the price of health care for everyone. Therefore, society is justified in taking measures to keep people from becoming obese.

One of the most famous recent efforts to combat obesity through public policy was New York City mayor Michael Bloomberg's efforts to ban the sale of foods containing trans fats and to cap the portion sizes of sugar-sweetened drinks. In 2005, Bloomberg and the NYC city council succeeded in prohibiting city restaurants and vendors from selling foods with artificial trans fats, manufactured lipids that have been shown to cause heart disease and obesity. Despite complaints from restaurant associations, the policy was successful and has served as a model for municipalities across the country. Bloomberg's efforts to ban sugar-sweetened drinks larger than sixteen ounces, however, proved much more controversial.

In the rollout of the latter policy, Bloomberg presented research findings that sugary drinks represent the largest single source of increased calories in the American diet over the past forty years. He also pointed to dramatic increases in the size of soda containers and evidence that consumers don't reduce their overall caloric intake to compensate for consuming such large quantities of sugar. (A *British Journal of Medicine* study found that consuming just one soda a day increases a child's risk of being overweight by 55% and an adult's risk by 27%.) Noting that a majority of New York's adults and 40 percent of its K–8 students were obese or overweight, Bloomberg presented the sugary drinks portion cap as a commonsense public health measure, not unlike popular bans on smoking in bars, restaurants, and most parks.

But the soda industry—and many New Yorkers—didn't see it that way. In addition to a negative public relations campaign and lawsuits launched by PepsiCo Inc., the Coca-Cola Company, and the Dr. Pepper Snapple Group, the policy was also opposed by the New York State Conference of the NAACP and the Hispanic Federation (both of which, it should be noted, have strong ties to soda companies). In addition, many New Yorkers objected to the policy as an overreach by "Nanny Bloomberg" that interfered with their personal choices. Eventually, a state court agreed with them, arguing that the city had overstepped its regulatory authority by wading into "complex value judgments concerning personal autonomy and economics."

Did the soda portion cap compromise New Yorkers' autonomy any more than the trans fat ban—or, for that matter, any more than the extensive regulations about how and where they could smoke or purchase cigarettes? Many critics said the only difference was that in this case the city took on a more powerful industry, one whose products are not as unpopular as tobacco but also pose serious health risks. (A 2010 meta-analysis published by the American Diabetes Association found that drinking one to two sweetened beverages a day increased diabetes risk by 26%.) Other critics suggested that by banning—rather than steeply taxing—large-portion sugary drinks, Bloomberg had moved beyond the legitimate sphere of public health incentives and into shaky ethical territory.

Determining where an incentive for better lifestyle choices becomes a violation of personal autonomy is one of the most ambiguous and vexing questions in public health. Take, for example, a wellness pilot program for Medicaid patients introduced in 2007 by West Virginia—a state with some of the country's highest rates of smoking, obesity, diabetes, and heart disease. The program asked Medicaid recipients to sign a pledge to do their "best" to stay healthy, to attend "health improvement programs as directed," to go for regularly scheduled preventative screenings, to take the medicines as prescribed, and to go to an emergency room only for an event like a heart attack, stroke, or seizure. Those who stuck to the plan received "enhanced benefits" such as diabetes management, cardiac rehabilitation, mental health counseling, more covered prescriptions, and home-health visits from a nurse as needed. Those who did not or who refused to sign up received only the benefits mandated by the federal government. (Medicaid is a joint federal–state program.) They were not eligible for the advanced benefits and their prescriptions were limited to four a month.

Critics of the West Virginia program argued that in attempting to reward some for health care success, the state was punishing others for health care failure—perhaps those who needed the extra benefits the most. They charged that it violated fundamental obligations of health care professionals to promote patient welfare and respect patient autonomy. Others, including officials in the federal Centers for Medicare & Medicaid Services, asked whether it was appropriate for the government to define and promote healthy behaviors. Based on these and other concerns, the program was eventually phased out, leaving a host of unresolved questions about how far Americans are willing to "incentivize" government benefit programs.

Information and Autonomy

A less controversial approach to improving public health involves providing the public with accurate information about the health impacts of various behaviors and letting them make their own decisions about whether or not to continue them. The United States was the first country to require warning labels about the serious health risks of smoking cigarettes, despite protracted efforts by the tobacco industry to oppose or water down such labels. (Studies suggest that warning labels have contributed to substantial reductions in U.S. smoking rates.) As research accumulates regarding the serious health risks associated with sugar-sweetened beverages, it seems possible that the soda industry may be forced to accept labels on its products regarding associated risks of obesity, diabetes, and tooth decay. (Legislation requiring such labels was introduced in the California legislature in 2014.)

In recent years, consumer groups have also succeeded in securing federal policies that mandate far more detailed—and accurate—nutritional information on food packaging and restaurant menus than was previously required. Knowing that a bacon double cheeseburger, fries, and a large milk shake usually contains more than half the calories an average person should consume in a day may help consumers make healthier choices. Similarly, new FDA standards require that food makers stop using notoriously unrealistic serving sizes for their products and instead base nutritional information on typical consumption. (Frosted Flakes, for example, lists its serving size as ¾ cup [110 calories], but two cups [293 calories] is more likely to be an actual serving.)

Finally, public health advocates can turn to an obvious avenue for educating the public about obesity, exercise, and nutrition: the public schools. Since 2003, the Arkansas State Board of Education has required that schools provide parents with a (confidential) health evaluation for their children, in addition to an academic report card. The goal is that when the report is accompanied by nutritional counseling and information, children and their parents will be able to make informed choices to avoid childhood obesity. Local school districts in a number of states—California, Massachusetts, and Oregon among them—have initiated similar programs.

Perhaps the most important factor in avoiding obesity—regular exercise—can also be emphasized through public education. For decades, budget cuts at the state and local level have decreased the amount of physical activity in the school day, shortening or eliminating recess and PE classes. To help address this issue and the broader epidemic of childhood obesity, programs such as First Lady Michelle Obama's "Let's Move!" campaign have promoted physical education programs in public schools, along with healthier food in school lunches, and better nutritional labeling on vending machines and food packaging. While the voluntary aspects of the campaign have proved popular, such as inviting local chefs to schools to teach kids about nutrition and incorporating movement into classroom activities, the administration's new nutritional requirements for school lunches have generated partisan conflict in Washington. Republican critics charged the administration with making school lunches too bland and too small, while Democrats accused Republican legislators of classifying pizza tomato sauce as a "vegetable" at the behest of the frozen foods industry. The political scuffle is a reminder that almost every public health decision involves value judgments about how to define such concepts as *health*, *sickness*, and *freedom of choice*.

How Far Is Too Far?

Examples such as the soda portion cap and West Virginia's wellness program raise important questions about how far we would like our government to go in the name of protecting the public health. Was the Bloomberg administration justified in banning unhealthy trans fats from restaurant meals and attempting to limit soda container sizes? If we categorize this as an example of excessive government interference, how do we distinguish it from other examples—such as smoking bans and limits on drug and alcohol use—where we seem to have accepted a fairly high degree of government regulation of our personal choices? If soda were definitively shown to be as harmful to public health as cigarettes, would this justify greater government intervention? Following the model of smoking, should foods that contribute to obesity and diabetes be heavily taxed to discourage their consumption and promote alternatives?

Similarly, we can ask whether West Virginia was justified in rewarding Medicaid beneficiaries for enrolling in programs to control their weight and help them quit smoking. Is it acceptable for a government benefit program to reward some choices it defines as healthy with better benefits? What about punishing choices it considers unhealthy with reduced benefits? These questions become even more vexing when the definitions of healthy and unhealthy choices are not made by a representative government, but instead by private corporations and individuals. Are insurance companies justified in charging higher premiums to tobacco smokers? What about soda drinkers or motorcyclists? Should employees be required to maintain their weight within specified limits, or suffer a penalty, or even lose their jobs? What if their employers consider all alcohol consumption unhealthy and make temperance a condition of employment?

These questions should remind us that definitions of healthy and unhealthy behavior often shift over time, reflecting different states of democratic consensus. In the early 1910s, for example, a significant portion of Americans decided that use of cocaine (an original ingredient in Coca-Cola) was too addictive and deadly for society to tolerate its legal consumption. They decided that restrictions on individual liberty were worth the public health benefits. Americans reached a similar conclusion about alcohol in 1920, with prohibition, only to change their minds thirteen years later. Increased restrictions on the sale and consumption of tobacco products suggest that Americans are increasingly willing to give up some autonomy to reduce the death toll from lung cancer, emphysema, and the other diseases that make smoking the single largest cause of preventable death in America. It remains to be seen whether the high death toll from obesity will eventually elicit a similar response.

But while it seems possible that Americans might eventually embrace some restrictions on the most "drug-like" and addictive causes of obesity, such as high-fructose corn syrup and trans fats, it seems unlikely that majorities of Americans would ever accept more extensive government or corporate management of their dietary and exercise choices. Few Americans would tolerate a government agency taking on the difficult task of getting them to lose weight or even "incentivizing" them to do it on their own. For most citizens in democratic societies, what people eat, how much they eat, how much or how little they exercise, and how fat or thin they become is a purely private matter. In their view, government is not justified in interfering with the nutritional aspect of their lives, any more than it would be justified in interfering with the religious aspect. While the examples of illegal drugs and smoking restrictions make it clear that most Americans are not libertarians—which is to say they accept government limitations on personal autonomy for some public health goods—it is clear that such acceptance has limits. Talk of penalizing or firing individuals for conditions such as obesity that are already highly stigmatized runs counter to most Americans' sense of fairness—not least because genetic, socioeconomic, and other arbitrary factors clearly make losing weight more difficult for some than for others.

A Treatable Epidemic

Ultimately, obesity is better regarded as a treatable medical problem than a moral one caused by a lack of willpower. Without encroaching on personal autonomy, government can help people acquire a better understanding of nutrition and can make it easier for people to seek medical advice regarding weight reduction. Most obese people aren't happy with their condition and would welcome appropriate help in changing it. They would not welcome being threatened with losing their jobs if they don't lose weight.

One of the most perverse aspects of the American health care system in past decades was that insurance providers tended to pay for expensive obesity-related treatments (e.g., stroke care, laser therapy for retinal bleeding, and foot amputations), while paying little or nothing for preventative care that might have helped patients avoid obesity and

diabetes in the first place. One of the most hopeful developments in American health care is a new emphasis on preventative care, in part generated by requirements in the 2010 Affordable Care Act (which we will discuss in greater detail in Chapter 9). Better coverage for nutritional counseling, exercise programs, monitoring by a specialist in metabolic medicine, or care of the feet by a podiatrist are all modest forms of government intervention that are likely to pay off not just for patients, but for insurers and for society as a whole.

CASE PRESENTATION
The Psychology of Torture

In the spring of 2002, the Central Intelligence Agency hired two clinical psychologists to design and implement what would become one of the most important—and infamous—interrogation programs in American history. Developed for use on suspects detained after the 9/11 terrorist attacks, the program was unprecedented both in its methods and in the backgrounds of the men who designed it.

Bruce Jessen and James Mitchell were retired military trainers who had never carried out a field interrogation nor were they experts on interrogation science. (Their psychology dissertations were on family therapy and hypertension, respectively.) They lacked language skills and specialized cultural knowledge for working with suspected members of Al Qaeda and the Taliban. What distinguished them, however, was a willingness to employ interrogation tactics that Americans had once assumed would be used only by their most brutal enemies. Drawing on techniques developed by the Nazi and Chinese Communist regimes of the 1940s and 1950s, along with a psychological theory of "learned helplessness," Jessen and Mitchell went on to develop "enhanced interrogation" methods that were used in Guantanamo Bay, Cuba, and secret CIA detention facilities, as well as in military prisons in Afghanistan and Iraq. When the details of the program emerged in the mid-2000s and early 2010s, they generated worldwide outrage and raised serious

questions about the participation of health care professionals in coercive interrogations. After reviewing the evidence, most congressional committees, medical societies, and media outlets found there was a much simpler name for "enhanced interrogation." It was called torture.

Theory

For decades before September 11, 2001, skilled intelligence officers and FBI agents had generally employed a "rapport building" approach to interrogation, one which prompts suspects to talk, lower their guard, and inadvertently disclose vital information. This is the psychological approach that American intelligence services had successfully used on thousands of high-level Nazi and Japanese prisoners of war during World War II, eliciting key data on troop movements, military leadership, and weaponry. The CIA's 1963 interrogation manual had rejected the infliction of pain as "quite likely to produce false confessions" and the 1992 Army Field Manual dismissed the use of force because it "yields unreliable results, may damage subsequent collection efforts, and can induce the source to say whatever he thinks the interrogator wants to hear."

But in the highly emotional and chaotic aftermath of the 9/11 terrorist attacks, some in the CIA and the administration of George W. Bush decided the established techniques were insufficient for hundreds of newly captured "high value" detainees. Officials such as Justice Department lawyer John Yoo argued that such detainees should be deprived of the protection of the Geneva Conventions and held in special "black site" facilities rather than the POW camps required by the laws of war. A memorandum from the CIA general counsel's office argued that when it came to terrorism, there might be situations in which "torture was necessary."

When the CIA captured a suspect known as Abu Zubaydah, who was at the time believed (mistakenly) to be Al Qaeda's third-in-command, the agency dismissed the government interrogators who initially questioned Zubaydah and had already obtained vital intelligence using rapport-building. To replace them, they called in Jessen and Mitchell, two little-known trainers for the Air Force's Survival, Evasion, Resistance and Escape (SERE) program.

SERE had been developed as a way to give potential American POWs a taste of the torture methods that might be used on them if captured by America's enemies. So-called "enhanced" or "sharpened" interrogation methods (*Verschärfte Vernehmung*) had been named and pioneered by the German Gestapo during World War II, as a form of torture that would leave no marks. It included sleep deprivation, hypothermia, strategic beatings, and stress positions. German and Japanese interrogators also employed *waterboarding*, a controlled drowning technique developed during the Spanish Inquisition that brings a prisoner close to unconsciousness or death. (After World War II, the United States convicted Japanese officials of torture and war crimes for waterboarding American POWs.) These "enhanced interrogation" techniques had then been refined by the North Koreans and their Chinese allies during the Korean War, often using them to extract false confessions from American POWs that could be used for propaganda purposes.

Jessen and Mitchell's job at SERE had been to try to teach American soldiers how they might withstand these torture techniques, often using simulations. In early 2002, they were both retired from the military and on the lookout for new business opportunities. They told the CIA they could "reverse engineer" their training methods, using the brutal techniques of America's former enemies as the basis for a new U.S. interrogation program.

Mitchell, in particular, was interested in a theory of "learned helplessness" developed by Martin Seligman, a prominent psychologist and former president of the American Psychological Association (APA). In the 1960s, Seligman had found that dogs who had been taught there was nothing they could do to avoid a series of electric shocks would become passive and listless, doing nothing to escape further shocks even when it was quite easy to do so. Mitchell became convinced that he could produce the same effect with human interrogation subjects and used the psychological theory as the cornerstone of his interrogation program. (Seligman later said that Mitchell had misunderstood and distorted his theory, and that inducing learned helplessness in interrogation subjects would make them more likely to lie and "compliantly tell the interrogator what he wants to hear.")

Mitchell and Jessen's ideas quickly met with approval at the highest levels of the U.S. government. Just weeks after the proposal for an "alternative set of interrogation procedures" had been made, it was discussed at a high level meeting attended by Vice President Dick Cheney, Defense Secretary Donald Rumsfeld, National Security Advisor Condoleezza Rice, and Attorney General John Ashcroft, among others. Although Ashcroft asked, "Why are we talking about this in the White House? History will not judge this kindly," the majority of the group endorsed the proposal. Just months after Jessen and Mitchell's names had first been mentioned at the CIA, their ideas had been legally codified in a series of memos written by Yoo and others, and the psychologists were brought in to oversee the interrogations of key 9/11 detainees such as Khalid Sheikh Mohammed. The speed of the process surprised even Jessen and Mitchell, who later argued that they hadn't sought out such weighty responsibilities.

"I never knew how that happened. I just got a phone call," Mitchell later recalled. "I didn't knock on the gate and say, 'Let me torture people.'"

Practice

Mitchell and Jessen were given permanent desks in the CIA's Counterterrorism Center and later granted a $180 million contract to start their own interrogation services company, which eventually employed over sixty people. The "menu" of interrogation techniques they adapted from the SERE training included waterboarding, stress positions, sleep deprivation, dietary manipulation, slapping, slamming against walls ("walling"), exposure to temperature extremes, high-decibel noise bombardment, forced nudity, sexual humiliation, confinement boxes, and "mock burials," in which detainees would be led to believe they were being buried alive. With the exception of the last item, which the CIA deemed too extreme, all of these techniques would be among those employed on detainees and detailed in landmark reports by the Senate Select Committee on Intelligence (SSCI) and the International Committee of the Red Cross (ICRC).

Perhaps by design, the names of the interrogation methods listed above have a tendency to obscure their intensity in practice. (The conservative radio personality Rush Limbaugh famously compared them to "fraternity pranks.") Subsequent reports, however, have filled in the details on a set of procedures that the CIA's chief of interrogations called a "train wreck" and the CIA's chief counsel John Rizzo later termed "sadistic and terrifying."

Waterboarding. As described above, waterboarding is a controlled drowning technique in which a prisoner is bound to a declined board and then slowly asphyxiated by pouring water over a cloth covering his nose and mouth. It typically causes choking, vomiting, water in the lungs, distension of the belly, and often produces unconsciousness and convulsions. The SSCI report found that Abu Zubaydah, the first prisoner Mitchell and Jessen personally waterboarded, was subjected to the procedure eighty-three times in twenty days, nearly dying during one session after he stopped breathing. (A videotape of that session, among others, was later destroyed by the CIA.) Other detainees, such as 9/11 planner Khalid Sheikh Mohammed, were waterboarded hundreds of times in the first weeks of their captivity, to the point where medical officers became concerned about water poisoning and recommended that interrogators switch to a saline solution.

Stress Positions and Sleep Deprivation.
Detainees were routinely shackled to cell walls or ceilings to keep them awake for as much as 180 hours (over one week) at a time. Frequently, this involved chaining detainees' arms above their heads and then forcing them to stand, uninterrupted, for several days at a time. In addition to visual and auditory

hallucinations, panic attacks, and self-harm episodes, these techniques caused intense pain and swelling in the legs—which CIA physicians treated with blood thinners and Ace bandages. The SSCI report found that four detainees were shackled into standing positions on broken or otherwise injured feet or legs. As these stress positions were adopted by CIA and contract interrogators at military prisons in Iraq and Afghanistan, they also began to involve handcuffing detainees' wrists behind their backs and suspending them this way from the ceilings or windows of their cells— hyperextending the shoulders and putting pressure on the chest. Subsequent investigations found that at least three detainees died struggling to breathe while hanging in these positions with hoods over their heads.

Slapping and "Walling." These techniques were originally authorized only as "attention-getting" maneuvers, but soon evolved into "rough takedowns" in which detainees would be dragged from their cells while being slapped and punched by screaming interrogators who would cut off detainees' clothing and bind them with tape. Detainees also had to be treated for head injuries resulting from being slammed repeatedly into walls. At military sites, these "startle" techniques sometimes took the form of severe and repeated beatings, especially in the legs. (In one of the deaths mentioned above, the military coroner found that the tissue in the detainee's legs "had basically been pulpified," creating blood clots that became the primary cause of death.)

Temperature Extremes. Detainees were commonly forced to stand naked or diapered in cells kept as cold as 50 degrees Fahrenheit. They were also frequently doused with cold water to accelerate heat loss. One detainee, Gul Rahman, was found to have died of hypothermia under such conditions, after being doused with cold water, chained to the wall, stripped from the waist down, and made to sit overnight on the bare concrete of his cell.

Confinement Boxes. When not being kept standing or being waterboarded, some of the high-value detainees were locked into coffins and small boxes to try to elicit claustrophobia and panic. Some were standard-sized coffins, while others were smaller than two-and-a-half cubic feet. During his initial interrogation, Abu Zubaydah was locked in these cramped spaces for a total of nearly three hundred hours.

Dietary Manipulation and "Rectal Feeding."

To further shift detainees into a "dependent" state of learned helplessness, the CIA originally authorized replacing solid food with liquid supplements, and at least thirty detainees were fed a diet of Ensure™ and water. With uncooperative detainees, however, the approach shifted to naso-gastric tubes, IV drips, and "rectal feeding," in which pureed food was pumped into the rectum via a tube. Although this last technique had been used in nineteenth-century medicine, it has no contemporary medical legitimacy and CIA officials reported using it on at least five detainees as a way to achieve "total control" and reduce "unnecessary conversation." Given evidence that medical officers took steps to maximize the discomfort of these procedures, as well as that of rectal exams, many observers have concluded that these punitive and involuntary anal penetrations constituted rape. (At least one detainee subject to these procedures was later diagnosed with "chronic hemorrhoids, an anal fissure, and symptomatic rectal prolapse.")

Sexual Humiliation.

The SERE training program had caused controversy in the 1990s for putting Air Force cadets through simulated rapes and other forms of sexual humiliation. Many of these techniques appear to have been carried forward in Jessen and Mitchell's "reverse engineering" of their program, in an effort to deepen detainees' sense of learned helplessness. In addition to routine forced nudity before female officers, the SSCI report found that detainees were repeatedly made to soil themselves or wear diapers, at least one was sexually threatened with a broomstick, and others were told how their mothers or children would be killed or sexually abused. As these techniques migrated to non-CIA facilities, they became more lurid and extreme—most infamously at Abu Ghraib prison in Iraq, where photographic evidence documented rapes of detainees by guards, detainees being sodomized with phosphorescent tubes and truncheons, and detainees being made to masturbate or simulate sexual acts in front of guards and contract interrogators.

Other Practices.

In addition to the authorized techniques, the SSCI report found that the CIA conducted at least two mock executions of prisoners. Detainees were also threatened with handguns and, on at least one occasion, a buzzing electric drill held near the head. Conditions were bleak, especially at CIA "black sites" in eastern Europe and Afghanistan, with detainees "kept shackled in complete darkness and isolation, with a bucket for human waste, and without notable heat" in winter. One detainee was found to have been forgotten for seventeen days, chained to a wall in a standing position. A 2006 study of mortality among detainees in U.S. custody from 2002 to 2005 found that homicide was the single largest cause of death, killing at least forty-three detainees.

Although Mitchell, Jessen, and CIA officials disavowed responsibility for these and other departures from their approved "enhanced interrogation" program, a 2008 bipartisan report from the Senate Armed Services Committee found that Secretary of Defense Donald Rumsfeld's authorization of interrogation techniques drawn from the SERE program had led directly to the abuses and killings at Abu Ghraib and other military facilities. As lower-level commanders adopted the new policies from SERE, "[w]hat followed was an erosion in standards dictating that detainees be treated humanely," the report concluded.

Torture and Medicine

As we have seen above, one of the notable features of the interrogation practices detailed in the SSCI, ICRC, and other reports is that they took place with the active participation and cooperation of health care professionals. In addition to being designed by two clinical psychologists, the procedures were implemented by dozens of other psychologists and physicians from the CIA's Office of Medical Services (OMS), who monitored the mental and physical health of detainees, calibrated distress levels to achieve better results, and studied the overall effectiveness of the procedures. Medical professionals also withheld standard care to increase pressure on detainees, allowing gunshot wounds to fester untreated, approving stress positions despite broken or dislocated limbs, and preparing a detainee for waterboarding shortly after abdominal surgery.

Many have argued that these acts violated basic ethical and professional obligations to do no harm, to protect those in their care from injury and brutality, and to prevent and report torture. (For a related philosophical argument, see this chapter's essay by Gerald Dworkin on "Patients and Prisoners.") Critics have also charged that the health care professionals involved may have violated the Nuremberg Code and other international prohibitions on torture and exploitative human subject research, and may thus have committed war crimes or crimes against humanity. In 2006, the UN Commission on Human Rights condemned American health professionals for "systematically" violating professional ethics and participating in widespread detainee abuse "amounting to torture." Groups such as Physicians for Human Rights have also pointed to an inherent conflict of interest in Jessen and Mitchell's formal evaluation of their own interrogation methods—methods that each was being paid as much as $1,800 a day to implement.

Since the 1980s, the American Medical Association (AMA) ethics code has prohibited physicians from participating in or facilitating torture in any way, nor are they allowed to be involved in any coercive interrogations that cause "harm through physical injury or mental suffering." While the AMA leadership has condemned some of the CIA's practices as torture and used the occasion of the 2014 SSCI report to remind physicians of their obligations not to participate in it, the organization has so far declined to censure any of its members for their participation in the program.

In recent years, the American Psychological Association (APA) has been particularly vocal in its assessment that the CIA's "enhanced interrogation" techniques constituted torture, and it has developed a specific "no torture" policy that prohibits psychologists from direct or indirect participation in waterboarding, stress positions, sexual humiliation, or phobia exploitation. (The APA's ethics code has also long emphasized the duty of *nonmalificence,* or "do no harm.") The organization's 2014 president, Nancy Kaslow, called the application of "learned helplessness" to interrogations a "perversion of psychological science" and expressed shock that the two psychologists had been paid more than $80 million to develop a torture program.

But investigations by *New York Times* reporter James Risen and an independent study requested by the APA board found that the organization took a strikingly different approach to "enhanced interrogation" in the early 2000s, and that it may have helped facilitate the very practices it now condemns. In 2002, for example, the APA revised its ethics policies to say that if there was a conflict between its ethics code and the "governing legal authority," psychologists could choose to follow lawful orders rather than their ethical obligations. (This change was widely criticized as echoing the defense at the Nuremberg trials and was removed in 2008.) Similarly, after a series of secret high-level meetings between APA and CIA officials in 2004, an APA task force revised its ethics policies to read that "it is consistent with the APA Ethics Code for psychologists to serve in consultative roles to interrogation and information-gathering processes for national security-related purposes."

In contrast to the American Psychiatric Association, which prohibited its members from playing any role in interrogations and thus kept psychiatrists out of Guantanamo and CIA "black sites," the APA ethics task force maintained close contacts with intelligence officials who were working with—and ultimately for—Jessen and Mitchell. (One former president of the APA ended up owning a 1 percent stake in Mitchell Jessen and Associates.) Critics charge that the APA allowed psychologists to provide legal and ethical "cover" for torture, and the APA's independent investigator found that its ethics office had "prioritized the protection of psychologists—even those who might have engaged in unethical behavior—above the protection of the public."

Ends and Means

Two days after taking office, on January 22, 2009, President Barack Obama signed an executive order that rescinded the Bush administration's exemption of interrogators from compliance with the Geneva Conventions, the Convention Against Torture, and the Army Field Manual. The order closed CIA's "black sites" and is widely perceived to have ended its "enhanced interrogation" practices. Three months later, the CIA abruptly cancelled Mitchell and Jessen's contracts, effectively dissolving their company after having paid them $81 million. (The CIA is still covering $5 million of Mitchell and Jessen's legal fees.)

Defenders of the "enhanced interrogation" program, such as former Vice President Dick Cheney, argue that the brutal means it employed were justified by the intelligence it produced, which they claim disrupted terrorist plots and saved lives. It has been difficult to assess such claims, since they often rest on classified information which Cheney, among others, says he cannot release. But the SSCI report reviewed twenty of the counterterrorism successes most often attributed to "enhanced interrogation" and found that in each case there was either "no relationship" between the success and information provided during such interrogations or the interrogations simply produced information that interrogators already knew. The only usable intelligence Abu Zubaydah provided, for example—

which helped in the capture of Ramzi bin al-Shibh and Khalid Sheikh Mohammed—had already been given to FBI inspectors using the rapport-building approach. Although some of the evidence that led to the location and killing of Osama bin Laden came from an Al Qaeda operative who was subsequently tortured, he voluntarily provided all of his actionable intelligence before the techniques were applied to him, and none during or after their application.

In addition, the SSCI investigation found that torture tactics sent the CIA on wild goose chases, as multiple detainees "provided fabricated information on critical intelligence issues, including the terrorist threats which the CIA identified as its highest priorities." This result echoes the findings of a new body of research on interrogation developed by the U.S. government's interagency High-Value Detainee Interrogation Group (HIG), demonstrating that rapport-building is dramatically more effective than threatening or coercive practices.

Ironically, one clear result of the government's "enhanced" interrogation practices is that they have made it profoundly difficult, in the view of many American military judges, to prosecute some of the central planners and would-be participants in the 9/11 attacks, such as Khalid Sheikh Mohammed and Mohammed al-Qahtani. The SSCI report also concluded that as many as twenty-six detainees held by the CIA were victims of mistaken identity, area dragnets, or lies told by informants; some, such as a man named Abu Hadhaifa, were released after having been subjected to days of "enhanced interrogation" techniques. Others, such as Abu Zubaydah, turned out to have been low-level figures in the Al Qaeda orbit, and may not even have been members of the organization.

Such outcomes may make intelligence agencies think twice before renewing any program of "enhanced" interrogation and also make health care professionals think twice about assisting them. For they are a reminder that torture, like other departures from basic standards of morality and professional ethics, can come with unintended and irrevocable consequences.

CASE PRESENTATION
Healing the Hmong

The Hmong are a Southeast Asian mountain people who were recruited by the U.S. government to fight the North Vietnamese during the Vietnam War of the 1960s and 1970s. At the end of the war, tens of thousands Hmong sought asylum in the United States, in part due to fear of reprisals from their former enemies, who had taken power in Laos and Vietnam. In the United States, most of the Hmong immigrants settled in California, and more than 35,000 now live in or near Fresno.

The Hmong (pronounced "mung") brought their culture with them and have not abandoned it in favor of prevailing Western or American cultural traditions. This adherence to culture has been largely unproblematic so far as matters such as dress, food preferences, and modes of worship are concerned. But some Hmong practices have brought them into conflict with U.S. law. Over the years, the Fresno police have been called in to deal with complaints about the Hmong slaughtering pigs and other animals in their apartments, and they have raided patches of ground where the Hmong were growing opium poppies. The city of Fresno was also prompted to launch an educational campaign to discourage some Hmong men from engaging in a rare but traditional practice of abducting teenage girls to be brides.

Hmong beliefs about illness, its causes, and its treatment have led to even more conflicts, sometimes with tragic results. Adhering to their traditional perspective, the Hmong generally don't accept the picture of the world depicted by Western science. They are animists who see the everyday world as a place shared with spirits, and they regard the interactions between spirits and humans as factors that shape the course of life. Spirits can be angered or seek revenge for insults or wrongs, and often the vengeful actions of the spirits are manifested as diseases. Propitiation of spirits may involve praying, performing healing rituals, burning incense, or carrying out animal sacrifices.

Hmong and Western cultures have come into especially sharp conflict over the treatment of sick children. In one famous case in Fresno from the late 1980s, Hmong parents of a child with severe clubfeet refused to have the problem surgically corrected because they thought the child's feet were deformed as punishment for an ancestor's wrongdoing. To try to correct the problem might, in their view, result in another family member's becoming sick. (The parents' refusal of treatment for the boy's condition, even though it meant he could lose the ability to walk, was upheld by a Fresno judge in 1990.)

Other Hmong parents have refused to allow surgery for their children because they believe surgery maims the body and makes it impossible for the child to be reincarnated. Others have treated childhood illnesses with traditional drinks that contain high levels of lead. In the rest of this case, we will examine two prominent examples of conflict between Hmong cultural beliefs and Western medicine, in which Hmong efforts to care for their children with traditional methods ran counter to Western legal and scientific norms.

Lee Lor

Lee Lor, a fifteen-year-old Hmong girl, was admitted to Valley Children's Hospital in late September of 1994 with a complaint of severe abdominal pains. Her physicians made a diagnosis of acute appendicitis and operated on her immediately. During the operation, however, the surgeon discovered that Lee Lor had what turned out to be an eight-inch cancerous tumor in her abdomen. To remove the tumor, he also had to take out an ovary and part of one of her fallopian tubes. Her family maintained that it wasn't until three days after the surgery that they were told about the cancer and the removal of the ovary. A hospital spokesman said that the parents were told, but he suggested that they may not have understood because of problems with the translation.

In any event, the damage had already been done. "At 12 years old, Hmong girls begin to marry," said Cheng Vang, Lee's uncle, who acted as the family's spokesman. "When the parents find out that they removed ovary and not just appendix, they didn't trust the doctors anymore." Meanwhile, Lee's physicians insisted that further treatment would not damage Lee's fertility and defended their removal of the ovary. "It was a matter of life and death," said Stephen Stephenson, a pediatric oncologist at the hospital. "To do otherwise would have been malpractice."

As a result of the conflict, the family refused to let Lee have the rounds of chemotherapy that her doctors recommended. (Her physicians estimated that with this treatment she had an 80% chance of survival, but without it her chances dropped to 10%.) Failing to get permission from Lee Lor's family to initiate chemotherapy, the hospital notified the Fresno County Department of Social Services. The agency obtained an order from Juvenile Court requiring Lee Lor's parents to submit to the treatment on child protection grounds. When they refused, the Fresno police removed the girl from the home, strapped to a stretcher. On the way out, the police were pelted with stones by a group of Hmong and wrestled a knife out of the hands of Lee Lor's father after he threatened to kill himself. A guard was later posted outside Lee's room in the hospital.

In the coming days, the situation in Fresno remained tense. To protest Lee Lor's forced treatment, several hundred Hmong marched through the city on two occasions. At a town meeting, they accused the county and the hospital of racism.

Lee Lor was given chemotherapy for a week in the hospital, then allowed to return home. On the day of her discharge, a court hearing was initiated to determine whether she should be placed in a foster home until the completion of her course of chemotherapy.

But Lee Lor made her own decision by running away from home. She left with little or no money, but she took with her a supply of herbal medicines. Her parents notified the police when they discovered she was gone. They also called in the family shaman, who said she had a vision of Lee Lor out in the open and well.

Some two months later, Lee Lor returned home. She had spent the time wandering around the state and was apparently in decent health. While she was gone, the Department of Social Services had dropped its efforts to force her to continue her chemotherapy. In one sense, Lee Lor's family and the Hmong community had won an initial round in their conflict with Western medicine.

Lia Lee

A second pivotal case in the history of the Hmong people's encounter with Western medicine involved the Lees, a family in Merced, California, whose experiences with their infant daughter Lia are chronicled in Anne Fadiman's book, *The Spirit Catches You and You Fall Down.*

Lia Lee was born in July of 1982 and had her first seizure three months later. She was eventually diagnosed with a severe seizure disorder at a county medical center. But the Lee family, in accordance with Hmong tradition, believed Lia's condition was caused by spirits called *dabs*. In their eyes, Lia's seizures involved the dabs catching hold of their child and separating her soul from her body. (The title of Fadiman's book is a literal translation of the Hmong word for epilepsy.) From the Lees' perspective, the only remedy for Lia's condition was to sacrifice animals and persuade the dabs to release her soul. They also interpreted Lia's condition as a kind of spiritual gift, which indicated she might have a vocation as a traditional Hmong shaman. Based on these beliefs, Lia's parents were reluctant to accept her doctor's prescription of a drug regimen to bring her seizures under control, and they often disregarded medical advice.

Largely unchecked by medication, Lia's seizures became worse over time and she eventually suffered irreversible brain damage from a catastrophic seizure when she was four. She lapsed into a persistent vegetative state and remained in that condition for the next twenty-six years, until her death from pneumonia at age thirty.

In many of their early interactions, Lia's doctors and her parents found themselves in conflict. After Lia's parents sacrificed a rooster and tied strings around Lia's wrist rather than give her medications, her doctors called Child Protective Services, who placed the child in foster care for a year. After Lia's brain damage, her physicians attributed her condition to her parent's failure to give her the drugs that could have helped her, while her parents attributed it to the drugs her physicians gave her during her hospital stays.

"I was trying to provide a way of controlling her seizures with Western methods and Western medicines," recalled Neil Ernst, one of Lia's physicians. "And in some sense, the Lees were giving up control of their child to a system that they didn't understand." The conflict reflected two radically different conceptual worlds.

Over time, however, understanding grew between the two sides. Lia's physicians were impressed by the extraordinary love and care that Lia's parents lavished on their daughter, and how Lia remained in the center of family life, even after her severe brain damage. One of Lia's sisters went on to become a clinical health educator and over time her parents forgave and developed relationships with her physicians. (They were even invited to Lia's traditional three-day Hmong funeral, in 2012.) Merced County has also taken steps to engage with Hmong culture more sensitively, training better interpreters and allowing Hmong shamans to perform some rituals in the hospital.

Are Good Intentions Enough?

A striking feature of the conflicts between Hmong families and Western medicine is that almost all the parties were clearly well intentioned and wished the best for the children in question. The physicians in Merced and Fresno wanted the best possible outcome for their patients, but their limited knowledge of Hmong culture meant that they sometimes antagonized the people they were trying to help. The Lees and the Lors were clearly devoted to their daughters, but they were operating within the conceptual framework of the Hmong culture. They found the framework of Western scientific medicine unintelligible and came to distrust it, as well as the doctors who represented it.

Such conflicts do not only come up with regard to non-Western cultures like that of the Hmong. Previously discussed examples such as the Church of the First Born and Christian Scientists (see this chapter's Case Presentation: Faith and Medicine) should remind us that cultures are neither monolithic nor consistent. Indeed, the entity we call "Western culture" contains many strands and subdivisions in which well-meaning individuals may also come into conflict with the beliefs of evidence-based medicine.

Do these conflicting sets of good intentions leave us in a scientific and ethical stalemate, in which there are no grounds for evaluating the different perspectives? One tempting ethical position, called *cultural relativism*, would say yes. On this view, the truth of scientific frameworks, as well as ethical frameworks, are *relative* to particular cultures (or even individuals) rather than *objective*. Thus, there is no objective truth about medicine or morality, only a range of equally valid cultural positions. Relativism is tempting because it often seems like a more tolerant and open-minded stance than *objectivism*—the view that there are some scientific truths and ethical values that apply to everyone whether or not they like or believe in them. But relativism has some notorious problems. For one thing, it renders us incapable of criticizing many culturally specific practices such as slavery (in nineteenth-century America or contemporary Africa) or the cultural beliefs that justified stoning witches or colonizing "subhuman" races. Ironically, relativists also have no way of criticizing aggressive intolerance, so long as the aggressor's culture endorses intolerance as a value. (We will discuss relativism and objectivism in greater detail in Chapter 11.)

If we reject relativism, however, it does not mean that we are obliged to view our own cultural perspective as infallible or to force it on others. Indeed, one of the lessons of the Lia Lee case is that greater humility and better communication can allow cultures in conflict to find things they value in common—such as unconditional love and care for children. They can also help us identify which fundamental values and premises about reality are truly necessary for the functioning of a decent society, and which may be less important than fostering an inclusive culture.

Autonomy and Pluralism

Medical conflicts involving Hmong, Christian Scientists, and other groups are challenging because they seem to pit the values of individual autonomy and cultural pluralism against concern for the welfare of society's most vulnerable members. On the one hand, respect for other cultures and individual autonomy suggests that society should respect alternative viewpoints on medicine and illness. Especially when the beliefs of an entire culture

such as that of the Hmong are concerned, no one wants to be thought guilty of cultural chauvinism or arrogance. On the other hand, concern for the welfare of the most vulnerable, particularly children, seems like a cornerstone of any decent society. Child welfare laws are premised on the idea that children are not the mere property of their parents, and that no matter how good the intentions of parents may be, society has a responsibility to stop them from inflicting lasting harm or unnecessary suffering on their children.

These insights seem particularly relevant when it comes to life-and-death medical decisions. It is one thing for an adult to choose a treatment with little or no chance of success, or to refuse treatment altogether—as most adult patients in the United States are now able to do. It is quite another thing for an adult to make such a decision on behalf of a child, since children are dependent on their parents and are not considered legally competent to make such decisions for themselves. Does society, recognizing this difference, have a duty to intervene when parents make what is generally acknowledged to be the wrong choice about their child's medical treatment?

As you explore the discussion of ethical theories and readings that make up the rest of this chapter, you'll want to reflect on the profound questions raised by the cases discussed above. Pay particular attention to situations in which medical crises bring important values into conflict.

BRIEFING SESSION

Consider the following examples:

1. A state decides to require that all behavioral therapists (that is, all professionals who make use of psychological conditioning techniques to alter behavior patterns) be either licensed psychologists or psychiatrists.

2. A member of the Jehovah's Witnesses religion, which is opposed to the transfusion of blood and blood products, refuses to consent to a needed appendectomy. But when his appendix

ruptures and he lapses into unconsciousness, a surgical resident operates and saves his life in a procedure that involves a transfusion.

3. A physician decides not to tell the parents of an infant who died shortly after birth that the cause of death was an unpredictable genetic condition, because he does not wish to diminish their desire to have another child.

4. A clinical psychologist uses his professional expertise to design and implement interrogation methods for the CIA that include waterboarding, extreme

temperatures, and hanging by hands and feet. He claims he has not violated the American Psychological Association's code of ethics, which requires that psychologists "do no harm."

5. A janitor employed in an elementary school consults a psychiatrist retained by the school board and tells her that he has molested young children on two occasions. The psychiatrist decides that it is her duty to inform the school board.

6. While in kindergarten, a six-year-old develops a high fever accompanied by violent vomiting and convulsions, and is rushed to a nearby hospital. The attending physician makes a diagnosis of meningitis and telephones the parents for permission to initiate treatment. Both parents are Christian Scientists, however, and they insist that no medical treatment be given to her. The physician initiates treatment anyway, and the parents later sue the physician and the hospital.

7. A thirty-year-old woman who is twenty-four-weeks pregnant is involved in an automobile accident that leaves her with a spinal cord injury. Her physician tells her that she would have a greater chance of recovery if she were not pregnant. She then requests an abortion. The hospital disagrees with her decision and gets a court order forbidding the abortion.

There is perhaps no single moral issue that is present in all these examples. Rather, there is a complex of related issues regarding the relationships between patients and caregivers. Each example involves actions on the behalf of someone else—another individual, the public at large, or a special group. And each action comes into conflict with the autonomy, wishes, or expectations of some person or persons. Even though the issues are related, it will be most useful to discuss them under separate headings. We will begin with a brief account of autonomy, then turn to a discussion of paternalism, informed consent, the principle of nonmaleficence, and imposed restrictions on autonomy.

Autonomy

We are said to act autonomously when our actions are the outcome of our deliberations and choices. To be autonomous is to be self-determining. Hence, our autonomy is violated when we are coerced to act by actual force or by explicit and implicit threats, or when we act under misapprehension or under the influence of factors that impair our judgment.

We associate autonomy with the status we ascribe to rational agents as *persons* in the moral sense. Many moral theories are committed to the idea that persons are, by their nature, uniquely qualified to decide what is in their own best interest. This is because they are ends in themselves, not means to some other end. As such, persons have inherent worth, rather than instrumental worth. Others have a duty to recognize this worth and to avoid treating persons as though they were only instruments to be employed to achieve a goal chosen by someone else. To treat someone as if she lacks autonomy is thus to treat her as less than a person.

All the cases previously listed can be construed as involving encroachments on the autonomy of the individuals concerned. (1) Laws requiring a license to provide therapy restrict the actions of individuals who do not qualify for a license. (2) The Jehovah's Witness receives a blood transfusion he has previously refused. (3) Information crucial to decision making is withheld from the parents of the child with the genetic disease, so their future decision cannot be a properly informed one. (4) Those subjected to torture clearly do not consent to the psychological "treatment" they receive to extract information from them; at the same time, the APA code of ethics restricts the professional behavior of its members. (5) By breaking confidentiality, the psychiatrist is denying the prerogative of the janitor to keep secret information that may harm him. (6) By treating the girl with meningitis, the physician claims an exception to the generally recognized right of parents to make decisions concerning their children's welfare. (7) By refusing the woman's request for an abortion, the hospital and the court are forcing her to remain pregnant against her will and against medical advice.

The high value we place on autonomy is based on the realization that without it we can make very little of our lives. In its absence, we become the creatures of others, and our lives assume the forms others choose for us. Without being able to act in ways that shape our own destiny by pursuing our aims and making our own decisions, we are not realizing the potential we have as human beings. Autonomy gives us the opportunity to make decisions ourselves; even if we are dissatisfied with the result, we have the satisfaction of knowing that the mistakes were our own. We at least acted as rational agents.

One of the traditional problems of social organization is how to structure society in such a way that the autonomy of individuals will be preserved and promoted. However, autonomy is not an absolute or unconditional value, but just one among others. For example, few would wish to live in a society in which you could do whatever you wanted if you had enough physical power to get your way. Because one person's exercise of autonomy is likely to come into conflict with another's, we are willing to accept some restrictions to preserve as much of our own freedom as possible. We commonly accept restrictions that are necessary to safeguard our lives and

enable us to pursue our life plans in peace. We may also accept such restrictions because they protect the lives, welfare, and goals of others in our society.

Because autonomy is so basic to us, we usually view it as not requiring any justification. This predisposition in favor of autonomy means that in order to violate someone's autonomy—to set aside that person's wishes and render impotent her power of action—requires that we offer a strong justification. Various principles have been proposed to justify conditions under which we are warranted in restricting autonomy.

The most relevant principle in discussing the relationships among physicians, patients, and society is that of *paternalism*. The role of paternalism in the physician–patient relationship and how it relates to truth telling and confidentiality in medical settings is discussed in the next section. (For a fuller account of autonomy, as well as the principles invoked to justify restricting its exercise, see Part VI: Foundations of Bioethics.)

Paternalism

The definition of paternalism is itself a matter of dispute. Roughly speaking, we can say that paternalism consists of acting in a way that is believed to protect or advance the interest of a person, even if acting in this way goes against the person's own immediate desires or limits the person's freedom of choice. Oversimplifying, we could say that paternalism is the view that "Father knows best." (The word "parentalism" is now sometimes preferred to "paternalism" because of the latter's gender-specific origin. See Part VI for the distinction between the weak and strong versions of the principle of paternalism.) Examples 1, 2, 3, 6, and 7 at the start of this Briefing are all clear instances of paternalistic behavior.

It is useful to distinguish what we can call "state paternalism" from "personal paternalism." State paternalism, as the name suggests, is the control exerted by a legislature, agency, or other governmental body over particular kinds of practices or procedures. Such control is typically exercised through laws, licensing requirements, technical specifications, and operational guidelines and regulations. (Examples 1 and 7 can both be construed as instances of state paternalism.)

By contrast, personal paternalism consists in an individual's deciding, on the basis of his own principles or values, that he knows what is best for another person. The individual then acts in a way that deprives the other person of genuine and effective choice. (Examples 2, 3, and 6 represent this approach.) Paternalism is personal when it is not a matter of public or semipublic policy, but is a result of private moral decision making.

The line between public and private paternalism is often blurred. For example, suppose a physician on the staff of a hospital believes a pregnant patient should have surgery to improve the chances of normal development for the fetus. After the patient refuses, the physician presents his view to the hospital's attorney, and, agreeing with him, the attorney goes to court to request an order for the surgery. The judge is persuaded and issues the order. Although the order is based on arguments that certain laws are applicable in the case, the order itself is neither a purely personal decision nor a matter of public policy. The order reflects the judgment of a physician who has succeeded in getting others to agree.

Despite the sometimes blurred distinction between state and personal paternalism, the distinction is useful. It permits us to separate decisions about public policies affecting classes of people (for example, those needing medication) from individual decisions that impact specific persons.

State Paternalism in Medicine

At first sight, state paternalism seems wholly unobjectionable in the medical context. We are likely to feel more confident in consulting a physician when we know that he or she has had to meet standards of education, competency, and character set by a state licensing board and professional organizations such as the American Medical Association. We feel relatively sure that we aren't putting ourselves in the hands of an incompetent quack.

Indeed, that we can feel such assurance can be regarded as one of the marks of social progress in medicine. As late as the early twentieth century in the United States, the standards for physicians were low, and licensing laws were either nonexistent or poorly enforced. It was possible to qualify as a physician with as little as four months' formal schooling and a two-year apprenticeship.

Rigorous standards and strictly enforced laws have undoubtedly done much to improve medical care in the United States. At the very least, they have made it less dangerous to consult a physician. At the same time, however, they have also placed restrictions on individual freedom of choice. In the nineteenth century, a person could choose among a wide variety of medical viewpoints from licensed physicians. That is no longer so today.

Through the application of the scientific method and research standards to medical practice, our society has decided that some medical viewpoints are simply wrong and, if implemented, can put patients in grave danger. Unlike people in the nineteenth century, our society has reached a broad consensus (within limits) about what kinds of medical therapies are effective and what kinds are useless or harmful. It is the scientific character of contemporary medicine that has produced this consensus. It has demonstrated, for example, that antibiotics are generally effective in fighting bacterial infections, while bleeding patients or rubbing mercury into wounds is not.

Secure in these beliefs, our society generally endorses paternalism by the state in the regulation of medical practice. We believe it is important to protect sick people from quacks and charlatans, from those who raise false hopes and take advantage of human suffering. We generally accept, then, that the range of choice in health therapies ought to be limited to what scientific research has shown to be safe and reasonably effective.

This approach to medicine has its detractors, of course. In particular, those seeking treatment for cancer have sometimes wanted to try drugs that are rumored to be miracle cures but are not approved by the Food and Drug Administration (FDA). Such drugs cannot be legally prescribed in the United States, and those wishing to gain access to them must typically travel to foreign clinics, often at considerable discomfort and expense. Some have claimed that FDA regulations make it impossible for them to choose the therapy they wish and that this is an unwarranted restriction of their rights. It should be enough, they claim, for the government to issue a warning if it determines one is necessary. But after that, physicians and patients should be free to act as they choose.

The debate about unapproved therapies raises a more general question: To what extent is it legitimate for a government to restrict the actions and choices of its citizens for their own good? It is perhaps not possible to give a wholly satisfactory general answer to this question. People do not object that they are not permitted to drink polluted water from the city water supply or that they are not able to buy candy bars contaminated with rodent feces. Yet some do object if they have to drink water that contains fluorides or if they cannot buy candy bars that contain saccharine. As we saw earlier in this chapter, New Yorkers seemed to accept Mayor

Bloomberg's trans fat ban but many chafed at his efforts to cap soda container sizes. (See Social Context: The Obesity Epidemic.)

All such limitations can be seen as governmental attempts to protect the health of citizens. Seeing to the well-being of its citizens certainly must be recognized as one of the fundamental aims of a government. And protecting their lives and physical health certainly seems to fall under this prerogative. So state paternalism with respect to health seems, in general, to be justifiable. Yet the laws and regulations through which the paternal concern is expressed are certain to come into conflict with the exercise of individual liberties. Perhaps the only way in which such conflicts can be resolved is on an issue-by-issue basis. (Later, we will discuss some of the limitations that moral theories place on state paternalism.)

State paternalism in medical and health care matters may be more pervasive than it seems at first sight. Laws regulating medical practice, the licensing of physicians and medical personnel, regulations governing the licensing and testing of drugs, and guidelines that must be followed in scientific research are some of the more obvious expressions of paternalism. Less obvious is the fact that government research funds can be expended only in prescribed ways and that only certain approved forms of medical care and therapy will be paid for under government-sponsored health programs. For example, it was a political and social triumph for chiropractors and Christian Science practitioners when some of their services were included under Medicare coverage. Thus, government money, as well as laws and regulations, can be used in paternalistic ways.

Personal Paternalism in Medicine

That patients occupy a dependent role with respect to their physicians seems to be true historically, sociologically, and psychologically.

The patient is sick; the physician is generally assumed to be well. The patient is in need of the knowledge and skills of the physician, but the physician does not need those of the patient. The patient seeks out the physician to ask for help, but the physician does not seek out the patient. The patient is a single individual, while the physician represents the institution of medicine with its hospitals, nurses, technicians, consultants, and so on. In his dependence on the physician, the patient willingly surrenders some of his autonomy. Explicitly or implicitly, he agrees to allow the physician to make certain decisions for him that he would ordinarily make for himself.

The physician tells the patient what to eat and drink and what to avoid, what medicine he should take and when to take it, how much exercise he should get and what kind it should be. The patient consents to run at least part of his life by "doctor's orders" in the hope that he will regain his health or at least improve his condition.

The physician acquires a great deal of power in this relationship. But she also takes on a great responsibility. It has been recognized at least since the time of Hippocrates that the physician has an obligation to act in the best interest of the patient. The patient is willing to transfer part of his autonomy because he is confident that the physician will act in that way. If this analysis of the present form of the physician–patient relationship is roughly correct, two questions are appropriate.

First, should the relationship be one in which the patient is so dependent on the paternalistic decisions of the physician? Perhaps it would be better if patients did not think of themselves as transferring any of their autonomy to physicians. Physicians might better be thought of as people offering advice rather than as ones issuing "orders." Thus, patients, free to accept or reject advice, would retain fully their power to govern their own lives. If this is a desirable goal, it is clear that the traditional model of the physician–patient relationship needs to be drastically altered.

One problem with this point of view is that the patient is frequently not in a position to judge the advice that is offered. Even when a patient has thoroughly researched his own condition, a primary reason for consulting a physician is to gain the advantage of her knowledge and judgment. Moreover, courses of medical therapy are often complicated ones involving many interdependent steps. A patient could not expect the best treatment if he insisted on accepting some of the steps and rejecting others. As a practical matter, a patient who expects good medical care must to a considerable extent put himself in the hands of his physician.

For this reason, the second question is perhaps based on a more realistic assessment of the nature of medical care: How much autonomy must be given up by the patient? The power of the physician over the patient cannot be absolute. The patient cannot become the slave or creature of the physician—this is not what a patient consents to when he agrees to place himself under the care of a physician. What, then, are the limits of the paternalism that can be legitimately exercised by the physician?

Informed Consent and Medical Interests

Traditionally, many physicians believed they could do almost anything to a patient so long as it was in the patient's best interest. Indeed, many thought they could act even against the patient's wishes because they considered themselves to know the patient's interest better than the patient himself and thought that eventually the patient would thank them for taking charge and making hard decisions about treatment. (See Case Presentation: Donald (Dax) Cowart Rejects Treatment, for what has become the standard example of this way of thinking.)

Although some physicians may still wish to press treatments on patients for the patients' own good, patients need not choose to do as they are advised. Some people refuse to take medications, change their diets, quit smoking, exercise more, or undergo surgical procedures that their doctors believe will improve their health or extend their lives. Valuing autonomy requires recognizing that people do not always choose to do what is best for their health, and accepting this outcome as a consequence of their exercise of autonomy.

As we have seen in the case of Dax Cowart, people may even choose to reject treatment that is clearly necessary to save their lives. Over the past two decades, the courts have recognized repeatedly and explicitly that the right to refuse or discontinue medical treatment has a basis in the Constitution and in common law. To receive medical treatment, people must first give their consent, and if they wish to reject treatment, even after it has been started, they are legally and morally entitled to do so.

Both ethicists and the courts have understood consent (in the context of agreeing to treatment) to mean that several specific conditions must be fulfilled. For consent to be morally and legally meaningful, individuals must be (1) competent to understand what they are told about their condition and capable of exercising judgment; (2) provided with relevant information about their illness and the proposed treatment for it in an understandable form and allowed the opportunity to ask questions; (3) given information about alternative treatments, including no treatment at all; and (4) allowed the freedom to make a decision about their treatment without coercion.

If any one of these criteria is not fulfilled, informed consent has not been obtained. In the following sections, we will consider some specific types of situations in which consent may be violated by physicians and evaluate the moral status of each.

Informed Consent and "Do No Harm"

Perhaps the most obvious examples of consent violations are coercive situations that involve "the healing hand acting as the hurting hand," as Gerald Dworkin puts it in one of this chapter's readings. The insistence that doctors "above all, do no harm" is the most famous ethical maxim in medicine, enshrined both in professional codes of ethics and the ancient Greek Hippocratic Oath, which physicians have taken for centuries at the conclusion of a medical education. (We will discuss this maxim as the *principle of nonmaleficence* in Part VI of this text.)

When health professionals actively assist in such practices as torture or capital punishment (as discussed in the Readings section of this chapter, as well as example 4 above) they are generally taken to not only violate the principle of nonmaleficence, but also the principle of informed consent. In such situations, health professionals use their medical skills *against* the health interests of the persons involved, and do so against their will. (Note how this contrasts with interventions such as a kidney donation, where a physician may act against a person's health interests *with* her consent.) In such situations, health care professionals turn the traditional objectives of medicine on their head, taking skills developed to heal, to reduce suffering, and to build strength, and using them in the service of injuring, increasing suffering, or weakening resistance. It should be no surprise that major medical organizations such as the American Medical Association and the American Public Health Association have clearly prohibited their members from participating in torture, "enhanced interrogations," or capital punishment, since the principle of nonmaleficence is central to their codes of ethics.

Prohibitions on medical participation in torture and other deliberately harmful practices grew out of World War II, when Nazi physicians were found to have conducted coercive experiments on large numbers of prisoners, mainly Jews in concentration camps, which resulted in death, disfigurement, and permanent disability. These experiments came to be considered prime examples of medical torture and prompted the development of the Nuremberg Code of medical ethics. (In the next chapter, we will explore these and other violations of consent in research contexts.)

Whose Consent? Whose Interests?

In the situations we have just discussed, medical professionals clearly disregarded both lack of consent and medical interests, and violated the "do no harm" standard. In at least one sense, such examples are ethically straightforward, since neither the absence of consent nor the failure to advance medical interests are in question. But what about situations in which a patient's wishes or her best medical interests are the subject of controversy? And what of situations in which someone besides a patient claims to speak for the medical interests of the party or parties involved?

Later in this text, we will explore several different ways in which a patient's consent or lack thereof can become controversial. Many classic examples of such dilemmas involve patients in persistent vegetative states or suffering from dementia, whose family members come to disagree with each other or with physicians about what medical interventions the patient would accept. While mentally competent adults have a well-established right to refuse medical treatment, there are still difficult questions about how far physicians ought

to follow patients' requests that are contrary to their own medical interests and may even produce death. (We will explore these questions in greater detail in Chapter 8: Euthanasia and Physician-Assisted Death.)

There are many different ways in which a patient's best medical interests can become a subject of controversy, as we will see throughout this text. But matters of consent and patient autonomy become especially complicated when someone besides the patient endeavors to speak for the medical interests of the persons (or potential persons) involved. Since children are not considered competent to consent to medical treatments, decisions about their best interests generally fall to their parents or guardians—whose beliefs about illness and medicine may, as we have seen, conflict with those of physicians or society at large. And as we saw in example 7 at the start of this Briefing, there are also situations in which individuals or government bodies claim to speak for the interests of a developing fetus—sometimes in direct conflict with the health interests or decisions of the pregnant woman who carries it. We will conclude our discussion of consent and medical interest by briefly exploring each type of situation in turn.

Parents and Children. In most situations, the medical goals of parents and their children's physicians are complementary. The duty of the physician is to provide the child with the best medical care possible. The duty of the parent is to protect and promote the welfare of the child. Ordinarily, these two duties are congruent with respect to a course of medical action. The parent asks the physician "what is best" for the child, while the physician discusses various options and risks with the parent and secures his or her consent on behalf of the child.

However, these complementary roles are dependent on physicians and parents sharing some fundamental beliefs about the nature of disease and the efficacy of medical therapy in controlling it. When these beliefs are not shared, the outcome is a divergence of opinion about what should be done in the best interest of the child. The actions favored by the physician may be incompatible with the actions favored by the parents.

As we have seen in the Case Presentations and example 6 above, some Christian Scientist parents believe that illness has no material reality but is instead a manifestation of fearful or disordered thinking. Adherents of other religious and cultural traditions, such as the Hmong, may view illness as the work of spirits who must be propitiated or exorcised. Parents with such beliefs often have deep convictions that the appropriate response to illness is to seek spiritual healing rather than to employ medical modalities.

What about the children of parents who hold such beliefs? Their parents can legitimately claim that by refusing to seek or accept medical treatment for their children, they are doing what they consider best. It is a recognized legal principle that parents should determine the best interests of their children except in very special circumstances, usually involving neglect, abuse, drug dependency, or mental illness. Should Christian Scientists and others with similar beliefs be put into the category of incompetent parents and forced to act against their beliefs?

In some situations, a strong case can be made for answering in the affirmative. If mentally competent adults wish to avoid or reject medical treatment for themselves, the principle of autonomy supports a public policy permitting this. But since children lack a legally recognized right to deliberate and decide for themselves, it seems reasonable to favor policies that will protect them from widely recognized risks of lasting harm and unnecessary suffering. Child welfare laws are based on the idea that children are not their parents'

property, to dispose of as they wish, but citizens whose basic safety and health are entrusted to their parents. In general, we consider a legitimate function of the state to be the protection of its citizens, especially its most vulnerable. When parents fail to take reasonable steps to secure the welfare of their children, doing so becomes a matter of interest to the state.

To justify restrictions on the generally recognized right of parents to promote the welfare of their children as they see fit, we can appeal to the harm principle. (This principle is discussed in greater detail in Part VI.) We might say, for example, that if a parent's action or failure to take action tends to result in serious harm to a child, then society is justified in restricting his or her freedom to make decisions on behalf of the child. In these situations, someone else—a court or an appointed guardian—may be better equipped to promote the child's best interest. But in such cases society must also weigh the potential harms, psychological and otherwise, that may befall a child who is forced into medical treatment against her parents' wishes, or, in extreme situations, removed from her parents' care.

Pregnancy and Autonomy. Pregnancy is a second type of situation in which the state or other individuals sometimes make proxy claims to medical interests. These situations typically involve some actual or potential conflict between the health interests or decisions of a pregnant woman and the health or continued development of the fetus she is carrying. (Example 7 above presents such a situation.)

Note that to frame such a conflict as one between two medical "interests" is already to privilege the viewpoint that the fetus is a person with its own interests—a controversial position that we will discuss in greater detail in Chapters 4 and 5. Indeed, one way of dealing with such conflicts is to deny that they are possible. If one holds that the fetus, at every developmental stage, is simply part of the woman's body, then others have no right to advocate for its interests—no more than they would have a right to speak for the "interests" of her appendix or her ovaries. The woman is simply making her own health decisions, and it would be an unjustifiable violation of her autonomy to regulate her actions in ways that the actions of men or nonpregnant women are not regulated.

However, a number of difficulties are associated with this position. The most significant one is that as a fetus continues to develop, it becomes increasingly problematic to hold that it is no different from any other part of a woman's body. Certainly at the early stages of development, advocates of fetal "interests" are often hard-pressed to explain how the supposed interests of a dividing ball of cells differ substantially from those of the sperm and egg that preceded conception. But at the later stages of pregnancy, it becomes harder to consistently deny a moral status to a fetus that one would grant to a newborn infant. As we will see in subsequent chapters, the problem of fetal personhood is one that plagues both the abortion debate (Chapter 5) and broader discussions of reproductive autonomy (Chapter 4), and it is no less relevant to the issue at hand.

Even if one is not prepared to say that the fetus has the status of a person at any time during a pregnancy, ethical problems can still arise with regard to the *potential* of the fetus to develop into a person. Indeed, if a woman intends to carry her pregnancy to term and has no reason to expect a miscarriage, then certain actions on her part come to seem morally inconsistent with reasonable care for the future welfare of a child.

Suppose, for example, a woman learns of a pregnancy and decides to carry it to term, then continues a binge drinking habit, despite her knowledge that alcohol increases the risks that her child will suffer birth defects, such as fetal alcohol syndrome. On most interpretations, it seems both inconsistent and wrong for her to disregard the potential consequences of her actions. If she has decided against (or failed to secure) an abortion, she may be morally obligated to accept some basic responsibilities of a pregnancy that will most likely end in the birth of a child. These responsibilities would include avoiding some actions that she knows will increase the risk of birth defects.

Still, as we will see throughout this text, determining that an action is morally objectionable does not mean that it is right or practical to make it illegal. The question of whether a pregnant woman has a moral responsibility to protect the welfare of a fetus is thus separate from the question of whether society is justified in regulating the woman's actions. Some local jurisdictions, for example, have detained and prosecuted pregnant women for drinking alcohol, for failing to follow a physician's directive to stay in bed or to refrain from sex during pregnancy, or for refusing a caesarean section. They have also used child abuse and drug distribution laws to supplement prosecutions of pregnant women for what would otherwise be crimes of minor drug possession. Such prosecutions reflect special restrictions on pregnant women's legal autonomy. Is it legitimate for society to require that women, by virtue of being pregnant, are subject to laws not applicable to other people? (See Case Presentation: Policing Pregnancy in Chapter 10.)

Several considerations make such a question difficult to answer. One is the issue of fetal personhood, as we saw above. If personhood begins at conception, then perhaps cases of "fetal neglect" or "fetal abuse" are no different from cases of child neglect or abuse. On this view, a pregnant woman should have similar legal responsibilities to those of a parent of a minor child. Just as parents are subject to laws and rules that don't apply to other people, so then are pregnant women—although questions remain about how far society should go in regulating their behavior. Should society enforce some minimum standards of fetal care? Should they apply throughout pregnancy? If women still have a constitutional right to abortion, how would such law enforcement establish a woman's abiding intent to carry her pregnancy to term? Such questions are considerably more complicated than those that surround child welfare laws.

At the same time, many interventions on behalf of "fetal interests" would appear to go beyond what is demanded of parents of minor children, especially when they compromise a pregnant woman's health or safety, as we saw in example 7 above. When courts or hospitals insist that women carry life-threatening pregnancies to term or deny them other medically recommended procedures out of concern for fetal health or viability, they appear to make demands on pregnant women that would never be made on parents of minors. While many people would consider it laudable for a father to risk his life or his health to save the life or health of his child, no one suggests that he should be legally required to do so. And while society might remove children from mothers or fathers whose alcohol abuse clearly endangers them, it does not rescind the parents' right to purchase alcohol. These and other factors demonstrate the difficulty of developing social policies to reduce the incidence of such problems as fetal alcohol syndrome and prenatal drug exposure while also protecting the autonomy of pregnant women. Such trade-offs between autonomy and desirable social goals will be a recurrent theme in the chapters that follow.

Truth Telling in Medicine

Questions regarding patient autonomy and medical paternalism arise with special force when physicians deceive patients. When, if ever, is it justifiable for a physician to deceive his patient?

The paternalistic answer is that deception by the physician is justified when it is in the best interest of the patient. Suppose, for example, that a transplant surgeon detects signs of tissue rejection in a patient who has just received a donor kidney. The surgeon is virtually certain that within a week the kidney will have to be surgically removed and the patient put on dialysis again. Although in no immediate clinical danger, the patient is suffering from postoperative depression. It is altogether possible that if the patient is told at this time that the transplant appears to be a failure, his depression will become more severe. This, in turn, might lead to a worsening of the patient's physical condition, perhaps even to a life-threatening extent.

Eventually the patient will have to be told of the need for another operation. But by the time that need arises, his psychological condition may have improved. Is the surgeon justified in not giving a direct and honest answer to the patient when he asks about his condition? In the surgeon's assessment of the situation, the answer is likely to do the patient harm. His duty as a physician, then, seems to require that he deceive the patient, either by lying to him (an act of commission) or by allowing him to believe that his condition is satisfactory and the transplant was successful (an act of omission).

Yet doesn't the patient have a right to know the truth from his physician? After all, it is his life that is being threatened. Should he not be told how things stand with him so that he will be in a position to make decisions that affect his own future? Is the surgeon not exceeding the bounds of the powers granted to him by the patient? The patient surely had no intention of completely turning over his autonomy to the surgeon.

The issue is one of truth telling. Does the physician always owe it to the patient to tell the truth? Some writers make a distinction between lying to the patient and merely being nonresponsive or evasive. But is this really a morally relevant distinction? In either case, the truth is being kept from the patient. Both are instances of medical paternalism.

Some insight into the attitudes of physicians and patients with respect to disturbing medical information can be gathered from a 2005 study by the Rand Corporation and Harvard Medical School. Researchers asked 509 oncologists how candid they were in giving a prognosis to cancer patients whom they expected to die in six to twelve months. Some 98 percent said they told these patients that their cancer would eventually kill them, but only 5 percent gave their patients an estimate of their remaining time. Yet 75 percent of these oncologists said that they themselves would want such an estimate. This might be viewed prima facie as an expression of medical paternalism.

Placebos

The use of placebos in medical therapy is another issue that raises questions about the legitimate limits of paternalism in medicine. The "placebo effect" is a well-documented phenomenon: a significant percentage of patients, even those who are seriously ill, will show improvement when they are given any kind of treatment or medication (even a sugar pill). This can occur even when the medication or treatment is irrelevant to their condition.

The placebo effect can be exploited by physicians for the (apparent) good of their patients. Many patients with mysterious, vague, or intractable symptoms are reluctant

to accept that their physician may be unable to help them. It can seem cruel or counterproductive to tell such patients that their condition is currently untreatable with modern medicine or that testing found no evidence of an underlying organic condition. Such harsh conclusions may cause patients to despair and continue to ail. They may cause them to lose confidence in their physicians or be less inclined to seek medical advice in the future.

One way to avoid these consequences is for the physician to prescribe a placebo for the patient. This practice has often been taken to be justified in situations where no effective treatment options exist or in which the physician suspects that a condition is primarily psychosomatic. Due to the placebo effect, a patient may actually find himself relieved of the symptoms that caused him to seek medical help. He may also benefit from having his complaint addressed rather than dismissed, and be more likely to seek medical attention in the future. So long as the placebo does not take the place of a potentially effective or untried treatment option and does the patient no harm, it may have few practical drawbacks.

However, since the placebo effect is not likely to be produced if the patient knows he is being given an ineffective medication, the physician cannot be candid about the "treatment" prescribed. She must either be silent, say something indefinite like "I think this might help your condition," or lie. Since the placebo effect is more likely to be achieved if the medication is touted as highly effective for conditions such as the patient's, there is a considerable incentive for the physician to lie. Because the patient may stand to gain a considerable amount of good from placebo therapy, the physician may think of herself as acting in the best interest of the patient.

Despite its apparent advantages, placebo therapy is open to at least two ethical criticisms. First, we can ask whether giving placebos is really in the best interests of patients. For patients with chronic or currently untreatable ailments, it may divert them from correctly assessing their conditions or researching new strategies for treating them. For patients with mysterious or possibly psychosomatic symptoms, giving a placebo may encourage a dependent assumption that there is a pill for every problem. It may prevent these patients from pursuing more genuinely beneficial strategies such as exercise, talk therapy, relaxation techniques, and dietary changes. Also, not all placebos are harmless (see Social Context: Placebos and Paternalism). Some contain active chemicals that produce side effects, so a physician who prescribes a "fake" placebo may be subjecting her patient to genuine risks.

Second, by deceiving her patient the physician is depriving him of the chance to make informed decisions about his own life and thus illegitimately undermining his autonomy. Because the physician is not directly or sincerely trying to treat the patient's condition, she does not seem to uphold her end of the physician–patient bargain. As a result, can we really say the patient has legitimately surrendered some of his autonomy and authorized the physician to act in his behalf?

Some of the traditional defenses of placebos as a form of treatment rest, in part, on the assumption that placebos can function as an effective form of therapy. But at least one influential study analyzing the use of placebos in experimental research has cast doubt on the genuineness of the placebo effect. Even if we assume that placebos sometimes work, we still must address the issue of whether it is ever morally legitimate to mislead a patient by giving her an inactive or irrelevant substance in the guise of an effective medication.

Dignity and Consent

Deception is probably not the first issue that most patients think about in the context of medical paternalism. Another important consideration has to do with something more elusive: the overall attitude and behavior of physicians toward their patients. Patients often report that their physicians deal with them in a way that is more literally paternalistic—that physicians treat them like children.

Contemporary physicians are still often invested with an aura of almost magical power and authority. To a considerable extent, they act as figures of power and mystery, whose esoteric knowledge relieves suffering and restores health. Like priests or potentates, their opinions are often delivered without explanation or debate, and their potential for ignorance or confusion is rarely acknowledged. Some physicians enjoy occupying these powerful positions and act in accordance with them. They resent having their authority questioned and fail to treat their patients with dignity and respect.

Some of these dynamics take the form of subtle or not-so-subtle expressions of condescension or arrogance. For example, many physicians call their patients by their first names, while expecting patients to address them with "Doctor" and their last names. Others brusquely interrupt patients' accounts of their symptoms or dismiss their interpretations of them without explanation. A 1999 study found that doctors let their patients speak, on average, only twenty-three seconds before redirecting them, with only 25 percent of patients getting to finish their statements. (A 2001 study found patients only got to speak twelve seconds before being interrupted, with female patients getting significantly less time to speak than their male counterparts.) Many patients say their doctors assume their own external observations are always more legitimate than their patients' first-hand reports about what it is like to live in their bodies. (There is a well-documented history of male physicians, in particular, belittling their female patients' conditions as hysterical or attention-seeking—a topic we will explore in greater detail in Chapter 10.) Others complain that physicians expect them to accept long wait times, poor customer service, and bureaucratic inefficiencies that would be unacceptable in any other business. They say doctors make them feel like supplicants or sufferers rather than valued customers. (The word *patient* literally means "one who suffers.") Such complaints are not entirely surprising, given our complicated insurance and fee-for-service system, which still generally pays doctors on the basis of how many patients they can squeeze into their schedules or how many tests they can order, rather than on how well they serve their patients.

One of the most damaging manifestations of medical paternalism is the fact that many physicians do not make a genuine effort to educate patients about the state of their health, the significance of laboratory findings, or the reasons that medication or other therapy is being prescribed. Patients are not only expected to follow orders but to do so without questioning them. Patients are, in effect, denied an opportunity to refuse treatment; consent is taken for granted.

As suggested above, one reason that physicians do not attempt to provide such information is that almost all physicians are extremely short on time. It is all too common for physicians to be scheduled to see a new patient every fifteen minutes or less, although visit times have gotten slightly longer in recent years. As we will explore in greater detail in Chapter 9: Distributing Health Care, much of this time crunch developed in the 1990s, when the rise of managed care resulted in lower reimburse-

ment fees from insurers. In order to maintain their incomes, doctors were forced to schedule more patients per day or join large practices that required them to meet ever-larger quotas of patients seen and billed. The result is a system in which careful listening and explaining on the part of doctors is often in short supply. Patients are not only provided insufficient information but are also discouraged from asking questions or revealing their doubts about care decisions.

There is no question that explaining complicated medical information to patients who lack a medical background is a challenge, especially when a physician barely has enough time to listen to their complaints. But is this challenge sufficient justification for adopting a paternalistic approach, in which physicians make decisions for patients without allowing patients to know the basis for them?

Explanations are not given, physicians sometimes say, because patients "wouldn't understand" or "might draw the wrong conclusions about their illness" or "might worry needlessly." But such well-intentioned justifications for paternalism can also slide into disdain or lack of empathy, especially when patients and doctors are in a tug-of-war over time. Recent books by physicians on the state of U.S. health care describe physicians routinely referring to persistent patients as "whiners," obese patients as "beached whales," and others as suffering from "Hispanic Hysterical Syndrome." While some of this talk may reflect doctors blowing off steam in stressful and overburdened medical environments, failures of empathy can have serious medical consequences. A famous 2011 study showed that diabetic patients of physicians who scored in the top third on a standard test of empathy have 40 percent fewer complications from the disease than those with physicians who scored the bottom third.

The moral questions here concern the most basic responsibilities of the physician to try to benefit patients. Is it ultimately beneficial for patients that physicians play the role of a distant and mysterious figure of power? Do patients have a right to ask that physicians treat them with the same dignity as physicians treat one another? Should a physician attempt to educate her patients about their illnesses? Or is a physician's only real responsibility to provide patients with needed medical treatment?

Furthermore, is it always obvious that the physician knows what will count as the overall best treatment for a patient? Patients, being human, have values of their own, and they may not rank their best chance for effective medical treatment above all other considerations. A patient with a recurrence of lung cancer might prefer palliative treatments to reduce suffering and allow her to spend time with her family, rather than a second round of chemotherapy and an extended hospital stay. Her oncologist, whose specialty has led him to focus on fighting cancer to the exclusion of other considerations, may not see the value of this alternative approach. Is it legitimate for him to withhold from her knowledge of alternative options and so allow her no choice? Can he make the decision about treatment himself on the grounds that it is a purely medical matter, one about which the patient has no expert knowledge?

Even this last assumption, that patients have no expert knowledge about their own conditions, may rest on increasingly shaky ground. Although many physicians are justifiably skeptical about "internet self-diagnosis," broader online access to medical journals now frequently means that patients are learning how to read the same research studies their physicians use to make diagnoses. New initiatives, such as OpenNotes, which give patients real-time access to notes on their medical charts, further reduce the information asymmetry between providers and patients.

Ultimately, if patients have a right to decide about their treatment, physicians have an obligation to provide them with an account of their options and with the information they need to make a reasonable choice. Thus, treating patients with dignity requires recognizing their status as autonomous agents and securing their free and informed consent.

Confidentiality

"Whatever I see or hear, professionally or privately, which ought not be divulged, I will keep it secret and tell no one," runs one of the pledges in the Hippocratic Oath.

The tradition of medical practice in the West has taken this injunction very seriously. That it has done so is not entirely due to the high moral character of physicians, for the pledge to secrecy also serves an important practical function. Physicians need to have information of an intimate and highly personal sort to make diagnoses and prescribe therapies. If physicians were known to reveal such personal information, then patients would be reluctant to cooperate, and the practice of medicine would be adversely affected.

Furthermore, because psychological factors play a role in medical therapy, the chances of success in medical treatment are improved when patients can place trust and confidence in their physicians. This aspect of the physician–patient relationship actually forms a part of medical therapy. It is particularly so for the "talking cures" characteristic of some forms of psychiatry and psychotherapy.

Breaching Confidentiality

A number of states recognize the need for "privileged communication" between physician and patient and have laws to protect physicians from being compelled to testify about their patients in court. Yet physicians are also members of the broader society and subject to its government, which is charged with protecting the lives and general interests of citizens. This sometimes places the physician in the middle of a conflict between the interest of the individual and the interest of society.

For example, physicians are often required by law to act in ways that force them to reveal information about their patients. The clearest instance of this is the legal obligation to report to health departments the names of patients who are carriers of such communicable diseases as Ebola or active tuberculosis. This permits health authorities to warn those with whom the carriers have come into contact and to guard against the spread of the diseases. Thus, the interest of society is given precedence over physician–patient confidentiality.

Confidentiality may also be breached in cases when the interest of the patient is at stake. State laws frequently require physicians and other *mandated reporters* who work with vulnerable populations to alert authorities if they suspect physical or sexual abuse, as well as child neglect or financial exploitation. Thus, a woman seeking medical attention for trauma resulting from abuse by a husband or boyfriend may have no choice about whether the police are notified. Similarly, physicians usually have no discretion about whether to report cases of suspected child abuse. Although the parents of the child may deny responsibility for the child's injuries, if the physician suspects the parents of abuse, she must make a report notifying police of her suspicions.

Few people question society's right to demand that physicians violate a patient's confidence when the health and safety of vulnerable populations is at stake. More open to question are laws that require physicians to report gunshot wounds or other injuries that might be connected with criminal actions. (In some states, before abortion became legal, physicians were required to report cases of attempted abortion.) Furthermore, as citizens, physicians may have a legal duty to report information they may have about a crime, unless they are protected by a privileged-communications law. Such legal requirements can place physicians in conflicted positions. If they act to protect patients' confidences, then they run the risk of legal sanction. If they act in accordance with the law, then they must violate the confidences of their patients.

Similar conflicts can arise for health care workers employed by government or private industry. Should a physician who works for a government agency, for example, tell her superiors if one of the employees she treats confides in her that he is a drug addict? If she does not, the employee may be subject to blackmail or bribery, or cause other problems for the agency. If she does, then she must violate the patient's confidence. Or what if a psychiatrist retained by a company decides one of its employees is so psychologically disturbed that she cannot function effectively in her job? Should the psychiatrist inform the employer, even if it means going against the wishes of the patient? (Consider also the scenario discussed in example 5, at the start of this Briefing Session.)

Duty to Warn?

Even more serious problems arise in psychiatry and have produced a number of pivotal legal decisions. Suppose, for example, that a patient expresses to his psychiatrist feelings of extreme anger against an acquaintance and even announces that he intends to kill her. What should the psychiatrist do? Should he report the threat to the police? Does he have an obligation to warn the person being threatened? This was the fundamental issue addressed by the California Supreme Court in the 1976 case *Tarasoff v. Regents of the University of California*. The majority in *Tarasoff* ruled that therapists at the student health service of the University of California, Berkeley, were negligent in their duty to warn student Tatiana Tarasoff that Prosenjit Poddar, one of their patients, had threatened her life. The therapists reported the threat to the police, but they did not warn Tarasoff. Two months later she was murdered by Poddar.

Poddar was tried and convicted of second-degree murder, but he was later released after his conviction was overturned on technical grounds. The parents of Tatiana Tarasoff sued the university for damages and took their case to the California Supreme Court. In *Tarasoff*, the court ruled that not only were the therapists justified in breaking Poddar's confidentiality, but they also had a duty to warn Tarasoff that her life was in danger. Since this ruling, many psychiatrists and other therapists have argued that this second requirement goes too far.

Health Insurance and Confidentiality

With the pervasive role that health insurers play in U.S. medical care—a role that has, if anything, been enhanced by the Affordable Care Act (ACA)—concerns have arisen about the release of confidential patient information to these companies. For patients to have their medical bills paid, their physicians may have to reveal to their insurers information concerning such matters as a patient's diabetes diagnosis or cancer treatment, sexual history and practices, and even such things as addiction treatments or psychiatric diagnoses. One ethical objection to such disclosures is that insurers are not medical professionals and it seems problematic for them to gain access to such intimate medical information about patients.

A second objection involves the use that insurers may make of this personal medical information. Before the passage of the ACA, many states allowed insurers to deny customers coverage on the basis of *preexisting conditions*, which could be as serious as a cancer diagnosis or as common and arbitrary as having diabetes or hyperthyroidism or even being pregnant or experiencing domestic violence. (A 2010 study found that large insurers denied coverage to one out of seven applicants based on such conditions—a phenomena we will discuss in greater detail in Chapter 9.) Due to such denials of coverage, many patients became reluctant to tell their physicians about serious medical symptoms, out of fear that this information would reach insurers and cause them to cancel their policies or deny coverage for necessary procedures.

While the ACA prohibits insurance companies from denying coverage based on preexisting conditions, many patients are still concerned that their insurers may try to drop their coverage based on information in their medical records. At the very least, few still believe that what one tells one's physician will remain private. The result is that many patients are still unwilling to tell their physicians anything that might cause them harm if it were known to their spouse, employer, or insurance company.

HIPAA Regulations

The Health Insurance Portability and Accountability Act (HIPAA) was passed in 1996 and was originally enacted to protect the integrity of medical records when patients changed insurers, physicians, or jobs. But over the years, the HIPAA law has been amended by Congress to contain some of the most comprehensive medical privacy protections available to Americans.

The law now includes provisions that establish patients' rights to examine and correct their medical records and that grant parents "appropriate access" to the records of their minor children. HIPAA also prohibits disclosure of patient medical records to third parties (such as employers) without patient consent, but it does allow such disclosures for treatment, payment, and insurance purposes. (Thus, a physician can consult with other health care providers about a patient's condition, bill insurance companies based on a patient's diagnoses, or call in prescriptions to a pharmacy.) Under HIPAA, medical consultants, laboratories, lawyers, and business associates connected with the care of patients must sign contracts agreeing to protect the patients' confidentiality. The law also restricts the information available to hospital staff and other health care workers to a bare minimum necessary to performing their tasks.

Some lesser-known provisions of the HIPAA law include those that allow re-searchers to use medical records for epide-miological studies (provided they remove all uniquely identifying information), and those that forbid pharmacists from disclosing patient prescription data to drug companies. (The pharmaceutical industry has repeat-edly tried to purchase access to prescription data to use in marketing campaigns aimed at physicians.)

When many of these HIPAA provisions were first proposed, critics in the health care and insurance industries claimed they would hinder physicians from questioning their patients without written consent and would impose a catastrophically heavy burden of paperwork on providers, pharmacists, and others. While many of the more dire predictions do not appear to have come to pass, HIPAA has clearly imposed some additional costs on health care providers and forced them to change some long-standing practices. Even a moderate-sized hospital, for example, may

have to negotiate confidentiality contracts with hundreds of business associates, and even small doctor's offices must document that they have made a "good faith" effort to notify patients of their HIPAA rights.

In addition, patients, as well as their families and friends, have had mixed reactions to the changes imposed by HIPAA. Some object to the fact that under HIPAA, lists of persons admitted to a hospital are no longer available without permission from patients. Thus, without prior authorization, a hospital may not be able to inform an adult son that his mother was taken to the emergency room with a stroke, was stabilized, and is now unconscious in the ICU. Families of patients with mental illness have also raised serious concerns about HIPAA regulations that hinder them from locating their loved ones, stopping them from harming themselves or others, and, if necessary, having them involuntarily committed to psychiatric facilities. But some patients appreciate rules that prevent their diagnoses and treatment from being disclosed to others without their consent. When family members are in conflict or have divergent views on such topics as end-of-life decisions, sexuality, mental health treatment, or specific procedures such as abortion, the disclosure of confidential medical information can be traumatic. This is especially true if there is a history of violence or abuse in the family. As noted above, however, HIPAA regulations do grant parents access to their minor children's medical records.

Some critics of HIPAA regulations say that they are still inadequate to protect pa-tients from the breaches of privacy made possible by computers and the electronic storage of information, and should include more opportunities for patients to stop the disclosure of their records. Even if this is true, HIPAA has undeniably done a great deal to protect and promote the medical privacy of individuals. It has made everyone involved in health care, including patients, aware of the importance of confidentiality and the legitimacy of demanding it.

Ethical Theories: Autonomy, Truth Telling, Confidentiality

Our current understanding of concepts such as autonomy, truth telling, and confidentiality are rooted in the history of philosophy and religion, and spring from a wide range of traditions and epochs. The application of these concepts to modern medicine, however, has been decisively shaped by a number of influential theories and thinkers, such as utilitarianism and the moral philosophy of Immanuel Kant. In the final section of this Briefing, we will examine how some of the specific concepts we have discussed here relate to these major ethical theories. To fully grasp the material in this and subsequent sections on ethical theories, we encourage readers to consult Part VI of this text.

We will begin this chapter's exploration of ethical theories with a discussion of utilitarianism, which evaluates actions or rules based on their tendency to increase or decrease the net quantity of happiness. According to the principle of utility, if laws, policies, practices, or regulations serve the general interest and promote the greatest happiness, then they are justified. At first glance, what we have called state paternalism and personal paternalism seem to be compatible with utilitarian ethical theory. Indeed, it can be argued that such practices can be justified on utilitarian grounds even if they restrict the individual's freedom of choice or action. This is because, for utilitarianism, autonomy has no absolute value. Personal paternalism can be justified in a similar way. If a physician believes that she can protect her patient from unnecessary

suffering or relieve his pain by keeping him in ignorance, by lying to him, by giving him placebos, or by otherwise deceiving him, these actions are morally legitimate.

It is important to note, however, that one of utilitarianism's founders, John Stuart Mill, did not take this view of paternalism. Mill argued that freedom of choice (autonomy) is of such importance that it can be justifiably restricted only when it can be shown that unregulated choice would cause harm to other people. Mill claimed that compelling people to act in certain ways "for their own good" is never legitimate. Since individuals are the best judges of their own interests and happiness, the principle of utility requires that they be free to pursue them without paternalistic interference. It follows that free and informed consent is a prerequisite for medical treatment, since physicians cannot make legitimate judgments about anyone's happiness but their own. These divergent conclusions about the legitimacy of paternalism suggest utilitarianism does not offer a single straightforward answer on this topic.

What we have said about paternalism applies also to confidentiality. Generally speaking, if violating confidentiality seems necessary to produce a state of affairs in which happiness is increased, then the violation is justified on utilitarian grounds. This might be the case when, for example, someone's life is in danger or someone is being tried for a serious crime and the testimony of a physician is needed to help establish her innocence. Yet it also might be argued from the point of view of rule utilitarianism that confidentiality is such a basic ingredient in the physician–patient relationship that, in the long run, more good will be produced if confidentiality is never violated.

The Kantian view of paternalism, truth telling, and confidentiality is more clear-cut. According to Immanuel Kant, every person is a rational and autonomous agent.

As such, he is entitled to make decisions that affect his own life. This means that a person is entitled to receive information relevant to making such decisions and is entitled to the truth, no matter how painful it might be. Thus, for treatment to be justified, the informed consent of the individual is required.

The use of placebos or any other kind of deception in medicine is morally illegitimate in a standard Kantian view, because this would involve denying a person the respect and dignity to which she is entitled. The categorical imperative also rules out lying, for the maxim involved in such an action produces a contradiction. (There are special difficulties in applying the categorical imperative, however, that are discussed in Part VI: Foundations of Bioethics. When these are taken into account, Kant's view is perhaps not quite so straightforward and definite as it first appears.)

It can be argued that Kant's principles also establish that confidentiality should be regarded as absolute. When a person becomes a patient, she does so with the expectation that with regard to what she tells her physician, there is an implicit promise of confidentiality. If this analysis is correct, then the physician is under an obligation to preserve confidentiality, because keeping promises is an absolute duty. Here, as in the case of lying, there are difficulties connected with the way a maxim is stated.

W. D. Ross's system of ethics recognizes that everyone has a moral right to be treated as an autonomous agent who is entitled to make decisions affecting her own life. Thus, free and informed consent to medical treatment is required. Also, everyone is entitled to know the truth and to be educated in helpful ways. Similarly, if confidentiality is a form of promise keeping, everyone is entitled to expect that it will be maintained. Thus, paternalism, lying, and violation of confidence are prima facie morally objectionable. Nevertheless,

it is possible to imagine circumstances in which these practices might be justified on Ross's view. The right course of action that a physician must follow is one that can be determined only on the basis of the physician's knowledge of the patient, the patient's problem, and the general situation. Only then can the relevant principles be weighed against each other.

John Rawls's theory of social and political morality is compatible with state paternalism of a restricted kind. No laws, practices, or policies can legitimately violate the basic rights of individuals. At the same time, however, a society, viewing arrangements from the original position, might decide to institute a set of practices that would promote what they agreed to be their best interests. If, for example, health is agreed to be an interest, then they might be willing to grant to the state the power to regulate a large range of matters connected with the promotion of health. Establishing standards for physicians would be an example of such regulation.

The rational agents in the original position might also go so far as to give the state power to decide (on the advice of experts) what medical treatments are legitimate, what drugs are safe and effective to use, what substances should be controlled or prohibited, and so on. So long as the principles of justice are not violated and so long as the society can be regarded as imposing these regulations on itself for the promotion of its own good (and particularly, the good of its worst-off members), then such paternalistic practices are unobjectionable.

With respect to personal paternalism, consent, deception, and confidentiality, Rawls's general theory offers few specific answers. But since Rawls endorses a version of Ross's account of prima facie duties, it seems reasonable to believe that Rawls's view on these matters would be comparable to Ross's.

The natural law doctrine of Roman Catholicism suggests that paternalism in both its forms is legitimate. If the state is organized to bring about such "natural goods" as health, then laws and practices that promote those goods are morally right. Individuals do have a worth in themselves and should be free to direct and organize their own lives. Thus, they generally should be informed and should make their own medical decisions. Yet at the same time, individuals may be ignorant of sufficient relevant information, lack the intellectual capacities to determine what is really in their best interest, or be moved by momentary passions and circumstances. For these reasons, the state may act to protect people from their own shortcomings and to foster their more genuine desires for their "natural ends."

Thus, natural law doctrine concludes that because each individual has an inherent worth, she is entitled to be told the truth in medical situations and not deceived. But the doctrine also holds that because a physician has superior knowledge, she may perceive the interest of the patient better than the patient himself. Accordingly, natural law suggests that although the physician should avoid lying, she is still under an obligation to act for the best interest of her patient. That may mean allowing the patient to believe something that is not so (as in placebo therapy) or withholding information from the patient. In the matter of confidentiality, the natural law doctrine recognizes that the relationship between physician and patient is one of trust, and a physician has a duty not to betray the confidences of her patients. But the relationship is not sacrosanct and the duty is not absolute. When the physician finds herself in a situation in which a greater wrong will be done if she does not reveal a confidence entrusted to her by a patient, she has a duty to reveal the confidence.

Contemporary ethical theories focused on capabilities, care, virtue, or socio-political identity will respond to questions of paternalism, truth-telling, and confidentiality in a variety of ways. But all of these approaches will tend to emphasize the ways in which the autonomous patient of traditional theory is always already caught up in a web of interpersonal relationships and socio-political structures, such as the family or religion, class or caste, gender or race. Going beyond merely formal autonomy, many of these approaches will ask what people are actually able to do or to be in their specific circumstances, and whether the results are compatible with basic human dignity. Such theories may question what securing informed consent or preserving confidentiality means if a female patient, for example, comes from a culture or religion in which she expects male relatives to make medical decisions for her. Different questions about confidentially and truth-telling might arise if a patient is potentially subject to domestic violence or genital cutting.

Imposing a formal standard of autonomous informed consent or confidentiality on some patients may be unethical, because other values—such as living out one's conception of a virtuous life in caring relationships with others—may sometimes take precedence over biomedical autonomy. At the same time, these theories suggest that physicians should be attentive to the ways in which familial, cultural, and other structures can impede human dignity and flourishing. Something more than informed consent or truth-telling may be required in light of social structures that have kept patients in subordinate roles, eroded their trust in medical benificence, or made them ashamed of their bodies or sexuality. Requests to discontinue treatment may be less than autonomous if they are conditioned by a cultural devaluation of women's lives or a lack of services that leaves disabled people isolated and dehumanized. All of these theories tend to challenge the mechanistic application of formal ethical principles to biomecical cases and call for attention to the specific historical and social circumstances that shape interactions between physicians and patients.

We have only sketched an outline of the possible ways in which ethical theories might deal with the issues involved in autonomy, paternalism, consent to treatment, truth telling, and confidentiality. Some of the views presented are open to challenge, and none has been worked out completely. The various roles and relationships among healthcare providers and patients are bound together in a complicated web of moral issues. We have not identified all the strands of the web, nor have we traced out their connections with one another. We have, however, mentioned enough difficulties to reveal the seriousness of the issues we will explore in this text.

READINGS

Section 1: Patient Autonomy and Medical Ethics

Paternalism and Partial Autonomy

Onora O'Neill

O'Neill argues that traditional views of autonomy in medical ethics fail to recognize that most patients fall short (to varying degrees) of the ideal rationality assumed as the basis of genuinely informed consent. Serious respect for autonomy, she claims, requires more than getting patients to sign consent forms. Physicians must make it possible for patients to understand the basics of their diagnosis and the proposed treatment, then make sure that they are secure enough to refuse the treatment or insist that it be changed.

Autonomous action, understood literally, is self-legislated action. It is the action of agents who can understand and choose what they do. When cognitive or volitional capacities, or both, are lacking or impaired, autonomous action is reduced or impossible. Autonomy is lacking or incomplete for parts of all lives (infancy, early childhood), for further parts of some lives (unconsciousness, senility, some illness and mental disturbance) and throughout some lives (severe retardation). Since illness often damages autonomy, concern to respect it does not seem a

From Onora O'Neill, "Paternalism and Partial Autonomy," *Journal of Medical Ethics* 10, no. 4 (1996): 173–178. Copyright © 1984 BMJ PUBLISHING GROUP. Reproduced by permission. (Notes omitted.)

promising fundamental principle for medical ethics. Medical concern would be strangely inadequate if it did not extend to those with incomplete autonomy. Concern for patients' well-being is generally thought a more plausible fundamental principle for medical ethics.

But it is also commonly thought implausible to make beneficence the only fundamental aim of medical practice, since it would then be irrelevant to medical treatment whether patients possessed standard autonomy, impaired autonomy or no capacity for autonomous action. All patients, from infants to the most autonomous, would be treated in ways judged likely to benefit them. Medical practice would be through and through paternalistic, and would treat patients as persons only if beneficence so required.

Recurrent debates about paternalism in medical ethics show that the aim of subordinating concern for autonomy to beneficence remains controversial. The group of notions invoked in these debates—autonomy, paternalism, consent, respect for persons, and treating others as persons—are quite differently articulated in different ethical theories. A consideration of various ways in which they can be articulated casts some light on issues that lie behind discussions of medical paternalism.

1. Paternalism and autonomy in result-oriented ethics

Most consequential moral reasoning does not take patients' autonomy as a fundamental constraint on medical practice. Utilitarian moral reasoning takes the production of welfare or well-being (variously construed) as the criterion of right action. Only when respect for patients' autonomy (fortuitously) maximises welfare is it morally required. Paternalism is not morally wrong; but some acts which attempt to maximise welfare by disregarding autonomy will be wrong if in fact non-paternalistic action (such as showing respect for others or seeking their consent to action undertaken) would have maximised welfare. Only some 'ideal' form of consequentialism, which took the maintenance of autonomy as an independent value, could regard the subordination of autonomy to beneficence as wrong. In utilitarian ethical thinking autonomy is of marginal ethical importance, and paternalism only misplaced when it reflects miscalculation of benefits.

This unambiguous picture is easily lost sight of because of an historical accident. A classical and still highly influential utilitarian discussion of autonomy and paternalism is John Stuart Mill's *On Liberty*. Mill believed both that each person is the best judge of his or her own happiness and that autonomous pursuit of goals is itself a major source of happiness, so he thought happiness could seldom be maximised by action which thwarted or disregarded others' goals, or took over securing them. Paternalists, on this view, have benevolent motives but don't achieve beneficent results. They miscalculate.

Mill's claims are empirically dubious. Probably many people would be happier under beneficent policies even when these reduce the scope for autonomous action. Some find autonomous pursuit of goals more a source of frustration and anxiety than of

satisfaction. In particular, many patients want relief from hard decisions and the burden of autonomy. Even when they don't want decisions made for them they may be unable to make them, or to make them well. The central place Mill assigns autonomy is something of an anomaly in result-oriented ethical thought. It is open to challenge and shows Mill's problem in reconciling liberty with utility rather than any success in showing their coincidence.

2. Paternalism and autonomy in action-oriented ethics

Autonomy can have a more central place only in an entirely different framework of thought. Within a moral theory which centres on action rather than on results, the preconditions of agency will be fundamental. Since autonomy, of some degree, is a presupposition of agency, an action-centred ethic, whether its fundamental moral category is that of human rights, or of principles of obligation or of moral worth, must make the autonomy of agents of basic rather than derivative moral concern. This concern may be expressed as concern not to use others, but to respect them or 'treat them as persons', or to secure their consent and avoid all (including paternalistic) coercion.

A central difficulty for all such theories is once again empirical. It is obvious enough that some human beings lack cognitive and volitional capacities that would warrant thinking of them as autonomous. But where autonomous action is ruled out what can be the moral ground for insisting on respect or support for human autonomy? The question is sharply pointed for medical ethics since patients *standardly* have reduced cognitive and volitional capacities.

Yet most patients have some capacities for agency. Their impairments undercut some but not all possibilities for action. Hence agent-centred moral theories may be relevant to medical ethics, but only if based on an accurate view of human autonomy. The central tradition of debate in agent-centred ethics has not been helpful here because it has tended to take an abstract and inaccurate view of human autonomy. The history of these discussions is revealing.

Enlightenment political theory and especially Locke's writings are classical sources of arguments against paternalism and for respect for human autonomy. Here the consent of citizens to their governments is held to legitimate government action. In consenting citizens become, in part, the authors of government action: the notion of the sovereignty of the people can be understood as the claim that they have consented to, and so authorised, the laws by which they are ruled. In obeying such laws they are not mere subjects but retain their autonomy.

This picture invited, and got, a tough focus on the question 'What constitutes consent?' An early and perennial debate was whether consent has to be *express*—explicitly declared in speech or writing—or can be *tacit*—merely a matter of going along with arrangements. In a political context the debate is whether legitimate government must have explicit allegiance, or whether, for example, continued residence can legitimate government action. A parallel debate in medical ethics asks whether legitimate medical intervention requires explicit consent, recorded by the patient's signing of consent forms, or whether placing oneself in the hands of the doctor constitutes consent to whatever the doctor does, provided it accords with the standards of the medical profession.

The underlying picture of human choice and action invoked by those who advocate the 'informed consent' account of human autonomy is appropriate to a contractual model of human relations. Just as parties to commercial contracts consent to specific action by others, and have legal redress when this is not forthcoming, and citizens consent to limited government action (and may seek redress when this is exceeded), so patients consent to specified medical procedures (and have cause for grievance if their doctors do otherwise). Those who argue that informed consent criteria are not appropriate in medical practice sometimes explicitly reject the intrusion of commercial and contractual standards in medical care.

The contractual picture of human relations is clearly particularly questionable in medicine. We may think that citizenship and commerce are areas where we are autonomous decision-makers, enjoying what Mill would have called 'the maturity of our faculties'. In these areas, if anywhere, we come close to being fully rational decision-makers. Various well-known idealisations of human rationality—'rational economic man', 'consenting adults', 'cosmopolitan citizens', 'rational choosers'—may seem tolerable approximations. But the notion that we could be 'ideal rational patients' cannot stand up to a moment's scrutiny. This suggests that we cannot plausibly extend the enlightenment model of legitimating consent to medical

contexts. Where autonomy is standardly reduced, paternalism must it seems be permissible; opposition to medical paternalism appears to reflect an abstract and inaccurate view of human consent which is irrelevant in medical contexts.

3. The opacity of consent: a reversal of perspective

However, the same picture might be seen from quite a different perspective. Human autonomy is limited and precarious in many contexts, and the consent given to others' actions and projects is standardly selective and incomplete. *All* consent is consent to some proposed action or project *under certain descriptions*. When we consent to an action or project we often do not consent even to its logical implications or to its likely results (let alone its actual results), nor to its unavoidable corollaries and presuppositions. Put more technically, consenting (like other proposition attitudes) is *opaque*. When we consent we do not necessarily 'see through' to the implications of what we consent to and consent to these also. When a patient consents to an operation he or she will often be unaware of further implications or results of that which is consented to. Risks may not be understood and post-operative expectations may be vague. But the opacity of patients' consent is not radically different from the opacity of all human consenting. Even in the most 'transparent', highly-regulated, contractual arrangements, consent reaches only a certain distance. This is recognised whenever contracts are voided because of cognitive or volitional disability, or because the expectations of the 'reasonable man' about the further implications of some activity do not hold up. Medical cases may then be not so much anomalies, with which consent theory cannot adequately deal, as revealing cases which highlight typical limits of human autonomy and consent.

Yet most discussions of consent theory point in the other direction. The limitations of actual human autonomy aren't taken as constraints on working out the determinate implications of respect for autonomy in actual contexts, but often as *aberrations* from ideally autonomous choosing. The rhetoric of the liberal tradition shows this clearly. Although it is accepted that we are discussing the autonomy of '*finite* rational beings', finitude of all sorts is constantly forgotten in favour of loftier and more abstract perspectives.

4. Actual consent and 'ideal' consent

There are advantages to starting with these idealised abstractions rather than the messy incompleteness of human autonomy as it is actually exercised. Debates on consent theory often shift from concern with dubious consent actually given by some agent to a proposed activity or arrangement to concern with consent that would hypothetically be given by an ideally autonomous (rational and free) agent faced with that proposal. This shift to hypothetical consent allows us to treat the peculiar impairments of autonomy which affect us when ill as irrelevant: we can still ask what the (admittedly hypothetical) ideally autonomous patient would consent to. This line of thought curiously allows us to combine ostensible concern for human autonomy with paternalistic medical practice. Having reasoned that some procedure would be consented to by ideally autonomous patients we may then feel its imposition on actual patients of imperfect autonomy is warranted. But by shifting focus from what has (actually) been consented to, to what would (ideally) be consented to, we replace concern for others' autonomy with concern for the autonomy of hypothetical, idealised agents. This is not a convincing account of what it is not to use others, but rather to treat them as persons.

If we don't replace concern for actual autonomy with concern for idealised autonomy, we need to say something definite about when actual consent is genuine and significant and when it is either spurious or misleading, and so unable to legitimise whatever is ostensibly consented to. Instead of facing the sharp outlines of idealised, hypothetical conceptions of human choosing we may have to look at messy actual choosing. However, we don't need to draw a sharp boundary between genuine, morally significant consent and spurious, impaired consent which does not legitimate. For the whole point of concern for autonomy and hence for genuine consent is that it is not up to the *initiator* of action to choose what to impose: it is up to those affected to choose whether to accept or to reject proposals that are made. To respect others' autonomy requires that we make consent *possible* for them, taking account of whatever partial autonomy they may have. Medical practice respects patients' autonomy when it allows patients as they actually are to refuse or accept what is proposed to them. Of course, some impairments prevent refusal or acceptance.

The comatose and various others have to be treated paternalistically. But many patients can understand and refuse or accept what is proposed over a considerable range. Given some capacities for autonomous action, whatever can be made comprehensible to and refusable by patients, can be treated as subject to their consent—or refusal. This may require doctors and others to avoid haste and pressure and to counteract the intimidation of unfamiliar, technically bewildering and socially alien medical environments. Without such care in imparting information and proposing treatment the 'consent' patients give to their treatment will lack the autonomous character which would show that they have not been treated paternally but rather as persons.

5. 'Informed consent' and legitimating consent

There is a long-standing temptation, both in medical ethics and beyond, to find ways in which consent procedures can be formalised and the avoidance of paternalism guaranteed and routinised. But if the ways in which human autonomy is limited are highly varied, it is not likely that any set procedures can guarantee that consent has been given. Early European colonialists who 'negotiated treaties' by which barely literate native peoples without knowledge of European moral and legal traditions 'consented' to sales of land or cession of sovereignty reveal only that the colonialists had slight respect for others' autonomy. Medical practice which relies on procedures such as routine signing of 'consent forms' may meet conditions for avoiding litigation, but does not show concern for human autonomy as it actually exists. Such procedures are particularly disreputable given our knowledge of the difficulties even the most autonomous have in assimilating distressing information or making unfamiliar and hard decisions.

Serious respect for autonomy, in its varied, limited forms, demands rather that patients' refusal or consent, at least to fundamental aspects of treatment, be made possible. The onus on practitioners is to see that patients, as they actually are, understand what they can about the basics of their diagnosis and the proposed treatment, and are secure enough to refuse the treatment or to insist on changes. If the proposal is accessible and refusable for an actual patient, then (but only then) can silence or going along with it reasonably be construed as consent. The notions of seeking consent and respecting autonomy are brought into disrepute when the 'consent' obtained does not genuinely reflect the patient's response to proposed treatment.

6. Partial autonomy, coercion and deception

Once we focus on the limited autonomy of actual patients it becomes clear that consent to *all* aspects and descriptions of proposed treatment is neither possible nor required. Only the ideally, unrestrictedly autonomous could offer such consent. In human contexts, whether medical or political, the most that we can ask for is consent to the more *fundamental* proposed policies, practices and actions. Patients can no more be asked to consent to every aspect of treatment than citizens can be asked to consent to every act of government. Respect for autonomy requires that consent be possible to *fundamental* aspects of actions and proposals, but allows that consent to trivial and ancillary aspects of action and proposals may be absent or impossible.

Treatment undertaken without consent when a patient could have reached his or her own decisions if approached with care and respect may fail in many ways. In the most serious cases the action undertaken uses patients as tools or instruments. Here the problem is not just that some partially autonomous patient couldn't (or didn't) consent, but that the treatment precluded consent even for ideally autonomous patients. Where a medical proposal hinges fundamentally on coercion or deception, not even the most rational and independent can dissent, or consent. Deceivers don't reveal their fundamental proposal or action; coercers may make their proposal plain enough but rob *anyone* of choice between consent or dissent. In deception 'consent' is spurious because cognitive conditions for consent are not met: in coercion 'consent' is spurious because volitional conditions for consent are not met.

However, some non-fundamental aspects of treatment to which consent has been given may have to include elements of deception or coercion. Use of placebos or of reassuring but inaccurate accounts of expected pain might sometimes be non-fundamental but indispensable and so permissible deceptions. Restraint of a patient during a painful procedure might be a non-fundamental but indispensable and so permissible coercion. But using patients as unwitting experimental subjects or concealing fundamental aspects of their illness or prognosis or treatment from them, or imposing medical treatment and ignoring or preventing its refusal, would always use patients, and so fail to respect autonomy. At best such imposed treatment might, if benevolent, constitute impermissible paternalism; at worst, if non-benevolent, it might constitute assault or torture.

7. Partial autonomy, manipulation and paternalism

Use of patients is an extreme failure to respect autonomy; it precludes the consent even of the ideally autonomous, let alone of those with cognitive or volitional impairments. Respect for partial autonomy would also require medical practice to avoid treatment which, though refusable by the ideally autonomous, would not be refusable by a particular patient in his or her present condition. Various forms of manipulation and of questionable paternalism fail to meet these requirements. Patients are manipulated if they are 'made offers they cannot refuse', given their actual cognitive and volitional capacities. For example, patients who think they may be denied further care or discharged without recourse if they refuse proposed treatment may be unable to refuse it. To ensure that 'consent' is not manipulated available alternatives may have to be spelled out and refusal of treatment shown to be a genuine option. 'Consent' which is achieved by relying on misleading or alarmist descriptions of prognosis or uninformative accounts of treatment and alternatives does not show genuine respect. Only patients who are quite unable to understand or decide need complete paternalist protection. When there is a relationship of unequal power, knowledge or dependence, as so often [exists] between patients and doctors, avoiding manipulation and unacceptable paternalism demands a lot.

Avoiding unacceptable paternalism demands similar care. Manipulators use knowledge of others and their weaknesses to impose their own goals; paternalists may not recognise either others' goals, or that they are *others'* goals. Patients, like anyone with limited understanding and capacity to choose, may be helped by advice and information, and may need help to achieve their aims. But if it is not the patients' but others' aims which determine the limits and goals of medical intervention, the intervention (even if neither deceptive nor coercive) will be unacceptably paternalistic. Handicapped patients whose ways of life are determined by others may not be deceived or coerced—but they may be unable to refuse what others think appropriate for them. This means that patients' own goals, medical and non-medical, and their plans for achieving these, are constraints on any medical practice which respects patients' autonomy. Since return to health is often central to patients' plans, this constraint may require little divergence from the treatment that paternalistic medical practice would select, except that patients would have to be party to fundamental features of their treatment. But where patients' goals differ from doctors' goals—perhaps they value quality of life or avoiding pain or dependence more than the doctor would—respect for the patient requires that these goals not be overridden or replaced by ones the patient does not share and that the patient's own part in achieving them not be set aside.

Debates on medical paternalism often assume that the goals of medical action can be determined independently of patients' goals. But in action-oriented ethical thinking morally required goals are not given independently of agents' goals. Paternalism in this perspective is simply the imposition of others' goals (perhaps those of doctors, nursing homes or relatives) on patients. These goals too must be taken into account if we are to respect the autonomy of doctors, nursing homes and relatives. But imposing their goals on patients capable of some autonomy does not respect patients. The contextually-sensitive, action-oriented framework discussed here does not reinstate a contractual or consumer-sovereignty picture of medical practice, in which avoiding deceit and coercion is all that respect requires. On the contrary, it insists that judgements of human autonomy must be contextual, and that what it takes to respect human autonomy will vary with context. When patients' partial autonomy constrains medical practice, respect for patients may demand action which avoids not only deceit and coercion but also manipulation and paternalism; but where autonomy is absent there is no requirement that it be respected.

8. Respecting limited autonomy

Medical paternalism has been considered within three frameworks. Within a result-oriented framework of the standard utilitarian type it is not only permissible but required that concern for human autonomy be subordinated to concern for total welfare. Within an action-oriented framework that relies on an abstract, 'idealising' account of human autonomy, medical practice is too readily construed as ruling out all paternalism and permitting only treatment that would be consented to by 'idealised' autonomous agents. Within an action-oriented framework that takes account of the partial character of human autonomy we can sketch patterns of reasoning which draw boundaries in given contexts between permissible and impermissible forms of paternalism. This account yields no formula, such as the requirement to avoid coercion and deception may be thought to yield for abstract approaches. But the inadequacies of that formula for guiding action when impairment is severe speak in favour of a more accurate and contextual view of human autonomy.

By trying to incorporate concern for actual, partial capacities for autonomous action into an account of respect for patients and medical paternalism we find that we are left without a single boundary-line between acceptable and unacceptable medical practice. What we have are patterns of reasoning which yield different answers for different patients and for different proposals for treatment. One patient can indeed be expected to come to an informed and autonomous (if idiosyncratic) decision; another may be too confused to take in what his options are. A third may be able to understand the issues but too dependent or too distraught to make decisions. Attempts to provide uniform guidelines for treating patients as persons, respecting their autonomy and avoiding unacceptable medical paternalism are bound to be insensitive to the radical differences of capacity of different patients. A theory of respect for patients must rely heavily and crucially on actual medical judgements to assess patient's current capacities to absorb and act on information given in various ways. But it does not follow that 'professional judgement' or 'current medical standards' *alone* can provide appropriate criteria for treating patients as persons. For if these do not take the varying ways in which patients can exercise autonomy as constraints on permissible treatment, they may institutionalise unjustifiable paternalism. Professional judgement determines what constitutes respect for patients only when guided by concern to communicate effectively what patients can understand and to respect the decisions that they can make.

9. Issues and contexts

Sections 1, 2 and 3 above discussed some ways in which treatment of autonomy, paternalism and respect for patients are articulated in result-oriented ethics and in action-oriented approaches which take an abstract view of cognition and volition, and hence of autonomy. The alternative account proposed in sections 4 to 8 is that only consideration of the determinate cognitive and volitional capacities and incapacities of particular patients at particular times provides a framework for working out boundaries of permissible medical paternalism. If such judgements are contextual, there is no way to demarcate unacceptable paternalism in the abstract. The following headings only point to contexts in which these issues arise and have to be resolved. Which resolutions are justifiable will depend not only on following a certain pattern of reasoning but on the capacities for autonomous action particular patients have at the relevant time.

A. Temporarily Impaired Capacity For Autonomy

If respect for autonomy is morally fundamental, restoring (some) capacities is morally fundamental. Survival is necessary for such restoration; but not sufficient. If patients' autonomy constrains practice, survival can never be foregone in favour of autonomy, but it is an open question whether survival with no or greatly reduced capacities for autonomy can be a permissible goal. Risky surgery may sometimes reasonably be imposed for the sake of restoring capacities, even when mere survival would be surer without surgery.

Temporary loss of autonomy offers grounds for paternalistic intervention to restore autonomy—but not for all paternalistic interventions. It might be better for an unconscious sportsman if advantage were taken of his temporary incapacity to perform some non-urgent operation or to make some non-medical intervention—in his affairs. But if restoration of autonomy is likely, an action-oriented ethic offers no ground for such paternalism.

B. Long Term Or Permanent Impairment Of Autonomy

This is the standard situation of children, and so the original context of paternalism. Those with long and debilitating illnesses, physical as well as mental, may suffer very varied impairments of autonomy. Hence consideration of parental paternalism may illuminate these cases. While the law has to fix an age to end minority, parents have to adapt their action to a constantly altering set of capacities for autonomous action. Choices which cannot be made at one stage can at another; autonomy develops in one area of life and lags in another. Unfortunately, medical trajectories may not be towards fuller capacities. Medical and other decisions may then have to be to some extent imposed. But there is no general reason to think that those who are unable to make some decisions are unable to make any decisions, and even when full return of capacities is unlikely, patients, like children, may gain in autonomy when an optimistic view is taken of their capacities.

C. Permanent Loss Of Autonomy

Here decisions have (eventually) to be made that go beyond what is needed for restoring (some) autonomy. Sometimes medical staff and relatives may be able to make some use of a notion of hypothetical consent. But what they are likely to be asking is not 'What would the ideally autonomous choose in this situation?', but rather 'What would this patient have chosen in this situation?' If this can be answered, it may be possible to maintain elements of respect for the particular patient as he or she was in former times. But usually this provides only vague indications for medical or other treatment, and respect for absent autonomy can be at best vestigial.

D. Lifelong Incapacity For Autonomy

For those who never had or will have even slight capacities for autonomous action the notion of respect is vacuous. There is no answer to the hypothetical question 'What would he or she have chosen if able to do so?' and the hypothetical question 'What would the ideally autonomous choose in this situation?' may have determinate answer. Here, unavoidably, paternalism must govern medical practice indefinitely and the main questions that arise concern the appropriate division of authority to make paternalistic decisions between relatives and medical staff and legally appointed guardians.

Paternalism

Gerald Dworkin

Dworkin attempts to show that even if we place an absolute value on individual choice, a variety of paternalistic policies can still be justified. In consenting to a system of representative government, we understand that it may act to safeguard our interests in certain ways. But under what conditions would rational individuals agree to limit their liberty, even when exercise of that liberty does not affect other people's interests?

Dworkin suggests that such conditions are satisfied in cases that involve a "good" such as health—one that everybody needs in order to pursue other goods. Rational people would agree that attaining such a good should be promoted by the government even when individuals don't recognize it as a good at a particular time. There is a sense, Dworkin argues, in which we are not imposing such a good on people. What we are really saying is that if people knew the facts and assessed them properly, this is what they would choose. As humans, we are susceptible to distraction, depression, and sometimes choose immediate gratification over long-term benefit. Thus, a person might approve of laws that restrict cigarette sales because she knows she should stop smoking.

It is plausible, Dworkin suggests, that rational people would grant to a legislature the right to impose such restrictions on their conduct. But the government has to demonstrate the exact nature of the harmful effects to be avoided. Also, if there is an alternative way of accomplishing the end without restricting liberty, then the society should adopt it.

Neither one person, nor any number of persons, is warranted in saying to another human creature of ripe years, that he shall not do with his life for his own benefit what he chooses to do with it.   Mill

I do not want to go along with a volunteer basis. I think a fellow should be compelled to become better and not let him use his discretion whether he wants to get smarter, more healthy or more honest.

General Hershey

I take as my starting point the "one very simple principle" proclaimed by Mill in *On Liberty* . . . "That principle is, that the sole end for which mankind are warranted, individually or collectively, in interfering with the liberty of action of any of their

From Gerald Dworkin, "Paternalism," *The Monist*, LaSalle, IL, vol. 56, no. 1 (1973): 64–84, by permission of Oxford University Press/on behalf of General Philosophical Inquiry. (Notes omitted.)

number, is self-protection. That the only purpose for which power can be rightfully exercised over any member of a civilized community, against his will, is to prevent harm to others. He cannot rightfully be compelled to do or forbear because it will be better for him to do so, because it will make him happier, because, in the opinion of others, to do so would be wise, or even right."

This principle is neither "one" nor "very simple." It is at least two principles; one asserting that self-protection or the prevention of harm to others is sometimes a sufficient warrant and the other claiming that the individual's own good is *never* a sufficient warrant for the exercise of compulsion either by the society as a whole or by its individual members. I assume that no one with the possible exception of extreme pacifists or anarchists questions the correctness of the first half of the principle. This essay is an examination of the negative claim embodied in Mill's principle—the objection to paternalistic interferences with a man's liberty.

I

By paternalism I shall understand roughly the interference with a person's liberty of action justified by reasons referring exclusively to the welfare, good, happiness, needs, interests or values of the person being coerced. One is always well-advised to illustrate one's definitions by examples but it is not easy to find "pure" examples of paternalistic interferences. For almost any piece of legislation is justified by several different kinds of reasons and even if historically a piece of legislation can be shown to have been introduced for purely paternalistic motives, it may be that advocates of the legislation with an anti-paternalistic outlook can find sufficient reasons justifying the legislation without appealing to the reasons which were originally adduced to support it. Thus, for example, it may be that the original legislation requiring motorcyclists to wear safety helmets was introduced for purely paternalistic reasons. But the Rhode Island Supreme Court recently upheld such legislation on the grounds that it was "not persuaded that the legislature is powerless to prohibit individuals from pursuing a course of conduct which could conceivably result in their becoming public charges," thus clearly introducing reasons of a quite different kind. Now I regard this decision as being based on reasoning of a very dubious nature but it illustrates the kind of problem one has in finding examples. The following is a list of the kinds of interferences I have in mind as being paternalistic.

II

1. Laws requiring motorcyclists to wear safety helmets when operating their machines.

2. Laws forbidding persons from swimming at a public beach when lifeguards are not on duty.

3. Laws making suicide a criminal offense.

4. Laws making it illegal for women and children to work at certain types of jobs.

5. Laws regulating certain kinds of sexual conduct, e.g. homosexuality among consenting adults in private.

6. Laws regulating the use of certain drugs which may have harmful consequences to the user but do not lead to anti-social conduct.

7. Laws requiring a license to engage in certain professions with those not receiving a license subject to fine or jail sentence if they do engage in the practice.

8. Laws compelling people to spend a specified fraction of their income on the purchase of retirement annuities. (Social Security)

9. Laws forbidding various forms of gambling (often justified on the grounds that the poor are more likely to throw away their money on such activities than the rich who can afford to).

10. Laws regulating the maximum rates of interest for loans.

11. Laws against duelling.

In addition to laws which attach criminal or civil penalties to certain kinds of action there are laws, rules, regulations, decrees, which make it either difficult or impossible for people to carry out their plans and which are also justified on paternalistic grounds. Examples of this are:

1. Laws regulating the types of contracts which will be upheld as valid by the courts, e.g. (an example of Mill's to which I shall return) no man may make a valid contract for perpetual involuntary servitude.

2. Not allowing as a defense to a charge of murder or assault the consent of the victim.

3. Requiring members of certain religious sects to have compulsory blood transfusions. This is made possible by not allowing the patient to have recourse to civil suits for assault and battery and by means of injunctions.

4. Civil commitment procedures when these are specifically justified on the basis of preventing the person being committed from harming himself. (The D.C. Hospitalization of the Mentally Ill Act provides for involuntary hospitalization of a person who "is mentally ill, and because of that illness, is likely to injure *himself* or others if allowed to remain at liberty." The term injure in this context applies to unintentional as well as intentional injuries.)

5. Putting fluorides in the community water supply.

All of my examples are of existing restrictions on the liberty of individuals. Obviously one can think of interferences which have not yet been imposed. Thus one might ban the sale of cigarettes, or require that people wear safety-belts in automobiles (as opposed to merely having them installed) enforcing this by not allowing motorists to sue for injuries even when caused by other drivers if the motorist was not wearing a seat-belt at the time of the accident. . . .

III

Bearing these examples in mind let me return to a characterization of paternalism. I said earlier that I meant by the term, roughly, interference with a person's liberty for his own good. But as some of the examples show the class of persons whose good is invoked is not always identical with the class of persons whose freedom is restricted. Thus in the case of professional licensing it is the practitioner who is directly interfered with and it is the would-be patient whose interests are presumably being served. Not allowing the consent of the victim to be a defense to certain types of crime primarily affects the would-be aggressor but it is the interests of the willing victim that we are trying to protect. Sometimes a person may fall into both classes as would be the case if we banned the manufacture and sale of cigarettes and a given manufacturer happened to be a smoker as well.

Thus we may first divide paternalistic interferences into "pure" and "impure" cases. In "pure" paternalism the class of persons whose freedom is restricted is identical with the class of persons whose benefit is intended to be promoted by such restrictions. Examples: the making of suicide a crime, requiring passengers in automobiles to wear seat-belts, requiring a Christian Scientist to receive a blood transfusion. In the case of "impure" paternalism in trying to protect the welfare of a class of persons we find that the only way to do so will involve restricting the freedom of other persons besides those who are benefitted. Now it might be thought that there are no cases of "impure" paternalism since any such case could always be justified on non-paternalistic grounds, i.e. in terms of preventing harm to others. Thus we might ban cigarette manufacturers from continuing to manufacture their product on the grounds that we are preventing them from causing illness to others in the same way that we prevent other manufacturers from releasing pollutants into the atmosphere, thereby causing danger to the members of the community. The difference is, however, that in the former but not the latter case

the harm is of such a nature that it could be avoided by those individuals affected if they so chose. The incurring of the harm requires, so to speak, the active co-operation of the victim. It would be mistaken theoretically and hypocritical in practice to assert that our interference in such cases is just like our interferences in standard cases of protecting others from harm. At the very least someone interfered with in this way can reply that no one is complaining about his activities. It may be that impure paternalism requires arguments or reasons of a stronger kind in order to be justified since there are persons who are losing a portion of their liberty and they do not even have the solace of having it be done "in their own interest." Of course in some sense, if paternalistic justifications are ever correct then we are protecting others, we are preventing some from injuring others, but it is important to see the differences between this and the standard case.

Paternalism then will always involve limitations on the liberty of some individuals in their own interest but it may also extend to interferences with the liberty of parties whose interests are not in question.

IV

Finally, by way of some more preliminary analysis, I want to distinguish paternalistic interferences with liberty from a related type with which it is often confused. Consider, for example, legislation which forbids employees to work more than, say, 40 hours per week. It is sometimes argued that such legislation is paternalistic for if employees desired such a restriction on their hours of work they could agree among themselves to impose it voluntarily. But because they do not the society imposes its own conception of their best interests upon them by the use of coercion. Hence this is paternalism.

Now it may be that some legislation of this nature is, in fact, paternalistically motivated. I am not denying that. All I want to point out is that there is another possible way of justifying such measures which is not paternalistic in nature. It is not paternalistic because as Mill puts it in a similar context such measures are "required not to overrule the judgment of individuals respecting their own interest but to give effect to that judgment they being unable to give effect to it except by concert, which concert again cannot be effectual unless it receives validity and sanction from the law."

The line of reasoning here is a familiar one first found in Hobbes and developed with great sophistication by contemporary economists in the last decade or so. There are restrictions which are in the interests of a class of persons taken collectively but are such that the immediate interest of each individual is furthered by his violating the rule when others adhere to it. In such cases the individuals involved may need the use of compulsion to give effect to their collective judgment of their own interest by guaranteeing each individual compliance by the others. In these cases compulsion is not used to achieve some benefit which is not recognized to be a benefit by those concerned, but rather because it is the only feasible means of achieving some benefit which is recognized as such by all concerned. This way of viewing matters provides us with another characterization of paternalism in general. Paternalism might be thought of as the use of coercion to achieve a good which is not recognized as such by those persons for whom the good is intended. Again while this formulation captures the heart of the matter—it is surely what Mill is objecting to in *On Liberty*—the matter is not always quite like that. For example when we force motorcyclists to wear helmets we are trying to promote a good—the protection of the person from injury—which is surely recognized by most of the individuals concerned. It is not that a cyclist doesn't value his bodily integrity; rather, as a supporter of such legislation would put it, he either places, perhaps irrationally, another value or good (freedom from wearing a helmet) above that of physical well-being or, perhaps, while recognizing the danger in the abstract, he either does not fully appreciate it or he underestimates the likelihood of its occurring. But now we are approaching the question of possible justifications of paternalistic measures and the rest of this essay will be devoted to that question.

V

I shall begin for dialectical purposes by discussing Mill's objections to paternalism and then go on to discuss more positive proposals.

An initial feature that strikes one is the absolute nature of Mill's prohibitions against paternalism. It is so unlike the carefully qualified admonitions of Mill and his fellow Utilitarians on other moral issues. He speaks of self-protection as the *sole* end warranting coercion, of the individual's own goals as *never* being a sufficient warrant. . . . The structure of Mill's argument is as follows:

1. Since restraint is an evil the burden of proof is on those who propose such restraint.

2. Since the conduct which is being considered is purely self-regarding, the normal appeal to the protection of the interests of others is not available.

3. Therefore we have to consider whether reasons involving reference to the individual's own good, happiness, welfare, or interests are sufficient to overcome the burden of justification.

4. We either cannot advance the interests of the individual by compulsion, or the attempt to do so involves evil which outweighs the good done.

5. Hence the promotion of the individual's own interests does not provide a sufficient warrant for the use of compulsion.

Clearly the operative premise here is 4 and it is bolstered by claims about the status of the individual as judge and appraiser of his welfare, interests, needs, etc.

> With respect to his own feelings and circumstances, the most ordinary man or woman has means of knowledge immeasurably surpassing those that can be possessed by any one else.
>
> He is the man most interested in his own well-being: the interest which any other person, except in cases of strong personal attachment, can have in it, is trifling, compared to that which he himself has.

These claims are used to support the following generalizations concerning the utility of compulsion for paternalistic purposes.

> The interferences of society to overrule his judgment and purposes in what only regards himself must be grounded in general presumptions; which may be altogether wrong; and even if right are as likely as not to be misapplied to individual cases.
>
> But the strongest of all the arguments against the interference of the public with purely personal conduct is that when it does interfere, the odds are that it interferes wrongly and in the wrong place.
>
> All errors which the individual is likely to commit against advice and warning are far outweighed by the evil of allowing others to constrain him to what they deem his good.

Performing the utilitarian calculation by balancing the advantages and disadvantages we find that:

Mankind are greater gainers by suffering each other to live as seems good to themselves, than by compelling each other to live as seems good to the rest.

From which follows the operative premise 4.

This is clearly the main channel of Mill's thought and it is one which has been subjected to vigorous attack from the moment it appeared—most often by fellow Utilitarians. The link that they have usually seized on is, as Fitzjames Stephen put it, the absence of proof that the "mass of adults are so well acquainted with their own interests and so much disposed to pursue them that no compulsion or restraint put upon them by any others for the purpose of promoting their interest can really promote them."

Now it is interesting to note that Mill himself was aware of some of the limitations on the doctrine that the individual is the best judge of his own interests. In his discussion of government intervention in general (even where the intervention does not interfere with liberty but provides alternative institutions to those of the market) after making claims which are parallel to those just discussed, e.g.

People understand their own business and their own interests better, and care for them more, than the government does, or can be expected to do.

He goes on to an intelligent discussion of the "very large and conspicuous exceptions" to the maxim that:

Most persons take a juster and more intelligent view of their own interest, and of the means of promoting it than can either be prescribed to them by a general enactment of the legislature, or pointed out in the particular case by a public functionary.

Thus there are things

of which the utility does not consist in ministering to inclinations, nor in serving the daily uses of life, and the want of which is least felt where the need is greatest. This is peculiarly true of those things which are chiefly useful as tending to raise the character of human beings. The uncultivated cannot be competent judges of cultivation. Those who most need to be made wiser and better, usually desire it least, and, if they desired it, would be incapable of finding the way to it by their own lights.

. . . A second exception to the doctrine that individuals are the best judges of their own

interest, is when an individual attempts to decide irrevocably now what will be best for his interest at some future and distant time. The presumption in favor of individual judgment is only legitimate, where the judgment is grounded on actual, and especially on present, personal experience; not where it is formed antecedently to experience, and not suffered to be reversed even after experience has condemned it.

The upshot of these exceptions is that Mill does not declare that there should never be government interference with the economy but rather that

. . . in every instance, the burden of making out a strong case should be thrown not on those who resist but on those who recommend government interference. Letting alone, in short, should be the general practice: every departure from it, unless required by some great good, is a certain evil.

In short, we get a presumption not an absolute prohibition. The question is why doesn't the argument against paternalism go the same way?

I suggest that the answer lies in seeing that in addition to a purely utilitarian argument Mill uses another as well. . . . A consistent Utilitarian can only argue against paternalism on the grounds that it (as a matter of fact) does not maximize the good. It is always a contingent question that may be refuted by the evidence. But there is also a non-contingent argument which runs through *On Liberty*. When Mill states that "there is a part of the life of every person who has come to years of discretion, within which the individuality of that person ought to rein uncontrolled either by any other person or by the public collectively" he is saying something about what it means to be a person, an autonomous agent. It is because coercing a person for his own good denies this status as an independent entity that Mill objects to it so strongly and in such absolute terms. To be able to choose is a good that is independent of the wisdom of what is chosen. A man's "mode" of laying out his existence is the best, not because it is the best in itself, but because it is his own mode.

It is the privilege and proper condition of a human being, arrived at the maturity of his faculties, to use and interpret experience in his own way.

As further evidence of this line of reasoning in Mill consider the one exception to his prohibition against paternalism.

In this and most civilised countries, for example, an engagement by which a person should sell himself, or allow himself to be sold, as a slave, would be null and void; neither enforced by law nor by opinion. The ground for thus limiting his power of voluntarily disposing of his own lot in life, is apparent, and is very clearly seen in this extreme case. The reason for not interfering, unless for the sake of others, with a person's voluntary acts, is consideration for his liberty. His voluntary choice is evidence that what he so chooses is desirable, or at least endurable, to him, and his good is on the whole best provided for by allowing him to take his own means of pursuing it. But by selling himself for a slave, he abdicates his liberty; he foregoes any future use of it beyond that single act.

He therefore defeats, in his own case, the very purpose which is the justification of allowing him to dispose of himself. He is no longer free; but is thenceforth in a position which has no longer the presumption in its favour, that would be afforded by his voluntarily remaining in it. The principle of freedom cannot require that he should be free not to be free. It is not freedom to be allowed to alienate his freedom.

Now leaving aside the fudging on the meaning of freedom in the last line it is clear that part of this argument is incorrect. While it is true that *future* choices of the slave are not reasons for thinking that what he chooses then is desirable for him, what is at issue is limiting his immediate choice; and since this choice is made freely, the individual may be correct in thinking that his interests are best provided for by entering such a contract. But the main consideration for not allowing such a contract is the need to preserve the liberty of the person to make future choices. This gives us a principle—a very narrow one, by which to justify some paternalistic interferences. Paternalism is justified only to preserve a wider range of freedom for the individual in question. How far this principle could be extended, whether it can justify all the cases in which we are inclined upon reflection to think paternalistic measures justified remains to be discussed. What I have tried to show so far is that there are two strains of argument in Mill—one a straight-forward Utilitarian mode of reasoning and one which relies not on the goods which free choice leads to but on the absolute value of the choice itself. The first cannot establish any absolute prohibition but at most a

presumption and indeed a fairly weak one given some fairly plausible assumptions about human psychology; the second while a stronger line of argument seems to me to allow on its own grounds a wider range of paternalism than might be suspected. I turn now to a consideration of these matters.

VI

We might begin looking for principles governing the acceptable use of paternalistic power in cases where it is generally agreed that it is legitimate. Even Mill intends his principles to be applicable only to mature individuals, not those in what he calls "non-age." What is it that justifies us in interfering with children? The fact that they lack some of the emotional and cognitive capacities required in order to make fully rational decisions. It is an empirical question to just what extent children have an adequate conception of their own present and future interests but there is not much doubt that there are many deficiencies. For example it is very difficult for a child to defer gratification for any considerable period of time. Given these deficiencies and given the very real and permanent dangers that may befall the child it becomes not only permissible but even a duty of the parent to restrict the child's freedom in various ways. There is however an important moral limitation on the exercise of such parental power which is provided by the notion of the child eventually coming to see the correctness of his parent's interventions. Parental paternalism may be thought of as a wager by the parent on the child's subsequent recognition of the wisdom of the restrictions. There is an emphasis on what could be called future-oriented consent—on what the child will come to welcome, rather than on what he does welcome.

The essence of this idea has been incorporated by idealist philosophers into various types of "real-will" theory as applied to fully adult persons. Extensions of paternalism are argued for by claiming that in various respects, chronologically mature individuals share the same deficiencies in knowledge, capacity to think rationally, and the ability to carry out decisions that children possess. Hence in interfering with such people we are in effect doing what they would do if they were fully rational. Hence we are not really opposing their will, hence we are not really interfering with their freedom. The dangers of this move has been sufficiently exposed by Berlin in his "Two Concepts of Liberty." I see no gain in theoretical clarity nor in practical advantage in trying to pass over the real nature of the interferences with liberty that we impose on others. Still the basic notion of consent is important and seems to me the only acceptable way of trying to delimit an area of justified paternalism.

Let me start by considering a case where the consent is not hypothetical in nature. Under certain conditions it is rational for an individual to agree that others should force him to act in ways which, at the time of action, the individual may not see as desirable. If, for example, a man knows that he is subject to breaking his resolves when temptation is present, he may ask a friend to refuse to entertain his requests at some later stage.

A classical example is given in the Odyssey when Odysseus commands his men to tie him to the mast and refuse all future orders to be set free because he knows the power of the Sirens to enchant men with their songs. Here we are on relatively sound ground in later refusing Odysseus' request to be set free. He may even claim to have changed his mind but since it is just such changes that he wishes to guard against we are entitled to ignore them.

A process analogous to this may take place on a social rather than individual basis. An electorate may mandate its representatives to pass legislation which when it comes time to "pay the price" may be unpalatable. I may believe that a tax increase is necessary to halt inflation though I may resent the lower pay check each month. However in both this case and that of Odysseus the measure to be enforced is specifically requested by the party involved and at some point in time there is genuine consent and agreement on the part of those persons whose liberty is infringed. Such is not the case for the paternalistic measures we have been speaking about. What must be involved here is not consent to specific measures but rather consent to a system of government run by elected representatives, with an understanding that they may act to safeguard our interests in certain limited ways.

I suggest that since we are all aware of our irrational propensities, deficiencies in cognitive and emotional capacities and avoidable and unavoidable ignorance it is rational and prudent for us to in effect take out "social insurance policies." We may argue for and against proposed paternalistic measures in terms of what fully rational individuals would accept as forms of protection. Now, clearly since the initial agreement is not about specific measures we are

dealing with a more-or-less blank check and therefore there have to be carefully defined limits. What I am looking for are certain kinds of conditions which make it plausible to suppose that rational men could reach agreement to limit their liberty even when other men's interests are not affected.

Of course as in any kind of agreement schema there are great difficulties in deciding what rational individuals would or would not accept. Particularly in sensitive areas of personal liberty, there is always a danger of the dispute over agreement and rationality being a disguised version of evaluative and normative disagreement.

Let me suggest types of situations in which it seems plausible to suppose that fully rational individuals would agree to having paternalistic restrictions imposed upon them. It is reasonable to suppose that there are "goods" such as health which any person would want to have in order to pursue his own good—no matter how that good is conceived. This is an argument that is used in connection with compulsory education for children but it seems to me that it can be extended to other goods which have this character. Then one could agree that the attainment of such goods should be promoted even when not recognized to be such, at the moment, by the individuals concerned.

An immediate difficulty that arises stems from the fact that men are always faced with competing goods and that there may be reasons why even a value such as health—or indeed life—may be overridden by competing values. Thus the problem with the Christian Scientist and blood transfusions. It may be more important for him to reject "impure substances" than to go on living. The difficult problem that must be faced is whether one can give sense to the notion of a person irrationally attaching weights to competing values.

Consider a person who knows the statistical data on the probability of being injured when not wearing seat-belts in an automobile and knows the types and gravity of the various injuries. He also insists that the inconvenience attached to fastening the belt every time he gets in and out of the car outweighs for him the possible risks to himself. I am inclined in this case to think that such a weighing is irrational. Given his life plans which we are assuming are those of the average person, his interests and commitments already undertaken, I think it is safe to predict that we can find inconsistencies in his calculations at some point. I am assuming that this is not a man who for some conscious or unconscious reasons is trying to injure himself nor is he a man who just likes to "live dangerously." I am assuming that he is like us in all the relevant respects but just puts an enormously high negative value on inconvenience—one which does not seem comprehensible or reasonable.

It is always possible, of course to assimilate this person to creatures like myself. I, also, neglect to fasten my seat-belt and I concede such behavior is not rational but not because I weigh the inconvenience differently from those who fasten the belts. It is just that having made (roughly) the same calculation as everybody else I ignore it in my actions. [Note: a much better case of weakness of the will than those usually given in ethics texts.] A plausible explanation for this deplorable habit is that although I know in some intellectual sense what the probabilities and risks are I do not fully appreciate them in an emotionally genuine manner.

We have two distinct types of situation in which a man acts in a non-rational fashion. In one case he attaches incorrect weights to some of his values; in the other he neglects to act in accordance with his actual preferences and desires. Clearly there is a stronger and more persuasive argument for paternalism in the latter situation. Here we are really not—by assumption—imposing a good on another person. But why may we not extend our interference to what we might call evaluative delusions? After all in the case of cognitive delusions we are prepared, often, to act against the expressed will of the person involved. If a man believes that when he jumps out the window he will float upwards—Robert Nozick's example— would not we detain him, forcibly if necessary? The reply will be that this man doesn't wish to be injured and if we could convince him that he is mistaken as to the consequences of his action he would not wish to perform the action. But part of what is involved in claiming that a man who doesn't fasten his seat-belts is attaching an irrational weight to the inconvenience of fastening them is that if he were to be involved in an accident and severely injured he would look back and admit that the inconvenience wasn't as bad as all that. So there is a sense in which if I could convince him of the consequences of his action he also would not wish to continue his present course of action. Now the notion of consequences being used here is covering a lot of ground. In one case it's being used to indicate what will or can happen as a result of a course

of action and in the other it's making a prediction about the future evaluation of the consequences—in the first sense—of a course of action. And whatever the difference between facts and values—whether it be hard and fast or soft and slow—we are genuinely more reluctant to consent to interferences where evaluative differences are the issue. Let me now consider another factor which comes into play in some of these situations which may make an important difference in our willingness to consent to paternalistic restrictions.

Some of the decisions we make are of such a character that they produce changes which are in one or another way irreversible. Situations are created in which it is difficult or impossible to return to anything like the initial stage at which the decision was made. In particular some of these changes will make it impossible to continue to make reasoned choices in the future. I am thinking specifically of decisions which involve taking drugs that are physically or psychologically addictive and those which are destructive of one's mental and physical capacities.

I suggest we think of the imposition of paternalistic interferences in situations of this kind as being a kind of insurance policy which we take out against making decisions which are far-reaching, potentially dangerous and irreversible. . . .

A second class of cases concerns decisions which are made under extreme psychological and sociological pressures. I am not thinking here of the making of the decision as being something one is pressured into—e.g. a good reason for making duelling illegal is that unless this is done many people might have to manifest their courage and integrity in ways in which they would rather not do so—but rather of decisions such as that to commit suicide which are usually made at a point where the individual is not thinking clearly and calmly about the nature of his decision. In addition, of course, this comes under the previous heading of all-too-irrevocable decision. Now there are practical steps which a society could take if it wanted to decrease the possibility of suicide—for example not paying social security benefits to the survivors or as religious institutions do, not allowing such persons to be buried with the same status as natural deaths. I think we may count these as interferences with the liberty of persons to attempt suicide and the question is whether they are justifiable.

Using my argument schema the question is whether rational individuals would consent to such limitations. I see no reason for them to consent to an absolute prohibition but I do think it is reasonable for them to agree to some kind of enforced waiting period. Since we are all aware of the possibility of temporary states, such as great fear or depression, that are inimical to the making of well-informed and rational decisions, it would be prudent for all of us if there were some kind of institutional arrangement whereby we were restrained from making a decision which is (all too) irreversible. What this would be like in practice is difficult to envisage and it may be that if no practical arrangements were feasible then we would have to conclude that there should be no restriction at all on this kind of action. But we might have a "cooling off" period, in much the same way that we now require couples who file for divorce to go through a waiting period. Or, more far-fetched, we might imagine a Suicide Board composed of a psychologist and another member picked by the applicant. The Board would be required to meet and talk with the person proposing to take his life, though its approval would not be required.

A third class of decisions—these classes are not supposed to be disjoint—involves dangers which are either not sufficiently understood or appreciated correctly by the persons involved. Let me illustrate, using the example of cigarette smoking, a number of possible cases.

1. A man may not know the facts—e.g. smoking between 1 and 2 packs a day shortens life expectancy 6.2 years, the costs and pain of the illness caused by smoking, etc.

2. A man may know the facts, wish to stop smoking, but not have the requisite willpower.

3. A man may know the facts but not have them play the correct role in his calculation because, say, he discounts the danger psychologically because it is remote in time and/or inflates the attractiveness of other consequences of his decision which he regards as beneficial.

In case 1 what is called for is education, the posting of warnings, etc. In case 2 there is no theoretical problem. We are not imposing a good on someone who rejects it. We are simply using coercion to enable people to carry out their own goals. (Note: There obviously is a difficulty in that only a subclass of the individuals affected wish to be prevented from doing what they are doing.) In case 3 there is a sense in which we are imposing a good on someone since given his current appraisal of the facts he doesn't wish to be restricted. But in another sense we are not imposing a good since what is being claimed—and what must be shown or at least argued for—is that an accurate accounting on his part would lead him to reject his current course of action. Now we all know that such cases exist, that we are prone to disregard dangers that are only possibilities, that immediate pleasures are often magnified and distorted.

If in addition the dangers are severe and far-reaching we could agree to allowing the state a certain degree of power to intervene in such situations. The difficulty is in specifying in advance, even vaguely, the class of cases in which intervention will be legitimate.

A related difficulty is that of drawing a line so that it is not the case that all ultra-hazardous activities are ruled out, e.g. mountain-climbing, bullfighting, sports-car racing, etc. There are some risks—even very great ones—which a person is entitled to take with his life.

A good deal depends on the nature of the deprivation—e.g. does it prevent the person from engaging in the activity completely or merely limit his participation—and how important to the nature of the activity is the absence of restriction when this is weighed against the role that the activity plays in the life of the person. In the case of automobile seat-belts, for example, the restriction is trivial in nature, interferes not at all with the use or enjoyment of the activity, and does, I am assuming, considerably reduce a high risk of serious injury. Whereas, for example, making mountain climbing illegal prevents completely a person engaging in an activity which may play an important role in his life and his conception of the person he is.

In general the easiest cases to handle are those which can be argued about in the terms which Mill thought to be so important—a concern not just for the happiness or welfare, in some broad sense, of the individual but rather a concern for the autonomy and freedom of the person. I suggest that we would be most likely to consent to paternalism in those instances in which it preserves and enhances for the individual his ability to rationally consider and carry out his own decisions.

I have suggested in this essay a number of types of situations in which it seems plausible that rational men would agree to granting the legislative powers of a society the right to impose restrictions on what Mill calls "self-regarding" conduct. However, rational men knowing something about the resources of ignorance, ill-will and stupidity available to the lawmakers of a society—a good case in point is the history of drug legislation in the United States—will be concerned to limit such intervention to [a] minimum. I suggest in closing two principles designed to achieve this end.

In all cases of paternalistic legislation there must be a heavy and clear burden of proof placed on the authorities to demonstrate the exact nature of the harmful effects (or beneficial consequences) to be avoided (or achieved) and the probability of their occurrence. The burden of proof here is twofold— what lawyers distinguish as the burden of going forward and the burden of persuasion. That the authorities have the burden of going forward means

that it is up to them to raise the question and bring forward evidence of the evils to be avoided. Unlike the case of new drugs where the manufacturer must produce some evidence that the drug has been tested and found not harmful, no citizen has to show with respect to self-regarding conduct that it is not harmful or promotes his best interests. In addition the nature and cogency of the evidence for the harmfulness of the course of action must be set at a high level. To paraphrase a formulation of the burden of proof for criminal proceedings—better 10 men ruin themselves than one man be unjustly deprived of liberty.

Finally I suggest a principle of the least restrictive alternative. If there is an alternative way of accomplishing the desired end without restricting liberty then although it may involve great expense, inconvenience, etc. the society must adopt it.

Confronting Death: Who Chooses, Who Controls? A Dialogue

Dax Cowart and Robert Burt

Dax Cowart and Robert Burt agree that the principle of autonomy gives competent patients the right to refuse or discontinue medical treatment. Burt suggests, however, that the physician should stop treatment only after a time during which the physician explores the patient's reasons for refusing it and perhaps even argues with him to get him to set aside any preconceptions that may be influencing his decision.

Cowart does not reject Burt's general views, but he is inclined to see the need for physicians to accept patients' decisions relatively quickly. Mentioning his own experiences, Cowart stresses that severe pain permits little delay and that patients should not be forced to endure what they do not wish to endure. That they may later be glad to be alive does not justify violating their autonomy and forcing treatment on them. For Cowart, respecting autonomy means recognizing that a patient is free to make wrong choices, as well as right ones.

Robert Burt: Let me start at a place where I think we agree. Before 1974, the dominant attitude of physicians toward patients was by and large

From Dax Cowart and Robert Burt, "Confronting Death: Who Chooses, Who Controls? A Dialogue Between Dax Cowart and Robert Burt," *Hastings Center Report* 28, no. 1, (1998): 14–17. Copyright © 1998 Hastings Center Report. All rights reserved. Reproduced by permission.

intensely disrespectful of patients' autonomy. The basic posture was paternalistic. Physicians knew what was best for patients, and the patient's job was just to go along. Dax himself has been a critically important actor and symbol in identifying the wrongdoing in that attitude, and raising into high social visibility the proposition that autonomy is a vitally important value; patients are the central actors here and physicians must attend to them in a respectful and careful way. On that point we agree.

The place at which I get troubled or confused is what exactly follows if we embrace this important norm of autonomy. Start with a simple version of two alternatives, perhaps extreme alternatives, to try and sharpen what the issues are. One version of autonomy says: well, it's the physician's job, like it's anybody's job who needs to respect autonomy, to say to a patient, "What do you want?"; the patient says "I want A, B, C," or "I don't want A, B, and C," and then it's just the physician's job to implement that. That is a possible interpretation of the law and way of proceeding.

I find that interpretation of the law, however, to be quite unsatisfactory. It is not only permissible, but important—I would even say essential—that a somewhat different step be taken by a physician (or anyone dealing with a patient). "What do you want?" Dax says, "I don't want treatment." At that point I think it is not only permissible but imperative that whoever hears that respond not with "OK, great, let's go ahead," but instead with, "Well, why exactly do you want that? Why have you come to that conclusion? I want to explore that with you." Now imagine the next step. Dax says, "None of your business." I think it is then both permissible and essential for the doctor to say, "No, no, it is my business, and not because I'm a doctor but because I am another human being who is necessarily involved in your life. We define one another in important kinds of ways, and while, of course, I can't define you, we have to negotiate together what our shared meanings are about, what it is that you want me to do or not to do." It is correct not only for me to say, "Why do you want to do that?" but also permissible for me to argue with you if I disagree, and to argue strenuously with you on a variety of grounds.

Now come the end of the day, yes, it's your life, it's not my life. But the question is, When have we reached the end of the day? When may we terminate this conversation so that I believe that the choice that you're making is as considerate a choice as I think it is morally obligatory for you to make? I know that this can become a kind of trick, and it shouldn't be that this is only the first step in a conversation.

Why do I think it's not just important but imperative that anybody hearing such a request on Dax's part explore it with him and even quarrel with him? I think we define one another for one another. We are not isolated creatures, popped into this world, who chart ourselves only by what's in our head. We are

intensely social creatures. Dax himself has become more than just an individual, he has become a symbol and independent force that shapes our way of thinking about ourselves when we imagine ourselves to be patients. We are mutually shaped by our expectation in lots of ways.

There is one way I want to particularize that in Dax's case. All of us, as members of a society, have attitudes toward people with disabilities. Those of us who are able-bodied or, as they say correctly among disability advocates, those of us who are temporarily able-bodied, often spend an enormous amount of energy denying the fact that our able-bodied status is, in fact, temporary. It is for many, many of us an unattractive, if not to say frightening, possibility to think of ourselves as significantly disabled. Many people in this society, for lots of different reasons, have stereotypical views of disabled people and what their possibilities are. You correct me if I misstep here, Dax, but just on the face of the matter, it seems to me that until your accident you were a member of the able-bodied community, and a very able-bodied member at that, for whom your physical prowess was a matter of great importance and pride to you. Suddenly and deeply beyond your control, in a way that can happen frighteningly to any of us, you found yourself pushed over this divide between the able-bodied and the not-able-bodied. But you inevitably brought with you attitudes that were shaped at a time when you were comfortably, happily, proudly a member of the able-bodied community.

Now it seems to me that having been pushed over that divide in physical terms, there still was a question, at least, about your attitudinal concerns, your attitudinal shift.

Let me read one passage from this initial conversation that Dax had with Dr. White.[1] Dr. White said to Dax, "From the very beginnings according to what you've told me, and what's been written in your hospital record, you had very strong feelings that you didn't want the doctors to go on with your treatment, that you wanted them to leave you alone and not attempt to sustain your life. How do you feel about that at this point?" Dax said in response, "At this point I feel much the same way. If I felt that I could be rehabilitated to where I could walk and do other things normally, I might have a different feeling about it. I don't know. But being blind itself is one big factor that influences my thinking on the matter. I know that there's no way that I want to go on as a blind and a cripple."

Now human communication is a chancy and somewhat crude thing. I only have your words. Dr. White only had Dax's words. Reading those words and putting myself imaginatively in the shoes of your physician, or your lawyer asked to represent you, I have a whole series of questions. How realistic was your perception at that point, just a few months after your accident? How realistic was it of the full range of capacities that could be held out to you, even if you were permanently blind, and even if you were permanently unable to walk (which it turns out, of course, you were not)? How much contact had you had with people with significant disabilities of these sorts? How much were you devaluing your own capacity, thinking that in fact you would be able to do nothing more than your mother's observation in the subsequent videotape interview. She said that you said at one point, "You know, all I'm going to be able do is to sit on a street corner and sell pencils." Well, of course we see today that you are very active and don't sell pencils. But this is a very common fear of able-bodied people who have had no substantial contact with people with disabilities.

So I would ask myself first of all, how realistic is someone like Dax's sense of the real possibilities open for him? But then second of all, how can I as a helper, someone who wants to be useful and helpful to him, communicate in a way that is fully understandable and believable what the real range of options are to him, disabled, that he, formerly able-bodied and now still able-bodied in his image of himself, is not able to see. What do you do? There are many possibilities. You bring people to talk, you discuss, you challenge. All this takes time. It's not something that you can just say to Dax, "Well, how realistic are you? Let's have a brief discussion." In the kind of immensely difficult, immensely traumatic situation in which he found himself, in the midst of his treatment and with the physical pain that he was feeling, and with the psychological pain of his losses including the loss of his father in the same accident, this is not a conversation that can take place in ten minutes or one day. Over how much time and with what kind of constraints?

Dax Cowart: Now I know how it feels to be killed. It makes it more difficult to take the opposing position, but being the good lawyer that I am I will do my best (audience laughter).

The right to control your own body is a right you're born with, not something that you have to ask anyone else for, not the government, not your treating physician, not your next-of-kin. No one has the right to amputate your arms or your legs without your consent. No one has the right to remove your internal organs without your consent. No one has the right to force other kinds of medical treatment upon you without your consent. There is no legitimate law, there is no legitimate authority, there is no legitimate power anywhere on the face of this earth that can take the right away from a mentally competent human being and give it to a state, to a federal government, or to any other person.

A number of quotations constitute a brief overview of what others have said throughout history and also give insight into my own feelings. In *A Connecticut Yankee in King Arthur's Court*, the leading character and one of his companions come across a whole family which has almost died of smallpox. The mother appears to be the only one still alive. Later on they discover she has a fifteen-year-old daughter up in a sleeping loft who is in a near-comatose state and almost dead. So they rushed the young girl down and began administering aid to her. I'll pick up the quotation there. "I snatched my liquor flask from my knapsack, but the woman forbade me and said: 'No, she does not suffer; it is better so. It might bring her back to life. None that be so good and kind as ye are would do her that cruel hurt. Thou go on thy way, and be merciful friends that will not hinder.' "

I was asking my own physicians to be merciful friends who go on their way and do not hinder. But they would not listen. In the first part of this century, Justice Louis Brandeis wrote in one of his Supreme Court opinions: "The makers of our Constitution sought to protect Americans, and their beliefs, their thoughts, their emotions, and their sensations. They conferred as against the government the right to be left alone, the most comprehensive of rights and the right most valued by civilized man."

Warren Burger, who later became chief justice, referred to Justice Brandeis: "Nothing suggests that Justice Brandeis thought an individual possessed these rights only as to sensible beliefs, valid thoughts, reasonable emotions or well-founded sensations. I suggest that he intended to include a great many foolish, unreasonable and even absurd ideas that do not conform, such as refusing medical treatment even at great risk."

Justice Burger did not want to encourage foolish, unreasonable, or absurd conduct, but he did recognize the importance that the individual has in making his or her own decision. He understood that what some of us might think of as foolish, unreasonable, or absurd can also be something that is very precious and dear to someone else.

The English poet John Keats, almost 200 years ago, wrote simply, "Until we are sick, we understand not." That is so true—until we are the ones who are feeling the pain, until we are the ones who are on the sick bed, we cannot fully appreciate what the other person is going through. And even having been there myself today I cannot fully appreciate what someone who has been badly burned is going through on the burn ward. Our mind mercifully blocks out much of that pain.

When I was in the second grade, a popular joke concerned a mother who severely reprimanded her young son for coming home late from school. He said, "Mom, now that I'm a Boy Scout, I stopped to do my good deed for the day and helped this little old granny lady cross the street." She said, "Young man, it sure doesn't take an hour to help one little old granny lady cross the street." He said, "Well, it sure did this one, 'cause she didn't want to go." I was like that little old granny lady; I didn't want to go. And even today there are many patients who are being forced to endure things that they do not wish to endure, while being taken places that they don't even want to go.

John Stuart Mill, the English philosopher, in his essay *On Liberty*, came down on the side of the right to self-determination by dividing acts into those that are self-regarding and those that are other-regarding in nature. Mill concluded that when the act is self-regarding in nature, the individual should be left to make his or her own decisions. That is precisely my view. In a medical context, I am saying that before a physician is allowed to pick up a saw and saw off a patient's fingers or pick up a scalpel and cut out a patient's eyes, we must make sure that the physician has first obtained that patient's informed consent. I always like to stick the word "voluntary" in there—informed and voluntary consent—because consent that is obtained through coercion or by telling half-truths or withholding the full measure of risk and benefit is not truly consent. Medical providers need to understand that patients do not lose their constitutional rights simply because they find themselves behind a hospital wall. They have the same constitutional rights that the rest of us have, that we expect and enjoy outside hospital walls.

Fortunately today we have many protections that we did not have when I was in the hospital in 1973 and 1974. We have legally enforceable advance directives such as durable power of attorney and other health care proxies. Studies, though, have shown that even when these advance directives are part of the patient's hospital records, over half the time they are ignored by the patient's physician.

When I was in the hospital there were many reasons I wanted to refuse treatment, but one was overriding—the pain. The pain was so excruciating, it was so far beyond any pain that I ever knew was possible, that I simply could not endure it. I was very naive. I had always thought in that day and age, 1973, that a doctor would not let his or her patient undergo that kind of pain; they would be given whatever was needed to control it. Then I found out that was not true. I found out later that much more could have been done for my pain.

There were other important issues, too. One, though it was a distant second, was what Dr. Burt mentioned, my quality of life. I just did not feel that living my life blind, disfigured, with my fingers amputated and at that time not even able to walk, would be worthwhile. With that quality of life it did not seem that I would ever want to live. I have freely admitted for many years now that I was wrong about that.

I want to clarify this, though. Freedom, true freedom, not only gives us the right to make the correct choices; it also has to give us the right sometimes to make the wrong choices. In my case, however, it was a moot point whether I was wrong as far as my quality of life went, because that was a secondary issue. The immediate issue, the urgent issue, was that my pain was not being taken care of. That was why I wanted to die.

Today I'm happy; in fact I even feel that I'm happier than most people. I'm more active physically than I thought I ever would be. I've taken karate for a couple of years, I've climbed a 50-foot utility pole with the assistance of a belay line on the ropes course. I do other mental things, like write poetry and practice law. That is not to say, though, that the doctors were right. To say that would reflect a mentality that says, all's well that ends well, or the ends justify the means—whatever means necessary to achieve the results are okay to use. That totally ignores the pain that I had to go through. I check myself on this very often, several times a year, since I do speak so much. I ask if the same thing were to happen today under identical circumstance, would I still want the freedom? Knowing what I know now, would I still want the freedom to refuse treatment and die? And the answer is always yes, a resounding yes. If I think about having to go through that kind of pain again, I know that it's not something I would want. Another individual may well make a different decision. That's the beauty of freedom; that's his or her choice to do so. . . .

Note

1. From the transcript made of the initial videotape and published as an appendix to Robert Burt, *Taking Care of Strangers: The Rule of Law in Doctor–Patient Relations* (New York: The Free Press, 1979), pp. 174–80.

Patients and Prisoners: The Ethics of Lethal Injection

Gerald Dworkin

Dworkin argues that health professionals' obligations to obtain consent and "do no harm" prohibits them from assisting in such practices as capital punishment and torture. This prohibition is not based on the premise that these practices are wrong (although Dworkin believes they are), but because they involve a perversion of medical practice, with "the healing hand acting as the hurting hand." To take skills developed to save lives and reduce suffering and use them to cause death or create pain is to make a mockery of both medical ethics and professional obligations.

Nevertheless, Dworkin is not arguing that medical professionals have an absolute duty not to harm their patients. Indeed, doing harm may be permissible to advance a patient's broader health interests or at a patient's request, as in a kidney donation. Instead, Dworkin's prohibition applies to a narrower set of cases in which (1) health care workers are using their medical skills; (2) do so against someone's health interests; and (3) do so without consent.

In the United States there are at least ten states which permit execution by lethal injection. Prison doctors do not themselves administer the lethal injection, but they do supervise the technicians who do so and pronounce the prisoner dead. In this essay I want to explore, from the perspective of a moral philosopher, the ethics of physician participation in administering capital punishment. Is it a violation of medical ethics for a doctor to participate directly in lethal injection? Does it matter exactly what the nature of that participation is? What is the connection between the existence of a professional code of ethics and one's moral duties and responsibilities? How do one's moral views about lethal injection fit in with other controversial medical practices such as euthanasia?

From Gerald Dworkin, "Patients and Prisoners: The Ethics of Lethal Injection," *Analysis* 62.2, April 2002, 181–189. Copyright © Gerald Dworkin (References omitted.)

1

Let me begin, in typical philosophical fashion, by making a distinction. I want to keep separate, for the sake of this discussion, two issues which, in practice, and for good reasons, are linked. The issue I do not want to address is that of the moral legitimacy of capital punishment itself. Let me simply state that I am opposed to capital punishment. I am opposed, not because of some general view that nobody deserves to be killed, nor even on the empirical grounds (which I accept) that there is no convincing evidence that capital punishment deters differentially with respect to, say, life imprisonment. I oppose capital punishment because the problems of mistake and arbitrariness are inherent in the administration of the death penalty. Any system of arrest, prosecution, conviction, sentencing, and appeal that is at all similar to that in the United States will inevitably involve making life and death decisions that are either not subject to legal standards at all, or are subject to standards that are more or less arbitrary in their application. Having made my view known, but of course not thinking that I have argued for it, I want to set the issue to one side. In doing so I will not be able to use a line of argument that I find weighty, but which will only appeal to those who already agree with me about the morality of capital punishment. The argument claims that the participation of physicians in the act of execution serves to legitimize an activity which ought to be condemned; to add a medical veneer and professional sanction to an unjust practice of the state.

Suppose, however, one thought that the death penalty was a legitimate mode of punishment for some range of offences, either because it was intrinsically just or because it produced desirable effects; that it was capable of being administered fairly and that it was not inhumane or degrading. There would still remain moral issues concerning the ways in which the penalty is carried out—including the techniques proposed, the manner and place of the execution, and the nature of the personnel who did the killing.

2

I take it to be relatively uncontroversial that painful, degrading, and brutal methods of execution are to be avoided even if one approves of capital punishment. I say relatively uncontroversial, because one New Jersey assemblyman objected to the use of lethal injections on the grounds that they were 'too humane'. In his opinion, 'this amounts to mollycoddling vicious killers and I object to giving them euphoric drugs'. But I suspect even he would not prefer the method of execution used in 1531 for Richard Roose, an English cook convicted of poisoning. He was publicly boiled to death in a huge cauldron and suffered for two hours in agony before he succumbed. Indeed, one of the arguments in favour of the lethal injection is that it is a more humane method of execution than alternatives such as the electric chair or the firing squad. And the medical community has been historically involved in reforming methods of execution. It was, after, all, Dr. Guillotine (himself opposed to the death penalty) who invented the device which bears his name as a more humane method of execution. In the United States it was a commission of physicians in 1887 that recommended the electric chair as superior to hanging. I will assume that lethal injection is a less painful way to kill somebody than, say, electrocution. My question then can be refined and put thus: Assuming that capital punishment is morally legitimate, and given that execution by lethal injection is more humane than an alternative mode of execution, what ought the role of the physician to be with respect to this method of execution?

3

One's first thought would be that the actions of a physician who participated in an execution, say by inserting the needle or by pushing the plunger, would be in violation of the Hippocratic Oath—the oath which for centuries has been taken by physicians upon completion of their medical education. It is a fascinating historical exercise to trace the code from its origins (which are Pythagorean and date from a later period than the fifth century when Hippocrates lived), through a Christian version of the oath found in an eleventh century manuscript entitled 'From the oath according to Hippocrates in so far as a Christian may swear it', which deletes the mention of pagan deities and makes substantive changes, such as replacing the pledge of secrecy with one to teach the art of medicine 'to those who require to learn it', to the contemporary version. Among other things, such an investigation shows that there are many elements of the original oath that are no longer accepted as binding on the profession. For example, to teach the art of medicine only to one's sons or the sons of one's teacher, and to pupils who have taken the physician's oath, or to refrain from surgery on 'sufferers from stone'. If one is going to appeal to the actual taking of an oath, then the only relevant clause is the following: 'I will use treatment to help the sick according to my ability and judgement, but never with a view to injury and wrongdoing. Neither will I administer a poison to anyone when asked to do so, nor will I suggest such a course.'

The reference to poison ('deadly drug' would be the best translation of the original Greek) is almost certainly to patients who were seeking to end their lives, and possibly to schemes for homicide. In addition to the oath, there is a body of code literature which has accumulated and which is certainly relevant to how physicians conceive of their moral obligations. We have Percival's *Medical Ethics* in the eighteenth century, the

American Medical Association code of ethics in 1847, the World Medical Association's 1948 *Declaration of Geneva*, and the same organization's *International Code of Ethics* adopted in 1949. The relevant text from the last is the following: 'An act, or advice, which could weaken physical or mental resistance of a human being may be used only in his interest.'

I believe it is incontrovertible that there is sufficient explicit text, whether in specific oaths taken by physicians or in the principles explicitly adopted by the medical community or in the code literature, to ensure that direct participation in lethal injection by physicians would be contrary to their professional code of ethics. Or, to be slightly more cautious, the only way I can see to avoid this conclusion would be to adopt the rather Platonic notion that it is in the interests of certain wicked people that they suffer death.

The only question that remains an open one, in terms of conformity with the code, is where to draw the line in terms of degree of participation. May a doctor order the drugs, train the personnel, supervise the cutting down of the veins for catheterization, pronounce death, without violating the code?

But before I turn to this, I want to consider a preliminary question, namely: What force does the presence of a professional code of ethics have in the determination of what it is proper for a member of the profession to do? Answers to this question cover a spectrum ranging from the belief that the existence of a code is irrelevant in determining moral responsibilities, to the view that (clear) provisions of a code are definitive of one's duties.

I believe that either of the extreme views are mistaken, the former for at least two reasons. First, to the extent that a code is incorporated into an explicit oath taken by the professional, this, like any other promise or commitment, must at least be relevant to her obligations. What is the point of an oath which, if not binding, does not at least constrain one's thinking about moral matters? And even if the code is not incorporated into an oath, it represents the relevant community's shared understandings of its role and attendant responsibilities. While the idea of tacit consent is subject to misuse, this is a legitimate application of the doctrine. To the extent that code material is used as binding in legal disputes, in the socialization of the professional, to the extent that the material is explicitly adopted by representative professional organizations, and to the extent that

the professional does not take steps to indicate her objection to particular provisions of the code, she is, in the lawyer's terminology, estopped from denying that they present a claim on her.

Yet, even if this is all true, it is also the case that the presence of either an explicit oath or a set of shared understandings may not be determinative of one's obligations. The situation is quite parallel to that which occurs with the positive law. A citizen of a democratic society cannot regard the existence of an authorized law as irrelevant to her obligations. But citizens also retain the right and duty to critically evaluate the law and its impact in specific situations in order to form a judgement on its justice. As there are unjust laws, there may be codes which contain unjust or immoral provisions. The provisions of a professional code have to be judged in the light of general ethical considerations which are binding on persons independent of their particular professional status.

I would argue, but it is a long and complicated argument, that there is no special set of principles and considerations which are independent of, or inconsistent with, principles and considerations which are binding on those who are not members of the profession. This is not meant to deny that, in virtue of the specific circumstances or specific tasks, or specific training of a professional, there are obligations which apply to her qua professional. Indeed she may have obligations which are specific to her professional role. However, all this is true of the duties of parents with respect to their children, or citizens with respect to their nations. This does not mean that there is a distinct and irreducible set of principles of Parent's Ethics or Australian Ethics.

My view is that the existence of a code or a set of shared understandings is relevant to, but not definitive of, one's moral responsibilities. This implies that a doctor, for example, in considering the morality of the lethal injection must first be aware of the commitments that she has undertaken (either by oath or by being a member of a community) and then ask herself whether those commitments are binding in the light of critical reflection upon the provisions of the code. The existence of a set of shared understandings is important, but also important is whether those understandings can withstand critical scrutiny. Are the provisions of the code merely a reflection of the narrow self-interest of the professional community, or can they be justified to the wider public as furthering common purposes or promoting a common interest? I want to argue now that the code is justified in its emphasis on the special nature of the doctor-patient relationship and on the special obligation of physicians to be single-minded in their concern for the health interests of their patients.

4

I shall begin with what I regard as an analogous issue—the participation of doctors in the interrogation and torture of prisoners. In 1975 the World Medical Assembly of the World Medical Association adopted 'Guidelines for Medical Doctors Concerning Torture and Other Cruel, Inhuman, or Degrading Treatment or Punishment in Relation to Detention and Imprisonment', otherwise known as the *Declaration of Tokyo*. This *Declaration* states that a doctor is prohibited from providing: the premises, instruments, substances, or knowledge to facilitate the practice of torture or other forms of cruel, inhuman or degrading treatment or to diminish the ability of the victim to resist such treatment.

The *Declaration* does not deal directly with capital punishment, but many interpret the *Declaration of Toyko* to be inconsistent with the administration of a lethal injection. Those who disagree with such an interpretation would claim that capital punishment is not torture as defined by the *Declaration* (the deliberate systematic or wanton infliction of physical or mental suffering) and that it does not fall under the residual heading of inhuman or degrading procedures.

I do not need to argue that capital punishment is a special case of torture or inhuman procedures. Instead, I want to assume that it would be wrong for doctors to participate in torture, and argue by analogy that it would be wrong for doctors to participate in a lethal injection. It might be thought that there is a glaring asymmetry in the two cases which defeats any attempt to argue by analogy. Most of us agree—subject perhaps to very special counter-examples (such as that of the nuclear terrorist)—that torture is wrong. It is inconsistent with any notion of treating others as ends, to attempt to undermine the self-respect of a person, to destroy his humanity. But, for the sake of argument, I have been assuming that capital punishment is legitimate, that one could conceive of punishment, even that involving the death of a victim, as not

inconsistent with respecting another person. How then can an analogy be drawn?

It can be drawn because there is an argument against the participation of a doctor in torture that is not predicated on torture itself being morally forbidden. It is predicated on the impermissibility of the healing hand acting as the hurting hand. It is a perversion of a role which is defined in terms of healing, of alleviating pain, of increasing the patient's resistance to injury, to use one's skills, training and education to increase the pain and weaken the resistance of those to whom one administers these skills. I use this circumlocution because to call those receiving such skills patients would be false descriptively, and a mockery normatively. Such a reversal affects the entire vocabulary we use to appraise physicians.

Consider the virtues, for example. Is it compassion that a doctor manifests when she attends to the injuries of a battered prisoner so that she can face further torture? Medicine, like any other human practice, is understood in terms of positively valued ends which it seeks to promote. What makes a good doctor can only be defined in terms of a set of understandings about the use to which her skills, and knowledge, are put. What counts as the virtues of a physician, that is, the possession and exercise of those qualities which enable her to achieve goals, is only defined relative to an understanding of such goals. Imagine, for example, what the training of a physician, the kinds of criticism that are made of what she does, would look like if the ends of medicine were quite different from what they are.

I am not claiming that the ends of medicine are simple or clear or uncontroversial. Moral progress within a profession often takes the form of political and intellectual struggle over defining those ends. In recent years we have seen moral and legal debate over what forms the ends should take. Must a doctor always act in the interest of her patient, ignoring those of other persons? What about the failure of a psychiatrist to warn the intended victim of a homicidal patient? Must the doctor never act against the wishes of the patient? Consider the hypochondriacal patient who wants an expensive series of diagnostic tests for an imaginary illness.

The most dramatic contemporary case of a debate about the proper ends of medicine is occurring in the context of the debate about physician-assisted suicide. Those who assert that doctors must not kill, wish to limit the ends of medicine to the treatment of medical disability and the relief of painful symptoms. Those who wish to advocate the permissibility of medically-assisted dying argue that the ends of medicine are more various and should include assisting a dying patient in the time and manner of his death.

5

The principle I want to rely on is a narrowly defined one. It denies the legitimacy of the use of medical skills and training when they run counter to the health interests of the person (whether patient or other) to whom they are applied, and are counter to the wishes of that person. Notice that all three factors must be present: use of medical skills, adverse effect on health interests, and non-consent.

This principle is compatible with a doctor acting in a manner that results in harm to somebody, but not through the use of her medical training. Thus, a doctor might serve on a jury which imposes the death penalty. There may be harm but it is not brought about by using the medical skills of the doctor.

A slightly more difficult case is whether a psychiatrist may certify that a prisoner is of sufficiently sound mind to understand the nature of her execution. Here there is harm to the patient, and the doctor uses his medical abilities (perhaps against the will of the patient). But I am inclined to say that, although the doctor's use of medical training may clear the way for the death of the prisoner, her skills are aimed at diagnosis and do not directly undermine health interests. Something like the principle of double-effect is necessary to make sense of many cases of role-responsibility.

A more complicated case is that of a person accused of a capital offence. The prisoner is currently in a psychotic state and not capable of being tried. However, with the proper medication he can participate in his trial. The defendant's lawyers, reasonably enough, do not wish their client to be forcibly medicated against his will. Leaving aside the legal issues, what should the doctor do? In terms of the health interests of the patient he ought to be on medication, so if the doctor forcibly medicates he does not violate my principle. There may be other applicable principles which nevertheless rule out forced medication. Certainly in the case of competent patients there is an absolute right to refuse unwanted medical treatment.

What does the principle say about failing to medicate? If the doctor fails to medicate then he may be injuring the health interests of the patient. Does the refusal of treatment count as an instance of the use of medical skills? It would seem that physicians use their medical skills both in giving and refusing treatment. So two of the conditions are satisfied. What about the absence of consent? Does the will of a psychotic patient count? If it does, then the principle does not apply since the patient declines to advance his medical needs.

Suppose the patient's will does not count as valid and there is no valid refusal of consent. Then the principle would apply and rule out failing to medicate. But the absence of competency to decide means that the prohibition against imposed treatment might not apply.

Notice that it is the patient's consent to being harmed that legitimates a doctor taking a kidney from a living donor who wishes to donate his kidney even though the doctor does use medical skills to harm the health interests of his patient.

6

To return to the issue of lethal injection, the principle would draw the line concerning the role of the doctor in lethal injection as follows. The ordering and preparation of either the toxic substance or the analgesics, the administering of the medication, the cutting down of the veins, would all be impermissible. Similarly for the supervision and training of other personnel to perform these specific tasks in this context. If it is improper for the physician to use her skills and training to harm a person against her will, it is similarly inconsistent with her role to advise or train others to do so. On the other hand, simply being present to pronounce the death of a prisoner would not be impermissible. Here medical skills are not being used to bring about death but merely to ascertain its presence.

I believe, then, that the relevant provisions of the oaths and codes of ethics can survive critical scrutiny and provide a sound basis for determining the moral responsibilities of the physician. The code is grounded in an understanding of the physician as serving the health interests of her patients and of role-responsibilities which are single-minded in their focus on such interests.

Section 2:   Children and Informed Consent

The Dilemma of Jehovah's Witness Children Who Need Blood to Survive

Anita Catlin

Catlin presents the case of a child given a blood transfusion even though his parents, both Jehovah's Witnesses, refused to consent to the procedure and tried to prevent it. The parents believed, on biblical grounds, that blood transfusions are forbidden and that, as punishment for violating God's commandment, their child would be separated from them for eternity. Catlin explores the ethical and legal issues relevant to the decisions of both medical staff and parents when the question of transfusion arises for a child whose parents are Jehovah's Witnesses.

She argues that although the blood transfusion was judged by a physician as medically necessary to serve the best interest of the child, the possibility of effective alternative treatments not requiring the use of blood products should have been explored. This is the approach that should be taken in all similar cases, the author holds, and the exploration of treatment alternatives could be facilitated by a knowledgeable ethics consultant.

The Story

In 1993, at a major medical center in the Midwest, parents were handcuffed and removed from their son's bedside and their child was taken into custody by the attending physician. What was the crime that these parents committed, resulting in the father's incarceration and the child being made a ward of the state for the following year? The case was a refusal by Jehovah's Witnesses parents to allow blood transfusion to their six-year-old child. The child was in a sickle cell crisis, with a stroke in progress, hemiplegia, and a hemoglobin so low that death was imminent. This essay examines the case as it progressed, the norms and values involved, the positions of the attending doctors and nurses, and the legal actions that took place, and makes recommendations for nursing and ethics committee considerations for the future.

From Anita Catlin, "The Dilemma of Jehovah's Witness Children Who Need Blood to Survive," *HEC Forum* 8, issue 4 (1996): 195–207. Copyright © 1996 by Kluwer Academic Publishers. With kind permission of Springer Science+Business Media. (Notes omitted.)

Persons who practice the Jehovah's Witnesses faith accept medical and surgical treatment. However, they are deeply religious people who believe that blood transfusion is forbidden for them. This prohibition is construed from the following biblical passages: "Only flesh with its soul—its blood—you must not eat" (Genesis 9:3–4); "Abstain from . . . fornication and from what is strangled and from blood" (Acts 15: 19–21). "You must not eat the blood of any sort of flesh, because the soul of every sort of flesh is its blood. I will set my face against that person who eats blood. . . . Anyone eating it will be cut off" (Leviticus 17:10, 13–14). Jehovah's Witnesses interpret these passages as forbidding the transfusion of whole blood, packed red blood cells, plasma, white blood cells, and platelets. Jehovah's Witnesses are allowed to decide for themselves, as a matter of conscience, whether or not to accept albumin, immune globulins, cryoprecipitate, and organ transplants. Non-blood plasma expanders such as saline solution, Ringer's lactate, and hetastarch are acceptable. When a Jehovah's Witness patient receives blood, this constitutes a grave sin. By disobeying God and being "cut off," they are denied life through resurrection. If a person's life is extended by a transfusion, it may become meaningless and lack spiritual purpose because the hope of everlasting life may be forfeited.

In sickle cell anemia, the red blood cells become damaged and are unable to deliver oxygen. The standard treatment for this condition is hydration, oxygenation, blood replacement and exchange transfusion. When parents of the little boy presented to the emergency room, they said, "We want you to treat and save our child, but you may not administer blood to him." When the child was admitted to the pediatric intensive care unit and found to be in critical condition, the parents were told, "There is no option, your child needs to have blood. If you wish to call in a specialist who treats Jehovah's Witnesses without blood, or wish to transfer him elsewhere, we will support that. If you would like to call your church elders to provide support or advice, you may do that. It will take two hours to type and cross match the blood. At the end of two hours, if alternative arrangements have not been made, we will transfuse your child."

Two hours passed. Phone calls were made but no transfer or alternative care was found. The parents held the child in their arms, lay across his bed, and said "you may not transfuse our child." Attempts to gain their cooperation failed. The hospital legal department advised the physician to proceed with the transfusion. Two hospital security guards physically removed the parents from the child's room. When the father would not cooperate with the separation from his child, he was handcuffed, taken into custody and remanded to the local jail facility. The mother was allowed to remain on the ward, but continued to protest. The blood was administered and the child's life was saved.

Goals of Medicine and Conflicting Principles

Healthcare personnel are trained to be true to the virtue of helping others. Their mission is to achieve the goals of medicine, which include: promoting health; preventing disease; relieving symptoms, pain, and suffering; curing disease; preventing untimely death; improving functional status; counseling patients and families; and avoiding harm to the patient. In this case, giving blood met every goal of medicine, and withholding blood constituted doing harm and causing the untimely death of a child. The organizational mission of a pediatrics unit supports the ethical principle of beneficence.

A case like this, however, brings out competing principles. Non-maleficence is the ethical principle which urges us to refrain from actions that would cause harm. For the healthcare team, the parents' refusal to allow the child to receive blood is seen as serious harm. For the parents, disobeying a religious commandment and having the child's soul in jeopardy was considered serious harm. Quintero, writing in *Pediatric Nursing*, pointed out that "what is right in the eyes of Jehovah's Witness parents is the need to ensure a life for their child after death, even if this means an early end to the child's life on earth." The dilemma of the case is the harm of the child's death lying in balance with the harm of not honoring the parents' beliefs.

Ethical Principles Regarding Children

Social historian M. Steinfels traced how thinking about children has changed over time. Historically, parents' desires and authority dominated and children had no interests apart from their parents'. Then there was a period when parents had duties to raise a child to fulfill a religiously, socially, or professionally agreed upon role, which did not necessarily represent the direct self-interests of the parents or the child. And presently, the child has individual interests and needs that must be given consideration apart from those of the parents and others who purport to define children's interests.

The principle of non-maleficence becomes more complex when the interests of children are involved. Attorney J. Goldstein reviewed the case law regarding parents and children:

1. To be an *adult* is to be a risk taker, independent, and with capacity and authority to decide and to do what is best for oneself.

2. To be an *adult who is a parent* is to be presumed by law to have the capacity, authority, and responsibility to determine and to do what is good for one's children.

3. The law is designed to assure for each child an opportunity to meet and master the developmental crises on the way to adulthood—to that critical age when he or she is presumed by the state to be qualified to determine what is best for oneself.

4. It is the function of the law to protect family privacy as a means of safeguarding parental autonomy in child rearing. At the same time the

law attempts to safeguard each child's entitlement to autonomous parents who care and who feel responsible and who can be held accountable for continually meeting the child's . . . needs.

Goldstein wrote that there can be state supervention of parental autonomy in health care matters only if three conditions are met: a) the medical profession is in agreement about the treatment, b) the expected outcome of the treatment is what society agrees to be right for any child (one which would give a chance for a normal healthy life or a life worth living), and c) the expected outcome of denial of that treatment would mean death for the child. Here the definition of society for those who would override parental autonomy is the "mainstream" society, which unfortunately is not inclusive of an individual religious group's dissenting opinion.

Jonsen, Siegler, and Winslade maintain that freedom of religion is highly valued and is protected by the U.S. Constitution, but that this freedom does not extend to making decisions about children. Parents are granted wide discretion about the values they believe their children's lives should embody, but parental discretion is limited in medical care when certain beliefs would disadvantage the child's health. This opinion was upheld in a 1978 Court decision in which Jehovah's Witnesses were told that it was not unconstitutional for the State to insist on blood transfusion for children in appropriate cases.

Ruth Macklin notes that the invasion of family privacy must be weighed against a lifetime of health, well being, or bodily integrity for the child on whose behalf the state seeks to intervene. The potential harm to the family must be weighed against the potential harm to the child. Macklin states that it is possible to accord a great deal of respect to family autonomy and integrity, and "at the same time recognize that close and loving family units are not destroyed by an occasional outside intervention aimed at serving the best interest of a child." Macklin's opinion, however, appears to downplay the potential for psychological harm that forcing a transfusion could cause.

What Did the Key Players Think?

The pediatrician in charge of the pediatric intensive care unit, Dr. B., recalled the case matter-of-factly, reciting the medical facts in a clinical manner. It was the agreement of consults from medicine, neurology, and hematology that this child would die if blood was not given. The parents, due to religious teachings, would not consent. Dr. B. stated that there was no alternative treatment and no other options available. When questioned about the use of hyperbaric oxygen and hypothermia to treat the anemia, as described by Akingbola et al., he stated that these cooling methods could not be used with sickle cell patients, as cooling increases the sickling. If the child was to live, he would have to be given transfused blood over parental objection.

Dr. B. recounted the call made to the legal affairs officer on duty that day. The legal opinion was given that [1] the emergency was reasonable and correct, [2] giving blood to Jehovah's Witness children over parental objection was well established in the courts, and [3] that Dr. B. himself must take personal, immediate, legal custody of the child. Dr. B. indicated that he was apprehensive about this responsibility, and that he was on the phone once every hour with the legal affairs attorney. He was advised by the attorney that the child could not be transferred and must be immediately treated, as he, Dr. B., was now the guardian of the child.

Both Dr. B. and the clinical nurse specialist described the pain of the moment. They recounted the tears shed by nurses who had to assist security guards to pull the parents off the child's bed when the parents were trying physically to prevent the transfusion. When asked what their ethical thinking was at the time, both mentioned the principle of the child's best interest. Perhaps they were recalling the ruling of the Supreme Court in *Prince v. Commonwealth of Massachusetts*, which states: "Parents may make martyrs of themselves, but it does not follow that they are free, in identical circumstances, to make martyrs of their children. . . ." When questioned about the sanctity of the commandment the parents were trying to uphold, or the seriousness of the harm of violating this commandment, both Dr. B. and Nurse C. could not reply. Protecting the child from death was the job that was to be done, and to them no argument existed that held greater moral weight.

When Dr. B. was later called to court to testify in the parental custody hearing, the judge stated that there was no need even to evaluate the case, that the correct legal actions had been taken. In fact, custody was not immediately returned to the parents, as the child would need on-going transfusion in the years ahead, and the judge wished to prevent further such occurrences. . . .

What Can the Literature Add?

Many physicians have written in opposition to treating children against their parents' wishes. In 1976, surgeons Gardner *et al.* posed the following question: "Who would benefit if the [adult] patient's corporal malady is cured but the spiritual life with God, as he sees it, is compromised, which leads to a life that is meaningless and perhaps worse than death itself. . . .

Richard Spence, in *Critical Care Medicine*, wrote: "Physicians must understand the severe consequences of transfusion to the Jehovah's Witness. The action is not considered by the church to be a minor infraction, punishable by a simple reprimand. The Jehovah's Witness may suffer excommunication from the church, which means forfeiture of a chance for eternal life and severance of the individual's relationship with God. Although it may be difficult for the physician to accept this position, especially in a situation in which transfusion can be lifesaving, he/she must contrast saving a life with the potential loss of everlasting life and redemption, as understood by the Jehovah's Witness."

Writing in the *Journal of the American Medical Association*, Dixon and Smalley state: Witness parents ask that therapies be used that are not religiously prohibited. This accords with the medical tenet of treating the "whole person," not overlooking the possible lasting psychosocial damage of an invasive procedure that violates a family's fundamental beliefs."

A number of legal actions in the United States and Canada have allowed parents to refuse blood and seek alternative therapies for their children. In the case of *In Re: E.G., a Minor*, physicians went to court to insist that a 17-year-old girl be treated with blood for her leukemia. The court upheld her right to refuse blood. The Illinois Appellate Court ruled in 1989, and upheld the ruling in 1990, that teenage children could decide whether or not to receive blood, and that parents were not neglectful when they did not allow blood transfusion for their children. In *Re Children's Aid Society of Metropolitan Toronto versus F.R.* Witness parents were allowed to refuse transfusion for their four-year-old child who was bleeding after a tonsillectomy.

At times, children themselves were asked what they wished to do. In Fox, a 13-year-old child injured in a car accident refused blood. In Robb, a 16-year-old with leukemia refused blood. In Akingbola et al., a 12-year-old with renal failure refused blood. In each of these cases, the physicians were supportive of the child's view and did not insist on overruling. In each case, other treatment modalities were found and were successful. The children's long term prognoses without transfusion were not certain. Dr. Mary Scully, attending physician of the child with leukemia has observed:

> *I was convinced that overall he did have very strong spiritual beliefs and that he was very anxious to maintain his personal integrity. . . . I was concerned what damage would be done to him and his psyche and his relationship with his family if that was disturbed . . . going against his will would seriously jeopardize his chances of recovery.*

A contrasting view can be found in the *Journal of Christian Nursing*. Here Rita Swan, a mother whose own child died because of parental religious convictions, wrote adamantly about how wrong she was, and how wrong the state was in not overruling her wishes. "Other children have inherent rights to appropriate medical care and their parents have a duty to provide them," Swan states, but "religious immunity laws are perpetrating crimes against children, the nursing profession and society." [Swan has been active in supporting legislative changes to repeal religious exemption laws from the child abuse statutes in the U.S.]

May describes the recent attempts by the American Academy of Pediatrics to remove these religious exemptions from the child abuse statute laws. Hawaii, South Dakota, and Massachusetts have already done so. May also notes that in a pluralistic society like America's, which was founded on the basis of religious freedom, it is hard to reconcile the imposition of the dominant society's values upon a religious group's values. I agree with May and find painful the idea that one group can say that another groups' deeply held beliefs are wrong and should not be followed.

What Could an Ethics Consultant Have Done?

In this case, the staff was very clear that there was to be no mediating, arbitrating, or negotiating, and they had obtained their own legal opinion. An ethics consultation was not requested at the time. But there are other roles that the ethics consultant could assist with, such as educating, problem solving, providing family advocacy, and helping to support the providers.

Education includes making sure that the most up-to-date medical care was available. Ethics consultants must keep up-to-date on the literature regarding controversial issues. Strokes in sickle cell children are frequent (6–9%) and at an increased risk in the 5 to 10 year old age group. A Jehovah's Witness child with stroke was likely to appear again in a hospital treating large numbers of sickle cell children. There are many recent studies which describe how to handle severe anemia in the Jehovah's Witness patient, but in this case, the physician stated that no alternative treatment would work. . . .

The consultant could also supply the clinicians with the 24-hour Jehovah's Witness hospital assistance phone line located in Brookline, Massachusetts. There is on file a data bank of 21,000 U.S. physicians who are trained in the care of patients without transfusion, and multiple hospitals that have special Bloodless Medicine and Surgery programs. The ethics consultant could suggest a physician-to-physician referral using this data bank, rather than relying on parents to find someone to care for their child in an emergency situation, as was done in this case. . . .

Providing advocacy for the family is the third of the ethics consultant's roles. In this case, the family is in great need of support. An ethics consultation early in the case may have been able to prevent the physical nature of the confrontation. In future cases, parents must be comforted in a much more pro-active way. A quiet place, such as the hospital chapel, should be found for prayer with their minister and friends. The nurse ethicist can advocate by "bridging, negotiating, and mediating between these two systems, (acting as) a middle man—a culture broker." A psychiatric nurse liaison could be called on the unit. The ethicist could say to the family "You are *not* consenting, you are *not* responsible, this is *not* voluntary, and your God knows that"—and this might help. I believe that under no circumstances should anyone be allowed to try convincing the parents to give up their beliefs. What nurses can do is assist parents with the guilt and pain they will feel. . . .

Summary

Medical researchers must continue to develop and test non-blood oxygen-transport products. Resources provided by the Jehovah's Witness Hospital Assistance Line must be consulted. Sickle cell researchers must continue to test non-blood treatment. Information about non-blood treatments must be disbursed. Ways to enhance parental comfort as the laws further and further support children's best interest must be provided. Information regarding cultural diversity must be disseminated. Hospitals and healthcare agencies that have not done so must institute the use of ethics consulting or ethics committees. Nurse ethicists must continue development of the role of educating staff; mediation, arbitration and negotiation; problem solving; obtaining legal opinion; providing patient, family, or staff advocacy; and helping to reduce suffering on the part of the providers. Difficult ethical decisions should continue to be debated.

Were the staff at X Med Center correct in overriding parental wishes and breaking tenets of their faith? In the doctor's, nurse's, lawyer's, and judge's view they were. The child, now eight years old, is alive and well. The stroke resolved, and imminent death averted. The parents' and child's views are not presently available. Whether the family is suffering from the child's loss of his relationship with God, or are secretly relieved in their hearts that they are not, like Rita Swan, mourning their dead son, is unknown. What is known, is that this was a difficult case for all involved, and that such cases will continue to present themselves in the future.

Reply to Anita Catlin
Eugene Rosam

Rosam, in his reply to Catlin, points out that Jehovah's Witness parents do not believe that children should be allowed to die and are not against medical treatment for their children. The parents seek medical treatment for their children, just not treatment that involves blood transfusion. Also, Rosam claims, we must recognize that a transfusion has the potential to cause medical harm, not just medical benefit.

From Eugene Rosam, "Reply to Anita Catlin," *HEC Forum* 8, issue 4 (1996): 208–211. Copyright © 1996 by Kluwer Academic Publishers. With kind permission of Springer Science+Business Media. (Notes omitted.)

Thus, giving a child blood, contrary to Catlin, does not necessarily "meet every goal of medicine."

Some laws and recent court decisions, Rosam points out, do not require that a child receive the "best" treatment, but only a treatment that is "adequate" or "reasonable." Thus, if a treatment does not involve the use of blood, even if some do not consider it the best treatment, there are no grounds for interfering with parental decision making. Like Catlin, Rosam thinks it is unacceptable to try to convince Jehovah's Witness parents to give up their beliefs.

We have read with interest the well researched article by Anita Catlin. We agree with her that the case she mentions is one that would pose a dilemma for the healthcare community as it indeed does for Jehovah's Witnesses themselves. Of all the conditions in adults and children that we find most difficult to deal with, and admittedly have few answers for, a sickle cell crisis, with a stroke in progress, is indeed a challenge. The case presents multiple problems.

We, too, like the author, would never recommend that the child be allowed to die. What we would ask is that the doctor do everything he can to save the life of the child *without* using a blood transfusion. The situation with Jehovah's Witnesses is not one of parents refusing all medical treatment, but simply differing with the doctor as to what *kind* of treatment is preferred. We often see both child and adult cases described in such a way as to indicate that when blood transfusion was administered the life was saved. One has to ask what the eventual outcome of these "saved" lives will be? What will be the quality of life in the years ahead? Could this child suffer from the potential adverse effects of blood transfusion, such as iron overload, hepatitis or other viral transmission? Thus, we cannot agree with the author that giving blood "meets every goal of medicine." Is blood the only thing that saves lives? In the majority of our cases there are new medical modalities that "save lives," such as erythropoietin, desmopressin, hemodilution, or the use of a blood salvage device. If one is going honestly to say that withholding blood constitutes doing harm, then one would have also to honestly admit that giving blood can also do harm. If there is a risk both ways, who should decide for the child which risk is to be taken?

Although the doctor said that nothing else would do but blood (granting that was his sincere judgment), another doctor may have felt differently. At least, we have often found this to be the case in many other situations where a controversy arose over whether blood should be given. In fact, in a growing number of cases, judges are now asking doctors to try the non-blood alternatives preferred by the parents first, and then give blood if the alternatives fail. These children are going home healthy and in good condition without blood transfusions.

It is unfortunate that the writer in *Pediatric Nursing* claimed that "what is right in the eyes of Jehovah's Witness parents is the need to insure life for their child after death, even if this means an early end to the child's life on earth." This puts the emphasis on the negative. The parents want the child to live, or they would not have brought it to the hospital and put it in the care of a doctor. They simply asked for alternative treatment. True, in this case there may not have been effective alternatives, but the statement in *Pediatric Nursing* is not correct. We do not wish to make martyrs of our children and we are not exercising a right to die.

Some articles that deal with this subject refer to what is called "the best interests standard." We find that the most relevant statutes do not mandate what is "best" for a child in need of medical care, but what is "adequate" or "reasonable." Thus, if non-blood care provides what is adequate or reasonable, then there is no basis to interfere with parental decision making in this regard.

On this point, the New York Court of Appeals said *In re Hofbauer*: "The most significant factor in determining whether a child is being deprived of adequate medical care . . . is whether the parents have provided an acceptable course of medical treatment . . . in light of all the surrounding circumstances. This inquiry cannot be posed in terms of whether the parent has made a 'right' or 'wrong' decision, for the present state of the practice of medicine, despite its vast advances, very seldom permits such definitive conclusions. Nor can a court assume the role of surrogate parent and establish as the objective criteria with which to evaluate a parent's decision its own judgement as to the exact method or degree of medical treatment which should be provided, for such standard is fraught with subjectivity."

Also pertinent is what was observed in Guides to the Judge in Medical Orders Affecting Children:

> *Although an emergency may exist from the physician's point of view, the person may not in fact be in extremis. This does not imply that doctors do not testify in good faith as to a person's likelihood of surviving a crisis without undergoing a particular procedure. It means, rather, that medical knowledge is not sufficiently advanced to enable a physician to predict with reasonable certainty that his patient will live or die or will suffer a permanent physical impairment or deformity. Doctors tend to urge the imposition of a treatment when, in their expert opinion, death or permanent physical impairment is more likely to occur if the treatment is not given than if it is. However, it is the duty of the court to determine the seriousness of the emergency in a particular case, to press the testifying physician on the imminent likelihood of death or impairment, the chance of survival or of alleviation of prolonged agonizing pain if the proposed treatment is given, and the danger of the treatment itself.*

There are many lawyers who are convinced that doctors and hospitals do not have official standing under the *parens patriae* provision of the law. That is for the State to exercise, not the hospital or doctor. If the State appoints a doctor as guardian, we would accept that. But we believe that if the court had time to hear the parents, *ex parte* orders for transfusion could be avoided.

No reasonable person would want to support a religious belief that is interpreted as bringing death to children. But there is a lot of interpretation involved in supporting such a position. For example, there have been harmful effects resulting from circumcisions performed for religious reasons. Are we to curb that practice? Is it an invasion of the child's right for its parents to insist upon

this surgical procedure for male children without the knowledge and consent of the infant? Should we have to wait until the child is of a legal age to see what he would like to do about circumcision?

We are not suggesting that these situations are simple ones to handle. But we are convinced that there is a greater need for more communication with the Hospital Liaison Committees for Jehovah's Witnesses in a sincere effort to avoid blood transfusions where this is humanly possible. We agree with the idea that an ethics consultation early in the case can make a difference. It was this type of dialogue that has been missing in our cases for decades. *Ex parte* orders were issued without any possibility for the parents to have their rights recognized where possible. Working with the Liaison Committee and with ethics consultation will take care of the greater number of cases, leaving only the unusual and rare medical problems to be worked out on a case-by-case basis. Some time ago it was thought that one would never get remissions in cases of leukemia without using blood transfusions to combat the anemia created by the chemotherapy, but there has been some success at this at M.D. Anderson Cancer Center (Houston, Texas).

I agree with the author of this article who contends that under no circumstances should anyone be allowed to try convincing the parents to give up their beliefs. This effort is frequently made. Though many do not appreciate the fact, what we often encounter is people who want to impose their religious beliefs on others, while asking parents not to impose their religious beliefs on their own children! Does it end up as a matter of whose religious beliefs are imposed upon the child? At least this illustrates how some get off track in reflecting on these matters. We would like to see these cases dealt with in an objective fashion, working out what can be done within the realm of good medicine, and to look after these children without blood transfusions wherever possible.

Section 3:   Truth Telling and Confidentiality

Is Honesty Always the Best Policy?

Michelle Gold

Gold argues for an expanded notion of patient autonomy that includes the right to remain ignorant of one's medical condition, if one chooses, or to delegate informed consent and treatment decisions

From M. Gold, "Is Honesty Always the Best Policy? Ethical Aspects of Truth Telling," *Internal Medicine Journal* 34 (2004): 578–580. Copyright © 2004 Internal Medicine Journal. (Notes omitted.)

to others. In a multicultural society, physicians should refrain from forcing one version of "truth-telling" on all patients, but should instead tailor the amount of information provided to the specific needs and preferences of individuals. Ultimately, this means relinquishing the idea that value-neutral data gives physicians a monopoly on truth, to be disclosed or withheld. Gold suggests that truth-telling should instead be viewed as dialogue among moral agents (patient, physician, and society) with a range of different values rooted in personal, cultural, and religious convictions.

Overheard in the oncology ward of a major teaching hospital:

Intern A: Mrs P's daughter doesn't want her to be told that the cancer has spread

Intern B: But if she asks us about the test results, don't we have to tell her?

Registrar C: Well, if she doesn't know her diagnosis then the oncologists won't give her any chemotherapy because she can't give consent.

Intern B: That's not fair—the cancer has a good chance of responding to chemotherapy.

Request such as that from Mrs P's daughter are not uncommon in circumstances where there is a diagnosis of an incurable malignancy and/or a patient from a non-English speaking background. For most western clinicians this will cause some discomfort as it challenges our commitment to honest disclosure of information. However, although very few physicians would exclude the patient from discussions about a diagnosis of cardiac failure, discussion relating to a poor prognosis may be more likely to be held with family members, out of hearing of the patient. The issue of truth telling touches on many areas, including topics such as autonomy, consent and working in a multicultural society.

Autonomy

In the first part of the twentieth century, the predominant principles in medical ethics were paternalism and beneficence. Subsequently, the overarching ethical principle influencing western thought became a respect for patient autonomy, the right or freedom of individuals to make decisions on their own behalf. A person's freedom to make informed choices should be respected. As a general rule, by explaining the truth about diagnosis, prognosis and treatment options we generate the basis for that freedom and expect patients to make appropriate decisions about their treatment.

Autonomous individuals are free to use their autonomy as they see fit—even to delegate it when this seems right or if they find themselves unwilling or unable to cope with the choices. Thus, an elderly Greek patient, when asked if he would like to know about the results of his biopsy, is exercising his autonomy by asking that we discuss the diagnosis and treatment with his son instead. To 'force' the truth on someone who might not be prepared to deal with the impact can be as insensitive as withholding the truth, and can damage the relationship between the physician and the patient/family.

One hundred years ago, treatment options were limited and the physician exercised his judgement to determine which course of action would be likely to produce the best outcome for the individual. The progressive availability of new, aggressive treatments, especially in the context of incurable disease, has resulted in increased difficulty in evaluating the cost-benefit ratio for individual patients, and has required patients to take on a greater role in decision-making. The patient needs more information about the natural history of the condition as well as the risks and benefits of the treatment in order to be able to participate in this process.

Medical information has become increasingly complex and specialists draw on a vast amount of training and experience to arrive at a decision or recommendation. Clearly, it is impossible to provide the patient/relative with knowledge equivalent to that of the doctor, and in many cases this would be incomprehensible. Thus, some guidance is necessary. Butow *et al.* observe that a majority of cancer patients want the doctor to have an equal or dominant role in decision-making. This is consistent with the concept of autonomy as the patient is exercising his/her own choice in seeking a recommendation from the doctor. Indeed, some might argue that leaving complex decision-making entirely in the hands of the patient is an abdication of the doctors' responsibilities.

Consent

As discussed, information is vital for patients to make decisions about their medical treatment. Additionally, there is a legal requirement for doctors to obtain consent from their patients prior to procedures, and to inform patients of their condition, treatment options and material risks of treatment. The most common exception to this rule is in an emergency situation where a patient cannot provide consent (e.g. an unconscious patient) and where delay in treatment would result in death, in which cases therapy can be commenced on the grounds that most reasonable persons would consent to this treatment.

For consent to medical treatment to be considered *legally* valid, a patient must (usually) be 18 years or older, fully informed and have the cognitive capacity to understand all aspects of their diagnosis, recommended treatment and likely outcomes with or without treatment. From an ethical point of view, this consent should also be freely given, as stated both in the Nuremburg Code and later in the World Medical Association declaration of Helsinki.

Cultural Influences

A significant volume of work documents the practices of physicians at various times and in diverse cultures regarding truth telling, and also examines the needs and preferences of lay-populations and patients. In western countries, overall approximately 80–90% of patients are given the truth about their diagnosis, whereas in other cultures, figures can range from 0 to 50%. Practices of western physicians have changed over time, as illustrated by two similar surveys conducted in the USA. In 1961, 88% of physicians did not routinely discuss a diagnosis of cancer with their patients, whereas in 1979, 98% of those surveyed generally did discuss the diagnosis.

Surveys in western populations have found that 83–99% of those surveyed would like to be informed of their diagnosis, with a somewhat lower figure in non-western countries of 24–74%. Many predictors of the desire for information have been identified, including age, level of education, ethnicity, a religious locus of control and in some studies, gender. However, it must be stressed that the studies provide as much evidence for variation within cultural groups as between different cultures.

The majority of doctors in Australia undoubtedly have a 'western' pattern of thinking. Part of this includes the belief that *'truth only belongs to science'*. Young doctors are cautioned against making 'value judgements' and we are all exhorted to practise evidence-based medicine. There is a belief that knowledge worthy of the name must transcend the particulars of experience to achieve objective purity and value neutrality. Therefore, in medicine and the patient/doctor relationship, we emphasize the 'objective' dimension of disease (computed tomography report, liver function tests—anything quantifiable) and tend to minimize the subjective dimension. This 'subjective' dimension of disease can't be measured with scientific methodology so we prefer to discard it.

In relation to truth telling, Hinton makes the point that asking the question 'Should the doctor tell?' implies that the doctor is the one who has all the knowledge about the patient's illness and prognosis, and the patient knows nothing. The act of truth telling in medicine is, instead, an exchange involving moral agents (the patient, the doctor and society), each with their sets of values and norms. The doctor alone should not make the decision about how much to tell an individual patient, even a doctor who is well informed about the likely cultural preferences of the person seeking care. The needs of each person must be evaluated individually because illness is, in the first instance, a subjective experience, influenced by cultural, personal and religious beliefs and traditions.

Can the Truth Be Harmful?

Perhaps one of the oldest and best known tenets of medicine is the supposed obligation to do no harm —described in various ways from the ancient Latin phrase 'primum-non-nocere' to the XIIIth law in Samuel Shem's *The House of God*, 'The delivery of medical care is to do as much nothing as possible'.

Physicians in the past voiced concern that revealing a cancer diagnosis would result in the loss of hope for a patient. Families are still often fearful that knowledge of cancer will result in despair, depression or result in increased suffering. Few studies have directly examined this question but it is likely that any increase in anxiety is transient. There is some evidence to support the notion that informing patients truthfully about a life-threatening disease does not result in a greater incidence of anxiety, despair, sadness, depression, insomnia or fear. On the contrary, informed patients have better communication with relatives and treating staff and greater trust in the care provided.

Insensitivity to the cultural norms or personal preferences of a patient can result in the provision of information to someone who is not willing or ready to hear it and, thus, be a source of distress. Too much information can be overwhelming and most physicians will recall instances of patients abandoning a successful treatment after hearing of a rare potential adverse effect. Families who feel their beliefs are not respected might fail to bring a patient for further follow up or treatment, with the potential for harm as a result.

Conclusion

The goal of truth telling in medicine is to achieve therapeutic efficacy. The amount of information provided to an individual should be tailored to their specific needs and might change with time. A dialogue is required, with the patient speaking and the doctor listening, enabling the patient to control the pace and the content of the conversation. Freedman details such an approach and terms it 'offering truth'.

In this way, patients maintain their autonomy and choose how much 'truth' they wish to hear, the physician does not compromise his/her commitment to honesty, and cultural or personal differences can be respected. The right to autonomy does not necessarily correspond to a universal desire for detailed factual information or total patient control over treatment decisions. As physicians working within a multicultural society, we should be prepared to tailor our approach to individual needs.

When offered information, Mrs P already knew her diagnosis (to her daughter's surprise) but did not wish to hear the details of treatment options. She requested that her daughter make that decision on her behalf, surprising the interns but adding to their appreciation of patient individuality.

'Today I bent the truth to be kind, and I have no regret, for I am far surer of what is kind than I am of what is true.'
                                                    ROBERT BRAULT

Respect for Patients, Physicians, and the Truth

Susan Cullen and Margaret Klein

Cullen and Klein argue that a respect for persons makes it wrong for physicians to deceive patients. Lying to patients outright or withholding crucial information about their medical condition violates their autonomy and prevents them from making informed choices about their lives. Telling the truth, they claim, should be the "default position" for physicians.

In reviewing three "critical questions," the authors hold, first, that a patient's wish not to be informed should be respected, except when a serious harm to others may result. Second, they claim, only a confusion between the "whole truth" and "wholly true" makes it plausible to believe it is impossible for physicians to tell patients "the truth." Finally, they maintain a physician may legitimately deceive a patient only in rare cases in which the deception is brief and the end sought is of great importance (for example, saving the patient's life) and is likely to be achieved. Deceiving a patient "for his own good" shows disrespect for the person and thus is, in general, an unacceptable way for physicians to try to help patients.

A long tradition in medicine holds that because medicine aims to promote the health of patients, it is permissible for a physician to deceive a patient if the deception would contribute to that end. "The crucial question," as one writer observes, "is whether the deception is intended to benefit the patient."

Thus, according to this view, if Dr. Allison tells Mr. Barton he is making a good recovery from a kidney transplant, when in fact the transplanted kidney is not functioning well and his recovery is slower than expected, Dr. Allison's action is justified on the grounds that she is trying to keep up her patient's spirits and encouraging him to fight to regain his health. A sick person isn't made better by gloomy assessments.

This deception-to-benefit-the-patient (DBP) view has a prima facie appeal. At the least it is motivated by the physician's effort to do something to help the patient. Were a physician to tell a healthy patient he had a vitamin deficiency so she could sell him vitamin supplements or recommend unneeded surgery so she could collect a fee for performing it, we would condemn such actions outright. The physician is practicing deception in such cases to benefit herself, not the patient.

We all realize that a physician wouldn't be justified in engaging in just any form of action to benefit her patients. We reject as morally grotesque, for example, the notion that a surgeon should remove the vital organs from a healthy person and use them to save the lives of four others. Having the aim of benefiting a patient does not license using any means whatsoever. Rather, the physician must use means that are morally acceptable. While deceiving a patient for his own good is very different from killing an innocent person to provide the patient a benefit, we will argue that such deception is nonetheless wrong. In all but the rarest cases, deceiving a patient "for his own good" is an unacceptable way for a physician to try to help her patient.

Respect for Persons

While the DBP view seems unobjectionable at first sight, it is wrong for the same reason it is wrong for a physician to tell a healthy patient he needs vitamins so she can benefit from selling them to him. Such behavior is wrong (in both cases), because it doesn't treat a human being with respect.

Humans are, at the very least, rational beings. We have the capacity to guide our actions on the basis of deliberation, rather than being moved only by instinct or psychological conditioning. Our ability to reason makes all of us worth more than a tree, a dog, or maybe anything else, in the natural world.

If we are each special because of our ability to make choices, then others should not destroy this ability or interfere with our exercise of it. All of us have an equal right to choose how to lead our lives, and others have a responsibility to respect that right. (Working out arrangements allowing each person maximum freedom while also guaranteeing the freedom of others is a major task of social and political philosophy.) Treating humans with respect means recognizing their autonomy by allowing them the freedom to make choices about their lives. By contrast, to disrespect people means taking away their freedom to live as they choose.

Disrespect and the Physician's Good

If Dr. Mires, a gynecological surgeon, tells Ms. Sligh she needs a hysterectomy, when in fact the medical indications are insufficient to justify the surgery and he is recommending it only for the money he will receive for the operation, Dr. Mires is treating Ms. Sligh with disrespect. By lying to Ms. Sligh, Dr. Mires is damaging her autonomy. She is put in the position of having to make a decision on the basis of the false information Dr. Mires provides to her. Hence, the option of deciding to do what is most likely to contribute to protecting and promoting her health is closed off to her. She can only *believe* she is making that decision, for Dr. Mires has forced her to deliberate on the basis of a false assumption.

When knowledge is power, ignorance is slavery. When Dr. Mires deliberately misinforms Ms. Sligh, he cripples her ability to carry out any plans she might have. It doesn't matter if she decides she doesn't want to have a hysterectomy and so avoids the risks, pain, and expense of surgery. Not only has she been made to worry needlessly and perhaps agonize over her decision, Dr. Mires' deception has put her in a false position with respect to making decisions about her life. Unknown to her, he has restricted her freedom to make meaningful choices. He has discounted her ability to reason and make decisions, and in this way, he has treated her with disrespect.

Disrespect and the Patient's Good

The most serious cases in which physicians have traditionally considered themselves justified (and perhaps even obligated) to deceive a patient are ones in which the patient is dying and the disease can no longer be treated effectively. In the past, the question was most often one of whether to tell a patient he had cancer. Now that cancer treatments have become more effective, the question has usually become one of whether to tell a patient a treatment is not likely to be effective in extending his life. The central issue remains the same, because the physician must still decide whether to deceive the patient.

Consider the following case. Susan Cruz, a thirty-four-year-old single mother of a six-year-old boy, suffered for more than two months from excruciating headaches that were often accompanied by vomiting and dizziness. Yet it wasn't until after she lost control of the left side of her body and collapsed in the bathroom in what she thought of as a fit that she went to see her HMO doctor. He immediately referred her to Dr. Charles Lambert, a neurologist, who, after a detailed examination, ordered an MRI of her brain. Susan had two seizures in the hospital, right after the scan. She was admitted, and the MRI was followed by a brain biopsy performed by Dr. Clare Williams, a neurosurgeon.

The results of the tests showed Susan had an aggressive form of malignant brain cancer affecting the glial cells. The cancer was so extensive Dr. Williams advised Dr. Lambert that not only was a surgical cure out of the question, surgery to reduce the amount of cancerous tissue would not be worth the risk of additional brain damage. Radiation treatments might shrink some of the tumor, but Susan's disease was so far advanced they would have little effect on the outcome.

After reviewing all the information in Susan's case, Dr. Lambert concluded it was not likely that whatever was done would extend Susan's life to an appreciable extent. Most likely, she would be dead within a few weeks, a month or two at the most. But should he tell her this? Wouldn't it be better to allow her to spend her last days free of the dread and anxiety that knowledge of the imminence of her death was sure to cause her? She and her son, Bryan, could share sometime together free from the worst kind of worry. She could do nothing to prevent her death, so shouldn't he leave her feeling hopeful about the future? After all, he couldn't *know* she would die in a few weeks.

"You have a disease of the supporting cells in the brain," Dr. Lambert told Susan. "That's the reason for the headaches, dizziness, vomiting, muscular weakness, and seizures."

"Is there a treatment?" Susan asked. "Will I have to have brain surgery?"

"Not for your stage of the disease," Dr. Lambert said. To avoid explaining why, he quickly added, "Radiation therapy is the best treatment we can offer, because X-rays will help kill off the abnormal tissue putting pressure on your brain."

"Will that make the headaches and all the rest go away?"

"It will help," Dr. Lambert said. "But we have medications that will help also. I can give you steroids to reduce the brain swelling and an anticonvulsant to control your seizures. I can also treat the headaches with effective drugs."

"When do my treatments start?"

"I'll prescribe some drugs today and set you up with the therapeutic radiologists," Dr. Lambert said. "I imagine they can start your treatments in a day or so."

"Great," Susan said. "I've got to get well so I can take care of Bryan. He's staying with my mom, and she's got a heart problem. A six-year-old boy can be a real handful."

Susan followed the treatment plan outlined by Dr. Lambert. She took the drugs prescribed and, with the help of her friend Mandy, showed up at the hospital for her radiation treatments for four weeks. She missed the fifth treatment, because she began having uncontrollable seizures and was taken to the hospital. She died the day after her admission.

Dr. Lambert never told Susan she had brain cancer, nor that the reason surgery wasn't appropriate was that the disease was so far advanced it would be useless. He didn't tell her that, by his estimation, she had only a few weeks of life remaining. Dr. Lambert didn't lie to Susan, but he deceived her. What he told her about her medical condition was vague and limited. He didn't share with her information he possessed that was relevant to her condition. He chose his words so that she would believe she had a disease that might be either cured or controlled by the treatments he prescribed.

While Susan did not (we may suppose) press Dr. Lambert for more information than he provided or ask him questions about her illness, this does not mean Dr. Lambert was not engaged in deception. Susan (like many people) may not have known enough about medicine or her own body to ask the right sort of questions, may have been so intimidated by doctors not to dare to ask questions, or may have been psychologically incapable of asking questions about her illness, preferring to leave everything in the hands of her physician. Dr. Lambert, at the least, should have found out from Susan how much she wanted to know. A willful ignorance is, after all, quite different from an enforced ignorance.

It was also disingenuous for Dr. Lambert to reason that because he cannot be *certain* Susan will die of her disease within a few weeks, he should withhold information from her. Uncertainty of that kind is an ineliminable part of medical practice, and Dr. Lambert has every reason to believe Susan has a relatively short time to live. Judges instructing juries in death penalty cases often distinguish between real doubt and philosophical doubt in explaining the meaning of "reasonable doubt." Dr. Lambert has no real doubt about Susan's fate, and she is entitled to his best medical judgment.

Dr. Lambert's deception of Susan Cruz, like Dr. Mires' deception of Ms. Sligh, is morally wrong. Dr. Lambert deceives Susan with the aim of doing something good for her, while Dr. Mires deceives Ms. Sligh with the aim of doing something good for himself. We might thus say that the deception practiced by Dr. Mires is morally worse than that practiced by Dr. Lambert. Even so, Dr. Lambert's deception of Susan Cruz is still wrong because it treats her disrespectfully.

By failing to provide Susan with crucial information, Dr. Lambert violates Susan's right to shape what is left of her own life. He deceives her into believing that, with the treatments he prescribes, she can go back to living a normal life and might eventually become healthy again. Because this is not so, Susan is thus denied the opportunity to decide how to spend the final weeks of her life.

She is unable to do what she might prefer to do, if she knew she had a fatal disease and a relatively short time left to live. She might reestablish a connection with her ex-husband, complete the novel she was writing or visit New York. Most important, she might arrange for someone to take care of her six-year-old son. Prevented by Dr. Lambert's deception from knowing she may soon die, Susan is barred from pursuing what she values most in the time she has remaining.

Respect for persons bars the deception of patients. When the deception is for the physician's benefit, the wrong is obvious. Yet even when the deception is intended to benefit the patient, the physician's good intention doesn't alter the fact that the deception violates the patient's autonomy.

Three Critical Questions

Three questions about physicians' telling the truth to their patients arise with sufficient frequency as to warrant their being addressed explicitly.

1. What if a Patient Doesn't Want to Know About His Disease or the State of His Health?

Some writers have argued that many patients don't want to know what's wrong with them. Although they may say they do, some don't mean it. Part of the physician's job is to assess how much information and what sort a patient can handle, then provide him with an appropriate amount and kind. Thus, a physician may decide that a man in his mid-thirties doesn't want to know he is showing the first symptoms of (say) Huntington's disease. Although the disease is invariably fatal and essentially untreatable, it is slow acting, and the patient may have another ten or fifteen years of more-or-less normal life before the worst symptoms of the disease manifest themselves. The physician may decide to spare the patient the anguish of living with the knowledge that he is eventually going to develop a fatal and particularly nasty disease. The patient, she judges, really wants her to protect him from the years of agony and uncertainty.

But with no more than her own assessment to guide her, in making judgments about what a patient wants to know, the physician is taking too much on herself. Huntington's disease is a genetic disorder that occurs when a parent passes on the HD gene to a child. Someone with one parent who has HD may already know he has a fifty-fifty chance of developing the disorder. He may want to know whether the problems he is experiencing are symptoms of the disease. If they are, he may choose to live his life in a way very different than he might if the problems are not symptoms. He might decide, for example, not to have a child and to avoid the risk of passing on the gene for the disease. Or if he and his partner decide to have a child, they might opt for artificial insemination and embryo screening to eliminate embryos carrying the HD gene. The physician is generally in no position to decide what information needs to be withheld from a patient. Full disclosure should be the default position for physicians.

The Patient Is Explicit. If a patient clearly and explicitly expresses the wish not to know the truth about his medical condition physicians should generally respect this desire. No disrespect is involved in not telling the truth (not providing information) to someone who decides he does not want to know it. The ignorance he imposes on himself may be necessary for him to go on with his life in the way he wishes.

Thus, someone may know himself well enough to realize that if he were diagnosed with inoperable cancer, he wouldn't be able to think about anything else, and the remainder of his life would be a misery of anxiety and fear. His physician should respect such a wish to remain ignorant, for it is as much an expression of autonomy as is the wish to be informed.

When a patient expresses the desire not to be informed about his medical condition, this does not justify his physician's *deceiving* him about his condition. The physician is warranted in withholding the truth from a patient who has asked to be kept ignorant, but the physician is not warranted in telling the patient nothing is wrong with him when there is or falsely assuring him he doesn't have metastatic prostate cancer.

Overriding Considerations? Cases in which patients do not wish to know about their medical condition may not be as rare as they once were. Some patients don't want to know if they are infected with HIV, for example, and request that they not be informed of test results that might show they are HIV-positive.

Such cases raise the question of whether the respect for persons that grounds the physician's obligation to allow a patient to make his own decisions requires the physician always to be bound by a patient's explicit wish not to be informed about his medical condition. We think not.

Where HIV or some other contagious disease is involved, the patient has a need to know, not necessarily for his own sake, but for the sake of others. Those who do not want to know they are HIV-positive lack information crucial to decisions concerning their own behavior with respect to others. The physician has an obligation to a particular patient, but she also has an obligation to prevent harm to others who may come into contact with that patient. Failing to tell a patient he is HIV-positive, even if he has requested not to know, makes her complicitous in the spread of the disease. She is not responsible for her patient's actions, but she is responsible for making sure he has information relevant to decisions affecting others. Violating his autonomy to the extent needed to inform him is justified by the possibility that it may save the lives of others. (If she discovered an airline pilot suffered from a seizure disorder, it would be morally wrong for her not to make sure the airline was informed.)

A question similar to that about infectious diseases arises about the "vertical transmission" of, genetic diseases. Suppose a thirty-four-year-old man whose mother died of Huntington's doesn't want to be tested to find out whether he is carrying the gene (and so will develop the disease). He is bothered by some movement problems and episodes of mental confusion. He wants his physician to treat him for these but not tell him whether they are symptoms of the onset of Huntington's. The man is about to be married, and he has told his physician he and his wife intend to have children.

After examination and testing, the physician believes the patient's problems are symptoms of HD and are likely to get progressively worse. Moreover, the physician knows that offspring of the man have a fifty percent chance of inheriting the gene that causes the disease. Should the physician go against the patient's explicit request and inform him it is likely he has HD?

Once again, violating a patient's autonomy to the extent of telling him something he does not want to hear seems warranted. If the patient knows he may have HD, he might decide either not to have children or to employ embryo screening to avoid having a child that inherits the HD gene. In the absence of this knowledge, he may be more likely to have a child who will inherit the gene and eventually develop a painful, lingering, and fatal disease. Decreasing the likelihood of bringing a child into the world who will eventually develop such a disease justifies the physician's going against her patient's wishes. (Before reaching this stage, the physician might talk to the patient and attempt to get him to change his mind by telling him what might be at stake and making sure he understands his reproductive options.)

In summary, we hold that while a physician has a prima facie obligation to withhold the truth about a patient's condition from the patient at the patient's request, in some circumstances the physician may have a duty to ignore the request and provide the patient with information he doesn't want to hear.

Patients Who Don't Say. What about patients like Susan Cruz who express neither a desire to be fully informed nor a wish to be kept ignorant? Physicians are justified in presuming that patients want to know about the state of their health, diseases they may have, and the appropriate treatments for them. This presumption is no less than the recognition that patients are persons, that they are rational agents who may be assumed to want to make informed decisions about matters affecting their lives. Setting aside this prior presumption requires that a patient explicitly inform a physician that he or she wishes to remain in ignorance. Informing patients about their medical condition is again, the default position for physicians.

Further, if a physician has doubts about whether a patient wants to be informed about her medical condition (as we discussed earlier in connection with Susan Cruz), he should make an effort to determine at the beginning of the relationship whether the patient wants to know about the nature and seriousness of her disease. "Don't ask, don't tell" is by no means an appropriate model for physician–patient communication, and because the physician holds the stronger position in the relationship, it is up to him to find out about how much his patient wants to know.

Studies indicate that a significant majority of patients do want to know about the state of their health. In most studies, over eighty percent of patients surveyed reported that they would want to be informed if they were diagnosed with cancer or some other seri- . ous disease. Thus, telling a patient the truth can be regarded as the default position for the physician on grounds that are empirical as well as moral.

2. What if a Physician Is Unable to Tell a Patient the Truth?

Physicians cannot tell patients what they don't know themselves. Nothing is wrong with a physician's admitting that little is known about the patient's disease or that the patient's symptoms don't point to a clear diagnosis. Patients are aware that physicians aren't omniscient, and a physician who confesses to ignorance or puzzlement may be showing respect for the patient. A physician must recognize his own limitations, as distinct from the limitations of the state of medicine, and be prepared to refer a patient to someone more able to address the patient's problem.

Actual ignorance and the consequent impossibility of telling a patient the truth is not the issue that physicians and patients typically focus on in the conflict over truth-telling. The issue is usually about whether physicians, when they know the truth, are able to tell it to their patients.

A complaint often expressed by physicians about the need to get a patient's informed consent before carrying out a surgical procedure is that patients are unable to understand their explanations. The notion underlying this complaint is that, even when physicians try, it is impossible to inform patients about their medical condition.

This notion lies at the base of the argument that physicians, even when they do their best, cannot tell their patients the truth. Patients (the argument goes) lack the technical background and experience of physicians, so even intelligent and educated patients are not able to understand the medical terms and concepts physicians must use to describe a patient's condition. Physicians, if they are to communicate at all with the patient, must then switch to using terms and concepts that neither adequately nor accurately convey to the patient what is wrong with him. Thus, it is impossible for physicians to tell patients the truth.

Critics have pointed out that this argument that physicians are not able even in principle to tell patients "the truth" rests on a confusion between "whole truth" and "wholly true." Physicians, we can agree, cannot tell patients the "whole truth," meaning that no patient is going to be able to understand all the known details of a disease process as it affects him. Medicine is an information-rich enterprise, and even physicians are quickly out of their depth in areas beyond their expertise. How many of us really understand the pancreas?

Even so, the explanation of a complicated situation in ways a layperson can understand is not a challenge unique to physicians. The same problem is faced by lawyers, electricians, automobile mechanics, and computer help-line workers. In none of these fields, including medicine, is it necessary to provide the layperson with a complete explanation (the "complete truth") of a situation. All a patient requires is an understanding adequate to appreciate the nature and seriousness of his illness and the potential benefits and risks of the available therapies. A diabetic need not know the stages of oxidative phosphorylation to grasp the importance of insulin and role of diet in maintaining her health.

The argument also does not support the claim endorsed by some writers that, because a physician cannot tell their patients "the truth" (the "whole truth"), it's all right to tell them what is not "wholly true"—that is, to deceive them. Such deception may involve using vague language to explain a patient's medical condition. Thus, Dr. Lambert tells Susan Cruz, "You have a disease of the supporting cells in the brain," when he should have explained to her that she had a particular kind of brain cancer, one that was aggressive and that had advanced to an inoperable stage. The view that the impossibility of telling a patient "the whole truth" makes it all right to tell the patient something not wholly true is analogous to saying, "Because I can't pay you the money I owe you, it's okay for me to rob you." Not being able to tell "the truth" is not a license to deceive.

Respect for persons requires that physicians tell their patients the relevant facts about their medical condition in a comprehensible way. It doesn't require trying to tell patients all the facts. Telling the truth is no more an impossibility for physicians than it is for automobile mechanics.

3. Don't Physicians Sometimes Have a Duty to Lie to Their Patients?

Some writers have argued that respect for persons and their autonomy sometimes permits physicians to deliberately deceive their patients. Granting that a sick patient desires to regain his health, then if that desire can most likely be attained by his physician's deceiving him, the physician is justified in carrying out the deception. Deceiving the patient in such a case assists him in securing his goal, so a respect for the patient's goal makes the deception permissible. The physician violates the patient's autonomy a little while the patient is sick so that he will regain his health.

This is not a view that can be dismissed as obviously flawed, but it is one we ought to be cautious about adopting without qualification.

First, it is easy to overestimate the extent to which lying to a patient will be useful in helping him regain his health. We certainly don't have any data that show the relative advantage of deceiving patients about their illnesses. The old notion that if a patient with a serious illness is protected from anxiety and worry about his condition, he will heal faster is no more than speculation. As such, it will not justify our infringing someone's autonomy for the sake of what is at best a hypothetical gain.

Second, it is easy to underestimate the benefits of informing patients about the character of disease and the aim of the treatment. Most treatments for serious diseases require the full cooperation of the patient. A woman diagnosed with metastatic breast cancer must go through a rigorous course of therapy, ranging from surgery through chemotherapy and radiation treatments. If she knows that her cancer has spread from the breast to other places in her body and knows her chances of survival, she is more likely to adhere to the treatment plan mapped out by her oncologist. Deceiving the patient about her medical problem is probably, in most cases, more likely to work against her goal of preserving her life and regaining her health. Thus, deception may not only violate her autonomy, it may contribute to the loss of her life.

Let us suppose, however, that in some cases we can know with reasonable certainty that if we deceive someone about her illness this will contribute to her recovery. Is it acceptable to use deception and violate autonomy in the short run, if the deception can be expected to promote autonomy in the longer run?

Recalling an example mentioned earlier should make us wary of answering this question in the affirmative. It would be wrong, we said, to kill one healthy person to obtain organs to save the lives of four people. Such examples suggest it is wrong to interfere with autonomy (that of the healthy person) for the sake of promoting autonomy (that of the four sick ones).

Yet we generally agree it is acceptable for the federal government to tax people with a certain income, then use part of the money to help feed starving foreigners. This suggests it is *not* wrong to interfere with autonomy (that of taxpayers) to promote autonomy (that of the starving). Are our responses in these two cases inconsistent, or is there a difference between the cases? We suggest there is a difference.

In both cases, the gain in autonomy is great (lives saved), but in the tax case, the infringement of autonomy needed to achieve a great gain is minor. Taxing us as citizens takes away some of our resources and thus counts as an infringement of our autonomy.

Yet we still retain a substantial degree of control over the important parts of our lives.

The contrast between these two cases suggests the following principle: It does not show a disrespect for persons to violate their autonomy, if the violation is minor and the potential gain is both probable and significant. Thus, for example, if a physician is confident she can save a patient's life by deceiving him for a short while, it is not wrong for her to deceive him. Suppose Ms. Cohen has an irrational fear of taking antibiotics, yet if she is not treated for a bacterial lung infection, she will almost certainly die. Her physician, in such circumstances, would be justified in telling her something like, "The pills I'm giving you will help your body fight the infection."

Such cases are sure to be rare, however. In most cases, either the stakes will not be high enough (someone's life) to justify deception or deception will not be likely to help. Most often, the physician's only legitimate course is to respect her patient's status as an autonomous agent. This means not trying to deceive him and helping him make decisions by providing him with information relevant to his disease and the treatment options open to him.

Conclusion

We have argued that a principle of respect for persons requires that physicians not engage in deceiving patients. It is clearly wrong for physicians to tell patients they need surgery that they don't need. Such a lie is wrong, we have contended, because it prevents patients from making informed choices about their lives. This is also true of deception intended to benefit a patient. In all but the rarest cases, deceiving a patient "for his own good" is an unacceptable way for physicians to try to help their patients.

Confidentiality in Medicine—A Decrepit Concept

Mark Siegler

Mark Siegler calls attention to the impossibility of preserving the confidentiality traditionally associated with the physician–patient relationship. In the modern hospital, a great many people have legitimate access to a patient's chart and so to all medical, social, and financial information the patient has provided. Yet the loss of confidentiality is a threat to good medical care. Confidentiality protects a patient at a time of vulnerability and promotes the trust that is necessary for effective diagnosis and treatment. Siegler concludes by suggesting some possible solutions for preserving confidentiality while meeting the needs of others to know certain things about the patient.

Medical confidentiality, as it has traditionally been understood by patients and doctors, no longer exists. This ancient medical principle, which has been included in every physician's oath and code of ethics since Hippocratic times, has become old, worn-out, and useless; it is a decrepit concept. Efforts to preserve it appear doomed to

From *The New England Journal of Medicine,* Mark Siegler, "Confidentiality in Medicine — A Decrepit Concept," *New England Journal of Medicine* 307, no. 24 (1982): 1518–521. Copyright © 1982 Massachusetts Medical Society. Reprinted with permission from Massachusetts Medical Society. Supported by a grant (OSS-8018097) from the National Science Foundation and by the National Endowment for the Humanities. The views expressed are those of the author and do not necessarily reflect those of the National Science Foundation or the National Endowment for the Humanities.

failure and often give rise to more problems than solutions. Psychiatrists have tacitly acknowledged the impossibility of ensuring the confidentiality of medical records by choosing to establish a separate, more secret record. The following case illustrates how the confidentiality principle is compromised systematically in the course of routine medical care.

A patient of mine with mild chronic obstructive pulmonary disease was transferred from the surgical intensive-care unit to a surgical nursing floor two days after an elective cholecystectomy. On the day of transfer, the patient saw a respiratory therapist writing in his medical chart (the therapist was recording the results of an arterial blood gas analysis) and became concerned about the confidentiality of his hospital records. The patient threatened to leave the hospital prematurely unless I could guarantee that the confidentiality of his hospital record would be respected.

The patient's complaint prompted me to enumerate the number of persons who had both access to his hospital record and a reason to examine it. I was amazed to learn that at least 25 and possibly as many as 100 health professionals and administrative personnel at our university hospital had access to the patient's record and that all of them had a legitimate need, indeed a professional responsibility, to open and use that chart. These persons included 6 attending physicians (the primary physician, the surgeon, the pulmonary consultant and others); 12 house officers (medical, surgical, intensive-care unit, and "covering" house staff); 20 nursing personnel (on three shifts); 6 respiratory therapists; 3 nutritionists; 2 clinical pharmacists; 15 students (from medicine, nursing, respiratory therapy, and clinical pharmacy); 4 unit secretaries; 4 hospital financial officers; and 4 chart reviewers (utilization review, quality assurance review, tissue review, and insurance auditor). It is of interest that this patient's problem was straightforward, and he therefore did not require many other technical and support services that the modern hospital provides. For example, he did not need multiple consultants and fellows, such specialized procedures as dialysis, or social workers, chaplains, physical therapists, occupational therapists, and the like.

Upon completing my survey I reported to the patient that I estimated that at least 75 health professionals and hospital personnel had access to his medical record. I suggested to the patient that these people were all involved in providing or supporting his health-care services. They were, I assured him, working for him. Despite my reassurances the patient was obviously distressed and retorted, "I always believed that medical confidentiality was part of a doctor's code of ethics. Perhaps you should tell me just what you people mean by 'confidentiality'!"

Two Aspects of Medical Confidentiality

Confidentiality and Third-Party Interests

Previous discussions of medical confidentiality usually have focused on the tension between a physician's responsibility to keep information divulged by patients secret and a physician's legal and moral duty, on occasion, to reveal such confidences to third parties, such as families, employers, public health authorities, or police authorities. In all these instances, the central question relates to the stringency of the physician's obligation to maintain patient confidentiality when the health, well-being, and safety of identifiable others or of society in general would be threatened by a failure to reveal information about the patient. The tension in such cases is between the good of the patient and the good of others.

Confidentiality and the Patient's Interest

As the example above illustrates, further challenges to confidentiality arise because the patient's personal interest in maintaining confidentiality comes into conflict with his personal interest in receiving the best possible health care. Modern high-technology health care is available principally in hospitals (often, teaching hospitals), requires many trained and specialized workers (a "health-care team"), and is very costly. The existence of such teams means that information that previously had been held in confidence by an individual physician will now necessarily be disseminated to many members of the team. Furthermore, since health-care teams are expensive and few patients can afford to pay such costs directly, it becomes essential to grant access to the patient's medical record to persons who are responsible for obtaining third-party payment. These persons include chart reviewers, financial officers, insurance auditors, and quality-of-care assessors. Finally, as medicine expands from a narrow, disease-based model to a model that encompasses psychological, social, and economic problems, not only will the size of the health-care team and medical costs increase, but more sensitive information (such as one's personal habits and financial condition) will now be included in the medical record and will no longer be confidential.

The point I wish to establish is that hospital medicine, the rise of health-care teams, the existence of third-party insurance programs, and the expanding limits of medicine all appear to be responses to the wishes of people for better and more comprehensive medical care. But each of these developments necessarily modifies our traditional understanding of medical confidentiality.

The Role of Confidentiality in Medicine

Confidentiality serves a dual purpose in medicine. In the first place, it acknowledges respect for the patient's sense of individuality and privacy. The patient's most personal physical and psychological secrets are kept confidential in order to decrease a sense of shame and vulnerability. Secondly, confidentiality is important in improving the patient's health care—a basic goal of medicine. The promise of confidentiality permits people to trust (i.e., have confidence) that information revealed to a physician in the course of a medical encounter will not be disseminated further. In this way patients are encouraged to communicate honestly and forthrightly with their doctors. This bond of trust between patient and doctor is vitally important both in the diagnostic process (which relies on an accurate history) and subsequently in the treatment phase, which often depends as much on the patient's trust in the physician as it does on medications and surgery. These two important functions of confidentiality are as important now as they were in the past. They will not be supplanted entirely either by improvements in medical technology or by recent changes in relations between some patients and doctors toward a rights-based, consumerist model.

Possible Solutions to the Confidentiality Problem

First of all, in all nonbureaucratic, noninstitutional medical encounters—that is, in the millions of doctor–patient encounters that take place in physicians' offices, where more privacy can be preserved—meticulous care should be taken to guarantee that patients' medical and personal information will be kept confidential.

Secondly, in such settings as hospitals or large-scale group practices, where many persons have opportunities to examine the medical record, we should aim to provide access only to those who have "a need to know." This could be accomplished through such administrative changes as dividing the entire record into several sections—for example, a medical and financial section—and permitting only health professionals access to the medical information.

The approach favored by many psychiatrists—that of keeping a psychiatric record separate from the general medical record—is an understandable strategy but one that is not entirely satisfactory and that should not be generalized. The keeping of separate psychiatric records implies that psychiatry and medicine are different undertakings and thus drives deeper the wedge between them and between physical and psychological illness. Furthermore, it is often vitally important for internists or surgeons to know that a patient is being seen by a psychiatrist or is taking a particular medication. When separate records are kept, this information may not be available. Finally, if generalized, the practice of keeping a separate psychiatric record could lead to the unacceptable consequence of having a separate record for each type of medical problem.

Patients should be informed about what is meant by "medical confidentiality." We should establish the distinction between information about the patient that generally will be kept confidential regardless of the interest of third parties and information that will be exchanged among members of the health-care team in order to provide care for the patient. Patients should be made aware of the large number of persons in the modern hospital who require access to the medical record in order to serve the patient's medical and financial interests.

Finally, at some point most patients should have an opportunity to review their medical record and to make informed choices about whether their entire record is to be available to everyone or whether certain portions of the record are privileged and should be accessible only to their principal physician or to others designated explicitly by the patient. This approach would rely on traditional informed-consent procedural standards and might permit the patient to balance the personal value of medical confidentiality against the personal value of high-technology, team health care. There is no reason that the same procedure should not be used with psychiatric records instead of the arbitrary system now employed, in which everything related to psychiatry is kept secret.

Afterthought: Confidentiality and Indiscretion

There is one additional aspect of confidentiality that is rarely included in discussions of the subject. I am referring here to the wanton, often inadvertent, but avoidable exchanges of confidential information that occur frequently in hospital rooms, elevators, cafeterias, doctors' offices, and at cocktail parties. Of course, as more people have access to medical information about the patient the potential for this irresponsible abuse of confidentiality increases geometrically.

Such mundane breaches of confidentiality are probably of greater concern to most patients than the broader issue of whether their medical records may be entered into a computerized data bank or whether a respiratory therapist is reviewing the results of an arterial blood gas determination. Somehow, privacy is violated and a sense of shame is heightened when intimate secrets are revealed to people one knows or is close to—friends, neighbors, acquaintances, or hospital roommates—rather than when they are disclosed to an anonymous bureaucrat sitting at a computer terminal in a distant city or to a health professional who is acting in an official capacity.

I suspect that the principles of medical confidentiality, particularly those reflected in most medical codes of ethics, were designed principally to prevent just this sort of embarrassing personal indiscretion rather than to maintain (for social, political, or economic reasons) the absolute secrecy of doctor–patient communications. In this regard, it is worth noting that Percival's Code of Medical Ethics (1803) includes the following admonition: "Patients should be interrogated concerning their complaint in a tone of voice which cannot be overheard" [Leake, C. D., ed., *Percival's Medical Ethics*, Baltimore: Williams and Wilkins, 1927]. We in the medical profession frequently neglect these simple courtesies.

Conclusion

The principle of medical confidentiality described in medical codes of ethics and still believed in by patients no longer exists. In this respect, it is a decrepit concept. Rather than perpetuate the myth of confidentiality and invest energy vainly to preserve it, the public and the profession would be better served if they devoted their attention to determining which aspects of the original principle of confidentiality are worth retaining. Efforts could then be directed to salvaging those.

Decision in the *Tarasoff* Case

Supreme Court of California

This ruling of the California Supreme Court has been of particular concern to psychiatrists and psychotherapists. The court ruled that therapists at the student health center of the University of California, Berkeley, were negligent in their duty to warn Tatiana Tarasoff that Prosenjit Poddar, one of their patients, had threatened her life. Although the therapists reported the threat to the police, Tarasoff herself was not warned, and she was murdered by Poddar.

The ruling and dissenting opinions in this case weigh the state's interest in protecting its citizens from injury against the interest of patients and therapists in preserving confidentiality. Does a therapist have a duty to warn at all? Should a patient be informed that not everything she tells her therapist will be held in confidence? Is a therapist obliged to seek a court order committing a patient involuntarily to an institution if the patient poses a serious threat to herself or others?

In the majority opinion, Justice Matthew Tobriner argues that a therapist whose patient poses a serious danger to someone has a legal obligation to use "reasonable care" to protect the intended victim. This may involve warning the person, but if it is reasonable to believe that a warning is not enough, then the therapist has a duty to seek to have the patient involuntarily institutionalized.

From California Supreme Court, Tarasoff v. Regents of the University of California, 131 *California Reporter* 14 (July 1, 1976).

In the dissenting opinion, Justice William Clark argues that the law should not interfere with the confidentiality between therapist and patient for three reasons. Without the guarantee of confidentiality, (1) those needing treatment may not seek it; (2) violence may increase, because those needing treatment were deterred from getting it; and (3) therapists, to protect their interest, may seek more involuntary commitments, thus violating the rights of their patients and undermining the trust needed for effective treatment.

Justice Matthew O. Tobriner (Majority Opinion)

On October 27, 1969, Prosenjit Poddar killed Tatiana Tarasoff. Plaintiffs, Tatiana's parents, allege that two months earlier Poddar confided his intention to kill Tatiana to Dr. Lawrence Moore, a psychologist employed by the Cowell Memorial Hospital at the University of California at Berkeley. They allege that on Moore's request, the campus police briefly detained Poddar, but released him when he appeared rational. They further claim that Dr. Harvey Powelson, Moore's superior, then directed that no further action be taken to detain Poddar. No one warned plaintiffs of Tatiana's peril. . . .

We shall explain that defendant therapists cannot escape liability merely because Tatiana herself was not their patient. When a therapist determines, or pursuant to the standards of his profession should determine, that his patient presents a serious danger of violence to another, he incurs an obligation to use reasonable care to protect the intended victim against such danger. The discharge of this duty may require the therapist to take one or more of various steps, depending upon the nature of the case. Thus it may call for him to warn the intended victim or others likely to apprise the victim of the danger, to notify the police, or to take whatever other steps are reasonably necessary under the circumstances. . . .

1. Plaintiff's Complaints

. . . Plaintiffs' first cause of action, entitled "Failure to Detain a Dangerous Patient," alleges that on August 20, 1969, Poddar was a voluntary outpatient receiving therapy at Cowell Memorial Hospital. Poddar informed Moore, his therapist, that he was going to kill an unnamed girl, readily identifiable as Tatiana, when she returned home from spending the summer in Brazil. Moore, with the concurrence of Dr. Gold, who had initially examined Poddar, and Dr. Yandell, assistant to the director of the department of psychiatry, decided that Poddar should be committed for observation in a mental hospital. Moore orally notified Officers Atkinson and Teel of the campus police that he would request commitment. He then sent a letter to Police Chief William Beall requesting the assistance of the police department in securing Poddar's confinement.

Officers Atkinson, Brownrigg, and Halleran took Poddar into custody, but, satisfied that Poddar was rational, released him on his promise to stay away from Tatiana. Powelson, director of the department of psychiatry at Cowell Memorial Hospital, then asked the police to return Moore's letter, directed that all copies of the letter and notes that Moore had taken as therapist be destroyed, and "ordered no action to place Prosenjit Poddar in 72-hour treatment and evaluation facility."

Plaintiffs' second cause of action, entitled "Failure to Warn on a Dangerous Patient," incorporates the allegations of the first cause of action, but adds the assertion that defendants negligently permitted Poddar to be released from police custody without "notifying the parents of Tatiana Tarasoff that their daughter was in grave danger from Prosenjit Poddar." Poddar persuaded Tatiana's brother to share an apartment with him near Tatiana's residence; shortly after her return from Brazil, Poddar went to her residence and killed her. . . .

2. Plaintiffs Can State a Cause of Action Against Defendant Therapists for Negligent Failure to Protect Tatiana

The second cause of action can be amended to allege 'that Tatiana's death proximately resulted from defendants' negligent failure to warn Tatiana or others likely to apprise her of her danger. Plaintiffs contend that as amended, such allegations of negligence and proximate causation, with resulting damages, establish a cause of action. Defendants, however, contend that in the circumstances of the present case they owed no duty of care to Tatiana or her parents and that, in the absence of such duty, they were free to act in careless disregard of Tatiana's life and safety.

. . . In analyzing this issue, we bear in mind that legal duties are not discoverable facts of nature, but merely conclusory expressions that, in cases of a particular type, liability should be imposed for damage done. As stated in *Dillon* v. *Legg* (1968): . . . "The assertion that liability must . . . be denied because defendant bears no 'duty' to plaintiff begs the essential question—whether the plaintiff's interests are entitled to legal protection against the defendant's conduct. . . . [Duty] is not sacrosanct in itself, but only an expression of the sum total of those considerations of policy which lead the law to say that the particular plaintiff is entitled to protection." . . .

In the landmark case of *Rowland* v. *Christian* (1968), . . . Justice Peters recognized that liability should be imposed "for an injury occasioned to another by his want of ordinary care or skill" as expressed in section 1714 of the Civil Code. Thus, Justice Peters, quoting from *Heaven* v. *Pender* (1883) . . . stated: "'whenever one person is by circumstances placed in such a position with regard to another . . . that if he did not use ordinary care and skill in his own conduct . . . he would cause danger of injury to the person or property of the other, a duty arises to use ordinary care and skill to avoid such danger.'"

. . . We depart from "this fundamental principle" only upon the "balancing of a number of considerations"; major ones "are the foreseeability of harm to the plaintiff, the degree of certainty that the plaintiff suffered injury, the closeness of the connection between the defendant's conduct and the injury suffered, the moral blame attached to the defendant's conduct, the policy of preventing future harm, the extent of the burden to the defendant and consequences to the community of imposing a duty to exercise care with resulting liability for breach, and the availability, cost and prevalence of insurance for the risk involved."

The most important of these considerations in establishing duty is foreseeability. As a general principle, a "defendant owes a duty of care to all persons who are foreseeably endangered by his conduct, with respect to all risks which make the conduct unreasonably dangerous." As we shall explain, however, when the avoidance of foreseeable harm requires a defendant to control the conduct of another person, or to warn of such conduct, the common law has traditionally imposed liability only

if the defendant bears some special relationship to the dangerous person or to the potential victim. Since the relationship between a therapist and his patient satisfies this requirement, we need not here decide whether foreseeability alone is sufficient to create a duty to exercise reasonable care to protect a potential victim of another's conduct. . . .

Although plaintiffs' pleadings assert no special relation between Tatiana and defendant therapists, they establish as between Poddar and defendant therapists the special relation that arises between a patient and his doctor or psychotherapist. Such a relationship may support affirmative duties for the benefit of third persons. Thus, for example, a hospital must exercise reasonable care to control the behavior of a patient which may endanger other persons. A doctor must also warn a patient if the patient's condition or medication renders certain conduct, such as driving a car, dangerous to others.

. . . Although the California decisions that recognize this duty have involved cases in which the defendant stood in a special relationship *both* to the victim and to the person whose conduct created the danger, we do not think that the duty should logically be constricted to such situations. Decisions of other jurisdictions hold that the single relationship of a doctor to his patient is sufficient to support the duty to exercise reasonable care to protect others against dangers emanating from the patient's illness. The courts hold that a doctor is liable to persons infected by his patient if he negligently fails to diagnose a contagious disease, . . . or, having diagnosed the illness, fails to warn members of the patient's family.

Since it involved a dangerous mental patient, the decision in *Merchants Nat. Bank Trust Co. of Fargo* v. *United States* . . . comes closer to the issue. The Veterans Administration arranged for the patient to work on a local farm, but did not inform the farmer of the man's background. The farmer consequently permitted the patient to come and go freely during nonworking hours; the patient borrowed a car, drove to his wife's residence and killed her. Notwithstanding the lack of any "special relationship" between the Veterans Administration and the wife, the court found the Veterans Administration liable for the wrongful death of the wife.

In their summary of the relevant rulings Fleming and Maximov conclude that the "case law should dispel any notion that to impose on the therapists a duty to take precautions for the safety of persons threatened by a patient, where due care so requires, is in any way opposed to contemporary ground rules on the duty relationship. On the contrary, there now seems to be sufficient authority to support the conclusion that by entering into a doctor–patient relationship the therapist becomes sufficiently involved to assume some responsibility for the safety, not only of the patient himself, but also of any third person whom the doctor knows to be threatened by the patient." . . .

Defendants contend, however, that imposition of a duty to exercise reasonable care to protect third persons is unworkable because therapists cannot accurately predict whether or not a patient will resort to violence. In support of this argument amicus representing the American Psychiatric Association and other professional societies cites numerous articles which indicate that therapists, in the present state of the art, are unable reliably to predict violent acts; their forecasts, amicus claims, tend consistently to overpredict violence, and indeed are more often wrong than right. . . .

We recognize the difficulty that a therapist encounters in attempting to forecast whether a patient presents a serious danger of violence. Obviously we do not require that the therapist, in making that determination, render a perfect performance; the therapist need only exercise "that reasonable degree of skill, knowledge, and care ordinarily possessed and exercised by members of [that professional specialty] under similar circumstances." Within the broad range of reasonable practice and treatment in which professional opinion and judgment may differ, the therapist is free to exercise his or her own best judgment without liability; proof, aided by hindsight, that he or she judged wrongly is insufficient to establish negligence.

In the instant case, however, the pleadings do not raise any question as to failure of defendant therapists to predict that Poddar presented a serious danger of violence. On the contrary, the present complaints allege that defendant therapists did in fact predict that Poddar would kill, but were negligent in failing to warn.

. . . Amicus contends, however, that even when a therapist does in fact predict that a patient poses a serious danger of violence to others, the therapist should be absolved of any responsibility for failing to act to protect the potential victim. In our view, however, once a therapist does in fact determine, or under applicable professional standards reasonably should have determined, that a patient poses a serious danger of violence to others, he bears a duty to exercise reasonable care to protect the foreseeable victim of that

danger. While the discharge of this duty of due care will necessarily vary with the facts of each case, in each instance the adequacy of the therapist's conduct must be measured against the traditional negligence standard of the rendition of reasonable care under the circumstances. . . . As explained in Fleming and Maximov, *The Patient or His Victim: The Therapist's Dilemma* (1974): " . . . the ultimate question of resolving the tension between the conflicting interests of patient and potential victim is one of social polity, not professional expertise. . . . In sum, the therapist owes a legal duty not only to his patient, but also to his patient's would-be victim and is subject in both respects to scrutiny by judge and jury." . . .

The risk that unnecessary warnings may be given is a reasonable price to pay for the lives of possible victims that may be saved. We would hesitate to hold that the therapist who is aware that his patient expects to attempt to assassinate the President of the United States would not be obligated to warn the authorities because the therapist cannot predict with accuracy that his patient will commit the crime.

Defendants further argue that free and open communication is essential to psychotherapy; . . . that "Unless a patient . . . is assured that . . . information [revealed by him] can and will be held in utmost confidence, he will be reluctant to make the full disclosure upon which diagnosis and treatment . . . depends." . . . The giving of a warning, defendants contend, constitutes a breach of trust which entails the revelation of confidential communications.

. . . We recognize the public interest in supporting effective treatment of mental illness and in protecting the rights of patients to privacy, . . . and the consequent public importance of safeguarding the confidential character of psychotherapeutic communication. Against this interest, however, we must weigh the public interest in safety from violent assault. . . .

We realize that the open and confidential character of psychotherapeutic dialogue encourages patients to express threats of violence, few of which are ever executed. Certainly a therapist should not be encouraged routinely to reveal such threats; such disclosures could seriously disrupt the patient's relationship with his therapist and with the persons threatened. To the contrary, the therapist's obligations to his patient require that he not disclose a confidence unless such disclosure is necessary to avert danger to others, and even then that he do so discreetly, and in a fashion that would preserve the privacy of his patient to the fullest extent compatible with the prevention of the threatened danger.

The revelation of a communication under the above circumstances is not a breach of trust or a violation of professional ethics; as stated in the Principles of Medical Ethics of the American Medical Association (1957), section 9: "A physician may not reveal the confidence entrusted to him in the course of medical attendance . . . *unless he is required to do so by law or unless it becomes necessary in order to protect the welfare of the individual or of the community.*" (Emphasis added.) We conclude that the public policy favoring protection of the confidential character of patient–psychotherapist communications must yield to the extent to which disclosure is essential to avert danger to others. The protective privilege ends where the public peril begins. . . .

For the foregoing reasons, we find that plaintiffs' complaints can be amended to state a cause of action against defendants Moore, Powelson, Gold, and Yandell and against the Regents as their employer, for breach of a duty to exercise reasonable care to protect Tatiana.

Justice William P. Clark (Dissenting Opinion)

Until today's majority opinion, both legal and medical authorities have agreed that confidentiality is essential to effectively treat the mentally ill, and that imposing a duty on doctors to disclose patient threats to potential victims would greatly impair treatment. Further, recognizing that effective treatment and society's safety are necessarily intertwined, the Legislature has already decided effective and confidential treatment is preferred over imposition of a duty to warn.

The issue whether effective treatment for the mentally ill should be sacrificed to a system of warnings is, in my opinion, properly one for the Legislature, and we are bound by its judgment. Moreover, even in the absence of clear legislative direction, we must reach the same conclusion because imposing the majority's new duty is certain to result in a net increase in violence. . . .

Overwhelming policy considerations weigh against imposing a duty on psychotherapists to warn a potential victim against harm. While offering virtually no benefit to society, such a duty will frustrate psychiatric treatment, invade fundamental patient rights and increase violence. . . .

Assurance of confidentiality is important for three reasons.

Deterrence from Treatment

First, without substantial assurance of confidentiality, those requiring treatment will be deterred from seeking assistance. It remains an unfortunate fact in our society that people seeking psychiatric guidance tend to become stigmatized. Apprehension of such stigma—apparently increased by the propensity of people considering treatment to see themselves in the worst possible light—creates a well-recognized reluctance to seek aid. This reluctance is alleviated by the psychiatrist's assurance of confidentiality.

Full Disclosure

Second, the guarantee of confidentiality is essential in eliciting the full disclosure necessary for effective treatment. The psychiatric patient approaches treatment with conscious and unconscious inhibitions against revealing his innermost thoughts. "Every person, however well-motivated, has to overcome resistance to therapeutic exploration. These resistances seek support from every possible source and the possibility of disclosure would easily be employed in the service of resistance." . . . Until a patient can trust his psychiatrist not to violate their confidential relationship, "the unconscious psychological control mechanism of repression will prevent the recall of past experiences." . . .

Successful Treatment

Third, even if the patient fully discloses his thoughts, assurance that the confidential relationship will not be breached is necessary to maintain his trust in his psychiatrist—the very means by which treatment is effected. "[T]he essence of much psychotherapy is the contribution of trust in the external world and ultimately in the self, modelled upon the trusting relationship established during therapy." . . . Patients will be helped only if they can form a trusting relationship with the psychiatrist. . . . All authorities appear to agree that if the trust relationship cannot be developed because of collusive communication between the psychiatrist and others, treatment will be frustrated.

Given the importance of confidentiality to the practice of psychiatry, it becomes clear the duty to warn imposed by the majority will cripple the use and effectiveness of psychiatry. Many people, potentially violent—yet susceptible to treatment— will be deterred from seeking it; those seeking it will be inhibited from making revelations necessary to effective treatment; and, forcing the psychiatrist to violate the patient's trust will destroy the interpersonal relationship by which treatment is effected.

Violence and Civil Commitment

By imposing a duty to warn, the majority contributes to the danger to society of violence by the mentally ill and greatly increases the risk of civil commitment—the total deprivation of liberty—of those who should not be confined. The impairment of treatment and risk of improper commitment resulting from the new duty to warn will not be limited to a few patients but will extend to a large number of the mentally ill. Although under existing psychiatric procedures only a relatively few receiving treatment will ever present a risk of violence, the number making threats is huge, and it is the latter group—not just the former—whose treatment will be impaired and whose risk of commitment will be increased.

Both the legal and psychiatric communities recognize that the process of determining potential violence in a patient is far from exact, being fraught with complexity and uncertainty. In fact precision has not even been attained in predicting who of those having already committed violent acts will again become violent, a task recognized to be of much simpler proportions. . . .

This predictive uncertainty means that the number of disclosures will necessarily be large. As noted above, psychiatric patients are encouraged to discuss all thoughts of violence, and they often express such thoughts. However, unlike this court, the psychiatrist does not enjoy the benefit of overwhelming hindsight in seeing which few, if any, of his patients will ultimately become violent. Now, confronted by the majority's new duty, the psychiatrist must instantaneously calculate potential violence from each patient on each visit. The difficulties researchers have encountered in accurately predicting violence will be heightened for the practicing psychiatrist dealing for brief periods in his office with heretofore nonviolent patients. And, given the decision not to warn or commit must always be made at the psychiatrist's civil peril, one can expect most doubts will be resolved in favor of the psychiatrist protecting himself.

Neither alternative open to the psychiatrist seeking to protect himself is in the public interest. The warning itself is an impairment of the psychiatrist's ability to treat, depriving many patients of adequate treatment. It is to be expected that after disclosing their threats, a significant number of patients, who would not become violent if treated according to existing practices, will engage in violent conduct as a result of unsuccessful treatment. In short, the majority's duty to warn will not only impair treatment of many who would never become violent but worse, will result in a net increase in violence.

The second alternative open to the psychiatrist is to commit his patient rather than to warn. Even in the absence of threat of civil liability, the doubts of psychiatrists as to the seriousness of patient threats have led psychiatrists to overcommit to mental institutions. This overcommitment has been authoritatively documented in both legal and psychiatric studies. This practice is so prevalent that it has been estimated that "as many as twenty harmless persons are incarcerated for every one who will commit a violent act." . . .

Given the incentive to commit created by the majority's duty, this already serious situation will be worsened, contrary to Chief Justice Wright's admonition "that liberty is no less precious because forfeited in a civil proceeding than when taken as a consequence of a criminal conviction."

DECISION SCENARIOS

The questions following each decision scenario are intended to prompt reflection and discussion. In deciding how to answer them, you should consider the information provided in the Social Context and Case Presentations, as well as in the Briefing Session. You should also make use of the ethical theories and principles presented in Part VI: Foundations of Bioethics, and the arguments and criticisms offered in the relevant readings in this chapter.

DECISION SCENARIO 1

When Prayer Is Not Enough

"You'll feel better soon," Marylyn Tauber told her eight-year-old son Madison. "God doesn't let bad things happen to people who believe in Him with all their heart, all their mind, and all their strength."

Madison said nothing, but from his bed, he looked up at her with eyes that were dull. His lips were dry and cracked, and his face a dusky red. He didn't seem to understand her. Marylyn put a hand on Madison's cheek. He was burning with fever, and she wondered if it would be all right for her to put a cool washcloth on his forehead.

Madison had been ill for three days. He had come home from school with a flushed face and a sore throat. His mother thought it was just another one of those summer colds he was always getting. But he'd gotten worse, not better. And his temperature was 102°F the last time she had taken it. She had given him ice and tried to get him to drink some Coke, but he hadn't wanted anything since.

"I've been praying for you night and day," Marylyn said. She tried to sound cheerful so she could lift Madison's spirits. "I know God loves little boys, and he is going to heal you before long."

She had to keep believing that, she told herself, because she couldn't face the possibility that Madison might die. He might, of course, if that were

God's will. But she wasn't sure she was a good enough person to accept God's will without complaint. She was frightened, but she knew she had to do the right thing. Taking Madison to a doctor would mean that her faith in God had failed when put to the test.

1. We can assume that Marylyn loves Madison and wants to do what is best for him. She believes that prayer, not seeking medical attention, is the best thing for Madison. Should parents always be the ones to decide what is in the best interest of their child?

2. If Madison dies, should Marylyn be charged with a crime?

3. The state places some limits on the expression of religious beliefs. We do not, for example, permit human or animal sacrifices. Should we require parents to seek medical assistance for their child when the child becomes ill, even if this means violating their religious beliefs?

DECISION SCENARIO 2

Protecting against Disease

First-time parents Bob and Susan Slocombe (as we will call them) were distressed when their fourteen-month-old son Cooper seemed to undergo a sudden change in character.

Cooper had been a happy and babbling infant who loved to play peek-a-boo with them, laughing and kicking with delight whenever he caught his parents' eyes. Then, in what seemed to the Slocombes like an overnight transformation, Cooper stopped making eye contact and smiling. He would cry uncontrollably when they picked him up, as if they were causing him pain, and he became easily startled by household noises.

The Slocombes initially thought that Cooper was only going through a new phase of development—after all, babies were always changing. But by the time Cooper was eighteen months old, they realized that he was never going to change back to being anything like the baby he had been before. In fact, Cooper seemed to have become more withdrawn and unresponsive. The babbling noises they used to think were his way of talking went away and were replaced by fretting and crying, and he no longer seemed to understand peek-a-boo. The

delight that the Slocombes had once taken in caring for their baby had turned into a nightmare of exhaustion, frustration, depression, and worry.

Cooper's pediatrician, Dr. Judith Nathan, had been vague, but generally reassuring, when they first expressed concern about his transformation. But eventually she became concerned enough herself to run some tests. She asked the Slocombes dozens of detailed questions about how Cooper behaved with them, responded to others, reacted to noises and smells, as well as what upset him and what soothed him. She then took a detailed history of both families, asking if anyone on either side had suffered from learning or language difficulties, neurological problems, or an illness like schizophrenia. Her interest was piqued when she discovered that Bob's brother and two of his cousins had been diagnosed with learning disabilities.

Dr. Nathan then tested Cooper's blood for the presence of lead, but as she had predicted, the test was negative. She sent a cheek swab from Cooper to a genetics lab to be tested for chromosomal abnormalities, but it, too, didn't turn up anything unusual. Finally, she referred the Slocombes to a pediatric otologist for an auditory assessment, but he assured them that Cooper's hearing was normal.

Almost a month passed before the Slocombes got a call from Dr. Nathan's office asking them to make an appointment to see her. Their hopes that Cooper's problems were not serious were destroyed the moment they heard Dr. Nathan's diagnosis. "Cooper has autism," she told them. "It's too early to say how severe it will be, but he should begin treatment and behavioral therapy as soon as possible."

"Could this have been caused by one of the vaccinations he had last year?" Bob asked. "My chiropractor said that some of those vaccines, especially the ones for measles, are dangerous for kids."

"I've heard that, too," Susan said. "I read that they're the reason autism is increasing."

"I wish I'd listened to my chiropractor." Bob sounded exhausted and sad. "He told me I shouldn't get Cooper vaccinated, that he'd be all right without his shots."

1. What evidence, if any, is there to support the belief that autism may be the result of childhood vaccinations?

2. What evidence, if any, is there to support the claim that autism rates are on the rise? Discuss the difference between an increase in number of diagnosed cases and an increase in the number of actual cases.

3. What might account for the increase in diagnosed autism cases?

4. Is there a social duty for parents to have their children vaccinated against infectious diseases such as pertussis (whooping cough), mumps, measles, and rubella?

5. Should childhood vaccinations be required by law, or should parents be able to opt out on behalf of their children?

DECISION SCENARIO 3

Weight Cops

"I'm referring you to the Bariatrics Clinic," Dr. Himmer said. He glanced at Carla Tolar, then quickly bent his head to write something in her record. "They're very helpful."

"The *what* clinic?" Carla Tolar asked. She was sorry she had insisted on taking her shoes off before she was weighed, because now she was struggling to get them on. She couldn't bend over far enough to use a finger to slip on the heel, and she was twisting her right foot, trying to work it into the shoe. She was only halfway paying attention to Himmer.

"It specializes in weight loss." He still avoided looking at her. "It's federally financed, so it's not going to cost you anything."

"I told you, I can lose weight on my own." Carla pressed her lips together.

"You've been saying that for two years." Himmer finally looked up. He gave her an artificial smile. "But now you are more than 150 pounds over your proper weight, and it's out of my hands. I'm required by law to refer you to the Bariatrics Clinic."

"Oh, my God," Carla said. "I never heard that. What if I don't go?" She straightened up in the chair, forgetting about her shoe. "I don't want to go. I won't go."

"You don't have a choice, really," Himmer said. "It's sort of like if you have a car, you've got to get

a license for it. It's for your protection and for society's. Do you know how much money obesity costs American taxpayers every year? If you don't go to the clinic, you become subject to fines."

"And if I don't pay?" Carla was stunned.

"I think you can be sent to jail," Dr. Himmer said. "Just the way you can be for driving without a license."

1. Could the government justifiably establish weight-loss clinics to assist people in losing weight? Why or why not? How would such clinics be different from current government-sponsored programs to help people conquer addictions to cocaine or cigarettes, or to manage their anger?

2. If such clinics were established, to what extent would the government be justified in requiring those who are overweight to participate in weight-control programs? (Fines are possible, but so, too, are rewards like tax credits or cash bonuses.)

3. Is Dr. Himmer's driver's license analogy a good one? Can overweight people impose such costs on society that the government would be justified in requiring them to make an effort to control their weight?

4. If considerations of autonomy are sufficient to bar society from using the powers of government to require adults to participate in weight-loss programs, would it be legitimate for society to require children to take steps to control their weight?

DECISION SCENARIO 4

Maternal–Fetal Conflict

Angela Carder was diagnosed with bone cancer when she was thirteen years old. Over the following years, she received a variety of treatments and underwent surgery several times. In one operation, her leg was amputated. By the time she was twenty-seven, the cancer had been in remission for three years, and she married and became pregnant. Twenty-five weeks into the pregnancy, however, she went for a routine checkup, and her physician discovered a large tumor in a lung. She was told she might have only days to live. She was admitted to George Washington Hospital, and five days later her condition took a turn for the worse.

Despite the objections of Carder, her husband, and even her physician, the hospital decided to attempt to save the developing fetus. The hospital went to court, and at a hearing a staff physician who had not examined Carder stated that, despite the fact that the fetus was only twenty-six weeks old, there was a 50 to 60 percent chance that it would survive if a caesarean section was performed. Furthermore, the physician estimated that there was less than a 20 percent chance that the child would be severely disabled, although she acknowledged that the surgery would increase the chances of Angela Carder's death.

The hospital obtained a court order for a caesarean, which was immediately appealed by Carder's family. Because the case demanded a quick resolution, the three judges on the appeals court consulted by telephone. The whole process, hearing and appeal, took less than six hours. During this time, the hospital had ordered Carder prepared for surgery.

The appeals court let the lower court ruling stand, and Angela Carder underwent the court-ordered caesarean section. The child, a girl, lived for only two hours. Carder lived for two days. The surgery was listed on her death certificate as a contributing cause of her death.

1. On what grounds might one object to this court-ordered surgery? On what grounds might one support it?

2. How is this case different from ones involving drug abuse by pregnant women? How might it be seen to involve similar issues?

3. Suppose Angela Carder had been further along in her pregnancy, so that the chance of her child's survival was virtually certain, and that she refused to have a caesarean surgery. Would it be right to force her to have a caesarean against her will?

4. Consider the following: A woman has a constitutional right to seek an abortion, but if she decides to carry her fetus to term, she may be forced to take steps (some at considerable cost to herself) to promote its interests. Is there a contradiction here?

DECISION SCENARIO 5

Pregnancy vs. Autonomy?

For five years, the hospital of the Medical University of South Carolina followed a controversial policy with respect to pregnant women. Pregnant women admitted to the hospital were asked to sign a consent form agreeing to drug testing if their physicians decided they needed it. Those who tested positive for cocaine were turned in to local police and were arrested, unless they agreed to take part in a drug rehabilitation program. Forty-two women were turned in. Some agreed to drug treatment, while others were charged with distributing drugs to minors—their fetuses. (These charges were later dropped.)

Critics of the policy claimed that it focused on poor, African American women, who form a large proportion of the hospital's patient population. Furthermore, the policy violated the confidentiality of the physician–patient relationship and the women's right to privacy.

In September 1994, responding to pressure from the federal government, the hospital agreed to change its policy. Had the hospital not complied with federal demands, it stood to lose $18 million of federal research money.

1. What are the potential dangers in adopting a policy like the hospital's? Do they outweigh the potential benefits?

2. Under what conditions, if any, would the hospital's policy be justified?

3. Are there policies that the hospital might pursue that would help prevent prenatal harm while also avoiding violations of pregnant women's autonomy and their patient–physician confidentiality?

DECISION SCENARIO 6

Should Doctors Take "No" for an Answer?

"I don't want to be treated," Alicia Nuvo said. "According to the statistics you gave me, even with the best treatment I've got no more than a 10 percent chance of surviving for another year."

"Pancreatic cancer is a tough customer," Dr. Cervando Lupe said. "I wish the numbers were better."

"So why should I suffer the pain and nausea of chemotherapy and then radiation if I'm going to die anyway?" Nuvo laughed grimly. "It's absurd. I'd rather spend the remaining time with my husband and two daughters, then die in peace, instead of puking up my guts in some hospital."

"We can use drugs to control the nausea from the chemotherapy," Lupe said. "And we don't know that the statistics apply to you. They apply to a whole group of people, and I never tell a patient that *she* has a 10 percent chance."

"Just give me something to control the pain and let me go home," Nuvo said. "I don't want to talk about it anymore."

1. Should Dr. Lupe argue with Alicia Nuvo and try to persuade her to undergo treatment? Why or why not?

2. If Lupe thinks Nuvo is making the wrong decision, how far should he go to try to persuade her to accept the treatment?

3. What methods are morally acceptable for getting patients to give their informed consent to treatment? What methods would be morally unacceptable?

4. Is it possible to justify forcing treatment on someone who refuses it? Why or why not?

DECISION SCENARIO 7

Vampire Confession

"Sometimes I think that what I really want to do is to kill people and drink their blood."

Dr. Wolfe looked at the young man in the chair across from him. The face was round and soft and innocent looking, like that of a large baby. But the body had the powerful shoulders of a college wrestler. There was no doubt that Hal Crane had the strength to carry out his fantasies.

"Any people in particular?" Dr. Wolfe asked.

"Women. Girls about my age. Maybe in their early twenties."

"But no one you're personally acquainted with."

"That's right. Just girls I see walking down the street or getting off a bus. I have a tremendous urge to stick a knife into their stomachs and feel the blood come out on my hands."

"But you've never done anything like that?"

Crane shook his head. "No, but I'm afraid I might."

Dr. Wolfe considered Crane a paranoid schizophrenic with compulsive tendencies, someone who might possibly act out his fantasies. He was a potentially dangerous person.

"Would you be willing to take my advice and put yourself in a hospital under my care for a while?"

"I don't want to do that," Crane said. "I don't want to be locked up like an animal."

"But you don't really want to hurt other people, do you?"

"I guess not," Crane said. "I haven't done anything yet."

"But you might," Dr. Wolfe said. "I'm afraid you might let yourself go and kill someone."

Crane smiled. "That's just the chance the world will have to take, isn't it?"

1. Suppose that you are Dr. Wolfe. To take the legal steps necessary to have Crane committed against his will requires that you violate his confidentiality. What justification might you offer for doing this?

2. As a health care professional, how would you justify acting to protect others while going against the wishes of your patient?

3. Should psychologists and psychiatrists be required by law to act to protect the welfare of people who are not their patients?

4. How does this case compare to the *Tarasoff* case?

DECISION SCENARIO 8

Nurse or Executioner?

Gary had been waiting at Denny's for a good forty-five minutes when Shawn Harrison finally walked in the door. The two men had been housemates in nursing school and later worked together at a public health clinic in Houston, before Shawn had been laid off. It had been over a year since they had met.

"Sorry, man. I had to work late last night and overslept." Shawn's eyes were bloodshot and he looked thinner than Gary remembered.

"That sucks," Gary said. "Are you back in the ER these days?"

"Naw. I've been working up at Huntsville."

"The prison?"

"Yup, it was the only full-time job I could find. They've got me—well, I don't really like to talk about it, but they've got me working on the death unit. Ordering the meds, cutting down veins, inserting IVs. It can be pretty intense."

"Whoa. I can imagine—or maybe I can't." Gary took a sip of his coffee. "But I got to ask, does the work ever bother you?"

"Sometimes it does. Those guys up there did some terrible things, but it's still hard to look them in the eye when I strap that tube around their arm." Shawn nodded to the waitress for a cup of coffee. "I figure, though, they're going to die anyway, and I've got the skills to make it as painless as possible." He seemed like he wanted to change the subject.

Gary started to ask about Shawn's family, but found he couldn't let it go.

"Shawn, no offense, man, but do you still see yourself as a nurse? I mean, we were trained to save people's lives and to 'do no harm,' right? It's not like those guys consented to your 'treatment.'"

"I never understood that kind of talk," Shawn said. "We used to harm patients all the time when we pumped them full of chemo. That hurts for a hell of a lot longer than this does. Besides, if I don't do this job, somebody else will. Now, what are you having for breakfast?"

1. Is Shawn still acting as a nurse or has he become an executioner? Is his response to Gary's questions persuasive? Why or why not?

2. Under what circumstances, if any, is a medical professional justified in acting against a patient's best medical interests? Why?

3. What about acting against a person's consent as well as against her best medical interests? Are there any situations in which that might be justified? Describe them.

4. Evaluate Shawn's argument that he is reducing suffering by making executions less painful. What if he made the same argument about helping a torturer extract information more quickly from a detainee? Would the substance of his position be any different?

Chapter 2

Research Ethics and Informed Consent

CHAPTER CONTENTS

CASES AND CONTEXTS

CASE PRESENTATION

The Afterlife of Henrietta Lacks: Consent, Research, and Race

In February of 1951, a young mother named Henrietta Lacks was diagnosed with cervical cancer and admitted for surgical treatment at Johns Hopkins Hospital in Baltimore, MD. While Lacks was under anesthesia there, her physician removed tissue from her cervix without her knowledge or consent, and allowed researchers to grow a line of cells from it. Although Lacks died later that year, at age 31, those cells would go on to alter the course of medical history.

Code-named "HeLa," for Lacks's first and last names, they would become the first human cells to survive in a laboratory, and indeed they are still thriving today. From a nickel-sized piece of tissue removed from Lacks's cervix, HeLa cells have been continuously dividing for the past sixty-four years, growing to an estimated fifty million metric tons that could wrap around the earth three times. HeLa cells are aggressively cancerous, which is part of what makes them so hardy and easy to grow. Otherwise they resemble normal human cells, which makes them ideal

for medical research that can't be performed on humans. Cultivated by scientists around the world, HeLa cells have played a pivotal role in the development of the polio vaccine, chemotherapy drugs, HIV therapies, and in vitro fertilization. They were widely used in the space program and atomic weapons tests, and in the groundbreaking research that led to the mapping of human genes and animal cloning. While initially distributed for free by Hopkins tissue culture researcher George Gey, HeLa cells were quickly transformed into commercial products, forming the basis of the multibillion-dollar industry we now know as biotech.

Despite these impressive achievements, the story of HeLa's development is also a disturbing and cautionary tale. Indeed, the experiences of Henrietta Lacks and her family can be seen to foreshadow many of the major problems in biomedical research ethics that we will discuss in this chapter. The harvesting of Lacks's cells without her knowledge or permission was just the first of many instances in which scientists would bypass informed consent and confidentiality in their dealings with the Lacks family. After Henrietta's agonizing death from her cancer in October 1951, it took twenty years before anyone told her family about the widespread use of her cells in medical research. In the 1970s, Hopkins scientists obtained blood samples from the Lacks children without disclosing that they would be used in further research. They also released Henrietta Lacks's medical records to journalists, who published them without the family's consent and exposed to the general public the painful details of her illness, death, and autopsy. Even as recently as 2013, a major research laboratory in Europe published the entire DNA sequence of HeLa—and thus, much of the Lacks family DNA—again without seeking the family's consent.

Henrietta Lacks was an African American woman with little formal education, who entered a medical system deeply influenced by segregation, institutional racism, and medical paternalism. Her family's story is thus a quintessentially American one, which involves both the frontiers of medical progress and the bitter legacies of race and class.

Race and Research

Henrietta Lacks was born in 1920 and raised in a log cabin that had been built as slave quarters on her white great-grandfather's plantation in Clover, Virginia. (Lacks, like most other African Americans in Clover, was descended from the plantation's white owners and their female slaves.) She grew up in extreme poverty, picking tobacco in the same fields her parents and grandparents had worked as sharecroppers and slaves, and her education at the local "colored" school ended after sixth grade so she could spend more time in the fields. She had her first child at fourteen, her second at eighteen, and she married their father, David "Day" Lacks, in 1941.

That same year, Henrietta and Day left Virginia with their children and moved to Baltimore County, Maryland, where Day had secured a job at a steel mill. Like other African Americans in the twentieth-century's "Great Migration," they hoped to escape poverty and the pervasive racism of the South, but encountered many of the same problems in the North. At the steel mill, black men were given dangerous jobs white men wouldn't touch and were exposed to toxic coal dust and asbestos. In Baltimore County, African Americans were still forced into separate (and usually inferior) schools, housing, restaurants, pools, and hospitals. Indeed, the reason that Henrietta Lacks

ended up at Johns Hopkins Hospital was because it was the only major medical facility for miles around that would treat black people. Even Hopkins treated such patients in "colored" wards, and segregated its water fountains, bathrooms, blood supply, operating rooms, and morgue.

This history helps explain the pattern of miscommunication and mistrust that hampered almost every interaction between the Lacks family and medical professionals. Physicians and researchers did not conspire to withhold informed consent from Lacks or hide the use of her cells from her family. It simply didn't occur to them to share the information. They often assumed that Lacks and her family were incapable of understanding their aims, and some admitted they didn't quite see her as "a real person."

Although her physicians later insisted that Lacks received the same treatment as white cancer patients—many of whom also had tissue samples taken without consent—such paternalistic practices appear to have been more intense in the case of Lacks and other African American patients. Her physicians failed to warn her that her cancer treatment would leave her infertile, for example, a warning that was standard for white patients at the time. When researchers later obtained blood samples from the Lacks family for further study, they left them with the impression that they were being "tested for cancer," when no such test existed. Such paternalism was often rationalized as necessary for the greater aims of science, but with respect to African Americans it also appears to have done serious harm. Retrospective studies on segregated medicine reveal that, compared to whites, black patients were typically hospitalized at later stages in their illnesses, received less pain medication, and had higher mortality rates.

The Lacks family had its own share of misconceptions and fears about the white medical establishment. In her best-selling book on the Lacks case, the science writer Rebecca Skloot suggests that for Henrietta Lacks, going to Hopkins was like "entering a foreign country where she didn't speak the language." After the Lacks family was finally told how Henrietta's "immortal" cells were still being used in research, Skloot describes their dismay and confusion about this disclosure. Some family members came to believe that white researchers had experimented on Henrietta and "sacrificed" her in order to obtain the cells; others were left with the impression scientists had created monstrous clones and chimeras from her tissue; still others believed "night doctors" from Hopkins routinely snatched black people off the street to use in research.

Although such beliefs may sound far-fetched, Skloot points out that for African Americans such horror stories have often been rooted in horrible realities. During the nineteenth century, many physicians tested drugs on slaves and tried new surgical techniques on them, often without anesthesia. Well into the 1900s, medical schools routinely used black corpses exhumed without family consent in their research and anatomy classes, often relying on an underground market that shipped cadavers in barrels. At the time the Lacks family was told about Henrietta's cells, news had just broken of the forty-year Tuskegee syphilis study, in which U.S. Public Health Service researchers had recruited hundreds of African American men with syphilis, then studied the excruciating and often fatal progression of their disease—even after it was discovered that penicillin could cure them. (Ironically, the Tuskegee Institute was also the site of the first "factory" to produce HeLa cells for research, before private companies took over that role.)

Unfortunately, the Tuskegee study (discussed later in this chapter and in Chapter 10) was not unique in the history of twentieth-century medical research. Perhaps the most disturbing aspect of the Lacks story involves another case of medical experimentation without consent. It took place in a facility built (using patient labor) as the "Maryland Hospital for the Negro Insane" and later called Crownsville State Hospital. Crownsville was one of the most crowded and understaffed mental hospitals in the state, with only one physician for every 225 patients, drains on the floors instead of toilets, and African American children, women, and men (some of them sex offenders) packed into the same dilapidated wards.

In the 1940s and 1950s, physicians at Crownsville conducted a series of troubling studies on patients without their families' consent. These included infecting syphilitic patients with malaria as experimental treatment and testing LSD and other experimental drugs on patients. They also drilled holes in the heads of hundreds of epileptic adults and children, draining the cerebrospinal fluid and replacing it with oxygen or helium to facilitate brain X-rays. Side effects of this procedure, called *pneumoencephalography*, could include headaches, vomiting, brain damage, and paralysis, and it was abandoned in the 1970s. As Skloot and the Lacks family later determined, Henrietta's eldest daughter, Elsie—who had been born deaf and mute, with a diagnosis of epilepsy—had been committed to Crownsville around 1950. She was almost certainly subject to such experiments before her death there in 1955.

Whose Tissue Is It, Anyway?

One of the most difficult questions raised by the Lacks case is that of who "owns" the tissue, DNA, and other human materials used in medical research. Although the Lacks family has never sued anyone over the use of their mother's cells, they have often wondered why none of the millions (more likely, billions) of dollars generated by HeLa has never reached them.

"I always have thought it was strange, if our mother cells done so much for medicine, how come her family can't afford to see no doctors?" asked Henrietta's younger daughter Deborah, who played a key role in the development of Skloot's book. Sonny, Henrietta's second son, recalled the surgeon for his 2003 quintuple bypass telling him that his mother's cells were "one of the most important things that had ever happened to medicine," but Sonny still woke up from the surgery $125,000 in debt because he lacked health insurance.

The question of property rights in one's own body was addressed in a landmark 1990 case decided by the California Supreme Court. The plaintiff was John Moore, a pipeline surveyor whose physician diagnosed him with a rare form of leukemia, then (without his knowledge or consent) used Moore's spleen and subsequent tissue samples to patent a therapeutic cell line called "Mo," which was ultimately valued at $3 billion. Despite the court's conclusion that his physician had violated informed consent by concealing his financial interest in taking the samples, it ruled against Moore's claim that his tissue had been stolen. Moore had abandoned his tissue as "waste," whereas his physician had used "human ingenuity" to produce the cell line. Moore, unlike the physician, thus had no potential patent rights to the "naturally occurring raw materials" in his body.

As critics of the Moore decision have pointed out, if someone discovers and refines valuable minerals on your land, you generally have a right to at least some of her profits. But courts have generally been reluctant to grant such rights to patients, partly out of fear it would impede the pace of scientific research. (See Case Presentation: Genae Girard and Gene Patents in Chapter 3 for a discussion of the positive and negative role of proprietary rights in biomedical research.) Other critics of the Moore decision have noted that by the time it was decided, many patients had already launched commercial ventures based on "raw materials" in their bodies. In the 1970s, a hemophilia patient named Ted Slavin learned from his physician that his blood contained antibodies that could be instrumental in developing a hepatitis B vaccine. Slavin then not only sold his blood serum to pharmaceutical companies but formed a company of his own, teaming up with other people who had rare and valuable biological materials in their bodies. Although Slavin never tried to patent his serum, he did retain control over it and collaborated with a Nobel Prize–winning scientist who eventually developed the hepatitis B vaccine.

As Rebecca Skloot points out, the difference between a patient like Ted Slavin and patients like John Moore and Henrietta Lacks is that Slavin was *informed* about what he had in his body, so he was able to make choices and *consent* to what was done with it. Moore and Lacks were never given that choice. Although the principle of informed consent is enshrined in professional codes (and recognized in the Moore decision) there is no law that enforces it today, just as there was no law enforcing it in 1951. Ultimately, what may matter most to the Lacks family and other unwitting subjects of medical research is that scientists demonstrate respect for their autonomy and privacy.

"It's weird to say everybody gets money except the people providing the raw material," said Ellen Wright Clayton, director of Vanderbilt University's Center for Genetics and Health Policy. "But the fundamental problem here isn't the money; it's the notion that the people these tissues come from don't matter."

An Unprecedented Agreement

A familiar disregard for the human sources of medical research appeared to be at play when it was revealed, in the spring of 2013, that a European research lab had sequenced and published the HeLa genome, and that a team at the University of Washington was about to do the same thing in the journal *Nature*. Without alerting the Lacks family, much less asking their permission, the researchers had effectively put their entire DNA sequence on public display. What's more, they had already presented their research at conferences and received a National Institutes of Health grant, a process during which no one seems to have raised questions about consent or confidentiality.

As we will see in the next chapter, posting genetic information can reveal sensitive medical information and constitute a serious violation of privacy. Researchers have recently proven that even anonymous genetic donors can be identified, by cross-referencing their

samples with genealogical DNA databases. Although the European lab initially claimed that no personal information about the Lacks family could be gleaned from the billions of letters that make up HeLa's genetic code, Skloot and a number of scientists quickly proved them wrong. Entering the HeLa genome into a publicly available website, they soon generated a report of personal medical information about the Lacks family—which they have kept confidential. In the ensuing outcry, the European lab apologized and took the full genetic data offline. The University of Washington paper—which pinpointed the exact genetic changes that made Lacks's cancer so prolific and deadly—was revised to avoid privacy violations. And NIH officials acknowledged they should have contacted the Lacks family before approving the grant. Then, they took an unprecedented step.

On April 8, 2013, NIH director Francis Collins traveled to Baltimore for the first of three meetings with Henrietta Lacks's children and grandchildren. They met on the Johns Hopkins campus, and they discussed the family's difficult experiences with HeLa research and how it should be handled in the future.

"The biggest concern was privacy," said Jeri Lacks Whye, one of the Lacks grandchildren. "What information was actually going to be out there about our grandmother, and what information they can obtain from her sequencing that will tell them about her children and grandchildren and going down the line."

In the end, the NIH and the Lacks family reached an agreement that future HeLa research requests will be handled by a six-person panel that includes two Lacks family representatives and that future research publications will include an acknowledgement of Henrietta Lacks as the source of the cells. Access to the HeLa genome will require an application and agreement to use the information for biomedical research only.

The NIH HeLa agreement may have marked a watershed in federal policy on informed consent and biological specimens. In 2015, the Department of Health and Human Services proposed changes to the Common Rule regulating human-subjects research that would require written consent for the use of biospecimens in current and future research. Nevertheless, there are still more than 600 million stored tissue samples from routine procedures in the United States alone, according to an estimate by the RAND Corporation. Research on these samples cannot be handled on a case-by-case basis like HeLa studies, but will require broad policies to try to uphold confidentiality and consent. The NIH agreement also does not address the question of who should profit when a person's biological materials prove to be immensely valuable. (The Lacks family will receive no monetary compensation under the agreement, although Skloot has set up a foundation that provides grants to Lacks descendants and others who were subject to medical

research without their knowledge.) Clearly, the conversation about the ethical use of human tissues in research is far from over, just as the conversation about race in America is far from over. But perhaps the story of Henrietta Lacks, with its pattern of scientific achievement and moral failure, can teach us something about how such conversations ought to proceed in the future.

CASE PRESENTATION

Abigail Alliance v. FDA: Do Terminally Ill People Have a Right to Take Experimental Drugs?

Abigail Burroughs was nineteen years old in 1999, the year she was diagnosed with squamous cell cancer of the head and neck. She was treated with chemotherapy and radiation at Johns Hopkins Hospital, but the cancer was not driven into remission.

A cytological study of the cells of her tumor conducted at Hopkins showed an excess of epidermal growth factor reception (EGFR) on the surfaces of the cell membranes. Two drugs were then being tested against EGFR: gefitinib and cetuximab. Burroughs's oncologist thought she might benefit from being treated with one of these drugs, but neither had been approved for use by the FDA. According to the manufacturers, the only way for Abigail to receive either drug was to qualify as a participant in a clinical trial in which they were being used. But the gefitinib trial was restricted to lung cancer patients, while the cetuximab trial was restricted to patients with colon cancer. Burroughs's oncologist was as frustrated and as helpless as she was.

Burroughs eventually met the criteria required to be included in a clinical trial of a third drug (erlotinib). By then, however, she was too sick for the drug to help her. Abigail Burroughs died from her disease on June 9, 2001.

Abigail Alliance

Shortly before Burroughs died, she gave a television interview in which she expressed her frustration at not being able to gain access to a drug her physician thought might help her. She and her family had petitioned the FDA and talked to members of Congress in an effort to get FDA policy changed. "This is not just about me," she told the interviewer. "I'm trying to help so many others."

Frank Burroughs, Abigail's father, wanted to honor his daughter's words and decided he needed to continue the fight Abigail had begun. Burroughs founded the Abigail Alliance for Better Access to Developmental Drugs in November 2001. The Alliance's goal was to change FDA policies to give terminally ill people easier access to investigational drugs that might benefit them. This brought the group into conflict with some of the most fundamental procedures of clinical research.

Since the 1960s, the FDA has mandated that all drugs and other treatments be vetted in a rigorous three-stage process before they can be prescribed. In Phase I of a trial, researchers administer a treatment for the first time to a small group of healthy volunteers, to test its safety, dosage levels, and side effects. (This is often the first time a drug is given to humans.) In Phase II, the treatment is given to a larger group to test its effectiveness and monitor safety, while in Phase III, the treatment is given to large groups to confirm its effectiveness, compare it to other therapies, and establish safety procedures. (We will discuss clinical trials in greater detail in this chapter's Briefing Session.)

Traditionally, investigational drugs are available only to patients enrolled in clinical trials in which the drugs are being tested. (Even these patients may not get these drugs; depending on how the trial is designed, they may receive the standard drug or even a placebo.) But in 1990, largely in response to the AIDS crisis, the FDA approved a "compassionate use" policy that makes it possible for a patient to be treated with a drug under development if the following conditions are met: (1) the drug is already being tested in a clinical trial; (2) no comparable alternative treatment is available; (3) the drug's developer has applied for FDA approval; and (4) available evidence suggests that the drug may be effective for the intended use and that it is not likely to pose a significant risk of harm to the patient. Although this "expanded access" policy has changed over the years, it is generally not available until Phase III of a trial, and only in Phase II if there is already compelling evidence for a drug's safety and efficacy.

Frank Burroughs and the Abigail Alliance claimed that the FDA had made its requirements for compassionate use so stringent that few patients could qualify for access to investigational drugs. As a result, drug developers manufactured only enough of an investigational drug to meet the needs of researchers conducting clinical trials. The restricted supply of drugs thus made it almost impossible for patients who were not in a clinical trial to get the drugs. The Alliance argued that patients should get access to drugs after they pass Phase I.

Lawsuit and Appeal

The Alliance was joined by the Washington Legal Foundation in petitioning the FDA to make more investigational drugs available under its compassionate-use policy. Before the FDA responded to the petition, the petitioners filed suit in the Washington, DC, Federal District Court. The suit claimed that the FDA violated terminally ill patients' constitutional right to privacy (self-defense), as well as their right to due process. (Under the due process clause of the Constitution's Fifth Amendment, no citizen can be deprived of life, liberty, or property without due process of the law.)

The Alliance's case was initially dismissed, but in May 2006, a panel from the U.S. Court of Appeals for the District of Columbia ruled in their favor—finding, in a 2–1 decision, that the due process clause gives terminally ill patients a "fundamental right" to access investigational drugs. (Versions of the majority and the dissenting opinion are given in this chapter's readings.) This was not the end of the matter, however: the full Appeals Court reconsidered the case and ruled against the Alliance in an 8–2 decision. In upholding the original decision, the Appeals Court ruled, in effect, that terminally ill patients have no right to access investigational drugs and that a right to self-defense "doesn't include assuming any level of risk without regard to the scientific and medical judgment expressed through the clinical testing process." The Alliance appealed the decision to the Supreme Court, which declined to hear the case. This meant that the Abigail Alliance had exhausted all possible legal remedies.

FDA Eases—but Does Not End—Restrictions

In 2006, the FDA revised its regulations to make it somewhat easier for patients to receive treatment with investigational drugs under its "compassionate use" and "expanded access" policies. Patients must have serious or immediately life-threatening diseases or conditions, lack other therapeutic options, and have a chance of benefiting from the drug. Also, the drug must be available in sufficient supply, the drug's manufacturer must agree to supply the drug, and the patient must have a way to pay for the associated costs. (These can be expensive if frequent monitoring of the patient is needed.)

But patient groups such as the Abigail Alliance have not given up. In many states, patients groups have successfully lobbied for "Right to Try" laws, which permit terminally ill patients who have exhausted other treatment options to try new therapies that have passed Phase I. Such laws appear to have had little impact, however, since most manufacturers still follow the FDA guidelines.

Defenders of FDA policies call "Right to Try" laws a "cruel sham." Dr. David Gorski, a surgeon in Michigan, warns that accessing drugs after Phase I is likely to increase suffering and hasten death, and says that it is "far more likely to harm patients than to help them." (Only 33 percent of drugs make it past Phase II testing and only 10 percent of Phase I drugs are ultimately approved.) Defenders of the current policy also argue that if patients were allowed access to unproven drugs, it would be very difficult to persuade enough patients to enroll in clinical trials in the first place, which would undermine the development of effective treatments for everyone. Indeed, one study shows that clinical trials of drugs that are also available outside the trial take much longer to complete (forty-eight months) than drugs available only in the trial (twenty-six weeks). The FDA, which has not taken a position on "Right to Try" laws, emphasizes the flexibility of its new expanded access program and points to emergency access grants available over the phone.

But desperate patients and their advocates are unlikely to be persuaded by such arguments or by the FDA's new, more relaxed policies. They will not be satisfied until seriously ill patients have the legal right to be treated with the drugs their physicians think might help them.

CASE PRESENTATION
Jesse Gelsinger: The First Gene-Therapy Death

When Jesse Gelsinger was three months short of his third birthday, he was watching cartoons on TV when he fell asleep. Except it was a sleep from which his parents were unable to rouse him. Panicked, they rushed him to a local hospital.

When Jesse was examined, he responded to stimuli but didn't awaken. The physicians classified him as being in a level-one coma. Laboratory tests showed he had a high level of ammonia in his blood, but it was only after several days and additional blood assays that Jesse's physicians were able to bring him out of the coma and arrive at a diagnosis: Jesse had ornithine transcarbamylase deficiency, or OTCD.

OTCD is a rare genetic disorder in which the enzyme ornithine transcarbamylase, one of the five involved in the body's urea cycle, is either missing or in short supply. The urea cycle primarily takes place in the liver. Enzymes in the cycle break down the ammonia that is a by-product of normal protein metabolism.

A deficiency of OTC means the body cannot get rid of the ammonia, and it gradually accumulates in the blood. When the ammonia reaches a crucial level, it can cause coma, brain damage, and eventually death. The disease typically results from a mutation on the X chromosome; thus females are carriers of the gene, which they pass on to their sons. The disorder occurs in one of every forty thousand births. Infants with the mutation usually become comatose and die within seventy-two hours of birth. Half die within a month of birth and half of those who remain die before age five.

Although OTCD is a genetic disease, no one else in Jesse's immediate family or ancestry had ever been diagnosed with the disease. His disease was probably the result of a spontaneous mutation. He was a genetic "mosaic," which meant his body contained a mixture of normal and mutated cells. For this reason, Jesse had a comparatively mild form of OTCD. His body produced enough of the enzyme that he could remain in stable health if he stuck to a low-protein diet and took his medications. These included substances, such as sodium benzoate, that chemically bind to ammonia and make it easier for the body to excrete it.

At age ten, after an episode of consuming too much protein, Jesse once again fell into a coma and was hospitalized. But five days later, he was back home with no apparent neurological damage. During his teens, Jesse's condition was monitored by semiannual visits to a metabolic clinic in his hometown of Tucson, Arizona.

In 1998, Jesse, now seventeen, and his father, Paul Gelsinger, heard from Randy Heidenreich, a doctor at the clinic, about a clinical trial at the University of Pennsylvania in Philadelphia. Researchers at the university's Institute for Human Gene Therapy were trying to introduce healthy genes into the livers of OTCD patients, to offset the deficiencies caused by their genetic mutation. Success would not constitute a cure for the disease, but it could be a treatment to bring OTCD babies out of comas and to prevent their suffering brain damage.

The Gelsingers were interested, but Jesse needed to be eighteen in order to consent to the trial. In April 1999, they again discussed the issue with Dr. Heidenreich, and Paul mentioned that the family would be taking a trip to New Jersey in June. They would be able to make a side trip to Philadelphia and meet with the researchers.

Heidenreich contacted an investigator at the gene therapy institute, who wrote Paul Gelsinger that same month. He said Jesse could be interviewed and tested at the university hospital on June 22 to determine whether he met the criteria for becoming a research participant.

Originally, the U. Penn OTCD trial was designed for infant subjects, rather than older patients like Jesse. But a bioethicist at the university, Arthur Caplan, had advised the researchers against using infants born with OTCD as participants in the gene-therapy trial. Because such infants could not be expected to live, Caplan reasoned, their parents would be driven by desperation and their consent to the trial would not be free. Instead, appropriate participants would be women who were carriers of the gene or men in stable health with only a mild form of the disease. Jesse fit these criteria, and he would turn eighteen the day the family flew to the East Coast.

On June 22, 1999, Jesse and Paul Gelsinger met with Dr. Steven Raper for forty-five minutes to review the consent forms and discuss the procedures that Jesse might undergo if he qualified and volunteered for the trial. Raper, a surgeon, would be the one performing the gene-therapy procedure.

According to Paul Gelsinger's recollections, Raper explained that Jesse would be sedated and two catheters inserted: one in the artery leading to Jesse's liver, the second in the vein leaving it. A weakened strain of adenovirus (the virus that causes colds), genetically modified to include the missing OTC gene, would be injected into the hepatic artery. Blood would then be taken from the vein to monitor whether the viral particles were being taken up by Jesse's liver cells.

To reduce the risk of a blood clot's breaking loose from the infusion site, Jesse would have to remain in bed for eight hours after the procedure. Most likely, he would develop flu-like symptoms lasting for a few days. He might even develop hepatitis, an inflammation of the liver. The consent form noted that if hepatitis progressed, Jesse might need a liver transplant. The consent form also mentioned death as a possible outcome.

Paul Gelsinger later said that Jesse's physicians had downplayed the seriousness of liver inflammation, and that he had ended up more concerned about a needle biopsy of the liver to be performed a week after the procedure. The risk of death from the biopsy was given as one in ten thousand. Paul urged Jesse to read the consent document carefully and to make sure he understood it. Paul thought the odds looked very good.

Dr. Raper explained that Jesse couldn't expect to derive any personal medical benefit from participating in the clinical trial. Even if the genes became incorporated into his cells and produced OTC, the effect would only be transitory. His immune system would attack the viral particles and destroy them within a month to six weeks.

Jesse, at the end of the information session, agreed to undergo tests to determine how well the OTC he produced got rid of ammonia in his blood—a measure of OTC efficiency. Samples of his blood were taken; then he drank a small amount of radioactively tagged ammonia. Later, samples of his blood and urine were taken to see how much of the ingested ammonia had been eliminated. The results showed his body's efficiency was only 6 percent of the normal level.

A month later, the Gelsingers received a letter from Mark Bratshaw, the pediatrician at the institute who had proposed the clinical trial. Bratshaw confirmed the

6 percent efficiency figure from additional test results and expressed his hope that Jesse would take part in the study. A week later, Bratshaw called and spoke to Jesse and his father. Bratshaw told them that treatment had worked well in mice, preventing the deaths of those given an otherwise lethal injection of ammonia. Also, the most recent human patient treated had shown a 50 percent increase in her ability to excrete ammonia. Paul Gelsinger later recalled his reaction as, "Wow! This really works. So, with Jesse at 6 percent efficiency, you may be able to show exactly how well this works."

Bratshaw said their real hope was to find a treatment for newborns lacking any OTC efficiency and with little chance of survival. Also, another twenty-five liver disorders could potentially be treated with the same gene-therapy technique. The promise, then, was that hundreds of thousands, if not millions, of lives might be saved. Bratshaw never talked about the dangers to Jesse of becoming a subject in the clinical trial.

In the end, Paul discussed participation with Jesse and both agreed that it was the right thing to do. Jesse would be helping babies stay alive and perhaps, in the long run, he might even be helping himself.

Approval

The clinical trial was supported by a National Institutes of Health grant awarded to Dr. James Wilson, the head of the gene therapy institute, and Mark Bratshaw. Their protocol had been reviewed by the federal Recombinant-DNA Advisory Committee (RAC) and the FDA. The animal studies Bratshaw had mentioned to Paul included twenty studies on mice to show the efficacy of the proposed technique. Wilson and his group had also conducted studies on monkeys and baboons to demonstrate the safety of the procedure.

Three of the treated monkeys had died of severe liver inflammation and a blood-clotting disorder when they had been given a strain of adenovirus twenty times stronger than that proposed in the human trial. As a result, both of the scientists assigned by the RAC to review the proposal concluded that the trial was too dangerous to include stable, asymptomatic volunteers such as Jesse. But Wilson and Bratshaw, employing Caplan's argument, convinced the panel that using subjects capable of giving consent was morally preferable to using newborns with OTCD.

The protocol called for the modified viruses to be introduced directly into the right lobe of the patient's liver. The thinking was that if the treatment caused damage, the right lobe could be removed and the left lobe spared. Despite RAC objections to this procedure as too risky, the FDA concluded that no matter where the viruses were injected, they would end up in the liver, so a direct injection would be safer. (The RAC was never informed of this decision.)

Protocol

The study was a Phase I clinical trial. According to its protocol, eighteen patients were to receive an infusion of the genetically modified adenovirus. The aim of the study was to determine "the maximum tolerated dose." The investigators wanted to find the maximum level of OTC production the genes could induce without creating intolerable side effects.

The eighteen patients were divided into six groups of three. Each successive group was to receive a slightly higher dose than the preceding one. The idea behind this common procedure is to protect the safety of the study participants. By increasing doses slightly, the hope is to spot the potential for serious side effects in time to avoid causing harm to the participants.

Preparation

On September 9, Jesse Gelsinger caught a plane for Philadelphia, carrying one suitcase full of clothes and another of the wrestling videos he loved. He checked into the hospital alone. His father, who was a self-employed handyman, stayed in Tucson to work. Paul planned to arrive on the eighteenth to be present for what he considered the most dangerous part of the trial—the liver biopsy.

The level of ammonia in Jesse's blood was tested on Friday and again on Sunday. That night he called his father, worried. His ammonia level was high and his physicians had put him on IV medication to lower it. Paul reassured his son, reminding him that the doctors at the institute knew more about OTCD than anyone else.

Tragedy

On the morning of Monday, September 13, Jesse Gelsinger became the eighteenth patient treated in the gene therapy trial. He was transported from his room to the hospital's interventional radiology suite, where a catheter was snaked through an artery in his groin to the hepatic artery. A second catheter was placed in the vein exiting the liver.

Dr. Raper then slowly injected thirty milliliters of the genetically altered virus into Jesse's catheter. This was the highest dose given to any participant. Patient 17, however, had received the same-size dose from a different lot of the virus and had, according to the researchers, done well. The procedure was completed around noon, and Jesse was returned to his room.

That evening Jesse, as expected, began to develop flu-like symptoms. He was feeling ill and feverish when he talked to his father and his stepmother, Mickie. "I love you, Dad," Jesse told his father. They all said what turned out to be their last good-byes.

During the night, Jesse's fever soared to 104.5 degrees. A nurse called Dr. Raper at home, and when he arrived at the hospital around six that morning, the whites of Jesse's eyes had a yellowish tinge. This was a sign of jaundice, not something the doctors had encountered with the other trial participants. Laboratory findings revealed that Jesse's bilirubin, the product of red blood cell destruction, was four times the normal level.

Raper called Bratshaw, who was in Washington, to tell him their patient had taken a serious turn, and he also called Paul Gelsinger to explain the situation. The jaundice was worrying to Jesse's physicians. Either his liver was not functioning adequately or his blood was not clotting properly and his red blood cells were breaking down faster than his liver could process them. Such a breakdown was life threatening for someone with OTCD, because the destroyed cells released protein the body would have to metabolize. Jesse was showing the same problem as the monkeys that had been given the stronger strain of the virus.

On Tuesday afternoon Paul Gelsinger received a call from Dr. Bratshaw. Jesse's blood-ammonia level had soared to 250 micromoles per deciliter, compared to a normal level of 35. He had slipped into a coma and had been put on dialysis to try to clear the ammonia from his blood. Paul said he would catch a plane and be at the hospital the next morning.

By the time Paul arrived at eight o'clock on Wednesday and met Bratshaw and Raper, Jesse had additional problems. Dialysis had brought his ammonia level down to 70 from its peak of 393, but he was definitely having a blood-clotting problem. Also, although placed on a ventilator, Jesse continued to breathe for himself, causing hyperventilation. This raised his blood pH, which increased the level of ammonia circulating to his brain. Paul gave his permission for the team to give Jesse medications that would paralyze his breathing muscles and allow the machine to take over completely.

By 10:30 that evening, however, Jesse's lungs were failing. Even by putting him on pure oxygen, they were unable to get an adequate amount of oxygen into his blood. Out of options, Raper, Bratshaw, and Wilson suggested a then experimental procedure called extracorporeal membrane oxygenation (ECMO). The ECMO technique would remove carbon dioxide from Jesse's blood and supply it with the needed oxygen, but only half of the thousand people ever placed on ECMO had lived. Informed by Raper that Jesse had only a 10 percent chance of surviving without ECMO, Paul Gelsinger agreed to the procedure.

"If we could just buy his lungs a day or two," Raper later told a reporter, "maybe he would go ahead and heal up."

Initially, the ECMO appeared to be working. But Paul was told that Jesse's lungs were so severely damaged that, if he survived, it would take months or years for him to recover. When Paul finally saw his son at midmorning the next day, he found Jesse still comatose and bloated beyond recognition. Only the tattoo on his right calf and a scar on his elbow assured Paul that the person in the bed was Jesse.

The next morning, Friday, September 17, Raper and Bratshaw met with Paul and Mickie to give them the news that they now expected. Jesse had suffered irreversible brain damage, and the team wanted Paul's permission to turn off the ventilator. At Paul's request, he and Mickie were left alone for a few minutes. He then told the doctors he wanted to bring in his family and hold a brief service for Jesse.

Later that day, Paul and Mickie, seven of Paul's siblings and their spouses, and about ten staff members crowded into Jesse's room. Paul leaned over Jesse, then turned and told those assembled that, "Jesse was a hero." The chaplain said a prayer; then Paul gave a signal. Someone flipped one switch to turn off the ventilator and flipped a second to turn off the ECMO unit.

Dr. Raper watched the heart monitor. When the line went flat, he put his stethoscope against Jesse's chest. At 2:30 P.M., Raper officially pronounced him dead. "Goodbye, Jesse," he said. "We'll figure this out."

Gathering Storm

James Wilson, the head of the Institute for Human Gene Therapy, immediately reported Jesse's death to the FDA. Paul Gelsinger, sad as he was, didn't blame the institute or Jesse's physicians for what had happened. Indeed, he supported them in the face of an initial round of criticism. "These guys didn't do anything wrong," he told reporters.

Then journalists began to bring to light information that raised questions about whether Jesse and his father had been adequately informed about the risks of the trial. They also raised questions about a conflict of interest that might have led researchers to minimize the risks. The FDA initiated an investigation, and the University of Pennsylvania conducted an internal inquiry.

Paul Gelsinger decided to attend the December 1999 RAC meeting that discussed his son's death. He learned for the first time at that meeting, according to his account, that gene therapy had never been demonstrated to work in humans. He had been misled, not necessarily deliberately, by the researcher's accounts of success in animals. As Paul listened to criticisms of the clinical trial, his faith in the researchers waned and was replaced by anger and a feeling of betrayal.

Other information fed his anger. When, a month earlier, he had asked James Wilson, "What is your financial position in this?" Wilson's reply, as Paul recalled, was that he was an unpaid consultant to Genovo, the biotech company that was partially funding the institute. Paul later learned that both Wilson and the University of Pennsylvania were major stockholders in Genovo and that Wilson had founded the company, then sold his 30 percent share for $13.5 million. What is more, Genovo had good reason to pursue the OTCD study, not for its own sake, but to test therapies for more common liver and lung diseases that it had already been paid tens of millions of dollars to develop.

Wilson and the university, as Paul Gelsinger now saw it, had ulterior motives for recruiting volunteers for the clinical trial and producing positive results, even at the expense of safety. Thus, they might not have been as careful as they should have been in warning the Gelsingers about the risks of the study. Also, the bioethicist approving the trial, Arthur Caplan, held an appointment in the department headed by Wilson. This, in effect, made Wilson his superior and thus automatically raised a question about the independence of his judgment.

A year and a day after Jesse's death, the Gelsinger family filed a wrongful-death lawsuit against the people conducting the clinical trial and the University of Pennsylvania. The university eventually settled the suit out of court. The terms of the settlement were not disclosed.

Federal Investigation

A subsequent investigation by the FDA pointed to several flaws in the way the gene therapy trial was conducted. First, the institute failed to follow protocol by not reporting liver toxicity in four patients treated prior to Gelsinger. At least two of those earlier volunteers had suffered "Grade 3" liver damage, which should have prompted the researchers to immediately halt the trial and notify the FDA. Second, the researchers had altered the FDA-approved patient consent form to omit the deaths of two rhesus monkeys injected with a high level of a similar vector. Perhaps most crucially, the FDA concluded that Jesse Gelsinger's liver function when he was injected was not at the minimal level that regulators had required for inclusion in the study.

Wilson's response was that he had sent the FDA the liver-toxicity information prior to the final approval of the protocol, although his report had been late. Further, the two monkeys that died were part of another study that used a different, stronger virus. He contended that Jesse's liver function only had to meet the minimum requirements when he was "enrolled," not when he was actually infused.

The government rejected these explanations and the Justice Department filed civil suits against the University of Pennsylvania team. In 2005, an agreement was reached in which the researchers admitted no wrongdoing and were fined a combined $1 million. Wilson was barred from leading research on humans for a decade, but Paul Gelsinger was not satisfied.

"I wanted some accountability, and that's not going to happen," he said.

Outcome

What caused the death of Jesse Gelsinger? Even after the autopsy, the answer wasn't entirely clear. Supporters of the institute noted that Jesse had abnormal cells in his bone marrow. This may have been a preexisting condition, and it may account for why his immune system reacted in an unpredicted way to the viral injection. Critics of the institute approach argued that Jesse simply had the same massive immune response that had killed the two primates and injured other trial subjects.

After Jesse's death, the FDA temporarily shut down all gene-therapy operations for review. The federal Office for Human Research Protections (OHRP) launched a major effort to educate researchers about requirements for the protection of trial participants and the need for institutional review boards. And the NIH, after making a nationwide appeal, received 652 additional reports of "adverse events," including deaths, in gene-therapy experiments similar to the one at U. Penn. Since some of these deaths were unexplained, they raised the possibility that Jesse Gelsinger was not the first person killed by gene therapy, as most researchers had assumed. Many other patients, it turned out, had suffered fevers, clotting abnormalities, and serious drops in blood pressure. The failure of researchers to report hundreds of additional adverse events led to congressional hearings in 2000.

Some critics, however, have argued that such outrage is disingenuous, since federal law still prohibits the FDA itself from distributing information about adverse events if industry sponsors successfully claim such information as proprietary. This, critics say, puts participants in the position of having to take risks that they know nothing about, even if a similar study is reporting serious adverse events to the government. In their view, the law favors protection of the pharmaceutical industry's investments more than protecting human subjects. (See Case Presentation: From Vioxx to the ASR Implant for more on this topic.)

Fifteen years later, Jesse Gelsinger's death continues to inspire debate over informed consent in medical research, particularly in cases where researchers fail to disclose pertinent information or rely on participants' vulnerabilities to get access to new trial subjects.

CASE PRESENTATION

From Vioxx to the ASR Implant: Do Research Sponsors Suppress Bad News?

Kim Horbas knew there was something wrong when she began to hear a clicking sound as she walked.

For the first month after her recovery from hip replacement surgery in February 2008, her stride had been smooth and pain-free. But early that summer, she began to hear a sharp *click* with each step she took.

"It got louder and louder, so you could hear me coming from a pretty far distance," recalled Horbas, a fifty-five-year-old woman from Champaign, Illinois, whose physician had recommended the hip replacement for her arthritis pain.

Horbas's orthopedic surgeon, Robert Bane, was concerned enough about the clicking and other symptoms that he decided to reopen her hip for a look inside. What he found was alarming. The muscle tissue around the replacement hip was extensively damaged and stained by metallic debris from the implant. Ten months after her first hip replacement, Horbas was forced to undergo a "revision" surgery to have a different type of artificial hip installed. And she was not alone.

During the mid 2000s, tens of thousands of hip replacement patients around the world started returning to their physicians complaining of pain, inflammation, and clicking or grinding sensations when they walked. Some came in with fluid-filled lumps on their hips the size of grapefruits. When surgeons operated, they often found a "biological dead zone," with "matted strands of tissue stained gray and black," and hip muscles that had deteriorated so much they could no longer contract. They also found shards of metal debris in the surrounding tissue and fluid. Blood tests on the patients revealed extremely high concentrations of cobalt and chromium, sometimes as much as six hundred times the normal levels in human blood.

All these patients had received a new type of "metal-on-metal" hip implant, in which both the femoral head and the "cup" it fits into are made of a cobalt-chromium alloy. In contrast to traditional hip implants, which use a ceramic or plastic cup that eventually wears out and often has to be replaced, these all-metal devices were supposed to last a lifetime. From their introduction in 1997, they were marketed

to younger patients as a prosthesis that would keep them active for the rest of their lives without requiring subsequent surgery. But for many, these all-metal devices seemed to be having the opposite effect, leaving them permanently disabled even after their failed implants had been replaced.

That's what happened to Mary Anne Doornbos, a former IBM employee from the Chicago area who got a "metal-on-metal" hip implant for arthritis in 2007, when she was fifty-three. Like Kim Horbas, Mary Anne Doornbos soon suffered extensive damage to the muscles, tendons, and other tissue surrounding her implant and a large mass formed around her hipbone. Years after a surgeon removed the mass and replaced the implant, she was still in acute pain, couldn't stand or walk without a cane, and was unable to return to work.

"Even before I get out of bed it's just pain, constant pain," Doornbos said. "And I can't understand how or when it's going to stop." She said that her physicians had advised her she should be prepared for the pain to last the rest of her life.

Design Flaws and Toxic Ions

Both Mary Anne Doornbos and Kim Horbas had received a popular all-metal hip implant called the Articular Surface Replacement (ASR). The ASR was introduced in 2004 by DePuy Synthes, a medical device division of Johnson & Johnson. Before its worldwide recall in 2010, the ASR was one of the most widely used artificial hips on the market, implanted in about ninety-three thousand patients worldwide, with about thirty thousand of those in the United States.

What Doornbos and Horbas didn't know when they received their hip implants in the late 2000s was that design problems in the ASR meant that it had an astonishingly high failure rate. Shortly after the ASR recall was announced in 2010, an internal analysis conducted by Johnson & Johnson estimated that its device could be expected to fail for nearly 40 percent of patients in the first five years of use. A study that same year in the British *Journal of Bone and Joint Surgery* found an even higher failure rate of 48.8 percent in the first six years of use.

These nearly even odds of joint failure are at least eight times greater than the 3.3 to 4.9 percent failure rate for traditional hip replacements in the first six years.

Retrospective studies of the ASR's design revealed that the interior surface of the hip's "cup" was unusually thin and had been designed to work with only one angle of implantation. This, combined with a protruding groove inside the cup and greater torque on the connection point meant that it was particularly vulnerable to a phenomenon called "edge loading," in which the joint's ball strikes against the cup's edge, chiseling off tiny metallic shards that can destroy tissue and bone.

Kim Horbas's doctors believe that is what caused the clicking noise she heard as she walked. It was likely the sound of metal grinding on metal, roughening the surfaces of her implant and sending cobalt and chromium debris into the surrounding tissue. Although the ASR design was far more prone to this problem than other all-metal implants, a propensity for internal friction and edge loading appears to be common in metal-on-metal hips. Experts say that may explain why, as a class, all-metal implants have been shown to have average failure rates above 10 percent, or at least twice as high as traditional implants made from other materials.

Edge loading may also help explain why patients like Mary Anne Doornbos were still experiencing problems even after their implants had been removed. All types of cobalt–chromium prostheses are known to release some metal ions into the surrounding tissue, but metal-on-metal hip implants like the ASR appear to do so to an unprecedented degree. Most healthy people have cobalt levels in their blood of about 0.5 micrograms per liter, but many patients with the ASR and other all-metal hips have been tested with cobalt levels over 300 micrograms per liter. Patients have also presented highly elevated levels of trivalent chromium, which has been listed by the World Health Organization as a potential carcinogen. A 2008 study found that 20 percent of patients with Johnson & Johnson's flagship Pinnacle hip system had metal ion concentrations over the limit accepted by occupational health experts.

Although there is uncertainty about the long-term effects of cobalt and chromium, implant studies from as early as 1975 warned about these metal ions causing reactions that damage surrounding muscle and bone. Studies in the 1990s also found cobalt and chromium

seeping into the bloodstream and spreading to the lymph nodes, liver, kidneys, and spleen. At high levels, cobalt and chromium toxicity can produce endocrine, respiratory, cardiac, and neurological problems, many of which have been reported by ASR patients. The FDA now recommends that ASR and other all-metal implant patients should be monitored for such systemic effects, especially cardiovascular, neurological, kidney, and thyroid problems.

The exposure of such issues and the subsequent recall of Johnson & Johnson's ASR system quickly gave rise to legal action. In the United States alone, ten thousand patients filed lawsuits against the company, or about one third of the total who had received the device. In 2013, the company reached a $2.5 billion global settlement with eight thousand plaintiffs, but new patients have continued to come forward and further settlements are expected. Critics of the 2013 agreement point to annual revenues for Johnson & Johnson that exceed $74 billion, and say that a payout of $2.5 billion represents a slap on the wrist for the company, which still argues that the ASR's design was not defective.

In the aftermath of a scandal that has been called "one of the biggest disasters in orthopaedic history," far fewer physicians are recommending all-metal hip replacements, and an editorial in the *Journal of Arthroplasty* urged surgeons to use the implants with "great caution, if at all." But journalists and researchers also began asking pointed questions. How could manufacturers and regulators not have known about these conspicuous problems? Subsequent reporting revealed that Johnson & Johnson had used regulatory loopholes to put the ASR on the market without device-specific clinical testing. And court filings showed that Johnson & Johnson executives had been warned about the ASR's design problems as early as 2005, often by their own consultants and internal analyses.

"A Large Uncontrolled Experiment"

In 2007, the same year Mary Anne Doornbos got her hip implant, a British orthopedic surgeon named Tony Nargol started receiving complaints of groin pain from his ASR hip implant patients. Initially, he assumed that his surgical technique had caused the problems and not the ASR device. After all, Nargol was a believer in the ASR's effectiveness; in 2003 he had been convinced by Johnson &

Johnson sales representatives that the ASR was superior to its competitors, and he had served as a consultant to the company for a study it presented to the FDA. But the problems kept cropping up.

"I started seeing patients come to the clinic complaining of groin pain and I saw this once, then twice, then again and again," Nargol said. "Then I thought something is wrong here. Then when we opened some of these patients up, we got the same thing, this fluid under pressure, sometimes it was milky, sometimes it was greeny-grey. It looked awful. But associated with necro[sis] and the muscle was just being eaten. It was just rotten."

So Nargol consulted with colleagues and studied the outcomes for hundreds of implant patients. The results, which they presented in 2008, showed that many ASR patients had elevated blood concentrations of cobalt and chromium, and that the failures of the joints did not appear to be linked to surgical errors. Working with an engineer at Newcastle University, they also identified design problems in the ASR cup that produced edge loading and internal friction. But when they presented their results to Johnson & Johnson executives, they were told they were the only physicians who were seeing such problems. The documentary evidence later suggested otherwise.

As early as 2006, a group of physicians recruited by Johnson & Johnson as "key opinion leaders" had stopped using the ASR, warning the company that the device was failing quickly after implantation. In 2007, the device failed an internal stress test in which Johnson & Johnson engineers measured how quickly the ASR would wear down compared to a competitor. But the company was also pursuing a successful marketing campaign in the United States and had persuaded tens of thousands of surgeons to switch to the ASR from its competitors. So they concluded that fixing the design flaws needed to wait.

"We will ultimately need a cup redesign, but the short-term action is manage perceptions," a top Johnson & Johnson sales official wrote a colleague in 2008.

The company used a similar approach when they were confronted by regulators at the Australian National Joint Replacement Registry, who contacted them seventeen times over two years, with increasing alarm about high ASR failure rates. Taking the same tack it would later take with Nargol and his colleagues, the company issued a worldwide safety warning in 2007 that blamed surgeons for "sub-optimal patient selection and surgical technique," but gave no hint there might be any problems with the ASR's design.

In the United States, the regulatory situation was more complicated. In 2005, the FDA had allowed the flawed ASR cup onto the U.S. market without clinical testing, because the rest of the device was "substantially similar" to one already on the market. This regulatory loophole is how Doornbos and Horbas came to be implanted with the ASR cup at the same time the FDA was evaluating a shorter "resurfacing" version of the implant with the same flawed mechanism. In 2009, the FDA would reject that version of the implant, citing, among other concerns, "high concentration of metal ions" in the blood of patients who received it. But that conclusion came too late for patients like Doornbos and Horbas. (The FDA has since taken steps to try to close the "substantially similar" device loophole.) It would be another year before Johnson & Johnson would recall the ASR, still maintaining that the device was safe.

When researchers looked back at the history of the ASR and other all-metal implants, they found that none of the world's medical regulators had required that the devices be tested in human clinical trials. Instead, from the time of their introduction in 1997, these all-metal implants had been categorized as devices that require only "simulator testing," using machines that put the hip through a series of mechanical tests. In other words, the clinical testing of the ASR took place out in the market, which a consumer advocacy group later called "one very large uncontrolled experiment exposing millions of patients to an unknown risk." Even Johnson & Johnson officials seemed concerned about this lack of oversight, acknowledging that although their laboratory data was promising, "the ultimate test is the long term human experience." Other J&J executives were more blunt, exclaiming with regard to the international rollout of the devices, "You could literally implant a tent rod if you wanted!"

Transparency and Cooperation

It is easy to hold up such comments to confirm a Hollywood portrait of industry executives as evil or greedy, conspiring to make money at the expense of patient health. But to do so would miss a more complicated and serious conversation about the environment in which physicians, regulators, and executives function. The

ASR saga is not a story of sinister industry conspirators in a smoke-filled room, but one in which physicians, regulators, sales reps, and executives were actively cooperating with each other in a highly competitive health care landscape. Many of the players faced competing and sometimes conflicting incentives, such as concern for good patient outcomes and concern for competitive advantage.

Take the design surgeons and other "key opinion leaders" who received stock options and other benefits from Johnson & Johnson to promote the ASR in conferences, journals, and educational programs—some of whom later notified the company about ASR's early failure rate. Or take Tony Nargol, who first served as a consultant for Johnson & Johnson's FDA request and ended up as a consultant to the lawyers suing Johnson & Johnson. Jesse Gelsinger's physicians (see this chapter's Case Presentation on gene therapy) faced equally complicated allegiances and agendas. Such ambiguous and conflicting roles are especially confusing because industry now funds most medical research that is not basic science.

The health care landscape has not always been so complicated. Industry also funded plenty of research in the 1980s, for example, but through a grant system in which the principle investigators were left to design studies, analyze data, and publish results without guidance from the sponsor. It was also rare for authors of studies to have independent financial ties to their sponsors. Today, the industry funders of research often play an integral role in designing and analyzing studies and making decisions about how, and whether, to publish the results.

Supporters of this new system, such as patient advocate Emma D'Arcy, believe it reflects a consumer-driven economy which gives patients, as well as physicians, a direct say in how treatments are developed. (See D'Arcy's essay later in this chapter.) In her view, industry professionals, no less than medical professionals and scientists, have an abiding interest in making sure that treatments are safe and effective. (The ASR recall, after all, will likely cost Johnson & Johnson more than $3 billion.) Rather than fear collaboration with industry, D'Arcy argues that physicians should embrace it as an opportunity to provide customer feedback and increase transparency.

Critics of the new system, such as former *New England Journal of Medicine* editor Marcia Angell, argue that commercial aims do not always lead to good patient outcomes, particularly when industry executives may

be motivated by short-term considerations such as quarterly earnings and shareholder dividends. Given such pressures, it might actually have been in Johnson & Johnson's best interest to suppress bad news about the ASR, even if that meant allowing more patients to receive failing devices. For Angell, the health care industry, which is often estimated to be the most profitable in the world, has too much power and influence to allow for neutral, objective collaboration with researchers and physicians.

Vioxx and Clinical Trials

One example often cited by critics such as Angell is the role that the pharmaceutical giant Merck played in safety and effectiveness research on its "blockbuster" painkiller rofecoxib, usually known by its commercial name, Vioxx®. The cox-2 inhibitor drug was taken by eighty million people worldwide and earned Merck $2.3 billion in 2003 alone. But the company voluntarily took Vioxx off the market in 2004, after studies indicated that the drug doubled long-term users' risk of heart attack and stroke. A 2005 study published in the *Lancet* estimated that during its time on the market, Vioxx caused between 88,000 and 140,000 excess heart attacks in the United States alone, killing 38,000 people.

In the spring of 2008, the *Journal of the American Medical Association* (*JAMA*) published two papers and an editorial on Merck and Vioxx research. In one retrospective analysis, the *JAMA* authors found that Merck had "minimized the appearance of any mortality risk" by undercounting the number of deaths in a preapproval trial it had funded and submitted to the FDA. (Merck's internal analyses, by contrast, had "clearly identified an increased risk of mortality associated with rofecoxib.") In the second paper, a different group of authors examined hundreds of research publications related to Vioxx and found that Merck had engaged in a pattern of "guest authorship and ghostwriting" in academic journals, presenting papers authored by its employees or contractors as if they had been written by independent academic scientists. In some instances, subpoenaed documents showed that Merck's marketing department was directly involved in analyzing and presenting medical research.

Merck disputed the integrity of the *JAMA* studies and noted that one of their authors had only been able to access the documents because he had worked as a consultant on Vioxx lawsuits. But in 2009, they acknowledged paying the publisher Elsevier to create a publication called the *Australasian Journal of Bone and Joint Medicine* (*AJBJM*), which was made to look like an actual medical journal and distributed to tens of thousands of physicians. In fact, it was a compilation of articles, some peer-reviewed and some of unknown origin, which made positive references to Vioxx and another Merck drug, a bone treatment called Fosamax. Elsevier later apologized for this and other publications that they acknowledged "were made to look like medical journals and lacked the proper disclosures" of drug company sponsorship.

Supporters of research cooperation between industry and academic medicine argue that such marketing ploys as the *AJBJM* are obvious and that physicians and patients are good at distinguishing brand promotion from useful medical information. The editors of *JAMA*, by contrast, contend that the problem is much more serious and reflects widespread "data misrepresentation, data analysis, and selective reporting in industry sponsored studies." In the scathing editorial that accompanied the Vioxx studies, the *JAMA* editors said such practices were "not the sole purview of one company" and called for broad changes, such as prospective registration of all trials and limits on sponsors' involvement in data collection and manuscript preparation.

Since many of the materials that detailed Johnson & Johnson's and Merck's actions were internal company documents that only came out through litigation, it is difficult to assess how widespread such practices are. But there is substantial evidence that the funding source of medical research has an impact on its outcome.

A 2010 study published in the *Annals of Internal Medicine* reviewed over five hundred drug trials in five major classes of drugs. They found that 85 percent of industry-funded studies reached positive conclusions about the drug in question, but only 50 percent of government-funded trials reached such conclusions. A 2007 review of 192 statin trials found that industry-sponsored trials for that class of drugs were twenty times more likely to reach positive conclusions about the test drug than those funded by independent sources. And a 2006 review of 542 psychiatric drug trials found that industry sponsors ended up with a positive result for their own drug 78 percent of the time, compared to 48 percent of the time with independent funding. Similarly, two different systemic reviews of the literature on this topic, published in *JAMA* and the *British Medical Journal* (*BMJ*), found that across the spectrum, industry-funded studies are four times

more likely to report positive results than independently funded ones. Given the fact that industry now funds about 60 percent of medical research (compared to about 30 percent in 1980), these results have generated significant concern among bioethicists, journalists, and health care providers.

Again, these and other stakeholders have raised questions about the integrity of research practices. Many of the papers discussed above have identified design weaknesses that might allow for bias to creep into medical research, including arbitrary start points and cutoffs for data collection, failures of randomization, and comparison of drugs to placebos rather than currently accepted best treatments. But one of the primary factors that may explain such results is that many trials with negative outcomes simply aren't published. A huge study on publication bias commissioned by the British government and published in 2010 found that about half of all medical trials never publish results and that those with positive results were twice as likely to be published as those with negative ones. One problem with so many trials going unpublished is that it offers opportunities for selection bias, or "cherry-picking" favorable or novel outcomes. And that can have an impact that extends far beyond the pages of a medical journal.

All Trials?

Debates over the integrity of medical research can be overwhelmingly complex, and it is no surprise that many physicians are tempted to give up and simply take a few published studies or a sales rep's recommendation at face value. But as we saw in the ASR and Vioxx cases above, such decisions can have a serious impact on patient outcomes.

This is one of the reasons why the World Medical Association's *Declaration of Helsinki* on medical research ethics now calls for every study involving human subjects to be registered in a publicly accessible database and insists that "Negative and inconclusive as well as positive results must be published or otherwise made publicly available." (See the rest of the *Helsinki* declaration later in this chapter.) It is also why the U.S. Congress, in 2007, enacted a law that requires that clinical trials beyond Phase I for new drugs and devices be registered on a federal website called clinicaltrials.gov and report results within a year of their conclusion.

But current evidence suggests that compliance with the 2007 law has been minimal. A 2012 study published in the *BMJ* found that only 22 percent of completed trials covered by the law had complied with the registration and reporting requirements. And a 2015 Duke University study of the more than 13,000 completed or terminated trials found that only 13 percent had reported results to clinicaltrials.gov. (The Duke study, it should be noted, found that NIH-funded trials were no better about reporting results than industry-sponsored ones, and some of the missing industry data involved exemptions to preserve competitive advantage.) In spite of this noncompliance, the enforcement rules for the 2007 law have, as of this writing, never been finalized. The law included provisions for offenders to be fined as much as $10,000 a day, but no such fines have ever been issued. In addition, most of the drugs and other treatments that physicians use today rely on trials that were conducted before 2007.

To try to address this situation, an initiative called the "All Trials" campaign was launched in 2013 under the direction of the *BMJ*, Oxford's Center for Evidence-Based Medicine, Dartmouth's Geisel School of Medicine, and a number of other professional organizations and individuals, including the physician and *BMJ* columnist Ben Goldacre. The campaign calls for "all past and present clinical trials to be registered and their full methods and summary results reported," a platform that may be gaining momentum. In 2013, GlaxoSmithKline (GSK) was the first pharmaceutical company to endorse the All Trials campaign, pledging to publish the results of "clinical outcomes trials for all approved medicines dating back to the formation of GSK." In 2014, the European Parliament overwhelmingly passed a new Clinical Trials Regulation that requires all EU trials to be registered and to publicly report results that are clear and accessible to lay readers. The law also includes stiff penalties for noncompliance.

Of course, it is unlikely that any single campaign or piece of regulation will be able to fully guarantee the integrity of medical research. The ASR and Vioxx cases demonstrate the challenge of identifying risky treatments, along with potential conflicts of interest, in time to protect patients from harm. They also demonstrate an ongoing lack of consensus about the proper role of industry sponsorship in medical research, and at what point efficient collaboration becomes unethical collusion. But consensus may be building that transparency is necessary in medical research, to provide sound evidence for the vast majority of treatments that are safe and effective, and to protect patients from those questionable treatments that do more harm than good.

SOCIAL CONTEXT

Prisoners as Test Subjects?

In a 1966 interview, Dr. Albert Klingman, professor of dermatology at the University of Pennsylvania, recalled his impression of Holmesburg State Prison in Philadelphia on his first visit. He looked around at the prisoners, many of them shirtless, and "All I saw before me were acres of skin. It was like a farmer seeing a fertile field for the first time."

Klingman went on to conduct a large number and variety of clinical trials at Holmesburg, using prisoners as research subjects. He was not, however, the only scientist to see the prison as a field of potential subjects. Allen Hornblum's 1998 book *Acres of Skin: Human Experiments at Holmesburg Prison* documents hundreds of cases of human research carried out at the prison from 1951 to 1974. The University of Pennsylvania established a research clinic and laboratory at the prison, and it was under its auspices that many investigations were carried out. University scientists conducted research supported by contracts from more than thirty private companies (such as Johnson & Johnson and Dow Chemical), as well as from the U.S. Army and thirty federal agencies, including the Central Intelligence Agency.

Numerous clinical trials were undertaken to determine the safety and effectiveness of dermatological products. Thus, prisoners were recruited to test skin creams, shampoos, moisturizers, deodorants, and foot powders. (Klingman's Holmesburg research established the effectiveness of Retin-A in treating acne.) Trials were not limited to skin products, and prisoners were also enrolled to test toothpaste, eyedrops, and liquid diets. Although most of the tests were carried out to develop products with commercial value, clinical trials of experimental drugs were also conducted at Holmesburg. Over the years, thirty-three drug companies employed prisoners as subjects in testing more than three hundred drugs.

Although some substances studied at Holmesburg were relatively benign, others posed a serious risk to the safety of the human subjects. Thus, more than seventy prisoners were exposed to dioxin, a toxic component of Agent Orange—the infamous defoliant used during the Vietnam War that was later linked to cancers and neurological disorders. Other prisoners were exposed to potentially harmful doses of radioactive materials and to chemicals that left some with lifelong problems. Edward Anthony, an inmate in 1962, was one of the many who were permanently harmed by serving as a research subject. He told reporter Jan Urbina in a 2006 interview that "When they put the chemicals on me, my hands swelled up like eight-ounce boxing gloves, and they've never gone back to normal."

One of several Army projects at Holmesburg involved administering powerful psychotropic (mind-altering) drugs such as LSD to more than 300 subjects. The aim of the research, conducted during the Cold War, was to find the minimum dose of a drug that would be effective in disabling half the population receiving it. Psychotropic drugs are highly dangerous, with the potential to cause death or trigger psychosis. It is almost certain that some inmates who served as test subjects for these drugs were irreversibly harmed.

Informed Consent?

Researchers recruited prisoners to participate in the Holmesburg experiments, and no one was forced to participate. In this sense, the subjects were all volunteers. (For examples of non-voluntary research subjects, see Case Presentation: The Tuskegee Syphilis Study in Chapter 10 and Case Presentation: STD Research in Guatemala in Chapter 11.) Hornblum and others familiar with the circumstances of the Holmesburg recruiting, however, doubt that the conditions required for legitimate informed consent were satisfied. Evidence suggests that prisoners were not supplied with relevant information in a form they could understand, and that their autonomy was compromised by their incarceration and by monetary and other inducements to disregard their own best interests.

First, many prisoners at Holmesburg either couldn't read or read poorly, making it unlikely that they were able to fully appreciate the risks of becoming subjects in the research. Such prisoners had to depend on explanations provided by the researchers conducting the investigations, who cannot be assumed to have provided unbiased information. It is doubtful that a prisoner's signature on an informed-consent document indicated that he had an adequate understanding of the nature of the clinical trial and the risk he might run as a participant.

Second, prisoners at Holmesburg, like those elsewhere, lived a grim and narrow existence, marked by the absence of even minor luxuries and by the ever-present threat of violence. Participating in a clinical trial not only offered prisoners a welcome distraction from routine, but also a chance to spend time in the safer and more comfortable environment of the study clinic. While there, they would receive better food, have more opportunities to socialize, and would be asked about their experiences by researchers. In prison, even such small benefits were likely to motivate some inmates to take risks they otherwise wouldn't agree to take.

Third, Holmesburg inmates were given the chance to earn, by prison standards, a significant amount of money. Inmates ordinarily worked in the prison's industries, making shoes and clothes or doing carpentry or laundry. For such work, they were paid fifteen to twenty-five cents a day. By contrast, an inmate volunteering to be a research subject might earn as much as $300 to $400 a month. Inmates who started out volunteering for relatively safe trials paying fifty or seventy-five dollars a month sometimes worked toward earning more money by volunteering for research that increased their risks. Thus, in the circumstance of prison life, the potential to earn a substantial sum of money served as an inducement to become a research subject.

These and other factors appear to have compromised the decisions of inmates and rendered their consent invalid. Indeed, informed consent at Holmesburg and many other prisons seems to have been more of a formal ritual than a genuine effort to protect the inmates' autonomy and dignity.

Other Prison Experiments

Research of the sort conducted at Holmesburg also took place at other prisons throughout the United States. During the 1950s, researchers in Oregon and Washington state prisons exposed the testicles of 130 inmates to radiation, to try to determine its effects on reproductive tissue. In 1963, prisoners in Ohio and Illinois were injected with blood from leukemia patients to determine whether the disease could be transmitted.

During the Second World War, prisons were sites of considerable research activity. Most able-bodied men were in the armed forces, and an unprecedented number of women had entered the workforce. Prisoners were encouraged to demonstrate

their patriotism by becoming "guinea pigs" in one of the many research projects conducted under military auspices. Some experiments required exposure to extreme temperatures to test survival clothing, while others involved skin grafting, nutritional deficiencies, and induced dysentery. Others tested human blood substitutes for use in transfusions. Hornblum cites the case of one prison trial in which filtered beef blood was injected into sixty-four inmate volunteers as part of a transfusion study. The experiment was ended when twenty people were afflicted by an immune reaction. Eight of those who fell ill developed high fever, rashes, and joint pain, and one of them died.

The best-known prison experiment during the war years was the study of malaria conducted in 1944 at Illinois State Penitentiary in Statesville. University of Chicago researchers, working under a contract with the U.S. Army, infected five hundred healthy volunteers with malaria. The study was conducted to test the effectiveness of various drugs in preventing relapses among those already infected with malaria. Because the United States and Allied forces were fighting in malaria-plagued regions of the world, finding effective treatments was crucial to the war efforts. Participants in the study were rewarded with time served for good behavior, making early release possible in some cases.

When the war ended, with prison experimentation an established practice, pharmaceutical companies began to recruit prisoners as subjects for Phase I clinical trials of experimental drugs. As discussed above and in this chapter's Briefing Session, Phase I trials are conducted to discover a new drug's side effects and establish a safe dose. Phase I trials are required by the FDA as part of the drug-approval process, but a Phase I trial does not have a therapeutic aim. Because of this, it has always been difficult to enroll an adequate number of people as test subjects. Prisons offered a solution to the problem. As one researcher observed in 1973, "Phase I is very big in prisons. FDA prefers Phase I to be on an in-patient basis—the only place available for large-scale toxicity studies is prison." The FDA estimates that from the end of the war until the early 1970s, about 90 percent of new drugs were first tested on prison inmates.

An experiment conducted by Robert E. Hodges in 1970 is typical of the nontherapeutic research carried out with prison inmates at the time. By withholding ascorbic acid from the diet of his research subjects, Hodges experimentally induced scurvy in five inmates from Iowa State Prison. The men developed hemorrhages under the skin, swollen and severely painful joints, bleeding gums, and weight gain, followed later by swelling of the legs, hair loss, tooth decay, shortness of breath, scaly skin, and depression. Hodges's results did no more than confirm what was already known about a lack of ascorbic acid in the diet. For volunteering, inmates earned a dollar a day during the course of the experiment. All the inmates suffered, and it appeared doubtful that the youngest of the five inmates would ever recover fully from the induced disease.

New Regulations

In 1972, information about the Tuskegee syphilis study became public. (For further details, see this chapter's Briefing Session as well as the Case Presentation in Chapter 10.) Revelations about the deception, exploitation, and harm caused to individuals in this federally sponsored study produced a public and political scandal. It also led to demands that regulations governing research involving human subjects be strengthened so that something like the Tuskegee experiment could never happen again.

Institutional review boards (IRBs) were established to review human research projects, and rules to protect confidentiality and enable informed consent were introduced. The general protections extended to prison inmates, but in 1978 the Department of Health and Human Services (DHHS) issued a set of regulations that applied specifically to federally funded research involving prisoners.

A major aim of the regulations was to protect the autonomy of prisoners by preventing them from being coerced into becoming research subjects. IRBs were instructed to consider the following four criteria before approving a research proposal: (1) Compensation must not be coercive. Even the opportunity to live in greater comfort or receive better food may be coercive in a prison environment. (2) Risks of participating in the research should be acceptable to potential subjects who are not prisoners. (3) Prisoners who decide against participation must not suffer such consequences as being denied parole or privileges to which they would otherwise be entitled. (4) Participants, after the end of the research, must be provided with medical care needed for any condition associated with the research.

In 2001, these regulations were expanded to require that IRBs for prison experiments include a prisoner or prisoner representative and that the majority of non-prisoner IRB members not have any other association with the prison. The DHHS also recognized prisoners as constituting a "vulnerable population," a formal category that also includes children and the mentally ill. This means that IRB oversight of the research in which prisoners are involved is required to be especially vigilant.

The new federal regulations effectively ruled out the participation of prisoners in Phase I and Phase II trials of experimental drugs. The "acres of skin" viewed with scientific excitement by Albert Klingman and other researchers became forbidden territory.

The new, more stringent rules made it extremely difficult for new drugs to be tested on prisoners. More and more often, pharmaceutical companies began to test the safety and effectiveness of potentially useful drugs in Asian, African, and Eastern European countries. The rules for protecting human subjects are less strict in many of those countries, and "offshore" testing has become a common practice. (See Chapter 11 for more on this topic.)

Change Current Restrictions?

In 2006, the National Institute of Medicine was commissioned by the federal Office for Human Research Protections (OHRP) to review the ethical considerations in research involving prisoners. The institute's report made recommendations to expand the protections accorded prisoners, while also permitting prisoners to gain potential benefits from research. These included an expansion of the definition of "prisoner" to include the millions of people under "adult correction supervision" such as probation, who thus remain a vulnerable population for research. Rather than excluding prisoners from research by category, the institute recommended that proposed research should be vetted on the basis of its potential benefit to prisoners. Thus pesticide or cosmetics testing might be excluded but testing on an HIV vaccine might be allowed, given the high rate of HIV infection in the prison population.

The report concluded that even if regulations were shifted to consider potential risk–benefit outcomes, using prisoners in Phase I or II clinical trials of drugs should not be permitted. Since such trials test for "safety and effectiveness," it is difficult to determine whether the benefit of giving the drug to a prisoner would exceed the risk. Phase III trials (which use drugs shown to have therapeutic benefits) would be allowable, but only when the ratio of prisoners to nonprisoners in the study doesn't exceed 50 percent.

This last restriction minimizes the possibility of using prisoners because they are convenient and accessible. The benefits to be considered in decisions about such research must be benefits that accrue to the prisoners themselves, not to some other group or to society. Behavioral or epidemiological studies may use a greater percentage of prisoners, however, if the risks are very low (e.g., filling out a questionnaire) and the knowledge obtained may benefit prisoners as a class (e.g., prevent the spread of disease).

The recommendations also called for the OHRP research protections to be applied more broadly, to include privately funded research, as well as research funded by all federal and state agencies. This is not the case now, but giving OHRP an oversight role in all human research would afford participants more protection than they currently enjoy.

Nevertheless, prisoners currently make up a small percentage of research subjects in the United States, and the Institute of Medicine's recommendations have yet to be implemented. Critics of the recommendations argue that if they are accepted, an increasing number of prisoners may be recruited as research subjects and may again run the risk of exploitation. There is too much demand for research subjects and too much money is at stake, critics say, for a marginalized and unsympathetic population to receive reliable protection from even the most stringent regulations. Deals will be made, shortcuts taken, and people exploited. Many of these concerns are based in the fundamental perception that informed consent is difficult to achieve among incarcerated populations. Prison, after all, is based on a radical restriction of a person's autonomy, and obtaining genuine consent in that context may simply be too much of a challenge.

The Cold-War Radiation Experiments

Amelia Jackson was a cook at Pogue's department store in Cincinnati when she was diagnosed with terminal colon cancer in September 1966. In October of that year, she was treated with 100 rads of full-body radiation—the equivalent of 7,500 chest X-rays. Until her exposure to radiation, Ms. Jackson had been a strong and hard-working fifty-two-year-old, but after the treatment, she bled and vomited for days. She was never again able to care for herself and died in March 1967.

Ms. Jackson was treated as part of a program operated by the University of Cincinnati and supported in part by funds from the Pentagon. She was one of several cancer patients in a research program that subjected dozens of people to radiation in massive doses to determine its biological effects.

The aim of the study, according to researchers, was to develop more effective cancer treatments. However, the study's military sponsors had another agenda: to determine how much radiation exposure military personnel could endure before becoming disoriented and unable to function effectively.

A Patchwork of Radiation Experiments

The Cincinnati project was only one of a patchwork of human experiments involving radiation that were carried out with funding from a variety of military and civilian agencies of the U.S. government over a period of at least thirty years. The experiments took place at government laboratories and university hospitals and research centers. Some experiments involved exposing patients to high-energy beams of radiation, while others involved injecting them with such dangerous radioactive substances as plutonium.

The experiments began near the end of World War II. They were prompted by both scientific interest and the military's practical need to know more about the damaging effects of radiation on humans. The escalating Cold War between the United States and the Soviet Union—in which the threat of a full-scale nuclear exchange loomed behind each political development—lent urgency to the project. At the start of the research, little was known about the harmful effects of radiation, and researchers believed their experiments not only would contribute to scientific understanding but would also provide the basis for more effective medical therapies. This lack of knowledge about the effects of radiation led to experiments that would be unthinkable today:

- In the late 1940s, Vanderbilt University exposed about eight hundred pregnant women to radiation to determine its effects on fetal development. A follow-up study of the children born to the women showed a higher-than-average rate of cancer.

- At a state residential school in Waltham, Massachusetts, from 1946 to 1956, nineteen teenaged boys were fed radioactive iron and calcium in their breakfast oatmeal. The research, conducted by MIT and Quaker Oats, was designed to prove that Quaker oatmeal traveled throughout the body, a finding that would bolster its advertising claims against competitors. In the consent form mailed to parents of the boys, no mention was made of radiation.

- At Columbia University and Montefiore Hospital in New York, during the late 1950s, twelve terminally ill cancer patients were injected with concentrations of radioactive calcium and strontium-85 to measure the rate at which the substances are absorbed by various types of tissues.

- From 1963 to 1971, experiments were conducted at Oregon State Prison in which the testicles of sixty-seven inmates were exposed to X-rays to determine the effects of radiation on sperm production. Prisoners signed consent statements that mentioned some of the risks of the radiation. However, the possibility that the radiation might cause cancer was not mentioned. A similar experiment was conducted on sixty-four inmates at Washington State Prison.

- Starting in the mid-1960s, patients with leukemia and other forms of cancer at the Oak Ridge National Laboratory in Tennessee were exposed to extremely high levels of radiation from isotopes of cesium and cobalt. Almost two hundred patients, including a six-year-old boy, were subjected to such treatment, until the experiment was ended in 1974 by the Atomic Energy Commission. The study had provided data to NASA about how much radiation astronauts could withstand and was later determined to have little patient benefit.

The Experiments Become Public

The American public did not learn of the radiation experiments until 1993, when reporters for the *Albuquerque Tribune* tracked down five of the eighteen subjects who had been injected with plutonium in an experiment conducted from 1945 to 1957. These experiments had been conducted at the University of Rochester, Oak Ridge Laboratory, the University of Chicago, and the University of California, San Francisco Hospital. Apparently, some of the patients did not receive information about their treatment and were injected with radioactive materials without first giving consent.

Relying on Freedom of Information Act requests, a reporter for the *Tribune* named Eileen Welsome attempted to get documents from the Department of Energy concerning the radiation research, including those listing the names of subjects. However, her requests produced little solid information, and Tara O'Toole, then Assistant Secretary of Energy, expressed reservations about releasing documents that named the subjects. "Does the public's right to know include releasing names?" O'Toole asked. "It is not clear to me that it is part of the ethical obligation of the Government."

Did Participants Give Their Informed Consent?

O'Toole's superior had a different view of government's obligations. Shortly after becoming Secretary of Energy in 1993, Hazel R. O'Leary had committed herself to greater transparency and an end to the department's "atmosphere of secrecy." O'Leary soon committed her department to a full investigation of the long-rumored U.S. radiation experiments. A major focus of the inquiry was whether patients were fully informed about the risks of the treatments they received and whether they gave meaningful consent to them.

In a number of cases, the government discovered, the experimental subjects were not informed of the risks they faced and did not consent to participate in the research. Patients were sometimes misled about the character of the treatments, and in some cases the signatures on consent forms appear to have been forged. Amelia Jackson's granddaughter argued that although her grandmother was illiterate, she could sign her name, and the signature on the form used by the University of Cincinnati was not hers. The same claim was made by other relatives of subjects in the study, many of whom, like Jackson, were African American and poor.

In a few instances, evidence indicates that researchers had found the radiation experiments to be morally suspect and had warned their colleagues against pursuing them. C. E. Newton at the Hanford nuclear weapons plant wrote in an internal memorandum about the work done with prisoners at Washington State Prison: "The experiments do not appear to have been in compliance with the criminal codes of the state of Washington, and there is some question as to whether they were conducted in compliance with Federal laws."

Similarly, in a 1950 memorandum, Joseph G. Hamilton, a radiation biologist, warned his supervisors that the experiments "might have a little of the Buchenwald touch." Hamilton warned that the Atomic Energy Commission would be "subject to considerable criticism."

But most researchers appeared to believe the experiments were justified, for patriotic or other reasons, and did not raise objections. Some contemporary observers claim that work carried out twenty or thirty years ago cannot be judged by ethical standards we would use today. Robert Loeb, speaking for Strong Memorial Hospital, where some of the studies were carried out, put the point this way: "In the 1940s, what was typical in research involving human subjects was for physicians to tell the patients that they would be involved in a study and not always give full details. That is not the standard today. Many of these studies would be impossible to conduct today."

By contrast, David S. Egilman, who has investigated research with human subjects conducted by the military and the Atomic Energy Commission, claims there is adequate evidence to conclude that the researchers and their supporting agencies knew they were conducting immoral experiments. "They called the work, in effect, Nazi-like," he says. "The argument we hear is that these experiments were ethical at the time they were done. It's simply not true."

With respect to the radiation experiments, Representative David Mann of Ohio summed up the views of many citizens: "I believe we have no choice but to conclude that the radiation experiments were simply wrong and that the Government owes a huge apology to the victims, their families, and the nation."

Over time, the initial investigation into the radiation experiments conducted under the auspices of what is now the Department of Energy was expanded to include those conducted by several other federal agencies. Taking these other experiments into account, investigators concluded at least one thousand people were exposed to varying levels of radiation in experiments conducted over a number of years at various locations. Some observers believe the actual figures are much higher.

The President's Advisory Committee on Human Radiation Experiments reviewed records from the Energy Department, Defense Department, Central Intelligence Agency, NASA, and federal health agencies in an attempt to locate research projects involving radiation and to identify the experimental subjects. After eighteen months of investigation, the committee reported in 1995 that many of the government-sponsored experiments had been illegal and that their survivors ought to be compensated.

Compensation

In November 1996, the federal government agreed to pay $4.8 million as compensation for injecting twelve people with plutonium or uranium. At the time of the settlement, only one of the twelve was still alive, and a $400,000 award was paid to the families of each of the other test subjects. In 1998, the Quaker Oats Company and MIT agreed to pay $1.85 million to the more than one hundred men who, as boys, had been fed radioactive oatmeal at the Fernald School and other study sites. A large number of claims from other experiments involving radiation exposures were also filed against the federal government, universities, and hospitals.

Advocates for those whose rights may have been violated charge the government with an insufficient effort to identify and contact individuals who were subjected to the various radiation experiments. (Names and addresses were frequently not included in the experiments' records.) The National Archives has placed all of the hundreds of thousands of pages of records acquired by the Presidential Commission in files available to the public, and individuals must come forward on their own initiative if they believe they have a legal claim for compensation.

New Regulations

In 1997, President Clinton endorsed a more stringent set of policies governing all human research receiving federal support. Under those rules, explicit informed consent is required, the sponsor of the experiment must be identified to the subject, the subject must be told whether the experiment is classified, and permanent records of the experiment and the subjects must be kept. Further, an external review must be conducted before the experiment can proceed. The hope was that these rules would reduce the chance of future governments and institutions conducting secret experiments in which humans are exposed to radioactive, chemical, or other dangerous substances without their knowledge or consent.

CASE PRESENTATION

The Willowbrook Hepatitis Experiments

The Willowbrook State School in Staten Island, New York, was an institution devoted to housing and caring for mentally disabled children. In 1956, a research group led by Saul Krugman and Joan P. Giles of the New York University School of Medicine initiated a long-range study of viral hepatitis at Willowbrook. The children confined there were made experimental subjects of the study.

Hepatitis, a disease affecting the liver, is now known to be caused by one of at least three separate viruses. Although the magnitude of the symptoms varies, all types of hepatitis involve the same underlying process. The liver becomes inflamed and increases in size as the invading viruses replicate themselves. Also, part of the tissue of the liver may be destroyed and the liver's normal functions impaired. Often the flow of bile through the ducts is blocked, and bilirubin (the major pigment in bile) is forced into the blood and urine. This produces the symptom of yellowish or *jaundiced* skin.

Although some cases of hepatitis are fairly mild, serious problems, such as permanent liver damage or even death can result. The symptoms are usually flu-like: fever, fatigue, and inability to keep food down. The viruses causing the disease are transmitted orally through contact with the feces and bodily secretions of infected people.

Krugman and Giles were interested in determining the natural history of viral hepatitis—the mode of infection

and the course of the disease over time. They also wanted to test the effectiveness of gamma globulin as an agent for inoculation against hepatitis. (Gamma globulin is a protein complex extracted from blood serum that contains antigens—substances that trigger the production of specific antibodies to counter infectious agents.)

Endemic Hepatitis

Krugman and Giles considered Willowbrook to be a good site for a study because viral hepatitis occurred more or less constantly in the institution. In the jargon of medicine, the disease was *endemic* there. This phenomenon, likely aggravated by unsanitary and overcrowded conditions, had been recognized as early as 1949, and it continued as the number of children in the school increased to more than five thousand by 1960. (By 1965, Willowbrook housed six thousand residents, despite having a maximum capacity of four thousand.)

Krugman and Giles claimed that "under the chronic circumstances of multiple and repeated exposure ... most newly admitted children became infected within the first six to twelve months of residence in the institution." Over a fourteen-year period, Krugman and Giles collected more than twenty-five thousand serum specimens from more than seven hundred patients at Willowbrook. Samples were taken before exposure, during the incubation period of the virus, and for periods after the infection. Then, in an effort to get the kind of precise data they considered most useful, Krugman and Giles decided to deliberately infect some of the incoming children with the strain of the hepatitis virus prevalent at Willowbrook.

Justifying Deliberate Infection

The researchers justified their decision in the following way: It was inevitable that susceptible children would become infected in the institution, given the overall prevalence of the disease. Hepatitis was especially mild in the three- to ten-year age group at Willowbrook. Studies on deliberately infected children would be carried out in a special unit with optimum isolation facilities to protect the children from other infectious diseases, such as shigellosis (dysentery caused by a bacillus) and parasitic and respiratory infections, which were also prevalent in the institution.

Most important, Krugman and Giles claimed that being an experimental subject was in the best medical interest of the child, for not only would the child receive special care, but infection with the milder form of hepatitis would provide protection against the more virulent and damaging forms. In their words: "It should be emphasized that the artificial induction of hepatitis implies a 'therapeutic' effect because of the immunity which is conferred."

Consent

Having decided upon a course of deliberate infection, Krugman and Giles next obtained what they considered to be adequate consent from the parents of the children used as subjects. Where they were unable to obtain consent, they did not include the child in the experiment. In the earlier phases of the study, parents were provided with relevant information either by letter or orally, and written consent was secured from them. In the later phases, a group procedure was used:

> First, a psychiatric social worker discusses the project with the parents during a preliminary interview. Those who are interested are invited to attend a group session at the institution to discuss the project in greater detail. These sessions are conducted by the staff responsible for the program, including the physician, supervising nurses, staff attendants, and psychiatric social workers.... Parents in groups of six to eight are given a tour of the facilities. The purposes, potential benefits, and potential hazards

> of the program are discussed with them, and they are encouraged to ask questions. Thus, all parents can hear the response to questions posed by the more articulate members of the group. After leaving this briefing session parents have an opportunity to talk with their private physicians who may call the unit for more information. Approximately two weeks after each visit, the psychiatric social worker contacts the parents for their decision. If the decision is in the affirmative, the consent is signed but parents are informed that signed consent may be withdrawn any time before the beginning of the program. It has been clear that the group method has enabled us to obtain more thorough informed consent. Children who are wards of the state or children without parents have never been included in our studies.

Krugman and Giles later pointed out that their studies were reviewed and approved by the New York State Department of Mental Hygiene, the New York State Department of Mental Health, the Armed Forces Epidemiological Board, and the human experimentation committees of the New York University School of Medicine and the Willowbrook School. They also stressed that, although they were under no obligation to do so, they chose to meet the World Medical Association's Draft Code on Human Experimentation.

Ethical Concerns

The value of the research conducted by Krugman and Giles has been recognized as significant in furthering a scientific understanding of viral hepatitis and methods for treating it. Yet serious moral doubts have been raised about the nature and conduct of the experiments. In particular, many have questioned the use of disabled children as experimental subjects, some claiming children should never be experimental subjects in investigations that are not directly therapeutic. Others have raised questions about the ways in which approval was obtained from the parents of the children, suggesting that they were implicitly blackmailed into giving their consent.

Some the most persistent objections to the experiments were directed at the institutional circumstances in which they were conducted. In response to widely publicized and long-standing concerns about overcrowding, unsanitary conditions, and the sexual and physical abuse of residents, the Willowbrook School was finally closed in 1987.

CASE PRESENTATION
Baby Fae

On October 14, 1984, a baby was born in a community hospital in Southern California with a malformation known as hypoplastic left heart syndrome (HLHS). In such a condition, the mitral valve or aorta on the left side of the heart is underdeveloped, and only the right side of the heart functions properly. Some three hundred to two thousand infants a year are born with this defect, and most die from it within a few weeks.

The infant, who to protect her family's privacy became known to the public as "Baby Fae," was taken to a small hospital at Loma Linda University. There, on October 26, a surgical team headed by Leonard Bailey performed a heart transplant. Baby Fae became the first human infant to receive a baboon heart. She died twenty days later.

Baby Fae was not the first human to receive a so-called *xenograft*, or cross-species transplant. In early 1964, a deaf and mute upholsterer named Boyd Rush had been transplanted with a chimpanzee heart at the University of Mississippi Medical Center, after he had been brought to the hospital on the verge of death. The heart failed after only an hour, and Rush died. Before Baby Fae, three other cross-species transplants had also ended in patient deaths.

Moral Questions

In the case of Baby Fae, questions about the moral and scientific legitimacy of the transplant were raised almost immediately. Hospital officials revealed that no effort had been made to find a human donor before implanting the baboon heart, and this led some critics to wonder if research interests were not being given priority over the welfare of the patient. Others questioned whether the parents were adequately informed about an alternative corrective surgery for HLHS, the Norwood procedure, which was available in Boston and Philadelphia. The quality of the parents' informed consent was also questioned, since they lacked health insurance and could not have afforded either a transplant or the Norwood procedure. (The xeno-transplant was offered for free.)

Other observers wondered whether the nature of the surgery and its limited value had been properly explained to the parents. Also, some critics raised objections to sacrificing a healthy young primate as part of an experiment

not likely to bring any lasting benefit to Baby Fae. They argued that if we would not kill an anencephalic infant, lacking a brain or cognitive ability, for such a procedure, then we should not sacrifice a healthy, responsive primate, who was cognitively closer to a healthy human. (It was later revealed that Baby Fae's heart had come from a nine-month-old female baboon named "Goobers.")

Scientific critics charged that not enough is known about crossing the species barrier to warrant the use of transplant organs from nonhuman animals. The previous record of failures, with no major advances in understanding, did not make the prospect of another such transplant reasonable. Furthermore, critics said, chimpanzees and gorillas are genetically more similar to humans than baboons, so the choice of a baboon heart was not appropriate. The only advantage of using baboons is that they are easier to breed in captivity. Other critics claimed Dr. Bailey was engaged in "wishful thinking" in believing that Baby Fae's immune system was too immature to produce a severe rejection response. They also criticized the science behind the antigen-typing tests that Bailey's team performed before selecting Goobers as the best transplant match.

Postmortem

An autopsy on Baby Fae showed that her death was caused by the incompatibility of her blood with that of the baboon heart. Baby Fae's blood was type O, the baboon's type AB. This mismatch resulted in the formation of blood clots and the destruction of kidney function. There was also evidence that the baby's kidneys had been poisoned by the massive doses of cyclosporin she had received to prevent rejection. The heart itself showed only mild signs of rejection.

In an address before a medical conference after Baby Fae's death, Dr. Bailey commented on some of the criticisms. He is reported to have said that it was "an oversight on our part not to search for a human donor from the start." Bailey also told the conference that he and his team believed that the difference in blood types between Baby Fae and the baboon would be less important than other factors and that the immunosuppressive drugs used to prevent rejection would also solve the problem of blood incompatibility. "We came to regret those assumptions," Bailey said. The failure to match blood types was "a tactical error that came back to haunt us."

On other occasions, Bailey reiterated his view that, because infant donors are extremely scarce, animal-to-human transplants offer a realistic hope for the future. Before the Baby Fae operation, Bailey had transplanted organs in more than 150 animals. None of his results were in published papers, however, and he performed all his work on local grants. He had never performed a human heart transplant before. After Baby Fae's death, Bailey indicated that he would use the information obtained from the case to conduct additional animal experiments. He never performed another xenograft, but did complete several successful allografts (human-to-human transplants).

NIH Report

In March of 1985, the National Institutes of Health released the report of a committee that had visited Loma Linda to review the Baby Fae case. The committee found that the informed-consent process was generally satisfactory, in that "the parents were given an appropriate and thorough explanation of the alternatives available, the risks and benefits of the procedure and the experimental

nature of the transplant." Moreover, consent was obtained in an "atmosphere which allowed the parents an opportunity to carefully consider, without coercion or undue influence, whether to give permission for the transplant."

The committee also pointed out certain flaws in the consent document. First, it "did not include the possibility of searching for a human heart or performing a human heart transplant." Second, the expected benefits of the procedure "appeared to be overstated," because the consent document "stated that 'long-term survival' is an expected possibility with no further explanation." Finally, the document did not discuss "whether compensation and medical treatment were available if injury occurred." Officials at Loma Linda University Medical Center promised that, before performing another such transplant, they would first seek a human infant heart donor.

As with other cases we have discussed, the Baby Fae story raises questions about the distinction between therapeutic and nontherapeutic research, and whether the latter is ever appropriate for children. (See this chapter's Briefing Session for more on this distinction.) Although Bailey claimed he always had a "therapeutic intent," critics have questioned whether he was ultimately more interested in performing a landmark research experiment.

BRIEFING SESSION

In 1947, an international tribunal meeting in Nuremberg, Germany, convicted fifteen Nazi physicians of "war crimes and crimes against humanity." The physicians were charged with taking part in "medical experiments without the subjects' consent." But the language of the charge fails to indicate the cruel and barbaric nature of the experiments:

- At the Ravensbrueck concentration camp, experiments were conducted to test the therapeutic powers of the drug sulfanilamide. Cuts were deliberately made on the bodies of prisoners; then the wounds were infected with bacteria. The infection was aggravated by forcing wood shavings and ground glass into the cuts. Then sulfanilamide and other drugs were tested for their effectiveness in combating the infection.

- At the Dachau concentration camp, healthy inmates were injected with extracts from the mucous glands of mosquitoes to produce malaria. Various drugs were then used to determine their relative effectiveness.

- At Buchenwald, numerous healthy prisoners were deliberately infected with the spotted-fever virus merely for the purpose of keeping the virus alive. Over 90 percent of those infected died as a result.

- Also at Buchenwald, various kinds of poisons were secretly administered to a number of inmates to test their efficacy. The inmates either died or they were immediately killed so that autopsies could be performed. Some experimental subjects were shot with poisoned bullets.

- At Dachau, to help the German air force, investigations were made into the limits of human endurance and survival at high altitudes. Prisoners were placed in sealed chambers and subjected to very high and very low atmospheric pressures. As the indictment puts it, "Many victims died as a result of these experiments and others suffered grave injury, torture, and ill-treatment."

The Nuremberg "doctors trial" only represented a portion of the medical experimentation carried out by the Nazi regime, with its widespread focus on eugenics and "racial hygiene." For example, it did not attempt to address the notorious experiments of Josef Mengele, a physician with a doctorate in genetics who also handled the "selection" process at the Auschwitz concentration camp that sent hundreds of thousands to their deaths in the gas chambers. (Mengele was in hiding at the time of the Nuremberg trials and eventually escaped to South America.) At Auschwitz, Mengele and his staff conducted experiments that included deliberate infection with typhus, unnecessary amputations and transfusions, ocular injections to try to change eye color, and routine murder for the sake of autopsies and dissections. (In one of his most notorious experiments, Mengele reportedly sewed a pair of twins together to see if he could make them conjoined.) Also at Auschwitz, physicians performed thousands of sterilization experiments, many involving radiation, chemical douches, or castration; indeed, forced sterilization was a pervasive hallmark of the Third Reich's emphasis on genetic purity.

Although the "doctors trial" at Nuremberg discussed only part of the Nazi regime's medical crimes, it marked a new era in accountability for such misconduct. Seven of the convicted Nuremberg physicians were hanged, and another eight received long prison terms. From the trial there emerged the "Nuremberg Code," a statement of the principles to be followed in conducting medical research with human subjects.

Despite the moral horrors that were revealed at Nuremberg, few people doubt the need for medical research involving human subjects. The extent to which contemporary medicine has become effective in the treatment of disease and illness is due almost entirely to the fact that it has become scientific. This means that contemporary medicine must conduct inquiries in which data are gathered to test hypotheses and general theories related to disease processes and their treatment. Investigations involving nonhuman organisms are essential to this process, but the ultimate tests of the effectiveness of medical treatments and their side effects must involve human research subjects. Human physiology and psychology are sufficiently distinctive to make animal studies inadequate on their own.

The German physicians tried at Nuremberg were charged with conducting experiments without the consent of their subjects. The notion that consent must be given before a person becomes a research subject is still considered the most basic requirement that must be met for an experiment to be morally legitimate. Moreover, it is not merely consent—saying yes—but *informed consent* that is demanded. Informed consent requires that a person's decision to participate in research is made only after he or she has been provided with the background information.

This notion of informed consent is also a requirement that must be satisfied before a person can legitimately be subjected to medical treatment. Thus, people are asked to formally consent to such ordinary medical procedures as blood transfusions, as well as to more complex interventions such as organ transplants or radiation therapy.

The underlying idea of informed consent in both research and treatment is that people have a right to control what is done to their bodies. The notion of informed consent is thus a recognition of an individual's autonomy—of the right to make decisions governing one's own life. This right is recognized both in practice and in the laws of our society. (Quite often, malpractice suits turn on the issue of whether a patient's informed consent was valid.)

In the abstract, informed consent seems a clear and straightforward notion. After all, we all have an intuitive grasp of what it is to make a decision after we have been supplied with relevant information. Yet, in practice, informed consent has proved to be a slippery and troublesome concept. We will identify later some of the moral and practical issues that can make the application of the concept particularly difficult and controversial.

Our focus in this chapter will be on informed consent in the context of research involving human subjects. But most of the issues that arise here also arise in connection with giving and securing informed consent for the application of medical therapies. (They also arise in special forms in practices such as abortion and euthanasia.)

Before discussing the details of informed consent, however, it will be useful to have an idea of what takes place in a typical clinical trial—one of the most common settings in which the concept is applied. Clinical trials account for the great majority of all medical research involving human subjects.

CLINICAL TRIAL PHASES

Testing a new drug, surgical procedure, or other therapy takes place in the sequence of phases that follows. Animal testing, when appropriate, is done before human studies begin, although additional animal testing may be performed parallel to research on humans.

Phase I: Investigators test the therapy in a small number of people (10–80) to evaluate its safety, identify its side effects, and (if a drug) determine the range of a safe dose. Testing the effectiveness of the therapy is not the aim of the trial.

Phase II: Investigators test the treatment in a larger group of people (100–300) to determine whether the therapy is effective and to further test its safety. Both effectiveness and safety are usually measured statistically.

Phase III: Investigators test the therapy in a significantly larger number of people (1,000–3,000) to confirm its effectiveness, monitor its side effects, and compare it with accepted therapies. Investigators also collect data that may be relevant to improving the therapy or increasing its safety.

Phase IV: Investigators collect data about the therapy's effects after the therapy has become established as a standard treatment. The aim is to refine the use of the therapy and improve its safety.

Clinical Trials

The United States spends over $100 billion per year on medical research, and a large proportion of the money goes to fund clinical trials. A clinical trial is a form of research in which the effectiveness and side effects of a treatment are tested by administering it to human subjects. The treatment may be a drug, surgical procedure, special diet, medical device, or even a form of behavior, such as getting out of bed or listening to music. The most common clinical trials are those in which the effectiveness of a new drug is tested, so we will now discuss briefly just what this involves.

Traditions of medical research and the regulations of the U.S. Food and Drug Administration typically require that the development of new drugs follows a set procedure. The procedure consists of two major parts: *preclinical* and *clinical testing*. When investigators think that a particular chemical compound might be useful in treating a particular disorder, they conduct animal experiments to determine how toxic it is. They use these tests to estimate the drug's *therapeutic index* (the ratio of a dose producing toxic effects to a dose producing desired effects). The effects of the substance on particular organs and tissues, as well as on the whole animal and its behavior, are also studied. In addition, the investigators make an effort to determine the drug's potential side effects and hazards. (Does it produce liver or kidney damage? Is it carcinogenic? Does it cause heart arrhythmias?) If a drug shows promise in animal testing and if its side effects are acceptable, it is then tested on humans in randomized clinical trials.

Clinical testing of the substance occurs in three phases. In Phase I, healthy human volunteers are used to determine whether the drug can be tolerated and whether its side effects are acceptable. If it causes serious *adverse events* (e.g., severe headaches, rashes, anemia, or a suppressed immune response), it may be too dangerous to give to people. The aim of a Phase I trial is to answer questions about safety and side effects, not to determine whether the drug is effective.

In a Phase II trial, the drug is administered to a limited number of patients who might be expected to benefit from it. If the drug produces desirable results and causes no serious side effects, then Phase III studies are initiated.

In Phase III, the drug is administered to a larger number of patients by (typically) a larger number of clinical investigators. Such multicenter trials usually take place at teaching hospitals or in large public institutions, although, like earlier phase trials, they are often sponsored by the drug's manufacturer. Successful results achieved in this phase ordinarily lead to the licensing of the drug for general use. If this happens, a Phase IV study may be conducted to gather more data about the drug and determine whether it is more effective—or perhaps more dangerous—for certain types of patients.

In the clinical part of testing, careful procedures must be followed to attempt to exclude bias in the results. Investigators want their tests to be successful and patients want to get well, and either or both of these factors may influence test results. Investigators may perceive a patient as "improved" because they want or expect him to be. Furthermore, medications themselves may produce a *placebo effect*. That is, when patients are given inactive substances (placebos), they nevertheless may show improvement. Their hopes and expectations may affect how their bodies respond and how they feel. (In one pain-relief study, for example, patients responded better to a placebo they were told cost $2.50 a pill than to one said to cost $0.10.)

To rule out these kinds of influences, a common procedure followed in clinical trials is the *double-blind* test design. In the classic version of this design, a certain number of patients are given the drug being tested and the remainder of the test group is given placebos. Patients are assigned to the treatment group or the placebo group in a random fashion (e.g., by the flip of a coin or a computer algorithm). Neither the investigators nor the patients are allowed to know who is receiving the drug and who is not—both are kept "blind." The two groups are often referred to as the *arms* of the study. (A variant of the double-blind trial is a trial with *three arms*: part of the test group gets placebos all of the time, part gets them only some of the time, and part gets genuine medication all of the time. Another variation is the "single blind" study, in which researchers, but not subjects, know who receives the new treatment and who does not.)

Placebos may be no more than sugar pills. Yet, frequently, substances are prepared to produce side effects that resemble those of the drug being tested. If, for example, the drug causes drowsiness, a placebo will be used that produces drowsiness. In this way, investigators will not be able to learn, on the basis of irrelevant observations, which patients are being given placebos.

In recent decades, clinical trials involving placebos are often designed so that a patient with a serious medical problem is never given only a placebo. Rather, patients in one group are given a placebo *plus* a drug established as effective, while those in another group are given the established drug *plus* an experimental drug. The established drug represents the *standard of care* and the aim of the trial is to determine whether the new drug is more effective than the old. In this design, no patient is denied the standard of care—that is, the best available treatment.

Such approaches are often seen to derive from the principle of *clinical equipoise,* which demands that there be genuine uncertainty in the expert medical community about whether one of the interventions being compared is superior to the others. The requirement of clinical equipoise is rooted in the notion that researchers should not knowingly disadvantage subjects in any arm of a study. Critics of the equipoise principle argue that it confuses therapeutic ethics with research ethics. They insist that researchers have no obligation to promote the best interests of research subjects, but only to serve the broader public good.

The theoretical issue of clinical equipoise remains unsettled, but in 2008, the FDA dropped the requirement that clinical trials compare a new drug with one recognized as the most effective currently available. This allows the pharmaceutical and biotech industries, which conduct the vast majority of clinical trials, to study their new drugs and interventions against placebos. Critics have charged that by dropping the old requirement, the FDA is failing to provide the most effective protection for patients who volunteer to participate in studies. Other critics argue that allowing placebo comparison facilitates the approval of "me-too" drugs, which differ only slightly from established drugs whose patents have expired. (Me-too drugs can then be marketed as new brand-name drugs, which are typically far more expensive than generic, off-patent drugs.)

Randomized clinical trials are typically referred to as constituting the "gold standard" of medical research. The double-blind test design is employed in many kinds of clinical investigations, not just in drug testing. Thus, the testing of new vaccines and even surgeries often follows the same procedure, and a treatment or drug that has not gone through the process of such a trial is often regarded with suspicion or considered unproven. Some critics consider this view too extreme and point to cases in which decades or even centuries of experience have shown certain treatments to be effective.

Clinical trials may also fail to establish a treatment as effective for a whole population if those who participated as subjects failed to represent the population. Thus, if the subjects in a clinical trial for prostate cancer are predominately men in their fifties, a treatment shown to be effective might not work for men in their seventies. Similarly, if 90 percent of the participants in a trial were adult women, the results may not apply to men or children. Clinical trials—even those that are well designed—don't always produce trustworthy results, unless they include very large and diverse groups of participants.

The "Informed" Part of Informed Consent

Consent, at first glance, is no more than agreement. A person consents when he or she says "yes" when asked to become a research subject. But legitimate or valid consent cannot be merely saying yes. If people are to be treated as autonomous agents, they must have the opportunity to *decide* whether they wish to become participants in research.

Deciding, whatever else it may be, is a process in which we reason about an issue at hand. We consider such matters as the risks of our participation, its possible advantages to ourselves and others, the risks and advantages of other alternatives that are offered to us, and our own values. In short, valid consent requires that we *deliberate* before we decide.

But genuine deliberation requires both information and understanding. These two requirements are a source of difficulties and controversies. After all, medical research and treatment are highly technical enterprises. They are based on complicated scientific theories that are expressed in a special vocabulary and involve unfamiliar concepts.

For this reason, some physicians and investigators have argued that it is virtually useless to provide patients with relevant scientific information about research and treatment. Patients without the proper scientific background, they argue, simply don't know what to make of the information. Not only do patients find it puzzling, but they may also find it frightening. Thus, some have suggested, informed consent is at worst a pointless charade and at best a polite fiction. The patient's interest is best served by allowing a physician to make the decision.

This clearly paternalistic point of view (see Chapter 1) implies, in effect, that all patients are incompetent to determine their best interest and that physicians must assume the responsibility of acting for them.

One immediate objection to this view is its assumption that, because patients lack a medical background, they cannot be given information in a form they can understand— one that is at least adequate to allow them to decide how they are to be treated. Thus, proponents of this view confuse difficulty of communication with impossibility of communication. While it is true that it is often hard for physicians to explain technical medical matters to a layperson, this hardly makes it legitimate for them to disregard patient autonomy. Rather, it imposes on physicians and researchers the obligation to find a way to explain medical matters to their patients in a comprehensible form.

The information provided to patients must be usable. That is, patients must understand enough about the proposed research and treatment to deliberate and reach a decision. From the standpoint of the researcher, the problem here is to determine when the patient has sufficient understanding to make informed consent valid. Patients, like other people, are often reluctant to acknowledge when they don't understand an explanation. Also, they may believe that they understand a physician's meaning when, in fact, they do not.

Until recently, little effort was made to deal with the problem of determining when a patient understands the information provided and is competent to assess it. In the last few years, researchers have investigated situations in which individuals have been asked to consent to become research subjects. Drawing upon these data, some writers have attempted to formulate criteria for assessing competency for giving informed consent. The complicated nature of this problem is still resistant to ideal solutions, but with additional empirical investigation and philosophical analysis, practical strategies to address the problem may be developed.

The "Consent" Part of Informed Consent

We have spoken thus far as if the issue of gaining someone's legitimate agreement to be a research subject or patient involves only providing information to an ordinary person in ordinary circumstances and then allowing the person to decide. But the matter is more complicated than this, because often either the person or the circumstances possess special features. These features can call into question the very possibility of valid consent.

It is generally agreed that consent, in order to be valid, must be voluntary. The person must of his or her "own free will" agree to become a research subject. This means that the person must be capable of acting voluntarily. In other words, the person must be *competent*.

This is an obvious and straightforward requirement accepted by almost all contemporary societies. But the difficulty lies in specifying just what it means to be competent. One answer is that a person is competent if he or she is capable of acting rationally. Because we have some idea of what it is to act rationally, this might seem to bring us closer to a definition.

The problem, however, is that people sometimes decide to act for the sake of moral (or religious) principles in ways that may not seem reasonable to others. For example, someone may volunteer to be a subject in a potentially hazardous experiment because she believes the experiment holds out the promise of helping countless others. In terms of self-interest alone, such an action would not be reasonable.

Vulnerable Populations

Even in the best of circumstances, it is not always easy to determine who is competent to consent and who is not. Yet researchers and ethicists must also face the issue of how to approach consent with respect to children, the mentally impaired, prisoners, and those suffering from psychiatric illnesses.

Should no one in any of these vulnerable populations be considered capable of giving consent? If so, then is it ever legitimate to secure consent from some third party, such as a parent or legal guardian?

One possibility is simply to rule out all research that involves such people as subjects. But this has the undesirable consequence of severely hampering efforts to gain the knowledge that might be of use either to the people themselves or to others in a similar condition. Later in this chapter we will consider some of the special problems that arise with children and other vulnerable groups as research subjects.

The circumstances in which research is conducted can also call into question the voluntariness of consent. This is particularly so with research conducted in prisons, nursing homes, and mental hospitals. These are all what the sociologist Erving Goffman called "total institutions," for within them, all aspects of a person's life are connected with the social structure. People have a definite place

---

FDA REGULATIONS

1906   **Pure Food and Drug Act:** Makes it illegal to sell adulterated or mislabeled medicines.

1938   **Food, Drug, and Cosmetics Act (FDCA):** Requires the FDA to test drugs for safety. The FDCA was prompted by deaths and illnesses caused by a pharmaceutical company's distribution of an elixir of acetaminophen that used diethylene glycol, an ingredient in antifreeze, as the flavoring syrup.

1962   **Kefauver–Harris Amendment to the FDCA:** Requires pharmaceutical companies to present data to the FDA demonstrating the effectiveness of a drug and gives the FDA the power to regulate clinical trials. The amendment was prompted by the 1960 refusal of Frances Kelsey, an FDA physician–pharmacologist, to approve the drug thalidomide on the basis of the safety data submitted by the manufacturer. Thalidomide had been approved in forty-two European countries as an antinausea agent and sedative, and prescribed widely to pregnant women to treat morning sickness. The drug turned out to produce severe arm and leg deformities, gum anomalies, and undeveloped ear canals in children born to women who had taken the drug. The United States was spared the epidemic.

1987   **FDA "compassionate use" and "expanded access" program:** Allows doctors to provide drugs that have completed Phase II clinical trials to patients who are too debilitated to participate in clinical trials or too far away from a center conducting a trial. The program was championed by AIDS activists who argued that people with AIDS not in clinical trials should not be denied access to potentially lifesaving drugs. At the time, no effective treatment for AIDS was available.

and particular social roles in the structure. Moreover, there are social forces at work that both pressure and encourage an inmate to do what is expected of him or her.

Elsewhere in this chapter, we discuss some of the special problems that arise in research with prisoners. Here we need only point out that gaining voluntary consent from inmates in institutions may not be possible, even in principle. If it is possible, these individuals still require safeguards to protect them from the inherent pressures associated with being inmates. Those who suffer from psychiatric illnesses may be considered capable of giving consent to research, but here too safeguards to protect them from institutional and other pressures need to be specified.

In recent years, researchers have expanded the testing of new drugs and drug regimens into developing countries. The citizens of these countries often have a limited education in biomedical science and may lack the medical sophistication of their counterparts in industrialized nations. They may also be more likely to trust that what they are asked to do by medical authorities will be in their best interest. Hence, securing genuine informed consent from them presents particular difficulties.

It is important to keep in mind that ordinary patients in hospitals may also be subject to pressures that call into question the voluntariness of the consent that they provide. Patients are often psychologically predisposed to act in ways that please physicians. Not only are physicians often considered figures of authority, but an ill person feels particularly dependent on those who may possess the power to make her well.

The ordinary patient, like the inmate in an institution, needs protection from the social and psychological pressures that are exerted by circumstances. Otherwise, the voluntariness of consent will be compromised, and the patient cannot act as a free and autonomous agent.

Medical Research and Medical Therapy

Medical therapy aims to relieve people's suffering and restore them to health. It attempts to cure diseases, correct disorders, and improve bodily functioning. Its focus is on the individual patient, and his or her welfare is its primary concern.

Medical research, by contrast, is a scientific enterprise. Its aim is to acquire a better understanding of the biochemical and physiological processes involved in human functioning. It is concerned with the effectiveness of therapies in ending disease processes and restoring functioning. But this concern is not for the patient as an individual. Rather it is directed toward establishing biomedical theories. The hope, of course, is that this theoretical understanding can be used as a basis for treating individuals. But helping individual patients get well is not a goal of medical research.

The related but distinct objectives of medical research and medical therapy are a source of conflict in human subjects research. It is not unusual for a physician to be acting both as a researcher and as a therapist. This means that although she must be concerned with the welfare of her patient, her goals must also include acquiring data that are important to her research project. It is possible, then, that she may, quite unconsciously, encourage her patients to volunteer to be research subjects, provide them with inadequate information for medical decision-making, or minimize the risks to which they are likely to be subject.

Medical research is a large-scale operation around the world and affects a great many people. It has been estimated that as many as 2.2 million people a year are involved in clinical trials. Since 1980, the number of clinical studies each year has increased more than 30 percent. Under these circumstances, informed consent is more than an abstract moral issue.

The competing aims of therapy and research may also cause moral difficulties for the physician that go beyond the question of consent. This is particularly so for certain kinds of research, which we will now examine in greater detail.

Investigators and Financial Conflict

The case of Jesse Gelsinger, who died in a clinical trial of gene therapy, raises serious questions about ulterior motives researchers may have had to disregard safety standards—in part because they were major stockholders in a biotech company sponsoring the research. (See Case Presentation: Jesse Gelsinger in this chapter for more details.) Similarly, the failure of the trial and testing process to identify risks associated with Vioxx and the ASR hip implant has been widely attributed to the shareholder-focused agendas of the research sponsors. (See Case Presentation: Do Research Sponsors Suppress Bad News?)

Private industry now sponsors more than 58 percent of biomedical research, compared to the 33 percent sponsored by government. (In the 1980s, these proportions were roughly reversed.) Private industry supports academic research to the tune of about $3.2 billion a year and one study of 50 leading research universities found that private industry covers roughly 30 percent of their research budgets. Such sponsors are typically pharmaceutical, medical-device, and biotech companies that expect to profit from patents based on the research.

It is not unusual, as was the case with the researcher conducting Jesse Gelsinger's trial, for an investigator to have a financial stake in the outcome of medical research. The stake may be slight or, when the investigator is a major shareholder in the company sponsoring the research, it may be significant.

A 2007 study found that 28 percent of physicians have received payments from industry for research or consulting and that 83 percent of them had received gifts from biomedical companies. Another study showed that one-fifth to one-third of all physicians providing patient care in clinical trials had financial ties to drug or device makers. Some were paid to be speakers (at fees ranging from $250 to $20,000 a year), while 32 percent of them held positions on the company's advisory committee or board of directors.

An investigator who stands to earn a considerable sum of money from the success of the clinical trial he is conducting has a clear conflict of interest. He may (even quite unconsciously) minimize the risks of participating when seeking the consent of a volunteer. Or he may be inclined to delay reporting adverse events associated with the trial to a regulatory agency or institutional review board (IRB), to avoid having the agency or IRB halt the study. He may also be prone to overestimating the value of the treatment or device being tested. A 2003 meta-analysis published in *JAMA* found that industry-sponsored studies were 3.6 times more likely to produce results favorable to the sponsor than those that were publicly funded.

Federal agencies and the IRBs of most institutions now require investigators to reveal whether they have a financial stake in the outcome of the research. Yet having such a stake does not automatically disqualify an investigator from conducting the research, and IRBs typically work to accommodate the interest of the investigator.

A 2009 study by the Department of Health and Human Services found that 90 percent of universities relied completely on researchers themselves to decide whether the money they earned as private consultants constituted a potential conflict of interest with respect to their research on behalf of the public. Also, almost half of the universities didn't require researchers to disclose the amount of money they were paid. Yet in the absence of such information, it is hard to determine the extent of an investigator's personal stake in the outcome of the research.

When research is funded privately, rather than by federal grants, institutions may not require disclosure to potential participants that the investigator has a financial interest in the research. Further, even when investigators are required to reveal a potential conflict of interest, the consequences for failure to do so often consist only of a notice of violation or a warning letter. Many universities do not see it as in their interest to press researchers to avoid conflicts of interest. Even if a university does not stand to make money from research projects, increased ethical restrictions on its leading researchers may prompt these scientists to take jobs elsewhere or leave academia to start their own companies.

Because more and more investigators are acquiring a financial stake in the results of their research, there is growing consensus about the need to develop national regulations for avoiding financial conflicts of interest and effective mechanisms for enforcing the regulations. It may not be wise to completely forbid researchers from profiting financially from the success of their research, but the practice does raise serious questions that must be addressed.

Placebos and Research

As we saw above, placebos are sometimes considered essential to determine the true effectiveness of a drug or other treatment being tested. In practice, this means that during all or some of the time they are being "treated," some patients who are also subjects in a research program will not be receiving genuine medication. They will not, then, receive the best available treatment for their specific condition.

This is one of the risks that a patient needs to know about before consenting to become a research subject. After all,

most people consult physicians in order to be cured of their ailments, not to further science. The physician-as-therapist seeks to provide appropriate medical care to patients, in accordance with her professional obligations. But the physician-as-researcher will know that a certain number of patients will be receiving a treatment that cannot be expected to help their condition. Thus, medical and research objectives can again come into conflict.

This conflict is particularly severe for cases in which it is reasonable to believe (on the basis of animal experimentation or in vitro research, for example) that an effective disease preventative exists, yet scientific rigor may require the use of placebos.

Such was the case with the development of a polio vaccine by Thomas Weller, John F. Enders, and Frederick C. Robbins in 1960. The initial phase of the clinical testing involved injecting thirty thousand children with a substance known to be useless in the prevention of polio—a placebo injection. The researchers realized that some of those children would, most likely, get polio and die from it.

Since Weller, Enders, and Robbins believed they had an effective vaccine, they can hardly be regarded as acting in the best interests of the children who received the placebo. But they succeeded in proving the safety and effectiveness of the polio vaccine. The moral question is whether they were justified in failing to provide thirty thousand children with a vaccine they believed to be effective, even though it had not been widely tested on humans. That is, did they correctly resolve the conflict between their roles as researchers and their roles as physicians?

Placebos also present physician–researchers with a different dilemma. As we noted in the earlier discussion, placebos are not always just "sugar pills." They often contain active ingredients that produce effects that resemble those caused by the medication being tested—nervousness, vomiting, loss of appetite, and so on. This means that a patient getting a placebo not only fails to receive any medication for his illness, but also receives a substance that may do him some harm. Do the aims of scientific research and its potential benefits to others justify treating patients in this fashion?

As discussed above, one way to avoid the moral dilemmas posed by placebos is for researchers to compare a standard treatment whose effectiveness is known to a new treatment with possible but unproven effectiveness. Although the control arm of such studies lacks the scientific clarity of that in a placebo trial, this approach is often seen to present fewer ethical difficulties and to uphold the principle of equipoise.

Nevertheless, this way of proceeding is associated with yet another moral question. If early statistical results indicate that the treatment being tested is more effective than the standard of care being used for comparison, should the trial be stopped so that all the patients in the study can gain the benefits of the test drug? Or does the informed consent of the participants warrant continuing the trial until the therapeutic value of the test drug is fully established? Many ethicists argue that if the evidence strongly indicates that a treatment being tested is more effective than the standard one, researchers have an obligation to discontinue the trial and offer the new treatment to all participants.

Therapeutic and Nontherapeutic Research

Some research holds out the possibility of a direct and immediate advantage to those patients who agree to become subjects. A new drug may, on the basis of limited trials, promise to be more effective in treating an illness than drugs in standard use. Or a new surgical procedure may turn out

to give better results than one that would ordinarily be used. By agreeing to participate in research involving such a drug or procedure, a patient may have a chance of obtaining medical benefits she would not otherwise receive.

Yet the majority of medical research projects do not offer any direct therapeutic advantages to patients who consent to be subjects. The research may eventually benefit many patients, but seldom does it bring more than minor therapeutic benefit to research participants. Ordinarily, the most that participants can expect to gain are the advantages of having the attention of physicians who are experts on their illness and receiving close observation and supervision from researchers.

Some patients do not even receive this much advantage. Pharmaceutical companies may pay physicians in private practice to conduct a study of a drug they manufacture in order to get the physician to prescribe the drug more frequently. Such studies are often poorly designed, with an insufficient number of participants for statistical significance, and they are rarely published. The physician gets paid and the company advances its marketing goals, but the patient is unlikely to benefit. Indeed, the patient may not even get the drug that is best for her.

A responsible investigator ought to present such risks and limitations to patients who contemplate participating in a trial. The patient must then decide whether he or she is willing to become a participant, even if there are serious risks involved and no special therapeutic advantages to be gained. It is in making this decision that a patient's moral beliefs may play a role. Some people volunteer to become research subjects without hope of reward because they believe that their action may eventually be beneficial to others. (For an example, see Case Presentation: Jesse Gelsinger earlier in this chapter.)

Medical Research in a Pluralistic Society

Developing a practice of medical research that both reflects and serves a globalized society, in all its complexity and diversity, is one of the great moral challenges of our time. In many different societies, medical research has tended to embody the injustices and asymmetries that have shaped the world around it, uncritically reflecting its prejudices and assumptions. The relationship between personal and social identity and the practice of both research and therapeutic medicine is a large and contested topic, one that we address in greater detail in Chapters 10 and 11 of this text. But our discussion of medical research ethics would be incomplete without a brief discussion of some of the topics that we will address more thoroughly in those chapters.

Medical Research and Identity

This chapter's Case Presentation on Henrietta Lacks provides a brief overview of the complicated dynamic between racial categories and research medicine. It touches on some of the ways that American medical research worked in concert with the institutions of slavery and Jim Crow, and adopted paternalistic practices that generated mistrust and fear in families such as the Lackses and in the African American community more generally. Such paternalism was often accompanied by a pseudoscience of race and ethnicity, one that aimed to justify social arrangements such as slavery and segregation on the grounds of the supposed inferiority of African Americans and other ethnic groupings. When African Americans and other non-white groups were included in clinical research, it was often conducted in a transparently biased fashion, aimed at affirming racial or ethnic inferiority and difference. (Similar research projects were conducted by the Nazi doctors to establish the racial inferiority of Jews, gypsies, and other groups.) The idea that race itself reflects anything more than a political and social category is still a highly controversial notion, a problem that informs the debate over "race-based" medical treatments such as BiDil.

Perhaps no single incident in the history of race and medicine in the United States has more ongoing resonance than the Tuskegee syphilis study, conducted under the auspices of the U.S. Department of Public Health (USPH). From 1932 to 1970, hundreds of African American men suffering from the later stages of syphilis were studied at regular intervals to track the course of the disease. The men in the study were poor, with little formal education, and believed that they were receiving proper medical care from the state and local public health clinics.

In fact, they were given either no treatment or inadequate treatment, and at least forty of them died as a result of factors connected with syphilis. Their consent was never obtained, and the nature of the study, its risks, and the alternatives open to them were never explained. It was well known when the study began that those with untreated syphilis have a higher death rate than those whose condition is treated. Although the study was started before the advent of penicillin (which is highly effective against syphilis), other drugs were available and were not used or used improperly. When penicillin did become widely available, it still was not employed to treat the men's deteriorating condition.

The Tuskegee study clearly violated the Nuremberg Code, but it was not stopped even after the 1947 "doctors trial." The study was finally reviewed in 1969 by a USPH ad hoc committee, and it was decided that the research should be phased out. The reasons for ending the experiment were not moral ones. Rather, it was concluded that little information of scientific value could be obtained by continuing the study. In 1973, a USPH advisory panel, which had been established as a result of public and congressional pressure, presented its final report on the Tuskegee study. It condemned the study both on moral grounds and because of its lack of scientific value and rigor. (See Case Presentation: The Tuskegee Syphilis Study in Chapter 10 as well as Case Presentation: STD Research in Guatemala for more information.)

* * *

As we will see in subsequent chapters, gender, no less than race, has often played a pivotal and controversial role in medical research. Feminist critics have long noted a tendency to approach women as an exotic and specialized subject of medical research and practice, rather than half the human population. Similarly, a pseudoscience of sex and gender often helped justify unequal social arrangements on the grounds that women were less rational, more animalistic, and more burdened by their reproductive systems than men. Such specious claims were not entirely surprising, given that medical research traditionally failed to include women as experimental subjects, even when women might stand to benefit from the results.

As recently as 1993, women of childbearing age were banned by the FDA from participation in clinical trial research. As a result, many of the landmark studies of the twentieth century are reflective of male physiology in ways that may not be fully applicable to women. A famous study showing the effectiveness of small doses of aspirin in reducing the risk of heart attack, for instance, was called into question when it was pointed out that all 22,071 of the subjects were men. Subsequent analysis could not reproduce the same effect in women and left the FDA "with doubts about whether aspirin was, in fact, effective in women for these indications."

In the past two decades, research has shown that women and men respond differently to a wide range of treatments, from sleeping pills to anesthesia, and that safe dosing levels can differ dramatically by sex. As a result, the FDA has taken steps to address some of these differences. It recently approved a recommended dosage of the sleeping aid zolpidem that is twice as high for men as for women, after research showed men metabolize the drug twice as fast as women do. Differential reactions to antibiotics, antimalarials, and cholesterol-lowering drugs are also being reflected in medical research and practice, but many believe that women still face a disproportionate share of adverse side effects because of a traditional research model based on the male body. Conducting medical research that serves and reflects over half of the human population is a relatively obvious imperative of social fairness, but its connection with informed consent is perhaps more subtle. Contemporary scientific medicine is still shaped by the fact that it developed as an almost exclusively male profession, and that many of its most paternalistic practices were directed at female patients assumed to be hysterical, irrational, or suffering from hypochondria. Many of those practices effectively robbed women of their autonomy in medical decision-making, and thus their informed consent. As we will see in Chapter 10, there is a still a lively debate about how medical research might better address the specific social and physiological conditions that affect women and men.

* * *

Just as one sex has often served as the standard for the pursuit of biomedical research, so too has one form of sexuality. It was not until 1973 that the American Psychiatric Association voted to remove homosexuality from its *Diagnostic and Statistical Manual of Mental Disorders* (*DSM*), which it had previously listed as a "socio-pathic personality disturbance." The history of medical research is marked by repeated efforts to "treat" non-heterosexual people for same-sex attractions, often with brutal techniques such as electroshock therapy and castration. As with race and gender, homosexuality also generated a pseudoscientific research literature that attempted to link gays and lesbians to criminality, promiscuity, and other social ills, with little empirical justification. (Such claims were another eugenic preoccupation of Nazis, who sterilized and experimented upon large numbers of gay men and lesbians, and murdered tens of thousands of them in concentration camps.)

Even today, with same-sex marriage legalized across the country, there is still ongoing debate over licensure for "conversion therapy" practices, which are premised on the possibility (and desirability) of converting homosexual orientations into heterosexual ones. There is also debate over surgeries to "normalize" infants with atypical genitalia and other physiological markers of sex, on the assumption that *intersexuality* is a medical illness that must be cured. A similar debate is taking place over efforts to pin down or reverse gender identity, particularly as it relates to those who do not fit into traditional gender categories or who have a *transgender* social identity.

* * *

The preceding discussion demonstrates how biomedical definitions of human and subhuman, normal and abnormal, health and sickness, have shifted over time. It shows how these divisions can be quite arbitrary and may reflect existing social and political arrangements as much as objective scientific categories. This insight is one of the primary starting points of the *disability rights movement*, which argues that the division between ability and disability is arbitrary and contextual, and that most humans are only

temporarily "able-bodied."

It also informs critiques of the *DSM* and other efforts to define mental health and mental illness. In Chapter 10, we will explore this problem of shifting biomedical categories as it relates to both therapeutic and research medicine in a pluralistic society.

In the rest of the current chapter, we will focus on a number of other categories that ethicists have traditionally agreed upon as requiring special care and attention in the pursuit of medical research. Many constitute *vulnerable populations,* such as children or the incarcerated, or raise special ethical issues, such as human fetuses and animals. While the definitions of these categories are still subject to debate, there is broad consensus that medical researchers need to take special care when conducting research in these areas.

Research Involving Children

One of the most controversial areas of all medical research has been that involving children as subjects. The Willowbrook study discussed in this chapter's Case Presentation is one among many investigations that have drawn intense criticism and, quite often, court action.

Why Study Children at All? Why should children ever be made research subjects? Children clearly lack the physical, psychological, and intellectual maturity of adults. They are unlikely to be as capable as adults of giving informed consent, and they can hardly be expected to grasp the nature of the research and the possible risks they face.

Furthermore, because children have not yet developed their capacities, it seems wrong to subject them to risks that might alter the course of their lives for the worse. They are in a position of relative dependency, relying upon adults to provide the conditions for their existence and development. It could be construed as a betrayal of trust to allow children to be subjected to treatment that has potential to harm them.

Such considerations help explain why we typically regard research involving children with deep suspicion. It is easy to imagine children being exploited and harmed by callous researchers. Some writers have thus advocated an end to all research with children as subjects.

But there is another perspective on this issue. Biologically, children are not just small adults. Their bodies are developing, growing systems. Not only are they anatomically different from adults; there are also differences in metabolism and biochemistry. For example, some drugs are absorbed and metabolized much more quickly in children than in adults, whereas other drugs continue to be active for a longer time. Some drugs produce dramatically different effects when administered to children. Furthermore, children are prone to certain kinds of diseases (measles or mumps, for example) that either are less common in adults or occur in different forms. It is important to know the kinds of therapies that are most successful in the treatment of children with these conditions. Findings based on adult subjects cannot simply be extrapolated to children, any more than results based on animal studies can be extrapolated to human beings.

Children are also susceptible to a range of serious medical problems that are not seen in adults. Various heart anomalies, for example, must be corrected to keep children alive. Thus, they must be involved in the development of new surgical techniques for these conditions. Even familiar surgical procedures cannot be employed in a straightforward fashion with children. Their developing organ systems are sufficiently different that special pediatric techniques must often be devised. For many medical purposes, children must be approached as physiologically distinct from adults. To gain the kind of knowledge and understanding required for effective medical treatment of children, it is often impossible to limit research solely to adults.

Furthermore, if children were completely excluded from investigations, then the development of pediatric medicine would be severely hindered. For example, in the 1940s, the use of pure oxygen in incubators for prematurely born babies resulted in hundreds of cases of blindness and retinal impairment. It was not until a controlled study using infants was conducted that the retinal damage was traced to the effects of oxygen. Had the research not been allowed, chances are good that the practice would have continued and thousands more infants would have been blinded.

Ethical Issues.   Even if we agree that not all research involving children should be forbidden, we still must address the issues that such research generates. Without attempting a complete account, we can mention the following three issues as among the more prominent:

Who Is a Child? Who is to be considered a child? For infants and children in elementary school, this question is not a difficult one. But what about patients in their teens? Then the line becomes hard to draw and any cut-off may seem arbitrary.

The concern behind the question is with the acquisition of autonomy—of self-direction and responsibility. It is obvious on the basis of ordinary experience that people develop at different rates, and some at sixteen are more capable of taking charge of their own lives than others are at twenty. Some teenagers are more capable of understanding the nature and hazards of a research project than are many people who are much older.

This suggests that many individuals who are legally children may be quite capable of giving their informed consent. Of course, many others probably are not, so decisions about this capability would seem to rest on an assessment of the individual. Where medical procedures that have a purely therapeutic aim are concerned, an individual who is capable of identifying his or her best interest should probably be the one to decide. The issue may be somewhat different when the aim is research. In such cases, a better policy might be to set a lower limit on the age at which consent can be given, and those below that limit should not be permitted to participate. The problem is, of course, what should that limit be?

Parental Consent.   Can anyone else consent on behalf of a child? Parents or guardians have a duty to act for the welfare of a child in their care. In effect, they have a duty to substitute their judgment for that of the child. We generally agree to this because most often we consider the judgment of an adult more mature and informed than a child's. It is almost as though the adult's autonomy is being shared with the child—as though the child were an extension of the adult.

Still, society and its courts have recognized limits on the power of adults to decide for children. When it seems that the adult is acting in an irresponsible or unreasonable manner, society steps in to act as a protector of the child's interests. Thus, courts have ordered that lifesaving procedures or blood transfusions be performed on children even when their parents or guardians have decided against it. The criterion used in such judgments is "the best interest of the child."

What sort of limits should govern a parent's or guardian's decision to allow a child to become a research subject? Is it reasonable to believe that if a parent would allow herself to be the subject of research, then it is also right for her to consent to her child's becoming a subject? Or should something more be required before consent for a child's participation can be considered legitimate?

Therapeutic Benefits.   Perhaps the "something more" that parents or guardians ought to require before consenting on behalf of a child is the genuine possibility that the research will bring the child direct therapeutic benefit. This would seem to accord with a parent's duty to advance the welfare of the child. It is also a way of recognizing that the parent's autonomy is not identical with that of the child: one may have the right to take a risk oneself without having the right to impose the risk on someone else.

This seems like a reasonable limitation, and it has been advocated by some writers. Yet there are difficulties with the position. Some research that is virtually free from risk (coordination tests, for example) might be stopped because of its lack of a "direct therapeutic value."

More important, however, much research promising long-term benefits would have to be halted. Research frequently involves the withholding of accepted therapies without any guarantee that the experimental therapy will be as effective. Sometimes the withholding of accepted treatment is beneficial. Thus, in the research on the incidence of blindness in premature infants in the 1940s, it turned out that premature infants who were not kept in a pure oxygen environment were better off than those who received ordinary treatment. If such research had been prohibited because of its uncertain therapeutic value, the standard treatment would have continued with its ordinary course of harmful results.

By contrast, in research that involves the substitution of placebos for medications or vaccines that are acknowledged to be effective, researchers know in advance that some children will not receive medical care considered to be best. A child who participates in such research is then subjected to a definite hazard. The limitation on parental consent that we are considering would rule out such research. But the consequence of doing this would be to restrict the development of new and potentially more effective medications and treatment techniques.

These are merely a few of the issues that we face in determining an ethical approach to the role of children in research. Like other vulnerable populations, children may appeal to medical investigators as cooperative research subjects who are often accessible in relatively controlled environments such as schools and other institutions. It would be unfair to characterize such research as inherently exploitative, but at the same time, careful controls are needed to see that research involving children is legitimate and carried out in a morally appropriate manner.

Guidelines.   In response to some of these difficulties, the Department of Health and Human Services has issued guidelines designed specifically to protect children as research subjects. First, for children to become participants, permission must be obtained from parents or guardians, and children must give their "assent." Second, an institutional review board is assigned the responsibility of considering the "ages, maturity, and psychological states" of the children and determining whether they are capable of assenting. (A failure to object cannot be construed as assent.)

Third, children who are wards of the state or of an institution can become participants only if the research relates to their status as wards or takes place in circumstances in which the majority of subjects are not wards. Each child must also be supplied with a legal advocate to represent her or his interest.

Research Involving Prisoners

Prisoners are frequently treated as social outcasts. They have been found guilty of breaking the laws of society and, as a consequence, are removed from it. Stigmatized and isolated, prisoners have often been treated as if they were less than human. To some, it has seemed reasonable and fitting that they should be used as the subjects of experiments that might bring benefits to the members of the society that they have wronged.

Accordingly, in the early part of the twentieth century, tropical medicine expert Richard P. Strong obtained permission from the governor of the Philippines to inoculate a number of convicted criminals with plague bacillus. The prisoners were not asked for their consent, but they were rewarded by being provided with cigarettes and cigars. Similarly, U.S. public health researchers deliberately infected hundreds of Guatemalan prisoners with syphilis and gonorrhea during the 1940s, in a non-consensual study of STD transmission and treatment. (See Case Presentation: STD Research in Guatemala in Chapter 11.)

Episodes of this sort were relatively common during the late nineteenth and early twentieth centuries. But as theories about the nature of crime and criminals changed, it became standard practice, at least in most U.S. prisons, to use only volunteers and to secure the consent of the prisoners themselves.

In the 1940s, for example, the University of Chicago infected more than four hundred prisoners with malaria in an attempt to discover new drugs to treat and prevent the disease. A committee set up by the governor of Illinois recommended that potential volunteers be informed of the risks, be permitted to refuse without fear of such reprisals as withdrawal of privileges, and be protected from unnecessary suffering. The committee also suggested that volunteering to be a subject in a medical experiment be considered a form of good conduct that should be taken into account in deciding whether a prisoner should be paroled or have his sentence reduced.

But the committee also called attention to a problem of great moral significance. They pointed out that if a prisoner's motive for volunteering is the wish to contribute to human welfare, then a reduction in his sentence would be a reward. But if his motive is to obtain a reduction in sentence, then the possibility of obtaining such a reduction is really a form of duress. In this case, the prisoner cannot be regarded as making a free decision. The issue of duress, or "undue influence," as it is called in law, is central to the question of deciding whether and under what conditions valid informed consent can be obtained for research involving prisoners. Some ethicists have argued that, to avoid undue influence, prisoners should never be promised any substantial advantages for volunteering to be research subjects. If they volunteer, they should do so for primarily moral or humane reasons.

Others have claimed that becoming research subjects offers prisoners personal advantages that they should not be denied. For example, participation in a research project frees them from the boredom of prison life, gives them an opportunity to enhance their sense of self-worth, and allows them to exercise their autonomy as moral agents. It has been argued, in fact, that prisoners have a right to participate in research if the opportunity is offered to them and they wish to do so. To forbid the use of prisoners as research subjects is thus to deny to them, without adequate grounds, a right that other citizens possess. As a denial of their basic autonomy—of their right to take risks and control their own bodies—prohibiting their participation might constitute a form of cruel and unusual punishment.

By contrast, it can also be argued that prisoners do not deserve to be allowed to exercise such autonomy. Because they have been sentenced for crimes against society, they should be deprived of the right to volunteer to be research subjects: that right belongs to free citizens. Being deprived of the right to act autonomously is part of their punishment. This is the position taken by the House of Delegates of the American Medical Association. The delegates passed a resolution in 1952 expressing disapproval of the use as research subjects of people convicted of "murder, rape, arson, kidnapping, treason, and other heinous crimes."

A more worrisome consideration is the question of whether prisoners can be sufficiently free of undue influence or duress to make their consent legitimate. As we mentioned earlier, prisons are total institutions and the institutional framework itself puts pressures on people to do what is desired or expected of them. There need not be either promises of rewards (such as reduced sentences) or overt threats (such as withdrawal of ordinary privileges) for coercion to be present. That people may volunteer to relieve boredom is itself an indication that they may be acting under duress. That "good conduct" is a factor in deciding whether to grant parole may function as another source of pressure.

The problem presented by prisoners is fundamentally the same as that presented by inmates in other institutions, such as nursing homes and mental hospitals. In all these cases, once it has been determined that potential subjects are mentally competent to give consent, then it must also be decided whether the institutional arrangements allow the consent to be "free and voluntary."

To protect prisoners from exploitation, the FDA instituted stringent regulations governing research conducted in prisons. The regulations constituted substantial barriers such that most academic investigators and pharmaceutical companies stopped using prisoners as research subjects. In 2006, the National Institute of Medicine issued a report that aimed to protect prisoners as research subjects, while also making it easier for prisoners to participate in research that might benefit them. Critics of the report charged that the prison environment alone makes it impossible for inmates to act autonomously and provide informed consent. (See Social Context: Prisoners as Test Subjects?)

Research Involving the Poor

In the eighteenth century, Princess Caroline of England requested the use of six "charity children" as subjects in the smallpox vaccination experiments she was directing. Then, and well into the twentieth century, poor people, like prisoners, were regarded by some medical researchers as ideal research subjects.

Few people would argue today that disadvantaged people ought to be made subjects of research simply because of their social or economic status. The "back wards" in hospitals whose poor patients once served as a source of research subjects have mostly disappeared as a result of such programs as Medicare and Medicaid. Each person is now supposed to be entitled to his or her own physician and is not under the general care of the state or of a private charity.

Yet many federally funded research projects continue to be based in large public or municipal hospitals. These hospitals serve a higher percentage of economically disadvantaged patients than do private institutions. At the same time, the growth of the pharmaceutical industry has dramatically increased the number of trials, so that some 70 percent of them now take place away from academic medical centers. These trials often take place in motels or strip malls, and typically involve paying subjects for their participation, sometimes as much as $2,000 a week for Phase I trials. Some pharmaceutical companies have acknowledged using homeless people and undocumented workers for such research, and semiprofessional "guinea pigs" make their living through participation in many trials each year. (See Decision Scenario: Guinea-Pigging at the end of this chapter.) These developments raise serious questions about whether the participation of poor and low-income subjects in such trials is genuinely free and informed. While FDA rules require that payments to subjects must not be "coercive" or exert "undue influence," there has been little enforcement of violations. Some companies do now require that test subjects provide proof of residency, but there are indications that considerable numbers of trial subjects, especially those in Phase I, live at or below the poverty line.

Offshore Research. In recent years, researchers have also expanded the testing of new drugs and drug regimens into other countries, many of them with substantially lower standards of living than the United States. (See Chapter 11 for more on this topic.) A 2009 study showed that, from 1995 to 2005, almost half of Phase III clinical trials sponsored by drug companies were carried out somewhere other than the United States. Favored countries included Eastern Europe and Russia, as well as Malaysia and India.

Several reasons lie behind the increase in offshore drug testing. First, in the United States it can be difficult to get subjects to volunteer for clinical trials. In recent years, only half the trials sponsored by the National Cancer Institute enrolled the number of participants needed to produce statistically significant results. Second, the United States has more stringent requirements for human-subject studies, especially in Phases II and III, and these requirements slow the testing process. The result is that drugs both take longer to test and are more expensive to test in the United States than in many other countries.

The cost of a clinical trial conducted in a major medical center in India is $1,500–$2,000. By contrast, a trial conducted in the United States at a second-tier institution costs $15,000–$20,000. Testing a drug in a clinical trial is a major part of the expense of drug development.

However, offshore testing raises significant ethical questions. In poorer countries, even a small amount of money can serve as an inducement for people to ignore their best interest and participate in trials they would otherwise avoid. Citizens in developing nations may not understand what the clinical trial of a drug requires of them and what the risks are. Or they may put their trust in the researchers, even though those researchers can have substantial conflicts of interest.

Many of the countries in which companies conduct drug tests lack strong regulations to protect human subjects. Hence, questions arise about whether the conditions for legitimate informed consent have been satisfied. Furthermore, participants in offshore trials may not be carefully monitored. Even serious adverse events (e.g., kidney damage) may not be caught and the trial ended before others are harmed. If serious adverse events are detected, they might be ignored so that the trial can continue as planned. Participants are thus put at greater risk.

Such considerations are relevant to the decisions that must be made by federal agencies and professional organizations in the United States about accepting the results of clinical trials conducted abroad. If the research was carried out in an impoverished country that lacks strong and enforced regulations to protect human subjects, should U.S. scientific and medical institutions accept the results without raising ethical questions about how they were obtained? If the trial doesn't meet standards established by the FDA or the *Helsinki Declaration*, should the results be rejected as morally tainted?

This might mean that a potentially life-saving drug shown to be effective in a trial would not be available to patients who need it. But accepting the results of an offshore drug trial without regard for the autonomy and safety of participants also has a cost associated with it. Patients in the United States could benefit immediately from a drug proved effective in the trial, but the benefit might come as a result of exploiting poor people in another country. Trials conducted under such circumstances may also have questionable scientific validity.

Research Involving the Terminally Ill

People who have been diagnosed with a terminal illness characteristically experience overwhelming feelings of despair. Within a few days or weeks, some are able to accept the situation, but others feel a sense of ongoing desperation at the imminent prospect of death. When these patients learn that conventional therapies offer little hope of prolonging their lives, they vow to fight their diseases by other means. They look for hope in a situation that seems hopeless, and with the encouragement of family and friends, they often seek new therapies.

Some of these patients turn to alternative therapies and some to dubious "miracle cures" offered by exploitative physicians. But many others seek out clinical trials of new drugs for their diseases. They seek acceptance into trials from the hospitals, universities, and pharmaceutical companies conducting the research.

Critics of the policy of accepting terminally ill patients into clinical trials base their objections on the vulnerability of these patients. Most often, critics charge, such patients are not sufficiently aware of what they are getting into, nor are they aware of how little personal benefit they may reasonably expect to receive from an experimental therapy.

To be enrolled in a drug trial, patients must satisfy the study's research protocol. They must meet diagnostic criteria for having a particular disease, or their disease must be at a certain stage in its natural history. Most trials require that patients be tested on a regular basis. The testing may involve only drawing blood for analysis, but it may also require submitting to painful and potentially harmful surgical procedures such as biopsies and spinal taps. A patient who qualifies for admission to a study may have a difficult and expensive road ahead. She may experience additional stress and expenses, particularly if the trial is located in another part of the country, and in the end she may receive very little benefit.

Critics charge that many patients go into experimental trials with unreasonable expectations about the effectiveness of the new therapies. Patients may assume, for example, that a drug has at least some record of success, when in fact the therapeutic benefits of the drug may be uncertain at best. Indeed, in the initial stage of drug testing with human subjects, the aim is not to determine the therapeutic effectiveness of the drug, but to determine such matters as its toxicity, rate of metabolism, or most effective mode of administration.

The chance that a drug under investigation will actually prolong the life of a patient in the final stages of a terminal illness is small. One study reviewed the results of forty-two preliminary reports on drugs used to treat colon cancer and thirty-three on drugs used to treat non-small-cell lung cancer—and found that only *one* of these trial drugs had therapeutic effects.

Furthermore, critics charge, patients may not realize the extent to which an experimental drug may turn out to cause unpleasant, painful, or harmful side effects. Patients may suffer nausea, vomiting, chills, fevers, neurological damage, or lowered immunological functioning. Such effects may not even be known to the investigators, so they cannot inform patients about them at the time consent is sought. The last weeks or months of a terminally ill patient's life may thus involve more stress and suffering than if he had instead enrolled in hospice—and in fact, the patient may even shorten his life by becoming a research subject.

Finally, critics point out that dying patients are often dropped from the studies they have been hoping will save their lives. The aim of a clinical trial of a new drug, for example, is to discover such medically important characteristics of the drug as its side effects, what constitutes an effective dosage, and whether the drug has therapeutic benefits. Patients in the study are sources of data, and if a patient who is receiving no therapeutic benefit from a drug turns out to be of no value to the study, she may be dismissed from it. Dying patients may be hit particularly hard by such a rejection.

In the view of critics, the desperation of terminally ill patients makes them too vulnerable to be able to give meaningful consent to participate in experimental trials. Even if they are informed that a drug trial will offer them only a remote possibility of prolonging their lives, they are under such duress from their illness that they may not be genuinely free to consent. Patients and their families may be so frightened and emotionally distraught that they hear only what they want to hear about an experimental therapy. They may be unable to grasp the reality that the therapy probably will not benefit them and may even cause harm. In this, critics see grounds for the possible exploitation of terminally ill patients that should exclude them as potential research subjects.

Supporters of the current policy of including the terminally ill in clinical trials argue that such patients may still have something to gain. The very act of trying a new drug might make some patients feel better, even if it is only a placebo effect. Patients and their families can feel that they are doing everything possible to improve the patient's health. Moreover, the drug might be of some therapeutic benefit to the patient, even if the chance of its prolonging the patient's life is remote.

Defenders also claim that dying patients deserve to be given a chance to do something for others. In fact, they argue that researchers should emphasize the contribution that dying patients' participation might make to helping others, rather than any therapeutic benefit they might personally receive. It is unclear, however, how many terminally ill patients would be motivated by such altruistic impulses, and the research on this topic does not suggest it is a primary motive.

Research Involving Fetuses

In 1975, legal charges were brought against several physicians in Boston. They had injected antibiotics into fetuses scheduled to be aborted. The aim of the research was to determine (by autopsy) how much of the drug got into the fetal tissues.

Such information might be considered of prime importance because it could increase our knowledge of how to provide medical treatment for a developing fetus that the mother plans to carry to term. It might also help determine ways in which drugs taken by a pregnant woman may affect a fetus and so could point the way to improved prenatal care. Other kinds of fetal research also promise to provide important knowledge. Effective vaccines for preventing viral diseases, techniques for treating children with defective immune-systems, and hormonal measurements that indicate the status of the developing fetus are just some of the potential advances that are partially dependent on fetal research.

But a number of moral questions emerge in connection with such research, especially when it involves fetuses scheduled for abortion. Does the fact that the fetus is going to be aborted alter the moral situation in any way? Or should such a fetus be treated with the same concern for its well-being as a fetus that will be carried to term?

According to CDC surveillance, 90 percent of abortions take place well before any possibility of fetal viability, at less than thirteen weeks. But as a pregnancy approaches the point at which a fetus could possibly survive outside the womb, new questions arise about any research that might be conducted. Even if it is highly unlikely that a fetus could live, physicians could experience conflicting imperatives as researchers and therapists. On the one hand, many physicians feel obligated to do everything they can to protect the life of a viable fetus. On the other hand, prenatal experiments may threaten viability. Does this mean that it is wrong to do anything before abortion to threaten the life or health of the fetus, even though we do not expect it to live?

These are difficult questions to answer without first settling the question of whether the fetus is to be considered a person. (See the discussion of this issue in the Briefing Session in Chapter 5.) If the fetus is a person, then it is entitled to the same moral considerations that we extend to other persons. If we decide to take its life, then we must be prepared to offer justification. Similarly, if we are to perform experiments on a fetus, even one expected to die, then we must also be prepared to offer justification. Whether the importance of the research is adequate justification is still being debated.

If the fetus is not a person, then the question of fetal experimentation becomes less important morally. Because, however, the fetus may be regarded as a potential person, we may still believe it is necessary to treat it with consideration and respect. The burden of justification may be somewhat less weighty, but it may still be there.

Let us assume that the fetus is aborted and is apparently not viable. Depending on how far it has developed, such a fetus may have a functional heart and lungs, which may keep working, for a time, after abortion. Is it morally permissible to conduct research on such a fetus, since it is virtually certain of dying, whether or not it is made a subject of research? The knowledge that can be gained, particularly of lung functions, might be used to help save the lives of premature infants.

After the death of a fetus that is either deliberately or spontaneously aborted, are there any moral restraints on what is done with the remains? Like other human tissues, it is possible to culture fetal tissues and use them for research purposes. These tissues might, in fact, be commercially grown and distributed by biological supply companies as a variety of adult human and animal tissues are. In 2015, controversy erupted over a short video clip that purported to show Planned Parenthood executives illegally profiting from donated fetal tissue. Although the full video of the meeting showed that the executives were only discussing the $30–100 fees to cover collection and transportation, the clip renewed debate over fetal tissue research.

Scientists have long been concerned about federal guidelines and state laws regulating fetal research. Most investigators feel that they are forced to operate under such rigid restrictions that research is slowed and, in some instances, even prohibited. Most researchers agree, however, that fetal research involves important moral and social issues.

To some critics, it seems peculiar to say that a woman who has decided to have an abortion is also the one who should grant consent to research involving her fetus. It could be argued that in deciding to have an abortion, she has renounced all interest and responsibility with respect to the fetus. Yet if her pregnancy miscarried at any stage, she would mostly likely be consulted about how the fetal tissue should be used. And if she gave birth to an extremely premature infant who lived, she would, as a parent, be considered legally and morally responsible for its continued well-being. But if a pregnant woman is the one who must give consent for fetal experimentation, are there limits to what she can consent to on behalf of the fetus?

This question brings us back to where we began. It is obvious that fetal research raises both moral and social issues. We need to decide, then, what is right as a matter of personal conduct and what is right as a matter of social policy. For the foreseeable future, issues in each of these areas remain highly controversial.

Research Involving Animals

The seventeenth-century philosopher René Descartes doubted whether animals experience pain. They may act as if they are in pain, but perhaps they are only reacting like complicated pieces of clockwork. If the view of animals represented by Descartes and others in the mechanistic tradition he initiated is correct, we need not have moral concern about the use of animals in research. Animals of whatever species have the status of any other piece of delicate and often expensive lab equipment. They may be used in any way for any purpose, and indeed the history of medical experimentation on animals sometimes seems to reflect such a view.

Here are some of the ways in which animals are being or have been used in biomedical research:

- A standard test for determining the toxicity of drugs or chemicals is the "lethal dose-50" (LD-50) test. The LD-50 is the amount of a substance that, when administered to a group of experimental animals, will kill 50 percent of them.

- The Draize test, once widely used in the cosmetics industry, involves dripping a chemical substance into the lidless eyes of rabbits to determine its potential to cause eye damage.

- The effects of cigarette smoking were investigated in a series of experiments using beagles with tubes inserted into holes cut in their tracheas so that, when breathing, they were forced to inhale cigarette smoke. The dogs were then killed and autopsied to look for significant changes in cells and tissues.

- Surgical procedures are both developed and acquired by using animals as experimental subjects. Surgical residents spend much time in "dog labs" learning to perform standard surgical procedures on live dogs. Limbs may be deliberately broken and organs damaged or destroyed to test the usefulness of surgical repair techniques.

- A traditional medical-school demonstration consisted in exsanguinating (bleeding to death) a dog to illustrate the circulation of the blood. High school and college biology courses sometimes require that students destroy the brains of frogs with long needles (pithing) and then dissect the frogs to learn about physiological processes.

■ Chimpanzees and other primates have served as experimental subjects for the study of the induction and treatment of infectious diseases. Perfectly healthy chimps and monkeys have been inoculated with viruses resembling the AIDS virus; then the course of the resulting diseases is studied.

A list of the ways in which animals are used would include virtually all basic biomedical research. The discovery of an "animal model" of a disease typically signals a significant advancement in research. It means that the disease can be studied in ways it cannot be in humans. The assumption is that animals can be subjected to experimental conditions and treatments that humans cannot be subjected to without violating basic moral principles.

Is the assumption that we have no moral obligation toward animals warranted? Certainly the crude "animal machine" view of Descartes has been rejected, and no one is prepared to argue that no nonhuman animal can experience pain.

Exactly which animals have the capacity for suffering is a matter of dispute. Mammals undoubtedly do, and vertebrates in general seem to experience pain, but what about insects, worms, lobsters, and clams? Is the identification of endorphins, naturally occurring substances associated with pain relief in humans, adequate grounds for saying that an organism that produces endorphins therefore experiences pain?

Once it is acknowledged that at least some animals can suffer, most philosophers agree that we have some moral responsibilities with respect to them. Some (such as W. D. Ross) argue that since we have a prima facie duty not to cause unnecessary suffering, we should not inflict needless pain on animals.

This does not necessarily mean that biomedical research should discontinue its use of animals. Strictly construed, it means only that the animals should be treated in a humane way. For example, surgical techniques should be practiced only on dogs that have been anesthetized. Understood in this way, the principle raises no objection to humanely conducted animal research, even if its purpose is relatively trivial.

Philosophers such as Kant and most in the natural law tradition would deny that we have any duties to animals at all. The only proper objects of duty are rational agents; unless we are prepared to argue that animals are rational, we have to refuse them the status of moral persons. We might treat animals humanely because we are magnanimous, but they are not in a position to lay claims against us. Animals have no rights, on this view.

Some contemporary philosophers (Tom Regan, in particular) have argued that, although animals are not rational agents, they have preferences. This gives them an autonomy that makes them "moral patients." Like humans, animals possess the right to respectful treatment, and this entails that they not be treated only as a means to some other end. They are ends in themselves, and this intrinsic worth makes it wrong to use them as subjects in research, even when alternatives to animal research are not available.

In contrast to Regan's argument, a number of philosophers have taken a utilitarian approach to the issue of animal experimentation. Some (such as Peter Singer) have argued that, although animals cannot be said to have rights, they have interests. If we recognize that the interests of humans are deserving of consideration, then so, too, are the interests of nonhuman animals. Hence, we can recognize that animals have inherent worth without assigning them rights, but this does not mean that we must treat them exactly as we treat humans.

Most people, whether utilitarians or not, argue that at least some forms of animal experimentation can be justified by the benefits produced. After all, they point out, the understanding of biological processes we have acquired since the time of Aristotle has been heavily dependent on animal experimentation. This understanding has given us insights into the causes and processes of diseases, and, most important, it has put us in a position to invent and test new therapies and modes of prevention.

Without animal experimentation, the identification of the role played by insulin, the development of the polio vaccine, and the refinement of hundreds of major surgical techniques surely would not have been possible. The list could be extended to include virtually every accomplishment of medicine and surgery. Millions of human lives have been saved by using the knowledge and understanding gained from animal studies.

Animals, too, have benefited from the theoretical and practical knowledge derived from such research. An understanding of nutritional needs has led to healthier domestic animals, and an understanding of organisms' roles in ecosystems has produced a movement to protect and preserve many species of wild animals. At the conceptual and scientific levels, veterinary medicine is not really distinct from human medicine. The same sorts of surgical procedures, medicines, and vaccines that benefit the human population also benefit many other species.

However, even from a broadly utilitarian perspective, accepting the general principle that the results justify the methods, does not mean that every experiment with animals is warranted. Some experiments might be trivial, unnecessary, or poorly designed. Others might hold no promise of yielding the kind or quantity of knowledge sufficient to justify causing animal subjects to suffer pain or death.

Furthermore, the utilitarian approach (like Regan's rights-based one) motivates a search for alternatives to animal experimentation, wherever possible. If good results can be obtained, for example, by conducting experiments with cell cultures (in vitro), rather than with whole organisms (in vivo), then in vitro experiments are to be preferred. However, if alternatives to animal testing are not available and if the benefits secured promise to outweigh the costs, animal testing may be morally legitimate.

The utilitarian justification faces what some writers see as a major difficulty. It is generated by the fact that animals such as chimpanzees and even dogs and pigs can be shown to possess mental abilities superior to those of humans suffering from severe brain damage and retardation. If experiments on mammals can be justified by appeal to biomedical benefits, then why aren't experiments on humans with serious mental impairments equally justified? Indeed, shouldn't we experiment on a human in a chronic vegetative state, rather than on a healthy and alert dog?

One way out of this dilemma might be to reject the utilitarian metric (or any other univocal metric) and instead focus on the basic capabilities and functions that both human and non-animals need to live with the basic dignity appropriate to their species. This approach, as advanced by thinkers such as Martha Nussbaum, would likely rule out experiments on mentally impaired humans, as incompatible with their human dignity and pursuit of central capabilities. But it might also exclude some animal research, as infringing too greatly on the dignified flourishing of animal lives.

The use made of animals in biomedical research is a significant issue, but it is only one aspect of the general philosophical question about the status of animals. Do animals have rights? If so, what grounds can be offered for them? Do animals have a right to coexist with humans? Do animals have a right to be free? Is it wrong to eat animals or use products made from their remains? These questions and many others like them are now being given the most careful scrutiny they have received since the nineteenth century. How they are answered will do much to shape the moral character both of medical research and of our society as a whole.

Summary

There are other areas of biomedical experimentation that present special moral problems. We have not discussed, for example, research involving military personnel, online consumers, corporate employees, or college students. Moreover, we mentioned only a few of the special difficulties presented by research on the mentally disabled, psychiatric patients, and geriatric patients confined to institutions.

We have, however, raised such a multiplicity of questions about consent and human research that it is perhaps worthwhile to attempt to restate some of them in a general form.

Basic Issues. Three issues are particularly noteworthy:

1. Who is competent to consent? (Are children? Are mental patients? If a person is not competent, who—if anyone—should have the power to consent for him or her? Given that animals, for example, have no power to consent, is research involving them legitimate?)

2. When is consent voluntary? (Is any institutionalized person in a position to offer free consent? How can even hospitalized patients be freed from pressures to consent?)

3. When are information and understanding adequate for genuine informed consent? (Can complicated medical information ever be adequately explained to laypersons? Should we attempt to devise tests for understanding?)

Standards. Although we have concentrated on the matter of consent in research, there are other morally relevant matters connected with research that we have only minimally discussed. These often relate to research criteria, such as the following:

1. Is the research of sufficient scientific and medical value to justify the human risk involved? Research that involves trivial aims or that is unnecessary (e.g., merely confirms what is already well established) cannot be used to justify causing serious threats to human well-being.

2. Can the knowledge sought be obtained without human clinical research? Can it be obtained without animal experimentation?

3. Have animal (and other) studies been done to minimize as much as possible the risk to human subjects? A great deal can be learned about the effects of drugs, for example, by using "animal models," and the knowledge gained can be used to minimize the hazards in human trials. (Ethical issues involving animals in research may also be raised here, of course.)

4. Does the design of the research meet accepted scientific standards? Sloppy research that is scientifically dubious means that people have been subjected to risks for no legitimate purpose and that animals have been harmed or sacrificed needlessly.

5. Do the investigators have the proper medical or scientific background to conduct the research effectively?

6. Is the research designed to minimize the risks and suffering of the participants? As we noted earlier, new drugs can be tested without using placebos. Thus, research subjects in need of medication may not be forced to forego treatment for their conditions.

7. Have the aims and the design of the research and the qualifications of the investigators been reviewed by a group or committee that is competent to judge them? Such "peer review" is intended to ensure that only research that is worthwhile and that meets accepted scientific standards is conducted. And although such review groups can fail to do their job properly—as in, for example, the Tuskegee syphilis study—they are still necessary instruments of control.

Most writers on experimentation would agree that these are among the questions that must be answered satisfactorily before research involving human subjects can be morally acceptable. Obviously, however, a patient who is asked to give his or her consent is in no position to judge whether the research project meets the standards implied by these questions. For this reason, it is important that there be social policies and practices governing research. Everyone should be confident that a research project is, in general, a legitimate one before having to decide whether to volunteer to become a participant.

Ethical Theories: Medical Research and Informed Consent

We have raised too many issues in too many areas of experimentation to discuss how each of several ethical theories might apply to them all. We must limit ourselves to considering a few suggestions about the general issues of human experimentation and informed consent.

Utilitarianism

Utilitarianism's principle of utility tells us, in effect, to choose those actions that will produce the greatest amount of benefit. Utilitarianism must approve human research in general, since there are cases in which the sacrifices of a few bring great benefits to many. We might, for example, design policies to make it worthwhile for people to volunteer for experiments, with the view that if subjects are paid for any risks and compensated for any suffering or harm that results from research, then society as a whole might still benefit.

The principle of utility also tells us to design experiments to minimize suffering and the chance of harm. Further, it forbids us to do research of an unnecessary or trivial kind—research that is not worth its cost in either human or economic resources.

As for the matter of informed consent, utilitarianism does not seem to require it. If more social good is to be gained by making people research subjects without securing their agreement, then this may be morally legitimate on some utilitarian accounts. It is not, of course, necessarily the best procedure to follow. A system of rewards to induce volunteers might be more likely to lead to an increase in general happiness. Furthermore, the principle of utility might suggest that the best research subjects would be "less valuable" members of the society, such as the mentally disabled, the violently criminal, or the dying. This, again, is not a necessary consequence of utilitarianism, although it is a possible one. If the recognition of rights and dignity would produce a better society in general, then a utilitarian might also say that these should be taken into account in experimentation with human beings.

For utilitarianism, that individual is competent to give consent who can balance benefits and risks and decide what course of action is best for him or her. Thus, if informed consent is taken to be a requirement supported by the principle of utility, those who are mentally ill or mentally disabled or demented may be excluded from the class of potential research subjects. Furthermore, investigators must provide enough relevant information to allow competent people to make a meaningful decision about what is most likely to serve their own interests.

Kant

For Kant, an individual capable of giving consent is one who is rational and autonomous. Kant's principles would thus rule out as research subjects people who are not able to understand experimental procedures, aims, risks, and benefits. People may volunteer for clinical trials if they expect to receive therapeutic benefits, or they may act out of duty and volunteer, thus discharging their imperfect obligation to advance knowledge or to improve human life.

Yet, for Kant, there are limits to the risks that potential subjects should take. We have a duty to preserve our lives, so no one should agree to become a subject in an experiment in which the likelihood of death is high. In addition, no one should subject himself or others to research in which there is considerable risk that the capacity for rational thought and autonomy will be destroyed.

Kant's principles also rule out as potential research participants those who are not in a position to act voluntarily, that is, those who cannot exercise their autonomy. This makes it important to determine, from a Kantian point of view, whether children and institutionalized people (including prisoners) can be regarded as free agents capable of moral choice.

Kant's view of people as autonomous rational beings requires that informed consent be obtained for both medical treatment and research. We cannot be forced to accept treatment for "our own good," nor can we be turned into research subjects for "the good of others." We must always be treated as ends and never as means only. To be treated in this way requires that others never deliberately deceive us, no matter how good their intentions. In short, we have

a right to be told what we are getting into so that we can decide whether or not we want to participate in biomedical research.

Ross

Ross's theory imposes on researchers prima facie duties to patients that are similar to Kant's requirements. The nature of people as autonomous moral agents requires that their informed consent be obtained. Researchers ought not to deceive their subjects, and protocols should be designed in ways that minimize suffering and the risk of injury or death.

These are all prima facie duties, of course, and it is possible to imagine situations in which other duties might take precedence over them.

In general, however, Ross, like Kant, tells us that human research cannot be based on what is useful; it must be based on what is right. Ross's principles, like Kant's, do not tell us, however, how we are to deal with such special problems as research involving children or prisoners.

Natural Law

The principle of double effect and the principle of totality, which are based on the natural law theory of morality, have specific applications to experimentation. Because we hold our bodies in trust, we are responsible for assessing the degree of risk associated with becoming a research subject. Thus, others have an obligation to supply us with the information that we need in order to make our decision. If we decide to give our consent, it must be given freely and not be the consequence of deception or coercion.

In general, the likelihood of a person's benefiting from research participation must exceed the danger of the person's suffering greater losses. The four requirements that govern the application of the principle of double effect determine what is and what is not a morally acceptable experiment. (See Part VI: Foundations of Bioethics, for a discussion of these requirements.)

People can volunteer for experiments from which they expect no direct benefits. The good they seek in doing so is not their own good but the good of others. But there are limits to what they can subject themselves to. A dying patient, for example, cannot be made the subject of a useless or trivial experiment. The probable value of the knowledge to be gained must balance out the patient's exposure to risk and suffering, and there must be no likelihood that the experiment will seriously injure or kill the patient.

These same restrictions also apply to experiments involving healthy people. The principle of totality prohibits a healthy person from submitting to an experiment that involves a high probability of serious injury, impaired health, mutilation, or death.

The status of the fetus is clear in the Roman Catholic version of the natural law theory: the fetus is a person. As such, the fetus is entitled to the same dignity and respect we accord to other persons. Experiments that involve harm to a fetus or lessening its chances of survival are morally prohibited. But not all fetal research is ruled out. That which may be of therapeutic benefit or which does not directly threaten the fetus's well-being could be allowed. Furthermore, research involving fetal tissue or remains may be permissible, if it is done for a serious and valuable purpose.

Rawls

From Rawls's point of view, the difficulty with utilitarianism with respect to human experimentation is that it would permit the exploitation of some groups (the dying, prisoners, the mentally disabled) for the sake of others. By contrast, Rawls's principles of justice would forbid all research that involves violating a liberty to which a person is entitled by virtue of being a member of society.

As a result, all experiments that make use of coercion or deception are ruled out. And since a person has a right to decide what risks she is willing to subject herself to, voluntary informed consent is required of all subjects. A just society might, as in utilitarianism, decide to reward those who volunteer to become research subjects. As long as this is a possibility open to all, it is not objectionable.

It would never be right, according to Rawls, to take advantage of those in the society who are least well off to benefit those who are better off. Inequalities must be arranged so that they bring benefits (ideally) to everyone or, at least, to those who are most disadvantaged. Research involving direct therapeutic benefits is clearly acceptable (assuming informed consent), but research that takes advantage of the sick, the poor, the disabled, or the institutionalized without benefiting them is unacceptable.

Theories of Identity, Care, and Capability

Identity-based ethical theories often focus on the ways in which both researchers and their subjects are influenced by cultural dynamics and by pervasive power structures such as gender and race. Thus abstract concern for the autonomy and informed consent of research subjects may be insufficient if female subjects, for example, are still primarily viewed (and excluded) on the basis of their reproductive capacities—or if non-white subjects are studied primarily for "race-based" interventions (rather than serving as adequate models for humanity in general). These theorists insist that biomedical research reflect a range of human bodies and historical experiences, and that their inclusion go beyond tokenism or exoticism in relation to a "neutral" (but often white male) subject.

At the same time, theories of virtue, care, and capability challenge the idea that comprehensive abstract principles (such as utility, autonomy, or justice) capture the ethical complexities of biomedical research. That such research furthers the realization of central capabilities and virtues compatible with human dignity and flourishing—such as bodily integrity, affiliation, generosity and courage—may be more relevant than the net utility of the research.

Although the capabilities approach is primarily concerned with creating opportunities for a wide range of human functioning, it insists that we look beyond narrow definitions of autonomy, and also examine the relationships of dependency and asymmetry that shape at least part of most people's lives. Familial and cultural relationships may require that researchers look beyond a signed consent form to evaluate a subject's voluntary (or less than voluntary) participation. Conversely, the dependent status of many elderly and disabled people need not exclude them from research, since participation may further their health and their engagement in civil society. One recurrent theme is that an abstract ideal of rational autonomy (whether Kantian or Rawlsian) is too narrow a standard to capture how medical research limits or extends what people can be or do.

Clearly, we have been able to provide only the briefest sketch of some of the ways in which our moral theories might apply to major issues in human experimentation. The preceding remarks are not meant to be anything more than suggestive. A satisfactory moral theory of human experimentation requires working out the application of principles to problems in detail, as well as resolving such issues as the status of children and fetuses and the capability of institutionalized people to act freely. In this chapter's Social Context and Case Presentations, the issues we have raised here are illustrated as moral problems that require decisions about both general policies and specific interventions.

READINGS

Section 1: Consent and Experimentation

The Willowbrook Letters: Criticism and Defense

Stephen Goldby, Saul Krugman, M. H. Pappworth, and Geoffrey Edsall

"The Willowbrook Letters," by Stephen Goldby, Saul Krugman, M. H. Pappworth, and Geoffrey Edsall, concern the moral legitimacy of a study of viral hepatitis that was conducted at the Willowbrook School by Krugman and his associates. (See Case Presentation: The Willowbrook Hepatitis Experiments in this chapter.) Goldby charges that the study was unjustified because it was morally wrong to infect children

From Stephen Goldby, Saul Krugman, M. H. Pappworth, and Geoffrey Edsall, "The Willowbrook Letters: Criticism and Defense," *The Lancet* 297 and 298, April 10, May 8, June 5, and July 10, 1971. Copyright © 1971, with permission from Elsevier.

when no benefit to them could result. Krugman defends himself by claiming that his results demonstrated a "therapeutic effect" for the children involved, as well as for others. He presents four reasons for holding that the deliberate infection of the children was justified.

Pappworth claims that Krugman's defense is presented only after the fact, whereas an experiment is ethical or not in its inception. Moreover, he asserts, consent was obtained through the use of coercion. Parents who wished to put their children in the institution were told there was room only in the "hepatitis unit."

In the final letter, Edsall defends the Krugman study. The experiments, he asserts, involved no greater risk to the children than they would have otherwise faced. He further contends that the results obtained were of general benefit.

Sir.—You have referred to the work of Krugman and his colleagues at the Willowbrook State School in three editorials. In the first article the work was cited as a notable study of hepatitis and a model for this type of investigation. No comment was made on the rightness of attempting to infect mentally retarded children with hepatitis for experimental purposes, in an institution where the disease was already endemic.

The second editorial again did not remark on the ethics of the study, but the third sounded a note of doubt as to the justification for extending these experiments. The reason given was that some children might have been made more susceptible to serious hepatitis as the result of the administration of previously heated icterogenic material.

I believe that not only this last experiment, but the whole of Krugman's study, is quite unjustifiable, whatever the aims, and however academically or therapeutically important are the results. I am amazed that the work was published and that it has been actively supported editorially by the *Journal of the American Medical Association* and by Ingelfinger in the 1967–68 *Year Book of Medicine.* To my knowledge only the *British Journal of Hospital Medicine* has clearly stated the ethical position on these experiments and shown that it was indefensible to give potentially dangerous infected material to children, particularly those who were mentally retarded, with or without parental consent, when no benefit to the child could conceivably result.

Krugman and Giles have continued to publish the results of their study, and in a recent paper go to some length to describe their method of obtaining parental consent and list a number of influential medical boards and committees that have approved the study. They point out again that, in their opinion, their work conforms to the World Medical Association Draft Code of Ethics on Human Experimentation. They also say that hepatitis is still highly endemic in the school.

This attempted defense is irrelevant to the central issue. Is it right to perform an experiment on a normal or mentally retarded child when no benefit can result to that individual? I think that the answer is no, and that the question of parental consent is irrelevant. In my view the studies of Krugman serve only to show that there is a serious loophole in the Draft Code, which under General Principles and Definitions puts the onus of consent for experimentation on children on the parent or guardian. It is this section that is quoted by Krugman. I would class his work as "experiments conducted solely for the acquisition of knowledge," under which heading the code states that "persons retained in mental hospital[s] or hospitals for mental defectives should not be used for human experiment." Krugman may believe that his experiments were for the benefit of his patients, meaning the individual patients used in the study. If this is his belief he has a difficult case to defend. The duty of a pediatrician in a situation such as exists at Willowbrook State School is to attempt to improve that situation, not to turn it to his advantage for experimental purposes, however lofty the aims.

Every new reference to the work of Krugman and Giles adds to its apparent ethical respectability and in my view such references should stop, or at least be heavily qualified. The editorial attitude of *The Lancet* to the work should be reviewed and openly stated. The issue is too important to be ignored.

If Krugman and Giles are keen to continue their experiments I suggest that they invite the parents of the children involved to participate. I wonder what the response would be.   STEPHEN GOLDBY

Sir.—Dr. Stephen Goldby's critical comments about our Willowbrook studies and our motives for conducting them were published without extending us the courtesy of replying in the same issue of *The Lancet*. Your acceptance of his criticisms without benefit of our response implies a blackout of all comment related to our studies. This decision is unfortunate because our recent studies on active and passive immunization for the prevention of viral hepatitis, type B, have clearly demonstrated a "therapeutic effect" for the children involved. These studies have provided us with the first indication and hope that it may be possible to control hepatitis in this institution. If this aim can be achieved, it will benefit not only the children, but also their families and the employees who care for them in the school. It is unnecessary to point out the additional benefit to the worldwide populations which have been plagued by an insoluble hepatitis problem for many generations.

Dr. Joan Giles and I have been actively engaged in studies aimed to solve two infectious-disease problems in the Willowbrook State School—measles and viral hepatitis. These studies were investigated in this institution because they represented major health problems for the 5000 or more mentally retarded children who were residents. Uninformed critics have assumed or implied that we came to Willowbrook to "conduct experiments on mentally retarded children."

The results of our Willowbrook studies with the experimental live attenuated measles vaccine developed by Enders and his colleagues are well documented in the medical literature. As early as 1960 we demonstrated the protective effect of this vaccine during the course of an epidemic. Prior to licensure of the vaccine in 1963 epidemics occurred at two-year intervals in this institution. During the 1960 epidemic there were more than 600 cases of measles and 60 deaths. In the wake of our ongoing measles vaccine programme, measles has been eradicated as a disease in the Willowbrook State School. We have not had a single case of measles since 1963. In this regard the children at the Willowbrook State School have been more fortunate than unimmunized children in Oxford, England, [and] other areas in Great Britain, as well as certain groups of children in the United States and other parts of the world.

The background of our hepatitis studies at Willowbrook has been described in detail in various publications. Viral hepatitis is so prevalent that newly admitted susceptible children become infected within 6 to 12 months after entry in the institution. These children are a source of infection for the personnel who care for them and for their families if they visit with them. We were convinced that the solution of the hepatitis problem in this institution was dependent on the acquisition of new knowledge leading to the development of an effective immunizing agent. The achievements with smallpox, diphtheria, poliomyelitis, and more recently measles represent dramatic illustrations of this approach.

It is well known that viral hepatitis in children is milder and more benign than the same disease in adults. Experience has revealed that hepatitis in institutionalized, mentally retarded children is also mild, in contrast with measles, which is a more severe disease when it occurs in institutional epidemics involving the mentally retarded. Our proposal to expose a small number of newly admitted children to the Willowbrook strains of hepatitis virus was justified in our opinion for the following reasons: (1) they were bound to be exposed to the same strains under the natural conditions existing in the institution; (2) they would be admitted to a special, well-equipped, and well-staffed unit where they would be isolated from exposure to other infectious diseases which were prevalent in the institution—namely, shigellosis, parasitic infections, and respiratory infections—thus, their exposure in the hepatitis unit would be associated with less risk than the type of institutional exposure where multiple infections could occur; (3) they were likely to have a subclinical infection followed by immunity to the particular hepatitis virus; and (4) only children with parents who gave informed consent would be included.

The statement by Dr. Goldby accusing us of conducting experiments exclusively for the acquisition of knowledge with no benefit for the children cannot be supported by the true facts.   SAUL KRUGMAN

Sir.—The experiments at Willowbrook raise two important issues: What constitutes valid consent and do ends justify means? English law definitely forbids experimentation on children, even if both parents consent, unless done specifically in the interests of each individual child. Perhaps in the U.S.A. the law is not so clear-cut. According to Beecher, the parents of the children at Willow-brook were informed that, because of overcrowd-ing, the institution was to be closed; but only a week or two later they were told that there would be vacancies in the "hepatitis unit" for children whose parents allowed them to form part of the hepatitis research study. Such consent, ethically if not legally, is invalid because of its element of coercion, some parents being desperately anxious to institutionalize their mentally defective chil-dren. Moreover, obtaining consent after talking to parents in groups, as described by Krugman, is extremely unsatisfactory because even a single enthusiast can sway the diffident who do not wish to appear churlish in front of their fellow citizens.

Do ends justify the means? Krugman maintains that any newly admitted children would inevitably have contracted infective hepatitis, which was rife in the hospital. But this ignores the statement by the head of the State Department of Mental Hygiene that during the major part of the 15 years these ex-periments have been conducted, a gamma-globulin inoculation programme had already resulted in over an 80 percent reduction of that disease in that hos-pital. Krugman and Pasamanick claim that subse-quent therapeutic effects justify these experiments. This attitude is frequently adopted by experimenters and enthusiastic medical writers who wish us to for-get completely how results are obtained but instead enjoy any benefits that may accrue. Immunization was not the purpose of these Willowbrook experi-ments but merely a by-product that incidentally proved beneficial to the victims. Any experiment is ethical or not at its inception, and does not become so because it achieved some measure of success in extending the frontiers of medicine. I particularly object strongly to the views of Willey, "...risk be-ing assumed by the subjects of the experimenta-tion balanced against the potential benefit to the subjects *and* [Willey's italics] to society in general." I believe that experimental physicians never have

the right to select martyrs for society. Every human being has the right to be treated with decency, and that right must always supersede every consid-eration of what may benefit mankind, what may advance medical science, what may contribute to public welfare. No doctor is ever justified in placing society or science first and his obligation to patients second. Any claim to act for the good of society should be regarded with distaste because it may be merely a highflown expression to cloak outrageous acts.

M.H. Pappworth

Sir.—I am astonished at the unquestioning way in which *The Lancet has* accepted the intemper-ate position taken by Dr. Stephen Goldby con-cerning the experimental studies of Krugman and Giles on hepatitis at the Willowbrook State School. These investigators have repeatedly ex-plained for over a decade that natural hepatitis infection occurs sooner or later in virtually 100% of the patients admitted to Willowbrook, and that it is better for the patient to have a known, timed, controlled infection than an untimed, uncontrolled one. Moreover, the wisdom and human justification of these studies have been repeatedly and carefully examined and verified by a number of very distinguished, able individu-als who are respected leaders in the making of such decisions.

The real issue is: Is it not proper and ethical to carry out experiments in children, which would apparently incur no greater risk than the children were likely to run by nature, in which the chil-dren generally receive better medical care when artificially infected than if they had been naturally infected, and in which the parents as well as the physician feel that a significant contribution to the future well-being of similar children is likely to re-sult from the studies? It is true, to be sure, that the W.M.A. code says, "Children in institutions and not under the care of relatives should not be the sub-jects of human experiments." But this unqualified *obiter dictum* may represent merely the well-known inability of committees to think a problem through. However, it has been thought through by Sir Austin Bradford Hill, who has pointed out the unfortunate effects for these very children that would have re-sulted, were such a code to have been applied over the years.

Geoffrey Edsall

Judgment on Willowbrook

Paul Ramsey

Ramsey reviews the justifications offered for the Willowbrook experiments presented by Krugman. He observes that there is nothing about hepatitis that requires that research be conducted on children. He points out that no justification except the needs of the experiment is given for withholding gamma globulin from the subjects and that nothing is said about attempting to control the low-grade epidemic by other means. Furthermore, Ramsey questions the morality of the consent secured from the parents of the children at Willowbrook. His basic recommendation is that the use of institutionalized children in research ought to be legally prohibited.

In 1958 and 1959 the *New England Journal of Medicine* reported a series of experiments performed upon patients and new admittees to the Willowbrook State School, a home for retarded children in Staten Island, NewYork. These experiments were described as "an attempt to control the high prevalence of infectious hepatitis in an institution for mentally defective patients." The experiments were said to be justified because, under conditions of an existing uncontrolled outbreak of hepatitis in the institution, "knowledge obtained from a series of suitable studies could well lead to its control." In actuality, the experiments were designed to duplicate and confirm the efficacy of gamma globulin in immunization against hepatitis, to develop and improve or improve upon that inoculum, and to learn more about infectious hepatitis in general.

The experiments were justified—doubtless, after a great deal of soul searching—for the following reasons: there was a smoldering epidemic throughout the institution and "it was apparent that most of the patients at Willowbrook were naturally exposed to hepatitis virus"; infectious hepatitis is a much milder disease in children; the strain at Willowbrook was especially mild; only the strain or strains of the virus already disseminated at Willowbrook were used; and only those small and incompetent patients whose parents gave consent were used.

The patient population at Willowbrook was 4478, growing at a rate of one patient a day over a three-year span, or from 10 to 15 new admissions per week. In the first trial the existing population was divided into two groups: one group served as uninoculated controls, and the other group was inoculated with 0.01 ml of gamma globulin per pound of body weight. Then for a second trial new admittees and those left uninoculated before were again divided: one group served as uninoculated controls and the other was inoculated with 0.06 ml of gamma globulin per pound of body weight. This proved that Stokes et al. had correctly demonstrated that the larger amount would give significant immunity for up to seven or eight months.

Serious ethical questions may be raised about the trials so far described. No mention is made of any attempt to enlist the adult personnel of the institution, numbering nearly 1000 including nearly 600 attendants on ward duty, and new additions to the staff, in these studies whose excusing reason was that almost everyone was "naturally" exposed to the Willowbrook virus. Nothing requires that major research into the natural history of hepatitis be first undertaken in children. Experiments have been carried out in the military and with prisoners as subjects. There have been fatalities from the experiments; but surely in all these cases the consent of the volunteers was as valid or better than the proxy consent of these children's "representatives." There would have been no question of the understanding consent that might have been given by the adult personnel at Willowbrook, if significant benefits were expected from studying that virus.

Second, nothing is said that would warrant withholding an inoculation of some degree of known efficacy from part of the population, or for withholding in the first trial less than the full amount of gamma globulin that had served to immunize in previous tests, except the need to test, confirm, and improve the inoculum. That, of course, was a desirable goal;

but it does not seem possible to warrant withholding gamma globulin for the reason that is often said to justify controlled trials, namely, that one procedure is *as likely* to succeed as the other.

Third, nothing is said about attempts to control or defeat the low-grade epidemic at Willowbrook by more ordinary, if more costly and less experimental, procedures. Nor is anything said about admitting no more patients until this goal had been accomplished. This was not a massive urban hospital whose teeming population would have to be turned out into the streets, with resulting dangers to themselves and to public health, in order to sanitize the place. Instead, between 200 and 250 patients were housed in each of 18 buildings over approximately 400 acres in a semi-rural setting of fields, woods, and well-kept, spacious lawns. Clearly it would have been possible to secure other accommodation[s] for new admissions away from the infection, while eradicating the infection at Willowbrook building by building. This might have cost money, and it would certainly have required astute detective work to discover the source of the infection. The doctors determined that the new patients likely were not carrying the infection upon admission, and that it did not arise from the procedures and routine inoculations given to them at the time of admission. Why not go further in the search for the source of the epidemic? If this had been an orphanage for normal children or a floor of private patients, instead of a school for mentally defective children, one wonders whether the doctors would so readily have accepted the hepatitis as a "natural" occurrence and even as an opportunity for study.

The next step was to attempt to induce "passive–active immunity" by feeding the virus to patients already protected by gamma globulin. In this attempt to improve the inoculum, permission was obtained from the parents of children from 5 to 10 years of age newly admitted to Willowbrook, who were then isolated from contact with the rest of the institution. All were inoculated with gamma globulin and then divided into two groups: one served as controls while the other group of new patients were fed the Willowbrook virus, obtained from feces, in doses having 50 percent infectivity, i.e., in concentrations estimated to produce hepatitis with jaundice in half the subjects tested. Then twice the 50 percent infectivity was tried. This proved, among other things, that hepatitis has an "alimentary-tract phase" in which it can be transmitted from one person to another while still "inapparent" in the first person. This, doubtless, is exceedingly

important information in learning how to control epidemics of infectious hepatitis. The second of the two articles mentioned above describes studies of the incubation period of the virus and of whether pooled serum remained infectious when aged and frozen. Still the small, mentally defective patients who were deliberately fed infectious hepatitis are described as having suffered mildly in most cases: "The liver became enlarged in the majority, occasionally a week or two before the onset of jaundice. Vomiting and anorexia usually lasted only a few days. Most of the children gained weight during the course of hepatitis."

That mild description of what happened to the children who were fed hepatitis (and who continued to be introduced into the unaltered environment of Willowbrook) is itself alarming since it is now definitely known that cirrhosis of the liver results from infectious hepatitis more frequently than from excessive consumption of alcohol! Now, or in 1958 and 1959, no one knows what may be other serious consequences of contracting infectious hepatitis. Understanding human volunteers were then and are now needed in the study of this disease, although a South American monkey has now successfully been given a form of hepatitis, and can henceforth serve as our ally in its conquest. But not children who cannot consent knowingly. If Peace Corps workers are regularly given gamma globulin before going abroad as a guard against their contracting hepatitis, and are inoculated at intervals thereafter, it seems that this is the least we should do for mentally defective children before they "go abroad" to Willowbrook or other institutions set up for their care.

Discussions pro and con of the Willowbrook experiments that have come to my attention serve only to reinforce the ethical objections that can be raised against what was done simply from a careful analysis of the original articles reporting the research design and findings. In an address at the 1968 Ross Conference on Pediatric Research, Dr. Saul Krugman raised the question, Should vaccine trials be carried out in adult volunteers before subjecting children to similar tests? He answered this question in the negative. The reason adduced was simply that "a vaccine trial may be a more hazardous procedure for adults than for children." Medical researchers, of course, are required to minimize the hazards, but not by moving from consenting to unconsenting subjects. This apology clearly shows that adults and children have become interchangeable in face of the overriding importance of obtaining the research goal. This means that the special moral claims of children for care and protection are forgotten, and especially the claims of children who are most weak and vulnerable. (Krugman's reference to the measles vaccine trials is not to the point.)

The *Medical Tribune* explains that the 16-bed isolation unit set up at Willowbrook served "to protect the study subjects from Willowbrook's other endemic diseases—such as shigellosis, measles, rubella and respiratory and parasitic infections—while exposing them to hepatitis." This presumably compensated for the infection they were given. It is not convincingly shown that the children could by no means, however costly, have been protected from the epidemic of hepatitis. The statement that Willowbrook "had endemic infectious hepatitis and a sufficiently open population so that the disease could never be quieted by exhausting the supply of susceptibles" is at best enigmatic.

Oddly, physicians defending the propriety of the Willowbrook hepatitis project soon began talking like poorly instructed "natural lawyers"! Dr. Louis Lasagna and Dr. Geoffrey Edsall, for example, find these experiments unobjectionable—both, for the reason stated by Edsall: "the children would apparently incur no greater risk than they were likely to run by nature." In any case, Edsall's example of parents consenting with a son 17 years of age for him to go to war, and society's agreements with minors that they can drive cars and hurt themselves were entirely beside the point. Dr. David D. Rutstein adheres to a stricter standard in regard to research on infectious hepatitis: "It is not ethical to use human subjects for the growth of a virus for any purpose."

The latter sweeping verdict may depend on knowledge of the effects of viruses on chromosomal difficulties, mongolism, etc., that was not available to the Willowbrook group when their researches were begun thirteen years ago. If so, this is a telling point against appeal to "no discernible risks" as the sole standard applicable to the use of children in medical experimentation. That would lend support to the proposition that we always know that there are unknown and undiscerned risks in the case of an invasion of the fortress of the body—which then can be consented to by an adult in behalf of a child only if it is in the child's behalf medically.

When asked what she told the parents of the subject children at Willowbrook, Dr. Joan Giles replied, "I explain that there is no vaccine against infectious hepatitis.... I also tell them that we can modify the disease with gamma globulin but we can't provide lasting immunity without letting them get the disease."

Obviously vaccines giving "lasting immunity" are not the only kinds of vaccine to be used in caring for patients.

Doubtless the studies at Willowbrook resulted in improvement in the vaccine, to the benefit of present and future patients. In September 1966, "a routine program of GG [gamma globulin] administration to every new patient at Willowbrook" was begun. This cut the incidence of icteric hepatitis 80 to 85 percent. Then follows a significant statement in the *Medical Tribune* article: "A similar reduction in the icteric form of the disease has been accomplished among the employees, who began getting routine GG earlier in the study." Not only did the research team (so far as these reports show) fail to consider and adopt the alternative that new admittees to the staff be asked to become volunteers for an investigation that might improve the vaccine against the strain of infectious hepatitis to which they as well as the children were exposed. Instead, the staff was routinely protected earlier than the inmates were! And, as we have seen, there was evidence from the beginning that gamma globulin provided at least some protection. A "modification" of the disease was still an inoculum; even if this provided no lasting immunization and had to be repeated. It is axiomatic to medical ethics that a known remedy or protection—even if not perfect or even if the best exact administration of it has not been proved—should not be withheld from individual patients. It seems to a layman that from the beginning various trials at immunization of all new admittees might have been made, and controlled observation made of their different degrees of effectiveness against "nature" at Willowbrook. This would doubtless have been a longer way round, namely, the "anecdotal" method of investigative treatment that comes off second best in comparison with controlled trials. Yet this seems to be the alternative dictated by our received medical ethics, and the only one expressive of minimal care of the primary patients themselves.

Finally, except for one episode, the obtaining of parental consent (on the premise that this is ethically valid) seems to have been very well handled. Wards of the state were not used, though by law the administrator at Willowbrook could have signed consent for them. Only new admittees whose parents were available were entered by proxy consent into the project. Explanation was made to groups of these parents, and they were given time to think about it and consult with their own family physicians. Then late in 1964 Willowbrook was closed to all new admissions because of overcrowding. What then happened can most impartially be described in the words of an article defending the Willowbrook project on medical and ethical grounds:

> Parents who applied for their children to get in were sent a form letter over Dr. Hammond's signature saying that there was no space for new admissions and that their name was being put on a waiting list.

> But the hepatitis program, occupying its own space in the institution, continued to admit new patients as each new study group began. "Where do you find new admissions except by canvassing the people who have applied for admission?" Dr. Hammond asked.

> So a new batch of form letters went out saying that there were a few vacancies in the hepatitis research unit if the parents cared to consider volunteering their child for that. In some instances the second form letter apparently was received as closely as a week after the first letter arrived.

Granting—as I do not—the validity of parental consent to research upon children not in their behalf medically, what sort of consent was that? Surely, the duress upon these parents with children so defective as to require institutionalization was far greater than the duress on prisoners given tobacco or paid or promised parole for their cooperation! I grant that the timing of these events was inadvertent. Since, however, ethics is a matter of criticizing institutions and not only of exculpating or making culprits of individual men, the inadvertence does not matter. This is the strongest possible argument for saying that even if parents have the right to consent to submit the children who are directly and continuously in their care to nonbeneficial medical experimentation, this should not be the rule of practice governing institutions set up for their care.

Such use of captive populations of children for purely experimental purposes ought to be made legally impossible. My view is that this should be stopped by legal acknowledgement of the moral invalidity of parental or legal proxy consent for the child to procedures having no relation to a child's own diagnosis or treatment. If this is not done, canons of loyalty require that the rule of practice (by law, or otherwise) be that children in institutions and not directly under the care of parents or relatives should *never* be used in medical investigations having present pain or discomfort and unknown present and future risks to them, and promising future possible benefits only for others.

Principles of the Nuremberg Code

1. The voluntary consent of the human subject is absolutely essential.

   This means that the person involved should have legal capacity to give consent; should be so situated as to be able to exercise free power of choice, without the intervention of any element of force, fraud, deceit, duress, over-reaching, or other ulterior form of constraint or coercion; and should have sufficient knowledge and comprehension of the elements of the subject matter involved as to enable him to make an understanding and enlightened decision. This latter element requires that before the acceptance of an affirmative decision by the experimental subject there should be made known to him the nature, duration, and purpose of the experiment; the method and means by which it is to be conducted; all inconveniences and hazards reasonably to be expected; and the effects upon his health or person which may possibly come from his participation in the experiment.

   The duty and responsibility for ascertaining the quality of the consent rests upon each individual who initiates, directs or engages in the experiment. It is a personal duty and responsibility which may not be delegated to another with impunity.

2. The experiment should be such as to yield fruitful results for the good of society, unprocurable by other methods or means of study, and not random and unnecessary in nature.

3. The experiment should be so designed and based on the results of animal experimentation and a knowledge of the natural history of the disease or other problem under study that the anticipated results will justify the performance of the experiment.

4. The experiment should be so conducted as to avoid all unnecessary physical and mental suffering and injury.

From "Permissible Medical Experiments," Trials of War Criminals Before the Nuremberg Military Tribunals Under Control Council Law No. 0: Nuremberg, October 1946–April 1949 (Washington, DC: Government Printing Office, n.d., vol. 2), 181–182.

5. No experiment should be conducted where there is an *a priori* reason to believe that death or disabling injury will occur; except, perhaps, in those experiments where the experimental physicians also serve as subjects.

6. The degree of risk to be taken should never exceed that determined by the humanitarian importance of the problem to be solved by the experiment.

7. Proper preparations should be made and adequate facilities provided to protect the experimental subject against even remote possibilities of injury, disability, or death.

8. The experiment should be conducted only by scientifically qualified persons. The highest degree of skill and care should be required through all stages of the experiment of those who conduct or engage in the experiment.

9. During the course of the experiment the human subject should be at liberty to bring the experiment to an end if he has reached the physical or mental state where continuation of the experiment seems to him to be impossible.

10. During the course of the experiment the scientist in charge must be prepared to terminate the experiment at any stage, if he has probable cause to believe, in the exercise of the good faith, superior skill and careful judgment required of him that a continuation of the experiment is likely to result in injury, disability, or death to the experimental subject.

Declaration of Helsinki—Ethical Principles for Medical Research Involving Human Subjects

World Medical Association

Preamble

1. The World Medical Association (WMA) has developed the Declaration of Helsinki as a statement of ethical principles for medical research involving human subjects, including research on identifiable human material and data.

    The Declaration is intended to be read as a whole and each of its constituent paragraphs should be applied with consideration of all other relevant paragraphs.

2. Consistent with the mandate of the WMA, the Declaration is addressed primarily to physicians. The WMA encourages others who are involved in medical research involving human subjects to adopt these principles.

General Principles

3. The Declaration of Geneva of the WMA binds the physician with the words, "The health of my patient will be my first consideration," and the International Code of Medical Ethics declares that, "A physician shall act in the patient's best interest when providing medical care."

4. It is the duty of the physician to promote and safeguard the health, well-being and rights of patients, including those who are involved in medical research. The physician's knowledge and conscience are dedicated to the fulfilment of this duty.

5. Medical progress is based on research that ultimately must include studies involving human subjects.

6. The primary purpose of medical research involving human subjects is to understand the causes, development and effects of diseases and improve preventive, diagnostic and therapeutic interventions (methods, procedures and treatments). Even the best proven interventions must be evaluated continually through research for their safety, effectiveness, efficiency, accessibility and quality.

7. Medical research is subject to ethical standards that promote and ensure respect for all human subjects and protect their health and rights.

8. While the primary purpose of medical research is to generate new knowledge, this goal can never take precedence over the rights and interests of individual research subjects.

9. It is the duty of physicians who are involved in medical research to protect the life, health, dignity, integrity, right to self-determination, privacy,

and confidentiality of personal information of research subjects. The responsibility for the protection of research subjects must always rest with the physician or other health care professionals and never with the research subjects, even though they have given consent.

10. Physicians must consider the ethical, legal and regulatory norms and standards for research involving human subjects in their own countries as well as applicable international norms and standards. No national or international ethical, legal or regulatory requirement should reduce or eliminate any of the protections for research subjects set forth in this Declaration.

11. Medical research should be conducted in a manner that minimises possible harm to the environment.

12. Medical research involving human subjects must be conducted only by individuals with the appropriate ethics and scientific education, training and qualifications. Research on patients or healthy volunteers requires the supervision of a competent and appropriately qualified physician or other health care professional.

13. Groups that are underrepresented in medical research should be provided appropriate access to participation in research.

14. Physicians who combine medical research with medical care should involve their patients in research only to the extent that this is justified by its potential preventive, diagnostic or therapeutic value and if the physician has good reason to believe that participation in the research study will not adversely affect the health of the patients who serve as research subjects.

15. Appropriate compensation and treatment for subjects who are harmed as a result of participating in research must be ensured.

Risks, Burdens and Benefits

16. In medical practice and in medical research, most interventions involve risks and burdens.

    Medical research involving human subjects may only be conducted if the importance of the objective outweighs the risks and burdens to the research subjects.

17. All medical research involving human subjects must be preceded by careful assessment of predictable risks and burdens to the individuals and groups involved in the research in comparison with foreseeable benefits to them and to other individuals or groups affected by the condition under investigation.

    Measures to minimise the risks must be implemented. The risks must be continuously monitored, assessed and documented by the researcher.

18. Physicians may not be involved in a research study involving human subjects unless they are confident that the risks have been adequately assessed and can be satisfactorily managed.

    When the risks are found to outweigh the potential benefits or when there is conclusive proof of definitive outcomes, physicians must assess whether to continue, modify or immediately stop the study.

Vulnerable Groups and Individuals

19. Some groups and individuals are particularly vulnerable and may have an increased likelihood of being wronged or of incurring additional harm.

    All vulnerable groups and individuals should receive specifically considered protection.

20. Medical research with a vulnerable group is only justified if the research is responsive to the health needs or priorities of this group and the research cannot be carried out in a non-vulnerable group. In addition, this group should stand to benefit from the knowledge, practices or interventions that result from the research.

Scientific Requirements and Research Protocols

21. Medical research involving human subjects must conform to generally accepted scientific principles, be based on a thorough knowledge of the scientific literature, other relevant sources of information, and adequate laboratory and, as appropriate, animal experimentation. The welfare of animals used for research must be respected.

22. The design and performance of each research study involving human subjects must be clearly described and justified in a research protocol.

    The protocol should contain a statement of the ethical considerations involved and should indicate how the principles in this Declaration have been addressed. The protocol should include information regarding funding, sponsors, institutional affiliations, potential conflicts of interest, incentives for subjects and information regarding provisions for treating and/or compensating subjects who are harmed as a consequence of participation in the research study.

In clinical trials, the protocol must also describe appropriate arrangements for post-trial provisions.

Research Ethics Committees

23. The research protocol must be submitted for consideration, comment, guidance and approval to the concerned research ethics committee before the study begins. This committee must be transparent in its functioning, must be independent of the researcher, the sponsor and any other undue influence and must be duly qualified. It must take into consideration the laws and regulations of the country or countries in which the research is to be performed as well as applicable international norms and standards but these must not be allowed to reduce or eliminate any of the protections for research subjects set forth in this Declaration.

The committee must have the right to monitor ongoing studies. The researcher must provide monitoring information to the committee, especially information about any serious adverse events. No amendment to the protocol may be made without consideration and approval by the committee. After the end of the study, the researchers must submit a final report to the committee containing a summary of the study's findings and conclusions.

Privacy and Confidentiality

24. Every precaution must be taken to protect the privacy of research subjects and the confidentiality of their personal information.

Informed Consent

25. Participation by individuals capable of giving informed consent as subjects in medical research must be voluntary. Although it may be appropriate to consult family members or community leaders, no individual capable of giving informed consent may be enrolled in a research study unless he or she freely agrees.

26. In medical research involving human subjects capable of giving informed consent, each potential subject must be adequately informed of the aims, methods, sources of funding, any possible conflicts of interest, institutional affiliations of the researcher, the anticipated benefits and potential risks of the study and the discomfort it may entail, post-study provisions and any other relevant aspects of the study. The potential subject must be informed of the right to refuse to participate in the study or to withdraw consent to participate at any time without reprisal. Special attention should be given to the specific information needs of individual potential subjects as well as to the methods used to deliver the information.

After ensuring that the potential subject has understood the information, the physician or another appropriately qualified individual must then seek the potential subject's freely-given informed consent, preferably in writing. If the consent cannot be expressed in writing, the non-written consent must be formally documented and witnessed.

All medical research subjects should be given the option of being informed about the general outcome and results of the study.

27. When seeking informed consent for participation in a research study the physician must be particularly cautious if the potential subject is in a dependent relationship with the physician or may consent under duress. In such situations the informed consent must be sought by an appropriately qualified individual who is completely independent of this relationship.

28. For a potential research subject who is incapable of giving informed consent, the physician must seek informed consent from the legally authorised representative. These individuals must not be included in a research study that has no likelihood of benefit for them unless it is intended to promote the health of the group represented by the potential subject, the research cannot instead be performed with persons capable of providing informed consent, and the research entails only minimal risk and minimal burden.

29. When a potential research subject who is deemed incapable of giving informed consent is able to give assent to decisions about participation in research, the physician must seek that assent in addition to the consent of the legally authorised representative. The potential subject's dissent should be respected.

30. Research involving subjects who are physically or mentally incapable of giving consent, for example, unconscious patients, may be done only if the physical or mental condition that prevents giving informed consent is a necessary characteristic of the research group. In such circumstances the physician must seek informed consent from the legally authorised representative. If no such representative is available and if the research cannot be delayed, the study may proceed without informed consent provided that the specific reasons for involving subjects with a condition that renders them unable to give informed consent have been stated in the research protocol and the study has been approved by a research ethics committee. Consent to remain in the research must be obtained as soon as possible from the subject or a legally authorised representative.

31. The physician must fully inform the patient which aspects of their care are related to the research. The refusal of a patient to participate in a study or the patient's decision to withdraw from the study must never adversely affect the patient-physician relationship.

32. For medical research using identifiable human material or data, such as research on material or data contained in biobanks or similar repositories, physicians must seek informed consent for its collection, storage and/or reuse. There may be exceptional situations where consent would be impossible or impracticable to obtain for such research. In such situations the research may be done only after consideration and approval of a research ethics committee.

Use of Placebo

33. The benefits, risks, burdens and effectiveness of a new intervention must be tested against those of the best proven intervention(s), except in the following circumstances:

    Where no proven intervention exists, the use of placebo, or no intervention, is acceptable; or

    Where for compelling and scientifically sound methodological reasons the use of any intervention less effective than the best proven one, the use of placebo, or no intervention is necessary to determine the efficacy or safety of an intervention and the patients who receive any intervention less effective than the best proven one, placebo, or no intervention will not be subject to additional risks of serious or irreversible harm as a result of not receiving the best proven intervention.

    Extreme care must be taken to avoid abuse of this option.

Post-Trial Provisions

34. In advance of a clinical trial, sponsors, researchers and host country governments should make provisions for post-trial access for all participants who still need an intervention identified as beneficial in the trial. This information must also be disclosed to participants during the informed consent process.

Research Registration and Publication and Dissemination of Results

35. Every research study involving human subjects must be registered in a publicly accessible database before recruitment of the first subject.

36. Researchers, authors, sponsors, editors and publishers all have ethical obligations with regard to the publication and dissemination of the results of research. Researchers have a duty to make publicly available the results of their research on human subjects and are accountable for the completeness and accuracy of their reports. All parties should adhere to accepted guidelines for ethical reporting. Negative and inconclusive as well as positive results must be published or otherwise made publicly available. Sources of funding, institutional affiliations and conflicts of interest must be declared in the publication. Reports of research not in accordance with the principles of this Declaration should not be accepted for publication.

Unproven Interventions in Clinical Practice

37. In the treatment of an individual patient, where proven interventions do not exist or other known interventions have been ineffective, the physician, after seeking expert advice, with informed consent from the patient or a legally authorised representative, may use an unproven intervention if in the physician's judgement it offers hope of saving life, re-establishing health or alleviating suffering. This intervention should subsequently be made the object of research, designed to evaluate its safety and efficacy. In all cases, new information must be recorded and, where appropriate, made publicly available.

Belmont Report

National Commission for the Protection of Human Subjects

The 1974 National Research Act mandated that every institution receiving federal funding for human subjects research establish an institutional review board (IRB) to provide oversight. The act was prompted by revelations about the federally-sponsored Tuskegee syphilis study (see Chapter 10), in which investigators enrolled patients without consent and failed to offer them standard-of-care treatment. The act also established the National Commission for the Protection of Human Subjects of Biomedical and Behavioral Research and charged it with identifying ethical principles and guidelines.

The resulting 1979 *Belmont Report* provides a framework for identifying, discussing, and settling ethical issues. It distinguishes medical practice from research and identifies three principles—respect for persons, beneficence, and justice—as generally accepted and most relevant for evaluating the ethical legitimacy of human-subjects research. To implement the *Report's* principles, in 1981 federal agencies adopted the Common Rule, which mandates IRBs and informed consent in federally-funded research. In 2015, major reforms were proposed to make risks and benefits to subjects more explicit, require written consent for the use of cells and tissues, reduce multiple IRB approvals, and expand IRB oversight to more institutions.

Ethical Principles and Guidelines for Research Involving Human Subjects

A. Boundaries Between Practice and Research

It is important to distinguish between biomedical and behavioral research, on the one hand, and the practice of accepted therapy on the other, in order to know what activities ought to undergo review for the protection of human subjects of research. The distinction between research and practice is blurred partly because both often occur together (as in research designed to evaluate a therapy) and partly because notable departures from standard practice are often called "experimental" when the terms "experimental" and "research" are not carefully defined.

Belmont Report from The National Commission for the Protection of Human Subjects of Biomedical and Behavioral Research, The Belmont Report: Ethical Principles and Guidelines for the Protection of Human Subjects of Research (April 18, 1979), http://ohsr.od.nih.gov/guidelines/belmont.html. (Notes omitted.)

For the most part, the term "practice" refers to interventions that are designed solely to enhance the well-being of an individual patient or client and that have a reasonable expectation of success. The purpose of medical or behavioral practice is to provide diagnosis, preventive treatment or therapy to particular individuals. By contrast, the term "research" designates an activity designed to test an hypothesis, permit conclusions to be drawn, and thereby to develop or contribute to generalizable knowledge (expressed, for example, in theories, principles, and statements of relationships). Research is usually described in a formal protocol that sets forth an objective and a set of procedures designed to reach that objective.

When a clinician departs in a significant way from standard or accepted practice, the innovation does not, in and of itself, constitute research. The fact that a procedure is "experimental," in the sense of new, untested or different, does not automatically place it in the category of research. Radically new procedures of this description should, however, be made the object of formal research at an early stage in order to determine whether they are safe and effective. Thus, it is the responsibility of medical practice committees, for example, to insist that a major innovation be incorporated into a formal research project.

Research and practice may be carried on together when research is designed to evaluate the safety and efficacy of a therapy. This need not cause any confusion regarding whether or not the activity requires review; the general rule is that if there is any element of research in an activity, that activity should undergo review for the protection of human subjects.

B. Basic Ethical Principles

The expression "basic ethical principles" refers to those general judgments that serve as a basic justification for the many particular ethical prescriptions and evaluations of human actions. Three basic principles, among those generally accepted in our cultural tradition, are particularly relevant to the ethics of research involving human subjects: the principles of respect of persons, beneficence and justices.

1. Respect for Persons. Respect for persons incorporates at least two ethical convictions: first, that individuals should be treated as autonomous agents, and second, that persons with diminished autonomy are entitled to protection. The principle of respect for persons thus divides into two separate moral requirements: the requirement to acknowledge autonomy and the requirement to protect those with diminished autonomy.

An autonomous person is an individual capable of deliberation about personal goals and of acting under the direction of such deliberation. To respect autonomy is to give weight to autonomous persons' considered opinions and choices while refraining from obstructing their actions unless they are clearly detrimental to others. To show lack of respect for an autonomous agent is to repudiate that person's considered judgments, to deny an individual the freedom to act on those considered judgments, or to withhold information necessary to make a considered judgment, when there are no compelling reasons to do so.

However, not every human being is capable of self-determination. The capacity for self-determination matures during an individual's life, and some individuals lose this capacity wholly or in part because of illness, mental disability, or circumstances that severely restrict liberty. Respect for the immature and the incapacitated may require protecting them as they mature or while they are incapacitated.

Some persons are in need of extensive protection, even to the point of excluding them from activities which may harm them; other persons require little protection beyond making sure they undertake activities freely and with awareness of possible adverse consequence. The extent of protection afforded should depend upon the risk of harm and the likelihood of benefit. The judgment that any individual lacks autonomy should be periodically reevaluated and will vary in different situations.

In most cases of research involving human subjects, respect for persons demands that subjects enter into the research voluntarily and with adequate information. In some situations, however, application of the principle is not obvious. The involvement of prisoners as subjects of research provides an instructive example. On the one hand, it would seem that the principle of respect for persons requires that prisoners not be deprived of the opportunity to volunteer for research. On the other hand, under prison conditions they may be subtly coerced or unduly influenced to engage in research activities for which they would not otherwise volunteer. Respect for persons would then dictate that prisoners be protected. Whether to allow prisoners to "volunteer" or to "protect" them presents a dilemma. Respecting persons, in most hard cases, is often a matter of balancing competing claims urged by the principle of respect itself.

2. Beneficence. Persons are treated in an ethical manner not only by respecting their decisions and protecting them from harm, but also by making efforts to secure their well-being. Such treatment falls under the principle of beneficence. The term "beneficence" is often understood to cover acts of kindness or charity that go beyond strict obligation. In this document, beneficence is understood in a stronger sense, as an obligation. Two general rules have been formulated as complementary expressions of beneficent actions in this sense: (1) do not harm and (2) maximize possible benefits and minimize possible harms.

The Hippocratic maxim "do no harm" has long been a fundamental principle of medical ethics. Claude Bernard extended it to the realm of research, saying that one should not injure one person regardless of the benefits that might come to others.

However, even avoiding harm requires learning what is harmful; and, in the process of obtaining this information, persons may be exposed to risk of harm. Further, the Hippocratic Oath requires physicians to benefit their patients "according to their best judgment." Learning what will in fact benefit may require exposing persons to risk. The problem posed by these imperatives is to decide when it is justifiable to seek certain benefits despite the risks involved, and when the benefits should be foregone because of the risks.

The obligations of beneficence affect both individual investigators and society at large, because they extend both to particular research projects and to the entire enterprise of research. In the case of particular projects, investigators and members of their institutions are obliged to give forethought to the maximization of benefits and the reduction of risk that might occur from the research investigation. In the case of scientific research in general, members of the larger society are obliged to recognize the longer term benefits and risks that may result from the improvement of knowledge and from the development of novel medical, psychotherapeutic, and social procedures.

The principle of beneficence often occupies a well-defined justifying role in many areas of research involving human subjects. An example is found in research involving children. Effective ways of treating childhood diseases and fostering healthy development are benefits that serve to justify research involving children—even when individual research subjects are not direct beneficiaries. Research also makes it possible to avoid the harm that may result from the application of previously accepted routine practices that on closer investigation turn out to be dangerous. But the role of the principle of beneficence is not always so unambiguous. A difficult ethical problem remains, for example, about research that presents more than minimal risk without immediate prospect of direct benefit to the children involved. Some have argued that such research is inadmissible, while others have pointed out that this limit would rule out much research promising great benefit to children in the future. Here again, as with all hard cases, the different claims covered by the principle of beneficence may come into conflict and force difficult choices.

3. Justice. Who ought to receive the benefits of research and bear its burdens? This is a question of justice, in the sense of "fairness in distribution" or

"what is deserved." An injustice occurs when some benefit to which a person is entitled is denied without good reason or when some burden is imposed unduly. Another way of conceiving the principle of justice is that equals ought to be treated equally. However, this statement requires explication. Who is equal and who is unequal? What considerations justify departure from equal distribution? Almost all commentators allow that distinctions based on experience, age, deprivation, competence, merit and position do sometimes constitute criteria justifying differential treatment for certain purposes. It is necessary, then, to explain in what respects people should be treated equally. There are several widely accepted formulations of just ways to distribute burdens and benefits. Each formulation mentions some relevant property on the basis of which burdens and benefits should be distributed. These formulations are (1) to each person an equal share, (2) to each person according to individual need, (3) to each person according to individual effort, (4) to each person according to societal contribution, and (5) to each person according to merit.

Questions of justice have long been associated with social practice[s] such as punishment, taxation and political representation. Until recently these questions have not generally been associated with scientific research. However, they are foreshadowed even in the earliest reflections on the ethics of research involving human subjects. For example, during the 19th and early 20th centuries the burdens of serving as research subjects fell largely upon poor ward patients, while the benefits of improved medical care flowed primarily to private patients. Subsequently, the exploitation of unwilling prisoners as research subjects in Nazi concentration camps was condemned as a particularly flagrant injustice. In this country, in the 1940's, the Tuskegee syphilis study used disadvantaged, rural black men to study the untreated course of a disease that is by no means confined to that population. These subjects were deprived of demonstrably effective treatment in order not to interrupt the project, long after such treatment became generally available.

Against this historical background, it can be seen how conceptions of justice are relevant to research involving human subjects. For example, the selection of research subjects needs to be scrutinized in order to determine whether some classes (e.g., welfare patients, particular racial and ethnic minorities, or persons confined to institutions) are being systematically selected simply because of their easy availability, their compromised position, or their manipulability, rather than for reasons directly related to the problem being studied. Finally, whenever research supported by public funds leads to the development of therapeutic devices and procedures, justice demands both that these not provide advantages only to those who can afford them and that such research should not unduly involve persons from groups unlikely to be among the beneficiaries of subsequent applications of the research.

Philosophical Reflections on Experimenting with Human Subjects

Hans Jonas

Jonas argues that if we justify experiments by considering them a right of society, then we are exposing individuals to dangers for the general good. This, for Jonas, is inherently wrong, and no individual should be forced to surrender himself or herself to a social goal.

Any risk that is taken must be voluntary; but obtaining informed consent, Jonas claims, is not sufficient to justify the experimental use of human beings. Two other conditions must be met: first, subjects must be recruited from those who are most knowledgeable about the circumstances of research and most capable of grasping its purposes and procedures; second, the experiment must be undertaken for an adequate cause. Jonas cautions us that the progress which may come from research is not necessarily worth our efforts or approval, and he reminds us that there are moral values which we ought not to abandon in the pursuit of science.

Experimenting with human subjects is going on in many fields of scientific and technological progress. It is designed to replace the overall instruction by natural, occasional experience with the selective information from artificial, systematic experiment which physical science has found so effective in dealing with inanimate nature. Of the new experimentation with man, medical is surely the most legitimate; psychological, the most dubious; biological (still to come), the most dangerous. I have chosen here to deal with the first only, where the case *for* it is strongest and the task of adjudicating conflicting claims hardest....

From Hans Jonas, "Philosophical Reflections on Experimenting with Human Subjects." Reprinted by permission of *Daedalus, Journal of the American Academy of Arts and Sciences*, Spring 1969, Boston, Mass. This essay is included, on pp. 105–131, in a 1980 re-edition of Jonas's *Philosophical Essays: From Current Creed to Technological Man*, published by the University of Chicago Press. Notes omitted.

The Melioristic Goal, Medical Research, and Individual Duty

Nowhere is the melioristic goal [of working toward improvement] more inherent than in medicine. To the physician, it is not gratuitous. He is committed to curing and thus to improving the power to cure. Gratuitous we called it (outside disaster conditions) as a *social* goal, but noble at the same time. Both the nobility and the gratuitousness must influence the manner in which self-sacrifice for it is elicited, and even its free offer accepted. Freedom is certainly the first condition to be observed here. The surrender of one's body to medical experimentation is entirely outside the enforceable "social contract."

Or can it be construed to fall within its terms—namely, as repayment for benefits from past experimentation that I have enjoyed myself? But I am indebted for these benefits not to society, but to the past "martyrs" to whom society is indebted itself, and society has no right to call in my personal debt by way of adding new to its own. Moreover, gratitude is not an enforceable social obligation; it anyway does not mean that I must emulate the deed. Most of all, if it was wrong to exact such sacrifice in the first place, it does not become right to exact it again with the plea of the profit it has brought me. If, however, it was not exacted, but entirely free, as it ought to have been, then it should remain so, and its precedence must not be used as a social pressure on others for doing the same under the sign of duty. . . .

The "Conscription" of Consent

The mere issuing of the appeal, the calling for volunteers, with the moral and social pressures it inevitably generates, amounts even under the most meticulous rules of consent to a sort of *conscripting*. And some soliciting is necessarily involved. . . . And this is why "consent," surely a nonnegotiable minimum requirement, is not the full answer to the problem. Granting then that soliciting and therefore some degree of conscripting are part of the situation, who may conscript and who may be conscripted? Or less harshly expressed: Who should issue appeals and to whom?

The naturally qualified issuer of the appeal is the research scientist himself, collectively the main carrier of the impulse and the only one with the technical competence to judge. But his being very much an interested party (with vested interests, indeed, not purely in the public good, but in the scientific enterprise as such, in "his" project, and even in his career) makes him also suspect. The ineradicable dialectic of this situation—a delicate incompatibility problem—calls for particular controls by the research community and by public authority that we need not discuss. They can mitigate, but not eliminate the problem. We have to live with the ambiguity, the treacherous impurity of everything human.

Self-Recruitment of the Community

To whom should the appeal be addressed? The natural issuer of the call is also the first natural addressee: the physician-researcher himself and the scientific confraternity at large. With such a coincidence—indeed, the noble tradition with which the whole business of human experimentation started—almost all of the associated legal, ethical, and metaphysical problems vanish. If it is full, autonomous identification of the subject with the purpose that is required for the dignifying of his serving as a subject—here it is; if strongest motivation—here it is; if fullest understanding—here it is; if freest decision—here it is; if greatest integration with the person's total, chosen pursuit—here it is. With the fact of self-solicitation the issue of consent in all its insoluble equivocality is bypassed per se. Not even the condition that the particular purpose be truly important and the project reasonably promising, which must hold in any solicitation of others, need be satisfied here. By himself, the scientist is free to obey his obsession, to play his hunch, to wager on chance, to follow the lure of ambition. It is all part of the "divine madness" that somehow animates the ceaseless pressing against frontiers. For the rest of society, which has a deep-seated disposition to look with reverence and awe upon the guardians of the mysteries of life, the profession assumes with this proof of its devotion the role of a self-chosen, consecrated fraternity, not unlike the monastic orders of the past, and this would come nearest to the actual, religious origins of the art of healing. . . .

"Identification" as the Principle of Recruitment in General

If the properties we adduced as the particular qualifications of the members of the scientific fraternity itself are taken as general criteria of selection, then one should look for additional subjects where a maximum of identification, understanding, and spontaneity can be expected—that is, among the most highly motivated, the most highly educated, and the least "captive" members of the community. From this naturally scarce resource, a descending order of permissibility leads to greater abundance and ease of supply, whose use should become proportionately more hesitant as the exculpating criteria are relaxed. An inversion of normal "market" behavior is demanded here—namely, to accept the lowest quotation last (and excused only by the greatest pressure of need); to pay the highest price first.

The ruling principle in our considerations is that the "wrong" of reification can only be made "right" by such authentic identification with the cause that it is the subject's as well as the researcher's cause—whereby his role in its service is not just permitted by him, but *willed*. That sovereign will of his which embraces the end as his own restores his personhood to the otherwise depersonalizing context. To be valid it must be autonomous and informed. The latter condition can, outside the research community, only be fulfilled by degrees; but the higher the degree of understanding regarding the purpose and the technique, the more valid becomes the endorsement of the will. A margin of mere trust inevitably remains. Ultimately, the appeal for volunteers should seek this free and generous endorsement, the appropriation of the research purpose into the person's own scheme of ends. Thus, the appeal is in truth addressed to the one, mysterious, and sacred source of any such, generosity of the will—"devotion," whose forms and objects of commitment are various and may invest different motivations in different individuals. The following, for instance, may be responsive to the "call" we are discussing: compassion with human sufferings, zeal for humanity, reverence for the Golden Rule, enthusiasm for progress, homage to the cause of knowledge, even longing for sacrificial justification (do not call that "masochism," please). On all these, I say, it is defensible and right to draw when the research objective is worthy enough; and it is a prime duty of the research community (especially in view of what we called the "margin of trust") to see that this sacred source is never abused for frivolous ends. For a less than adequate cause, not even the freest, unsolicited offer should be accepted.

The Rule of the "Descending Order" and Its Counterutility Sense

We have laid down what must seem to be a forbidding rule to the number-hungry research industry. Having faith in the transcendent potential of man, I do not fear that the "source" will ever foil a society that does not destroy it—and only such a one is worthy of the blessings of progress. But "elitistic" the rule is (as is the enterprise of progress itself), and elites are by nature small. The combined attribute of motivation and information, plus the absence of external pressures, tends to be socially so circumscribed that strict adherence to the rule might numerically starve the research process. This is why I spoke of a descending order of permissibility which is itself permissive, but where the realization that it is a *descending* order is not without pragmatic import. Departing from the august norm, the appeal must need shift from idealism to docility,

from high-mindedness to compliance, from judgment to trust. Consent spreads over the whole spectrum. I will not go into the casuistics of this penumbral area. I merely indicate the principle of the order of preference: The poorer in knowledge, motivation, and freedom of decision (and that alas, means the more readily available in terms of numbers and possible manipulation), the more sparingly and indeed reluctantly should the reservoir be used, and the more compelling must therefore become the countervailing justification.

Let us note that this is the opposite of a social utility standard, the reverse of the order by "availability and expandability": The most valuable and scarcest, the least expendable elements of the social organism, are to be the first candidates for risk and sacrifice. It is the standard of *noblesse oblige,* and with all its counterutility and seeming "wastefulness," we feel a rightness about it and perhaps even a higher "utility," for the soul of the community lives by this spirit. It is also the opposite of what the day-to-day interests of research clamor for, and for the scientific community to honor it will mean that it will have to fight a strong temptation to go by routine to the readiest sources of supply—the suggestible, the ignorant, the dependent, the "captive" in various senses. I do not believe that heightened resistance here must cripple research, which cannot be permitted; but it may indeed slow it down by the smaller numbers fed into experimentation in consequence. This price—a possibly slower rate of progress—may have to be paid for the preservation of the most precious capital of higher communal life.

Experimentation on Patients

So far we have been speaking on the tacit assumption that the subjects of experimentation are recruited from among the healthy. To the question "Who is conscriptable?" the spontaneous answer is: Least and last of all the sick—the most available of all as they are under treatment and observation anyway. That the afflicted should not be called upon to bear additional burden and risk, that they are society's special trust and the physician's trust in particular—these are elementary responses of our moral sense. Yet the very destination of medical research, the conquest of disease, requires at the crucial stage trial and verification on precisely the sufferers from the disease, and their total exemption would defeat the purpose itself. In acknowledging this inescapable necessity, we enter the most sensitive area of the whole complex, the one most keenly felt and most searchingly discussed by the practitioners themselves. No wonder, it touches the heart of the doctor–patient relation, putting its most solemn obligations to the test. There is nothing new in what I have to say about the ethics of the doctor–patient relation, but for the purpose of confronting it with the issue of experimentation some of the oldest verities must be recalled.

The Fundamental Privilege of the Sick

In the course of treatment, the physician is obligated to the patient and to no one else. He is not the agent of society, nor of the interests of medical science, nor of the patient's family, nor of his co-sufferers, nor of future sufferers from the same disease. The patient alone counts when he is under the physician's care. By the simple law of bilateral contract (analogous, for example, to the relation of lawyer to client and its "conflict of interest" rule), the physician is bound not to let any other interest interfere with that of the patient in being cured. But manifestly more sublime norms than contractual ones are involved. We may speak of a sacred trust; strictly by its terms, the doctor is, as it were, alone with his patient and God.

There is one normal exception to this—that is, to the doctor's not being the agent of society vis-à-vis the patient, but the trustee of his interests alone: the quarantining of the contagious sick. This is plainly not for the patient's interest, but for that of others threatened by him. (In vaccination, we have a combination of both: protection of the individual and others.) But preventing the patient from causing harm to others is not the same as exploiting him for the advantage of others. And there is, of course, the abnormal exception of collective catastrophe, the analogue to a state of war. The physician who desperately battles a raging epidemic is under a unique dispensation that suspends in a nonspecifiable way some of the structures of normal practice, including possibly those against experimental liberties with his patients. No rules can be devised for the waiving of rules in extremities. And as with the famous shipwreck examples of ethical theory, the less said about it the better. But what is allowable there and may later be passed over in forgiving silence cannot

serve as a precedent. We are concerned with non-extreme, non-emergency conditions where the voice of principle can be heard and claims can be adjudicated free from duress. We have conceded that there are such claims, and that if there is to be medical advance at all, not even the superlative privilege of the suffering and the sick can be kept wholly intact from the intrusion of its needs. About this least palatable, most disquieting part of our subject I have to offer only groping, inconclusive remarks.

The Principle of "Identification" Applied to Patients

On the whole, the same principles would seem to hold here as are found to hold with "normal subjects": motivation, identification, understanding on the part of the subject. But it is clear that these conditions are peculiarly difficult to satisfy with regard to a patient. His physical state, psychic preoccupation, dependent relation to the doctor, the submissive attitude induced by treatment—everything connected with his condition and situation makes the sick person inherently less of a sovereign person than the healthy one. Spontaneity of self-offering was almost to be ruled out; consent is marred by lower resistance or captive circumstance, and so on. In fact, all the factors that make the patient, as a category, particularly accessible and welcome for experimentation at the same time compromise the quality of the responding affirmation that must morally redeem the making use of them. This, in addition to the primacy of the physician's duty, puts a heightened onus on the physician-researcher to limit his undue power to the most important and defensible research objectives and, of course, to keep persuasion at a minimum.

Still, with all the disabilities noted, there is scope among patients for observing the rule of the "descending order of permissibility" that we have laid down for normal subjects, in vexing inversion of the utility order of quantitative abundance and qualitative "expendability." By the principle of this order, those patients who most identify with and are cognizant of the cause of research—members of the medical profession (who after all are sometimes patients themselves)—come first; the highly motivated and educated, also least dependent, among the lay patients come next; and so on down the line. An added consideration here is seriousness of condition, which again operates in inverse proportion. Here the profession must fight the tempting sophistry that the hopeless case is expendable (because in prospect already expended) and therefore especially usable; and generally the attitude that the poorer the chances of the patient the more justifiable his recruitment for experimentation (other than for his own benefit). The opposite is true.

Nondisclosure as a Borderline Case

Then there is the case where ignorance of the subject, sometimes even of the experimenter, is of the essence of the experiment (the "double-blind"–control group–placebo syndrome). It is said to be a necessary element of the scientific process. Whatever may be said about its ethics in regard to normal subjects, especially volunteers, it is an outright betrayal of trust in regard to the patient who believes that he is receiving treatment. Only supreme importance of the objective can exonerate it, without making it less of a transgression. The patient is definitely wronged even when not harmed. And ethics apart, the practice of such deception holds the danger of undermining the faith in the *bona fides* of treatment, the beneficial intent of the physician—the very basis of the doctor–patient relationship. In every respect it follows that concealed experiment on patients—that is, experiment under the guise of treatment—should be the rarest exception, at best, if it cannot be wholly avoided.

This has still the merit of a borderline problem. The same is not true of the other case of necessary ignorance of the subject—that of the unconscious patient. Drafting him for nontherapeutic experiments is simply and unqualifiedly impermissible; progress or not he must never be used, on the inflexible principle that utter helplessness demands utter protection.

When preparing this paper, I filled pages with a casuistic of this harrowing field, but then scrapped most of it, realizing my dilettante status. The shadings are endless, and only the physician-researcher can discern them properly as the cases arise. Into his lap the decision is thrown. The philosophical rule, once it has admitted into itself the idea of a sliding scale, cannot really specify its own application. It can only impress on the practitioner a general maxim or attitude for the exercise of his judgment and conscience in the concrete occa-

sions of his work. In our case, I am afraid, it means making life more difficult for him.

It will also be noted that, somewhat at variance with the emphasis in the literature, I have not dwelt on the element of "risk" and very little on that of "consent." Discussion of the first is beyond the layman's competence; the emphasis on the second has been lessened because of its equivocal character. It is a truism to say that one should strive to minimize the risk and to maximize the consent. The more demanding concept of "identification," which I have used, includes "consent" in its maximal or authentic form, and the assumption of risk is its privilege.

No Experiments on Patients Unrelated to Their Own Disease

Although my ponderings have, on the whole, yielded points of view rather than definite prescriptions, premises rather than conclusions, they have led me to a few unequivocal yeses and nos. The first is the emphatic rule that patients should be experimented upon, if at all, *only* with reference to *their disease*. Never should there be added to the gratuitousness of the experiment as such the gratuitousness of service to an unrelated cause. This follows simply from what we have found to be the only excuse for infracting the special exemption of the sick at all—namely, that the scientific war on disease cannot accomplish its goal without drawing the sufferers from disease into the investigative process. If under this excuse they become subjects of experiment, they do so *because,* and only because, of *their* disease.

This is the fundamental and self-sufficient consideration. That the patient cannot possibly benefit from the unrelated experiment therapeutically, while he might from experiment related to his condition, is also true, but lies beyond the problem area of pure experiment. I am in any case discussing nontherapeutic experimentation only, where *ex hypothesi* the patient does not benefit. Experiment as part of therapy—that is, directed toward helping the subject himself—is a different matter altogether and raises its own problems but hardly philosophical ones. As long as a doctor can say, even if only in his own thought: "There is no known cure for your condition (or: You have responded to none); but there is promise in a new treatment still under investigation, not quite tested yet as to effectiveness and safety;

you will be taking a chance, but all things considered, I judge it in your best interest to let me try it on you"—as long as he can speak thus, he speaks as the patient's physician and may err, but does not transform the patient into a subject of experimentation. Introduction of an untried therapy into the treatment where the tried ones have failed is not "experimentation on the patient."

Generally, and almost needless to say, with all the rules of the book, there is something "experimental" (because tentative) about every individual treatment, beginning with the diagnosis itself and he would be a poor doctor who would not learn from every case for the benefit of future cases, and a poor member of the profession who would not make any new insights gained from his treatments available to the profession at large. Thus, knowledge may be advanced in the treatment of any patient, and the interest of the medical art and all sufferers from the same affliction as well as the patient himself may be served if something happens to be learned from his case. But his gain to knowledge and future therapy is incidental to the *bona fide* service to the present patient. He has the right to expect that the doctor does nothing to him just in order to learn.

In that case, the doctor's imaginary speech would run, for instance, like this: "There is nothing more I can do for you. But you can do something for me. Speaking no longer as your physician but on behalf of medical science, we could learn a great deal about future cases of this kind if you would permit me to perform certain experiments on you. It is understood that you yourself would not benefit from any knowledge we might gain; but future patients would." This statement would express the purely experimental situation, assumedly here with the subject's concurrence and with all cards on the table. In Alexander Bicker's words: "It is a different situation when the doctor is no longer trying to make [the patient] well, but is trying to find out how to make others well in the future."

But even in the second case, that of the non-therapeutic experiment where the patient does not benefit, at least the patient's own disease is enlisted in the cause of fighting that disease, even if only in others. It is yet another thing to say or think: "Since you are here—in the hospital with its facilities—anyway, under our care and observation anyway, away from your job (or, perhaps, doomed) anyway, we wish to profit from your being available for some other research of great interest we are presently engaged in." From the standpoint of merely medical ethics, which has only to consider risk, consent, and the worth of the objective, there may be no cardinal difference between this case and the last one. I hope that the medical reader will not think I am making too fine a point when I say that from the standpoint of the subject and his dignity there is a cardinal difference that crosses the line between the permissible and the impermissible, and this by the same principle of "Identification" I have been invoking all along. Whatever the rights and wrongs of any experimentation on any patient—in the one case, at least that residue of identification is left him that it is his own affliction by which he can contribute to the conquest of that affliction, his own kind of suffering which he helps to alleviate in others; and so in a sense it is his own cause. It is totally indefensible to rob the unfortunate of this intimacy with the purpose and make his misfortune a convenience for the furtherance of alien concerns.

Conclusion

…I wish only to say in conclusion that if some of the practical implications of my reasonings are felt to work out toward a slower rate of progress, this should not cause too great dismay. Let us not forget that progress is an optional goal, not an unconditional commitment and that its tempo in particular, compulsive as it may become, has nothing sacred about it. Let us also remember, that a slower progress in the conquest of disease would not threaten society, grievous as it is to those who have to deplore that their particular disease be not yet conquered, but that society would indeed be threatened by the erosion of those moral values whose loss, possibly caused by too ruthless a pursuit of scientific progress, would make its most dazzling triumphs not worth having. Let us finally remember that it cannot be the aim of progress to abolish the lot of mortality. Of some ill or other, each of us will die. Our mortal condition is upon us with its harshness but also its wisdom—because without it there would not be the eternally renewed promise of the freshness, immediacy, and eagerness of youth; nor would there be for any of us the incentive to number our days and make them count. With all our striving to wrest from our mortality what we can, we should bear its burden with patience and dignity.

Section 2:   The Ethics of Randomized Clinical Trials

Of Mice but Not Men: Problems of the Randomized Clinical Trial

Samuel Hellman and Deborah S. Hellman

Samuel and Deborah Hellman show how randomized clinical trials (RCTs) in medicine may create an ethical dilemma for the physician who is also acting as a scientist. A physician is committed to the interest of an individual patient, while a scientist may have to sacrifice the interests of a present patient to benefit future ones, thus undermining the physician–patient relationship.

The Hellmans reject a utilitarian argument that would sacrifice the interests of individual patients for the benefit of future ones. They argue that the physician–patient relationship implies that patients have a right to receive a physician's best judgment and care, and that physicians have a duty to provide them. The methods typically used in a RCT may require a physician to violate this duty by remaining ignorant of whether a patient is receiving the best available therapy. An RCT may also prompt a physician to continue a therapy she no longer believes is most beneficial for a patient.

The Hellmans conclude with a discussion of the ways in which problems such as observer bias and patient selection might be overcome with out resorting to RCTs.

As medicine has become increasingly scientific and less accepting of unsupported opinion or proof by anecdote, the randomized controlled clinical trial has become the standard technique for changing diagnostic or therapeutic methods. The use of this technique creates an ethical dilemma. Researchers participating in such studies are required to modify their ethical commitments to individual patients and do serious damage to the concept of the physician as a practicing, empathetic professional who is primarily concerned with each patient as an individual. Researchers using a randomized clinical trial can be described as physician-scientists, a term that expresses the tension between the two roles. The physician, by entering into a relationship with an individual patient, assumes certain obligations, including the commitment always to act in the patient's best interests.

From The *New England Journal of Medicine*, Samuel Hellman and Deborah S. Hellman, "Of Mice but Not Men: Problems of the Randomized Clinical Trial," 324, no. 22 (1991): 1585–1589. Copyright © 1991. Massachusetts Medical Society. Reprinted with permission from Massachusetts Medical Society. (References omitted.)

As Leon Kass has rightly maintained, "the physician must produce unswervingly the virtues of loyalty and fidelity to his patient." Though the ethical requirements of this relationship have been modified by legal obligations to report wounds of a suspicious nature and certain infectious diseases, these obligations in no way conflict with the central ethical obligation to act in the best interests of the patient medically. Instead, certain nonmedical interests of the patient are preempted by other social concerns.

The role of the scientist is quite different. The clinical scientist is concerned with answering questions — i.e., determining the validity of formally constructed hypotheses. Such scientific information, it is presumed, will benefit humanity in general. The clinical scientist's role has been well described by Dr. Anthony Fauci, director of the National Institute of Allergy and Infectious Diseases, who states the goals of the randomized clinical trial in these words: "It's not to deliver therapy. It's to answer a scientific question so that the drug can be available for everybody once you've established safety and efficacy." The demands of such a study can conflict in a number of ways with the physician's duty to minister to patients. The study may create a false dichotomy in the physician's opinions: according to the premise of the randomized clinical trial, the physician may only know or not know whether a proposed course of treatment represents an improvement; no middle position is permitted. What the physician thinks, suspects, believes, or has a hunch about is assigned to the "not knowing" category, because knowing is defined on the basis of an arbitrary but accepted statistical test performed in a randomized clinical trial. Thus, little credence is given to information gained beforehand in other ways or to information accrued during the trial but without the required statistical degree of assurance that a difference is not due to chance. The randomized clinical trial also prevents the treatment technique from being modified on the basis of the growing knowledge of the physicians during their participation in the trial. Moreover, it limits access to the data as they are collected until specific milestones are achieved. This prevents physicians from profiting not only from their individual experience, but also from the collective experience of the other participants.

The randomized clinical trial requires doctors to act simultaneously as physicians and as scientists. This puts them in a difficult and sometimes untenable ethical position. The conflicting moral demands arising from the use of the randomized clinical trial reflect the classic conflict between rights-based moral theories and utilitarian ones. The first of these, which depend on the moral theory of Immanuel Kant (and seen more recently in neo-Kantian philosophers, such as John Rawls), asserts that human beings, by virtue of their unique capacity for rational thought, are bearers of dignity. As such, they ought not to be treated merely as means to an end; rather, they must always be treated as ends in themselves. Utilitarianism, by contrast, defines what is right as the greatest good for the greatest number—that is, as social utility. This view, articulated by Jeremy Bentham and John Stuart Mill, requires that pleasures (understood broadly, to include such pleasures as health and well-being) and pains be added together. The morally correct act is the act that produces the most pleasure and the least pain overall.

A classic objection to the utilitarian position is that according to that theory, the distribution of pleasures and pains is of no moral consequence. This element of the theory severely restricts physicians from being utilitarians, or at least from following the theory's dictates. Physicians must care very

deeply about the distribution of pain and pleasure, for they have entered into a relationship with one or a number of individual patients. They cannot be indifferent to whether it is these patients or others that suffer for the general benefit of society. Even though society might gain from the suffering of a few, and even though the doctor might believe that such a benefit is worth a given patient's suffering (i.e., that utilitarianism is right in the particular case), the ethical obligation created by the covenant between doctor and patient requires the doctor to see the interests of the individual patient as primary and compelling. In essence, the doctor-patient relationship requires doctors to see their patients as bearers of rights who cannot be merely used for the greater good of humanity.

As Fauci has suggested, the randomized clinical trial routinely asks physicians to sacrifice the interests of their particular patients for the sake of the study and that of the information that it will make available for the benefit of society. This practice is ethically problematic. Consider first the initial formulation of a trial. In particular, consider the case of a disease for which there is no satisfactory therapy—for example, advanced cancer or the acquired immunodeficiency syndrome (AIDS). A new agent that promises more effectiveness is the subject of the study. The control group must be given either an unsatisfactory treatment or a placebo. Even though the therapeutic value of the new agent is unproved, if physicians think that it has promise, are they acting in the best interests of their patients in allowing them to be randomly assigned to the control group? Is persisting in such an assignment consistent with the specific commitments taken on in the doctor-patient relationship? As a result of interactions with patients with AIDS and their advocates, Merigan recently suggested modifications in the design of clinical trials that attempt to deal with the unsatisfactory treatment given to the control group. The view of such activists has been expressed by Rebecca Pringle Smith of Community Research Initiative in New York: "Even if you have a supply of compliant martyrs, trials must have some ethical validity."

If the physician has no opinion about whether the new treatment is acceptable, then random assignment is ethically acceptable, but such lack of enthusiasm for the new treatment does not augur well for either the patient or the study. Alternatively, the treatment may show promise of beneficial results but also present a risk of undesirable complications. When the physician believes that the severity and likelihood of harm and good are evenly balanced, randomization may be ethically acceptable. If the physician has no preference for either treatment (is in a state of equipoise), then randomization is acceptable. If, however, he or she believes that the new treatment may be either more or less successful or more or less toxic, the use of randomization is not consistent with fidelity to the patient.

The argument usually used to justify randomization is that it provides, in essence, a critique of the usefulness of the physician's beliefs and opinions, those that have not yet been validated by a randomized clinical trial. As the argument goes, these not-yet-validated beliefs are as likely to be wrong as right. Although physicians are ethically required to provide their patients with the best available treatment, there simply is no best treatment yet known.

The reply to this argument takes two forms. First, and most important, even if this view of the reliability of a physician's opinions is accurate, the ethical constraints of an individual doctor's relationship with a particular patient require the doctor to provide individual care. Although physicians must take pains to make clear the speculative nature of their views, they cannot withhold these views from the patient. The patient asks from the doctor both knowledge and judgment. The relationship established between them rightfully allows patients to ask for the judgment of their particular physicians, not merely that of the medical profession in general. Second, it may not be true, in fact, that the not-yet-validated beliefs of physicians are as likely to be wrong as right. The greater certainty obtained with a randomized clinical trial is beneficial, but that does not mean that a lesser degree of certainty is without value. Physicians can acquire knowledge through methods other than the randomized clinical trial. Such knowledge, acquired over time and less formally than is required in a randomized clinical trial, may be of great value to a patient.

Even if it is ethically acceptable to begin a study, one often forms an opinion during its course—especially in studies that are impossible to conduct in a truly double-blinded fashion—that makes it ethically problematic to continue. The inability to remain blinded usually occurs in studies of cancer or AIDS, for example, because the therapy is associated by nature with serious side effects. Trials attempt to restrict the physician's access to the data in order to prevent such unblinding. Such restrictions should make physicians eschew the trial, since their ability to act in

the patient's best interests will be limited. Even supporters of randomized clinical trials, such as Merigan, agree that interim findings should be presented to patients to ensure that no one receives what seems an inferior treatment. Once physicians have formed a view about the new treatment, can they continue randomization? If random assignment is stopped, the study may be lost and the participation of the previous patients wasted. However, if physicians continue the randomization when they have a definite opinion about the efficacy of the experimental drug, they are not acting in accordance with the requirements of the doctor-patient relationship. Furthermore, as their opinion becomes more firm, stopping the randomization may not be enough. Physicians may be ethically required to treat the patients formerly placed in the control group with the therapy that now seems probably effective. To do so would be faithful to the obligations created by the doctor-patient relationship, but it would destroy the study.

To resolve this dilemma, one might suggest that the patient has abrogated the rights implicit in a doctor-patient relationship by signing an informed-consent form. We argue that such rights cannot be waived or abrogated. They are inalienable. The right to be treated as an individual deserving the physician's best judgment and care, rather than to be used as a means to determine the best treatment for others, is inherent in every person. This right, based on the concept of dignity, cannot be waived. What of altruism, then? Is it not the patient's right to make a sacrifice for the general good? This question must be considered from both positions—that of the patient and that of the physician. Although patients may decide to waive this right, it is not consistent with the role of a physician to ask that they do so. In asking, the doctor acts as a scientist instead. The physician's role here is to propose what he or she believes is best medically for the specific patient, not to suggest participation in a study from which the patient cannot gain. Because the opportunity to help future patients is of potential value to a patient, some would say physicians should not deny it. Although this point has merit, it offers so many opportunities for abuse that we are extremely uncomfortable about accepting it. The responsibilities of physicians are much clearer; they are to minister to the current patient.

Moreover, even if patients could waive this right, it is questionable whether those with terminal illness would be truly able to give voluntary informed consent.

Such patients are extremely dependent on both their physicians and the health care system. Aware of this dependence, physicians must not ask for consent, for in such cases the very asking breaches the doctor-patient relationship. Anxious to please their physicians, patients may have difficulty refusing to participate in the trial the physicians describe. The patients may perceive their refusal as damaging to the relationship, whether or not it is so. Such perceptions of coercion affect the decision. Informed-consent forms are difficult to understand, especially for patients under the stress of serious illness for which there is no satisfactory treatment. The forms are usually lengthy, somewhat legalistic, complicated, and confusing, and they hardly bespeak the compassion expected of the medical profession. It is important to remember that those who have studied the doctor-patient relationship have emphasized its empathetic nature.

> [The] relationship between doctor and patient partakes of a peculiar intimacy. It presupposes on the part of the physician not only knowledge of his fellow men but sympathy.... This aspect of the practice of medicine has been designated as the art; yet I wonder whether it should not, most properly, be called the essence.

How is such a view of the relationship consonant with random assignment and informed consent? The Physician's Oath of the World Medical Association affirms the primacy of the deontologic view of patients' rights: "Concern for the interests of the subject must always prevail over the interests of science and society."

Furthermore, a single study is often not considered sufficient. Before a new form of therapy is generally accepted, confirmatory trials must be conducted. How can one conduct such trials ethically unless one is convinced that the first trial was in error? The ethical problems we have discussed are only exacerbated when a completed randomized clinical trial indicates that a given treatment is preferable. Even if the physician believes the initial trial was in error, the physician must indicate to the patient the full results of that trial.

The most common reply to the ethical arguments has been that the alternative is to return to the physician's intuition, to anecdotes, or to both as the basis of medical opinion. We all accept the dangers of such a practice. The argument states that we must therefore accept randomized, controlled clinical trials regardless of their ethical problems because of the great social benefit they make possible, and we salve our conscience

with the knowledge that informed consent has been given. This returns us to the conflict between patients' rights and social utility. Some would argue that this tension can be resolved by placing a relative value on each. If the patient's right that is being compromised is not a fundamental right and the social gain is very great, then the study might be justified. When the right is fundamental, however, no amount of social gain, or almost none, will justify its sacrifice. Consider, for example, the experiments on humans done by physicians under the Nazi regime. All would agree that these are unacceptable regardless of the value of the scientific information gained. Some people go so far as to say that no use should be made of the results of those experiments because of the clearly unethical manner in which the data were collected. This extreme example may not seem relevant, but we believe that in its hyperbole it clarifies the fallacy of a utilitarian approach to the physician's relationship with the patient. To consider the utilitarian gain is consistent neither with the physician's role nor with the patient's rights.

It is fallacious to suggest that only the randomized clinical trial can provide valid information or that all information acquired by this technique is valid. Such experimental methods are intended to reduce error and bias and therefore reduce the uncertainty of the result. Uncertainty cannot be eliminated, however. The scientific method is based on increasing probabilities and increasingly refined approximations of truth. Although the randomized clinical trial contributes to these ends, it is neither unique nor perfect. Other techniques may also be useful.

Randomized trials often place physicians in the ethically intolerable position of choosing between the good of the patient and that of society. We urge that such situations be avoided and that other techniques of acquiring clinical information be adopted. For example, concerning trials of treatments for AIDS, Byar et al. have said that "some traditional approaches to the clinical-trials process may be unnecessarily rigid and unsuitable for this disease." In this case, AIDS is not what is so different; rather, the difference is in the presence of AIDS activists, articulate spokespersons for the ethical problems created by the application of the randomized clinical trial to terminal illnesses. Such arguments are equally applicable to advanced cancer and other serious illnesses. Byar et al. agree that there are even circumstances in which uncontrolled clinical trials may be justified: when there is no effective treatment to use as a control, when the prognosis is uniformly poor, and when there is a reasonable expectation of benefit without excessive toxicity. These conditions are usually found in clinical trials of advanced cancer.

The purpose of the randomized clinical trial is to avoid the problems of observer bias and patient selection. It seems to us that techniques might be developed to deal with these issues in other ways. Randomized clinical trials deal with them in a cumbersome and heavy-handed manner, by requiring large numbers of patients in the hope that random assignment will balance the heterogeneous distribution of patients into the different groups. By observing known characteristics of patients, such as age and sex, and distributing them equally between groups, it is thought that unknown factors important in determining outcomes will also be distributed equally. Surely, other techniques can be developed to deal with both observer bias and patient selection. Prospective studies without randomization, but with the evaluation of patients by uninvolved third parties, should remove observer bias. Similar methods have been suggested by Royall. Prospective matched-pair analysis, in which patients are treated in a manner consistent with their physician's views, ought to help ensure equivalence between the groups and thus mitigate the effect of patient selection, at least with regard to known

covariates. With regard to unknown covariates, the security would rest, as in randomized trials, in the enrollment of large numbers of patients and in confirmatory studies. This method would not pose ethical difficulties, since patients would receive the treatment recommended by their physician. They would be included in the study by independent observers matching patients with respect to known characteristics, a process that would not affect patient care and that could be performed independently any number of times.

This brief discussion of alternatives to randomized clinical trials is sketchy and incomplete. We wish only to point out that there may be satisfactory alternatives, not to describe and evaluate them completely. Even if randomized clinical trials were much better than any alternative, however, the ethical dilemmas they present may put their use at variance with the primary obligations of the physician. In this regard, Angell cautions, "If this commitment to the patient is attenuated, even for so good a cause as benefits to future patients, the implicit assumptions of the doctor–patient relationship are violated." The risk of such attenuation by the randomized trial is great. The AIDS activists have brought this dramatically to the attention of the academic medical community. Techniques appropriate to the laboratory may not be applicable to human. We must develop and use alternative methods for acquiring clinical knowledge.

Clinical Trials: Are They Ethical?

Eugene Passamani

Passamani argues that randomized clinical trials (RCTs) are the most reliable means of evaluating new therapies. Without RCTs, chance and bias may affect our conclusions.

Passamani rejects the argument that the physician–patient relationship demands that physicians recommend the "best" therapy for patients, no matter how poor the data on which the recommendation is based. He acknowledges that RCTs pose ethical problems for physician–researchers but suggests the difficulties can be overcome by employing three procedural safeguards.

First, all participants must give their informed consent. They must be told about the goals of the research and its potential benefits and risks. Moreover, they must be informed about alternatives to their participation, and they must be permitted to withdraw from the trial

From The *New England Journal of Medicine*, Eugene Passamani, "Clinical Trials: Are They Ethical?" 324, no. 22 (1991): 1589–1591. Copyright © 1991. Massachusetts Medical Society. Reprinted with permission from Massachusetts Medical Society. (References omitted.)

at any time they choose. Second, for an RCT to be legitimate, a state of *clinical equipoise* must exist. Competent physicians must be genuinely uncertain about which of the alternative therapies in the trial is superior and content to allow their patients to be treated with any of them. Finally, the clinical trial must be designed as a critical test of the therapeutic alternatives. Properly carried out, RCTs should protect physicians and patients from therapies that are ineffective or toxic.

Biomedical research leads to better understanding of biology and ultimately to improved health. Physicians have for millenniums attempted to understand disease, to use this knowledge to cure or palliate, and to relieve attendant suffering. Improving strategies for prevention and treatment remains an ethical imperative for medicine. Until very recently, progress depended largely on a process of carefully observing groups of patients given a new and promising therapy; outcome was then compared with that previously observed in groups undergoing a standard treatment. Outcome in a series of case patients as compared with that in nonrandomized controls can be used to assess the treatment of disorders in which therapeutic effects are dramatic and the pathophysiologic features are relatively uncomplicated, such as vitamin deficiency or some infectious diseases. Observational methods are not very useful, however, in the detection of small treatment effects in disorders in which there is substantial variability in expected outcome and imperfect knowledge of complicated pathophysiologic features (many vascular disorders and most cancers, for example). The effect of a treatment cannot easily be extracted from variations in disease severity and the effects of concomitant treatments. Clinical trials have thus become a preferred means of evaluating an ever increasing flow of innovative diagnostic and therapeutic maneuvers. The randomized, double-blind clinical trial is a powerful technique because of the efficiency and credibility associated with treatment comparisons involving randomized concurrent controls.

The modern era of randomized trials began in the early 1950s with the evaluation of streptomycin in patients with tuberculosis. Since that time trial techniques and methods have continuously been refined. In addition, the ethical aspects of these experiments in patients have been actively discussed.

In what follows I argue that randomized trials are in fact the most scientifically sound and ethically correct means of evaluating new therapies. There is

potential conflict between the roles of physician and physician-scientist, and for this reason society has created mechanisms to ensure that the interests of individual patients are served should they elect to participate in a clinical trial.

Clinical Research

The history of medicine is richly endowed with therapies that were widely used and then shown to be ineffective or frankly toxic. Relatively recent examples of such therapeutic maneuvers include gastric freezing for peptic ulcer disease, radiation therapy for acne, MER-29 (triparanol) for cholesterol reduction, and thalidomide for sedation in pregnant women. The 19th century was even more gruesome, with purging and bloodletting. The reasons for this march of folly are many and include, perhaps most importantly, the lack of complete understanding of human biology and pathophysiology, the use of observational methods coupled with the failure to appreciate substantial variability between patients in their response to illness and to therapy, and the shared desire of physicians and their patients for cure or palliation.

Chance or bias can result in the selection of patients for innovative treatment who are either the least diseased or the most severely affected. Depending on the case mix, a treatment that has no effect can appear to be effective or toxic when historical controls are used. With the improvement in diagnostic accuracy and the understanding of disease that has occurred with the passage of time, today's patients are identified earlier in the natural history of their disease. Recently selected case series therefore often have patients who are less ill and an outcome that is considerably better than that of past case series, even without changes in treatment.

Randomization tends to produce treatment and control groups that are evenly balanced in both known and unrecognized prognostic factors, which permits a more accurate estimate of treatment effect in groups of patients assigned to experimental and standard therapies. A number of independent randomized trials with congruent results are powerful evidence indeed.

A physician's daily practice includes an array of preventive, diagnostic, and therapeutic maneuvers, some of which have been established by a plausible biologic mechanism and substantial evidence from randomized clinical trials (e.g., the use of beta-blockers, thrombolytic therapy, and aspirin in patients with myocardial infarction). It is unlikely that our distant descendants in medicine will discover that we late 20th-century physicians were wrong in these matters. However, new therapeutic maneuvers that have not undergone rigorous assessment may well turn out to be ineffective or toxic. Every therapy adopted by common consent on the basis of observational studies and plausible mechanism, but without the benefit of randomized studies, may be categorized by future physicians as useless or worse. Physicians are aware of the fragility of the evidence supporting many common therapies, and this is why properly performed randomized clinical trials have profound effects on medical practice. The scientific importance of randomized, controlled trials is in safeguarding current and future patients from our therapeutic passions. Most physicians recognize this fact.

Like any human activity, experimentation involving patients can be performed in an unethical and even criminal fashion. Nazi war crimes led to substantial efforts to curb abuse, beginning with the Nuremberg Code and the Helsinki Declaration and culminating in the promulgation of clearly articulated regulations in the United States and elsewhere. There are abuses more subtle than those of the Gestapo and the SS. Involving patients in experiments that are poorly conceived and poorly executed is unethical. Patients who participate in such research may incur risk without the hope of contributing to a body of knowledge that will benefit them or others in the future. The regulations governing human experimentation are very important, as is continuing discussion and debate to improve the scientific and ethical aspects of this effort.

Several general features must be part of properly designed trials. The first is informed consent, which involves explicitly informing a potential participant of the goals of the research, its potential benefits and risks, the alternatives to participating, and the right to withdraw from the trial at any time. Whether informed consent is required in all trials has been debated. I believe that patients must always be aware that they are part of an experiment. Second, a state of

clinical equipoise must exist. Clinical equipoise means that on the basis of the available data, a community of competent physicians would be content to have their patients pursue any of the treatment strategies being tested in a randomized trial, since none of them have been clearly established as preferable. The chief purpose of a data-monitoring committee is to stop the trial if the accumulating data destroy the state of clinical equipoise—that is, indicate efficacy or suggest toxicity. Finally, the trial must be designed as a critical test of the therapeutic alternatives being assessed. The question must be clearly articulated, with carefully defined measures of outcome; with realistic estimates of sample size, including probable event rates in the control group and a postulated and plausible reduction in the event rates in the treatment group; with Type I and II errors specified[*]; and with subgroup hypotheses clearly stated if appropriate. The trial must have a good chance of settling an open question.

Ethical Dimensions of Properly Constituted Trials

Experimentation in the clinic by means of randomized, controlled clinical trials has been periodically attacked as violating the covenant between doctor and patient. Critics have charged that physicians engaged in clinical trials sacrifice the interests of the patient they ask to participate to the good of all similarly affected patients in the future. The argument is that physicians have a personal obligation to use their best judgment and recommend the "best" therapy, no matter how tentative or inconclusive the data on which that judgment is based. Physicians must play their hunches. According to this argument, randomized clinical trials may be useful in seeking the truth, but carefully designed, legitimate trials are unethical and perhaps even criminal because they prevent individual physicians from playing their hunches about individual patients. Therefore, it is argued, physicians should not participate in such trials.

It is surely unethical for physicians to engage knowingly in an activity that will result in inferior therapy for their patients. It is also important that the community of physicians be clear in distinguishing between established therapies and those that are

---

[*] A Type I error consists in deciding that therapy A is better than therapy B when, in fact both are of equal worth (i.e., a true null hypothesis is rejected). A Type II error consists in deciding that the treatments are equally good when A is actually better than B (i.e., a false null hypothesis is accepted).[—Eds.]

promising but unproved. It is this gulf between proved therapies and possibly effective therapies (all the rest) that defines the ethical and unethical uses of randomized clinical trials. Proved therapies involve a consensus of the competent medical community that the data in hand justify using a treatment in a given disorder. It is this consensus that defines an ethical boundary. The physician-investigator who asks a patient to participate in a randomized, controlled trial represents this competent medical community in asserting that the community is unpersuaded by existing data that an innovative treatment is superior to standard therapy. Arguments that a physician who believes that such a treatment *might be* useful commits an unethical act by randomizing patients are simply wrong. Given the history of promising but discarded therapies, hunches about potential effectiveness are not the ideal currency of the patient–doctor interchange.

Lest readers conclude that modern hunches are more accurate than older ones, I have selected an example from the current cardiovascular literature that reveals the problems inherent in relying on hunches to the occlusion of carefully done experiments.

The Cardiac Arrhythmia Suppression Trial

Sudden death occurs in approximately 300,000 persons in the United States each year and is thus a problem worthy of our best efforts. In the vast majority of cases the mechanism is ventricular fibrillation superimposed on a scarred or ischemic myocardium. It had been observed that the ventricular extrasystoles seen on the ambulatory electrocardiographic recordings of survivors of myocardial infarction were independently and reproducibly associated with an increased incidence of subsequent mortality. It had been established that a variety of antiarrhythmic drugs can suppress ventricular extrasystoles. Accordingly, physicians had the hunch that suppressing ventricular extrasystoles in the survivors of myocardial infarction would reduce the incidence of ventricular fibrillation and sudden death.

The Cardiac Arrhythmia Suppression Trial (CAST) investigators decided to test this hypothesis in a randomized, controlled trial. They sought survivors of myocardial infarction who had frequent extrasystoles on electrocardiographic recordings. The trial design included a run-in period during which one of three active drugs was administered and its effect on

extrasystoles noted. Those in whom arrhythmias were suppressed were randomly assigned to active drug or placebo. The trial had to be stopped prematurely because of an unacceptable incidence of sudden death in the treatment group. During an average follow-up of 10 months, 56 of 730 patients (7.7 percent) assigned to active drug and 22 of 725 patients (3.0 percent) assigned to placebo died. Clinical equipoise was destroyed by this striking effect. It is quite unlikely that observational (nonrandomized) methods would have detected this presumably toxic effect.

The CAST trial was a major advance in the treatment of patients with coronary disease and ventricular arrhythmia. It clearly revealed that the hunches of many physicians were incorrect. The trial's results are applicable not only to future patients with coronary disease and ventricular arrhythmia but also to the patients who participated in the study. By randomizing, investigators ensured that half the participants received the better therapy—in this case placebo—and, contrary to intuition, most of them ultimately received the better therapy after the trial ended prematurely and drugs were withdrawn.

To summarize, randomized clinical trials are an important element in the spectrum of biomedical research. Not all questions can or should be addressed by this technique; feasibility, cost, and the relative importance of the issues to be addressed are weighed by investigators before they elect to proceed. Properly carried out, with informed consent, clinical equipoise, and a design adequate to answer the question posed, randomized clinical trials protect physicians and their patients from therapies that are ineffective or toxic. Physicians and their patients must be clear about the vast gulf separating promising and proved therapies. The only reliable way to make this distinction in the face of incomplete information about pathophysiology and treatment mechanism[s] is to experiment, and this will increasingly involve randomized trials. The alternative—a retreat to older methods—is unacceptable.

Physicians regularly apply therapies tested in groups of patients to an individual patient. The likelihood of success in an individual patient depends on the degree of certainty evident in the group and the scientific strength of the methods used. We owe patients involved in the assessment of new therapies the best that science and ethics can deliver. Today, for most unproved treatments, that is a properly performed randomized clinical trial.

Section 3: Conflicts of Interest

Drug Companies and Medicine: What Money Can Buy

Marcia Angell

Angell contends that academic medicine and the pharmaceutical industry have fundamentally incompatible missions: one is charged with educating doctors, caring for patients, and conducting scientifically valid research; the other is charged, first and foremost, with increasing shareholder value. She argues that industry's growing role in medical research, education, and clinical practice distorts scientific objectivity and impedes genuine innovation. It teaches academics to scramble for low-quality patents and convinces physicians that there is a new drug for every ailment and minor discontent. To address rampant conflicts of interest, Angell argues that industry sponsors should relinquish control over the design and interpretation of medical research, that physicians should refuse gifts from drug companies, and that discoveries made by academic medical researchers should be placed in the public domain or licensed inexpensively, as they were in the 1980s.

The boundaries between academic medicine—medical schools, teaching hospitals, and their faculty—and the pharmaceutical industry have been dissolving since the 1980s, and the important differences between their missions are becoming blurred. Medical research, education, and clinical practice have suffered as a result.

Academic medical centers are charged with educating the next generation of doctors, conducting scientifically important research, and taking care of the sickest and neediest patients. That's what justifies their tax-exempt status. In contrast, drug companies—like other investor-owned businesses—are charged with increasing the value of their shareholders' stock. That is their fiduciary responsibility, and they would be remiss if they didn't uphold it. All their other activities are means to that end. The companies are supposed to develop profitable drugs, not necessarily important or innovative ones, and paradoxically enough, the most profitable drugs are the least innovative. Nor do drug companies aim to educate doctors, except as a means to the primary end of selling drugs. Drug companies don't have education budgets; they have marketing budgets from which their ostensibly educational activities are funded.

From Marcia Angell, "Big Pharma, Bad Medicine," *Boston Review*, May–June 2010. Used by permission of the author.

This profound difference in missions is often deliberately obscured—by drug companies because it's good public relations to portray themselves as research and educational institutions, and by academics because it means they don't have to face up to what's really going on.

Industry and Academia

No area of overlap between industry and academia is more important than clinical trials. Unlike basic medical research, which is funded mainly by the National Institutes of Health (NIH), most clinical trials are funded by the pharmaceutical industry. In fact, that is where most pharmaceutical research dollars go. That's because the Food and Drug Administration (FDA) will not approve a drug for sale until it has been tested on human subjects. Pharmaceutical companies must show the FDA that a new drug is reasonably safe and effective, usually as compared with a placebo. That requires clinical trials, in which treatments are compared under rigorous conditions in a sample of the relevant population. The results of drug trials (there may be many) are submitted to the FDA, and if one or two are positive—that is, they show effectiveness without serious risk—the drug is usually approved, even if all the other trials are negative.

Since drug companies don't have direct access to human subjects, they've traditionally contracted with academic researchers to conduct the trials on patients in teaching hospitals and clinics. That practice continues, but over the past couple of decades the terms and conditions have changed dramatically.

Until the mid-1980s, drug companies simply gave grants to medical centers for researchers to test their products, and then waited for the results and hoped their products looked good. Usually the research was investigator-initiated, that is, the question was something the academic researcher thought scientifically important. Sponsors had no part in designing or analyzing the studies, they did not claim to own the data, and they certainly did not write the papers or control publication. Grants were at arm's length.

Thanks to the academy's increasing dependence on industry, that distance is a thing of the past. The major drug companies are now hugely profitable, with net incomes consistently several times the median for *Fortune* 500 companies. In fact, they make more in profits than they spend on research and development (R&D), despite their rhetoric about high prices being necessary to cover their research costs. (They also spend twice as much on marketing and administration as they do on R&D.) The reasons for the astonishing profitability of these companies aren't relevant here, but suffice it to say that as a result the industry has acquired enormous power and influence. In contrast, medical centers have fallen on difficult times (or so they believe), mainly because of shrinking reimbursements for their educational and clinical missions. To a remarkable extent, then, medical centers have become supplicants to the drug companies, deferring to them in ways that would have been unthinkable even twenty years ago.

Often, academic researchers are little more than hired hands who supply human subjects and collect data according to instructions from corporate paymasters. The sponsors keep the data, analyze it, write the papers, and decide whether and when and where to submit them for publication. In multi-center trials, researchers may not even be allowed to see all of the data, an obvious impediment to science and a perversion of standard practice.

While some new companies—called contract research organizations (CROs)—do clinical research for the drug manufacturers by organizing doctors in private practice to enroll their patients in clinical trials, the manufacturers typically prefer to work with academic medical centers. Doing so increases the chances of getting research published, and, more importantly, provides drug companies access to highly influential faculty physicians—referred to by the industry as "thought leaders" or "key opinion leaders." These are the people who write textbooks and medical-journal papers, issue practice guidelines (treatment recommendations), sit on FDA and other governmental advisory panels, head professional societies, and speak at the innumerable meetings and dinners that take place every day to teach clinicians about prescription drugs.

In addition to grant support, academic researchers may now have a variety of other financial ties to the companies that sponsor their work. They serve as consultants to the same companies whose products they evaluate, join corporate advisory boards and speakers bureaus, enter into patent and royalty arrangements, agree to be the listed authors of articles ghostwritten by interested companies, promote drugs and devices at company-sponsored symposia, and allow themselves to be plied with expensive gifts and trips to luxurious settings. Many also have equity interest in sponsoring companies.

Much of the time, the institutional conflict-of-interest rules ostensibly designed to control these relationships are highly variable, permissive, and loosely enforced. At Harvard Medical School, for example, few conflicts of interest are flatly prohibited; they are only limited in various ways. Like Hollywood, academic medical centers run on a star system, and schools don't want to lose their stars, who are now accustomed to supplementing their incomes through deals with industry.

Schools, too, have deals with industry. Academic leaders, chairs, and even deans sit on boards of directors of drug companies. Many academic medical centers have set up special offices to offer companies quick soup-to-nuts service. Harvard's Clinical Research Institute (HCRI), for example, originally advertised itself as led by people whose "experience gives HCRI an intimate understanding of industry's needs, and knowledge of how best to meet them"—as though meeting industry's needs is a legitimate purpose of an academic institution.

Much of the rationalization for the pervasive research connections between industry and academia rests on the Bayh-Dole Act of 1980, which has acquired the status of holy writ in academia. Bayh-Dole permits—but does not require, as many researchers claim—universities to patent discoveries that stem from government-funded research and then license them exclusively to companies in return for royalties. (Similar legislation applies to work done at the NIH itself.) In this way, academia and industry are partners, both benefiting from public support.

Until Bayh-Dole, all government-funded discoveries were in the public domain. The original purpose of Bayh-Dole was to speed technology transfer from the discovery stage to practical use. It was followed by changes in patent law that loosened the criteria for granting patents. As a consequence, publicly funded discoveries of no immediate practical use can now be patented and handed off to start-up companies for early development. The start-up companies are often founded by the researchers and their institutions, and they usually either license their promising products to larger companies or are bought by large companies outright.

The result of Bayh-Dole was a sudden, huge increase in the number of patents—if not in their quality. And the most prestigious academic centers now have technology-transfer offices and are ringed by start-up companies. Most technology-transfer offices at academic medical centers don't make much money, but every now and then one strikes it rich. Columbia University, for example, received nearly $300 million in royalties from more than 30 biotech companies during the seventeen-year life of its patent on a method for synthesizing biological products. Patenting and licensing the fruits of academic research has the character of a lottery, and everyone wants to play.

A less-appreciated outcome of Bayh-Dole is that drug companies no longer have to do their own creative, early-stage research. They can, and increasingly do, rely on universities and start-up companies for that. In fact, the big drug companies now concentrate mainly on the late-stage development of drugs they've licensed from other sources, as well as on producing variations of top-selling drugs already on the market—called "me-too" drugs. There is very little innovative research in the modern pharmaceutical industry, despite its claims to the contrary.

Over the past two or three decades, then, academia and industry have become deeply intertwined. Moreover, these links, though quite recent, are now largely accepted as inherent in medical research. So what's wrong with that? Isn't this just the sort of collaboration that leads to the development of important new medical treatments?

Medical Research

Increasingly, industry is setting the research agenda in academic centers, and that agenda has more to do with industry's mission than with the mission of the academy. Researchers and their institutions are focusing too much on targeted, applied research, mainly drug development, and not enough on non-targeted, basic research into the causes, mechanisms, and prevention of disease.

Moreover, drug companies often contract with academic researchers to carry out studies for almost entirely commercial purposes. For example, they sponsor trials of drugs to supplant virtually identical ones that are going off patent. And academic institutions are increasingly focused on the Bayh-Dole lottery. A few years ago, the Dana Farber Cancer Institute sent Harvard faculty an invitation to a workshop called "Forming Science-Based Companies." It began:

> *So you want to start a company? Join the Provost, Harvard's Office for Technology and Trademark Licensing (OTTL), leading venture capitalists, lawyers and entrepreneurs for a conference on the basics of forming a start-up based on university technology.*

There's a high scientific opportunity cost in serving the aims of the pharmaceutical industry. For example, new antibiotics for treating infections by resistant organisms are an urgent medical need, but are not economically attractive to industry because they are not likely to generate much return on investment.

In addition to distorting the research agenda, there is overwhelming evidence that drug-company influence biases the research itself. Industry-supported research is far more likely to be favorable to the sponsors' products than is NIH-supported research. There are many ways to bias studies—both consciously and unconsciously—and they are by no means always obvious. I saw a good number of them during my two decades as an editor of the *New England Journal of Medicine*. Often, when we rejected studies because of their biases, they turned up in other journals essentially unchanged. And looking back, I now realize that despite our best efforts, we sometimes published biased studies without knowing it. One problem is that we thought that if studies were subjected to rigorous peer review, it was sufficient to disclose authors' commercial ties—essentially to tell readers *caveat emptor*…. I no longer believe that's enough.

An important cause of bias is the suppression of negative results. But clinical trials are also biased through research protocols designed to yield favorable results for sponsors. There are many ways to do that. The sponsor's drug may be compared with another drug administered at a dose so low that the sponsor's drug looks more powerful. Or a drug that's likely to be used by older people will be tested in young people, so that side effects are less likely to emerge. The standard practice of comparing a new drug with a placebo, when the relevant question is how it compares with an existing drug, is also misleading. Supporters of the status quo claim that attempts to regulate conflicts of interest will slow medical advances, but the truth is that conflicts of interest distort medical research, and advances occur *in spite* of them, not because of them.

To be clear, I'm not objecting to all research collaboration between academia and industry—only to terms and conditions that threaten the independence and impartiality essential to medical research. Research collaboration between academia and industry can be fruitful, but it doesn't need to involve payments to researchers beyond grant support. And that support, as I have argued, should be at arm's length.

Expert Advice

Conflicts of interest affect more than research. They also directly shape the way medicine is practiced, through their influence on practice guidelines issued by professional and governmental bodies and through their effects on FDA decisions.

Consider three examples I've written about before: first, in a survey of 200 expert panels that issued practice guidelines, one third of the panel members acknowledged that they had some financial interest in the drugs they assessed. Second, in 2004, after the NIH National Cholesterol Education Program called for sharply lowering the acceptable levels of "bad" cholesterol, it was revealed that eight of nine members of the panel writing the recommendations had financial ties to the makers of cholesterol-lowering drugs. Third, of the 170 contributors to the most recent edition of the American Psychiatric Association's Diagnostic and Statistical Manual of Mental Disorders (DSM-IV), 95 had financial ties to drug companies, including all of the contributors to the sections on mood disorders and schizophrenia.

Perhaps most important, many members of the eighteen standing committees of experts that advise the FDA on drug approvals also have financial ties to the industry. After the painkiller Vioxx was removed from the market in 2005 (it increased the risk of heart attacks), the FDA convened a panel consisting of two of these committees to consider whether painkillers of the same class as Vioxx should also be removed from the market. Following three days of public hearings, the combined panel decided that, although these drugs—called COX-2 inhibitors—did increase the risk of heart attacks, the benefits outweighed the risks. It therefore recommended that all three of the drugs, including Vioxx, be permitted to remain on the market, perhaps with strong warnings on the labels.

A week after the panel's decision, however, *The New York Times* revealed that of the 32 panel members, ten had financial ties to the manufacturers, and that if their votes had been excluded, only one of the drugs would have been permitted to stay on the market. As a result of this embarrassing revelation, the FDA reversed the panel and left only one of the drugs, Celebrex, on the market, with a warning on the label.

Medical Education

Conflicts of interest are equally troubling in medical education, where industry influence is perhaps greatest and least justified. The pharmaceutical industry devotes much, if not most, of its vast marketing budget to what it calls the "education" of doctors. The reason is obvious: doctors write the prescriptions, so they need to be won over.

Drug companies support educational programs even within our best medical schools and teaching hospitals, and are given virtually unfettered access to young doctors to ply them with gifts and meals and promote their wares. In most states doctors are required to take accredited education courses, called continuing medical education (CME), and drug companies contribute roughly half the support for this education, often indirectly through private investor-owned medical-education companies whose only clients are drug companies. CME is supposed to be free of drug-company influence, but incredibly these private educators have been accredited to provide CME by the American Medical Association's Accreditation Committee for Continuing Medical Education—a case of the fox not only guarding the chicken coop, but living inside it.

…If drug companies and medical educators were really providing education, doctors and academic institutions would pay them for their services. When you take piano lessons, you pay the teacher, not the other way around. But in this case, industry pays the academic institutions and faculty, and even the doctors who take the courses. The companies are simply buying access to medical school faculty and to doctors in training and practice.

This is marketing masquerading as education. It is self-evidently absurd to look to companies for critical, unbiased education about products they sell. It's like asking a brewery to teach you about alcoholism, or a Honda dealer for a recommendation about what car to buy. Doctors recognize this in other parts of their lives, but they've convinced themselves that drug companies are different. That industry-sponsored education is a masquerade is underscored by the fact that some of the biggest Madison Avenue ad agencies, hired by drug companies to promote their products, also own their own medical-education companies. It's one-stop shopping for the industry.

But doctors do learn something from all the ostensible education they're paid to receive. Doctors and their patients come to believe that for every ailment and discontent there is a drug, even when changes in lifestyle would be more effective. And they believe that the newest, most expensive brand-name drugs are superior to older drugs or generics, even though there is seldom any evidence to that effect because sponsors don't usually compare their drugs with older drugs at equivalent doses. In addition, doctors are encouraged to prescribe drugs for uses not approved by the FDA (known as "off-label" prescriptions).

While I favor research collaboration between industry and academia under certain terms and conditions, I believe the pharmaceutical industry has no legitimate role in graduate or post-graduate medical education. That should be the responsibility of the profession. In fact, responsibility for its own education is an essential part of the definition of a learned profession.

No Excuses

It's easy to fault drug companies for much of what I've described, and they certainly deserve a great deal of blame. Most of the big drug companies have paid huge fines to settle charges of illegal activities. Last year Pfizer pleaded guilty and agreed to pay $2.3 billion to settle criminal and civil charges of marketing drugs for off-label uses—the largest criminal fine in history. The fines, while enormous, are still dwarfed by the profits generated by these activities, and are therefore not much of a deterrent. Still, apologists might argue that, despite its legal transgressions, the pharmaceutical industry is merely trying to do its primary job—furthering the interests of its investors—and sometimes it simply goes a little too far.

Doctors, medical schools, and professional organizations have no such excuse; the medical profession's only fiduciary responsibility is to patients and the public.

What should be done about all of this? So many reforms would be necessary to restore integrity to medical research, education, and practice that they can't all be summarized here. Many would involve congressional legislation and changes in the FDA, including its drug-approval process. But the medical profession also needs to wean itself from industry money almost entirely.

For some time now, I've been recommending these three essential reforms:

First, members of medical school faculties who conduct clinical trials should not accept any payments from drug companies except research support, and that support should have no strings attached. In particular, drug companies should have no control over the design, interpretation, and publication of research results. Medical schools and teaching hospitals should rigorously enforce this rule and should not themselves enter into deals with companies whose products are being studied by members of their faculty.

Second, doctors should not accept gifts from drug companies, even small ones, and they should pay for their own meetings and continuing education. Other professions pay their own way, and there is no reason for the medical profession to be different in this regard.

Finally, academic medical centers that patent discoveries should put them in the public domain or license them inexpensively and non-exclusively, as Stanford does with its patent on recombinant DNA technology based on the work of Stanley Cohen and Herbert Boyer. Bayh-Dole is now more a matter of seeking windfalls than of transferring technology. Some have argued that it actually impedes technology transfer by enabling the licensing of early discoveries, which encumbers downstream research. Though the legislation stipulates that drugs licensed from academic institutions be made "available on reasonable terms" to the public, that provision has been ignored by both industry and academia. I believe medical research was every bit as productive before Bayh-Dole as it is now, despite the lack of patents. I'm reminded of Jonas Salk's response when asked whether he had patented the polio vaccine. He seemed amazed at the very notion. The vaccine, he explained, belonged to everybody. "Could you patent the sun?" he asked.

I'm aware that my proposals might seem radical. That is because we are now so drenched in market ideology that any resistance is considered quixotic. But academic medical centers are not supposed to be businesses. They now enjoy great public support, and they jeopardize that support by continuing along the current path.

And to those academic researchers who think the current path is just fine, I have this to say: no, it is not necessary to accept personal payments from drug companies to collaborate on research. There was plenty of innovative research before 1980—at least as much as there is now—when academic researchers began to expect rewards from industry. And no, you are not entitled to anything you want just because you're very smart. Conflicts of interest in academic medicine have serious consequences, and it is time to stop making excuses for them.

A Partnership Worth Promoting

Emma D'Arcy

D'Arcy contends that pharmaceutical and medical professionals have equally strong motivations to develop safe and effective treatments. She argues for more collaboration between industry and medical researchers, as a way of fostering transparency and consumer feedback in the medical marketplace. D'Arcy suggests that pharmaceutical companies should be more involved in medical education, to increase physician's knowledge of drugs and to address medical school funding problems. Ultimately, she argues, patients and doctors are capable of acting as informed health care consumers, distinguishing "overt brand promotion" from scientifically valid data, and using social media tools to improve drug development and research.

The relationship between doctors and drug companies continues to draw scrutiny, skepticism, and suspicion, despite the absence of proof of harm. The rhetoric and conjecture are not merely false, but corrosive of medical professionalism and toxic for patients.

This sanctimony continues, unchecked, thanks to the efforts of a small cohort of anti-relationship puritans who seem oblivious to three simple facts.

First, we live and work in an era of "consumer conversation" in which top-down marketing is increasingly outdated. Thanks in part to the user-generated power of the Internet, there has been an unprecedented rise in the demand for product and company transparency in all business sectors: it is now the customer (physician, patient, the public) who is in charge, and that customer wants insights on existing and future products. Consumers are adept at distinguishing between overt brand promotion and useful information that helps them to live longer, healthier, and happier lives. The pharmaceutical industry is struggling to adapt to this new environment because its activities are already so heavily policed that

From Emma D'Arcy, "A Partnership Worth Promoting," *Boston Review*, May–June 2010. Used by permission of the author.

attempting to participate in the conversation leads into a regulatory minefield.

Second, medical and pharmaceutical professionals aspire to the same goals. It is in everyone's interest that medicines are safe and effective. Physicians who collaborate with industry are not simply duped—and many, rightly, find the implication offensive. Instead, they see an opportunity to help patients through an ethical exchange, and they don't allow sensationalized media scare stories about fraudulent trials, dangerous drugs, and corrupt doctors to sway them.

Since the medical community recognizes the value of knowledgeable engagement with industry, it has begun to incorporate education geared toward responsible cooperation. New courses and codes of practice at a number of American medical schools teach students how to interact with the pharmaceutical industry, and similar efforts are being considered in the United Kingdom.

In February 2009 the Royal College of Physicians (RCP) in London published recommendations from an eighteen month-long review of interactions between the pharmaceutical industry, physicians, academia, and the National Health Service that argues for a more collaborative culture between industry and physicians. The review points out that more funding from industry would allow medical students better training in prescription, a process marred by high error rates in the first few years after graduation from medical schools. The distrust of industry means that education is persistently underfunded. The RCP reviewers seem to have no trust deficit. "Industry has a distinctive voice that students deserve to hear," they contend.

The failure adequately to train medical students in the workings and literature of pharmaceutical development persists into the professional ranks. A 2008 study in *Psychological Science in the Public Interest* points out that "many doctors ... do not understand what health statistics mean." Prescribers misunderstand efficacy and safety reports about pharmaceutical products, and the resulting excesses in enthusiasm and concern surrounding drugs can have devastating consequences for patients. Harmonious physician-pharma interaction demands a clinical community that comprehends data. Physicians' statistical illiteracy is not the fault of the drug industry, but drug industry money could help mitigate it, if we gave it a chance.

The third fact that anti-relationship advocates miss is that a better-educated patient population expects its physicians to engage in a dramatically altered physician-patient dialogue. Again thanks in large part to the Internet, doctors no longer hold a monopoly on medical information. Patients research symptoms and semi-self-diagnose ahead of their initial meeting with their physicians. They also research therapeutic recommendations and include peer-recommendations in their decisions to embark on courses of treatment, pharmaceutical or otherwise. Patients review products, rate doctors, and rank companies as part of a process of managing their conditions.

We are witnessing patients assert a consumer-like approach to medicine, with pioneers such as the community members at PatientsLikeMe.com. In exchange for expedited solutions to the challenges their conditions pose, they willingly abandon confidentiality and openly deliberate about medicines not necessarily licensed for those conditions. These patients thereby support the aims and intents of industry and are even starting to influence the direction of research.

Doctors should be involved in this new frontier of medicine, but opponents of physician-industry collaboration need to appreciate that the arguments purporting bias and influence by pharma are outdated. They are

yesterday's news. The balance of power over company and product transparency has shifted significantly to patients, who have been efficiently using social-media tools to aggregate their voices and expand their influence. Critics and commentators on directional influence are, quite simply, looking in the wrong place.

Ultimately, the anti-relationship puritans, in ignoring these three facts, are stifling the translation of scientific innovations into health gains. Their concern is for medical professionalism and academic integrity, yet those will more likely be compromised if we stymie interactions between industry and academy by attempting to enforce draconian rules of engagement. Tomorrow's medical experts will not understand the drug development pipeline, and patients will suffer physicians' and academics' commercial illiteracy. Medical innovation may be hindered if we further limit interactions, and medical professionals and industry researchers may find it equally frustrating if restrictions on interactions limit their professional aspirations. If pharma-sponsored education, interaction, and strategic alliances are vanquished, we may witness tomorrow's doctors practicing yesterday's medicine.

Accordingly, Web 2.0 tools, which rely on "user-generated content," should be part of the infrastructure to develop more, not less, collaborative communities. The popularity of patient forums (which outnumber brand/industry-sponsored forums by five-to-one), established physician-only network sites such as Sermo, and pharma-physician conduits is overwhelming evidence that we are online, we want to engage, we need to connect. As co-founder of the new site MedPharmaConnect, I have seen that desire in action: I was compelled to create the site by physicians, academics, and patients who have repeatedly sought an environment in which they can expand their professional alliances with pharma and engage confidently and openly. Pharma is not influencing these experts—these experts are seeking to align with equanimity.

Loathe it or love it, this connected generation will continue to insist that the immediacy of blogs, podcasts, and discussion boards usurp the dinosaur of the medical journal, and physicians and academics will have more and more complex relationships with industry. We must embrace the value of these relationships rather than seek to stop them. Because—headlines, bickering, and utopian ideals aside—patients and the public simply want relationships that generate results.

Section 4:   Access to Experimental Drugs

Abigail Alliance v. FDA Majority Opinion: Patients Have a Right to Have Access to Experimental Drugs

Judith W. Rogers

Judge Rogers argues that terminally ill adult patients should have access to investigational drugs if (a) they have no better treatment options and (b) the drugs have completed Phase I trials and been found safe enough for additional human testing. She bases much of her argument on two claims: first, there has been no long-standing tradition in the United States of government concern with the effectiveness of drugs. Second, the right to access lifesaving drugs can be inferred from the *Cruzan* decision (see Chapter 7), in which the Supreme Court established a right to refuse lifesaving treatment.

The Abigail Alliance for Better Access to Developmental Drugs seeks to enjoin the Food and Drug Administration from continuing to enforce a policy barring the sale of new drugs that the FDA has determined, after Phase I trials on human beings, are sufficiently safe for expanded human testing.... More specifically, the Alliance seeks access to potentially life-saving post-Phase I investigational new drugs on behalf of mentally competent, terminally ill adult patients who have no alternative government approved treatment options....

The Alliance contends that the FDA's policy violates the substantive due process rights to privacy, liberty, and life of its terminally ill members. The complaint presents the question of whether the Due Process Clause protects the right of terminally ill patients to decide, without FDA interference, whether to assume the risks of using potentially life-saving investigational new drugs that the FDA has yet to approve for commercial marketing but that the FDA has determined, after Phase I clinical human trials, are safe enough for further testing on a substantial number of human beings....

United States Court of Appeals for the District of Columbia Circuit, No. 04-5350 (Decided May 2, 2006). *Abigail Alliance for Better Access to Developmental Drugs and Washington Legal Foundation, Appellants v. Andrew C. von Eeschenbach, M.D., in His Official Capacity as Acting Commissioner, Food and Drug Administration, and Michael O. Leavitt, in his Official Capacity as Secretary of the U.S. Department of Health and Human Services, Appellees.* Appeal from the United States District Court for the District of Columbia (No. 03cv01601). (Headings added by editors.)

Government Permits Liberty

We find, upon examining "our Nation's history, legal traditions, and practices," that the government has not blocked access to new drugs throughout the greater part of our Nation's history. Only in recent years has the government injected itself into consideration of the effectiveness of new drugs. [Moreover], Supreme Court precedent on liberty indicates that the right claimed by the Alliance can be inferred from the Court's conclusion in *Cruzan v. Director, Missouri Department of Health* that an individual has a due process right to refuse life-sustaining medical treatment.... Here, the claim implicates a similar right—the right to access potentially life-sustaining medication where there are no alternative government-approved treatment options. In both instances, the key is the patient's right to make the decision about her life free from government interference....

[T]he Supreme Court has employed two distinct approaches when faced with a claim to a fundamental right. In some cases, the Court has discerned the existence of fundamental rights by probing what "personal dignity and autonomy" demand.... In other cases, the Court has derived fundamental rights by reference to the Nation's history and legal tradition.... Because we conclude, upon applying the seemingly more restrictive analysis of *Glucksberg* [which held that there is no right to physician-assisted suicide], that the claimed right warrants protection under the Due Process Clause, we need not decide whether the line of cases construing the concept of "personal dignity and autonomy" would also lend protection to the claimed right....

Alliance Claim

The Alliance claims neither an unfettered right of access to all new or investigational new drugs nor a right to receive treatment from the government or at government expense. The Alliance's claim also does not challenge the Controlled Substances Act or the government's authority to regulate substances deemed harmful to public health, safety, and welfare. Rather, the Alliance contends that the fundamental due process rights to privacy, liberty, and life include the right of terminally ill patients, acting on a doctor's advice, to obtain potentially lifesaving medication when no alternative treatment approved by the government is available. Recognizing that the effectiveness and side effects of the investigational new drugs may still be in question after the Phase I trials have been completed, the Alliance asks only that the decision to assume these known or unknown risks be left to the terminally ill patient and not to the FDA....

Roots of Control Over Body

A right of control over one's body has deep roots in the common law. The venerable commentator on the common law William Blackstone wrote that the right to "personal security" includes "a person's legal and uninterrupted enjoyment of his life, his limbs, his body, [and] his health," as well as "the preservation of a man's health from such practices as may prejudice or annoy it." This right included the right to self-defense and the right to self-preservation. "For whatever is done by a man, to save either life or member, is looked upon as done upon the highest necessity and compulsion." As recognized throughout Anglo-American history and law, when a person is faced with death, necessity often warrants extraordinary measures not otherwise justified.... Barring a terminally ill patient from the use of a potentially lifesaving treatment impinges on this right of self-preservation. Such a bar also puts the FDA in the position of interfering with efforts that could save a terminally ill patient's life. Although the common law imposes no general duty to rescue or to preserve a life, it does create liability for interfering with such efforts....

Control Over Drugs

In contrast to these ancient principles, regulation of access to new drugs has a history in this country that is of recent origin.... For over half of our Nation's history, ...a person could obtain access to any new drug without any government interference whatsoever. Even after enactment of the FDCA [Food, Drug, and Cosmetic Act] in 1938, Congress imposed no limitation on the commercial marketing of new drugs based upon the drugs' effectiveness. Rather, at that time, the FDA could only interrupt the sale of new drugs based on its determination that a new drug was unsafe. Government regulation of drugs premised on concern over a new drug's efficacy, as opposed to its safety, is of recent origin. And even today, a patient may use a drug for unapproved purposes even where the drug may be unsafe or ineffective for the off-label purpose.... Therefore, it cannot be said that government control of access to potentially lifesaving medication "is now firmly ingrained in our understanding of the appropriate role of government," so as to overturn the long-standing tradition of the right of self-preservation.

The Alliance's ... claimed right is implied by the Court's conclusion in *Cruzan* that due process protects a person's right to refuse life-sustaining treatment.... Chief Justice Rehnquist noted in examining the origins of the doctrine of informed consent that the Court had observed early on that "[n]o right is held more sacred, or is more carefully guarded, by the common law, than the right of every individual to the possession and control of his own person, free from all restraint or interference of others, unless by clear and unquestionable authority of law." The Court reasoned that "[t]he logical corollary of the doctrine of informed consent is that the patient generally possesses the right not to consent, that is, to refuse treatment." The Court turned to the language of the Fourteenth Amendment and its precedent to determine whether "the United States Constitution grants what is in common parlance referred to as a 'right to die.' " Without qualification, the Court stated: "It cannot be disputed that the Due Process Clause protects an interest in life as well as an interest in refusing life-sustaining medical treatment."

A similar analysis leads to the conclusion that the Due Process Clause protects the liberty interest claimed by the Alliance for its terminally ill members.... The text of the Due Process Clause refers to protecting "liberty" and "life." Although there is no similarly clear textual basis for a "right to die" or [to refuse] life-sustaining medical treatment, the Supreme Court in *Cruzan* recognized, in light of the common law and constitutionally protected liberty interests based on the inviolability of one's body, that an individual has a due process right to make an informed decision to engage in conduct, by withdrawing treatment, that will cause one's death. The logical corollary is that an individual must also be free to decide for herself whether to assume any known or unknown risks of taking a medication that might prolong her life.... Much as the guardians of the comatose patient in *Cruzan* did, the Alliance seeks to have the government step aside by changing its policy so the individual right of self-determination is not violated. The Alliance claims that there is a protected right of terminally ill patients to choose to use potentially lifesaving investigational new drugs that have successfully cleared Phase I. If there is a protected liberty interest in self-determination that includes a right to refuse life-sustaining treatment, even though this will hasten death, then the same liberty interest must include the complementary right of access to potentially life-sustaining medication, in the light of the explicit protection accorded "life."...

Ruling

Accordingly, we hold ... that where there are no alternative government-approved treatment options, a terminally ill, mentally competent adult patient's informed access to potentially lifesaving investigational new drugs determined by the FDA after Phase I trials to be sufficiently safe for expanded human trials warrants protection under the Due Process Clause.

Abigail Alliance v. FDA Dissenting Opinion: Patients Have No Right to Experimental Drugs

Thomas B. Griffith

Judge Griffith argues that Rogers's opinion is based on a series of faulty inferences: (1) that government has not always regulated drugs does not imply a recognition of a constitutional right to be free of such regulation; (2) the traditions of the necessity defense and the prohibition of forced medication do not imply a right of access to medication; (3) that a drug has completed Phase I testing does not imply that it has a medical benefit and a minimal risk. In fact, the government has long regulated drugs through the executive and legislative branches. To ignore this and give the judicial branch the role of deciding which drugs are safe and beneficial enough for use would burden the courts with a task both practically and logically impossible to carry out. Griffith concludes by agreeing with the lower court decision that even terminally ill patients have no right to access drugs that are still in the testing stage.

Inferential Basis of Claimed Right

... The majority creates a fundamental right by making a series of inferences.... From the fact that

United States Court of Appeals for the District of Columbia Circuit, No. 04-5350 (Decided May 2, 2006). *Abigail Alliance for Better Access to Developmental Drugs and Washington Legal Foundation, Appellants v. Andrew C. von Eeschenbach, M.D. in His Official Capacity as Acting Commissioner, Food and Drug Administration and Michael O. Leavitt, in his Official Capacity as Secretary of the U.S. Department of Health and Human Services, Appellees.* Appeal from the United States District Court for the District of Columbia (No. 03cv01601). (Headings added by editors.)

the Government has not always regulated drugs, the majority infers a constitutional right to be free from such regulation. From the common law defense of necessity and the tradition prohibiting battery and forced medication, the majority infers a fundamental right of access to medication. From the fact that drugs in the first phase of FDA testing have undergone some testing, the majority infers that those drugs will probably have a medical benefit with sufficiently minimal risk. But there is no evidence in this Nation's history and traditions of a right to access experimental drugs. Balancing the risks and benefits found at the forefront of uncertain science and medicine has been, for good reason, the historical province of the democratic branches. Because I can find no basis in the Constitution or judicial precedents to remove that function from the elected branches, I respectfully dissent.

Safety and Post-Phase-I Testing

…In the Alliance's view, the Due Process Clause of the Constitution guarantees terminally ill patients a fundamental "right of access to drugs that have cleared Phase I trials" because those drugs are "safe enough to be tested in humans" and "simply ha[ve] not yet met FDA's standards." Based upon that argument, the majority creates a fundamental right and concludes that, under the Constitution, "a terminally ill, mentally competent adult patient's informed access to potentially lifesaving investigational new drugs determined by the FDA after Phase I trials to be sufficiently safe for expanded human trials warrants protection under the Due Process Clause."…

The Alliance's proposed new constitutional right would exempt terminally ill patients from much of the legislative and regulatory approval process created by Congress and the FDA for new experimental drugs…. Testing a new drug for safety and effectiveness in treating humans generally requires three or sometimes four phases…. The majority and I differ in our understanding of the importance of the testing that occurs after Phase I. The majority implies that the FDA is primarily concerned with effectiveness after Phase I and that the right argued for by the Alliance would only override FDA regulation for effectiveness. Contrary to the majority's suggestion, all phases of the FDA's testing process for new drugs involve testing for safety….

Thus, at issue today is whether terminally ill patients have a fundamental right to procure and use an experimental drug before the FDA and the scientific community have evaluated its scientific and medical risks and corresponding benefits as called for in the FDCA [Food, Drug, and Cosmetics Act] and its accompanying regulations….

The Doctrine of Necessity

[T]he Supreme Court's guidance in *Oakland* indicates that the common law doctrine of necessity is not deeply rooted in this Nation's history and traditions. In *Oakland*, a group of patients seeking

access to marijuana for medicinal purposes argued that "because necessity was a defense at common law, medical necessity should be read into the Controlled Substances Act."… [T]he Court noted that…"under any conception of legal necessity, one principle is clear: The defense cannot succeed when the legislature itself has made a determination of values." The structure of the FDCA does just that: Congress has prohibited general access to experimental drugs, … and has prescribed in detail how experimental drugs may be studied and used by the scientific and medical communities…. Given the Supreme Court's conclusion that the common law defense of necessity remains controversial and cannot override a value judgment already determined by the legislature, I cannot see how the majority's proposed right is supported by the common law doctrine of necessity….

Ordered Liberty

The majority never provides evidence…that the Alliance's *asserted* right is deeply rooted and implicit in ordered liberty. Instead, the majority infers its new right from several broad principles…. The majority concludes that these principles are deeply rooted based upon a passage from Blackstone describing an individual's interest in being free from battery at common law, and a provision … discussing when one person will be liable under the common law for preventing aid from reaching another. The majority infers from these principles a liberty interest in procuring and using experimental drugs. But *Glucksberg* [which held that there is no right to physician-assisted suicide] does not authorize courts to create substantive due process rights by inference. These principles are precisely the type of "abstract concepts of personal autonomy" that do not constitute evidence of a fundamental right….

History of Government Drug Regulation

The remainder of the majority's analysis sets out to prove an unremarkable proposition: the federal government has only regulated drugs for approximately 100 years. From the lack of federal regulation prior to 1906, the majority infers a constitutional right to be free from regulation. It is not difficult to see the sweeping claims of fundamental rights that such an analysis would support. Because Congress did not significantly regulate marijuana until relatively late in the constitutional day, there must be a tradition of protecting marijuana use. Because Congress did not regulate narcotics until 1866 when it heavily taxed opium, a drug created long before our Nation's founding, it must be that individuals have a right to acquire and use narcotics free from regulation. But this is not the law....

The history of drug regulation in this country does not evidence a tradition of protecting a right of access to drugs; instead, it evidences government responding to new risks as they are presented.... The majority's historical analysis of the FDCA demonstrates that Congress has expressed a keen interest in regulating drugs as science has progressed. Congress has responded to evolving medical technology with evolving regulation. But, unlike the majority, I do not see how the decision by Congress to regulate an area of concern in the early part of the twentieth century demonstrates a fundamental right to be free from regulation today.

Tradition of Prohibiting Battery

Nor does the majority's analogy to *Cruzan* ... and [to] forced medication at common law explain why there is a fundamental, deeply rooted right to "self-preservation" protecting a "terminally ill, mentally competent adult patient's informed access to potentially life-saving investigational new drugs determined by the FDA after Phase I trials to be sufficiently safe for expanded human trials." The Court's assumption that there is a right to refuse lifesaving treatment in some circumstances was predicated upon "the common-law rule that forced medication was a battery and the long legal tradition protecting the decision to refuse unwanted medical treatment." But a tradition protecting individual *freedom* from life-saving, but forced, medical treatment does not evidence a constitutional tradition of providing affirmative *access* to a potentially harmful, and even fatal, commercial good.

In light of *Cruzan's* discussion of the "right of a *competent* individual to refuse medical treatment," the majority attempts to limit its new right to a patient who is "mentally competent" and has "informed access" to experimental drugs. The majority never explains what mental competence, in this context, would require. As the FDA noted in response to the Alliance's proposal, "with so little data available, it is hard to understand how a patient could be truly informed about the risks—or potential benefits—associated with the drug." By injecting patients into an early stage of the FDA's process for testing experimental drugs, the majority's approach allows terminally ill patients to take experimental drugs unknowingly—that is, without anyone having knowledge of potential risks and benefits. I fail to see how such a right is supported by *Cruzan*. *Cruzan* rejected an argument that an incompetent person has a right to withdraw treatment absent intent expressed while competent. Under the majority's decision, terminally ill patients seem to have a right to make an uninformed and involuntary choice....

Vexing Questions

The majority's new right to procure and use experimental drugs raises a number of vexing questions.... If a terminally ill patient has such a right, are patients with serious medical conditions entitled to the benefit of the same logic and corresponding access? If an indigent cannot afford potentially lifesaving treatment, would the Constitution mandate access to such care under the right recognized by the majority? Can a patient access any drug (i.e., marijuana for medicinal purposes), if she believes, in consultation with a physician, it is potentially lifesaving? Would the majority's right guarantee access to federally-funded stem cell research and treatment? Perhaps most significantly, what potential must a treatment have in order for the Constitution to mandate access? ...

Because the majority does not answer this last question, the District Court faces an impossible task on remand. The majority concludes that the District Court must "determine whether the FDA's policy barring access to post-Phase I investigational new drugs by terminally ill patients is narrowly tailored to serve a compelling governmental interest." Under the majority's approach on the face of it, the District Court must examine every drug undergoing FDA testing and every drug that may ever undergo FDA testing.... [T]he unknown risks and benefits of these experimental drugs will make nearly impossible a judicial examination of whether some level of access short of a prohibition would be more narrowly tailored to protect the majority's constitutional right of access.

Moreover, the level of benefit a patient will have to show, in order to demonstrate that under the majority's right a drug is potentially lifesaving, remains an enigma. Whatever the majority means by "potentially," its use of that term suggests that some drugs will not demonstrate enough potential benefit, while simultaneously presenting extraordinary risks.

Considering the potential benefits of an experimental drug in light of its risks will require the District Court to step into the role of the FDA....

Conclusion

Because the Alliance has failed to present objective evidence establishing a deeply rooted right to procure and use experimental drugs, I would apply rational basis review to its due process challenge.... For the terminally ill, as for anyone else, a drug is unsafe if its potential for inflicting death or physical injury is not offset by the possibility of therapeutic benefit. Although terminally ill patients desperately need curative treatments, their death can certainly be hastened by the use of a toxic drug. Prior to distribution of a drug outside of controlled studies, the Government has a rational basis for ensuring that there is a scientifically and medically acceptable level of knowledge about the risks and benefits of such a drug. I would affirm the decision of the District Court [barring access to experimental drugs].

Section 5: Animal Experimentation

Animal Experimentation

Peter Singer

Singer argues that the vast majority of animal experiments cannot be justified. They exact an extraordinary cost in animal suffering, while producing little or no knowledge—and whatever knowledge they do produce can usually be obtained in other ways. Singer provides multiple examples of painful, pointless experiments leading to the death of animal subjects. He argues that our willingness to tolerate such experiments can be explained only by our "speciesism"—the notion that the interests of nonhuman animals need not be considered. Speciesism, Singer holds, is analogous to racism and is just as indefensible.

Singer argues that the fundamental issue in determining how we may treat animals is whether they suffer and that the pains of animals and humans deserve equal consideration. Many animals are more intelligent than severely disabled or infant humans, so if deficient intelligence justifies painful animal experiments, it would also justify the same experiments on some humans. Because it is immoral to subject humans to such experiments, we have good reason to believe it is also wrong to subject animals to them. Singer concludes that research ethics committees should include members representing the welfare of animals and that investigators should be required to demonstrate that the benefits of their research will outweigh the suffering of the animals involved.

There has been opposition to experimenting on animals for a long time. This opposition has made little headway because experimenters, backed by commercial firms that profit by supplying laboratory animals and equipment, have been able to convince legislators and the public that opposition comes from uninformed fanatics who consider the interests of animals more important than the interests of human beings. But to be opposed to what is going on now it is not necessary to insist that all animal experiments stop immediately. All we need to say is that experiments serving no direct, and urgent purpose should stop immediately,

From Peter Singer, *Animal Liberation*, 2nd ed. (Random House/*New York Review of Books*, New York, 1990), 31–33, 40, 45–46, 48, 61–63, 65, 90–92. (Notes and references omitted.)

and in the remaining fields of research, we should, whenever possible, seek to replace experiments that involve animals with alternative methods that do not....

Professor [Harry] Harlow, who worked at the Primate Research Center in Madison, Wisconsin, was for many years editor of a leading psychology journal, and until his death a few years ago was held in high esteem by his colleagues in psychological research. His work has been cited approvingly in many basic textbooks of psychology, read by millions of students taking introductory psychology courses over the last twenty years. The line of research he began has been continued after his death by his associates and former students.

In a 1965 paper, Harlow describes his work as follows:

> For the past ten years we have studied the effects of partial social isolation by raising monkeys from birth onwards in bare wire cages.... These monkeys suffer total maternal deprivation.... More recently we have initiated a series of studies on the effects of total social isolation by rearing monkeys from a few hours after birth until 3, 6, or 12 months of age in [a] stainless steel chamber. During the prescribed sentence in this apparatus the monkey has no contact with any animal, human or sub-human.

These studies, Harlow continues, found that

> sufficiently severe and enduring early isolation reduces these animals to a social–emotional level in which the primary social responsiveness is fear.

In another article Harlow and his former student and associate Stephen Suomi described how they were trying to induce psychopathology in infant monkeys by a technique that appeared not to be working. They were then visited by John Bowlby, a British psychiatrist. According to Harlow's account, Bowlby listened to the story of their troubles and then toured the Wisconsin laboratory. After he had seen the monkeys individually housed in bare wire cages he asked, "Why are you trying to produce psychopathology in monkeys? You already have more psychopathological monkeys in the laboratory than have ever been seen on the face of the earth."

Bowlby, incidentally, was a leading researcher on the consequences of maternal deprivation, but his research was conducted with children, primarily war orphans, refugees, and institutionalized children. As far back as 1951, before Harlow even began his research on nonhuman primates, Bowlby concluded:

> The evidence has been reviewed. It is submitted that evidence is now such that it leaves no room for doubt regarding the general proposition that the prolonged deprivation of the young child of maternal care may have grave and far-reaching effects on his character and so on the whole of his future life.

This did not deter Harlow and his colleagues from devising and carrying out their monkey experiments.

In the same article in which they tell of Bowlby's visit, Harlow and Suomi describe how they had the "fascinating idea" of inducing depression by "allowing baby monkeys to attach to cloth surrogate mothers who could become monsters":

> The first of these monsters was a cloth monkey mother who, upon schedule or demand, would eject high-pressure compressed air. It would blow the animal's skin practically off its body. What did the baby monkey do? It simply clung tighter and tighter to the mother, because a frightened infant clings to its mother at all costs. We did not achieve any psychopathology.
>
> However, we did not give up. We built another surrogate monster mother that would rock so violently that the baby's head and teeth would rattle. All the baby did was cling tighter and tighter to the surrogate. The third monster we built had an embedded wire frame within its body which would spring forward and eject the infant from its ventral surface. The infant would subsequently pick itself off the floor, wait for the frame to return into the cloth body, and then cling again to the surrogate. Finally, we built our porcupine mother. On command, this mother would eject sharp brass spikes over all of the ventral surface of its body. Although the infants were distressed by these pointed rebuffs, they simply waited until the spikes receded and then returned and clung to the mother.

These results, the experimenters remark, were not so surprising, since the only recourse of an injured child is to cling to its mother....

Harlow is now dead, but his students and admirers have spread across the United States and continue to perform experiments in a similar vein....

Since Harlow began his maternal deprivation experiments some thirty years ago, over 250 such experiments have been conducted in the United States.

These experiments subjected over seven thousand animals to procedures that induced distress, despair, anxiety, general psychological devastation, and death....

An equally sad tale of futility is that of experiments designed to produce what is known as "learned helplessness"—supposedly a model of depression in human beings. In 1953 R. Solomon, L. Kamin, and L. Wynne, experimenters at Harvard University, placed forty dogs in a device called a "shuttlebox," which consists of a box divided into two compartments, separated by a barrier. Initially the barrier was set at the height of the dog's back. Hundreds of intense electric shocks were delivered to the dogs' feet through a grid floor. At first the dogs could escape the shock if they learned to jump the barrier into the other compartment. In an attempt to "discourage" one dog from jumping, the experimenters forced the dog to jump one hundred times onto a grid floor in the other compartment that also delivered a shock to the dog's feet. They said that as the dog jumped he gave a "sharp anticipatory yip which turned into a yelp when he landed on the electrified grid." They then blocked the passage between the compartments with a piece of plate glass and tested the dog again. The dog "jumped forward and smashed his head against the glass." The dogs began by showing symptoms such as defecation, urination, yelping and shrieking, trembling, attacking the apparatus, and so on; but after ten or twelve days of trials dogs who were prevented from escaping shock ceased to resist. The experimenters reported themselves "impressed" by this, and concluded that a combination of the plate glass barrier and foot shock was "very effective" in eliminating jumping by dogs.

This study showed that it was possible to induce a state of hopelessness and despair by repeated administration of severe inescapable shock. Such "learned helplessness" studies were further refined in the 1960s. One prominent experimenter was Martin Seligman of the University of Pennsylvania. He electrically shocked dogs through a steel grid with such intensity and persistence that the dogs stopped trying to escape and "learned" to be helpless. In one study, written with colleagues Steven Maier and James Geer, Seligman describes his work as follows:

When a normal, naive dog receives escape/avoidance training in a shuttlebox, the following behavior typically occurs: at the onset of electric shock the dog runs frantically about, defecating, urinating, and howling until it scrambles over the barrier and

so escapes from shock. On the next trial the dog, running and howling, crosses the barrier more quickly, and so on, until efficient avoidance emerges.

Seligman altered this pattern by strapping dogs in harnesses and giving them shocks from which they had no means of escape. When the dogs were then placed in the original shuttlebox situation from which escape was possible, he found that

such a dog reacts initially to shock in the shuttlebox in the same manner as the naive dog. However in dramatic contrast to the naive dog it soon stops running and remains silent until shock terminates. The dog does not cross the barrier and escape from shock. Rather it seems to "give up" and passively "accept" the shock. On succeeding trials the dog continues to fail to make escape movements and thus takes 50 seconds of severe, pulsating shock on each trial.... A dog previously exposed to inescapable shock ... may take unlimited shock without escaping or avoiding at all....

Electric shock has also been used to produce aggressive behavior in animals. In one study at the University of Iowa, Richard Viken and John Khutson divided 160 rats into groups and "trained" them in a stainless steel cage with an electrified floor. Pairs of rats were given electric shocks until they learned to fight by striking out at the other rat while facing each other in an upright position or by biting. It took an average of thirty training trials before the rats learned to do this immediately on the first shock. The researchers then placed the shock-trained rats in the cage of untrained rats and recorded their behavior. After one day, all the rats were killed, shaved, and examined for wounds. The experimenters concluded that their "results were not useful in understanding the offensive or defensive nature of the shock-induced response...."

When experiments can be brought under the heading "medical" we are inclined to think that any suffering they involve must be justifiable because the research is contributing to the alleviation of suffering. But...the testing of therapeutic drugs is less likely to be motivated by the desire for maximum good to all than by the desire for maximum profit. The broad label "medical research" can also be used to cover research that is motivated by a general intellectual curiosity. Such curiosity may be acceptable as part of a basic search for knowledge when it involves no suffering, but should not be tolerated if it causes pain. Very often, too, basic medical research has been going on for decades and much of it, in the long run, turns out to have been quite pointless. As an illustration, consider the following series of experiments stretching back nearly a century, on the effects of heat on animals:

In 1880 H.C. Wood placed a number of animals in boxes with glass lids and placed the boxes on a brick pavement on a hot day. He used rabbits, pigeons, and cats. His observations on a rabbit are typical. At a temperature of 109.5 degrees Fahrenheit the rabbit jumps and "kicks hind legs with great fury." The rabbit then has a convulsive attack. At 112 degrees Fahrenheit the animal lies on its side slobbering. At 120 degrees Fahrenheit it is gasping and squealing weakly. Soon after it dies.

In 1881 a report appeared in *The Lancet* on dogs and rabbits whose temperatures had been raised to 113 degrees Fahrenheit. It was found that death could be prevented by cool air currents, and the results were said to indicate "the importance of keeping down the temperature in those cases in which it exhibits a tendency to rise to [an] extreme height."

In 1927 W.W. Hall and E.G. Wakefield of the U.S. Naval Medical School placed ten dogs in a hot humid chamber to produce experimental heatstroke. The animals first showed restlessness, breathing difficulties, swelling and congestion of the eyes, and thirst. Some had convulsions. Some died early in the experiment. Those who did not had severe diarrhea and died after removal from the chamber.

In 1954 at Yale University School of Medicine, M. Lennox, W. Sibley, and H. Zimmerman placed thirty-two kittens in a "radiant-heating" chamber. The kittens were "subjected to a total of 49 heating periods.... Struggling was common, particularly as the temperature rose." Convulsions occurred on nine occasions: "Repeated convulsions were the rule." As many as thirty convulsions occurred in rapid sequence. Five kittens died during convulsions, and six without convulsions. The other kittens were killed by the experimenters for autopsies. The experimenters reported: "The findings in artificially induced fever in kittens conform to the clinical and EEG findings in human beings and previous clinical findings in kittens...."

In 1969 S. Michaelson, a veterinarian at the University of Rochester, exposed dogs and rabbits to heat-producing microwaves until their temperatures reached the critical level of 107 degrees Fahrenheit or greater. He observed that dogs start panting shortly after microwave exposure begins. Most "display increased activity varying from restlessness to extreme agitation." Near the point of death, weakness and prostration occur. In the case of rabbits "within 5 minutes, desperate attempts are made to escape the cage," and the rabbits die within forty minutes. Michaelson concluded that an increase in heat from microwaves produces damage "indistinguishable from fever in general...."

In 1984 experimenters working for the Federal Aviation Administration, stating that "animals occasionally die from heat stress encountered during shipping in the nation's transportation systems," subjected ten beagles to experimental heat. The dogs were isolated in chambers, fitted with muzzles, and exposed to 95 degrees Fahrenheit combined with high humidity. They were given no food or water, and were kept in these conditions for twenty-four hours. The behavior of the dogs was observed; it included "deliberate agitated activity such as pawing at the crate walls, continuous circling, tossing of the head to shed the muzzle, rubbing the muzzle back and forth on the floor of the crate, and aggressive acts on the sensor guards." Some of the dogs died in the chambers. When the survivors were removed, some vomited blood, and all were weak and exhausted. The experimenters refer to "subsequent experiments on more than 100 beagles...."

Here we have cited a series of experiments going back into the nineteenth century—and I have had space sufficient to include only a fraction of the published literature. The experiments obviously caused great suffering; and the major finding seems to be the advice that heatstroke victims should be cooled....Similar series of experiments are to be found in many other fields of medicine. In the New York City offices of United Action for Animals there are filing cabinets full of photocopies of experiments reported in the journals. Each thick file contains reports on numerous experiments, often fifty or more, and the labels on the files tell their own story: "Acceleration," "Aggression," "Asphyxiation," "Blinding," "Burning," "Centrifuge," "Compression," "Concussion," "Crowding," "Crushing," "Decompression," "Drug Tests," "Experimental Neurosis," "Freezing," "Heating," "Hemorrhage," "Hindleg Beating," "Immobilization," "Isolation," "Multiple Injuries," "Prey Killing," "Protein Deprivation," "Punishment," "Radiation," "Starvation," "Shock," "Spinal Cord Injuries," "Stress," "Thirst," and many more. While some of the experiments may have led to advances in medical knowledge, the value of this knowledge is often questionable, and in some cases the knowledge might have been gained in other ways. Many of the experiments appear to be trivial or misconceived, and some of them were not even designed to yield important benefits....

When are experiments on animals justifiable? Upon learning of the nature of many of the experiments carried out, some people react by saying that all experiments on animals should be prohibited immediately. But if we make our demands as absolute as this, the experimenters have a ready reply: Would we be prepared to let thousands of humans die if they could be saved by a single experiment on a single animal?

This question is, of course, purely hypothetical. There has never been and never could be a single experiment that saved thousands of lives. The way to reply to this hypothetical question is to pose another. Would the experimenters be prepared to carry out their experiment on a human orphan under six months old if that were the only way to save thousands of lives?

If the experimenters would not be prepared to use a human infant then their readiness to use non-human animals reveals an unjustifiable form of discrimination on the basis of species, since adult apes, monkeys, dogs, cats, rats, and other animals are more aware of what is happening to them, more self-directing, and, so far as we can tell, at least as sensitive to pain as a human infant. (I have specified that the human infant be an orphan, to avoid the complications of the feeling of parents. Specifying the case in this way is, if anything, overgenerous to those defending the use of nonhuman animals in experiments, since mammals intended for experimental use are usually separated from their mothers at an early age, when the separation causes distress for both mother and young.)

So far as we know, human infants possess no morally relevant characteristic to a higher degree than adult nonhuman animals, unless we are to count the infants' potential as a characteristic that makes it wrong to experiment on them. Whether this characteristic should count is controversial—if we count it, we shall have to condemn abortion along with experiments on infants, since the potential of the infant and the fetus is the same. To avoid the complexities of this issue, however, we can alter our original question a little and assume that the infant is one with irreversible brain damage so severe as to rule out any mental development beyond the level of a six-month-old infant. There are, unfortunately, many such human beings, locked away in special wards throughout the country, some of them long since abandoned by their parents and other relatives, and, sadly, sometimes unloved by anyone else. Despite their mental deficiencies, the anatomy and physiology of these infants are in nearly all respects identical with those of normal humans. If, therefore, we were to force-feed them with large quantities of floor polish or drip concentrated solutions of cosmetics into their eyes, we would have a much more reliable indication of the safety of these products for humans than we now get by attempting to extrapolate the results of tests on a variety of other species. The LD50 tests, the Draize eye tests, the radiation experiments, the heatstroke experiments, and many others could have told us more about human reactions to the experimental situation if they had been carried out on severely brain-damaged humans instead of dogs or rabbits.

So whenever experimenters claim that their experiments are important enough to justify the use of animals, we should ask them whether they would be prepared to use a brain-damaged human being at a similar mental level to the animals they are planning to use. I cannot imagine that anyone would seriously propose carrying out the experiments described in this chapter on brain-damaged human beings. Occasionally it has become known that medical experiments have been performed on human beings without their consent; one case did concern institutionalized intellectually disabled children, who were given hepatitis. When such harmful experiments on human beings become known, they usually lead to an outcry against the experimenters, and rightly so. They are, very often, a further example of the arrogance of the research worker who justifies everything on the grounds of increasing knowledge. But if the experimenter claims that the experiment is important enough to justify inflicting suffering on animals, why is it not important enough to justify inflicting suffering on humans at the same mental level? What difference is there between the two? Only that one is a member of our species and the other is not? But to appeal to that difference is to reveal a bias no more defensible than racism or any other form of arbitrary discrimination.

The analogy between speciesism and racism applies in practice as well as in theory in the area of experimentation. Blatant speciesism leads to painful experiments on other species, defended on the grounds of their contribution to knowledge and possible usefulness for our species. Blatant racism has led to painful experiments on other races, defended on the grounds of their contribution to knowledge and possible usefulness for the experimenting race. Under the Nazi regime in Germany, nearly two hundred doctors, some of them eminent in the world of medicine, took part in experiments on Jews and

Russian and Polish prisoners. Thousands of other physicians knew of these experiments, some of which were the subject of lectures at medical academies. Yet the records show that the doctors sat through verbal reports by doctors on how horrible injuries were inflicted on these "lesser races," and then proceeded to discuss the medical lessons to be learned from them, without anyone making even a mild protest about the nature of the experiments. The parallels between this attitude and that of experimenters today toward animals are striking. Then, as now, subjects were frozen, heated, and put in decompression chambers. Then, as now, these events were written up in dispassionate scientific jargon. The following paragraph is taken from a report by a Nazi scientist of an experiment on a human being, placed in a decompression chamber:

> *After five minutes spasms appeared; between the sixth and tenth minute respiration increased in frequency, the TP [test person] losing consciousness. From the eleventh to the thirtieth minute respiration slowed down to three inhalations per minute, only to cease entirely at the end of that period.... About half an hour after breathing ceased, an autopsy was begun.*

Decompression chamber experimentation did not stop with the defeat of the Nazis. It shifted to nonhuman animals. At the University of Newcastle on Tyne, in England, for instance, scientists used pigs. The pigs were subjected to up to eighty-one periods of decompression over a period of nine months. All suffered attacks of decompression sickness, and some died from these attacks. The example illustrates only too well what the great Jewish writer Isaac Bashevis Singer has written: "In their behavior towards creatures, all men [are] Nazis...."

We have still not answered the question of when an experiment might be justifiable. It will not do to say "Never!" Putting morality in such black-and-white terms is appealing, because it eliminates the need to think about particular cases; but in extreme circumstances, such absolutist answers always break down. Torturing a human being is almost always wrong, but it is not absolutely wrong. If torture were the only way in which we could discover the location of a nuclear bomb hidden in a New York City basement and timed to go off within the hour, then torture would be justifiable. Similarly, if a single experiment could cure a disease like leukemia, that experiment would be justifiable. But in actual life the benefits are always

more remote, and more often than not they are nonexistent. So how do we decide when an experiment is justifiable?

We have seen that experimenters reveal a bias in favor of their own species whenever they carry out experiments on nonhumans for purposes that they would not think justified them in using human beings, even brain-damaged ones. This principle gives us a guide toward an answer to our question. Since a speciesist bias, like a racist bias, is unjustifiable, an experiment cannot be justified unless the experiment is so important that the use of a brain-damaged human would also be justifiable.

This is not an absolutist principle. I do not believe that it could never be justifiable to experiment on a brain-damaged human. If it really were possible to save several lives by an experiment that would take just one life, and there were no other way those lives could be saved, it would be right to do the experiment. But this would be an extremely rare case. Certainly none of the experiments described in this chapter could pass this test. Admittedly, as with any dividing line, there would be a gray area where it was difficult to decide if an experiment could be justified. But we need not get distracted by such considerations now. As this chapter has shown, we are in the midst of an emergency in which appalling suffering is being inflicted on millions of animals for purposes that on any impartial view are obviously inadequate to justify the suffering. When we have ceased to carry out all those experiments, then there will be time enough to discuss what to do about the remaining ones which are claimed to be essential to save lives or prevent greater suffering....

In the United States, where experimenters can do virtually as they please with animals, one way of making progress might be to ask those who use this argument to defend the need for animal experiment whether they would be prepared to accept the verdict of an ethics committee that, like those in many other countries, includes animal welfare representatives and is entitled to weigh the costs to the animals against the possible benefits of the research. If the answer is no, the defense of animal experimentation by reference to the need to cure major diseases has been proved to be simply a deceitful distraction that serves to mislead the public about what the experimenters want: permission to do whatever they like with animals. For otherwise why would the experimenter not be prepared to leave the decision on carrying out the experiment to an ethics committee, which would surely be as keen to see major diseases ended as the rest of the community? If the answer is yes, the experimenter should be asked to sign a statement asking for the creation of such an ethics committee.

Suppose that we were able to go beyond minimal reforms of the sort that already exist in the more enlightened nations. Suppose we could reach a point at which the interests of animals really were given equal consideration with the similar interests of human beings. That would mean the end of the vast industry of animal experimentation as we know it today. Around the world, cages would empty and laboratories would close down. It should not be thought, though, that medical research would grind to a halt or that a flood of untested products would come onto the market. So far as new products are concerned it is true, as I have already said, that we would have to make do with fewer of them, using ingredients already known to be safe. That does not seem to be any great loss. But for testing really essential products, as well as for other kinds of research, alternative methods not requiring animals can and would be found....

The defenders of animal experimentation are fond of telling us that animal experimentation has greatly increased our life expectancy. In the midst of the debate over reform of the British law on animal experimentation, for example, the Association of the British Pharmaceutical Industry ran a full-page advertisement in the *Guardian* under the headline "They say life begins at forty. Not so long ago, that's about when it ended." The advertisement went on to say that it is now considered to be a tragedy if a man dies in his forties, whereas in the nineteenth century it was commonplace to attend the funeral of a man in his forties, for the average life expectancy was only forty-two. The advertisement stated that "it is thanks largely to the breakthroughs that have been made through research which requires animals that most of us are able to live into our seventies."

Such claims are simply false. In fact, this particular advertisement was so blatantly misleading that a specialist in community medicine, Dr. David St. George, wrote to *The Lancet* saying "the advertisement is good teaching material, since it illustrates two major errors in the interpretation of statistics." He also referred to Thomas McKeown's influential book *The Role of Medicine*, published in 1976, which set off a debate about the relative contributions of social and environmental changes, as compared with medical intervention, in

improvements in mortality since the mid-nineteenth century; and he added:

> *This debate has been resolved, and it is now widely accepted that medical interventions had only a marginal effect on population mortality and mainly at a very late stage, after death rates had already fallen strikingly.*

J. B. and S. M. McKinley reached a similar conclusion in a study of the decline of ten major infectious diseases in the United States. They showed that in every case except poliomyelitis the death rate had already fallen dramatically (presumably because of improved sanitation and diet) before any new form of medical treatment was introduced. Concentrating on the 40 percent fall in crude mortality in the United States between 1910 and 1984, they estimated "conservatively" that

> *perhaps 3.5 percent of the fall in the overall death rate can be explained through medical interventions for the major infectious diseases. Indeed, given that it is precisely for these diseases that medicine claims most success in lowering mortality, 3.5 percent probably represents a reasonable upper-limit estimate of the total contribution of medical measures to the decline in infectious disease mortality in the United States.*

Remember that this 3.5 percent is a figure for all medical intervention. The contribution of animal experimentation itself can be, at most, only a fraction of this tiny contribution to the decline in mortality....

Finally, it is important to realize that the major health problems of the world largely continue to exist, not because we do not know how to prevent disease and keep people healthy, but because no one is putting enough effort and money into doing what we already know how to do. The diseases that ravage Asia, Africa, Latin America, and the pockets of poverty in the industrialized West are diseases that, by and large, we know how to cure. They have been eliminated in communities that have adequate nutrition, sanitation, and health care. It has been estimated that 250,000 children die each week around the world, and that one quarter of these deaths are by dehydration caused by diarrhea. A simple treatment, already known and needing no animal experimentation, could prevent the deaths of these children. Those who are genuinely concerned about improving health care would probably make a more effective contribution to human health if they left the laboratories and saw to it that our existing stock of medical knowledge reached those who need it most.

The Case for the Use of Animals in Biomedical Research

Carl Cohen

Cohen rejects arguments by those who favor severely curbing or eliminating animal experimentation, then defends the position that we have a strong duty to conduct such experiments to alleviate human suffering and extend human lives.

Animals have no rights, Cohen claims. To have a right is to have a moral claim against others. This means having the capacity to recognize conflicts between one's self-interest and what is right and being able to restrain one's self-interest when appropriate. Animals lack these capacities. Hence, they are not the sort of beings who can possess rights, and lacking rights, their interests may be sacrificed for the welfare of others.

Cohen rejects Peter Singer's argument that the pleasures and pains of animals deserve consideration equal to those of humans in calculating the overall benefits of animal experiments, because to do otherwise is "speciesism." Singer's analogy with racism and sexism does not hold, Cohen claims, because animals lack autonomy and membership in the moral community. Indeed, speciesism is "essential to right conduct," because those who fail to make the relevant distinctions between humans and nonhumans will fail to recognize their moral duties.

Using animals as research subjects in medical investigations is widely condemned on two grounds: first, because it wrongly violates the *rights* of animals, and second, because it wrongly imposes on sentient creatures much avoidable *suffering*. Neither of these arguments is sound. The first relies on a mistaken understanding of rights; the second relies on a mistaken calculation of consequences. Both deserve definitive dismissal.

Why Animals Have No Rights

A right, properly understood, is a claim, or potential claim, that one party may exercise against another. The target against whom such a claim may be registered can be a single person, a group, a community, or (perhaps) all humankind. The content of rights claims also varies greatly: repayment of loans, nondiscrimination by employers, noninterference by the state, and so on. To comprehend any

genuine right fully, therefore, we must know *who* holds the right, *against whom* it is, held, and *to what* it is a right.

Alternative sources of rights add complexity. Some rights are grounded in constitution and law (e.g., the right of an accused to trial by jury); some rights are moral but give no legal claims (e.g., my right to your keeping the promise you gave me); and some rights (e.g., against theft or assault) are rooted both in morals and in law.

The differing targets, contents, and sources of rights, and their inevitable conflict, together weave a tangled web. Notwithstanding all such complications, this much is clear about rights in general: they are in every case claims, or potential claims, within a community of moral agents. Rights arise, and can be intelligibly defended, only among beings who actually do, or can, make moral claims against one another. Whatever else rights may be, therefore, they are necessarily human; their possessors are persons, human beings.

The attributes of human beings from which this moral capability arises have been described variously by philosophers, both ancient and modern: the inner consciousness of a free will (Saint Augustine); the grasp, by human reason, of the binding character of moral law (Saint Thomas); the self-conscious participation of human beings in an objective ethical order (Hegel); human membership in an organic moral community (Bradley); the development of the human self through the consciousness of other moral selves (Mead); and the underivative, intuitive cognition of the rightness of an action (Prichard). Most influential has been Immanuel Kant's emphasis on the universal human possession of a uniquely moral will and the autonomy its use entails. Humans confront choices that are purely moral; humans—but certainly not dogs or mice—lay down moral laws, for others and for themselves. Human beings are self-legislative, morally *autonomous*.

Animals (that is, nonhuman animals, the ordinary sense of that word) lack this capacity for free moral judgment. They are not beings of a kind capable of exercising or responding to moral claims. Animals therefore have no rights, and they can have none. This is the core of the argument about the alleged rights of animals. The holders of rights must have the capacity to comprehend rules of duty, governing all including themselves. In applying such rules, the holders of rights must recognize possible conflicts between what is in their own interest and what is just. Only in a community of beings capable of self-restricting moral judgments can the concept of a right be correctly invoked.

Humans have such moral capacities. They are in this sense self-legislative, are members of communities governed by moral rules, and do possess rights. Animals do not have such moral capacities. They are not morally self-legislative, cannot possibly be members of a truly moral community, and therefore cannot possess rights. In conducting research on animal subjects, therefore, we do not violate their rights, because they have none to violate.

To animate life, even in its simplest forms, we give a certain natural reverence. But the possession of rights presupposes a moral status not attained by the vast majority of living things. We must not infer, therefore, that a live being has, simply in being alive, a "right" to its life. The assertion that all animals, only because they are alive and have interests, also possess the "right to life" is an abuse of that phrase, and wholly without warrant.

It does not follow from this, however, that we are morally free to do anything we please to animals. Certainly not. In our dealings with animals, as in our dealings with other human beings, we have obligations that do not arise from claims against us based on rights. Rights entail obligations, but many of the things one ought to do are in no way tied to another's entitlement. Rights and obligations are not reciprocals of one another, and it is a serious mistake to suppose that they are.

Illustrations are helpful. Obligations may arise from internal commitments made: physicians have obligations to their patients not grounded merely in their patients' rights. Teachers have such obligations to their students, shepherds to their dogs, and cowboys to their horses. Obligations may arise from differences of status: adults owe special care when playing with young children, and children owe special care when playing with young pets. Obligations may arise from special relationships: the payment of my son's college tuition is something to which he may have no right, although it may be my obligation to bear the burden if I reasonably can; my dog has no right to daily exercise and veterinary care, but I do have the obligation to provide these things for her. Obligations may arise from particular acts or circumstances: one may be obliged to another for a special kindness done, or obliged to put an animal out of its misery in view of its condition—although neither the human benefactor nor the dying animal may have had a claim of right.

Plainly, the grounds of our obligations to humans and to animals are manifold and cannot be formulated simply. Some hold that there is a general obligation to do no gratuitous harm to sentient creatures (the principle of nonmaleficence); some hold that there is general obligation to do good to sentient creatures when that is reasonably within one's power (the principle of beneficence). In our dealings with animals, few will deny that we are at least obliged to act humanely—that is, to treat them with the decency and concern that we owe, as sensitive human beings, to other sentient creatures. To treat animals humanely, however, is not to treat them as humans or as the holders of rights.

A common objection, which deserves a response, may be paraphrased as follows:

> If having rights requires being able to make moral claims, to grasp and apply moral laws, then many humans—the brain-damaged, the comatose, the senile—who plainly lack those capacities must be without rights. But that is absurd. This proves [the critic concludes] that rights do not depend on the presence of moral capacities.

This objection fails; it mistakenly treats an essential feature of humanity as though it were a screen for sorting humans. The capacity for moral judgment that distinguishes humans from animals is not a test to be administered to human beings one by one. Persons who are unable, because of some disability, to perform the full moral functions natural to human beings are certainly not for that reason ejected from the moral community. The issue is one of kind. Humans are of such a kind that they may be the subject of experiments only with their voluntary consent. The choices they make freely must be respected. Animals are of such a kind that it is impossible for them, in principle, to give or withhold voluntary consent or to make a moral choice. What humans retain when disabled, animals have never had.

A second objection, also often made, may be paraphrased as follows:

> *Capacities will not succeed in distinguishing humans from the other animals. Animals also reason; animals also communicate with one another; animals also care passionately for their young; animals also exhibit desires and preferences. Features of moral relevance—rationality, interdependence, and love—are not exhibited uniquely by human beings. Therefore [this critic concludes] there can be no solid moral distinction between humans and other animals.*

This criticism misses the central point. It is not the ability to communicate or to reason, or dependence on one another, or care for the young, or the exhibition of preference, or any such behavior that marks the critical divide. Analogies between human families and those of monkeys, or between human communities and those of wolves, and the like, are entirely beside the point. Patterns of conduct are not at issue. Animals do indeed exhibit remarkable behavior at times. Conditioning, fear, instinct, and intelligence all contribute to species survival. Membership in a community of moral agents nevertheless remains impossible for them. Actors subject to moral judgment must be capable of grasping the generality of an ethical premise in a practical syllogism. Humans act immorally often enough, but only they—never wolves or monkeys—can discern, by applying some moral rule to the facts of a case, that a given act ought or ought not to be performed. The moral restraints imposed by humans on themselves are thus highly abstract and are often in conflict with the self-interest of the agent. Communal behavior among animals, even when most intelligent and most endearing, does not approach autonomous morality in this fundamental sense.

Genuinely moral acts have an internal as well as an external dimension. Thus, in law, an act can be criminal only when the guilty deed, the actus reus, is done with a guilty mind, mens rea. No animal can ever commit a crime; bringing animals to criminal trial is the mark of primitive ignorance. The claims of moral right are similarly inapplicable to them. Does a lion have a right to eat a baby zebra? Does a baby zebra have a right not to be eaten? Such questions, mistakenly invoking the concept of right where it does not belong do not make good sense. Those who condemn biomedical research because it violates "animal rights" commit the same blunder.

In Defense of "Speciesism"

Abandoning reliance on animal rights, some critics resort instead to animal sentience—their feelings of pain and distress. We ought to desist from the imposition of pain insofar as we can. Since all or nearly all experimentation on animals does impose pain and could be readily forgone, say these critics, it should be stopped. The ends sought may be worthy, but those ends do not justify imposing agonies on humans, and by animals the agonies are felt no less. The laboratory use of animals (these critics conclude) must therefore be ended—or at least very sharply curtailed.

Argument of this variety is essentially utilitarian, often expressly so; it is based on the calculation of the net product, in pains and pleasures, resulting from experiments on animals. Jeremy Bentham, comparing horses and dogs with other sentient creatures, is thus commonly quoted: "The question is not, Can they reason? nor Can they talk? but, Can they suffer?"

Animals certainly can suffer and surely ought not to be made to suffer needlessly. But in inferring, from these uncontroversial premises, that biomedical research causing animals distress is largely (or wholly) wrong, the critic commits two serious errors.

The first error is the assumption, often explicitly defended, that all sentient animals have equal moral standing. Between a dog and a human being, according to this view, there is no moral difference; hence the pains suffered by dogs must be weighed no differently from the pains suffered by humans. To deny such equality, according to this critic, is to give unjust preference to one species over another; it is "speciesism." The most influential statement of this moral equality of species was made by Peter Singer:

> *The racist violates the principle of equality by giving greater weight to the interests of members of his own race when there is a clash between their*

interests and the interests of those of another race. The sexist violates the principle of equality by favoring the interests of his own sex. Similarly the speciesist allows the interests of his own species to override the greater interests of members of other species. The pattern is identical in each case.

This argument is worse than unsound; it is atrocious. It draws an offensive moral conclusion from a deliberately devised verbal parallelism that is utterly specious. Racism has no rational ground whatever. Differing degrees of respect or concern for humans for no other reason than that they are members of different races is an injustice totally without foundation in the nature of the races themselves. Racists, even if acting on the basis of mistaken factual beliefs, do grave moral wrong precisely because there is no morally relevant distinction among the races. The supposition of such differences has led to outright horror. The same is true of the sexes, neither sex being entitled by right to greater respect or concern than the other. No dispute here.

Between species of animate life, however— between (for example) humans on the one hand and cats or rats on the other—the morally relevant differences are enormous, and almost universally appreciated. Humans engage in moral reflection; humans are morally autonomous; humans are members of moral communities, recognizing just claims against their own interest. Human beings do have rights; theirs is a moral status very different from that of cats or rats.

I am a speciesist. Speciesism is not merely plausible; it is essential for right conduct, because those who will not make the morally relevant distinctions among species are almost certain, in consequence, to misapprehend their true obligations. The analogy between speciesism and racism is insidious. Every sensitive moral judgment requires that the differing natures of the beings to whom obligations are owed be considered. If all forms of animate life—or vertebrate animal life?—must be treated equally, and if therefore in evaluating a research program the pains of a rodent count equally with the pains of a human, we are forced to conclude (1) that neither humans nor rodents possess rights, or (2) that rodents possess all the rights that humans possess. Both alternatives are absurd. Yet one or the other must be swallowed if the moral equality of all species is to be defended.

Humans owe to other humans a degree of moral regard that cannot be owed to animals. Some humans take on the obligation to support and heal others, both humans and animals, as a principal duty in their lives; the fulfillment of that duty may require the sacrifice of many

animals. If biomedical investigators abandon the effective pursuit of their professional objectives because they are convinced that they may not do to animals what the service of humans requires, they will fail, objectively, to do their duty. Refusing to recognize the moral differences among species is a sure path to calamity. (The largest animal rights group in the country is People for the Ethical Treatment of Animals; its codirector, Ingrid Newkirk, calls research using animal subjects, "fascism" and "supremacism." "Animal liberationists do not separate out the *human* animal," she says, "so there is no rational basis for saying that a human being has special rights. A rat is a pig is a dog is a boy. They're all mammals.")

Those who claim to base their objection to the use of animals in biomedical research on their reckoning of the net pleasures and pains produced make a second error, equally grave. Even if it were true—as it is surely not—that the pains of all animate beings must be counted equally, a cogent utilitarian calculation requires that we weigh all the consequences of the use, and of the nonuse, of animals in laboratory research. Critics relying (however mistakenly) on animal rights may claim to ignore the beneficial results of such research, rights being trump cards to which interest and advantage must give way. But an argument that is explicitly framed in terms of interest and benefit for all over the long run must attend also to the disadvantageous consequences of not using animals in research, and to all the achievements attained and attainable only through their use. The sum of the benefits of their use is utterly beyond quantification. The elimination of horrible disease, the increase of longevity, the avoidance of great pain, the saving of lives, and the improvement of the quality of lives (for humans and for animals) achieved through research using animals is so incalculably great that the argument of these critics, systematically pursued, establishes not their conclusion but its reverse: to refrain from using animals in biomedical research is, on utilitarian grounds, morally wrong.

When balancing the pleasures and pains resulting from the use of animals in research, we must not fail to place on the scales the terrible pains that would have resulted, would be suffered now, and would long continue had animals not been used. Every disease eliminated, every vaccine developed, every method of pain relief devised, every surgical procedure invented, every prosthetic device implanted—indeed, virtually every modern medical therapy is due, in part or in whole, to experimentation using animals. Nor may we ignore, in the balancing process, the predictable gains in human (and animal) well-being that are probably achievable in the future but that will not be achieved if the decision is made now to desist from such research or to curtail it.

Medical investigators are seldom insensitive to the distress their work may cause animal subjects. Opponents of research using animals are frequently insensitive to the cruelty of the results of the restrictions they would impose. Untold numbers of human beings—real persons, although not now identifiable— would suffer grievously as the consequence of this well-meaning but shortsighted tenderness. If the morally relevant differences between humans and animals are borne in mind, and if all relevant considerations are weighed, the calculation of long-term consequences must give overwhelming support for biomedical research using animals.

Concluding Remarks

Substitution

The humane treatment of animals requires that we desist from experimenting on them if we can accomplish the same result using alternative methods—in vitro experimentation, computer simulation, or others.

Critics of some experiments using animals rightly make this point.

It would be a serious error to suppose, however, that alternative techniques could soon be used in most research now using live animal subjects. No other methods now on the horizon—or perhaps ever to be available—can fully replace the testing of a drug, a procedure, or a vaccine, in live organisms. The flood of new medical possibilities being opened by the successes of recombinant DNA technology will turn to a trickle if testing on live animals is forbidden. When initial trials entail great risks, there may be no forward movement whatever without the use of live animal subjects. In seeking knowledge that may prove critical in later clinical applications, the unavailability of animals for inquiry may spell complete stymie. In the United States, federal regulations require the testing of new drugs and other products on animals, for efficacy and safety, before human beings are exposed to them. We would not want it otherwise.

Every advance in medicine—every new drug, new operation, new therapy of any kind—must sooner or later be tried on a living being for the first time. That trial, controlled or uncontrolled, will be an experiment. The subject of that experiment, if it is not an animal, will be a human being. Prohibiting the use of live animals in biomedical research, therefore, or sharply restricting it, must result either in the blockage of much valuable research or in the replacement of animal subjects with human subjects. These are

the consequences—unacceptable to most reasonable persons—of not using animals in research.

Reduction

Should we not at least reduce the use of animals in biomedical research? No, we should increase it, to avoid when feasible the use of humans as experimental subjects. Medical investigations putting human subjects at some risk are numerous and greatly varied. The risks run in such experiments are usually unavoidable, and (thanks to earlier experiments on animals) most such risks are minimal or moderate. But some experimental risks are substantial.

When an experimental protocol that entails substantial risk to humans comes before an institutional review board, what response is appropriate? The investigation, we may suppose, is promising and deserves support, so long as its human subjects are protected against unnecessary dangers. May not the investigators be fairly asked, Have you done all that you can to eliminate risk to humans by the extensive testing of that drug, that procedure, or that device on animals? To achieve maximal safety for humans we are right to require thorough experimentation on animal subjects before humans are involved.

Opportunities to increase human safety in this way are commonly missed; trials in which risks may be shifted from humans to animals are often not devised, sometimes not even considered. Why? For the investigator, the use of animals as subjects is often more expensive, in money and time, than the use of human subjects. Access to suitable human subjects is often quick and convenient, whereas access to appropriate animal subjects may be awkward, costly, and burdened with red tape. Physician-investigators have often had more experience working with human beings and know precisely where the needed pool of subjects is to be found and how they may be enlisted. Animals, and the procedures for their use, are often less familiar to these investigators. Moreover, the use of animals in place of humans is now more likely to be the target of zealous protests from without. The upshot is that humans are sometimes subjected to risks that animals could have borne, and should have borne, in their place. To maximize the protection of human subjects, I conclude, the wide and imaginative use of live animal subjects should be encouraged rather than discouraged. This enlargement in the use of animals is our obligation.

Consistency

Finally, inconsistency between the profession and the practice of many who oppose research using animals deserves comment. This frankly *ad homi-nem* observation aims chiefly to show that a coherent position rejecting the use of animals in medical research imposes costs so high as to be intolerable even to the critics themselves.

One cannot coherently object to the killing of animals in biomedical investigations while continuing to eat them. Anesthetics and thoughtful animal husbandry render the level of actual animal distress in the laboratory generally lower than that in the abattoir. So long as death and discomfort do not substantially differ in the two contexts, the consistent objector must not only refrain from all eating of animals but also protest as vehemently against others eating them as against others experimenting on them. No less vigorously must the critic object to the wearing of animal hides in coats and shoes, to employment in any industrial enterprise that uses animal parts, and to any commercial development that will cause death or distress to animals.

Killing animals to meet human needs for food, clothing and shelter is judged entirely reasonable by most persons. The ubiquity of these uses and the virtual universality of moral support for them confront the opponent of research using animals with an inescapable difficulty. How can the many common uses of animals be judged morally worthy, while their use in scientific investigation is judged unworthy?

The number of animals used in research is but the tiniest fraction of the total used to satisfy assorted human appetites. That these appetites, often base and satisfiable in other ways, morally justify the far larger consumption of animals, whereas the quest for improved human health and understanding cannot justify the far smaller, is wholly implausible. Aside from the numbers of animals involved, the distinction in terms of worthiness of use, drawn with regard to any single animal, is not defensible. A given sheep is surely not more justifiably used to put lamb chops on the supermarket counter than to serve in testing a new contraceptive or a new prosthetic device. The needless killing of animals is wrong; if the common killing of them for our food or convenience is right, the less common but more humane uses of animals in the service of medical science are certainly not less right.

Scrupulous vegetarianism, in matters of food, clothing, shelter, commerce, and recreation, and in all other spheres, is the only fully coherent position the critic may adopt. At great human cost, the lives of fish and crustaceans must also be protected, with equal vigor, if speciesism has been forsworn. A very few consistent critics adopt this position. It is the *reductio ad absurdum* of the rejection of moral distinctions between animals and human beings.

Opposition to the use of animals in research is based on arguments of two different kinds—those relying on the alleged rights of animals and those relying on the consequences for animals. I have argued that arguments of both kinds must fail. We surely do have obligations to animals, but they have, and can have, no rights against us on which research can infringe. In calculating the consequences of animal research, we must weigh all the long-term benefits of the results achieved—to animals and to humans—and in that calculation we must not assume the moral equality of all animate species.

DECISION SCENARIOS

The questions following each decision scenario are intended to prompt reflection and discussion. In deciding how to answer them, you should consider the information provided in the Social Context and Case Presentations, as well as in the Briefing Session. You should also make use of the ethical theories and principles presented in Part VI: Foundations of Bioethics, and the arguments offered in the relevant readings in this chapter.

DECISION SCENARIO 1

A Right to Try?

For three days now, she had returned from lunch to find the man with the sign standing quietly next to the bank of elevators. Security wouldn't allow protesters to come any closer to the lab. Connie decided it was time to talk to him.

"Mr. Haberstrom?"

He looked at her blankly and flipped his sign around. "Benuvo Kills" became "Open the Trial!"

"Mr. Haberstrom, my name is Connie Desner. I'm head of research at Benuvo."

"Have you decided to open the ziaxa trial?" His eyes met hers. "If not, I don't want to talk to you."

"Mr. Haberstrom, I want you to know how sorry I was to hear about your daughter. She was an amazing person and we wish we could have helped her."

"You could have let her into the ziaxa trial," Haberstrom said. "You had lymphoma patients in an earlier round."

"You know, only about a third of drugs make it past Phase II testing. Usually, they aren't effective and sometimes they do more harm than good."

What Connie knew, but could not tell him, was that the lymphoma patients in the earlier ziaxa trial had gotten no benefit from the drug, and some of them had gotten worse. The drug was effective, just not for lymphoma.

"Yeah, I've heard that all before," Haberstrom said. "But who are you to tell my daughter that she couldn't try a drug her doctor recommended? She knew there were risks involved. But she was nineteen. She had the right to decide for herself."

1. The FDA guidelines for "compassionate use" of investigational drugs say that patients must have a chance of benefitting from their use. Because a drug's effectiveness isn't tested until Phase II, these trials are generally off-limits to patients who don't meet the criteria. Is this fair? Should patients like Haberstrom's daughter be allowed into such trials?

2. How might allowing broader access to investigational drugs make it harder to find subjects for a double-blind study? If you were a patient, would you be willing to risk getting a placebo or an established (standard of care) treatment, when you knew you could get the promising new treatment outside of the trial?

3. Investigational drugs are expensive to research and produce. How might cost considerations factor into a company's decision about whether or not to open a trial for "compassionate use"? Are such concerns appropriate?

DECISION SCENARIO 2

Genuine Consent?

"You realize," Dr. Thorne said, "that you may not be in the group that receives medication. You may be in the placebo group for at least part of the time."

"Right," Ada Ross said. "You're just going to give me some medicine."

"And do you understand the aims of the research?"

"You want to help me get better," Ross suggested hesitantly.

"We hope you get better, of course. But that's not what we're trying to accomplish here. We're trying to find out if this medication will help other people with your condition if we treat them earlier than we were able to treat you."

"You want to help people," Ross said.

"That's right. But you do understand that we may not be helping you in this experiment?"

"But you're going to try?"

"Not exactly. I mean, we aren't going to try to harm you. But we aren't necessarily going to be giving you the preferred treatment for your complaint either. Do you know the difference between research and therapy?"

"Research is when you're trying to find something out. You're searching around."

"That's right. And we're asking you to be part of a research effort. As I told you, there are some risks. Besides the possibility of not getting treatment that you need, the drug may produce limited hepatic portal damage. We're not sure how much."

"I think I understand," Ross said.

"I'm sure you do," said Thorne. "I understand that you are freely volunteering to participate in this research."

"Yes, sir. Ms. Woolerd, she told me if I volunteered, I'd get a letter put in my file and I could get early release."

"Ms. Woolerd told you the review board would take your volunteering into account when they considered whether you should be put on work-release."

"And I'm awfully anxious to get out of here. I've got two children staying with my aunt, and I need to get out of this place as quick as I can."

"I understand. We can't promise you release, of course. But your participation will look good on your record. Now I have some papers here I want you to sign."

1. Discuss some of the difficulties involved in explaining research procedures to non-expert subjects and determining whether they are aware of the nature and risks of their participation.

2. List some possible reasons for doubting that Ada Ross fully understands what she is volunteering for?

3. Discuss the problems involved in securing free and voluntary consent from a person involuntarily confined to an institution (a prisoner, for example).

4. Is it possible to obtain genuine consent from patients in Phase I cancer treatment trials, even if they are not in prison?

DECISION SCENARIO 3

Guinea-Pigging

Jordan Lee held his head still and tried to concentrate on *Oprah* reruns. His right knee was jiggling uncontrollably and he felt a wave of nausea building in the pit of his stomach.

"Got the spins again?" Jordan nodded and Rabbit handed him the hotel wastebasket.

Rabbit's real name was Desmond, but no one in the trial called him that. Jordan and Rabbit had been sharing a room at the Winston Suites for three days now, watching TV and loading up trays at the motel's all-you-can-eat buffet, along with eighteen other trial subjects. Each morning, a tech from Rejuvian Pharmaceuticals would arrive with pale-green pills for them to swallow. She'd take blood and urine samples, measure blood pressure, and make some notes on her laptop. Forty-five minutes later, the nausea would begin.

"I know you're hating life right now," said Rabbit. "But seriously, this trial is pretty good. Decent food, no IVs or nose tubes, free cable. You just have to learn how to ride out the side effects." As he listened to Rabbit, Jordan closed his eyes and felt the room begin to lurch and spin.

The flyer had read "Spare time this summer?" and it had seemed like a perfect solution to Jordan's money problems. For a week's participation in a Phase I trial of a new antidepressant, he'd be paid $2,000 by Rejuvian. That would cover next month's rent, plus the back rent he owed, plus his textbooks for next semester. There had been a list of possible side effects, such as hypertension, insomnia, dizziness, and psychosis, but Jordan hadn't paid much attention. Now he wasn't sure he could make it through the week.

"You've been doing this for a while?" Jordan asked, when the dry heaves finally stopped.

"Ever since I got off probation," Rabbit said. "It pays my bills and I get some free health care. You just have to know which trials pay well and which ones to avoid."

"So this is like an actual career for you?"

"Damn right. There are tons of us who do it. We've got our own magazine, called *Guinea Pig Zero*. They call us 'professional volunteers.'"

"You're not worried about your health?"

"I got jaundice one time and my eyes stayed yellow for months. Another time I started having nightmares about birds. That was kind of weird. But I'm tough. And I'd never make this kind of money flipping burgers."

1. The FDA guidelines for trial review boards say that payments to subjects should not be "coercive" or exert "undue influence." Could paying indigent subjects $2,000 for a week-long study undermine informed consent?

2. What is your assessment of Rabbit and other semiprofessional "guinea pigs"? Should people volunteer for Phase I trials for more altruistic reasons? Would unpaid trials attract volunteers in sufficient numbers to maintain the pace of medical research?

3. Are Rabbit and other "professional volunteers"—many of whom enroll in five or six studies a year—essentially selling their bodies to researchers? Might their ability to tolerate so many clinical trials make them unrepresentative subjects?

4. Roughly 70 percent of drug trials now take place in the private sector, away from academic health centers. What are the benefits or risks for trial subjects such as Rabbit and Jordan in this (relatively new) situation? What are the potential advantages and disadvantages for the general public?

DECISION SCENARIO **4**

Facebook Lab Rats?

Janine threw down her book bag and slid into the booth opposite Chandra.

"I'm sorry I'm late," Janine said. "But you won't believe what I just found out. Do you remember how depressed I was last January, when I posted all those angry status updates and almost broke up with Kim?"

"Yeah, you were a mess. I was pretty worried about you," Chandra said.

"It turns out that Facebook was conducting a psychology study on, like, seven hundred thousand users. They manipulated some people's news feeds to feature more positive information and other people's to feature more sad and depressing stuff. They wanted to see if it would change what people posted—if they would experience 'massive-scale emotional contagion.' " Janine sighed in disgust.

"And you think that's what happened to you?"

"I looked back at my news feed for that month and it was full of negative information. Maybe it's a coincidence, but I don't think so. They used us as lab rats without our consent! We could never get away with that in psych lab. What if I was already depressed and it made me suicidal?"

"First of all, you don't know you were picked for the experiment," said Chandra. "Even though you *are* on Facebook all the time, you had some other reasons to be upset, as I recall. Second, it's not like Facebook used federal funds for the study, right? They're a private company. Didn't you click through a user agreement when you joined?"

"The user agreement I accepted said nothing about subjecting users to secret research. Where was my informed consent?"

1. Was the Facebook research on "emotional contagion" unethical? Why or why not?

2. Institutional review boards do, on rare occasions, allow research without informed consent if the "rights and well-being" of subjects are not threatened by the study. Did Facebook's efforts to alter its users' moods violate that standard?

3. The Facebook study apparently made no effort to exclude minors or other vulnerable populations (such as the mentally ill). Were they morally obligated to do so? Why or why not?

4. It is not clear to what use, if any, Facebook put its research on "emotional contagion." But what if they used similar news feed manipulations to make users feel happier after buying certain products or voting for certain candidates? Would it change your opinion of the original research?

DECISION SCENARIO **5**

Phase I and Consent

"Mrs. Wilkins," Ellen Blake said, "I want to ask you to participate in what we call a Phase I trial of a new drug called Novaltin. The aim of this trial, it is my duty to tell you, isn't to treat your disease, but to help us determine how toxic Novaltin is. What we learn may help us figure out how to help other people."

"You mean Novaltin won't help me?" Mrs. Wilkins asked.

"I can't say that it won't," Blake said. "Quite frankly, we just don't know. That possibility is always there, but that's not why you should agree to participate. If you do agree, that is."

"I've been told my disease is terminal," Mrs. Wilkins said. "I'm in the last stage of life right now.

So it looks to me like I don't have anything to lose and, potentially, I've got something to gain. It's a gamble and I'm ready to take it."

"So long as you know Novaltin isn't likely to help you," Blake said. "I'll get the consent forms, and you can ask me any other questions that occur to you."

1. Should Mrs. Wilkins's consent to participate in a Phase I trial be regarded as informed?

2. Is Mrs. Wilkins an appropriate candidate to participate in a Phase I clinical trial?

3. How should investigators go about getting people to consent legitimately to Phase I trials?

DECISION SCENARIO 6

Using Nazi Data

During World War II, the Nazis conducted experiments on human beings to test the effects of phosgene gas, which had been used in chemical warfare. The experiments were carried out on prisoners in concentration camps and caused fatal pulmonary edemas. In 1988, the Environmental Protection Agency decided to exclude the Nazi data from a study it had commissioned on phosgene. Those favoring the exclusion held that data obtained by unethical means should never be used. Opponents of this view held that making use of such data is a way of honoring and remembering those who were sacrificed to obtain it.

1. Does using data from research conducted by the Nazis make one complicit in their crimes? Does it matter if one is using the data for broadly beneficial applications (e.g., developing cancer treatments) versus more self-interested ones (e.g., patenting a cosmetics line)?

2. Suppose the data had never been published but were available as research notes. Would this make any difference to the question of whether the data ought to be used?

DECISION SCENARIO 7

Tissue Theft?

Ben Ramirez didn't get suspicious until Dr. Piser mailed him the consent form for the third time. "Just sign this, Ben," read a note stuck to the top of the page. "Don't be difficult."

Piser had removed part of Ben's thyroid over a year ago, after he diagnosed him with a rare form of thyroid cancer. But in the past six months, Piser had called Ben back to the University Medical Center three times for blood tests, a bone-marrow sample, and a postoperative biopsy. He had mailed Ben a new consent form that asked him to grant Piser and the university rights to his tissue and blood samples, along with "any cell line or other potential products that might be derived."

Piser had described the new consent form as a "mere formality," but something had made Ben hesitate. Now Piser's note raised his suspicions. The next day, he called a lawyer named Vera Levin, who said she'd look into the matter and meet with him in a week.

"Your doctor has been a busy guy," said Levin, after Ben took a seat in her office. "He's filed a patent on a new cell line called 'BeRa,' which the biotech company Syncia has valued at $2.7 billion. Apparently, your thyroid cells produce a rare protein that can be used to develop treatments for Parkinson's and HIV. Piser has already been paid $2 million in Syncia stock to develop the BeRa cell line."

"Piser never said anything about proteins or Parkinson's," Ben said. "He just said my cancer was aggressive and that he was making sure it didn't grow back. I mean, I'm happy that my cells might help treat those diseases. But I feel betrayed. I feel like he stole my cells to make a fortune. And I can't even afford my co-pays."

"Unfortunately, the most we can hope for is to try to get his license revoked," Levin said. "The courts have ruled that when you give a doctor a tissue sample, you are 'abandoning' it like trash and so relinquish property rights. If Piser found oil in your backyard, I could sue to get you some of his profits, but for something he finds in your body, I don't have a case."

1. Should Ben have a right to some of the profits that will be derived from his cells, or should the profits belong to Piser alone, for identifying and growing the cell line?

2. Did Piser disregard Ben's informed consent when he didn't disclose his financial interest in taking blood and tissue samples? Should such consent violations be punishable by law?

3. What if Ben worked with other researchers to develop a cell line from his remaining thyroid tissue? Should Piser be allowed to sue him for patent infringement?

DECISION SCENARIO 8

Boyd Rush: The First Animal–Human Transplant

The first human-to-human heart transplant was performed in 1967 by a South African surgeon named Christiaan Barnard. However, this was not the first heart transplanted to a human being. In January 1964, James Hardy, of the University of Mississippi, transplanted a chimpanzee heart into a patient named Boyd Rush.

Rush was deaf and mute, a retired upholsterer who was brought to the University of Mississippi Medical Center unconscious and on the verge of death. A stepsister, the only relative who could be located, signed a consent form permitting, if necessary, "the insertion of a suitable heart transplant." The form made no reference to the sort of heart that might be employed. Rush lived for two hours after the transplant.

Hardy justified the use of the chimpanzee heart on the grounds that it was impossible to obtain a human heart in time Also, he was encouraged by the limited success obtained by Tulane University surgeon Keith Reentsma in transplanting chimpanzee kidneys into a man dying of glomerulonephritis. The kidney recipient had lived for two months.

Leonard Bailey, the surgeon who transplanted the baboon heart into the child known as Baby Fae, expressed his view of James Hardy in an interview: "He's an idol of mine because he followed through and did what he should have done…he took a gamble to try to save a human life."

1. Evaluate the quality of the consent that was secured for Boyd Rush's transplant surgery.

2. Suppose Rush's stepsister did know that a chimpanzee heart might be used. Should anyone be permitted to give consent to such a transplant on behalf of someone else?

3. If the only way to save Rush's life was to transplant a chimpanzee heart, was the surgery justified?

4. Suppose the transplant had been expected to postpone Rush's death for only a short period of time. Could the sacrifice of a baboon be justified?

5. Evaluate the criticism that Hardy was simply performing a medical experiment in which Boyd Rush was the unknowing and unconsenting subject.

DECISION SCENARIO 9

When the Numbers Are Small, Can a Trial Be Ethical?

"The Human Subjects Committee has reviewed your protocol for using KM-47 to treat patients with Napier's syndrome," the chair informed Dr. Tom Kline. "We can't approve it, because it would be unethical to enroll only six patients, as you propose. Such a clinical trial would involve so few patients as to have no statistical significance."

1. Suppose Napier's syndrome (a fictitious disease) is relatively common. Provide an argument that

might support the decision of the Human Subjects Committee.

2. Suppose KM-47 is a drug that anecdotal evidence suggests may be appropriate for treating Napier's syndrome. Would this be grounds for approving the protocol?

3. Suppose Napier's syndrome is a rare disease. What sort of evidence might the committee require Dr. Kline to present to persuade them to approve his protocol?

DECISION SCENARIO 10

Primate Head Trauma

During the two years he had worked for the Bioplus Foundation, Kieran Quade had visited many labs. Before he could renew the funding of a grant, he was required to make an on-site inspection of the facilities and review the work of the investigators. Now he was sitting in a small, chilly conference room about to watch a video of the new work being done at Carolyn Sing's lab.

Sing herself was sitting at the table with him, and she leaned forward and pushed the play button. "The experimental subjects we used are baboons," she told him. "We think they possess facial and cranial structures sufficiently similar to humans to make them the best animal models." Kieran nodded, then watched the monitor in silence. He was appalled by what he saw. An adult animal, apparently limp from anesthesia, was strapped to a stainless-steel table. Its head was fitted into a viselike device, and several clamps were tightened to hold it immobile. The upper-left side of the baboon's head had been shaved and the area painted with a faintly purple antiseptic solution. A dark circle had been drawn in the center of the painted area.

The white-coated arms of an assistant appeared in the frame. The assistant was holding a device that looked like an oversized electric drill. A transparent plastic sleeve protruded from the chuck end of the device, and through it Kieran could see a round, stainless-steel plate. A calibrated dial was visible on the side of the device, but Kieran couldn't read the marks.

"That's an impact hammer," Dr. Sing said. "We thought at first we were going to be able to use one off the shelf, but we had to modify one. That's an item we didn't anticipate in our initial budget."

The assistant centered the plastic tube over the spot marked on the baboon's head, then pulled the trigger of the impact hammer. The motion of the steel plate was too swift for Kieran to see, but he saw the results. The animal's body jerked in spasm, and a froth of blood, brain tissue, and bone fragments welled up from the purple spot.

Kieran Quade turned away from the monitor, unable to stand the images any longer.

"Through induced head trauma studies, we have been able to learn an enormous amount," Carolyn Sing said. "Not only do we know more about what happens to brain tissue during the first few minutes after trauma, but we've used that knowledge to develop some new management techniques that may save literally tens of thousands of people from permanent brain damage."

Kieran Quade nodded.

1. On what grounds might someone oppose experiments such as Sing's? Suppose it is true that they could help reduce or eliminate traumatic brain damage in thousands of people. Would this change the ethics of the situation?

2. If you knew that the information gained from the study described would prevent your child from suffering brain damage, should this count in your decision about whether such an experiment is justifiable?

3. Is there any reason to suppose that a human life (of any sort) is worth more than an animal life (of any sort)? On what moral grounds, if any, might one object to using patients in a chronic vegetative state as experimental subjects in the study?

4. In 2011, a major NIH study criticizing primate research as unnecessary and inhumane prompted the United States to dramatically scale back such studies, especially those involving chimpanzees. Was this the right decision? Should a distinction be drawn between primate research and other animal research?

Part II

Controls

Chapter 3

Genetic Control

CHAPTER CONTENTS

CASES AND CONTEXTS

CASE PRESENTATION
Genae Girard and Gene Patents

Genae Girard was only thirty-six years old in 2006, when she was diagnosed with breast cancer. Girard was an entrepreneur, building a veterinary supply business in Austin, Texas, and the cancer caught her off guard. She felt she still had many more things to accomplish in her life, but cancer threatened to destroy all her plans.

Following the advice of her doctor, Girard agreed to a genetic test, and the results showed that she was positive for the BRCA2 gene mutation. Inheriting either the BRCA2 or BRCA1 mutation makes it five times more likely that a woman will develop breast cancer. To prevent Girard from developing cancer in her other breast and to treat her current disease, her doctor recommended that she have a double mastectomy.

Then the bad news got worse. Girard was told that BRCA2 also substantially increases the risk of ovarian cancer. By some estimates, women who carry one of the known BRCA mutations have a 60 percent chance of developing ovarian cancer by age sixty-five. To improve her chances of remaining alive, Girard would need to have her ovaries surgically removed.

Girard did not have children and losing her ovaries would effectively prevent her from doing so in the future. This caused her to wonder, What if the test was wrong? What if she didn't have the BRCA2 mutation? Then maybe she wouldn't have to have the double mastectomy, and she wouldn't have to lose her ovaries. After all, she later

recalled, "There is human error, and labs make mistakes." She was being asked to make a major decision about her future on the basis of a single laboratory test.

Girard told her doctor that she wanted to have another test, one performed by another lab. That was when she learned—to her surprise—that there was no other test available, because a company called Myriad Genetics owned a patent on the BRCA1 and BRCA2 genes. This gave Myriad the sole right to test for the presence of the mutations. Thus, Girard learned, Myriad was not merely the only game in town, it was the only game legally allowed.

Patenting Life?

The idea of securing a patent on a human gene strikes many people as absurd. Common sense seems to suggest that genes have the same status as other natural phenomena, such as oak trees, granite boulders, sheet lightning, and the law of gravity. How could anyone patent such things?

No one can. The patent laws of the United States explicitly rule out patents on natural objects, processes, or laws of nature. Nor is it possible to patent naturally occurring organisms such as the oak tree, grizzly bear, army ant, or *E. coli* bacterium. With the development of molecular biology in the 1960s and recombinant DNA technology in the 1970s, however, the line between "naturally occurring" organisms and altered or "manufactured" organisms began to blur.

Consider the story of Ananda Chakrabarty's modification of the bacteria *Pseudomonas*. The bacteria is found in soil the world over, is known to metabolize hydrocarbons, and for decades it was referred to as the "oil-eating" microbe. *Pseudomonas* does its metabolic work very slowly, however, and Chakrabarty, a microbiologist employed by General Electric, saw the need for a strain of the bacterium that would degrade oil more efficiently. Over six years of research, Chakrabarty manipulated the bacteria's natural plasmid transfer process to genetically modify *Pseudomonas*. The result was a new strain of the bacteria that would degrade oil ten to one hundred times faster than any naturally occurring strains. This made it environmentally valuable, due to its potential use in cleaning up oil spills. This "superbug" would also be valuable financially, Chakrabarty realized, if it were possible to secure a patent on it. It could then be licensed, and the patent owners could demand a fee every time the modified bacterium was employed.

Chakrabarty (along with General Electric) applied for a patent on the superbug. The application was initially rejected on the grounds that the law does not permit living things to be patented. But Chakrabarty filed an appeal, which eventually brought the case to the U.S. Supreme Court. On June 16, 1980, the Court, in a five to four decision, ruled in favor of Chakrabarty. Citing U.S. patent law, which states that "Whoever invents or discovers any new and useful process, machine, manufacture, or composition of matter, or any new and useful improvement thereof, may obtain a patent therefore," a majority of the Court decided that Chakrabarty's "microorganism constitutes a 'manufacture' or 'composition of matter' within the meaning of the law." The fact that Chakrabarty's microorganisms were alive was considered a matter without legal significance. The case marked a legal precedent and opened the door to thousands of new biotech patents, especially when it was combined with earlier court rulings that had already upheld patents on products found in the human body.

Human Products

The first U.S. patent for a naturally occurring product was granted to Jokichi Takamine, a Japanese chemist who spent most of his professional life in New York. In 1906, Takamine and his sponsor, the drug company Parke-Davis, applied for a patent on "a blood pressure raising" substance that he had isolated and purified from glandular secretions. Parke-Davis gave the substance the trade name *adrenaline*. (It was later found to be a combination of the neurotransmitter hormones epinephrine and norepinephrine.)

The patent was challenged in court by a rival drug company, on the grounds that the substance was a part of nature and not something invented or manufactured. In 1911, the influential circuit-court judge Learned Hand ruled that adrenaline could be patented, and his decision established the legal precedent that patents could be issued on "isolated and purified" versions of substances found in the human body. Such versions of the substances, Hand reasoned, wouldn't be available without the procedures chemists performed to produce them.

Human insulin, as soon as it was available in a purified form, was patented in 1923. A variety of other biological products, including vaccines, medical tests, and medical treatments, were patented in the decades that followed. Such patents became so common that it was striking news in 1955 when Jonas Salk, the developer of the first effective polio vaccine, announced that he wouldn't seek a patent on it, because it was owned by the people. "Could you patent the sun?" Salk asked.

Human Genes

The steady stream of patents for human and other biological materials became a flood with the advent of *recombinant DNA* techniques, which allowed scientists to create new proteins and therapies by splicing together DNA strands from different organisms.

In 1977, three years before the Chakrabarty decision, the University of California applied for a patent on genes for the production of human insulin and human growth hormone by genetically modified bacteria. The patents were granted in 1982 and 1987, and in 1985 the Cetus Corporation was granted a patent for the protein interleukin-2, an immune system activator used in the treatment of some cancers.

Patents were also issued for specific antibodies, various human hormones and growth factors, and blood factors used in the treatment of hemophilia, as well as for a variety of genetically engineered viruses. Many of the specialized viruses are vaccines, while others are used to transport genes into cells in gene-therapy experiments. Animals that have been genetically modified to allow the study of human diseases (animal models) have also been patented. (Transgenic organisms that include genes from other species, including humans, are themselves a source of controversy.)

At the turn of the twenty-first century, the Human Genome Project inaugurated the widespread sequencing of the human genome, and as large numbers of human genes were identified, they were quickly patented. (See Social Context: The Human Genome Project in this chapter.) The new patents included DNA sequences that encode instructions for making particular proteins and for regulating the way a gene is expressed, but they also encompassed variants of normal genes associated with diseases. The BRCA1 and BRCA2 mutations patented by Myriad Genetics fall into this category. So does the HHF gene, a mutation leading to hemochromatosis (a disease in which so much iron accumulates in the blood as to cause organ damage). Patents have also been issued for RNA sequences, such as those which function as "switches" to turn genes off or on.

Some experts estimate that about 20 percent of the human genome, involving more than four thousand genes, are now covered by at least one U.S. patent. In addition, as many as fifty thousand patents involving genetic material—RNA sequences, transgenic animals, and modified bacteria—have been issued.

Myriad Flexes its Patents

The deluge of new patents on genes and other biological materials soon moved beyond commercial research applications and began to spill over into clinical practice. Because such patents covered tests designed to detect the presence of a gene or a mutation, many became concerned that patent enforcement might not only impede scientific research but also health care delivery.

A 2003 survey found that 53 percent of U.S. laboratories had stopped developing or offering one or more genetic tests because of patent enforcement actions and 67 percent of respondents at those labs said patents interfered with medical research. In order to use the HHF gene (discussed above) in medical research, academic scientists were forced pay the patent holder $25,000 to license it. (Commercial scientists had to pay as much as

$250,000.) On the other hand, the company that owned the patent to the cystic fibrosis gene CFTR was praised for inexpensively licensing a test to dozens of laboratories.

The most glaring instance of a patent monopoly in genetic testing, however, involved Myriad Genetics. In 2001, the company sent letters to biological and medical researchers in industrialized countries, informing them that Myriad owned the rights to BRCA1 and BRCA2 and that all testing for the presence of these genes had to be done in a laboratory operated or licensed by Myriad.

Canada refused to recognize the terms of Myriad's patents, and in Europe the patents were challenged in court. As a result, Myriad's patent claims on BRCA1 were largely abandoned there, and a BRCA2 patent was granted to the British Cancer Research Campaign, a research organization that pledged to offer unrestricted access to scientists.

But in the United States, as Genae Girard discovered, Myriad had established a monopoly on testing for the breast-cancer genes. Critics argued that the nearly $4,000 fee that Myriad charged for its BRCA tests could be substantially reduced if Myriad was not stifling competition. Other labs might also be able to perform the tests more quickly, but so long as Myriad asserted its patent rights, hospitals and clinical laboratories did not want to risk a lawsuit. Before Myriad started sending out its warning letters, some physician-researchers had been testing breast-cancer patients for the mutations, but they soon stopped.

Patent enforcement in genetic testing can have a serious personal impact on patients. Genae Girard, as discussed above, was unable to get a second opinion on her BRCA status before she agreed to have a double mastectomy and her ovaries removed. Since breast cancer kills more women in Western societies than any other type of cancer, second opinions matter a great deal. (A 2006 article in *JAMA* found that the Myriad test was wrong 12 percent of the time.) Others, such as Lisbeth Ceriani, a single mother from Newton, Massachusetts, were unable to afford the test in the first place. Following her double mastectomy for breast cancer, Ceriani wanted to be tested for BRCA1 and BRCA2 to see if she should have her ovaries removed as well. Myriad refused to accept her insurance, and Ceriani was unable to come up with the cash. (Myriad also refused to accept Medicaid insurance, as other patients had discovered.) Ceriani hesitated to have a surgery she might not need; but as the mother of an eight-year-old daughter, she also wanted to know if her child might have inherited gene mutations predisposing her to breast cancer and ovarian cancer. "No one invented my gene," Ceriani told a reporter. "All they're doing is looking at it. It's crazy."

Con and Pro

As concern grew over stories such as Ceriani's and Girard's, some began to question the entire rationale for allowing monopoly patents on naturally occurring genes. Critics pointed to its potentially negative impact on patients, as well as on biomedical research. Forty-nine percent of members of the American Society of Human Genetics, for example, said they had to limit their research due to gene patents, and others noted a "chilling effect" resulting from patents such as Myriad's. Researchers who attempted to explore the mechanisms by which genetic variants operated to produce disease risked lawsuits for patent infringement if they failed to secure permission to use the genes in question.

In the case of Myriad, researchers could not even compare a normal stretch of DNA with one containing mutated genes without Myriad's permission. Rather than risk legal entanglements, research institutions, universities, and scientists often opted to focus on research areas in which patents were less pervasive. In the view of a representative of the American Civil Liberties Union, Myriad's patent claims constituted restrictions on the free exchange of ideas and thus violated the First Amendment.

Defenders of gene patents argued that without patent protection, genetic research could not flourish. Researchers, institutions, and venture capitalists would not invest the talent, time, and money that are necessary to advance such research without the promise of a significant financial payoff. The very purpose of a patent system, they pointed out, is to encourage innovation and effort by rewarding those who succeed in acquiring potentially useful knowledge. If the processes and materials involved in the production of microchips could not be patented, they argued, the computer industry would still be in its infancy. If we want to see biotech industries flourish in a similar way, we need to recognize the importance of the patent system in providing financial incentives.

Opponents responded that Myriad and other companies' mere isolation of a naturally occurring substance did not constitute the kind of invention that patent law

is designed to protect. They argued that granting DNA patents is inconsistent with the rest of U.S. patent law as well as the *Chakrabarty* case—which prohibited the patenting of naturally occurring substances, such as newly discovered minerals, and of other natural phenomena, such as the law of gravity. They also pointed out that the discovery of BRCA1 and BRCA2 was largely achieved with public funding at the University of California and the University of Utah, which only brought in Myriad as a later-stage collaborator.

Genae Girard's Day in Court

In 2009, Genae Girard, Lisbeth Ceriani, and other patients, along with a group of prominent physicians and researchers, filed a lawsuit against Myriad Genetics, challenging several of its BRCA1 and BRCA2 patent claims. Supported by the American Civil Liberties Union and the Association for Molecular Pathology, the suit eventually reached the U.S. Supreme Court, which announced its decision on June 13, 2013.

In a unanimous ruling, the Court rejected Myriad's patent claims on the BRCA1 and BRCA2 genes and effectively ended the thirty-year-old practice of granting patents on naturally occurring human genes.

"Myriad did not create anything," Justice Clarence Thomas wrote on behalf of the Court. "A naturally occurring DNA segment is a product of nature and not patent eligible merely because it has been isolated." The Court thus largely accepted arguments, such as those made by the ACLU's Chris Hansen, that "[t]he human genome, like the structure of blood, air or water, was discovered, not created."

Nevertheless, the Court emphasized that *modifications* of genetic material may constitute legitimate inventions deserving of patent protections. For example, the synthetic DNA created in a laboratory—often known as *complementary DNA* or *cDNA*—is still eligible for patents. The Court also emphasized that Myriad's patents on specific aspects of its screening and testing process (which had not been challenged by the plaintiffs) were not implicated in its decision.

Genae Girard praised the ruling as a landmark that would "further research in medicine by opening up the door and not having these monopolies that gouge patients and insurance companies." Mary-Claire King, the geneticist who first demonstrated the genetic basis of breast cancer and identified the BRCA1 gene in 1990, called the decision "a fabulous result for patients, physicians, scientists, and common sense."

Aftermath

In the wake of the Supreme Court's decision, three companies said they would immediately begin offering competing BRCA tests, some for under $1,000. Although Myriad Genetics initially filed suit against these companies based on its other patents, it had abandoned such efforts by 2015 and was shifting its business model toward a comprehensive test of twenty-five genes associated with cancer risk. In an effort to overcome Myriad's still robust data-analysis advantage in the field, an advocacy group is building a public database of BRCA1 variants based on patient-submitted data.

The Supreme Court's decision was widely interpreted to have invalidated most of the patents held on four thousand human genes, or 20 percent of the genome. But many of those patents were acquired in the late 1990s and were already close to expiring. Ironically, the *Myriad* decision may have more of an impact on nonhuman DNA research, and some have argued that the inability to patent unmodified bacterial genes will slow innovation. Patent lawyers have complained that there is a substantial "gray area" between modified and unmodified DNA, and some have admitted they plan to advise biotech clients to introduce random modifications into naturally occurring DNA to help them obtain patents.

Despite these ambiguities, the *Myriad* ruling decisively intervened in a long-standing debate over patents on nature. The conclusion that unmodified natural phenomena cannot be patented sets a precedent with broad legal and scientific implications that will unfold in the decades to come.

SOCIAL CONTEXT
The Promise of Precision Medicine

Clinical medicine as it has developed over the last two centuries has become more and more refined in both its diagnostic categories and in its treatments. The dozens of "fevers" of the eighteenth and early nineteenth centuries (fever with sweating, fever with a rash, fever with swelling of the throat) were, by the end of the twentieth century, recognized as symptoms of particular diseases such as the flu, measles, and diphtheria. Treatments such as bleeding, blistering, and purging for all diseases were replaced by specific remedies for specific diseases.

Even so, physicians recognized that not all cases of heart failure are alike, and that even within specific categories of cancer, tumors are different and respond differently to treatment. At the same time, there is growing awareness that many intractable diseases—including autism, type 2 diabetes, heart disease, and many cancers—arise from a complex interaction of genetic, environmental, immunologic, and other factors. These *multifactorial diseases*, as they are often called, may be caused by a different combination of factors in each case. This can make trying to treat or prevent these conditions particularly challenging. Trial and error, guesswork, and unexplained failures are typical of medicine when the specific causes of disease remain elusive or intractably complicated.

The development of molecular genetics and information technology now offers such new tools as the rapid and inexpensive sequencing of individual genomes and the identification of genes associated with particular diseases. These developments suggest we may be entering a new era of *personalized* or *precision medicine*, one that will eventually allow physicians to understand the character of a disease as it is manifested in a particular individual. Bringing together specific data on a patient's genes, health, environment, lifestyle, and other factors, physicians hope to create targeted tools for better prevention and better treatment.

Precision Medicine Initiative

On January 30, 2015, President Obama announced a major precision medicine initiative in the East Room of the White House. He was joined by Republican senator Lamar Alexander, National Institutes of Health (NIH) director Francis Collins, and a group of patients who have benefited from targeted genetic therapies.

The president's initiative would devote $215 million in fiscal year 2016 to a range of precision medicine projects to be implemented by the NIH, the FDA, and the Office of the National Coordinator for Health Information Technology (ONC). The initiative includes:

- $130 million to the NIH, to develop a research cohort of a million volunteers for a long-term study of their genes, environment, lifestyle, and other factors. The subjects would get continuous access to their health data and any research that makes use of it.

- $70 million to the National Cancer Institute, to expand efforts to identify the genetic drivers of cancer—including the genomic "signatures" of specific tumors—and to use the data in developing targeted cancer treatments.

- $10 million to the FDA, to develop and monitor the diagnostic tests and complex databases necessary for offering individualized clinical care to the general public.

- $5 million to the ONC, to protect patient privacy and data security, and to ensure interoperability among the various precision medicine projects.

The spending in the president's proposal was relatively modest—just $215 million out of a $4 trillion budget—but it was accompanied by ambitious language. Obama spoke of "delivering the right treatment at the right time, every time, to the right person," while Collins envisioned a "true revolution in medicine, one that promises to transform the traditional 'one size fits all' approach into a much more powerful strategy." Some critics were unconvinced, however, arguing that personalized genomic medicine fails to the account for the ambiguity and complexity of genetic information and may produce unintended consequences. To better evaluate the arguments for and against precision medicine, we will briefly examine some of its stated goals, along with its record of success and failure.

P4 Medicine

Precision medicine advocates argue that our current medical system is inefficient and reactive, focused on trial-and-error and "one size fits all" treatments for late-stage diseases. Instead they recommend a "P4" approach that is *personalized*, *predictive*, *preventive*, and *participatory*.

Personalized. Advocates of precision medicine acknowledge that physicians have always tailored treatments to specific patients, and have, at least since the discovery of human blood types, identified individual factors that condition disease and treatment response.

But advocates argue that we can now harness information technology and genomic sequencing to tailor treatments more precisely. They note that the cost of sequencing a human genome has fallen from $400 million to $1,000 in just over a decade. They also point to mobile device technology that allows patients to refine their medical histories, providing real-time data on such parameters as pulse and blood pressure, glucose levels, diet, and exercise. By synthesizing all this information, physicians will be able treat two people with the same condition very differently, based on genetically influenced variations in metabolism, allergies, drug response, and other factors.

To date, this type of individualized treatment has been most widely used with cancer patients, many of whom have had the genetic "signature" of their tumors analyzed for targeted treatments. It has also been employed at the Mayo Clinic's Center for Individualized Medicine, which develops profiles of the microbial colonies in patients' bodies, as well as of the various *epigenetic* mechanisms that shape how genes are expressed.

Critics argue that as useful as such individualized data may be, it will not be genuinely personalized without the intelligent listening and compassionate concern that effective practitioners must show their patients. They also point out that behaviors surrounding such things as diet and exercise are more complicated and personal than just logging data into a smartphone, and that those who fall behind on these parameters may feel stigmatized and more inclined to give up.

Predictive. Accurately predicting the way in which genes (in combination with other factors) produce disease states is notoriously tricky. Although some diseases, such as cystic fibrosis and sickle-cell anemia, arise from single genetic mutations, most have a more complicated genetic backstory, in which a range of different mutations can contribute to disease risk. To be able to draw inferences about how genetic and other risk factors might combine to produce disease requires painstaking analysis of data from large groups of people. This is why a central goal of Obama's Precision Medicine Initiative is to assemble a massive volunteer research cohort. With over a million subjects, it would constitute the largest genetic health data bank of its kind.

Skeptics about precision medicine contend that its ability to predict disease risk has been exaggerated. They argue that for most common diseases, such as diabetes and many cancers, there is no clear set of genetic causes, only hundreds of variations that slightly increase risk. They suggest that parameters such as age, sex, and body weight, along with exercise and diet, remain the best predictors of disease and health. Even the somatic expression of "high risk" genes is often dependent on factors such as environment, behavior, and culture.

PRECISION MEDICINE TODAY: BRAIN CANCER AND GENETIC MARKERS

Beau Biden, the son of Vice President Joseph Biden, died of brain cancer at age forty-six on May 30, 2015. The Biden family did not make public the kind of cancer responsible for Beau's death, but chances are that it was a glioma.

Gliomas are a group of cancers involving the glial cells, which form the network of tissue that supports neurons in the brain and spinal cord. Gliomas are classified by the subtype of the glial cells involved and the grade and location of the tumor. Some gliomas start as low-grade, then become more malignant, while others are highly aggressive. About ten thousand Americans a year are diagnosed with gliomas. These cancers are treated with surgery, radiation, and chemotherapy, but they are rarely curable. Even so, treatments can extend lives, sometimes for years.

Pathologists classify gliomas and make a judgment about their aggressiveness on the basis of biopsied brain tissue. Despite a standard system of classification, enough subjectivity is involved that experts don't always agree on the best form of treatment. Nor can they say how well patients will respond to particular treatments.

continued

Some of this uncertainly will change as a result of studies conducted by a group at the National Institutes of Health and a second group from the Mayo Clinic and the University of California, San Francisco. The researchers analyzed 1,380 gliomas and found that they could use specific genetic variations to divide gliomas into three distinct categories:

1. Slow-growing but responsive to drugs, making chemotherapy alone likely to be sufficient;

2. Slow-growing but less responsive to drugs, making radiation plus chemotherapy necessary to get the best result;

3. Most aggressive and unlikely to have a good long-term prognosis, no matter what the treatment. (Knowing this would give patients a chance to search for clinical trials offering more promise.)

Some experts consider the use of genetic markers to classify gliomas and predict the outcome of their treatment to be a significant advance in precision medicine. It is an important example of how genetic information can guide research and how the genetic profiles of patients can turn precision medicine into personalized medicine.

Nevertheless, the predictive capacity of genetic research appears to be growing, particularly when it draws on large data sets. In 2015, an Icelandic genetics firm announced that it sequenced the genomes of 2,636 Icelanders and accurately inferred those of 100,000 more, representing nearly a third of the country. This collection of genetic data—the largest ever analyzed from a single population—has already allowed the Icelandic researchers to identify new mutations that apparently elevate risks for Alzheimer's disease, gallstones, and atrial fibrillation. Using a combination of health records and genetic information, they have also been able to identify new patterns of genetic influence—such as a mutation that stimulates more or less thyroid hormone depending on whether the mutation has been handed down from one's mother or one's father. Drawing on a technique called "imputation," they were also able to infer full genomes and mutations for hundreds of thousands of individuals beyond their original subject pool—identifying, for example, those who carry BRCA breast cancer mutations before they have even been tested for them.

Defenders of precision medicine argue that its predictive power will continue to grow, particularly as it factors in more epigenetic mechanisms that influence gene expression, along with individualized data on a person's microbial biome, environment, diet, and exercise. Drawing on large genetic research cohorts, such as the one proposed by President Obama, precision medicine will become part of a larger effort to redefine diseases based on their actual molecular and environmental mechanisms, rather than on external symptoms.

Preventive. Precision medicine research has already led to a number of novel approaches to disease prevention. In 2015, for example, researchers based at the University of Michigan examined seventeen combined factors that predicted diabetes risk—including family history, blood sugar data, and body measurements. Depending on how prediabetic patients scored on each factor, the researchers were able to determine those who stood the best chance of preventing diabetes through lifestyle changes versus those who stood the best chance using a diabetes drug. It turned out there was substantial variation in the likelihood that different prediabetic patients would benefit from these different treatments, something that a "one size fits all" approach could not have addressed.

Participatory. Precision medicine is often described as a "patient centered" approach, one in which patients are "empowered" to take charge of their own care.

Certainly, the volunteer cohort proposed by Obama and Collins, in which patients would be granted ongoing access to data and research, reflects a shift away from paternalistic practices of the past. The initiative's emphasis on privacy protections and data security also reflects a recognition that patients must retain control over their genetic and health records.

Still, critics of the precision medicine concept have argued it might disempower patients as much as it empowers them. Some have raised concerns that patients might be "profiled" at the molecular level, then prevented by physicians or insurers from accessing treatments that work infrequently in people with similar profiles. Some defenders respond that such limits on patient autonomy might be preferable to the way our current system rations care and limits patient choice— typically on the basis of how much health insurance a person can afford. (See Chapters 8 and 9 for more on the topic of rationing.) Other precision medicine skeptics suggest that knowing more about genetic predispositions may actually make patients more complacent—or fatalistic— about behavior and lifestyle habits. They emphasize precision medicine's potential to create both false reassurance and stigmatizing fear about disease risk.

Pharmacogenomics

One area in which precision medicine has already made substantial strides is in the field of *pharmacogenomics*—which individualizes treatment by using genetic information to predict a patient's likely response to different drugs and doses. Roughly 10 percent of drug labels in the United States now include information on genetic drug response, and increasing numbers of drugs are designed for specific genetic groupings. The "Dx–Rx" model (a genetic test before a prescription) is becoming an accepted clinical paradigm.

Of course, physicians have long identified allergic drug reactions among certain patients and individualized treatments to try to prevent their recurrence. But precision medicine offers the hope of personalizing treatment *before* such adverse reactions occur. Most patients can take the HIV drug abacavir, for example, but 6 percent have a potentially lethal allergic reaction. That reaction correlates almost exactly with a single genetic variation for which the FDA now recommends patients be tested before they take the drug.

One of the earliest pharmacogenomic treatments was the use of trastuzumab (brand name Herceptin® [Genentech]) to treat breast cancer. The drug targets the 15 to 20 percent of breast cancer tumors that are associated with excess levels of a protein called human epidermal growth factor 2 (HER2), which is part of the system that regulates cell growth. Tumors identified as HER2 positive tend to be aggressive and to respond poorly to standard treatment. By binding to HER2 receptors in cell surfaces, trastuzumab can be extraordinarily effective in killing tumors and preventing cancer recurrence. The drug is useless and potentially dangerous, however, for women whose tumors do not express the HER2 protein. A genetic analysis of the gene responsible for production of the protein has been shown to be a good (though far from perfect) predictor of which women will respond to the drug.

Critics of these and other pharmacogenetic strategies argue that most cancers have too much "genetic heterogeneity" for targeted treatment. Rather than resulting from a few simple genetic mutations, these cancers develop from incremental genomic damage over the course of a life, and some will mutate further, developing "resistance" to targeted treatments. In addition, there is often no "bright line" between patients who are genetically predisposed to respond best to certain drugs and those who get less benefit. Instead there is a "ragged edge" or continuum that may require controversial cost-benefit analyses to determine who gets the targeted drug and who doesn't. Such "rationing" (either by genetic profile or ability to pay) is likely, since the market for such drugs is small and manufacturers may charge over $300,000 for a course of treatment.

Nevertheless, advocates point out, some of the new pharmacogenomic treatments have produced impressive results. The launch of President Obama's Precision Medicine Initiative featured a cystic fibrosis patient named William Elder, Jr., who had been able to breathe out of his nose for the first time in his life after just one day on ivacaftor—a new drug focused on the roughly 5 percent of cystic fibrosis patients whose disease is caused by a specific genetic mutation. In recent years, genetic analysis of tumors has been used to target drug treatments for lung and colorectal cancer, as well as leukemia and lymphoma, and some hos-pitals conduct such analysis on the tumors of all new cancer patients. Despite the current expense of such treatments, precision medicine advocates believe they will prove worthwhile in the long run. They point to studies showing that for every dollar spent on mapping the human genome, $140 has been added to the U.S. economy. (See Social Context: The Human Genome Project.)

Envoi

In many respects, the goals of precision medicine can be seen as a logical extension of those of traditional medicine: to accurately analyze specific disease mechanisms in specific patients, then target those mechanisms in a way that "does no harm" to the patient's overall health. But projects such as the Precision Medicine Initiative will still have to grapple with the overwhelming complexity of our DNA and bodily systems. It remains to be seen whether our current medical technologies are powerful—and precise—enough to match it.

CASE PRESENTATION
The CRISPR Revolution

In March 2015, a group of eighteen leading biologists took a highly unusual step. Writing in the journal *Science,* they warned that a powerful new genome-editing technology could be used to modify the human germ line, making changes to the DNA in our reproductive cells that could be passed down to future generations. They called for a worldwide moratorium on such uses of the technology, which is known by the acronym CRISPR-Cas9, and for an open discussion of its implications for society, the environment, and ethics.

CRISPR-Cas9 could allow us to "take control of our genetic destiny, which raises enormous peril for humanity," one of the *Science* paper's coauthors, George Daley, later told a reporter. Others warned that even therapeutic changes to reproductive DNA, to fix a disease-causing mutation for example, could open the door to nontherapeutic genetic enhancement.

Yet despite these warnings, the biologists also stressed the revolutionary benefits that could be derived from CRISPR-Cas9, a technology so powerful and effective that it has been called a "biological version of find and replace." Simple and inexpensive, it has already been used to cure mice of metabolic liver disease by fixing a specific genetic mutation, while other researchers have used it to engineer pest-resistant crops and malaria-resistant mosquitoes by making precise "edits" to existing DNA. Novartis has announced plans to use CRISPR to engineer immune cells to attack tumors, while a group of scientists at Harvard Medical School are rewriting elephant genomes to make them resemble those of wooly mammoths.

So what is CRISPR, a technology that the *MIT Technology Review* has called "the biggest biotech discovery of the century" and that has raised so much ethical alarm and therapeutic hope? How was it developed and by whom?

The short answer is that it wasn't developed by humans at all. Instead, it was developed by bacteria, to protect themselves from their enemies.

An Adaptive Immune System

In 1987, Japanese researchers studying the genome of the bacteria *E. coli* discovered patterns of strange genetic "spacers" in the microbe's DNA. The spacers contained unique genetic sequences that differed sharply from *E. coli*'s normal DNA. No one had seen anything like them before, and the researchers ultimately concluded that the "biological significance of these sequences is not known."

But as DNA research on bacteria accelerated in the 1990s and early 2000s, these repetitive "spacer" patterns kept cropping up in microbe after microbe, and they were given a descriptive name: "clustered regularly interspaced short palindromic repeats"—a.k.a. CRISPR. Scientists also noticed that the CRISPR patterns always appeared with genes for powerful enzymes that could cut DNA. But as with the spacers themselves, no one could figure out what purpose these "CRISPR-associated" or *Cas* enzymes served.

It wasn't until the mid-2000s that three independent teams of scientists noticed that the unique snippets of DNA in the CRISPR spacers looked a lot like the DNA in viruses. And that is when the pieces of the CRISPR puzzle fell into place.

CRISPR, the scientists realized, is a powerful *adaptive immune system* that evolved in bacteria to protect them from viruses and other pathogens. The "spacers" are snippets of genetic code from viruses that have previously attacked the bacterium or its ancestors. This collection of "genetic mug shots" allows the bacterium to identify recurring threats and then take them out with the DNA-cutting *Cas* enzymes.

CRISPR thus resembles the human adaptive immune system, in that it "remembers" past threats and develops immunity, just as humans do once exposed to or vaccinated for viruses such as measles. But unlike the human immune system, CRISPR is built into the DNA of bacteria, which means that its "memory" of past threats can be passed on to future generations of the bacteria.

The solution to the CRISPR mystery was a triumph of basic research. But no one realized that it might have practical applications until a UC Berkeley biologist named Jennifer Doudna began to work on CRISPR in 2012, with a Swedish colleague named Emmanuelle Charpentier. Doudna and Charpentier are authorities on RNA, the single-strand corollary of DNA that helps build proteins and control gene activity. They soon realized that they could synthesize strands of "guide" RNA and use them to reprogram the CRISPR immune system. Instead of attacking past viruses, CRISPR could be made to seek out *any* specific strand of DNA that corresponded to the guide RNA the scientists had introduced—giving it a precise genetic address for the *Cas* enzyme to cut. Not only could Doudna and Charpentier use the CRISPR-Cas system to effectively "knock out" any DNA sequence they chose, they could also use it to insert a "patch"—a piece of similar DNA with desired changes—that would be incorporated as the cell repaired the cut.

The result was a powerful gene-editing tool. Although CRISPR-Cas sometimes cuts DNA in the wrong place (due in part to the relatively short snippets of RNA it uses to locate targets), its speed and simplicity were unprecedented. Utilizing the CRISPR system from the strep throat bacteria, along with its specific DNA-cutting enzyme, *Cas9*, Doudna and Charpentier published a paper that explained how to use CRISPR-Cas9 to cheaply and efficiently edit DNA. The result, Doudna recalled, "was like firing a starting gun in a race."

Animal Models and Gene Surgery

As soon as Doudna and Charpentier's paper was published in 2012, scientists around the world began using CRISPR-Cas9 to edit DNA in a wide variety of cells. Earlier gene modification tools such as zinc finger nucleases (ZFNs) and transcription activator-like effector nucleases (TALENs) had required months or years to develop proteins that would bind to longer DNA sequences. But CRISPR-Cas9 could be programmed to seek out a specific genetic address in a matter of days.

The pace of scientific discovery since the introduction of CRISPR technologies has been astonishing. Less than a year after Doudna and Charpentier's paper, researchers at MIT and Harvard demonstrated that CRISPR-Cas9 could be used to edit genes in animal cells, including those of humans. They also showed how CRISPR could be used to edit multiple genes at the same time, by using several different RNA guides to direct Cas9 to multiple locations.

Researchers such as MIT's Feng Zhang soon found they could easily recreate genetic variants found in autism and schizophrenia, and do so in both lab mice and human cell cultures. Researchers could then quickly compare specific genomic edits with resulting changes in cultured neurons and live animal behavior—a key procedure for unraveling the complicated interplay of genetic factors involved in such diseases. CRISPR-Cas9 also allowed researchers to create genetically modified laboratory animals—including fruit flies, rats, rabbits, and frogs—who could "model" a wide range of genetic conditions. They also started assembling "libraries" of CRISPRs, each targeting a different human gene, for use by researchers.

But advances using CRISPR soon progressed beyond disease modeling and began to move toward therapeutic applications. Traditional gene therapy has serious limitations. (See Case Presentation: Gene Therapy in this chapter and Case Presentation: Jesse Gelsinger in Chapter 2.) It must introduce new genetic material only at a random location in the cell and it can only add genes, not subtract them. As a bacterial immune system, CRISPR evolved to actively "police" cells, targeting specific DNA locations and knocking out genes. Thus, CRISPR-Cas9 can perform a kind of "microsurgery" on DNA at the level of individual base pairs.

One obvious starting place for therapeutic CRISPR applications are diseases like sickle-cell anemia, which is caused by a single mutation in one of a person's three billion DNA base pairs. (See this chapter's Briefing Session for more on this condition.)

Researchers at the Georgia Institute of Technology quickly established that CRISPR-Cas9 could correct sickle-cell mutations in human cell cultures. They also sketched out what a therapeutic application in humans might look like: harvesting red blood stem cells from the bone marrow of sickle-cell patients, using CRISPR to correct the mutation, then returning them to the patient's bone marrow, where they could be prompted to produce healthy cells. Gang Bao, the lead Georgia Tech researcher, estimates that replacing 70 percent of a patient's blood cells this way would constitute a cure for sickle cell disease. Similar treatments for cystic fibrosis and muscular dystrophy have been envisioned, and several have been successfully tested in mice. Scientists have also successfully altered human cell cultures to make them apparently immune to HIV infection, using CRISPR and earlier gene-editing tools.

These applications of CRISPR, along with similar uses of ZFNs and TALENs, are all considered part of *somatic* gene therapy, which would target genetic problems in existing individuals. These applications are not without controversy, particularly regarding the potential for "off-target" DNA cuts, a problem to which CRISPR seems particularly prone. But a more acute controversy surrounding CRISPR is how easy it makes it for scientists to "cross the germ line" and modify the DNA in human and animal reproductive cells—making changes to sperm, eggs, and embryos that could be passed down to offspring and subsequent generations. In fact, scientists have already been using CRISPR to make changes to germ cells for several years.

Crossing the Germ Line

In November of 2014, a pair of twin female monkeys were born in Kunming, in southwestern China. While the twins, named Mingming and Lingling, appear to be normal and healthy, they are the first primates born with specific genetic modifications using CRISPR technology. Researchers at Kunming Biomedical International used CRISPR-Cas9 to modify three genes in monkey embryos created through in vitro fertilization (IVF) and then implanted them in a surrogate. (See Chapter 4 for more on IVF and related reproductive technologies.) While the researchers are still studying the impacts of the CRISPR edits—which targeted genes regulating metabolism, immune cells, and sex selection—these "designer monkeys" may have marked a tipping point in the use of CRISPR technology in reproductive cells.

In April 2015, another group of Chinese researchers announced they had altered the DNA of eighty-five human embryos with CRISPR technology. The embryos used had chromosomal defects and were not implanted to produce pregnancies. Instead, the study was an effort to edit a specific gene, linked to the blood disorder beta thalassemia, in every cell of the developing embryos. But the results of the CRISPR alterations showed how unpredictable and potentially harmful such uses of the technology can be. The intervention produced a slew of unintentional DNA mutations beyond the beta thalassemia gene and caused the deaths of many of the embryos.

"Their study should give pause to any practitioner who thinks the technology is ready for testing to eradicate diseases during I.V.F." said the Harvard researcher George Daley.

Still, germ-line applications of CRISPR and related gene-editing tools are particularly tempting for scientists. Not only do they allow them to genetically engineer animal models of key disease states, as described above, but they suggest more ambitious animal and environmental projects, such as the potential "de-extinction" of the wooly mammoth. Using CRISPR to make pest-resistant food crops or malaria-resistant mosquitoes also involves germ-cell changes, and researchers have recently demonstrated how CRISPR edits could be induced to spread throughout an entire population or even an entire species, using a technique called "gene drive." There is even a new Harvard-associated company called OvaScience whose cofounder David Sinclair has spoken of eliminating Huntington's disease in families, using CRISPR and other technologies to "correct those mutations before we generate your child."

Therapy or Eugenics?

For many Americans, statements such as Sinclair's represent laudable or at least acceptable therapeutic goals. A 2014 Pew Research Center poll found that 46 percent of adults consider genetic engineering of babies to reduce serious disease risk to be "appropriate." By contrast, 83 percent said engineering babies to make them smarter would be "taking medical advances too far."

For many critics of crossing the germ line, however, even therapeutic interventions such as those described by Sinclair put us on a "slippery slope" toward nontherapeutic genetic enhancement. They question whether there is any real therapeutic need to alter the human germ line, since IVF technology already allows concerned parents to sequence the DNA of created embryos and select those free from mutations for Huntington's and other heritable diseases. They see projects such as Sinclair's as disingenuous attempts to profit from *positive eugenics*, a field that might eventually allow some (perhaps very wealthy) parents to design their children for greater-than-average intelligence, health, or beauty. (Julian Savulescu, the author of one of this chapter's readings, embraces a different version of positive eugenics. So does George Church, who has worked closely with Sinclair at Harvard and whose lab has been instrumental in CRISPR research.)

For others concerned about using CRISPR to cross the germ line, the fear is less that it will lead to a eugenic dystopia and more that it could produce serious unintended consequences for the individuals involved, for society, and for the environment. This is the position taken by the *Science* paper described at the beginning of this discussion. (The lead author of that paper, ironically, is Jennifer Doudna, the codiscoverer of CRISPR-Cas9.) The *Science* authors do not call for a ban on modifying human reproductive cells in the lab, which they believe could, in fact, have therapeutic value. But they insist that modified germ cells not be used to initiate a pregnancy and call for a moratorium on crossing the germ line in clinical practice.

"We worry about people making changes without the knowledge of what those changes mean in terms of the overall genome," said David Baltimore, the Nobel Prize–winning former president of Caltech and another coauthor of the paper. "I personally think we are just not smart enough—and won't be for a very long time—to feel comfortable about the consequences of changing heredity, even in a single individual."

Testing for Genetic Risk: The Angelina Jolie Effect

In May 2013, the actress and director Angelina Jolie made a highly publicized announcement about a personal medical decision. Writing in the *New York Times*, she described her decision to have a preventive double mastectomy earlier that year. It turned out that Jolie had tested positive for a dangerous defect in the BRCA1 gene, a rare mutation that gives women, on average, a 60 percent risk of developing breast cancer. Due to the specific form of Jolie's BRCA1 mutation, her physicians estimated that she actually had an 87 percent chance of developing breast cancer and a 50 percent chance of developing ovarian cancer. Jolie's decision to undergo preemptive surgery was also influenced by the fact that her mother had died of ovarian cancer at age 56 and her aunt had died of breast cancer.

"Once I knew that this was my reality, I decided to be proactive and to minimize the risk as much as I could," Jolie wrote. She said she was making her surgery public to help other women fight the sense of powerlessness often associated with cancer. As a result of her surgery, Jolie's estimated chance of developing breast cancer fell below 5 percent, and she said that she could now confidently assure her children that they would not lose her to the disease. While acknowledging that only a fraction of cancers are caused by inherited genetic mutations, Jolie expressed hope that more women would get genetic testing, as a way to "take on and take control" of the challenges posed by serious illness.

In the weeks and months after Jolie's high-profile announcement, genetic counselors and testing centers around the world reported sharply increased demand for their services. The influential medical writer and cardiologist Eric Topol went so far as to call Jolie's announcement a "tipping point in medicine" that would inspire patients to take charge of their health care decisions through direct-to-consumer genetic testing. A resurgence of this "Jolie effect" was widely expected following the actress's subsequent announcement, in March 2015, that she had her ovaries and fallopian tubes surgically removed, as a further step to address her genetically elevated risk of developing ovarian cancer.

It may be tempting to dismiss the public's response to these announcements as little more than "recreational genetics" driven by prurient interest in the private life of a celebrity. Certainly, some of the public's increased interest in genetic disease risks appeared to be based on misconceptions about BRCA mutations and genetic testing in general. But two retrospective studies of the "Jolie effect" found that it had roughly doubled the number of referrals for women who were genuinely at high risk for hereditary breast cancer. It also appeared to have decreased stigma associated with prophylactic surgery.

Despite its Hollywood backdrop, the story of Angelina Jolie Pitt (as she is now known) exemplifies many of the challenges faced by those who choose to be tested for genetic disease risks. As Jolie Pitt discovered, such testing can provide patients with empowering knowledge that allows them to take decisive action to protect their health. But it can also present patients with difficult life-and-death choices, which must be made on the basis of probabilities and limited information. Making sense of genetic testing results can be even more challenging if they are obtained through a direct-to-consumer testing service such as 23andMe, which do not provide face-to-face genetic counseling. As these services offer an increasing number of FDA-approved medical tests, it is more important than ever for patients and physicians to take stock of what genetic testing can and cannot tell us about our risk of disease.

Genetic Disease: A Blurred Concept?

Since the 1990s, the discovery of hundreds of disease-predisposing genes has been accompanied by the development of dozens of new genetic tests. Given the increasing sophistication of biotechnology, tests that were complex and expensive just a few years ago have become simple and cheap. Automated processes using intricate arrays of genetic probes can efficiently test a saliva or blood sample for the presence of hundreds of genetic variations.

Researchers have identified an expanding cata- logue of genetic anomalies and associated diseases, but the concept of a genetic disease is not as clear-cut as it may seem. Although single-gene disorders such as sickle-cell anemia, cystic fibrosis, and Huntington's disease have been at the focus of much research, they account for only about 2 percent of genetically influenced disorders. Most diseases result from a multiplicity of conditions, including (1) the particular form of a gene (many genes can have hundreds, even thousands, of potential mutations); (2) the simultane- ous presence or absence of other specific genes; and (3) the presence or absence of specific environmental factors. These complications can raise a number of challenging questions about the benefits and draw- backs of genetic testing.

Individual Choice

Recent studies have indicated that roughly 60 percent of Americans say they would be interested in genetic test- ing to determine if they or their children are at risk for se- rious diseases. While this figure reflects an increase over polls from two decades ago, which showed an even split on the question, many Americans are clearly still ambiva- lent about testing for genetic predispositions, particularly if they feel there is nothing they can do about the results. Patients such as Angelina Jolie Pitt, by contrast, believe that "knowledge is power" and argue that "it is possible to take control and tackle head-on any health issue" by learning about the options and making "choices that are right for you."

There is no question that information about genetic disease predispositions can be powerfully beneficial. It can prompt patients to seek medical evaluation so that they can receive appropriate and early treatment for a disease, should it develop. Further, such informa- tion can help patients avoid environmental factors that may trigger the expression of a genetic condition. For example, those with the genetic mutation that causes xeroderma pigmentosum are extremely sensitive to ul- traviolet radiation, and exposure to it is likely to lead to a form of skin cancer (melanoma) that is often incur- able. However, if those with the gene avoid prolonged exposure to sunlight, they have a better chance of avoiding melanoma.

By contrast, in the case of some single-gene diseases such as Huntington's, the knowledge that one is a carrier of the gene opens up few options for altering the outcome of the disease. Huntington's is currently not preventable and treatment options are limited to the temporary mitigation of symptoms. Although some patients might want to know whether they are carriers of the gene in order to make in- formed plans about such matters as childbearing, marriage, and careers, others might prefer to live their lives without knowing. (See Case Presentation: Hun- tington's Disease in this chapter.)

Even the dangerous genetic mutation that prompted Jolie Pitt's prophylactic surgeries can leave patients un- certain about what course of action to take—a problem that is exacerbated by the complexity of the treatment options and underlying genetics.

The mutated gene BRCA1, located on chromosome 17, was identified in 1994 as responsible for breast and ovarian cancer susceptibility in families with multiple incidences of those diseases. A second gene, BRCA2, located on chromosome 13, was identified in 1995 as causing increased susceptibility to breast cancer and was later also linked to ovarian cancer.

When functioning properly, the BRCA1 and BRCA2 genes produce tumor suppressor proteins that repair damaged DNA. But when parts of these genes are mu- tated or deleted in such a way that they fail to produce effective proteins, DNA damage can run rampant in cells. While thousands of mutations have been identified on BRCA genes, many of which have no negative effects, researchers have identified a number of mutations, par- ticularly those on BRCA1, which are strongly associated with cancer in younger women. Some studies have indicated that women who carry these mutated BRCA1 genes are estimated to have an 85 percent chance of developing breast cancer and a 60 percent chance of developing ovarian cancer by age 65. (This may account for the 87 percent risk of breast cancer estimated by Jolie Pitt's physicians.)

While BRCA mutations are likely responsible for the majority of hereditary breast and ovarian cancers, they do not appear to play a role in the 85 to 90 percent of these cancers that are "sporadic," with no known link to inherited susceptibilities. In addition, even the most dangerous BRCA mutations do not guarantee that a

A Sample of DNA Tests Currently Available

Disease	Description
Huntington's disease	Progressive neurological disorder, onset in forties or fifties
Polycystic kidney disease	Multiple kidney cysts leading to loss of kidney function
Cystic fibrosis	Mucus clogs lungs and pancreas; death in thirties is common
Sickle-cell disease	Hemoglobin defect; anemia, strokes, and heart damage
Familial adenomatous polyposis	Colon polyps by age thirty-five, often leading to cancer
Muscular dystrophy	Progressive muscle deterioration
Hemophilia	Blood fails to clot properly
Tay-Sachs disease	Lipid metabolism disorder causing death in first one to four years of life
Phenylketonuria	Enzyme deficiency producing mental disabilities
Retinitis pigmentosa	Progressive retinal degeneration leading to blindness
Hereditary breast and ovarian cancer (HBOC)	10 to 15 percent of breast and ovarian cancers
Familial hypercholesterolemiaboc	High levels of cholesterol leading to early heart disease
Spinocerebellar ataxia	Neurological disorder producing lack of muscle control

patient will develop cancer. Other factors, including diet, exercise, alcohol consumption, and other bodily systems may play a significant role in whether above-average odds translate into disease.

Nevertheless, about a third of women diagnosed with dangerous BRCA1 mutations opt for prophylactic double mastectomies and even more start with surgery to remove their ovaries and fallopian tubes. As Jolie Pitt has noted, these surgical interventions have been shown to bring cancer risks for women with BRCA mutations back into the single digits—close to average levels of risk. But they also come with serious consequences and side effects.

Mastectomies, as Jolie Pitt has noted, are usually long and complicated surgeries, particularly when they involve techniques aimed at artificially reconstructing the breasts. But the long-term physical and mental side effects are relatively minor. Breasts serve no biological function apart from breastfeeding, and most women who get mastectomies report high satisfaction with the decision years later. By contrast, *oophorectomies*, or removal of the ovaries, are now relatively simple laparoscopic procedures, but can come with substantial side effects. In addition to eliminating the capacity to conceive children, oophorectomy forces a woman's body into menopause.

The abrupt shift can increase risk of heart disease, high blood pressure, and stroke, while interfering with sleep, cognition, and libido. While these side effects can be mitigated by hormone treatments, they should not be taken lightly.

Getting tested for BRCA mutations can thus present women with a set of complicated dilemmas. If they test positive for one of the riskier mutations, their best treatment option may involve a surgery that causes sterility and long-term side effects. If they decide to forego surgery, they may have to live with decades of expensive, ambiguous, and anxiety-provoking tests aimed at detecting early onset cancers. Thus, even though the CDC recommends that women with a strong family history of breast and ovarian cancer be tested for BRCA1 and BRCA2, some may choose not to. The high cost of BRCA screening may also pose an obstacle for these patients. (See Case Presentation: Genae Girard and Gene Patents for more on this topic.)

Other women, such as Jolie Pitt, see the knowledge that comes with genetic screening as inherently useful and empowering. Even if they have ruled out surgery, what they learn from the test can help them make informed choices about career, family, and lifestyle—something which they see as valuable in its own right. If they test negative for BRCA defects, knowing that they are no more likely than other women to develop breast or ovarian cancer can provide peace of mind and a chance to focus on standard cancer prevention strategies. If they test positive, they are in a position to reevaluate the full range of aggressive prevention procedures and screening protocols.

Direct-to-Consumer Genetic Testing

Patients such as Angelina Jolie Pitt believe that "knowledge is power" when it comes to obtaining and taking action based on genetic information. Some proponents of patient-driven medicine see direct-to-consumer genetic testing companies as the ultimate way of empowering patients, allowing them access to their genetic information without interference from (potentially paternalistic) gatekeepers such as physicians and insurers.

From the time of their rollout in the mid-2000s, however, direct-to-consumer genetic testing companies such as 23andMe, deCODE Genetics, and Navigenics faced questions about their scientific accuracy and legality. The companies typically provided non-disease-related genetic analysis of ancestry and paternity, along with characteristics such as male-pattern baldness, "supertasting" ability, and ear wax consistency. But they also claimed to provide information about genetic "risk factors" for diseases, which brought charges from state and federal regulators that they were providing medical advice without meeting the standards required for clinical laboratories. Their methods of assessing disease risk were also challenged by scientists.

SNPs and Risks. Unlike the genetic test that revealed Jolie Pitt's BRCA1 defect, most direct-to-consumer genetic tests have not generally tested for individual genes, nor sequenced the billions of DNA base pairs in an individual's entire genome—a more expensive process typically carried out in academic laboratories. Instead, direct-to-consumer tests have often focused on the hundreds of thousands of segments of DNA known as *single-nucleotide polymorphisms*, or *SNPs* (pronounced "snips").

PERSONAL GENOMICS AT BERKELEY

The University of California, Berkeley, announced in 2010 that it will mail a DNA-collecting kit, consisting of a cotton swab and a plastic tube, to all members of incoming freshmen classes.

Returning the DNA sample is voluntary, but those returned will be tested for three genetic markers associated with the ability to metabolize alcohol, lactose, and folates. The three genes were selected because the students who test positive for them could use the information to live healthier lives by consuming less alcohol, avoiding dairy products, and eating more leafy green vegetables. The privacy of students will be protected using an anonymous bar code system.

Jasper Rine, the geneticist heading the project, sees it as an opportunity for students to learn about personalized medicine and their own genetic traits. "The history of genetics is the history of finding bad things," he is quoted as saying. "But in the future, nutritional genetics is probably going to be the sweet spot."

Critics worry that because genetic information can be cause distress, it ought to be provided only by physicians and in a setting in which counseling is offered. Defenders consider such a view paternalistic and argue that people should be able to learn about their own genes.

SNPs are variations in nucleotides (the adenine, cytosine, guanine, or tyrosine on a DNA strand) that occur together in a genome. (For a more detailed discussion, see Social Context: The Human Genome Project.) These variations may be harmless, simply reflecting ancestral and regional differences. But because SNPs can be identified in gene mutations (as well as in nongene segments of DNA), they also have been associated with problems in gene expression—such as the failure to produce certain enzymes or proteins.

In this sense, SNPs have been said to function as genetic markers. Whether or not they are responsible for a disease or trait, particular SNPs have been shown to be associated with diseases like breast cancer, asthma, bipolar disorder, macular degeneration, cluster headaches, Crohn's disease, amyotrophic lateral sclerosis (ALS), diabetes, and colon cancer.

To make use of these associations between specific SNPs and specific diseases, direct-to-consumer companies have typically used biochips programmed to detect common SNP variations along a DNA strand. The chip creates, in effect, a catalogue of an individual's SNPs, which are then compared with those in a database linking particular SNPs with particular diseases. (The same process is used to associate SNPs with particular traits, such as hair color and lactose intolerance.) Combining the accumulated disease risk associated with multiple SNPs, the companies then typically provided customers with a risk percentage for specific diseases—such as a 65 percent chance of developing arteriosclerosis before age seventy.

One problem with this procedure is that there were wide variations in the databases different companies use to make SNP–disease associations, as well as in the methods different companies use to calculate risk. Based on these variations, two different companies sometimes offered different—or even diametrically opposed—estimates of specific disease risks for the same individual. A deeper problem is that many scientists question the reliability of SNPs as disease predictors, since they often appear in nongene or "junk" sections of a person's DNA, which are not expressed. The correlation between certain diseases and certain SNPs may not reflect a causal (or even a particularly reliable) relationship. While a few of the companies offered some form of counseling to help customers make sense of these complexities, experts generally dismissed them as an inadequate substitute for the advice of a personal physician.

Regulation and Renewal. Based on these and other concerns, state and federal regulators began to crack down on direct-to-consumer genetic testing companies. New York and California sent letters to dozens of the companies in 2008, warning them that they must obtain state licenses or conform to federal standards for laboratory tests, which were henceforth to be considered a form of medical advice. But little changed until 2013, when the FDA sent out a strongly worded warning to the companies that any health-related testing would require the agency's approval before they could be marketed.

Partly in response to the threat of being put out of business by federal and state regulation, the major genetic-testing companies agreed to stop performing disease-risk assessments. They also made a commitment to develop their own industry-wide standards and shared guidelines to reduce the inconsistency in their results. In February of 2015, 23andMe received approval from the FDA to market its first medical test since 2013, for a rare genetic condition called Bloom syndrome, which causes short stature, red skin, and cancer susceptibility. Unlike its previous "risk factor" screening, the 23andMe Bloom syndrome test is a "carrier test" that seeks to identify the presence of an abnormal gene in prospective parents. In this it resembles other medically established carrier tests for cystic fibrosis and sickle-cell disease. But it does constitute the first FDA approval of a genetic test to be directly marketed to consumers, and thus suggests a new direction for the industry.

Genetic Knowledge and Patient Autonomy

To the extent that direct-to-consumer genetic testing adopts the more rigorous standards of "brick and mortar" clinical laboratories, it may help support the type of informed and empowered patient championed by Angelina Jolie Pitt and others. Being able to access quick, affordable, and reliable information about genetic disease predispositions might prove highly appealing to Jolie Pitt's model patient who can "take control and tackle head-on any health issue."

But other patients will likely see little point in going outside traditional medical avenues of genetic testing, particularly now that GINA (Genetic Information Nondiscrimination Act) and the ACA (Affordable Care Act) have banned genetic discrimination by employers and most health insurers. Indeed many wonder if direct-to-consumer genetic testing will survive now that patients have much less reason to hide genetic information from their physicians. Another group of patients will look at the treatment and prevention options for genetically conditioned diseases and simply decide that it is better not to know.

SOCIAL CONTEXT
Prenatal Genetic Testing

The ability to detect serious genetic conditions at the fetal or even embryonic stage of development is often considered one of the triumphs of contemporary biomedical science. Prenatal genetic testing offers physicians and prospective parents a new level of control over difficult genetic outcomes that they once approached with resignation.

Not everyone takes such a positive view of prenatal genetic testing, however. The optimistic view celebrates the idea that genetic testing can grant parents a certain measure of control over what their child will be like or have to endure. But critics worry about the use of this power and about its consequences for people born with certain genetic traits or disorders.

Don't Test

First, critics ask, which conditions are sufficiently serious to justify a decision to have an abortion (or, alternatively, avoid implanting an embryo with a certain gene)? Those who accept the legitimacy of abortion may agree that the prospect of having a child with a disease such as Tay-Sachs, which is untreatable and fatal in early childhood, would warrant an abortion.

By contrast, people with the Huntington's gene do not develop the disease until middle age, and the lives of those with cystic fibrosis can be extended into their thirties or even forties. Can these lives justifiably be prevented by abortion or embryo selection? Moreover, what about other hereditary conditions, including some forms of deafness and blindness? Should we even consider these diseases,

much less view them as conditions that justify terminating a pregnancy or rejecting an embryo?

Second, some critics maintain that genetic testing with the aim of screening out embryos or fetuses considered in some way "abnormal" is a form of discrimination against people with disabilities. It is, they say, an implicit endorsement of the notion that someone who has Down syndrome or is born blind, deaf, or with dwarfism is not the equal of (or less valuable than) someone who is "normal." Thus, genetic testing can be seen as a socially approved eugenics program that devalues the worth of people with disabilities.

Third, critics worry that diminishing the number of people with conditions such as cystic fibrosis, Down syndrome, muscular dystrophy, and hereditary deafness will have a negative impact on those now living with those conditions. In addition to potentially increasing their social isolation, reduced numbers might cost the members of such groups much of their political influence. Public programs established to move disabled people into the mainstream of school and civic life might face funding cuts and logistical problems. For example, school districts can generally institute a program in special athletics only if three or more people qualify to participate.

Finally, critics say, a drastic reduction in the number of people born with genetic diseases or conditions will mean that researchers will no longer be motivated to develop new drugs or treatments for such conditions. If cystic fibrosis can be eliminated by early genetic screening and the number of people with the disease falls below some crucial level, researchers are not likely to devote their careers to improving the lot of the handful of people who still have it. Rather, cystic fibrosis will become an "orphan" disease—one affecting so few people that it can't command the resources and talent needed to find a better way to treat it.

Test

The preceding criticisms are unconvincing for those who believe that prenatal genetic testing, combined with abortion or preimplantation embryo selection, offers a way to reduce suffering and sickness by preventing the birth of children who will have to live with devastating and incurable diseases.

Advocates of prenatal genetic testing answer the critics' first point by arguing that potential parents are the ones who should decide whether they want to accept the burden of caring for a child with a debilitating disease. Someone with cystic fibrosis may live thirty or even forty years, but this is not likely to happen unless parents make keeping their child alive their central priority and devote the majority of their time and effort to that task. Typically, such devotion shortchanges other children in the family and requires great sacrifice from parents. There are examples of parents in their eighties who must still provide extensive care to their fifty- or sixty-year-old children with Down syndrome. Some prospective parents feel called to devote their lives to such care, but others do not.

Also, defenders of testing argue that it may be morally irresponsible to bring a child into the world with a disease or condition that can significantly shorten his life or seriously reduce its quality. Yes, someone with Huntington's disease may live more than forty years, but the final years will be spent in a condition of intense physical and mental impairment. The person will suffer greatly and become a burden to himself and others. Some defenders of testing carry this argument a step further. If we identify a gene in an embryo that, if implanted in a women's uterus, will lead to the birth of a blind child, why should the woman not ask that a different embryo lacking that gene be implanted? Such a limiting condition as blindness may make the child's life harder in general and eliminate many possibilities of both pleasure and accomplishment. A blind child also imposes special burdens on the parents, the family, and society. In these and similar cases, defenders of testing say that we may have an obligation to both prevent suffering and protect an individual's range of possibilities in life.

Defenders of genetic testing are equally unconvinced by the second criticism regarding devaluation of or discrimination against disabled people. In their view, this criticism involves two errors. First, critics assume that an embryo or a fetus has the same moral status as a person. Some people believe this, but it is not an idea accepted by everyone and so cannot be used as a general objection to genetic testing. Second, the critics are confusing disabled people with their condition. That prospective parents don't want a child to be born with muscular dystrophy (MD) does not mean they don't value people with the disease. We value people with muscular dystrophy because they are *people,* not because they have MD. Those with muscular dystrophy often have impaired capacities (in walking, balancing, and breathing) that limit their ability to explore and cope with the world. The world would be better, in this respect, if people who currently have MD did not experience these symptoms. Yet to say it would be a better world if there were no muscular dystrophy does not devalue the people who have it or wish them out of existence. On this view, embryo selection or selective abortion is on par with other steps parents take to prevent suffering in their future children, such as prenatal care and nutrition. As Bonnie Steinbock argues in one of this chapter's readings, taking folic acid during pregnancy to prevent spina bifida does not imply that one devalues the lives of people with spina bifida.

Most defenders of prenatal genetic testing also reject the idea that there is anything *eugenic* about deciding not to implant an embryo that will lead to the birth of a child with a serious disease or disability. Such a practice can be regarded as negative eugenics in a narrow, technical sense, but it isn't what we usually think of as eugenic. It is not, that is, part of a social policy intended to improve the human race. Typically, the use of prenatal genetic testing is only an effort by prospective parents to have a child as free as possible from burdensome diseases and conditions. Although people who seek genetic testing in connection with reproduction are sometimes criticized as attempting to have a "perfect baby," the great majority say they want only a healthy baby.

Defenders of genetic testing reject the third and fourth criticisms as little more than expressions of self-interest. The critics are often individuals (and their families) with conditions that are decreasing in frequency as genetic testing becomes more widely used in reproductive decisions. Thus, the advocacy-focused Cystic Fibrosis Foundation does not promote prenatal testing for the CF gene. By contrast, the American College of Obstetrics and Gynecology recommends it to pregnant women.

According to this argument, critics of testing simply want to maintain the number of similarly affected people so that they or their family members won't lose benefits gained by political activism. These benefits may be directly personal (medical expenses, educational mainstreaming, etc.) or they may include improved treatments that benefit everyone with the condition. Defenders of prenatal testing say this approach is both unimaginative and morally dubious.

So far as benefits are concerned, wouldn't it be better for critics to advocate for reforms in education and health care that would provide all people in society with the level of support they need? Similarly, instead of seeking to maintain or increase the number of people born with (say) cystic fibrosis to attract research money and talent, wouldn't it be better to advocate a change in the way that medical research takes place? Defenders argue that encouraging research on "orphan" diseases is a more reasonable approach than trying to ensure that a constant or increased number of people are born with cystic fibrosis. Finally, defenders of prenatal testing question whether it is morally defensible to promote the birth of more children with debilitating diseases in order to benefit oneself, one's family, or the members of one's community.

Research Results

Instead of favoring or objecting to reproductive genetic testing in a wholesale fashion, prospective parents often make more nuanced decisions. A 2002 study of the choices of fifty-three thousand women, published in *Obstetrics and Gynecology,* showed that when prenatally diagnosed anomalies would have no impact on the quality of a child's life, the pregnancy termination rate was only about 1 percent. However, when the conditions would have a serious negative impact on life quality, the rate rose to 50 percent.

When testing indicated a disability likely to affect cognitive functioning, the women in the study were much more likely to choose to terminate their pregnancies. If a condition was predicted that would require surgery or special medical treatment, the abortion rate was 16 percent. This rate doubled, though, when the condition was likely to cause some form of mental dysfunction, such as cognitive impairment.

This emphasis on cognitive abilities also seems to hold when decisions are made about Down syndrome. That condition invariably involves, among other traits, mental disability. While the statistics are not wholly reliable, physicians in reproductive medicine estimate that when prenatal tests show that a fetus will develop Down syndrome, about 80 percent of women decide to terminate their pregnancies. Such

decisions have become embroiled in abortion politics in recent years, as legislators in states such as Ohio have introduced bills that would ban abortions if Down Syndrome is the reason.

The issues connected with prenatal genetic testing, embryo testing, and abortion are complicated and contentious. Advocates on one side of the debate sometimes find themselves behaving at odds with it when their own circumstances force them to make a decision. When an issue becomes personal, abstract ideological commitments are frequently discarded.

CASE PRESENTATION
Huntington's Disease: Deadly Disorder, Personal Dilemmas

Huntington's disease (HD) is a particularly cruel and frightening genetic disorder. It has no effective treatment and is invariably fatal. Furthermore, each child of an affected parent has a 50 percent chance of developing the disease.

HD typically makes its appearance between the ages of thirty-five and forty-five in men and women who have shown no previous symptoms. The signs of its onset may be quite subtle—a certain clumsiness in performing small tasks, a slight slurring of speech, a few facial twitches. But the disease is progressive. Over time, the small changes develop into devastating physical and mental impairments. Walking becomes jerky and unsteady, the face contorts into wild grimaces, the hands repeatedly clench and relax, and the whole body writhes with involuntary muscle spasms. The patient becomes disoriented, volatile, and impulsive, and eventually loses the power of speech. Death may occur fifteen or twenty years after the onset of symptoms. Usually, it results from massive infection and malnutrition—as the disease progresses, the patient loses the ability to swallow normally.

In the United States, at any given time, some 30,000 people are living with an HD diagnosis, and as many as

150,000 more have the gene responsible for it. The incidence of the disease is only one in ten thousand, but for the child of someone with the disease, the chances of having it are one in two.

Gene Identified

The gene associated with Huntington's disease was identified in 1993 after ten years of intensive research carried out in six laboratories in the United States, England, and Wales. Following clues provided by genetic markers, scientists finally located the gene near the tip of chromosome 4. When the researchers sequenced the nucleotides making up the gene, they discovered a mutation known as a trinucleotide repeat. In healthy individuals, the nucleotides CAG are repeated eleven to thirty-four times, whereas in individuals with HD, the repetitions typically range from thirty-seven to eighty-six. Some evidence suggests that higher numbers of repetitions are associated with earlier onset.

When the HD gene was identified, it was expected that this would speed the development of effective treatments for the disease. This has not occurred, in part because the mechanism of the gene's action is still not fully understood. Furthermore, the HD gene was expected to be found functioning only in the brain, but in fact radioactive tagging has shown that the gene operates in virtually every tissue of the body, including the colon, liver, pancreas, and testes. The protein that the gene codes for is believed to be involved in nerve cell development and function, so it has its most devastating impact on the brain.

Before the HD gene was identified or a marker for it discovered, the disease was known to be transmitted from generation to generation in the sort of hereditary pattern indicating that it is caused by a single gene. However, because the disease makes its appearance relatively late in life, an unsuspecting carrier may already have passed on the gene to a child before showing any sign of the disease. In the absence of a genetic test to detect the gene, the individual could not know whether he or she was a carrier.

In 1983, a major step toward the development of such a test was announced by James F. Gusella and his group at Massachusetts General Hospital. The team did not locate the gene itself, but discovered a "genetic marker" indicating its presence. They began by studying the DNA taken from members of a large American family with a history of Huntington's disease, then employed recombinant DNA techniques to attempt to locate DNA segments that might be associated with the HD gene.

The techniques involved using proteins known as restriction enzymes. A particular enzyme, when mixed with a single strand of DNA, cuts the strand at specific locations known as recognition sites. After the DNA strand has been cut up by restriction enzymes, short sections of radioactive, single-stranded DNA are added to serve as probes. The probes bind to particular segments of the DNA. Because the probes are radioactive, the segments to which they are attached can be identified. The various fragments of DNA produced by the restriction enzymes and identified by probes form a pattern that is typical of specific individuals. Thus, if the pattern of someone who does not have the disease is compared with the pattern of a family member who does, the fragments that include the faulty gene can be identified, even when the gene itself is unknown. The pattern serves as a marker for the presence of the gene, and Gusella's group found such a marker.

The group faced the problem of finding a marker consistently inherited by those with Huntington's disease but not by those free of the disease. This meant identifying perhaps as many as eight hundred markers and determining whether one could serve as the marker for the HD gene. After twelve attempts, the team identified a good candidate marker, found in all members of the family they were studying. Those with the disease had the same form of the marker, while those free of the disease had some other form.

Gusella and other researchers were supported in their work by the Hereditary Disease Foundation. The organization was founded by Milton Wexler after his wife was diagnosed with Huntington's. Wexler hoped a treatment for the disease could be found that might benefit his daughters, Nancy and Alice, who stood a 50 percent chance of developing the disease. Nancy Wexler soon became an active participant in research activities aimed at discovering a genetic marker for HD.

In collaboration with the Hereditary Disease Foundation, plans were made to test Gusella's candidate marker in a large population. It was known that a large family with a high incidence of HD lived along the shores of Lake Maracaibo in Venezuela. Nancy Wexler led a team to this remote location to collect a family history and to obtain blood and skin samples for analysis. The Venezuelan family included some 100 people with the disease and 1,100 children with the risk of developing it. Analysis of the samples showed that those with the disease also carried the same form of the marker as their American counterparts. Subsequent work by Susan Naylor and others indicated that the marker was on chromosome 4.

Genetic Test Available

Once the location of the gene for Huntington's disease was known, a genetic test for its presence was quickly developed. The availability of the test, however, raises a number of serious ethical and social issues. A study conducted in Wales revealed that more than half of those whose parents or relatives were afflicted by Huntington's would *not* want to be tested for the HD gene. Considering that the disease cannot be effectively treated and is invariably fatal, this is not a particularly surprising result.

Nancy Wexler told a reporter that she and her sister had assumed that once a test for the HD gene was available, they would both take it. However, when they met with their father to work out the details for a test based on the genetic marker, he asked, "What are we doing here? Are we sure we want to do this?" The sisters, Nancy recalled, "had a visceral understanding that either one of us could get bad news and that it would certainly destroy my father."

One argument for at-risk individuals getting tested for the HD gene is based on their obligations to others. Now that a test is widely available, is it fair to contemplate marriage or childrearing without finding out whether one is a carrier of the HD gene and informing others of the result? One may be willing to take the chance that one's offspring will have HD. But the tremendous burden the disease places on the entire family of those afflicted suggests that getting tested for the condition may be morally necessary for the sake of others. Should a potential carrier of the gene impose on his or her family the risk of having a child who will inherit the gene? Should such a risk be imposed on the child?

Prenatal Testing and Embryo Screening

The HD test now in use can also be employed in conjunction with amniocentesis to determine whether a developing fetus carries the relevant mutation. This fact raises problems for potential parents. A child born with the HD gene will inevitably develop the disease but may not do so for three, four, or even five or more decades. Does that delay make abortion less justifiable in the event of a positive test? But if prospective parents aren't prepared to seek an abortion, why administer the test in the first place? Finally, is the fact that the fetus can be expected to develop into an adult who will eventually succumb to the disease reason enough to make an abortion morally obligatory?

One alternative for prospective parents who have reason to fear that they carry the HD gene is to make use of the techniques of assisted reproduction. Once

embryos have been produced by artificial insemination from the parents' donated ova and sperm, the embryos can be tested for the HD gene. Only embryos without the gene can then be transferred to the woman's uterus for implantation.

Personal Risks

The advent of a standard, inexpensive test for the HD gene raises various other personal and social issues. For example, insurance companies may refuse to provide life or long-term care insurance to individuals whose relatives have Huntington's disease, unless they prove that they are not carriers of the gene. (The Genetic Information Nondiscrimination Act and the Affordable Care Act do not forbid such specialized insurers from using genetic information in underwriting policies.) Adoption agencies have requested that infants up for adoption be tested to assure prospective parents that the children are not at risk for HD. As Nancy Wexler put the point, "In our culture, people assume that knowledge is always good. . . . But our experience with Huntington's has shown that some things may be better left unknown."

Informing someone that he or she carries the gene can also be devastating, both to the person and to the person's family. Evidence indicates that the suicide rate among those with HD is as much as ten times the rate in the general population. One study found that out of 4,527 patients who tested positive for the HD gene at major medical centers, 5 killed themselves, 21 attempted suicide, and 18 were hospitalized for psychiatric reasons. Thus, the mere act of conveying the information that someone will later develop HD can itself constitute a threat to life. Nancy Wexler has refused to disclose publicly whether she has been tested for the HD gene. "I don't want to influence anyone's decision," she says.

Envoi

In an ideal world, an effective means of preventing the onset of Huntington's disease or treating it effectively would be available. Then the moral, social, and personal issues associated with a genetic test for it would disappear without having to be resolved. Regrettably, that world still lies in the future.

CASE PRESENTATION
The Threat of Genetic Discrimination

Judith Berman Carlisle was forty-eight years old and in the process of setting up a therapy practice when she realized that she had reasons to be worried about her health.

The year before, her sister had been diagnosed with ovarian cancer and her aunt had died of the disease. Prior to that, her grandmother and another aunt had died of breast cancer. Carlisle knew that she could be tested for the BRCA1 or BRCA2 gene mutations to learn whether she was predisposed to develop breast or ovarian cancer.

She decided against the test, however. She was going to be self-employed, and if she tested positive for either of the genes, she might not be able to get health insurance. Instead, she decided to tell her doctor about her family history and request surgery to remove her ovaries.

Carlisle suspected that the surgery wouldn't raise a red flag the way genetic information would. As she told reporter Amy Harmon, she saw an important difference between saying "I have a strong family history predisposing me to breast cancer" and saying "I only have a thirteen percent chance of not getting breast cancer during the time you are insuring me."

Carlisle had the surgery to remove her ovaries; then, after she got health insurance and couldn't be turned down because of a "preexisting condition," she had herself tested for BRCA1 and BRCA2. The test results were negative. She hadn't needed to have her ovaries removed after all, but she hadn't dared to be tested to find that out.

Preexisting Conditions

For much of the past three decades, stories like Judith Carlisle's were common in the American health care system. That was because health insurers, who had come to dominate the health care landscape, were legally allowed to discriminate on the basis of *preexisting conditions*. This meant that a diagnosis of one or more common but potentially expensive conditions such as high blood pressure, asthma, or diabetes could render a patient effectively uninsurable—

subject to unaffordable premiums, no coverage for the condition, or outright denial of coverage. With out-of-pocket expenses for some of these conditions costing tens, if not hundreds, of thousands of dollars a year, medical debt soared, to the point that it became a key factor in about half of all U.S. bankruptcies. While insurers claimed that they would not treat a person's genetic information as a preexisting condition, a 2007 study by Georgetown University researchers found that over 10 percent of insurance underwriters surveyed said they would deny coverage, exclude coverage for certain disorders, or charge higher premiums if a customer's genetic data indicated increased disease risk.

Employers, too, were tempted to limit their insurance costs by denying coverage to employees on the grounds that their genetic makeup constituted a preexisting condition. The Burlington Northern Railroad Company took this path when it required each employee making an insurance claim for carpal tunnel syndrome to have blood drawn by a company doctor. Without telling the employees, the railway had the blood tested to see if genetic factors predisposing them to carpal tunnel syndrome could be found. Based on such factors, the company could then deny coverage on the grounds that carpal tunnel was a preexisting condition, already present in the employee's genes. (Due to this practice, the railway was sued by the Equal Employment Opportunities Commission, and the case was settled out of court in 2002.)

Widespread concern over these and other preexisting condition policies has played a significant role in how Americans approach genetic testing. They have been extremely cautious about agreeing to tests that could become part of their medical records and perhaps lead to health insurance coverage being denied or even canceled.

Protecting Themselves

To avoid putting themselves in a position that would allow their employer or insurer to use genetic information to their disadvantage, Americans have sometimes avoided genetic screening or tried to ensure that its results would not become part of their medical record. Consider the following illustrations:

- People who have a parent or sibling with Huntington's disease (HD) have a 50 percent chance of also having the gene that causes the disease. HD typically appears between the ages of thirty-five and forty-four. It is a progressive neurological disorder that cannot be effectively treated and is invariably fatal. (See Case Presentation: Huntington's Disease in this chapter.)

Some people at risk for HD prefer not to know whether they are carrying the gene; others want the information so that they can better plan their lives. Comparative data suggest, however, that decisions about learning one's genetic HD status may have more to do with fears about keeping health insurance than individual preferences. In the United States, only 5 percent of those at risk for HD choose to be tested for the gene. In Canada, by contrast, 20 percent of those at risk decide to have the test. Although it is possible that this fourfold difference can be ascribed to a cultural divergence, the most likely explanation is that Canada's national health care system has never denied treatment on the basis of preexisting conditions.

- The head of breast cancer research at NYC's Weil–Cornell Medical Center estimated in 2008 that 20 percent of the patients who chose to be tested for BRCA1 and BRCA2 paid for the tests in cash. This meant that they would not have to file an insurance claim and thus tip off their insurer that they might be predisposed to develop breast or ovarian cancer.

- Thousands of people who worry they might have genes predisposing them to specific diseases avoid consultation with physicians. Instead, they pay private companies such as DNA Direct and deCode Genetics for genetic testing. The companies promise confidentiality, and thus the test results do not become a part of their clients' medical records—the primary evidence for insurance denials based on preexisting conditions.

Hindering Medicine

In the late 2000s, concern began to grow about the impact that preexisting condition policies were having on medical practice. Physicians need reliable information about their patients to make accurate diagnoses and prescribe effective treatments. When, for whatever reason, a patient withholds relevant information, the physician is hindered from providing sound medical care. But such hindrance can be especially dangerous when it comes to genetic diseases, as the case of Katherine Anderson demonstrates.

Katherine's parents were told by their doctor that Katherine might have inherited from her father the gene for Factor V Leiden, a disorder that can cause life-threatening blood clots. But if Katherine tested positive for the gene, the doctor warned, she might later find it difficult to get insurance. The Andersons decided not to have her tested.

When Katherine turned sixteen and began having irregular periods, her gynecologist prescribed a birth-control drug to regulate them, unaware that she might be positive for the Factor V Leiden gene. The result was life threatening. She developed a massive blood clot that stretched from her abdomen to her knee. The drug her doctor had prescribed was a hormone, and it, in combination with her genetic predisposition, had raised Katherine's chance of developing blood clots to thirty times the average risk.

Katherine Anderson eventually recovered, but her case illustrates what can happen when patients fail to provide physicians with information relevant to diagnosis or treatment. If employers or insurers can use genetic or other health information as grounds for firing them or denying them insurance, it makes sense for patients to want to keep that information private. A society with policies that encourage such secrecy, however, is not one in which safe and effective medicine can be practiced.

In an effort to address these and other problems in the U.S. health care system, Congress eventually passed two landmark pieces of legislation: the 2008 Genetic Information Nondiscrimination Act (GINA) and the 2010 Affordable Care Act (ACA).

GINA

The Genetic Information Nondiscrimination Act took effect on November 21, 2009. GINA was designed to address preexisting condition fears like those discussed above and to make it possible for people to keep their genetic information private without suffering a penalty.

Through its major provisions and accompanying regulations, GINA:

- Prohibits employers from requiring any genetic test as a condition of hiring, firing, promotion, setting compensation, or determining other terms, conditions, or privileges of employment.

- Prohibits employers from requesting or purchasing genetic information about an employee or any member of an employee's family.

- Prohibits insurers from requiring or requesting that an individual take any genetic test.

- Prohibits insurers from using genetic information to determine an individual's eligibility for health insurance or to set the amount of an individual's premium for either individual or group health care coverage.

- Prohibits both employers and health insurers from disclosing genetic information about an individual.

The "genetic information" that employers and insurers are prohibited from acquiring, using, or revealing encompasses more than the results of genetic tests. It includes, for example, family histories of breast cancer, heart disease, or Huntington's disease. It also includes information about prescribed medications that might suggest someone is being treated for a particular genetic disorder.

What GINA Permits

The Congressional framers of GINA were concerned that the law's prohibitions not be so broad as to impede legitimate uses of genetic information. In the series of compromises that shaped the legislation, they granted exemptions for a number of practices and policies. Some of these have been relatively uncontroversial. For instance, under GINA:

- A health care professional treating a patient is free to ask the patient or the patient's family members to take a genetic test.

- Genetic data can be collected for the purposes of monitoring toxic conditions in the workplace, auditing employer-sponsored wellness programs, and administering federal and state family leave laws. Data about individuals, however, may not be disclosed to the employer.

- Health plans and insurers that operate "wellness programs" are free to notify employees about genetic testing and discuss its potential usefulness to them. They are also allowed to ask employees to provide family health histories for purposes of the program, but they cannot use such information for decisions regarding insurance coverage or any other penalty or reward.

Other exemptions granted under the law have proved more controversial. For example:

- Under GINA, life, disability, and long-term care insurers can still discriminate against applicants based on genetic information. Someone with a genetic predisposition for Alzheimer's disease who seeks (quite logically) to obtain long-term care coverage can still be denied on genetic grounds. In fact, a long-term care insurer can require her to take a genetic test before applying.

- Employers and insurers are not held accountable under GINA for the accidental acquisition of genetic information. (For example, an employer may hear gossip that an employee's father died from a heart attack at age forty-eight or read an obituary that notes an employee's oldest child died at age twenty from cystic fibrosis.) While insurers and employers are prohibited from making use of such knowledge in coverage or employment decisions, it is quite difficult to prove that the information hasn't influenced these choices. Like discrimination on the basis of age, gender, or race, genetic discrimination can be difficult to prove.

- Before the passage of the Affordable Care Act, GINA also allowed insurers to evaluate applicants for health insurance on the grounds of the applicant's current health status, and employers can still do so. This means that some people with manifest (but not disabling) genetic illnesses can still be denied jobs or promotions on the basis of their disease—even if it does not impact their work performance.

The Affordable Care Act

The Patient Protection and Affordable Care Act (ACA) was passed by Congress in March 2010 and fully took effect in 2014. The most substantial reform of the U.S. health care system since the advent of Medicare and Medicaid in 1965, the ACA was designed to increase health insurance affordability and quality, and to reduce the number of Americans lacking health insurance, who constituted some 20 percent of the population. To do this, the law employs mechanisms such as tax subsidies, regulated insurance marketplaces, expansions of Medicaid, and an individual mandate to purchase health insurance. As of spring 2015, the law had reduced the uninsured rate from 20 to 13.2 percent, the biggest drop in forty years. (See Chapter 9 for a detailed discussion of the ACA and the broader issues involved in health care distribution.)

One of the most popular (and least controversial) provisions of the ACA is that it prohibits health insurers from denying coverage or charging higher rates on the basis of preexisting conditions, including genetic screening results. This part of the act appears to be largely successful, although there is some evidence that insurers are using so-called "adverse tiering" in drug pricing to make coverage for certain diseases (such as HIV) nearly impossible to obtain. The ACA also does not close the loophole in GINA that allows long-term care, disability, and life insurers to deny coverage based on preexisting genetic and other conditions, nor does it address employment issues, such as GINA's exemption for discrimination based on manifest diseases.

Some critics of GINA and the ACA argue that their antidiscrimination provisions go too far. For example, it has been argued that certain genetic predispositions could be highly relevant to an individual's ability to perform certain jobs, and thus constitute a *bona fide occupational qualification* (BFOQ). If genetic testing could reveal, for example, that a bus driver had a condition that made her prone to accidents or seizures, her employer might be justified in requiring such screening and considering the results in hiring decisions. It remains unclear how Americans would respond to such genetic BFOQs as an exception to GINA's privacy and antidiscrimination provisions. The ACA and GINA's bans on preexisting condition policies in health insurance, however, seem unlikely to be rolled back, as they appear to be popular even among fierce congressional opponents of the ACA.

Retrospect and Prospect

Consider again the cases of Judith Carlisle and Katherine Anderson—people who put themselves at risk so that an insurance company wouldn't be able to deny them health insurance on the basis of their genetic inheritance.

GINA and the ACA have changed the health care system that generated such cases. Americans have been largely freed from the fear that a genetic test will stand in the way of their getting or keeping their health insurance, getting or keeping a job, or winning a promotion. They no longer need to get genetic tests in secret out of concern that the results will find their way into their medical records.

It is becoming increasingly clear that all people carry genetic variants that predispose them to certain diseases and disorders. Medical treatments are also utilizing genetic information and technology to an unprecedented degree. In this environment, GINA and other laws may become an important shield against a new and potentially pervasive form of discrimination.

CASE PRESENTATION
Gene Therapy: Risks and Rewards

On September 14, 1990, at the National Institutes of Health in Bethesda, Maryland, a four-year-old girl became the first patient to be treated by gene therapy under an approved protocol. The child, whose parents initially asked that her identity not be made public, lacked the gene for producing adenosine deaminase

(ADA), an enzyme required to keep immune cells alive and functioning.

The girl's life expectancy was low, because, without ADA, she would almost certainly develop cancers and opportunistic infections that cannot be effectively controlled by conventional treatments. The aim of the therapy was to provide her with genetically altered cells cells that would boost her immune system and increase the production of essential antibodies. During the months that followed, she received four injections of such cells.

The treatment, under the direction of W. French Anderson, R. Michael Blaese, and Kenneth Culver, involved taking blood from the patient, isolating the T-cells, and then growing a massive number of them. These cells were infected with a weakened retrovirus into which a copy of the human gene for ADA had been spliced. The cells were then injected back into the patient via blood transfusion.

The Therapy

The idea behind this therapy was for the ADA gene to migrate to the patient's cellular DNA, become functional, and begin producing ADA. If the cells produced enough of the enzyme, the child's immune system would recover. Because most T-cells live for only weeks or months, however, the process had to be repeated at regular intervals.

The girl's parents later revealed their daughter's identity. She is Ashanthi Desilva, and more than a decade later she is alive and doing well. Soon after Desilva's treatment, on January 30, 1991, nine-year-old Cynthia Cutshall became the second person to receive gene therapy for ADA deficiency.

Laboratory tests showed that both children's immune systems were functioning effectively after treatment. But the need to replace short-lived T-cells meant that Ashanthi and Cynthia had to continue to receive regular injections of altered cells. Anderson and his collaborators had long hoped to find a way around this requirement, and the break came several years later, when an NIH group developed a procedure for isolating stem cells from the bone marrow. If enough of a patient's stem cells could be obtained and genetically altered, these cells might, when reintroduced, generate enough T-cells for an adequately functioning immune system.

In May 1993, Cynthia Cutshall's stem cells were harvested, exposed to the retrovirus containing the normal ADA gene, and reinjected. She tolerated the procedure with no apparent ill effects, and later that year essentially the same procedure was repeated with Ashanthi Desilva. The immune systems of both children continued to function within the normal range.

This may seem to be an unequivocal success for gene therapy, but the value of the experiment in establishing this is difficult to assess. Both subjects continued to be treated with a standard drug regimen, so was it gene therapy or the drugs that saved their lives? Although gene therapy can't be said to have produced a cure for ADA, advocates believe that eventually it will.

Definitive Evidence, Potential Risks

More definitive evidence for the effectiveness of gene therapy comes from results of clinical trials conducted at Paris's Necker Hospital in 2000 by Alain Fischer. Fischer's group treated eleven patients (ten infants and a teenager) with severe combined immunodeficiency disease (SCID), a disorder caused by a defect on the X chromosome. Nine of those treated by using a retrovirus to insert new genes were cured. This is an astounding outcome, considering that most children born with the defect die from the disease by the end of their first year. Bone marrow transplants, the standard treatment, are successful only about 75 percent of the time.

In 2002, however, a three-year-old boy in the study developed leukemia-like symptoms. The clinical trial was immediately halted, and the outcome had a chilling effect on gene therapy research around the world. Regulatory agencies in the United States were already particularly inclined to caution after the death of eighteen-year-old Jesse Gelsinger in a gene therapy trial. (See the Case Presentation on Gelsinger in Chapter 2). After a period of suspension to permit a safety review, the FDA once again allowed gene therapy trials to go forward, focused on a number of debilitating conditions:

Parkinson's Disease. Parkinson's disease, which affects more than five hundred thousand people in the United States, is a progressive disorder in which cells in the part of the brain called the substantia nigra die off, resulting in a lack of the neurotransmitter dopamine.

This condition leads to symptoms such as hand tremors, impaired balance, and "freezing" in place. As more cells die, the symptoms become progressively worse, and the disease may have a fatal outcome.

In August 2007, the *Lancet* published the results of a Phase I clinical trial that used gene therapy to increase the amount of gamma-aminobutyric acid (GABA) in the brain. GABA is one of the major inhibitory neurotransmitters in the central nervous system, and in Parkinson's patients it is in short supply. By using a retrovirus to introduce billions of copies of the gene that encodes GABA into brain cells, a team led by Michael Kaplitt was able to increase the amount of the neurotransmitter present in the brains of the trial's subjects. This resulted in a reduction of the tremors and other unchecked movements characteristic of the disease.

The trial involved twelve patients, and all of them continued to take their prescribed medications. They also continued to have some of the symptoms of the disease. Even so, over a year of evaluation, patients showed general improvement in symptoms, such as less difficulty walking, less muscular rigidity, and fewer hand tremors. Most important for gene therapy, none of the patients showed significant side effects from the treatment.

Inherited Retinal Degeneration. The retina is the light-sensitive tissue layer that covers the inside of the eye. Photoreceptors in the retina convert light energy into electrical impulses that travel along the optic nerve to the brain. Retinol, a form of vitamin A that plays a key role in the process of converting light into a nerve impulse, is active in the pigmented epithelium—the layer of cells under the photoreceptors. Retinol is kept available by an enzyme (the protein RPE65) that recycles it as it is used by cells, and when retinol is missing, the photoreceptors can't do their job.

Leber's congenital amaurosis (LCA) is a genetic disorder in which mutations in the gene RPE65 result in a shortage or the complete absence of the enzyme required to recycle retinol. Children with the mutated gene are born with impaired vision, and what sight they have continues to deteriorate. Over time, photoreceptors deteriorate, and the outcome is significant, if not total, blindness.

In May 2007, a team at Moorfields Eye Hospital in London used a virus to transfer healthy copies of the RPE65 gene into the cells of the pigmented epithelium of seventeen-year-old Robert Johnson. Johnson, diagnosed with LCA, had been steadily losing his sight, but within months of the gene therapy, his vision improved measurably. The same procedure was carried out on eleven other LCA patients, and they, too, showed improvement.

In 2009, an American study reported results similar to the British study. Researchers used viruses to introduce normal copies of RPE65 into areas of the pigmented epithelium in which photoreceptor cells seemed most intact. Within two weeks, the five children and seven adults treated began to show significant improvement in their vision. Children improved the most, but the oldest participant, a forty-four-year-old woman who was once largely housebound, began to see well enough to meet her children coming home from school.

AIDS Treatment. In 2009, many researchers lauded the results of a Phase II clinical trial that used gene therapy to treat AIDS. A patient's blood stem cells were first cultured with OZ1, a genetically altered mouse virus. The goal was to get the gene for the so-called hairpin ribozyme incorporated into the DNA of the blood stem cells. The ribozyme chemically slices up RNA, and because HIV depends on RNA for replication, blood cells with the altered DNA prevent the virus from reproducing. The idea was for the genetically altered stem cells to populate the bone marrow of the patient and then begin producing blood cells containing the ribosome. When enough altered blood cells are generated in an HIV-positive person, her viral load would be lowered.

The trial involved seventy-four patients; thirty-eight were transfused with genetically altered blood stem cells, and thirty-six were transfused with an inactive placebo solution. All patients had HIV infections, which were being kept under control by highly active antiretroviral therapy (HAART).

During the hundred-week period of the trial, patients receiving altered stem cells had a higher number of CD4 T-cells, which indicated that HIV wasn't killing those cells off at the same rate as before.

During nontreatment intervals, treated patients had higher CD4 counts and a lower HIV load than those patients in the placebo group. Also, when HAART was stopped, those in the treatment group were able to wait longer before starting the drugs again than those in the placebo group.

Treating Genetic Disorders

Gene therapy holds enormous promise for treating a variety of genetic disorders. Experimental clinical protocols for the treatment of a wide range of relatively common diseases such as cystic fibrosis, hemophilia, phenylketonuria, sickle-cell disease, hypercholesterolemia, cardiovascular disease, cancer, lupus erythematous, and blood-clotting disorders are either underway or in the planning stage. Following are a few examples:

Sickle-Cell Disease. Sickle-cell disease, which affects about one in four hundred African Americans, among other groups, is produced by a gene that affects the folding of the two chains making up the hemoglobin molecule. In a proposed treatment, molecular fragments called chimeraplasts will be induced to enter the stem cells in the bone marrow that produce red blood cells.

If a stem cell incorporates the chimeraplast into the nucleus, the cell's own repair system may eliminate the gene for the defective hemoglobin chain and substitute that provided by the chimeraplast. If enough stem cells are altered and function properly, the amount of red blood cells produced should eliminate the heart damage and strokes that can cause early death in sickle-cell patients.

Malignant Melanoma. In one experimental cancer treatment, researchers make trillions of copies of the gene for the antigen HLA-B7 and then inject them directly into the tumors of those with melanoma. The gene enters the cells of the tumor, inserts itself in their nuclear DNA, and triggers the production of HLA-B7. The antigen then extrudes from the cells, causing the tumor to be attacked by the immune system's killer T-cells. Two patients were successfully treated by this approach in 2006, demonstrating that gene therapy can be used as a cancer treatment.

Leukemia. A genetic abnormality known as the Philadelphia chromosome triggers cancerous changes in stem cells in the bone marrow. The resulting disease is chronic myelogenous leukemia, which affects about 4,600 people a year and is annually responsible for about 1,000 deaths. The best standard treatment is to inject patients with stem cells from a bone marrow donor. Sometimes, however, a compatible donor can't be located; also, the therapy has a lower level of success in people over fifty-five.

A gene-based therapy is being developed to alter the patient's own stem cells by adding an antisense RNA sequence to the cellular DNA. The sequence is designed to block the formation of the protein leading to cancerous growth, thereby making the cancer cells behave like normal cells. The sequence will also include a gene making the altered cells more resistant to the chemotherapeutic drug methotrexate. Thus, when a patient receives chemotherapy, the cancerous cells will be killed while the altered ones will survive and reproduce. The altered stem cells should then produce normal red blood cells.

Collateral Blood Vessel Growth. Every year, thirty to forty thousand people in the United States develop almost complete blockage of the arteries in their legs. Shut off from blood supply, the tissues in the leg develop ulcers that don't heal, a problem that can lead to gangrene, amputation, and death. Indeed, twenty percent of these patients die in the hospital, and 40 percent die within the next year. No effective drugs are available to increase the blood flow to the legs.

A new treatment under development uses the gene for vascular endothelial growth factor (VEGF), a protein that stimulates the growth of collateral blood vessels. When billions of VEGF genes are injected into leg muscle, about 5 percent of them are incorporated into muscle cells, causing them to start producing the relevant proteins. When the VEGF molecule attaches to the surface of the cells beyond the blockage, they begin to produce tiny new blood vessels that grow around the blockage.

Trials are also underway to test the effectiveness of the therapy in heart disease. If VEGF can establish collateral circulation in the heart, the need for coronary bypass surgery might be reduced or even eliminated.

Those too frail or sick to undergo a bypass or even angioplasty might eventually be helped by the new technique.

Genome Editing and Germ-Line Therapy

The gene therapy with the longest track record of use in humans is *somatic cell therapy*, which involves genetic modification of patients' body cells, as opposed to their sex cells. This means that even if the therapy can eliminate disease in an individual with a defective gene, the therapy will do nothing to alter the probability that the patient's children will inherit the same defective gene. To permanently disrupt this genetic transmission, germ-line cells might have to be altered. That is, the defective gene in an ovum or sperm cell would have to be replaced.

It so happens that in recent years, new technologies have been developed that directly insert, replace, or remove DNA from the human genome using "molecular scissors" at specific locations in the double helix. These *genome-editing* tools include zinc finger nucleases (ZFN), transcription activator-like effector nucleases (TALENs), and, most recently, CRISPR-Cas9, which uses a bacterial immune system to identify and cut specific DNA regions. Unlike previous gene therapies, these genome-editing tools can disable specific mutations, sometimes down to the level of individual nucleotide base pairs. This means that they have far greater potential than previous technologies to effect germ-line changes in human DNA, generating both excitement and alarm.

For one thing, the clinical value of germ-line therapy remains in question. If the aim is to eliminate heritable diseases from a family, the most direct and effective way to achieve this is to screen embryos and avoid implanting those which carry the flawed gene. This process is currently available at fertility clinics and doesn't involve the risks and uncertainties of tinkering with the DNA of germ cells.

Germ-line therapy, unlike somatic cell therapy, includes a potential application that has made it the focus of sustained ethical criticism. Germ-line therapy holds out the prospect of genetically engineering sex cells to produce offspring with virtually any set of desired characteristics. This possibility has led many critics to warn that genomic editing threatens to create a dystopian future in which we practice eugenics and manufacture our children to order. (See the Briefing Session in this chapter and Case Presentation: The CRISPR Revolution for a fuller discussion.)

Envoi

For the time being, both somatic and germ-line gene therapy continues to be experimental. But some of its forms are likely to become standard treatments in the next few decades. Other forms will for some time remain experimental and, as such, will raise the same sorts of moral questions that are typical of any experimental procedure. These include questions of informed consent, medical benefit, and personal risk.

SOCIAL CONTEXT

The Human Genome Project: Genes, Diseases, and the Personal Genome

For a half-century, scientists considered sequencing the human genome so important a task that they referred to it as the "Holy Grail" of biology. The Holy Grail, in medieval Christian legend, is the lost cup used by Jesus Christ at the Last Supper. Because the Grail delivers salvation to whomever possesses it, finding the Grail was the aim in many medieval quest stories.

Deciphering the human genome never offered the promise of eternal life, but it has unlocked a vast store of genetic knowledge, including the possibility of understanding genetic diseases and bringing them under control. This last objective has turned out to be more elusive than those who set out on the quest believed, yet sequencing the genome has at least brought that goal within sight.

Genome Success

On June 26, 2000, Francis Collins, then director of the National Genome Research Institute, and J. Craig Venter, president of Celera Genetics, announced that, thanks to the joint work of the two groups, the human genome had finally been mapped.

This meant that the estimated 3.2 billion base pairs making up human DNA had been identified and sequenced; that is, the precise order of the base pairs had been established. Human DNA is now thought to contain about thirty thousand genes. Earlier estimates had put this figure around one hundred thousand, so the lower number came as a considerable surprise.

The complete set of genes contained in the forty-six human chromosomes is known as the *genome*. One way of looking at the genome is that it is the total set of encoded instructions for assembling a human being that is stored in the nucleus of each cell. About 75 percent of the genome is thought to be "junk" (as geneticists call it), consisting of repetitive DNA sequences accumulated during evolution and contributing nothing to human development or functioning. Yet biologists are also quick to say that we don't yet know enough to declare the junk DNA absolutely useless. It may contain sequences that in the future we will realize are crucially important.

Background

In 1985, biologist Robert Sinsheimer began promoting the idea that the entire human genome should be mapped and its genes sequenced. Because the genome was recognized to contain some three billion base pairs, the proposed Human Genome Project (HGP) would operate on a scale unprecedented in the biological sciences. It would compare with the efforts of physicists to develop the atomic bomb during World War II and with the manned space project of the 1960s.

The sheer size of the genome project made many scientists skeptical about supporting it. Some believed it would drain money away from smaller projects of immediate value in favor of one with only distant and uncertain promise. Also, some feared the genome project would turn out to be too much like the space project, emphasizing solutions to engineering problems rather than the advancement of basic science.

Attitudes changed in 1988, when the National Research Council endorsed the HGP and outlined a gradual approach of coordinated research that would protect the interest of the basic sciences. When James Watson (who, along with Francis Crick, worked out the structure of DNA in 1953) agreed to be director of the project, most critics dropped their opposition. Watson headed the project with great success until he resigned in 1993, when the position was taken over by Francis Collins.

Mapping and sequencing the human genome was expected to take fifteen to twenty years and to cost between $3 and $5 billion. In 1989, Congress approved $31 million to initiate the program, but the project eventually came to cost about $200 million per year. (Most biological and medical scientists view the money as wisely spent; recent estimates suggest that $140 have been put back into the U.S. economy for every $1 spent mapping the genome.)

The HGP was divided among nine different centers at both national laboratories and universities, with the result that hundreds of scientists participated in the research and contributed to the final product. The HGP was expected to be completed by 2005, but in response to a challenge by a commercial enterprise, it was completed as a public–private partnership five years ahead of schedule.

Biologist J. Craig Venter, head of Celera Corporation, had claimed he would begin sequencing in 1999 and finish in 2001. Venter's group took an approach different from that of the federal project. Celera sequenced millions of DNA fragments, then used a computer program to piece them together on the basis of their overlaps. Unlike the HGP approach, Celera did not break DNA into fragments and then create a map of each piece's location.

The results of the Human Genome Project are considered by most biological and medical researchers to be of inestimable worth. The information has already provided us with a dramatically enhanced understanding of the patterns and processes of human evolution and clarified our genetic relatedness to other organisms. The detailed genetic information acquired by the HGP continues to give us a much-improved understanding of the links between specific genes and specific diseases. This information is a crucial step along the path to understanding genetic diseases and devising treatments that will eliminate or control them.

Early Successes

In the wake of the HGP's completion, researchers began to identify with astonishing rapidity the genes responsible for a large number of human diseases. The following sample from a list of several thousand conditions gives some idea of the success genetics researchers have had in linking genes or gene markers to particular diseases:

Colon Cancer. For the hereditary form of colon cancer, a marker was found on the upper end of chromosome 2 for a "repair" gene that corrects minor errors in cellular DNA. In its mutant form, the gene seems to trigger hundreds of thousands of mutations in other genes. One person in two

hundred has the gene; 65 percent of the carriers are liable to develop cancer. The heredity form accounts for about 15 percent of all colon tumors.

Amyotrophic Lateral Sclerosis. The hereditary form of ALS (Lou Gehrig's disease) results from a mutation of a gene on chromosome 21 that encodes the enzyme superoxide dismutase, which plays a role in eliminating free radicals. It is believed that if these radicals aren't controlled, they may damage motor neurons, which will then lead to muscle degeneration. The familial form of the disease accounts for only about 10 percent of cases, but those with a family history of the disease can now be screened for the defective gene.

Type 2 (Adult-Onset) Diabetes. A gene on chromosome 7 encodes glucokinase, an enzyme that stimulates the pancreas to produce insulin. At least twenty-three mutated forms of the gene may cause diabetes by encoding for a faulty enzyme that impedes insulin production. A screening test for the mutated genes is available.

Alzheimer's Disease. The gene ApoE on chromosome 19 encodes a protein that transports cholesterol. People who have both alleles for the form of the protein known as E4 have eight times the risk of developing Alzheimer's; those with one allele have two to three times the risk. The gene could account for as many as half of those with Alzheimer's, although the causal role of E4 in producing it is not yet established.

X-Linked SCID. Severe combined immunodeficiency disease (SCID) is caused by a defective gene passed from mothers to sons on the X chromosome. The normal gene encodes part of the receptor of interleukin-2, which is part of the cytokine messenger system that keeps the body's protective T-cells functioning. Newborns with the mutated gene have few or no T-cells in their immune systems, and even a mild infection is life threatening. The disease occurs in only one out of a hundred thousand births. (The cells used in the study were from a child known as "David," who died in Houston after he was removed from the sterile plastic bubble where he had spent almost twelve years of his life. Because of the publicity surrounding him, SCID is sometimes called "the Bubble Boy disease.")

This list of genetically linked diseases can be expanded to include spinocerebellar ataxia (a degenerative disease associated with a gene on chromosome 6); Huntington's disease (see Case Presentation: Huntington's Disease in this chapter); Lorenzo's disease (adrenoleukodystrophy, or ALD, which involves the degeneration of the myelin sheath around nerves); Canavan disease (a rare and fatal brain disorder similar to ALD); achondroplastic dwarfism (the FGR3 gene causes about one-third of the cases of dwarfism); sickle-cell disease (see this chapter's Briefing Session); and cystic fibrosis (in which mucus accumulates in the lungs and pancreas).

HapMap

Genomic sequencing is a powerful tool for understanding the disease-causing role of genes that in the past could be located only by determined research and good luck. Unlike cystic fibrosis or sickle-cell disease, however, most diseases are not the result of a single gene mutation. Breast cancer, for example, is sometimes caused by a mutated BRCA gene, but it occurs more frequently due to the spontaneous, nonhereditary mutations that are termed "sporadic."

In 2002, an international project was launched to supplement the HGP by assembling a haplotype map (HapMap). A *haplotype* is a stretch of alleles of different genes that lie closely together on the same chromosome and tend to be inherited together. The idea behind the HapMap was to chart molecular differences in haplotypes. These differences could then be linked with particular diseases by comparing the genomes of individuals with the disease to the genomes of those who don't have it.

Such studies did not compare entire genomes. Rather, they relied on analyzing hundreds of thousands of segments of DNA known as *single-nucleotide polymorphisms*, or SNPs (pronounced "snips"). SNPs are common variations in nucleotides (the adenine, cytosine, guanine, or tyrosine molecules on a DNA strand) that occur at the same location in a genome. In one person's genome, for example, cytosine might occur where most genomes have guanine. Alternatively, at that location, the nucleotide might be missing or an additional nucleotide may be present.

These substitutions, deletions, and insertions may be harmless human variants that reflect ancestral or regional differences. SNPs themselves are not genes, but they can occur within genes. Thus, they may be found in a gene mutation (a variant form of a gene) that may alter the way a gene is expressed. The gene could fail to make a particular enzyme, for example, and the result could be a disease such as Tay-Sachs. Based on these findings, scientists have been able to correlate specific SNPs with specific diseases, although these correlations do not necessarily imply any causal relationship.

The analysis of SNPs is made possible by biochips programmed to detect nucleotide differences at locations along a DNA strand. The biochip assembles, in effect, a catalogue of the variants displayed by an individual's DNA. The SNPs in the catalogue are then compared with those in a database of past associations between particular SNPs and particular diseases. The location of the gene containing the SNP variant can then be mapped onto the genome. The idea, in principle, was to use SNPs to create a complete catalogue of all genetic diseases and the genetic mutations responsible for them.

Many researchers have subsequently concluded, however that the main assumption behind the HapMap was wrong. Although some two thousand SNPs are found at sites on the human genome that are linked to diseases such as asthma, bipolar disorder, Crohn's disease, ALS, and diabetes, these SNPs often occur as well in nongene segments of DNA—that is, in the so-called "junk DNA." This suggests that the association between a SNP and a disease may often be no more than a statistical artifact. Thus the HapMap approach has turned out to be not completely wrong, but more limited in value than researchers first believed.

Personal Genomes

In contrast to the earlier assumption that "[m]utations causing common diseases are common," most researchers now believe that "[c]ommon diseases are caused by rare mutations," as the health journalist Nicholas Wade puts it. This suggests that the best way to find the gene responsible for a disease is to compare the entire genome of someone with the disease with the entire genome of someone who does not have it. Unlike the HapMap approach, which used common SNP variations as samples, this process involves searching for rare mutations in complete genomes, made up of about three billion nucleotides. The genomes must be sequenced—the whole string of nucleotides must be listed in the order in which they occur. Thus, if the entire genome of someone with a disease is compared with that of someone lacking the disease, variants in the nucleotides will show up.

A paradigmatic example of this approach is Richard A. Gibbs's analysis of the genome of James R. Lupski. Gibbs and Lupski are colleagues at Baylor College of Medicine, and Lupski, a medical geneticist, has an inherited neurological disorder called Charcot-Marie-Tooth (CMT) disease. The disease involves dysfunction of nerve cells and myelin (the insulating sheath around nerves), and leads to a progressive loss of control of the feet, legs, hands, and arms. A single normal copy of the gene involved is enough to prevent a full-blown version of the disease, although those who inherit one normal and one mutated copy may experience mild symptoms. Mutations in any one of thirty-nine (known) genes can cause CMT.

Gibbs had already sequenced the genomes of ten healthy people before he asked Lupski to serve as a test case. When Lupski's genome was compared with those of the healthy people, Gibbs found that Lupski had mutations in both copies (alleles) of the gene SH3TC2. Nor did each allele have the same mutation. The one Lupski had inherited from his father was different from the one he inherited from his mother. His mother had one normal gene and one mutated, and his father had one normal and one with a different mutation.

Lupski was one of eight children, and the way the two mutations were distributed from the parents determined whether each child was free of CMT, mildly affected, or like Lupski, had a full-blown version of the disease. Two children inherited normal copies of the genes—one from each parent. Two others inherited the mother's mutation and the father's normal copy. Four, including Lupski, inherited each parent's mutated copy and thus developed CMT.

The cost of sequencing Lupski's genome in 2010 was $50,000. Because of its cost, sequencing the genomes of individuals was then still a rarely used research tool. In 2009, only seven human genomes had been sequenced. But by 2014, the cost of sequencing a complete genome had fallen to about $1000, and an estimated 228,000 had already been sequenced by researchers around the world. This leap forward has been facilitated by new biochip microarrays and powerful computer programs that work faster and require fewer people to run them.

This lowered cost has enabled researchers to analyze the DNA of multigenerational families, identify disease-causing genes, and trace the way they are inherited. The payoff has been an increasingly detailed understanding of how genes cause particular diseases.

Epigenetics and Precision Medicine

Being able to locate a gene is a crucial step toward understanding the complex function of DNA, but a knowledge of where genes appear in the human (or in an individual's) genome is incomplete in a crucial way. Such knowledge must be accompanied by an understanding of the proteins that chemically interact with DNA and regulate gene transcription. These mechanisms, which do not involve changes in the nucleotide sequence, nevertheless have a significant impact on the cellular and physiological expression of our genetics. They are thus often called *epigenetic* mechanisms.

Genes do most of their work by producing proteins. The proteins interact with other proteins to regulate human development, cell division, physiological functioning, immunological responses, tissue repair, and so on. Since the epigenetic features of these proteins can be passed on when cells divide, they can have a profound influence on cellular behavior, including the growth

of cancers. This may help explain the origins of the many "sporadic" cancers people develop that cannot be traced to a single gene mutation or combination of mutations. Diagnosing and treating such diseases will not involve comparing a "healthy" genome with a "sick" one and looking for a few key mutations. Rather it involves monitoring the genome-wide distribution of epigenetic "biomarkers" that are linked to specific variations in gene expression.

Tracking epigenetic markers in the development of cancer and other diseases is a new and highly complicated field—in part because the distribution of such markers is so highly individualized. This is why epigenetics is often considered a part of *precision medicine*, which seeks to tailor treatments to the specific combination of factors that produce disease in individual cases. These factors may involve genetic and epigenetic mechanisms, as well as such things as diet, exercise, environment, immunology, and the colonies of microbes that live in our bodies. (See Social Context: Precision Medicine for a more detailed discussion.)

We can expect researchers in the future to unravel more connections between genetics and *multifactorial* diseases, which have more than one cause. We can then hope to see new approaches to diagnosing and treating diseases that have often been mysterious and lacking effective therapies. Instead of a broad diagnostic category like "breast cancer," for example, the disease may be subdivided into many more specific categories, and each may have its own prognosis and its own therapy. Indeed, pharmaceutical companies have already begun to design drugs that are specific to particular physiological and genetic makeups. By tailoring an individual treatment to an individual version of a disease, scientists can make some drugs much more effective. They can also avoid some of the worst side effects of "one size fits all" treatments aimed at an average population of patients.

Envoi

When we better understand the interplay among genes, proteins, developmental processes, and environmental factors, we will be far closer to grasping the molecular origins of disease. Understanding this complex array of causes will also help us find effective measures for prevention, treatments, and cures. Almost all of these new strategies will depend, at some level, on the analysis of the human genome. That is the new promise of the scientific Holy Grail.

SOCIAL CONTEXT

Stem Cells: The End of the Battle?

In November 1998, research groups headed by John Gearhart of Johns Hopkins University and James Thomson of the University of Wisconsin announced that they had succeeded in isolating and culturing human embryonic stem cells.

Embryonic stem cells are undifferentiated cells produced after a fertilized egg has divided several times and developed into a hollow ball of cells called a *blastocyst*. The blastocyst—which is itself a tiny speck barely visible to the human eye—contains a small lump called the *inner-cell mass* that consists of fifteen to twenty embryonic stem cells.

As development proceeds, embryonic stem cells become specialized or *differentiated*. Responding to DNA-coded cues in combination with epigenetic factors, they turn into specialized "adult" cells. These cells go on to produce the approximately 120 different cell types that form tissues and organs such as the blood, brain, bone, and liver. Adult stem cells have been found in the bone marrow and the brain, and there is evidence that specific adult stem cells are associated with every organ system, where they act as a kind of "internal repair system" for the tissue.

Before embryonic stem cells begin to differentiate, they have the potential to become any of the specialized cells. For this reason,

they are called *pluripotent* (based on the same root as "plural"). Afterward, their fate is largely determined, and they do not go back to their previous state. When specialized heart cells divide, for example, they can produce only heart cells or cells for related tissues. They cannot be turned into neurons or liver cells. These "adult" stem cells are termed *differentiated* or *multipotent*.

Due to the flexibility and generative power of pluripotent stem cells, they have long generated hope among researchers for developing new treatments for a wide range of diseases. But starting with Gearhart and Thomson's research, the use of embryonic stem cells has also generated intense political and ethical controversy.

Stem Cells and the Law

In 1995, Congress passed the Dickey-Wicker Amendment, which prohibits use of federal funds to create human embryos for research purposes or to support research in which a human embryo is destroyed. (The amendment, which has the status of law, has been subsequently attached to appropriation bills that fund the National Institutes of Health.)

Since Thomson and Gearhart's research was privately funded, it did not violate federal law, but it did generate immediate controversy. Thomson had retrieved embryonic stem cells from "surplus" embryos produced for fertility treatments—after obtaining consent from the egg and sperm donors. Gearhart, by contrast, had cultured his embryonic stem cells using gonadal tissue samples from early aborted fetuses (a practice which few have emulated).

When Gearhart and Thomson announced their success, the question of the moral legitimacy of obtaining and using embryonic stem cells quickly became a topic of national debate.

The National Conference of Catholic Bishops and other socially conservative groups and politicians denounced the research and vehemently opposed federal funding for stem-cell research. The opposition included many traditional opponents of abortion. They argued that human embryos have the status of persons, so retrieving their stem cells, and thus killing them, would be morally wrong.

By contrast, many disease-advocacy groups, seeing the possibilities of stem-cell therapies, proposed making such research eligible for federal funds. Without such funding, they argued, progress on effective treatments for a number of devastating diseases would be seriously hampered. While private and state funds soon allowed some researchers to initiate embryonic stem cell lines, the ban on participation by NIH or any other federal-funded researchers held back progress on the basic science.

Many people, politicians included, found it hard to object to removing stem cells from embryos that had been created at reproductive clinics and then not used. Ordinarily, such embryos are discarded anyway. If so, then why not retrieve the stem cells and use them to develop treatments for diseases? Social conservatives—Roman Catholics in particular—did not find this argument persuasive. So far as they were concerned, it was already morally wrong to create embryos for the purpose of assisted reproduction. Hence, destroying them to acquire stem cells would also be wrong.

In August 2001, President Bush tried to navigate these treacherous political waters with a new policy on federal funding of research involving human embryonic stem cells. His decision allowed federally funded work on the sixty-four embryonic stem-cell lines already established, but prohibited federal funds from being used to acquire new stem cells if it involved the destruction of embryos.

The new policy met with a mixed response. It was denounced by the National Conference of Catholic Bishops as "morally unacceptable," while many researchers and patient advocates viewed the policy as placing unwarranted restrictions on essential research. Scientists were particularly concerned about limiting research to existing stem cell lines. No one could say in advance, they pointed out, exactly how many genetically different kinds of stem cells would be adequate for treating diseases, and it was not clear that all sixty-four lines were even viable or available.

Although the remaining years of the Bush administration saw some loosening of the ban on federally funded researchers working on new embryonic stem-cell lines, the mandatory red tape and duplication kept much of the progress at bay. But through a combination of private and state funds, including a $3 billion ballot measure passed by Californians in 2004, therapeutic stem-cell research gradually began to gather momentum.

Treatment Dreams

From the beginning, the identification of embryonic stem cells and the ability to culture them have been viewed as important steps in developing powerful new treatments for chronic, debilitating, and life-threatening diseases. In this respect, they may usher in a new era of treatment. *Regenerative medicine,* a collection of therapies aimed at producing new tissues and perhaps entirely new organs, holds out the promise of cures for dozens of currently untreatable conditions.

Cultures of pluripotent stem cells appear to be what biologists call *immortal* cell lines. That is, the cells can replicate for an indefinite number of generations without dying or accumulating genetic errors. This capacity reduces, but does not eliminate, the need to acquire new stem cells. Cell lines can be established and maintained to supply the needs of researchers and physicians. As we learn how to control the system of chemical messengers and receptors that regulate the development of "blank" embryonic stem cells into specialized brain, heart, liver, or pancreas cells, it may be possible to repair those organs with stem-cell therapies.

This approach may make it possible, for example, to treat Parkinson's disease by injecting stem cells into the substantia nigra in the brain to boost the production of the neurotransmitter dopamine. (The lack of dopamine produces the symptoms of the disease.) Or diabetes might be brought under control by inducing the pancreas to incorporate insulin-producing islet cells developed from stem cells.

Because pluripotent stem cells have the capacity to become cells of any type, scientists have long wondered if they could be used to produce the specialized categories of cells needed to treat currently irreversible conditions. Damaged spinal nerves that prevent patients from walking or moving their bodies might be repaired, and faulty retinas that cause blindness might be replaced with functional ones.

The study of pluripotent stem cells has already helped scientists understand more about how genes are turned on and off during the process of development. This, in turn, may eventually help us control the gene expression process at work in such diseases as cystic fibrosis and muscular dystrophy. We might also be able to treat certain forms of cancer through a better understanding of stem cell development.

An even more dramatic prospect is that stem cells might be used to grow body tissues and even whole organs for transplantation. People could be provided with bone or skin grafts, liver segments, lung lobes, or even new kidneys or hearts. The problems caused by the current shortage of transplant organs would simply disappear. (See Chapter 8 for more on this topic.)

The problem of the rejection of tissue and organ transplants is currently managed only by the use of powerful immunosuppressive drugs. Stem cells may offer several innovative means of mitigating tissue rejection. These include (1) *stem cell banks*, which could house a "library" of cell lines with different antigen properties matched to different patients; (2) *suppression of markers*, which involves growing stem cells with suppressed or disguised "markers" that provoke immune responses; and (3) *cloning* or *somatic cell nuclear transfer*. This last and most controversial option involves removing the nucleus from a donor egg, then replacing it with DNA taken from one of the patient's somatic (body) cells. The egg will thus contain DNA only from the patient's somatic cell. When the egg develops into an embryo and the stem cells are removed, they will be genetically identical to those of the individual contributing the DNA and should not trigger an immune rejection. This process, technically known as somatic cell nuclear transfer, is often called *therapeutic cloning*, in contrast to *reproductive cloning*. (For details on the moral and legal status of cloning, see Social Context: Advances in Reproductive Cloning in Chapter 4.)

Treatments with Adult Stem Cells

The therapeutic promise of pluripotent stem cells have been matched, and in some cases exceeded, by the research—and even some therapies—that use differentiated or "adult" stem cells.

Evidence from a growing number of animal studies suggests, for example, that cardiac muscle damaged by a heart attack can be effectively treated by an injection of multipotent adult stem cells. These cells can be induced to form normal heart cells, creating new tissue to replace damaged cardiac muscle. (See below for a discussion of induced pluripotent stem cells.) Some of these studies used cardiac stem cells that naturally occur in the heart. But more strikingly, some of the most successful studies used blood stem cells (derived from bone marrow and other tissue), which appeared to respond to the biochemical environment of the heart and began producing cardiac muscle cells. There have even been a few small studies on humans, in which such stem cells were injected during open-heart surgery—and appeared to boost cardiac function and the formation of new capillaries.

In January 1999, Swedish scientists identified neural stem cells. These are brain cells that have differentiated to become cavity-lining cells, yet when they divide, their progeny can differentiate into either glial (structural) cells or neurons. When the brain is injured, the cavity-lining cells begin reproducing and the neural stem cells produce glial cells that form scars. If a way could be found to induce the neural stem cells to produce more neurons at the site of the injury, more brain function might be preserved. In recent years, clinical trials have been approved in Britain and the United States to test both blood and neural stem cells as a treatment for stroke-related brain damage.

The most extensively studied stem cell treatments, however, involve the use of blood stem cells to treat diseases of the blood and immune systems. Clinical trials have been conducted using blood stem cells from donated umbilical cords to treat children with type 1 diabetes. Preliminary results suggest that an infusion of these blood stem cells may slow the loss of insulin production in these children. In 2012, Canadian regulators approved Prochymal,® manufactured by Osiris Therapeutics, as the first stem cell drug to be authorized for market use. Made from bone marrow stem cells, the drug is designed to treat a deadly inflammatory immune response to bone marrow transplants called *graft-versus-host disease* (GvHD). In early 2015, it was also in Phase III trials for treatment of Crohn's disease and was being studied for treatment of type 1 diabetes and heart disease.

Despite these successes, many researchers believe that medical use of stem cells will be limited if restricted to differentiated "adult" stem cells. They argue that embryonic cells have more potential for radically regenerative treatments. But such projects are likely to generate continued conflict over the moral status of the embryos.

Ethical Issues over Acquiring Embryos

For many who oppose abortion or believe that embryos have a special moral status, the retrieval of embryonic stem cells from human embryos can constitute a serious moral wrong. From their perspective, each fertilized egg (embryo) has the potential to develop into a human being, and that entitles it (in a strong version of the position) to be treated as a person in the moral sense. Because it is wrong to kill an innocent person, it is thus wrong to destroy a human embryo. (See the discussion of this stance in Chapter 5.)

Accordingly, such critics also object to the instrumental use of donated embryos or fetal tissue, rather than according them the dignity of full (or potential) persons. Taking embryonic stem cells from donated

IVF embryos or from an aborted fetus (as some of the earliest stem cell research did) is also seen as morally wrong. Because abortion is viewed as an immoral act, it is considered wrong to benefit from it in any way. Some also object to using human eggs and sperm to produce embryos for research, or to IVF itself, since it is seen as treating eggs and sperm as commodities with an instrumental value. The purpose of the research may be laudable, these critics say, but even so, the eggs and sperm are being put to a use that is contrary to their natural purpose, which is to play a role in reproduction.

Defenders of the use of embryonic stem cells challenge the ascription of personhood to the blastocyst, which is a hollow ball of cells smaller than the dot on an "i." They point out that embryos are constantly "sacrificed" in natural reproduction, since 75–80 percent of embryos produced by sexual intercourse fail to implant in the uterus and are expelled by women's bodies. Also, many of the embryos donated by fertility clinics for stem cell research are of poor quality and thus could not produce a pregnancy anyway—although they can produce stem cells.

Alternative Sources for Embryonic Stem Cells

Stem-cell opponents typically object more to the ways embryonic stem cells are acquired than to the ways the cells are used. Hence, if it were possible to acquire stem cells without violating moral prohibitions, some critics might drop their opposition. Following are three alternative sources of stem cells that most critics have found unobjectionable. A fourth source, induced pluripotent stem cells, will be discussed in further detail in the next section.

1. **Miscarriages.** Those who consider the destruction of an embryo to obtain stem cells immoral may (but do not

necessarily) consider it legitimate to obtain stem cells from spontaneously aborted fetuses. If no one did anything to cause the miscarriage, the stem cells cannot be seen as acquired as the result of a morally wrong action. Practically speaking, however, this means of getting stem cells is difficult, uncertain, and expensive.

2. **Parthenogenesis.** Some who oppose acquiring stem cells from embryos or aborted fetuses would find stem cells produced by a process of *parthenogenesis*, or cell growth without fertilization, morally acceptable. That is, if an unfertilized human egg could be induced by biochemical means to divide and produce stem cells, the stem cells recovered could be legitimately used. Because the unfertilized egg would lack the genetic information needed for development, it would have no special moral status.

3. **Blastomeres.** Some might find it acceptable to use stem cells if they could be obtained from fertilized eggs that are not destroyed in the process. In a technique developed in 2006 at Advanced Cell Technology, researchers removed embryonic stem cells from a two-day-old embryo without destroying it. At this stage of development, a fertilized egg comprises eight cells, or blastomeres. Researchers removed one of the blastomeres and took the stem cells from it. This blastomere was destroyed, but the other seven blastomeres retained the capacity to develop. (There is no reason to believe that a single blastomere, even if implanted, could ever develop into a fetus.) But since this process was developed through the practice of preimplantation genetic screening, it might still be objectionable to Roman Catholics and others who oppose that practice.

These three alternative proposals for obtaining embryonic stem cells have been superseded by a newer method that has already had substantial success in generating pluripotent stem cells without provoking serious moral objections.

Induced Pluripotent Stem Cells. In 2007, Shinya Yamanaka and Kazutoshi Takahashi of Kyoto University published a paper in which they identified four genes essential to restoring a somatic cell to a pluripotent state. In a process known as *cell conversion*, they used a retrovirus to insert the four genes into the DNA of mouse skin cells, and the incorporated genes then reprogrammed the skin cells into embryonic stem cells. The genes, in effect, restored the cells to their "unspecialized" pluripotent state, thereby creating an *induced pluripotent stem cell* (iPSC). Their research was widely replicated and earned Yamanaka a Nobel Prize in 2012.

Induced pluripotent stem cells, like embryonic stem cells, apparently have the capacity to develop into any of the 120 kinds of cells that form tissues and organs. Studies with converted mouse cells, for example, have shown that when they are injected into mouse embryos, they form different types of tissue that are indistinguishable from those produced by embryonic stem cells.

The possibilities of using the induced pluripotent cells pioneered by Yamanaka are currently being explored at the level of basic science and applied research. Already, iPSCs derived from human skin cells are being used widely to test drugs and to model diseases in the laboratory, including Down syndrome and polycystic kidney disease. iPSCs have also been used to synthesize blood cells and grow human "liver buds" in the laboratory that performed basic metabolizing and protein production functions. In September 2014, Japanese researchers treated a woman with macular degeneration with an implanted sheet of retinal pigment epithelium cells that had been created, via iPSCs, from her own skin cells.

Cell conversion to iPSCs can be used to create tissue that is genetically compatible with the rest of a person's cells. Thus, they can be used to repair tissues and organs without the risk of immune system rejection. Until now, the only way scientists could imagine achieving this result was through therapeutic cloning (see above).

Nevertheless, some difficulties may have to be overcome before the full promise pluripotent stem cells can be realized. One of the genes used by Yamanaka in his original work, for example, is known to cause cancerous tumors. Yamanaka later showed that he could achieve cell conversion without the gene, but concern that pluripotent cells could produce cancer still troubles some researchers. The more serious concern is that the viruses still currently used to introduce most of the "reprogramming" factors into adult cells have a risk of inducing mutations that can lead to cancer or other health problems.

Acceptance by Critics?

One obvious appeal of being able to acquire human embryonic stem cells by converting somatic cells is the possibility that researchers will no longer need to create or destroy human embryos. It does appear that the debate over the moral legitimacy of stem-cell research has significantly abated, if not wholly disappeared, since iPSCs began to be employed

"You should have a solution here that will address the moral objections that have been percolating for years," said Tadeusz

Pacholczyk of the National Catholic Bioethics Center.

Yet some observers are not so sure that the debate can be resolved so easily. They point out, first, that if researchers can produce pluripotent cells from somatic cells, then they will eventually be able to convert somatic cells into totipotent cells, which would have all the capacities of a fertilized egg. This would start the argument about potential human life all over again, and might introduce the possibility that *any* human cell could become an embryo—a disturbing possibility for many.

From this point of view, the stem-cell debate is not resolved by our new capacity to convert body cells into pluripotent cells. Rather, the debate becomes even more complicated. Meanwhile, the old issues will continue to be debated, because scientists still need to conclusively establish that stem cells produced by somatic cell conversion are exactly the same as the pluripotent cells extracted from an embryo. (Ironically, the research needed to prove the equivalence will require the destruction of embryos, and those who consider the destruction of embryos the moral equivalent of murder will argue for its abolition.)

For some, these new techniques have only complicated the moral debate. Even so, such discoveries still point in the direction of a resolution. Faced with the reality of converted pluripotent cells, those who hold that an embryo is a person may be compelled to rethink their view. They may decide that what they took as the criterion for personhood (having the developmental capacity to become a child) is not so clear a category as they assumed. They may have to look for other criteria, and it is possible that these will exclude embryos from the category of persons.

Envoi

In 2009, President Barack Obama issued an executive order instructing the NIH to draft guidelines lifting some of the Bush rules governing stem-cell research. The most important change in the regulations was to make research on thirteen new human embryonic stem-cell lines eligible for federal funding and to initiate a review of dozens more new lines.

Today, all human embryonic stem cell lines used in research come from four- to five-day-old embryos donated after IVF fertility treatments. It remains illegal to perform federally-funded research using stem cells from human embryos created solely for research purposes. (Human cloning for therapeutic purposes, the process of somatic cell nuclear transfer, also remains illegal. See Chapter 4 for more on this topic.)

Under the new rules, donors of embryos for stem-cell research must be informed that the embryos will be destroyed and that there are other ways of disposing of them. Donors must provide written consent, retain the right to change their minds, and receive no payment.

Many researchers and advocates for developing regenerative medicine were disappointed at the comparatively limited changes in federal policy, while critics of stem-cell research were quick to condemn the Obama policy. Because the new rules permit the disposal of discarded embryos, some saw them as a major step toward permitting embryos to be created and destroyed to serve the needs of research.

For now, the controversies over stem cells will continue to simmer. But advances in both iPSC and adult stem cell research have shifted the focus away from embryos and reduced their importance in medical breakthroughs. For the first time since human embryonic stem cells were identified and isolated in 1998, an end to the stem-cell wars can be imagined.

BRIEFING SESSION

The two great triumphs of nineteenth-century biology were Darwin's formulation of the theory of organic evolution and Mendel's statement of the laws of transmission genetics. One of the twentieth century's outstanding accomplishments was the analysis of the molecular structures and processes involved in genetic inheritance. All three achievements give rise to moral and social issues of considerable complexity. The theories are abstract, but the problems they generate are concrete and immediate.

Significant ethical problems have arisen from our increased knowledge of inheritance and genetic change. One class of problems concerns the use of this knowledge and its impact on individuals. We now know a great deal about the ways genetic diseases are transmitted and the sorts of anomalies that can occur in human development. We have the means to make reliable predictions about an individual's chance of developing certain diseases, and we have the medical technology to detect some disorders before birth. We are closer than ever to developing technologies that can correct or "edit" the human genetic code.

To what extent should we employ this knowledge? One possibility is that we might use it to actively detect, treat, or prevent genetic disorders. Thus, our society might recommend genetic screening and counseling to all couples before they have children and give them the option of selective abortion if fetuses show signs of debilitating genetic diseases. We might recommend that children be tested either prenatally or immediately after birth. For some prospective parents, we might suggest in vitro fertilization, followed by selection and implantation of the embryos that are free from certain disease-producing genes. Using some combination of these methods, we might be able to bring many genetic diseases under control (although we could never eliminate them) in the way we have brought many contagious diseases under control.

Making such screening and interventions mandatory might suggest an even more ambitious and controversial goal, one that involves a broader agenda with respect to human genetics. Eliminating genetic disease might become part of a broader plan for deliberately improving the entire species. Should we attempt to control human evolution by formulating policies and practices designed to alter the genetic composition of the human population? Should we make use of "gene editing" tools and recombinant DNA technology to shape the physical and mental attributes of our species? That is, shall we practice some form of eugenics?

Another class of problems has to do with the wider social and environmental consequences of genetic research and technology. Research in molecular genetics concerned with recombinant DNA has already revealed to us how the machinery of cells can be beneficially altered. We are able to make bacteria synthesize such important biological products as human insulin, and we are able to alter bacteria to serve as vaccines against diseases. In effect, recombinant DNA technology produces life-forms that have never existed before. Should biotech industries be allowed to patent these creations in the way that new inventions are patented? Or do such genetically altered organisms belong to us all?

A related question concerns the development and distribution of genetically modified organisms (GMOs). When it comes to crops and livestock, GMOs may not seem substantially different than the countless other ways humans have "modified" nature for millennia, through selective breeding of plants and animals. But they also reflect a new level of human control over this process that—while it has enormous potential for doing good—could also cause substantial harm. We have already witnessed the harm that pesticides and chemical pollution can inflict on the environment and human health.

In the next three sections, we shall focus attention on the issues raised by both the actual and potential use of genetic information and technology. Our topics are these: genetic intervention (screening, counseling, and prenatal diagnosis), eugenics, and genetic research (therapy, technology, and biohazards).

Genetic Intervention: Screening, Counseling, and Diagnosis

Our genes play a major role in making us what we are. The biological systems that encode and implement our genetic information work amazingly well to produce healthy, functional human organisms. But sometimes things go wrong, and when they do, the results can be tragic.

Over six thousand human diseases have been identified as involving genetic factors. Some of the diseases are quite rare, whereas others are relatively common. Some are invariably fatal, whereas others are comparatively minor. Some respond well to treatment, whereas others do not. The use of genetic information in predicting and diagnosing diseases has significantly increased during the last few decades. New scientific information, new medical techniques, and new social programs have all contributed to this increase.

Three approaches in particular have been adopted by the medical community as means of acquiring and making use of genetic information related to diseases: genetic screening, genetic counseling, and prenatal genetic diagnosis. Each approach has generated significant ethical and political debate, but before examining the approaches and the problems associated with them, we need to look more closely at what we mean when we call something a genetic disease.

Genetic Disease

The concept of a *genetic disease* is far from clear. Roughly speaking, a genetic disease is one in which genes or the ways in which they are expressed are causally responsible for specific biochemical, cellular, or physiological defects. Rather than rely upon this general definition, however, we can better understand genetic diagnosis if we consider some of the various roles that genes play in producing disease.

Gene Defects. In these situations, the information coded in a person's DNA is damaged or disrupted, usually due to an inherited or spontaneous mutation. (That is, a particular gene may have been lost or damaged, or a new gene added.) Consequently, when the DNA code is "read" and its instructions are followed by the body's cells, the individual may develop with impairments that correspond to these genetic "errors."

For example, a number of diseases, such as phenylketonuria (PKU), are the result of inborn errors of metabolism. (For a description of PKU, see Genetic Screening later in this Briefing Session.) Such diseases are produced by the lack of a particular enzyme necessary for ordinary metabolic functioning. The genetic coding required for the production of the enzyme is simply not present—the gene for the enzyme is missing.

A missing or defective gene may be due to a new or "spontaneous" mutation, but more often the condition has been inherited.

It has been transmitted to the offspring through the genetic material contributed by the parents. Because defective genes can be passed on in this way, the diseases they produce are themselves described as heritable. (Thus, PKU is a genetically transmissible disease.) The diseases follow regular patterns through generations, and tracing out those patterns has been one of the great accomplishments of modern biology and medicine.

Developmental Defects.   The biological development of a human being from a fertilized egg to a newborn child is an immensely complicated process. It involves an interplay between both genetic and environmental factors, and as a result there are many different ways in which the developmental process can go astray.

Mistakes that result as part of the developmental process are ordinarily called "congenital." Such defects are not in the original coding (genes) but result either from subsequent genetic damage or from improper implementation of the code. When either happens, problems can arise in the manufacture and assembly of the biological materials required for normal fetal development.

Radiation, drugs, chemicals, and nutritional deficiencies can all cause changes in the developmental process. Also, biological disease agents, such as certain viruses, may intervene. They may alter the machinery of the cells, interfere with the formation of tissues, and defeat the carefully calibrated processes of healthy human development.

Finally, factors internal to fetal development may also alter the process and lead to problems. The most common form of Down syndrome, for example, is caused by a failure of chromosomes to separate normally. The result is a child who fails to develop normally and displays physical anomalies and some degree of mental impairment. Defects occurring during the developmental

process are not themselves the results of inheritance. Consequently, they cannot be passed on to the next generation.

Genetic Carriers.   Some diseases are produced only when an individual inherits two copies of a gene (two *alleles*) for the disease, one from each parent. Parents who possess only one copy of the gene generally show none of the disease's symptoms. Sometimes these parents may have similar, but less severe, symptoms of the kind that are associated with the full-fledged disease.

In the metabolic disease PKU, for example, individuals who have inherited only one allele (i.e., who are *heterozygous*, rather than *homozygous*) may show a greater-than-normal level of phenylalanine in their blood. Such people are somewhat deficient in the enzyme required to metabolize this substance, but the level may not be high enough to cause them any damage. At the same time, they are *carriers* of a gene that, when passed on with another copy of the same gene from the other parent, can cause PKU in their offspring. (As we will see later, this is also true for carriers of the sickle-cell trait.) The individual who receives both alleles for PKU definitely has the disease, but what about the parents? The point at which a condition becomes a disease is often uncertain.

Genetic Predisposition.   It has been suggested that every disease involves a genetic component in some way or other. Even when different people are exposed to the same virus, their bodies will react differently: some will destroy the virus, while others will become infected. Genetic variations can play a significant role in these differences. For example, although AIDS researchers noted in the 1980s that some HIV-positive patients seemed especially slow to develop AIDS, it wasn't until a mutation in the gene called CCR5 was identified that a potential explanation was found.

The mutation—which alters the function of the immune system's T-cells— is present in 4 to 10 percent of people with European ancestry but is extremely rare in people of Asian and African descent.

In some cases, genes play a larger role in producing disease than in others. We have good evidence that hypertension, heart disease, various forms of cancer, and differential responses to environmental agents (such as sunlight, molds, and chemical pollutants) all run in families, and the genetic makeup of particular individuals may predispose them to specific diseases.

For example, women who carry the BRCA1 gene are more likely to develop breast cancer at an early age than others in the population. Of course, not every woman who carries the gene develops breast cancer. What distinguishes the two groups? Their diet? Possessing other genes? No one knows, and what's true for familial breast cancer holds for dozens of other diseases.

Even granting the role of genes in producing diseases, it is important to keep in mind that predispositions are not themselves diseases. At best, they can be regarded only as causal conditions that may produce disease in conjunction with other conditions, many of them unknown.

The action of genes in disease processes is even more complicated than described here. Nevertheless, our general categories are now sufficient for us to move on to some of the issues associated with the diagnosis of genetic diseases.

Genetic Screening

In 1962, Robert Guthrie of the State University of New York at Buffalo developed an automated blood test procedure to screen newborns for the disease PKU. (He was prompted to develop the test after his own child was born with PKU.) Although a diagnostic test for PKU had been available since 1934, it was time-consuming and labor-intensive. The Guthrie "neonatal heel prick" test made it practical to diagnose a large number of infants at a relatively low price.

As described above, PKU is a serious metabolic disorder. Infants affected are deficient in the enzyme phenylalanine hydroxylase. Because the enzyme is necessary to convert the amino acid phenylalanine into tyrosine as part of the normal metabolic process, a deficiency of the enzyme leads to a high concentration of phenylalanine in the blood. Without early treatment, the almost invariable result is severe mental impairment.

If the high level of phenylalanine in an infant's blood is detected very early, however, the child can be put on a diet low in that amino acid. Keeping children on the diet until they are around the age of six significantly reduces the severity of the impairment that is otherwise inescapable.

The availability of the Guthrie test and the prospect of saving newborn children from irreparable damage encouraged state legislatures to pass mandatory screening laws. Massachusetts passed the first such law in 1963, and by 1967 similar legislation had been adopted by forty-one states. All fifty states now have such laws.

The term *genetic screening* is sometimes used broadly to refer to any activity having to do with identifying or advising people with genetically conditioned diseases. We will restrict the term's application here and use it to refer only to public health programs that survey or test target populations with the aim of detecting individuals at risk of disease for genetic reasons.

The Massachusetts PKU law pointed the way to the development of other genetic screening programs. PKU was the first disease tested for, but before long others were added to the list. All fifty states now require screening for at least twenty-one of a standard panel of twenty-nine diseases. Some 96 percent of the four million babies born in the United States each year are routinely tested, often using a single drop of blood to test for as many as forty disease conditions.

Although genetic screening is relatively new as a social program, the concept is historically connected with public health measures for the detection and prevention of communicable diseases such as tuberculosis, syphilis, and HIV infection. If an individual with such a disease is identified, he will not only receive treatment, but, more importantly, he can be prevented from spreading the disease to other members of the population.

It is possible to think of diseases with a genetic basis as resembling contagious diseases. Individuals are affected and they can pass on the disease to others. Unlike infectious diseases, which spread *horizontally* through a population, genetic diseases spread *vertically* down through the generations.

To continue the analogy, public health measures similar to those that control contagious diseases can be used to help bring genetic diseases under control. When screening locates an individual with a genetic disorder, steps can be taken to ensure that she receives appropriate therapy. Furthermore, when carriers of genes that produce diseases are identified, they can be warned about their risk of having children who are genetically impaired. Thus, a limited amount of control over the spread of genetic disease can be exercised, and the suffering of at least some at-risk individuals can be reduced or eliminated. Public health experts estimate that about three thousand babies a year are born with diseases for which early intervention can save lives or prevent serious disabilities.

The justification for laws mandating genetic screening can be sought in the power and responsibility of government to protect the welfare of its citizens. Here again, the public health measures employed to control infectious disease might be looked to as a model. Although some states allow religious or philosophical exemptions, the general rule is that vaccinations are required before children can attend school, unless contraindicated by a medical condition. Except in special circumstances, we do not permit the parents of a child in school to decide whether or not the child should be vaccinated against measles, for example. (See the Case Presentation on vaccines in Chapter 1.) We believe that society, operating through its government, has a duty to protect the child and the general public. By analogy, some argue that society owes it to a child with PKU to ensure that the condition is discovered as quickly as possible so that treatment can be instituted.

Critics of screening programs, however, are not convinced that a contagious-disease model is appropriate for genetic diseases. Given the way genetic diseases are spread, only a very small part of the population can be said to suffer any risk at all. By contrast, an epidemic of smallpox may threaten millions of people. Furthermore, some genetic screening programs don't include follow-up or counseling services, so participants may receive little tangible benefit. Merely informing clients that they are the carriers of a genetic disease may do them more harm than good.

Whether the benefits of screening programs are sufficient to outweigh their liabilities remains a serious question. In particular, are screening programs so beneficial as to justify the restriction of autonomy entailed by mandatory participation? What if parents don't want to know whether their child has the genes responsible for a particular disease? Is it legitimate for the state, in the interest of protecting the child, to require parents to be informed of this genetic information?

NEONATAL SCREENING: TARGET CONDITIONS

PKU Metabolic disorder causing seizures and mental disability; 1 in 25,000 births.

MCAD Enzyme needed to convert fat to energy is missing; causes seizures, respiratory failure, cardiac arrest, and death; 1 in 15,000 newborns.

Congenital hypothyroidism Deficiency of thyroid hormone retards growth and brain development; 1 in 5,000 births.

Congenital adrenal hyperplasia Defects in the synthesis of the adrenal hormones; can alter sexual development, and in severe cases, metabolic disturbance results in death; 1 in 25,000 births.

Biotinidase deficiency Results in failure to synthesize biotin (a B vitamin), causing seizures, uncontrolled movements, deafness, and mental disabilities; 1 in 75,000 births.

Maple-syrup urine disease (branched-chain ketoaciduria) Inborn metabolic error causing mental disability and death; 1 in 180,000 births.

Galactosemia Missing enzyme needed to convert galactose sugar into glucose, causing mental disability, blindness, and death; 1 in 34,000 births.

Sickle-cell disease Disorder of the red blood cells; causes damage to vital organs, can result in heart attack and stroke, pain, ulceration, and infection; 1 in 500 births among African Americans; at least 1 in 1,400 births among Latino Americans and several other groups.

These and related issues become more pressing when considered in the context of particular kinds of screening programs. We'll discuss briefly two programs that have been both important and controversial.

PKU Screening. Screening for PKU was the first mass testing program to be mandated by state law, as is now the case in all fifty U.S. states. It is also widely considered to be a successful program, in part because early intervention in PKU typically has good outcomes, allowing infants with the disease to grow into healthy adulthood.

As noted above, PKU is a relatively rare disease. It accounts for only about 0.8 percent of mentally disabled people who are institutionalized; among all the infants screened each year in each state, only three or four cases of PKU are typically discovered. Given this relatively low incidence, critics have argued that the abrogation of autonomy required by mandatory PKU screening is not justified by the benefits.

This is particularly true, they suggest, because of some difficulties with the testing procedure itself. The level of phenylalanine in the blood may fluctuate so that not all infants with a higher-than-normal level at the time of the test actually have PKU. Such "false positives" could lead to healthy infants being harmed by the restricted PKU diet and other treatments. More refined testing is available, but it increases the cost of screening programs considerably, even if employed only when the first test is positive. From the statistical standpoint of public health, then, the cost of preventing a few cases of PKU may be much greater than allowing these cases to remain undetected and untreated. Of course, from the perspective of a parent whose child has PKU, these and other additional costs are clearly worthwhile.

Sickle Cell. Sickle-cell disease is a group of genetic disorders involving the hemoglobin in red blood cells. Because of faulty hemoglobin, the cells assume a characteristic "sickle" shape and do not transport oxygen as well as normal red cells. They are also fragile and break apart more frequently. The result is anemia, excruciating pain, and, frequently, the blocking of blood vessels by fragments of ruptured cells. Life-threatening infections can develop in tissues that have broken down due to oxygen deprivation. Associated stroke and heart disease can cause early deaths.

Sickle-cell occurs only in individuals who have inherited both alleles for the disease from their parents. (That is, the gene for the disease is *recessive*, and those who are *homozygous* for the gene are the ones who develop the disease.) People with only one allele for the disease (that is, those who are *heterozygous*) are said to have sickle-cell *trait*. Sickle-cell disease may develop in infancy, or it may manifest itself later in life, sometimes with painful and debilitating symptoms. Those with sickle-cell trait rarely show any of the more serious clinical symptoms.

In the United States, sickle-cell disease is most common among African Americans, but it is also found among those of Mediterranean, Caribbean, South Asian, and Central and South American ancestry. The trait is carried by about 7 to 9 percent of African Americans (about three million people), and the disease occurs in about 0.3 percent of the U.S. population. Many people with the disease are not severely affected and can live relatively normal lives. However, the disease may also be fatal, and at present there is no cure for it. It can be diagnosed prenatally, however.

In 1970, a relatively inexpensive and accurate test for sickle-cell hemoglobin was developed, making it possible to identify the carriers of sickle-cell trait. This technological development, combined with political activism associated with the civil rights movement, led to the passage of various state laws mandating sickle-cell screening. During 1971 and 1972, twelve states enacted sickle-cell screening legislation.

The results, however, were highly controversial. Some laws required African Americans (but not others) who applied for a marriage license to undergo sickle-cell screening. Because at the time the only way to reduce the incidence of the disease was for two carriers to avoid having children, many charged that the mandatory screening laws represented an effort to reduce the African American population—a kind of slow-motion genocide. Such fears were not entirely unreasonable, given the recent history of forced sterilization laws in the United States, many of which had been disproportionately and arbitrarily imposed on African American women. (See Chapter 10 for more on this topic.)

Medical reports that carriers of sickle-cell trait sometimes suffer pain and disability also came to serve as a thinly veiled instrument of racial discrimination. Some employers and insurance companies began to require tests of African American employees, frequently closing off job opportunities to those with sickle-cell trait.

In order to address some of these abuses, Congress passed the National Sickle-Cell Anemia Control Act in 1972. In order to qualify for federal grants under the act, states were required to make sickle-cell screening voluntary, provide genetic counseling, and take steps to protect the confidentiality of participants. The most significant impact of the act was to force states to modify their laws to bring them into conformity with the act's requirements. In response, thirty-four states with sickle-cell screening laws began to require universal screening, regardless of ancestry. The National Genetic Diseases Act, passed in 1976 and funded annually since then, provides testing and counseling for the diagnosis and treatment of a number of genetic diseases. The act further strengthens the commitment to voluntary participation and to guarantees of confidentiality.

One lesson to be learned from the early sickle-cell screening programs is that genetic information can be used in ways that are harmful to the interests of individuals. Furthermore, such information can be used to reinforce patterns of systematic discrimination.

In April 1993, an expert panel assembled by the Agency for Health Care and Policy recommended that all newborns, regardless of race, be screened for sickle cell. In making its recommendations, the panel stressed that sickle cell is not uniquely a disease of African Americans and that people of non-African origin are also at risk. Targeted screening of high-risk groups is not adequate to identify infants with sickle-cell disease, the panel concluded, because ancestry information is often inaccurate or subject to privacy concerns. Targeted screening, according to one study, may miss as many as 20 percent of cases.

One advantage of universal screening that the panel did not mention is that it permits individuals needing treatment to be identified without stigmatization. The broader problem, however, of certain diseases or traits giving rise to social stigma—often for arbitrary or prejudiced reasons—is not a matter that can be resolved by an expert panel. It is something that must be addressed by law, social policy, and public education.

Genetic Counseling

Many genetic diseases are passed down to offspring following a clear and predictable pattern of inheritance. Conditions such as PKU, sickle cell, and Tay-Sachs follow the well-established laws of Mendelian genetic inheritance. Given relevant information, it is thus often possible to determine how likely it is that a particular couple will have a child with a certain disease.

Suppose, for example, an African American couple is concerned about the possibility of having a child with sickle-cell disease. They can seek testing to discover whether either or both of them are carriers of sickle-cell trait. As noted above, sickle-cell disease occurs only when two recessive alleles are present—one inherited from the mother, one from the father. If only one of the parents is a carrier of the trait, any resulting child will be heterozygous for the s (sickle cell) trait and will not develop the disease. If both

parents are carriers of the trait, however, the chances are one in four that their child will have sickle-cell disease. (This is determined simply by considering which combinations of the two genes belonging to each parent will produce a combination that is homozygous recessive. The combination of Ss and Ss will produce ss in only 25 percent of the possible cases.)

Such information can help potential parents assess the disease risks their children might face. But, as the case of sickle-cell disease illustrates, it is often difficult for individuals to decide how to use such information.

Is a 25 percent risk of having a child with sickle-cell disease sufficiently high that parents ought to adopt, seek a sperm or egg donor, or forego having children? If the parents are opposed to abortion, the questions raised by these odds become especially crucial. Answering them is made more difficult by the fact that sickle-cell disease varies greatly in severity. A child with the disease may be reasonably healthy, or doomed to a short life filled with suffering. No one can say in advance of the child's birth which possibility is more likely.

If the parents are not opposed to abortion, is a 25 percent risk high enough to warrant prenatal testing for the disease? Alternatively, the parents could avoid making a selective abortion decision by relying on artificial insemination so the embryos could be screened before one is implanted. This option would be expensive, however, and probably not covered by insurance.

The question of whether or not to have a child when serious health risks are involved is a complicated personal decision, one that no one else can make for a parent. A counselor may provide information about disease risk, and—just as important—about medical therapies that are available for children born with genetic diseases. In the case of diseases for which prenatal diagnosis is possible, having the option of selective abortion may reassure some prospective parents. Here, too, the object of counseling is to help clients get accurate information that is relevant to their needs and values.

Prenatal Genetic Diagnosis

A variety of technological developments make it possible to secure increasingly detailed information about a developing embryo or fetus while it is still in the uterus. Ultrasound, radiography, and fiber optics allow examination of soft-tissue and skeletal development. Anatomical abnormalities can be detected early enough to permit an abortion to be safely performed if that is the decision of the pregnant patient.

Amniocentesis and CVS. The most common methods of prenatal diagnosis are still amniocentesis and chorionic villus sampling (CVS), which involve direct cell studies. In *amniocentesis*, the *amnion* (the membrane surrounding the fetus) is punctured with a needle and some of the amniotic fluid is removed for study. The procedure cannot be safely and effectively performed until fourteen to sixteen weeks into a pregnancy. Until that time, there is an insufficient quantity of amniotic fluid. The risk to the woman and to the fetus from the procedure is relatively small, usually less than 1 percent. (The risk that the procedure will result in a miscarriage is about one in two hundred.) However, a 1998 study showed that if amniocentesis is performed early, eleven to twelve weeks after conception, it can increase the risk of childhood foot deformities or miscarriage.

Chorionic villus sampling (CVS) involves retrieving hairlike villi cells from the developing placenta. The advantage of the test is that it can be employed six to ten weeks after conception. Although the procedure is as safe as amniocentesis, a 1994 study by the Centers for Disease Control found that

infants whose mothers had undergone CVS from 1988 to 1992 had a slightly elevated (0.03%–0.1%) risk of missing or undeveloped fingers or toes. A later study questioned this finding and found no reason to believe that the risk of fetal damage is greater than normal.

Amniocentesis came into wide use only in the early 1960s. At first, it was mostly restricted to testing pregnancies with a risk of Rh incompatibility. When the mother's body lacks a group of blood proteins called the Rh (or Rhesus) factor, and the fetus does have such proteins, the immune system of the mother may produce antibodies against the fetus. The result for the fetus may be anemia, brain damage, and even death, and amniocentesis can help predict this problem.

But it was soon realized that additional information about the fetus could be gained from analysis of the amniotic fluid and the fetal cells present in it. The fluid can be chemically assayed, and the cells can be grown in cultures for study. DNA analysis can show whether there are any known abnormalities that are likely to cause serious physical or mental disorders. Some metabolic disorders (such as Tay-Sachs disease) can be detected by chemical analysis of the amniotic fluid. Other genetic conditions, however, such as PKU and muscular dystrophy, require an analysis of genetic material. Finally, because of the chromosomal differences between males and females, it is impossible to examine fetal cells without also discovering the sex of the embryo or fetus—information which, controversially, is sometimes used for sex-selective abortions.

Procedures such as amniocentesis and CVS do have some associated risks. Accordingly, prenatal genetic diagnosis is not regarded as a routine step to be taken in every pregnancy. There must usually be some indication that the fetus is at risk from a genetic or developmental disorder. One common indication is the age of the mother;

Down syndrome, for example, is much more likely to occur in fetuses conceived by women over the age of thirty-five.

Noninvasive Prenatal Testing.

Relatively new tests for Down syndrome and other chromosomal abnormalities fall into the category of *noninvasive prenatal testing* (NIPT). These increasingly accurate tests analyze fetal DNA circulating in a blood sample from the pregnant woman to determine if it carries risk of Down syndrome, trisomy 13 or 18, and sex chromosome anomalies such as Turner syndrome. They can also identify sex and Rhesus blood type.

Typically, a positive NIPT test will prompt a physician to recommend amniocentesis or CVS to confirm the result. NIPT techniques, such as the cell-free DNA blood test, pose no risk for the woman or the fetus and can be performed as early as ten weeks into a pregnancy. Other blood tests, such as those for estriol and alpha-fetoprotein (AFP), can also provide an early diagnosis for Down syndrome, as well as for neural tube disorders such as spina bifida or anencephaly.

Familial Screening.

As discussed above, familial genetic screening and counseling can also provide an indication of the need to perform amniocentesis. For example, Tay-Sachs disease is a metabolic disorder that occurs ten times more frequently among people with central and eastern European Jewish (Ashkenazi) ancestry than it does in the general population. The disease is invariably fatal and follows a sad course, by which an apparently normal child progressively develops blindness and brain damage, then dies at an early age. Carriers of the Tay-Sachs gene can be identified by a blood test, and couples who are both carriers of the trait run a 25 percent risk of having a child with the disease. In such a case, there might be a good reason to perform amniocentesis.

When Is a Test Justified?

Our ability to test for the presence of certain genes can give rise to cases that some people find troubling. Suppose, for example, a woman with a family history of breast and ovarian cancer wants to know whether the fetus she is carrying has the BRCA1 gene. If the gene is present, she plans to have an abortion, then attempt to get pregnant again.

Chances are good that no clinic or testing center would agree to test the fetus for the BRCA1 gene. After all, its presence only increases the probability that a woman will develop breast and ovarian cancer. Unlike, say, the gene for Huntington's disease, the BRCA1 gene doesn't inevitably produce the disease. Hence, a testing center would be likely to reject the woman's request, on the grounds that it is not in the business of helping parents create "perfect" babies.

Yet the woman, not the center, is the one who will have responsibility for her child. Hence, if she wants to have a child who, so far as can be determined by the tests available, is free from the threat of disease, shouldn't she be allowed to pursue that aim? What's so wrong about trying to have a baby lacking the gene predisposing her to two forms of cancer?

Another controversy has developed as pregnant women and couples younger than thirty-five, with no particular risk factors in their background, have increasingly sought prenatal screening. These clients often argue that even though their risk of having a child with a detectable genetic abnormality is small, the financial and emotional consequences of raising an impaired child are so serious that they should be allowed to take advantage of the technology available to minimize even slight risk.

Opponents of this view point out that the risk of a miscarriage from a diagnostic procedure can be as high as 1 in 200, while the risk of a woman below the age of forty having an impaired child is about 1 in 192.

Hence, the chance of losing a healthy pregnancy to miscarriage is almost as great as the chance of having an impaired child. Further, amniocentesis can cost from $1,000 to $2,500 to perform, and the money spent on such screening procedures contributes to the overall rise in health care costs.

Such replies are not convincing to those advocating wider access to prenatal testing. Some see the issue as one of women's right to make choices affecting their bodies and lives. For many, the distress caused by a miscarriage seems relatively minor compared to the lifelong burdens of caring for a disabled child. Most ethicists believe, in any event, that women and their co-parents have to make their own assessments about what risks and burdens they are willing to bear. Such decisions should certainly not be made unilaterally by physicians, hospitals, and health-policy planners.

Advocates of access to prenatal testing argue that when compared to the lifetime costs of caring for an impaired child, the money that individuals and society spend on testing is insignificant. It costs about $100,000 to support a Down syndrome child during just the first year of life, and expenditures in the millions may be required to meet the needs of a severely impaired person over a lifetime.

Some parents are also reassured by the added sense of control that prenatal screening can provide. Such tests can offer information that will put them in a position to make a decision about abortion, depending on the results; it can also offer peace of mind and the knowledge that a pregnancy is proceeding with only a small likelihood of serious anomalies. The general perspective in favor of such testing is that the technology to secure relevant information exists and should be available to anyone who wants to make use of it. It thus should not be paternalistically controlled physicians who will not have to live with the choices and outcomes involved.

Selective Abortion. In most cases in which prenatal diagnosis indicates that a fetus suffers from a genetic disorder or developmental defect, the only means of avoiding the birth of an impaired child is abortion. Because those who go through prenatal screening are typically focused on having a child, abortion performed under such circumstances is called *selective*. That is, the woman decides to have an abortion to avoid producing a child with birth impairments, not just to terminate a pregnancy.

Those who oppose abortion in principle (see Chapter 5) also generally oppose selective abortion. In the view of some, the fact that a child will be born with severe impairment is in no way a justification for terminating the development of the fetus.

Those who believe in the moral legitimacy of abortion typically approve of selective abortion as an acceptable way to reduce suffering. In their view, it is better that the potential person—the fetus—not become an actual person, afflicted with pain, disease, and disability.

The choice between having an abortion or giving birth to an impaired child may also be avoided by employing ova, sperm, or embryo screening. But this entails using the techniques of assisted reproduction (see Chapter 4), and the cost in time, frustration, and money can be considerable.

More recently, another way to avoid abortion has opened up as the techniques of fetal surgery have been employed to correct at least some abnormal physical conditions. Repairs to the heart, the insertion of shunts to drain off excess brain fluids, and the placement of tubes to inflate collapsed lungs are some of the intrauterine surgical procedures now being performed. As new surgical techniques for the treatment of fetuses are perfected and extended, the reliance on abortion to avoid the birth of impaired children may decline to some degree. Of course, surgery cannot provide a remedy for a large number of hereditary disorders. For example, it can do nothing for a child with Tay-Sachs, sickle cell, cystic fibrosis, muscular dystrophy, or PKU.

Helplessness in this regard is balanced by the hope that in future years pharmaceutical and biochemical therapies will be able to compensate for genetic conditions that involve missing enzymes or proteins. There are also some indications that traditional gene therapy or "gene editing" tools such as CRISPR-Cas9 will make it possible to insert the proper gene for manufacturing a needed biochemical into the DNA of fetal cells. (See Case Presentation: The CRISPR Revolution.)

Embryo Selection. Potential parents who learn that they are carriers of genes responsible for lethal or life-threatening diseases may decide to use the techniques of assisted reproduction to avoid having a child afflicted with the disease. Their embryos, produced by in vitro fertilization, can be genetically screened, and then only those free of disease-causing genes can be transferred to the woman's uterus. (See Chapter 4 for a fuller discussion.)

Embryo screening allows couples to manage the risk their genetic heritage poses for their offspring. Those carrying the Tay-Sachs gene or the gene responsible for cystic fibrosis, for example, can be sure they do not have children with these diseases. It also makes selective abortion unnecessary. (However, some consider destroying embryos, for whatever reason, the moral equivalent of abortion.)

Ethical Difficulties with Genetic Intervention

Genetic screening, counseling, prenatal diagnosis, and embryo selection represent positive developments for those who see value in exercising rational control over the accidents of birth and disease. They see

preventing the births of children who would suffer from crippling impairments as one of the triumphs of contemporary medicine. They are also drawn to the possibility of wholly eliminating some genetic diseases through counseling and reproductive control. For example, if people who are carriers of diseases caused by a dominant gene (such as Huntington's) produced no children who carry the gene, the disease would soon disappear entirely. The gene causing the disease would simply not be passed on to the next generation.

A vision of a world without the suffering caused by genetic defects is a primary motivation for those who strongly advocate for genetic intervention programs. It is difficult to reject this perspective out of hand, given the devastating and excruciating effects of some genetic conditions. Yet whether or not one shares this view and is prepared to use it as a basis for social action, serious ethical questions about genetic intervention must be faced.

We've already mentioned some of the issues in connection with particular programs and procedures. We can now add some more general questions to that list. The moral issues connected with genetic intervention are woven into a complicated fabric of personal and social life; here we will merely examine a few key questions:

Is there a right to have children who are likely to be impaired? Suppose a woman is informed, after an alpha-fetoprotein (AFP) test and amniocentesis, that the child she's carrying will be born with a severe (and often fatal) neural tube defect such as open spina bifida or anencephaly. Does she have the right to refuse an abortion and have the child anyway?

Those opposed to all abortion on the grounds of natural law would favor the woman's having the child. By contrast, a utilitarian might argue that the decision would be wrong. The amount of suffering the potential child might be expected to undergo outweighs any parental loss. For different reasons, a Kantian might endorse this same point of view. Even assuming that the fetus is a person, a Kantian might argue that we are obliged to prevent its suffering.

Suppose we decide that the woman does have a right to have a child who is almost certain to be severely impaired. If so, then is society obligated to bear the expense of caring for the child? On the natural law view, the answer is almost certainly yes. The child, impaired or not, is a person and, as such, is entitled to the support and protection of society.

If we agree that the impaired child is a person, he or she is also a person disadvantaged in ways that are "arbitrary from a moral point of view." Thus, an argument based on Rawls's principles of justice might also support the view that the child is entitled to social support.

Is society justified in requiring that people submit to genetic screening, counseling, or prenatal diagnosis? Children born with genetic diseases and defects typically require the expenditure of large amounts of public funds. The question arises whether society is justified in mitigating these costs by recommending or requiring genetic screening. (A related question is whether society ought to make available genetic testing to all who wish it, regardless of their ability to pay.) Such mandatory diagnosis need not imply any recommendation of abortion or abstention from bearing children.

On utilitarian grounds, it might be argued that society has a legitimate interest in seeing to it that, no matter what people ultimately decide, they should at least have information about the likelihood that they will produce an impaired child.

If mandatory screening is adopted, then a number of specific practical and moral questions become relevant. For example, who should be screened? It is impractical and unnecessary to screen everyone. For example, need we screen schoolchildren or prisoners, those who are sterile, or those past the age of childbearing?

This is closely connected with a second question: What should people be screened for? Should everyone be screened for Tay-Sachs disease, even though the Ashkenazi Jewish population is most at risk? Should everyone be screened for the cystic-fibrosis gene, even though the disease occurs primarily among those of European ancestry?

Those who accept the contagious-disease model for widespread genetic screening frequently defend it on the utilitarian grounds that screening promotes the general social welfare. However, one might argue that screening can also be justified on deontological grounds. It could be claimed that we owe it to developing fetuses, regarded as persons, to see to it they receive the opportunity for the most effective treatment. For example, it might be said that we have an obligation to provide a child with PKU the immediate therapy required to save him or her from severe mental disability. The restriction of the autonomy involved in requiring screening might be regarded as justified by this obligation. If screening is voluntary, the welfare of the child is made to depend on ignorance and accident.

Do patients have a right to be informed of all of the results of a genetic test? Ethical theories based on respect for the autonomy of the individual (such as Kant's and Ross's) strongly suggest that patients are entitled to know all that has been learned from their genetic screening.

But what if, in addition to a negative result for serious impairments, the test reveals that a fetus carries risks for a minor genetically transmissible condition? Is the physician obligated to disclose all these details when she suspects it will merely fuel the parents' quest for a "perfect" baby through selective abortion or embryo selection? Or are such suspicions and concerns simply none of the physician's business?

Similarly, we might ask if the physician is obligated to disclose the sex of the fetus or embryo, if it is revealed through genetic screening. Are prospective parents entitled to this information? Are physicians obliged to provide it if the parents plan to use it to choose against females or males through embryo selection or selective abortion? If a genetic basis of sexual orientation were discovered and available through prenatal screening, would physicians also be obliged to disclose this information?

It might be argued on both utilitarian and deontological grounds that the sex of the fetus simply isn't relevant to the genetic health of the fetus or the parents. Accordingly, the physician is under no obligation to reveal such information. Indeed, the physician might be under an obligation *not* to reveal a fetus's sex, to avoid its termination for trivial reasons. But, again, is this really a decision for the physician to make?

Should public funds be used to pay for genetic tests when an individual is unable to pay? This is a question that holders of various ethical theories may not be prepared to answer in a simple yes-or-no fashion, and may depend on other moral commitments. Those who oppose abortion on natural law grounds might limit provision of public funds to genetic testing and counseling. That is, they might favor providing prospective parents with information they might use to refrain from having children. Yet other opponents of abortion might oppose spending any public money on tests that might encourage the use of abortion to prevent the birth of an impaired child.

Proponents of Rawlsian justice and utilitarianism might support the use of public funds for genetic testing as part of a more general egalitarian health care system. Whether and how much genetic testing programs are to be funded would then depend on judgments about their anticipated value in comparison with other health care initiatives.

A number of ethical and social dilemmas spring from the fact that while federal funds may be employed to pay for genetic screening and testing, they cannot legally be used to pay for abortions. Consequently, it is possible for a low-income woman to discover she is carrying a fetus with a serious genetic disease, opt to have an abortion, yet be prevented from doing so by her poverty.

Issues about the confidentiality of test results, informed consent, the use of genetic testing to gather epidemiological information, and a variety of other matters might be mentioned here in connection with genetic intervention. (Confidentiality issues, for example, become particularly tricky when genetic information may be relevant to multiple members of a family.) The questions that have been raised here are sufficient to indicate that the difficulties presented by genetic intervention are at least as numerous as the benefits it promises.

Eugenics

Like other organisms, we are the products of millions of years of evolutionary development. This process has taken place through the operation of natural selection on randomly produced genetic mutations. Individual organisms are successful in an evolutionary sense when they contribute a number of genes to the gene pool of their species that is proportionately greater than the number contributed by others.

Most often, this means that the evolutionarily successful individuals are those with the largest number of offspring. These are the individuals favored by natural selection. That is, they possess the genes for certain properties that are favored by existing environmental factors. (This favoring of properties is natural selection.) In subsequent generations, the genes of "favored" individuals will thus occur with greater frequency than the genes of others. If the same environmental factors continue to operate, these genes will spread through the entire population.

With the development of agriculture, human beings began to protect themselves from the brute forces of natural selection and to change their relationship to their environment. This change was extended by the development of tools and medicine, which further slowed and changed the course of human evolution.

It was not until Darwin, however, and the biologists who came after him, that humans arrived at a sound understanding of the evolutionary processes and the mechanisms that shaped them. This understanding puts us in a position to deliberately and systematically intervene in human evolution. As the evolutionary biologist Theodosius Dobzhansky expressed the point: "Evolution need no longer be a destiny imposed from without; it may conceivably be controlled by man, in accordance with his wisdom and values."

Those who advocate eugenics accept exactly this point of view. They favor social policies and practices that, over time, offer the best possibility of increasing the number of genes in the human population responsible for producing or improving intelligence, morality, creativity, beauty, strength, and other valued traits.

The aim of increasing the number of favorable genes in the human population is called *positive eugenics*. By contrast, *negative eugenics* aims at decreasing the number of undesirable or harmful genes. Those who advocate negative eugenics are most interested in eliminating or reducing from the population genes responsible for various kinds of genetic diseases.

Both positive and negative eugenics require instituting or extending existing controls over human reproduction. Several kinds of policies and procedures have been advocated, and we will discuss a few of the possibilities.

Negative and Positive Eugenics

The preceding discussion of genetic screening, counseling, prenatal genetic diagnosis, and embryo selection has already explored some of our current capacity for predicting and diagnosing genetic diseases. As we have seen, given information about the genetic makeup and background of potential parents, many genetic diseases can be predicted with a fairly high degree of accuracy. Additionally, the presence of specific disease-causing genes can be determined by genetic analysis of DNA. This is true of such diseases as PKU, sickle-cell anemia, hemophilia, Huntington's disease, Tay-Sachs, and muscular dystrophy.

When genetic information is not adequate for reliable disease prediction, information about the developing fetus can often be obtained by employing one of several procedures of prenatal diagnosis. These procedures may provide information about active disease states and developmental defects that are not reflected in genetic testing. Thus, in addition to predicting the genetic disorders named previously, prenatal tests can be performed to identify such developmental defects as neural tube anomalies and Down syndrome. Other tests for genetic and developmental problems can be performed on ova, sperm, and embryos.

A proponent of negative eugenics might advocate that a screening process be encouraged or required by law for all (or some) currently detectable genetic diseases and developmental disorders. When the probability of disease or impairment is high (however that is defined), the potential parents might be encouraged to adopt or seek reproductive alternatives such as egg or sperm donation. Indeed, the law might even require that such a couple either abstain from having children or rely on embryo selection. If those carrying the genes for certain genetic diseases could be prevented from passing those genes on to their offspring, the incidence of the diseases would decrease over time. In cases when the disease is the result of a dominant gene (as it is in Huntington's disease), the disease would eventually disappear. (It could appear again with new mutations, however.)

When the disease is of the sort that can be detected only after a child is conceived, selective abortion might be encouraged if the results of a prenatal diagnosis show that the developing fetus has a heritable disease. Alternatively, at-risk couples might be encouraged to seek such alternatives as artificial insemination and embryo testing and transfer.

Short of mandatory laws, a variety of social policies might be instituted to make selective abortion or embryo selection more attractive options. (For example, the cost of a selective abortion might be subsidized or the costs of embryo selection might be covered under a federal program.) Eugenic advocates point out that discarding an embryo or aborting a fetus found to have a transmissible genetic disease not only prevents the birth of an impaired infant, but also eliminates potential carriers of disease in subsequent generations. In this way, the number of disease-causing genes in the population would be proportionately reduced.

Of course, no state or federal law currently penalizes couples for passing on genetic risks to their offspring or directly encourages them to avoid doing so. Yet

there are some signs of increased genetic regulation. Screening newborns for genetic conditions that respond well to early treatment is established medical practice. And state-sponsored genetic screening is frequently offered for free to encourage people to seek information about particular diseases.

At present, adult genetic testing and counseling are voluntary services. They aim to provide information and then leave reproductive decisions up to the individuals concerned. Most often, they are directed toward the immediate goal of decreasing the number of children suffering from birth defects and genetic diseases. Yet genetic testing and counseling might also be viewed as an instrument of negative eugenics. To the extent that they indirectly discourage the birth of children carrying deleterious genes, they also discourage the spread of those genes in the human population.

Genetic testing and genetic counseling programs might also be used to promote positive eugenics. Individuals possessing genes for traits society values might be encouraged to have large numbers of children. In this way, the relative frequency of genes for those traits would increase in the general population.

No programs of positive eugenics currently operate in the United States. It is not difficult to imagine, however, how a variety of social and economic incentives (such as tax breaks) might be introduced as part of a plan to promote the spread of certain genes.

Germ Cell Selection and Engineering

In recent decades, developments in reproductive technology have opened up biomedical options once considered the stuff of science fiction. Artificial insemination and in-vitro fertilization (IVF) using donated and frozen sperm has become common-place. So, too, has the use of donor eggs and embryos. While most of these embryos are "backups" produced in the IVF process, others are produced in infertility clinics by combining gametes from commercial sperm and ova banks. The developing embryos can be divided into several genetically identical embryos and implanted in surrogates or donors. We may also already the capacity to clone a human being from a single body cell. (See Chapter 4 for detailed discussion of all these topics.)

Those wishing to have a child now have the option of selecting donor eggs or sperm from online catalogs of individuals with traits they consider desirable. Alternatively, they may select a frozen embryo based on descriptions of the donors who produced it.

At present, we clearly have the ability to practice both negative and positive eugenics on an individual and societal basis. If we wished, we could encourage some individuals to avoid having their own biological children and, instead, make use of the "superior" sperm, ova, and embryos currently offered at sperm banks and infertility centers. In this way, we could increase the number of genes for desirable traits in the population.

Ethical Difficulties with Eugenics

Critics have been quick to point out that many of the proposals mentioned above suffer from serious drawbacks. First, on a practical level, negative eugenics is not likely to effect much of a change in the species as a whole. Most hereditary diseases are genetically recessive and so occur only when both parents possess the same defective gene. Even though a particular couple might be counseled (or required) not to have children, the gene will still be widespread in the population.

For a similar reason, sterilization and even embryo selection would have few long-range effects.

Critics point out that on average, everyone carries recessive genes for at least five genetic defects or diseases. Genetic counseling and the use of assisted reproduction techniques may help individuals, but they are unlikely to further the broad societal goals of negative eugenics.

Positive eugenics involves even greater difficulties. It is difficult to imagine that citizens in our pluralistic society would agree on what traits we would like to see increased in the human species. But even if we could agree, it is not clear that we would be able to increase these traits in the general population.

For one thing, we have little understanding of the genetic basis of traits such as "intelligence," "honesty," "creativity," "beauty," and so on. It is clear that they are not the result of single genes. Instead, they appear to be the result of a complicated interplay among genetic endowments and social and environmental factors. Consequently, the task of increasing the frequency of such traits is quite different from that of, say, increasing the frequency of shorthorn cattle. Furthermore, desirable traits may be accompanied by less desirable ones, and we may not be able to increase the first without also increasing the second.

Quite apart from these practical problems, eugenics also raises a host of ethical questions. Have we indeed become the "business manager of evolution," as the eugenicist Julian Huxley once claimed? If so, do we have a responsibility to future generations to "improve" the human race? Would this responsibility justify requiring genetic screening and testing? Would it justify establishing a program of positive eugenics?

Affirmative answers to these questions may generate conflicts with values such as individual dignity and self-determination.

They also raise serious questions about pluralism and social justice. Even a negative genetics program would elicit serious objections from many who see at least some genetically influenced conditions (such as Down syndrome, hereditary deafness, and autism) as contributing to a valuable diversity of human lives and perspectives. Many contemporary theories of identity and care would also question aggressive campaigns to eliminate certain forms of disability, rather than trying to help disabled individuals participate in civic life with dignity and autonomy.

Of the traditional ethical theories we have discussed, it seems likely that only utilitarianism might be construed as favoring a program of positive eugenics. The possibility of increasing the frequency of desirable traits in the human species might, in terms of the principle of utility, justify placing restrictions on reproduction. Yet the goal of an improved society or human race might be regarded as too distant and uncertain to warrant the imposition of restrictions that would increase the current sum of human unhappiness.

As far as negative eugenics is concerned, the principle of utility could be appealed to in order to justify social policies that would discourage or prohibit potential parents from passing on genes for serious diseases. The remote aim of improving the human population might be less relevant here than the more immediate goal of preventing the pain and suffering experienced by severely impaired children and their families.

The natural law doctrines of Roman Catholicism forbid abortion, sterilization, and embryo selection. Thus, these means of practicing negative eugenics are ruled out. Further, the view that reproduction is the natural purpose of sexual capacities would seem, at least prima facie, to rule out negative eugenics as a deliberate policy. It could be argued, however, that voluntary abstinence from sexual intercourse or some other acceptable form of birth control would be a legitimate means of practicing negative eugenics.

Ross's prima facie duty of causing no harm might be invoked to justify negative eugenics. If there is good reason to believe a child is going to live a life of genetically-induced suffering, we might have a duty to help reduce the chance of that child being born. Although Rawls's theory might be seen to permit some form of negative eugenics as a means of benefiting those worst off in society, his emphasis on "free and equal" citizens would strongly limit the kinds of restrictions that negative eugenics could place on reproduction. Similarly, Kantian ethics would be likely to view regulated conception or forced sterilization as serious violations of the dignity and autonomy of individuals. Nevertheless, programs of genetic screening and counseling might be considered to be legitimate on Kantian grounds, since rational moral agents require accurate information on which to base their reproductive decisions.

Genetic Research, Therapy, and Technology

By replacing natural selection with an artificial selection directly under our control, we can, over time, alter the genetic composition of populations of organisms. Such changes have been achieved for thousands of years by animal and plant breeders, and our improved understanding of genetics allows breeding programs to proceed with greater efficacy and accuracy. Yet such genetic modifications take a relatively long time to achieve. New technologies of molecular genetics offer the prospect of immediate and lasting genetic change. For decades, such technology has been applied to bacteria, plants, and animals, and it is increasingly being applied to humans.

The Double Helix

The information required for genetic inheritance is coded in the two intertwined strands of DNA (deoxyribonucleic acid) found in plant and animal cells—the famous double helix. The strands of DNA are made up of four kinds of chemical units called nucleotides, and the genetic "code" is determined by the particular sequence of nucleotides. Three nucleotides in sequence form a triplet *codon*. Each codon directs the synthesis of a particular amino acid and determines the place it will occupy in making up a protein molecule. Since virtually all properties of organisms (enzymes, organs, eye color, and so on) depend on proteins, the processes directed by DNA are fundamental to the growth of living organisms.

Alterations in the nucleotide sequence of DNA occur naturally as mutations—random changes introduced as "copying errors" when DNA replicates (reproduces) itself. These alterations result in changes in the properties of organisms, because the properties are under the control of DNA. Much current research in molecular genetics is directed toward bringing about desired changes by finding different ways to manipulate the nucleotide sequences in DNA.

Recombinant DNA

The first major steps toward altering DNA nucleotides involved the development of techniques for "recombining" DNA from different sources. Recombinant DNA molecules are sometimes called *chimeric* because they frequently combine material from two different species, like the *chimera* of mythology.

The recombinant process typically begins by taking proteins known as restriction enzymes from bacteria and mixing them with DNA that has been removed from the cells of a particular organism. These enzymes cut open the DNA strands at particular nucleotide locations. DNA nucleotide sequences from another source can then be added, and some of these will attach to the cut ends. Thus, DNA from two distinct sources can be recombined to form a single molecule. This recombinant DNA can then be made to enter a host cell.

The organism most widely employed in this process is the one-celled bacterium *E. coli*, which inhabits the human intestine by the billions. In addition to the DNA in its nucleus, *E. coli* has small circular strands of DNA known as *plasmids*. The plasmid DNA can be recombined with DNA from an outside source and returned to the cell. When the plasmid replicates, it will make copies of both the original nucleotides and the added segments. Thus, a strain of bacteria can be produced that will make limitless copies of the foreign DNA.

This complicated feat of bioengineering has had a profound effect on basic research, agriculture, and industry. Over the past forty years, it has led to a better understanding of the molecular processes involved in such diseases as cancer, diabetes, and hemophilia. It has led to the development of new breeds of plants able to utilize nitrogen from the air and requiring less fertilizer and pesticides. It has helped researchers create bacterial "superbugs" capable of breaking down oil, toxic chemicals, and other environmental pollutants. And it has been used in industry to create stronger paper, food thickeners, and petrochemical substitutes.

But the most immediate benefit of recombinant DNA technology is that it has allowed researchers to create chemical "factories" from bacteria, to produce biological materials of medical importance. These include:

- *Recombinant human growth hormone.* A number of conditions, including hypopituitary dwarfism, are caused by a deficiency in growth hormone. The hormone itself consists of molecules too large and structurally complex to synthesize in the laboratory, but as early as 1979 researchers employed recombinant DNA technology to induce bacteria to produce the hormone. It is now available in quantities large enough to be used as a therapy.

- *Recombinant human insulin.* Modified bacteria now produce human insulin in quantities large enough to meet the need of most diabetics, many of whom are allergic to the swine or bovine insulin that was used in the past.

- *Recombinant blood clotting factor VIII.* Genetically engineered clotting factor has revolutionized the treatment of hemophilia, which used to rely on large quantities of donated blood, putting patients at risk for HIV and hepatitis B and C.

- *Recombinant vaccines.* Genetically engineered bacteria have been used to produce a vaccine against hepatitis B and against a strain of genital herpes.

- *Recombinant cancer treatments.* In 1985, the Cetus Corporation was awarded the first patent for an altered form of the protein interleukin-2. This protein activates the immune system and is used in the treatment of some cancers. It occurs naturally but in very small amounts; thus, it wasn't possible to use it therapeutically until it was produced in quantity by genetically altered bacteria.

- *Recombinant heart medicine.* Substances occurring in the human body in trace amounts can serve as powerful drugs when produced in large quantities through recombinant engineering. For example, tissue plasminogen activator (TPA), which is naturally found in blood vessels, can be synthesized and used to treat blood clots and heart attacks.

- *Recombinant animal models.* In 1997, researchers genetically engineered mice to serve as an animal model for sickle-cell disease, by combining mouse DNA with human genes for the defective hemoglobin that causes the disease. In subsequent years genetically modified animals have modeled cancers, AIDS, Alzheimer's, and many other conditions, accelerating the testing of new drugs and treatments.

Gene Therapy and Gene Editing

Rapid advances in genetic knowledge over the past four decades has led to the use of recombinant DNA and other genetic tools in a range of medical treatments. Therapies in which a missing or nonfunctioning gene is inserted into a patient's cells has been employed to treat debilitating diseases such as ADA deficiency. Genetically altered cells have been used to treat conditions such as non-healing leg ulcers and coronary artery blockages. (See Case Presentation: Gene Therapy for more details.)

In the past decade, a new set of technologies has been developed that directly insert, replace, or remove DNA from the human genome using "molecular scissors" to create double-strand breaks at specific locations in the double helix. These *genome-editing* tools include zinc finger nucleases (ZFNs) and transcription activator-like effector nucleases (TALENs), which use synthesized proteins to locate and cut specific regions of DNA. Another new genome-editing tool is CRISPR, which uses a bacterial immune system to identify and cut specific DNA regions. Unlike previous gene therapies, these genome-editing tools can disable specific mutations, sometimes down to the level of individual nucleotide base pairs, and can be precision-guided to specific areas in cells. They have already been used to treat a range of genetic diseases in animal models and to engineer new pest- and virus-resistant plants and animals. (See Case Presentation: The CRISPR Revolution earlier in this chapter.)

The ability to precisely alter and repair the basic machinery of life is one of the most lofty aspirations of medicine. The first therapeutic tasks of gene-editing tools such as CRISPR have been to delete or replace genes in human body cells that control the production of specific substances. Diseases such as PKU that are caused by the absence of an enzyme might thus be corrected by inducing the patient's cells to manufacture that enzyme. Many other genetic diseases involve dozens or even hundreds of genes, and often the mechanism by which the genes produce the disease is not understood. Consequently, it may be a long while before most genetic diseases can be treated by gene therapy or editing. Even so, the effective treatment of single-gene disorders is a promising possibility.

When it comes to the genetic "editing" of somatic (body) cells, ethical concerns have been primarily focused on safety issues. (These include the risk of "off-target" cuts to DNA.) But the moral stakes are raised considerably by the prospect of genetically modifying human *germ-line* (reproductive) cells, such as those in sperm, eggs, and embryos. Somatic cell changes cannot be inherited, but germ-line changes can be. This possibility holds out the benign prospect of eliminating forever a number of genetic diseases, as well as the malign chance of introducing harmful new mutations into human DNA. Many question the need to take such risks with germ-line therapy, however. Embryo testing and selection before implantation, a technology already in widespread use, is a simpler way to achieve many of the same goals.

While germ-line therapy may at present have no legitimate medical use, it already offers an alarming prospect. With their increased efficacy and ease of use, genome-editing tools make it increasingly likely that researchers will attempt to "engineer" human beings by making specific genetic changes to germ cells. While much of the talk about such "edited" people involves proposed therapeutic applications, many fear a quick transition from fixing disease-causing mutations to "engineering" babies to meet predetermined specifications. The ease with which the new tools could be used for eugenics-focused applications is one of the reasons that a group of leading biologists have called for a worldwide moratorium on the implantation of genomically "edited" embryos.

Biohazards and GMOs

A similar moratorium on genetic technology applications was called for (and largely respected) in 1975, following a now famous conference at the Asilomar Center in Monterey County, California. Based on concerns about unpredictable environmental and public health impacts, a group of influential biologists issued a report recommending that scientists suspend work on recombinant DNA experiments involving tumor viruses, antibiotic resistance, and toxic bacteria. The discussion that ensued resulted in the formulation of new research guidelines by the National Institutes of Health.

An initial concern at the Asilomar conference was that recombinant techniques might be employed to produce essentially new organisms that would threaten human health. Suppose that the nucleotide sequence for manufacturing a lethal toxin were combined with the DNA of *E. coli.* Then this usually harmless inhabitant of our intestines might be transformed into a deadly organism that would threaten the entire human population. (In recent years we've seen how naturally occurring *E. coli* mutations can be deadly when they enter the food supply.)

Or, to take another scenario, suppose nucleotide sequence that transforms normal cells into cancerous ones is introduced into the human gene pool and triggers an epidemic of cancer. Without a thorough knowledge of the molecular mechanisms involved, little could be done to halt the outbreak. Indeed, it is far from clear what would happen if one of today's bacterial strains engineered to produce insulin were to escape from the lab and spread through the human population.

Perhaps most famously, recombinant or "chimeric" DNA also offers scientists the ability to create new crops and organisms by splicing together DNA from two or more sources. Critics of this process have suggested that these *genetically modified organisms* (GMOs) could wreak havoc with the world's ecosystems and ultimately human health, because they are not the natural products of evolution. Defenders of the GMO process argue that it is simply a more precise (and beneficial) form of the crossbreeding of plants and animals that humans have engaged in for millennia. Exotic fruits and flowers, as well as dog breeds and mules (the sterile chimeric offspring of a donkey and a horse) are all "genetically modified" departures from evolution, they point out.

Despite the scenarios envisioned by some scientists and anti-GMO activists, almost two decades of recombinant DNA research have passed without the occurrence of a major biological catastrophe. Some observers regard this as sufficient proof of the essential safety of the research, while others see it as creating a false sense of

security. Almost no one advocates that the research be abandoned, but a number of high-profile geneticists have argued that we still do not know enough about the mechanisms of genetics to accurately estimate the potential for dire, unintended consequences.

Quite apart from the possible hazards associated with genetic engineering, people continue to be uneasy about the ethical implications of the research. In a world where genomic editing tools are effectively applied to human germ cells, some will be tempted to pursue eugenic dreams of human perfectibility. Combined with the form of asexual reproduction known as cloning, we might produce copies of ourselves and others engineered to suit our needs or ideals. (See Chapter 4 for more on cloning.) Many fear the impact these developments could have on ethical values such as autonomy, diversity, and the inherent worth of the individual. In the most dystopic visions of a genetically engineered society, those with sufficient funds to enhance their own and their children's intelligence, health, and physical prowess would come to dominate, leaving behind a class of service-industry workers who cannot afford to enhance their DNA.

It is little wonder that molecular biologists have become concerned about the nature and direction of their research. As Robert Sinsheimer says, "Biologists have become, without wanting it, custodians of great and terrible power."

Ethical Difficulties with Genetic Research, Therapy, and Technology

The risks involved in such technologies as genomic editing and gene therapy are not entirely unique. In many respects, they parallel those involved in any new medical treatment. Thus many of the same ethical standards and concerns for patient and social welfare that are relevant to the use of other therapies may apply to these new genetic technologies.

The principles of Kant and Ross suggest that the autonomy and dignity of the individual must be respected and preserved. Accordingly, the individual ought not to be viewed as an experimental case for testing genetic interventions that may only later have therapeutic benefit. If a subject is adequately informed and competent to consent, and if no alternative therapy is likely to be effective, it may be morally legitimate to proceed. However, if the hazards of genetic interventions are great or largely unknown, it is doubtful whether the patient would be justified in risking his or her life.

On utilitarian principles, by contrast, if the outcome of genetic therapy can be reasonably expected to produce more benefit than harm, its use might be considered justifiable. Since each case treated is likely to increase potentially beneficial medical knowledge, genetic interventions may be justified by the principle of utility even when they are unlikely to help the individual.

Few currently believe we should call a halt to research in molecular genetics and forego the advances in medicine and basic science it has already helped produce. However, some forms of genetic engineering may have the potential to profoundly alter our society and to distort some of our most cherished values. These are the possibilities that require us to make careful ethical evaluations of our progress in genetic research at each step of the way.

The natural law view of ethics would not necessarily seek to restrict scientific inquiry in genetics. For, on this view, there is a natural inclination (and hence a natural duty) to seek knowledge. Yet certain types of experiments and genetic engineering would probably be prohibited. Those that aim at improving human beings or creating new species from recombinant DNA are most likely to be seen to violate the natural development and goals of our species. On the Roman Catholic view, such a violation of nature would run counter to God's plan and purpose and so be immoral.

The principle of utility might also be invoked to justify limiting, directing, or even ending some research in molecular genetics. If the research or its results are likely to bring about more harm than benefit, regulation would be called for. On the utilitarian view, knowledge may be recognized as a good, but it is only one good among others. Possessing knowledge that could be used for eugenic "engineering" or to create new species must be evaluated for its overall costs and benefits.

Such an analysis also seems to be consistent with Rawls's principles. For Rawls, there is no absolute right to seek knowledge, nor is there any obligation to employ knowledge that is available. Restrictions might well be imposed on scientific research and on the technological possibilities it presents if they threaten the basic goods to be enjoyed by free and equal citizens. Similarly, genetic applications that conflict with the central capabilities that allow us to lead lives of human dignity would be rejected by the capabilities approach. This approach, like several of the identity-based theories discussed in Part VI, would also be critical of aggressive eugenic policies that attempt to impose one standard of functioning on the human population—particularly when it comes to the contested categories of disability. Genetic screening and selection should be available to parents who seek them but broader efforts to "perfect" the human genome conflicts with value pluralism. Genetic technology should primarily be

directed to helping all, disabled and non-disabled, access basic opportunities that allow them to pursue to their various conceptions of a good life.

READINGS

Section 1: Dilemmas of Genetic Choice

The Morality of Screening for Disability
Jeff McMahan

McMahan reviews four common objections to prenatal or preimplantation screening for disabilities: screening is discriminatory, has harmful consequences for disabled people, expresses a hurtful view of disabled people, and reduces human diversity. If these objections are sufficient to show that screening is wrong, McMahan argues, they also imply that it is permissible to cause oneself to have a disabled child.

Indeed, those who accept these objections to screening and claim that certain forms of disability are no worse than non-disability seem committed to accepting the deliberate prenatal selection of disabilities, even for a trivial reason. If we find this view unacceptable, McMahan argues, then we also cannot accept the objections to prenatal screening for disability.

My topic is the morality of using screening technologies to enable potential parents to avoid having a disabled child. The relevant techniques include preconception genetic and non-genetic testing of potential parents, preimplantation genetic diagnosis (PGD), and prenatal screening with the option of abortion. Many people use these techniques and are grateful to have them. Others, however, object to their use, even when abortion is not an issue. The most common objections can be grouped into four basic types.

First, the opponents of screening and selection urge that these practices are perniciously discriminatory, in that their aim is to rid the world of people of a certain type, people who have increasingly come to share a sense of collective identity and solidarity. Some might even argue that for society to endorse

From Jeff McMahan, "The Morality of Screening for Disability," *Ethics, Law and Moral Philosophy of Reproductive Biomedicine* 1, no. 1 (2005): 129–132. Copyright © 2005, permission from Elsevier.

and support screening for disability is analogous to promoting efforts to prevent the births of people of a particular racial group.

Second, the practices of screening and selection are not just detrimental to the disabled as a group but may also be harmful to individual disabled people in various ways. They may, for example, reinforce or seem to legitimize forms of discrimination against existing disabled people. And, if effective, they also reduce the *number* of disabled people, thereby making each disabled person a bit more unusual and a bit more isolated. The reduction in numbers may, in addition, diminish the visibility and political power of disabled people generally.

Third, it is often held that a reduction in the number of disabled people would have an adverse effect on human diversity. To eliminate the disabled would be to eliminate a type of human being who makes a unique contribution to the world. For the disabled themselves, and indeed their mere presence among the rest of us, teach valuable lessons about respect for difference, about the nobility of achievement in the face of grave obstacles, and even about the value of life and what makes a life worth living.

Fourth, it is often held that practices of screening and selection express a view of disabled people that is hurtful to existing disabled people. Efforts to prevent disabled people from existing are said to express such views as that disabled people ought not to exist, that it is bad if disabled people exist, or at least worse than if normal people exist, that disabled people are not worth the burdens they impose on their parents and on the wider society, and so on. Screening and selection, in other words, seem to say to existing disabled people: The rest of us are trying to prevent the existence of other people like you.

One can respond to these objections to screening and selection, as some of the speakers at this conference have done, by appealing to rights of individual liberty. One could grant that the practices are objectionable for the reasons given but argue that those reasons are overridden by rights to reproductive freedom and by the benefits to those who are able to exercise those rights. But I want to advance a reason for scepticism about the force of the objections themselves.

The objections do of course express serious and legitimate concerns, concerns that must be addressed in appropriate ways. But I will argue that they're insufficiently strong to show that screening and selection are wrong or should be prohibited. For if they were taken to show that, they would also have implications beyond the practices of screening and selection. They would also imply the permissibility of certain types of action that most people believe are impermissible.

Consider this hypothetical example: Suppose there is a drug that has a complex set of effects. It is an aphrodisiac that enhances a woman's pleasure during sexual intercourse. But it also increases fertility by inducing ovulation. If ovulation has recently occurred naturally, this drug causes the destruction of the egg that is present in one of the fallopian tubes but also causes a new and different egg to be released from the ovaries. In addition, however, it has a very high probability of damaging the new egg in a way that will cause any child conceived through the fertilization of that egg to be disabled. The disability caused by the drug is, let us suppose, one that many potential parents seek to avoid through screening. But it is also, like virtually all disabilities, not so bad as to make life not worth living. Suppose that a woman takes this drug primarily

to increase her pleasure but also with the thought that it may increase the probability of conception—for she wants to have a child. She is aware that the drug is likely to cause her to have a disabled child but she is eager for pleasure and reflects that it might be rather nice to have a child who might be more dependent than children usually are. Although she does not know it, she has in fact just ovulated naturally so the drug destroys and replaces the egg that was already present but also damages the new egg, thereby causing the child she conceives to be disabled.

Note that because the drug causes the woman's ovaries to release a new egg, the disabled child she conceives is a different individual from the child she would have had if she hadn't taken the drug.

Many people think that this woman's action is morally wrong. It is wrong to cause the existence of a disabled child rather than a child without a disability, just for the sake of one's own sexual pleasure. There are, of course, some who think that rights to reproductive freedom make it permissible to choose to have a disabled child just as they also make it permissible to try to avoid having a disabled child. But most of us do not share that view. Most of us think that if it would be wrong to cause an already born child to become disabled, and if it would be wrong to cause a future child to be disabled through the infliction of prenatal injury, it should also be wrong to cause a disabled child to exist rather than a child without a disability.

There are of course differences. Whether they are morally significant and if so to what extent are matters to which I will return shortly. For the moment, the important point to notice is that if the arguments I cited earlier show that screening and selection are wrong, they should also show that the action of the woman who takes the aphrodisiac is permissible. This is because if it is morally *mandatory* to *allow* oneself to have a disabled child rather than to try, through screening, to have a child who would not be disabled, then it must be at least *permissible* to *cause* oneself to have a disabled rather than a non-disabled child.

Let me try to explain this in greater detail. If it is wrong for the woman to take the aphrodisiac, that must be because there is a moral objection to voluntarily having a disabled child—an objection that's strong enough to make it wrong to cause oneself, by otherwise permissible means, to have a disabled rather than a non-disabled child. But if there is such an objection, it must surely be strong enough to make it at least permissible for people to try, by morally acceptable means, to avoid having a disabled child and to have a non-disabled child instead, and to make it impermissible for others to prevent them from making this attempt.

Yet the critics of screening believe not only that it is wrong for people to try to avoid having a disabled child and to have a non-disabled child instead, but even that it is permissible for others to prevent them from having a non-disabled rather than a disabled child. It would be inconsistent for these critics to condemn the woman in this example for causing herself to have a disabled rather than a non-disabled child and to condemn those who try to cause themselves *not* to have a disabled rather than a non-disabled child.

The crucial premise here is that if it would be morally objectionable to try to *prevent* a certain outcome, and permissible to deprive people of the means of preventing that outcome, then it ought to be permissible to *cause* that outcome, provided one does so by otherwise permissible means.

Note also that if we were to assert publicly that it would be wrong for this woman to do what would cause her to have a disabled child rather than a non-disabled child, or if we were to attempt to prevent her from taking the drug—for example, by making the drug illegal on the ground that it causes "birth defects"—our action would be vulnerable to the same objections that opponents of screening and selection urge against those practices.

If, for example, we were publicly to state the reasons why it would be objectionable for the woman to take the drug—that the disabled child's life might be likely to contain more hardship and less good than the life of a non-disabled child, that provision for the disabled child's special needs would involve greater social costs, and so on—the evaluations of disability and of disabled people that might be thought to be implicit in these claims could be deeply hurtful to existing disabled people, and if we were to prevent this woman and others from being able to take the drug, this would reduce the number of disabled people relative to the number there would otherwise have been, thereby threatening the collective identity and political power of existing disabled people.

In short, the arguments of the opponents of screening seem to imply not only that it would be permissible for the woman to take the aphrodisiac, thereby causing herself to have a disabled child, but also that it would be wrong even to voice objections to her action.

Some opponents of screening and selection may be willing to accept these implications. They might argue that there are relevant differences between causing oneself to have a disabled child rather than a different non-disabled child and causing an existing individual to be disabled. For example, in the latter case but not the former, there is a victim, someone for whom one's act is worse. So there are objections to causing an existing individual to be disabled that do not apply to merely causing a disabled person to exist, and to assert these objections merely expresses the view that it can be worse to be disabled than not to be, which seems unobjectionable, since it does not imply any view of disabled people themselves. Screening and selection, by contrast, are held to express a pernicious and degrading view of disabled people.

Thus, opponents of screening and selection typically think that they can draw the line between action by a woman that may cause her to conceive a child who will be disabled and, for example, action taken by a pregnant woman that injures her fetus, causing it to be disabled when it otherwise would not have been. But in fact many people, especially among the disabled themselves, contend that it is no worse to be disabled than not to be. They claim that disabilities are "neutral" traits. So, for example, Harriet McBryde Johnson (2003), a disabled lawyer, emphatically repudiates the "unexamined assumption that disabled people are inherently 'worse off,' that we 'suffer,' that we have lesser 'prospects of a happy life.'"

The view that it is not bad to be disabled, apart from any ill effects caused by social discrimination, would be very difficult to sustain if it implied that to cause a person to become disabled would not harm that person, or that it is irrational to be averse to becoming disabled. But in fact those who claim that it is not bad in itself to *be* disabled can accept without inconsistency that it can be bad to *become* disabled. They can appeal to the *transition costs*. It is bad to become disabled because this can involve loss and discontinuity, requiring that one abandon certain goals and projects and adapt to the pursuit of different ones instead. It is these effects that make it rational to fear becoming disabled and they are a major part of the explanation of why it is wrong to cause someone to become disabled. The other major part is that the causation of disability involves a violation of the victim's autonomy.

But notice that these considerations do not count against causing disability through prenatal injury. For congenital disability does not have transition costs, and fetuses are not autonomous.

It seems, therefore, that opponents of screening and selection who also claim that it is not worse to be disabled have no basis for objecting to the infliction of prenatal injury that causes congenital disability. Moreover, to object to the infliction of disabling prenatal injury or to enact measures to prevent it would seem to express a negative view of disability and perhaps of the disabled themselves. At a minimum, it expresses the view that it is bad to be disabled, or at least worse than not to be disabled. And, if effective, efforts to prevent disabling prenatal injury would have other effects comparable to those of prohibiting or restricting screening for disability and selection, such as reducing the number of disabled people who would be born, thereby also threatening the sense of collective identity and solidarity among the disabled as well as diminishing their visibility and political power. Finally, prevention of prenatal injury would also threaten human diversity. It would deprive those who would have had contact with the person if he had been disabled of the unique benefits that disabled people offer to others.

So for those opponents of selection who also hold that it is not a harm or misfortune to be disabled, it seems that there are not only no reasons to object to the infliction of disabling prenatal injury but even positive reasons not to object to it and not to try to prevent it.

Suppose there were an aphrodisiac that would greatly enhance a woman's pleasure during sex but would, if taken during pregnancy, injure the fetus in a way that would cause it to be congenitally severely disabled. Those who oppose screening and selection for the reasons I cited earlier and who also hold that it is not bad in itself to be disabled are logically committed by their own arguments to accept that it would be permissible for a pregnant woman to take this aphrodisiac just to increase her own pleasure, and they are further committed to accept that it would be wrong to try to prevent the woman from taking the aphrodisiac or even to criticize her for doing so.

If we think that these conclusions are mistaken, which they surely are, we must reject some part of the case against screening and selection.

I will conclude by briefly suggesting a more positive way of addressing the concerns of those who oppose screening and selection. My sense is that the chief worry of those opposed to screening and selection has

to do with the expressive effects of these practices. The worry is, as I noted earlier, that these practices give social expression to a negative view of disabled people, thereby reinforcing other forms of discrimination against them.

But notice that it is usually only people who have not had a disabled child who are averse to doing so. Those people who actually have a disabled child tend overwhelmingly to be glad that they had the particular child they had. If any child they might have had would have been disabled, they tend to prefer having had their actual disabled child to having had no child at all. If they could have had a non-disabled child but it would have been a different child, they tend to prefer their actual disabled child. Of course, what they would usually most prefer is that their actual child had not been disabled. But it is almost invariably the case that any action that would have enabled them to avoid having a disabled child would have caused them to have a different child. When the parents appreciate this fact, they cease to wish that anything had been different in the past, and focus their hopes on the possibility of a cure.

In short, most people who currently have or have had a disabled child in the past do not regret having done so. They are, instead, glad to have had their actual child and frequently testify to the special joy and illumination afforded by being bound to a disabled child. This very different evaluation of having a disabled child by those who actually have experience of it is no less rational and no less authoritative than the evaluation that many people make prospectively that it would be bad or worse to have a disabled child.

We could therefore try to offset any negative expressive effects of screening and selection by giving public expression to these different and equally valid evaluations. I do not have any suggestions for how we might do this. That's a matter for specialists in public policy, not philosophers. But the crucial point is that it would be morally and strategically better for disabled people and their advocates to focus their efforts on positive proposals of this sort rather than to stigmatize and to seek to restrict or suppress practices such as screening and selection. By crusading against screening and selection, they risk making themselves appear to the wider public as fanatics bent on imposing harmful restrictions on others. That would certainly not serve the cause of obtaining justice for the disabled.

Genetic Dilemmas and the Child's Right to an Open Future

Dena S. Davis

Davis asks whether genetic counselors must assist couples who wish to have a child with deafness or achondroplastic dwarfism. Taking deafness as an example, she argues that although counselors are professionally committed to an ethic of patient autonomy, they may reject such a request, on the ground that it would limit the future autonomy of any child that might be born.

Davis compares the situation with one in which Jehovah's Witnesses refuse to consent to a lifesaving blood transfusion for their child and one in which Amish parents remove their children from school after the eighth grade. While courts have allowed the second, Davis sees both as unjustifiably denying children an "open future."

Whether or not deafness is considered a disability in a culture, being born deaf significantly restricts the choices open to a child. Thus, if it is chosen before birth by the child's parents, it must be considered a harm. For this reason, genetic counselors should not help parents produce deaf children.

The profession of genetic counseling is strongly characterized by a respect for patient autonomy that is greater than in almost any other area of medicine. When moral challenges arise in the clinical practice of genetics, they tend to be understood as conflicts between the obligation to respect patient autonomy and other ethical norms, such as doing good and avoiding harm. Thus, a typical counseling dilemma exists when a person who has been tested and found to be carrying the gene for Tay-Sachs disease refuses to share that information with siblings and other relatives despite the clear benefits to them of having that knowledge, or when a family member declines to participate in a testing protocol necessary to help another member discover his or her genetic status.

This way of looking at moral issues in genetic counseling often leaves both the counselors and commentators frustrated, for two reasons. First, by elevating respect for patient autonomy above all other values, it may be difficult to give proper weight to other factors, such as human suffering. Second, by privileging patient autonomy and by defining the

patient as the person or couple who has come for counseling, there seems no "space" in which to give proper attention to the moral claims of the future child who is the endpoint of many counseling interactions.

These difficulties have been highlighted of late by the surfacing of a new kind of genetic counseling request: parents with certain disabilities who seek help in trying to assure that they will have a child who shares their disability. The two reported instances are in families affected by achondroplasia (dwarfism) and by hereditary deafness. This essay will focus on deafness.

Such requests are understandably troubling to genetic counselors. Deeply committed to the principle of giving clients value-free information with which to make their own choices, most counselors nonetheless make certain assumptions about health and disability—for example, that it is preferable to be a hearing person rather than a deaf person. Thus, counselors typically talk of the "risk" of having a child with a particular genetic condition. Counselors may have learned (sometimes with great difficulty) to respect clients' decisions not to find out if their fetus has a certain condition or not to abort a fetus which carries a genetic disability. But to respect a parental value system that not only favors what most of us consider to be a disability, but actively expresses that preference by attempting to have a child with the condition, is "the ultimate test of nondirective counseling."

To describe the challenge primarily as one that pits beneficence (concern for the child's quality of life) against autonomy (concern for the parents' right to decide about these matters) makes for obvious difficulties. These are two very different values, and comparing and weighing them invites the proverbial analogy of "apples and oranges." After all, the perennial critique of a principle-based ethics is that it offers few suggestions for ranking principles when duties conflict. Further, beneficence and respect for autonomy are values that will always exist in some tension within genetic counseling. For all the reasons I list below, counselors are committed to the primacy of patient autonomy and therefore to nondirective counseling. But surely, most or all of them are drawn to the field because they want to help people avoid or at least mitigate suffering.

Faced with the ethical challenge of parents who wish to ensure children who have a disability, I suggest a different way to look at this problem. Thinking this problem through in the way I suggest will shed light on some related topics in genetics as well, such as sex selection. I propose that, rather than conceiving this as a conflict between autonomy and beneficence, we recast it as a conflict between parental autonomy and the child's future autonomy: what Joel Feinberg has called "the child's right to an open future."

New Challenges

The Code of Ethics of the National Society of Genetic Counselors states that its members strive to:

- Respect their clients' beliefs, cultural traditions, inclinations, circumstances, and feelings.

- Enable their clients to make informed independent decisions, free of coercion, by providing or illuminating the necessary facts and clarifying the alternatives and anticipated consequences.

Considering the uncertain and stochastic nature of genetic counseling, and especially in light of the difficulty physicians experience in sharing uncertainty with patients, it is remarkable that medical geneticists have hewed so strongly to an ethic of patient autonomy. This phenomenon can be explained by at least five factors: the desire to disassociate themselves as strongly as possible from the discredited eugenics movement; an equally strong desire to avoid the label of "abortionist," a realistic fear if counselors are perceived as advocates for abortion of genetically damaged fetuses; the fact that few treatments are available for genetic diseases; an awareness of the intensely private nature of reproductive decisions; and the fact that genetic decisions can have major consequences for entire families. As one counselor was quoted, "I am not going to be taking that baby home—they will."

The commitment to patient autonomy faces new challenges with the advances arising from the Human Genome Project. The example of hereditary deafness is reported by Walter E. Nance, who writes:

> It turns out that some deaf couples feel threatened by the prospect of having a hearing child and would actually prefer to have a deaf child. The knowledge that we will soon acquire [due to the Human Genome Project] will, of course, provide us with the technology that could be used to assist such couples in achieving their goals. This, in turn, could lead to the ultimate test of nondirective counseling. Does adherence to the concept of nondirective counseling actually require that we assist such a couple in terminating a pregnancy with a hearing child or is this nonsense?

Several issues must be unpacked here. First, I question Nance's depiction of deaf parents as feeling "threatened" by the prospect of a hearing child. From Nance's own depiction of the deaf people he encounters, it is at least as likely that deaf parents feel that a deaf child would fit into their family better, especially if the parents themselves are "deaf of deaf" or if they already have one or more deaf children. Or perhaps the parents feel that Deafness (I use the capital "D," as Deaf people do, to signify Deafness as a culture) is an asset—tough at times but worthwhile in the end—like belonging to a racial or religious minority.

Second, I want to avoid the issue of abortion by discussing the issue of "deliberately producing a deaf child" as distinct from the question of achieving that end by aborting a hearing fetus. The latter topic is important, but it falls outside the purview of this paper. I will focus on the scenario where a deaf child is produced without recourse to abortion. We can imagine a situation in the near future where eggs or sperm can be scrutinized for the relevant trait before fertilization, or the present situation in which preimplantation genetic diagnosis after in vitro fertilization allows specialists to examine the genetic makeup of the very early embryo before it is implanted.

Imagine a Deaf couple approaching a genetic counselor. The couple's goals are to learn more about the cause(s) of their own Deafness, and, if possible, to maximize the chance that any pregnancy they embark upon will result in a Deaf child. Let us suppose that the couple falls into the 50% of clients whose Deafness has a genetic origin. The genetic counselor who adheres strictly to the tenets of client autonomy will respond by helping the couple to explore the ways in which they can achieve their goal: a Deaf baby. But as Nance's depiction of this scenario suggests, the counselor may well feel extremely uneasy about her role here. It is one thing to support a couple's decision to take their chances and "let Nature take its course," but to treat as a goal what is commonly considered to be a risk may be more pressure than the value-neutral ethos can bear. What is needed is a principled argument against such assistance. This refusal need not rise to a legal prohibition, but could become part of the ethical norms and standard of care for the counseling profession.

The path I see out of this dilemma relies on two steps. First, we remind ourselves why client autonomy is such a powerful norm in genetic counseling. Clients come to genetic counselors with questions that are simultaneously of the greatest magnitude and of the greatest intimacy. Clients not only have the right to bring their own values to bear on these questions, but in the end they must do so because they—and their children—will live with the consequences. As the President's Commission said in its 1983 report on Screening and Counseling for Genetic Conditions:

> The silence of the law on many areas of individual choice reflects the value this country places on pluralism. Nowhere is the need for freedom to pursue divergent conceptions of the good more deeply felt than in decisions concerning reproduction. It would be a cruel irony, therefore, if technological advances undertaken in the name of providing information to expand the range of individual choices resulted in unanticipated social pressures to pursue a particular course of action. Someone who feels compelled to undergo screening or to make particular reproductive choices at the urging of health care professionals or others or as a result of implicit social pressure is deprived of the choice-enhancing benefits of the new advances. The Commission recommends that those who counsel patients and those who educate the public about genetics should not only emphasize the importance of preserving choice but also do their utmost to safeguard the choices of those they serve.

Now let us take this value of respect for autonomy and put it on both sides of the dilemma. Why is it morally problematic to seek to produce a child who is deaf? Being deaf does not cause one physical pain or shorten one's life span, two obvious conditions which it would be prima facie immoral to produce in another person. Deaf people might (or might not) be less happy on average than hearing people, but that is arguably a function of societal prejudice. The primary argument against deliberately seeking to produce deaf children is that it violates the child's own autonomy and narrows the scope of her choices when she grows up; in other words, it violates her right to an "open future."

The Child's Right to an Open Future

Joel Feinberg begins his discussion of children's rights by noticing that rights can ordinarily be divided into four kinds. First, there are rights that adults and children have in common (the right not to be killed, for example). Then, there are rights that are generally possessed only by children (or by "childlike" adults). These "dependency-rights," as Feinberg calls them, derive from the child's dependence on others for such basics as food, shelter, and protection. Third, there are rights that can only be exercised by adults (or at least by children approaching adulthood), for example, the free exercise of religion. Finally, there are rights that Feinberg calls "rights-in-trust," rights which are to be "saved for the child until he is an adult." These rights can be violated by adults now, in ways that cut off the possibility that the child, when it achieves adulthood, can exercise them. A striking example is the right to reproduce. A young child cannot physically exercise that right, and a teenager might lack the legal and moral grounds on which to assert such a right. But clearly the child, when he or she attains adulthood, will have that right, and therefore the child now has the right not to be sterilized, so that the child may exercise that right in the future. Rights in this category include a long list: virtually all the important rights we believe adults have, but which must be protected now to be exercised later. Grouped together, they constitute what Feinberg calls "the child's right to an open future."

Feinberg illustrates this concept with two examples. The first is that of the Jehovah's Witness child who needs a blood transfusion to save his life but whose parents object on religious grounds. In this case, the parents' right to act upon their religious beliefs and to raise their family within the religion of their choice conflicts with the child's right to live to adulthood and to make his own life-or-death decisions. As the Supreme Court said in another (and less defensible) case involving Jehovah's Witnesses:

> *Parents may be free to become martyrs themselves. But it does not follow that they are free in identical circumstances to make martyrs of their children before they have reached the age of full and legal discretion when they can make that decision for themselves.*

The second example is more controversial. In 1972, in a famous Supreme Court case, a group of Old Order Amish argued that they should be exempt from Wisconsin's requirement that all children attend school until they are either sixteen years old or graduate from high school. The Amish didn't have to send their children to public school, of course; they were free to create a private school of their own liking. But they framed the issue in the starkest manner: to send their children to any school, past eighth grade, would be antithetical to their religion and their way of life, and might even result in the death of their culture.

The case was framed as a freedom of religion claim on the one hand, and the state's right to insist on an educated citizenry on the other. And within that frame, the Amish won. First, they were able to persuade the Court that sending their children to school after eighth grade would potentially destroy their community, because it

> *takes them away from their community, physically and emotionally, during the crucial and formative adolescent period. During this period, the children must acquire Amish attitudes favoring manual work and self-reliance and the specific skills needed to perform the adult role of an Amish farmer or housewife. In the Amish belief higher learning tends to develop values they reject as influences that alienate man from God. (p. 211)*

Second, the Amish argued that the state's concerns—that children be prepared to participate in the political and economic life of the state—did not apply in this case. The Court listened favorably to expert witnesses who explained that the Amish system of home-based vocational training—learning from your parent—worked well for that community, that the community itself was prosperous, and that few Amish were likely to end up unemployed. The Court said:

> *the value of all education must be assessed in terms of its capacity to prepare the child for life. . . . It is one thing to say that compulsory education for a year or two beyond the eighth grade may be necessary when its goal is the preparation of the child for life in modern society as the majority live, but it is quite another if the goal of education can be viewed as the preparation of the child for life in the separated agrarian community that is the keystone of the Amish faith. (p. 222)*

What only a few justices saw was that the children themselves were largely ignored in this argument. The Amish wanted to preserve their way of life. The state of Wisconsin wanted to make sure that its citizens could vote wisely and make a living. No justice squarely faced the question of whether the liberal democratic state owes all its citizens, especially children, a right to a basic education that can serve as a building block if the child decides later in life that she wishes to become an astronaut, a playwright, or perhaps to join the army. As we constantly hear from politicians and educators, without a high school diploma one's future is virtually closed. By denying them a high school education or its equivalent, parents are virtually ensuring that their children will remain housewives and agricultural laborers. Even if the children agree, is that a choice parents ought to be allowed to make for them?

From my perspective, the case was decided wrongly. If Wisconsin had good reasons for settling on high school graduation or age sixteen as the legal minimum to which children are entitled, then I think that the Amish children were entitled to that minimum as well, despite their parents' objections. In deciding the issue primarily on grounds that the Amish were not likely to create problems for the state if allowed to keep their children out of school, the Court reflected a rather minimalist form of liberalism. In fact, the abiding interest of this case for many political philosophers lies in the deep conflict it highlights between two different concepts of liberalism: commitment to autonomy and commitment to diversity. William Galston, for example, argues that:

A standard liberal view (or hope) is that these two principles go together and complement one another: the exercise of autonomy yields diversity, while the fact of diversity protects and nourishes autonomy. By contrast, my . . . view is that these principles do not always, perhaps even do not usually, cohere; that in practice, they point in quite different directions in currently disputed areas such as education. . . . Specifically: the decision to throw state power behind the promotion of individual autonomy can weaken or undermine individuals and groups that do not and cannot organize their affairs in accordance with that principle without undermining the deepest sources of their identity.

Galston claims that "properly understood, liberalism is about the protection of diversity, not the valorization of choice. . . . To place an ideal of autonomous choice . . . at the core of liberalism is in fact to narrow the range of possibilities available within liberal societies" (p. 523).

One can see this conflict quite sharply if one returns to the work of John Stuart Mill. On the one hand, there is probably no philosopher who gives more weight to the value of individual choice than does Mill. In *On Liberty*, he claims that the very measure of a human being is the extent to which he makes life choices for himself, free of societal pressure:

The human faculties of perception, judgment, discriminative feeling, mental activity, and even moral preference, are exercised only in making a choice. He who does anything because it is the custom makes no choice.

Mill would abhor a situation like that of the Amish communities in *Yoder*, which unabashedly want to give their children as few choices as possible. But, on the other hand, it is clear from both common sense and from Mill's own statements that in order for people to have choices about the pattern of their lives (and to be inspired to create new patterns) there must be more than one type of community available to them. To quote Mill again, "There is no reason that all human existence should be constructed on some one or some small number of patterns" (p. 64).

As we look at the last three centuries of American history, we see what an important role different community "patterns" have played, from the Shakers to the Mormons to Bronson Alcott's Fruitlands to the communal experiments of the 1960s. If those patterns are to exhibit the full range of human endeavor and experiment, they must include communities that are distinctly antiliberal. Not only does the panoply of widely different communities enrich our culture, but it also provides a welcome for those who do not fit into the mainstream. As Mill says, "A man cannot get a coat or pair of shoes to fit him unless they are either made to his measure, or he has a whole warehouseful to choose from: and is it easier to fit him with a life than with a coat[?]" (p. 64). Some of us are geniuses who make our lives to "fit our measure," others are happy enough to fit into the mainstream, but for others, the availability of a "warehouseful" of choices increases the possibility of finding a good fit. And for some, a good fit means an authoritarian community based on tradition, where one is freed from the necessity of choice. Thus Galston is correct in pointing to the paradox: if the goal of a liberal democracy is to actively promote something like the greatest number of choices for the greatest number of individuals, this seems to entail hostility toward narrow-choice communities like the Amish. But if the Amish, because of that hostility, fail to flourish, there will be fewer choices available to all.

The compromise I promote is that a liberal state must tolerate even those communities most unsympathetic to the liberal value of individual choice. However, this tolerance must exist within a limiting context, which is the right of individuals to choose which communities they wish to join and to leave if they have a mind to. Even Galston begins with the presumption that society must "defend . . . the liberty not to be coerced into, or trapped within, ways of life. Accordingly, the state must safeguard the ability of individuals to shift allegiances and cross boundaries." Thus, I argue that the autonomy of the individual is ethically prior to the autonomy of the group. Both deals have powerful claims on us, but when group rights would extinguish the abilities of the individuals within them to make their own life choices, then the liberal state must support the individual against the group. This is especially crucial when the individual at issue is a child, who is particularly vulnerable to adult coercion and therefore has particular claims on our protection.

Unfortunately, it is precisely where children are concerned that groups are understandably most jealous of their prerogatives to guide and make decisions. The Amish are an example of a group guarding its ability to shape the lives of its children; Deaf parents wishing to ensure Deaf children are an example of families pursuing the same goals. Of course, groups and families ought to—in fact, they must—strive to shape the values and lives of the children in their care; not to do so leads to social and individual pathology. But when that shaping takes the form of a radically narrow range of choices available to the child when she grows up, when it impinges substantially on the child's right to an open future, then liberalism requires us to intervene to support the child's future ability to make her own choices about which of the many diverse visions of life she wishes to embrace.

But I concede one problem with this point of view. As a liberal who believes that the state should not dictate notions of "the good life," Feinberg believes that the state must be neutral about the goals of education, skewing the question neither in favor of Amish lifestyle nor in favor of the "modern," technological life most Americans accept. The goal of education is to allow the child to make up its own mind from the widest array of options; the best education is the one which gives the child the most open future. A neutral decision would assume only that education should equip the child with the knowledge and skills that will help him choose whichever sort of life best fits his native endowment and matured disposition. It should send him out into the adult world with as many open opportunities as possible, thus maximizing his chances for self-fulfillment.

The problem here is that an education which gave a child this array of choices would quite possibly make it impossible for her to choose to remain Old Order Amish. Her "native endowment and matured disposition" might now have taken her away from the kind of personality and habits that would make Amish life pleasant. Even if she envies the peace, warmth, and security that a life of tradition offers, she may find it impossible to turn her back on "the world," and return to her lost innocence. To quote the Amish, she may have failed irreversibly to "acquire Amish attitudes" during "the crucial and formative adolescent period." This problem raises two issues. First, those of us who would make arguments based on the child's right to an open future need to be clear and appropriately humble about what we are offering. Insisting

on a child's right to a high school education may open a future wider than she otherwise could have dreamed, but it also may foreclose one possible future: as a contented member of the Amish community. Second, if the Amish are correct in saying that taking their children out of school at grade eight is crucial for the child's development into a member of the Amish community, then there is no "impartial" stance for the state to take. The state may well be impartial about whether the "better life" is to be found within or without the Amish community, but it cannot act in an impartial fashion. Both forcing the parents to send their children to school or exempting them from the requirement has likely consequences for the child's continued existence within the community when she grows up and is able to make a choice. Feinberg seeks to avoid this second problem by claiming that the neutral state would act to

> let all influences . . . work equally on the child, to open up all possibilities to him, without itself influencing him toward one or another of these. In that way, it can be hoped that the chief determining factor in the grown child's choice of a vocation and life-style will be his own governing values, talents, and propensities. (pp. 134–35)

The problem with this is that, as I understand the Amish way of life, being Amish is precisely not to make one's life choices on the basis of one's own "talents and propensities," but to subordinate those individual leanings to the traditions of the group. If one discovers within oneself a strong passion and talent for jazz dancing, one ought to suppress it, not nurture it.

Is Creating a Deaf Child a Moral Harm?

Now, as we return to the example of the couple who wish to ensure that they bear only deaf children, we have to confront two distinctly different issues. The first is, in what sense is it ever possible to do harm by giving birth to a child who would otherwise not have been born at all? The second is whether being deaf rather than hearing is in fact a harm.

The first issue has been well rehearsed elsewhere. The problem is, how can it be said that one has harmed a child by bringing it into the world with a disability, when the only other choice was for the child not to have existed at all? In the case of a child whose life is arguably not worth living, one can say that life itself is a cruelty to the child. But when a child is born in less than ideal circumstances, or is partially disabled in ways that do not entail tremendous suffering, there seems no way to argue that the child herself has been harmed. This may appear to entail the conclusion, counter to our common moral sense, that therefore no harm has been done. "A wrong action must be bad for someone, but [a] choice to create [a] child with its handicap is bad for no one."

All commentators agree that there is no purely logical way out of what Dan Brock calls the "wrongful handicap" conundrum (p. 272). However, most commentators also agree that one can still support a moral critique of the parents' decision. Bonnie Steinbock and Ron McClamrock argue for a principle of "parental responsibility" by which being a good parent entails refraining from bringing a child into the world when one cannot give it "even a decent chance at a good life." Brock, following Parfit, distinguishes same person from same number choices. In same person choices, the same person exists in each of the alternative courses of action the agent chooses, but the person may exist more or less harmed. In same number choices, "the choice affects who, which child, will exist." Brock claims that moral harms can exist in both instances, despite the fact that in same number choices the moral harm cannot be tied to a specific person. Brock generates the following principle:

Individuals are morally required not to let any possible child . . . for whose welfare they are responsible experience serious suffering or limited opportunity if they can act so that, without imposing substantial burdens or costs on themselves or others, any alternative possible child . . . for whose welfare they would be responsible will not experience serious suffering or limited opportunity. (pp. 272–73)

While agreeing with Brock, Steinbock, and others, I locate the moral harm differently, at least with respect to disabled persons wishing to reproduce themselves in the form of a disabled child. Deliberately creating a child who will be forced irreversibly into the parents' notion of "the good life" violates the Kantian principle of treating each person as an end in herself and never as a means only. All parenthood exists as a balance between fulfillment of parental hopes and values and the individual flowering of the actual child in his or her own direction. The decision to have a child

is never made for the sake of the child—for no child then exists. We choose to have children for myriad reasons, but before the child is conceived those reasons can only be self-regarding. The child is a means to our ends: a certain land of joy and pride, continuing the family name, fulfilling religious or societal expectations, and so on. But morally the child is first and foremost an end in herself. Good parenthood requires a balance between having a child for our own sakes and being open to the moral reality that the child will exist for her own sake, with her own talents and weaknesses, propensities and interests, and with her own life to make. Parental practices that close exits virtually forever are insufficiently attentive to the child as end in herself. By closing off the child's right to an open future, they define the child as an entity who exists to fulfill parental hopes and dreams, not her own.

Having evaded the snares of the wrongful handicap conundrum, we must tackle the second problem: is being deaf a harm? At first glance, this might appear as a silly question. Ethically, we would certainly include destroying someone's hearing under the rubric of "harm"; legally, one could undoubtedly receive compensation if one were rendered deaf through someone else's negligence. Many Deaf people, however, have recently been claiming that Deafness is better understood as a cultural identity than as a disability. Particularly in the wake of the Deaf President Now revolution at Gallaudet University in 1988, Deaf people have been asserting their claims not merely to equal access (through increased technology) but also to equal respect as a cultural minority. As one (hearing) reporter noted:

So strong is the feeling of cultural solidarity that many deaf parents cheer on discovering that their baby is deaf. Pondering such a scene, a hearing person can experience a kind of vertigo. The surprise is not simply the unfamiliarity of the views; it is that, as in a surrealist painting, jarring notions are presented as if they were commonplace.

From this perspective, the use of cochlear implants to enable deaf children to hear, or the abortion of deaf fetuses, is characterized as "genocide." Deaf pride advocates point out that as Deaf people they lack the ability to hear, but they also have many positive gains: a cohesive community, a rich cultural heritage built around the various residential schools, a growing body of drama, poetry, and other artistic traditions, and, of course, what makes all this possible, American

Sign Language. Roslyn Rosen, the president of the National Association of the Deaf, is Deaf, the daughter of Deaf parents, and the mother of Deaf children. "I'm happy with who I am," she says, "and I don't want to be 'fixed.' Would an Italian-American rather be a WASP? In our society everyone agrees that whites have an easier time than blacks. But do you think a black person would undergo operations to become white?"

On the other side of the argument is evidence that deafness is a very serious disability. Deaf people have incomes thirty to forty percent below the national average. The state of education for the deaf is unacceptable by anyone's standards; the typical deaf student graduates from high school unable to read a newspaper.

However, one could also point to the lower incomes and inadequate state of education among some racial and ethnic minorities in our country, a situation we do not (or at least ought not) try to ameliorate by eradicating minorities. Deaf advocates often cite the work of Nora Ellen Groce, whose oral history of Martha's Vineyard, *Everyone Here Spoke Sign Language*, tells a fascinating story. For over two hundred years, ending in the middle of the twentieth century, the Vineyard experienced a degree of hereditary deafness exponentially higher than that of the mainland. Although the number of deaf people was low in noncomparative terms (one in 155), the result was a community in which deaf people participated fully in the political and social life of the island, had an economic prosperity on par with their neighbors, and communicated easily with the hearing population, for "everyone here spoke sign language." So endemic was sign language for the general population of the island that hearing islanders often exploited its unique properties even in the absence of deaf people. Old-timers told Groce stories of spouses communicating through sign language when they were outdoors and did not want to raise their voices against the wind. Or men might turn away and finish a "dirty" joke in sign when a woman walked into the general store. At church, deaf parishioners gave their testimony in sign.

As one Deaf activist said, in a comment that could have been directly related to the Vineyard experience, "When Gorbachev visited the U.S., he used an interpreter to talk to the President. Was Gorbachev disabled?" Further, one might argue that, since it is impossible to eradicate deafness completely even if

that were a worthy goal, the cause of deaf equality is better served when parents who are proud to be Deaf deliberately have Deaf children who augment and strengthen the existing population. Many of the problems that deaf people experience are the result of being born, without advance warning, to hearing parents. When there is no reason to anticipate the birth of a deaf child, it is often months or years before the child is correctly diagnosed. Meanwhile, she is growing up in a world devoid of language, unable even to communicate with her parents. When the diagnosis is made, her parents first must deal with the emotional shock, and then sort through the plethora of conflicting advice on how best to raise and educate their child. Most probably, they have never met anyone who is deaf. If they choose the route recommended by most Deaf activists and raise their child with sign language, it will take the parents years to learn the language. Meanwhile, their child has missed out on the crucial development of language at the developmentally appropriate time, a lack that is associated with poor reading skills and other problems later (p. 43).

Further, even the most accepting of hearing parents often feel locked in conflict with the Deaf community over who knows what is best for their child. If Deafness truly is a culture rather than a disability, then raising a deaf child is somewhat like white parents trying to raise a black child in contemporary America (with a background chorus of black activists telling them that they can't possibly make a good job of it!). Residential schools, for example, which can be part of the family culture for a Deaf couple, can be seen by hearing parents as Dickensian nightmares or, worse, as a "cultlike" experience in which their children will be lost to them forever.

By contrast, deaf children born to Deaf parents learn language (sign) at the same age as hearing children. They are welcomed into their families and inculcated into Deaf culture in the same way as any other children. Perhaps for these reasons, by all accounts the Deaf of Deaf are the acknowledged leaders of the Deaf Pride movement, and the academic crème de la crème. In evaluating the choice parents make who deliberately ensure that they have Deaf children, we must remember that the statistics and descriptions of deaf life in America are largely reflective of the experience of deaf children born to hearing parents, who make up the vast majority of deaf people today.

But if Deafness is a culture rather than a disability, it is an exceedingly narrow one. One factor that does not seem clear is the extent to which children raised with American Sign Language as their first language ever will be completely comfortable with the written word. (Sign language itself has no written analogue and has a completely different grammatical structure from English.) At present, the conflicted and politicized state of education for the deaf, along with the many hours spent (some would say "wasted") on attempting to teach deaf children oral skills, makes it impossible to know what is to blame for the dismal reading and writing skills of the average deaf person. Some deaf children who are raised with sign language from birth do become skilled readers. But there is reason to question whether a deaf child may have very limited access to the wealth of literature, drama, and poetry that liberals would like to consider every child's birthright.

Although Deaf activists rightly show how many occupations are open to them with only minor technological adjustments, the range of occupations will always be inherently limited. It is not likely that the world will become as Martha's Vineyard, where everyone knew sign. A prelingually deafened person not only cannot hear, but in most instances cannot speak well enough to be understood. This narrow choice of vocation is not only a harm in its own sake but also is likely to continue to lead to lower standards of living. (Certainly one reason why the Vineyard deaf were as prosperous as their neighbors was that farming and fishing were just about the only occupations available.)

Either Way, a Moral Harm

If deafness is considered a disability, one that substantially narrows a child's career, marriage, and cultural options in the future, then deliberately creating a deaf child counts as a moral harm. If Deafness is considered a culture, as Deaf activists would have us agree, then deliberately creating a Deaf child who will have only very limited options to move outside of that culture, also counts as a moral harm. A decision, made before a child is even born, that confines her forever to a narrow group of people and a limited choice of careers, so violates the child's right to an open future that no genetic counseling team should acquiesce in it. The very value of autonomy that grounds the ethics of genetic counseling should preclude assisting parents in a project that so dramatically narrows the autonomy of the child to be.

Coda

Although I rest my case at this point, I want to sketch out some further ramifications of my argument. Are there other, less obvious, ways in which genetic knowledge and manipulation can interfere with the child's right to an open future?

The notion of the child's right to an open future can help in confronting the question of whether to test children for adult-onset genetic diseases, for example Huntington disease. It is well known that the vast majority of adults at risk for Huntington disease choose not to be tested. However, it is not uncommon for parents to request that their children be tested; their goals may be to set their minds at rest, to plan for the future, and so on. On one account, parental authority to make medical decisions suggests that clinicians should accede to these requests (after proper counseling about possible risks). A better account, in my opinion, protects the child's right to an open future by preserving into adulthood his own choice to decide whether his life is better lived with that knowledge or without.

Finally, a provocative argument can be made that sex selection can be deleterious to the child's right to an open future. I am ignoring here all the more obvious arguments against sex selection, even when accomplished without abortion. Rather, I suspect that parents who choose the sex of their offspring are more likely to have gender-specific expectations for those children, expectations that subtly limit the child's own individual flowering. The more we are able to control our children's characteristics (and the more time, energy, and money we invest in the outcome), the more invested we will become in our hopes and dreams for them. It is easy to sympathize with some of the reasons why parents might want to ensure a girl or boy. People who already have one or two children of one sex can hardly be faulted for wanting to "balance" their families by having one of each. And yet, this ought to be discouraged. If I spent a great deal of time and energy to get a boy in the hope of having a football player in the family, I think I would be less likely to accept it with good grace if the boy hated sports and spent all his spare time at the piano. If I insisted on having a girl because I believed that as a grandparent I would be more likely to have close contact with the children of a daughter than of a son, I think I would find it much harder to raise a girl who saw motherhood as a choice rather than as a foregone conclusion. Parents whose preferences are compelling enough for them to take active steps to control the outcome, must, logically, be committed to certain strong gender-role expectations. If they want a girl that badly, whether they are hoping for a Miss America or the next Catherine McKinnon, they are likely to make it difficult for the actual child to resist their expectations and to follow her own bent.

Section 2:   Genetic Interventions: A New Eugenics?

Procreative Beneficence: Why We Should Select the Best Children

Julian Savulescu

Savulescu argues that if tests for nondisease genes become available, we have a moral obligation to use them in making decisions about reproduction. Because disease-causing genes reduce the well-being of a person, what he calls the "principle of Procreative Benevolence" directs us to select against them. It isn't the disease itself we are selecting against, Savulescu claims, but its impact on a life. But nondisease genes can also have an impact. Intelligence, for example, can also affect well-being. Thus, genetic information about specific qualities should be used to select the embryo or fetus, with the aim of producing a life of the greatest well-being.

Procreative Beneficence, Savulescu holds, must be balanced against Procreative Autonomy. Even so, doctors should try to persuade potential parents to seek out and use genetic information that will let them select for the greatest possible well-being in the life to be created.

Introduction

Imagine you are having in vitro fertilization (IVF) and you produce four embryos. One is to be implanted. You are told that there is a genetic test for predisposition to scoring well on IQ tests (let's call this intelligence). If an embryo has gene subtypes (alleles) A, B there is a greater than 50% chance it will score more than 140 if given an ordinary education and upbringing. If it has subtypes C, D there is a much lower chance it will score over 140. Would you test the four embryos for these gene subtypes and use this information in selecting which embryo to implant?

Many people believe intelligence is a purely social construct and so it is unlikely to have a significant

From Julian Savulescu, "Procreative Beneficence: Why We Should Select the Best Children," *Bioethics* 15 (Oct. 2001): 414–426. Copyright © 2001 Wiley-Blackwell Ltd. Reprinted by permission. (References omitted.)

genetic cause. Others believe there are different sorts of intelligence, such as verbal intelligence, mathematical intelligence, musical ability and no such thing as general intelligence. Time will tell. There are several genetic research programs currently in place which seek to elucidate the genetic contribution to intelligence. This paper pertains to any results of this research even if it only describes a weak probabilistic relation between genes and intelligence, or a particular kind of intelligence.

Many people believe that research into the genetic contribution to intelligence should not be performed, and that if genetic tests which predict intelligence, or a range of intelligence, are ever developed, they should not be employed in reproductive decision-making. I will argue that we have a moral obligation to test for genetic contribution to nondisease states such as intelligence and to use this information in reproductive decision-making.

Imagine now you are invited to play the Wheel of Fortune. A giant wheel exists with marks on it from 0–$1,000,000, in $100 increments. The wheel is spun in a secret room. It stops randomly on an amount. That amount is put into Box A. The wheel is spun again. The amount which comes up is put into Box B. You can choose Box A or B. You are also told that, in addition to the sum already put in the boxes, if you choose B, a [die] will be thrown and you will lose $100 if it comes up 6.

Which Box Should You Choose?

The rational answer is Box A. Choosing genes for non-disease states is like playing the Wheel of Fortune. You should use all the available information and choose the option most likely to bring about the best outcome.

Procreative Beneficence: The Moral Obligation to Have the Best Children

I will argue for a principle which I call Procreative Beneficence:

> *couples (or single reproducers) should select the child, of the possible children they could have, who is expected to have the best life, or at least as good a life as the others, based on the relevant, available information.*

I will argue that Procreative Beneficence implies couples should employ genetic tests for non-disease traits in selecting which child to bring into existence and that we should allow selection for non-disease genes in some cases even if this maintains or increases social inequality.

By "should" in "should choose," I mean "have good reason to." I will understand morality to require us to do what we have most reason to do. In the absence of some other reason for action, a person who has good reason to have the best child is morally required to have the best child.

Consider the following three situations involving normative judgements.

1. "You are 31. You will be at a higher risk of infertility and having a child with an abnormality if you delay child-bearing. But that has to be balanced against taking time out of your career now. That's only something you can weigh up."

2. "You should stop smoking."

3. "You must inform your partner that you are HIV positive or practise safe sex."

The "should" in "should choose the best child" is that present in the second example. It implies that persuasion is justified, but not coercion, which would be justified in the third case. Yet the situation is different from the more morally neutral (1).

Definitions

A disease gene is a gene which causes a genetic disorder (e.g. cystic fibrosis) or predisposes to the development of disease (e.g. the genetic contribution to cancer or dementia). A non-disease gene is a gene which causes or predisposes to some physical or psychological state of the person which is not itself a disease state, e.g. height, intelligence, character (not in the subnormal range).

Selection

It is currently possible to select from a range of possible children we could have. This is most frequently done by employing fetal selection through prenatal testing and termination of pregnancy. Selection of embryos is now possible by employing in vitro fertilization and preimplantation genetic diagnosis (PGD). There are currently no genetic tests available for non-disease states except sex. However, if such tests become available in the future, both PGD and prenatal testing could be used to select offspring on the basis of non-disease genes. Selection of sex by PGD is now undertaken in Sydney, Australia. PGD will also lower the threshold for couples to engage in selection since it has fewer psychological sequelae than prenatal testing and abortion.

In the future, it may be possible to select gametes according to their genetic characteristics. This is currently possible for sex, where methods have been developed to sort X and Y bearing sperm . . . .

An Argument for Procreative Beneficence

Consider the *Simple Case of Selection for Disease Genes.* A couple is having IVF in an attempt to have a child. It produces two embryos. A battery of tests for common diseases is performed. Embryo A has no abnormalities on the tests performed. Embryo B has no abnormalities on the tests performed except its genetic profile reveals it has a predisposition to developing asthma. Which embryo should be implanted?

Embryo B has nothing to be said in its favour over A and something against it. Embryo A should (on pain of irrationality) be implanted. This is like choosing Box A in the Wheel of Fortune analogy.

Why shouldn't we select the embryo with a predisposition to asthma? What is relevant about asthma is that it reduces quality of life. Attacks cause severe breathlessness and in extreme cases, death. Steroids may be required to treat it. These are among the most dangerous drugs which exist if taken long term. Asthma can be lifelong and require lifelong drug treatment. Ultimately it can leave the sufferer wheel chair bound with chronic obstructive airways disease. The morally relevant property of "asthma" is that it is a state which reduces the well-being a person experiences.

Parfitian Defence of Voluntary Procreative Beneficence in the Simple Case

The following example, after Parfit, supports Procreative Beneficence. A woman has rubella. If she conceives now, she will have a blind and deaf child. If she waits three months, she will conceive another different but healthy child. She should choose to wait until her rubella is passed.

Or consider the Nuclear Accident. A poor country does not have enough power to provide power to its citizens during an extremely cold winter. The government decides to open an old and unsafe nuclear reactor. Ample light and heating are then available. Citizens stay up later, and enjoy their lives much more. Several months later, the nuclear reactor melts down and large amounts of radiation are released into the environment. The only effect is that a large number of children are subsequently born with predispositions to early childhood malignancy.

The supply of heating and light has changed the lifestyle of this population. As a result of this change in lifestyle, people have conceived children at different times than they would have if there had been no heat or light, and their parents went to bed earlier. Thus, the children born after the nuclear accident would not have existed if the government had not switched to nuclear power. They have not been harmed by the switch to nuclear power and the subsequent accident (unless their lives are so bad they are worse than death). If we object to the Nuclear Accident (which most of us would), then we must appeal to some form of harmless wrong-doing. That is, we must claim that a wrong was done, but no one was harmed. We must appeal to something like the Principle of Procreative Beneficence.

An Objection to Procreative Beneficence in the Simple Case

The following objection to Procreative Beneficence is common.

> *"If you choose Embryo A (without a predisposition to asthma), you could be discarding someone like Mozart or an Olympic swimmer. So there is no good Reason to select A."*

It is true that by choosing A, you could be discarding a person like Mozart. But it is equally true that if you choose B, you could be discarding someone like Mozart without asthma. A and B are equally likely (on the information available) to be someone like Mozart (and B is more likely to have asthma).

Other Principles of Reproductive Decision-Making Applied to the Simple Case

The principle of Procreative Beneficence supports selecting the embryo without the genetic predisposition to asthma. That seems intuitively correct. How do other principles of reproductive decision-making apply to this example?

1. *Procreative Autonomy:* This principle claims that couples should be free to decide when and how to procreate, and what kind of children to have. If this were the only decision-guiding principle, it would imply couples might have reason to choose the embryo with a predisposition to asthma, if for some reason they wanted that.

2. *Principle of Non-Directive Counselling:* According to this principle, doctors and genetic counselors should only provide information about risk and options available to reduce that risk. They should not give advice or other direction. Thus, if a couple wanted to transfer Embryo B, and they knew that it would have a predisposition to asthma, nothing more is to be said according to Non-Directive Counselling.

3. *The "Best Interests of the Child" Principle:* Legislation in Australia and the United Kingdom related to reproduction gives great weight to consideration of the best interests of the child. For example, the Victorian Infertility Treatment Act 1995 states *"the welfare and interests of any person born or to be born as a result of a treatment procedure are paramount."* This principle is irrelevant to this choice. This couple could choose the embryo with

the predisposition to asthma and still be doing everything possible in the interests of *that* child.

None of the alternative principles give appropriate direction in the Simple Case.

Moving from Disease Genes to Non-Disease Genes: What Is the "Best Life"?

It is not asthma (or disease) which is important, but its impact on a life in ways that matter which is important. People often trade length of life for non-health related well-being. Non-disease genes may prevent us from leading the best life.

By "best life," I will understand the life with the most well-being. There are various theories of well-being: hedonistic, desire-fulfilment, objective list theories. According to hedonistic theories, what matters is the quality of our experiences, for example, that we experience pleasure. According to desire-fulfilment theories, what matters is the degree to which our desires are satisfied. According to objective list theories, certain activities are good for people, such as achieving worthwhile things with your life, having dignity, having children and raising them, gaining knowledge of the world, developing one's talents, appreciating beautiful things, and so on.

On any of these theories, some non-disease genes will affect the likelihood that we will lead the best life. Imagine there is a gene which contributes significantly to a violent, explosive, uncontrollable temper, and that state causes people significant suffering. Violent outbursts lead a person to come in conflict with the law and fall out of important social relations. The loss of independence, dignity and important social relations are bad on any of the three accounts.

Buchanan et al. argue that what is important in a liberal democracy is providing people with general purpose means, i.e. those useful to any plan of life. In this way we can allow people to form and act on their own conception of the good life. Examples of general purpose means are the ability to hear and see. But similarly the ability to concentrate, to engage with and be empathetic towards other human beings may be all purpose means. To the degree that genes contribute to these, we have reason to select those genes.

Consider another example. Memory (M) is the ability to remember important things when you want to. Imagine there is some genetic contribution to M:

Six alleles (genes) contribute to M. IVF produces four embryos. Should we test for M profiles?

Does M relate to well-being? Having to go to the supermarket twice because you forgot the baby formula prevents you doing more worthwhile things. Failing to remember can have disastrous consequences. Indeed, forgetting the compass on a long bush walk can be fatal. There is, then, a positive obligation to test for M and select the embryo (other things being equal) with the best M profile.

Does being intelligent mean one is more likely to have a better life? At a folk intuitive level, it seems plausible that intelligence would promote well-being on any plausible account of well-being. On a hedonistic account, the capacity to imagine alternative pleasures and remember the salient features of past experiences is important in choosing the best life. On a desire-fulfilment theory, intelligence is important to choosing means which will best satisfy one's ends. On an objective list account, intelligence would be important to gaining knowledge of the world, and developing rich social relations. Newson has reviewed the empirical literature relating intelligence to quality of life. Her synthesis of the empirical literature is that "intelligence has a high instrumental value for persons in giving them a large amount of complexity with which to approach their everyday lives, and that it equips them with a tool which can lead to the provision of many other personal and social goods."

Socrates, in Plato's Philebus, concludes that the best life is a mixture of wisdom and pleasure. Wisdom includes thought, intelligence, knowledge and memory. Intelligence is clearly a part of Plato's conception of the good life:

> *without the power of calculation you could not even calculate that you will get enjoyment in the future; your life would be that not of a man, but of a sea-lung or one of those marine creatures whose bodies are confined by a shell.*

Choice of Means of Selecting

This argument extends in principle to selection of fetuses using prenatal testing and termination of affected pregnancy. However, selection by abortion has greater psychological harms than selection by PGD and these need to be considered. Gametic selection, if it is ever possible, will have the lower psychological cost.

Objections to the Principle of Procreative Beneficence Applied to Non-Disease Genes

1. Harm to the Child. One common objection to genetic selection for non-disease traits is that it results in harm to the child. There are various versions of this objection, which include the harm which arises from excessive and overbearing parental expectations, using the child as a means, and not treating it as an end, and closing off possible future options on the basis of the information provided (failing to respect the child's "right to an open future").

There are a number of responses. Firstly, in some cases, it is possible to deny that the harms will be significant. Parents come to love the child whom they have (even a child with a serious disability). Moreover, some have argued that counselling can reduce excessive expectations.

Secondly, we can accept some risk of a child experiencing some state of reduced well-being in cases of selection. One variant of the harm to child objection is: "If you select embryo A, it might still get asthma, or worse, cancer, or have a much worse life than B, and you would be responsible." Yet selection is immune to this objection (in a way which genetic manipulation is not).

Imagine you select Embryo A and it develops cancer (or severe asthma) in later life. You have not harmed A unless A's life is not worth living (hardly plausible) because A would not have existed if you had acted otherwise. A is not made worse off than A would otherwise have been, since without the selection, A would not have existed. Thus we can accept the possibility of a bad outcome, but not the probability of a very bad outcome. (Clearly, Procreative Beneficence demands that we not choose a child with a low predisposition to asthma but who is likely to have a high predisposition to cancer.)

This is different from genetic manipulation. Imagine you perform gene therapy to correct a predisposition to asthma and you cause a mutation which results in cancer later in life. You have harmed A: A is worse off in virtue of the genetic manipulation than A would have been if the manipulation had not been performed (assuming cancer is worse than asthma).

There is, then, an important distinction between:

- interventions which are genetic manipulations of a single gamete, embryo or fetus

- selection procedures (e.g., sex selection) which select from among a range of different gametes, embryos and fetuses.

2. Inequality. One objection to Procreative Beneficence is that it will maintain or increase inequality. For example, it is often argued that selection for sex, intelligence, favourable physical or psychological traits, etc. all contribute to inequality in society, and this is a reason not to attempt to select the best.

In the case of selection against disease genes, similar claims are made. For example, one version of the *Disability Discrimination Claim* maintains that prenatal testing for disabilities such as Down syndrome results in discrimination against those with those disabilities both by:

- the statement it makes about the worth of such lives.

- the reduction in the numbers of people with this condition.

- Even if the Disability Discrimination Claim were true, it would be a drastic step in favour of equality to inflict a higher risk of having a child with a disability on a couple (who do not want a child with a disability) to promote social equality.

- Consider a hypothetical rubella epidemic. A rubella epidemic hits an isolated population. Embryos produced prior to the epidemic are not at an elevated risk of any abnormality but those produced during the epidemic are at an increased risk of deafness and blindness. Doctors should encourage women to use embryos which they have produced prior to the epidemic in preference to ones produced during the epidemic. The reason is that it is bad that blind and deaf children are born when sighted and hearing children could have been born in their place.

- This does not necessarily imply that the lives of those who now live with disability are less deserving of respect and are less valuable. To attempt to prevent accidents which cause paraplegia is not to say that paraplegics are less deserving of respect. It is important to distinguish between disability and persons with disability. Selection reduces the former, but is silent on the value of the latter. There are better ways to make statements about the equality of people with disability (e.g., we could direct savings from selection against embryos/fetuses with genetic abnormalities to improving well-being of existing people with disabilities).

■ These arguments extend to selection for non-disease genes. It is not disease which is important but its impact on well-being. In so far as a non-disease gene such as a gene for intelligence impacts on a person's well-being, parents have a reason to select for it, even if inequality results.

■ This claim can have counter-intuitive implications. Imagine in a country women are severely discriminated against. They are abandoned as children, refused paid employment and serve as slaves to men. Procreative Beneficence implies that couples should test for sex, and should choose males as they are expected to have better lives in this society, even if this reinforces the discrimination against women.

■ There are several responses. Firstly, it is unlikely selection on a scale that contributes to inequality would promote well-being. Imagine that 50% of the population choose to select boys. This would result in three boys to every one girl. The life of a male in such a society would be intolerable.

■ Secondly, it is social institutional reform, not interference in reproduction, which should be promoted. What is wrong in such a society is the treatment of women, which should be addressed separately to reproductive decision-making. Reproduction should not become an instrument of social change, at least not mediated or motivated at a social level.

■ This also illustrates why Procreative Beneficence is different from eugenics. Eugenics is selective breeding to produce a better *population*. A *public interest* justification for interfering in reproduction is different from Procreative Beneficence which aims at producing the best child, of the possible children, a couple could have. That is an essentially private enterprise. It was the eugenics movement itself which sought to influence reproduction, through involuntary sterilisation, to promote social goods.

■ Thirdly, consider the case of blackmail. A company says it will only develop an encouraging drug for cystic fibrosis (CF) if there are more than 100,000 people with CF. This would require stopping carrier testing for CF. Should the government stop carrier testing?

■ If there are other ways to fund this research (e.g., government funding), this should have priority. In virtually all cases of social inequality, there are other avenues to correct inequality than encouraging or forcing people to have children with disabilities or lives of restricted genetic opportunity.

Limits on Procreative Beneficence: Personal Concern for Equality or Self Interest

Consider the following cases. David and Dianne are dwarfs. They wish to use IVF and PGD to select a child with dwarfism because their house is set up for dwarfs. Sam and Susie live in a society where discrimination against women is prevalent. They wish to have a girl to reduce this discrimination. These choices would not harm the child produced if selection is employed. Yet they conflict with the Principle of Procreative Beneficence.

We have here an irresolvable conflict of principles:

■ personal commitment to equality, personal interests and Procreative Autonomy.

■ Procreative Beneficence.

Just as there are no simple answers to what should be done (from the perspective of ethics) when respect for personal autonomy conflicts with other principles such as beneficence or distributive justice, so too there are no simple answers to conflict between Procreative Autonomy and Procreative Beneficence.

For the purposes of public policy, there should be a presumption in favour of liberty in liberal democracies. So, ultimately, we should allow couples to make their own decisions about which child to have. Yet this does not imply that there are no normative principles to guide those choices. Procreative Beneficence is a valid principle, albeit one which must be balanced against others.

The implication of this is that those with disabilities should be allowed to select a child with disability, if they have a good reason. But the best option is that we correct discrimination in other ways, by correcting discriminatory social institutions. In this way, we can achieve both equality and a population whose members are living the best lives possible.

Conclusions

With respect to non-disease genes, we should provide:

- information (through PGD and prenatal testing)
- free choice of which child to have
- non-coercive advice as to which child will be expected to enter life with the best opportunity of having the best life.

Selection for non-disease genes which significantly impact on well-being is *morally required* (Procreative Beneficence). "Morally required" implies moral persuasion but not coercion is justified.

If, in the end, couples wish to select a child who will have a lower chance of having the best life, they should be free to make such a choice. That should not prevent doctors from attempting to persuade them to have the best child they can. In some cases, persuasion will not be justified. If self-interest or concern to promote equality motivate a choice to select less than the best, then there may be no overall reason to attempt to dissuade a couple. But in cases in which couples do not want to use or obtain available information about genes which will affect well-being, and their desires are based on irrational fears (e.g., about interfering with nature or playing God), then doctors should try to persuade them to access and use such information in their reproductive decision-making.

The Case Against Perfection

Michael J. Sandel

Sandel argues that genetic engineering and human enhancement are morally problematic, but not because they undermine human autonomy or deprive children of their right to an "open" future. Instead, the danger Sandel sees in the genomic revolution is a type of "hyper-agency," a drive to master and perfect nature to serve our purposes. In so doing, we lose a humble appreciation of children, natural talents, and life itself as a gift, rather than products of our will and design. For Sandel, a central problem with the "liberal eugenics" offered by thinkers such as Julian Savulescu is that it undermines compassion and social solidarity with the less fortunate, those with worse luck in the social or natural lotteries. In embracing the illusion that we can claim responsibility for our genetic and other endowments, we forget how much our own lives are shaped by contingency and chance. The risk of such eugenic enhancement lies not in state-imposed coercion but in an individualistic hubris that narrows our sympathies, dulls our sense of appreciation, and makes us see children as extensions of our own will.

Breakthroughs in genetics present us with a promise and a predicament. The promise is that we may soon be able to treat and prevent a host of debilitating diseases. The predicament is that our newfound genetic knowledge may also enable us to manipulate our own nature—to enhance our muscles, memories, and moods; to choose the sex, height, and other genetic traits of our children; to make ourselves "better than well." When science moves faster than moral understanding, as it does today, men and women struggle to articulate their unease. In liberal societies they reach first for the language of autonomy, fairness, and individual rights. But this part of our moral vocabulary is ill equipped to address the hardest questions posed by genetic engineering. The genomic revolution has induced a kind of moral vertigo.

Consider cloning. The birth of Dolly the cloned sheep, in 1997, brought a torrent of concern about the prospect of cloned human beings. There are good medical reasons to worry. Most scientists agree that cloning is unsafe, likely to produce offspring with serious abnormalities. (Dolly recently died a premature death.) But suppose technology improved to the point where clones were at no greater risk than naturally conceived offspring. Would human cloning still be objectionable? Should our hesitation be moral as well as medical? What, exactly, is wrong with creating a child who is a genetic twin of one parent, or of an older sibling who has tragically died—or, for that matter, of an admired scientist, sports star, or celebrity?

Some say cloning is wrong because it violates the right to autonomy: by choosing a child's genetic makeup in advance, parents deny the child's right to an open future. A similar objection can be raised against any form of bioengineering that allows parents to select or reject genetic characteristics. According to this argument, genetic enhancements for musical talent, say, or athletic prowess, would point children toward particular choices, and so designer children would never be fully free.

At first glance the autonomy argument seems to capture what is troubling about human cloning and other forms of genetic engineering. It is not persuasive, for two reasons. First, it wrongly implies that absent a designing parent, children are free to choose their characteristics for themselves. But none of us chooses his genetic inheritance. The alternative to a cloned or genetically enhanced child is not one whose future is unbound by particular talents but one at the mercy of the genetic lottery.

Second, even if a concern for autonomy explains some of our worries about made-to-order children, it cannot explain our moral hesitation about people who seek genetic remedies or enhancements for themselves. Gene therapy on somatic (that is, nonreproductive) cells, such as muscle cells and brain cells, repairs or replaces defective genes. The moral quandary arises when people use such therapy not to cure a disease but to reach beyond health, to enhance their physical or cognitive capacities, to lift themselves above the norm.

Like cosmetic surgery, genetic enhancement employs medical means for nonmedical ends—ends unrelated to curing or preventing disease or repairing injury. But unlike cosmetic surgery, genetic enhancement is more than skin-deep. If we are ambivalent about surgery or Botox injections for sagging chins and furrowed brows, we are all the more troubled by genetic engineering for stronger bodies, sharper memories, greater intelligence, and happier moods. The question is whether we are right to be troubled, and if so, on what grounds.

In order to grapple with the ethics of enhancement, we need to confront questions largely lost from view—questions about the moral status of nature, and about the proper stance of human beings toward the given world. Since these questions verge on theology, modern philosophers and political theorists tend to shrink from them. But our new powers of biotechnology make them unavoidable.

It is commonly said that genetic enhancements undermine our humanity by threatening our capacity to act freely, to succeed by our own efforts, and to consider ourselves responsible—worthy of praise or blame—for the things we do and for the way we are. It is one thing to hit seventy home runs as the result of disciplined training and effort, and something else, something less, to hit them with the help of steroids or genetically enhanced muscles. Of course, the roles of effort and enhancement will be a matter of degree. But as the role of enhancement increases, our admiration for the achievement fades—or, rather, our admiration for the achievement shifts from the player to his pharmacist. This suggests that our moral response to enhancement is a response to the diminished agency of the person whose achievement is enhanced.

Though there is much to be said for this argument, I do not think the main problem with enhancement and genetic engineering is that they undermine effort and erode human agency. The deeper danger is that they represent a kind of hyperagency—a Promethean aspiration to remake nature, including human nature, to serve our purposes and satisfy our desires. The problem is not the drift to mechanism but the drive to mastery. And what the drive to mastery misses and may even destroy is an appreciation of the gifted character of human powers and achievements.

To acknowledge the giftedness of life is to recognize that our talents and powers are not wholly our own doing, despite the effort we expend to develop and to exercise them. It is also to recognize that not everything in the world is open to whatever use we may desire or devise. Appreciating the gifted quality of life constrains the Promethean project and conduces to a certain humility. It is in part a religious sensibility. But its resonance reaches beyond religion.

It is difficult to account for what we admire about human activity and achievement without drawing upon some version of this idea. Consider two types of athletic achievement. We appreciate players like Pete Rose, who are not blessed with great natural gifts but who manage, through striving, grit, and determination, to excel in their sport. But we also admire players like Joe DiMaggio, who display natural gifts with grace and effortlessness. Now, suppose we learned that both players took performance-enhancing drugs. Whose turn to drugs would we find more deeply disillusioning? Which aspect of the athletic ideal—effort or gift—would be more deeply offended?

Some might say effort: the problem with drugs is that they provide a shortcut, a way to win without striving. But striving is not the point of sports; excellence is. And excellence consists at least partly in the display of natural talents and gifts that are no doing of the athlete who possesses them. This is an uncomfortable fact for democratic societies. We want to believe that success, in sports and in life, is something we earn, not something we inherit. Natural gifts, and the admiration they inspire, embarrass the meritocratic faith; they cast doubt on the conviction that praise and rewards flow from effort alone. In the face of this embarrassment we inflate the moral significance of striving, and depreciate giftedness. This distortion can be seen, for example, in network-television coverage of the Olympics, which focuses less on the feats the athletes perform than on heartrending stories of the hardships they have overcome and the struggles they have waged to triumph over an injury or a difficult upbringing or political turmoil in their native land.

But effort isn't everything. No one believes that a mediocre basketball player who works and trains even harder than Michael Jordan deserves greater acclaim or a bigger contract. The real problem with genetically altered athletes is that they corrupt athletic competition as a human activity that honors the cultivation and display of natural talents. From this standpoint, enhancement can be seen as the ultimate expression of the ethic of effort and willfulness—a kind of high-tech striving. The ethic of willfulness and the biotechnological powers it now enlists are arrayed against the claims of giftedness.

The ethic of giftedness, under siege in sports, persists in the practice of parenting. But here, too, bioengineering and genetic enhancement threaten to dislodge it. To appreciate children as gifts is to accept them as they come, not as objects of our design or products of our will or instruments of our ambition. Parental love is not contingent on the talents and attributes a child happens to have. We choose our friends and spouses at least partly on the basis of qualities we find attractive. But we do not choose our children. Their qualities are unpredictable, and even the most conscientious parents cannot be held wholly responsible for the kind of children they have.

That is why parenthood, more than other human relationships, teaches what the theologian William F. May calls an "openness to the unbidden."

May's resonant phrase helps us see that the deepest moral objection to enhancement lies less in the perfection it seeks than in the human disposition it expresses and promotes. The problem is not that parents usurp the autonomy of a child they design. The problem lies in the hubris of the designing parents, in their drive to master the mystery of birth. Even if this disposition did not make parents tyrants to their children, it would disfigure the relation between parent and child, and deprive the parent of the humility and enlarged human sympathies that an openness to the unbidden can cultivate.

To appreciate children as gifts or blessings is not, of course, to be passive in the face of illness or disease. Medical intervention to cure or prevent illness or restore the injured to health does not desecrate nature but honors it. Healing sickness or injury does not override a child's natural capacities but permits them to flourish.

Nor does the sense of life as a gift mean that parents must shrink from shaping and directing the development of their child. Just as athletes and artists have an obligation to cultivate their talents, so parents have an obligation to cultivate their children, to help them discover and develop their talents and gifts. As May points out, parents give their children two kinds of love: accepting love and transforming love. Accepting love affirms the being of the child, whereas transforming love seeks the well-being of the child. Each aspect corrects the excesses of the other, he writes: "Attachment becomes too quietistic if it slackens into mere acceptance of the child as he is." Parents have a duty to promote their children's excellence.

These days, however, overly ambitious parents are prone to get carried away with transforming love—promoting and demanding all manner of accomplishments from their children, seeking perfection. "Parents find it difficult to maintain an equilibrium between the two sides of love," May observes. "Accepting love, without transforming love, slides into indulgence and finally neglect. Transforming love, without accepting love, badgers and finally rejects." May finds in these competing impulses a parallel with modern science: it, too, engages us in beholding the given world, studying and savoring it, and also in molding the world, transforming and perfecting it.

The mandate to mold our children, to cultivate and improve them, complicates the case against enhancement. We usually admire parents who seek the best for their children, who spare no effort to help them achieve happiness and success. Some parents confer advantages on their children by enrolling them in expensive schools, hiring private tutors, sending them to tennis camp, providing them with piano lessons, ballet lessons, swimming lessons, SAT-prep courses, and so on. If it is permissible and even admirable for parents to help their children in these ways, why isn't it equally admirable for parents to use whatever genetic technologies may emerge (provided they are safe) to enhance their children's intelligence, musical ability, or athletic prowess?

The defenders of enhancement are right to this extent: improving children through genetic engineering is similar in spirit to the heavily managed, high-pressure child-rearing that is now common. But this similarity does not vindicate genetic enhancement. On the contrary, it highlights a problem with the trend toward hyperparenting. One conspicuous example of this trend is sports-crazed parents bent on making champions of their children. Another is the frenzied drive of overbearing parents to mold and manage their children's academic careers.

As the pressure for performance increases, so does the need to help distractible children concentrate on the task at hand. This may be why diagnoses of attention deficit and hyperactivity disorder have increased so sharply. Lawrence Diller, a pediatrician and the author of *Running on Ritalin*, estimates that five to six percent of American children under eighteen (a total of four to five million kids) are currently prescribed Ritalin, Adderall, and other stimulants, the treatment of choice for ADHD. (Stimulants counteract hyperactivity by making it easier to focus and sustain attention.) The number of Ritalin prescriptions for children and adolescents has tripled over the past decade, but not all users suffer from attention disorders or hyperactivity. High school and college students have learned that prescription stimulants improve concentration for those with normal attention spans, and some buy or borrow their classmates' drugs to enhance their performance on the SAT or other exams. Since stimulants work for both medical and nonmedical purposes, they raise the same moral questions posed by other technologies of enhancement.

However those questions are resolved, the debate reveals the cultural distance we have traveled since the debate over marijuana, LSD, and other drugs a generation ago. Unlike the drugs of the 1960s and 1970s,

Ritalin and Adderall are not for checking out but for buckling down, not for beholding the world and taking it in but for molding the world and fitting in. We used to speak of nonmedical drug use as "recreational." That term no longer applies. The steroids and stimulants that figure in the enhancement debate are not a source of recreation but a bid for compliance—a way of answering a competitive society's demand to improve our performance and perfect our nature. This demand for performance and perfection animates the impulse to rail against the given. It is the deepest source of the moral trouble with enhancement.

Some see a clear line between genetic enhancement and other ways that people seek improvement in their children and themselves. Genetic manipulation seems somehow worse—more intrusive, more sinister—than other ways of enhancing performance and seeking success. But morally speaking, the difference is less significant than it seems. Bioengineering gives us reason to question the low-tech, high-pressure child-rearing practices we commonly accept. The hyperparenting familiar in our time represents an anxious excess of mastery and dominion that misses the sense of life as a gift. This draws it disturbingly close to eugenics.

The shadow of eugenics hangs over today's debates about genetic engineering and enhancement. Critics of genetic engineering argue that human cloning, enhancement, and the quest for designer children are nothing more than "privatized" or "free-market" eugenics. Defenders of enhancement reply that genetic choices freely made are not really eugenic—at least not in the pejorative sense. To remove the coercion, they argue, is to remove the very thing that makes eugenic policies repugnant.

Sorting out the lesson of eugenics is another way of wrestling with the ethics of enhancement. The Nazis gave eugenics a bad name. But what, precisely, was wrong with it? Was the old eugenics objectionable only insofar as it was coercive? Or is there something inherently wrong with the resolve to deliberately design our progeny's traits?

James Watson, the biologist who, with Francis Crick, discovered the structure of DNA, sees nothing wrong with genetic engineering and enhancement, provided they are freely chosen rather than state-imposed. And yet Watson's language contains more than a whiff of the old eugenic sensibility. "If you really are stupid, I would call that a disease," he recently told The Times of London. "The lower

10 percent who really have difficulty, even in elementary school, what's the cause of it? A lot of people would like to say, 'Well, poverty, things like that.' It probably isn't. So I'd like to get rid of that, to help the lower 10 percent." A few years ago Watson stirred controversy by saying that if a gene for homosexuality were discovered, a woman should be free to abort a fetus that carried it. When his remark provoked an uproar, he replied that he was not singling out gays but asserting a principle: women should be free to abort fetuses for any reason of genetic preference—for example, if the child would be dyslexic, or lacking musical talent, or too short to play basketball.

Watson's scenarios are clearly objectionable to those for whom all abortion is an unspeakable crime. But for those who do not subscribe to the pro-life position, these scenarios raise a hard question: If it is morally troubling to contemplate abortion to avoid a gay child or a dyslexic one, doesn't this suggest that something is wrong with acting on any eugenic preference, even when no state coercion is involved?

A number of political philosophers call for a new "liberal eugenics." They argue that a moral distinction can be drawn between the old eugenic policies and genetic enhancements that do not restrict the autonomy of the child. "While old-fashioned authoritarian eugenicists sought to produce citizens out of a single centrally designed mould," writes Nicholas Agar, "the distinguishing mark of the new liberal eugenics is state neutrality." Government may not tell parents what sort of children to design, and parents may engineer in their children only those traits that improve their capacities without biasing their choice of life plans. A recent text on genetics and justice, written by the bioethicists Allen Buchanan, Dan W. Brock, Norman Daniels, and Daniel Wikler, offers a similar view. The "bad reputation of eugenics," they write, is due to practices that "might be avoidable in a future eugenic program." The problem with the old eugenics was that its burdens fell disproportionately on the weak and the poor, who were unjustly sterilized and segregated. But provided that the benefits and burdens of genetic improvement are fairly distributed, these bioethicists argue, eugenic measures are unobjectionable and may even be morally required.

The libertarian philosopher Robert Nozick proposed a "genetic supermarket" that would enable parents to order children by design without imposing a single design on the society as a whole:

"This supermarket system has the great virtue that it involves no centralized decision fixing the future human type(s)."

Even the leading philosopher of American liberalism, John Rawls, in his classic *A Theory of Justice* (1971), offered a brief endorsement of noncoercive eugenics. Even in a society that agrees to share the benefits and burdens of the genetic lottery, it is "in the interest of each to have greater natural assets," Rawls wrote. "This enables him to pursue a preferred plan of life." The parties to the social contract "want to insure for their descendants the best genetic endowment (assuming their own to be fixed)." Eugenic policies are therefore not only permissible but required as a matter of justice. "Thus over time a society is to take steps at least to preserve the general level of natural abilities and to prevent the diffusion of serious defects."

But removing the coercion does not vindicate eugenics. The problem with eugenics and genetic engineering is that they represent the one-sided triumph of willfulness over giftedness, of dominion over reverence, of molding over beholding. Why, we may wonder, should we worry about this triumph? Why not shake off our unease about genetic enhancement as so much superstition? What would be lost if biotechnology dissolved our sense of giftedness?

From a religious standpoint the answer is clear: To believe that our talents and powers are wholly our own doing is to misunderstand our place in creation, to confuse our role with God's. Religion is not the only source of reasons to care about giftedness, however. The moral stakes can also be described in secular terms. If bioengineering made the myth of the "self-made man" come true, it would be difficult to view our talents as gifts for which we are indebted, rather than as achievements for which we are responsible. This would transform three key features of our moral landscape: humility, responsibility, and solidarity.

In a social world that prizes mastery and control, parenthood is a school for humility. That we care deeply about our children and yet cannot choose the kind we want teaches parents to be open to the unbidden. Such openness is a disposition worth affirming, not only within families but in the wider world as well. It invites us to abide the unexpected, to live with dissonance, to rein in the impulse to control. A Gattaca-like world in which parents became accustomed to specifying the sex and genetic traits of their children would be a world inhospitable to the unbidden, a gated community writ large.

The awareness that our talents and abilities are not wholly our own doing restrains our tendency toward hubris.

Though some maintain that genetic enhancement erodes human agency by overriding effort, the real problem is the explosion, not the erosion, of responsibility. As humility gives way, responsibility expands to daunting proportions. We attribute less to chance and more to choice. Parents become responsible for choosing, or failing to choose, the right traits for their children. Athletes become responsible for acquiring, or failing to acquire, the talents that will help their teams win.

One of the blessings of seeing ourselves as creatures of nature, God, or fortune is that we are not wholly responsible for the way we are. The more we become masters of our genetic endowments, the greater the burden we bear for the talents we have and the way we perform. Today when a basketball player misses a rebound, his coach can blame him for being out of position. Tomorrow the coach may blame him for being too short. Even now the use of performance-enhancing drugs in professional sports is subtly transforming the expectations players have for one another; on some teams players who take the field free from amphetamines or other stimulants are criticized for "playing naked."

The more alive we are to the chanced nature of our lot, the more reason we have to share our fate with others. Consider insurance. Since people do not know whether or when various ills will befall them, they pool their risk by buying health insurance and life insurance. As life plays itself out, the healthy wind up subsidizing the unhealthy, and those who live to a ripe old age wind up subsidizing the families of those who die before their time. Even without a sense of mutual obligation, people pool their risks and resources and share one another's fate.

But insurance markets mimic solidarity only insofar as people do not know or control their own risk factors. Suppose genetic testing advanced to the point where it could reliably predict each person's medical future and life expectancy. Those confident of good health and long life would opt out of the pool, causing other people's premiums to skyrocket. The solidarity of insurance would disappear as those with good genes fled the actuarial company of those with bad ones.

The fear that insurance companies would use genetic data to assess risks and set premiums recently led the Senate to vote to prohibit genetic discrimination in health insurance. But the bigger danger, admittedly more speculative, is that genetic enhancement, if routinely practiced, would make it harder to foster the moral sentiments that social solidarity requires.

Why, after all, do the successful owe anything to the least-advantaged members of society? The best answer to this question leans heavily on the notion of giftedness. The natural talents that enable the successful to flourish are not their own doing but, rather, their good fortune—a result of the genetic lottery. If our genetic endowments are gifts, rather than achievements for which we can claim credit, it is a mistake and a conceit to assume that we are entitled to the full measure of the bounty they reap in a market economy. We therefore have an obligation to share this bounty with those who, through no fault of their own, lack comparable gifts.

A lively sense of the contingency of our gifts—a consciousness that none of us is wholly responsible for his or her success—saves a meritocratic society from sliding into the smug assumption that the rich are rich because they are more deserving than the poor. Without this, the successful would become even more likely than they are now to view themselves as self-made and self-sufficient, and hence wholly responsible for their success. Those at the bottom of society would be viewed not as disadvantaged, and thus worthy of a measure of compensation, but as simply unfit, and thus worthy of eugenic repair. The meritocracy, less chastened by chance, would become harder, less forgiving. As perfect genetic knowledge would end the simulacrum of solidarity in insurance markets, so perfect genetic control would erode the actual solidarity that arises when men and women reflect on the contingency of their talents and fortunes.

Thirty-five years ago Robert L. Sinsheimer, a molecular biologist at the California Institute of Technology, glimpsed the shape of things to come. In an article titled "The Prospect of Designed Genetic Change" he argued that freedom of choice would vindicate the new genetics, and set it apart from the discredited eugenics of old.

> *To implement the older eugenics . . . would have required a massive social programme carried out over many generations. Such a programme could not have been initiated without the consent and co-operation of a major fraction of the population,*

and would have been continuously subject to social control. In contrast, the new eugenics could, at least in principle, be implemented on a quite individual basis, in one generation, and subject to no existing restrictions.

According to Sinsheimer, the new eugenics would be voluntary rather than coerced, and also more humane. Rather than segregating and eliminating the unfit, it would improve them. "The old eugenics would have required a continual selection for breeding of the fit, and a culling of the unfit," he wrote. "The new eugenics would permit in principle the conversion of all the unfit to the highest genetic level."

Sinsheimer's paean to genetic engineering caught the heady, Promethean self-image of the age. He wrote hopefully of rescuing "the losers in that chromosomal lottery that so firmly channels our human destinies," including not only those born with genetic defects but also "the 50,000,000 'normal' Americans with an IQ of less than 90." But he also saw that something bigger than improving on nature's "mindless, age-old throw of dice" was at stake. Implicit in technologies of genetic intervention was a more exalted place for human beings in the cosmos. "As we

enlarge man's freedom, we diminish his constraints and that which he must accept as given," he wrote. Copernicus and Darwin had "demoted man from his bright glory at the focal point of the universe," but the new biology would restore his central role. In the mirror of our genetic knowledge we would see ourselves as more than a link in the chain of evolution: "We can be the agent of transition to a whole new pitch of evolution. This is a cosmic event."

There is something appealing, even intoxicating, about a vision of human freedom unfettered by the given. It may even be the case that the allure of that vision played a part in summoning the genomic age into being. It is often assumed that the powers of enhancement we now possess arose as an inadvertent by-product of biomedical progress—the genetic revolution came, so to speak, to cure disease, and stayed to tempt us with the prospect of enhancing our performance, designing our children, and perfecting our nature. That may have the story backwards. It is more plausible to view genetic engineering as the ultimate expression of our resolve to see ourselves astride the world, the masters of our nature. But that promise of mastery is flawed. It threatens to banish our appreciation of life as a gift, and to leave us with nothing to affirm or behold outside our own will.

Section 3: Genetics and Abortion

Disability, Prenatal Testing, and Selective Abortion
Bonnie Steinbock

Steinbock examines the view that selective abortion on the basis of fetal abnormalities is a form of discrimination against the disabled. According to this perspective, prenatal screening and selective abortion embody the idea that the disabled are "better off unborn" and is comparable to terminating a pregnancy based on sex. Steinbock rejects this view, arguing that it is reasonable for parents to wish to prevent disability in their children and that doing so does not imply a devaluation of disabled people. Instead, it reflects a wish to avoid genuinely heavy burdens for developmentally disabled children and their parents. If abortion is morally acceptable in other contexts, then it is no more discriminatory than taking other steps during a pregnancy (such as taking folic acid) to avoid giving birth to a child with serious disabilities.

When Bob Dole addressed the international convention of B'nai B'rith a few years ago, he said that, as a member of a minority group himself—the disabled—he understands the wrong of discrimination. Some listeners were offended by this comparison. A professor of theology at Georgetown University was quoted in The New York Times as saying, "Most Jews today don't regard being Jewish as a handicap. They regard it as a privilege; it gives them roots and depth and a mission."

But some disabled people would argue that they do not regard their disabling condition as a handicap. It is not their medical condition that puts limits on what they can do, but rather the way in which society is organized. Some would go farther, arguing that disability makes one part of a community or culture, and that identification with that culture is as important to identity as being a member of a race or ethnic group. Erik Parens has characterized the position this way:

> Some people in the disability-rights community argue that so-called disabilities are forms of variation, which ought to be affirmed in the same way that most liberals want to affirm any other form of variation (such as being female or black).

Let us call this the "forms of variation" argument. Parens goes on to draw out an implication of this view for what physicians call "abortion for fetal indications":

> Some people in the disability-rights community argue that just as most liberals deplore sex selection (at least in part) on the grounds that it exacerbates discrimination against women, so should they deplore other sorts of selective abortion on similar grounds. While we can accept that being a woman in this culture can be disadvantageous (can in its way be "disabling"), we think that we ought to change the culture, not aggressively pursue the elimination of female fetuses. According to this line, having a "traditional disability" is like being a woman: the disadvantages it brings are largely socially constructed; we should change how the culture treats people with disabilities, not try to eliminate fetuses with "disabling" traits.[1]

Let us call this view "the disability perspective on abortion."[2] The disability perspective on abortion is independent of the form of variation argument: it is possible to reject the form of variation argument while still holding the disability perspective on abortion. It is also important to note that the opposition to aborting fetuses likely to have a disability is not derived from a generally "pro-life" perspective. Some of the most passionate advocates of the disability perspective on abortion are generally "pro-choice." However, they regard abortion for "fetal indications" as discriminatory and pernicious in a way that abortion for other reasons is not.

Needless to say, the disability perspective on abortion is not a mainstream view. For most people who regard abortion as justifiable, a serious disabling condition[3] in the fetus is regarded as one of the strongest reasons for terminating a pregnancy, far stronger than reasons like inability to afford a child, having to drop out of school, not wanting to marry the father, and so forth. Even among those who are almost always opposed to abortion, a severe disability in the fetus, like rape and incest, is often regarded as justifying abortion. The disability perspective challenges this popular view, and therefore must be addressed.

Are Prenatal Testing and Selective Abortion Morally Acceptable Ways of Preventing Disability?[4]

The disability perspective holds that prenatal testing for disability is as destructively discriminatory as sex selection. It maintains that the view that "fetal indications" justify abortion (or embryo discard) stems from the ignorant and prejudiced belief that having a disability makes life unbearable, and that those who are disabled are "better off unborn." Moreover, since prenatal screening cannot prevent all disability, e.g., disabilities caused during or after birth, an attitude of inclusion is better than an attitude of removal. Furthermore, prenatal screening leads parents to expect a "perfect baby." It increases intolerance of imperfection, and thus increases discriminatory attitudes toward disability.

Adrienne Asch is one writer who finds abortion for "fetal indications" profoundly troubling. This is not because she regards fetuses as persons and abortion as seriously morally wrong. Her view is that abortion is morally acceptable if the woman does not want to become a mother. However, she distinguishes between abortion to prevent having a child (any child) and abortion to prevent having this child. Why, Asch asks, would someone who wants to be a mother reject this pregnancy and this (future) child because of one thing about that child: that is, that he or she will have, or is likely to have, a disability? She believes that such rejection is likely to stem from inaccurate and prejudiced ideas about what it is like to have a disability or to parent a child with a disability.

Asch considers aborting to avoid having a child with a disability morally on a par with abortion to avoid having a child of the "wrong" sex. It embodies the view that there is something undesirable about being a person with a disability; so undesirable that it is better that such people do not get born. George Annas agrees that this is the rationale for prenatal testing, but does not think that this makes such testing wrong. This is because he thinks that prenatal testing is used only to prevent the births of individuals whose lives would be so awful that they are better off not being born. He writes:

> *Historically, prenatal screening has been used to find life-threatening or severely debilitating disease where a reasonable argument can be made that actually the fetus is better off dead than living a, usually, short life (Annas, 1994, p. 265).*

But this is simply false. Prenatal testing has not been, and is not today, used only or even primarily to detect life-threatening, extremely severe fetal anomalies. One of the most common reasons for screening women over 35 in the U.S. is to detect trisomy 21 (Down syndrome). Down syndrome is not a fatal disease; many people with Down's live into their fifties and sixties. Moreover, it is compatible with a good quality of life, with appropriate medical treatment and educational opportunities. It is simply not true that someone who has Down syndrome would be better off dead or unborn.

What, then, should we say about most prenatal testing, which is used to screen for conditions that are serious but compatible with a life worth living? Should we say that such screening is wrong, comparable to screening for sex?[5] I do not think we need to concede this. There is another way to defend prenatal screening, one that does not require the fiction that it is used only to prevent the births of children whose lives will be so awful that they are better off unborn. Prenatal screening, along with abortion and embryo selection, can be seen as a form of prevention. It enables prospective parents to prevent an outcome they reasonably want to avoid: the birth of a child who will be sick or have a serious disability.

Admittedly, abortion prevents this outcome by terminating a pregnancy, by killing a fetus. In this respect, it differs from giving the pregnant woman folic acid, which does not kill, but rather promotes healthy development in, the fetus. Obviously, if fetuses have the same moral status as born children, then this difference is crucial. It is permissible to reduce the incidence disability by keeping people healthy; it is not permissible to reduce the incidence of disability by killing people with disabilities. But if embryos and fetuses are not people (something a pro-choicer like Asch concedes), then the impermissibility of killing people to prevent or reduce the incidence of disability is irrelevant to the permissibility of abortion or embryo selection.

At the same time, most people find the termination of a wanted pregnancy troubling. Having an abortion at 16 weeks, after an amniocentesis that reveals a serious, but not life-threatening, condition in the fetus, is not psychologically comparable to taking a folic acid supplement during pregnancy, and probably is not morally identical either. Even if fetuses are not people and do not have full moral status, they are potential people with some claim to our moral attention and concern, a claim that grows stronger as the fetus grows and develops. Most abortions for fetal indications take place in the second or even third trimester, when the fetus has many of the characteristics of a newborn, including human form, perhaps sentience, and some brain activity in the neocortex. All of these developments may incline us to extend the protection granted newborns to the late-gestation fetus.[6] For late abortions to be morally justifiable, the reason for having the abortion must be serious. In my view, abortion for fetal indications meets this requirement. It is reasonable for parents to wish to avoid having a child with a serious disability, like spina bifida or Down syndrome or cystic fibrosis, because these conditions may involve undesirable events, such as pain, repeated hospitalizations and operations, paralysis, a shortened life span, limited educational and job opportunities, limited independence, and so forth. This is not to say that everyone with a serious disability will experience these difficulties, only that they may, and that these are problems parents reasonably wish their children not to have. If abortion is permissible at all, it is permissible to avoid such outcomes, or the risk of such outcomes.

Asch rejects the idea that prenatal testing and abortion (or embryo selection) can be viewed as "prevention." She writes:

> *What differentiates ending pregnancy after learning of impairment from striving to avoid impairment before life has begun is this: At the point one ends such a pregnancy, one is indicating that one cannot accept and welcome the opportunity to nurture a life that will have a potential set of characteristics—impairments perceived as deficits and problems (Asch, 1988, p. 82).*

This suggests that there is something morally deficient in not being able to accept and welcome the opportunity to nurture a child with disabilities, a suggestion I want to rebut. First, the impairments may not merely be perceived as creating problems. This may be a realistic assessment of the situation. We do no one, not disabled individuals, not women, not families, a service by minimizing the physical, mental, and emotional burdens that may result from parenting children with disabilities.

Wertz and Fletcher outline some of these burdens in a discussion of the probable impact of having a mentally retarded child (Wertz and Fletcher, 1993). First, most of the care of the child tends to fall on the mother. Since most people with mental retardation live at home, she may have to stop working and adopt motherhood as her primary identification. She may have this role for the rest of her life. "It is not uncommon for parents in their eighties to be caring for children with Down syndrome who are in their fifties." (Wertz and Fletcher, 1993, p. 175) These are not trivial burdens, and the desire to avoid them does not indicate a character flaw, any more than wanting to avoid an hiatus in one's education or career. Whether a woman wants to terminate a pregnancy to avoid the burdens that come with being a mother, or whether she wants to terminate a pregnancy to avoid the burdens that come with being the mother of this child, the rationale for the abortion is the same: the avoidance of burdens that she finds unacceptable.

Asch points out that prospective parents cannot protect themselves from all burdens. A child may become disabled during or after birth. If a woman is unwilling to expend the extra effort to parent a child with a disability, how good a parent will she be? But even if we agree that a good parent will be willing to undergo burdens and sacrifices for a child, it doesn't follow that it is impermissible to try to avoid such sacrifices and burdens before becoming a parent. From a pro-choice perspective at least, a fetus is not a child and a pregnant woman is not yet a mother. Therefore, she does not have the same obligations to her fetus as she would to a born child.

In my view, a pregnant woman still has a choice whether or not to continue her pregnancy. She may change her mind because her circumstances change (e.g., the couple divorces). Although the pregnancy was wanted, she may not want to become a mother if this means being a single parent. Similarly, she may prefer to terminate a wanted pregnancy, because she wants a healthy, non-disabled child. Terminating the pregnancy gives her and her husband the chance to try again.

We can all agree that prospective parents should be fully informed about the problems and challenges they are likely to face, and that the decision to terminate should not be based on fear or ignorance. However, we can also recognize that parenthood itself is a very difficult job, even raising children without disabilities. If a woman or couple prefer not to accept the burdens and challenges that go with raising a child with special needs, that is a morally acceptable choice, and not one for which they need feel guilty or inadequate as prospective parents.

The Discrimination Argument

Another argument from the disability community focuses on the symbolic meaning of prenatal testing and its implications for people with disabilities. Sometimes this is expressed by saying that prenatal testing "sends a message" that "we don't want any more of your kind." Prenatal testing is seen, on this view, as a public statement that the lives of the disabled are worth less than those of the able-bodied. As John Robertson characterizes the view, "In short, it engenders or reinforces public perceptions that the disabled should not exist, making intolerance and discrimination toward them more likely" (Robertson, 1996, p. 453)

This is a powerful charge and one that needs to be taken seriously. If prenatal testing actually causes harm to disabled people by increasing discrimination or reducing opportunities, that is a strong policy reason against prenatal testing. Even if prenatal testing does not cause tangible harm to discreet individuals, but only makes a symbolic statement that the lives of disabled people are worth less, that is a reason to be troubled by prenatal testing.

However, I do not think that the argument is persuasive. From the fact that a couple wants to avoid the birth of a child with a disability, it just does not follow that they value less the lives of existing people with disabilities, any more than taking folic acid to avoid spina bifida indicates a devaluing of the lives of people with spina bifida. The wish to avoid having a child with disabilities does not imply that if that outcome should occur, the child will be unwanted, rejected, or loved less. There is no inconsistency in thinking, "If I have a child who has a disability, or becomes ill, or has special needs, I will love and care for that child; but this is an outcome I would much prefer to avoid." Allen Buchanan illustrates this point with a thought experiment:

> *Suppose God tells a couple: "I'll make a child for you. You can have a child that has limited opportunities due to a physical or cognitive defect or one who does not. Which do you choose?" Surely, if the couple says they wish to have a child without defects, this need not mean that they devalue persons with disabilities, or that they would not love and cherish their child if it were disabled. Choosing to have God make a child who does not have defects does not in itself in any way betray negative judgments or attitudes about the value of individuals with defects(Buchanan, 1996, pp. 33–34).*

Disability activists have a laudable goal: to change society so that it is welcoming and accepting of people with disabilities. However, there is no reason why society cannot both attempt to prevent disability and to provide for the needs of those who are disabled. As a matter of fact, the rise of prenatal screening has coincided with more progressive attitudes toward the inclusion of people with disabilities, as evidenced in the United States by the passage of the Americans with Disabilities Act.

Conclusion

Prejudice and discrimination against people with disabilities is no more acceptable than racial or gender prejudice and discrimination. The socio-political model can help nondisabled (or temporarily-abled) individuals see how the world might be changed to make it more accessible to those with disabilities. The result might be a greater willingness on the part of prospective parents to accept the risk of having a child with a serious disability, and might reduce the desire for prenatal testing.

On the other hand, it might not. Some couples will prefer not to have a child with a serious disability, no matter how wonderful the social services, no matter how inclusive the society. In my view, this is a perfectly acceptable attitude, one that does not impugn their ability to be good parents. Nor does this attitude imply a devaluing of the lives of existing people with disabilities, any more than programs to vaccinate children against polio or ensure that pregnant women get enough folic acid. There is no conflict between respecting the rights of people with disabilities, and respecting the rights of women to make their own informed decisions about whether to have prenatal testing, and if they have it, how to respond to the results of that testing.

Notes

1. Letter to the author.
2. In calling this "the disability perspective on abortion, " I do not mean to suggest that all people with disabilities embrace this view, or even that all people who are disability rights advocates take this view. At a meeting of the Society for Disability Studies (SDS), I heard one woman speak in favor of prenatal testing on the ground that it would not benefit a child with a disability to be born to parents who felt unwilling or unable to cope with raising such a child. Nevertheless, I think that the more prevalent view among disability activists is that abortion to prevent the birth of a person with disabilities is morally wrong, comparable to abortion for sex selection.
3. I limit myself in this paper to "serious disabilities," leaving aside the question of abortion for trivial conditions. People will differ on what they consider a "serious" disability and I do not attempt to define the term. In general, I consider a disability serious if most people would make strenuous efforts to prevent its occurrence.
4. Some of the material in this section comes from my paper, "Preimplantation Genetic Diagnosis and Embryo Selection, " in Justine Burley and John Harris, eds., *A Companion to Genetics: Philosophy and the Genetic Revolution* (Blackwell Publishers, forthcoming 1999).
5. While most people find sex selection generally morally problematic, there might be situations in which screening for sex would be morally permissible. Some genetic diseases affect only one sex, so it is reasonable to screen for sex to avoid having a child with the disease. In addition, there may be cultures in which being female is a disability. Ideally, those cultures should change, but until they do, I do not think it would be wrong for a woman to screen for sex, rather than undergo multiple pregnancies which might be damaging to her own health until she produces the required male child. Moreover, bringing female children into the world knowing they will be deprived of food and medical care is not necessarily a strike for feminism.
6. See Nancy Rhoden, "Trimesters and Technology: Revamping *Roe v. Wade*," *Yale Law Journal* 95:4 (1986), 639–697, for a good explanation of the moral significance of late-gestation.

Implications of Prenatal Diagnosis for the Human Right to Life

Leon R. Kass

Kass expresses concern that the practice of "genetic abortion" will strongly affect our attitudes toward all who are "defective" or abnormal. Those who escape the net of selective abortion might receive less care and might even come to think of themselves as second-class citizens. Furthermore, on Kass's view, genetic abortion might encourage us to accept the general principle that "defectives" of any kind ought not to be born. This in turn would threaten our commitment to the basic moral principle that each person, despite any physical or mental disability, is the inherent equal of every other person.

Kass presents six criteria that he suggests ought to be satisfied to justify the abortion of a fetus for genetic reasons. In the remainder of his paper, he focuses on the question raised by the last criterion: According to what standards should we judge a fetus with genetic abnormalities unfit to live? As candidates for such standards, Kass examines the concepts of social good, family good, and the "healthy and sound" fetus. He finds difficulty with all, and in the end he professes himself unable to provide a satisfactory justification for genetic abortion.

I wish to focus on the special ethical issues raised by the abortion of "defective" fetuses (so-called "abortion for fetal indications"). I shall consider only the cleanest cases, those cases where well-characterized genetic diseases are diagnosed with a high degree of certainty by means of amniocentesis, in order to sidestep the added moral dilemmas posed when the diagnosis is suspected or possible, but unconfirmed. However, many of the questions I shall discuss could also be raised about cases where genetic analysis gives only a statistical prediction about the genotype of the fetus, and also about cases where the defect has an infectious or chemical rather than a genetic cause (e.g. rubella, thalidomide). . . .

Precisely because the quality of the fetus is central to the decision to abort, the practice of genetic abortion has implications which go beyond those raised by abortion in general. What may be at stake here is the belief that all human beings possess equally and independent of merit certain fundamental rights, one among which is, of course, the right to life.

To be sure, the belief that fundamental human rights belong equally to all human beings has been but an ideal, never realized, often ignored, sometimes shamelessly. Yet it has been perhaps the most powerful moral idea at work in the world for at least two centuries. It is this idea and ideal that animates most of the current political and social criticism around the globe. It is ironic that we should acquire the power to detect and eliminate the genetically unequal at a time when we have finally succeeded in removing much of the stigma and disgrace previously attached to victims of congenital illness, in providing them with improved care and support, and in preventing, by means of education, feelings of guilt on the part of their parents. One might even wonder whether the development of amniocentesis and prenatal diagnosis may represent a backlash against these same humanitarian and egalitarian tendencies in the practice of medicine, which, by helping to sustain to the age of reproduction persons with genetic disease, has itself contributed to the

Reprinted from *Ethical Issues in Human Genetics: Genetic Counseling and the Use of Genetic Knowledge*, edited by Bruce Hilton, Daniel Callahan, Maureen Harris, Peter Condliffe, and Burton Berkely (New York: Plenum, 1973), pp. 186–199. A revised version of this essay ("Perfect Babies: Prenatal Diagnosis and the Equal Right to Life") appears in Kass's book *Toward a More Natural Science: Biology and Human Affairs* (New York: Free Press, 1985). (Notes omitted).

increasing incidence of genetic disease, and with it, to increased pressures for genetic screening, genetic counseling, and genetic abortion.

No doubt our humanitarian and egalitarian principles and practices have caused us some new difficulties, but if we mean to weaken or turn our backs on them, we should do so consciously and thoughtfully. If, as I believe, the idea and practice of genetic abortion points in that direction, we should make ourselves aware of it. And if, as I believe, the way in which genetic abortion is described, discussed, and justified is perhaps of even greater consequence than its practice for our notions of human rights and of their equal possession by all human beings, we should pay special attention to questions of language and in particular, to the question of justification. Before turning full attention to these matters, two points should be clarified.

First, my question "What decision, and why?" is to be distinguished from the question "Who decides, and why?" There is a tendency to blur this distinction and to discuss only the latter, and with it, the underlying question of private freedom versus public good. I will say nothing about this, since I am more interested in exploring what constitutes "good," both public and private. Accordingly, I would emphasize that the moral question—What decision, and why?—does not disappear simply because the decision is left in the hands of each pregnant woman. It is the moral question she faces. I would add that the moral health of the community and of each of its members is as likely to be affected by the aggregate of purely private and voluntary decisions on genetic abortions as by a uniform policy imposed by statute. We physicians and scientists especially should refuse to finesse the moral question of genetic abortion and its implications and to take refuge behind the issue, "Who decides?" For it is we who are responsible for choosing to develop the technology of prenatal diagnosis, for informing and promoting this technology among the public, and for the actual counseling of patients.

Second, I wish to distinguish my discussion of what ought to be done from a descriptive account of what in fact is being done, and especially from a consideration of what I myself might do, faced with the difficult decision. I cannot know with certainty what I would think, feel, do, or want done, faced with the knowledge that my wife was carrying a child branded with Down's syndrome or Tay-Sachs disease. But an understanding of the issues is not advanced by

personal anecdote or confession. We all know that what we and others actually do is often done out of weakness, rather than conviction. It is all-too-human to make an exception in one's own case (consider, e.g., the extra car, the "extra" child, income tax, the draft, the flight from cities). For what it is worth, I confess to feeling more than a little sympathy with parents who choose abortions for severe genetic defect. Nevertheless, as I shall indicate later, in seeking for reasons to justify this practice, I can find none that are in themselves fully satisfactory and none that do not simultaneously justify the killing of "defective" infants, children, and adults. I am mindful that my arguments will fall far from the middle of the stream, yet I hope that the oarsmen of the flagship will pause and row more slowly, while we all consider whither we are going.

Genetic Abortion and the Living Defective

The practice of abortion of the genetically defective will no doubt affect our view of and our behavior toward those abnormals who escape the net of detection and abortion. A child with Down's syndrome or with hemophilia or with muscular dystrophy born at a time when most of his (potential) fellow sufferers were destroyed prenatally is liable to be looked upon by the community as one unfit to be alive, as a second-class (or even lower) human type. He may be seen as a person who need not have been, and who would not have been, if only someone had gotten to him in time.

The parents of such children are also likely to treat them differently, especially if the mother would have wished but failed to get an amniocentesis because of ignorance, poverty, or distance from the testing station, or if the prenatal diagnosis was in error. In such cases, parents are especially likely to resent the child. They may be disinclined to give it the kind of care they might have before the advent of amniocentesis and genetic abortion, rationalizing that a second-class specimen is not entitled to first-class treatment. If pressed to do so, say by physicians, the parents might refuse, and the courts may become involved. This has already begun to happen.

In Maryland, parents of a child with Down's syndrome refused permission to have the child operated on for an intestinal obstruction present at birth. The physicians and the hospital sought an injunction to require the parents to allow surgery. The judge ruled in favor of the parents, despite what I understand to be the weight of precedent to the contrary, on the grounds that the child was Mongoloid; that is, had the child been "normal," the decision would have gone the other way. Although the decision was not appealed to and hence not affirmed by a higher court, we can see through the prism of this case the possibility that the new powers of human genetics will strip the blindfold from the lady of justice and will make official the dangerous doctrine that some men are more equal than others.

The abnormal child may also feel resentful. A child with Down's syndrome or Tay-Sachs disease will probably never know or care, but what about the child with hemophilia or with Turner's syndrome? In the past decade, with medical knowledge and power over the prenatal child increasing and with parental authority over the postnatal child decreasing, we have seen the appearance of a new type of legal action, suits for wrongful life. Children have brought suit against their parents (and others) seeking to recover damages for physical and social handicaps inextricably tied to their birth (e.g., congenital deformities, congenital syphilis, illegitimacy). In some of the American cases, the courts have recognized the justice of the child's claim (that he was injured due to parental negligence), although they have so far refused to award damages, due to policy considerations. In other countries, e.g., in Germany, judgments with compensation have gone for the plaintiffs. With the spread of amniocentesis and genetic abortion, we can only expect such cases to increase. And here it will be the soft-hearted rather than the hard-hearted judges who will establish the doctrine of second-class human beings, out of compassion for the mutants who escaped the traps set out for them.

It may be argued that I am dealing with a problem which, even if it is real, will affect very few people. It may be suggested that very few will escape the traps once we have set them properly and widely, once people are informed about amniocentesis, once the power to detect prenatally grows to its full capacity, and once our "superstitious" opposition to abortion dies out or is extirpated. But in order even to come close to this vision of success, amniocentesis will have to become part of every pregnancy—either by making it mandatory, like the test for syphilis, or by making it "routine medical practice," like the Pap smear. Leaving aside the other problems with universal amniocentesis, we

would expect that the problem for the few who escape is likely to be even worse precisely because they will be few.

The point, however, should be generalized. How will we come to view and act toward the many "abnormals" that will remain among us—the retarded, the crippled, the senile, the deformed, and the true mutants—once we embark on a program to root out genetic abnormality? For it must be remembered that we shall always have abnormals—some who escape detection or whose disease is undetectable *in utero,* others a result of new mutations, birth injuries, accidents, maltreatment, or disease—who will require our care and protection. The existence of "defectives" cannot be fully prevented, not even by totalitarian breeding and weeding programs. Is it not likely that our principle with respect to these people will change from "We try harder" to "Why accept second best?" The idea of "the unwanted because abnormal child" may become a self-fulfilling prophecy, whose consequences may be worse than those of the abnormality itself.

Genetic and Other Defectives

The mention of other abnormals points to a second danger of the practice of genetic abortion. Genetic abortion may come to be seen not so much as the prevention of genetic disease, but as the prevention of birth of defective or abnormal children—and, in a way, understandably so. For in the case of what other diseases does preventive medicine consist in the elimination of the patient-at-risk? Moreover, the very language used to discuss genetic disease leads us to the easy but wrong conclusion that the afflicted fetus or person is rather than has a disease. True, one is partly defined by his genotype, but only partly. A person is more than his disease. And yet we slide easily from the language of possession to the language of identity, from "He has hemophilia" to "He is a hemophiliac," from "She has diabetes" through "She is diabetic" to "She is a diabetic," from "The fetus has Down's syndrome" to "The fetus is a Down's." This way of speaking supports the belief that it is defective persons (or potential persons) that are being eliminated, rather than diseases.

If this is so, then it becomes simply accidental that the defect has a genetic cause. Surely, it is only because of the high regard for medicine and science, and for the accuracy of genetic diagnosis, that genotypic defectives are likely to be the first to go. But once the principle, "Defectives should not be born," is established, grounds other than cytological and biochemical may very well be sought. Even ignoring racialists and others equally misguided—of course, they cannot be ignored—we should know that there are social scientists, for example, who believe that one can predict with a high degree of accuracy how a child will turn out from a careful, systematic study of the socio-economic and psycho-dynamic environment into which he is born and in which he grows up. They might press for the prevention of socio-psychological disease, even of "criminality," by means of prenatal environmental diagnosis and abortion. I have heard a rumor that a crude, unscientific form of eliminating potential "phenotypic defectives" is already being practiced in some cities, in that submission to abortion is allegedly being made a condition for the receipt of welfare payments. "Defectives should not be born" is a principle without limits. We can ill-afford to have it established.

Up to this point, I have been discussing the possible implications of the practice of genetic abortion for our belief in and adherence to the idea that, at least in fundamental human matters such as life and liberty, all men are to be considered as equals, that for these matters we should ignore as irrelevant the real qualitative differences amongst men, however important these differences may be for other purposes. Those who are concerned about abortion fear that the permissible time of eliminating the unwanted will be moved forward along the time continuum, against newborns, infants, and children. Similarly, I suggest that we should be concerned lest the attack on gross genetic inequality in fetuses be advanced along the continuum of quality and into the later stages of life.

I am not engaged in predicting the future; I am not saying that amniocentesis and genetic abortion will lead down the road to Nazi Germany. Rather, I am suggesting that the principles underlying genetic abortion simultaneously justify many further steps down that road. . . .

Perhaps I have exaggerated the dangers; perhaps we will not abandon our inexplicable preference for generous humanitarianism over consistency. But we should indeed be cautious and move slowly as we give serious consideration to the question "What price the perfect baby?"

Standards for Justifying Genetic Abortion

. . . According to what standards can and should we judge a fetus with genetic abnormalities unfit to live, i.e., abortable? It seems to me that there are at least three dominant standards to which we are likely to repair.

The first is societal good. The needs and interest of society are often invoked to justify the practices of prenatal diagnosis and abortion of the genetically abnormal. The argument, full blown, runs something like this. Society has an interest in the genetic fitness of its members. It is foolish for society to squander its precious resources ministering to and caring for the unfit, especially for those who will never become "productive," or who will never in any way "benefit" society. Therefore, the interests of society are best served by the elimination of the genetically defective prior to their birth.

The societal standard is all-too-often reduced to its lowest common denominator: money. Thus one physician, claiming that he has "made a cost–benefit analysis of Tay-Sachs disease," notes that "the total cost of carrier detection, prenatal diagnosis and termination of at-risk pregnancies for all Jewish individuals in the United States under 30 who will marry is $5,730,281. If the program is setup to screen only one married partner, the cost is $3,122,695. The hospital costs for the 990 cases of Tay-Sachs disease these individuals would produce over a thirty-year period in the United States is $34,650,000." Another physician, apparently less interested or able to make such a precise audit has written: "Cost–benefit analyses have been made for the total prospective detection and monitoring of Tay-Sachs disease, cystic fibrosis (when prenatal detection becomes available for cystic fibrosis) and other disorders, and in most cases, the expenditures for hospitalization and medical care far exceed the cost of prenatal detection in properly selected risk populations, followed by selective abortion." Yet a third physician has calculated that the costs to the state of caring for children with Down's syndrome is more than three times that of detecting and aborting them. (These authors all acknowledge the additional non-societal "costs" of personal suffering, but insofar as they consider society, the costs are purely economic.)

There are many questions that can be raised about this approach. First, there are questions about the accuracy of the calculations. Not all the costs have been reckoned. The aborted defective child will be "replaced" by a "normal" child. In keeping the ledger, the "costs" to society of his care and maintenance cannot be ignored—costs of educating him, or removing his wastes and pollutions, not to mention the "costs" in non-replaceable natural resources he consumes. Who is the greater drain on society's precious resources, the average inmate of a home for the retarded or the average graduate of Harvard College? I am not sure we know or can even find out. Then there are the costs of training the physicians and genetic counselors, equipping their laboratories, supporting their research, and sending them and us to conferences to worry about what they are doing. An accurate economic analysis seems to me to be impossible, even in principle. And even if it were possible, one could fall back on the words of that ordinary language philosopher, Andy Capp, who, when his wife said that she was getting really worried about the cost of living, replied: "Sweet 'eart, name me one person who wants t'stop livin' on account of the cost."

A second defect of the economic analysis is that there are matters of social importance that are not reducible to financial costs, and others that may not be quantifiable at all. How does one quantitate the costs of real and potential social conflict, either between children and parents, or between the community and the "deviants" who refuse amniocentesis and continue to bear abnormal children? Can one measure the effect on racial tensions of attempting to screen for and prevent the birth of children homozygous (or heterozygous) for sickle cell anemia? What numbers does one attach to any decreased willingness or ability to take care of the less fortunate, or to cope with difficult problems? And what about the "costs" of rising expectations? Will we become increasingly dissatisfied with anything short of the "optimum baby"? How does one quantify anxiety? humiliation? guilt? Finally, might not the medical profession pay an immeasurable price if genetic abortion and other revolutionary activities bring about changes in medical ethics and medical practice that lead to the further erosion of trust in the physician?

An appeal to social worthiness or usefulness is a less vulgar form of the standard of societal good. It is true that great social contributions are unlikely to be forthcoming from persons who suffer from most serious genetic diseases, especially since many of them

die in childhood. Yet consider the following remarks of Pearl Buck (1968) on the subject of being a mother of a child retarded from phenylketonuria:

> *"My child's life has not been meaningless. She has indeed brought comfort and practical help to many people who are parents of retarded children or are themselves handicapped. True, she has done it through me, yet without her I would not have had the means of learning how to accept the inevitable sorrow, and how to make that acceptance useful to others. Would I be so heartless as to say that it has been worthwhile for my child to be born retarded? Certainly not, but I am saying that even though gravely retarded it has been worthwhile for her to have lived.*

> *"It can be summed up, perhaps, by saying that in this world where cruelty prevails in so many aspects of our life, I would not add the weight of choice to kill rather than to let live. A retarded child, a handicapped person, brings its own gift to life, even to the life of normal human beings. That gift is comprehended in the lessons of patience, understanding, and mercy, lessons which we all need to receive and to practice with one another, whatever we are."*

The standard of potential social worthiness is little better in deciding about abortion in particular cases than is the standard of economic cost. To drive the point home, each of us might consider retrospectively whether he would have been willing to stand trial for his life while a fetus, pleading only his worth to society as he now can evaluate it. How many of us are not socially "defective" and with none of the excuses possible for a child with phenylketonuria? If there is to be human life at all, potential social worthiness cannot be its entitlement.

Finally, we should take note of the ambiguities in the very notion of societal good. Some use the term "society" to mean their own particular political community, others to mean the whole human race, and still others speak as if they mean both simultaneously, following that all-too-human belief that what is good for me and mine is good for mankind. Who knows what is genetically best for mankind, even with respect to Down's syndrome? I would submit that the genetic heritage of the human species is largely in the care of persons who do not live along the amniocentesis frontier. If we in the industrialized West wish to be really serious about the genetic future of the species, we would concentrate our attack on mutagenesis, and especially on our large contribution to the pool of environmental mutagens.

But even the more narrow use of society is ambiguous. Do we mean our "society" as it is today? Or do we mean our "society" as it ought to be? If the former, our standards will be ephemeral, for ours is a faddish "society." (By far the most worrisome feature of the changing attitudes on abortion is the suddenness with which they changed.) Any such socially determined standards are likely to provide too precarious a foundation for decisions about genetic abortion, let alone for our notions of human rights. If we mean the latter, then we have transcended the societal standard, since the "good society" is not to be found in "society" itself, nor is it likely to be discovered by taking a vote. In sum, societal good as a standard for justifying genetic abortion seems to be unsatisfactory. It is hard to define in general, difficult to apply clearly to particular cases, susceptible to overreaching and abuse (hence, very dangerous), and not sufficient unto itself if considerations of the good community are held to be automatically implied.

A second major alternative is the standard of parental or familial good. Here the argument of justification might run as follows. Parents have a right to determine, according to their own wishes and based upon their own notions of what is good for them, the qualitative as well as the quantitative character of their families. If they believe that the birth of a seriously deformed child will be the cause of great sorrow and suffering to themselves and to their other children and a drain on their time and resources, then they may ethically decide to prevent the birth of such a child, even by abortion.

This argument I would expect to be more attractive to most people than the argument appealing to the good of society. For one thing, we are more likely to trust a person's conception of what is good for him than his notion of what is good for society. Also, the number of persons involved is small, making it seem less impossible to weigh all the relevant factors in determining the good of the family. Most powerfully, one can see and appreciate the possible harm done to healthy children if the parents are obliged to devote most of their energies to caring for the afflicted child.

Yet there are ambiguities and difficulties perhaps as great as with the standard of societal good. In the first place, it is not entirely clear what would be good for the other children. In a strong family, the experience with a suffering and dying child might help the healthy siblings learn to face and cope with adversity. Some have even speculated that the lack of experience with death and serious illness in our affluent young people is an important element in their difficulty in trying to find a way of life and in responding patiently yet steadily to the serious problems of our society (Cassell, 1969). I suspect that one cannot generalize. In some children and in some families, experience with suffering may be strengthening, and in others, disabling. My point here is that the matter is uncertain, and that parents deciding on this basis are as likely as not to be mistaken.

The family or parental standard, like the societal standard, is unavoidably elastic because "suffering" does not come in discontinuous units, and because parental wishes and desires know no limits. Both are utterly subjective, relative, and notoriously subject to change. Some parents claim that they could not tolerate having to raise a child of the undesired sex; I know of one case where the woman in the delivery room, on being informed that her child was a son, told the physician that she did not even wish to see it and that he should get rid of it. We may judge her attitude to be pathological, but even pathological suffering is suffering. Would such suffering justify aborting her normal male fetus?

Or take the converse case of two parents, who for their own very peculiar reasons, wish to have an abnormal child, say a child who will suffer from the same disease as grandfather or a child whose arrested development would preclude the threat of adolescent rebellion and separation. Are these acceptable grounds for the abortion of "normals"?

Granted, such cases will be rare. But they serve to show the dangers inherent in talking about the parental right to determine, according to their wishes, the quality of their children. Indeed, the whole idea of parental rights with respect to children strikes me as problematic. It suggests that children are like property, that they exist for the parents. One need only look around to see some of the results of this notion of parenthood. The language of duties to children would be more in keeping with the heavy responsibility we bear in affirming the continuity of life with life and in trying to transmit what wisdom we have acquired to the next generation. Our children are not our children. Hopefully, reflection on these matters could lead to a greater appreciation of why it is people do and should have children. No better consequence can be hoped for from the advent of amniocentesis and other technologies for controlling human reproduction.

If one speaks of familial good in terms of parental duty, one could argue that parents have an obligation to do what they can to ensure that their children are born healthy and sound. But this formulation transcends the limitation of parental wishes and desires. As in the case of the good society, the idea of "healthy and sound" requires an objective standard, a standard in reality. Hard as it may be to uncover it, this is what we are seeking. Nature as a standard is the third alternative.

The justification according to the natural standard might run like this. As a result of our knowledge of genetic diseases, we know that persons afflicted with certain diseases will never be capable of living the full life of a human being. Just as a no-necked giraffe could never live a giraffe's life, or a needle-less porcupine would not attain true "porcupine-hood," so a child or fetus with Tay-Sachs disease or Down's syndrome, for example, will never truly be human. They will never be able to care for themselves, nor have they even the potential for developing the distinctively human capacities for thought or self-consciousness. Nature herself has aborted many similar cases, and has provided for the early death of many who happen to get born. There is no reason to keep them alive; instead, we should prevent their birth by contraception or sterilization if possible, and abortion if necessary.

The advantages of this approach are clear. The standards are objective and in the fetus itself, thus avoiding the relativity and ambiguity in societal and parental good. The standard can be easily generalized to cover all such cases and will be resistant to the shifting sands of public opinion.

This standard, I would suggest, is the one which most physicians and genetic counselors appeal to in their heart of hearts, no matter what they say or do about letting the parents choose. Why else would they have developed genetic counseling and amniocentesis? Indeed, the notions of disease, of abnormal, of defective, make no sense at all in the absence of a natural norm of health. This norm is the foundation of the art of the physician and of the inquiry of the health scientist. Yet, as Motulsky and others [1971] . . . have pointed out, the standard is elusive. Ironically, we are gaining increasing power to manipulate and control our own nature at a time in which we are increasingly confused about what is normal, healthy, and fit.

Although possibly acceptable in principle, the natural standard runs into problems in application when attempts are made to fix the boundary between potentially human and potentially not human. Professor Lejeune (1970) has clearly demonstrated the difficulty, if not the impossibility, of setting clear molecular, cytological, or developmental signposts for this boundary. Attempts to induce signposts by considering the phenotypes of the worst cases is equally difficult. Which features would we take to be the most relevant in, say, Tay-Sachs disease, Lesch-Nyhan syndrome, Cri du chat, Down's syndrome? Certainly, severe mental retardation. But how "severe" is "severe"? As . . . I argued earlier, mental retardation admits of degree. It too is relative. Moreover it is not clear that certain other defects and deformities might not equally foreclose the possibility of a truly or fully human life. What about blindness or deafness? Quadriplegia? Aphasia? Several of these in combination? Not only does each kind of defect admit of a continuous scale of severity, but it also merges with other defects on a continuous scale of defectiveness. Where on this scale is the line to be drawn after mental retardation? blindness? muscular dystrophy? cystic fibrosis? hemophilia? diabetes? galactosemia? Turner's syndrome? XYY? club foot? Moreover, the identical two continuous scales—kind and severity—are found also among the living. In fact, it is the natural standard which may be the most dangerous one in that it leads most directly to the idea that there are second-class human beings and subhuman human beings.

But the story is not complete. The very idea of nature is ambiguous. According to one view, the one I have been using, nature points to or implies a peak, a perfection. According to this view, human rights depend upon attaining the status of humanness. The fetus is only potential; it has no rights, according to this view. But all kinds of people fall short of the norm: children, idiots, some adults. This understanding of nature has been used to justify not only abortion and infanticide, but also slavery.

There is another notion of nature, less splendid, more humane and, though less able to sustain a notion of health, more acceptable to the findings of modern science. Animal nature is characterized by impulses of self-preservation and by the capacity to feel pleasure and to suffer pain. Man and other animals are alike on this understanding of nature. And the right to life is ascribed to all such self-preserving and suffering creatures. Yet on this understanding of nature, the fetus—even a defective fetus—is not potential, but actual. The right to life belongs to him. But for this reason, this understanding of nature does not provide and may even deny what it is we are seeking, namely a justification for genetic abortion, adequate unto itself, which does not simultaneously justify infanticide, homicide, and enslavement of the genetically abnormal.

There is a third understanding of nature, akin to the second, nature as sacrosanct, nature as created by a Creator. Indeed, to speak about this reminds us that there is a fourth possible standard for judgments about genetic abortion: the religious standard. I shall leave the discussion of this standard to those who are able to speak of it in better faith.

Now that I am at the end, the reader can better share my sense of frustration. I have failed to provide myself with a satisfactory intellectual and moral justification for the practice of genetic abortion. Perhaps others more able than I can supply one. Perhaps the pragmatists can persuade me that we should abandon the search for principled justification, that if we just trust people's situational decisions or their gut reactions, everything will turn out fine. Maybe they are right. But we should not forget the sage observation of Bertrand Russell: "pragmatism is like a warm bath that heats up so imperceptibly that you don't know when to scream." I would add that before we submerge ourselves irrevocably in amniotic fluid, we take note of the connection to our own baths, into which we have started the hot water running.

Section 4: Embryonic Stem Cells

Ontological and Ethical Implications of Direct Nuclear Reprogramming

Gerard Magill and William B. Neaves

Magill and Neaves argue that the creation of induced pluripotent stem cells (iPS cells or iPSCs) from human skin cells has ethical implications for how we regard natural human embryos, as well as embryos produced by cloning (i.e., somatic cell nuclear transfer).

The iPS cells share with embryos the potential to develop, given the right conditions, into a viable fetus. Further research may show that iPS cells, like embryos, can also make their own placentas. This would make them indistinguishable in relevant ways from embryos (however produced). Thus, logically speaking, those who consider an embryo the moral equivalent of a person and seek to protect it must either extend the same protection to iPS cells or change the criteria for personhood to rely on features from a later state of embryonic development. Otherwise, defenders of the embryo-as-person view must reject using iPS cells for therapeutic purposes, in the same way that they reject the destruction of embryos and cloning.

From Gerard Magill and William B. Neaves, "Ontological and Ethical Implications of Direct Nuclear Reprogramming," *Kennedy Institute of Ethics* 19, no. 1 (2009): 23–32. © 2009 The Johns Hopkins University Press. Reprinted with permission of the Johns Hopkins University Press. (Notes omitted.)

A combination of two recent scientific breakthroughs may transform the ethical landscape of stem cell research. The discoveries deal with direct nuclear reprogramming of human skin cells and with the progression of reprogrammed mouse cells into fetuses. The laboratories of Yamanaka and of Thomson crossed a threshold to highlight a crucial aspect of cellular life. They demonstrated that direct nuclear reprogramming can drive back the development of human skin cells to yield induced pluripotent stem (iPS) cells—i.e., cells that resemble and behave like embryonic stem cells in their developmental potential, despite not being derived from embryos. The production of human iPS cells resulted from a prior breakthrough in reprogramming mouse cells.

A simultaneously published study on reprogrammed mouse cells by the Jaenisch laboratory in Boston demonstrated that these cells can develop into live late-term fetuses if provided a placenta by injecting them into a tetraploid blastocyst four cell and implanting the resulting cell mass in a uterus. This procedure, also known as tetraploid complementation, was developed by Andras Nagy and Janet Rossant to characterize the full developmental potential of embryonic stem cells. Tetraploid complementation combines ordinary diploid embryonic stem cells with developmentally compromised tetraploid blastocysts, which are formed by fusing the two diploid cells from the first cell division after fertilization and growing the resulting tetraploid cell into a blastocyst. When these aggregates composed of embryonic stem cells inserted into tetraploid blastocysts are implanted in a uterus, the embryo proper forms entirely from the diploid embryonic stem cells, while the tetraploid component contributes only to the extraembryonic membranes and placenta.

The tetraploid complementation procedure has become the definitive method for proving cellular pluripotency, and it was in this context that the Jaenisch lab employed it to demonstrate pluripotency of mouse iPS cells. It would be impractical and unethical to ascertain if human iPS cells could develop into a late-term fetus. However, the combined results of these studies provide persuasive evidence that reprogrammed human cells could develop into a human fetus if they were placed in an environment that would provide a placenta and uterine support. No evidence indicates that anyone has attempted tetraploid complementation with primate cells, but there is likewise no basis for believing it would not work.

This new science reveals that every cell in the human body has the biological capacity or natural potentiality, given appropriate supportive interventions and the right circumstances, of becoming a fetus. Previously,

the beginning of early human life was associated with the process of fertilization. The technology known as somatic cell nuclear transfer (SCNT) made it possible to unlock the developmental potential of an ordinary body cell by exposing its nucleus to factors found in an unfertilized egg, a zygote, or embryonic stem cells. Now with direct reprogramming, pluripotent cells can be generated with the potential to form a clone of the cell donor if the reprogrammed cells are placed in an environment that would allow formation of a placenta and are gestated in a uterus. Hence, directly reprogrammed cells can form cloned organisms capable of developing into fetuses just as can occur in the case of SCNT. Of course, no responsible scientist would try to reproduce a human being from either SCNT or from direct nuclear reprogramming—there is no substantive dispute over that issue.

The significance of reprogrammed cells, whether produced by SCNT or by the direct method of Yamanaka, is that the beginning of what could become personal human life is associated with any ordinary cell in the body. This reality reflects the presence of the entire human genome—the genetic code for the development of a completely formed human being—inside the nucleus of each of trillions of cells in the adult human body. The genes responsible for embryonic and fetal development reside in every ordinary body cell. The technology of direct nuclear reprogramming can unlock the expression of these genes and with appropriate manipulation such as that employed by the Jaenisch lab, enable any body cell to become a fetus that is a clone of the donor of the reprogrammed skin cell. Therefore, iPS cells have the biological capacity to develop into a fetus and indeed possibly to be born as an individual person.

This natural capacity can be construed as referring to what is described in the philosophical argument of natural potentiality as "the potential encoded in, and expressive of, one's nature or kind," or "basic natural capacity."

Now ordinary body cells can develop into a fetus without involving an enucleated egg. Because it is technically possible to develop a fetus from reprogrammed human cells, the question of their ontological status arises with ensuing ethical implications for research. By ontological status we mean the assignment of either personal or potentially personal life in the sense of having full moral respect. The new scientific data on iPS cells raises fundamental philosophical questions about the ontological status of cellular activity at the beginning of human life. Addressing these questions within the framework of an ethical analysis that focuses upon consistency could challenge philosophical arguments to assign full moral respect for human cellular development from its inception.

Ethical Analysis

Proponents of the philosophical argument of natural potentiality seek to protect human cellular development from its inception as personal. The basic rationale for this stance is that a human embryo directs its own integral organismic function from its beginning, developing its underlying natural potentiality by virtue of the entity it is. From the point at which it comes into being, there is a whole, albeit immature, and distinct human organism that is intrinsically valuable with the status of inviolability and deserving full moral respect (understanding inviolability and moral respect synonymously). The basis for this moral respect is the embryo's inherent natural capacity, or natural potentiality, as described above. Hence, it is argued that the human embryo is an end in itself and should not be used merely as a means to benefit others such as occurs in research that entails its destruction. Proponents of this stance prohibit research on embryos arising from natural fertilization, somatic cell nuclear transfer, and "other cloning technologies." The question is whether the consistency that has appeared so robust in this stance is placed in jeopardy by the demonstration of the Jaenisch lab that iPS cells can produce a cloned fetus.

The realization that any adult body cell could engender a fetus was first established by SCNT. This knowledge is now reinforced by the new cloning technology using iPS cells. Both technologies show that any ordinary body cell has the potential to become a late-term fetus. This information provides sharper contours to the consistency challenge that the natural potentiality argument must address.

The critical question is whether the natural potentiality argument pertains to the use of iPS cells as a cloning technology. A leading proponent of the natural potentiality argument explains as follows: In SCNT scientists "are doing more than merely placing the somatic cell in an environment hospitable to its continuing maturation and development. They are generating a wholly distinct, self-integrating, entirely new organism—an embryo." The same argument pertains to iPS cells. Direct reprogramming, like SCNT, initiates a cellular process that, with appropriate supportive interventions, can generate an organism intrinsically capable of developing into a late-term fetus.

If the natural potentiality argument applies to cells produced by SCNT, consistency appears to demand its application to iPS cells. However, accepting natural potentiality in the case of cells made either by SCNT or by direct reprogramming leads logically to the conclusion that these cells merit ethical protection. But if the natural potentiality argument should be invoked to prohibit research on iPS cells because they have the biological capacity or natural potentiality of becoming a late-term fetus, such a prohibition is likely to appear absurd given its reach to every cell in the body. The appearance of absurdity lies in preventing science from exploiting the potential of ordinary body cells through direct nuclear reprogramming for life-saving medical research.

It may be argued that human iPS cells do not merit ethical protection because they are merely pluripotent and must be artificially provided with a placenta to develop into a fetus, unlike fertilized eggs and cells made by SCNT that are totipotent and can develop their own placenta. But that argument may not be convincing for at least two reasons. First, although the placenta provides sustenance and a supportive environment that includes growth factor signals to the inner cell mass, such interaction is bidirectional and typical of signaling between cells and tissues throughout embryonic development. Indeed, the trophoblast depends on signals from the inner cell mass to proliferate and differentiate into the placenta. Most significantly, the placenta contributes no genetic or cellular elements to the substance of the embryo or fetus, and it is completely discarded at the end of gestation. Second, the natural potentiality argument that requires protection of IVF embryos also seems to apply to iPS cells. The former need artificial support during cultivation *in vitro* and insertion into the uterus as the indispensable environment for their natural potential to be realized, while the latter also would need to be supported artificially by the provision of a placenta via tetraploid complementation.

A reprogrammed human cell is not fundamentally different from a nuclear-transfer or natural fertilization zygote in its ability to become a fetus. The zygote makes its own placenta, while the reprogrammed skin cell must be provided with one, but the placenta never becomes part of the embryo itself. Both the reprogrammed skin cells and the cells of the blastocyst's inner cell mass solely form the respective embryos. That is, reprogrammed skin cells have the same developmental potential as do the cells of the inner cell mass of the blastocyst formed by a zygote. Hence, an iPS cell in an appropriate environment can from its beginning direct its own integral organismic development into a fully-formed, late-term fetus, which is the basic rationale of the natural potentiality argument.

Furthermore, one must recognize that efforts at direct reprogramming of adult somatic cells have focused on making pluripotent cells, not totipotent cells. The research community has devoted intense effort to making induced pluripotent stem cells (iPS cells) because of the therapeutic potential offered by their ability to develop into any ordinary body cell. No known effort has been directed to making induced totipotent stem cells (iTS cells), since there is no apparent therapeutic advantage gained by adding the ability to make a placenta. If the objective were to study development of the placenta's precursor, the trophoblast, this can be accomplished by treating either human embryonic stem cells or human iPS cells with a specific cell signaling factor, bone morphogenetic protein 4. If the only advantage of induced totipotent cells were in facilitating reproductive cloning, scientists would universally condemn such an objective in the context of human application.

However, if making totipotent cells by direct reprogramming were seriously attempted for future research purposes, it is likely that a combination of transcription factors could be found that would activate the genes required for making a placenta as well as an embryo. Each somatic cell does, after all, contain the complete human genome, including the genes required for making the trophoblast, which becomes the placenta, as well as the inner cell mass, which becomes the embryo proper. The fact that human iPS cells can be induced to differentiate into trophoblastic cells makes this point clearly. Some might argue that iPS cells are morally different from embryonic stem cells made by SCNT because they are merely pluripotent while the latter are totipotent. However, such an argument will fail as soon as someone discovers a combination of transcription factors and chemical agents that directly activate a somatic cell's genes for making both trophoblast and inner cell mass simultaneously.

Hence, for the natural potentiality argument, consistency must recognize a continuum between natural fertilization, SCNT, and iPS cells. And applying the

natural potentiality argument here would also extend to totipotent derivatives if iTS cells were developed. Each involves similar personal ontological status and entails similar claims to protection from research that disrupts their cellular development. The recent production of iPS cells enhances the awareness of this continuum, but in so doing, it highlights a *prima facie* absurdity for the natural potentiality argument, as described previously.

Consistency also suggests a challenging alternative to the natural potentiality argument. An alternative to protecting human embryonic development along this continuum—natural fertilization, SCNT, iPS cells, and iTS cells if ever developed—avoids the concern about *prima facie* absurdity by applying insights gained from reprogrammed human cells back across the continuum to SCNT and to natural fertilization. The production of reprogrammed human cells may provide support for a philosophical viewpoint opposed by the natural potentiality argument—a viewpoint that earliest human embryogenesis basically deals with the biological matter of cellular development, matter that is inadequate for the so-called form of human personhood. This nuanced idea is supported by the commonsense recognition that manipulating body cells to exploit their inherent pluripotency for medical research is justifiable and laudable. Indeed, that common-sense recognition seems initially to have been the basis of nearly universal public support for iPS cell research, even among proponents of the so-called natural potentiality argument who advocate protecting human life as personal from its inception.

This alternative viewpoint does not oppose the ethical protection of the early stages of human life, but it postpones the beginning of that protection to a point later than its cellular inception. Of course, determining when that subsequent point of protection should begin continues to be a debated question in secular and religious discourse that relates science, ethics, and policy.

Mistaken or Insightful Relief

The initial relief over the direct reprogramming of human cells voiced by some who protect human life from its earliest stages of cellular development appears to have been premised on a mistaken assumption that iPS cells were unrelated to embryogenesis. The misplaced relief was motivated by the desire to find an escape hatch for obtaining embryonic-like stem cells without destroying embryos. However, it is now clear that reprogrammed human cells have the integral potential to become an embryo and, in due course, a fetus. Hence, direct nuclear reprogramming can be placed on a continuum with the processes of natural fertilization and SCNT. And each process on this continuum should be addressed with consistency.

Perhaps the most significant breakthrough resulting from direct nuclear reprogramming of human cells may not be an alternative source of embryonic-like stem cells, although that is indeed a superb accomplishment. Rather, the greatest significance might be its clarification of the ontological status of all forms of early cellular development along the continuum of natural potentiality that can result in the formation of a fetus. From this perspective, there may have been instinctive perspicacity in the initial sense of relief occasioned by the discovery of how ordinary body cells can be reprogrammed into iPS cells.

Declaration on the Production and the Scientific and Therapeutic Use of Human Embryonic Stem Cells

Pontifical Academy for Life

The declaration by the Pontifical Academy sets out the official Roman Catholic position on the moral aspects of acquiring and using human embryonic stem cells. The Academy declares it is not morally legitimate to produce or use human embryos as a source of stem cells, nor is it acceptable to use stem cells from cell lines already established. The Academy endorses the idea of using adult stem cells to receive medical benefits that many hope to derive from embryonic stem cells. In 2008, the Congregation for the Doctrine of the Faith issued "Instruction *Dignitas Personae* on Certain Bioethical Questions," in which it reaffirmed these positions and justifications.

Given the nature of this article, the key ethical problems implied by these new technologies are presented briefly, with an indication of the responses which emerge from a careful consideration of the human subject from the moment of conception. It is this consideration which underlies the position affirmed and put forth by the Magisterium of the Church.

The **first ethical problem**, which is fundamental, can be formulated thus: *Is it morally licit to produce and/or use living human embryos for the preparation of ES cells?*

The answer is negative, for the following reasons:

1. On the basis of a complete biological analysis, the living human embryo is—from the moment of the union of the gametes—a *human subject* with a well defined identity, which from that point begins its own *coordinated, continuous and gradual development,* such that at no later stage can it be considered as a simple mass of cells.

2. From this it follows that as a *"human individual"* it has the *right* to its own life; and therefore every intervention which is not in favour of the embryo is an act which violates that right. Moral theology has always taught that in the case of *"jus certum tertii"* the system of probabilism does not apply.

3. Therefore, the ablation of the inner cell mass (ICM) of the blastocyst, which critically and irremediably damages the human embryo, curtailing its development, is a *gravely immoral* act and consequently is *gravely illicit.*

4. *No end believed to be good,* such as the use of stem cells for the preparation of other differentiated cells to be used in what look to be promising therapeutic procedures, *can justify an intervention of this kind.* A good end does not make right an action which in itself is wrong.

From Pontifical Academy for Life, Vatican City, August 25, 2000.

5. For Catholics, this position is explicitly confirmed by the Magisterium of the Church which, in the Encyclical *Evangelium Vitae,* with reference to the Instruction *Donum Vitae* of the Congregation for the Doctrine of the Faith, affirms: "The Church has always taught and continues to teach that the result of human procreation, from the first moment of its existence, must be guaranteed that unconditional respect which is morally due to the human being in his or her totality and unity in body and spirit: The human being is to be respected and treated as a person from the moment of conception; and therefore from that same moment his rights as a person must be recognized, among which in the first place is the inviolable right of every innocent human being to life."

The **second ethical problem** can be formulated thus: *Is it morally licit to engage in so-called "therapeutic cloning" by producing cloned human embryos and then destroying them in order to produce ES cells?*

The answer is negative, for the following reason: Every type of therapeutic cloning, which implies producing human embryos and then destroying them in order to obtain stem cells, is illicit; for there is present the ethical problem examined above, which can only be answered in the negative.

The **third ethical problem** can be formulated thus: *Is it morally licit to use ES cells, and the differentiated cells obtained from them, which are supplied by other researchers or are commercially obtainable?*

The answer is negative, since: prescinding from the participation—formal or otherwise—in the morally illicit intention of the principal agent, the case in question entails a proximate material cooperation in the production and manipulation of human embryos on the part of those producing or supplying them.

In conclusion, it is not hard to see the seriousness and gravity of the ethical problem posed by the desire to extend to the field of human research the production and/or use of human embryos, even from an humanitarian perspective.

The possibility, now confirmed, of using **adult stem cells** to attain the same goals as would be sought with embryonic stem cells—even if many further steps in both areas are necessary before clear and conclusive results are obtained—indicates that adult stem cells represent a more reasonable and humane method for making correct and sound progress in this new field of research and in the therapeutic applications which it promises. These applications are undoubtedly a source of great hope for a significant number of suffering people.

DECISION SCENARIOS

The questions following each decision scenario are intended to prompt reflection and discussion. In deciding how to answer them, you should consider the information provided in the Social Context and Case Presentations, as well as in the Briefing Session. You should also make use of the ethical theories and principles presented in Part VI: Foundations of Bioethics, and the arguments offered in the relevant readings in this chapter.

DECISION SCENARIO 1

Improving the Society One Embryo at a Time

"The concept behind the bill is very simple, Senator," said Jill Laude. "We want to improve the nation, and we know how to begin. Thousands of couples each year rely on assisted reproduction, and they can tell the specialists to implant only embryos with genes for traits like intelligence and creativity."

"So we can increase the number of smart and creative people who are born each year?"

"Exactly," Laude said. "Over time, those numbers will add up. Then those talented kids will start having their own talented kids."

"I see what you mean, but how does the bill you want me to sponsor make that possible?"

"By a system of financial incentives," Laude said. "We start by paying half the costs of assisted reproduction for those who agree to select embryos with traits specified by the legislation."

"I'm guessing that at stage two we pay the full amount."

"Good guess." Laude smiled. "Then after ten years we start rewarding people for using assisted reproduction, even when they don't need to."

"This will be very controversial, you know," said the senator.

"We know," Laude said. "But we think it's the most important piece of legislation imaginable. We need to keep our society competitive, and in the long run the whole human race will benefit."

1. Given the state of genetic knowledge at this time, is such a program feasible?

2. Assuming the program is feasible, is there anything objectionable about it in principle?

3. If you opted to have a child by means of assisted reproduction, would you want the embryos tested to be sure that they are free from serious genetic diseases?

4. If it were possible to test for traits you view as positive, would you want the embryos tested for these traits before they are implanted?

DECISION SCENARIO 2

A Child Like Us

"Carl and I wouldn't know how to raise an average-sized child," Olivia Padrone said. "We know what it's like to be little people, and we know we could help a child who shared our stature."

"So you want me to help arrange for the genetic test, then counsel you on the results?" Dallas Stratford asked.

"Exactly, we want a child just like us," Olivia said. "We're proud members of the dwarf community, and we're both active in helping people see that our culture and way of life is as good as anyone else's. Having an average-size child would betray our ideals and be false to our view of life."

"I don't know what to say," Dallas said. "Usually, people want to avoid having a child with the mutation that produces dwarfism."

1. Genetic counselors are taught to be "value neutral," withholding judgment about the characteristics of embryos and fetuses revealed to potential parents. Should they maintain neutrality about parental wishes, such Olivia's, to select *for* specific birth anomalies, such as dwarfism, deafness, or blindness?

2. Compare the situation of parents who actively seek a deaf child to that of parents who knowingly give birth to children with Tay-Sachs or Down syndrome. Is one choice more acceptable than the other? What role should the potential child's suffering and/or limitations play in such decisions?

3. If dwarfism, deafness, or blindness is a way of life and a culture, is it wrong to discourage the birth of more people who can belong to that culture?

4. Do we have a duty to select embryos that will produce the "best" children possible?

DECISION SCENARIO 3

Screening for Marriage

In 1983, a group of Orthodox Jews in New York and Israel initiated a screening program with the aim of eliminating from their community diseases transmitted as recessive genes. The group called itself Dor Yeshorim, "the generation of the righteous."

Because Orthodox Jews do not approve of abortion in most instances, the program does not employ prenatal testing. Instead, people are given a blood test to determine whether they carry the genes for Tay-Sachs, cystic fibrosis, or Gaucher's disease. Each person is given a six-digit identification number, and if two people consider dating, they are encouraged to call a hotline. They are told either that they are "compatible" or that they each carry a recessive gene for one of the three diseases. Couples who are carriers are offered genetic counseling.

During 1993, eight thousand people were tested, and eighty-seven couples who were considering marriage decided against it after they learned that they were both carriers of recessive genes. The number of people tested has steadily increased, and some view the Dor Yeshorim program as a model that might be followed by other groups or by society in general.

The tests were initially only for Tay-Sachs, but over time other diseases were added. By 2010, the organization was testing for ten diseases, all of them lethal or severely debilitating. However, some critics regard it as a mistake to have moved beyond testing for untreatable, almost invariably lethal diseases such as Tay-Sachs to include tests for diseases such as cystic fibrosis. Individuals may feel pressured into being tested, and those who are carriers of one or more disease-predisposing genes may become social outcasts. Considering that most genetic diseases manifest themselves in varying degrees of severity,

some individuals may face poor marriage prospects based on prejudice and fear. For example, Gaucher's disease, which involves an enzyme defect producing anemia and an enlarged liver and spleen, manifests itself only after age forty-five in half the diagnosed cases. Further, although the disease may be fatal, it often is not, and the symptoms can be treated.

1. Is the Dor Yeshorim screening program a form of eugenics? If so, does this make it unacceptable?

2. Is the program a good model for a national screening program? If not, why not?

3. Is it reasonable to screen for nonlethal genetic diseases?

4. What are some dangers inherent in any screening program?

DECISION SCENARIO 4

DNA Dragnet?

"You want a sample of what?" Dan Macallister was still shaking off sleep and wasn't sure he'd heard the officer correctly.

"A DNA sample, sir. Just a painless cheek swab," said Officer Deena Suh.

"Is this about my brother?"

"Yes, sir. We believe he left DNA evidence at the scene of an armed robbery. We need your sample to confirm he was there."

"I haven't spoken to my brother in over a decade," Macallister said. "Now you want me to help put him in prison?"

"You're not under suspicion, Mr. Macallister. But you and your brother will share enough genetic markers to help us build a profile."

"What happens to my DNA sample afterward?"

"Well, it might become part of the FBI's Combined DNA Index. But that's a private system. It's not like having a criminal record."

"I've been trying to get away from him my whole life. I just want to be left in peace. You can't force me to give a sample, right?"

"No, but we can easily get one from your trash or your next cigarette butt." Suh smiled at him. "Why don't you save us the effort?"

1. Should efforts like those of Officer Suh be prohibited by genetic privacy laws such as GINA? What about the "surreptitious sampling" methods she threatens to use?

2. U.S. law enforcement databases contain over 5.6 million DNA profiles, mostly from convicted felons, but also from others picked up in the course of arrests and investigations. Would it be ethical for those samples to be used in genetic research on criminality or aggression?

DECISION SCENARIO 5

A Duty Not to Reproduce?

"I'm sorry I wasn't able to bring you better news," Dr. Valery Mendez said.

Timothy Schwartz shook his head. "We gambled and lost," he said. "We can't say we didn't know what we were doing."

"That doesn't make it much easier," Judith Schwartz said. "When you said we were both Tay-Sachs carriers, I thought, well, it won't happen to us. But I was wrong. What about this new test? Can we really trust the results?"

"I'm afraid so," said Dr. Mendez. "The fetal cells were cultured, and the chromosome study showed that the child you're carrying will have Tay-Sachs."

"What do you recommend?" Mr. Schwartz asked.

"It's not for me to recommend. I can give you some information—tell you the options—but you've got to make your own decision."

"Is abortion the only solution?" Mrs. Schwartz asked.

"If you call it a solution," Mr. Schwartz said.

"The disease is invariably fatal," Dr. Mendez said. "And there is really no effective treatment for it. A lot of people think there may be in the future, but that doesn't help right now."

"So what does it involve?" Mr. Schwartz asked.

"At first your child will seem quite normal, but that's only because it takes time for a particular chemical to build up in the brain. After the first year or so, the child will start to show signs of deterioration. He'll start losing his sight. Then, as brain damage progresses, he'll lose control over his muscles, and eventually he will die."

"And we just have to stand by and watch that happen?" Mrs. Schwartz asked.

"Nothing can be done to stop it," Dr. Mendez said. "It's a terrible and sad disease."

"We certainly do want to have a child," Mr. Schwartz said. "But we don't want to have one that is going to suffer all his life. I don't think I could stand that."

1. In this case, how persuasive is the argument that "genetic abortion" constitutes a threat to the principle that all persons are of equal value?

2. Could the argument that every child deserves an opportunity for a good life be used to justify recommending or even requiring abortion in a case such as this?

3. Some philosophers argue that a child's right to an "open future" are grounds for refusing to assist deaf parents in having a deaf child. Could this same notion be used to justify abortion when the Tay-Sachs gene has been identified in the fetus?

4. Are there genetic circumstances under which parents might be said to have a duty *not* to reproduce? To what extent is the seriousness of a predicted genetic disease relevant to the answer?

DECISION SCENARIO 6

A Duty to Tell or to Remain Silent?

"Dr. Gress, two of the people we tested for heart disease also turned out positive for the APOe gene," Clara Chang said. "Do we have an obligation to notify them that they are at risk of developing Alzheimer's?"

"Absolutely not," Charles Gress said. "We have an obligation *not* to notify them. What good would it do for them to know they're at risk for a disease that can't be prevented and can't be treated? It would only cause them distress and unhappiness."

1. Is Gress's position morally legitimate?

2. Does the fact that genetic information was acquired accidentally as part of a research program, and not at the request of the individuals, relieve the investigators of an obligation to inform the test subjects about their disease risks?

3. Could Gress's position be considered paternalistic? If so, how might we recommend that the genetic information about individual patients be handled?

4. Some hold that patients may have a duty to learn their genetic disease status, even if they would prefer not to. Might an investigator have a duty to inform a patient of her status, even if the patient has said she doesn't want to know the outcome of a test?

DECISION SCENARIO 7

Choosing Sexual Orientation?

"I haven't told you what we're doing in the lab," Amy Lamont said. "Because I worry you might not approve." She sighed and sat down next to her brother on the porch swing.

"I know what you're doing," said Dave Lamont-Burke, who was visiting Amy from out-of-state with his husband and twin daughters. "You've identified key genes involved in sexual orientation. You already know I approve."

"We didn't just identify the genes, Dave. We figured out a way to edit them, using CRISPR technology." She took a deep breath. "We think we'll soon be able to give parents a choice about whether their kids are gay or straight."

"I see why you didn't tell me," Dave said quietly. He turned to look at her. "You know I believe in parents trying to prevent genetic diseases in their children. Bill and I did that with the twins. But being gay isn't a preventable genetic condition, it's who we are."

"All we're doing is giving parents a choice," said Amy. "If I ever have kids, I might choose that they be gay, because I love you so much and love who you are."

"That's sweet of you, Amy, but you know most heterosexual parents aren't like you. When you give people a choice, you imply there is something wrong with what they have. Would you give African American parents the choice of making their children look white?"

"If they wanted to, who are we to tell them they can't?"

"That sounds like old-fashioned eugenics to me," Dave said. "Just because it isn't imposed by the government doesn't make it any better."

1. If technology made it possible, should parents be allowed to choose their children's sexual orientation? What about their skin color and other characteristics?

2. Summarize Amy's argument. Would it be stronger or weaker if she were talking about changing a disability, such as hereditary blindness, rather than sexual orientation?

3. Does giving parents the option to choose against homosexuality imply there is something wrong with it? Does giving them the option to choose against heterosexuality balance out the equation?

4. Does the choice Amy defends amount to a kind of eugenics? Does it make a difference if the choice is not determined by government or others in authority?

5. In the twentieth century, "old-fashioned" eugenics was often based on prejudice against Jews, homosexuals, Roma, and other non-white groups; it also viewed the disabled as less than human. Could a new eugenics avoid being influenced by societal prejudices?

CHAPTER CONTENTS

CASES AND CONTEXTS

CASE PRESENTATION
Brave New Families

In the spring of 2015, the fashion designers Domenico Dolce and Stefano Gabbana took a high-profile stand on the issues of assisted reproduction and the traditional family.

"You are born and you have a mother and a father, or at least that's how it should be," Dolce told the Italian magazine *Panorama.* "I am not convinced by those I call children of chemistry, synthetic children, rented wombs, semen chosen from a catalog. Life has a natural flow, there are things that should not be changed."

Dolce's comments (along with similar statements by Gabbana) provoked immediate and angry responses on the Internet and beyond. Families whose children were conceived through in vitro fertilization (IVF) and other techniques of assisted reproduction flooded Twitter and Facebook with photos of their offspring and condemnation of the comments. The British singer Elton John called for a boycott of Dolce & Gabbana, writing, "How dare you refer to my beautiful children as 'synthetic.' And shame on you for wagging your judgmental little fingers at IVF.... Your archaic thinking is out of step with the times." Within twenty-four hours, the hashtag #BoycottDolceGabbana had topped the "trending" list on Twitter.

Of course, it is possible to view the controversy over Dolce and Gabbana's comments as little more than a soon-to-be-forgotten celebrity scuffle. But it is clear that the comments also touched a nerve with the general public. For one thing, the "traditional" family that the designers championed—a married mother and father living with biologically related children—has been decreasing as a share of the U.S. population for over half a century. To take just a few well-known statistics, 50 percent of all American children will live with a single mother before they are eighteen and 8 percent of households with children are headed by a single father. Fifty percent of births to American women under thirty occur outside of marriage, and 41 percent of *all* babies in the United States are now born out of wedlock—a fourfold increase from 1970. Since 1996, the number of cohabiting couples has increased 170 percent.

Social scientists find it hard to ascribe these massive shifts to traditional categories of social dysfunction. Indeed, most unmarried parents today are middle class and in their twenties and thirties, while both the teen birth rate and the divorce rate have declined from peaks in the 1980s and early 1990s. Today's overall birth rate is half the 1960 level, with 10 percent fewer women choosing to give birth than they did in the 1970s. Those who do choose to have children are doing so increasingly later in life. As traditional couples have fewer children, singles and same-sex couples are having more, with 25 percent of all same-sex couples in the United States now raising children, according to the 2010 census.

Many of these changes, especially the increasing number of older, single, and gay parents, have been facilitated by the assisted reproductive technologies condemned by Dolce and Gabbana as "synthetic." IVF, artificial insemination, and donated sperm and eggs have helped thousands of otherwise infertile couples start families with genetically related children. They have facilitated new family configurations such as "single parents by choice" as well as "voluntary kin"—who may raise children together without ever being romantically involved. And they have also introduced new potential for conflict over custody, exploitation, and informed consent, as third parties such as donors and surrogates get involved in reproduction.

For all of these reasons, it is no surprise that Domenico Dolce's comments about "synthetic children" generated controversy. For they touch on fundamental questions about what constitutes a family and what we mean by the word *natural*. Neither this case nor this chapter can fully address those questions or the myriad complexities of contemporary family life. Instead, we will examine here just a few of the new family configurations that assisted reproductive technologies (ART) have helped make possible.

Same-Sex Couples and ART

When Aaron Bell and Sid Cuecha met and fell in love in 1996, neither one of them so much as considered having children together.

"It was just assumed that two men in a relationship together, it wasn't an option," Bell said. But after fourteen years together, they gradually discovered that they both dreamed of becoming fathers and, like most straight couples, hoped for biological children. "What we both wanted more than anything was a family."

Cuecha and Bell were not alone, and by 2010 they had new options for starting a family. In 2009, the Ethics Committee of the American Society for Reproductive Medicine (ASRM) had issued a statement that fertility programs have an ethical obligation "to treat all persons equally, regardless of their marital status or sexual orientation." The committee cited three decades of social science evidence that children of gay and lesbian couples do as well or better than those of straight couples on such metrics as personality development, social adjustment, health, happiness, and family cohesion. The research also showed no differences in the development of sexual identity between such children and those of heterosexual couples.

Of course, by the time that the ASRM issued its recommendation, significant numbers of same-sex couples were already raising children in the United States. Many of these parents had adopted children—adoptions by same-sex couples tripled from 2001 to 2011, and studies showed them more likely than heterosexual couples to take on minority, older, and special needs adoptees. But there was also a long tradition of same-sex couples using assisted reproduction to start families.

In the 1970s, lesbian couples began using artificial insemination (AI) with donor sperm from friends or sperm banks. This usually involved a traditional AI method called *intracervical insemination* (ICI) and was often performed at home, due to refusals by fertility clinics to assist women without husbands. Similarly, gay male couples also began to arrange with surrogate mothers to conceive and bear children, typically using ICI with sperm from one member of the couple. Since the resulting child would be genetically related to the surrogate, she would then have to give the child up for adoption. (See this chapter's Briefing Session for more on ICI and surrogacy.)

Starting in the late 1990s and early 2000s, however, increased social acceptance and legal recognition gave same-sex couples greater access to mainstream fertility programs. This helped generate what is now widely considered a same-sex "baby boom." In addition to using artificial insemination techniques, female couples also began to employ *reciprocal IVF*, in which an egg is harvested from one woman (the genetic mother), fertilized with donor sperm, and then implanted into the uterus of her partner (the birth mother). The technique allows both mothers to have a biological connection to the child.

During the 2000s, courts also began to recognize *gestational surrogacy* agreements, in which a surrogate gestates a donor egg, fertilized through IVF or related techniques, that is *not* genetically related to her.

Like many infertile straight couples, gay male couples began to use this method to conceive biological children, because it offered greater legal protections than traditional surrogacy. (For more on this topic see the Calvert and Baby M Case Presentations.)

Gestational surrogacy was the route that Aaron Bell and Sid Cuecha decided to take to have their own children, and in 2010 they began to try to find a surrogate and an egg donor online. The two men lived in Arizona, however, which at the time allowed neither same-sex marriage nor surrogacy arrangements. So that summer, they drove to California to meet Heidi and Jeremy Grosser.

Heidi Grosser had started exploring surrogacy around the same time Cuecha and Bell did, inspired by an acquaintance who had worked as a gestational surrogate. She had been moved by Cuecha and Bell's promise in their online profile that "our child will be the center of our lives," and she decided to make contact. Heidi and Jeremy had been married eleven years and already had two boys. They had decided against more children but they liked the idea of helping someone else start a family. When the two couples met in August 2010 to speak with a fertility program case worker, they felt an immediate connection and decided to move forward with surrogacy. But they also faced challenging questions from the case worker, such as how they would handle health problems for Heidi or multiple gestations.

The questions turned out to be important, because Heidi Grosser would eventually became pregnant with triplets. Until recently, the IVF process has generally involved the implantation of multiple fertilized eggs, to improve the chances that at least one of them will result in a pregnancy. (See this chapter's Briefing Session for more on IVF.) The risk of this procedure is that all the embryos will implant in the uterus, creating twins, triplets, or more. Such was the case with the three embryos that were transferred to Heidi Grosser's uterus in January 2011, created from donor eggs and Aaron Bell's sperm.

Despite a difficult pregnancy and some health scares for the triplets and Heidi, the Grossers decided, in consultation with Cuecha and Bell, to carry all three fetuses to term. The two couples also grew closer as the pregnancy developed, going to ultrasound and doctor's appointments together, and cooking each other meals. All three men were at the hospital for the successful delivery of the babies, six weeks premature, on August 26, 2011.

Four years later, Cuecha and Bell are raising three rambunctious children in Phoenix—a boy and two girls—while the Grossers still live in California. But the two couples have stayed close, calling or texting regularly, visiting each other's extended families, and vacationing together in San Diego.

"The first time I saw them with their babies, it just made it all worth it," said Heidi Grosser. Cuecha and Bell also have no regrets, as they told a reporter from the *Arizona Republic.*

"It's the best thing we've done our entire lives," said Bell. "The journey of going through surrogacy is definitely overwhelming…. But looking at the kids now, there is not a single thing I would have done differently."

Parents and Third Parties

The story of the Grosser and Cuecha-Bell families is an example of *third-party reproduction*, meaning that third parties (in this case Heidi Grosser and the anonymous egg donor) helped the intended parents have children. In cases like the one just described, third parties can have a demonstrably positive impact on family life, expanding the circle of care and support for children and parents. In many other cases, such as most sperm and egg donation, third parties simply remain anonymous and have little impact beyond the genetic legacy they leave their offspring.

But in some cases, the involvement of third parties can also generate unexpected complication and conflict. There have been instances (such as the Baby M and Calvert cases discussed later in this chapter) where either surrogates or intended parents have changed their minds about their prior agreements, leading to legal battles and emotional strife. Given surrogacy fees as high as $30,000, there is also increasing concern about potential exploitation of surrogates, particularly financially struggling women and those in developing nations. (See the Briefing Session for more on this topic.) Even sperm and egg donors may produce unexpected complications, either from genetic conditions missed by screening or from their own shifting intentions.

In 2014, Sheena and Tierra Yates, a married lesbian couple in New Jersey, were forced to grant visitation rights to the sperm-donor fathers of their two children, after both men challenged prior legal agreements they had signed, specifying they would have no involvement with the children beyond the genetic donation. In a related case, the state of Kansas is seeking to have a man named William Marotta pay child support and assume legal paternity of a girl he fathered through a sperm donation, after one of the child's mothers briefly went on public assistance. The relevant issue in these cases is not the legal validity of the signed contracts waiving paternity, which in the Yates case was also signed by a physician. The trouble, instead, is that in both cases, the artificial inseminations took place at home, rather than in the clinical setting recognized by New Jersey and Kansas. Thus the states can ask (some say disingenuously) whether the men were, in fact, sexual partners of the women and thus subject to the rights and responsibilities that come with traditional paternity. (The Yates' donors were also ordered to pay child support.)

It is unclear whether such cases would have moved forward if the parents involved had been heterosexuals. The common law "presumption of paternity" that protects traditional marriages would certainly have placed the burden of proof on the Yates' donors and on the state of Kansas, which likely would not have identified a legal issue to pursue. Whether these cases were brought justly or unjustly, however, they underscore the importance in third-party reproduction of thoroughly documenting the intentions and obligations of everyone involved. While the New Jersey and Kansas cases may be no worse than the average custody battle when a traditional marriage falls apart, such disputes can cause instability for children and unnecessary complexity for adults.

Single Parents by Choice

One way that some have tried to reduce the complexity of contemporary parenting is to separate it entirely from romantic relationships. In recent decades, a substantial number of women (and a small but growing number of men) have started using assisted reproduction to become *single parents by choice*. The "by choice" part of this phrase is meant to signal a distinction from the "unchosen" type of single parenthood—the more common kind that results from divorce, breakups, death, or accidental pregnancy. For many of the women, "by choice" is also a way to distinguish themselves from the stock image of single mothers as young, uneducated, and impoverished.

By contrast, this new breed of single parent runs counter to social stereotype. These are frequently women (and men) in their thirties or forties who occupy the upper tiers of income, education, and occupations. For many of these women and men, trying to find a compatible romantic partner while working stressful, high-powered jobs comes to seem like an impossible task. For women, whose fertile years end earlier than those of most men, the pressure to "settle"—to accept a mediocre romantic relationship in order to become a mother—can feel overwhelming. (Indeed, several popular self-help books have been published in recent years that exhort women to do just that.) For women who are sure they want to have children, the result can be anxiety, despair, and a distorted dating life.

"I certainly never thought I would be the last one standing," an executive named Karyn told the reporter and novelist Jennifer Egan. "You feel a little bit resentful, like, Gosh, how did I get here? Blind date after blind date—why can't it be easy for me like it was for other people? Right up until I ordered the sperm and made the doctor's appointment, I was filled with anxiety. I felt sad, overwhelmed. Now I'm completely at peace with it."

Like many other single mothers by choice, Karyn used a sperm bank and artificial insemination to pursue her lifelong dream of starting a family. The typical anonymity of sperm bank donors—and the lack of emotional and financial entanglement that comes with it—is often seen as an advantage. Rather than approach a friend or an ex about fathering a child, with all the potential negotiation and miscommunication that might entail, sperm banks offer a more reliable transaction.

There is no question that today's tools for picking out both donor sperm and ova can resemble the "catalogue" shopping criticized by Domenico Dolce. But so, for that matter, can contemporary dating itself. Indeed, the websites for both sperm and ova services have come to resemble nothing so much as online dating sites, with photos, videos, and information about career, hobbies, health, ethnicity, and appearance. Sperm banks and ova agencies like to point out that they provide even more data than anyone could reasonably demand from a potential mate, such as IQ and genetic predispositions. But much like online dating profiles, sperm and ova service profiles are designed to present the best side of the person profiled. Some donors have turned out to be much less accomplished or successful than advertised, when located years later by their children. More disturbing, some men have passed on genetic conditions that sperm banks do not typically screen for. Other "popular" donors have, contrary their wishes, become biological fathers to dozens, even hundreds of children. (See Case Presentation: Egg and Sperm Donors for more on these issues.) But for many women who see motherhood as a central life goal, such risks may be worth the benefits when fertility is on the wane.

Although men pursuing single fatherhood face less of a time crunch, they express similar certainty about wanting to reproduce and similar frustration with the dating market.

"I thought I would meet the right person but I didn't want to force anything," said Conrad Cean, a forty-three-year-old physician who recently became the father to twins through IVF and a gestational surrogate. Growing up in a close-knit family in Queens, Cean had always assumed he would become a father, but when he reached forty without finding the right woman, he decided to focus on children first. B. J. Holt, another "choice father" of two, found that his focus on having children just gradually eclipsed his desire to find the right man—a sentiment expressed by many of the women pursuing single motherhood.

The sheer expense of donor eggs and surrogacy arrangements, as discussed above, will likely keep the number of "choice dads" significantly lower than the number of "choice moms." Critics also point out that the logistical and financial burdens of raising a child alone make it unlikely that any form of single parenthood by choice will appeal to many beyond America's educational and economic elite. Ironically, that elite group is the only one in which the "traditional" family model— two married parents living with biological children—is thriving. The rest of American children are increasingly likely to live in households headed by a single parent, but it is not clear that this reflects a lifestyle choice, so much as the complicated dynamics of cohabitation, divorce, custodial arrangements, and economic insecurity. It is also difficult to tell from census data how many single parents are actually "going it alone" and how many rely on complicated *co-parenting* arrangements with family, friends, and neighbors.

Voluntary Kin

Dawn Pieke might have seemed like a good candidate for single motherhood by choice. She was a sales executive nearing forty who knew she wanted a child but was fed up with relationship fiascos and uninspiring profiles on Match.com:

"I thought, 'These guys look like jerks.... I just want a kid, why can't I just have a baby and not worry about if it's *the* guy?' "

But Pieke was raised by a single mother and had grown up haunted by her father's absence. If possible, she wanted her child to know both parents—something an anonymous sperm donation would preclude. So she turned to one of a growing number of "co-parenting" websites, which connect people who want to raise children together, but without a romantic relationship. Within a few months, she had started developing an intense connection with an American hotel manager named Fabian Blue, who was then working in Australia. The connection was not romantic and Blue is gay, but it was about shared values—particularly their similar ideas about how to parent. The two began talking every day on Skype, discussing their fears and hopes about parenting, and finding they agreed about almost everything.

"It felt like speaking to an old family member," said Blue.

After months of this online "courtship" the two met in person in Omaha, where Pieke lives, and decided they wanted to start a family. Blue moved back from Australia and they began the process of trying to get pregnant through intracervical insemination (ICI). (See Briefing Session for more on artificial insemination.) After two months of trying, Pieke became pregnant and gave birth to a daughter in October 2012.

Today, Pieke and Blue are raising their two-year-old together, with some of the complexity that defines contemporary family life. Pieke is caring for her ailing mother with Alzheimer's while Blue's work often takes him away from Omaha for extended periods, but they split childcare costs fifty-fifty. In addition, both are open to finding a romantic partner, provided it does not interfere with their child-rearing commitments. Critics of platonic parenting arrangements (as well as nonmonogamous ones) argue that they are inherently unstable and therefore bad for children. Supporters respond that many traditional marriages soon become platonic with no apparent harm—a point often emphasized by "just settle" self-help books.

In a broader sense, the Blue–Pieke family may also be more representative of the average American family configuration than most of the examples discussed above. Social scientists suggest that many of the "single parent" households that are swiftly becoming the new American norm actually involve extensive co-parenting by grandparents, aunts, uncles, and exes, as well as by *voluntary kin*, such as lifelong friends. These arrangements are not pre-planned like Pieke and Blue's, nor do they typically involve assisted reproduction. But they do reflect a struggle to give children the support and care they need at a time when the traditional nuclear family has become a "luxury good" mostly reserved for economic and educational elites. There is no question that the stable nuclear family has a great deal of social science evidence in its favor, as the most reliable guarantor of good outcomes for children, but the other approaches may have more time on their side.

"Throughout history, the model that has worked for humankind was extended family—a village, a tribe," said Rachel Hope, author of a book on platonic parenting. "It's only recently that we've started doing the nuclear family, with one mom and one dad."

Envoi

One fundamental objection that Domenico Dolce and Stefano Gabbana raise with regard to "synthetic children," "rented wombs," and "semen chosen from a catalog" is that they are *unnatural* while the traditional family is *natural*. While this idea has much intuitive plausibility, the historical evidence suggests that the two-parent nuclear family is a relatively recent invention. As we will see in our discussion of natural law (see Part VI), there is also considerable difficulty in distinguishing what is natural from what is synthetic.

If natural human development ought to resemble the self-generated growth of an oak tree from an acorn, for example, then assisted reproductive technologies may be less of a "crime against nature" than the many other ways that technology and medicine have reshaped the human species. After all, ART still primarily relies on the natural mechanisms of human *gametes*, sperm and eggs. Some have likened this to simply watering and cultivating an acorn—rather than trying to grow an oak tree from a brick or a microchip. On the other hand, perhaps there is an intuitive abhorrence to tampering with human reproduction that should be respected. (Leon Kass's essay in this chapter, "The Wisdom of Repugnance" offers such a perspective.)

Finally, perhaps the question that Dolce and Gabbana raise is best viewed as an empirical, rather than a philosophical, one. Namely, do alternative families, including those made possible by assisted reproduction, provide children with as much stability, love, and support as the "traditional" model? This remains a difficult and controversial question. But millions of Americans are currently engaged in a vast experiment to help answer it.

CASE PRESENTATION
Louise Brown: The First "Test-Tube Baby"

Under other circumstances, the birth announcement would have been perfectly ordinary, the sort appearing in newspapers every day: *Born to John and Lesley Brown: a baby girl, Louise, 5 lbs. 12 ozs., 11:47 p.m., July 25, 1978, Oldham (England) General Hospital.*

But the birth of Louise Brown was far from being an ordinary event, and the announcement of its occurrence made headlines throughout the world. For the first time in history, a child was born who had been conceived outside her mother's body under controlled laboratory conditions. Louise Brown was the world's first "test-tube baby."

For John and Lesley Brown, the birth of Louise was a truly marvelous event. "She's so small, so beautiful, so perfect," her mother told a reporter. Her father said, "It was like a dream. I couldn't believe it."

The Browns' elation was understandable. From the time of their marriage in 1969, they had both very much wanted to have a child. Then they discovered that Lesley Brown was unable to conceive because of blocked fallopian tubes—the ova would not descend, so fertilization could not occur. In 1970, she had surgery to correct the condition, but the procedure was unsuccessful.

The Browns decided they would adopt a child, because they couldn't have one of their own. After two years on a waiting list, they gave up that plan. But the idea of having their own child was rekindled when they were referred to the gynecologist Patrick Steptoe and the embryologist Robert Edwards.

New Methods

For the previous twelve years, Steptoe and Edwards had been working on the medical and biochemical techniques required for embryo transfer. Steptoe developed techniques for removing a mature ovum from a woman's ovaries, then reimplanting it in the uterus after it had been fertilized. Edwards improved the chemical solutions needed to keep ova functioning and healthy outside the body and perfected a method of external fertilization with sperm.

Using these techniques, Steptoe and Edwards had successfully produced a pregnancy in one of their patients in 1975, but it had resulted in a miscarriage. They considered Lesley Brown a superb candidate for an embryo transfer. She was in excellent general health; at thirty-one, she was within the usual age range for pregnancy; and she was highly fertile. In 1976, Steptoe found through exploratory surgery that Lesley Brown's fallopian tubes were not functional and could not be surgically repaired. He removed them so he would have unimpeded access to her ovaries.

In November 1977, Lesley Brown was given injections of a hormone to increase the maturation rate of her egg cells. Then, in a small private hospital in Oldham, Dr. Steptoe performed a minor surgical procedure. Using a laparoscope—a tube with a built-in eyepiece and light source that is inserted through a tiny slit in the abdomen—he extracted an ovum with a suction needle from a ripened follicle.

The ovum was then placed in a small glass vessel containing biochemical nutrients and sperm secured from John Brown. Once the egg was fertilized, it was transferred to another nutrient solution. More than fifty hours later, the ovum had reached the eight-cell stage of division. Guided by their previous experience and research, Steptoe and Edwards had decided that it was at this stage an ovum should be returned to the womb. Although in normal human development the ovum has divided to produce sixty-four or more cells before it completes its descent down the fallopian tube and becomes attached to the uterine wall, Steptoe and Edwards had learned that implantation is possible at an earlier stage. The difficulties in creating and maintaining the proper biochemical environment for a multiplying cell made it reasonable to reduce the ovum's time outside the body as much as possible.

Lesley Brown had been given another series of hormone injections to prepare her uterus. Two and a half days after the ovum was removed, the fertilized egg was reimplanted. Using a laparoscope and a hollow plastic tube (a *cannula*), Dr. Steptoe introduced the small sphere of cells into Brown's uterus. It successfully attached itself to the uterine wall.

Success

Lesley Brown's pregnancy proceeded normally, but about a week before the birth was expected, the baby was delivered by caesarean section. Brown had developed toxemia, a condition associated with high blood pressure that can lead to stillbirth.

The baby was healthy, however, and all concerned were jubilant. "The last time I saw the baby, it was just eight cells in a test tube," Dr. Edwards said. "It was beautiful then, and it's still beautiful now." After the delivery, Dr. Steptoe said, "She came out crying her head off, a beautiful normal baby."

When John Brown learned of the successful delivery, he ran down the halls of the hospital telling people he passed, "It's a girl! I've got a baby daughter."

To calm down, he went outside and stood in the rain. It was there that a reporter from a London newspaper captured John Brown's view of the event. "The man who deserves all the praise is Dr. Steptoe," he said. "What a man to be able to do such a wonderful thing."

Life as Usual

On July 25, 2003, Louise Brown celebrated her twenty-fifth birthday at a party with three thousand guests; a thousand of them were others also born by in vitro fertilization (IVF). Patrick Steptoe had died in 1988, but Robert Edwards, then 77, was there to mark the occasion. So was Louise's twenty-year-old sister, Natalie, who had the distinction of being the first person conceived via IVF to have children of her own.

Despite dire predictions by opponents of IVF, Louise Brown did not turn out to be either physically impaired or psychologically scarred. (This is not to say that questions have not been raised about the safety of IVF; see the Briefing Session for a discussion.) Brown's life has primarily been distinguished by her fame and by a trust fund in her name, derived from the books and television projects her story has inspired. Since her birth, more than a million other babies have been born through the techniques of assisted reproduction. Such births have become so commonplace that they no longer attract attention.

In December 2006, three years after her enormous birthday party, Louise Brown gave birth to a boy whom she and her husband named Cameron. Some observers had started to speculate that if she waited too long, she might have to rely on the assisted-reproduction techniques required for her own birth. Presumably, this wouldn't bother her. "I want to have my own children, whatever it takes," she told a reporter from London's *Daily Mail* when she was twenty-three. "I would use the in vitro method if I couldn't have a baby."

CASE PRESENTATION
Egg and Sperm Donors: Risks and Rewards

In the late 1990s, when Wendie Wilson was an undergraduate at the University of Washington, she first noticed ads soliciting human egg donation in the campus newspaper. The ads offered women willing to sell their ova to fertility clinics as much as $10,000, which seemed to Wilson an exorbitant amount of money.

A few years later, at age twenty-three, Wilson decided to give egg donation a try. The $5,000 financial incentive was helpful but her primary motivation was to help others start families. Her eggs ended up being donated to a woman who had become infertile after being treated for breast cancer. The process took about five weeks and was physically challenging at times, but Wilson came to view it as "the single most amazing experience of my life to date." Wilson would go on to become an egg donor four more times in the next decade. As she got to know more infertile and same-sex couples who desperately wanted to have children, Wilson decided to start her own egg donation and surrogacy agency. She also helped found an organization to help craft ethical standards for egg donation and surrogacy programs.

Since Wilson first donated her ova, demand for both sperm and eggs has risen in the United States, and so have the prices that prospective parents are willing to pay for donated reproductive tissue.

Supply and Demand
An ad in the Columbia University student newspaper several years ago offered students $35,000 for becoming an egg donor, and similar offers have appeared in

publications at Harvard, Princeton, and other Ivy League institutions. Ads in college newspapers throughout the country offer payments of as much as $15,000 to recruit female students to donate eggs, and some of the same ads appear on Craigslist and Facebook. In large cities, it is not unusual to see billboards with the headline "EGG DONORS NEEDED," followed by a telephone number and a promise of confidentiality.

Such advertisements follow decades of advertising from sperm banks, offering young men a chance to "Get Paid for What You're Already Doing!" and to make as much as $1,500 a month by donating sperm three times a week. As with ova donations, the ads are often targeted at undergraduates in college, although they increasingly offer premium payments to young men in doctoral programs or successful professional careers. It has been estimated that 40 percent of sperm donors are full-time students.

The ubiquity of such advertisements is an indicator that donations of genetic material are more in demand than ever before. The Centers for Disease Control reported that in 2012 (the most recent figures), fresh and frozen donor eggs were used in the birth of some ten thousand children in the United States alone. From 2003 to 2012, the number of assisted reproduction cycles using donor eggs or embryos increased nearly 40 percent, from 14,323 to 19,847. While there is comparatively little research on sperm donation, it has been estimated that as many as sixty thousand children are born each year using donated sperm, a number that appears to be on the rise.

Donor Risks

The significant increase in the use of donated eggs, as well as donated sperm, raises a number of ethical and social issues. For women, the substantial financial rewards for allowing their eggs to be harvested, combined with the genuine health risks of doing so, poses serious questions about informed consent. (Men receive lower financial rewards and face no health risks in sperm donation, but the practice raises other ethical questions, which we will discuss below.)

In the early years of assisted reproduction, most egg donors were relatives or close friends of those seeking assistance, and money typically was not involved. Today, most donors are unrelated to the recipients and have no contact with them, since the process is generally handled by fertility clinics or ova banks. While egg donors (unlike sperm donors) are generally encouraged to think of their contributions as a "gift" rather than a "sale," there is considerable evidence that these women, many of whom are college students, are motivated to donate their eggs for financial reasons.

Age, relative inexperience, and the need for money may undermine the quality of donors' informed consent. They may not be adequately informed about both the foreseeable and unpredictable risks of donation. Under financial pressure, ova donors may discount the seriousness of the health risks they will be taking or not appreciate the implications of creating biological children to be raised by others—an issue that also comes up with sperm donors.

Sperm banks typically require that the men they accept as donors contribute sperm on a regular (usually weekly) basis for at least a year. While women who donate ova typically have to invest only a few weeks, they may experience significant pain and discomfort in the process and face potentially serious health risks.

The egg donation process begins when donors are injected with a series of hormones to stimulate their ovaries. These hormones can produce such symptoms as nausea, bloating, weight gain, depression, and fatigue. Such common side effects are temporary, but in 6 percent of cases the injections may also cause ovarian hyperstimulation syndrome (OHSS), a condition that can result in blood clots, kidney failure, and even death. After hormone treatment, women undergo a series of blood tests and ultrasound scans to determine when their ova

are ready to be harvested. They must then be anesthetized while the eggs are retrieved from their follicles. This may be performed via a small surgical incision or (most often) by aspiration through a hollow needle inserted through the vagina. The rare but serious risks of this final procedure include adverse reactions to anesthesia, organ damage, and hemorrhaging.

The entire ova donation process often takes slightly over a month. The chance that an egg donor may be injured by the procedures used to cause ovulation and retrieve eggs is relatively small, but it is real. A 2008 study of 973 egg donation cycles at a single NYC clinic found serious complications in 0.7 percent of the cycles and minor complications prompting donors to seek medical attention in 8.5 percent of the cycles. The 6 percent chance of ovarian hyperstimulation syndrome has been well established in studies of IVF patients, who are given the same hormonal treatments.

The long-term risks of egg donation are difficult to establish because ova donors, like sperm donors, are not tracked in a central registry and no major scientific studies on them have been performed. (Although the CDC tracks the number of donated eggs used in infertility treatments, it is not known how many individual donors this represents.) Some express concern about the long-term cancer risk the ovary-stimulating hormones pose to donors. But there is conflicting evidence about the cancer risks that infertility patients face in taking the same types of drugs. Some studies have found increases in uterine and ovarian cancer to be associated with these hormonal treatments, but it is unclear whether these can be generalized to egg donors, who are usually younger and healthier than infertility patients. (Women experiencing problems with fertility already have a higher than average rate of ovarian cancer.) So far, no studies have been done to determine whether ovum donors are at a higher risk for infertility, which is another concern raised by critics.

Informed consent for potential ovum donors is usually limited to mentioning the possibility of immediate harms. But a 2008 study found that 34 percent of former egg donors did not recall being informed about the risk of OHSS and 20 percent said they did not know there were *any* physical risks posed by egg donation. A 2012 Columbia University study of agencies and clinics recruiting ova donors found that more than half omitted the procedure's potential risks on their websites. They also found that 34 percent of the sites mentioned paying donors more for certain intellectual and physical traits and 64 percent paid more to women who had donated before. Forty-one percent of the sites said they accepted donors younger than twenty-one, the minimum age for egg donation set by the American Society for Reproductive Medicine (ASRM). Such findings raise questions about the quality of the informed consent obtained by ova donation programs.

Furthermore, the differential pay structures for different egg (and sperm) donors suggest that they are being paid for specific qualities in their reproductive tissues, rather than for their time and discomfort. Under U.S. law, only the latter type of compensation is allowed, which is part of why we still refer to these individuals as "donors."

Personal Eugenics

The screening and marketing process for both donated ova and donated sperm has been the subject of considerable ethical controversy in recent years. Fertility clinics, egg donor agencies, and sperm banks all solicit clients with marketing tools such as video and photo galleries of donors that resemble online dating profiles. Couples and individuals are encouraged to shop (and pay more for) sperm and ova they consider "superior" in particular respects.

What do they look for? Traits sought include an unproblematic family medical history (no schizophrenia, cancer, diabetes, sickle cell, and so on), evidence of intellectual accomplishment (admission to a highly selective college and high SAT scores serve as markers), and specific physical features involving height, weight, hair and eye color, and conventional attractiveness.

While fixed cutoffs for physical characteristics (such as height) or intellectual ones (such as a college degree) are far more common among sperm banks than ova agencies, the practices of both sides of the fertility industry raise ethical questions. Our society is generally thought to have rejected the institutional practice of eugenics, but does such shopping for "perfect" maternal or paternal characteristics amount to a sort of *personal* eugenics? On the other hand, is attempting to find a sperm or egg donor who embodies characteristics we would like to see in our children substantially different (in an ethical sense) from pursing a specific spouse or partner with whom we would like to have children? (For more on this issue, see Michael Sandel's essay "The Case Against Perfection" in Chapter 3.)

Perhaps it is the *commodification* of desirable traits, putting a price tag on them rather than merely pursuing them, that makes the relevant ethical difference. Sperm banks routinely set up different payment tiers based on the academic degrees, height, health, and sperm quality of donors. Similarly, a 2010 study found that the advertised fees for ova donation were strongly correlated with average SAT scores at the university in whose campus paper the ad was placed. The study's author, Aaron Levine, also found that more than half of the advertisements soliciting ova donation offered fees larger than the $10,000 maximum recommended by the American Society for Reproductive Medicine. One ad offered $50,000 for "an extraordinary egg donor," a payment $40,000 over the ASRM maximum.

Self-Regulation and Potential Harms

As the example above indicates, many of the ethical issues associated with the fertility industry stem from the fact that it is largely *self-regulated*. Although fertility clinics are more likely than sperm banks or ova agencies to abide by professional guidelines such as those of the American Society of Reproductive Medicine, enforcement of such guidelines is limited due to lack of mandatory reporting. Thus, despite ASRM health recommendations that women donate eggs no more than six times in their lives, no one knows how often the fertility industry abides by these limits. And despite ASRM guidelines limiting conception by individual sperm donors to no more than twenty-five births per population of eight hundred thousand, there is substantial evidence that this limit is sometimes ignored for "popular" sperm donors. In one famous example, a single sperm donor was found to have fathered more than 150 children in the Washington, DC area.

Such stories have provided fodder for late-night comedians and Hollywood movies, but they can have serious consequences for both donors and recipients. In cases of "popular" sperm donors, these include the increased chance of accidentally incestuous unions between half brothers and sisters, which could result in birth defects and other problems. (See this chapter's Briefing Session for more on this topic.) Such departures from industry guidelines also frequently violate the informed consent of sperm donors, who are often promised that their sperm will be used to father no more than a handful of children.

Another promise that is frequently made to women and men who donate ova and sperm is that they can remain anonymous, if they choose. But with inexpensive DNA testing and online ancestry services such as Family Tree DNA, it is increasingly easy for children genetically fathered or mothered by third parties to track the donors down. This can produce unexpected emotional (and perhaps even legal) consequences for donors who were assured that their privacy would be respected.

The families of children conceived through third-party reproduction have their own reasons for questioning both the promise of anonymity and self-regulation by the fertility industry. In recent years, a number of high-profile cases have arisen in which donors passed on serious genetic conditions to their offspring. In one particularly tragic case, a sperm donor passed on a serious genetic heart defect called hypertrophic cardiomyopathy (HCM) to nine of his twenty-four children. Two of the children had to get pacemakers and one died of HCM, which causes a dangerous thickening of the heart muscle that makes it harder to pump blood. Other donors have passed on genetic predispositions for spinal muscular atrophy, neurofibromatosis, and cystic fibrosis to their offspring. Although most reputable fertility clinics perform genetic testing on donated reproductive tissue, the only current federal requirement is that such tissue be tested for communicable diseases such as HIV and hepatitis. Since sperm banks often buy and sell frozen sperm from each other, sometimes years after a donation, it can also be difficult to verify the integrity of genetic and other kind of testing—a situation that critics see as intolerable.

"We have more rules that go into place when you buy a used car than when you buy sperm," said Debora L. Spar, Barnard College president and author of a book on the fertility market. "It's very clear that the dealer can't sell you a lemon, and there's information about the history of the car. There are no such rules in the fertility industry right now."

Registry and Reform

In 2000, Wendy Kramer and her son Ryan founded the Donor Sibling Registry (DSR) to help people conceived through sperm, egg, or embryo donation make "mutually desired" contact with half-siblings and donors. (Ryan had been conceived by a sperm donor with whom he later developed a connection.) The DSR soon grew into one of the largest databases of information on reproductive tissue donation, with forty-five thousand members posting information. It has been through the DSR that many large groups of half-siblings, such as the 150-person group mentioned earlier, have been identified. It has also provided one of the primary means for the families of donor-conceived children with genetic conditions to compare notes and, at times, identify their donors.

The DSR has become a model for reformers and researchers who would like to be able to track both the health outcomes of donor-conceived children and the health of male and female donors. They argue that a national registry would benefit not just recipients but also donors—allowing for long-term study of inherited diseases as well as the health effects of such practices as ova donation. There is growing evidence that a majority of donors might be open to such a registry, particularly if it included an option to keep the health data anonymous. But Kramer's published research has also indicated that large majorities of donors are open to at least limited contact with their biological offspring.

In the past decade, there have been a number of conflicting legislative efforts to reform the practices associated with reproductive tissue donation. Several states have prohibited the sales of human ova, for example, while others have endorsed it as appropriate compensation for the burdens and risks of donating. In 2009, California passed a law requiring that potential egg donors be informed of the risks as part of an informed consent process. But for the most part, the states continue to leave medical and professional organizations to police the reproductive tissue market on their own.

Critics argue that guidelines like those of the ASRM will always be violated, because they lack the force of law. If a physician is censured or kicked out of the professional organization, she can still continue to practice. In the multi-billion-dollar fertility business, it is success in producing pregnancies that counts, not professional status. Critics argue that the donation process is complicated by the fact that everyone involved—clinics, physicians, donor agencies, and donors—has a financial stake in the donation. They point to the British government's stricter regulation of the human egg and sperm market, including a firm limit (ten) on how many children a sperm donor can father.

By contrast, supporters of fertility industry self-regulation argue that both women and men should be allowed to donate their reproductive tissues without paternalistic oversight, and they find the notion that young women are being coerced to donate condescending.

"I think the biggest misconceptions about egg donation is that women are used as commodities or lured in only by financial motivation," said Wendie Wilson, the egg donor and agency CEO whose story opened this case. "The money I made from my donations is long gone, but the joy of knowing someone has a family and children because of a choice I made is priceless."

SOCIAL CONTEXT
Advances in Reproductive Cloning

On February 3, 1997, Ian Wilmut of the Roslin Institute in Edinburgh, Scotland, made public the information that he and his research group had successfully produced a clone of an adult sheep. The younger genetic twin, the clone they named Dolly, had been born about seven months earlier and appeared to be healthy and normal in every respect.

The procedure Wilmut followed had a cookbook simplicity but was scientifically highly sophisticated. He took cells from the mammary tissue of a Finn Dorset ewe and got them to stop ordinary cell division by culturing them in a medium with a low level of nutrients. Retrieving egg cells from a Scottish Blackface ewe, he removed their nuclei (and hence the DNA) and then mixed these "enucleated" egg cells with the mammary cells. By passing a weak current of electricity through the mixture, Wilmut got some of the egg cells and mammary cells to fuse together. He then used a second pulse of electricity to activate the machinery responsible for cell division. (The process of transferring the nucleus of a somatic cell into an egg cell from which the nucleus has been evacuated is now called *somatic cell nuclear transfer*. This descriptive phrase avoids the highly-charged word *cloning*.)

Six days later, some of the fused cells had divided to become embryos, just as fertilized eggs do. Using the technology of embryo transfer, Wilmut succeeded in implanting one of the embryos in the uterus of a third sheep, another Blackface ewe. At the end of her pregnancy, the ewe gave birth to a lamb that was the genetic twin of the Finn Dorset sheep that supplied the mammary cells.

Wilmut and his group made 277 attempts at fusing the nuclei of the body cells with the enucleated egg cells, but they managed to produce only twenty-nine embryos that lasted longer than six days—the usual time in vitro fertilization specialists allow for a fertilized egg to develop into an embryo before transferring it into the uterus. Of the embryos Wilmut implanted, Dolly was the sole success.

Most biologists were surprised by Wilmut's achievement. Although they acknowledged that the DNA in the nucleus of a body cell contains a complete set of genes and so, in principle, could be used to produce another genetically identical individual, they did not believe that our understanding of cells was detailed enough actually to do it. The view accepted by most researchers was that once a cell finds its place in the body, it switches off all the genes it contains except those it needs to do its job and to reproduce itself. But to become an embryo, the genes must be switched on again.

When the embryo is implanted in a uterus, the genes must be able to orchestrate the stunningly complicated process of development.

Wilmut demonstrated that what the majority of scientists considered only a distant possibility could be achieved in a relatively straightforward fashion. Placing the mammary cells in a culture low in nutrients seemed to return them to the state when their genetic potential is still open, and the pulse of electricity seemed to trigger them into dividing and developing. Wilmut showed that it wasn't necessary to understand the underlying biology of the process to control it. Under the right conditions, the DNA would reprogram itself to initiate and direct development.

Confirming Experiments

Wilmut's success was initially greeted with skepticism by some in the research community. Cloning was demonstrated as a phenomenon beyond doubt, however, when Ryuzo Yanagimachi and his team at the University of Hawaii reported in 1998 that they had produced more than fifty mouse clones. Some of the mice, moreover, were clones of clones.

Yanagimachi's technique was a variation of Wilmut's. Yanagimachi injected the genetic material from a mouse cumulus cell in the resting phase into an enucleated mouse egg and then used chemicals to get the cell to divide. After that, the cell was implanted into a surrogate mother and allowed to develop into a mouse. In one experiment, tan mice were used as genetic donors, black mice as egg donors, and white mice as gestational surrogates. The clones were all tan.

After Yanagimachi's demonstration, doubt about the reality of cloning evaporated. Scientists soon succeeded in cloning cows, goats, pigs, and cats. The first cat was cloned in 2002 only because researchers at

Texas A&M failed (as others had) to clone a dog. Called *cc*, for "carbon copy" or "copycat," the kitten was the only successful result of attempts using eighty-seven cloned embryos transferred to gestational surrogates.

Drawbacks

Despite cc's name, cc really isn't an exact copy of her biological mother, a two-year-old calico cat named Rainbow. Although the two are genetically identical, the color and pattern of cc's coat is different. Coat color results from the separation and distribution of pigmented cells. This takes place during development and is not completely determined by genes.

Although cc is apparently healthy and normal, some cloned animals have not been so fortunate. A number typically die soon after birth, while others suffer from a variety of birth anomalies. Developmental delays, defective hearts, underdeveloped lungs, neurological deficits, and faulty immune systems are the more common problems. Some cloned mice appear normal; then, as they grow, they become extremely obese. Developing calves become oversized and die prematurely.

Scientists don't know exactly what happens to cause these adverse results. Some speculate that cloning increases the occurrence of random genetic changes. During normal reproduction, both egg and sperm mature before they combine, but in cloning, eggs must be harvested and the DNA combined with them must be reprogrammed during a period of minutes or hours. During the process, researchers think, genes are altered and random errors occur. These cause unpredictable problems that can crop up at any time during development or after birth.

That cloning works at all is surprising to some researchers, given what needs to happen to make it possible. Even under the best laboratory conditions and in skilled hands, only about 3 percent of attempts at cloning mammals are successful. Only about one attempt in a hundred results in viable offspring.

When Dolly was born, some scientists speculated that it was likely she would age prematurely. The cell from which the nuclear DNA was removed had already undergone a number of cell divisions and, given that cells divide only about fifty times before they die, perhaps the clock for Dolly had already been ticking before she was born. Experience with cloned animals, however, has so far not shown that they age prematurely. Dolly herself was euthanized after she developed a serious lung infection on February 14, 2003. She was six years old, and the infection appeared to have nothing to do with the fact that she was a clone.

Practical Uses

Cloning was developed to be the foundation of a practice known as *pharming:* the use of animals to produce drugs. The Roslin Institute is an agricultural research center, and a third of Ian Wilmut's funding came from PPL Therapeutics, a biotechnology firm. Wilmut's aim, as well as PPL's, was to produce a flock of sheep genetically engineered to give milk containing such medically valuable and expensive substances as blood-clotting factor, insulin, and human growth hormone. If a single sheep could be genetically engineered to produce such a substance in her milk, she could then be cloned into a herd. Cloning would thus make it possible to produce animals for the pharmaceutical industry, ensuring a supply of useful substances at lower prices. Cloning has also been pursued in conventional agriculture, to create herds of cows with unusually high milk yields, for example. So far, studies have indicated that milk and meat from cloned animals is safe to consume.

The research that produced cc, the cloned cat, was supported by Genetics Saving and Clone, a biotech company that aims to profit from cloning valued pets. The company is already storing, for a fee, DNA samples from pets, with the expectation that cloning technology will soon be adequate to produce a genetic replica of a beloved pet.

Critics object to this enterprise, pointing to the millions of dogs and cats that are killed each year in animal shelters, and arguing that the company's clients should instead adopt one of them. They also argue that those who believe they will get an identical version of their cat or dog are simply mistaken. Developmental factors, including environmental ones, are likely to result in a very different animal, just as cc's coat color (as well as her personality) was different from those of Rainbow, the cat she "copied."

More people are enthusiastic about the possibility of using reproductive cloning to establish colonies of endangered species. In 2001, scientists in Italy reported that they had successfully cloned an endangered wild sheep known as a muflon. The sheep survived and was put into a wildlife sanctuary. Another research group cloned a gaur, a wild ox, in 2002, but the calf died from an infection. Zoos around the world are investigating the possibility of cloning animals such as the Siberian tiger, the Sumatran tiger, several species of antelope, and the giant panda to save them from extinction. Some research facilities are saving cell samples from many species in the hope that, if they become extinct, new populations can be established.

There are even efforts underway to take the completely preserved nucleus of an extinct animal (or piece together enough DNA fragments to form a complete set of genes), then transfer the nucleus into an enucleated egg cell and implant the embryo into the uterus of a similar species. Scientists at Harvard, for example, have initiated a project to resurrect the woolly mammoth by using an elephant as a gestational surrogate. (See Social Context: The CRISPR Revolution in Chapter 3.)

In 2002, Advanced Cell Technologies announced that it had cloned cow eggs and, when the embryos developed into fetuses, had removed kidney cells and transferred them to a sponge-like matrix. The cells developed into what researchers described as a small kidney. When the kidney was implanted into the cow contributing the DNA, it produced a small amount of urine. Although no one sees this as an acceptable procedure for use with human cells, it demonstrates the possibility of growing organs for transplantation without relying on stem cells. (For the controversy over embryonic stem cells, see Social Context: Stem Cells in Chapter 3.)

The possibility of using human embryonic stem cells to treat diseases, repair organs, and even grow whole organs makes cloning extremely important. Embryonic stem cells are obtained from embryos and can be induced to develop into almost any tissue in the human body—a capacity called *pluripotent*. If someone with (for example) diabetes needed stem cells for treatment, her DNA could be used to replace the nucleus in a donor egg. When the egg formed a blastocyst, the stem cells could be removed. They would be a perfect genetic match with her own tissue, thus avoiding the problem of tissue rejection. This is an example of *therapeutic cloning*. That is, the cloning is for the purpose of getting materials for treatment, not for the purpose of reproduction. Because embryos must be destroyed to secure the stem cells, however, those who consider human embryos to have the status of persons regard even therapeutic cloning as a serious moral wrong.

Cell Conversion

In 2007, Shinya Yamanaka showed that it is possible to use a retrovirus to insert four genes into a somatic cell and convert the cell into a pluripotent state. In effect, the genes can reprogram a skin cell into an embryonic stem cell. These so-called *induced pluripotent stem cells* may make it unnecessary to destroy embryos to acquire stem cells; thus, the major objection to cloning for therapeutic purposes may disappear. Indeed, converted cells may make it unnecessary to rely on somatic cell nuclear transfer even for reproductive purposes. Many difficulties must be overcome, however, before either of these possibilities can be realized in any practical way. (See Social Context: Stem Cells in Chapter 3.)

What about Humans?

Most of the public discussion of cloning has focused on human *reproductive cloning*. If sheep, mice, cattle, and cats can be successfully cloned, there seems to be no technical reason a human cannot also be cloned.

Assuming that human reproductive cloning were perfected, here are a few of the possibilities it opens up:

1. When one member of a couple carries a gene responsible for a devastating illness, such as Tay-Sachs disease, the couple could decide to clone a child and use only the genetic material from the noncarrier.

2. Women who have entered menopause as a result of chemotherapy, had their ovaries removed, or are postmenopausal could still have a genetically connected child by employing the DNA from their somatic cells. The child would be a genetically identical twin, as well as an offspring, of the woman.

3. Similarly, men who are sterile for any reason or who no longer are capable of producing undamaged sperm (e.g., as a result of cancer surgery or radiation

treatments) could still produce a cloned child.

4. The parents of a dying child could decide to have another who would be a genetically identical replacement.

5. Cells from a deceased spouse, partner, or relative could be used to create children who would be the lost loved one's twins.

6. To solve various fertility issues, a family could include offspring who are genetically identical with one of the parents. These children would be genetic twins of the parent, although separated by years.

These possibilities, which some regard as potentially neutral or beneficial, are shadowed by other possibilities that some see as offering more serious objections to human cloning.

1. The rich and the powerful might decide to clone themselves to perpetuate their unique combination of genes or extend their social or political influence.

2. The cellular DNA from popular figures such as athletes and movie stars might become marketed as commodities. Because cloning would make "popular" DNA valuable, it might be stolen and used to produce children without the consent of the "donor."

Not a Photocopy

Some fears about cloning seem to reflect the mistaken belief that the clone of an individual will grow up to be exactly the same as the individual—a sort of photocopy. But of course, genetic identity doesn't result in exact similarity: we already know that identical twins, even when brought up in the same family, may turn out to be quite distinct in personality, interests, and motivations. A child who develops in a different uterine environment, then grows up in a world filled with different people, practices, events, and experiences, is unlikely to be exactly like the person cloned.

The most serious objection to human reproductive cloning at the moment is that it would lead to so many tragic outcomes. With a success rate with mice hovering around a mere 3 percent, the number of failed pregnancies is not likely to be better. Also, the chance of children being born with either lethal or seriously debilitating impairments is unacceptably high. We know from cloned mammals that unpredictable genetic and developmental errors occur.

No serious researcher thinks it would be anything but premature and morally indefensible to attempt to clone a human at this point. Even if it is not wrong in principle, it seems wrong to produce a large number of children who would most likely be severely impaired, assuming that they did not die shortly after birth.

But what of the future? In what circumstances, if any, would the cloning of humans be legitimate? Are we willing to take the risks involved in the development of clones? Are we prepared to accept the alterations in our society that successful human cloning might produce?

Politics

Research involving cloning human embryos has been controversial from the start. On February 4, 1997, the day after Wilmut announced the cloning of Dolly, President Bill Clinton asked the National Bioethics Advisory Committee to report to him in ninety days "with recommendations on possible Federal actions" to prevent the "abuse" of cloning. Meanwhile, on March 4, President Clinton issued an executive order banning the use of federal funds to support research leading to the cloning of humans. On June 9, the committee made its report to the president, and he immediately called for legislation banning cloning "for the purpose of creating a child."

In August 2001, President George W. Bush announced that federally funded embryonic stem-cell research could proceed only on stem cells that had already been recovered from embryos. Federal money could not be used, however, to create new embryos and thus could not be used for therapeutic cloning. In March 2009, President Barack Obama issued an executive order instructing the NIH to draft guidelines lifting some of the Bush rules governing stem-cell research. The most important change was to make thirteen new human embryonic stem-cell lines eligible for research receiving federal funding and to evaluate dozens more lines for further funding.

Denounced in Principle

Cloning human embryos for the purpose of reproduction continues to be denounced, even in principle, by the entire scientific and medical community. Researchers have repeatedly assured the public that they have no plans to carry out experiments like those that have produced other mammals. The fundamental practical interest in human cloning is in therapeutic cloning: the creation of human embryos to acquire embryonic stem cells to treat diseases and injuries. Recent success in developing viable stem cell lines from adult cells through somatic cell nuclear transfer has lent greater scientific legitimacy to therapeutic cloning. It has also lent the practice greater political legitimacy, as it avoids the ongoing controversy surrounding both embryonic stem cells and reproductive cloning.

CASE PRESENTATION
Savior Sibling

Anissa Ayala was fifteen years old in 1988, when she was diagnosed with chronic myelogenous leukemia. She received radiation and chemotherapy to destroy diseased bone marrow and blood cells, but one outcome of such treatments is that the patient's bone marrow is unable to produce enough normal blood cells to sustain life. Anissa's parents, Mary and Andy Ayala, were informed that without a bone-marrow transplant of blood-producing stem cells, Anissa's chances of long-term survival were virtually zero, while with a transplant she would have a 70 to 80 percent chance.

Tests showed that neither the Ayala parents nor their nineteen-year-old son, Airon, had bone marrow sufficiently compatible for them to be donors for Anissa. The family then turned to a public bone-marrow registry, and for the next two years they searched for a donor. The odds of a match between two nonrelated people is only one in twenty thousand, and as time passed and no donor turned up, the Ayalas felt increasingly desperate. Anissa's health had stabilized, but that condition could not be expected to last.

Radical Solution

Mary and Andy Ayala decided that the only way they could do more to help save their daughter's life was to try to have another child. Anissa's physician tried to discourage them, pointing out that the odds were only one in four that the child would have the right tissue type to be a stem-cell donor. Furthermore, the probability of their conceiving another child was very low: Andy Ayala was forty-five and been sterilized by vasectomy sixteen years earlier; Mary was forty-two and thus past the period of peak female fertility. Nevertheless, the Ayalas decided to go ahead with their plan, and as the first step Andy Ayala had surgery to reverse the vasectomy. Then, against all the odds, Mary Ayala became pregnant.

Response

When word spread that the Ayalas planned to have a child because their daughter needed compatible bone marrow, they became the subjects of intense media attention and harsh criticism. Critics claimed that they were treating the baby Mary was expecting as a means only and not as a person of unique worth. Some said they were taking an irrevocable step down the path that ultimately would lead to conceiving children merely to be sources of tissues and organs needed by others.

A few opposed this outpouring of criticism by noting that people decide to have children for varied and complex reasons and sometimes for no reason at all. Furthermore, the reason for having a child need not determine how one regards or treats the child. In addition, those who condemned the Ayalas often emphasized the "child-as-an-organ-bank" notion but never mentioned the relative safety of a bone-marrow transplant.

The Ayalas were hurt by the criticisms. Mary said she had wanted a third child for a number of years but had been unable to get her husband to agree. Andy admitted that he wouldn't have wanted another child if Anissa hadn't become ill, but he said he also had in mind the comfort a child would bring to the family if Anissa should die. The whole family said they would want and love the child, whether or not its bone marrow was a good match for Anissa's.

Against All Odds

In February 1990, the Ayalas found that they had beaten the odds once more. Tests of the developing fetus showed that the stem cells were nearly identical with Anissa's. During an interview after the results were known, Anissa said, "A lot of people think 'How can you do this? How can you be having this baby for your daughter?' But she's my baby sister and we're going to love her for who she is, not for what she can give me."

On April 6, 1990, in a suburban Los Angeles hospital, more than a week before her due date, Mary Ayala gave birth to a healthy six-pound baby girl. The Ayalas named her Marissa Eve.

Anissa's physician, pediatric oncologist Patricia Konrad, collected and froze blood from the baby's umbilical cord. Umbilical blood contains a high concentration of stem cells, and she wanted the blood available should Anissa need it before Marissa was old enough to be a donor.

When Marissa Eve was fourteen months old and had reached an adequate weight, she was given general anesthesia and marrow was extracted from her hipbone. After preparation, the donated marrow was injected into one of Anissa's veins. The procedure was successful, and the stem cells migrated to Anissa's marrow and began to multiply. Anissa's own bone marrow once again began to produce normal blood cells.

Three years later, Anissa married Bryan Espinosa, and Marissa Eve was the flower girl at the wedding. Radiation treatments had destroyed Anissa's chances of having a child of her own, but she noted that the bond between her and Marissa Eve was especially close. "Marissa is more than a sister to me," Anissa told reporter Anni Griffiths Belt. "She's almost like my child, too."

"I was struck by the extraordinary bond between the sisters," Belt said, "The fact is, neither one would be alive today without the other."

Easier Than Ever

Mary and Andy Ayala beat the odds in several ways: Andy's vasectomy was successfully reversed, Mary became pregnant without medical intervention, and Marissa Eve turned out to be a good bone-marrow match for her sister. The odds of the first two events remain about the same today, but no longer is it necessary to gamble against the odds where bone-marrow compatibility is concerned.

Using eggs and sperm, embryos can be produced in vitro by artificial insemination, then screened for compatibility with an intended bone-marrow recipient. Only those embryos compatible with the recipient will then be introduced into the uterus of the mother. Thus, the same techniques used in preimplantation genetic screening for the purpose of preventing the transmission of a heritable disease can also be employed to select for such positive traits as bone-marrow compatibility. (For a discussion, see the Briefing Session in Chapter 3.)

Most often, this technique has been used to ensure that umbilical-cord blood, which contains blood-producing stem cells, is compatible with the tissue of the recipient. This procedure has been used in more than two thousand cases over the past decade. Those who object to preimplantation screening for genetic reasons also object when it is used to select for tissue donation.

Baby M and Mary Beth Whitehead: Surrogate Pregnancy in Court

On March 30, 1986, Elizabeth Stern, a professor of pediatrics, and her husband William accepted from Mary Beth Whitehead a baby who had been born four days earlier. The child's biological mother was Whitehead, but she had been engaged by the Sterns as a surrogate mother. Even so, it was not until almost exactly a year later that the Sterns were able to claim legal custody of the child.

The Sterns, working through the Infertility Center of New York, had first met with Whitehead and her husband Richard in January of 1985. Whitehead, who already had a son and a daughter, had indicated her willingness to become a surrogate mother when she registered with the Infertility Center. "What brought her there was empathy with childless couples who were infertile," her attorney later stated. (Whitehead's own sister had been unable to conceive.)

According to court testimony, the Sterns considered Mary Beth Whitehead a "perfect person" to bear a child for them. William Stern said it was "compelling" for him to have children, for he had no biological relatives left in the world. He and his wife had planned to have children, but they put off attempts to conceive until his wife completed her medical residency in 1981. In 1979, however, she was diagnosed with an eye condition that likely indicated she had multiple sclerosis. When she learned that the symptoms of the disease might be worsened by pregnancy and that she might become temporarily or even permanently paralyzed, the Sterns "decided the risk wasn't worth it." It was this decision that led them to the Infertility Center and to Mary Beth Whitehead.

The Sterns agreed to pay Whitehead $10,000 to be artificially inseminated with Mr. Stern's sperm and to bear a child. Whitehead would then turn the child over to the Sterns, and Elizabeth Stern would be allowed to adopt the child legally. The agreement was drawn up by a lawyer specializing in surrogacy. William Stern later testified that Whitehead seemed perfectly pleased with the agreement and expressed no interest in keeping the baby she was to bear. "She said she would not come to our doorstep," he said. "All she wanted from us was a photograph each year and a little letter on what transpired that year."

Birth and Strife

The baby was born on March 27, 1986. According to Elizabeth Stern, the first indication that Whitehead might not uphold the agreement was a statement she made to the Sterns in the hospital two days after the baby's birth. "She said she didn't know if 'I can go through with it,' " Dr. Stern testified. Although Whitehead did turn the baby over to the Sterns on March 30, she called a few hours later. "She said she didn't know if she could live any more," Stern said. Whitehead called again the next morning and asked to see the baby, and she and her sister arrived at the Sterns' house before noon.

According to Elizabeth Stern, Whitehead told her she "woke up screaming in the middle of the night" because the baby was gone, her husband was threatening to leave her, and she had "considered taking a bottle of Valium." Stern quoted Whitehead as saying, "I just want her for a week, and I'll be out of your lives forever." The Sterns allowed Whitehead to take the baby home with her.

But then Mary Beth Whitehead refused to return the baby and instead took the infant to her parents' home in Florida. The Sterns obtained a court order, and on July 31 the child was seized from Whitehead. The Sterns were granted temporary custody. Then Mr. Stern, as the father of the child, and Ms. Whitehead, as the mother, each sought permanent custody from the Superior Court of the State of New Jersey.

Trial

The seven-week trial attracted national attention, for the legal issues were without precedent. Whitehead was the first to challenge the legal legitimacy of a surrogate agreement in a U.S. court. Her lawyer argued that the agreement was "against public policy" and violated New Jersey prohibitions against selling babies. In contrast, William Stern was the first to seek a legal decision to uphold the "specific performance" of the terms of a surrogate contract. In particular, he argued that Whitehead should be ordered to uphold her agreement, surrendering her parental rights and permitting his wife to become the baby's legal mother. In addition to the contractual issues, the judge had to deal with the "best interest" of the child as required by New Jersey child-custody law. The "best interest" standard, which many critics saw as conceptually vague, had never been applied in a surrogacy case.

On March 31, 1987, Judge Harvey R. Sorkow announced his decision. He upheld the legality of the surrogate-mother agreement between the Sterns and Whitehead and dismissed all arguments that the contract violated public policy or prohibitions against selling babies.

Immediately after he read his decision, Judge Sorkow summoned Elizabeth Stern into his chambers and allowed her to sign documents permitting her to adopt the baby she and her husband called Melissa. The court decision effectively stripped Mary Beth Whitehead of all parental rights concerning the baby, whom she called Sara.

Appeal

The Baby M story did not stop with Judge Sorkow's decision. Whitehead's attorney appealed the ruling to the New Jersey Supreme Court, and on February 3, 1988, the seven members of the court, in a unanimous decision, reversed Judge Sorkow's ruling on the surrogacy agreement.

The court held that the agreement violated the state's adoption laws, because it involved a payment for a child. "This is the sale of a child, or at the very least, the sale of a mother's right to her child," Chief Justice Wilentz wrote. The agreement "takes the child from the mother regardless of her wishes and her maternal fitness…; and it accomplishes all of its goals through the use of money."

The court ruled that surrogacy agreements might be acceptable if they involved no payment and if a surrogate mother voluntarily surrendered her parental rights. In the present case, though, the court regarded paying for surrogacy as "illegal, perhaps criminal, and potentially degrading to women."

The court let stand the award of custody to the Sterns, because "their household and their personalities promise a much more likely foundation for Melissa to grow and thrive." (Whitehead, having divorced her husband three months earlier, was romantically involved with another man and was pregnant at the time of the court decision, which may have influenced the court's judgment against her.)

Despite awarding custody to the Sterns, the court set aside the adoption agreement signed by Elizabeth Stern. Whitehead remained a legal parent of Baby M, and the court ordered a lower court hearing to consider visitation rights for the mother.

The immediate future of the child known to the court and to the public as Baby M was finally settled. Neither the Sterns nor Mary Beth Whitehead had won exactly what they had sought, but neither had they lost all.

CASE PRESENTATION
The Calvert Case: A Gestational Surrogate Changes Her Mind

Disease forced Crispina Calvert of Orange County, California, to have a hysterectomy, but only her uterus was surgically removed, not her ovaries. She and her husband, Mark, wanted a child of their own, but without a uterus Crispina would not be able to bear it. So in January 1990, they arranged with a woman named Anna Johnson to act as a surrogate, for a fee of $10,000.

Unlike the "traditional" model of surrogate pregnancy, Johnson would have no genetic connection to the Calverts' child. The ovum that would be fertilized would not be Johnson's. This, the Calverts hoped, would help them avoid scenarios like the controversial "Baby M" case, in which the surrogate Mary Beth Whitehead had sued for custody of a child she had borne, and to whom she had made as much genetic contribution as the father.

By contrast, Johnson would be a *gestational surrogate*, a category that was new at the time but has since become the primary form of surrogacy in the United States. Gestational surrogacy relies on in vitro fertilization (IVF) to create an embryo from the sperm and egg of the intended parents, which is then implanted into the uterus of the surrogate. Accordingly, ova were extracted from Crispina Calvert and mixed with sperm from Mark Calvert. An embryo fertilized this way was then implanted in Anna Johnson's uterus, and a fetus began to develop.

Johnson's pregnancy proceeded normally, but in her seventh month she announced she had changed her mind about giving up the child. She filed suit against the Calverts to seek custody of the unborn child. "Just because you donate a sperm and an egg doesn't make you a parent," said Johnson's attorney. "Anna is not a machine, an incubator."

"That child is biologically Chris and Mark's," the Calverts' lawyer responded. "That contract is valid."

Critics of genetic surrogate pregnancy are often equally critical of gestational surrogate pregnancy. Both methods, some claim, exploit women, particularly poor women. Further, in gestational pregnancy the surrogate is the one who must run the risks and suffer the discomforts and dangers of pregnancy. She has a biological claim to be the child's mother, they argue, because it is her body that produces the child using the genetic information supplied by the implanted embryo.

Defenders of surrogate pregnancy respond to the first criticism by denying that surrogates are exploited. They enter freely into a contract to serve as a surrogate for pay, just as anyone might contract to perform any other service. Pregnancy has hazards and leaves its marks on the body, but so do many other paid occupations. As far as gestational surrogacy is concerned, defenders argue that since the surrogate makes no genetic contribution to the child, in no reasonable way can she be regarded as the child's parent.

For decades, the Ethics Committee of the American Society for Reproductive Medicine (ASRM) has endorsed a policy that use of gestational surrogates should be limited to intended parents who have a "true medical condition" that precludes the intended parent from carrying a pregnancy. The current policy lists such conditions as the absence of a uterus or uterine anomalies, absolute medical contraindications to pregnancy, and serious medical conditions exacerbated by pregnancy, as well as the biological inability to bear children of single men and same-sex male couples. The apparent aim of the policy is to permit the use of gestational surrogate pregnancy in cases like that of Crispina Calvert, while prohibiting it when its motivation is mere convenience or an unwillingness to have children via pregnancy. The ASRM Ethics Committee has also endorsed "fair and reasonable economic compensation" for gestational carriers that reflect the burdens and dangers of pregnancy, but do not constitute an "undue inducement" for women to take them on.

Birth and Resolution

The child carried by Anna Johnson, a boy, was born on September 19, and for a time Johnson and the Calverts shared visitation rights, in accordance with a court order. Then, in October 1990, a California Superior Court denied Johnson the parental rights she had sought. Justice R. N. Parslow awarded complete custody of the child to the Calverts and terminated Johnson's visitation rights.

"I decline to split the child emotionally between two mothers," the judge said. He said Johnson had nurtured and fed the fetus in the way a foster parent might take care of a child, but she was still a "genetic stranger" to the boy and could not claim parenthood because of surrogacy.

Justice Parslow found the contract between the Calverts and Johnson to be valid, and he expressed doubt about Johnson's contention that she had "bonded" with the fetus she was carrying. "There is substantial evidence in the record that Anna Johnson never bonded with the child till she filed her lawsuit, if then," he said. (While the trial was in progress, Johnson was accused of planning to sue the Calverts from the beginning, so she could make money from book and movie rights associated with a famous case.)

"I see no problem with someone getting paid for her pain and suffering," Parslow said. "There is nothing wrong with getting paid for nine months of what I understand is a lot of misery and a lot of bad days. They are not selling a baby; they are selling pain and suffering."

The Calverts were overjoyed by the decision.

BRIEFING SESSION

"Oh, brave new world that has such people in it!" exclaims Miranda in Shakespeare's *The Tempest*.

This is the line from which Aldous Huxley took the title for his dystopian novel *Brave New World*. A dystopia is the opposite of a utopia, and the future society depicted by Huxley is one that we are invited to view with shock and disapproval.

In Huxley's dystopia, "pregnancy" is a dirty word, sex is purely recreational, and children are produced according to explicit genetic standards in the artificial wombs of state "hatcheries." Furthermore, one's genetic endowment determines the social position and obligations one has within the society, and everyone is conditioned to believe that the role she finds herself in is the best one to have.

In some respects, the future society envisioned in the novel has arrived. The new and still developing technologies of human reproduction have reached a stage in which the innovations imagined by Huxley in 1932 are well within the limits of feasibility.

We have no state hatcheries and no artificial uteruses. But we do have sperm banks, donor ova, artificial insemination, frozen embryos, and surrogate pregnancies. It is common practice to remove an ovum from a woman's body, fertilize it, then place it in her uterus or that of a surrogate so that it may develop into a child. We can remove one or more of the cells of a growing embryo and allow them to develop into separate embryos. Because we have the power to clone mammals, producing a genetically identical twin, we most likely also have the power to clone humans. What we have yet to do is to employ these technologies as part of a deliberate social policy to collectively restructure our world along the lines imagined by Huxley.

On the one hand, our reproductive technologies have been largely used for individual and, many would say, benign purposes. They have been used by thousands of infertile couples to have children that are biologically related to them. They have given thousands of same-sex couples, as well as single men and women, opportunities to start families and raise children. They have provided new reproductive possibilities for women past the age of ovulation or who have lost their ovaries or uterus in surgery. They increasingly offer new tools for fighting debilitating diseases at the earliest stages of development. Far from the mechanistic and dehumanized future of *Brave New World*, these tools appear to offer new opportunities for building deep and meaningful family relationships, new structures of intimate care and concern.

But in the view of some, our current reproductive technologies merely mark a beginning, and the disturbing possibilities inherent in reproductive technology remain unrealized. It may be possible before long, for example, to avoid sexual reproduction and use in vitro fertilization and surrogate pregnancy to reproduce clones of an individual. When combined with other incipient technologies, such as germ-line genomic "editing," it is easy to imagine how reproductive technologies might come to undermine the basic fabric and pattern of our society.

Some of the core values associated with reproduction and family life—such as unconditional love and the inherent value of each individual—might come to seem quaint in a society populated by clones and "designer" children. In such a society, people might come to see their offspring as commodities or accessories to be perfected and enhanced rather than cherished for who they are. At the same time, increased reproductive control might prompt us to place the good of the species or society over the value of individual autonomy. This might justify the exploitation or oppression of clones or of individuals who do not (or cannot afford to) pursue reproduction for the greater good.

The possible loss of personal values is a legitimate and serious concern. Indeed, the technologies of human reproduction are sometimes viewed as "unnatural" interventions that will lead to a world of bleakness and loss. Yet it is important to remember that these same technologies also profoundly enrich the lives of those presently living and prevent considerable suffering and despair. Will our increased control over reproduction continue to be used to help nurture children and build meaningful family bonds? Or does our use of these technologies set us on a path toward a biological dystopia? One way of thinking about these general questions is to turn once more to Huxley.

In 1962, Huxley published a utopian novel, *Island*. Like the society in *Brave New World*, Huxley's ideal society also relies on the principles of science, but they are used to promote autonomy and personal development. For more than a hundred years, the society on the island of Pala has shaped itself in accordance with the principles of reason and science. Living is communal, sexual repression is nonexistent, children

are cared for by both biological parents and other adults, drugs are used to enhance perceptual awareness, and social obligations are assigned on the basis of personal interest and ability.

Reproductive technology is one of the means the society uses to achieve its ends. It practices contraception, eugenics, and artificial insemination. Negative eugenics to eliminate genetic diseases is considered only rational. But more than this, by the use of deep freeze and artificial insemination, sperm from donors with superior genetic endowments are available for the use of couples who wish to improve their chances of having a child with special talents or higher-than-usual intelligence.

Huxley's ideal *Island* is not above criticism, even from those sympathetic to the values he endorses. Yet it should remind us that *Brave New World*, with its powerful cautionary tale of science pressed into the service of repressive political goals, is only one of many possible futures for reproductive technology. Ultimately, how we apply such technologies will depend on what kind of society we wish to live in and what ethical values we want it to embody.

Techniques of Assisted Reproduction

The birth of Louise Brown in 1978 (see the Case Presentation in this chapter) was a major media event. Photographs, television coverage, interviews, and news stories presented the world with minute details of the lives of the people involved and of the procedures leading to Brown's conception through in vitro fertilization.

Despite the unprecedented character of the event, few people seemed surprised by it. The idea of a "test-tube baby" was one already familiar from fiction and folklore. Medieval alchemists were thought capable of

generating life in their flasks, and hundreds of science fiction stories depicted a future in which the creation of life in the laboratory was an ordinary occurrence. Thus, in some ways, the birth of Louise Brown was seen as merely a matter of science and medicine catching up with imagination.

While it is doubtful that the public appreciated the magnitude of the achievement that resulted in the birth of Louise Brown, it was one of considerable significance. The first embryo transfer was performed in rabbits in 1890, but it wasn't until the role of hormones in reproduction, the nutritional requirements of developing cells, and the reproductive process itself were better understood that it became possible to fertilize an egg outside a human mother's body and then implant it in her uterus for ordinary development.

An estimated 350,000 babies are born worldwide each year through the use of assisted reproductive technologies (ART). Since the birth of Louise Brown, more than five million children conceived using these technologies have entered the world, more than half of those since 2007. In the United States, a leader in fertility treatments, about sixty-two thousand infants a year are born as a result of ART. The number of such babies doubled from 1996 to 2004, and it continues to rise, representing by 2015 over 1.5 percent of all births in the United States. This is not surprising, given the fact that nearly 12 percent of women ages 15–44 now seek fertility treatments. The world we live in is more like the one Huxley wrote about than ever before.

IVF

In vitro is a Latin phrase that means "in glass," and in embryology, it is used in contrast with *in utero*, or "in the uterus." Traditional human fertilization takes place in utero (strictly speaking, in the fallopian tubes) when a sperm cell unites with an ovum. In vitro fertilization, then, is fertilization that is artificially performed outside the woman's body—in a test tube, so to speak.

The ovum that produced Louise Brown was fertilized in vitro. But the remainder of the process involved *embryo transfer.* After the ovum from her mother's body was fertilized and had become an embryo, it was transferred—returned for in utero development.

Robert Edwards and Patrick Steptoe, who were responsible for developing and performing the techniques that led to the birth of Louise Brown, followed an IVF process that, allowing for technical improvements, is basically the same as the one used today.

A woman is given a reproductive hormone to cause her ova to mature. Several of these eggs are extracted from the ovarian follicles and placed in a nutrient solution to which sperm is then added. With luck, sperm cells penetrate several ova, fertilizing them. The fertilized eggs are transferred to another nutrient solution where they undergo cell division. The embryo (also called a *zygote* or a *pre-embryo*) is then transferred back to the woman (or to a surrogate), who has been given injections of hormones to prepare her uterus to receive it.

Numerous modifications and extensions of Steptoe and Edwards's techniques have been introduced since 1978. One of the first was a nonsurgical procedure for securing ova. After hormones stimulate the ovarian follicles, ultrasound is used to locate the follicles, and a hollow needle is inserted through the vaginal wall and into a follicle. Fluid is withdrawn and egg cells are identified under the microscope. They are then fertilized with the sperm and cultured, and the resulting embryos implanted.

Since implantation does not guarantee that a fertilized embryo will attach to the uterine wall, IVF has often involved the implantation of multiple embryos at the same time. This makes it more likely that at least one will attach to the uterine wall and so eliminates the need for a woman to have eggs removed another time. Yet the practice also has the disadvantage of increasing the chances of multiple gestations, which can increase complications for both the woman and the resulting fetuses. (See this chapter's Decision Scenario on the Perils of Multiple Pregnancy.)

More recent innovations, such as the direct injection of sperm into ova and the freezing of embryos, have contributed to higher success rates for assisted reproduction. This has reduced the need, especially in younger women, to implant more than one embryo in the uterus at a time. We will discuss these and other variations on traditional IVF in the following section.

ICSI, PZD, DNA Transfer, GIFT, ZIFT, IVC, COH, and IUI

Intracytoplasmic sperm injection (ICSI), is a technique originally developed to reduce male infertility due to low quantity or quality of sperm. Sperm are examined microscopically and one that seems best shaped and most active is injected directly into the egg cell. Since it produces fertilization rates as high as 80 percent, it has become one of the most common techniques of assisted reproduction after IVF and is often used even when there is no diagnosis of male factor infertility.

Partial zona dissection (PZD), is another technique focused on male infertility. It involves using microtechniques to drill holes in the *zona*, or protective membrane surrounding an ovum, to facilitate the passage of sperm into the interior. This increases the chances of fertilization by reducing the egg's resistance to penetration, which is particularly useful when the sperm involved may be less active or fewer in number.

DNA transfer involves replacing the nucleus of a donor egg with one taken from the intended mother, who is then implanted with the resulting embryo. It has been used to treat infertility in older women by harnessing the cellular mechanisms of a (younger) donor ova to the nuclear DNA of the (older) patient. More recently, it has been used to prevent devastating mitochondrial diseases, by taking advantage of the healthy mitochondria (and mitochondrial DNA) from the donor ovum. This technique was legalized in Britain in 2015, despite concerns that it created "three parent" children with DNA from two different women—a combination which could be passed on to future offspring. Still, all 23 chromosome pairs come from the child's mother and father, not the egg donor.

Gamete intrafallopian transfer (GIFT), uses some of the same techniques as traditional IVF. It involves inserting both ova and sperm into the fallopian tubes through a small abdominal incision, so if fertilization takes place, it does so inside the woman's body. Some regard the procedure as being more "natural" than in vitro fertilization.

Zygote intrafallopian transfer (ZIFT), involves culturing eggs and sperm outside the body and then placing the zygotes into a woman's fallopian tubes. If the transfer is done at a particular developmental stage, it is called *pronuclear stage tubal transfer*. Both are variants of *tubal embryo transfer* and reflect the view that the fallopian tubes provide the most protective environment for embryo development.

Intravaginal culture (IVC), is another attempt to bring assisted reproduction closer to natural fertilization. Ova are placed in a tube into which sperm cells are added, and the tube is then inserted into the vagina and kept next to the cervix by a diaphragm. Sexual intercourse can take place with the tube in place. Two days later, the tube is removed, the contents decanted, and any fertilized ova transferred into the uterus.

Controlled ovarian hyperstimulation (COH) involves administering hormones to stimulate egg production by the ovaries. When ovulation occurs, *intrauterine insemination* (IUI) can be used to inject semen into the uterus. (See the Artificial Insemination section below for more on IUI.) Controlled ovarian hyperstimulation and IUI are less expensive ($2,000–$3,000) than IVF ($12,000–$15,000), and more likely to be covered by insurance. The pregnancy rate is lower, however, and the hormones used in COH are more likely to lead to a pregnancy involving multiple fetuses.

The use of ovarian stimulating hormones is believed to be responsible for 20 percent of multiple births (8 percent of which involve triplets, quadruplets, or more), and it is likely a major cause of the 12.8 percent rate of premature births. If some of the multiple embryos produced by COH–IUI are not eliminated by selective reduction, the likelihood of harm to the mother and the babies is considerable.

New techniques to assist reproduction are being developed at a rapid rate, and not all those in use are mentioned here. They include strategies as simple as shifts in nutrition and sexual positions, and as complicated as transplanting a uterus. That so many techniques are available means that if one doesn't work, prospective parents may try another. Yet having so many options makes it difficult for some people who wish to have children to stop trying, even after repeated failures to conceive.

Demand

The most common reason for seeking out assisted reproduction technologies is some form of male or female infertility, which is usually defined by a failure to conceive despite a year of unprotected intercourse. In 2010, the U.S. population included about 61 million women of reproductive age, and about 12 percent of them reported using infertility services for themselves or their partners. Nine percent of men aged 15–44 reported being subfertile or infertile, while 11 percent of women reported impaired fecundity and about 5 percent reported infertility. Although these figures actually represent a slight reduction in reported infertility rates from past decades, utilization of assisted reproductive technologies is increasing.

Assisted reproduction is not a solution to all problems of fertility, but it is the only solution possible in a large number of cases.

Figures show that as many as 45 percent of all cases of female infertility are caused by abnormal or obstructed fallopian tubes. Although normal ova are produced, they cannot move down the tubes to be fertilized. In some cases, tissue blocking the tubes can be removed or the tubes reconstructed. In other cases, however, the tubes may be impossible to repair or may be entirely absent. (Only 40 to 50 percent of infertile women can be helped through surgery.) This means that the only way in which these women can expect to have genetically related children is by means of assisted reproduction technologies. This is also true when a woman has no uterus or is postmenopausal and must rely on a donated ovum.

While heterosexual couples struggling with infertility still constitute the biggest group utilizing technologies such as IVF and ICSI, these techniques are also increasingly being used by singles and by same-sex couples. Single men and male same-sex couples use IVF in combination with donor eggs and gestational surrogates to start their own families. Single women and lesbian couples use IVF in combination with donor sperm to increase the odds of conceiving or in *reciprocal IVF* so that one partner can be the birth mother while the other is the genetic mother. (See Case Presentation: Brave New Families for more on these topics.)

Effectiveness

In 2014, the Centers for Disease Control reported the results of the agency's 2012 study (the most recent) on the effectiveness of assisted reproductive technology as employed in 456 infertility clinics. Attempts to produce pregnancy involve one-month cycles, and during 2012 the clinics intervened to produce pregnancy in 157,662 cycles. The interventions resulted in 51,267 live births (some of them multiple), for a success rate of 32.5 percent. Single births occurred in 72.6 percent of the live births, twins in 26.4 percent, and triplets or more in 1 percent.

The chance of a woman's becoming pregnant with the help of reproductive technology is on average now roughly the same (by some estimates) as that of a fertile couple attempting conception throughout the woman's regular cycle. But of course, not all the pregnancies result in births, and roughly half of the women treated in infertility programs never become pregnant.

Costs

The financial cost of an attempt to become pregnant with ART can be staggering. Each fertilization cycle can cost as much as $15,000, and most women who get pregnant go through three or four cycles before pregnancy occurs. (The average cost of a single in vitro fertilization attempt is about $12,000, not counting medications.) Only about fifteen states require insurers to cover infertility diagnosis and treatment, and many people go deeply into debt to pay for them. The costs can be even higher when donated reproductive tissue or surrogates are involved.

It is not unusual for someone to spend $25,000 to $35,000 attempting to get pregnant, and a few people spend as much as $200,000 or $300,000. By some estimates, the money spent on fertility-related medical services exceeds $3 billion a year. The cost of treatment has led some people to visit clinics abroad, where prices are significantly lower, even though the success rate may also be lower.

Although some clinics discourage women from repeated attempts at pregnancy to improve their own success rates, others are willing to go far beyond reasonable efforts. Not only is providing fertility assistance lucrative, but specialists often become invested in realizing the hopes of their patients.

Risks

Along with the tangible benefits, assisted reproductive technologies are also associated with a number of potential risks for the children conceived with them, as well as for prospective parents and third parties. As we will discuss later in the chapter, these risks can raise serious ethical concerns for the families and physicians involved.

Health concerns. While many of the early health concerns associated with "test tube babies" have been dispelled, several new issues have arisen to extend the debate on the safety of assisted reproduction.

For over a decade, studies found that babies conceived by ART procedures seemed to have a higher risk of serious birth impairments. An influential 2002 study published in the *New England Journal of Medicine* found that babies conceived by IVF or intracytoplasmic sperm injection (ICSI) had a 9 and 8.6 percent risk, respectively, of being diagnosed with such problems as heart abnormalities, cleft palate, or undescended testicles, whereas the risk in unassisted pregnancies was 4.2 percent. A second study in the same journal found that IVF and ICSI babies have 2.6 times the usual risk of low birth weight, a condition associated with heart and lung problems and poor cognitive development. A 2009 CDC study found that IVF–ICSI babies were more than twice as likely to have defects in the septum of the heart (a hole between the chambers), a cleft lip or cleft palate, or an incompletely developed esophagus. Such babies were also more than four times as likely to have a malformed rectum.

One of the immediate questions that arose with regard to these and other studies was whether the increased risk of birth defects was due to some aspect of the IVF or ICSI procedure or whether it was instead a result of preexisting biological factors—such as gene mutations—that might have contributed to the original infertility in the parents. In other words, the question was whether ART technologies caused the problems or were merely correlated with them.

On the causality side, one line of thought is that the culture medium in which embryos are grown in IVF and ICSI contains chemicals that cause *epigenetic* changes—that is, changes in the way genes are expressed. The medium may add methyl groups, which act as switches to turn genes on or off. Epigenetic changes are known to cause disorders such as Beckwith-Wiedemann syndrome (BWS) and are also associated with low-birth-weight babies. Both BWS—a genetic disorder that predisposes children to cancer and abnormal tissue growth—and low birth weight have been shown to be more common in children conceived with IVF. The epigenetic hypothesis was given more support by studies that linked an IVF conception to rare cancers in humans and behavioral anomalies in mice.

On the "mere correlation" side of the question, the first suggestive evidence came from a 2006 Danish study of fifty thousand births, which found that previously infertile parents who managed to conceive through sexual intercourse also gave birth to children with an increased prevalence of serious birth defects—including those of the nervous, digestive, and musculoskeletal systems. Then, in 2012, a large study of 308,974 Australian births published in *NEJM* found that the increased risk of birth defects associated with IVF disappeared when factors such as maternal age and health, as well as ancestry and socioeconomic status, were taken into account. The study still found a correlation between ICSI and increased birth defects, although the researchers lacked some information (such as paternal age) that might be relevant. Like the Danish study, the 2012 *NEJM* study found that a history of infertility, with or without ART conception, was significantly associated with birth defects.

Whether assisted reproductive technologies actively cause, rather than merely correlate to, increased birth anomalies is a question unlikely to be settled for some time. But, as we will see, the ethical question—whether the good of overcoming infertility is worth some increased risk of health problems for one's offspring—is one that remains for most people who use assisted reproductive technologies. (Of course, that question is irrelevant to the minority of IVF–ICSI users who typically don't have health-related fertility problems—such as singles or same-sex couples.)

Despite the health concerns related to ART, it should be pointed out that the chance of any baby having some sort of birth defect is about 3 percent. In addition, some researchers question the methodology of comparing children conceived with IVF–ICSI to those conceived through intercourse, which is how the correlation with birth anomalies was established. It is important to remember that the actual number of children conceived through ART who develop serious impairments or diseases is quite small.

Multiple births. One of the hazards of the newer forms of assisted reproduction is that the fertility drugs given to women to speed up the production of ova can increase the chances that the women will become pregnant with multiple fetuses. Also, the IVF practice of transferring several embryos at a time to improve the probability that at least one will implant may, in fact, cause several to implant.

A pregnancy with multiple fetuses puts the entire pregnancy at increased risk for miscarriage; the more fetuses in the womb, the greater the risk. A woman carrying quadruplets has a 25 percent chance of a miscarriage in the first trimester; a woman carrying quin- tuplets has a 50 percent chance. The only way to substantially reduce the miscarriage risk is a selective abortion technique known as *fetal reduction*. Even if a miscarriage does not oc- cur, a multiple pregnancy puts the newborn infants at risk. Sixty percent of multiple preg- nancies result in premature birth, compared to just 10 percent of *singleton* (one fetus) preg- nancies. While a full-term pregnancy typi- cally lasts forty weeks, triplets (on average) are born around thirty-three weeks and qua- druplets around thirty-one weeks. Because of their prematurity, babies born as multiples often suffer from such problems as blindness, stroke, brain damage, and impaired motor skills. Recent evidence indicates that even if impairments are not obvious, premature babies often grow up to have more difficul- ties in school and in life than those who were full-term babies.

From 1915 to 1980 the number of multi- ple births in the U.S. population was stable, at around one in every fifty births. But in the 1980s, the number began to rise steeply, so that by 2010, multiple births represented roughly one out of every thirty births, an increase of 76 percent. The vast major- ity of these births involved twins, but the number of triplets, quadruplets, and larger groups also rose. The shift has produced roughly a *million* more twins than there would have been if the 1915–1980 rate had held.

What accounts for this shift? Research- ers think that about a third of the change is attributable to more women in their thir- ties and forties bearing children, which is strongly correlated with multiple births. But they ascribe roughly two-thirds of the change to assisted reproduction, especially the use of infertility drugs in procedures such as controlled ovarian stimulation. Indeed, the biggest spike in multiple births can be seen to correspond to the fact that the number of women taking fertility drugs tripled in the decade from 1995–2005, rising from about one million to three million.

Nevertheless, there are signs that the number of multiple births is leveling off. The 2012 twin birth rate of 33.2 per thou- sand births was basically unchanged from the 2009–2011 rate. The rate of triplet and larger-group births has fallen more than one-third since its 1998 high of 1.93 per 1,000. Just as the increase in multiple births can be attributed to the rise in the use of re- productive technology, the decline can most likely be attributed to the guidelines that the American Society for Reproductive Medi- cine established in 1999. A major aim of the guidelines was to reduce the rate of triplet and higher pregnancies. Also, procedures for producing and selecting embryos have improved over the years, reducing the need to implant more than one embryo to achieve a pregnancy. These and other shifts already appear to have produced marked reduc- tions in the rates of premature birth, low birth weight, stillbirths, and other deaths among babies conceived through assisted reproduction.

Even with these improvements, about one-third of births in which reproductive technology is used are multiple ones. In- fertility specialists are under a great deal of pressure to produce results, both from fami- lies and competitors. The procedures they offer are expensive, and the families seeking to have children know that their chances may go down over time. The fertility busi- ness is a multi-billion-dollar industry, and the incentives to violate professional guide- lines can be considerable.

Critics point out that the social costs of multiple pregnancies can be substantial. It has been estimated that as many as 20 per- cent of the babies in neonatal intensive care units were conceived by reproductive tech- nology and born prematurely. Such tragic situations can produce higher health care costs for everyone.

Would society be justified in intervening in this situation? Should the use of ovulation stimulators be contingent upon agreeing to the selective fetal reduction of any multiple pregnancies that result? Should more insurers be required to cover IVF treatments, so that families would feel less financial pressure to achieve a pregnancy on the first try? Or does the problem lie with fertility clinics and their relatively low level of regulation in the United States? (See Case Presentation: Egg and Sperm Donors for more on this topic.) Perhaps giving professional guidelines the force of law would mitigate some of the problems that multiple births can produce for children, the families they are born to, and the larger society.

Artificial Insemination

Artificial insemination (AI) is the oldest and most basic technique of assisted reproduction. It has been employed in human reproduction since at least the nineteenth century and used with domesticated and lab animals for even longer. Compared to the ARTs discussed above, artificial insemination involves a relatively simple procedure.

AI is generally initiated when a woman's body temperature and other factors indicate that ovulation is going to take place in one or two days. It is then repeated once or twice more until ovulation is likely completed. Typically, three inseminations are performed during a monthly cycle.

There are two main methods of artificial insemination. The most common in medical settings is *intrauterine insemination* (IUI), which, as discussed above, involves the direct injection of sperm into the uterus. This method can employ semen collected by masturbation or medical extraction, or a thawed donation from a sperm bank. To avoid antigenic reactions in the uterus, the sample is generally "washed" in a laboratory, which concentrates it and separates it from seminal fluid. This sample is then injected into the uterus using a catheter that has been threaded through the cervical canal.

By contrast, *intracervical insemination* (ICI) is more commonly employed at home without medical professionals. It involves the injection of semen into the neck of the cervix using a needleless syringe. The semen is typically collected through masturbation and then allowed to liquefy. Sometimes the woman trying to conceive will also insert a cervical cap to hold semen in the vagina. ICI most closely resembles natural insemination and is generally thought to be less effective than IUI, though it is much less expensive.

Efficacy

The monthly chance of pregnancy with both AI methods is low, from 8 to 15 percent. But with persistence both methods produce high success rates, with IUI ultimately achieving pregnancy in 85 to 90 percent of cases. Success on the first attempt is rare, and the highest conception rate occurs in the third month. Such efforts are continued, however, only when a detailed examination shows that the woman is not suffering from some unrecognized problem preventing her from becoming pregnant. Since ICI is often attempted without medical consultation, research on its effectiveness is less reliable, but some studies suggest it is about a third as effective as IUI, at least in the early cycles.

Benefits and Risks

Both IUI and ICI are fast and usually painfree procedures, with few related health risks. IUI on its own is not associated with multiple births, which are only likely when IUI is combined with controlled ovarian hyperstimulation.

Other risks specific to AI also appear to be low. When sperm taken from a sperm bank is used, the rate of congenital abnormalities in offspring is actually slightly lower than the 2 to 4 percent common in the general population. (If the sperm donor *does* have a hereditary condition, however, he may father a large number of children with the condition. See Case Presentation: Sperm and Egg Donors.)

Artificial insemination may be sought for a variety of reasons. When a man and woman are involved, infertility or subfertility of some kind is the most common reason for seeking AI. Roughly 10 percent of all heterosexual married couples are considered infertile, and it is estimated that 40 percent of those cases are due to factors that involve the male.

A man may be unable to produce any sperm cells (a condition called *asospermia*), or the number he produces may be too low to make impregnation of a woman likely (a condition called *oligospermia*). In other cases, adequate numbers of sperm cells may be produced, but they may not function effectively. Hence, their chances of reaching and fertilizing an ovum are slight. Finally, a man may suffer from a neurological condition that makes ejaculation impossible or from a disease (such as diabetes) that renders him impotent. In such cases, sperm can be medically removed and used in artificial insemination, although ICSI and IVF now offer other options for addressing male infertility.

If a woman cannot ovulate or if her fallopian tubes are blocked so that ova cannot descend, artificial insemination will not be helpful. (In such cases IVF may be the best option.) Yet there are some problems affecting women's reproductive systems that artificial insemination can address. For example, if a woman has a vaginal environment that is biochemically inhospitable to sperm, artificial insemination may be a successful alternative to intercourse. Also, if a woman has a small cervix or if her uterus is atypically positioned, then artificial insemination may be used to increase the chances of sperm reaching the uterus.

A couple might also seek artificial insemination for genetic reasons. Both may be carriers of a recessive gene for a genetic disorder (e.g., Tay-Sachs disease), or the male may be the carrier of a dominant gene for a genetic disorder (e.g., Huntington's disease). In either case, they may not want to run the risk of their child's being born with a genetic disease, yet may also not be willing to accept embryo screening or prenatal testing and abortion. To avoid the possibility they fear, they may choose to make use of artificial insemination with sperm secured from a donor.

Since at least the 1970s, single women and female same-sex couples have also used artificial insemination as a means of starting their own families. Since the medical establishment was traditionally averse to helping women procreate without a male spouse or partner, many of these women focused on self-insemination at home using donated sperm from friends or sperm banks. Second-wave feminist organizations held workshops on artificial insemination as a way for women to reclaim control of their bodies from what they saw as inherently patriarchal institutions. (See Chapter 10 for more on these issues.) Although single women and lesbian couples now make up a significant portion of the demand for medical fertility services, some couples still prefer to use ICI at home or IUI with a midwife, rather than try to conceive in a physician's office or fertility clinic. While home insemination efforts are frequently effective and significantly less expensive than those managed by physicians, it should be noted that they are more likely to generate complicated legal and custodial issues with sperm donors— as a number of couples, both gay and straight, have discovered in recent years. (See Case Presentation: Brave New Families.) In the next section, we will discuss these and other specific issues related to the donation of sperm, eggs, and other reproductive tissues and capacities.

Donors, Recipients, and Surrogates

The donation of reproductive tissue (sperm, eggs, ovaries) as well as embryos is often referred to as *third-party reproduction*, since it involves a third person (the donor) who enables a couple or an individual (the recipients) to become parents. This category also includes *surrogacy* arrangements, in which a woman carries a pregnancy for another individual or couple. Third-party reproduction raises a number of complicated practical, legal, and ethical issues. As in the previous section, we will focus on practical and legal matters here, saving a full discussion of the ethical implications of these procedures until the end of the chapter. We will also defer a full discussion of the ethical issues associated with embryo donations until the next section.

Sperm and Egg Donors

Donors of sperm and ova are often undergraduate or graduate students. Commercial sperm banks and ova agencies also recruit among young professionals, but a general effort is made to employ donors who are in excellent health, with a high level of intellectual ability. Donors are frequently given psychological and basic fertility tests. Their family histories are reviewed to reduce the possibility of transmitting a genetic disorder, although actual genetic testing typically takes place only if there is an ancestry-based risk of a genetic disease such as Tay-Sachs or sickle cell. Donor blood types are tested for compatibility with recipients and donors must be tested for infectious diseases such as HIV, hepatitis, and syphilis. (Donations to sperm banks must also be quarantined for at least six months to avoid infectious disease

transmission.) Most institutional sperm and egg donors choose to remain anonymous, although increasing numbers choose *open* donations, which allow offspring to contact them at a later date. Both egg and sperm donors are also frequently *known donors* who volunteer to help friends or family members start a family.

Despite these basic similarities, the processes of sperm and egg donation differ from each other in many important respects. Sperm donors encounter almost no health risks and generally make no more than $1,000 a month for multiple semen samples—although they usually must commit to keep donating on a weekly basis for a year. Egg donors, by contrast, are frequently paid as much as $10,000 for a month-long cycle of ova extraction, but face significant health risks and side effects. The injection of ovary-stimulating hormones can cause nausea, depression, and fatigue, as well as *ovarian hyperstimulation syndrome*, a condition that may involve blood clots, kidney failure, and, in rare cases, death. The procedure to harvest eggs can also cause organ damage and hemorrhages. These risks, combined with high fees, raise questions about the quality of the informed consent that young (and often cash-strapped) women give before egg donations. (See Case Presentation: Egg and Sperm Donors for more discussion.)

These issues are complicated by the fact that both sperm and egg donation programs are largely self-regulating, bound by professional guidelines that the lucrative fertility industry sometimes ignores. There are many documented instances in which ova donors have been offered fees above the level that the American Society for Reproductive Medicine considers "coercive." Many agencies also offer differential fee structures for "superior" candidates, which seems to belie the notion that ova and sperm donors are simply being paid for their time and inconvenience.

Finally, sperm and egg donors may encounter unexpected psychological and other consequences from becoming genetic parents to children raised entirely (or primarily) by others. Despite promises of anonymity by fertility centers, DNA testing and online databases now usually make it possible for families with donor-conceived children to identify donors. Some sperm donors have discovered they are the fathers of dozens (and in a few cases, hundreds) of children.

Recipients

Like sperm and egg donors, the recipients of donated reproductive tissue are subject to health screening, to test for disease and for their capacity to conceive and/or carry a pregnancy to term. Singles and couples are also subject to some degree of psychological evaluation, especially in the case of embryo donation, which is regulated more closely by FDA guidelines.

In addition to opposite-sex couples with fertility issues, parents of donor-conceived children now include many lesbian couples and single women, as well as gay male couples and single men who rely on surrogates to gestate and give birth to their children. All of these parents can end up with complicated and occasionally antagonistic connections to their donors and surrogates, particularly if all the legal details of the arrangement are not spelled out in advance. Recent years have seen sperm donors granted visiting rights in New Jersey and sued by the state of Kansas for child support despite prior written agreements that their involvement would end with the donation. (See Case Presentation: Brave New Families.) The past decade has also seen a number of instances in which sperm donors have passed on serious genetic diseases to their numerous offspring, despite assurances by fertility clinics that they had been genetically screened.

Examples like these have prompted recipients to take greater legal precautions (even with known donors), to develop information-sharing databases with other families of donor-conceived children, and to lobby for greater regulatory oversight of the fertility industry—especially of the practice of buying and selling frozen sperm and eggs multiple times before they are implanted.

Such concerns apply even to the final category of recipients we will mention, sometimes known as "self-donors." Technologies that allow reproductive tissues and embryos to be frozen and banked have produced a large group of recipients who become, in effect, their own donors. These include women and men who are about to undergo cancer or other treatments that will likely render them infertile, those who are about to get a vasectomy or a tubal ligation, and those who fear they may not be ready or able to have children while they are still fertile. These "backup" strategies have been largely successful, with hundreds of children born from previously frozen ova since 1998 and even a growing number successfully born from previously frozen ovaries and ovarian tissue. (Frozen sperm have been the mainstay of the sperm banks for decades.) Still, there are lingering concerns about the long-term effects that freezing may have on reproductive tissue and embryos. (For more on ethical issues related to embryo donation, see the discussion later in this Briefing.)

Surrogates

In the context of reproduction, a *surrogate* denotes a woman who carries a pregnancy for another individual or a couple who intend to parent the child. But the category of surrogacy comprises two very different kinds of arrangements:

The older, now less common, arrangement is called *traditional* or *genetic surrogacy*. A traditional surrogate is typically inseminated artificially, with the sperm of a man who intends to parent the child, either as part of a couple or on his own. Such a surrogate is called *genetic* because her own ovum is fertilized and she is thus genetically and biologically related to the resulting child.

A *gestational surrogate*, by contrast, carries a pregnancy created by the egg and sperm of both intended parents—or that of just one intended parent in combination with a donor egg or sperm. A gestational surrogate is thus *not* genetically related to the resulting child, although she still has a strong biological influence over fetal development. Gestational surrogacies typically involve IVF or ICSI technology.

Both types of surrogates generally enter into legally binding contracts to surrender the infant to the intended parents after giving birth, but a gestational surrogate arrangement has a much better chance of being upheld by the courts if a dispute should arise. (See the Baby M and Calvert Case Presentations for more on this topic.)

Benefits and efficacy. It is difficult to know how often surrogates are used in assisted reproduction efforts, since such arrangements sometimes bypass major medical institutions. But the Society for Assisted Reproductive Technologies says that at least 1,100 children are born each year of gestational surrogacies; other estimates are substantially higher.

Gestational surrogates offer infertile couples and single women options for conceiving genetic children that are not possible with the methods previously discussed. For example, a woman who has had her uterus removed can still contribute an ovum that, after being fertilized in vitro, is implanted in the uterus of the gestational surrogate. The resulting child will then be genetically related to the infertile woman and her male partner (or to a sperm donor). Gestational surrogacy can also offer genetic

motherhood to women with medical conditions that contraindicate pregnancy or may be exacerbated by it. According to the CDC, IVF-ICSI cycles that involve gestational surrogates are as much as 10 percent more likely to result in a live birth than those in which the intended mother gestates the embryo.

Single men and same-sex male couples also increasingly turn to gestational surrogates to help them become genetic fathers. By working with the same egg donor and surrogate over two pregnancies, for example, gay male couples can conceive two half-siblings, one of whom is genetically related to one father and one of whom is genetically related to the other.

Risks. Despite the undeniable benefits that can come with surrogacy arrangements, they are also fraught with practical and ethical risks. The most obvious (through rare) risk is that the surrogate will change her mind about the agreement and fight the intended parents for custody of the child. A slightly more common risk is that the intended parents will change their minds and demand that the surrogate terminate the pregnancy. For these reasons, the ASRM Ethics Committee recommends that both the surrogate and the intended parents get lawyers and undergo extensive psychological, medical, and legal counseling. They must then create a detailed legal agreement that spells out the intentions of all parties for a variety of circumstances. It is particularly important that such prior agreements cover serious health problems that may arise in the fetus or the surrogate during the course of the pregnancy and what steps (including abortion) should or should not be taken. The ASRM Committee also insists that surrogates be at least twenty-one and have already delivered a child.

One particularly troubling risk of surrogacy is that women will be unduly induced to take on the substantial physical and emotional risks of pregnancy, especially if they are poor. Surrogates in the U.S. can typically earn between $20,000 and $35,000 per pregnancy, and critics of compensated surrogacy charge that this represents either an unacceptable commodification of women's bodies or of babies or both. Supporters of compensation, including the ASRM, argue that current fees are reasonable for the duration and burdens of pregnancy. They also point to other professions, such as mining and the military, that involve taking on serious bodily risks for money. In general, surrogates are assumed to be paid for their time and associated burdens, rather than for the baby or for their reproductive capacity. (This stipulation is especially important in cases of traditional surrogacy where the surrogate and intended parents are subject to adoption laws.)

A different, related risk is that surrogacy could become a way for fertile women who would simply prefer not to be pregnant to "outsource" the job to other (most likely less wealthy) women. To prevent this, the ASRM guidelines and some state laws limit surrogacy arrangements only to intended parents who have a "true medical condition" such as the absence of a uterus, medical contraindications to pregnancy, or biologic inability to bear children (as in the case of male singles and couples).

Due to a lack of consensus about these practical and ethical risks, state laws on surrogacy are an unpredictable patchwork. Some states, such as Arizona, Michigan, and New York, forbid all forms of commercial surrogacy and punish those who enter into such arrangements. (Surrogates can generally still be paid for their medical expenses in these states but must otherwise be "altruistic" volunteers.) Other states, such as

Illinois, New Jersey, and Tennessee, are supportive of commercial gestational surrogacy but forbid traditional surrogacy. Others, such as Florida and California, allow and regulate both forms.

On the international stage, the United States, with its "free-market" ethos, is more tolerant than most nations of compensated surrogacy. As a result, dozens of couples and individuals from overseas travel to the United States each year to enter into surrogacy arrangements—which can be hard to come by in nations, such as Britain, that only allow compensation for a surrogate's expenses. Critics charge that this amounts to "reproductive tourism" and point to other nations, such as Thailand and India, where surrogacy has, in some cases, produced fertility operations that resemble "baby factories," with dormitory housing and group medical care. Since poor women in the developing world can often earn as much as fifteen years worth of income in just nine months, informed consent to surrogacy becomes highly problematic in these situations. (See Chapter 11 for more on global health care disparities.)

Embryos

As we saw in the discussion of stem-cell treatment in Chapter 3, ethical objections have been raised with regard to the creation, storage, selection, and disposal of embryos in IVF and other assisted reproductive technologies. Although the embryos created for ART are invisible specks made up of just four to eight cells, some consider them full human persons or morally significant as potential persons—convictions that can raise a number of ethical issues.

IVF and ICSI, as discussed above, involve the creation of human embryos through either the mixing of sperm with an extracted ovum (IVF) or the direct injection of a sperm into an ovum (ICSI). Due to the high failure rate for the implantation of transferred embryos (almost always over 50 percent), physicians have generally created more embryos than were intended to produce pregnancies. (In this respect, ART is probably much more efficient than unassisted reproduction, since as many as 80 percent of all embryos created through intercourse fail to implant.)

An important development in assisted reproduction was the perfection of techniques for freezing embryos. One advantage of the procedure is that it eliminates the need for women to undergo the lengthy and uncomfortable process required to secure additional ova. If a woman fails to become pregnant in a first attempt, embryos saved from the initial fertilization can be employed in a subsequent effort.

The technique also makes it possible to delay an embryo transplant until the intended mother has reached the most favorable time in her menstrual cycle. Furthermore, because embryos survive storage very well, women about to undergo medical treatments (such as chemotherapy) can first have their ova harvested and fertilized, with the resulting embryos preserved for pregnancy years later. Evidence to date indicates that embryos can be stored in a frozen condition and then unfrozen and implanted without any damage to the chromosomes.

Each year about forty thousand embryos are frozen at fertility clinics and only those deemed most likely to successfully implant are used. The result is a vast and growing number of embryos in storage—one million is the current rough estimate for the U.S.—which has generated a number of practical and ethical dilemmas. Recent years have seen high-profile legal conflicts over what should be done with stored embryos after couples split up, with one side typically claiming a right to use the embryos for pregnancy

and the other demanding protection from involuntary parenthood. (The latter position has tended to prevail in court.) Other questions arise if both intended parents die or no surrogate can be found.

Fertility clinics typically offer the options of having excess embryos destroyed, used for stem-cell and other research, or offered to an infertile couple. Often, though, couples cannot be traced, and centers are unwilling to give away an embryo without permission. When embryos are unclaimed or the bills for storage (sometimes as much as $1200 a year) are left unpaid, frozen embryos are usually destroyed simply by being allowed to thaw. At times, this practice has generated intense protest, with the Vatican newspaper denouncing it as a "prenatal massacre."

At some fertility centers, another layer of complexity has been added by the practice of creating embryos from donated eggs and sperm from commercial tissue banks. The rationale is that donor eggs are relatively scarce, and when a surplus is available, they shouldn't be wasted. Having on hand a collection of embryos that don't belong to any person or couple allows the centers to offer what fertility specialists call *embryo adoption*. This means that individuals or couples can choose ("adopt") an embryo for transfer on the basis of a description of the gamete donors. Over 1,000 such donated embryos were transferred in 2013, up from 569 in 2009.

Some critics are troubled by the move from the creation of embryos in order to help particular people to the production of embryos as "inventory." They charge that reproductive technology is a step nearer treating human embryos as commercial products to be offered to discriminating consumers. This issue, as we have seen, can be raised with regard to our entire free-market approach to the fertility industry, including the "donation" of ova, sperm, and surrogacy services, and the typical limitation of ART to wealthy clients who can afford to pay out of pocket. As with most other aspects of ART, no laws govern the preservation or destruction of frozen embryos. Fertility centers set their own policies, and the rules followed by various centers are not uniform.

Cloning and Twinning

Cloning produces individuals from a DNA sample that are exact genetic "copies" of the donor from whom the DNA was obtained. Some animal cells have been cloned for more than five decades, but it wasn't until 1997 that the first mammal (a sheep) was cloned. Nothing in principle seems to stand in the way of cloning a human, but if human cloning became a practical reality, it would present serious moral and social challenges.

Cloning involves taking a somatic cell from a developed organism, extracting the DNA, and then growing a (genetically identical) embryo from it in an enucleated egg cell. (See Case Presentation: Advances in Reproductive Cloning for more details.) Although no researchers have yet admitted to human cloning, many have engaged in *twinning* procedures, in which dozens of genetically identical embryos can be produced from the *blastomeres* (individual cells) of existing embryos. (Twinning can increase the supply of implantable embryos for ART treatments.) Both cloning and twinning open up a number of surprising and controversial scenarios which society may, at some point, have to confront. These include:

1. The production of cloned or twinned embryos might generate a robust embryo market. If a child had already been born from one of the embryos and could be shown to have desirable qualities, the couple who had produced the embryos could conceivably try to sell the remainder. It would then be possible for someone to have a child genetically identical to the one with the desirable qualities.

2. Parents could have a family in which all their children were genetically identical. If several gestational mothers were employed, it would be possible to produce a dozen or more genetically identical children of the same age, although they would not, strictly speaking, be twins.

3. A couple might have a child while also freezing a clone or twin as a spare. If the child should die, then the genetic twin could be grown from the embryo, as a genetic "replacement."

4. If embryonic clones or twins were frozen and stored, they could be implanted in two different gestational mothers years apart. Thus, one might be sixty, while the other is only six.

5. Clones or twins of an individual might be stored so that if the person needed something like a bone-marrow or kidney transplant, the clone or twin could be implanted in a gestational surrogate and allowed to develop. The tissue match would be perfect, and the problem of rejection would not arise.

The issues raised by twinning differ little from those raised by cloning, and twinning is already a practical reality. Some of the uses are so benign as to be hardly debatable, while others might result in a morally objectionable cheapening or commercialization of human life. For now, they remain speculative moral problems.

Ethical and Social Questions

A number of aspects of the assisted reproductive technologies and their applications raise serious moral questions for critics. In this section we will address a few general objections to ART as well as some more targeted ethical criticisms not mentioned earlier. In the final section, we will discuss how such criticisms relate to major ethical theories.

General Criticisms of ART

Assisted reproduction is complicated, expensive, and requires a great investment of skill, knowledge, and resources. An obvious question is, What is to be gained by it? What benefits might justify the use of the technically difficult and expensive medical procedures involved? The most direct and perhaps most persuasive answer is that assisted reproduction makes it possible for many people to have children who would not otherwise be able to do so. For these intended parents, this is a crucial consideration.

While admitting the present and potential value of reproductive technology in assisting families who want to have children, many critics think the technology has been oversold. Despite their hopes, many who must rely on it don't achieve a pregnancy. Also, intended parents aren't always properly informed about their chances of success. A particular clinic may have an average success rate of 25 percent, but for a woman in her early forties, the rate may be only a 1 percent to 2 percent chance per month of trying. (Only about a quarter of those who seek to overcome infertility succeed in doing so.) This seems like a bad bargain, critics say, especially when ART procedures involve discomfort and risk. Although the risk of permanent injury is small, it cannot be dismissed.

Critics also point out that trying to become pregnant through ART can be prohibitively expensive, and a lack of insurance coverage typically limits ART to the wealthy. Each attempt costs $12,000 or more, and several attempts are usually required for success. For society to mandate that insurers cover ART, however, might seem to endorse the view that having a biologically related child is inherently superior to adopting one. Although adoption is also expensive and time-consuming, there is no doubt of the serious social need for more adoptive parents, especially for non-white, older, and special needs adoptees. The nation's foster care system is also overstrained, dysfunctional, and in dire need of dedicated foster parents.

Critics of assisted reproduction often argue there is no *right* to have a biologically related child and suggest that those unable to conceive, for whatever reason, should simply accept the fact and perhaps adopt or foster children. Proponents do not tend to justify assisted reproduction in terms of rights, however. They refer primarily to the strong desire some people have to become parents, and ask why these intended parents cannot attempt to create biological families as others do. Few people criticize fertile heterosexual couples for reproducing, they say, so why should infertile or same-sex couples be singled out to address broad social issues through their parenting? Perhaps instead everyone who seeks to parent should adopt at least one child. They also point out that assisted reproduction, as it is most often employed, is nothing more than a means of facilitating a natural function that cannot be carried out due to morally arbitrary biological factors. To criticize intended parents or deny them assisted reproduction on the basis of those factors is thus unfair or unjust, say defenders, especially if they are willing to pay for ART themselves.

Impact on Children

In 2010, the politically conservative Institute for American Values published the results of a study based on a survey of adults 18–45 who had been conceived by the use of donor sperm. The results, as the columnist Ross Douthat reports, depict a group of people who are grateful for the technology that made their lives possible, yet also feel regret about being the products of a technological and financial transaction.

IVF offspring are more likely to endorse the idea that everyone has a right to have a child, and they support the practice of assisted reproduction. (Indeed, some 20 percent say they are sperm or egg donors.) However, a substantial minority report that they are troubled by "the circumstances of my conception" and that "money was exchanged to conceive me." A larger percentage than that in the general population disapprove of the practice of paying for sperm or eggs and agree with the statement "It is wrong to deliberately conceive a fatherless/motherless child." A large minority say that if a friend were planning to get pregnant by paying for donor sperm, they would discourage her.

IVF offspring are almost twice as likely as adopted children to report envying those who knew their biological parents, twice as likely to worry that their parents "might have lied to me about important matters," and three times as likely to report feeling "confused about who is a member of my family and who is not." The children of sperm donors are also more likely than adopted children to agree that "when I see someone who resembles me, I often wonder if we are related."

Douthat, among others, recommends that U.S. laws be revised to make sperm and egg donation a more deliberate and serious process. As a medical procedure, assisted reproduction may resemble a blood transfusion, but its social and personal consequences more closely resemble adoption. Britain, Sweden, Norway, and Switzerland are among the countries that have banned anonymous sperm and egg donation. When children who are born as a result of assisted reproduction turn eighteen, they have the legal right to gain access to their biological parents.

Little information is available on the long-term psychological and social well-being of children born with the help of assisted reproduction. Like Louise Brown, many are on the brink of middle age, but many more are still young and developing. The Institute for American Values report suggests that more research should be done to understand the needs, attitudes, and problems of this growing segment of the population. The United States may need to consider changing its laws to mandate that children born from donated sperm, eggs, or embryos have access to information about their biological parentage. Broad access to DNA testing and ancestry databases, as well as citizen groups such as the Donor Sibling Registry (see Case Presentation: Egg and Sperm Donors) suggests that society is already moving away from traditional secrecy and anonymity when it comes to donor-assisted reproduction.

Impact on the Family

Critics sometimes charge that reproductive technology promotes a social climate in which having children becomes severed from the family. The procedures involved in ART depend upon the mechanics of conception in a medical setting and so minimize the significance of the shared love and commitment on the part of intended parents, they say. Others argue the technology dilutes the responsibilities of parenthood by involving third parties in reproduction. For example, as many as five people may become involved in having a child—if, for example, a couple uses donor sperm and eggs and then relies on the services of a gestational surrogate for pregnancy. Because there is no clear biological sense in which the child belongs to any of the parties, critics argue that parenthood becomes recreational or optional. Finally, many of these critics also object to single people and same-sex couples using ART to have biologically related children, on the grounds that this will undermine the traditional family.

Defenders of assisted reproduction respond that the love and commitment that parents offer a child has no inherent connection to the circumstances of the child's conception. They argue that, if anything, the time and expense of ART suggests that these intended parents will be more committed and secure in their relationships than many parents who conceive children through intercourse. They point to many ways in which "traditional" parenthood has the risk of becoming optional or recreational, particularly for fathers who avoid primary caregiving responsibilities or couples who accidentally conceive children before they are ready to parent.

Defenders also point to the extensive social science evidence that same-sex families tend to do as well (and often better) than heterosexual ones when it comes to rearing happy and well-adjusted children. Now that same-sex marriage is widespread in the United States and the Supreme Court has made it the law of the land, it is increasingly difficult to claim that such families are any less committed than heterosexual ones.

Although the current evidence is more worrisome when it comes to children reared by single parents, defenders of "single parenthood by choice" contend that evidence of negative financial and psychosocial outcomes is distorted by parents who become involuntarily single and are not prepared to take on the emotional and financial responsibilities this entails. (See Case Presentation: Brave New Families for more on these topics.)

Whether assisted reproduction leads to a weakening of the values associated with the family is partly an empirical question that only additional evidence will answer. Even if childbearing does become severed from traditional family structures, it still must be shown that this is in itself something of which we ought to disapprove. After all, alternative social structures for childbearing and childrearing might prove to be superior to ones that have been dominant in modern Western culture.

Eugenics

Some charge that the use of reproductive technology may encourage eugenic ambitions to improve the human species. Rather than accepting children shaped by the genetic combination of their own DNA, would-be parents might be motivated to seek out ova and sperm from people who possess physical and intellectual characteristics that they consider desirable. Thus, even without an organized plan of social eugenics (see Chapter 3), individuals might be tempted to pursue their own eugenic projects. Efforts to obtain "the perfect baby" would cheapen human life by promoting the view that babies are commodities produced to order rather than individuals to be cherished and accepted as they are.

These critics point to the websites for ova and sperm donor programs, many of which appear to offer a "catalogue shopping" experience for prospective parents. They question features that allow would-be parents to search for donors with specific ethnic backgrounds, those with specific intellectual or occupational achievements, or those who have specific physical attributes, such as eye or hair color or height.

Other critics point to the growing use of IVF and preimplantation screening to choose the sex of offspring, a practice that is still legal in the United States, Thailand, and South Africa but illegal in all other countries. Since males contain both an X and a Y chromosome and this genetic signature is detectable in the cells of the developing embryo, fertility clinics can easily opt to implant only male or only female embryos.

Thus, the ability to select sex is an almost inevitable by-product of IVF and preimplantation genetic screening, unless prohibited by law. Some object to the rejected male or female embryos being frozen or destroyed for trivial or discriminatory reasons. Others suggest that this extension of free-market choice to gender selection is another unacceptable commodification of human life.

Defenders of ART may respond that these eugenic and commodifying tendencies are part of a broader trend not limited to assisted reproduction. They may point out that the quest for a perfect child more commonly manifests itself in the "hyper-parenting" of traditionally conceived children, as when parents push for filial accomplishments and beauty as reflections on their own lives. Others defenders may simply embrace eugenic tendencies as good for humanity in the long run or legitimate expressions of free-market choice. Since these tendencies are not imposed by a central authority, they argue, they do not put us on a path to the society envisioned in *Brave New World*.

Dysgenics

Fertility clinics typically refuse to reveal the names of sperm and egg donors to their clients or to the children born from donated genetic material. Sperm banks also generally have no fixed limits on how many children one donor is able to father and tend to allow "popular" sperm from men with certain intellectual or physical characteristics to be given to many more intended parents. As a result, it is possible for sizable groups of half-siblings to end up living in the same geographic area without knowing they are related. If these half-siblings encounter each other socially, there is a small but real risk that they or their offspring will unknowingly engage in incestuous sex. (The same potential exists for children conceived from donor eggs, but is less likely due to smaller numbers of donations.)

Although the American Society for Reproductive Medicine recommends that conceptions by donors be limited to no more than twenty-five births per population of eight hundred thousand, there is strong evidence that fertility programs ignore these limits—allowing some donors to conceive dozens or even hundreds of children. (See Case Presentation: Egg and Sperm Donors for more on this.) Britain, by contrast, has a strict ten-per-donor limit on conceptions, based on recommendations from an influential 1982 bioethics commissions led by the prominent English philosopher Mary Warnock.

"It is quite unpredictable what the ultimate effect on the gene pool of a society might be if donors were permitted to donate as many times as they chose," Warnock concluded.

Defenders of self-regulation in the American fertility industry argue that these fears are overblown and that large pools of half-siblings in the same geographic area are unlikely. Others dismiss *dysgenic* fears such as Warnock's by pointing to evidence that the children of first cousins are no more likely to have impairments than those conceived by postmenopausal women. They contend that genetic concentrations created by donors are likely to be swiftly "diluted" by the influence of exogamous DNA.

Donors

Many of the ethical questions raised by ART critics involve third-party reproduction and the individual rights and responsibilities of donors and recipients. For example, does a man who has donated sperm have any special moral responsibilities? Some basic responsibilities seem obvious. For example, it would be wrong for him to lie about any genetic diseases in his family history. But does he have any responsibilities to a child that is conceived with his sperm? If donating sperm is no different from donating blood, then perhaps he does not. But is such a comparison apt? (Similar questions apply to egg donation.)

Can donor-conceived children legitimately demand to know the name of their donor parents? We need not assume that mere curiosity motivates such a request. Some seek family background information in order to determine if a potential child might have a genetic disorder. Others might want to rule out inadvertent incest if their current or potential partners are also donor-conceived. Perhaps the standard practice of maintaining the anonymity of sperm and egg donors is not one that can withstand critical scrutiny.

Other questions concerning fertility program policies and procedures are also of considerable moral significance. For example, how thoroughly must sperm and ova donors be screened for genetic defects? What physical, educational, or general social traits (if any) can individual donors be required to possess? At the same time, should sperm and ova donors have a right to know how many children their gametes may be used conceive before they consent to a donation? Should formal records be maintained and shared through a mandatory network, perhaps based on the Donor Sibling Registry, to share genetic information and avert problems?

Finally, there are questions about the potential exploitation and informed consent of donors. Given that egg donors, like sperm donors, are typically young and unsettled in life, large payments may have an undue or coercive influence, prompting women to disregard their health and other interests. Should payments to both ova and sperm donors thus be limited by law, to prevent exploitation and the commodification of "desirable" characteristics?

At present, these questions have been addressed only by individual physicians or clinics, if at all. No laws or policies govern most third-party reproduction, although the ASRM and other organizations offer ethical guidelines. Even if present practices are adequate, many people believe that we need to develop uniform policies to better regulate reproduction involving third parties.

Surrogacy

Arguments for both gestational and traditional surrogacy arrangements are often similar to those for the use of ART and donors. Couples and individuals who cannot have children due to infertility or their sex rely on surrogates as their sole means of conceiving biologically related children. Some rule out adoption because of the time, expense, and relative shortage of available infants; some simply want a genetic link with their children. Most fertile and heterosexual couples seek this biological connection to their children, so why should it be denied to others if they are willing to take on the expense and complications?

Critics have charged that surrogate pregnancy is "womb rental" or even a specialized form of prostitution. A woman, in effect, rents out her body for a period of time and is paid for doing so. Of course, such criticism rests on the assumption that prostitution is morally wrong, or more wrong than some of the other ways that employers use or even harm the bodies of their employees. The criticism also fails to take into account the differences in aims. Some surrogate mothers have volunteered their services with no expectation of monetary reward, and some women have agreed to be surrogate mothers at the request of a sister, friend, daughter, or son. Even those who are paid often mention that part of their motivation is to help couples who desperately want a child. Rather than condemning surrogacy as immoral, it is possible to view at least some versions as morally heroic given the benefit they bestow on others.

Perhaps the most serious objection to surrogacy arrangements stems from evidence that surrogates are likely to be recruited from the ranks of the economically disadvantaged. There is little history of upper- and middle-income women serving as pregnancy surrogates. Women with low-paying jobs or no jobs at all are prime candidates for recruiters. It might be charged, then, that women who become surrogate mothers are being exploited by those who have sufficient resources to pay for their services.

Merely paying someone in need of money to do something does not constitute exploitation, however. To make such a charge stick, it would be necessary to show that women who become surrogate mothers are under a great deal of social and economic pressure and thus their choices are not really free. (This case is particularly robust when it comes to surrogacy in the developing world.) Furthermore, it could be argued that, within limits, individuals have a right to do with their bodies as they choose. If a woman freely decides to earn money by serving as a surrogate mother, then we have no more reason to object to her decision than we would have to object to someone else's decision to earn money by working as a coal miner.

Cloning

As we have discussed, cloning is both a therapeutic and a reproductive issue, and some of the ethical debate over it has been addressed in other chapters. As discussed above, many of the issues related to reproductive cloning (and twinning) involve concern that an individual who is deliberately conceived as a genetic copy may be treated like a copy: as disposable, supplementary, or only valued for her use to someone else. Ethical objections range from concern that clones will be used for "replacement" children or transplant organs (see Case Presentation: Savior Sibling) to dystopian fears of clone armies or labor forces.

Since no reported cloning of humans beings has yet taken place, it is difficult to assess these speculative moral objections. One consideration is that different epigenetic and environmental factors, to say nothing of different gestational mothers, would be likely to make clones at least as different from each other as fraternal twins. Such differences might make it difficult to treat them as interchangeable or disposable beings. While some results might be incongruous, such as genetically identical individuals separated by fifty or sixty years, such phenomena are not necessarily objectionable on moral grounds.

Nevertheless, it is important to recall that practices such as embryonic sex selection and gestational surrogacy were once viewed as remote science fiction possibilities. Now they are contemporary realities posing serious moral questions. Cloning, like current ART practices, clearly has potential for exploitation and unintended consequences.

Ethical Theories and Reproductive Control

One of the themes of Mary Shelley's famous novel *Frankenstein* is that it is both wrong and dangerous to tamper with the natural forces of life. It is wrong because it disturbs the natural order of things, and it is dangerous because it unleashes forces beyond human control. The "monster" that is animated by Dr. Victor Frankenstein stands as a warning and reproach to all who seek to impose their will on the world through the powers of scientific technology.

One fundamental ethical question about the technology of human reproductive control is whether it ought to be employed at all. Is it simply wrong for us to use our knowledge of human biology to exercise power over the processes of human reproduction?

The natural law view, as represented by currently accepted doctrines of the Roman

Catholic Church, suggests that all the techniques for controlling human reproduction that we have discussed here are fundamentally wrong. On this view, children are the only legitimate goal of sexual union within marriage. However, if no measures are wrongfully taken to frustrate the possibility of their birth (contraception, for example), then a married couple has no obligation to attempt to conceive children by other means, such as artificial insemination or in vitro fertilization. Certainly, the couple has no reason to resort to donor ova or sperm—and the latter has the additional drawback of requiring masturbation, which is viewed as another departure from natural reproductive impulses. All these methods are seen to reduce conception to a mechanical act.

In vitro fertilization is open to similar natural law objections, not least because the process itself typically involves the destruction of fertilized ova. On the view that human conception takes place at the moment of fertilization, the discarding of unimplanted embryos amounts to the destruction of human life.

On the utilitarian view, no reproductive technology is in itself objectionable. The question that has to be answered is whether the use of any particular procedure, in general or in a certain case, is likely to lead to more good than harm. In general, it is reasonable to believe that a utilitarian might be able to approve of all the procedures we have discussed here, based on the benefits they provide new families.

According to Ross's ethical theory, we have prima facie duties of beneficence. That is, we have an obligation to assist others in bettering their lives. This suggests that the use of reproductive technology may be justified as a means to promote the well-being of others. For example, if a couple desires to have a child but is unable to conceive one, then either IVF procedures or artificial insemination might be employed to help

them satisfy their shared desire. Twinning might be used to increase the number of embryos, and even cloning seems prima facie unobjectionable.

Kantian principles do not seem to supply grounds for objecting to assisted reproduction or reproductive technology in general as inherently wrong. However, the imperative to treat rational humanity always as an end in itself and not just as a means might raise concerns about the instrumental use of donors and surrogates, as well as of "designer" children who might be conceived through ART. Many feminist philosophers would share this concern with instrumental or exploitative uses of individuals, but might add analysis of the gender-based social structures that could reinforce it. Policies and practices that treat women (but not men) as the focus of reproductive control and concern might come under particular scrutiny, for example, as setting up unjustified double standards.

By contrast, ethical theories of care are more likely to evaluate ART on the basis of how they impact (and potentially cheapen) familial and social relationships over time. None of the technologies discussed are inherently incompatible with the ethical ideal of sustained care in relation to the other, but the potential for alienation and commodification might cause the theory to object to certain forms of cloning or surrogacy, for example. This could only be assessed, however, on the basis of the affective states of concrete individuals in relationships of mutual dependency and care. And it would pay close attention to the domestic sphere in which ARTs probably have their most significant and long-lasting impact.

There is no doubt that the technologies of assisted reproduction have become a pervasive reality in American life. So far they have made our society into neither a dystopia nor a utopia. They may be seen as just one set of tools among the many that science and medicine have forged. Yet the tools are powerful ones, and we should beware of allowing familiarity to produce indifference. The moral and social issues raised by reproductive technology are just as real as the technology. So far, many of them have not been addressed with the seriousness they deserve.

READINGS

Section 1:   Assisted Reproduction and the Limits of Autonomy

"Give Me Children or I Shall Die!" New Reproductive Technologies and Harm to Children

Cynthia B. Cohen

Cohen points to evidence suggesting that the use of reproductive technologies produces serious deficits in a small number of children and asks whether, if this is so, it would be wrong to continue to use them. Cohen focuses on the "Interest in Existing" argument, which holds that producing deficits would not necessarily be wrong because, except in extreme cases, it is better to be alive than to not exist.

A flaw in the argument, Cohen claims, is that it assumes children are waiting in a world of nonexistence, where they are worse off than if they were born. A second flaw is that the argument would seem to justify any harm caused by reproductive technology, so long as it is preferable to death (i.e., does not produce a "wrongful life"). Cohen argues that this is to view the nonexistence of not being born (which is neither good nor bad) as the same as the nonexistence produced by death (which may be preceded by devastating or serious deficits).

Cohen addresses the issue of what counts as a serious deficiency and claims such judgments must be made in specific circumstances in particular cultures. She ends by considering how obligations to actual children differ from those to potential children and why potential parents must make informed choices about using reproductive technologies.

"Be fruitful and multiply," God urged newly created humans. Those who take this command to heart cherish the opportunity to procreate and nurture children, to pass on their individual traits and family heritage to their offspring. Having children, for many, is a deeply significant experience that offers

From Cynthia B. Cohen, " 'Give Me Children or I Shall Die!' New Reproductive Technologies and Harm to Children," *Hastings Center Report* 26, no. 2 (1996): 19–27. Copyright © 1996 Hastings Center Report. Reproduced by permission. (References omitted.)

overall meaning for their lives. Not all who wish to do so, however, can fulfill the biblical injunction to multiply. Those who cannot often experience a terrible sense of loss. Rachel, in Genesis, felt such despair over her failure to conceive that she cried out to Jacob, "Give me children, or I shall die!" Some who echo her cry today turn to the new reproductive technologies.

There are ethical limits, however, to what may be done to obtain long-sought offspring. Having a deep desire and even a need for something does not justify doing anything whatsoever to obtain it. If the means used to bring children into the world were to create substantial harm to others or to these very children, this would provide strong moral reason not to employ them. It would be wrong, for instance, for infertile couples to place women at risk of substantial harm by enticing those who are not in peak physical condition to "donate" eggs with handsome sums of money. By the same token, it would be wrong to use reproductive technologies to create children if this bore a significant chance of producing serious disease and impairments in these very children. Questions are being raised about whether in vitro fertilization (IVF) and other reproductive technologies do, in fact, create serious illness and deficits in a small but significant proportion of children who are born of them. If these technologies were found to do so, it would be wrong to forge ahead with their use.

Yet advocates of procreative liberty reject this seemingly inescapable conclusion. They contend that even if children were born with serious disorders traceable to their origin in the new reproductive technologies, this would not, except in rare cases, provide moral reason to refrain from using them. Those who conclude otherwise, they maintain, do not understand the peculiar sort of substantial harm to which children born of these novel reproductive means are susceptible. Surely, John Robertson and like-minded thinkers claim, it is better to be alive—even with serious disease and deficits—than not. And these children would not be alive, but for the use of the new reproductive techniques. Therefore, they argue, these children cannot be substantially harmed by the use of these means to bring them into the world. Only if they are caused by these technologies to suffer devastating illness that makes life worse than nonexistence can they be said to be substantially harmed by them.

This startling claim raises intriguing questions. What do we mean by substantial harm—particularly when children who might experience it have not yet been conceived? What degree of disease and suffering that a child would experience as a result of the application of these novel means of conception would make it wrong to use them? Would it be wrong if the child's life would be so terrible that nonexistence would be better? Few conditions would be excluded by this standard. Would it be wrong if the child's life would not be awful, but would include major physical impairments, severe mental disability, and/or considerable pain and suffering?

In responding to such questions, we must consider the possibility that different standards of substantial harm may apply to children at the time when we consider conceiving them and after conception and birth. If so, we must develop a standard of substantial harm that applies to children who might be conceived that is distinct from one that applies to those already born—and must explain how children who are not born can be harmed. We must also address the concern that decisions not to conceive children because they would have serious deficits devalue the lives of those already living who were born with such deficits. Finally, we must grapple with the question of what parents and infertility specialists ought to do in the current state of inadequate knowledge about the effects of the new reproductive technologies on the children who result from their use.

The Harm to Children Argument

To ask what it means to attribute substantial harm to children who result from the new reproductive technologies is not just to pose an interesting abstract question. Studies indicate this may be a very practical, real question, as they raise the possibility that these technologies may create serious deficits in some proportion of the children born of them. To get a sense of the harms at issue, let us consider the claims of critics of the use of these technologies about their effect on the children born of them.

A primary harm that they attribute to the use of the new reproductive technologies is physical damage. Few long-term studies have been undertaken of the kinds and rates of physical diseases and abnormalities incurred by children born of the new reproductive technologies. Moreover, the evidence these investigations provide is conflicting. Australia is the only country that has kept statistics on the condition at birth *and* subsequent progress of children born of IVF since the inception of this technique in the late 1970s. Data from that country indicate that these children are two or three times more likely to suffer such serious diseases as spina bifida and transposition of the great vessels (a heart abnormality). The Australian data also suggest that some drugs used to stimulate women's ovaries to produce multiple oocytes in preparation for IVF increase the risk of serious birth impairments in the resulting children. Other investigations and commentators support this finding. Still other reports, however, suggest that there is no increase in disorders at birth among children resulting from the use of the new reproductive technologies. One small American follow-up study of the health status of children born of IVF and gamete intrafallopian transfer (GIFT) could find no significant differences in the rate of physical or neurological abnormalities in children born of techniques of assisted conception. No controlled study to date, however, has incorporated an adequate sample size or sufficiently long follow-up monitoring period to determine accurately the risk of physical disorders associated with children born of IVF.

And little is known about the physiological impact on children who result from such other procedures as embryo freezing, gamete donation, zona drilling, and intracytoplasmic sperm injection.

It is well known that the higher rate of multiple births in IVF due to the implantation of several embryos in the uterus at a time contributes to an increased rate of preterm and low birth-weight babies. This, in turn, is associated with a higher incidence of perinatal, neonatal, and infant mortality in children conceived by IVF than those conceived coitally. In France, for instance, the rates of prematurity and intrauterine growth retardation among IVF births in a two-year period were 16 percent and 14 percent respectively, whereas the expected rates for the general population were 7 percent and 3 percent. An analysis of IVF outcome data from France between 1986 and 1990 indicated that perinatal mortality among IVF births also was higher than that in the general population, even when data were stratified according to gestational number. French neonatologists who had worked to prevent low birth weight, congenital anomalies, and genetic disorders among newborns observed that "[n]ow, we suddenly find our NICU filled with high-risk newborns … [as a result of the expansion of IVF services]."

Critics also express concern that the new reproductive technologies may jeopardize the psychological and social welfare of the children who result from them, particularly when they involve third parties in donor or surrogacy arrangements and depend on secrecy. These children, they hypothesize, will view themselves as manufactured products, rather than distinctive individuals born of love between a man and a woman. They will be denied the stable sense of identity that comes from knowing their biological heritage and family lineage should their rearing parents differ from their genetic parents. Moreover, the social stigma these children will experience when others learn that they were conceived by these novel means will

increase their difficulties, opponents contend. Little research is available on the effect of the use of assisted reproduction on the psychosocial development of the resulting children. In the first controlled study of family relationships and the psychological development of children created by the new reproductive technologies, no group differences in the emotions, behavior, or relationships with parents between children born of assisted reproduction and children conceived naturally or adopted could be found.

One commentator summarizes the issues of harm raised by the use of the new reproductive technologies as follows:

> The technology for both IVF and GIFT as well as adjunct technologies such as zona drilling, embryo freezing, and gamete donation have not been accompanied by careful scrutiny and analysis of the risks involved. Indeed, even when risks are clearly established (as with multiple pregnancy), there has been no discernible attempt to reduce these risks by altering procedures and protocols. There also has been an appalling lack of follow-up studies to determine the long-term health, psychological, and social consequence of these procedures.

In view of the current lack of systematic knowledge about difficulties these methods may create in children born of them, opponents of the new reproductive technologies maintain it is wrong to use them. Those who resort to these techniques, they claim, bear the burden of proof of their safety. They have an obligation to establish whether these ever-increasing methods of assisted reproduction do, in fact, harm a small but significant proportion of children before they are used. For ease of reference, we will call their claims the Harm to Children Argument against the use of the new reproductive technologies.

The Interest in Existing Argument

The basic response to the Harm to Children Argument by several proponents of the use of the new reproductive technologies, of whom John Robertson is a respected spokesperson, is that even if children born of the new reproductive technologies were to suffer serious impairments as a result of their origin, this would not necessarily render it wrong to use these techniques. We might call this response the Interest in Existing Argument: since it is, in almost all cases, better to be alive than not, and these children would not be alive but for the employment of these techniques, using them to bring these children into the world is justified. Robertson writes:

> [A] *higher incidence of birth defects in such offspring would not justify banning the technique in order to protect the offspring, because without these techniques these children would not have been born at all. Unless their lives are so full of suffering as to be worse than no life at all, a very unlikely supposition, the defective children of such a union have not been harmed if they would not have been born healthy.*

Only where "from the perspective of the child, viewed solely in light of his interests as he is then situated, any life at all with the conditions of his birth would be so harmful to him that from his perspective he would prefer not to live," could it be said to be a substantial harm to have been brought into existence by means of the new reproductive technologies.

Robertson here implicitly distinguishes between *devastating harm*—harm that brings such suffering into a person's life that this life is worse than no life at all—[and] *serious harm*—harm that does not render life worse than death, but that includes such detriments as major physical impairments, severe mental disability, and/or considerable pain and suffering. He labels only the former *substantial harm*. Indeed, at certain points, Robertson maintains that children damaged by their origin in the new reproductive technologies cannot be said to suffer harm at all, since their birth is an overriding benefit.

The Harm to Children Argument is logically flawed, Robertson and like-minded thinkers maintain, because the benefit of life that children born of these techniques receive outweighs almost any detriment they might experience as a result of their origins. Robertson notes:

> *Preventing harm would mean preventing the birth of the child whose interests one is trying to protect. Yet a child's interests are hardly protected by preventing the child's existence. If the child has no way to be born or raised free of that harm, a person is not injuring the child by enabling her to be born in the circumstances of concern.*

It is not open to children damaged by the use of the new reproductive technologies to live free of impairment, since they could not have existed without the use of these technologies. The alternative for them would have been not to live at all, a state which is not in their interests. Consequently, according to the Interest in Existing Argument, it is, in almost all instances, in the interests of children who might be born of the new reproductive technologies to be brought into the world by these means, even if this would risk serious harm to them.

This argument applies only to children who suffer harm that is a necessary result of the use of these techniques. Thus, if it were claimed that contract surrogacy creates psychological harm for a child because the biological mother and rearing parents would be in a constant state of conflict with each other, the Interest in Existing Argument could not be used in response. This is because the warring trio could behave in a different manner less likely to cause this sort of harm to the child. According to advocates of the Interest in Existing Argument it was not a necessary condition of the child's very existence that the conflict among these various parents occur.

The Harm of Not Existing

The Interest in Existing Argument assumes that children with an interest in existing are waiting in a spectral world of nonexistence where their situation is less desirable than it would be were they released into this world. This presupposition is revealed by such observations as "a child's interests are hardly protected by preventing the child's existence" and that it is a disadvantage to such children that they "have no way of being born." In the Interest in Existing Argument children who might be conceived are pictured as pale preexisting entities with an interest in moving into the more full-blooded reality of this world. Their admission into this realm is thwarted by the failure to use available new reproductive technologies. This failure negates their interest in existing and thereby harms them.

Before a person exists, however, he or she does not reside in some other domain. Prior to conception, there is *no one who waits to be brought into this world*. Joel Feinberg argues, "Since it is necessary to *be* if one is to *be better off*, it is a logical contradiction to say that someone could be better off though not in existence." To say that it was good for someone already in existence to have been born does not imply that his existence in this world is better than his life in some other realm. Nor does it imply that if he had not been caused to exist, this would have been bad for him. Although a wealth of possible children can be conceived, their interests cannot be diminished if they are not. Therefore, it cannot be coherently argued that it is "better" for children to be created by means of the new reproductive technologies, even when this would result in serious disorders to them, since there is no alternative state in which their lot could be worse.

Part of the confusion at the heart of the Interest in Existing Argument stems from an incoherence found in tort actions for "wrongful life," to which this argument has an acknowledged debt. In these suits, children born with impairments claim that their current condition is worse than the state of nonexistence they would have had were it not for negligence on the part of physicians, hospitals, or testing laboratories. The wrong done to them, they contend, is not that their impaired condition was negligently caused, but that their very existence was negligently caused. This, they maintain, is a serious injury, since they would have been better off not being born at all. They ask for compensation for the injury of being brought into this world.

In an early wrongful life case, *Gleitman v. Cosgrove*, a child born with impairments whose mother had been told erroneously that her exposure to German measles during pregnancy would not harm the fetus, brought suit for damages for the injury of being born. The traditional method of measuring damages in tort is to compare the condition of the plaintiff before and after an injury and to compensate for the difference. When the putative wrong done to the plaintiff is to have been brought into existence in an impaired state, the court must measure the difference between nonexistence and existence with impairments. In *Gleitman*, the court found it "logically impossible" to "weigh the value of life with impairments against the nonexistence of life itself." We cannot, according to the court, conceptualize a world in which the plaintiff did not exist and ask what benefits and burdens he experienced in that world in order to compare it with his situation in this world.

Even so, the *Gleitman* court concluded that the value of life, no matter how burdened, outweighs the disvalue of not existing, and that damages therefore could not be awarded to the child for "wrongful life." In drawing this conclusion, the court implicitly compared the world of existence with that of non-existence and declared the former always preferable to the latter. Yet this is precisely the step the court had said it could not take. Similarly, in another leading case, *Berman v. Allan*, the court ruled against

recognition of a "wrongful life" claim on grounds that "life—whether experienced with or without a major physical handicap—is more precious than non-life." These courts were concerned that award-ing damages for being alive would diminish the high value that the law places on human life. This public policy concern, however, caused them to lapse into incoherence. They claimed that the world of existence cannot be measured against that of nonexistence. However, if existence is better than nonexistence, as they also declared, nonexistence must be conceptu-ally accessible in some sense so that an intelligible comparison can be made between it and existence.

Proponents of the Interest in Existing Argument adopt the two-world view underlying the logically impossible thesis of the early wrongful life cases when they claim that children are harmed if they are not brought out of the world of nonexistence into the world of existence. This leaves them with two problems: (1) explaining how to conceptualize and comprehend nonexistence and (2) justifying the claim that it is better to exist than not. Moreover, their dependence on the wrongful life decisions causes them to overlook an essential feature of their oppo-nents' argument. The Harm to Children Argument is a *before-the-fact* one that applies to the time when a decision must be made about whether to employ the new reproductive technologies. *At this time, un-like the wrongful life cases, no child exists who could be harmed.* The Harm to Children Argument holds that at this preconception time, the morally right decision is not to use such technologies until further research establishes the degree of harm this might do to chil-dren who result. The Interest in Existing Argument, however, is an after-the-fact argument meant to apply at a time when children are already born. It must be used as a response to those who object to having al-ready brought children into the world. Since the harm posited by the critics has not yet occurred when the decision is made whether to employ them, it is not an adequate response to say that without these technolo-gies the resulting children would not have been born. That is precisely what is at issue—*whether these chil-dren ought to have been conceived and born.*

A further difficulty is that the Interest in Existing Argument justifies allowing the new reproductive technologies to create almost any harm to children conceived as a result of their use—as long as this is not devastating harm in which death is preferable to life with it. As Bonnie Steinbock and Ron McClamrock observe, "Very few lives meet the stringent conditions imposed by the wrongful life analysis.... Even the most dismal sorts of circumstances of opportunity (including, for example ... an extremely high chance of facing an agonizing death from starvation in the early years of life, severe retardation plus quadriplegia) fail to be covered" by the standard of devastating harm. Yet it would strike many as ethically objectionable to proceed with reproductive techniques should such serious, but not devastating harms result from them in a significant proportion of cases.

The "Wrongful Life" Standard of Substantial Harm

Those who present the Interest in Existing Argument, adopting the standard applied in wrongful life cases, describe substantial harm as that which, in Robertson's words, puts one in a condition that renders life so "horrible" and so "full of unavoidable suffering"... that it is worse than "no life at all." Robertson does not give a more precise definition of substantial harm, nor does he present specific examples of conditions which fall under that rubric in his discussion of harm to children and the new reproductive technologies. Feinberg expands on the "wrongful life" standard of substantial harm:

> Surely in most cases of suffering and impairment we think of death as even worse. This is shown by the widespread human tendency to "cling to life at all costs." And even for severe genetic handicaps and inherited maladies, most competent persons who suffer from them will not express regret that they were born in the first place.... In the most extreme cases, however, I think it is rational to prefer not to have come into existence at all, and while I cannot prove this judgment, I am confident that most people will agree that it is at least plausible. I have in mind some of the more severely victimized sufferers from brain malformation, spina bifida, Tay-Sachs disease, polycystic kidney disease, Lesch-Nyhan syndrome, and those who, from whatever cause, are born blind and deaf, permanently incontinent, severely retarded, and in chronic pain or near-total paralysis, with life-expectancies of only a few years.

To talk about death, both Feinberg and Robertson assume, is the same as to talk about "not coming into existence at all." They assimilate nonexistence before life and nonexistence after having lived. This is a mistake. *Nonexistence before coming into being* and *nonexistence after having lived* are two distinct concepts.

Lucretius observed that we do not express concern about nonexistence before creation, but we do fear our nonexistence after death. Why is this? The reason we perceive death as bad, Thomas Nagel proposes, is that it causes us to have fewer goods of this life than we would have had if we had continued to live. Frances Kamm further observes that it is not only the absence of future goods in this life that leads us to fear death, but that death "takes away what already was and would have continued to be." Preconception nonexistence, however, does not deprive us of what was ours already. In it there is no particular individual whose life ends and who thereby loses out on life's goods. Consequently, nonexistence before conception and birth does not seem as bad as death. We are indifferent to it.

Several other features of death that are also not characteristic of preconception nonexistence contribute to our assessment of it as bad. Death, for instance, happens to a person, whereas preconception nonexistence does not include an event in which nonexistence happens to a person. Death reveals our vulnerability in that through it a person is destroyed and deprived of life's goods. If a person does not exist, in contrast, this does not reflect negatively on "his" or "her" capacities. Because of significant differences between them, preconception and posthumous nonexistence are qualitatively distinct concepts that are not interchangeable. Death has characteristics that lead us to evaluate it as bad, whereas preconception nonexistence strikes us as neither good nor bad.

Do we, too, fall into the trap of positing a shadowy world of nonexistence by distinguishing between preconception and posthumous nonexistence? We do not claim that either of these forms of nonexistence is a metaphysical locale. Instead, we view both as logical constructs built out of what we know about being alive. For both Nagel and Kamm, the meaning of death is derived from what we know about our existence in this world. The same is true of preconception nonexistence. Although the multitude of children whom it is possible for us to bring into the world do not exist, we can conceptualize certain things about them and what their lives would be like were we to conceive and bear them. We can also comprehend certain things about the negation of their existence were they to be born. That is, we can understand what they would lose if we decided not to conceive them and bring them into the world. Thus, we can meaningfully compare preconception nonexistence with life. We can consider children who might be brought into existence and ask whether we ought to conceive them without having to postulate a separate sphere of nonexistence in which they wait as we ponder the question.

While we can make sense of the notion of preconception nonexistence, can we also intelligibly claim that children who have not yet been conceived can have interests? It might be argued that those who do not exist cannot have interests and that therefore possible children can have no interest in not being conceived and brought into the world with serious disorders. Yet possible children can have interests, if these are taken in the sense of what contributes to their good, rather than as psychological states. We can conceive of what would promote their welfare were they to be brought into the world. To deny them such interests is mistakenly to reason by analogy with the dead. It has been supposed that the dead can have no interests because we cannot perform any actions that will affect the condition of their lives. We cannot causally impinge on them for better or worse, it has been argued, for their lives have been completed. But this is not the case with possible children. We can affect them causally for better or worse by our present actions. Thus, we can ascribe to possible children certain interests that can be thwarted or fulfilled by actions that we take.

The interests of children who might be born of the new reproductive technologies are not adequately captured by the "wrongful life" standard. The comparison that parents and physicians must make when they assess whether use of these technologies would negatively affect the good of children who might result is not between *death* and the condition of these children were they to be born with certain deficits. The appropriate comparison is between *preconception nonexistence* and their condition were they to be born with certain deficits. If preconception nonexistence, unlike death, is neither good nor bad, then any life that will be worse than it *will not have to be as bad as the life of devastating deficits set out in the wrongful life standard.* A life with serious, but not devastating, deficits could be bad and therefore worse than preconception nonexistence, which is neither good nor bad. Therefore, we must modify the wrongful life standard of substantial harm to indicate that if new reproductive technologies were shown to cause a significant proportion of children born of them to suffer either devastating *or*

serious deficits, they would cause substantial harm to these children and consequently ought not be used.

The Inadequate Opportunity for Health Standard of Substantial Harm

How are we to identify the serious deficits that—along with devastating deficits—would constitute substantial harm to these children? The boundary between moderate, serious, and devastating deficits is sufficiently blurred that reasonable people can disagree about where it lies in particular cases. Many would disagree with Feinberg that children knowingly conceived with such disorders as spina bifida, blindness, deafness, severe retardation, or permanent incontinence should be considered to be suffering from devastating deficits that make their lives worse than death. However, they might well view these disorders as amounting to serious deficits that make their lives worse than preconception nonexistence. What is needed is a conceptual framework that marks off those deficits that have such a negative impact on children that reasonable people would agree that knowingly to conceive children with these disorders would be to impose substantial harm on them in the vast majority of cases.

Laura Purdy suggests that we cause substantial harm to future children and therefore ought not knowingly conceive them "when there is a high risk of transmitting a serious disease or defect [of a sort that would deny them] a normal opportunity for health." At points in Purdy's discussion, as when she states that "every parent should try to ensure normal health for his child," she can be taken to mean that having an abnormal state of health would constitute a disorder sufficiently serious to warrant not conceiving a child who would have it. On this approach, children with a particular biological, chemical, or mental state different from the norm would be said to lack "normal health" and therefore to suffer from a "serious disease or defect" that would justify not conceiving them. Yet it would not strike us as wrong knowingly to conceive children who are not "normal" because they have myopia or albinism. Normality does not appear to provide an adequate standard for deciding that a disorder is a serious deficit that substantially harms a child knowingly conceived with it.

At other points, however, Purdy seems to suggest that the focus for defining a serious deficit that falls under the substantial harm rubric should be on the failure to provide an adequate opportunity for a healthy life, as this is defined within a culture. Here she seems on the right track, for notions of health and disease—for better and for worse—are embedded within a society. What constitutes health and what represents a serious falling away from it varies from culture to culture and changes from time to time. As the notion of health and of an adequate opportunity for health vary according to the cultural context and conditions, so, too, does the meaning of a serious disease or deficit. Moreover, access to health services and the resulting opportunity for health—or lack of it—also affect what is meant by health, serious disorder, and substantial harm.

In our society, children who are color-blind are considered to have only a mild deficit and no diminution of their opportunity for health. However, in certain African cultures in which the capacity to distinguish a great variety of shades of green is needed to function at a minimal level for survival, color blindness is a serious deficit. Children born with this condition in such cultures do not have an adequate opportunity for health because their condition cannot be remedied. Thus, cultural values affect the meanings of health and of serious disorders. Stanley Hauerwas observes that "disease descriptions and remedies are relative to a society's values and needs. Thus 'retardation' might not 'exist' in a society which values cooperation more than competition and ambition." Further, medical practices in different cultures reflect different views of what constitutes health and serious disorders. In Germany children with blood pressure that differs from the norm for their age on both the high and low end are suspected to be at risk of serious disease, whereas in America only high blood pressure is considered an indicator of serious disease.

What makes a disorder serious, however, is not only a matter of cultural needs, expectations, constructions, and practices. Some children are born with remediable conditions that are transformed into serious deficits when they are not ameliorated due to circumstances of injustice and neglect within a culture. The child born with spina bifida to poor parents in the hills of Appalachia has a minimal opportunity for health and a more serious disorder than the child born with this same condition to professional parents in Los Angeles. It might not be unfair to a child knowingly to conceive him or her with paralysis of the lower limbs if that child, once born, would have access to support structures giving him or her adequate mobility. Nor

would we have grounds for considering it wrong for parents knowingly to conceive a blind child if that child would receive compensatory education and ameliorative instruments enabling him or her to have an adequate opportunity for health within a society.

This relativity of the notion of health and of an adequate opportunity for health means that no definition of serious disease or disorder amounting to substantial harm that would apply across all cultures, times, and places can be given. Instead, the assessment of serious disease amounting to substantial harm must be made under specific circumstances within particular cultures. It must be defined not only in terms of a given physical or mental condition that damages a child's ability to function within a culture, but also in terms of the failure or inability of a culture to provide a child with access to ameliorative resources.

Sidney Callahan maintains that a principle of proportionality should be applied when making decisions concerning reproduction. This would mean that the lower the risk and gravity of impairment to the child and the more would-be parents, family, and the institutional structures of a society are able and willing to ameliorate the impairment, the less the likelihood that a child would suffer a serious deficit and the more ethically justifiable it would be to conceive him or her. Should the probability and gravity of impairment be great, however, and the would-be parents, family, and social structure unwilling or unable to provide ameliorative measures for the child with such impairment, the higher the likelihood the child would suffer a serious deficit and the less ethically justifiable it would be to conceive that child. We do not end up with a black letter definition of a deficit serious enough to be termed substantial harm on this approach, but one that requires us to consider the nature of the disorder from which the child would suffer, the circumstances into which the child would be brought, and the ameliorative resources available for that child. Under current circumstances in our culture in which children born with disabling disorders have inadequate support, it would be morally questionable, at least, knowingly to conceive a child suffering from some of the deficits listed by Feinberg above.

Obligations to Actual and Possible Children

Although we consider it ethically necessary to provide treatment to keep children alive who have serious illnesses, we do not consider it ethically necessary knowingly to conceive children with those same disorders. Why is this? Why do we assume that our obligations to children who already exist differ from our obligations to children whom we might conceive?

The difference between an actual and possible child and between our evaluations of preconception nonexistence and death help to explain this distinction. Since we view death as an evil in relation to being alive, we tend to maintain that once children are born, only if they suffer devastating harms that make life worse than death would we be justified in not doing what we can to prevent their death. Being alive is better than being dead, except in rare circumstances. However, we do not believe that we have an obligation to do everything we can to conceive and bring into the world possible children who would suffer serious or devastating illness as a result. This is because no one exists who is wronged by not being conceived and also because preconception nonexistence does not strike us as being either bad or good. To fail to actualize a possible child, therefore, does not put that child in a worse situation or wrong that child.

Furthermore, we have no obligation to conceive children if this would detrimentally affect the good of the family or culture into which they would be born. We have no obligation, for instance, to conceive a sixth child if we believe our family can only function adequately with five. And we need not bring children into the world when this would contribute to a problem of overpopulation or of limited resources. It is morally acceptable, indeed, some would say, morally required, that *before* we bring children into the world, we consider not only their well-being were they to be born, but the good of those who would be affected by their birth. *After* birth, however, the interest in existing of the living child comes into play and morally outweighs remnants of a parental or societal interest in not having had that child.

These conclusions may appear to intimate that the lives of children born with serious or even devastating disorders are not valued or valuable. This conclusion does not follow from the preceding argument. Should parents, after receiving convincing evidence that use of the new reproductive technologies would harm the resulting children, decide against employing them, this could say one of two things to living children with serious or devastating disorders. It could suggest that it would have been better for their families if a different child had been born without these disorders and she was not. Or it could imply that it would have been better for this child to have been born without these disorders. The first implication suggests that it would be better for others if children with these disorders were not born, whereas the second maintains that it would be better for the children themselves if they had not been born with them. The first implies that it is regrettable that these children are alive instead of "normal" children. The second implies that it is regrettable that these children have these disorders. The second implication is the one on which we tend to act. This is exhibited by efforts we make to avoid serious or devastating disorders in children during pregnancy and to treat and care for children with such disorders after they are born. All of this suggests that it is not the children we disvalue, but the disorders that they have sustained. Consequently, it is not necessarily a reproach to disabled children who are already born if decisions are made against knowingly conceiving children who would have the same disabilities.

It is, however, a reproach to us and to our social institutions that once children with serious and devastating disorders are born, we provide woefully insufficient services and resources to them and their families. Does this contradict the claim that we value living children with disabilities and have their interests at heart? Hauerwas provides one perceptive explanation of our ambivalent and complex attitude toward those who live with serious disabilities in the course of discussing those who are developmentally delayed. He observes:

> After all, what we finally seek is not simply to help the retarded better negotiate their disability but to be like us: not retarded. Our inability to accomplish that frustrates and angers us, and sometimes the retarded themselves become the object of our anger. We do not like to be reminded of the limits of our power, and we do not like those who remind us.

We wish to remedy the disabilities with which children may be born, but find it difficult to cope with the recognition of our own vulnerability that they inadvertently call forth. Therefore, we relegate them to a separate domain within the world of existence where we believe unknown others will assist them to meet the special challenges they face. This is uncharitable and unjust. We have a responsibility to overcome our misplaced frustration about being unable to render those who have serious or devastating disorders more like those who do not. We have a responsibility to assist them to make their own way in the world unhampered by our irrational fears.

Taking Harms Seriously

The biblical injunction to multiply does not exhort us to do anything whatsoever to have children. It would be wrong to have children if it were known before conception that the means used to bring this about could inflict serious or devastating deficits on those very children. Yet the logic of the Interest in Existing Argument leads its proponents to brush aside the question whether these technologies might create such serious impairments. The thrust of this argument is that use of the new reproductive technologies provides its own justification—it produces children. This claim disregards the welfare of these children. Moreover, it creates a barrier to more extensive and detailed investigations of the effect of the new reproductive technologies on children born of them.

On the approach presented here, if it were known ahead of time that children conceived with the assistance of the new reproductive technologies would not have an adequate opportunity for health, it would be wrong to use them. Assessment of when and whether this would be the case would be carried out in light of the personal, familial, and social circumstances into which these children would be born. This means that would-be parents who consider resorting to the new reproductive technologies must be informed about the risks these techniques would present to the children born as a result of their use, the means available for ameliorating deficits these children might experience, and what social support would be available should they lack the resources to address such deficits on their own. Only then can they decide whether they ought to proceed with these techniques. To implement this recommendation, evidence for and against the contention that the new reproductive technologies cause serious or devastating physical, psychological, or social harm to the resulting children should be investigated more thoroughly than at present. Because of limited knowledge of the possible effects of these measures on their children, those who repeat Rachel's cry today face an agonizingly difficult decision when they consider whether to use the new reproductive technologies.

The Right to Lesbian Parenthood

Gillian Hanscombe

Hanscombe argues that same-sex couples are entitled to the same treatment from physicians and institutions as heterosexual couples. The objection that lesbian women should not be allowed to reproduce by artificial insemination is not one that can be supported by relevant evidence, Hanscombe points out. No studies have demonstrated that homosexual mothering is any different from heterosexual mothering or that children of two mothers "fall victim to negative psychosexual developmental influences." She concludes by citing instances of what she considers to be groundless prejudice against lesbian women by the medical establishment.

Anyone daring to address the subject of human rights faces both an appalling responsibility and being accused of an unnatural arrogance of utterance.

From Gillian Hanscombe, "The Right to Lesbian Parenthood," *Journal of Medical Ethics* 9 (1983): 133–135. Copyright © 1983 BMJ PUBLISHING GROUP. All rights reserved. Reproduced by permission. (Most notes omitted.)

I accept these risks not because I think myself expert on the subject of human rights, but because my experience is that human rights in the domain of parenthood are so very often denied existence.

I refer to a large minority in our population, that of lesbian women and gay men. Even at the most conservative estimate—which is that at least 1 in

20 adult people are homosexual—a group comprising 5 percent—we are dealing with a group larger than the 4 percent ethnic minorities group which already receives, as indeed it deserves to do, special attention. Lesbian women and gay men have to date, in all matters of social policy, been traditionally regarded as a deviant group.

It is the case, nonetheless, that the pathologising of this group is increasingly questioned, not only by members of the gay community themselves, but also by the agencies of our institutional life: that is, by medical practitioners, by teachers and social workers, and by working parties of religious and/or political orientation.

I am the co-author of a book about lesbian mothers. It is written for the general public, rather than for specialists, but is nevertheless the only book to date on the subject which I know of. It records the experiences of a selected group of lesbian mothers—selected to range over the varieties of social existence these parents and their children experience—from divorced women to single women who have deliberately chosen to conceive their children by artificial insemination by donor (AID).

The question asked by many heterosexual professionals who are charged with the theory or practice of social policy, is whether lesbian women, for example, should be (a) allowed, and (b) aided, to become mothers.

Objections to lesbian women being *allowed* to reproduce can only be social, since no physiological studies seeking to find physical differences between lesbian and non-lesbian women have ever succeeded in demonstrating such a difference.

Social objections fall into two categories: (a) the extent to which the psychopathology of the lesbian mother is assumed or demonstrated to deviate negatively from the norm. No studies to date have demonstrated that lesbian mothering is either significantly different from heterosexual mothering or that the lesbian mother is psychologically inadequately equipped to mother; (b) the extent to which the children of lesbian mothers are assumed to fall victim to negative psychosexual developmental influences. No study to date has succeeded in demonstrating such a phenomenon. There remain social objections issuing from prejudice, which in turn issues from ignorance. Since the medical profession forms a professional part of our social policy-making institutional life, it is required that medical practitioners do not form judgments based on ignorance. A mere assumption that because,

historically, lesbian women have been pathologised this somehow proves that they are "not normal" (and that in a negative sense) is, of course, unacceptable.

A good way of thinking about this is to begin with what is known about female sexuality. In the first place, it is clear that women, unlike men, are able to separate their sexual practice from their reproductive practice. It is possible, that is, for a woman (a) to become sexually aroused and reach orgasm without any possibility that she will become pregnant and (b) for a woman to be inseminated—either naturally or artificially—and become pregnant whether or not at the same time, she experiences any sexual pleasure. Whatever might be thought, therefore, about lesbian sexual practice, it is clear that lesbian women are able to conceive and bear children in the same way as non-lesbian women do.

Hence, attempting not to allow them to do so would be highly problematic, even apart from the massive dilemma—were such a decision taken—of not being able to enforce the sanction. Contrary to popular prejudice, it is the case that lesbian women, like other women, are quite capable of engaging in sexual intercourse with a man and, like other women, often solely for the reason that they intend to become pregnant.

Prejudice is not only rife within what are called the "helping professions," it is rife, too, in the courts. Lesbian mothers in dispute with husbands almost all lose custody of their children solely on the grounds of their lesbianism. Because of this, as well as for many other reasons, young women in the last decade have turned increasingly to the alternative of AID. They have found, by and large, that medical practitioners are not willing to provide AID for them, again solely on the grounds of their lesbianism. They have decided, increasingly, in response to this attitude, to conduct AID by themselves, with the assistance of sympathetic men. This is neither technically difficult nor is it illegal. Many AID daughters and sons of lesbian women are now in our nurseries and schools.

There are over two million lesbian mothers in the United States. Calculations for Britain are well-nigh impossible, owing to the professional nonrecognition of the existence of the group, together with the mothers' reticence in the face of prejudice. They are rightly anxious to conceal their sexuality since, like nearly all mothers, they love their children and will not willingly give them up, either to the courts or to any other social agency.

We might consider one case in particular. A lesbian woman, of middle-class background and professional standing in her own right, decided that she wanted to become a mother. It was, for her, a natural fulfillment of her womanhood, just as it is for millions of other women.

She became pregnant, deliberately, but unfortunately suffered a miscarriage, accompanied by much distress and depression. The usual practice of the hospital treating her was that, following the customary D & C, the patient should report to her own general practitioner. This she did, some six weeks later, wanting very much to know whether there were any clinical reasons why she might suffer further miscarriages. She asked the GP whether the hospital had sent her report.

"Yes, why?" came the reply.

"I want to know whether there is anything wrong with me which explains why I lost the baby," the woman explained.

"Why do you want to know?" persisted the GP.

"Because if there isn't, I want to become pregnant again," said the woman. "It was so dreadful losing the baby that I wouldn't knowingly go through it again. But if I can have a normal, full-term pregnancy, I want to try."

"But you can't have a baby," replied the GP, appalled; "you're not married!"

"What's that got to do with it?" asked the woman. And so ensued an embarrassing session of moralistic instruction from the GP to the silent woman. Her question remained unanswered.

She asked a friend who was a GP in a different area to write to the hospital for the information. This was done. There was no clinical reason for the miscarriage and the woman was pronounced normal and healthy.

The woman became pregnant again. But instead of feeling she could be cared for by her GP, she felt forced to opt for ante-natal care in the impersonal atmosphere of the hospital, where hundreds of women attended the clinic and where the same practitioner hardly ever appeared twice. At each visit, she was seen by different staff, which was comfortless but which at least ensured minimal questioning.

When she was nearly three months pregnant, the sister-in-charge said she must see the social worker. It was "hospital policy." But only, of course, for the unmarried. The woman felt angry and hurt, but didn't want to be accused of "making trouble." The social worker was sympathetic. "Just for the record, do you want your baby?" she asked. "Just for the record," the woman replied, "I planned my baby."

After delivery, she and her baby were not placed in an ordinary ward, but in one where mothers with handicapped babies were placed, together with mothers who had not had normal deliveries. In addition, she was "strongly advised" to stay for the full period, rather than go home after 48 hours. And yet both she and her baby were fit and healthy.

This mother keeps away from the "helping professionals." She is not open with her present GP, her child's school or the paramedical services, either about the circumstances of her child's birth or about her own sexuality. When she is offered contraception during her cervical smear tests, she simply declines it, not daring to explain that she is one of thousands of lesbian women who don't need it.

This woman is a proud and independent mother.[1] And her story is only one among scores. There is the mother who was refused AID by her local medical services and who then answered an advertisement in a lonely hearts column in order to find a man who would make her pregnant. She [charted] her ovulation cycle, and when she was fertile, dated the man, who only and clearly wanted casual sex. Her "experiment" worked and she bore a healthy child. There is the mother who came home from work one day to find a weeping partner who had to tell her that both her children—a son aged nine and a daughter aged seven—had been taken into care, because someone had told the social worker that the two women were lesbians.[2]

Hardly any histories of lesbian mothers and their children are on the record. But they are amongst us and they deserve the same care from professional caregivers as do other mothers and their children.

There are, too, gay men who parent and there are lesbian women and gay men who, though not biological parents themselves, are necessarily involved in childcare by virtue of their partners' parenthood. And there are men who donate semen for the insemination of women who take on themselves the responsibility of conception in order to exercise their rights to reproduce and bring up children. None of the considered and intricate planning undertaken by all these people is mentioned in the vast literature about the family, either in professional or popular publications. Hardly any of this material finds its way into discussions and seminars about family policy, about education, about poverty and so on.

In addition, cruel and heartless lobbying from powerful religious and political quarters—aimed against the human rights of adult homosexual women and men—is ongoing, despite its lack of scientific objectivity. Such pressure is also richly funded. The onus is therefore on the rational, well-informed and compassionate professionals in our caring institutions to consider how they will respond to those of our number born to homosexual parents. Removing the right to reproduce is both immoral and impractical. Neglecting the need of parents for normal support is both discriminatory and cruel. Removing their children from the natural custody of their parents—merely on grounds of the parents' sexuality—is a monstrous interference, with consequences for the children which are no better than the fate of children who are unwanted by their natural mothers. What is needed is education, not legislation.

There are no data—scientific, psychological, or social—which could support the thesis that homosexual people should not have the right to reproduce and to bring up their children. There are only differing opinions and prejudices, which are not capable of sustaining the rigorous intellectual analysis upon which any given body of knowledge must

rest. Hitler didn't like homosexuals. Or the handicapped. Or Jews. His answer was to attempt to exterminate them. Our cruelties are not so extreme. What we do is simply to ignore groups of people whose existence troubles us.

I submit, humbly but confidently, that using an argument to exclude adult people from parenthood which is based solely on the definition of an individual's sexual practice, is untenable and uncivilized. Adult people have in their gift the right to dispose of their own reproductive potential as they themselves think suitable. And the rest of us share, all of us, in the responsibility to care for all those committed to parenting and for the children for whom they care.

Notes

1. Identity and details withheld.
2. Identities and details withheld.

Instruction on Respect for Human Life in Its Origin and on the Dignity of Procreation: Replies to Certain Questions of the Day

Congregation for the Doctrine of the Faith

This "Instruction" was issued on February 22, 1987. It was approved and ordered published by Pope John Paul II and thus may be taken as representing the official position of the Roman Catholic Church on the issues addressed.

The document takes the position that a number of current or potential practices connected with reproductive technology are morally illegitimate. Included are the following:

- The use of human genetic material in procedures like cloning, parthenogenesis, and twin fission (the splitting of gametes)
- Attempts to manipulate genetic material for the purpose of sex selection or to promote desirable characteristics
- Artificial insemination involving unmarried individuals or the artificial insemination of an unmarried woman or a widow, even if the sperm is that of her deceased husband
- Acquiring sperm by means of masturbation
- Surrogate motherhood

Some techniques and practices, according to the document, are morally legitimate. Included are the following:

- Medical intervention to remove the causes of infertility
- The prescription of drugs to promote fertility

From "Instructions for the Congregation for the Doctrine of the Faith," February 22, 1987.

The document also makes a number of specific recommendations to governments to establish laws and policies governing reproductive technologies. It asks that civil laws be passed to prohibit the donation of sperm or ova between unmarried people. Laws should "expressly forbid" the use of living embryos for experimentation and protect them from mutilation and destruction. Further, legislation should prohibit "embryo banks, postmortem insemination and 'surrogate motherhood.'"

Some Roman Catholic theologians disagreed sharply with parts of the document. "The document argues that a child can be born only from a sexual act," Richard McCormick pointed out. "The most that can be argued is that a child should be born within a marriage from a loving act. Sexual intercourse is not the only loving act." Some suggested that individuals would make up their own minds on the issues, quite apart from the Vatican position. The significance of the document for non-Catholics is that these positions and arguments still affect the character of the discussion about reproductive technology. They also have an impact on legislation that would place restraints on research and practices many currently consider legitimate.

Interventions upon Human Procreation

By "artificial procreation" or "artificial fertilization" are understood here the different technical procedures directed towards obtaining a human conception in a manner other than the sexual union of man and woman. This Instruction deals with fertilization of an ovum in a test-tube (in vitro fertilization) and artificial insemination through transfer into the woman's genital tracts of previously collected sperm.

A preliminary point for the moral evaluation of such technical procedures is constituted by the consideration of the circumstances and consequences which those procedures involve in relation to the respect due the human embryo. Development of the practice of in vitro fertilization has required innumerable fertilizations and destructions of human embryos. Even today, the usual practice presupposes a hyper-ovulation on the part of the woman: a number of ova are withdrawn, fertilized and then cultivated in vitro for some days. Usually not all are transferred into the genital tracts of the woman; some embryos, generally called "spare," are destroyed or frozen. On occasion, some of the implanted embryos are sacrificed for various eugenic, economic or psychological reasons. Such deliberate destruction of human beings or their utilization for different purposes to the detriment of their integrity and life is contrary to the doctrine on procured abortion already recalled.

The connection between in vitro fertilization and the voluntary destruction of human embryos occurs too often. This is significant: through these procedures, with apparently contrary purposes, life and death are subjected to the decision of man, who thus sets himself up as the giver of life and death by decree. This dynamic of violence and domination may remain unnoticed by those very individuals who, in wishing to utilize this procedure, become subject to it themselves. The facts recorded and the cold logic which links them must be taken into consideration for a moral judgment on IVF and ET (in vitro fertilization and embryo transfer): the abortion-mentality which has made this procedure possible, thus leads, whether one wants it or not, to man's domination over the life and death of his fellow human beings and can lead to a system of radical eugenics.

Nevertheless, such abuses do not exempt one from a further and thorough ethical study of the techniques of artificial procreation considered in themselves, abstracting as far as possible from the destruction of embryos produced in vitro.

The present Instruction will therefore take into consideration in the first place the problems posed by heterologous artificial fertilization (II, 1–3),[1] and subsequently those linked with homologous artificial fertilization (II, 4–6).[2]

Before formulating an ethical judgment on each of these procedures, the principles and values which determine the moral evaluation of each of them will be considered.

A. Heterologous Artificial Fertilization

1. Why must human procreation take place in marriage? *Every human being is always to be accepted as a gift and blessing of God. However, from* the moral point of view a truly responsible procreation vis-a-vis the unborn child must be the fruit of marriage.

For human procreation has specific characteristics by virtue of the personal dignity of the parents and of the children: the procreation of a new person, whereby the man and the woman collaborate with the power of the Creator, must be the fruit and the sign of the mutual self-giving of the spouses, of their love and of their fidelity. *The fidelity of the spouses in the unity of marriage involves reciprocal respect of their right to become a father and a mother only through each other.*

The child has the right to be conceived, carried in the womb, brought into the world and brought up within marriage: it is through the secure and recognized relationship to his own parents that the child can discover his own identity and achieve his own proper human development.

The parents find in their child a confirmation and completion of their reciprocal self-giving: the child is the living image of their love, the permanent sign of their conjugal union, the living and indissoluble concrete expression of their paternity and maternity.

By reason of the vocation and social responsibilities of the person, the good of the children and of the parents contributes to the good of civil society; the vitality and stability of society require that children come into the world within a family and that the family be firmly based on marriage.

The tradition of the Church and anthropological reflection recognize in marriage and in its indissoluble unity the only setting worthy of truly responsible procreation.

2. Does heterologous artificial fertilization conform to the dignity of the couple and to the truth of marriage? Through IVF and ET and heterologous artificial insemination, human conception is achieved through the fusion of gametes of at least one donor other than the spouses who are united in marriage. *Heterologous artificial fertilization is contrary to the unity of marriage, to the dignity of the spouses, to the vocation proper to parents, and to the child's right to be conceived and brought into the world in marriage and from marriage....*

These reasons lead to a negative moral judgment concerning heterologous artificial fertilization: consequently fertilization of a married woman with the sperm of a donor different from her husband and fertilization with the husband's sperm of an ovum not coming from his wife are morally illicit. Furthermore, the artificial fertilization

of a woman who is unmarried or a widow, whoever the donor may be, cannot be morally justified.

The desire to have a child and the love between spouses who long to obviate a sterility which cannot be overcome in any other way constitute understandable motivations; but subjectively good intentions do not render heterologous artificial fertilization conformable to the objective and inalienable properties of marriage or respectful of the rights of the child and of the spouses.

3. Is "surrogate"[3] motherhood morally licit? *No, for the same reasons which lead one to reject heterologous artificial fertilization: for it is contrary to the unity of marriage and to the dignity of the procreation of the human person.*

Surrogate motherhood represents an objective failure to meet the obligations of maternal love, of conjugal fidelity and of responsible motherhood; it offends the dignity and the right of the child to be conceived, carried in the womb, brought into the world and brought up by his own parents; it sets up, to the detriment of families, a division between the physical, psychological and moral elements which constitute those families.

B. Homologous Artificial Fertilization

Since heterologous artificial fertilization has been declared unacceptable, the question arises of how to evaluate morally the process of homologous artificial fertilization: IVF and ET and artificial insemination between husband and wife. First a question of principle must be clarified.

4. What connection is required from the moral point of view between procreation and conjugal act? . . . In reality, the origin of a human person is the result of an act of giving. The one conceived must be the fruit of his parents' love. He cannot be desired or conceived as the production of an intervention of medical or biological techniques; that would be equivalent to reducing him to an object of scientific technology. No one may subject the coming of a child into the world to conditions of technical efficiency which are to be evaluated according to standards of control and dominion.

The moral relevance of the link between the meanings of the conjugal act and between the goods of marriage, as well as the unity of the human being and the dignity of his origin, demand that the procreation of a human person be brought about as the fruit of the conjugal act specific to the love between spouses. The link between procreation and the conjugal act is thus shown to be of great importance on the anthropological and moral planes, and it throws light on the positions of the Magisterium with regard to homologous artificial fertilization.

5. Is homologous "in vitro" fertilization morally licit?

The answer to this question is strictly dependent on the principles just mentioned. Certainly one cannot ignore the legitimate aspirations of sterile couples. For some, recourse to homologous IVF and ET appears to be the only way of fulfilling their sincere desire for a child. The question is asked whether the totality of conjugal life in such situations is not sufficient to insure the dignity proper to human procreation. It is acknowledged that IVF and ET certainly cannot supply for the absence of sexual relations and cannot be preferred to the specific acts of conjugal union, given the risks involved for the child and the difficulties of the procedure. But it is asked whether, when there is no other way of overcoming the sterility which is a source of suffering, homologous in vitro fertilization may not constitute an aid, if not a form of therapy, whereby its moral licitness could be admitted.

The desire for a child—or at the very least an openness to the transmission of life—is a necessary prerequisite from the moral point of view for responsible human procreation. But this good intention is not sufficient for making a positive moral evaluation of in vitro fertilization between spouses. The process of IVF and ET must be judged in itself and cannot borrow its definitive moral quality from the totality of conjugal life of which it becomes part nor from the conjugal acts which may precede or follow it.

It has already been recalled that, in the circumstances in which it is regularly practiced, IVF and ET involves the destruction of human beings, which is something contrary to the doctrine on the illicitness of abortion previously mentioned. But even in a situation in which every precaution were taken to avoid the death of human embryos, homologous IVF and ET dissociates from the conjugal act the actions which are directed to human fertilization. For this reason the very nature of homologous IVF and ET also must be taken into account, even abstracting from the link with procured abortion.

Homologous IVF and ET is brought about outside the bodies of the couple through actions of third parties whose competence and technical activity determine the success of the procedure. Such fertilization entrusts the life and identity of the embryo into the power of doctors and biologists and establishes the domination of technology over the origin and destiny of the human person. Such a relationship of domination is in itself contrary to the dignity and equality that must be common to parents and children.

Conception in vitro is the result of the technical action which presides over fertilization. *Such fertilization is neither in fact achieved nor positively willed as the expression and fruit of specific acts of the conjugal union. In homologous IVF and ET, therefore, even if it is considered in the context of "de facto" existing sexual relations, the generation of the human person is objectively deprived of its proper perfection: namely, that of being the result and fruit of a conjugal act* in which the spouses can become "cooperators with God for giving life to a new person."…

Certainly, homologous IVF and ET fertilization is not marked by all that ethical negativity found in extra-conjugal procreation; the family and marriage continue to constitute the setting for the birth and upbringing of the children. Nevertheless, in conformity with the traditional doctrine relating to the goods of marriage and the dignity of the person, *the Church remains opposed from the moral point of view to homologous "in vitro" fertilization. Such fertilization is in itself illicit and in opposition to the dignity of procreation and of the conjugal union, even when everything is done to avoid the death of the human embryo.*

Although the manner in which human conception is achieved with IVF and ET cannot be approved, every child which comes into the world must in any case be accepted as a living gift of the divine Goodness and must be brought up with love.

6. How is homologous artificial insemination to be evaluated from the moral point of view?

Homologous artificial insemination within marriage cannot be admitted except for those cases in which the technical means is not a substitute for the conjugal act but serves to facilitate and to help so that the act attains its natural purpose.

The teaching of the Magisterium on this point has already been stated. This teaching is not just an expression of particular historical circumstances but is based on the Church's doctrine concerning the connection between the conjugal union and procreation and on a consideration of the personal nature of the conjugal act and of human procreation. "In its natural structure, the conjugal act is a personal action, a simultaneous and immediate cooperation on the part of the husband and wife, which by the very nature of the agents and the proper nature of the act is the expression of the mutual gift which, according to the words of Scripture, brings about union 'in one flesh.'" Thus moral conscience "does not necessarily proscribe the use of certain artificial means destined solely either to the facilitating of the natural act or to insuring that the natural act normally performed achieves its proper end." If the technical means facilitates the conjugal act or helps it to reach its natural objectives, it can be morally acceptable. If, on the other hand, the procedure were to replace the conjugal act, it is morally illicit.

Artificial insemination as a substitute for the conjugal act is prohibited by reason of the voluntarily achieved dissociation of the two meanings of the conjugal act. Masturbation, through which the sperm is normally obtained, is another sign of this dissociation: even when it is done for the purpose of procreation, the act remains deprived of its unitive meaning. "It lacks the sexual relationship called for by the moral order, namely the relationship which realizes 'the full sense of mutual self-giving and human procreation in the context of true love.'"...

7. The suffering caused by infertility in marriage. *The suffering of spouses who cannot have children or who are afraid of bringing a handicapped child into the world is a suffering that everyone must understand and properly evaluate.*

On the part of the spouses, the desire for a child is natural: it expresses the vocation to fatherhood and motherhood inscribed in conjugal love. This desire can be even stronger if the couple is affected by sterility which appears incurable. Nevertheless, marriage does not confer upon the spouses the right to have a child, but only the right to perform those natural acts which are per se ordered to procreation.

A true and proper right to a child would be contrary to the child's dignity and nature. The child is not an object to which one has a right, nor can be considered as an object of ownership: rather, a child is a gift, "the supreme gift" and the most gratuitous gift of marriage, and is a living testimony of the mutual giving of his parents. For this reason, the child has the right, as already mentioned, to be the fruit of the specific act of the conjugal love of his parents; and he also has the right to be respected as a person from the moment of his conception ....

Notes

1. By the term heterologous artificial fertilization or procreation, the Instruction means techniques used to obtain a human conception artificially by the use of gametes coming from at least one donor other than the spouses who are joined in marriage. Such techniques can be of two types: (a) Heterologous IVF and ET: the technique used to obtain a human conception through the meeting in vitro of gametes taken from at least one donor other than the two spouses joined in marriage. (b) Heterologous artificial insemination: the technique used to obtain a human conception through the transfer into the genital tracts of the woman of the sperm previously collected from a donor other than the husband.

2. By artificial homologous fertilization or procreation, the Instruction means the technique used to obtain a human conception using the gametes of the two spouses joined in marriage. Homologous artificial fertilization can be carried out by two different methods: (a) Homologous IVF and ET: the technique used to obtain a human conception through the meeting in vitro of the gametes of the spouses joined in marriage. (b) Homologous artificial insemination: the technique used to obtain a human conception through the transfer into the genital tracts of a married woman of the sperm previously collected from her husband.

3. By "surrogate mother" the Instruction means: (a) the woman who carries in pregnancy an embryo implanted in her uterus and who is genetically a stranger to the embryo because it has been obtained through the union of the gametes of "donors." She carries the pregnancy with a pledge to surrender the baby once it is born to the party who commissioned or made the agreement for the pregnancy. (b) the woman who carries in pregnancy an embryo to whose procreation she has contributed the donation of her own ovum, fertilized through insemination with the sperm of a man other than her husband. She carries the pregnancy with a pledge to surrender the child once it is born to the party who commissioned or made the agreement for the pregnancy.

Section 2: Human Reproductive Cloning

The Wisdom of Repugnance

Leon R. Kass

Kass argues that the repulsion many people feel about the possibility of human cloning springs from a recognition that it violates our nature as embodied, engendered, and engendering beings and the social relations we have because of that nature. First, cloning would

From *The New Republic*, June 2, 1997, pp. 17–26. Reprinted by permission of the author.

distort the cloned person's sense of individuality and social identity. Second, like IVF and prenatal genetic testing, cloning would transform procreation into manufacture and children into commodities. Third, cloning would encourage parents to regard children as property.

In contrast to those who see cloning as simply another technique, like AI and IVF, for helping individuals exercise their "right" to reproduce, Kass regards cloning as a significant slide down the slippery slope toward the "sperm to term" production of genetically designed children. In view of all these considerations, Kass urges an international legal ban on human cloning.

…"Offensive." "Grotesque." "Revolting." "Repugnant." "Repulsive." These are the words most commonly heard regarding the prospect of human cloning. Such reactions come both from the man or woman in the street and from the intellectuals, from believers and atheists, from humanists and scientists. Even Dolly's creator has said he "would find it offensive" to clone a human being.

People are repelled by many aspects of human cloning. They recoil from the prospect of mass production of human beings, with large clones of look-alikes, compromised in their individuality, the idea of father–son or mother–daughter twins; the bizarre prospects of a woman giving birth to and rearing a genetic copy of herself, her spouse or even her deceased father or mother; the grotesqueness of conceiving a child as an exact replacement for another who has died; the utilitarian creation of embryonic genetic duplicates of oneself, to be frozen away or created when necessary, in case of need for homologous tissues or organs for transplantation; the narcissism of those who would clone themselves and the arrogance of others who think they know who deserves to be cloned or which genotype any child-to-be should be thrilled to receive; the Frankensteinian hubris to create human life and increasingly to control its destiny; man playing God. Almost no one finds any of the suggested reasons for human cloning compelling; almost everyone anticipates its possible misuses and abuses. Moreover, many people feel oppressed by the sense that there is probably nothing we can do to prevent it from happening. This makes the prospect all the more revolting.

Revulsion is not an argument; and some of yesterday's repugnances are today calmly accepted—though, one must add, not always for the better. In crucial cases, however, repugnance is the emotional expression of deep wisdom, beyond reason's power fully to articulate it. Can anyone really give an argument fully adequate to the horror which is father–daughter incest (even with consent), or having sex with animals, or mutilating a corpse, or eating human flesh, or even just (just!) raping or murdering another human being?

Would anybody's failure to give full rational justification for his or her revulsion at these practices make that revulsion ethically suspect? Not at all. On the contrary, we are suspicious of those who think that they can rationalize away our horror, say, by trying to explain the enormity of incest with arguments only about the genetic risks of inbreeding.

The repugnance at human cloning belongs in this category. We are repelled by the prospect of cloning human beings not because of the strangeness or novelty of the undertaking, but because we intuit and feel, immediately and without argument, the violation of things that we rightfully hold dear. Repugnance, here as elsewhere, revolts against the excesses of human willfulness, warning us not to transgress what is unspeakably profound. Indeed, in this age in which everything is held to be permissible so long as it is freely done, in which our given human nature no longer commands respect, in which our bodies are regarded as mere instruments of our autonomous rational wills, repugnance may be the only voice left that speaks up to defend the central core of our humanity. Shallow are the souls that have forgotten how to shudder.

The goods protected by repugnance are generally overlooked by our customary ways of approaching all new biomedical technologies. The way we evaluate cloning ethically will in fact be shaped by how we characterize it descriptively, by the context into which we place it, and by the perspective from which we view it. The first task for ethics is proper description. And here is where our failure begins.

Typically, cloning is discussed in one or more of three familiar contexts, which one might call the technological, the liberal and the meliorist.

Under the first, cloning will be seen as an extension of existing techniques for assisting reproduction and determining the genetic makeup of children. Like them, cloning is to be regarded as a neutral technique, with no inherent meaning or goodness, but subject to multiple uses, some good, some bad. The morality of cloning thus depends absolutely on the goodness or badness of the motives and intentions of the cloners: as one bioethicist defender of cloning puts it, "the ethics must be judged [only] by the way the parents nurture and rear their resulting child and whether they bestow the same love and affection on a child brought into existence by a technique of assisted reproduction as they would on a child born in the usual way."

The liberal (or libertarian or liberationist) perspective sets cloning in the context of rights, freedoms and personal empowerment. Cloning is just a new option for exercising an individual's right to reproduce or to have the kind of child that he or she wants. Alternatively, cloning enhances our liberation (especially women's liberation) from the confines of nature, the vagaries of chance, or the necessity for sexual mating. Indeed, it liberates women from the need for men altogether, for the process requires only eggs, nuclei and (for the time being) uteri—plus, of course, a healthy dose of our (allegedly "masculine") manipulative science that likes to do all these things to mother nature and nature's mothers. For those who hold this outlook, the only moral restraints on cloning are adequately informed consent and the avoidance of bodily harm. If no one is cloned without her consent, and if the clonant is not physically damaged, then the liberal conditions for licit, hence moral, conduct are met. Worries that go beyond violating the will or maiming the body are dismissed as "symbolic"—which is to say, unreal....

The meliorist perspective embraces valetudinarians and also eugenicists. The latter were formerly more vocal in these discussions, but they are now generally happy to see their goals advanced under the less threatening banners of freedom and technological growth. These people see in cloning a new prospect for improving human beings—minimally, by ensuring the perpetuation of healthy individuals by avoiding the risks of genetic disease inherent in the lottery of sex, and maximally, by producing "optimum babies," preserving outstanding genetic material, and (with the help of soon-to-come techniques for precise genetic engineering) enhancing inborn human capacities on many fronts. Here the morality of cloning as a means is justified solely by the excellence of the end, that is, by the outstanding traits or individuals cloned—beauty, or brawn, or brains....

The technical, liberal and meliorist approaches all ignore the deeper anthropological, social and, indeed, ontological meanings of bringing forth new life. To this more fitting and profound point of view, cloning shows itself to be a major alteration, indeed, a major violation, of our given nature as embodied, gendered and engendering beings—and of the social relations built on this natural ground. Once this perspective is recognized, the ethical judgment on cloning can no longer be reduced to a matter of motives and intentions, rights and freedoms, benefits and harms, or even means and ends. It must be regarded primarily as a matter of meaning: Is cloning a fulfillment of human begetting and belonging? Or is cloning rather, as I contend, their pollution and perversion? To pollution and perversion, the fitting response can only be horror and revulsion; and conversely, generalized horror and revulsion are prima facie evidence of foulness and violation. The burden of moral argument must fall entirely on those who want to declare the widespread repugnances of humankind to be mere timidity or superstition.

Yet repugnance need not stand naked before the bar of reason. The wisdom of our horror at human cloning can be partially articulated, even if this is finally one of those instances about which the heart has its reasons that reason cannot entirely know....

The Perversities of Cloning

Cloning creates serious issues of identity and individuality. The cloned person may experience concerns about his distinctive identity not only because he will be in genotype and appearance identical to another human being, but, in this case, because he may also be twin to the person who is his "father" or "mother"—if one can still call them that. What would be the psychic burdens of being the "child" or "parent" of your twin? The cloned individual moreover, will be saddled with a genotype that has already lived. He will not be fully a surprise to the world. People are likely always to compare his performances in life with that of his alter ego. True, his nurture and his circumstance in life will be different; genotype is not exactly destiny. Still, one must also expect parental and other efforts to shape this new life after the original—or at least to view the child with the original version always firmly in mind. Why else did they clone from the star basketball player, mathematician and beauty queen—or even dear old dad—in the first place?…

Troubled psychic identity (distinctiveness), based on all-too-evident genetic identity (sameness), will be made much worse by the utter confusion of social identity and kinship ties: For, as already noted, cloning radically confounds lineage and social relations, for "offspring" as for "parents." As bioethicist James Nelson has pointed out, a female child cloned from her "mother" might develop a desire for a relationship to her "father," and might understandably seek out the father of her "mother," who is after all also her biological twin sister. Would "Grandpa," who thought his paternal duties concluded, be pleased to discover that the clonant looked to him for paternal attention and support?

Social identity and social ties of relationship and responsibility are widely connected to, and supported by, biological kinship. Social taboos on incest (and adultery) everywhere serve to keep clear who is related to whom (and especially which child belongs to which parents), as well as to avoid confounding the social identity of parent-and-child (or brother-and-sister) with the social identity of lovers, spouses and co-parents. True, social identity is altered by adoption (but as a matter of the best interest of already living children: we do not deliberately produce children for adoption). True, artificial insemination and in vitro fertilization with donor sperm, or whole embryo donation, are in some way forms of "prenatal adoption"—a not altogether unproblematic practice. Even here, though, there is in each case (as in all sexual reproduction) a known male source of sperm and a known single female source of egg—a genetic father and a genetic mother—should anyone care to know (as adopted children often do) who is genetically related to whom.

In the case of cloning, however, there is but one "parent." The usually sad situation of the "single-parent child" is here deliberately planned, and with a vengeance. In the case of self-cloning, the "offspring" is, in addition, one's twin; and so the dreaded result of incest—to be parent to one's sibling—is here brought about deliberately, albeit without any act of coitus. Moreover, all other relationships will be confounded. What will father, grandfather, aunt, cousin, sister mean? Who will bear what ties and what burdens? What sort of social identity will someone have with

one whole side—"father's" or "mother's"—necessarily excluded? It is no answer to say that our society, with its high incidence of divorce, remarriage, adoption, extramarital childbearing and the rest, already confounds lineage and confuses kinship and responsibility for children (and everyone else), unless one also wants to argue that this is, for children, a preferable state of affairs.

Human cloning would also represent a giant step toward turning begetting into making, procreation into manufacture (literally, something "handmade"), a process already begun with in vitro fertilization and genetic testing of embryos. With cloning, not only is the process in hand, but the total genetic blueprint of the cloned individual is selected and determined by the human artisans. To be sure, subsequent development will take place according to natural processes; and the resulting children will still be recognizably human. But we here would be taking a major step into making man himself simply another one of the man-made things. Human nature becomes merely the last part of nature to succumb to the technological project, which turns all of nature into raw material at human disposal, to be homogenized by our rationalized technique according to the subjective prejudices of the day.

How does begetting differ from making? In natural procreation, human beings come together, complementarily male and female, to give existence to another being who is formed, exactly as we were, *by what we are:* living, hence perishable, hence aspiringly erotic, human beings. In clonal reproduction, by contrast, and in the more advanced forms of manufacture to which it leads, we give existence to a being not by what we are but by what we intend and design. As with any product of our making, no matter how excellent, the artificer stands above it, not as an equal but as a superior, transcending it by his will and creative prowess. Scientists who clone animals make it perfectly clear that they are engaged in instrumental making; the animals are, from the start, designed as means to serve rational human purposes. In human cloning, scientists and prospective "parents" would be adopting the same technocratic mentality to human children: human children would be their artifacts.

Such an arrangement is profoundly dehumanizing, no matter how good the product. Mass-scale cloning of the same individual makes the point vividly; but the violation of human equality, freedom and dignity are present even in a single planned clone. And procreation dehumanized into manufacture is further degraded by commodification, a virtually inescapable result of allowing babymaking to proceed under the banner of commerce. Genetic and reproductive biotechnology companies are already growth industries, but they will go into commercial orbit once the Human Genome Project nears completion. Supply will create enormous demand. Even before the capacity for human cloning arrives, established companies will have invested in the harvesting of eggs from ovaries obtained at autopsy or through ovarian surgery, practiced embryonic genetic alteration, and initiated the stockpiling of prospective donor tissues. Through the rental of surrogate-womb services, and through the buying and selling of tissues and embryos, priced according to the merit of the donor, the commodification of nascent human life will be unstoppable.

Finally, and perhaps most important, the practice of human cloning by nuclear transfer—like other anticipated forms of genetic engineering of the next generation—would enshrine and aggravate a profound and mischievous misunderstanding of the meaning of having children and of the parent–child relationship. When a couple now chooses to procreate, the partners are saying yes to the emergence of new life in its novelty, saying yes not only to having a child but also, tacitly, to having whatever child this child turns out to be. In accepting our finitude and opening ourselves to our replacement, we are tacitly confessing the limits of our control. In this ubiquitous way of nature, embracing the future by procreating means precisely that we are relinquishing our grip, in the very activity of taking up our own share in what we hope will be the immortality of human life and the human species. This means that our children are not *our* children: they are not our property, not our possessions. Neither are they supposed to live our lives for us, or anyone else's life but their own. To be sure, we seek to guide them on their way, imparting to them not just life but nurturing love, and a way of life; to be sure, they bear our hopes that they will live fine and flourishing lives, enabling us in small measure to transcend our own limitations. Still, their genetic distinctiveness and independence are the natural foreshadowing of the deep truth that they have their own and never-before-enacted life to live. They are sprung from a past, but they take an uncharted course into the future.

Much harm is already done by parents who try to live vicariously through their children. Children are sometimes compelled to fulfill the broken dreams of unhappy parents; John Doe Jr. or the III is under the burden of having to live up to his forebear's name. Still, if most parents have hopes for their children, cloning parents will have expectations. In cloning, such overbearing parents take at the start a decisive step which contradicts the entire meaning of the open and forward-looking nature of parent–child relations. The child is given a genotype that has already lived, with full expectation that this blueprint of a past life ought to be controlling of the life that is to come. Cloning is inherently despotic, for it seeks to make one's children (or someone else's children) after one's own image (or an image of one's choosing) and their fixture according to one's will. In some cases, the despotism may be mild and benevolent. In other cases, it will be mischievous and downright tyrannical. But despotism—the control of another through one's will—it inevitably will be.

Meeting Some Objections

The defenders of cloning, of course, are not wittingly friends of despotism. Indeed, they regard themselves mainly as friends of freedom: the freedom of individuals to reproduce, the freedom of scientists and inventors to discover and devise and to foster "progress" in genetic knowledge and technique. They want large-scale cloning only for animals, but they wish to preserve cloning as a human option for exercising our "right to reproduce"—our right to have children, and children with "desirable genes." As law professor John Robertson points out, under our "right to reproduce" we already practice early forms of unnatural, artificial and extramarital reproduction, and we already practice early forms of eugenic choice. For this reason, he argues, cloning is no big deal.

We have here a perfect example of the logic of the slippery slope, and the slippery way in which it already works in this area. Only a few years ago, slippery slope arguments were used to oppose artificial insemination and in vitro fertilization using unrelated sperm donors. Principles used to justify these practices, it was said, will be used to justify more artificial and more eugenic practices, including cloning. Not so, the defenders retorted, since we can make the necessary distinctions. And now, without even a gesture at making the necessary distinctions, the continuity of practice is held by itself to be justificatory.

The principle of reproductive freedom as currently enunciated by the proponents of cloning logically embraces the ethical acceptability of sliding down the entire rest of the slope—to producing children ectogenetically from sperm to term (should it become feasible) and to producing children whose entire genetic makeup will be the product of parental eugenic planning and choice. If reproductive freedom means the right to have a child of one's own choosing, by whatever means, it knows and accepts no limits.

But, far from being legitimated by a "right to reproduce," the emergence of techniques of assisted reproduction and genetic engineering should compel us to reconsider the meaning and limits of such a putative right. In truth, a "right to reproduce" has always been a peculiar and problematic notion. Rights generally belong to individuals, but this is a right which (before cloning) no one can exercise alone. Does the right then inhere only in couples? Only in married couples? Is it a (woman's) right to carry or deliver or a right (of one or more parents) to nurture and rear? Is it a right to have your own biological child? Is it a right only to attempt reproduction, or a right also to succeed? Is it a right to acquire the baby of one's choice?

The assertion of a negative "right to reproduce" certainly makes sense when it claims protection against state interference with procreative liberty, say, through a program of compulsory sterilization. But surely it cannot be the basis of a tort claim against nature, to be made good by technology, should free efforts at natural procreation fail. Some insist that the right to reproduce embraces also the right against state interference with the free use of all technological means to obtain a child. Yet such a position cannot be sustained: for reasons having to do with the means employed, any community may rightfully prohibit surrogate pregnancy, or polygamy, or the sale of babies to infertile couples, without violating anyone's basic human "right to reproduce." When the exercise of a previously innocuous freedom now involves or impinges on troublesome practices that the original freedom never was intended to reach, the general presumption of liberty needs to be reconsidered.

We do indeed already practice negative eugenic selection, through genetic screening and prenatal diagnosis. Yet our practices are governed by a norm of health. We seek to prevent the birth of children who suffer from known (serious) genetic diseases. When and if gene therapy becomes possible, such diseases could then be treated, in utero or even before implantation—I have no ethical objection in principle to such a practice (though I have some practical worries), precisely because it serves the medical goal of healing existing individuals. But therapy, to be therapy, implies not only an existing "patient." It also implies a norm of health. In this respect, even germline gene "therapy," though practiced not on a human being but on egg and sperm, is less radical than cloning, which is in no way therapeutic. But once one blurs the distinction between health promotion and genetic enhancement, between so-called negative and positive eugenics, one opens the door to all future eugenic designs. "To make sure that a child will be healthy and have good chances in life": this is Robertson's principle, and owing to its latter clause it is an utterly elastic principle, with no boundaries. Being over eight feet tall will likely produce some very good chances in life, and so will having the looks of Marilyn Monroe, and so will a genius-level intelligence....

Ban the Cloning of Humans

What, then, should we do? We should declare that human cloning is unethical in itself and dangerous in its likely consequences. In so doing, we shall have the backing of the overwhelming majority of our fellow Americans, and of the human race, and (I believe) of most practicing scientists. Next, we should do all that we can to prevent the cloning of human beings. We should do this by means of an international legal ban if possible, and by a unilateral national ban, at a minimum. Scientists may secretly undertake to violate such a law, but they will be deterred by not being able to stand up proudly to claim the credit for their technological bravado and success. Such a ban on clonal baby-making, moreover, will not harm the progress of basic genetic science and technology. On the contrary, it will reassure the public that scientists are happy to proceed without violating the deep ethical norms and intuitions of the human community....

The president's call for a moratorium on human cloning has given us an important opportunity. In a truly unprecedented way, we can strike a blow for the human control of the technological project, for wisdom, prudence and human dignity. The prospect of human cloning, so repulsive to contemplate, is the occasion for deciding whether we shall be slaves of unregulated progress, and ultimately its artifacts, or whether we shall remain free human beings who guide our technique toward the enhancement of human dignity.

The Ethics of Human Reproductive Cloning

Carson Strong

Strong addresses the question of whether, if human cloning does not produce birth defects, it would be morally legitimate for some infertile couples to employ cloning to have a genetically related child. The objections to human reproductive cloning, he claims, are of three kinds: those that appeal to the interest of the child, those based on the consequences to society, and those arising from teleological views. Strong examines objections of all three types and argues that each involves problems so serious as to keep it from being sufficiently compelling. He concludes that human reproductive cloning could be ethically justifiable in at least some situations.

Introduction

Many hold that human reproductive cloning would be wrong under any circumstances. Others have maintained that in certain situations reproductive cloning would be ethically permissible. One type of case in which it has been claimed that it would be permissible involves infertile couples. This paper focuses on infertility cases in order to address the question of whether human reproductive cloning could at least sometimes be ethically justifiable.

A caveat should be stated at the outset. The risk of congenital anomalies in the offspring makes it reasonable to hold that it would be wrong to attempt human reproductive cloning at this time. In the future, however, it might be possible to carry out cloning with no more risk of anomalies than the background risk in procreation by sexual intercourse. Let us assume, for sake of argument, that cloning technology has advanced to that point. Given this assumption, would cloning in infertility cases be ethically permissible?...

An example of the type of case in question is a scenario in which the woman is unable to produce ova and the man is unable to produce spermatozoa. Like many couples, they want to have a child genetically related to at least one of them. One approach to having genetically related children would involve using sperm and ova donated by family members, but

Reprinted from *Ethics, Law and Moral Philosophy of Reproductive Biomedicine* 1, no. 1 (2005): 45–49, Carson Strong, "The Ethics of Human Reproductive Cloning," Copyright © 2005, with permission from Elsevier. (References omitted.)

suppose that no family members are available in this case. Let us assume, in other words, that cloning using a cell nucleus from one member of the couple is the only way they could have a child genetically related to one of them....

Whether cloning in such scenarios is ethically justifiable rests on the following question: which should be considered weightier, infertile couples' freedom to use cloning or the arguments against human reproductive cloning? To address this question, let us begin with the importance of the freedom of infertile couples to use cloning.

Cloning and Procreative Freedom

Some have claimed that cloning is not procreation because it does not involve the joining of male and female gametes. In reply, to assess whether cloning in the infertility cases is procreation, we should compare it to the paradigm of procreation—what I shall call "ordinary procreation." I refer to the type of procreation in which a couple begets, by sexual intercourse, a child whom they then rear. In making this comparison, we need to look not only at the differences but also at the similarities, and it turns out that a number of similarities can be identified. First, in both types of situation there is a genetic connection between the child and at least one member of the couple. Second, assuming that the woman can gestate, there is gestating and childbirth. Third, the child is raised by the couple. Fourth, in both types of case, the overall purpose is to create a family or add a child to the family.

So, the similarities between the two situations are quite substantial. They both involve central features of the project of having children: genetic connection, gestation, childbirth, and rearing. Because of these similarities, it is reasonable to regard the use of cloning by infertile couples as procreation, even though it does not consist of the union of male and female gametes.

Based on these considerations, it is reasonable to hold that the freedom of infertile couples to use cloning is a form of procreative freedom. Procreative freedom is worthy of respect in part because freedom in general is worthy of respect. But more than this, procreative freedom is an especially important freedom because of the significance that procreative decisions can have for persons' lives. For these reasons, the freedom of infertile couples to use cloning is worthy of respect.

It might be objected that the desire to have genetically related children should be given relatively little weight. One might argue that this desire is a mere expression of vanity and is too frivolous to outweigh the objections to reproductive cloning, given that there are other options such as adoption or donor pre-embryos.... Let us consider whether there are reasons for desiring genetically related children that are not easy to dismiss.

To explore this, one strategy is to try to understand why having genetic children might be meaningful to people in "ordinary procreation" and then use this understanding in addressing reproductive cloning. It turns out that there are a number of reasons why people might find it meaningful to have genetic offspring in the ordinary type of procreation. It will suffice to discuss two of these reasons. First, having a genetic child might be valued because it involves participation in the creation of a person. When one has a child in ordinary procreation, a normal outcome is the creation of an individual with self-consciousness. Philosophers have regarded the phenomenon of self-consciousness with wonder.... One might say that in having children we participate in the mystery of the creation of self-consciousness. For this reason, some might regard creating a person as an important event, perhaps one with spiritual overtones.

Turning to the second reason, having genetic children in the ordinary situation might be valued as an affirmation of a couple's mutual love and acceptance. It can be a deep expression of acceptance to say to another, in effect, "I want your genes to contribute to the genetic makeup of my children." Moreover, in such a context there might be an anticipation that the emotional bond between the couple will grow stronger because of common children to whom each has a biological relationship. To intentionally seek the strengthening of their personal bond in this manner can be a further affirmation of mutual love and acceptance. In stating these two reasons, I do not mean to imply that one ought to desire to have genetic offspring, but only that the desire can be defended. These are examples of reasons that are not silly or confused. Rather, they are reasons that deserve consideration.

Now let us consider the applicability of these reasons to cloning. Would it be reasonable for the infertile couple to want to use cloning in part because it would enable them to participate in the creation of a person? It can be argued that it would be. The member of the couple who provides a somatic cell nucleus for cloning would participate by providing the nuclear genetic material for the new person, and regardless of who provides the cell nucleus, if the woman is capable of gestating, then she could participate by gestating and giving birth to the child. If she has ova, then she could participate genetically by providing mitochondrial DNA. In addition, the couple might value cloning because they interpret it as an affirmation of mutual love and acceptance. A biological partnership in creating the child is possible if a cell nucleus from the man is used and the woman is the gestational mother. In that situation, the child comes forth from their two bodies.

Assuming mutual love, the woman bears a child having the genes of the man who loves her and is loved by her. Alternatively, suppose that a cell nucleus from the woman is used. The man then can become the social father of a child having the genes of the woman who loves him and is loved by him. To seek to become social parents in this manner can be an affirmation of mutual acceptance. These considerations show that some of the important reasons for valuing the having of genetic children in the ordinary scenario also apply when cloning is used. Although not everyone in the infertile couple's situation would want to use cloning in order to have a genetically related child, some might.

Objections to Human Reproductive Cloning

A number of objections have been raised against human reproductive cloning, and they generally fall into three main categories—those that appeal to the interests of the child, those based on consequences for society, and those arising from teleological views. First we shall consider objections that focus on the child's interests. The main ones are of two kinds, consequentialist and deontological. Let us begin with the consequentialist type.

Harm to the Child

Consequentialist child-centred objections claim that cloning will harm the child. An example is the "life in the shadow" argument. It claims that people will expect the child to lead a life that follows in the footsteps of the older person who has the same DNA. These expectations will pressure her to follow in that person's footsteps, and this will be harmful because it will prevent her from following a different path that might be more conducive to her well-being. Another example is the argument that there will be confusion over family lineage and kinship. The nucleus donor will be both the social parent and the twin sibling of the child. This unusual relationship could result in some type of family turmoil that is harmful to the child, so the argument goes.

These consequentialist objections sometimes rest on the belief that persons with identical nuclear DNA will be identical. This belief is mistaken. For one thing, the imprinting of the DNA of parent and child might differ, resulting in phenotypic differences even though they have the same DNA. Even if the imprinting is the same, the parent and child will be exposed to different environments *in utero* and will be raised in different social environments. Different environments can result in different outlooks, ambitions, and life choices. In addition, cloning does not duplicate the brain. As a child's brain develops, neural connections are made in response to environmental stimuli. Different stimuli result in different patterns of connections. The child's brain will differ in many ways from the parent's.

Some authors who put forward these consequentialist objections acknowledge that the parent and child will not be identical. However, they hold that there will be a widespread *perception* that the parent and child are identical, based on the mistaken belief that people with identical nuclear DNA are identical, and that this perception will cause the harm in question. In reply, it is difficult to predict what people's perceptions will be when and if reproductive cloning becomes safe and feasible. That might be some distance into the future. Perhaps by then many people will have come to understand that genes alone do not

determine who one is. If there is a concern that some infertile couples who use cloning might expect the child to follow in the footsteps of the parent, this concern could be addressed by means of prepregnancy counselling. Psychological counselling is already widely used in preparing infertile couples for various methods of assisted reproduction. Couples planning to use cloning could be counselled about the psychosocial dimensions of this method of procreation, including a possible tendency to assume, erroneously, that genetics determine who the child will be.

There is an even more serious problem with this objection, a problem that all versions of the objection that have been put forward share in common. Namely, the objection focuses exclusively on harms to the child, without consideration of benefits to the child. It makes this mistake precisely because it overlooks the fact that without the cloning the child in question would not exist. If one holds that bringing a child into existence through cloning can result in harms to her, then one must also hold that bringing a child into existence through cloning can result in benefits to her. It would be arbitrary to make one claim but deny the other. In assessing the objection, we need to consider the benefits as well as the harms and there would be benefits in the infertility cases. After all, cloning gives the child a life. Life generally is a good thing. It is expected that the child will experience pleasures associated with being alive and that she will have many good experiences. Moreover, what counts in a consequentialist argument is the overall balance of harms and benefits, and it is reasonable to expect that the benefits are going to outweigh the harms—that the child is going to have a good life on balance. If the child benefits on balance, then no wrong is done in creating her, at least as far as harms and benefits are concerned.

Perhaps the opponents of cloning will claim that cloning is wrong because *some* harms will occur, although admittedly not a net harm. However, the claim that it is wrong to create children who will experience some harms, although not a net harm, leads to unacceptable conclusions. We would have to say, for example, that it is wrong for minorities who are subject to discrimination to have children because the children would experience harms caused by discrimination. Surely, this would be an incorrect conclusion. The objection amounts to saying that it is wrong to procreate when some ideal involving freedom from harm cannot be met. But there is no obligation to have children only if their lives will be free from harm, as this counterexample illustrates.

Deontological Objections

Deontological child-centred objections hold that creating a child through cloning amounts to treating her with insufficient respect. This might be expressed in various ways. Some claim that the child has a *right* to a unique genetic make-up, or a *right* to ignorance of the effect of one's genome on one's future. Others assert that cloning violates the Kantian categorical imperative by treating the child as a mere means. In reply, several points can be made. First, merely asserting that there is a right to a unique genetic make-up does not make it convincing, much less true, that there is such a right. An argument is needed supporting the claim that there is such a right, but opponents of reproductive cloning have not provided a successful argument for this. In the absence of a justification for the claim that there is such a right, the claim should be rejected. Second, to create a child through cloning can be consistent with respect for persons. It can be an instance of treating another as an end in herself and not as a mere means. We can imagine that the couple has purposes such that, in creating the child, they are not using her as a mere means but are acting, in part at least, in order to give her a life that will be her own. Third, in making a judgement about whether a child is treated with disrespect, it is not enough to look only at the technique of creation. It is also necessary to look at how the child is treated after she is born. Suppose she is brought into a loving family, with parents who nurture her, foster her discovery of her own interests and talents, and help her develop her autonomy as she grows older. In that scenario, the child is treated with respect. To put it differently, the problem with the objections that appeal to the categorical imperative is that they commit the fallacy of assuming that every case would be an instance of the worst case scenario—that every case would involve using the child as a mere means. This assumption seems rather extreme, and it is not reasonable.

Consequences for Society

Let us consider the objections that focus on adverse consequences for society. These too are expressed in various ways. It is argued that cloning and designing our children will transform procreation into a process similar to manufacturing, thereby altering the attitudes of parents toward their children and harming society. Another version is the argument that abuses might occur if cloning is used by totalitarian regimes or other unscrupulous persons. In reply, when these various objections are applied to the specific context of helping infertile couples, they lose whatever persuasiveness they might initially have had. The purpose of cloning in these cases is not to choose the characteristics of the child, but to have a genetically related child. There is no genetic manipulation to make the child "better" in some sense. In this context, cloning is not about designing the child. It is about helping the couple experience the personal meaning that procreation can have when it involves having genetically related children. If there were a plausible concern that a widespread practice of cloning would be harmful to society, there would be a middle ground that we could take. Cloning could be restricted to a relatively small number of cases, such as cases involving infertile couples. In that event it would be doubtful that the particular adverse consequences in question would occur.

Teleological Arguments

Finally, there are teleological objections. These too can be expressed in several ways. It is claimed that cloning is contrary to human dignity or contrary to the essence of being human. These objections are based on the view that humans have a natural essence or telos which they are meant to fulfil or strive for in order to be genuinely human. It is claimed that cloning prevents a human from achieving that essence and therefore it is contrary to human dignity.

In reply, several points are worth noting. First, within secular bioethics, teleological theories have become suspect, and for good reason. Teleological world views have been displaced by our scientific understanding of the world. Science gives us ways of understanding the workings of living organisms without appeal to a telos. One can see the consequences of this when one looks at secular bioethics. Approaches such as casuistry and principalism are widely discussed, and teleology is rarely mentioned. Second, even if one accepts a teleological world view, there are serious problems in specifying what the essence of a human is and in achieving a consensus on this matter.

Conclusion

None of the objections to human reproductive cloning discussed above appear to provide good reasons for claiming that cloning is wrong in the cases considered. The objections fail and therefore do not [outweigh] the procreative freedom of infertile couples to use cloning in the cases considered. Assuming these are the main objections, it appears that reproductive cloning would be ethically justifiable in at least some cases involving infertile couples.

Section 3: Surrogate Pregnancy

Surrogate Motherhood as Prenatal Adoption

Bonnie Steinbock

Steinbock reviews the "Baby M" case and maintains that the court decision was inconsistent in considering the best interest of the child. The aim of legislation, she claims, should be to minimize potential harms and prevent cases like that of Baby M from happening again. This can be so only if surrogacy is not intrinsically wrong.

This leads Steinbock to examine three lines of argument. She contends that neither paternalism of the sort outlined by Gerald Dworkin (see Chapter 1) nor such considerations as the threats of exploitation, loss of dignity, or harm to the child are adequate to show that surrogacy is inherently objectionable. In Steinbock's view, regulating surrogacy—and protecting liberty—is preferable to prohibiting it.

The recent case of "Baby M" has brought surrogate motherhood to the forefront of American attention. Ultimately, whether we permit or prohibit surrogacy depends on what we take to be good reasons for preventing people from acting as they wish. A growing number of people want to be, or hire, surrogates; are there legitimate reasons to prevent them? Apart from its intrinsic interest, the issue of surrogate motherhood provides us with an opportunity to examine different justifications for limiting individual freedom.

In the first section, I examine the Baby M case, and the lessons it offers. In the second section, I examine claims that surrogacy is ethically unacceptable because it is exploitive, inconsistent with human dignity, or harmful to the children born of such arrangements. I conclude that these reasons justify restrictions on surrogate contracts, rather than an outright ban.

From Bonnie Steinbock, "Surrogate Motherhood as Prenatal Adoption," *Law, Medicine and Health Care* 16, no. 1 (1988): 44–50. (Most notes omitted.)

I. Baby M

Mary Beth Whitehead, a married mother of two, agreed to be inseminated with the sperm of William Stern, and to give up the child to him for a fee of $10,000. The baby (whom Mrs. Whitehead named Sara, and the Sterns named Melissa) was born on March 27, 1986. Three days later, Mrs. Whitehead took her home from the hospital, and turned her over to the Sterns.

Then Mrs. Whitehead changed her mind. She went to the Sterns' home, distraught, and pleaded to have the baby temporarily. Afraid that she would kill herself, the Sterns agreed. The next week, Mrs. Whitehead informed the Sterns that she had decided to keep the child, and threatened to leave the country if court action was taken.

At that point, the situation deteriorated into a cross between the Keystone Kops and Nazi storm troopers. Accompanied by five policemen, the Sterns went to the Whitehead residence armed with a court order giving them temporary custody of the child. Mrs. Whitehead managed to slip the baby out of a window to her husband, and the following morning the Whiteheads fled with the child to Florida, where Mrs. Whitehead's parents lived. During the next three months, the Whiteheads lived in roughly twenty different hotels, motels, and homes to avoid apprehension. From time to time, Mrs. Whitehead telephoned Mr. Stern to discuss the matter: He taped these conversations on advice of counsel. Mrs. Whitehead threatened to kill herself, to kill the child, and falsely to accuse Mr. Stern of sexually molesting her older daughter.

At the end of July 1986, while Mrs. Whitehead was hospitalized with a kidney infection, Florida police raided her mother's home, knocking her down, and seized the child. Baby M was placed in the custody of Mr. Stern, and the Whiteheads returned to New Jersey, where they attempted to regain custody. After a long and emotional court battle, Judge Harvey R. Sorkow ruled on March 31, 1987, that the surrogacy contract was valid, and that specific performance was justified in the best interests of the child. Immediately after reading his decision, he called the Sterns into his chambers so that Mr. Stern's wife, Dr. Elizabeth Stern, could legally adopt the child.

This outcome was unexpected and unprecedented. Most commentators had thought that a court would be unlikely to order a reluctant surrogate to give up an infant merely on the basis of a contract. Indeed, if Mrs. Whitehead had never surrendered the child to the Sterns, but had simply taken her home and kept her there, the outcome undoubtedly would have been different. It is also likely that Mrs. Whitehead's failure to obey the initial custody order angered Judge Sorkow, and affected his decision.

The decision was appealed to the New Jersey Supreme Court, which issued its decision on February 3, 1988. Writing for a unanimous court, Chief Justice Wilentz reversed the lower court's ruling that the surrogacy contract was valid. The court held that a surrogacy contract which provides money for the surrogate mother, and which includes her irrevocable agreement to surrender her child at birth, is invalid and unenforceable. Since the contract was invalid, Mrs. Whitehead did not relinquish, nor were there any other grounds for terminating, her parental rights. Therefore, the adoption of Baby M by Mrs. Stern was improperly granted, and Mrs. Whitehead remains the child's legal mother.

The Court further held that the issue of custody is determined solely by the child's best interests, and it agreed with the lower court that it was in Melissa's best interests to remain with the Sterns. However, Mrs. Whitehead, as Baby M's legal as well as natural mother, is entitled to have her own interest in visitation considered. The determination of what kind of visitation rights should be granted to her, and under what conditions, was remanded to the trial court.

The distressing details of this case have led many people to reject surrogacy altogether. Do we really want police officers wrenching infants from their mothers' arms, and prolonged custody battles when surrogates find they are unable to surrender their children, as agreed? Advocates of surrogacy say that to reject the practice wholesale, because of one unfortunate instance, is an example of a "hard case" making bad policy. Opponents reply that it is entirely reasonable to focus on the worst potential outcomes when deciding public policy. Everyone can agree on at least one thing: This particular case seems to have been mismanaged from start to finish, and could serve as a manual of how not to arrange a surrogate birth.

First, it is now clear that Mary Beth Whitehead was not a suitable candidate for surrogate motherhood. Her ambivalence about giving up the child was recognized early on, although this information was not passed on to the Sterns.[1] Second, she had contact with the baby after birth, which is usually avoided in "successful" cases. Typically, the adoptive mother is actively involved in the pregnancy, often serving as the pregnant woman's coach in labor. At birth, the baby is given to the adoptive, not the biological, mother. The joy of the adoptive parents in holding their child serves both to promote their bonding, and to lessen the pain of separation of the biological mother.

At Mrs. Whitehead's request, no one at the hospital was aware of the surrogacy arrangement. She and her husband appeared as the proud parents of "Sara Elizabeth Whitehead," the name on her birth certificate. Mrs. Whitehead held her baby, nursed her, and took her home from the hospital—just as she would have done in a normal pregnancy and birth. Not surprisingly, she thought of Sara as her child, and she fought with every weapon at her disposal, honorable and dishonorable, to prevent her being taken away. She can hardly be blamed for doing so.[2]

Why did Dr. Stern, who supposedly had a very good relation with Mrs. Whitehead before the birth, not act as her labor coach? One possibility is that Mrs. Whitehead, ambivalent about giving up her baby, did not want Dr. Stern involved. At her request, the

Sterns' visits to the hospital to see the newborn baby were unobtrusive. It is also possible that Dr. Stern was ambivalent about having a child. The original idea of hiring a surrogate was not hers, but her husband's. It was Mr. Stern who felt a "compelling" need to have a child related to him by blood, having lost all his relatives to the Nazis.

Furthermore, Dr. Stern was not infertile, as was stated in the surrogacy agreement. Rather, in 1979 she was diagnosed by two eye specialists as suffering from optic neuritis, which meant that she "probably" had multiple sclerosis. (This was confirmed by all four experts who testified.) Normal conception was ruled out by the Sterns in late 1982, when a medical colleague told Dr. Stern that his wife, a victim of multiple sclerosis, had suffered a temporary paralysis during pregnancy. "We decided the risk wasn't worth it," Mr. Stern said.

Mrs. Whitehead's lawyer, Harold J. Cassidy, dismissed the suggestion that Dr. Stern's "mildest case" of multiple sclerosis determined their decision to seek a surrogate. He noted that she was not even treated for multiple sclerosis until after the Baby M dispute had started. "It's almost as though it's an afterthought," he said.

Judge Sorkow deemed the decision to avoid conception "medically reasonable and understandable." The Supreme Court did not go so far, noting that "her anxiety appears to have exceeded the actual risk, which current medical authorities assess as minimal." Nonetheless the court acknowledged that her anxiety, including fears that pregnancy might precipitate blindness and paraplegia, was "quite real." Certainly, even a woman who wants a child very much, may reasonably wish to avoid becoming blind and paralyzed as a result of pregnancy. Yet is it believable that a woman who really wanted a child would decide against pregnancy *solely* on the basis of *someone else's* medical experience? Would she not consult at least one specialist on her *own* medical condition before deciding it wasn't worth the risk? The conclusion that she was at best ambivalent about bearing a child seems irresistible.

This possibility conjures up many people's worst fears about surrogacy: That prosperous women, who do not want to interrupt their careers, will use poor and educationally disadvantaged women to bear their children. I will return shortly to the question of whether this is exploitive. The issue here is psychological: What kind of mother is Dr. Stern likely to

be? If she is unwilling to undergo pregnancy, with its discomforts, inconveniences, and risks, will she be willing to make the considerable sacrifices which good parenting requires? Mrs. Whitehead's ability to be a good mother was repeatedly questioned during the trial. She was portrayed as immature, untruthful, hysterical, overly identified with her children, and prone to smothering their independence. Even if all this is true—and I think that Mrs. Whitehead's inadequacies were exaggerated—Dr. Stern may not be such a prize either. The choice for Baby M may have been between a highly strung, emotional, over-involved mother, and a remote, detached, even cold one.

The assessment of Mrs. Whitehead's ability to be a good mother was biased by the middle-class prejudices of the judge and mental health officials who testified. Mrs. Whitehead left school at 15, and is not conversant with the latest theories on child rearing: She made the egregious error of giving Sara teddy bears to play with, instead of the more "age-appropriate," expert-approved pans and spoons. She proved to be a total failure at patty-cake. If this is evidence of parental inadequacy, we're all in danger of losing our children.

The Supreme Court felt that Mrs. Whitehead was "rather harshly judged" and acknowledged the possibility that the trial court was wrong in its initial award of custody. Nevertheless, it affirmed Judge Sorkow's decision to allow the Sterns to retain custody, as being in Melissa's best interests. George Annas disagrees with the "best interests" approach. He points out that Judge Sorkow awarded temporary custody of Baby M to the Sterns in May 1986 without giving the Whiteheads notice or an opportunity to obtain legal representation. That was a serious wrong and injustice to the Whiteheads. To allow the Sterns to keep the child compounds the original unfairness: "...justice requires that reasonable consideration be given to returning Baby M to the permanent custody of the Whiteheads."

But a child is not a possession, to be returned to the rightful owner. It is not fairness to all parties that should determine a child's fate, but what is best for her. As Chief Justice Wilentz rightly stated, "The child's interest comes first: We will not punish it for judicial errors, assuming any were made."

Subsequent events have substantiated the claim that giving custody to the Sterns was in Melissa's best interests. After losing custody, Mrs. Whitehead, whose husband had undergone a vasectomy, became pregnant by another man. She divorced her husband

and married Dean R. Gould last November. These developments indicate that the Whiteheads were not able to offer a stable home, although the argument can be made that their marriage might have survived, but for the strains introduced by the court battle, and the loss of Baby M. But even if Judge Sorkow had no reason to prefer the Sterns to the Whiteheads back in May 1986, he was still right to give the Sterns custody in March 1987. To take her away then, at nearly eighteen months of age, from the only parents she had ever known, would have been disruptive, cruel, and unfair to her.

Annas's preference for a just solution is premised partly on his belief that there is no "best interest" solution to this "tragic custody case." I take it that he means that however custody is resolved, Baby M is the loser. Either way, she will be deprived of one parent. However, a best interests solution is not a perfect solution.

It is simply the solution which is on balance best for the child, given the realities of the situation. Applying this standard, Judge Sorkow was right to give the Sterns custody, and the Supreme Court was right to uphold the decision.

The best interests argument is based on the assumption that Mr. Stern has at least a *prima facie* claim to Baby M. We certainly would not consider allowing a stranger who kidnapped a baby, and managed to elude the police for a year, to retain custody on the grounds that he was providing a good home to a child who had known no other parent. However, the Baby M case is not analogous. First, Mr. Stern is Baby M's biological father and, as such, has at least some claim to raise her, which no non-parental kidnapper has. Second, Mary Beth Whitehead agreed to give him their baby. Unlike the miller's daughter in *Rumpelstiltskin*, the fairy tale to which the Baby M case is sometimes compared, she was not forced into the agreement. Because both Mary Beth Whitehead and Mr. Stern have *prima facie* claims to Baby M, the decision as to who should raise her should be based on her present best interests. Therefore we must, regretfully, tolerate the injustice to Mrs. Whitehead, and try to avoid such problems in the future.

It is unfortunate that the Court did not decide the issue of visitation on the same basis as custody. By declaring Mrs. Whitehead Gould the legal mother, and maintaining that she is entitled to visitation, the Court has prolonged the fight over Baby M. It is hard to see how this can be in her best interests. This is no ordinary divorce case, where the child has a relation with both parents which it is desirable to maintain. As Mr. Stern said at the start of the court hearing to determine visitation, "Melissa has a right to grow and be happy and not be torn between two parents."

The court's decision was well-meaning but internally inconsistent. Out of concern for the best interests of the child, it granted the Sterns custody. At the same time, by holding Mrs. Whitehead Gould to be the legal mother, with visitation rights, it precluded precisely what is most in Melissa's interest, a resolution of the situation. Further, the decision leaves open the distressing possibility that a Baby M situation could happen again. Legislative efforts should be directed toward ensuring that this worse-case scenario never occurs.

II. Should Surrogacy Be Prohibited?

On June 27, 1988, Michigan became the first state to outlaw commercial contracts for women to bear children for others. Yet making a practice illegal does not necessarily make it go away: Witness black market adoption. The legitimate concerns which support a ban on surrogacy might be better served by careful regulation. However, some practices, such as slavery, are ethically unacceptable, regardless of how carefully regulated they are. Let us consider the arguments that surrogacy is intrinsically unacceptable.

A. Paternalistic Arguments

These arguments against surrogacy take the form of protecting a potential surrogate from a choice she may later regret. As an argument for banning surrogacy, as opposed to providing safeguards to ensure that contracts are freely and knowledgeably undertaken, this is a form of paternalism.

At one time, the characterization of a prohibition as paternalistic was a sufficient reason to reject it. The pendulum has swung back, and many people are willing to accept at least some paternalistic restrictions on freedom. Gerald Dworkin points out that even Mill made one exception to his otherwise absolute rejection of paternalism: He thought that no one should be allowed to sell himself into slavery, because to do so would be to destroy his future autonomy.

This provides a narrow principle to justify some paternalistic interventions. To preserve freedom in the long run, we give up the freedom to make certain choices, those which have results which are "far-reaching, potentially dangerous and irreversible." An example would be a ban on the sale of crack. Virtually everyone who uses crack becomes addicted and, once addicted, a slave to its use. We reasonably and willingly give up our freedom to buy the drug, to protect our ability to make free decisions in the future.

Can a Dworkinian argument be made to rule out surrogacy agreements? Admittedly, the decision to give up a child is permanent, and may have disastrous effects on the surrogate mother. However, many decisions may have long-term, disastrous effects (e.g., postponing childbirth for a career, having an abortion, giving a child up for adoption). Clearly we do not want the state to make decisions for us in all these matters. Dworkin's argument is rightly restricted to paternalistic interferences which protect the individual's autonomy or ability to make decisions in the future. Surrogacy does not involve giving up one's autonomy, which distinguishes it from both the crack and selling-oneself-into-slavery examples. Respect for individual freedom requires us to permit people to make choices which they may later regret.

B. Moral Objections

Four main moral objections to surrogacy were outlined in the Warnock Report.

1. It is inconsistent with human dignity that a woman should use her uterus for financial profit.

2. To deliberately become pregnant with the intention of giving up the child distorts the relationship between mother and child.

3. Surrogacy is degrading because it amounts to child-selling.

4. Since there are some risks attached to pregnancy, no woman ought to be asked to undertake pregnancy for another in order to earn money.

We must all agree that a practice which exploits people or violates human dignity is immoral. However, it is not clear that surrogacy is guilty on either count.

1. Exploitation. The mere fact that pregnancy is *risky* does not make surrogate agreements exploitive, and therefore morally wrong. People often do risky things for money; why should the line be drawn at undergoing pregnancy? The usual response is to compare surrogacy and kidney-selling.

The selling of organs is prohibited because of the potential for coercion and exploitation. But why should kidney-selling be viewed as intrinsically coercive? A possible explanation is that no one would do it, unless driven by poverty. The choice is both forced and dangerous, and hence coercive.

The situation is quite different in the case of the race car driver or stuntman. We do not think that they are *forced* to perform risky activities for money: They freely choose to do so. Unlike selling one's kidneys, these are activities which we can understand (intellectually, anyway) someone choosing to do. Movie stuntmen, for example, often enjoy their work, and derive satisfaction from doing it well. Of course they "do it for the money," in the sense that they would not do it without compensation; few people are willing to work "for free." The element of coercion is missing, however, because they enjoy the job, despite the risks, and could do something else if they chose.

The same is apparently true of most surrogates. "They choose the surrogate role primarily because the fee provides a better economic opportunity than alternative occupations, but also because they enjoy being pregnant and the respect and attention that it draws." Some may derive a feeling of self-worth from an act they regard as highly altruistic: providing a couple with a child they could not otherwise have. If these motives are present, it is far from clear that the surrogate is being exploited. Indeed, it seems objectionably paternalistic to insist that she is.

2. Human dignity. It may be argued that even if womb-leasing is not necessarily exploitive, it should still be rejected as inconsistent with human dignity. But why? As John Harris points out, hair, blood and other tissue is often donated or sold; what is so special about the uterus?

Human dignity is more plausibly invoked in the strongest argument against surrogacy, namely, that it is the sale of a child. Children are not property, nor can they be bought or sold. It could be argued that surrogacy is wrong because it is analogous to slavery, and so is inconsistent with human dignity.

However, there are important differences between slavery and a surrogate agreement. The child born of a surrogate is not treated cruelly or deprived of freedom or resold; none of the things which make slavery so awful are part of surrogacy. Still, it may be thought that simply putting a market value on a child is wrong. Human life has intrinsic value; it is literally priceless.

Arrangements which ignore this violate our deepest notions of the value of human life. It is profoundly disturbing to hear the boyfriend of a surrogate say, quite candidly in a television documentary on surrogacy, "We're in it for the money."

Judge Sorkow accepted the premise that producing a child for money denigrates human dignity, but he denied that this happens in a surrogate agreement. Mrs. Whitehead was not paid for the surrender of the child to the father: She was paid for her willingness to be impregnated and carry Mr. Stern's child to term. The child, once born, is his biological child. "He cannot purchase what is already his."

This is misleading, and not merely because Baby M is as much Mrs. Whitehead's child as Mr. Stern's. It is misleading because it glosses over the fact that the surrender of the child was part—indeed, the whole point—of the agreement. If the surrogate were paid merely for being willing to be impregnated and carrying the child to term, then she would fulfill the contract upon giving birth. She could take the money *and* the child. Mr. Stern did not agree to pay Mrs. Whitehead merely to *have* his child, but to provide him with a child. The New Jersey Supreme Court held that this violated New Jersey's laws prohibiting the payment or acceptance of money in connection with adoption.

One way to remove the taint of baby-selling would be to limit payment to medical expenses associated with the birth or incurred by the surrogate during pregnancy (as is allowed in many jurisdictions, including New Jersey, in ordinary adoptions). Surrogacy could be seen, not as baby-selling, but as a form of adoption. Nowhere did the Supreme Court find any legal prohibition against surrogacy when there is no payment, and when the surrogate has the right to change her mind and keep the child. However, this solution effectively prohibits surrogacy, since few women would become surrogates solely for self-fulfillment or reasons of altruism.

The question, then, is whether we can reconcile paying the surrogate, beyond her medical expenses, with the idea of surrogacy as prenatal adoption. We can do this by separating the terms of the agreement, which include surrendering the infant at birth to the biological father, from the justification for payment. The payment should be seen as compensation for the risks, sacrifice, and discomfort the surrogate undergoes during pregnancy. This means that if, through no fault on the part of the surrogate, the baby is stillborn, she should still be paid in full, since she has kept her part

of the bargain. (By contrast, in the Stern–Whitehead agreement, Mrs. Whitehead was to receive only $1,000 for a stillbirth.) If, on the other hand, the surrogate changes her mind and decides to keep the child, she would break the agreement, and would not be entitled to any fee, or compensation for expenses incurred during pregnancy.

C. The Right of Privacy

Most commentators who invoke the right of privacy do so in support of surrogacy. However, George Annas makes the novel argument that the right to rear a child you have borne is also a privacy right, which cannot be prospectively waived. He says:

> *[Judge Sorkow] grudgingly concedes that [Mrs. Whitehead] could not prospectively give up her right to have an abortion during pregnancy.... This would be an intolerable restriction on her liberty and under Roe v. Wade, the state has no constitutional authority to enforce a contract that prohibits her from terminating her pregnancy.*
>
> *But why isn't the same logic applicable to the right to rear a child you have given birth to? Her constitutional rights to rear the child she has given birth to are even stronger since they involve even more intimately, and over a lifetime, her privacy rights to reproduce and rear a child in a family setting.*

Absent a compelling state interest (such as protecting a child from unfit parents), it certainly would be an intolerable invasion of privacy for the state to take children from their parents. But Baby M has two parents, both of whom now want her. It is not clear why only people who can give birth (i.e., women) should enjoy the right to rear their children.

Moreover, we do allow women to give their children up for adoption after birth. The state enforces those agreements, even if the natural mother, after the prescribed waiting period, changes her mind. Why should the right to rear a child be unwaivable before, but not after birth? Why should the state have the constitutional authority to uphold postnatal, but not prenatal, adoption agreements? It is not clear why birth should affect the waivability of this right, or have the constitutional significance which Annas attributes to it.

Nevertheless, there are sound moral and policy, if not constitutional, reasons to provide a postnatal waiting period in surrogate agreements. As the Baby M case makes painfully clear, the surrogate may underestimate the bond created by gestation, and the emotional trauma caused by relinquishing the baby. Compassion requires that we acknowledge these feelings, and not deprive a woman of the baby she has carried because, before conception, she underestimated the strength of her feelings for it. Providing a waiting period, as in ordinary postnatal adoptions, will help protect women from making irrevocable mistakes, without banning the practice.

Some may object that this gives too little protection to the prospective adoptive parents. They cannot be sure that the baby is theirs until the waiting period is over. While this is hard on them, a similar burden is placed on other adoptive parents. If the absence of a guarantee serves to discourage people from entering surrogacy agreements, that is not necessarily a bad thing, given all the risks inherent in such contracts. In addition, this requirement would make stricter screening and counseling of surrogates essential, a desirable side effect.

D. Harm to Others

Paternalistic and moral objections to surrogacy do not seem to justify an outright ban. What about the effect on the offspring of such contracts? We do not yet have solid data on the effects of being a "surrogate child." Any claim that surrogacy creates psychological problems in the children is purely speculative. But what if we did discover that such children have deep feelings of worthlessness from learning that their natural mothers deliberately created them with the intention of giving them away? Might we ban surrogacy as posing an unacceptable risk of psychological harm to the resulting children?

Feelings of worthlessness are harmful. They can prevent people from living happy, fulfilling lives. However, a surrogate child, even one whose life is miserable because of these feelings, cannot claim to have been harmed by the surrogate agreement. Without the agreement, the child would never have existed. Unless she is willing to say that her life is not worth living because of these feelings, that she would be better off never having been born, she cannot claim to have been harmed by being born of a surrogate mother.

Children can be *wronged* by being brought into existence, even if they are not, strictly speaking, *harmed*. They are wronged if they are deprived of the minimally decent existence to which all citizens are entitled. We owe it to our children to see that they are not born with such serious impairments that their most

basic interests will be doomed in advance. If being born to a surrogate is a handicap of this magnitude, comparable to being born blind or deaf or severely mentally retarded, then surrogacy can be seen as wronging the offspring. This would be a strong reason against permitting such contracts. However, it does not seem likely. Probably the problems arising from surrogacy will be like those faced by adopted children and children whose parents divorce. Such problems are not trivial, but neither are they so serious that the child's very existence can be seen as wrongful.

If surrogate children are neither harmed nor wronged by surrogacy, it may seem that the argument for banning surrogacy on grounds of its harmfulness to the offspring evaporates. After all, if the children themselves have no cause for complaint, how can anyone else claim to reject it on their behalf? Yet it seems extremely counter-intuitive to suggest that the risk of emotional damage to the children born of such arrangements is not even relevant to our deliberations. It seems quite reasonable and proper—even morally obligatory—for policymakers to think about the possible detrimental effects of new reproductive technologies, and to reject those likely to create physically or emotionally damaged people. The explanation for this must involve the idea that it is wrong to bring people into the world in a harmful condition, even if they are not, strictly speaking, harmed by having been brought into existence. Should evidence emerge that surrogacy produces children with serious psychological problems, that would be a strong reason for banning the practice.

There is some evidence on the effect of surrogacy on the other children of the surrogate mother. One woman reported that her daughter, now 17, who was 11 at the time of the surrogate birth, "...is still having problems with what I did, and as a result she is still angry with me." She explains, "Nobody told me that a child could bond with a baby while you're still pregnant. I didn't realize then that all the times she listened to his heartbeat and felt his legs kick that she was becoming attached to him."

A less sentimental explanation is possible. It seems likely that her daughter, seeing one child given away, was fearful that the same might be done to her. We can expect anxiety and resentment on the part of children whose mothers give away a brother or sister. The psychological harm to these children is clearly relevant to a determination of whether surrogacy is contrary to public policy. At the same time, it should be remembered that many things, including divorce, remarriage, and even moving to a new neighborhood, create anxiety and resentment in children. We should not use the effect on children as an excuse for banning a practice we find bizarre or offensive.

Conclusion

There are many reasons to be extremely cautious of surrogacy. I cannot imagine becoming a surrogate, nor would I advise anyone else to enter into a contract so fraught with peril. But the fact that a practice is risky, foolish, or even morally distasteful is not sufficient reason to outlaw it. It would be better for the state to regulate the practice, and minimize

the potential for harm, without infringing on the liberty of citizens.

Notes

1. Had the Sterns been informed of the psychologist's concerns as to Mrs. Whitehead's suitability to be a surrogate, they might have ended the arrangement, costing the Infertility Center its fee. As Chief Justice Wilentz said, "It is apparent that the profit motive got the better of the Infertility Center." In the matter of Baby M, Supreme Court of New Jersey, A–39, at 45.
2. "[W]e think it is expecting something well beyond normal human capabilities to suggest that this mother should have parted with her newly born infant without a struggle…. We…cannot conceive of any other case where a perfectly fit mother was expected to surrender her newly born infant, perhaps forever, and was then told she was a bad mother because she did not." *Id.* at 79.

Is Women's Labor a Commodity?

Elizabeth S. Anderson

Anderson argues that commercial surrogacy should not be allowed. The practice of paying women to be surrogate mothers involves a "commodification" of both children and women. It treats women and their children as things to be used, instead of as persons deserving respect. Hence, surrogacy contracts should be unenforceable, and those who arrange them should be subject to criminal penalties.

Anderson holds that the introduction of market values and norms into a situation previously based on respect, consideration, and unconditional love has the effect of harming children and degrading and exploiting women. The values of the market contribute to a tendency to view children as property. When this happens, they are no longer valued unconditionally (as is the case with parental love), but are valued only because they possess characteristics with a market value.

Market values require that surrogate mothers repress whatever parental love they may feel for their children. Hence, the feelings of women are manipulated, degraded, and denied legitimacy. Further, women are exploited by having the personal feelings that incline them to become surrogates turned into something that can be marketed as part of a commercial enterprise.

In the past few years the practice of commercial surrogate motherhood has gained notoriety as a method for acquiring children. A commercial

From Elizabeth S. Anderson, "Is Women's Labor a Commodity?" *Philosophy & Public Affairs* 19, no. 1 (1990): 71–87, 91–92. Copyright © John Wiley & Sons-Blackwell. Reprinted by permission. (References omitted.)

surrogate mother is anyone who is paid money to bear a child for other people and terminate her parental rights, so that the others may raise the child as exclusively their own. The growth of commercial surrogacy has raised with new urgency a class of concerns regarding the proper scope of the market. Some critics have objected to commercial surrogacy on the ground that it improperly treats children and women's reproductive capacities as commodities. The prospect of reducing children to consumer durables and women to baby factories surely inspires revulsion. But are there good reasons behind the revulsion? And is this an accurate description of what commercial surrogacy implies? This article offers a theory about what things are properly regarded as commodities which supports the claim that commercial surrogacy constitutes an unconscionable commodification of children and of women's reproductive capacities.

What Is a Commodity?

The modern market can be characterized in terms of the legal and social norms by which it governs the production, exchange, and enjoyment of commodities. To say that something is properly regarded as a commodity is to claim that the norms of the market are appropriate for regulating its production, exchange, and enjoyment. To the extent that moral principles or ethical ideals preclude the application of market norms to a good, we may say that the good is not a (proper) commodity.

Why should we object to the application of a market norm to the production or distribution of a good? One reason may be that to produce or distribute the good in accordance with the norm is to *fail to value it in an appropriate way.* Consider, for example, a standard Kantian argument against slavery, or the commodification of persons. Slaves are treated in accordance with the market norm that owners may use commodities to satisfy their own interests without regard for the interests of the commodities themselves. To treat a person without regard for her interests is to fail to respect her. But slaves are persons who may not be merely used in this fashion, since as rational beings they possess a dignity which commands respect. In Kantian theory, the problem with slavery is that it treats beings worthy of *respect* as if they were worthy merely of *use.* "Respect" and "use" in this context denote what we may call different *modes of valuation....*

These considerations support a general account of the sorts of things which are appropriately regarded as commodities. Commodities are those things which are properly treated in accordance with the norms of the modern market. We can question the application of market norms to the production, distribution, and enjoyment of a good by appealing to ethical ideals which support arguments that the good should be valued in

some other way than use. Arguments of the latter sort claim that to allow certain market norms to govern our treatment of a thing expresses a mode of valuation not worthy of it. If the thing is to be valued appropriately, its production, exchange, and enjoyment must be removed from market norms and embedded in a different set of social relationships.

The Case of Commercial Surrogacy

Let us now consider the practice of commercial surrogate motherhood in the light of this theory of commodities. Surrogate motherhood as a commercial enterprise is based upon contracts involving three parties: the intended father, the broker, and the surrogate mother. The intended father agrees to pay a lawyer to find a suitable surrogate mother and make the requisite medical and legal arrangements for the conception and birth of the child, and for the transfer of legal custody to himself. The surrogate mother agrees to become impregnated with the intended father's sperm, to carry the resulting child to term, and to relinquish her parental rights to it, transferring custody to the father in return for a fee and medical expenses. Both she and her husband (if she has one) agree not to form a parent–child bond with her child and to do everything necessary to effect the transfer of the child to the intended father. At current market prices, the lawyer arranging the contract can expect to gross $15,000 from the contract, while the surrogate mother can expect a $10,000 fee.

The practice of commercial surrogacy has been defended on four main grounds. First, given the shortage of children available for adoption and the difficulty of qualifying as adoptive parents, it may represent the only hope for some people to be able to raise a family. Commercial surrogacy should be accepted as an effective means for realizing this highly significant good. Second, two fundamental human rights support commercial surrogacy: the right to procreate and freedom of contract. Fully informed autonomous adults should have the right to make whatever arrangements they wish for the use of their bodies and the reproduction of children, so long as the children themselves are not harmed. Third, the labor of the surrogate mother is said to be a labor of love. Her altruistic acts should be permitted and encouraged. Finally, it is argued that commercial surrogacy is no different in its ethical implications from many already accepted practices which separate genetic, gestational, and social parenting, such as artificial insemination by donor, adoption, wet-nursing and day care. Consistency demands that society accept this new practice as well.

In opposition to these claims, I shall argue that commercial surrogacy does raise new ethical issues, since it represents an invasion of the market into a new sphere of conduct, that of specifically women's labor—that is, the labor of carrying children to term in pregnancy. When women's labor is treated as a commodity, the women who perform it are degraded. Furthermore, commercial surrogacy degrades children by reducing their status to that of commodities. Let us consider each of the goods of concern in surrogate motherhood—the child, and women's reproductive labor—to see how the commercialization of parenthood affects people's regard for them.

Children as Commodities

The most fundamental calling of parents to their children is to love them. Children are to be loved and cherished by their parents, not to be used or manipulated by them for merely personal advantage. Parental love can be understood as a passionate, unconditional commitment to nurture one's child, providing it with the care, affection, and guidance it needs to develop its capacities to maturity. This understanding of the way parents should value their children informs our interpretation of parental rights over their children. Parents' rights over their children are trusts, which they must always exercise for the sake of the child. This is not to deny that parents have their own aspirations in raising children. But the child's interests beyond subsistence are not definable independently of the flourishing of the family, which is the object of specifically parental aspirations. The proper exercise of parental rights includes those acts which promote their shared life as a family, which realize the shared interests of the parents and the child.

The norms of parental love carry implications for the ways other people should treat the relationship between parents and their children. If children are to be loved by their parents, then others should not attempt to compromise the integrity of parental love or work to suppress the emotions supporting the bond between parents and their children. If the rights to children should be understood as trusts, then if those rights are lost or relinquished, the duty of those in charge of transferring custody to others is to consult the best interests of the child.

Commercial surrogacy substitutes market norms for some of the norms of parental love. Most importantly, it requires us to understand parental rights no longer as trusts but as things more like property rights—that is, rights of use and disposal over the things owned. For in this practice the natural mother deliberately conceives a child with the intention of giving it up for material advantage. Her renunciation of parental responsibilities is not done for the child's sake, nor for the sake of fulfilling an interest she shares with the child, but typically for her own sake (and possibly, if "altruism" is a motive, for the intended parents' sakes). She and the couple who pay her to give up her parental rights over her child thus treat her rights as a kind of property right. They thereby treat the child itself as a kind of commodity, which may be properly bought and sold.

Commercial surrogacy insinuates the norms of commerce into the parental relationship in other ways. Whereas parental love is not supposed to be conditioned upon the child having particular characteristics, consumer demand is properly responsive to the characteristics of commodities. So the surrogate industry provides opportunities to adoptive couples to specify the height, I.Q., race, and other attributes of the surrogate mother, in the expectation that these traits will be passed on to the child. Since no industry assigns agents to look after the "interests" of its commodities, no one represents the child's interests in the surrogate industry. The surrogate agency promotes the adoptive parents' interests and not the child's interests where matters of custody are concerned. Finally, as the agent of the adoptive parents, the broker has the task of policing the surrogate (natural) mother's relationship to her child, using persuasion, money, and the threat of a lawsuit to weaken and destroy whatever parental love she may develop for her child.

All of these substitutions of market norms for parental norms represent ways of treating children as commodities which are degrading to them. Degradation occurs when something is treated in accordance with a lower mode of valuation than is proper to it. We value things not just "more" or "less," but in qualitatively higher and lower ways. To love or respect someone is to value her in a higher way than one would if one merely used her. Children are properly loved by their parents and respected by others. Since children are valued as mere use-objects by the mother and the surrogate agency when they are sold to others, and by the adoptive parents when they seek to conform the child's genetic makeup to their own wishes, commercial surrogacy degrades children insofar as it treats them as commodities.

One might argue that since the child is most likely to enter a loving home, no harm comes to it from permitting the natural mother to treat it as property. So the purchase and sale of infants is unobjectionable, at least from the point of view of children's interests. But the sale of an infant has an expressive significance which this argument fails to recognize. By engaging in the transfer of children by sale, all of the parties to the surrogate contract express a set of attitudes toward children which undermine the norms of parental love. They all agree in treating the ties between a natural mother and her children as properly loosened by a monetary incentive. Would it be any wonder if a child born of a surrogacy agreement feared resale by parents who have such an attitude? And a child who knew how anxious her parents were that she have the "right" genetic makeup might fear that her parents' love was contingent upon her expression of these characteristics.

The unsold children of surrogate mothers are also harmed by commercial surrogacy. The children of some surrogate mothers have reported their fears that they may be sold like their half-brother or half-sister, and express a sense of loss at being deprived of a sibling. Furthermore, the widespread acceptance of commercial surrogacy would psychologically threaten all children. For it would change the way children are valued by people (parents and surrogate brokers)—from being loved by their parents and respected by others, to being sometimes used as objects of commercial profit-making.

Proponents of commercial surrogacy have denied that the surrogate industry engages in the sale of children. For it is impossible to sell to someone what is already his own, and the child is already the father's own natural offspring. The payment to the surrogate mother is not for her child, but for her services in carrying it to term. The claim that the parties to the surrogate contract treat children as commodities, however, is based on the way they treat the *mother's* rights over her child. It is irrelevant that the natural father also has some rights over the child; what he pays for is exclusive rights to it. He would not pay her for the "service" of carrying the child to term if she refused to relinquish her parental rights to it. That the mother regards only her labor and not her child as requiring compensation is also irrelevant. No one

would argue that the baker does not treat his bread as property just because he sees the income from its sale as compensation for his labor and expenses and not for the bread itself, which he doesn't care to keep.

Defenders of commercial surrogacy have also claimed that it does not differ substantially from other already accepted parental practices. In the institutions of adoption and artificial insemination by donor (AID), it is claimed, we already grant parents the right to dispose of their children. But these practices differ in significant respects from commercial surrogacy. The purpose of adoption is to provide a means for placing children in families when their parents cannot or will not discharge their parental responsibilities. It is not a sphere for the existence of a supposed parental right to dispose of one's children for profit. Even AID does not sanction the sale of fully formed human beings. The semen donor sells only a product of his body, not his child, and does not initiate the act of conception.

Two developments might seem to undermine the claim that commercial surrogacy constitutes a degrading commerce in children. The first is technological: the prospect of transplanting a human embryo into the womb of a genetically unrelated woman. If commercial surrogacy used women only as gestational mothers and not as genetic mothers, and if it was thought that only genetic and not gestational parents could properly claim that a child was "theirs," then the child born of a surrogate mother would not be hers to sell in the first place. The second is a legal development: the establishment of the proposed "consent–intent" definition of parenthood. This would declare the legal parents of a child to be whoever consented to a procedure which leads to its birth, with the intent of assuming parental responsibilities for it. This rule would define away the problem of commerce in children by depriving the surrogate mother of any legal claim to her child at all, even if it was hers both genetically and gestationally.

There are good reasons, however, not to undermine the place of genetic and gestational ties in these ways. Consider first the place of genetic ties. By upholding a system of involuntary (genetic) ties of obligation among people, even when the adults among them prefer to divide their rights and obligations in other ways, we help to secure children's interests in having an assured place in the world, which is more firm than the wills of their parents. Unlike the consent–intent rule, the principle of respecting genetic ties does not make the obligation to care for those whom one has created (intentionally or not) contingent upon an arbitrary desire to do so. It thus provides children with a set of preexisting social sanctions which give them a more secure place in the world. The genetic principle also places the children in a far wider network of associations and obligations than the consent–intent rule sanctions. It supports the roles of grandparents and other relatives in the nurturing of children, and provides children with a possible focus of stability and an additional source of claims to care if their parents cannot sustain a well-functioning household.

In the next section I will defend the claims of gestational ties to children. To deny these claims, as commercial surrogacy does, is to deny the significance of reproductive labor to the mother who undergoes it and thereby to dehumanize and degrade the mother herself. Commercial surrogacy would be a corrupt practice even if it did not involve commerce in children.

Women's Labor as a Commodity

Commercial surrogacy attempts to transform what is specifically women's labor—the work of bringing forth children into the world—into a commodity. It does so by replacing the parental norms which usually govern the practice of gestating children with the economic norms which govern ordinary production processes. The application of commercial norms to women's labor reduces the surrogate mothers from persons worthy of respect and consideration to objects of mere use.

Respect and consideration are two distinct modes of valuation whose norms are violated by the practices of the surrogate industry. To respect a person is to treat her in accordance with principles she rationally accepts—principles consistent with the protection of her autonomy and her rational interests. To treat a person with consideration is to respond with sensitivity to her and to her emotional relations with others, refraining from manipulating or denigrating these for one's own purposes....

The application of economic norms to the sphere of women's labor violates women's claims to respect and consideration in three ways. First, by requiring the surrogate mother to repress whatever parental love she feels for the child, these norms convert women's labor into a form of alienated labor. Second, by manipulating and denying legitimacy to the surrogate mother's evolving perspective on her own pregnancy, the norms of the market degrade her. Third, by taking advantage of the surrogate mother's noncommercial motivations without offering anything but what the norms of commerce demand in return, these norms leave her open to exploitation. The fact that these problems arise in the attempt to commercialize the labor of bearing children shows that women's labor is not properly regarded as a commodity.

The key to understanding these problems is the normal role of the emotions in noncommercialized pregnancies. Pregnancy is not simply a biological process but also a social practice. Many social expectations and considerations surround women's gestational labor, marking it off as an occasion for the parents to prepare themselves to welcome a new life into their family. For example, obstetricians use ultrasound not simply for diagnostic purposes but also to encourage maternal bonding with the fetus. We can all recognize that it is good, although by no means inevitable, for loving bonds to be established between the mother and her child during this period.

In contrast with these practices, the surrogate industry follows the putting-out system of manufacturing. It provides some of the raw materials of production (the father's sperm) to the surrogate mother, who then engages in production of the child. Although her labor is subject to periodic supervision by her doctors and by the surrogate agency, the agency does not have physical control over the product of her labor as firms using the factory system do. Hence, as in all putting-out systems, the surrogate industry faces the problem of extracting the final product from the mother. This problem is exacerbated by the fact that the social norms surrounding pregnancy are designed to encourage parental love for the child. The surrogate industry addresses this problem by requiring the mother to engage in a form of emotional labor. In the surrogate contract, she agrees not to form or to attempt to form a parent–child relationship with her offspring. Her labor is alienated, because she must divert it from the end which the social practices of pregnancy rightly promote—an emotional bond with her child. The surrogate contract thus replaces a norm of parenthood, that during pregnancy one create a loving attachment to one's child, with a norm of commercial production, that the producer shall not form any special emotional ties to her product....

Commercial surrogacy is also a degrading practice. The surrogate mother, like all persons, has an independent evaluative perspective on her activities and relationships. The realization of her dignity demands that the other parties to the contract acknowledge rather than evade the claims which her independent perspective makes upon them. But the surrogate industry has an interest in suppressing, manipulating, and trivializing her perspective, for there is an ever-present danger that she will see her involvement in her pregnancy from the perspective of a parent rather than from the perspective of a contract laborer.

How does this suppression and trivialization take place? The commercial promoters of surrogacy commonly describe the surrogate mothers as inanimate objects: mere "hatcheries," "plumbing," or "rented property"—things without emotions which could make claims on others. They also refuse to acknowledge any responsibility for the consequences of the mother's emotional labor. Should she suffer psychologically from being forced to give up her child, the father is not liable to pay for therapy after her pregnancy, although he is liable for all other medical expenses following her pregnancy.

The treatment and interpretation of surrogate mothers' grief raises the deepest problems of degradation. Most surrogate mothers experience grief upon giving up their children—in 10 percent of cases, seriously enough to require therapy. Their grief is not compensated by the $10,000 fee they receive. Grief is not an intelligible response to a successful deal, but rather reflects the subject's judgment that she has suffered a grave and personal loss. Since not all cases of grief resolve themselves into cases of regret, it may be that some surrogate mothers do not regard their grief, in retrospect, as reflecting an authentic judgment on their part. But in the circumstances of emotional manipulation which pervade the surrogate industry, it is difficult to determine which interpretation of her grief more truly reflects the perspective of the surrogate mother. By insinuating a trivializing interpretation of her emotional responses to the prospect of losing her child, the surrogate agency may be able to manipulate her into accepting her fate without too much fuss, and may even succeed in substituting its interpretation of her emotions for her own. Since she has already signed a contract to perform emotional labor—to express or repress emotions which are dictated by the interests of the surrogate industry—this might not be a difficult task. A considerate treatment of the mothers' grief, on the other hand, would take the evaluative basis of their grief seriously.

Some defenders of commercial surrogacy demand that the provision for terminating the surrogate mother's parental rights in her child be legally enforceable, so that peace of mind for the adoptive parents can be secured. But the surrogate industry makes no corresponding provision for securing the peace of mind of the surrogate. She is expected to assume the risk of a transformation of her ethical and emotional perspective on herself and her child with the same impersonal detachment with which a futures trader assumes the risk of a fluctuation in the price of pork bellies. By applying the market norms of enforcing contracts to the surrogate mother's case, commercial surrogacy treats a moral transformation as if it were merely an economic change.

The manipulation of the surrogate mother's emotions which is inherent in the surrogate parenting contract also leaves women open to grave forms of exploitation. A kind of exploitation occurs when one party to a transaction is oriented toward the exchange of "gift" values, while the other party operates in accordance with the norms of the market exchange of commodities. Gift values, which include love, gratitude, and appreciation of others, cannot be bought or obtained through piecemeal calculations of individual advantage. Their exchange requires a repudiation of a self-interested attitude, a willingness to give gifts to others without demanding some specific equivalent good in return each time one gives. The surrogate mother often operates according to the norms of gift relationships. The surrogate agency, on the other hand, follows market norms. Its job is to get the best deal for its clients and itself, while leaving the surrogate mother to look after her own interests as best as she can. The situation puts the surrogate agencies in a position to manipulate the surrogate mothers' emotions to gain favorable terms for themselves. For example, agencies screen prospective surrogate mothers for submissiveness, and emphasize to them the importance of the motives of generosity and love. When applicants question some of the terms of the contract, the broker sometimes intimidates them by questioning their character and morality: if they were really generous and loving they would not be so solicitous about their own interests....

Many surrogate mothers see pregnancy as a way to feel "adequate," "appreciated," or "special." In other words, these women feel inadequate, unappreciated, or unadmired when they are not pregnant. Lacking the power to achieve some worthwhile status in their own right, they must subordinate themselves to others' definitions of their proper place (as baby factories) in order to get from them the appreciation they need to attain a sense of self-worth. But the sense of self-worth one can attain under such circumstances is precarious and ultimately self-defeating. For example, those who seek gratitude on the part of the adoptive parents and some opportunity to share the joys of seeing their children grow discover all too often that the adoptive parents want nothing to do with them. For while the surrogate mother sees in the arrangement some basis for establishing the personal ties she needs to sustain her emotionally, the adoptive couple sees it as an impersonal commercial contract, one of whose main advantages to them is that all ties between them and the surrogate are ended once the terms of the contract are fulfilled. To them, her presence is a threat to marital unity and a competing object for the child's affections.

These considerations should lead us to question the model of altruism which is held up to women by the surrogacy industry. It is a strange form of altruism which demands such radical self-effacement, alienation from those whom one benefits, and the subordination of one's body, health, and emotional life to the independently defined interests of others.

The primary distortions which arise from treating women's labor as a commodity—the surrogate mother's alienation from loved ones, her degradation, and her exploitation—stem from a common source. This is the failure to acknowledge and treat appropriately the surrogate mother's emotional engagement with her labor. Her labor is alienated, because she must suppress her emotional ties with her own child, and may be manipulated into reinterpreting these ties in a trivializing way. She is degraded, because her independent ethical perspective is denied, or demoted to the status of a cash sum. She is exploited, because her emotional needs and vulnerabilities are not treated as characteristics which call for consideration, but as factors which may be manipulated to encourage her to make a grave self-sacrifice to the broker's and adoptive couple's advantage. These considerations provide strong grounds for sustaining the claims of women's labor to its "product," the child. The attempt to redefine parenthood so as to strip women of parental claims to the children they bear does violence to their emotional engagement with the project of bringing children into the world.

Commercial Surrogacy, Freedom, and the Law

In the light of these ethical objections to commercial surrogacy, what position should the law take on the practice? At the very least, surrogate contracts should not be enforceable. Surrogate mothers should not be forced to relinquish their children if they have formed emotional bonds with them. Any other treatment of women's ties to the children they bear is degrading.

But I think these arguments support the stronger conclusion that commercial surrogate contracts should be illegal, and that surrogate agencies who arrange such contracts should be subject to criminal penalties. Commercial surrogacy constitutes a degrading and harmful traffic in children, violates the dignity of women, and subjects both children and women to a serious risk of exploitation....

If commercial surrogate contracts were prohibited, this would be no cause for infertile couples to lose hope for raising a family. The option of adoption is still available, and every attempt should be made to open up opportunities for adoption to couples who do not meet standard requirements—for example, because of age. While there is a shortage of healthy white infants available for adoption, there is no shortage of children of other races, mixed-race children, and older and handicapped children who desperately need to be adopted. Leaders of the surrogate industry have proclaimed that commercial surrogacy may replace adoption as the method of choice for infertile couples who wish to raise families. But we should be wary of the racist and eugenic motivations which make some people rally to the surrogate industry at the expense of children who already exist and need homes.

The case of commercial surrogacy raises deep questions about the proper scope of the market in modern industrial societies. I have argued that there are principled grounds for rejecting the substitution of market norms for parental norms to govern the ways women bring children into the world. Such substitutions express ways of valuing mothers and children which reflect an inferior conception of human flourishing. When market norms are applied to the ways we allocate and understand parental rights and responsibilities, children are reduced from subjects of love to objects of use. When market norms are applied to the ways we treat and understand women's reproductive labor, women are reduced from subjects of respect and consideration to objects of use. If we are to retain the capacity to value children and women in ways consistent with a rich conception of human flourishing, we must resist the encroachment of the market upon the sphere of reproductive labor. Women's labor is *not* a commodity.

DECISION SCENARIOS

The questions following each decision scenario are intended to prompt reflection and discussion. In deciding how to answer them, you should consider the information provided in the Social Context and Case Presentations, as well as in the Briefing Session. You should also make use of the ethical theories and principles presented in Part VI: Foundations of Bioethics, and the arguments offered in the relevant readings in this chapter.

DECISION SCENARIO 1

The Perils of Multiple Pregnancy

"I still can't believe we're going to have six babies," Juliana Samaras said. "I don't even know what that's called." She laughed and took her husband's hand.

"It's called sextuplets," said her physician, Betsy Travers. "But that's part of why I wanted the two of you to come in today."

"Is there something wrong with the babies?" asked Andreas Samaras.

"Not yet," said Travers. "Your wife is only five weeks pregnant. But I need to warn you both that with a multiple pregnancy like this, the chance of a miscarriage is over 50 percent. There is also a greater risk of premature birth and lifelong impairments like blindness and brain damage."

"Isn't there something you can do?"

"There is. It's called multifetal pregnancy reduction. We could get the number of embryos down to a safer level. Your wife's health is also at risk."

"That sounds like a euphemism for abortion," Juliana said. "That's not an option. We're Orthodox Christians and our church teaches us that abortion is murder. Why didn't you tell us about this when you gave us the fertility drugs?"

"I wish we had."

1. Ovary-stimulating drugs such as menotropins have a high risk of creating multiple gestations. Should physicians be required to disclose this risk to patients before prescribing the drugs? Should patients agree to multifetal reduction, if necessary, before starting treatment?

2. Suppose both Juliana and Andreas Samaras are unemployed, have borrowed money to pay for infertility treatment, and will be supporting their children largely on public assistance. Should any of these factors be considered when prescribing them fertility drugs?

3. Another major cause of multiple gestations has been the transfer of multiple embryos after IVF. Should the number of transfers be limited by law, as it is in some countries but not in the United States?

DECISION SCENARIO 2

Looking for the Family Tree

The Donor Sibling Registry (DSR) makes it possible for people who were conceived from donated sperm and eggs to make contact with genetic relatives—such as half-siblings whose mothers used the same sperm donor. The site also makes it possible for a donor to shed his or her anonymity and make contact with biological offspring, although this is less common. Since its founding in 2000, the Registry's website has connected more than 12,000 half-siblings and other genetic relatives. (See Case Presentation: Egg and Sperm Donors for more on the DSR.)

The half-siblings connected through the DSR say that it helps them develop a different sense of family. Using the name of a sperm or ova donation program combined with a donor number, individuals conceived by donors can identify genetic relatives. It has also allowed them to pool information about genetic conditions that may have been passed along by their donor parents.

The number of donor-conceived children and adults in the United States has been estimated to be more than a million. In addition, the sperm of a single "popular" donor may be chosen dozens or even hundreds of times. Among other issues with this practice, it means that half-siblings in the same geographic area have a small, but genuine, chance of accidental incest.

1. Should sperm and egg donors be required to agree to reveal their identities to their biological children when the children turn eighteen?

2. Parents currently have no legal obligation to reveal to their children that they were conceived through the use of donor sperm or ova. Should this information be included on a child's birth certificate?

3. Should sperm and ova donation programs be required to keep a registry of children born from the same donors? This would allow donor-conceived children to determine whether they were related while preserving the anonymity of donors.

DECISION SCENARIO **3**

Embryo = Person?

"I'm curious," Lois Ramer said. "What happens to the eggs you take from me that get fertilized but not implanted?"

"We donate them to other families," Dr. Martha Herman said.

"Oh," Lois Ramer said, sounding surprised. "I don't want that to happen."

"Why is that?"

"Because they belong to my husband and me, and implanting them into other women would be like giving our children away."

"But a fertilized egg isn't a person," Dr. Herman said.

1. Is it necessary to think that a fertilized egg is equivalent to a person to agree with Lois Ramer's objection? Construct an argument supporting her position.

2. What position does the Catholic Church take on the question of the status of an egg that is fertilized for the purpose of implantation, but then not used? What are the strengths and weaknesses of this position?

3. List a set of criteria for personhood that would exclude newly fertilized eggs. Then identify criteria that would include them as persons. Which is more plausible?

DECISION SCENARIO **4**

Surrogacy and Morality

In January 1985, the British High Court took custody of a five-day-old girl, the first child known to be born in Britain to a woman paid to be a surrogate mother.

An American couple, known only as "Mr. and Mrs. A," were reported to have paid about $7,500 to a twenty-eight-year-old woman who was artificially inseminated with sperm from Mr. A. The woman, Kim Cotton, was prevented from turning the child over to Mr. and Mrs. A by a court order issued due to uncertainty over the legal status of a surrogate mother.

The court permitted "interested parties, including the natural father" to apply for custody of the child. Mr. A applied, and a judge ruled that the couple

could take the baby girl out of the country because they could offer her "a very good upbringing."

1. Are there moral reasons that might have made the court hesitate before turning over the child to her biological father? For example, could it be persuasively argued that Kim Cotton was in effect selling her baby to Mr. and Mrs. A?

2. Kim Cotton agreed to be a surrogate mother for the sake of the money. Is surrogate pregnancy a practice that tends to exploit the poor? Does it involve them in something resembling prostitution? Or is it a legitimate way to earn money by providing a needed service?

3. The case just described involved a *traditional* surrogacy arrangement, in which Kim Cotton became pregnant through the fertilization of one of her own eggs. How might the ethics of the case be different if she were a *gestational* surrogate and thus genetically unrelated to the child?

DECISION SCENARIO 5

A Matter of Autonomy?

Dr. Charles Davis quickly scanned the data sheet on his desk, then looked at the woman seated across from him. Her name was Nancy Callahan. She was twenty-five years old and worked as a print conservator at an art museum.

"I see that you're single," Dr. Davis said.

"That's right," Nancy Callahan said. "That's basically the reason I'm here." When Dr. Davis looked puzzled, she added, "I still want to have a child."

Dr. Davis nodded and thought for a moment. Nancy Callahan was the first unmarried person to come to the Bayside Fertility Clinic to request assisted reproduction. As the legal owner and medical director of the clinic, Dr. Davis was the one ultimately responsible for the clinic's policies.

"You're not engaged or planning to get married?"

"No, but I don't want to rule out the possibility that I will want to get married someday."

"Don't you know anybody you would want to have a child with in the ordinary sexual way?"

"I might be able to find someone," Callahan said. "But I honestly don't want to get involved with anybody right now. I'm ready to be a mother, but having a child in what you call 'the ordinary sexual way' would require compromises and negotiations that I see no need to accept."

"It's just somewhat unusual," Dr. Davis said.

"But it's not illegal, is it?"

"No," Davis said. "It's not illegal."

"So what's the problem? I'm healthy. I'm financially sound and mentally stable, and I'm both able and eager to accept the responsibility of being a mother."

"It's just that at the moment the policy of our clinic requires that patients be married and that both intended parents agree to the insemination procedure."

"But there's nothing magical about a policy," Nancy Callahan said. "It can be changed for good reasons, can't it?"

"Perhaps so," said Davis.

1. How might it be argued that respect for Nancy Callahan's autonomy makes it wrong to deny her the service she requests, when the same service would be provided to a married woman?

2. Would Dr. Davis have any legitimate grounds for offering assisted reproduction to Callahan but denying it to a single man who sought to become a father through IVF and gestational surrogacy?

DECISION SCENARIO 6

A Replacement Child?

"You've got to help us," Clarence Woody said. "Keith was our only child, and he meant the world to us. When the police came and told us he was dead, all Sara and I could think of was how we could get him back."

"But you can't get him back," Dr. Alma Lieu said. "Even if we prepared one of his cells and implanted it in your wife's uterus, the baby wouldn't be Keith."

"But he would be his genetic twin," Clarence said. "He would be as close as we can get to replacing our son." His eyes filled with tears. "Won't you help us?"

1. On what grounds do critics object to cloning a human?

2. Assuming the safety of the cloned person is not in question, would cloning in such a case as this be morally legitimate?

3. Does the cloning of a human necessarily lead to the commodification of human life?

4. How persuasive in a case like this is the objection that cloning is "repugnant" because it violates our nature as biological and social organisms?

DECISION SCENARIO 7

An Interest in Existing?

"You realize that the drugs we'll be using in preparing you for implanting the embryos will involve a slight, but significant, risk to any child you might have?" Dr. Gabriel Aaron asked.

"I certainly didn't," Stephanie Dalata said. "You mean we might have a child with a birth defect?"

"You might," Aaron said. "Or one who is premature or has a low birth weight. Or if we implant four embryos, all four of them might develop, and then all the babies would be at risk."

"I don't think we should go through with the treatments," said Alice Stimmons, Dalata's wife. "If assisted reproduction is going to produce a child with serious impairments, then, it's wrong."

"I don't know about that," Dalata said. "Maybe it's better for a child to have even serious impairments than to not exist at all."

1. Dalata has just articulated a version of what some call the "Interest in Existing" argument, discussed in the article by Cynthia Cohen earlier in this chapter. State the argument clearly and concisely. How persuasive is it?

2. Even births that don't involve assisted reproduction involve risks of serious and perhaps devastating harm to the child. Do objections to the "Interest in Existing" argument also apply to ordinary sexual (non-ART) pregnancies?

DECISION SCENARIO 8

Family Balance?

Ada Sing had just woken up from sedation when Dr. Sewell walked into the recovery room. He nodded to Ada's husband, Sudhir, and smiled at her two young daughters, Diya and Pari, who were assembling a Lego castle in the corner.

"Glad to see you're awake, Ada. I just wanted to let you know that the procedure was a success and we were able to extract enough ova to proceed with IVF."

"That's wonderful news," said Ada Sing. "Thank you, doctor."

"Just one question before we move forward." Sewell lowered his voice and turned to Sudhir Sing. "After we fertilize the ova in the lab, it's fairly easy for us to determine which embryos are male and which are female." Sewell paused. "We don't advertise this, but for an additional charge we can help you achieve the 'family balance' you might be seeking? It's perfectly legal in the U.S."

"What are you saying, Doctor Sewell?" asked Ada.

"I just noticed that you already have two girls and thought you might not want any more." Sewell cleared his throat and smiled. "Not that there is anything wrong with girls."

1. Should the Sings take Sewell's offer, if they would prefer a boy to another girl? What, if anything, might be morally questionable about the service Sewell offers?

2. It has been estimated that four thousand to six thousand gender-selection procedures take place through IVF and preimplantation genetic screening each year, with revenues of over $100 million. The practice is illegal everywhere except the United States, Thailand, and South Africa. Should it be banned in these countries?

3. Although China outlaws sex-selection practices like the one just described, its "one child" policy has led to the highest gender imbalance in the world, with 120 newborn boys for every 100 girls. Is it likely that a similar gender imbalance will develop in the United States? Or will as many parents seek girls as boys?

Part III

Terminations

Chapter 5

Abortion

CHAPTER CONTENTS

CASES AND CONTEXTS

When Abortion Was Illegal: The Odyssey of Sherri Finkbine

In the spring of 1962, Sherri Finkbine of Phoenix, Arizona, started having trouble sleeping. She was pregnant with her fifth child and was also experiencing morning sickness. So she started taking some sleeping pills her husband had brought back from a trip to Europe. The tranquilizers were widely used there; like aspirin or cough syrup, they could be bought over the counter in any pharmacy.

A few weeks after she began taking the tranquilizers, Finkbine read an article that discussed a substantial increase in the number of severely deformed babies being born in Europe. Many of the children's arms and legs failed to develop or developed with strange anomalies, such as having hands protruding directly from their shoulders. Other children were blind and deaf or had seriously defective internal organs. About half of them died before their first birthday. The impairments had already been traced to the use in pregnancy of a supposedly harmless and widely used tranquilizer. Its active ingredient was called thalidomide.

Finkbine was worried enough to ask her physician to find out if the pills she had been taking contained thalidomide. They did. What's more, she had been taking thalidomide during the first eight weeks of her pregnancy, when it appeared to be most harmful. When her physician learned this, he told her, "The odds for a normal baby are so against you that I am recommending termination of pregnancy."

In 1962, abortion was illegal in Arizona unless the mother's life was clearly endangered. Nevertheless, a small number of therapeutic abortions were approved each year by a three-doctor medical board in Phoenix, and Finkbine's physician believed that getting approval for an abortion would not be difficult.

Sherri Finkbine agreed with her doctor's advice. But then she began to think that perhaps it was her duty to inform other women who were taking thalidomide about its disastrous consequences. She called a local newspaper

and told her story to the editor. He agreed not to use her name, but on a front page, bordered in black, he used the headline "Baby-Deforming Drug May Cost Woman Her Child Here."

The story was picked up by the wire services, and Sherri Finkbine's identity was soon revealed. The medical board had already approved her request for an abortion, but because of the publicity that her case received, board members grew skittish and canceled their approval. When Finkbine's doctor asked for a court order to permit the abortion, she and her husband became the objects of international scrutiny and scorn.

Il Osservatore Romano, the official Vatican newspaper, condemned Finkbine and her husband as murderers. She and her husband received death threats and the FBI was called in to protect them. One letter said, "I hope someone takes the other four children and strangles them, because it is all the same thing." Another wrote from the perspective of the fetus: "Mommy, please dear Mommy, let me live. Please, please, I want to live. Let me love you, let me see the light of day, let me smell a rose, let me sing a song, let me look into your face, let me say Mommy." Finkbine was fired from her job in local television, and her husband was suspended from his high school teaching position.

After her physician's request for a court order was denied, Sherri Finkbine tried to obtain a legal abortion outside her own state, but she was unable to find a doctor who would help her. She and her husband tried to travel to Japan for an abortion but were denied a visa. Eventually, they got on a plane to Sweden, and Finkbine consulted a physician at a Swedish hospital. After an investigation by a medical board, Sherri Finkbine received the abortion she had traveled so far and struggled so hard to get. As she had feared, the thirteen-week-old fetus lacked legs and one arm and had been so severely deformed that its sex could not be determined. If carried to term, the Swedish doctors doubted it would have survived.

The Finkbines returned to Arizona and private life, but their story had started to change public opinion on abortion. A Gallup poll in late 1962 found that 52 percent of Americans thought Sherri Finkbine had done the right thing. Finkbine's story also drew attention to women who did not have the resources to fly to Sweden for an abortion, but instead turned to dangerous and unskilled "back-alley" providers, whose incompetence caused 17 percent of all pregnancy-related deaths in the 1960s. By 1966, Gallup found that 54 percent of Americans said abortion should be legal in cases of fetal abnormality and 77 percent said it should be legal to protect the health of the mother. By the early 1970s, sizable majorities of both men and women agreed with the statement: "The decision to have an abortion should be made solely by a woman and her physician."

CASE PRESENTATION
Roe v. Wade

Norma McCorvey of Dallas was single, poor, and pregnant. She was twenty-one years old and wanted to have an abortion, but under Texas law in 1970, abortion was a criminal offense, except when required to save a woman's life.

McCorvey's life had been hard. She had been abused both sexually and emotionally as a child, then raped at a reform school when she was a teenager. She married at sixteen, was physically abused by her husband, and developed problems with drugs and alcohol. Her first child, a daughter, was taken to be raised by her mother, and the father of her second child, also a daughter, assumed responsibility for the child's welfare.

When McCorvey found herself pregnant for the third time, she knew she did not want another child. The law in California was less restrictive than the law in Texas, and McCorvey believed she could get an abortion there, but she lacked the money for travel and expenses. She tried to visit an illegal abortion clinic in Dallas, but found it closed down.

The Case

While still pregnant, McCorvey was approached by Linda Coffee, a public-interest attorney who had been given McCorvey's name by a lawyer specializing in adoptions. Coffee and Sarah Weddington, also an attorney, met with McCorvey and asked her if she would agree to be the plaintiff in a class-action lawsuit. The suit would be filed against Henry Wade, the district attorney of Dallas County, and would challenge the constitutionality of the Texas abortion law. McCorvey readily consented. When the papers were filed, Norma McCorvey became "Jane Roe."

Although McCorvey was the plaintiff, the case was a class-action suit that Coffee and Weddington hoped would ultimately lead to the recognition of a constitutional right to seek an abortion. The federal courts ruled that the Texas statute was void, but Dallas district attorney Henry Wade appealed the District Court decision to the U.S. Supreme Court.

The legal case took time as it wound its way through the courts, and despite McCorvey's explicit wish not to have another child, she bowed to legal necessity and carried the fetus to term. She gave birth to a third daughter, then immediately gave up the baby for adoption.

The Decision

The Supreme Court handed down its ruling in *Roe v. Wade* on January 23, 1973. In a 7–2 decision, written by Justice Harry A. Blackmun, the Court found the Texas law to be unconstitutional. This ruling had the effect of decriminalizing abortion in the United States, because abortion laws in most other states differed little from the Texas statute.

The *Roe* decision did not hold that states could not regulate abortion. Rather, it placed limits on the regulations states could impose without violating a woman's constitutionally protected right to privacy. Physicians traditionally divided the nine months of pregnancy into three three-month trimesters, and the Court made use of these divisions to guide states in determining to what extent they could legitimately restrict abortion.

The ruling held that, during the first twelve weeks (the first trimester) of pregnancy, states cannot restrict a woman's decision to have an abortion. During the second trimester, states may place restrictions on abortion to protect the health or safety of the pregnant woman. In the final trimester, because the fetus may be considered viable and capable of an independent existence, states may restrict abortions, but only in ways that still preserve the health of the pregnant woman, as determined by her physician.

From Roe to McCorvey

"Jane Roe" went back to being Norma McCorvey, but her life remained troubled. A high-school dropout with no vocational training, McCorvey supported herself with various unskilled jobs, working as a waitress and a bartender. In the 1980s she began to acknowledge in public that she had been "Jane Roe," and this led to a brief flurry of attention from abortion-rights groups. She was introduced at meetings, gave interviews to the media, and gave some public talks. For a time, she became a celebrity of sorts.

Yet her celebrity did not pay the bills, and she continued to work at low-paying jobs. Her celebrity did help her get jobs in abortion clinics, however. While she was working in a women's clinic in Dallas, the antiabortion group Operation Rescue set up an office next door and protested the clinic's activities. McCorvey was hostile to them at first, but then she began to have conversations with Philip Benham, the group's director, during her cigarette breaks. Benham, an evangelical preacher, talked to her about Christianity, and McCorvey agreed to attend church with the daughter of one of the group's members.

McCorvey converted to Christianity on her first visit to the church. She was baptized by Benham on August 8, 1995, in a swimming pool belonging to one of Benham's followers. The event, considered a major publicity coup by Operation Rescue, was videotaped and released to the media. McCorvey renounced her previous support for abortion and took a job doing word processing for Operation Rescue.

With the help of a coauthor, Andy Meisler, she went public with the details of her story in *I Am Roe: My Life*, Roe v. Wade, *and Freedom of Choice*. With the help of another coauthor, she wrote *Won by Love*, an account of her conversion. She later converted to Roman Catholicism, founded an anti-abortion ministry called "Roe No More," and is still active in pro-life protests.

The Debate Continues

Linda Coffee and Sarah Weddington, McCorvey's lawyers, had achieved their aim. The *Roe* decision provided legal protections for most women seeking an abortion. Yet the decision also triggered fierce conflict between proponents of relatively unfettered reproductive choice ("pro-choice" advocates) and opponents of so-called abortion on demand ("pro-life" or "right-to-life" advocates), a conflict that shows no sign of abating.

Those who favor making abortion a private, personal decision were pleased by the *Roe* decision, but those who consider abortion a serious moral wrong were not. Many of the opponents resolved to work for a constitutional amendment prohibiting abortion or, alternatively, to get the Supreme Court ruling in *Roe v. Wade* overturned.

Within the limits of regulation imposed by the *Roe* decision, opponents of abortion have taken various legal measures over the years in an attempt to slow or halt its practice. Thus, they have often succeeded in getting state laws passed that impose requirements making it difficult for women to get an abortion—especially poor women and those living in rural areas. In response, advocates of reproductive rights have often charged that the laws are unconstitutional and filed suits that have ended up before the Supreme Court. *Roe v. Wade* marked the beginning of the legal skirmishes and battles centered on abortion, but four decades later, the end of the war is not in sight.

A Statistical Profile of Abortion in the United States

January 2013 marked the fortieth anniversary of the Supreme Court decision legalizing abortion in the United States. Yet more than four decades after the decision, abortion has not become a standard, uncontroversial medical procedure, as many abortion-rights advocates had hoped and expected.

Even though some one million abortions are performed every year in the United States, Americans remain ambivalent and divided on abortion's moral acceptability. To some extent, abortion has become less accepted than it was during the 1980s and 1990s.

The data that follow present a statistical profile of abortion in the United States.[1] The picture that emerges reveals a strong public commitment to the idea that abortion should remain a legal procedure, combined with a lesser, yet still vocal, belief that abortion should be severely restricted or outlawed.

Despite the enduring and often sharp political conflicts over abortion, public support for keeping the procedure legal, although perhaps more stringently regulated, remains high. Abortion as a procedure is not going to go away, yet neither are the moral and political issues associated with it.

How Many Abortions?

About 21 percent of all pregnancies among American women end with an abortion, according to a 2011 estimate. When the pregnancies aren't intended, this percentage rises to 40 percent. Each year,

seventeen out of every thousand women aged fifteen to forty-four have an abortion, and half of those who have an abortion have had one before. By age forty-five, about half of American women will have had an unintended pregnancy. By the same age, about 30 percent will have had an abortion.

In 2011 (the most recent statistics), 1.06 million abortions were performed. Public health experts estimate that during the 1950s and 1960s, before the 1973 Supreme Court decision in *Roe v. Wade* that legalized abortion, some 200,000 to 1.2 million illegal abortions were performed each year. The number of abortions increased after the procedure was made legal, peaking at 1.6 million in 1990. Since then, abortions have been declining, measured both as an absolute number and as a percentage of women of childbearing age who have them. (Nevertheless, it is beginning to look as if the number of abortions has stabilized at between 1.0 and 1.3 million a year.)

The reasons for the declining incidence of abortion are unclear, but some believe it is connected with the aging of the population, the wider availability of contraception, and fewer unwanted pregnancies. Others think the decline reflects a change of attitude toward abortion, as well as legal restrictions that make it more difficult for women to secure abortions in many states. Nevertheless, the same decline has occurred in states that have not adopted such restrictions and where the population is largely pro-choice. Although the number of abortions is likely to vary slightly from year to year, experts think it is unlikely that any increase will approach the peak levels of the early 1990s.

---

[1] The data cited here may sometimes be inconsistent from section to section. Some statistics are for the latest year for which complete data are available, while other numbers are for more recent years for which data are incomplete. The discrepancies are few and small, and do not substantially alter the general picture.

Who Has an Abortion?

Age. More than half (57 percent) of women who have an abortion are in their twenties. Women ages twenty to twenty-four account for 33 percent of all abortions, and teenagers account for another 18 percent.

Race. European Americans have 36 percent of the abortions performed in the United States, African Americans, 30 percent, and Hispanics, 25 percent.

Religion. Of women who have abortions, 37 percent say they are Protestants and 28 percent identify themselves as Catholics.

Marital status. About 45 percent of all abortions are obtained by women who have never been married.

Children. More than 61 percent of abortions are among women who have previously given birth to at least one child.

Why Abortion?

- 75 percent of women say they are choosing to have an abortion because having a child would interfere with their family responsibilities, education, or work.

- 75 percent say that they cannot afford to have a (or another) child for financial reasons.

- 50 percent say they don't want to be a single parent or that they aren't getting along with their spouse or partner and don't want to bring a child into this complicated situation.

- Each year, 19,500 women have abortions to end pregnancies that are the result of rape or incest.

Contraception and Abortion

Some critics of abortion claim that its availability encourages women to use it as a form of birth control. The statistics suggest, however, that the situation is more complicated than that. Nearly all women seeking an abortion have (at some time) used some form of contraception, and the majority used it during the month in which they became pregnant. The intention of the majority to avoid becoming pregnant is most often thwarted by a failure to employ contraception properly and consistently, and the relatively high failure rates of some methods.

- 8 percent of women having abortions in 2000 reported having never used any form of birth control. Those who are young, poor, African American, unmarried, or less educated are at greater risk of having never used contraception.

- 68 percent of sexually active women in their childbearing years use contraception consistently and correctly if they are not trying to become pregnant. They account for only 5 percent of unintended pregnancies.

- 18 percent of women in their childbearing years use contraception inconsistently, and they account for 41 percent of unintended pregnancies.

Obtaining an Abortion

Medication Abortion

In 2000, the federal Food and Drug Administration approved the drug mifepristone (RU-486) for inducing abortion, permitting women in the earlier stages of pregnancy to avoid a surgical abortion. The number of early medication abortions increased from 6 percent of the total number of abortions in 2001 to 23 percent in 2011.

Safety

- Less than 1 percent of women who have abortions experience major complications. A first trimester abortion has a less than 0.05 percent risk of such complications.

- Large studies have consistently shown no association between breast cancer and abortion, according to the National Cancer Institute.

- There is no greater prevalence of mental health problems among women who have had elective first trimester abortions than among the general population of women, according to a task force convened by the American Psychological Association.

- The risk of death associated with abortion is lower than many other medical procedures but increases with the length of pregnancy: up to 8 weeks, one death per million; 16–20 weeks, one per twenty-nine thousand; 21+ weeks, one per eleven thousand.

- The risk of death associated with childbirth is fourteen times as high as the risk associated with abortion.

Timing

The great majority of abortions (91 percent) take place during the first thirteen weeks of pregnancy. About 50 percent of the women who have an abortion after the fifteenth week of pregnancy say the delay was caused by problems in getting the money or in finding someone to perform the procedure. Teenagers are much more likely than older women to have an abortion after the fifteenth week.

When Women Have Abortions	
Before the 9th week	64.5%
9–13 weeks	26.9
14–15 weeks	3.5
16–17 weeks	1.9
18–20 weeks	1.9
21+ weeks	1.4

Providers

- During the period 2008–2011, the number of hospitals, clinics, and physicians providing abortion declined by 4 percent.

- 89 percent of counties in the United States lacked an abortion provider in 2011.

- 38 percent of all women fifteen to forty-four lived in a county without an abortion provider in 2011.

- In 2011, the average cost of a surgical abortion in the tenth week of pregnancy carried out with local anesthesia in a clinic or doctor's office was $480. The average amount for an early medication abortion before ten weeks was $504.

Public Payment

- Federal law prohibits the use of Medicaid funds (the state–federal program for the poor) to pay for abortion, except in cases in which the mother's life is endangered or the pregnancy is the result of rape or incest.

- Publicly funded family planning services (such as those provided by Planned Parenthood) prevent an estimated 1.3 million unplanned pregnancies a year through contraception and education. On the basis of the rate at which unplanned pregnancies are terminated, more than 632,000 abortions a year are thus avoided.

Ambivalence toward Abortion

Americans remain evenly split on the abortion question, as revealed by a May 2014 poll by the Gallup Organization. When people were asked, "With respect to the abortion issue, would you consider yourself to be pro-choice or pro-life?" 47 percent described themselves as pro-choice and 46 percent described themselves as pro-life. This result is essentially unchanged from 2009, when the pro-life position gained a few percentage points and for the first time represented a majority, albeit a slim one, since Gallup first asked the question in 1995.

Americans do appear to be becoming more polarized on the abortion issue. The middle position that abortion should be legal, but only under certain circumstances, has fallen from a high of 59 percent in 1998 to just 50 percent in 2014. Meanwhile, the percentage of those who believe abortion should be legal in all circumstances has increased in recent years, to 28 percent, while the percentage that say it should be illegal in all circumstances has held steady at 21 percent. Thus while Americans are divided and

polarized on the issue, a large majority (78 percent) still support the legalization of abortion established by *Roe v. Wade.* Fifty-three percent of those surveyed by Gallup in 2012 said that *Roe* should not be overturned, compared to 29 percent who said it should be. (Eighteen percent had no opinion.)

A Fragmented Middle

A large majority of Americans (78 percent) appear to believe that abortion should be legal in some or all cases. But polls have also found that support for legal abortion drops sharply when respondents are asked about it during the second trimester and even more so when asked about the third. Thus abstract statements such as "A woman has a right to choose to have an abortion for any reason at all" and "A fertilized egg is as much a person as a born child and has just as much right to life" do not accurately represent the opinions of the largest group of Americans on abortion.

Some of the ambiguity for Americans may spring from both increased control over and increased understanding of our reproductive capacities. The ability to screen for genetic diseases such as Tay-Sachs strikes many Americans as worth the sacrifice of embryos a few weeks old, and more than 70 percent of Americans aren't troubled by preventing implantation through the use of a drug like mifepristone. At the same time, advances in neonatal technology have given Americans more experience with premature infants delivered as early as twenty-four weeks of gestation. While such infants tend to do poorly and suffer lasting impairments, the fact that technology can sometimes keep them alive has made more Americans question late-stage abortions.

Thus it seems likely that a majority of Americans still think abortion should be

Abortion and Women's Characteristics

Age (rate per 1,000 women)	
Under 15	0.9
15–19	10.5
20–24	24.9
25–29	19.4
30–34	12.7
35–39	7.5
40–44	2.8
Race/Ethnicity (percent of all abortions)	
White	37.2%
Hispanic	19.7%
African American	36.2%
Race/Ethnicity and Marital Status (percent of abortions by group)	
White, married	16.0
White, unmarried	84.0
African American, married	7.8
African American, unmarried	92.2
Hispanic, married	17.4
Hispanic, unmarried	82.6

Source: Centers for Disease Control and Prevention, 2011

"safe, legal, and rare," to quote President Bill Clinton's famous phrase. But of course, agreement to such a general proposition does not translate into agreement about what restrictions are appropriate. Although abstract positions may have blurred for most people, debates over particular policies remain as divisive and acrimonious as ever.

Plan B and Emergency Contraception

Every year, Americans have 3.4 million unintended pregnancies, which represents more than half the total. About 40 percent of unintended pregnancies will end with an abortion. Although the teen pregnancy rate has reached its lowest point in more than thirty years, the vast majority (77 percent) of pregnancies to women under twenty are unintended. More than 25,000 women a year become pregnant as a result of sexual assault and about 19,500 will have abortions to end pregnancies that occur as a result of rape or incest.

One way to further decrease the number of abortions performed each year would be to decrease the number of unwanted pregnancies. One way to accomplish this is through *emergency contraception* drugs that prevent pregnancy *after* intercourse. They are sometimes called "morning after" pills, but this name is somewhat misleading. It generally takes one to two days (and sometimes up to five days) after intercourse for a sperm to fertilize an egg. During this period of time, emergency contraceptives delay ovulation and thicken cervical mucus to prevent fertilization. (Some abortion opponents charge that the drugs can also prevent implantation of fertilized ova, a topic we will address below.)

Plan B

The synthetic hormone levonorgestrel, commonly known by its original brand name, "Plan B," is the most well-known emergency contraceptive. Plan B One-Step® (Teva) consists of one 1.5-milligram dose of levonorgestrel, which is the same synthetic version of progesterone used in many birth control pills. If taken within seventy-two hours of unprotected intercourse, it is estimated to be about 89 percent effective at preventing pregnancy, and 95 percent effective if taken within twenty-four hours. (Some studies have indicated a higher failure rate for the drug, however.)

Since 2013, Plan B has been available over the counter without age restrictions. The most common side effects of the drug are headaches and nausea. About 20 percent of women taking Plan B experience headaches and around 10 percent nausea and vomiting, and an over-the-counter antinausea medication is often recommended to prevent such side effects.

Research has shown that Plan B (and similar drugs such as ella) prevent pregnancy by delaying or preventing ovulation and inhibiting the passage of sperm by thickening cervical mucus. What research has *not* demonstrated so far is that these drugs prevent pregnancy by impeding the implantation of fertilized eggs. Instead, multiple studies have shown that when Plan B is taken after ovulation occurs, women are just as likely to become pregnant as those who have not taken the drug. Women who take the drug before ovulating, however, successfully prevent pregnancy.

This might seem to be a relatively minor issue, since the standard medical and legal definition of the start of pregnancy is the implantation of a fertilized egg in the uterus. But for abortion opponents who argue that a fertilized ovum has the full moral standing of personhood, the days between fertilization and implantation are a crucial and perilous time for human life. Without any intervention, 50 to 80 percent of fertilized eggs naturally fail to implant in the uterine lining, a loss that is already a profound tragedy in the view of some abortion opponents. Taking steps that might prevent implantation would compound that natural tragedy with an active moral wrong, tantamount to abortion.

It is not surprising that some abortion opponents have focused on Plan B as potentially preventing implantation, since the original FDA label, drafted at the time of the drug's approval in 1999 and still in use as of early 2015, says that the drug "may also prevent fertilization or attachment of a fertilized egg to the uterus." But researchers at the NIH, along with the rest of the mainstream medical establishment, subsequently concluded that this language was inaccurate and out-of-date, modeled on labels for birth control pills from the 1960s, when scientists had little understanding of how the drugs worked. (The FDA approval process did not involve any studies about the drug's mechanism.) By 2012, both the NIH and the Mayo Clinic, as well as European regulators for the drug, had removed language on their websites about implantation disruption, and the International Federation of Gynecology and Obstetrics had issued a statement explicitly stating that levonorgestrel does not stop implantation.

Nevertheless, abortion opponents argue that further proof is needed and point out that if the current studies get further confirmation, Plan B's label should be changed to say that it is ineffective after ovulation. (This is a point on which both sides agree.) For now, Plan B, its generic equivalents, and the longer-acting drug, ella, continue to generate controversy. Indeed, they have done so for over a decade.

Conflict

In 1999, the FDA approved Plan B as a safe and effective prescription drug regimen. It originally involved two tablets to be taken within seventy-two hours of unprotected intercourse. Given the demonstrated safety of the drug and the practical difficulty of obtaining a prescription within the seventy-two-hour window, however, many physicians began to argue that Plan B should be made available over the counter (OTC). In October 2003, Barr Laboratories' application to sell the drug OTC was reviewed by an independent FDA advisory panel of scientists and physicians, which voted 23–4 for approval.

The FDA has generally taken the advice of its advisory panels, but this time the panel's recommendation was overruled by upper-level FDA officials. Plan B was controversial, and abortion opponents were lobbying Bush administration officials to deny Barr's application. Although the FDA's own scientific panel had already concluded that Plan B was a contraceptive agent, not an abortion drug, this finding was rejected by many social conservatives and the U.S. Conference of Catholic Bishops. They also objected to making the drug available OTC because, in their view, it might encourage sexual activity among unmarried women and teens who might otherwise avoid it due to the fear of pregnancy.

On the other side of the reproductive divide, the American Medical Association, American College of Gynecologists and Obstetricians, American Academy of Family Physicians, and American Academy of Pediatricians endorsed OTC sales of Plan B as serving the best medical interest of women.

As it turned out, Plan B was the only one of twenty-three applications to change a drug from prescription-required status to OTC to be turned down in the period 1994–2004. Some FDA staff claimed that Steven Galson, the head of the FDA's drug-review center, had told staff members that it did not matter what the independent advisory panel's recommendation was, because the decision would be made by top officials at the agency.

After the Plan B application was turned down, several members of Congress asked the Government Accountability Office (GAO) to conduct a review of what had taken place at the FDA. The GAO investigation discovered that the decision to reject the application had been made before the FDA's own scientific review of the application was finished.

Reapplication and Restriction

In his rejection of Barr's application, Steven Galson had argued that the original study on Plan B had not included enough teens fourteen to sixteen. So in July 2004, Barr resubmitted its application limiting OTC sales to females *older* than 16. But the FDA delayed action on the application for over a year, then announced in February 2005 that it was delaying its decision indefinitely for further study. In September of that year, Susan Wood, director of the FDA's Office of Women's Health, resigned to protest the agency's decision. "I feel very strongly that this shouldn't be about abortion politics," she said. She told a reporter that she could no longer serve at the FDA "when scientific and clinical evidence, fully evaluated and recommended by approval by the professional staff here, has been overruled."

In 2006, in response to congressional pressure and lawsuits, the FDA agreed that Plan B could be sold without a prescription to women ages eighteen and older. In August 2009, however, Judge Edward R. Korman of the New York Federal District

Court ruled that this decision again appeared to be determined by politics, not science. He gave the agency thirty days to lower the limit to age seventeen and recommended they consider dropping the age requirement altogether. The FDA complied with the order, inviting the manufacturer to submit a plan to market Plan B "without a prescription to women seventeen years of age or older."

In 2011, Barr Laboratories—now owned by Teva Pharmaceuticals—submitted an application to move Plan B from "dual label" use to full OTC status without age limits. The FDA's Center for Drug Evaluation and Research (CDER) studied the application and determined that Plan B was effective and safe for "all females of child-bearing potential." They also concluded that adolescents were capable of understanding and using the drugs without a physician's aid. But later that year, the Director of Health and Human Services, Kathleen Sebelius, overruled the decision, again citing insufficient evidence on use by younger patients.

Finally, in April 2013, Judge Korman overruled Sebelius's decision, concluding it had involved "bad faith and improper political influence" and confirming the CDER's findings. Later that month, the FDA complied with Korman's order and approved the use of Plan B as a nonprescription product without age or point-of-sale restrictions.

Coverage and Conscience

The FDA's approval of Plan B for OTC use was praised by organizations promoting the reproductive autonomy of women and condemned by conservative groups on the grounds that easier access to emergency contraception would encourage more sex outside of marriage and procreation. It has also led to further legal action.

In June 2014, the Supreme Court ruled in *Burwell v. Hobby Lobby* that family-run Christian corporations such as the craft store Hobby Lobby need not provide employees contraception coverage—including emergency contraception—under the Affordable Care Act. (See Chapter 9 for more on the ACA.) The plaintiffs had argued for a partial exemption from the ACA's coverage requirements, based on their religious beliefs that contraceptives such as the IUD and Plan B constituted a form of abortion. Despite the growing scientific consensus that neither of these methods prevents the implantation of fertilized eggs, the ruling posed a setback for those who advocate broader access to emergency contraception.

Studies also suggest that, despite FDA regulations, as many as 20 percent of pharmacies still refuse to allow adolescents to purchase emergency contraception over the counter and an equal number do not keep the drugs in stock. For these pharmacists, too, the refusal is frequently cast as a matter of religious conscience. If scientific evidence on levonorgestrel and related drugs continues to demonstrate that the drugs do not prevent the implantation of blastocysts, some of this reluctance may fade over time. There is also substantial evidence that as much as 70 percent of the American public does not see fertilization versus implantation as a serious moral issue. Nevertheless, opinions about emergency contraception, like opinions about abortion, are deeply rooted in beliefs about sex, procreation, and personhood. Therefore it is unlikely that the conflict over emergency contraception will disappear any time soon.

CASE PRESENTATION
The "Abortion Pill": The Rise of Medication Abortion

Sandra Crane, as we'll call her, became concerned after looking at her calendar. She was thirty-one years old and ordinarily her menstrual cycle was as regular as clockwork. Because her period was now a week overdue, she worried she might be pregnant.

The feeling was familiar. She had two children already: six-year-old Jennifer and two-year-old Thomas. She and her husband Carl had decided not to have any more kids. Their finances were tight and they had recently started caring for Carl's elderly mother in their home. They had already agreed that if the condoms they used for birth control ever failed, they would take steps to end the pregnancy.

Sandra paid a visit to her gynecologist's office to take a pregnancy test, and the day after that a nurse practitioner called to inform her that the test was positive. She was likely to be about two weeks pregnant. Sandra explained that she wanted to end the pregnancy as soon as possible, and the nurse made an appointment for her to see a doctor at a local women's health clinic. There, Sandra discussed her decision with Dr. Tina Merida, who also performed an ultrasound to confirm the date of Sandra's pregnancy. The next day, Sandra and Carl returned to the clinic, where Sandra was given one tablet to swallow—a 200-milligram dose of the hormone blocker mifepristone (formerly known as RU-486). She was also given a prescription for 400 micrograms of the prostaglandin misoprostol, to be administered at home the next day.

Just six hours after letting the misoprostol dissolve under her tongue, Sandra began to experience uterine cramping and bleeding. Eventually, the lining of her uterus was expelled, just as it would be in a miscarriage. Sandra felt some pain, but the experience differed little from a heavy menstrual period. After two days of rest, she felt almost her usual self again. Two weeks later, she returned to the clinic for an examination to confirm that the abortion was complete.

Sandra's experience appears to be representative of most medication abortions in the United States. Although they usually involve more discomfort than surgical abortions, serious complications are extremely rare. Like the vast majority of abortions in the United States, medication abortions take place very early in pregnancy. But since abortion in general remains a highly divisive issue in the United States, the "abortion pill" has been the subject of intense political and moral debate.

Background

Mifepristone, originally called RU-486, was developed by the French endocrinologist Étienne-Émile Baulieu. The drug works by blocking the action of progesterone, the hormone that prepares the uterine wall for the implantation of a fertilized egg. The dose of misoprostol (a kind of prostaglandin) then induces uterine contractions that expel the sloughed-off lining, including the embryo or fetus.

When it approved the drug in 2000, the FDA concluded it should be taken no later than seven weeks into a pregnancy, although a number of studies and systematic reviews later found it could be effective up to ten weeks. Subsequent research by the World Health Organization (WHO) and other researchers also demonstrated that the drug combination was effective at substantially lower doses than originally thought and that the misoprostol dose could be safely administered at home—recommendations that over 80 percent of U.S. providers have now adopted.

If mifepristone is taken soon after sexual intercourse, it also blocks the action of progesterone, and as a result, a fertilized egg won't be able to implant itself in the uterine wall. Hence, the drug also has the possibility of serving as a "morning-after pill" for preventing pregnancy. But the drug's main use lies in its power to induce an abortion. When taken on its own, the drug is roughly 95 percent effective at inducing abortion, a rate that rises to as much as 99 percent when combined with misoprostol.

Conflict

From the beginning, mifepristone was a source of intense controversy, condemned by abortion opponents and hailed by reproductive rights proponents. The French pharmaceutical company that developed it, Roussel-Uclaf, pulled the drug after boycott threats, only to reinstate it after the French health ministry threatened to transfer the patent to another company. Roussel licensed the drug for use in China, Sweden, and Britain, but its plans to market the drug in the United States were

abandoned because of opposition from antiabortion groups. The general position was stated by a representative of the National Right to Life Committee, who characterized the use of the drug as "chemical warfare against an entire class of innocent humans."

The Population Council, a nonprofit research organization committed to making medical abortion available to U.S. women, was frustrated by Roussel's decision and persuaded the company to grant it a license to manufacture and distribute the drug in the United States. The council conducted another clinical trial, which, like the French studies, showed high efficacy and few complications. The data were presented to the FDA, and in September 2000 the agency approved RU-486 (as it was then known) as a safe and effective prescription drug.

Reactions to the approval were predictably mixed. Abortion opponents denounced the FDA decision, calling mifepristone a "baby poison" and vowing to lobby for legislation to prohibit its use. Pro-choice advocates hoped that the approval of the drug would effectively defuse the public abortion debate by allowing women to make abortion decisions privately. Given the concentration of abortion clinics in urban areas, they also hoped that women living in rural and other areas far from such clinics would now have a safe and legal alternative.

Restriction and Risk

Only some of the hopes that pro-choice advocates pinned on medication abortion have materialized. For one thing, it turned out that the FDA's approval of mifepristone came with a number of restrictions that do not apply to most other prescription drugs. Before physicians can prescribe the drug, they must present special information about their qualifications. Patients must also take mifepristone at the doctor's office rather than obtaining it at a pharmacy.

As a result, many physicians still prefer the speed and reliability of surgical abortions. Those procedures take only a few minutes, and then the patient is on the way to recovery. Mifepristone is limited to use during the first seven to ten weeks of pregnancy, and once a woman is given the drug, the protocol approved by the FDA requires that she return to the office two more times.

Many physicians who thought they were likely to prescribe mifepristone also soon came to realize that abortion is regulated by a bewildering and complicated set of state laws. Many of these laws were lobbied for by abortion opponents who wanted to make it difficult for women to obtain abortions, and they apply to all abortion providers, including those prescribing mifepristone.

Some states require, for example, that a physician performing abortions have an ultrasound machine, life-support equipment, and an operating suite available. Other states have laws stipulating specific standards the facility must satisfy, including hall width, temperature of running water, and amount of ventilation. Others mandate that providers read patients long lists of scientifically controversial warnings about health risks. The laws of some states regulate abortion in general, but those in other states specifically mention drug-induced abortion. In 2015, for instance, Arizona enacted a law that physicians must tell patients that medication abortions are "reversible," a claim that the medical community has rejected as lacking scientific grounding. (See Social Context: State Abortion Laws.)

The political debate over abortion has also led to increased scrutiny of the safety of medication abortion. As with the highly charged debate over vaccine safety, this scrutiny has tended to focus on a small number of ambiguous cases whose causal relationship to the drugs in question is unclear. In 2008, after the drugs had been prescribed an estimated 915,000 times over the course of eight years, researchers identified seven deaths that might be attributable to them. One death was due to an undiagnosed ectopic pregnancy, while the other six involved rare bacterial infections of *Clostridium sordellii* and *Clostridium perfringens.* Some researchers suggested that misoprostol might have lowered women's immune response to these bacteria, while others suggested that the off-label administration of misoprostol as a vaginal suppository might be responsible. The possibility that a particular lot of the drugs had become contaminated was also suggested, since the deaths all occurred in 2005 and 2006 and no similar deaths were reported in other countries. A joint CDC–NIH–FDA investigation, however, later concluded that the evidence did not indicate that the drugs had caused the infections. Instead, they cited CDC studies and other research indicating that pregnancy itself, rather than the medication, was likely the critical risk factor. They pointed to another cluster of

ten fatal clostridial infections before 2001, eight of which occurred after childbirth.

Nevertheless, there is clearly some small risk of adverse reactions to medication abortion, particularly excess bleeding as well as other (nonfatal) infections. A study conducted by Princeton University and Planned Parenthood published in 2009 found that the very rare (0.93 in 1,000) risk of a serious infection after taking the drugs could be reduced to 0.06 in 1,000 if practitioners avoided the vaginal suppository approach and prescribed antibiotics with the drugs. Although subsequent studies have continued to find complication rates well below 1 percent for both the FDA protocol and the lower-dose approach adopted by most providers, some physicians still prefer surgical abortion. For one thing, a drug-induced abortion is five to ten times more likely to fail and then require a surgical procedure.

In addition, abortion opponents continue to cite safety when fighting efforts to make medication abortion more easily accessible—lobbying against videoconference consultations for patients in rural areas and administration of the drugs by nurses and physician's assistants. Abortion rights advocates argue that these expressions of concern for women's health are disingenuous efforts to fight abortion by fanning irrational fear. They also point to evidence that childbirth is fourteen times more likely to kill women than any form of abortion.

Despite this ongoing conflict, mifepristone has been used in 2.3 million procedures and now accounts for a third of all abortions that occur before ten weeks of gestation. Despite the fact that overall abortion rates in the United States continue to fall to their lowest levels since the mid-1970s, the proportion of abortions performed using medication is on the rise. The drug combination also appears to have accelerated the overall trend toward earlier abortions, 73 percent of which take place in the first nine weeks of pregnancy and 90 percent of which take place during the first trimester.

Still, fifteen years after the approval of mifepristone, it has not ended the abortion controversy in the United States, as some advocates had hoped it would. Nor has it provided a legal abortion route for women who live in rural areas and cannot afford to travel to the urban centers where most surgical and medication abortions are available. As a result of the dozens of new abortion restrictions that have been adopted on the state level, the number of clinics providing abortion of any kind has continued to fall precipitously in many states. (In just three years, the number of clinics in Texas fell from forty-four to nineteen, and there is now just one abortion provider in the entire state of Mississippi.) This situation has given rise to new uses of mifepristone and misoprostol that occupy a gray area in the law.

Mail-Order Abortion?

In September 2014, Jennifer Whalen, a thirty-nine-year-old mother of three from a small town in rural Pennsylvania, started serving a nine-to-eighteen-month prison term. Her crime was ordering mifepristone and misoprostol online and providing them to her sixteen-year-old daughter.

In the winter of 2012, Whalen's daughter had come to her and told her she was pregnant. Whalen told her daughter she would "support any decision she made," but the girl ultimately decided, "I can't have a baby right now."

When Whalen and her daughter began to research abortion clinics, however, they encountered problems. The closest clinic was seventy-five miles away, and Pennsylvania's twenty-four-hour abortion waiting period meant they would have to spend the night in Harrisburg before the procedure, which itself would cost as much as $600. Whalen was a personal care aide at a nursing home who shared one car with her husband, and she had no health insurance for her daughter. When she and her daughter found a reputable-looking European website that offered mifepristone and misoprostol for sale for $45, the choice seemed obvious.

They ordered the pills, which arrived and worked as promised. But Whalen became alarmed after her daughter experienced abdominal pains and took her to the hospital as a precaution. Her daughter turned out to be fine, but the hospital reported Whalen to the police after learning what her daughter had taken. Whalen later said she had no idea she needed a prescription to order the pills and her defenders argue that her prison sentence is unusual for personal online drug purchases. (Whalen's felony conviction was for offering abortion consultation without a medical license; she was also convicted of assault and endangering the welfare of a child.)

Whatever one makes of Jennifer Whalen's choices, they exemplify the fact that abortion has become considerably harder to access for millions of women in certain regions of the country. In the Rio Grande Valley of Texas, where the last abortion clinic closed in early 2014, women now regularly cross the border to buy misoprostol in Mexico, where it is legally sold over the counter, and volunteer groups have been organized to get women access to the drugs and monitor their reactions to them.

The organized provision of medication abortion across international borders is relatively new in the United States, but it has been going on elsewhere in the world for over a decade. Nearly 40 percent of the world's population lives in countries where abortion is either officially or effectively banned, and dangerous "back alley" abortions are still the only route available for ending unwanted pregnancies. As a result, several nonprofit groups have sprung up to offer medication abortion to women who cannot access it in their home countries. Women on Web, founded by the Dutch physician and activist Rebecca Gomperts, offers online medical consultations followed by mail-order prescriptions for mifepristone and misoprostol. The service is provided for free or for a donation and comes with detailed instructions on how to use the pills.

Women on Web's physicians advise women who experience any complications to seek local medical care but not disclose that they have taken the pills, since any treatment they need will be identical to that provided for spontaneous miscarriage. (The group does not operate in the United States and other countries where abortion is still legal.)

Envoi

The dream of many women's health groups in the 1980s was that mifepristone and misoprostol would make abortion safe, private, and easily secured by all women who sought one. The failure to achieve this dream reflects how contentious the abortion issue remains in the United States and how much progress opponents of abortion have made, especially at the state level. The fact that medication abortion is now being sought out illegally or quasi-legally reflects a familiar pattern: as abortions become more difficult to obtain, the steps women will take to end unintended pregnancies become more desperate and extreme.

The "Partial-Birth Abortion" Controversy

In the mid-1990s, a fierce public debate arose over abortions performed after twenty weeks of gestation, often focusing on a specific surgical procedure used to terminate pregnancy. Technically known as intact dilation and extraction, the procedure was dubbed "partial-birth abortion" by anti-abortion activists.

The debate, still simmering after more than twenty years, has been characterized to an unusual extent by a lack of information and a reliance on misinformation by participants on both sides. Instead of laying out the issues as the opponents present them, it may be more useful to begin by considering some of the facts relevant to evaluating the various positions taken.

Late-Term Abortion

While abortion opponents often portray "abortion doctors" as employing brutal procedures to destroy viable fetuses in order to satisfy the whims of pregnant women, those favoring abortion rights often present women as opting for late-term abortions in only desperate and extreme cases. The best estimates available suggest that neither picture is entirely accurate.

The length of a normal pregnancy is forty weeks from the first day of the pregnant woman's last menstrual cycle. More than half (64.5 percent) of all abortions are performed less than nine weeks after this point, and more than a quarter (26.9 percent) are performed in weeks nine through thirteen. Indeed, 98.6 percent of all abortions are performed within twenty weeks gestation. Thus, late-term abortion, defined as abortion after twenty weeks, is quite rare, accounting for only 1.4 percent of all abortions.

Few statistics are available on the reasons women have late-term abortions, although a number of small studies combined with the testimony of physicians presents a general picture. It suggests that one group of women has such abortions because the woman's own health is threatened by pregnancy. For example, the pregnancy may have triggered an autoimmune disease, or the woman may have developed cancer and need treatment with chemotherapy and radiation.

A second group has late-term abortions because the fetus has developed a severe defect. For example, ultrasound may reveal that the growing child's cerebral hemispheres have failed to develop. If the pregnancy continues, the child that is born not only will lack all cognitive capacity, but will die within a few days or weeks.

The third and largest group comprises those who have failed to get an early abortion for a variety of mostly social, economic, and logistical reasons. The group includes women who do not recognize a pregnancy due to a number of factors that may include irregular menstrual periods, obesity, or psychological denial. It also disproportionately includes younger women, indigent or homeless women, the mentally ill or disabled, and the unemployed. Women seeking late-term abortions are also more likely to be in conflict with their spouse or partner over their decision. Finally, lack of insurance, being turned away by a previous provider, and having to travel more than three hours to get to an abortion facility are all associated with late-term abortions.

Proponents of abortion rights tend to overlook this third group and focus instead on the other two. Being able to cite the pressing need of a pregnant woman to save her life or the cruelty of forcing a pregnant woman to carry to term a fetus with a serious developmental defect makes for a simpler and more appealing public relations campaign.

Opponents of abortion, by contrast, tend to discuss late-term abortion as if it were the general rule, rather than very much the statistical exception. When 98.6 percent of all abortions are performed before twenty weeks, it is misleading to condemn all abortion by focusing on the 1.4 percent as representative. They also tend to ignore powerful reasons that someone may have a late-term abortion, preferring to use cases producing the strongest negative emotional response.

Fetal Viability

Abortion opponents have focused on fetal viability as the crucial grounds for outlawing late-term abortion. In making their case, they have suggested that late abortions involve killing babies that otherwise would live and thrive. This has made the debate over late-term abortion particularly contentious, for determinations of viability cannot be made in a fixed and reliable fashion.

Perinatologists (specialists in newborns) say that too many factors are involved in determining viability to make reliable generalizations about which fetuses will live and which will die at any given stage of development. In addition to characteristics such as a fetus's weight and the developmental stage of the organs, factors such as the health of the mother, her socioeconomic status, and her access to health care also play a role. So do the ancestry and gender of the fetus. For example, a European American fetus developmentally lags a week behind an African American one of the same age and a male fetus lags about the same amount behind a female.

The viability of a fetus is also connected with the state of medical technology and management. At the time of the *Roe v. Wade* decision in 1973, fetal viability was around twenty-six weeks, but in recent decades it has averaged about twenty-four, with survival at twenty-two weeks being rare but possible. A severely premature *micropremie* weighs 500 to 600 grams (a bit over a pound) and is hardly larger than the palm of an adult's hand. Babies of this age and size, even if they survive, are likely to have irreversible physical and mental deficits. (See Chapter 6.)

The American College of Obstetrics and Gynecology estimates that less than 4 percent of babies are born during weeks twenty-three to twenty-five of the normal forty-week gestation period, and their survival is conditional on the factors mentioned. Some experts doubt that, even with aggressive intervention and intensive care, more than about 1 percent of twenty-five-week fetuses will survive. Some hospitals and state laws make twenty-three or twenty-four weeks the cutoff point for elective abortions, while others follow a more restrictive policy and make twenty weeks the limit. After these cutoffs, factors such as the health and safety of the mother or a fetal abnormality must be present to justify an abortion.

How viable a fetus is and how likely it is to survive without serious and permanent mental and physical deficits is a clinical judgment that can be made only case by case. Claims to the effect that hundreds or even thousands of viable fetuses are destroyed by abortion are not supported by the evidence.

Methods

Opponents of abortion have focused attention on a method to perform late-term abortion known as intact dilation and extraction. The procedure involves using a drug to dilate (widen) the pregnant woman's cervix, then manipulating the fetus by hand until it can be pulled through the birth canal. Usually, to ease the passage and make the procedure easier on the woman, the fetal brain is extracted by suction so that the skull can be collapsed (fenestrated). It is this procedure that abortion opponents have called "partial-birth abortion," a name coined for rhetorical purposes and not one used in medicine.

Intact dilation and extraction may also be performed by injecting digoxin into the uterus to stop the fetal heart. After the death of the fetus, the woman is induced into labor with a hormone injection and the fetus is delivered vaginally. Some obstetricians consider this form of the procedure too psychologically stressful for the patient. Others believe it is sufficiently well tolerated to make it the preferred method.

The third or classic method of dilation and extraction does not involve removing an intact fetus. After a woman's cervix is dilated, instruments are used to dismember the fetus and extract the parts through the birth canal. The fetus is killed either by a prior injection or by the process itself. Ultrasound may be used to guide the instruments, and the procedure may take twenty minutes or longer.

Surgeons who prefer intact dilation and extraction point to the time and risks associated with the classic procedure. The woman's uterus may be damaged by an instrument or punctured by a sharp bone fragment. It is safer for the woman if the intact fetus is pulled out by hand.

About 86 percent of abortions performed after twenty weeks are done by one of these three procedures, all of which are troubling for some practitioners. "Any procedure done at this stage is pretty gruesome," said one high-risk-pregnancy specialist.

Early Federal Attempts to Ban

In 1996, Congress passed legislation banning late-term abortion, along with intact dilation and extraction, but the bill was vetoed by President Clinton on the grounds that it made no provision for protecting the health of the pregnant woman. Abortion opponents claimed that allowing an exception for health would be equivalent to no regulation at all, because the health protections (particularly those for mental health) were too open-ended.

A revised version of the bill was then passed that was designed to reflect a proposal framed and endorsed by the American Medical Association. In the first endorsement of any position on abortion, the AMA proposal made it clear that dilation and *evacuation*, the procedure most often used in early abortions, was not banned. Also, the proposal protected physicians from criminal penalties if they had to perform a dilation and extraction because of unforeseen circumstances during a delivery. Finally, the proposal allowed physicians accused of violating the ban to appear before a state medical board instead of a trial court.

In contrast with the AMA, the American College of Obstetricians and Gynecologists and the American Academy of Pediatrics both opposed any ban on dilation and extraction. Some saw a danger in the AMA's position, suggesting that it invited politicians to make decisions about what medical procedures are appropriate.

State Attempts to Ban

Impatient with the slowness of Congress in passing a law banning "partial-birth abortion," about twenty-two states had passed their own laws by 1997. By 2005, however, most of these laws had been ruled unconstitutional by the courts. The most common flaw was that the language of the laws was so broad that it would also apply to abortions performed before the fetus could be viable. Also, like the original bill passed by Congress, the laws made no exception to protect the pregnant woman's health.

Ohio decision. In 1995, the Ohio legislature passed a law banning all abortion past the point of fetal viability. Viability was presumed to occur twenty-four weeks after conception. The only exception to the ban was for abortions a physician decided needed to be performed to "prevent the death of the pregnant woman or a serious risk of the substantial and irreversible impairment of a major bodily function of the pregnant woman." The law also included a provision making it a crime for a physician to end a pregnancy "by purposely inserting a suction device into the skull of a fetus to remove its brain."

In *Voinovich v. Women's Medical Professional Corporation*, a case brought to challenge the law, the U.S. Sixth Circuit Court of Appeals in Cincinnati ruled that the law unconstitutionally restricted a woman's right to abortion by defining the prohibited procedure so broadly that it had the consequence of banning the most common method of surgical abortion during the second trimester.

The ruling was appealed to the Supreme Court. In a 1998 decision (6–3), the Court refused to hear the case, letting the Appeals Court decision stand. In a dissenting opinion, Justice Clarence Thomas criticized the lower court's focus on whether prohibitions of late-term abortion could limit their health exemptions to physical health, while excluding mental health. (In the landmark 1973 decision *Doe v. Bolton*, the Court had held that physicians may consider "emotional" and "psychological" factors in deciding whether an abortion after fetal viability is necessary to preserve the health of the pregnant woman.)

Nebraska Decision

A 2000 ruling by the U.S. Supreme Court on a Nebraska law resulted in nullifying more than thirty state laws. The 1997 Nebraska law banned "an abortion procedure in which the person performing the abortion partially delivers vaginally a living unborn child before killing the unborn child and completing the delivery." The phrase "partial delivery" was defined as "deliberately and intentionally delivering into the vagina a living unborn child or a substantial proportion thereof."

In a 5–4 vote, the Supreme Court held that the government cannot prohibit physicians from employing an abortion procedure that may be the most medically appropriate way of terminating some pregnancies. The Nebraska law, the Court decided, also did not contain provisions for protecting the health and safety of the pregnant woman. Justice John Paul Stevens wrote in the majority opinion that it was "impossible for me to understand how a state has any legitimate interest in requiring a doctor to follow any procedure other than the one he or she reasonably believes will best protect the woman."

Partial-Birth Abortion Ban Act of 2003

Many observers believed that the earlier Supreme Court decisions had effectively declared that all legislation, state or federal, aimed at regulating abortion by outlawing specific procedures would be unconstitutional. Even so, in 2003, Congress passed the Partial-Birth Abortion Ban Act. The law makes it a crime for a doctor to perform an abortion in which "the entire fetal head" or "any part of the fetal trunk past the navel" is outside the woman's uterus at the time the fetal life is terminated.

Opponents of the law immediately challenged it in court, so the law did not take effect. In 2005, the Eighth Circuit U.S. Court of Appeals in St. Louis ruled that the law was unconstitutional. The act, the court held, contained an exception to protect a pregnant woman's life, but it made no exception to protect her health. This decision was in keeping with the Supreme Court's ruling against the 1997 Nebraska law.

Congress, in an attempt to avoid having the law overturned on just this ground, appended to the law a "finding" claiming that the "partial-birth" procedure is never needed to protect the health of a pregnant woman and that "there is no credible medical evidence that partial-birth abortions are safe or are safer than other abortion procedures." Both these claims have been challenged in court by expert medical testimony. One doctor testified, for example, that the health of some women could be preserved by avoiding such complications as the puncturing of the uterus in the course of alternative procedures.

The Bush administration immediately appealed the St. Louis ruling to the Supreme Court. The Court agreed to hear the case (*Gonzales v. Carhart*), and in 2007 it upheld the constitutionality of the Partial-Birth Abortion Ban Act of 2003. This came as a surprise to many observers, because the Court's 2000 decision had overturned a Nebraska law that was essentially the same as the 2003 act.

Need for a Law?

Many observers believe there was never a need for laws banning late-term abortion. In keeping with the *Roe v. Wade*, *Webster*, and *Casey* decisions, more than forty states passed laws banning abortion after fetal viability. (See Social Context: Supreme Court Decisions after *Roe v. Wade* in this chapter.) The problem of precisely fixing a point of fetal viability is vexing and perhaps unsolvable, but an additional law banning late-term abortion, even if constitutional, does not help resolve the issue.

Advocates for abortion rights and even some opponents of abortion have expressed the view that the controversy over late-term abortion is primarily a way to keep abortion issues at the forefront of political discussion and to pressure politicians to modify their endorsement of elective abortion. Some have also seen the controversy as a way to raise money for all antiabortion activities.

Although these analyses may be inaccurate, or even cynical, it seems fair to say that the debate over late-term abortion introduces no new ethical issues into the discussion. The old problems remain as complex and perhaps as intractable as before.

SOCIAL CONTEXT
Supreme Court Abortion Decisions after *Roe v. Wade*

The conflict over abortion has been expressed, in part, through a continuing series of legal battles and Supreme Court decisions that attempt to define abortion rights and restrictions. To get some sense of the way in which laws, regulations, and practices have changed since the *Roe* decision in 1973, it is useful to review a few of the Court's major abortion decisions. They provide a sense of the dramatic shifts in public policy with regard to abortion over the past few decades.

Doe v. Bolton (1973)
The Court rejected the requirement that abortions had to be performed in hospitals or approved by anyone (such as a hospital committee) besides a woman's physician, thus opening the way for abortion clinics. The Court also found that physicians could consider emotional and psychological factors connected with the health of a pregnant woman in deciding whether an abortion after viability was justified.

Planned Parenthood v. Danforth (1976)

A Missouri law requiring a husband's consent for an abortion was struck down. Also, parents were found not to have veto power over the abortion decisions of their daughters under age twenty-one.

Maher v. Roe (1977)

The Court ruled that states do not have a constitutional obligation to pay for abortions for the poor. Hence, states can decide whether they want to include abortion funding in their contribution to the Medicaid program.

Harris v. McRae (1980)

The Court upheld the Hyde Amendment, a federal law banning the use of federal Medicaid funds to pay for abortions. Hence, a woman who wants an abortion but is unable to pay for it must obtain the money from some other source. States may choose to provide the funds, but they have no constitutional obligation to do so.

City of Akron v. Akron Center for Reproductive Health (1983)

The Court struck down a law requiring that women seeking an abortion receive counseling that included the statement that "the unborn child is a human life from the moment of conception," then wait a minimum of twenty-four hours before reaffirming their decision.

Webster v. Reproductive Health Services (1989)

The Missouri law in the *Webster* case is similar to earlier state laws the Court had ruled unconstitutional, such as that in the *Akron* case. However, the law was carefully crafted by pro-life advocates to avoid the specific difficulties that had led the Court to reject previous statutes. The preamble of the law asserts

that "life begins at conception," but at issue were three provisions restricting abortion: (1) Public employees, including physicians and nurses, are forbidden to perform an abortion, except when necessary to save a woman's life. (2) Tax-supported facilities, including public hospitals, cannot be used to perform abortions, unless one is necessary to save a woman's life. (3) Physicians are required to conduct tests to determine the viability of a fetus if they have reason to believe the woman has been pregnant for at least twenty weeks.

On July 3, 1989, in a 5–4 decision, the Supreme Court upheld the constitutionality of the law. Chief Justice William Rehnquist, writing for the majority, held that the Court did not have to rule against the claim that life begins at conception, for such language is only an expression of a permissible value judgment. Furthermore, "Nothing in the Constitution requires States to enter or remain in the business of performing abortions. Nor...do private physicians and their patients have some kind of constitutional right of access to public facilities for the performance of abortions."

So far as viability is concerned, Rehnquist saw a problem not with the Missouri law, but with *Roe v. Wade*'s "rigid trimester analysis of a pregnancy." He found the Missouri law more sensitive to the issue of viability than the trimester rule in *Roe*, which holds that the state can regulate abortion in the second trimester to protect a woman's health, but can only prohibit abortion in the last trimester.

Justice Harry A. Blackmun, the author of the majority opinion in *Roe v. Wade*, wrote the dissenting opinion in *Webster*. Rehnquist, he argued, failed to consider the case on appropriate grounds—namely, the right to privacy or autonomy, on which *Roe* was decided. Instead, Rehnquist misread the Missouri law's unconstitutional intervention based on fetal interests during the second trimester and set up an artificial conflict with the *Roe* trimester system. He argued that allowing such pre-viability regulations would eventually render *Roe's* protection of procreative rights meaningless, and warned that "a chill wind blows."

Abortion opponents hoped that the Court would use the *Webster* case to overturn *Roe v. Wade*. The Court stopped short of that, but the *Webster* decision made it clear that the Court was willing to approve restrictions on abortion of a sort that it had held unconstitutional until then. Various new state and local regulations were then formulated and passed into law.

Planned Parenthood v. Casey (1992)

The 1989 Pennsylvania Abortion Control Act was also framed with the intention of making abortions more difficult to secure. It set forth the following restrictions: (1) A physician must inform a woman seeking an abortion about the procedure and its risks, the stage of her pregnancy, and the alternative of carrying the fetus to term. (2) The woman must wait at least twenty-four hours after receiving this information before having an abortion. (3) A girl under the age of eighteen must secure the informed consent of at least one parent before having an abortion, and a parent must accompany the girl to counseling. Alternatively, consent may be sought from a court. (4) A married woman must (except under certain circumstances) sign a statement that she has notified her husband of her intention to have an abortion.

The Pennsylvania law was challenged on constitutional grounds by Planned Parenthood and other plaintiffs, who sued the state and its Governor, Robert P. Casey. Given the *Webster* decision and a new conservative majority on the Court, many observers expected it to use the *Casey* decision to overturn *Roe v. Wade*—but this did not occur. The 5–4 *Casey* ruling upheld most sections of the Pennsylvania law, but it rejected the provision requiring a married woman to notify her husband of her intention. In the view of many, the most important result of the *Casey* decision was to reaffirm a constitutional right to an abortion, while introducing a new legal standard for testing the constitutional legitimacy of abortion regulations.

The Court considered the law's provisions in terms of whether they had the purpose or result of imposing an "undue burden" on a woman seeking an abortion. The Court defined a burden as "undue" if it places "substantial obstacles in the path of a woman seeking an abortion before the fetus attains viability." Only the spousal notification requirement, the Court held, imposed such a burden. The undue-burden standard thus made clear the Court's view that laws attempting to prohibit abortions outright or reduce the frequency of abortions by making them extraordinarily difficult to obtain are unconstitutional.

The Court explicitly endorsed *Roe v. Wade* as having established "a rule of law and a component of liberty that we cannot renounce." It held that *Roe* has acquired such a "rare precedential force" that it could be repudiated only "at the cost of both profound and unnecessary damage to the Court's legitimacy and to the nation's commitment to the rule of law."

Until the *Webster* decision, abortion was considered a fundamental right that could not be restricted, except to serve a compelling state interest. Thus, during the first two trimesters of pregnancy, almost all restrictions were considered unconstitutional. After *Webster*, abortion opponents saw that it might be possible to impose more and heavier regulations. But although the "undue-burden" standard introduced in *Casey* appears to permit considerable regulation during that period, it does not allow the practice to be regulated so heavily as to make it virtually unavailable.

Madsen v. Women's Health Center (1994)

In 1993, a Florida circuit court issued an injunction to protect access to the clinic operated by the Aware Woman Center for Choice in Melbourne, Florida. Demonstrators from Operation Rescue and other antiabortion organizations were made subject to the injunction. The order imposed a three-hundred-foot protected zone around the clinic, forbade the display of signs that could be seen from inside the clinic, and barred demonstrators from making excessive noise.

The case was appealed, and in a 6–3 ruling, the Supreme Court upheld the basic provisions of the injunction. It approved an approximately thirty-six-foot buffer zone to keep protesters away from the clinic's entrance and parking lot and off a public right-of-way. The buffer zone "burdens no more speech than necessary to accomplish the government's interest," Justice Rehnquist wrote.

Schenck v. Pro-Choice Network (1997)

In a New York State case in which a group opposed to abortion appealed an injunction ordering them to cease blockading the entrances to a clinic and stop harassing and intimidating the women seeking an abortion, the Supreme Court, in a 6–3 decision, upheld the lower court's decision to keep the protesters from blocking doorways and driveways.

The Court's tacit endorsement of a fixed buffer zone around abortion clinics is significant, because about three hundred of the nine hundred abortion clinics in the country are protected by buffer zones spelled out in court injunctions. Both the Florida and New York rulings are considered important indicators of the Court's view of the Freedom of Access to Clinic Entrances Act, which is designed to provide federal remedies, including criminal penalties, to restrict violent protests at abortion clinics.

Stenberg v. Carhart (2000)

A Nebraska law directed at prohibiting late-term (past twenty weeks) abortion banned any "abortion procedure in which the person performing the abortion partially delivers vaginally a living unborn child before killing the unborn child and completing the delivery." In a 5–4 vote, the Court held that the government cannot prohibit physicians from employing whatever abortion procedure may be the most medically appropriate. Also, in trying to regulate abortion, the law failed to include any provisions for protecting the health and safety of the pregnant woman.

Gonzales v. Carhart (2007)

Congress passed the Partial-Birth Abortion Ban Act in 2003, making it a crime to perform an abortion in which "the entire fetal head" or "any part of the fetal trunk past the navel" is outside the woman's uterus at the time fetal life is ended. The law was challenged before it went into effect, and federal appeals court rulings in St. Louis found it to be unconstitutional. The rulings were immediately appealed to the Supreme Court, which upheld the law in a 5–4 decision. The ruling effectively negated the impact of the 2000 *Stenberg v. Carhart* decision, which had found unconstitutional a law with virtually the same prohibitions as the 2003 Partial-Birth Abortion Ban Act.

SOCIAL CONTEXT

State Abortion Laws: Rolling Back *Roe*?

Although the Supreme Court has upheld (with some changes and limitations) the basic finding in *Roe v. Wade,* access to abortion in America has become increasingly challenging and complicated in recent years. This is especially true for rural and low-income women, and for those living in southern and midwestern states, and it is partly attributable to hundreds of new state regulations and restrictions that have been instituted in those regions. More laws restricting abortion were enacted in just three years (2011–2013) than in the entire previous decade.

For abortion opponents, these laws and regulations are key victories in a larger struggle to end what they view as a crime of genocidal proportions. Despite abortion rates at their lowest levels since 1973, with 89 percent of procedures taking place during the first twelve weeks of gestation, roughly a million abortions are still performed in the United States each year. For those with deep-seated convictions that moral standing begins at fertilization or implantation, this is an unacceptable state of affairs and there is value in any law or regulation that makes it harder for women to obtain abortions or that might persuade them to change their minds about the procedure.

For defenders of abortion, the new laws and regulations represent illegitimate encroachments on rights and liberties recognized by the Supreme Court and the Constitution. They argue that many violate basic standards affirmed by the *Roe* and *Casey* decisions: that abortions cannot be banned before fetal viability and that before that point states must not impose an "undue burden" on women seeking abortions. (See Social Context: Supreme Court Abortion Decisions after *Roe v. Wade*.) They also charge that many of these laws undermine the fiduciary responsibilities of physicians to their patients and curtail the free speech and autonomy of both pregnant women and their doctors. It is expected that several of these laws will result in new Supreme Court decisions in coming years.

For now, it will be useful to survey four categories of state abortion laws and regulations and to briefly mention some of the ethical and legal issues they raise.

Regulation of Abortion Providers

States have enacted dozens of new regulations in recent years focused on abortion providers. Twenty-two states, for example, now mandate that abortion clinics meet the regulatory standards for ambulatory surgical centers—the outpatient facilities that perform orthopedic knee, hip, and spine surgeries, as well as hernia operations and cataract removals. Many of these regulations include specific requirements on room size, corridor width, ventilation systems, and other structural features, as well as special relationships with and maximum distances from local hospitals.

Defenders of these laws say they are necessary to ensure the safety of women undergoing what they see as a risky procedure, although many acknowledge they would not be upset if the regulations forced abortion clinics out of business. Critics say the regulations are being inappropriately applied, especially to clinics that only provide early-stage abortions—procedures that typically take less than fifteen minutes and use only local anesthetic or mild sedation. They say that requiring admitting privileges and other special ties give hospital systems—many of which are affiliated with the Catholic Church and opposed to abortion—veto power over abortion clinics.

However one assesses these claims, it seems clear that these and related laws have contributed to a precipitous drop in the number of abortion clinics operating in large areas of the United States. Eighty-nine percent of U.S. counties now lack an abortion clinic, and a nationwide survey found that over fifty clinics in twenty-seven states had closed since 2010, when many of the first laws were passed. Thirty of the closures were in Texas, which in a single year went from having forty clinics operating to ten, after strict new regulations went into effect. Three states now have only one abortion clinic in the entire state.

Defenders of the new regulations say that they do not violate the "undue burden" standard, since women are free to travel to the remaining clinics. Critics point out that the burden is substantially heavier if one cannot afford the transportation, childcare, or time off work to reach a clinic. (Mandatory waiting periods of twenty-four hours or more also typically necessitate securing local accommodations before the procedure.) As with many other aspects of abortion, the impact of the regulations varies widely depending on socioeconomic status.

Counseling and Waiting Periods

Another set of regulations involve abortion decisions and how physicians discuss the procedure with patients. Thirty-five states require that women receive "counseling" before having an abortion, although in twenty-seven states this means that physicians must read aloud from a script mandated by the government. Some of the scripts state that personhood begins at conception while others suggest that abortion is linked to breast cancer, mental health problems, and infertility. Many of these states also mandate that women undergo an ultrasound exam, and in some states physicians are required to describe the ultrasound image aloud if patients refuse to look at it. In twenty-six states, women are required to wait a specific number of hours after counseling before they can obtain an abortion—usually twenty-four hours, but in some states as many as seventy-two.

Critics of these laws say they undermine physicians' fiduciary responsibilities by forcing them to transmit false medical information to their patients. They point to official statements from the National Cancer Institute finding no link between breast cancer and abortion, and from the American Psychological Association finding that abortion does not significantly impact women's mental health. They also cite studies from *Clinical Obstetrics and Gynecology* and *NEJM*

concluding that common first-trimester techniques such as vacuum aspiration and medication abortion pose no risk to future fertility. (There is evidence, however, that second-trimester use of dilation and evacuation may slightly increase future pregnancy complications.) Finally, critics of counseling laws note that physicians do not have to read a state-specified list of warnings before such serious and potentially dangerous procedures as prostate removal, breast augmentation, or open-heart surgery.

Abortion opponents argue such warnings are necessary to provide for women's full informed consent. But they also acknowledge that counseling laws are broadly focused on anything that may make women stop and reconsider an abortion decision. In the spring of 2015, for example, Arizona enacted a law mandating that medication abortion patients be told that the procedure may be "reversible." Although there is no scientific evidence that the progesterone regimen used by some physicians "reverses" medication abortions, it is well known that 30 to 50 percent of pregnancies will remain intact if medication abortion patients take only half of the prescribed two-drug regimen—as did the patients cited by the law's authors. The law is, in effect, another plea for women to change their minds. While there is little evidence that state-mandated counseling or ultrasound images actually have an impact on abortion decisions, it should not be surprising that abortion opponents advance such regulations, for they view themselves as obligated to do anything they can to prevent women from committing a serious and irrevocable moral wrong.

Pre-Viability Bans

Many new state abortion laws have also been focused on limiting the window of time during which women can obtain abortions. As of early 2015, thirteen states had enacted so-called "fetal pain" bills, which ban abortion as early as twenty weeks' gestation. The bills are premised on a controversial theory that a fetus can feel pain at this stage of development. (A 2005 systematic review published in the *Journal of the American Medical Association*, for example, concluded that "fetal perception of pain is highly unlikely before the third trimester," due to the absence of thalamocortical fibers involved in pain perception before twenty-nine to thirty weeks' gestation. Most medical associations and scientists say pain perception requires brain developments that only take place in the third trimester.)

Also controversial is the use, in many of the bills, of "fertilization" to date a pregnancy, rather than the start of a woman's last menstrual period (LMP) before pregnancy. Only in IVF pregnancies can physicians accurately determine when fertilization occurs. It is therefore standard medical practice to date the *gestational age* of a fetus from the first day of the woman's last period, assuming that ovulation and fertilization occurs approximately two weeks later. Twenty weeks *post-fertilization* thus roughly equals twenty-two weeks' gestation (LMP), using the standard system. But some providers in these states appear to be refusing abortion requests at twenty weeks' gestation, to protect themselves from prosecutors who may be confused about the law. (Two of the laws, in Mississippi and North Carolina, explicitly ban abortions after twenty weeks gestation.)

Some defenders of these laws point out that less than 1.4 percent of abortions take place after twenty-one weeks' gestation and that the bans impact relatively few women. Critics argue that these cases are particularly tragic, often involving severe fetal deformities or women afflicted with mental illness or disability, who should not be forced to bear a child. (Another criticism of the laws is that many grant exceptions only to preserve the life and *physical* health of the pregnant woman.)

It is unclear how many of these new bans on abortion will withstand constitutional scrutiny, and three have already been blocked by the courts. Fetal viability is generally considered to begin around twenty-four weeks' gestation, though even that must be confirmed by a physician in individual cases. Since the *Roe* and *Casey* decisions guarantee a right to abortion before fetal viability, critics say that these twenty- and twenty-two-week bans are flagrantly unconstitutional. Defenders of these and even earlier state bans have argued in court that since a fertilized ovum can survive in a lab for a few days after IVF, viability actually begins at conception.

Personhood Laws

Perhaps the most straightforward expression of the belief that moral standing begins with conception takes the form of so-called "personhood" laws, which either seek to redefine the legal conception of personhood to include fertilized eggs or to amend state criminal codes to define them as children. When proposed as ballot measures, such laws have failed to win approval even in deeply conservative states, due to concerns that in addition to criminalizing all abortions, they would be used to outlaw IVF and contraception methods such as the birth control pill, IUDs, and Plan B. (These contraceptive techniques are actually designed to prevent fertilization rather than implantation, but some abortion opponents have claimed they are similar to abortion and called for their prohibition.)

Abortion opponents have had much greater success in redefining "person" in state homicide codes to include "an unborn child in utero at any stage of development," as Alabama's statute has since 2006. Alaska, Kentucky, and North Dakota have similar laws, and some twenty-five other states have some form of "fetal homicide" law that applies throughout gestation. Defenders of these laws argue they are necessary to punish drunk driving, domestic violence, and murder that results in the loss of a pregnancy, and point to exemptions in the laws for legal abortions. Critics say that additional punishments are already available through laws against nonconsensual termination of pregnancy and that fetal homicide laws are indirect attempts to establish a fetus's right to life. They also cite hundreds of instances in which feticide laws have been used against pregnant women themselves rather than those who do them violence.

In Iowa, for instance, a pregnant woman was arrested in 2010 for attempted fetal homicide after she fell down a flight of stairs after an argument with her husband. In Louisiana, a woman who had arrived at a hospital with unexplained vaginal bleeding was jailed for over a year on second-degree murder charges until the discovery of medical records indicating she had suffered a miscarriage at no more than fifteen weeks' gestation. In Utah, a woman was arrested on fetal homicide charges and spent several months in jail after the stillborn birth of one of her twins was attributed to her decision to delay a caesarean section. In many other cases, pregnant women have been forced by judges and local police to undergo caesarean sections against their will. Notable instances include a critically ill pregnant woman in Washington, DC, who was forced by a judge to have a caesarean that neither she nor her fetus survived, and cases in Florida in which pregnant women were physically restrained by hospital staff or law enforcement until they had undergone C-sections. (See Case Presentation: Policing Pregnancy in Chapter 10.)

Defenders argue that such laws and practices are justified by the state's interest in protecting fetal life, and are generally supportive of other instances in which pregnant women have been detained to prevent them from using alcohol or drugs. Critics say that women do not lose their civil rights or right to refuse treatment when they become pregnant. They also express concern about the use of feticide laws to prosecute women who intentionally induce their own abortions during a period when viability is ambiguous—actions that resulted in a twenty-year prison sentence for an Indiana woman in early 2015. Questions have also been raised about a 2014 Alabama law that appoints a lawyer to represent the fetus in hearings on whether minors can obtain abortions with parental permission. Developments such as these ensure that fetal personhood will remain an area of intense ethical and legal debate in the years to come.

Envoi

The dramatic increase in state abortion regulations has occurred during two decades of steep decline in the U.S. abortion rate—which is now at its lowest point since 1973. Some have wondered if the two phenomena are connected—whether the surge in antiabortion legislation may have caused a decline in abortions. Although sharp reductions in the number of abortion providers has likely decreased the number of legally obtained abortions in some states and regions, it appears that the continuing decline in the abortion rate is most likely attributable to other factors. For one thing, the decline in abortions has been underway since 1990—long before the largest wave of state abortion regulations—and it has occurred to an equal extent in states that have imposed no new restrictions on abortion. Moreover, the decline in abortions has coincided with a decline in unwanted pregnancies—indicating that better contraception and care to avoid pregnancy in tough economic times may be the most likely explanation for the shift.

BRIEFING SESSION

The history of abortion in America is a story of bitter conflict and dramatic reversals.

From the time of the nation's founding until the mid-nineteenth century, abortion was legal in the United States until *quickening*—the point four to five months into a pregnancy at which a fetus's movements can be detected. This standard was derived from British common law and was reflected in the earliest state abortion laws, which criminalized the use of *abortifacient* ("abortion causing") drugs, but only if employed after quickening. For much of the nineteenth century, these and other abortion methods were both advertised and widely available, but could also be hazardous for the women who used them. When states began to restrict earlier abortions in the mid-1800s, it was partly a result of a campaign by the newly formed American Medical Association (AMA) against both the procedure and the unlicensed midwives who often facilitated it. Abortion restrictions also reflected the medical and moral concerns of a larger and more active federal government. In 1873, Congress passed the Comstock Law, drafted by Anthony Comstock of the New York Society for the Suppression of Vice, which banned the distribution of abortion drugs and contraceptives, along with pornography.

By 1900, every state in the union had made abortion a felony, although some granted exceptions in cases of rape or to save a woman's life. Nevertheless, these laws were rarely enforced, and abortion was still widely practiced. A late nineteenth-century estimate placed the annual number of abortions at two million (more than seven times the current number per capita). In the 1930s, it was estimated that at least eight hundred thousand abortions were performed every year in the United States, often by licensed physicians operating openly out of clinics.

Though widely practiced, abortion was still illegal and dangerous. In 1930, illegal abortion was listed as the official cause of 18 percent of all pregnancy-related maternal deaths, although the actual number was likely far higher. With the widespread introduction of antibiotics in the 1940s, deaths due to both childbirth and abortion fell dramatically, but illegal abortion was still the official cause of 17 percent of pregnancy-related deaths as late as 1965. The procedure was particularly dangerous for low-income and minority women who typically lacked access to physicians willing to risk their licenses to perform the procedure. These women instead often relied on self-induced abortions or "back-alley" abortionists who operated with poor sanitation and little medical expertise. (See Case Presentation: When Abortion Was Illegal for more on this topic.)

In the 1960s and 1970s, growing concern about the public health consequences of illegal abortion prompted the AMA, the American Public Health Association, and other medical groups to change course, declaring that abortion could be permitted "in accordance with good medical practice" and that a "rapid and simple abortion referral" should be available from public health departments. A resurgence of the women's rights movement also shaped a perception that if women were to be autonomous and equal citizens, they had to be able to exercise greater control over their reproductive lives.

One result of these shifts was a series of landmark Supreme Court cases, most famously *Roe v. Wade* in 1973. The decision prohibited states from placing restrictions on abortion during the first trimester (three months) of pregnancy and prohibited states from banning it before the point of fetal viability. Even after viability, states cannot prohibit abortions that are "necessary to preserve the life or health" of the woman, as determined by her physician.

Shortly after the *Roe* decision, many assumed that the abortion issue was largely settled in the United States. Americans appeared to have returned to a "moral continuum" view of abortion, in which it only becomes a matter of serious ethical and legal concern as pregnancy progresses toward its final stages. But far from resolving the abortion question, the four decades since *Roe* have given rise to a committed movement dedicated to overturning it, along with a committed countermovement dedicated to defending it. Although the constitutional rights established by *Roe* have been largely reaffirmed by the Supreme Court, abortion opponents have been increasingly successful at restricting access to abortion through state laws. (See Social Context: State Abortion Laws.)

Despite the bitter (and sometimes violent) conflict over its legal status, abortion remains a deeply personal issue, one that involves some of our deepest convictions about life, liberty, personhood, and moral responsibility. It is also personal because it touches the lives of so many Americans. More than half of the pregnancies in America are unintended, and 40 percent of those are ended by abortion. The result is that 30 percent of American women have had an abortion by the time they are forty-five. Although wider access to effective contraception has steadily reduced the abortion rate to its lowest levels since the 1970s, the procedure remains a common, albeit frequently hidden, experience in many American families.

Given all these factors, it should not be surprising that controversy over the legitimacy of abortion continues to flare. In the abortion question, major moral, legal, and social issues are intertwined to form a problem of great subtlety and complexity. Indeed, no other topic in medical ethics has attracted more attention or so polarized public opinion.

Before focusing on some of the specific issues raised by abortion, however, it is useful to have in hand some of the relevant factual information about human developmental biology and abortion techniques.

Gestational Development

While the abortion debate is often framed in terms of trimesters and months, the stages of gestational development are generally measured in weeks:

Weeks 1–3: Ovulation takes place roughly eleven to twenty-one days after the first day of a woman's most recent menstrual cycle. *Fertilization* occurs when an ovum is penetrated by a sperm cell and the nuclei of the two unite to form a single cell containing forty-six chromosomes. This normally occurs in the fallopian tubes, narrow ducts leading from each ovary into the uterus. The fertilized ovum—commonly known as a *zygote*—continues its passage down the fallopian tube, and during its two- to three-day passage, it undergoes a number of cell divisions. After reaching the uterus, the zygote floats free in the intrauterine fluid. Here it develops into a *blastocyst*, a microscopic ball of cells surrounding a fluid-filled cavity.

Weeks 3–8: Six to twelve days after fertilization, the blastocyst becomes embedded in the wall of the uterus. At this point and until the end of the eighth week, it is known as an *embryo*. During the fourth and fifth weeks, organ systems such as the heart and digestive tube begin to develop, as well as structural features such as arm and leg buds. At this stage, the embryo is about the size of a pen tip. By the end of the eighth week, some brain activity usually becomes detectable. At this time, the embryo is about the size of a kidney bean, and comes to be known as a *fetus*.

Weeks 12–20: By week twelve, the fetus is about two and a half inches long. It is a few weeks after this point that some pregnant women are first able to detect fetal movement or *quickening* (see above). For most first-time pregnancies, this doesn't take place until weeks eighteen to twenty, however.

Weeks 24–40: During the period around twenty-four weeks of gestation, some fetuses develop the capacity to survive outside the womb, although the chance of survival is roughly one in four and most who do survive will have severe lifelong disabilities. There is no scientifically defined threshold of *fetal viability*, only individual case assessments based on fetal lung development and other factors. The fetus's chance of being able to survive outside the womb starts to increase substantially, however, during the middle of the seventh month, although the premature infant will still require extensive medical intervention.

The time intervals given above are approximate and vary from pregnancy to pregnancy. In addition, there is no way (except via IVF) for women or physicians to determine when fertilization actually occurs. For this reason, a pregnancy is typically dated from the first day of a woman's *last menstrual period* (LMP), with the assumption that ovulation and fertilization took place roughly two weeks after that. The expected duration of most pregnancies is forty weeks from the first day of LMP, and it is the point from which the weeks of gestational development are measured, as described above.

The more colloquial understanding of pregnancy is that it lasts nine months, a duration which is then divided into three three-month periods or *trimesters*. This is a more approximate system of general benchmarks with several weeks' variability, however, and should not be taken to represent precise developmental stages.

At present, pregnancy can be diagnosed as early as seven to ten days after fertilization. Also, improvements in ultrasound imaging allow the gestational sac surrounding the embryo to be detected in its earliest stages. Hence, a woman may be able to find out she is pregnant even before she has missed an expected period.

Abortion and Pregnancy

Abortion is a general word for the termination of pregnancy. It can occur because of internal physiological factors or as a result of physical injury to the woman. Terminations from such causes are technically referred to as *spontaneous abortions*, but they are also commonly called *miscarriages*.

Abortion can also be *induced*, which is to say a deliberate process resulting from human intervention. The abortion methods used in contemporary medicine depend to a great extent on the stage of the pregnancy. Because newer tests and ultrasound make it possible to detect pregnancy as early as a week or ten days after fertilization, a pregnancy can be terminated at that point. This can be done through a *medication abortion*, which typically involves taking the hormone blocker mifepristone followed by the prostaglandin misoprostol. The drug combination causes the lining of the uterus to shed, as it does in a menstrual period, and expels it through the cervix, ending the pregnancy.

The other earliest option is *manual vacuum aspiration* (MVA), in which a physician *dilates* (widens) the cervix, then uses a hand-operated syringe to suction out the uterine lining. This procedure lasts approximately ten minutes and involves local anesthesia.

Subsequent intervention during the first trimester (up to about twelve weeks) commonly employs the same technique or *vacuum aspiration*. In this procedure, a small tube is inserted into the uterus and its contents are emptied by machine suction.

It is also known as *dilation and evacuation*. (The classical abortion procedure is *dilation and curettage*, in which the cervical contents are gently scraped out by the use of a curette, a spoon-shaped surgical instrument. The procedure has been almost wholly replaced by evacuation in developed countries.)

After approximately sixteen weeks' gestation, when the fetus is too large to make the other methods practical, the most common abortion technique involves dilating the cervix and extracting the fetus. (See Social Context: The "Partial-Birth Abortion" Controversy for discussion.)

These facts about pregnancy and abortion put us in a position to discuss some of the moral problems connected with them. We won't be able to untangle the complicated issues surrounding the abortion question. We'll only attempt to introduce a few of the more serious ones and to indicate the relevant lines of argument that have been put forward; afterward we'll sketch out some possible responses that might be offered on the basis of major ethical theories.

The Status of the Fetus

It is crucial for the application of the principles of any moral theory that we have a settled opinion about the objects and subjects of morality. Although principles are often stated with respect to an ideal rational individual, moral theories recognize that there are many sentient living beings—including animals, young children, the unconscious, and those with severe brain damage—who do not meet the standard of rationality. Still, most ethical theories recognize duties to those beings, particularly if they are categorized as *persons*.

This raises a basic problem: Who or what is to be considered a person? Are there any characteristics that we can point to and say that it is by virtue of possessing these

characteristics that an individual must be considered a person and thus accorded moral consideration?

The abortion issue raises this question most particularly with regard to the fetus. (We will use the term "fetus," for the moment, to refer to the developing organism at any stage.) Some writers on both sides of the abortion debate argue that we must reach a conclusion about the moral status of the fetus before we can resolve the general moral problem of abortion.

Let us consider some possible consequences of answering the question one way or the other. First, if a fetus is a person from the moment of conception, it has a serious claim to life throughout pregnancy. We can assert the claim on its behalf, for, like an unconscious person, the fetus is unable to do so. The claim of the fetus as a person must be given weight and respect in deliberating about any action that would terminate its life. Assuming that the fetus is a person, then, an abortion would be a case of killing and something not to be undertaken without reasons sufficient to override the fetus's right to life.

Of course, the right to life is not absolute. For no person is it construed as a right not to be killed or to be kept alive under any circumstances or at any cost to others' rights. Some will argue, as we will see in the next section, that even if a fetus is a person, it does not have an unqualified right against a pregnant woman to use her body to sustain its life. This point is easiest to see in cases that can be framed as self-defense (e.g., when a pregnancy threatens a woman's life) or when pregnancy is forced or otherwise involuntary (e.g., through rape or a failure of birth control). But however one evaluates these different situations, they set up a potential conflict between the rights of two persons, the fetus and the pregnant woman.

By contrast, if a fetus is not a person in a morally relevant sense, then the conflict diminishes or disappears, for abortion need not be considered a case of killing equivalent to the killing of an adult. In one view, it might be said that an abortion is not essentially different from an appendectomy. According to this way of thinking, a fetus is an extension of a woman's body, created almost entirely from her biological processes, and its removal is thus her prerogative. Alternatively, one might grant that the fetus is a sentient organism, as nonhuman animals are, but argue that it still lacks the essential features, such as consciousness, reason, and will, that would make it a part of the human moral community. There may be compelling reasons to refrain from terminating its life, but those reasons would not rise to the level of rights.

Another position in the debate argues that even though the fetus is not currently a person, it is a *potential* person, and thus endowed with a significant and morally relevant property. The fetus's potential human personhood makes it unique and distinguishes it from a rabbit or an appendix. Thus, because the fetus may become a person, abortion presents a moral problem, according to this view. A fetus can be destroyed only for serious reasons and may require justification comparable to that required for killing an adult.

Critics of this view argue that it puts our duties to potential people on par with our duties to *actual* people, and that in a conflict between the two, the latter should clearly prevail. Moreover, the notion that a fetus is a potential rather than an actual person calls our attention to the fact that human development is a process with many stages.

So far we have used the word "fetus" to cover the entire span of pregnancy, which has meant that claims to fetal personhood apply from the moment an egg is fertilized. But perhaps it is only in the later stages of development that a fetus achieves personhood. The difference between a fertilized ovum and a fully developed fetus just a few minutes before birth are considerable. To many, the ovum and the blastocyst seem just so much tissue. But the fetus presents a more serious claim to being a person. Should abortion be allowed until the fetus becomes visibly human, or until the fetus shows heartbeat and brain waves, or until the fetus has a reasonable chance of surviving outside the uterus (becomes viable)?

The process of development is continuous, and so far it has proved difficult to find differences between stages that can be generally accepted as morally relevant. Some writers on abortion have suggested that it is useless to look for such differences, because any place where the line is drawn will be arbitrary. Others have claimed that it is possible to draw the line by relying on criteria that can be rationally defended.

For some philosophers, such as John Noonan, Patrick Lee, and Robert George, the line can be clearly drawn at fertilization, when the blastocyst receives its distinct genetic code and develops new cells that are neither sperm nor egg. On their view, the blastocyst is a complete human organism, programmed to develop itself if properly nurtured, and thus qualifies for personhood. Other philosophers, such as Judith Jarvis Thomson, contend that although a fertilized egg is no more a person than an acorn is an oak tree, the fetus does become a person well before birth. Another position, advanced by philosophers such as Mary Anne Warren, holds that fetuses are never persons and that a reasonable set of criteria for determining who shall be considered a person might even deny that status to infants.

In all discussions of ethics, it is important to remember that moral positions do not necessarily correspond to legal or practical positions. So, for example, Warren's position need not commit her to tolerating infanticide, since there may be other serious ethical and social reasons, apart from personhood, for legally protecting the lives of infants. Similarly, Noonan, Lee, and George's position need not commit them to a legal ban on first trimester abortions or IVF. Believing something is wrong does not necessarily mean you think it should be illegal.

Pregnancy, Abortion, and the Rights of Women

Pregnancy and fetal development are normal biological processes, and most women who choose to have a child can carry it to term without severe difficulties. However, it is important to keep in mind that even a normal pregnancy involves risks and restrictions that are uniquely burdensome.

Once the process of fetal growth is initiated, a woman's entire physiology is altered by the new demands placed on it and by the biochemical changes taking place within her body. For example, her metabolic rate increases, her thyroid gland grows larger, her heart pumps more blood to meet fetal needs, and a great variety of hormonal changes take place. The growing fetus physically displaces the woman's internal organs and alters the size and shape of her body.

As a result of such changes, a pregnant woman may suffer a variety of ailments. More common ones include severe nausea and vomiting ("morning sickness"), muscle cramps, abdominal pain, anemia, fatigue, and headaches. For many women, such complaints are relatively mild or infrequent; for others, they are severe and constant. Nausea and vomiting can lead to dehydration and malnutrition so serious as to be life threatening. Women who suffer from diseases such as diabetes are apt to face special health problems as a result of pregnancy. In addition, complications such as high blood pressure, cervical changes, and multiple gestations cause hundreds of thousands of pregnant women each year to be prescribed strict bed rest. This can last for months at a time and is sometimes so strict as to require sponge baths and bedpans.

Anyone who intends to carry a child to term is also likely to have to alter her life in many ways. She may have to curtail the time she spends working or take a leave of absence, and she may even lose her job. Any career plans she has are likely to suffer. She may be unable to participate in social activities and unable to fulfill previous commitments and roles. In addition, if she recognizes an obligation to the developing fetus and is well informed, she may have to alter her diet, stop smoking, and limit the amount of alcohol she consumes.

Pregnancy is also often accompanied by burdensome psychological symptoms, including depression and anxiety. Such conditions are often rooted in quite realistic concerns about the life-long responsibilities and vulnerabilities that typically come with being a parent, as well as the changes in one's hormones, body image, and personal relationships. These burdens are all the more acute if a woman lacks the financial, emotional, or social resources and support systems that she deems necessary for responsibly bearing and raising a child.

Finally, childbirth involves its own serious risks and sacrifices. For example, a study in the *New England Journal of Medicine* found that 35–44 percent of vaginal births resulted in tears so severe that they damaged the anal sphincter, a problem that can cause lifetime incontinence, fissures, and pain. Caesarean sections can cause anesthesia reactions, infections, and blood clots, among other problems. While childbirth in the developed world is vastly safer than it was fifty or a hundred years ago, it still kills nearly six hundred American women every year. (The risk to women of dying in childbirth is about fourteen times greater than the risk of dying due to complications from an abortion.)

In sum, the physical and emotional price paid by a woman for a full-term pregnancy is high. Even a normal pregnancy, one that proceeds without any special difficulties, exacts a substantial toll of discomfort, stress, and restricted activity.

Women who wish to have children are generally willing to undergo the rigors of pregnancy to satisfy this desire. But is it a woman's duty to nurture and carry to term an unwanted child? If she lacks the financial or social resources to raise a child (or an additional child), is she obliged to give birth and then surrender the infant to an adoption system that many see as dysfunctional and harmful? Pregnancies resulting from rape and incest are frequently mentioned to emphasize the seriousness of the burden pregnancy imposes on women. But the question is also important when the conditions surrounding the pregnancy are less traumatic.

Suppose that a woman becomes pregnant unintentionally and concludes that raising the child will be harmful to her other children, her financial security, her relationships, or her way of life. Or suppose she simply does not wish to subject herself to the serious health risks and restrictions of pregnancy. Does a woman have a moral duty to see to it that the developing embryo or fetus comes to be born?

A number of writers have taken the position that women have an exclusive right to control their own reproductive lives. In the view of these writers, such a right is based upon the generally recognized right to control what is done to our bodies. Since pregnancy is something that involves a woman's body, the woman concerned may legitimately decide whether to continue the pregnancy or terminate it. The decision is hers alone, and social or legal policies that restrict the free exercise of her right are unjustifiable.

A related point is sometimes phrased by saying that women own their bodies. Because their bodies are their own "property," women alone have the right to decide whether to become pregnant and, if pregnant unintentionally, whether to have an abortion.

Critics have suggested that this general line of argument, which is associated with libertarian thought, does not support the strong conclusion that women should be free from all constraints in making abortion decisions. Even granting that our bodies are our own property, we nevertheless recognize some restrictions on exercising property rights. We may not arbitrarily shoot trespassers and we may have Good Samaritan obligations to help sick or dying individuals who show up at our door. Similarly, if any legitimate moral claims can be made on behalf of the fetus, then the right of women to decide whether to have an abortion may not be unrestricted.

In a famous article reprinted later in this chapter, Judith Jarvis Thomson engages this question using a number of analogies. Her conclusion indicates that just as a sick trespasser has no right to expect that we devote our own lives to preventing him from dying, a fetus also has no right against a pregnant woman to use her body to preserve its life. Even if we grant that a fetus is a person, its claim to life cannot be given unconditional precedence over a woman's claim to control her own life. She is entitled to autonomy and the right to arrange her life in accordance with her own concept of the good. She may refuse to help the fetus live and may have it removed from her body, knowing that decision will end its life.

Critics of this view have argued that when a woman becomes pregnant, she assumes a special responsibility for the life of the fetus. It is, after all, completely dependent on her for its continued existence. For some, this dependency relationship means that abortion is impermissible—equivalent to killing someone whose death brings one special benefits. For others, this dependency shows the folly of pitting the interests of embryos and fetuses against those of pregnant women in the first place. Since their well-being and interests cannot be clearly separated, only a pregnant woman can make the difficult moral decisions about whether or not to carry a pregnancy to term, given her specific moral circumstances, relationships, and responsibilities.

Others grant Thomson's primary conclusion but argue that it is only fully persuasive in cases of pregnancy due to rape, less so in cases of failed birth control, and perhaps not at all if a woman chooses to become pregnant and then changes her mind, especially late in a pregnancy. Thomson defends her conclusion that women are within their rights to choose to terminate pregnancies, but acknowledges that there are some abortion decisions, such as ending a late-term pregnancy for trivial reasons, that could violate standards of minimal decency.

Therapeutic Abortion

Abortion is sometimes required to save the life of a pregnant woman or in order to provide medical treatment considered essential to her health. Abortion performed for such a purpose is ordinarily regarded as a case of basic self-preservation and self-defense. For this reason, it is almost universally considered to be morally unobjectionable. (Strictly speaking, the Roman Catholic view condemns abortion in all of its forms. It does generally approve of providing essential medical treatment for the mother, however, even if this results in the death of the fetus. But the death of the fetus must never be intended and some Catholic hospitals refuse to perform even therapeutic abortions.)

If the principle of preserving the life and health of the mother justifies abortion, then what conditions fall under that principle? If a woman has cancer of the uterus and her life can be saved only by an operation that will result in the death of the fetus, then this clearly falls under the principle. But what about psychological conditions? Is mental health relevant to deciding whether an abortion is justified? What if a psychiatrist believes that a patient cannot face the physical rigors of pregnancy or bear the psychological stresses that go with it without developing severe psychiatric symptoms or committing suicide? Would such a judgment justify an abortion?

Consider, too, the welfare of the fetus. Suppose that prenatal tests indicate that the developing child suffers from serious abnormalities. (This was the case of the "thalidomide babies," as discussed in the Case Presentation: When Abortion Was Illegal.) Is abortion for the purpose of preventing the birth of such children justifiable?

It might be argued that an impaired fetus has as much right to its life as an impaired adult. We do not, after all, consider it legitimate to kill people who become seriously injured or suffer from diseases that render them helpless. Rather, we care for them and work to improve their lives—or at least we ought to.

Some might argue, however, that abortion in such cases is not only justifiable, but a duty. It is our duty to abort the fetus to spare the person it will become a life of unhappiness and suffering. We might even be said to be acknowledging the dignity of the fetus by doing what it might do for itself if it could—what any rational creature would do. Aborting such a fetus would spare future pain to the individual and his or her family and save the family and society enormous expense. Thus, perhaps we have not only a justification to terminate such a fetus, but also the positive obligation to do so.

In this chapter, we will not deal explicitly with the issues that are raised by the "selective" abortion of severely impaired fetuses. Because such issues are directly connected with prenatal genetic diagnosis and treatment, we discuss them more fully in Chapter 3. Nonetheless, in considering the general question of the legitimacy of abortion, it is important to keep such special considerations in mind.

Abortion and the Law

Abortion in our society has been a legal issue as well as a moral issue. From the late 1800s until the Supreme Court decision in *Roe v. Wade*, nontherapeutic abortion was illegal in virtually all states. The *Webster* decision (see Social Context: Supreme Court Abortion Decisions after *Roe v. Wade*) was an indication that the Court may be willing to accept more state restrictions than it originally did in the wake of *Roe*. However, even though groups still lobby for a constitutional amendment to protect a fetus's right to life and prohibit elective abortion, the position has limited popular support.

Ironically, there is some evidence that making abortion illegal may have the unintended consequence of making it more common. Several studies, including one published in the *Lancet* medical journal in 2012, have found that estimated abortion rates are higher in regions around the world where the procedure is mostly illegal (such as Latin America) and lower in those where abortion laws are least restrictive (such as Western Europe). This may have more to do with reliable access to contraception than abortion itself, but it does indicate some of the practical difficulties of outlawing the procedure. The history of abortion in the United States, as well as the current situation in some states, suggests that abortion restrictions tend to drive the practice underground, where it happens later in pregnancy and with greater risks to women. (The *Lancet* study also found that nearly half of all abortions worldwide are dangerous for women, killing 47,000 a year—a problem that is strongly correlated with abortion prohibitions.)

Of course, these empirical considerations can only guide our moral and legal determinations so far. Ultimately, the rightness or wrongness of abortion is an ethical matter, one whose issues may be best resolved by appeal to a moral theory. But different theories may yield incompatible answers, and even individuals who accept the same theory may arrive at different conclusions.

Such a state of affairs raises the question of whether the moral convictions or conclusions of some people should be embodied in laws that govern the lives of all people in the society. The question can be put succinctly: Should the moral beliefs of some people serve as the basis for laws that will impose those beliefs on everyone?

This question cannot be answered in a straightforward way. To some extent, which moral beliefs are at issue is a relevant consideration. So, too, are the political principles that we are willing to accept as basic to our society. Every ethical theory recognizes that there is a scope of action that must be left to individuals as moral agents acting freely on the basis of their own understanding and perceptions. Laws requiring the expression of benevolence or gratitude, for example, seem peculiarly inappropriate.

Yet, one of the major aims of a government is to protect the rights of its citizens. Consequently, a society must have just laws that recognize and enforce those rights. In a very real way, then, the moral theory we hold and the conclusions arrived at on the basis of it will determine whether we believe that certain types of laws are justified. They are justified when they protect the rights recognized in our moral theories—when political rights reflect moral rights. (See the Briefing Session in Chapter 9 for a fuller discussion of moral rights and their relation to political rights.)

An ethical theory that accords the status of a person to a fetus is likely to claim that the laws of the society should also recognize the rights of the fetus. A theory that does not grant the fetus this position is not likely to regard laws forbidding abortion as justifiable.

Ethical Theories and Abortion

Theories such as those of Mill, Kant, Ross, and Rawls attribute autonomy, or self-direction, to individuals. An individual is entitled to control his or her own life, and it seems reasonable to extend this principle to apply to one's own body. If so, then a woman should have the right to determine whether or not she wishes to have a child. If she becomes pregnant with an unwanted child, then, no matter how she came to be pregnant, she might legitimately decide on an abortion. Utilitarianism also suggests this answer, though on consequential grounds. In the absence of other considerations, if it seems likely that having a child will produce more unhappiness than an abortion would, then an abortion would be justifiable.

If the fetus is considered to be a person, however, the situation is different for some theories. The natural law view typically holds that the embryo or fetus is an innocent person and that direct abortion is never justifiable. Even if the pregnancy is due to rape, the fetus cannot be held responsible and must be carried to term. Even though she may not wish to have the child, the pregnant woman has a duty to preserve the life of the fetus on this view.

For deontological theories like those of Kant and Ross, the situation becomes more complicated. If the fetus is a person, it has an inherent dignity and worth. It is an innocent life that cannot be destroyed except for the weightiest moral reasons. Those reasons may include the interests and wishes of the woman, but deontological theories provide no clear answer as to how these factors are to be weighed. Of course, if fetal life does not rise to the level of personhood, then the problem disappears.

For utilitarianism, by contrast, even if the fetus is considered a person, the principle of utility may still justify an abortion. Killing a person is not, for utilitarianism, inherently wrong. (Yet it is compatible with rule utilitarianism to argue, for example, that permitting elective abortion as a matter of policy would produce more unhappiness than forbidding abortion altogether. Thus, utilitarianism does not offer a definite answer to the abortion issue.)

As we have already seen, both utilitarianism and deontological theories can be used to justify therapeutic abortion. When the pregnant woman's life or health is at stake, the situation may be construed as one of self-defense. Both Kant and Ross recognize that we each have a right to protect ourselves, even if it means taking the life of another person. For utilitarianism, preserving one's life is justifiable, for being alive is a necessary condition for all forms of happiness.

We have also indicated that abortion "for the sake of the fetus" can be justified by both utilitarianism and deontological theories. If aborting an embryo or fetus can spare it a life of suffering, minimize the sufferings of a family, and preserve the resources of society, then abortion is legitimate on utilitarian grounds. In the terms of Kant and Ross, destroying the fetus might also be a way of recognizing its dignity. If we assume that it is a person, then by sparing it a life of indignity and pain, we are treating it as a rational being would want to be treated.

The legitimacy of laws forbidding abortion is an issue that utilitarianism would resolve by considering their effects. If such laws promote the general happiness of the society, then they are justifiable. Otherwise, they are not. In general, Kant, Ross, Rawls, and natural law theory recognize intrinsic human worth and regard as legitimate laws protecting that worth, even if those holding this view are only a minority of the society. Thus, laws discriminating against African

Americans and women, for example, would be considered unjust on the basis of these theories. Laws enforcing equality, by contrast, would be considered just.

But what about embryos and fetuses? The Roman Catholic interpretation of natural law would regard the case as exactly the same. As full human persons, they are entitled to have their rights protected by law. Those who fail to recognize this are guilty of moral failure, and laws permitting abortion are the moral equivalent of laws permitting murder.

For Kant and other deontologists, the matter is less clear. As long as there is substantial doubt about the status of the fetus, it is not certain that it has interests or rights that should be recognized and protected by law. It is clear that the issue of whether or not the fetus is considered a person is crucial to many (but not all) approaches to the abortion controversy.

By contrast, feminist and care ethics often reject the focus on personhood and competing rights in discussions of abortion. Instead, they point out that the embryo or fetus only exists in a specific biological and moral relationship to a pregnant woman, and indeed, the two make up one integrated organism for most of gestation. Their well-being and interests cannot be evaluated separately or pitted against each other. Instead, abortion decisions must be evaluated in the context of the moral relationship and responsibilities that come with pregnancy and potential parenthood. How and whether a woman should assume these relational responsibilities depends on concrete moral factors (including her social, personal, and financial circumstances) that abstract legal and philosophical concepts are ill-equipped to handle. Thus, these theorists argue, the moral assessment of most—and perhaps all—abortion decisions should be left to pregnant women themselves, free from legal interference. Virtue and capabilities theories are also generally inclined to view the morality of abortion decisions within the broader personal and societal context of childbearing, childrearing, and parenthood—and to question the application of abstract legal standards to these concrete situations.

The battle over abortion is certain to continue in the courts, the streets, the media, and classrooms. The issues are of great social importance, yet highly personal and explosively emotional. The best hope for a resolution continues to rest with the condemnation of violence and an emphasis on the traditional strategies of verbal persuasion, rational argument, and the appeal to widely shared values.

READINGS

Section 1: The Abortion Debate: Beyond Personhood

A Defense of Abortion

Judith Jarvis Thomson

In this influential article, Thomson sets aside the problem of fetal personhood. For the sake of argument only, she grants the anti-abortion view that from conception, the embryo is a person with a right to life.

From Judith Jarvis Thomson, "A Defense of Abortion," *Philosophy & Public* Affairs 1, no. 1 (Fall 1971). Copyright © 1971 John Wiley & Sons-Blackwell. Reprinted by permission. (Some notes omitted.)

She points out, however, that this right is never absolute. It is not a right to have one's life sustained under any circumstances or at any cost to others' rights and interests. Using several moral analogies, Thomson attempts to show that a right to life does not consist in the right not to be killed, but in the right not to be killed unjustly.

The most famous of these analogies asks us to imagine we have been kidnapped, hospitalized, and attached to the circulatory system of a famous violinist, who will die if we don't detoxify his blood with our own kidneys for nine months or more. Although it would be generous to consent to this arrangement, Thomson argues, we are not morally obligated to be generous and are within our rights to detach ourselves, causing his death. Similarly, the fetus's claim to life is not an absolute one that must always be granted unconditional precedence over the interests of a pregnant woman.

In response to those who would say that a woman assumes special responsibility for the dependent fetus just by becoming pregnant, Thomson argues that we are not required to devote our lives to sustaining those of trespassers just because they manage to get into our houses and become dependent on us. Nevertheless, Thomson acknowledges that minimal decency may make some abortion decisions wrong, especially if made for trivial reasons late in a pregnancy. Thus while abortion is not, in general, morally impermissible, neither is it always permissible.

Most opposition to abortion relies on the premise that the fetus is a human being, a person, from the moment of conception. The premise is argued for, but, as I think, not well. Take, for example, the most common argument. We are asked to notice that the development of a human being from conception through birth into childhood is continuous; then it is said that to draw a line, to choose a point in this development and say "before this point the thing is not a person, after this point it is a person" is to make an arbitrary choice, a choice for which in the nature of things no good reason can be given. It is concluded that the fetus is, or anyway that we had better say it is, a person from the moment of conception. But this conclusion does not follow. Similar things might be said about the development of an acorn into an oak tree, and it does not follow that acorns are oak trees, or that we had better say they are. Arguments of this form are sometimes called "slippery slope arguments"—the phrase is perhaps self-explanatory—and it is dismaying that opponents of abortion rely on them so heavily and uncritically.

I am inclined to agree, however, that the prospects for "drawing a line" in the development of the fetus look dim. I am inclined to think also that we shall probably have to agree that the fetus has already become a human person well before birth. Indeed, it comes as a surprise when one first learns how early in its life it begins to acquire human characteristics. By the tenth week, for example, it already has a face, arms and legs, fingers and toes; it has internal organs, and brain activity is detectable. On the other hand, I think that the premise is false, that the fetus is not a person from the moment of conception. A newly fertilized ovum, a newly implanted clump of cells, is no more a person than an acorn is an oak tree. But I shall not discuss any of this. For it seems to me to be of great interest to ask what happens if, for the sake of argument, we allow the premise. How, precisely, are we supposed to get from there to the conclusion that abortion is morally impermissible? Opponents of abortion commonly spend most of their time establishing that the fetus is a person, and hardly any time explaining the step from there to the impermissibility of abortion. Perhaps they think the step too simple and obvious to require much comment. Or perhaps instead they are simply being economical in argument. Many of those who defend abortion rely on the premise that the fetus is not a person, but only a bit of tissue that will become a person at birth; and why pay out more arguments than you have to? Whatever the explanation, I suggest that the step they take is neither easy nor obvious, that it calls for closer examination than it is commonly given, and that when we do give it this closer examination we shall feel inclined to reject it.

I propose, then, that we grant that the fetus is a person from the moment of conception. How does the argument go from here? Something like this, I take it. Every person has a right to life. So the fetus has a right to life. No doubt the mother has a right to decide what shall happen in and to her body; everyone would grant that. But surely a person's right to life is stronger and more stringent than the mother's right to decide what happens in and to her body, and so outweighs it. So the fetus may not be killed; an abortion may not be performed.

It sounds plausible. But now let me ask you to imagine this. You wake up in the morning and find yourself in bed with an unconscious violinist. A famous unconscious violinist. He has been found to have a fatal kidney ailment, and the Society of Music Lovers has canvassed all the available medical records and found that you alone have the right blood type to help. They have therefore kidnapped you, and last night the violinist's circulatory system was plugged into yours, so that your kidneys can be used to extract poisons from his blood as well as your own. The director of the hospital now tells you, "Look, we're sorry the Society of Music Lovers did this to you—we would never have permitted it if we had known. But still, they did it, and the violinist is now plugged into you. To unplug you would be to kill him. But never mind, it's only for nine months. By then he will have recovered from his ailment, and can safely be unplugged from you." Is it morally incumbent on you to accede to this situation? No doubt it would be very nice of you if you did, a great kindness. But do you *have* to accede to it? What if it were not nine months, but nine years? Or longer still? What if the director of the hospital says, "Tough luck, I agree, but now you've got to stay in bed, with the violinist plugged into you, for the rest of your life. Because remember this. All persons have a right to life, and violinists are persons. Granted you have a right to decide what happens in and to your body, but a person's right to life outweighs your right

to decide what happens in and to your body. So you cannot ever be unplugged from him." I imagine you would regard this as outrageous, which suggests that something really is wrong with that plausible-sounding argument I mentioned a moment ago.

In this case, of course, you were kidnapped; you didn't volunteer for the operation that plugged the violinist into your kidneys. Can those who oppose abortion on the ground I mentioned make an exception for pregnancy due to rape? Certainly. They can say that all persons have a right to life, but that some have less of a right to life than others, in particular, that those who came into existence because of rape have less. But these statements have a rather unpleasant sound. Surely the question of whether you have a right to life at all, or how much of it you have, shouldn't turn on the question of whether or not you are a product of a rape. And in fact the people who oppose abortion on the ground I mentioned do not make this distinction, and hence do not make an exception in case of rape.

Nor do they make an exception for a case in which the mother has to spend the nine months of her pregnancy in bed. They would agree that would be a great pity, and hard on the mother; but all the same, all persons have a right to life, the fetus is a person, and so on. I suspect, in fact, that they would not make an exception for a case in which, miraculously enough, the pregnancy went on for nine years, or even for the rest of the mother's life.

Some won't even make an exception for a case in which continuation of the pregnancy is likely to shorten the mother's life; they regard abortion as impermissible even to save the mother's life. Such cases are nowadays very rare, and many opponents of abortion do not accept this extreme view. All the same, it is a good place to begin: a number of points of interest come out in respect to it.

1.

Let us call the view that abortion is impermissible even to save the mother's life "the extreme view." I want to suggest that it does not issue from the argument I mentioned earlier without the addition of some fairly powerful premises. Suppose a woman has become pregnant, and now learns that she has a cardiac condition such that she will die if she carries the baby to term. What may be done for her? The fetus, being a person, has a right to life, but as the mother is a person too, so has she a right to life. Presumably they have an equal right to life. How is it supposed to come out that an abortion may not be performed? If mother and child have an equal right to life, shouldn't we perhaps flip a coin? Or should we add to the mother's right to life her right to decide what happens in and to her body, which everybody seems to be ready to grant—the sum of her rights now outweighing the fetus's right to life?

The most familiar argument here is the following. We are told that performing the abortion would be directly killing[1] the child, whereas doing nothing would not be killing the mother, but only letting her die. Moreover, in killing the child, one would be killing an innocent person, for the child has committed no crime, and is not aiming at his mother's death. And then there are a variety of ways in which this might be continued. (1) But as directly killing an innocent person is always and absolutely impermissible, an abortion may not be performed. Or, (2) as directly killing an innocent person is murder, and murder is always and absolutely impermissible, an abortion may not be performed.[2] Or, (3) as one's duty to refrain from directly killing an innocent person is more stringent than one's duty to keep a person from dying, an abortion may not be performed. Or, (4) if one's only options are directly killing an innocent person or letting a person die, one must prefer letting the person die, and thus an abortion may not be performed.[3]

Some people seem to have thought that these are not further premises which must be added if the conclusion is to be reached, but they follow from the very fact that an innocent person has a right to life.[4] But this seems to me to be a mistake, and perhaps the simplest way to show this is to bring out that while we must certainly grant that innocent persons have a right to life, the theses in (1) through (4) are all false. Take (2) for example. If directly killing an innocent person is murder, and thus is impermissible, then the mother's directly killing the innocent person inside her is murder, and thus is impermissible. But it cannot seriously be thought to be murder if the mother performs an abortion on herself to save her life. It cannot seriously be said that she *must* refrain, that she *must* sit passively by and wait for her death. Let us look again at the case of you and the violinist. There you are, in bed with the violinist, and the director of the hospital says to you, "It's all most distressing, and I deeply sympathize, but you see this is putting an additional strain on your kidneys, and you'll be dead within the month. But you *have* to stay where you are all the same. Because unplugging you would

be directly killing an innocent violinist, and that's murder, and that's impermissible." If anything in the world is true, it is that you do not commit murder, you do not do what is impermissible, if you reach around to your back and unplug yourself from that violinist to save your life.

The main focus of attention in writings on abortion has been on what a third party may or may not do in answer to a request from a woman for an abortion. This is in a way understandable. Things being as they are, there isn't much a woman can safely do to abort herself. So the question asked is what a third party may do, and what the mother may do, if it is mentioned at all, is deduced, almost as an afterthought, from what it is concluded that third parties may do. But it seems to me that to treat the matter in this way is to refuse to grant to the mother that very status of person which is so firmly insisted on for the fetus. For we cannot simply read off what a person may do from what a third party may do. Suppose you find yourself trapped in a tiny house with a growing child. I mean a very tiny house, and a rapidly growing child—you are already up against the wall of the house and in a few minutes you'll be crushed to death. The child on the other hand won't be crushed to death; if nothing is done to stop him from growing he'll be hurt, but in the end he'll simply burst open the house and walk out a free man. Now I could well understand it if a bystander were to say, "There's nothing we can do for you. We cannot choose between your life and his, we cannot be the ones to decide who is to live, we cannot intervene." But it cannot be concluded that you too can do nothing, that you cannot attack it to save your life. However innocent the child may be, you do not have to wait passively while it crushes you to death. Perhaps a pregnant woman is vaguely felt to have the status of house, to which we don't allow the right of self-defense. But if the woman houses the child, it should be remembered that she is a person who houses it.

I should perhaps stop to say explicitly that I am not claiming that people have a right to do anything whatever to save their lives. I think, rather, that there are drastic limits to the right of self-defense. If someone threatens you with death unless you torture someone else to death, I think you have not the right, even to save your life, to do so. But the case under consideration here is very different. In our case there are only two people involved, one whose life is threatened, and one who threatens it. Both are innocent:

the one who is threatened is not threatened because of any fault, the one who threatens does not threaten because of any fault. For this reason we may feel that we bystanders cannot intervene. But the person threatened can.

In sum, a woman surely can defend her life against the threat to it posed by the unborn child, even if doing so involves its death. And this shows not merely that the theses in (1) through (4) are false; it shows also that the extreme view of abortion is false, and so we need not canvass any other possible ways of arriving at it from the argument I mentioned at the outset.

2.

The extreme view could of course be weakened to say that while abortion is permissible to save the mother's life, it may not be performed by a third party, but only by the mother herself. But this cannot be right either. For what we have to keep in mind is that the mother and the unborn child are not like two tenants in a small house which has, by an unfortunate mistake, been rented to both: the mother *owns* the house. The fact that she does adds to the offensiveness of deducing that the mother can do nothing from the supposition that third parties can do nothing. Certainly it lets us see that a third party who says "I cannot choose between you" is fooling himself if he thinks this is impartiality. If Jones has found and fastened on a certain coat, which he needs to keep him from freezing, but which Smith also needs to keep him from freezing, then it is not impartiality that says "I cannot choose between you" when Smith owns the coat. Women have said again and again "This body is *my* body!" and they have reason to feel angry, reason to feel that it has been like shouting into the wind. Smith, after all, is hardly likely to bless us if we say to him, "Of course it's your coat, anybody would grant that it is. But no one may choose between you and Jones who is to have it."

We should really ask what it is that says "no one may choose" in the face of the fact that the body that houses the child is the mother's body. It may be simply a failure to appreciate this fact. But it may be something more interesting, namely the sense that one has a right to refuse to lay hands on people, even where justice seems to require that somebody do so. Thus justice might call for somebody to get Smith's coat back from Jones, and yet you have a right to refuse to be the one to lay hands on Jones, a right to refuse to do the physical violence to him. This, I think, must be granted. But then what should be said is not "no one may choose," but only "I cannot choose," and indeed not even this, but "I will not *act*," leaving it open that somebody else can or should, and in particular that anyone in a position of authority, with the job of securing people's rights, both can and should. So this is no difficulty. I have not been arguing that any given third party must accede to the mother's request that he perform an abortion to save her life, but only that he may.

I suppose that in some view of human life the mother's body is only on loan to her, the loan not being one which gives her any prior claim to it. One who held this view might well think it impartiality to say "I cannot choose." But I shall simply ignore this possibility. My own view is that if a human being has any just, prior claim to anything at all, he has a just, prior claim to his own body. And perhaps this needn't be argued for here anyway, since, as I mentioned, the arguments against abortion we are looking at do grant that the woman has a right to decide what happens in and to her body.

But although they do grant it, I have tried to show that they do not take seriously what is done in granting it. I suggest the same thing will reappear even more clearly when we turn away from cases in which the mother's life is at stake, and attend, as I propose we now do, to the vastly more common cases in which a woman wants an abortion for some less weighty reason than preserving her own life.

3.

Where the mother's life is not at stake, the argument I mentioned at the outset seems to have a much stronger pull. "Everyone has a right to life, so the unborn person has a right to life." And isn't the child's right to life weightier than anything other than the mother's own right to life, which she might put forward as ground for an abortion?

This agreement treats the right to life as if it were unproblematic. It is not, and this seems to me to be precisely the source of the mistake.

For we should now, at long last, ask what it comes to, to have a right to life. In some views having a right to life includes having a right to be given at least the bare minimum one needs for continued life. But suppose that what in fact is the bare minimum a man needs for continued life is something he has no right at all to be given? If I am sick unto death, and the only thing that will save my life is the touch of Henry Fonda's cool hand on my fevered brow, then all the same, I have no right to be given the touch of Henry Fonda's cool hand on my fevered brow. It would be frightfully nice of him to fly in from the West Coast to provide it. It would be less nice, though no doubt well meant, if my friends flew out to the West Coast and carried Henry Fonda back with them. But I have no right at all against anybody that he should do this for me. Or again, to return to the story I told earlier, the fact that for continued life the violinist needs the continued use of your kidneys does not establish that he has a right to be given the continued use of your kidneys. He certainly has no right against you that *you* should give him continued use of your kidneys. For nobody has any right to use your kidneys unless you give him this right—if you do allow him to go on using your kidneys, this is a kindness on your part, and not something he can claim from you as his due. Nor has he any right against anybody else that *they* should give him continued use of your kidneys. Certainly he had no right against the Society of Music Lovers that they should plug him into you in the first place. And if you now start to unplug yourself, having learned that you will otherwise have to spend nine years in bed with him, there is nobody in the world who must try to prevent you, in order to see to it that he is given something he has a right to be given.

Some people are rather stricter about the right to life. In their view, it does not include the right to be given anything, but amounts to, and only to, the right not to be killed by anybody. But here a related difficulty arises. If everybody is to refrain from killing that violinist, then everybody must refrain from doing a great many different sorts of things. Everybody must refrain from slitting his throat, everybody must refrain from shooting him—and everybody must refrain from unplugging you from him. But does he have a right against everybody that they shall refrain from unplugging you from him? To refrain from doing this is to allow him to continue to use your kidneys. It could be argued that he has a right against us that *we* should allow him to continue to use your kidneys. That is, while he had no right against us that we should give him the use of your kidneys, it might be argued that he anyway has a right against us that we shall not now intervene and deprive him of the use of your kidneys. I shall come back to third-party interventions later. But certainly the violinist has no

right against you that you shall allow him to continue to use your kidneys. As I said, if you do allow him to use them it is a kindness on your part, not something you owe him.

The difficulty I point to here is not peculiar to the right to life. It reappears in connection with all the other natural rights, and it is something which an adequate account of rights must deal with. For present purposes it is enough just to draw attention to it. But I would stress that I am not arguing that people do not have a right to life—quite to the contrary, it seems to me that the primary control we must place on the acceptability of an account of rights is that it should turn out in that account to be a truth that all persons have a right to life. I am arguing only that having a right to life does not guarantee having either a right to be given the use of or a right to be allowed continued use of another person's body—even if one needs it for life itself. So the right to life will not serve the opponents of abortion in the very simple and clear way in which they seem to have thought it would.

4.

There is another way to bring out the difficulty. In the most ordinary sort of case, to deprive someone of what he has a right to is to treat him unjustly. Suppose a boy and his small brother are jointly given a box of chocolates for Christmas. If the older boy takes the box and refuses to give his brother any of the chocolates, he is unjust to him, for the brother has been given a right to half of them. But suppose that, having learned that otherwise it means nine years in bed with that violinist, you unplug yourself from him. You surely are not being unjust to him, for you gave him no right to use your kidneys, and no one else can have given him any such right. But we have to notice that in unplugging yourself, you are killing him; and violinists, like everybody else, have a right to life, and thus in the view we were considering just now, the right not to be killed. So here you do what he supposedly has a right you shall not do, but you do not act unjustly to him in doing it.

The emendation which may be made at this point is this: the right to life consists not in the right not to be killed, but rather in the right not to be killed unjustly. This runs a risk of circularity, but never mind: it would enable us to square the fact that the violinist has a right to life with the fact that you do not act unjustly toward him in unplugging yourself, thereby killing him.

For if you do not kill him unjustly, you do not violate his right to life, and so it is no wonder you do him no injustice.

But if this emendation is accepted, the gap in the argument against abortion stares us plainly in the face: it is by no means enough to show that the fetus is a person, and to remind us that all persons have a right to life—we need to be shown also that killing the fetus violates its right to life, i.e., that abortion is unjust killing. And is it?

I suppose we may take it as a datum that in a case of pregnancy due to rape the mother has not given the unborn person a right to the use of her body for food and shelter. Indeed, in what pregnancy could it be supposed that the mother has given the unborn person such a right? It is not as if there were unborn persons drifting about the world, to whom a woman who wants a child says "I invite you in."

But it might be argued that there are other ways one can have acquired a right to the use of another person's body than by having been invited to use it by that person. Suppose a woman voluntarily indulges in intercourse, knowing of the chance it will issue in pregnancy, and then she does become pregnant; is she not in part responsible for the presence, in fact the very existence, of the unborn person inside? No doubt she did not invite it in. But doesn't her partial responsibility for its being there itself give it a right to the use of her body? If so, then her aborting it would be more like the boy's taking away the chocolates, and less like your unplugging yourself from the violinist—doing so would be depriving it of what it does have a right to, and thus would be doing it an injustice.

And then, too, it might be asked whether or not she can kill it even to save her own life: If she voluntarily called it into existence, how can she now kill it, even in self-defense?

The first thing to be said about this is that it is something new. Opponents of abortion have been so concerned to make out the independence of the fetus, in order to establish that it has a right to life, just as its mother does, that they have tended to overlook the possible support they might gain from making out that the fetus is *dependent* on the mother, in order to establish that she has a special kind of responsibility for it, a responsibility that gives it rights against her which are not possessed by any independent person—such as an ailing violinist who is a stranger to her.

On the other hand, this argument would give the unborn person a right to its mother's body only if her pregnancy resulted from a voluntary act, undertaken in full knowledge of the chance a pregnancy might result from it. It would leave out entirely the unborn person whose existence is due to rape. Pending the availability of some further argument, then, we would be left with the conclusion that unborn persons whose existence is due to rape have no right to the use of their mothers' bodies, and thus that aborting them is not depriving them of anything they have a right to and hence is not unjust killing.

And we should also notice that it is not at all plain that this argument really does go even as far as it purports to. For there are cases and cases, and the details make a difference. If the room is stuffy, and I therefore open a window to air it, and a burglar climbs in, it would be absurd to say, "Ah, now he can stay, she's given him a right to the use of her house—for she is partially responsible for his presence there, having voluntarily done what enabled him to get in, in full knowledge that there are such things as burglars, and that burglars burgle." It would be still more absurd to say this if I had had bars installed outside my windows, precisely to prevent burglars from getting in, and a burglar got in only because of a defect in the bars. It remains equally absurd if we imagine it is not a burglar who climbs in, but an innocent person who blunders or falls in. Again, suppose it were like this: people-seeds drift about in the air like pollen, and if you open your windows, one may drift in and take root in your carpets or upholstery. You don't want children, so you fix up your windows with fine mesh screens, the very best you can buy. As can happen, however, and on very, very rare occasions does happen, one of the screens is defective, and a seed drifts in and takes root. Does the person-plant who now develops have a right to the use of your house? Surely not—despite the fact that you voluntarily opened your windows, you knowingly kept carpets and upholstered furniture, and you knew that screens were sometimes defective. Someone may argue that you are responsible for its rooting, that it does have a right to your house, because after all you could have lived out your life with bare floors and furniture, or with sealed windows and doors. But this won't do—for by the same token anyone can avoid a pregnancy due to rape by having a hysterectomy, or anyway by never leaving home without a (reliable!) army.

It seems to me that the argument we are looking at can establish at most that there are some cases in which the unborn person has a right to the use of its mother's body, and therefore *some* cases in which abortion is unjust killing. There is room for much discussion and argument as to precisely which, if any. But I think we should sidestep this issue and leave it open, for at any rate the argument certainly does not establish that all abortion is unjust killing.

5.

There is room for yet another argument here, however. We surely must all grant that there may be cases in which it would be morally indecent to detach a person from your body at the cost of his life. Suppose you learn that what the violinist needs is not nine years of your life, but only one hour: all you need do to save his life is to spend one hour in that bed with him. Suppose also that letting him use your kidneys for that one hour would not affect your health in the slightest. Admittedly you were kidnapped. Admittedly you did not give anyone permission to plug him into you. Nevertheless it seems to me plain you *ought* to allow him to use your kidneys for that hour—it would be indecent to refuse.

Again, suppose pregnancy lasted only an hour, and constituted no threat to life or health. And suppose that a woman becomes pregnant as a result of rape. Admittedly she did not voluntarily do anything to bring about the existence of a child. Admittedly she did nothing at all which would give the unborn person a right to the use of her body. All the same it might well be said, as in the newly amended violinist story, that she *ought* to allow it to remain for that hour—that it would be indecent of her to refuse.

Now some people are inclined to use the term "right" in such a way that it follows from the fact that you ought to allow a person to use your body for the hour he needs, that he has a right to use your body for the hour he needs, even though he has not been given that right by any person or act. They may say that it follows also that if you refuse, you act unjustly toward him. This use of the term is perhaps so common that it cannot be called wrong; nevertheless it seems to me to be an unfortunate loosening of what we would do better to keep a tight rein on. Suppose that box of chocolates I mentioned earlier had not been given to both boys jointly, but was given only to the older boy. There he sits, stolidly eating his way through the box, his smaller brother watching enviously. Here we are likely to say, "You ought not to be so mean. You ought to give your brother some of those chocolates."

My own view is that it just does not follow from the truth of this that the brother has any right to any of the chocolates. If the boy refuses to give his brother any, he is greedy, stingy, callous—but not unjust. I suppose that the people I have in mind will say it does follow that the brother has a right to some of the chocolates, and thus that the boy does act unjustly if he refuses to give his brother any. But the effect of saying this is to obscure what we should keep distinct, namely the difference between the boy's refusal in this case and the boy's refusal in the earlier case, in which the box was given to both boys jointly, and in which the small brother thus had what was from any point of view clear title to half.

A further objection to so using the term "right" that from the fact that A ought to do a thing for B, it follows that B has a right against A that A do it for him, is that it is going to make the question of whether or not a man has a right to a thing turn on how easy it is to provide him with it; and this seems not merely unfortunate, but morally unacceptable. Take the case of Henry Fonda again. I said earlier that I had no right to the touch of his cool hand on my fevered brow, even though I needed it to save my life. I said it would be frightfully nice of him to fly in from the West Coast to provide me with it, but that I had no right against him that he should do so. But suppose he isn't on the West Coast. Suppose he has only to walk across the room, place a hand briefly on my brow—and lo, my life is saved. Then surely he ought to do it, it would be indecent to refuse. Is it to be said, "Ah, well, it follows that in this case she has a right to the touch of his hand on her brow, and so it would be an injustice in him to refuse"? So that I have a right to it when it is easy for him to provide it, though no right when it's hard? It's rather a shocking idea that anyone's rights should fade away and disappear as it gets harder and harder to accord them to him.

So my own view is that even though you ought to let the violinist use your kidneys for the one hour he needs, we should not conclude that he has a right to do so—we should say that if you refuse, you are, like the boy who owns all the chocolates and will give none away, self-centered and callous, indecent in fact, but not unjust. And similarly, that even supposing a case in which a woman pregnant due to rape ought to allow the unborn person to use her body for the hour he needs, we should not conclude that he has a right to do so; we should conclude that she is self-centered, callous, indecent, but not unjust, if she refuses. The complaints are no less grave; they are just different. However, there is no need to insist on this point. If anyone does wish to deduce "he has a right" from "you ought," then all the same he must surely grant that there are cases in which it is not morally required of you that you allow that violinist to use your kidneys, and in which he does not have the right to use them, and in which you do not do him an injustice if you refuse. And so also for mother and unborn child. Except in such cases as the unborn person has a right to demand it—and we were leaving open the possibility that there may be such cases—nobody is morally *required* to make large sacrifices, of health, of all other interests and concerns, of all other duties and commitments, for nine years, or even for nine months, in order to keep another person alive.

6.

We have in fact to distinguish between two kinds of Samaritan: the Good Samaritan and what we might call the Minimally Decent Samaritan. The story of the Good Samaritan, you will remember, goes like this:

> *A certain man went down from Jerusalem to Jericho, and fell among thieves, which stripped him of his raiment, and wounded him, and departed, leaving him half dead.*
>
> *And by chance there came down a certain priest that way: and when he saw him, he passed by on the other side.*
>
> *And likewise a Levite, when he was at the place, came and looked on him, and passed by on the other side.*
>
> *But a certain Samaritan, as he journeyed, came where he was; and when he saw him he had compassion on him.*
>
> *And went to him, and bound up his wounds, pouring in oil and wine, and set him on his own beast, and brought him to an inn, and took care of him.*
>
> *And on the morrow, when he departed, he took out two pence, and gave them to the host, and said unto him, "Take care of him, and whatsoever thou spendest more, when I come again, I will repay thee." (Luke 10:30–35)*

The Good Samaritan went out of his way, at some cost to himself, to help one in need of it. We are not told what the options were, that is, whether or not

the priest and the Levite could have helped by doing less than the Good Samaritan did, but assuming they could have, then the fact they did nothing at all shows they were not even Minimally Decent Samaritans, not because they were not Samaritans, but because they were not even minimally decent.

These things are a matter of degree, of course, but there is a difference, and it comes out perhaps most clearly in the story of Kitty Genovese, who, as you will remember, was murdered while thirty-eight people watched or listened, and did nothing at all to help her. A Good Samaritan would have rushed out to give direct assistance against the murderer. Or perhaps we had better allow that it would have been a Splendid Samaritan who did this, on the ground that it would have involved a risk of death for himself. But the thirty-eight not only did not do this, they did not even trouble to pick up a phone to call the police. Minimally Decent Samaritanism would call for doing at least that, and their not having done it was monstrous.

After telling the story of the Good Samaritan, Jesus said, "Go, and do thou likewise." Perhaps he meant that we are morally required to act as the Good Samaritan did. Perhaps he was urging people to do more than is morally required of them. At all events it seems plain that it was not morally required of any of the thirty-eight that he rush out to give direct assistance at the risk of his own life, and that it is not morally required of anyone that he give long stretches of his life—nine years or nine months—to sustaining the life of a person who has no special right (we were leaving open the possibility of this) to demand it.

Indeed, with one rather striking class of exceptions, no one in any country in the world is *legally* required to do anywhere near as much as this for anyone else. The class of exceptions is obvious.

My main concern here is not the state of law in respect to abortion, but it is worth drawing attention to the fact that in no state in this country is any man compelled by law to be even a Minimally Decent Samaritan to any person; there is no law under which charges could be brought against the thirty-eight who stood by while Kitty Genovese died. By contrast, in most states in this country women are compelled by law to be not merely Minimally Decent Samaritans, but Good Samaritans to unborn persons inside them. This doesn't by itself settle anything one way or the other, because it may well be argued that there should be laws in this country—as there are in many European countries—compelling at least Minimally Decent Samaritanism. But it does show that there is a gross injustice in the existing state of the law. And it shows also that the groups currently working against liberalization of abortion laws, in fact working toward having it declared unconstitutional for a state to permit abortion, had better start working for the adoption of Good Samaritan laws generally, or earn the charge that they are acting in bad faith.

I should think, myself, that Minimally Decent Samaritan laws would be one thing, Good Samaritan laws quite another, and in fact highly improper. But we are not here concerned with the law. What we should ask is not whether anybody should be compelled by law to be a Good Samaritan, but whether we must accede to a situation in which somebody is being compelled—by nature, perhaps—to be a Good Samaritan. We have, in other words, to look now at third-party interventions. I have been arguing that no person is morally required to make large sacrifices to sustain the life of another who has no right to demand them, and this even where the sacrifices do not include life itself; we are not morally required to be Good Samaritans or anyway Very Good Samaritans to one another. But what if a man cannot extricate himself from such a situation? What if he appeals to us to extricate him? It seems to me plain that there are cases in which we can, cases in which a Good Samaritan would extricate him. There you are, you were kidnapped, and nine years in bed with that violinist lie ahead of you. You have your own life to lead. You are sorry, but you simply cannot see giving up so much of your life to the sustaining of his. You cannot extricate yourself, and ask us to do so. I should have thought that—in light of his having no right to the use of your body—it was obvious that we do not have to accede to your being forced to give up so much. We can do what you ask. There is no injustice to the violinist in our doing so.

7.

Following the lead of the opponents of abortion, I have throughout been speaking of the fetus merely as a person, and what I have been asking is whether or not the argument we began with, which proceeds only from the fetus's being a person, really does establish its conclusion. I have argued that it does not.

But of course there are arguments and arguments, and it may be said that I have simply fastened on the wrong one. It may be said that what is important is not merely the fact that the fetus is a person, but that it is a person for whom the woman has a special responsibility issuing from the fact that she is its mother. And it might be argued that all my analogies are therefore irrelevant—for you do not have that special kind of responsibility for that violinist, Henry Fonda does not have that special kind of responsibility for me. And our attention might be drawn to the fact that men and women both *are* compelled by law to provide support for their children.

I have in effect dealt (briefly) with this argument in section 4 above; but a (still briefer) recapitulation now may be in order. Surely we do not have any such "special responsibility" for a person unless we have assumed it, explicitly or implicitly. If a set of parents do not try to prevent pregnancy, do not obtain an abortion, but rather take it home with them, then they have assumed responsibility for it, they have given it rights, and they cannot *now* withdraw support from it at the cost of its life because they now find it difficult to go on providing for it. But if they have taken all reasonable precautions against having a child, they do not simply by virtue of their biological relationship to the child who comes into existence have a special responsibility for it. They may wish to assume responsibility for it, or they may not wish to. And I am suggesting that if assuming responsibility for it would require large sacrifices, then they may refuse. A Good Samaritan would not refuse—or anyway, a Splendid Samaritan, if the sacrifices that had to be made were enormous. But then so would a Good Samaritan assume responsibility for that violinist; so would Henry Fonda, if he is a Good Samaritan, fly in from the West Coast and assume responsibility for me.

8.

My argument will be found unsatisfactory on two counts by many of those who want to regard abortion as morally permissible. First, while I do argue that abortion is not impermissible, I do not argue that it is always permissible. There may well be cases in which carrying the child to term requires only Minimally Decent Samaritanism of the mother, and this is a standard we must not fall below. I am inclined to think it a merit of my account precisely that it does *not* give a general yes or a general no. It allows for and supports our sense that, for example, a sick and desperately frightened fourteen-year-old schoolgirl, pregnant due to rape, may *of course* choose abortion, and that any law which rules this out is an insane law. And it also allows for and supports our sense that in other cases resort to abortion is even positively indecent. It would be indecent in the woman to request an abortion, and indecent in a doctor to perform it, if she is in her seventh month, and wants the abortion just to avoid the nuisance of postponing a trip abroad. The very fact that the arguments I have been drawing attention to treat all cases of abortion, or even all cases of abortion in which the mother's life is not at stake, as morally on a par ought to have made them suspect at the outset.

Second, while I am arguing for the permissibility of abortion in some cases, I am not arguing for the right to secure the death of the unborn child. It is easy to confuse these two things in that up to a certain point in the life of the fetus it is not able to survive outside the mother's body; hence removing it from her body guarantees its death. But they are importantly different. I have argued that you are not morally required to spend nine months in bed, sustaining the life of that violinist; but to say that is by no means to say that if, when you unplug yourself, there is a miracle and he survives, you then have a right to turn around and slit his throat. You may detach yourself even if this costs him his life; you have no right to be guaranteed his death, by some other means, if unplugging yourself does not kill him. There are some people who will feel dissatisfied by this feature of my argument. A woman may be utterly devastated by the thought of a child, a bit of herself, put out for adoption and never seen or heard of again. She may therefore want not merely that the child be detached from her, but more, that it die. Some opponents of abortion are inclined to regard this as beneath contempt—thereby showing insensitivity to what is surely a powerful source of despair. All the same, I agree that the desire for the child's death is not one which anybody may gratify, should it turn out to be possible to detach the child alive.

At this place, however, it should be remembered that we have only been pretending throughout that the fetus is a human being from the moment of conception. A very early abortion is surely not the killing of a person, and so is not dealt with by anything I have said here.

Notes

1. The term "direct" in the arguments I refer to is a technical one. Roughly, what is meant by "direct killing" is either killing as an end in itself, or killing as a means to some end, for example, the end of saving someone else's life. See note [4] below, for an example of its use.

2. *Cf. Encyclical Letter of Pope Pius XI on Christian Marriage*, St. Paul Editions (Boston, n.d.), p. 32: "However much we may pity the mother whose health and even life is gravely imperiled in the performance of the duty allotted to her by nature, nevertheless what could ever be a sufficient reason for excusing in any way the direct murder of the innocent? This is precisely what we are dealing with here." Noonan (*The Morality of Abortion*, p. 43) reads this as follows: "What cause can ever avail to excuse in any way the direct killing of the innocent? For it is a question of that."

3. The thesis in (4) is in an interesting way weaker than those in (1), (2), and (3): they rule out abortion even in cases in which both mother *and* child will die if the abortion is not performed. By contrast, one who held the view expressed in (4) could consistently say that one needn't prefer letting two persons die to killing one.

4. Cf. the following passage from Pius XII, *Address to the Italian Catholic Society of Midwives*: "The baby in the maternal breast has the right to life immediately from God.—Hence there is no man, no human authority, no science, no medical, eugenic, social, economic or moral 'indication' which can establish or grant a valid juridical ground for a direct deliberate disposition of an innocent human life, that is a disposition which looks to its destruction either as an end or as a means to another end perhaps in itself illicit.—The baby, still not born, is a man in the same degree and for the same reason as the mother" (quoted in Noonan, *The Morality of Abortion*, p. 45).

Why Abortion Is Immoral

Don Marquis

Marquis offers what he considers to be an essentially new argument to establish the basic wrongness of abortion. The reason murder is wrong, according to Marquis, is that it deprives a person of the value of his or her future. Because an embryo or fetus, if not aborted, can be

From Don Marquis, "Why Abortion Is Immoral," *The Journal of Philosophy* 86, no. 4 (1989): 183–202. Copyright © 1989 THE JOURNAL OF PHILOSOPHY, INC. Reproduced by permission.

assumed to have a future like ours that is also of value, abortion, like any other kind of killing, can be justified only by the most compelling reasons. Contraception, by contrast, is not wrong, because there is no identifiable individual to be deprived of a future.

The view that abortion is, with rare exceptions, seriously immoral has received little support in the recent philosophical literature. No doubt most philosophers affiliated with secular institutions of higher education believe that the anti-abortion position is either a symptom of irrational religious dogma or a conclusion generated by seriously confused philosophical argument. The purpose of this essay is to undermine this general belief. This essay sets out an argument that purports to show, as well as any argument in ethics can show, that abortion is, except possibly in rare cases, seriously immoral, that it is in the same moral category as killing an innocent adult human being…

I

…[A] necessary condition of resolving the abortion controversy is a more theoretical account of the wrongness of killing. After all, if we merely believe, but do not understand, why killing adult human beings such as ourselves is wrong, how could we conceivably show that abortion is either immoral or permissible?

II

In order to develop such an account, we can start from the following unproblematic assumption concerning our own case: it is wrong to kill *us*. Why is it wrong? Some answers can be easily eliminated. It might be said that what makes killing us wrong is that a killing brutalizes the one who kills. But the brutalization consists of being inured to the performance of an act that is hideously immoral; hence, the brutalization does not explain the immorality. It might be said that what makes killing us wrong is the great loss others would experience due to our absence. Although such hubris is understandable, such an explanation does not account for the wrongness of killing hermits, or those whose lives are relatively independent and whose friends find it easy to make new friends.

A more obvious answer is better. What primarily makes killing wrong is neither its effect on the murderer nor its effect on the victim's friends and relatives, but its effect on the victim. The loss of one's life is one of the greatest losses one can suffer. The loss of one's life deprives one of all the experiences, activities, projects, and enjoyments that would otherwise have constituted one's future. Therefore, killing someone is wrong, primarily because the killing inflicts (one of) the greatest possible losses on the victim. To describe this as the loss of life can be misleading, however. The change in my biological state does not by itself make killing me wrong. The effect of the loss of my biological life is the loss to me of all those activities, projects, experiences, and enjoyments which would otherwise have constituted my future personal life. These activities, projects, experiences, and enjoyments are either valuable for their own sakes or are means to something else that is valuable for its own sake. Some parts of my future are not valued by me now, but will come to be valued by me as I grow older and as my values and capacities change. When I am killed, I am deprived both of what I now value which would have been part of my future personal life, but also what I would come to value. Therefore, when I die, I am deprived of all of the value of my future. Inflicting this loss on me is ultimately what makes killing me wrong. This being the case, it would seem that what makes killing *any* adult human being prima facie seriously wrong is the loss of his or her future.…

The claim that what makes killing wrong is the loss of the victim's future is directly supported by two considerations. In the first place, this theory explains why we regard killing as one of the worst of crimes. Killing is especially wrong, because it deprives the victim of more than perhaps any other crime. In the second place, people with AIDS or cancer who know they are dying believe, of course, that dying is a very bad thing for them. They believe that the loss of a future to them that they would otherwise have experienced is what makes their premature death a very bad thing for them. A better theory of the wrongness of killing would require a different natural property associated with killing which better fits with the attitudes of the dying. What could it be?

The view that what makes killing wrong is the loss to the victim of the value of the victim's future gains additional support when some of its implications are examined. In the first place, it is incompatible with the view that it is wrong to kill only beings who are biologically human. It is possible that there exists a different species from another planet whose members have a future like ours. Since having a future like that is what makes killing someone wrong, this theory entails that it would be wrong to kill members of such a species. Hence, this theory is opposed to the claim that only life that is biologically human has great moral worth, a claim which many anti-abortionists have seemed to adopt. This opposition, which this theory has in common with personhood theories, seems to be a merit of the theory.

In the second place, the claim that the loss of one's future is the wrong-making feature of one's being killed entails the possibility that the futures of some actual nonhuman mammals on our own planet are sufficiently like ours that it is seriously wrong to kill them also. Whether some animals do have the same right to life as human beings depends on adding to the account of the wrongness of killing some additional account of just what it is about my future or the futures of other adult human beings which makes it wrong to kill us. No such additional account will be offered in this essay. Undoubtedly, the provision of such an account would be a very difficult matter. Undoubtedly, any such account would be quite controversial. Hence, it surely should not reflect badly on this sketch of an elementary theory of the wrongness of killing that it is indeterminate with respect to some very difficult issues regarding animal rights.

In the third place, the claim that the loss of one's future is the wrong-making feature of one's being killed does not entail, as sanctity of human life theories do, that active euthanasia is wrong. Persons who are severely and incurably ill, who face a future of pain and despair, and who wish to die will not have suffered a loss if they are killed. It is, strictly speaking, the value of a human's future which makes killing wrong in this theory. This being so, killing does not necessarily wrong some persons who are sick or dying. Of course, there may be other reasons for a prohibition of active euthanasia, but that is another matter. Sanctity-of-human-life theories seem to hold that active euthanasia is seriously wrong even in an individual case where there seems to be good reason for it independently of public policy considerations. This consequence is most implausible, and it is a plus for the claim that the loss of a future of value is what makes killing wrong that it does not share this consequence.

In the fourth place, the account of the wrongness of killing defended in this essay does straightforwardly entail that it is prima facie seriously wrong to kill children and infants, for we do presume that they have futures of value. Since we do believe that it is wrong to kill defenseless little babies, it is important that a theory of the wrongness of killing easily account for this. Personhood theories of the wrongness of killing, on the other hand, cannot straightforwardly account for the wrongness of killing infants and young children. Hence, such theories must add special ad hoc accounts of the wrongness of killing the young. The plausibility of such ad hoc theories seems to be a function of how desperately one wants such theories to work. The claim that the primary wrong-making feature of a killing is the loss to the victim of the value of its future accounts for the wrongness of killing young children and infants directly; it makes the wrongness of such acts as obvious as we actually think it is. This is a further merit of this theory. Accordingly, it seems that this value of a future-like-ours theory of the wrongness of killing shares strengths of both sanctity-of-life and personhood accounts while avoiding weaknesses of both. In addition, it meshes with a central intuition concerning what makes killing wrong.

The claim that the primary wrong-making feature of a killing is the loss to the victim of the value of its future has obvious consequences for the ethics of abortion. The future of a standard fetus includes a set of experiences, projects, activities, and such which are identical with the futures of adult human beings and are identical with the future of young children. Since the reason that is sufficient to explain why it is wrong to kill human beings after the time of birth is a reason that also applies to fetuses, it follows that abortion is prima facie seriously morally wrong.

This argument does not rely on the invalid inference that, since it is wrong to kill persons, it is wrong to kill potential persons also. The category that is morally central to this analysis is the category of having a valuable future like ours; it is not the category of personhood. The argument to the conclusion that abortion is prima [facie] seriously morally wrong proceeded independently of the notion of person or potential person or any equivalent....

Of course, this value of a future-like-ours argument, if sound, shows only that abortion is prima facie wrong, not that it is wrong in any and all circumstances. Since the loss of the future to a standard fetus, if killed, is, however, at least as great a loss as the loss of the future to a standard adult human being who is killed, abortion, like ordinary killing, could be justified only by the most compelling reasons. The loss of one's life is almost the greatest misfortune that can happen to one. Presumably abortion could be justified in some circumstances, only if the loss consequent on failing to abort would be at least as great. Accordingly, morally permissible abortions will be rare indeed unless, perhaps, they occur so early in pregnancy that a fetus is not yet definitely an individual. Hence, this argument should be taken as showing that abortion is presumptively very seriously wrong, where the presumption is very strong—as strong as the presumption that killing another adult human being is wrong.

III

How complete an account of the wrongness of killing does the value of a future-like-ours account have to be in order that the wrongness of abortion is a consequence? This account does not have to be an account of the necessary conditions for the wrongness of killing. Some persons in nursing homes may lack valuable human futures, yet it may be wrong to kill them for other reasons. Furthermore, this account does not obviously have to be the sole reason killing is wrong where the victim did have a valuable future. This analysis claims only that, for any killing where the victim did have a valuable future like ours, having that future by itself is sufficient to create the strong presumption that the killing is seriously wrong.

One way to overturn the value of a future-like-ours argument would be to find some account of the wrongness of killing which is at least as intelligible and which has different implications for the ethics of abortion. Two rival accounts possess at least some degree of plausibility. One account is based on the obvious fact that people value the experience of living and wish for that valuable experience to continue. Therefore, it might be said, what makes killing wrong is the discontinuation of that experience for the victim. Let us call this the *discontinuation account*. Another rival account is based upon the obvious fact that people strongly desire to continue to live. This suggests that what makes killing us so wrong is that it interferes with the fulfillment of a strong and fundamental desire, the fulfillment of which is necessary for the fulfillment of any other desires we might have. Let us call this the *desire account*.

Consider first the desire account as a rival account of the ethics of killing which would provide the basis for rejecting the anti-abortion position. Such an account will have to be stronger than the value of a future-like-ours account of the wrongness of abortion if it is to do the job expected of it. To entail the wrongness of abortion, the value of a future-like-ours account has only to provide a sufficient, but not a necessary, condition for the wrongness of killing. The desire account, on the other hand, must provide us also with a necessary condition for the wrongness of killing in order to generate a pro-choice conclusion on abortion. The reason for this is that presumably the argument from the desire account moves from the claim that what makes killing wrong is interference with a very strong desire to the claim that abortion is not wrong because the fetus lacks a strong desire to live. Obviously, this inference fails if someone's having the desire to live is not a necessary condition of its being wrong to kill that individual.

One problem with the desire account is that we do regard it as seriously wrong to kill persons who have little desire to live or who have no desire to live or, indeed, have a desire not to live. We believe it is seriously wrong to kill the unconscious, the sleeping, those who are tired of life, and those who are suicidal. The value-of-a-human-future account renders standard morality intelligible in these cases; these cases appear to be incompatible with the desire account.

The desire account is subject to a deeper difficulty. We desire life, because we value the goods of this life. The goodness of life is not secondary to our desire for it. If this were not so, the pain of one's own premature death could be done away with merely by an appropriate alteration in the configuration of one's desires. This is absurd. Hence, it would seem that it is the loss of the goods of one's future, not the interference with the fulfillment of a strong desire to live, which accounts ultimately for the wrongness of killing....

The discontinuation account looks more promising as an account of the wrongness of killing. It seems just as intelligible as the value of a future-like-ours account, but it does not justify an anti-abortion position. Obviously, if it is the continuation of one's activities, experiences, and projects, the loss of which makes killing wrong, then it is not wrong to kill fetuses for that reason, for fetuses do not have experiences, activities, and projects to be continued or discontinued. Accordingly, the discontinuation account does not have the anti-abortion consequences that the value of a future-like-ours account has. Yet, it seems as intelligible as the value of a future-like-ours account, for when we think of what would be wrong with our being killed, it does seem as if it is the discontinuation of what makes our lives worthwhile which makes killing us wrong.

Is the discontinuation account just as good an account as the value of a future-like-ours account? The discontinuation account will not be adequate at all, if it does not refer to the *value* of the experience that may be discontinued. One does not want the discontinuation account to make it wrong to kill a patient who begs for death and who is in severe pain that cannot be relieved short of killing. (I leave open the question of whether it is wrong for other reasons.) Accordingly, the discontinuation account must be more than a bare discontinuation account. It must make some reference to the positive value of the patient's experience. But, by the same token, the value of a future-like-ours account cannot be a bare future account either. Just having a future surely does not itself rule out killing the above patient. This account must make some reference to the value of the patient's future experience and projects also. Hence, both accounts involve the value of experiences, projects, and activities. So far we still have symmetry between the accounts.

The symmetry fades, however, when we focus on the time period of the value of the experiences, etc., which has moral consequences. Although both accounts leave open the possibility that the patient in our example may be killed, this possibility is left open only in virtue of the utterly bleak future for the patient. It makes no difference whether the patient's immediate past contains intolerable pain, or consists of being in a coma (which we can imagine is a situation of indifference), or consists in a life of value. If the patient's future is a future of value, we want our account to make it wrong to kill the patient. If the patient's future is intolerable, whatever his or her immediate past, we want our account to allow killing the patient. Obviously, then, it is the value of that patient's future which is doing the work in rendering the morality of killing the patient intelligible.

This being the case, it seems clear that whether one has immediate past experiences or not does no work in the explanation of what makes killing wrong. The addition the discontinuation account makes to the value of a human future is otiose. Its addition to the value-of-a-future account plays no role at all in rendering intelligible the wrongness of killing. Therefore, it can be discarded with the discontinuation account of which it is a part.

IV

The analysis of the previous section suggests that alternative general accounts of the wrongness of killing are either inadequate or unsuccessful in getting around the anti-abortion consequences of the value of a future-like-ours argument. A different strategy for avoiding these anti-abortion consequences involves limiting the scope of the value-of-a-future argument. More precisely, the strategy involves arguing that fetuses lack a property that is essential for the value-of-a-future argument (or for any anti-abortion argument) to apply to them.

One move of this sort is based upon the claim that a necessary condition of one's future being valuable is that one values it. Value implies a valuer. Given this one might argue that, since fetuses cannot value their futures, their futures are not valuable to them. Hence, it does not seriously wrong them deliberately to end their lives.

This move fails, however, because of some ambiguities. Let us assume that something cannot be of value unless it is valued by someone. This does not entail that my life is of no value unless it is valued by me. I may think, in a period of despair, that my future is of no worth whatsoever, but I may be wrong because others rightly see value—even great value—in it. Furthermore, my future can be valuable to me even if I do not value it. This is the case when a young person attempts suicide, but is rescued and goes on to significant human achievements. Such young people's futures are ultimately valuable to them, even though such futures do not seem to be valuable to them at the moment of attempted suicide. A fetus's future can be valuable to it in the same way. Accordingly, this attempt to limit the anti-abortion argument fails....

V

In this essay, it has been argued that the correct ethic of the wrongness of killing can be extended to fetal life and used to show that there is a stronger presumption that an abortion is morally impermissible. If the ethic of killing adopted here entails, however, that contraception is also seriously immoral, then there would appear to be a difficulty with the analysis of this essay.

But this analysis does not entail that contraception is wrong. Of course, contraception prevents the actualization of a possible future of value. Hence it follows from the claim that futures of value should be maximized that contraception is prima facie immoral. This obligation to maximize does not exist, however; furthermore, nothing in the ethics of killing in this paper entails that it does. The ethics of killing in this essay would entail that contraception is wrong only if something were denied a human future of value by contraception. Nothing at all is denied such a future by contraception, however.

Candidates for a subject of harm by contraception fall into four categories: (1) some sperm or other, (2) some ovum or other, (3) a sperm and an ovum separately, and (4) a sperm and an ovum together. Assigning the harm to some sperm is utterly arbitrary, for no reason can be given for making a sperm the subject of harm rather than an ovum. Assigning the harm to some ovum is utterly arbitrary, for no reason can be given for making an ovum the subject of harm rather than a sperm. One might attempt to avoid these problems by insisting that contraception deprives both the sperm and the ovum separately of a valuable future like ours. On this alternative, too many futures are lost. Contraception was supposed to be wrong, because it deprived us of one future of value, not two. One might attempt to avoid this problem by holding that contraception deprives the combination of sperm and ovum of a valuable future like ours. But here the definite article misleads. At the time of contraception, there are hundreds of millions of sperm, one (released) ovum and millions of possible combinations of all of these. There is no actual combination at all. Is the subject of the loss to be a merely possible combination? Which one? This alternative does not yield an actual subject of harm either. Accordingly, the immorality of contraception is not entailed by the loss of a future-like-ours argument simply because there is no nonarbitrarily identifiable subject of the loss in the case of contraception.

VI

The purpose of this essay has been to set out an argument of the serious presumptive wrongness of abortion subject to the assumption that the moral permissibility of abortion stands or falls on the moral status of the fetus. Since a fetus possesses a property, the possession of which in adult human beings is sufficient to make killing an adult human being wrong, abortion is wrong....

Section 2:   Abortion and Personhood

On the Moral and Legal Status of Abortion

Mary Anne Warren

Warren argues that a woman's right to have an abortion is unrestricted. She attempts to show that there is no adequate basis for holding that the fetus has "a significant right to life" and that, whatever claims can be appropriately granted to the fetus, these can never override a woman's right to protect her own interests and well-being. Accordingly, laws that restrict access to abortion are an unjustified violation of a woman's rights.

Warren is critical of both Thomson and the jurist John T. Noonan, who had advanced an influential argument that human life begins at conception. Noonan, she claims, fails to demonstrate that whatever is genetically human (the fetus) is also morally human (a person).

Thomson, Warren argues, is mistaken in believing that it is possible both to grant that the fetus is a person and to produce a satisfactory defense of the right to obtain an abortion. Contrary to Thomson's aim, Thomson's central argument supports the right to abortion only in cases in which the woman is in no way responsible for her pregnancy.

Like Noonan, Warren conceives the basic issue in abortion to be the question of what properties something must possess to be a person in the moral sense. She offers five traits she believes anyone would accept as central and argues that the fetus, at all stages of development, possesses none of them. Since the fetus is not a person, it is not entitled to the full range of moral rights. That the fetus has the potential to become a person may give it a prima facie right to life, but the rights of an actual person always outweigh those of a potential person.

We will be concerned with both the moral status of abortion, which for our purposes we may define as the act which a woman performs in voluntarily terminating, or allowing another person to terminate, her pregnancy, and the legal status which is appropriate for this act. I will argue that, while it is not possible to produce a satisfactory defense of a woman's right to obtain an abortion without showing that a fetus is not a human being, in the morally relevant sense of that term, we ought not to conclude that the difficulties involved in determining whether or not a fetus is human make it impossible to produce any satisfactory solution to the problem of the moral status of abortion. For it is possible to show that, on the basis of intuitions which we may expect even the opponents of abortion to share, a fetus is not a person, hence not the sort of entity to which it is proper to ascribe full moral rights.

Of course, while some philosophers would deny the possibility of any such proof,[1] others will deny that there is any need for it, since the moral permissibility of abortion appears to them to be too obvious to require proof. But the inadequacy of this attitude should be evident from the fact that both the friends and foes of abortion consider their position to be morally self-evident. Because proabortionists have never adequately come to grips with the conceptual issues surrounding abortion, most if not all, of the arguments which they advance in opposition to laws restricting access to abortion fail to refute or even weaken the traditional antiabortion

argument, i.e., that a fetus is a human being, and therefore abortion is murder.

These arguments are typically of one of two sorts. Either they point to the terrible side effects of the restrictive laws, e.g., the deaths due to illegal abortions, and the fact that it is poor women who suffer the most as a result of these laws, or else they state that to deny a woman access to abortion is to deprive her of her right to control her own body. Unfortunately, however, the fact that restricting access to abortion has tragic side effects does not, in itself, show that the restrictions are unjustified, since murder is wrong regardless of the consequences of prohibiting it; and the appeal to the right to control one's body, which is generally construed as a property right, is at best a rather feeble argument for the permissibility of abortion. Mere ownership does not give me the right to kill innocent people whom I find on my property, and indeed I am apt to be held responsible if such people injure themselves while on my property. It is equally unclear that I have any moral right to expel an innocent person from my property when I know that doing so will result in his death . . . .

John Noonan is correct in saying that "the fundamental question in the long history of abortion is, How do you determine the humanity of a being?"[2] He summarizes his own antiabortion argument, which is a version of the official position of the Catholic Church, as follows:

> . . . it is wrong to kill humans, however poor, weak, defenseless, and lacking in opportunity to develop

their potential they may be. It is therefore morally wrong to kill Biafrans. Similarly, it is morally wrong to kill embryos.[3]

Noonan bases his claim that fetuses are human upon what he calls the theologians' criterion of humanity: that whoever is conceived of human beings is human. But although he argues at length for the appropriateness of this criterion, he never questions the assumption that if a fetus is human then abortion is wrong for exactly the same reason that murder is wrong.

Judith Thomson is, in fact, the only writer I am aware of who has seriously questioned this assumption; she has argued that, even if we grant the antiabortionist his claim that a fetus is a human being, with the same right to life as any other human being, we can still demonstrate that, in at least some and perhaps most cases, a woman is under no moral obligation to complete an unwanted pregnancy.[4] Her argument is worth examining, since if it holds up it may enable us to establish the moral permissibility of abortion without becoming involved in problems about what entitles an entity to be considered human, and accorded full moral rights. To be able to do this would be a great gain in the power and simplicity of the proabortion position, since, although I will argue that these problems can be solved at least as decisively as can any other moral problem, we should certainly be pleased to be able to avoid having to solve them as part of the justification of abortion.

On the other hand, even if Thomson's argument does not hold up, her insight, i.e., that it requires arguments to show that if fetuses are human then abortion is properly classified as murder, is an extremely valuable one. The assumption she attacks is particularly invidious, for it amounts to the decision that it is appropriate, in deciding the moral status of abortion, to leave the rights of the pregnant woman out of consideration entirely, except possibly when her life is threatened. Obviously, this will not do; determining what moral rights, if any, a fetus possesses is only the first step in determining the moral status of abortion. Step two, which is at least equally essential, is finding a just solution to the conflict between whatever rights the fetus may have, and the rights of the woman who is unwillingly pregnant. While the historical error has been to pay far too little attention to the second step,

Ms. Thomson's suggestion is that if we look at the second step first we may find that a woman has a right to obtain an abortion *regardless* of what rights the fetus has.

Our own inquiry will also have two stages. In Section I, we will consider whether or not it is possible to establish that abortion is morally permissible even on the assumption that a fetus is an entity with a full-fledged right to life. I will argue that in fact this cannot be established, at least not with the conclusiveness which is essential to our hopes of convincing those who are skeptical about the morality of abortion, and that we therefore cannot avoid dealing with the question of whether or not a fetus really does have the same right to life as a (more fully developed) human being.

In Section II, I will propose an answer to this question, namely, that a fetus cannot be considered a member of the moral community, the set of beings with full and equal moral rights, for the simple reason that it is not a person, and that it is personhood, and not genetic humanity, i.e., humanity as defined by Noonan, which is the basis for membership in this community. I will argue that a fetus, whatever its stage of development, satisfies none of the basic criteria of personhood, and is not even enough *like* a person to be accorded even some of the same rights on the basis of this resemblance. Nor, as we will see, is a fetus's *potential* personhood a threat to the morality of abortion, since, whatever the rights of potential people may be, they are invariably overridden in any conflict with the moral rights of actual people.

I

We turn now to Professor Thomson's case for the claim that even if a fetus has full moral rights, abortion is still morally permissible, at least sometimes, and for some reasons other than to save the woman's life. Her argument is based upon clever, but I think faulty, thinking. She asked us to picture ourselves waking up one day, in bed with a famous violinist. Imagine that you have been kidnapped, and your bloodstream hooked up to that of the violinist, who happens to have an ailment which will certainly kill him unless he is permitted to share your kidneys for a period of nine months. No one else can save him, since you alone have the right type of blood. He will be unconscious all that time, and you will have to stay in bed with him, but after the nine months are over he may be unplugged, completely cured, that is provided that you have cooperated.

Now then, she continues, what are your obligations in this situation? The antiabortionist, if he is consistent, will have to say that you are obligated to stay in bed with the violinist: for all people have a right to life, and violinists are people, and therefore it would be murder for you to disconnect yourself from him and let him die.[5] But this is outrageous, and so there must be something wrong with the same argument when it is applied to abortion. It would certainly be commendable of you to agree to save the violinist, but it is absurd to suggest that your refusal to do so would be murder. His right to life does not obligate you to do whatever is required to keep him alive; nor does it justify anyone else forcing you to do so. A law which required you to stay in bed with the violinist would clearly be an unjust law, since it is no proper function of the law to force unwilling people to make huge sacrifices for the sake of other people toward whom they have no such prior obligation.

Thomson concludes that, if this analogy is an apt one, then we can grant the antiabortionist his claim that a fetus is a human being, and still hold that it is at least sometimes the case that a pregnant woman has the right to refuse to be a Good Samaritan towards the fetus, i.e., to obtain an abortion. For there is a great gap between the claim that x has a right to life, and the claim that y is obligated to do whatever is necessary to keep x alive, let alone that he ought to be forced to do so. It is y's duty to keep x alive only if he has somehow contracted a *special* obligation to do so; and a woman who is unwillingly pregnant, e.g., who was raped, has done nothing which obligates her to make the enormous sacrifice which is necessary to preserve the conceptus.

This argument is initially quite plausible, and in the extreme case of pregnancy due to rape it is probably conclusive. Difficulties arise, however, when we try to specify more exactly the range of cases in which abortion is clearly justifiable even on the assumption that the fetus is human. Professor Thomson considers it a virtue of her argument that it does not enable us to conclude that abortion is *always* permissible. It would, she says, be "indecent" for a woman in her seventh month to obtain an abortion just to avoid having to postpone a trip to Europe. On the other hand, her argument enables us to see that "a sick and desperately frightened schoolgirl pregnant due to rape may *of course* choose abortion, and that any law which rules this out is an insane law" (p. 65). So far, so good; but what are we to say about the woman who becomes pregnant not through rape but as a result of her own carelessness, or because of contraceptive failure, or who gets pregnant intentionally and then changes her mind about wanting a child? With respect to such cases, the violinist analogy is of much less use to the defender of the woman's right to obtain an abortion.

Indeed, the choice of a pregnancy due to rape, as an example of a case in which abortion is permissible even if a fetus is considered a human being, is extremely significant; for it is only in the case of pregnancy due to rape that the woman's situation is adequately analogous to the violinist case for our intuitions about the latter to transfer convincingly. The crucial difference between a pregnancy due to rape and the normal case of an unwanted pregnancy is that in the normal case we cannot claim that the woman is in no way responsible for her predicament; she could have remained chaste, or taken her pills more faithfully, or abstained on dangerous days, and so on. If on the other hand, you are kidnapped by strangers, and hooked up to a strange violinist, then you are free of any shred of responsibility for the situation, on the basis of which it would be argued that you are obligated to keep the violinist alive. Only when her pregnancy is due to rape is a woman clearly just as nonresponsible.[6]

Consequently, there is room for the antiabortionist to argue that in the normal case of unwanted pregnancy a woman has, by her own actions, assumed responsibility of the fetus. For if x behaves in a way which he could have avoided, and which he knows involves, let us say, a 1 percent chance of bringing into existence a human being, with a right to life, and does so knowing that if this should happen then that human being will perish unless x does certain things to keep him alive, then it is by no means clear that when it does happen x is free of any obligation to what he knew in advance would be required to keep that human being alive.

The plausibility of such an argument is enough to show that the Thomson analogy can provide a clear and persuasive defense of a woman's right to obtain an abortion only with respect to those cases in which the woman is in no way responsible for her pregnancy, e.g., where it is due to rape. In all other cases, we would almost certainly conclude that it was necessary to look carefully at the particular circumstances in order to determine the extent of the woman's responsibility, and hence the extent of her obligation. This is an extremely unsatisfactory outcome, from the viewpoint of the opponents of restrictive abortion laws, most of whom are convinced that a woman has a right to obtain an abortion regardless of how and why she got pregnant.

Of course a supporter of the violinist analogy might point out that it is absurd to suggest that forgetting her pill one day might be sufficient to obligate a woman to complete an unwanted pregnancy. And indeed it is absurd to suggest this. As we will see, the moral right to obtain an abortion is not in the least dependent upon the extent to which a woman is responsible for her pregnancy. But unfortunately, once we allow the assumption that a fetus has full moral rights, we cannot avoid taking this absurd suggestion seriously. Perhaps we can make this point more clear by altering the violinist story just enough to make it more analogous to a normal unwanted pregnancy and less to a pregnancy due to rape, and then seeing whether it is still obvious that you are not obligated to stay in bed with the fellow.

Suppose, then, that violinists are peculiarly prone to the sort of illness the only cure for which is the use of someone else's bloodstream for nine months, and that because of this there has been formed a society of music lovers who agree that whenever a violinist is stricken they will draw lots and the loser will, by some means, be made the one and only person capable of saving him. Now then, would you be obligated to cooperate in curing the violinist if you had voluntarily joined this society, knowing the possible consequences, and then your name had been drawn and you had been kidnapped? Admittedly, you did not promise ahead of time that you would, but you did deliberately place yourself in a position in which it might happen that a human life would be lost if you did not. Surely this is at least a prima facie reason for supposing that you have an obligation to stay in bed with the violinist. Suppose that you had gotten your name drawn deliberately; surely *that* would be quite a strong reason for thinking that you had such an obligation.

It might be suggested that there is one important disanalogy between the modified violinist case and the case of an unwanted pregnancy, which makes the woman's responsibility significantly less, namely, the fact that the fetus *comes into existence* as the result of the woman's actions. This fact might give her a right to refuse to keep it alive, whereas she would not have had this right had it existed previously, independently, and then as a result of her actions become dependent upon her for its survival.

My own intuition, however, is that x has no more right to bring into existence, either deliberately or as a foreseeable result of actions he could have avoided, a being with full moral rights (y), and then refuse to do what he knew beforehand would be required to keep that being alive, than he has to enter into an agreement with an existing person, whereby he may be called upon to save that person's life, and then refuse to do so when so called upon. Thus x's responsibility for y's existence does not seem to lessen his obligation to keep y alive, if he is also responsible for y's being in a situation in which only he can save him.

Whether or not this intuition is entirely correct, it brings us back once again to the conclusion that once we allow the assumption that a fetus has full moral rights it becomes an extremely complex and difficult question whether and when abortion is justifiable. Thus the Thomson analogy cannot help us produce a clear and persuasive proof of the moral permissibility of abortion. Nor will the opponents of the restrictive laws thank us for anything less; for their conviction (for the most part) is that abortion is obviously *not* a morally serious and extremely unfortunate, even though sometimes justified act, comparable to killing in self-defense or to letting the violinist die, but rather is closer to being a morally neutral act, like cutting one's hair.

The basis of this conviction, I believe, is the realization that a fetus is not a person, and thus does not have a full-fledged right to life. Perhaps the reason why this claim has been so inadequately defended is that it seems self-evident to those who accept it. And so it is, insofar as it follows from what I take to be perfectly obvious claims about the nature of personhood, and about the proper grounds for ascribing moral rights, claims which ought, indeed, to be obvious to both the friends and foes of abortion. Nevertheless, it is worth examining these claims, and showing how they demonstrate the moral innocuousness of abortion, since this apparently has not been adequately done before.

II

The question which we must answer in order to produce a satisfactory solution to the problem of the moral status of abortion is this: How are we to define the moral community, the set of beings with full and equal moral rights, such that we can decide whether a human fetus is a member of this community or not? What sort of entity, exactly, has the inalienable rights to life, liberty, and the pursuit of happiness? Jefferson attributed these rights to all *men*, and it may or may not be fair to suggest that he intended to attribute them *only* to men. Perhaps he ought to have attributed them to all human beings. If so, then we arrive, first, at Noonan's problem of defining what makes a being human, and, second, at the equally vital question which Noonan does not consider, namely, What reason is there for identifying the moral community with the set of all human beings, in whatever way we have chosen to define that term?

1. On the Definition of "Human"

One reason why this vital second question is so frequently overlooked in the debate over the moral status of abortion is that the term "human" has two distinct, but not often distinguished, senses. This fact results in a slide of meaning, which serves to conceal the fallaciousness of the traditional argument that since (1) it is wrong to kill innocent human beings, and (2) fetuses are innocent human beings, then (3) it is wrong to kill fetuses. For if "human" is used in the same sense in both (1) and (2) then, whichever of the two senses is meant, one of these premises is question-begging. And if it is used in two different senses then of course the conclusion doesn't follow.

Thus, (1) is a self-evident moral truth,[7] and avoids begging the question about abortion, only if "human being" is used to mean something like "a full-fledged member of the moral community." (It may or may not also be meant to refer exclusively to members of the species *Homo sapiens.*) We may call this the *moral* sense of "human." It is not to be confused with what we will call the *genetic* sense; i.e., the sense in which *any* member of the species is a human being, and no member of any other species could be. If (1) is acceptable only if the moral sense is intended, (2) is non-question-begging only if what is intended is the genetic sense.

In "Deciding Who Is Human," Noonan argues for the classification of fetuses with human beings by pointing to the presence of the full genetic code, and the potential capacity for rational thought (p. 135). It is clear that what he needs to show, for his version

of the traditional argument to be valid, is that fetuses are human in the moral sense, the sense in which it is analytically true that all human beings have full moral rights. But, in the absence of any argument showing that whatever is genetically human is also morally human, and he gives none, nothing more than genetic humanity can be demonstrated by the presence of the human genetic code. And, as we will see, the *potential* capacity for rational thought can at most show that an entity has the potential for becoming human in the moral sense.

2. Defining the Moral Community

Can it be established that genetic humanity is sufficient for moral humanity? I think that there are very good reasons for not defining the moral community in this way. I would like to suggest an alternative way of defining the moral community, which I will argue for only to the extent of explaining why it is, or should be, self-evident. The suggestion is simply that the moral community consists of all and *only* people, rather than all and only human beings;[8] and probably the best way of demonstrating its self-evidence is by considering the concept of personhood, to see what sorts of entity are and are not persons, and what the decision that a being is or is not a person implies about its moral rights.

What characteristics entitle an entity to be considered a person? This is obviously not the place to attempt a complete analysis of the concept of personhood, but we do not need such a fully adequate analysis just to determine whether and why a fetus is or isn't a person. All we need is a rough and approximate list of the most basic criteria of personhood, and some idea of which, or how many, of these an entity must satisfy in order to properly be considered a person.

In searching for such criteria, it is useful to look beyond the set of people with whom we are acquainted, and ask how we would decide whether a totally alien being was a person or not. (For we have no right to assume that genetic humanity is necessary for personhood.) Imagine a space traveler who lands on an unknown planet and encounters a race of beings utterly unlike any he has ever seen or heard of. If he wants to be sure of behaving morally toward these beings, he has to somehow decide whether they are people, and hence have full moral rights, or whether they are the sort of thing which he need not feel guilty about treating as, for example, a source of food.

How should he go about making this decision? If he has some anthropological background, he might look for such things as religion, art, and the manufacturing of tools, weapons, or shelters, since these factors have been used to distinguish our human from our prehuman ancestors, in what seems to be closer to the moral than the genetic sense of "human." And no doubt he would be right to consider the presence of such factors as good evidence that the alien beings were people, and morally human. It would, however, be overly anthropocentric of him to take the absence of these things as adequate evidence that they were not, since we can imagine people who have progressed beyond, or evolved without ever developing, these cultural characteristics.

I suggest that the traits which are most central to the concept of personhood, or humanity in the moral sense, are, very roughly, the following:

1. consciousness (of objects and events external and/or internal to the being), and in particular the capacity to feel pain;

2. reasoning (the developed capacity to solve new and relatively complex problems);

3. self-motivated activity (activity which is relatively independent of either genetic or direct external control);

4. the capacity to communicate, by whatever means, messages of an indefinite variety of types, that is, not just with an indefinite number of possible contents, but on indefinitely many possible topics;

5. the presence of self-concepts, and self-awareness, either individual or racial, or both.

Admittedly, there are apt to be a great many problems involved in formulating precise definitions of these criteria, let alone in developing universally valid behavioral criteria for deciding when they apply. But I will assume that both we and our explorer know approximately what (1)–(5) mean, and that he is also able to determine whether or not they apply. How, then, should he use his findings to decide whether or not the alien beings are people? We needn't suppose that an entity must have *all* of these attributes to be properly considered a person; (1) and (2) alone may well be sufficient for personhood, and quite probably (1)–(3), if "activity" is construed so as to include the activity of reasoning.

All we need to claim, to demonstrate that a fetus is not a person, is that any being which satisfies *none* of (1)–(5) is certainly not a person. I consider this claim to be so obvious that I think anyone who denied it, and claimed that a being which satisfied none of (1)–(5) was a person all the same, would thereby demonstrate that he had no notion at all of what a person is—perhaps because he had confused the concept of a person with that of genetic humanity. If the opponents of abortion were to deny the appropriateness of these five criteria, I do not know what further arguments would convince them. We would probably have to admit that our conceptual schemes were indeed irreconcilably different, and that our dispute could not be settled objectively.

I do not expect this to happen, however, since I think that the concept of a person is one which is very nearly universal (to people), and that it is common to both proabortionists and antiabortionists, even though neither group has fully realized the relevance of this concept to the resolution of their dispute. Furthermore, I think that on reflection even the antiabortionists ought to agree not only that (1)–(5) are central to the concept of personhood, but also that it is a part of this concept that all and only people have full moral rights. The concept of a person is in part a moral concept; once we have admitted that x is a person we have recognized, even if we have not agreed to respect, x's right to be treated as a member of the moral community. It is true that the claim that x is a *human being* is more commonly voiced as part of an appeal to treat x decently than is the claim that x is a person, but this is either because "human being" is here used in the sense which implies personhood, or because the genetic and moral sense of "human" have been confused.

Now if (1)–(5) are indeed the primary criteria of personhood, then it is clear that genetic humanity is neither necessary nor sufficient for establishing that an entity is a person. Some human beings are not people, and there may well be people who are not human beings. A man or woman whose consciousness has been permanently obliterated but who remains alive is a human being which is no longer a person; defective human beings, with no appreciable mental capacity, are not and presumably never will be people; and a fetus is a human being which is not yet a person, and which therefore cannot coherently be said to have full moral rights. Citizens of the next century should be prepared to recognize highly advanced, self-aware robots or computers, should such be developed, and intelligent inhabitants of other worlds, should such be found, as people in the fullest sense, and to respect their moral rights. But to ascribe full moral rights to an entity which is not a person is as absurd as to ascribe moral obligations and responsibilities to such an entity.

3. Fetal Development and the Right to Life

Two problems arise in the application of these suggestions for the definition of the moral community to the determination of the precise moral status of a human fetus. Given that the paradigm example of a person is a normal adult being, then (1) How like this paradigm, in particular how far advanced since conception, does a human being need to be before it begins to have a right to life by virtue, not of being fully a person as of yet, but of being *like* a person? and (2) To what extent, if any, does the fact that a fetus has the *potential* for becoming a person endow it with some of the same rights? Each of these questions requires some comment.

In answering the first question, we need not attempt a detailed consideration of the moral rights of organisms which are not developed enough, aware enough, intelligent enough, etc., to be considered people, but which resemble people in some respects. It does seem reasonable to suggest that the more like a person, in the relevant respects, a being is, the stronger is the case for regarding it as having a right to life, and indeed the stronger its right to life is. Thus we ought to take seriously the suggestion that, insofar as "the human individual develops biologically in a continuous fashion . . . the rights of a human person might develop in the same way."[9] But we must keep in mind that the attributes which are relevant in determining whether or not an entity is enough like a person to be regarded as having some of the same moral rights are no different from those which are relevant to determining whether or not it is fully a person—i.e., are no different from (1)–(5)—and that being genetically human, or having recognizably human facial and other physical features, or detectable brain activity, or the capacity to survive outside the uterus, are simply not among these relevant attributes.

Thus it is clear that even though a seven- or eight-month fetus has features which makes it apt to arouse in us almost the same powerful protective instinct as is commonly aroused by a small infant, nevertheless it is not significantly more personlike than is a very small embryo. It is *somewhat* more personlike; it can apparently feel and respond to pain, and it may even have a rudimentary form of consciousness, insofar as its brain is quite active. Nevertheless, it seems safe to say that it is not fully conscious, in the way that an infant of a few months is, and that it cannot reason, or communicate messages of indefinitely many sorts, does not engage in self-motivated activity, and has no self-awareness. Thus, in the *relevant* respects, a fetus, even a fully developed one, is considerably less personlike than is the average mature mammal, indeed the average fish. And I think that a rational person must conclude that if the right to life of a fetus is to be based upon its resemblance to a person, then it cannot be said to have any more right to life then, let us say, a newborn guppy (which also seems to be capable of feeling pain), and that a right of that magnitude could never override a woman's right to obtain an abortion, at any stage of her pregnancy.

There may, of course, be other arguments in favor of placing legal limits upon the stage of pregnancy in which an abortion may be performed. Given the relative safety of the new techniques of artificially inducing labor during the third trimester, the danger to the woman's life or health is no longer such an argument. Neither is the fact that people tend to respond to the thought of abortion in the later stages of pregnancy with emotional repulsion, since mere emotional responses cannot take the place of moral reasoning in determining what ought to be permitted. Nor, finally, is the frequently heard argument that legalizing abortion, especially late in the pregnancy, may erode the level of respect for human life, leading, perhaps, to an increase in unjustified euthanasia and other crimes. For this threat, if it is a threat, can be better met by educating people to the kinds of moral distinctions which we are making here than by limiting access to abortion (which limitation may, in its disregard for the rights of women, be just as damaging to the level of respect for human rights).

Thus, since the fact that even a fully developed fetus is not personlike enough to have any significant right to life on the basis of its personlikeness shows that no legal restrictions upon the stage of pregnancy in which an abortion may be performed can be justified on the grounds that we should protect the rights of the older fetus; and since there is no other apparent justification for such restrictions, we may conclude that they are entirely unjustified. Whether or not it would be *indecent* (whatever that means) for a woman in her seventh month to obtain an abortion just to avoid having to postpone a trip to Europe, it would not, in itself, be *immoral*, and therefore it ought to be permitted.

4. Potential Personhood and the Right to Life

We have seen that a fetus does not resemble a person in any way which can support the claim that it has even some of the same rights. But what about its *potential*, the fact that if nurtured and allowed to develop naturally it will very probably become a person? Doesn't that alone give it at least some right to life? It is hard to deny that the fact that an entity is a potential person is a strong prima facie reason for not destroying it; but we need not conclude from this that a potential person has a right to life, by virtue of that potential. It may be that our feeling that it is better, other things being equal, not to destroy a potential person is better explained by the fact that potential people are still (felt to be) an invaluable resource, not to be lightly squandered. Surely, if every speck of dust were a potential person, we would be much less apt to conclude that every potential person has a right to become actual.

Still, we do not need to insist that a potential person has no right to life whatever. There may well be something immoral, and not just imprudent, about wantonly destroying potential people, when doing so isn't necessary to protect anyone's rights. But even if a potential person does have some prima facie right to life, such a right could not possibly outweigh the right of a woman to obtain an abortion, since the rights of any actual person invariably outweigh those of any potential person, whenever the two conflict. Since this may not be immediately obvious in the case of a human fetus, let us look at another case.

Suppose that our space explorer falls into the hands of an alien culture, whose scientists decide to create a few hundred thousand or more human beings, by breaking his body into its component cells, and using these to create fully developed human beings, with, of course, his genetic code. We may imagine that each of these newly created men will have all of the original man's abilities, skills, knowledge, and so on, and also have an individual self-concept, in short that each of them will be a bona fide (though hardly unique) person. Imagine that the whole project will take only seconds, and that its chances of success

are extremely high, and that our explorer knows all of this, and also knows that these people will be treated fairly. I maintain that in such a situation he would have every right to escape if he could, and thus to deprive all of these potential people of their potential lives; for his right to life outweighs all of theirs together, in spite of the fact that they are all genetically human, all innocent, and all have a very high probability of becoming people very soon, if only he refrains from acting.

Indeed, I think he would have a right to escape even if it were not his life which the alien scientists planned to take, but only a year of his freedom, or, indeed, only a day. Nor would he be obligated to stay if he had gotten captured (thus bringing all these people-potentials into existence) because of his own carelessness, or even if he had done so deliberately, knowing the consequences. Regardless of how he got captured, he is not morally obligated to remain in captivity for *any* period of time for the sake of permitting any number of potential people to come into actuality, so great is the margin by which one actual person's right to liberty outweighs whatever right to life even a hundred thousand potential people have. And it seems reasonable to conclude that the rights of a woman will outweigh by a similar margin whatever right to life a fetus may have by virtue of its potential personhood.

Thus, neither a fetus's resemblance to a person, nor its potential for becoming a person provides any basis whatever for the claim that it has any significant right to life. Consequently, a woman's right to protect her health, happiness, freedom, and even her life,[10] by terminating an unwanted pregnancy, will always override whatever right to life it may be appropriate to ascribe to a fetus, even a fully developed one. And thus, in the absence of any overwhelming social need for every possible child, the laws which restrict the right to obtain an abortion, or limit the period of pregnancy during which an abortion may be performed, are a wholly unjustified violation of a woman's most basic moral and constitutional rights.

Notes

1. For example, Roger Wertheimer, who in "Understanding the Abortion Argument" (*Philosophy and Public Affairs*, 1, No. 1 [Fall, 1971], 67–95), argues that the problem of the moral status of abortion is insoluble, in that the dispute over the status of the fetus is not a question of fact at all, but only a question of how one responds to the facts.
2. John Noonan, "Abortion and the Catholic Church: A Summary History," *Natural Law Forum*, 12 (1967), 125.

3. John Noonan, "Deciding Who Is Human," *Natural Law Forum*, 13 (1968), 134.

4. "A Defense of Abortion."

5. Judith Thomson, "A Defense of Abortion," *Philosophy and Public Affairs*, 1, No. 1 (Fall, 1971), 47–66.

6. We may safely ignore the fact that she might have avoided getting raped, e.g., by carrying a gun, since by similar means you might likewise have avoided getting kidnapped, and in neither case does the victim's failure to take all possible precautions against a highly unlikely event (as opposed to reasonable precautions against a rather likely event) mean that he is morally responsible for what happens.

7. Of course, the principle that it is (always) wrong to kill innocent human beings is in need of many other modifications, e.g., that it may be permissible to do so to save a greater number of other innocent human beings, but we may safely ignore these complications here.

8. From here on, we will use "human" to mean genetically human, since the moral sense seems closely connected to, and perhaps derived from, the assumption that genetic humanity is sufficient for membership in the moral community.

9. Thomas L. Hayes, "A Biological View," *Commonweal*, 85 (March 17, 1967), 677–78; quoted by Daniel Callahan, in *Abortion, Law, Choice, and Morality* (London: Macmillan & Co., 1970).

10. That is, insofar as the death rate, for the woman, is higher for childbirth than for early abortion.

The Wrong of Abortion

Patrick Lee and Robert P. George

Lee and George present evidence that the human embryo is a complete human organism at conception, based on its distinctive genetic makeup and intrinsic developmental path. They then attempt to show that any coherent definition of personhood must apply to this organism at any stage of development. Notions of personhood such as Warren's, which separate biological humanity from moral humanity, are based on a false identification of personhood with disembodied consciousness. Instead, the "I" of intentional consciousness is identical with the physical organism that senses objects, the same one that began developing at conception. Those who present personhood as a secondary attribute acquired by the embodied self are also mistaken, since one's right to life must not depend on an immediate capacity for higher cognitive functions, something young infants clearly lack. Such a capacity is only the realization of the underlying potential coded in our DNA. Since moral standing cannot be partial or gradual, it must be granted at conception—the only nonarbitrary cutoff point in the continuous development of a human being.

Much of the public debate about abortion concerns the question whether deliberate feticide ought to be unlawful, at least in most circumstances. We will lay that question aside here in order to focus first on the question: is the choice to have, to perform, or to help procure an abortion morally wrong?

We shall argue that the choice of abortion is objectively immoral. By "objectively" we indicate that we are discussing the choice itself, not the (subjective) guilt or innocence of someone who carries out

From Patrick Lee and Robert P. George, "The Wrong of Abortion," *Contemporary Debates in Applied Ethics*, second edition, edited by Andrew I. Cohen and Christopher Heath Wellman. Copyright © 2014 John Wiley & Sons. (References and some notes omitted.)

the choice: someone may act from an erroneous conscience, and if he is not at fault for his error, then he remains subjectively innocent, even if his choice is objectively wrongful.

The first important question to consider is: what is killed in an abortion? It is obvious that some living entity is killed in an abortion. And no one doubts that the moral status of the entity killed is a central (though not the only) question in the abortion debate. We shall approach the issue step by step, first setting forth some (though not all) of the evidence that demonstrates that what is killed in abortion—a human embryo—is indeed a human being, then examining the ethical significance of that point.

Human Embryos and Fetuses are Complete (though Immature) Human Beings

It will be useful to begin by considering some of the facts of sexual reproduction. The standard embryology texts indicate that in the case of ordinary sexual reproduction the life of an individual human being begins with complete fertilization, which yields a genetically and functionally distinct organism, possessing the resources and active disposition for internally directed development toward human maturity. In normal conception, a sex cell of the father, a sperm, unites with a sex cell of the mother, an ovum. Within the chromosomes of these sex cells are the DNA molecules which constitute the information that guides the development of the new individual brought into being when the sperm and ovum fuse. When fertilization occurs, the 23 chromosomes of the sperm unite with the 23 chromosomes of the ovum. At the end of this process there is produced an entirely new and distinct organism, originally a single cell. This organism, the human embryo, begins to grow by the normal process of cell division—it divides into 2 cells, then 4, 8, 16, and so on (the divisions are not simultaneous, so there is a 3-cell stage, and so on). This embryo gradually develops all of the organs and organ systems necessary for the full functioning of a mature human being. His or her development (sex is determined from the beginning) is very rapid in the first few weeks. For example, as early as eight or ten weeks of gestation, the fetus has a fully formed, beating heart, a complete brain (although not all of its synaptic connections are complete—nor will they be until sometime *after* the child is born), a recognizably human form and the fetus feels pain,* cries, and even sucks his or her thumb.

There are three important points we wish to make about this human embryo. First, it is from the start *distinct* from any cell of the mother or of the father. This is clear because it is growing in its own distinct direction. Its growth is internally directed to its own survival and maturation. Second, the embryo is *human:* it has the genetic makeup characteristic of human beings. Third, and most importantly, the embryo is a *complete* or *whole* organism, though immature. The human embryo, from conception onward, is fully programmed actively to develop himself or herself to the mature stage of a human being, and, *unless prevented by disease or violence, will actually do so, despite possibly significant variation in environment* (in the mother's womb). None of the changes that occur to the embryo after fertilization, for as long as he or she survives, generates a new direction of growth. Rather, *all* of the changes (for example, those involving nutrition and environment) either facilitate or retard the internally directed growth of this persisting individual.

Sometimes it is objected that if we say human embryos are human beings, on the grounds that they have the potential to become mature humans, the same will have to be said of sperm and ova. This objection is untenable. The human embryo is radically unlike the sperm and ova, the sex cells. The sex cells are manifestly not *whole* or *complete* organisms. They are not only genetically but also functionally identifiable as parts of the male or female potential parents. They clearly are destined either to combine with an ovum or sperm or die. Even when they succeed in causing fertilization, they do not survive; rather, their genetic material enters into the composition of a distinct, new organism.

Nor are human embryos comparable to somatic cells (such as skin cells or muscle cells), though some have tried to argue that they are. Like sex cells, a somatic cell is functionally only a part of a larger organism. The human embryo, by contrast, possesses from the beginning the internal resources and active disposition to develop himself or herself to full maturity; all he or she needs is a suitable environment and nutrition. The direction of his or her growth *is not extrinsically determined*, but the embryo is internally directing his or her growth toward full maturity.

So, a human embryo (or fetus) is not something distinct from a human being; he or she is not an individual of any nonhuman or intermediate species. Rather, an embryo (and fetus) is a human being at a certain (early) stage of development—the embryonic (or fetal) stage. In abortion, what is killed is a human being, a whole living member of the species *homo sapiens*, the same *kind* of entity as you or I, only at an earlier stage of development.

---

*It should be noted that the fetus's capacity to feel pain before the third trimester is a matter of intense political controversy and has not been scientifically established. A 2005 systematic review published in *JAMA*, for example, found that fetal pain perception is unlikely before six months gestation. —Eds.

No-Person Arguments:
The Dualist Version

Defenders of abortion may adopt different strategies to respond to these points. Most will grant that human embryos or fetuses are human beings. However, they then distinguish "human being" from "person" and claim that embryonic human beings are not (yet) *persons*. They hold that while it is wrong to kill persons, it is not always wrong to kill human beings who are not persons.

Sometimes it is argued that human beings in the embryonic stage are not persons because embryonic human beings do not exercise higher mental capacities or functions. Certain defenders of abortion (and infanticide) have argued that in order to be a person, an entity must be self-aware. They then claim that, because human embryos and fetuses (and infants) have not yet developed self-awareness, they are not persons.

These defenders of abortion raise the question: Where does one draw the line between those who are subjects of rights and those that are not? A long tradition says that the line should be drawn at *persons*. But what is a person, if not an entity that has self-awareness, rationality, etc.?

This argument is based on a false premise. It implicitly identifies the human person with a consciousness which inhabits (or is somehow associated with) and uses a body: the truth, however, is that we human persons are particular kinds of physical organisms. The argument here under review grants that the human organism comes to be at conception, but claims nevertheless that you or I, the human person, comes to be only much later, say, when self-awareness develops. But if this human organism came to be at one time, but *I* came to be at a later time, it follows that I am one thing and this human organism with which I am associated is another thing.

But this is false. We are not consciousnesses that *possess* or *inhabit* bodies. Rather, we are living bodily entities. We can see this by examining the kinds of action that we perform. If a living thing performs bodily actions, then it is a physical organism. Now, those who wish to deny that we are physical organisms think of *themselves*, what each of them refers to as "*I*," as the subject of self-conscious acts of conceptual thought and willing (what many philosophers, ourselves included, would say are non-physical acts). But one can show that this "I" is identical to the subject of physical, bodily actions, and so is a living, bodily being (an organism). Sensation is a bodily action. The act of seeing, for example, is an act that an animal performs with his eyeballs and his optic nerve, just as the act of walking is an act that he performs with his legs. But it is clear in the case of human individuals that it must be the same entity, the same single subject of actions, that performs the act of sensing and that performs the act of understanding. When I know, for example, that "That is a tree," it is by my understanding, or a self-conscious intellectual act, that I apprehend what is meant by "tree," apprehending what it is (at least in a general way). But the subject of that proposition, what I refer to by the word "That," is apprehended by sensation or perception. Clearly, it must be the same thing—the same I—which apprehends the predicate and the subject of a unitary judgment.

So, it is the same substantial entity, the same agent, which understands and which senses or perceives. And so what all agree is referred to by the word "I" (namely, the subject of conscious, intellectual acts) is identical with the physical organism which is the subject of bodily actions such as sensing or perceiving. Hence the entity that I am, and the entity that you are—what you and I refer to by the personal pronouns "you" and "I"—is in each case a human, physical organism (but also with non-physical capacities). Therefore, since you and I are *essentially* physical organisms, *we* came to be when these physical organisms came to be. But, as shown above, the human organism comes to be at conception. Thus you and I came to be at conception; we once were embryos, then fetuses, then infants, just as we were once toddlers, pre-adolescent children, adolescents, and young adults.

So, how should we use the word "person"? Are human embryos persons or not? People may stipulate different meanings for the word "person," but we think it is clear that what we normally mean by the word "person" is that substantial entity that is referred to by personal pronouns—"I," "you," "she," and so on. It follows, we submit, that a person is a distinct subject with the natural capacity to reason and make free choices. That subject, in the case of human beings, is identical with the human organism, and therefore that subject comes to be when the human organism comes to be, even though it will take him or her months and even years to actualize the natural capacities to reason and make free choices, natural capacities which are already present (albeit in radical, i.e. root, form) from the beginning. So it makes no sense to say that the human organism came to be at one point but the person—you or I—came to be at some later point. To have destroyed the human organism that you are or I am even at an early stage of our lives would have been to have killed you or me.

No-Person Arguments: The Evaluative Version

Let us now consider a different argument by which some defenders of abortion seek to deny that human beings in the embryonic and fetal stages are "persons" and as such, ought not to be killed. Unlike the argument criticized in the previous section, this argument grants that the being who is you or I came to be at conception, but contends that you and I became valuable and bearers of rights only much later, when, for example, we developed the proximate, or immediately exercisable, capacity for self-consciousness. Inasmuch as those who advance this argument concede that you and I once were human embryos, they do not identify the self or the person with a non-physical phenomenon, such as consciousness. They claim, however, that being a person is an accidental attribute. It is an accidental attribute in the way that someone's being a musician or basketball player is an accidental attribute. Just as you come to be at one time, but become a musician or basketball player only much later, so, they say, you and I came to be when the physical organisms we are came to be, but we became persons (beings with a certain type of special value and bearers of basic rights) only at some time later. Those defenders of abortion whose view we discussed in the previous section disagree with the pro-life position on an ontological issue, that is, on what *kind of entity* the human embryo or fetus is. Those who advance the argument now under review, by contrast, disagree with the pro-life position on an evaluative question.

Judith Thomson argued for this position by comparing the right to life with the right to vote: "If children are allowed to develop normally they will have a right to vote: that does not show that they now have a right to vote" (1995). According to this position, it is true that we once were embryos and fetuses, but in the embryonic and fetal stages of our lives we were not yet valuable in the special way that would qualify us as having a right to life. We acquired that special kind of value and the right to life that comes with it at some point after we came into existence.

We can begin to see the error in this view by considering Thomson's comparison of the right to life with the right to vote. Thomson fails to advert to the fact that some rights vary with respect to place, circumstances, maturity, ability, and other factors, while other rights do not. We recognize that one's right to life does not vary with place, as does one's right to vote. One

may have the right to vote in Switzerland, but not in Mexico. Moreover, some rights and entitlements accrue to individuals only at certain times, or in certain places or situations, and others do not. But to have the right to life is to have *moral status at all*; to have the right to life, in other words, is to be the sort of entity that can have rights or entitlements to begin with. And so it is to be expected that *this* right would differ in some fundamental ways from other rights, such as a right to vote.

In particular, it is reasonable to suppose (and we give reasons for this in the next few paragraphs) that having moral status at all, as opposed to having a right to perform a specific action in a specific situation, follows from an entity's being the *type of thing* (or substantial entity) it is. And so, just as one's right to life does not come and go with one's location or situation, so it does not accrue to someone in virtue of an acquired (i.e., accidental) property, capacity, skill, or disposition. Rather, this right belongs to a human being at all times that he or she exists, not just during certain stages of his or her existence, or in certain circumstances, or in virtue of additional, accidental attributes.

Our position is that we human beings have the special kind of value that makes us subjects of rights in virtue of *what* we are, not in virtue of some attribute that we acquire some time after we have come to be. Obviously, defenders of abortion cannot maintain that the accidental attribute required to have the special kind of value we ascribe to "persons" (additional to being a human individual) is an *actual* behavior. They, of course do not wish to exclude from personhood people who are asleep or in reversible comas. So, the additional attribute will have to be a capacity or potentiality of some sort.[1] Thus, they will have to concede that sleeping or reversibly comatose human beings will be persons because they have the potentiality or capacity for higher mental functions.

But human embryos and fetuses also possess, albeit in radical form, a capacity or potentiality for such mental functions: human beings possess this radical capacity in virtue of the kind of entity they are, and possess it by coming into being as that kind of entity (viz., a being with a rational nature). Human embryos and fetuses cannot of course *immediately* exercise these capacities. Still, they are related to these capacities differently from, say, how a canine or feline embryo is. They are the kind of being—a natural kind, members of a biological species—which, if not prevented by extrinsic causes, in due course develops by active self-development to the point at which capacities initially possessed in root form become immediately exercisable. (Of course, the capacities in question become immediately exercisable only some months or years after the child's birth.) Each human being comes into existence possessing the internal resources and active disposition to develop the immediately exercisable capacity for higher mental functions. Only the adverse effects on them of other causes will prevent this development.

So, we must distinguish two sorts of capacity or potentiality for higher mental functions that a substantial entity might possess: first, an immediately (or nearly immediately) exercisable capacity to engage in higher mental functions; second, a basic, natural capacity to develop oneself to the point where one does perform such actions. But on what basis can one require the first sort of potentiality—as do proponents of the position under review in this section—which is an accidental attribute, and not just the second? There are three decisive reasons against supposing that the first sort of potentiality is required to qualify an entity as a bearer of the right to life.

First, the developing human being does not reach a level of maturity at which he or she performs a type of mental act that other animals do not perform—even animals such as dogs and cats—until at least several months after birth. A six-week-old baby lacks the immediately (or nearly immediately) exercisable capacity to perform characteristically human mental functions. So, if full moral respect were due only to those who possess a nearly immediately exercisable capacity for characteristically human mental functions, it would follow that six-week-old infants do not deserve full moral respect. If abortion were morally acceptable on the grounds that the human embryo or fetus lacks such a capacity for characteristically human mental functions, then one would be logically committed to the view that, subject to parental approval, human infants could be disposed of as well.

Second, the difference between these two types of capacity is merely a difference between stages along a continuum. The proximate or nearly immediately exercisable capacity for mental functions is only the development of an underlying potentiality that the human being possesses simply by virtue of the kind of entity it is. The capacities for reasoning, deliberating, and making choices are gradually developed, or brought towards maturation, through gestation, childhood, adolescence, and so on. But the difference between a being that deserves full moral respect and a being that does not (and can therefore legitimately be disposed of as a means of benefiting others) cannot consist only in the fact that, while both have some feature, one has more of it than the other. A mere *quantitative* difference (having more or less of the same feature, such as *the development* of a basic natural capacity) cannot by itself be a justificatory basis for treating different entities in *radically* different ways. Between the ovum and the approaching thousands of sperm, on the one hand, and the embryonic human being, on the other hand, there *is* a clear difference in kind. But between the embryonic human being and that same human being at any later stage of its maturation, there is only a difference in degree.

Note that there *is* a fundamental difference (as shown) between the gametes (the sperm and the ovum), on the one hand, and the human embryo and fetus, on the other. When a human being comes to be, a substantial entity that is identical with the entity that will later reason, make free choices, and so on, begins to exist. So, those who propose an accidental characteristic as qualifying an entity as a bearer of the right to life (or as a "person" or being with "moral worth") are *ignoring* a radical difference among groups of beings, and instead fastening on to a mere quantitative difference as the basis for treating different groups in radically different ways. In other words, there are beings a, b, c, d, e, and so on. And between a and b groups on the one hand and c, d and e groups on the other hand, there is a fundamental difference, a difference in kind not just in degree. But proponents of the position that being a person is an accidental characteristic ignore that difference and pick out a mere difference in degree between, say, d and e, and make that the basis for radically different types of treatment. That violates the most basic canons of justice.

Third, being a whole human being (whether immature or not) is an either/or matter—a thing either is or is not a whole human being. But the acquired qualities that could be proposed as criteria for personhood come in varying and continuous degrees: there is an infinite number of degrees of the *development* of the basic natural capacities for self-consciousness, intelligence, or rationality. So, if human beings were worthy of full moral respect (as subjects of rights) only because of such qualities, and not in virtue of the kind of being they are, then, since such qualities come in varying degrees, no account could be given of why basic rights are not possessed by human beings in varying degrees. The proposition that all human beings are created equal would be relegated to the status of a superstition. For example, if developed self-consciousness bestowed rights, then, since some people are more self-conscious than others (that is, have developed that capacity to a greater extent than others), some people would be greater in dignity than others, and the rights of the superiors would trump those of the inferiors where the interests of the superiors could be advanced at the cost of the inferiors. This conclusion would follow no matter which of the acquired qualities generally proposed as qualifying some human beings (or human beings at some stages) for full respect were selected. Clearly, developed self-consciousness, or desires, or so on, are arbitrarily selected degrees of development of capacities that all human beings possess in (at least) radical form from the coming into existence of the human being until his or her death. So, it cannot be the case that some human beings and not others possess the special kind of value that qualifies an entity as having a basic right to life, by virtue of a certain degree of development. Rather, human beings possess that kind of value, and therefore that right, in virtue of what (i.e., the kind of being) they are: and *all* human beings—not just some, and certainly not just those who have advanced sufficiently along the developmental path as to be able immediately (or almost immediately) to exercise their capacities for characteristically human mental functions—possess that kind of value and that right.[2]

Since human beings are valuable in the way that qualifies them as having a right to life in virtue of what they are, it follows that they have that right, whatever

it entails, from the point at which they come into being—and that point (as shown in our first section) is at conception.

In sum, human beings are valuable (as subjects of rights) in virtue of what they are. But what they are are human physical organisms. Human physical organisms come to be at conception. Therefore, what is intrinsically valuable (as a subject of rights) comes to be at conception.

Notes

1. Some defenders of abortion have seen the damaging implications of this point for their position, and have struggled to find a way around it. There are two leading proposals. The first is to suggest a mean between a capacity and an actual behavior, such as a disposition. But a disposition is just the development or specification of a capacity and so raises the unanswerable question of why just that much development, and not more or less, should be required. The second proposal is to assert that the historical fact of someone having exercised a capacity (say, for conceptual thought) confers on her a right to life even if she does not now have the immediately exercisable capacity. But suppose we have baby Susan who has developed a brain and gained sufficient experience to the point that just now she has the immediately exercisable capacity for conceptual thought, but she has not yet exercised it. Why should she be in a wholly different category than say, baby Mary, who is just like Susan except she did actually have a conceptual thought? Neither proposal can bear the moral weight assigned to it. Both offer criteria that are wholly arbitrary.

2. In arguing against an article by Lee, Dean Stretton claims that the basic natural capacity of rationality also comes in degrees, and that therefore the argument we are presenting against the position that moral worth is based on having some accidental characteristic would apply to our position also. But this is to miss the important distinction between having a basic natural capacity (of which there are no degrees, since one either has it or one does not), and the *development of that capacity* (of which there are infinite degrees).

DECISION SCENARIOS

The questions following each decision scenario are intended to prompt reflection and discussion. In deciding how to answer them, you should consider the information provided in the Social Context and Case Presentations, as well as in the Briefing Session. You should also make use of the ethical theories and principles presented in Part VI: Foundations of Bioethics, and the arguments offered in the relevant readings in this chapter.

DECISION SCENARIO 1

Emergency Contraception

Samantha Williams was feeling desperate when she walked into Wall's Drugs. She hadn't used protection when she hooked up with Charlie, and Charlie

hadn't been prepared either. Neither of them had been expecting what happened to happen.

But it had, and now she was going to have to do something about it. She was only sixteen, and she couldn't have a baby. It would change the rest of her life. She wouldn't be able to go to college, and she would have to get a job. She knew she and Charlie weren't destined to start a family together. Charlie had no better ability to support himself than she did, and his family was even poorer than hers. She had already waited too long. She should have gone to the drugstore immediately.

Samantha hung back, waiting until no one else was standing in the alcove the pharmacy had set aside for consultations. She was relieved to see that the pharmacist on duty was a young red-haired woman with a nice smile. Her plastic name tag identified her as Monique Marquesa.

"I need a package of Plan B," Samantha told her. She then quickly added, "Or a bottle or however it comes."

"You think you need it?" The pharmacist gave her an appraising glance. "You know what it is?"

"I absolutely need it." Samantha felt herself blushing. "And I know people call it the morning-after pill."

"How old are you?" Monique Marquesa asked the question curtly.

"I'm sixteen." Samantha was not going to let herself be bullied. "But I know there is no age requirement to buy Plan B." She added, "I also have the money. In cash."

"I don't approve of girls your age taking Plan B." Marquesa gave Samantha a stern look, "You

shouldn't need it, and I'm not going to sell it to you. For me, it's a matter of conscience."

"But I need it." Samantha was so stunned she couldn't think of what to say. "You have to sell it to me."

"No I don't," the pharmacist said. "If you want the drug, you can go to a Planned Parenthood clinic and get it. There's one at the Millennium Plaza."

"But that's miles from here." Samantha couldn't believe what the woman was telling her. "It's already been a couple of days, and I'm sure the clinic is closed this time of night. I don't know if I can even get there."

"I'm sorry." The pharmacist didn't sound sorry. "That's all I can do. I've sent you to a place where you can get what you want. I'm not going to go against my principles just to please you."

1. Is Monique Marquesa acting within her rights in refusing to sell Samantha Plan B for reasons of conscience?

2. Do pharmacists have a professional duty to provide patients with the drugs they request, so long as it is legal to do so?

3. Would it be legitimate for a taxi driver to refuse to drive Samantha to Planned Parenthood on the grounds that he objects to contraception and abortion?

4. Should pharmacists be required by law to stock and sell Plan B?

DECISION SCENARIO 2

After the Concert

It happened after a concert. Sixteen-year-old Mary Kwon had gone with three of her friends to a Taylor Swift show at Chicago's KeyCorp Auditorium. After the concert, in a crowd estimated at eleven thousand, Mary became separated from the other three girls. She decided that the best thing to do was to meet them at the car.

But when she got to the eight-story parking building, Mary realized she wasn't sure what level they had parked on. She thought it might be somewhere in the middle, so she started looking on the fourth floor. While she was walking down the aisles of cars, two men in their early twenties stopped her and asked if she was having some kind of trouble.

Mary explained the situation to them, and one of the men suggested that they get his car and drive around inside the parking garage. Mary hesitated, but both seemed so polite and genuinely concerned to help that she decided to go with them.

Once they were in the car, however, the situation changed. They drove out of the building and toward an industrial area. Mary pleaded with them to let her out of the car. Then, some seven miles from the auditorium, the driver stopped the car in a dark area behind a vacant building. Mary was then raped by both men.

Mary was treated at Allenworth Hospital and released into the custody of her parents. She filed a complaint with the police, but her troubles were not yet over. Two weeks after she missed her menstrual period, tests showed that Mary was pregnant.

"How do you feel about having this child?" asked Sarah Ruben, the Kwon family physician.

"I hate the idea," Mary said. "I feel guilty about it, though. I mean, it's not the child's fault."

"Let me ask a delicate question," said Dr. Ruben. "I know from what you've told me before that you and your boyfriend have been having sex. Can you be sure this pregnancy is not really the result of that?"

Mary shook her head. "Not really. We're careful about using condoms but I know they don't give a hundred percent guarantee."

"That's right. Now, does it make any difference to you who the father might be, so far as a decision about terminating the pregnancy is concerned?"

"If I were sure it was Shawn, I guess the problem would be harder," Mary said.

"There are some tests we can use to give us that information," Dr. Ruben said. "But that would mean waiting for the embryo to develop into a fetus. It would be easier and safer to terminate the pregnancy now."

Mary's eyes filled with tears. "I don't want a child," she said. "I don't want any child. I don't care who's the father. It was forced on me, and I want to get rid of it."

"I'll make the arrangements," said Dr. Ruben.

1. If abortion can be justified in a case of rape, can a similar argument be used to justify it in a case in which the pregnancy was unintended?

2. Suppose an embryo or fetus is a person. Can abortion still be justified on the grounds that a woman is not obligated to sacrifice her own vital interests to sustain another's life?

3. Is depriving the fetus of a future justified by the conditions under which it was conceived?

DECISION SCENARIO 3

A Procedure by Another Name

In March 1995, Tammy Watts had been pregnant for eight months and was excited by the prospect of becoming a mother for the first time. Then her world fell apart. A routine ultrasound revealed that the fetus had trisomy 13, a chromosomal abnormality that causes severe deformities and no hope of survival for the fetus.

Tammy Watts's fetus was dying inside her, and this put her own life at risk. Because she could not help her child and feared for her own life, she chose to have the procedure known as intact dilation and extraction. This is the procedure called "partial-birth abortion" by abortion opponents.

"Losing my baby at the end of my pregnancy was agonizing," Watts said in congressional testimony in 1995. "But the way the right deals with the procedure makes it even worse. When I heard [President] Bush mention 'partial-birth abortion' during the debates, I thought, 'How dare you stand there and tell flat-out lies?' There is no such thing as this procedure."

Watts's comments were accompanied by additional testimony from Viki Wilson, who had a late-term abortion because the brain of the fetus she was carrying was developing outside the skull. More testimony was given by Vikki Stella, whose fetus

had developed without a brain (was anencephalic [one word]) and had seven other serious abnormalities.

The women all testified that they owed their health to a late-term abortion and that a continuation of their ultimately futile pregnancies would have led to threats to their lives posed by strokes, blood clots, and infection. "No women have these procedures for trivial reasons," Stella testified.

1. "Partial-birth abortion" is a term coined by opponents of late-term abortion for its rhetorical power. Does the use of the term make it difficult to engage in informed public discussions of the relevant issues? (The Partial-Birth Abortion Act of 2003 gave the term a definition and legally-sanctioned status.)

2. Vikki Stella testified that women did not choose late-term abortion for "trivial reasons." Statistics indicate, however, that some women with normally developing fetuses seek late-term abortions because, for various reasons, they failed to seek an early abortion. Does this fact undercut the argument the three women advance in their testimony?

3. Does the testimony indicate that there is sufficient reason not to make late-term abortion illegal? (For more information, see the Social Context: The "Partial-Birth Abortion" Controversy in this chapter.)

DECISION SCENARIO 4

Mail Order Miscarriage

When Mona Trujillo emerged from the bathroom she was ashen and shaking. In her left hand was a plastic pregnancy test with two pink lines on the screen.

"How could this happen?" she asked her boyfriend, Caden Burke. "We've been so careful."

"Except for the time that the condom broke," Caden reminded her. "I'm sorry, babe. We'll figure this out." Mona burst into tears and began to sob against Caden's shoulder.

Mona had been the first member of her extended family to graduate from high school. She had a 4.0 GPA at McAllen community college and worked nights cleaning hotel rooms to pay rent and tuition. She had dreams of becoming a veterinarian. But now she could see it all slipping away. Getting pregnant too early—the same thing that had kept her mother and grandmother from escaping poverty—had somehow happened to her.

"I know I have to get an abortion," she said. "I love you and can see us having kids someday, but not now." Caden nodded and hugged her, and they began to look for a clinic online.

The trouble was, there weren't any. Texas had just enacted strict new regulations targeting abortion providers and the closest clinic was now over 250 miles away. Neither she nor Caden had a car or could take time off work, and when they added up the cost of bus fare, a motel, and the procedure, it was $1600 more than their combined savings. Finally, after a

sleepless night at her school's computer lab, Mona found a reputable-looking website offering medication abortion through the mail for $70.

"I don't know if this will work or if it's even legal, but I think it might be our only option," she told Caden the next morning.

"But what if something goes wrong or you don't stop bleeding?"

"I think that's unlikely. But if it happens we can go to the hospital and tell them I had a miscarriage. The treatment is the same."

1. Although research suggests that medication abortion has a very low risk of complications, ordering pills online is risky and could, in this case, be considered a crime. Setting aside the morality of abortion, do Mona's aspirations and circumstances justify taking such risks? (See Social Context: The Rise of Medication Abortion.)

2. The Supreme Court has ruled that states are not allowed to ban abortions or place an "undue burden" on those seeking them before the point of fetal viability. Do regulations like those in Texas constitute an "undue burden" for poor and small-town women like Mona? (See Social Context: State Abortion Laws for details.)

3. Roughly one in four pregnancies end in miscarriage. If any complications did result from Mona's medication abortion, would she be justified in lying about having a miscarriage to obtain treatment and avoid possible prosecution?

DECISION SCENARIO 5

Disabled and Pregnant

Clare Macwurter was twenty-two years old, but mentally she remained a child. As a result of a prolonged and difficult labor, Clare had been deprived of an adequate blood-oxygen supply during her birth. The consequence was that she suffered irreversible brain damage.

Clare enjoyed life and was generally a happy person. She couldn't read, but she liked listening to music and watching television, although she could rarely understand the stories. She was in good

health, physically attractive, and, with the help of her parents, she could care for herself.

Clare was also interested in sex. When she was seventeen, she and a fellow student at the special school they attended had been interrupted having intercourse in a supply closet. Clare's parents had been told about the incident, but after Clare left school the following year, they didn't discuss it with her. After all, she stayed at home with her mother every day, and, besides, it was a matter they preferred not to think about.

So the Macwurters were both surprised and upset when it became clear to them that Clare was pregnant. At first they couldn't imagine how it could have happened. Then they recalled that on several occasions Clare had been sent to stay at the house of Mr. Macwurter's brother and his wife while Mrs. Macwurter went shopping.

John Macwurter at first denied that he had had anything to do with Clare's pregnancy. But during the course of a long and painful conversation with his brother, he admitted to having sex with Clare.

"I wasn't wholly to blame," John Macwurter said. "I mean, I know I shouldn't have done it. But still, she was interested, too. I didn't really rape her. Nothing like that."

The Macwurters were at a loss about what they should do. At first, they considered filing charges against John, but decided they couldn't face the shame it would cause the family.

Then there was the matter of the pregnancy itself. The physician they consulted told them that Clare would probably have a perfectly healthy baby. But of course, Clare couldn't really take care of herself, much less a baby. Mrs. Macwurter, for her part, was not eager to assume the additional responsibilities of caring for another child. Mr. Macwurter would be eligible to retire in four more years, and the couple had been looking forward to selling their house and moving back to the small town in Oklahoma where they had met and married. The money they had managed to save, plus insurance and a sale of their property, would permit them to place Clare in a long-term care facility after their deaths. Being responsible for another child would both ruin their plans and jeopardize Clare's future well-being.

"I never thought I would say such a thing," Mrs. Macwurter told her husband, "but I think we should arrange for Clare to have an abortion."

"That's killing," Mr. Macwurter said.

"I'm not so sure it is. I don't really know. But even if it is, I think it's the best thing to do."

Mrs. Macwurter made the arrangements with Clare's physician for an abortion to be performed. When Mr. Macwurter asked his brother to pay for the procedure, John Macwurter refused. He explained that he was opposed to abortion and so it would not be right for him to provide money to be used in that way.

1. Could Thomson's defense of abortion be employed here to show that the proposed abortion is permissible?

2. Why might Lee and George oppose abortion in this case? Why might Marquis? What alternatives might they recommend? What if it were likely that the baby would be impaired? Would this alter the situation?

3. Do the traits Warren lists as central to the concept of personhood require that we think of Clare Macwurter as not being a person in a morally relevant sense? What combination of traits, in your view, are required for moral standing?

DECISION SCENARIO 6

Whose Life?

Daniel Bocker was worried. The message his secretary had taken merely said "Go to see Dr. Tai at 3:30 today." He hadn't been asked if 3:30 was convenient for him, and he hadn't been given a reason for coming in.

Bocker knew it would have to do with his wife, Devorah. She had been suffering a lot of pain during her pregnancy, and the preceding week she had been examined by a specialist that Edward Tai, her gynecologist, had sent her to see. The specialist had performed a thorough examination and taken blood, tissue, and urine samples.

"Thank you for coming in," Dr. Tai said. "I've already spoken to Devorah and she gave me permission to discuss the situation with you."

"The tests showed something bad, didn't they?" Mr. Bocker said. "Something is wrong with the baby."

"The baby is fine, but there is something wrong with your wife, something very seriously wrong. She has what we call uterine neoplasia."

"Is that cancer?"

"Yes, it is," said Dr. Tai. "But I don't want either of you to panic about it. It's not at a very advanced stage, and at the moment it's localized. If an operation is performed very soon, then she has a good chance to make a full recovery. The standard figures show an 80 percent success rate."

"But what about the baby?"

"The pregnancy will have to be terminated," Dr. Tai said. "And I should tell you that your wife will not be able to have children after the operation."

Bocker sat quietly for a moment. He had always wanted children; for him, a family without children was not a family at all. He and Devorah had talked about having at least three, and the one she was pregnant with now was the first.

"Is it possible to save the baby?" he asked Tai.

"Devorah is only in her fourth month; there is no chance that the child could survive outside her body."

"But what if she didn't have the operation? Would the baby be normal?"

"Probably so, but the longer we wait to perform the operation, the worse your wife's chances become. I don't want to seem to tell you what to do, but my advice is for your wife to have an abortion and to undergo the operation as soon as it is reasonably possible."

"But she might recover, even if she had the child and then had the operation, mightn't she?"

"It's possible, but her chances of recovery would be much less. I don't know what the exact odds would be, but she would be running a terrible risk."

Bocker understood what Dr. Tai was saying, but he also understood what he wanted.

"I'm going to encourage Devorah to refuse an abortion," he said. "I want her to have a child, and I think she wants that, too."

"What if she wants to have a better chance to live? I think the decision is really hers. After all, it's her life that is at stake."

"But it's not just her decision," Mr. Bocker said. "It's a family decision, hers and mine. She'll have the baby and then have the operation."

1. Would the doctrine of double effect justify taking steps to treat Devorah Bocker's illness, even at the cost of terminating her pregnancy?

2. Would both Marquis and Thomson see the situation as one in which considerations of self-defense are relevant?

3. It is sometimes argued that the father of a child also has a right to decide whether an abortion is to be performed. Would Daniel Bocker be justified in urging his wife to take the risk of delaying treatment and having the child?

DECISION SCENARIO **7**

Fetal Reduction

Lois Bishop (as we will call her) learned that she was carrying twins at the same time she learned that one of the twins had Down syndrome.

"There's no question in my mind," she said. "I want to have an abortion. I had the tests done in the first place to do what I could to guarantee that I would have a normal, healthy child. I knew from the first that there was a possibility that I would have to have an abortion, so I'm prepared for it."

Her obstetrician, George Savano, nodded. "I understand that," he said. "You are certainly within your rights to ask for an abortion, and I can arrange for you to have one. But there is another possibility, an experimental one, that you might want to consider as an option."

The possibility consisted of the destruction of the abnormally developing fetus. In the end, it was the possibility that Ms. Bishop chose. A long, thin needle was inserted through Ms. Bishop's abdomen and guided into the heart of the fetus. A solution was then injected directly into the fetal heart.

Although there was a risk that Ms. Bishop would have a miscarriage, she did not. The surviving twin continued to develop normally, and Ms. Bishop had an uneventful delivery.

Savano was criticized by some physicians as "misusing medicine," but he rejected such charges. Ms. Bishop also had no regrets, for if the procedure had not been performed, she would have been forced to abort both twins.

1. What sort of utilitarian argument might be offered to justify Dr. Savano's procedure in this case?

2. Would Marquis consider the destruction of the fetus with Down syndrome immoral? After all, it might be argued that persons with Down syndrome do not have "a future like ours."

3. The procedure leads to the death of a developing fetus, so one might say that it is morally equivalent to abortion. Are there any morally relevant factors that distinguish this case from more ordinary cases involving abortion?

DECISION SCENARIO 8

A Family Tragedy

For months, doctors told eleven-year-old Visna (as we will call her) and her parents that her abdominal pains were nothing but indigestion. Then, in July 1998, the truth finally emerged: Visna was twenty-seven weeks pregnant.

Visna's family had emigrated from India to the Detroit suburb of Sterling Heights, Michigan, only the previous summer. Her parents found factory jobs and rented a two-bedroom apartment, and Visna shared one of the rooms with Hari, her sixteen-year-old brother. Sometime during the winter after their arrival, Visna told her parents, Hari had raped her, but this emerged only after Visna, who had turned twelve, was found to be pregnant.

As soon as Visna's parents learned of her condition, they made plans to take her to Kansas for an abortion. Visna would have to have a late-term abortion, and because Michigan law bans almost all abortions after twenty-four weeks, her family would have to take her out of state. But their plans were frustrated when they were leaked to a family court judge. Charges of parental negligence were filed by prosecutors against her parents, and the court immediately removed Visna from her family and made her a ward of the state.

At a court hearing, Visna's doctor argued that if her pregnancy were allowed to continue, it could cause her both physical and psychological damage. A psychologist testified that, because Visna was from a traditional Hindu background, if she were forced to have a child out of wedlock, she might later be considered unfit for marriage. Her parents also expressed their worry that if Visna had a child, the child might suffer from genetic abnormalities and, in particular, might be mentally disabled.

At the end of the hearing, the prosecution announced that it was convinced that pregnancy might endanger Visna's life and dropped the negligence charge against her parents. Visna was reunited with her family, and her parents pursued their original plan of taking her to Kansas. In Wichita, Dr. George Tiller, who was later shot to death in his church by a pro-life activist, stopped the fetus's heart and used drugs to induce labor, thus performing a "partial-birth" abortion.

1. In what circumstances, if any, should late-term abortions be legally permitted?

2. Should ethics panels be established to decide on the legitimacy of cases of late-term abortion?

3. What, if any, are the differences between late-term abortion and infanticide?

4. If it could be proven that some late-term abortions kill viable fetuses, could these abortions still be justified? If so, under what circumstances?

DECISION SCENARIO 9

Unexpected News

Helen and John Kent waited nervously in the small consulting room while Laurie Stent, their genetic counselor, went to tell Dr. Charles Blatz that they had arrived to speak with him.

"I regret that I have some bad news for you," Blatz told them. "The karyotyping that we do after amniocentesis shows a chromosomal abnormality."

He looked at them, and Helen felt that she could hardly breathe. "What is it?" she asked.

"It's a condition known as trisomy 21, and it produces Down syndrome."

"Oh, God," John said. "How severe will it be?"

"Such children are always mentally disabled," Blatz said. "Some are severely impaired and others just twenty or so points below average IQ. They have some minor physical deformities, and they sometimes have heart damage. They typically don't live beyond their thirties, but they can have a good quality of life."

Helen and John looked at each other wearily. "What do you think we should do?" Helen asked. "Should I have an abortion, and then we could try again?"

"I don't know," John said. "I really don't know. You've had a hard time being pregnant these last five months, and you'd have to go through that again. Besides, there's no guarantee this wouldn't happen again."

"But this isn't the kind of parenting we imagined. We'll be caring for this child for the rest of our lives," Helen said. "Maybe in the long run we'll be even unhappier than we are now."

1. How might a utilitarian assess this situation? How might the potential unhappiness of the Kents be measured against the potential happiness of their child? What difference might the duration or quality of happiness or unhappiness make in this situation?

2. If one accepts Thomson's view, what factors are relevant to deciding whether an abortion is justifiable in this instance?

3. How might care ethics approach this situation? What might it focus on that the theories in 1 and 2 might disregard?

Chapter 6

The Dilemma of Impaired Infants

CHAPTER CONTENTS

CASES AND CONTEXTS

The Agony of Bente Hindriks

Bente Hindriks was diagnosed at birth with a severe form of a rare genetic disorder called Hallopeau-Siemens syndrome. The disorder involves a genetic defect that affects the collagen fibers that anchor the epidermis to the overlying dermis.

The defect in the collagen results in the formation of large blisters on the skin's outer layer, and even a light touch can rupture the blisters and make the skin slough off, causing excruciating pain. When a baby with Hallopeau-Siemens syndrome is fed, the mechanical action of her sucking and swallowing can tear off the mucosal layer lining her mouth and esophagus. The scar tissue that then forms can block the esophagus and restrict the motion of the tongue. Feeding through a surgically implanted gastric tube is then necessary. The delicate membrane (the conjunctiva) covering the eye and lining the eyelids and the cornea may also be affected, and the heavy scarring of these tissues can result in blindness. Webbing may also develop between the fingers or toes, resulting in mitten-like fingers or toes.

The gene responsible for Hallopeau-Siemens syndrome is recessive, and it may affect babies of both genders. The disorder is expressed either at birth or very soon afterward, and children with the syndrome die early. They may live for three or four years or, when the disorder is not so severe, nine or ten. But they remain in constant pain throughout their lives, no matter how short or how long. The longer they live, the more they will need surgery and medical intervention to keep them alive and functioning. If they don't die of infection, they eventually die of invasive skin cancer.

Bente's problem was obvious from the moment of birth. Her skin blistered as if it had been severely burned, and the blisters broke open when she was moved to an isolette or lifted to be cleaned. She lost fluids and proteins from the ruptured blisters and had to be kept hydrated by IV fluids. The raw patches of flesh from which the skin had fallen away made her subject to bacterial infections, so she had to be given IV antibiotics. Because of the scarring in her mouth and esophagus, she needed to be fed through a surgically implanted gastric tube.

Such problems were manageable, but the pain was not. Bente showed signs of extreme suffering: uncontrollable and unceasing shrieking, abnormally high blood pressure, a rapid pulse, and fast breathing. These are signs that experienced pediatricians recognize as indicating that a baby's body is under severe stress.

Does being under severe stress mean that the baby is experiencing severe pain? Because babies cannot say what they are feeling, answering the question requires drawing a conclusion from vital signs and behavior. The behavior that babies with the syndrome exhibit and the physiological signs that they manifest are the same as those displayed by older children and adults when they are suffering great pain. Infants also have much of the physiological equipment associated with pain in adults and older children—namely, a well-developed nervous system, brain, and neurotransmitters. Thus, despite the absence of direct or recollected reports on infants' suffering, most people assume they experience pain levels comparable to that of adults. (This discussion reflects a broader issue philosophers call the "problem of other minds.")

Bente was born in the Netherlands at Groningen University Medical Center. Her pediatrician, Eduard Verhagen, had no reasonable doubt that Bente was in unremitting pain. Yet, to his immense frustration, he could do nothing to help her. Even the most powerful painkilling drugs did no good. Day after day, Bente went on screaming in agony. The hospital staff bandaged her raw flesh where the skin had peeled away, but when they changed her bandages, they tore off even more skin. No medical intervention seemed to help.

"The diagnosis was extremely rare and impossible to treat," Dr. Verhagen recalled several years later. "We knew she would live a few years, but not more than five or six. Then she would die of skin cancer."

Karin and Edwin Hindriks, Bente's parents, could not bear to witness their daughter's unrelievable agony. Karin Hindriks asked Dr. Verhagen and the other physicians taking care of Bente to end her suffering.

"We said we didn't want this for our daughter," Mrs. Hindriks recalled. "Such a horrendous life." But without running the risk of criminal prosecution, the doctors were powerless to act. "The doctors said, 'We understand, but we can't do anything, because if we did, then it's murder.' "

The Hindriks took their daughter home. "We saw her getting worse and worse," Mrs. Hindriks remembered. "After five or six months, her toes began to mesh, to grow together." Mr. Hindriks recalled that "It was painful to watch. You want it to stop." But they could do nothing to help Bente. Most babies with fatal disorders can be made comfortable in the period leading up to their death, but not even this was possible for Bente.

The Hindriks thought about ending Bente's life themselves. In the end, though, she died in her father's arms, to both the relief and sadness of her parents. The death certificate says she died of natural causes, but the Hindriks acknowledge that Bente was given large doses of morphine in an effort to ease her pain. Most likely, her father believes, the drug ended her life, but he has no regrets about this. Bente's death, from the parents' point of view, was for the best, and the unnecessary tragedy is that she had to suffer such a long and pointless agony.

Dr. Verhagen suspects that throughout the world physicians administer large doses of morphine to suffering infants with fatal diseases to try to ease their pain, even though the physicians know that the drug will cause the infants' death. What is unfortunate, he claims, is that this must be done in a fashion that is surreptitious and not subject to discussion and decision-making that is both rational and compassionate.

Infants, Dr. Verhagen believes, are as much entitled to the benefit of euthanasia as adults. He wishes now that he had been able legally to act on the wishes of the Hindriks and provide Bente with a merciful death to end her suffering. Such regrets helped prompt Verhagen's formulation (with Pieter Sauer) of the influential Groningen Protocol for treating severely impaired infants. (See this chapter's readings for a discussion.)

SOCIAL CONTEXT
The Dilemma of Extreme Prematurity

When Jan Anderson went into labor, she was twenty-three weeks pregnant—seventeen weeks short of the normal forty-week pregnancy.

"They told me I had a beautiful baby boy," she said. But her son, Aaron, weighed only a little more than 750 grams (about 1.5 pounds), and when she finally saw him, he was in the neonatal intensive care unit. He was attached to a battery of monitors, intravenous lines, and a respirator. Surrounding him were people checking his heart and respiration rates, monitoring his blood gases, siphoning the mucus from his mouth and underdeveloped lungs, and injecting a variety of medications needed to keep his condition stable.

"It was pretty scary," Ms. Anderson told reporter Gina Kolata.

Aaron spent four months in the hospital before Anderson was allowed to take him home. Aaron's life was preserved, but despite all the treatment he received, he was left with permanent disabilities. By age two he was quadriplegic and virtually blind, had cerebral palsy, and appeared to be mentally impaired.

Statistical Profile of the Problem

Every year, more than four hundred thousand babies are born at least six weeks prematurely and about fifty-five thousand of them weigh less than 1,500 grams (about 3.3 pounds). In the United States, about one out of nine births are preterm, and although the rate has fallen in recent years, it still remains high compared to other industrialized nations. (The U.S. ranks 131st out of 184 countries on preterm birth rates, comparable to Somalia and Thailand.) Thanks to the development of new procedures and the use of new drugs, around 90 percent of preterm infants live long enough to leave the hospital (though many must return), but almost 10 percent will have lifelong physical or mental impairments.

Survival rate is closely connected with gestation time and prematurity accounts for 35 percent of all infant deaths, more than any other cause. The more premature an infant and the lower its birth weight, the more likely it is that the infant will die soon after birth or be severely physically and mentally impaired. About half of premature infants in the 500- to 750-gram (1- to 1.5-pound) range fail to survive, and more than 25 percent of babies under 750 grams have irreversible neurological damage. The risk of brain damage rises to between 40 and 50 percent for those with a birth weight between 500 and 600 grams, and below that weight only about 1 percent will be free from physical and mental disability. As many as 10 percent of very low-birth-weight babies will have cerebral palsy (CP), and a similar percentage will have IQs below 70, where 100 is average. Only about 34 percent of those born before 27 weeks are free from serious disabilities at age three.

The technological limit for preserving the lives of premature infants is about twenty-three to twenty-four weeks. Estimates of an infant's developmental stage may be off by a week or so because it is impossible to be certain when conception takes place. (For more on this topic, see the Briefing Session in Chapter 5.) Also, because female fetuses mature more quickly in utero than males, studies show that boys born prematurely are at consistently higher risk of death and disability than females born at the same stage of gestation.

Underdeveloped

Extremely premature babies have not spent enough time in the uterus, and as a result, they are physiologically underdeveloped and liable to life-threatening disorders. Many have problems eating, digesting food, and absorbing nutrients. Their lungs are small and brittle and fill up with secretions, making it impossible for them to breathe normally. They typically must be put on a mechanical ventilator, and they tend to suffer from respiratory infections. Poor prenatal development also makes smaller infants prone to cerebral hemorrhages, or "brain bleeds," that can result in a variety of devastating consequences. Such bleeds are strongly associated with seizure disorders, blindness, deafness, mental disability, and other cognitive problems that may show up only years later.

Because of aggressive interventions and the use of new drugs and technology, the survival rates of even the most premature infants have risen somewhat in recent years, approaching 25 percent for those born at 23 weeks. Artificial pulmonary surfactants can increase the breathing capacity of an infant's lungs and shorten the time a respirator is needed. Infants with underdeveloped lungs can also benefit from extracorporeal membrane oxygenation (ECMO), a treatment in which an artificial lung removes carbon dioxide from the blood and supplies it with oxygen. Better infection control and better nutrition have also contributed to survival.

Most important, corticosteroids are now used to treat pregnant women who are likely to give birth during the period from twenty-four to thirty-four weeks of gestation. The drug stimulates fetal development and speeds up the maturation of the lungs. The steroid therapy may reduce by as much as one-third the amount of time a premature infant must remain in neonatal intensive-care units (NICUs).

After Prematurity

Statistics about the effects of prematurity on infants who survive and mature are often confusing. Results from small studies of special populations rarely match the results of large studies. Even so, the studies mentioned next sketch a consistent picture.

A 2015 systematic review of nine studies of babies born between 22 and 25 weeks gestation found that as many as 43 percent ended up with moderate or severe impairment, including very low IQs and other neurological problems. Earlier studies have shown that those born extremely premature perform worse on executive function and other tests and as adults score an average of 8.4 points lower on IQ tests than those born at full term. Even those born at 37 or 38 weeks have been shown to have lower reading and math scores than those delivered later.

These studies confirm earlier findings on the lasting effects of premature birth. A 2005 U.S. study followed into their early school years 219 children born prematurely (with birth weights of 2.2 pounds or less) from 1992 to 1995 at Cleveland's Children's Hospital. The study found that although 70 percent of the babies survived, compared with 50 percent in the 1970s and 1980s, they were just as likely to suffer from serious disabilities as those born in the earlier decades. Some 38 percent of the children had IQs below 85, compared with 14 percent of normal-weight children; 21 percent had asthma, compared with 9 percent of full-term children. The premature children were also much more likely to suffer from cerebral palsy, hearing and vision deficits, social difficulties, and poor school performance.

What all the studies show is that premature infants who survive often struggle to outgrow their initial challenges. That said, most appear to rise to meet these challenges and take satisfaction in their lives. A 1996 study surveyed 150 surviving adolescents about the quality of their lives. Researchers found that, although 27 percent of the group was disabled, they rated their quality of life about as high as a comparison group that had been born after full-term development.

Costs

Greater success in neonatal care after premature birth has not come without financial costs. The average cost of keeping a premature infant alive during the first year is $49,000. A very low-birth-weight neonate may have to remain in intensive care for weeks or even months. The most premature infants may run up bills approaching $1 million. Sadly, these infants, despite having the highest treatment costs, are also the ones least likely to benefit from the care they are given. In-hospital care for preterm infants accounts for $18.1 billion in health care costs each year, according to the Institute of Medicine. A substantial percentage of these costs are likely to be passed on to taxpayers, for the mothers of very low-birth-weight babies are more likely to be uninsured and unemployed, with their care covered by federal- and state-funded programs. Many of these women have received no prenatal care, and a substantial number have substance abuse issues.

Some critics believe that too much money is being spent trying to save infants who are not likely to gain significant benefits, and that these funds would be better spent on preventative and prenatal care programs. According to Michael Rie, a neonatologist at the University of Kentucky, "The hundred highest users of Medicaid dollars in each state are preemies who end up for months on ventilators and end up with cerebral bleeds and extremely lousy outcomes." It costs three times as much to care for an infant under 750 grams as it does to care for a victim of serious burns in a burn unit. It costs 20 percent more to care for such an infant than it does to pay for heart transplant surgery. Most hospitals spend more money on very young patients than they do on the very old, the group often singled out in discussions of medical costs as consuming a disproportionate amount of health-care funds.

Treatment Decisions

One basic moral question about extremely low-birth-weight infants is whether they ought to be treated at all. Some neonatologists regard the treatment of all infants as a moral obligation. They resuscitate fully any infant showing the slightest signs of life at delivery, regardless of gestational age or weight. They believe this is the right course of action, even though they know that surviving infants will be likely to have severe mental and physical impairments.

Other neonatologists view the outcome of extraordinary efforts as likely to be so grim as to make resuscitation an unacceptable option. As one NICU physician states the policy at his hospital for dealing with infants weighing less than 500 grams, "We generally keep them warm and let them expire by themselves. These are not viable babies, and it's crazy to do anything more."

Because of these differences in beliefs about the right way to proceed, a premature infant may be the object of an all-out medical effort to save his life at one hospital, while at another hospital he might be provided only the care needed to keep him comfortable. At some U.S. hospitals, physicians try to save infants as young as twenty-two weeks or younger, but most European hospitals require a minimum of twenty-six weeks of gestation.

The same divergence of views about withholding treatment is found in the question of discontinuing treatment. Some physicians say that they seek a court order to preserve life if a parent asks that a respirator sustaining an infant be turned off. Others view discontinuing treatment as sometimes in the best interest of the child. As one physician put the point in a hypothetical case, "If a baby survives a major head bleed, we'll tell the parents he'll almost surely be damaged and he's suffering a great deal and we don't think we should do anything more."

Perhaps partly because of the development of NICUs and partly because of a misconstrual of federal regulations, there has been an increased tendency for physicians to make the basic decisions about whether a premature infant is treated and the extent of the treatment. Parents sometimes say that they were not even consulted about these decisions. Indeed, some report that although they did not want their child treated or wanted treatment discontinued, their wishes were disregarded by physicians, who did whatever they thought best.

Whose Decision?

This was the experience of Jan Anderson. Believing that further treatment would only produce a life of suffering and impairment for Aaron, she twice asked Aaron's physicians to turn off the ventilator. But no one would even discuss the possibility with her. According to Ms. Anderson, one physician screamed at her, "We're trying to save your child, not kill him."

After four months of hospitalization, Aaron went home, but with the severe impairments described above. (He is quadriplegic and blind, with severe cerebral palsy and mental disabilities.) Although Anderson loves him and takes care of him, she says that if she had been given the opportunity, she would have discontinued her baby's life support when he was born. She also says that if she were pregnant and went into labor again at twenty-three weeks, then "I would make sure there was no discussion about saving the child." In her view, "There is no need for anyone to suffer like this."

For some physicians and some disability rights activists, no one—not even a parent—should be able to decide for an impaired child that his or her life is not worth living. Some also believe that granting parents broad prerogatives to withhold or discontinue treatment from severely impaired infants will put society on a "slippery slope" toward the eugenic quest for "perfect" children and a general devaluing of the lives of the disabled. (See Chapters 3 and 10 for more on these topics.) It is the parents, however, who usually must bear the emotional, social, and financial burdens that a severely impaired child imposes. The courts have often recognized this and allowed the final decision about treatment to rest with families.

Nevertheless, many physicians are still reluctant to follow parental directives that will result in a child's death. Some appear to still be influenced by the so-called "Baby Doe laws" of the early 1980s. (See the Social Context: The Baby Doe Cases in this chapter.) These federal regulations required that all newborns, regardless of the degree of their impairment or the likelihood of their survival, receive lifesaving treatment and support. Physicians were threatened with federal prosecution for not following strict guidelines that prohibited ""Discriminatory failure to feed and care for handicapped infants." (A Supreme Court decision eventually overturned the regulations, and affirmed the earlier standard practice of making treatment decisions on a case-by-case basis.)

Physicians also have professional incentives to keep treating impaired neonates. Insurance companies or Medicaid typically pays the bills for premature infants that receive treatment in NICUs. Hence, physicians are generally insulated from the financial impact of treating extremely premature infants. Neonatologists may also want to explore the limits of new treatments and technologies, and these research interests may incline them to exclude parents from some treatment decisions.

Given these competing moral claims and incentives, some neonatologists and bioethicists argue that hospital ethics committees should play a larger (if not decisive) role in how premature infants should be treated. Such committees, having no vested interest in the outcome of a decision, might be able to weigh the issues more objectively than either physicians or the parents, and offer advice to all the parties concerned.

CASE PRESENTATION

Baby Owens: Down Syndrome and Duodenal Atresia

On a chilly December evening in 1976, Dr. Joan Owens pushed through the plate glass doors of Midwestern Medical Center and walked over to the admitting desk. Dr. Owens was a physician in private practice and regularly visited Midwestern to attend to her patients.

But this night was different. Dr. Owens was coming to the hospital to be admitted as a patient. She was pregnant, and shortly after 9:00 she began having periodic uterine contractions. Owens recognized them as the beginnings of labor pains. She was sure of this not only because of her medical knowledge but also because the pains followed the same pattern they had before her other three children were born.

While her husband, Phillip, parked the car, Dr. Owens went through the formalities of admission. She was not particularly worried, for the birth of her other children had been uneventful. But the pains were coming more frequently now, and she was relieved when she completed the admission process and was taken to her room. Phillip came with her, bringing a small blue suitcase of personal belongings.

At 11:30 that evening, Dr. Owens gave birth to a 4.5-pound baby girl. The plastic bracelet fastened around her wrist identified her as Baby Owens.

Bad News

Dr. Owens was groggy from exhaustion and from the medication she had received. But when the baby was shown to her, she saw at once that something was wrong. The baby's head was misshapen and the skin around her eyes strangely formed.

"Clarence," she called to her obstetrician. "Is the baby mongoloid?" (The term was then commonly used to refer to Down syndrome.)

"We'll talk about it after your recovery," Dr. Clarence Ziner said.

"Tell me now," said Owens. "Examine it!"

Dr. Ziner made a hasty examination of the child. He had already seen that Dr. Owens was right and was doing no more than making doubly certain. A more careful examination would have to be made later.

When Dr. Ziner confirmed Joan Owens's suspicion, she did not hesitate to say what she was thinking. "Get rid of it," she told Dr. Ziner. "I don't want a mongoloid child."

Dr. Ziner tried to be soothing. "Just sleep for a while now," he told her. "We'll talk about it later."

Four hours later, a little after 5:00 in the morning and before it was fully light, Joan Owens woke up. Phillip was with her, and he had more bad news to tell. A more detailed examination had shown that the child's small intestine had failed to develop properly and was closed off in one place—the condition known as duodenal atresia. It could be corrected by a relatively simple surgical procedure, but until surgery was performed the child could not be fed. Phillip had refused to consent to the operation until he had talked to his wife. Joan Owens had not changed her mind: she did not want the child.

"It wouldn't be fair to the other children to raise them with a mongoloid," she told Phillip. "It would take all of our time, and we wouldn't be able to give David, Sean, and Melinda the love and attention they need."

"I'm willing to do whatever you think best," Phillip said. "But what can we do?"

"Let the child die," Joan said. "If we don't consent to the surgery, the baby will die soon. And that's what we have to let happen."

Phillip put in a call for Dr. Ziner, and when he arrived in Joan's room, they told him of their decision. He was not pleased with it.

"The surgery has very low risk," he said. "The baby's life can almost certainly be saved. We can't tell how retarded she'll be, but most DS children get along quite well with help from their families. The whole family will grow to love her."

"I know," Joan said. "And I don't want that to happen. I don't want us to center our lives around a defective child. Phillip and I and our other children will be forced to lose out on many of life's pleasures and possibilities."

"We've made up our minds," Phillip said. "We don't want the surgery."

"I'm not sure the matter is as simple as that," Dr. Ziner said. "I'm not sure we can legally just let the baby die. I'll have to talk to the director and the hospital attorney."

Applying for a Court Order

At 6:00 in the morning, Dr. Ziner called Dr. Felix Entraglo, the director of Midwestern Medical Center, and Isaac Putnam, the head of the center's legal staff. They agreed to meet at 9:00 to talk over the problem presented to them by the Owenses.

They met for two hours. It was Putnam's opinion that the hospital would not be legally liable if Baby Owens were allowed to die because her parents refused to give consent for necessary surgery.

"What about getting a court order requiring surgery?" Dr. Entraglo asked. "That's the sort of thing we do when an infant requires a blood transfusion or immunization and his parents' religious beliefs make them refuse consent."

"This case is not exactly parallel," said Mr. Putnam. "Here we're talking about getting a court order to force parents to allow surgery to save the life of a defective infant. The infant will still be defective after the surgery, and I think a court would be reluctant to make a family undergo significant emotional and financial hardships when the parents have seriously deliberated about the matter and decided against surgery."

"But doesn't the child have some claim in this situation?" Dr. Ziner asked.

"That's not clear," said Mr. Putnam. "In general, we assume that parents will act for the sake of their child's welfare, and when they are reluctant to do so we look to the courts to act for the child's welfare. But in a situation like this . . . who can say? Is the Owens baby really a person in any legal or moral sense?"

"I think I can understand why a court would hesitate to order surgery," said Dr. Entraglo. "What sort of life would it be for a family when they had been pressured into accepting a child they didn't want? It would turn a family into a cauldron of guilt and resentment mixed in with love and concern. In this case, the lives of five normal people would be profoundly altered for the worse."

"So we just stand by and let the baby die?" asked Dr. Ziner.

"I'm afraid so," Dr. Entraglo said.

The Final Days

It took twelve days for Baby Owens to die. Her lips and throat were moistened with water, and in a small disused room set apart from other patients, she was allowed to starve to death.

Many nurses and physicians thought it was wrong that the Owens baby was forced to die such a lingering death. Yet they were cautioned by Dr. Entraglo that anything done to shorten the baby's life would probably constitute a criminal action. Thus, fear of being charged with a crime kept the staff from administering any medication to the Owens baby. (Like many disability advocates who would later condemn the hospital's decision, some staff members also felt it was wrong that this "defective" infant was being allowed to die in the first place.)

The burden of caring for the dying baby fell on the nurses in the obstetrics ward. The physicians avoided the child entirely, and it was the nurses who had to see to it that she received her water and was turned in her bed. This was the source of much resentment among the nursing staff, and a few nurses refused to have anything to do with the Owens baby. Most kept their ministrations to an absolute minimum.

But one nurse, Sara Ann Moberly, was determined to make Baby Owens's last days as comfortable as possible. She held the baby, rocked her, and talked soothingly to her when she cried. Doing all for the baby that she could do soothed Sara Ann as well.

But even Sara Ann was glad when Baby Owens died. "It was a relief to me," she said. "I almost couldn't bear the frustration of just sitting there day after day and doing nothing that could really help her."

SOCIAL CONTEXT

The Baby Doe Cases

In Bloomington, Indiana, in 1982, a child was born with Down syndrome and esophageal atresia—a condition in which the esophagus ends in a pouch rather than connecting to the stomach. The parents and the physicians of the infant, who became known as Baby Doe, decided against the surgery that would have been needed to open the esophagus and allow the baby to be fed. The decision was upheld by the courts, and six days after birth, Baby Doe died of starvation and dehydration.

A month later, in May 1982, the secretary of Health and Human Services (HHS) notified hospitals that any institution receiving federal funds could not lawfully "withhold from a handicapped infant nutritional sustenance or medical or surgical treatment required to correct a life-threatening condition if (1) the withholding is based on the fact that the infant is handicapped and (2) the handicap does not render treatment or nutritional sustenance contraindicated."

Baby Doe Hot Line

Ten months later, acting under instructions from President Reagan, an additional and more detailed regulation was issued. Hospitals were required to display a poster in NICUs and pediatric wards indicating that "Discriminatory failure to feed and care for handicapped infants in this facility is prohibited by Federal law." The poster also listed a toll-free, twenty-four-hour hot-line number for reporting suspected violations. In addition, the regulations authorized representatives of HHS to take "immediate remedial action" to protect infants. Further, hospitals were required to permit HHS investigators access to the hospital and to relevant patient records.

A group of associations, including the American Academy of Pediatrics, brought suit against HHS in an attempt to stop the regulations from becoming legally effective. Judge Gerhard Gesell of the U.S. District Court ruled, in April 1983, that HHS had not followed the proper procedures in putting the regulations into effect and so they were invalid. In particular, the regulations were issued without notifying and consulting with those affected by them, a procedure that is legally required to avoid arbitrary bureaucratic actions. The judge held that, although HHS had considered relevant factors in identifying a problem, it had failed to consider the effects of the use of the hot-line number. An "anonymous tipster" could cause "the sudden descent of Baby Doe squads" on hospitals, thus "monopolizing physician and nurse time, and making hospital charts and records unavailable during treatment."

Furthermore, Judge Gesell held, the main purpose of the regulations was apparently to "require physicians treating newborns to take into account wholly medical risk–benefit considerations and to prevent parents from having any influence upon decisions as to whether further medical treatment is desirable." The regulations explored no other ways to prevent "discriminatory medical care." In his conclusion, Judge Gesell held that federal regulations dealing with imperiled newborns should "reflect caution and sensitivity" and that "wide public comment prior to rule-making is essential."

HHS responded to the court decision by drafting another regulation that attempted to resolve the procedural objection that invalidated the first. Sixty days was allowed for the filing of written comments. Since the substance of the regulation was virtually the same, the proposal was widely contested, and in January 1984, another set of regulations was published. They too became an object of controversy.

Baby Jane Doe

Meanwhile, a second Baby Doe case had become the focus of public attention and legal action. On October 11, 1983, an infant who became known as Baby Jane Doe was born in Port Jefferson, New York. This infant suffered from meningomyelocele, anencephaly, and hydrocephaly. (See Briefing Session, this chapter, for an explanation of these conditions.) Her parents were told that without surgery she might live from two weeks to two years, but with surgery she might survive twenty years. However, she would be severely mentally disabled, epileptic, paralyzed, and likely to have constant urinary and bladder infections. The parents consulted with neurologists, a Roman Catholic priest, nurses, and social workers. They decided surgery was not in the best interest of the child and opted, instead, for the use of antibiotics to prevent infection of the exposed spinal nerves. "We love her very much," her mother said, "and that's why we made the decision we did."

Lawrence Washburn, Jr., a lawyer who for a number of years had initiated lawsuits on behalf of fetuses and impaired infants, somehow learned that Baby Jane Doe was being denied surgery and entered a petition on her behalf before the New York State Supreme Court. Because Washburn was not related to the infant, his legal standing in the case was questionable, and the court appointed another attorney, William Weber, to represent the interests of Baby Jane Doe. After a hearing, the judge ruled that the infant was in need of surgery to preserve her life and authorized Weber to consent.

This decision was reversed on appeal. The court held that the parents' decision was in the best interest of the infant. Hence, the state had no basis to intervene. The ruling was then appealed to the New York Court of Appeals and upheld. The court held that the parents' right to privacy was invaded when a person totally unrelated and with no knowledge of the infant's condition and treatment entered into litigation in an attempt to challenge the discharge of parental responsibility.

In the cases of both Baby Doe and Baby Jane Doe, the federal government went to court to demand the infants' medical records. The government charged that decisions against their treatment represented discrimination against disabled individuals. However, the courts consistently rejected the government's demands. In June 1985, the Supreme Court agreed to hear arguments to decide whether the federal laws that protect the disabled against discrimination also apply to the treatment of impaired newborns who are denied life-prolonging treatment.

Final Regulations

On May 15, 1985, the third anniversary of the death of Baby Doe, HHS's final "Baby Doe" regulation went into effect. The regulation was an implementation of an amendment to the Child Abuse Prevention and Treatment Act that was passed into law in October 1984 and the result of negotiations among some nineteen groups representing right-to-life activists, advocates for the disabled, the medical professions, and members of Congress.

The regulation extended the term "medical neglect" to cover cases of "withholding of medically indicated treatment from a disabled infant with a life-threatening condition." Withholding treatment, but not food and water, was not to be considered "medical neglect" in three kinds of cases: (1) the infant is chronically and irreversibly comatose; (2) the provision of such treatment would merely prolong dying, not be effective in ameliorating or correcting all the infant's life-threatening conditions; (3) the provision of such treatment would be virtually futile in terms of the survival of the infant, and the treatment itself under such circumstances would be inhumane.

The regulation defined "reasonable medical judgment" as "a medical judgment that would be made by a reasonably prudent physician knowledgeable about the case and the treatment possibilities with respect to the medical conditions involved." State child-protection service agencies were designated as the proper organizations to see to it that infants were not suffering "medical neglect," and, in order to receive any federal funds, such agencies were required to develop a set of procedures to carry out this function. Parents, physicians, and hospitals were thus no longer the direct subjects of the regulation.

Supreme Court Decision

On June 9, 1986, the Supreme Court, in a 5–3 ruling with one abstention, struck down the Baby Doe regulations. The Court held that there was no evidence that hospitals had discriminated against impaired infants or had refused treatments sought by parents. Accordingly, there was no basis for federal intervention.

Justice John Paul Stevens, in the majority opinion, stressed that no federal law requires hospitals to treat impaired infants without parental consent. Nor does the government have the right "to give unsolicited advice either to parents, to hospitals, or to state officials who are faced with difficult treatment decisions concerning handicapped children." Furthermore, state child-protection agencies "may not be conscripted against their will as the foot soldiers in a Federal crusade."

Hospitals and those directly involved in neonatal care were generally relieved by the Supreme Court decision. In their arguments before the Court, they had claimed that the federal government had second-guessed the agonizing decisions made by parents and physicians and that this had "a devastating impact on the parents."

The Court decision once again placed the responsibility for making decisions about withholding life-sustaining treatment from impaired newborns on families and physicians acting in consultation. Some hospitals now rely on ethics committees to recommend whether infants ought to be treated, but what powers these committees should have and who should be on them continues to be a matter of dispute.

CASE PRESENTATION

Baby K: An Anencephalic Infant and a Mother's Request

The female infant known in court records as Baby K was born in 1993 at Fairfax Hospital in Falls Church, Virginia. She was born with the catastrophic impairment called anencephaly. Her brain lacked both cerebral hemispheres, and she would never be capable of even a rudimentary form of thought. Only her brain stem was intact, and it would keep her breathing for a while.

The standard treatment for anencephalic infants is to make them comfortable, provide them with nourishment, and then wait until their organ systems fail and death ensues. Death usually comes within a few hours, days, or weeks from respiratory failure, because the brain stem does not adequately regulate breathing.

Baby K remained alive much longer than most babies with her impairment, primarily because of her mother's insistence that the baby's periodic respiratory crises be treated aggressively, including the use of a mechanical ventilator to breathe for her. The mother was described in court documents as "acting out of a firm Christian faith that all life should be protected."

By the age of sixteen months, Baby K was living in an extended-care facility so that she could receive the constant attention her survival required. She left the nursing home only to have respiratory treatment at Fairfax Hospital. After her second admission, the hospital went to federal district court to seek a ruling that it would not violate any state or federal law by refusing to provide Baby K with additional treatment. Physicians at the hospital held that further treatment would be futile, and a hospital ethics committee decided that withholding aggressive treatment would be legitimate. Nevertheless, the court ruled that the hospital had to provide the care required to preserve the infant's life.

Ruling Appealed

The hospital appealed the district court ruling to the U.S. Court of Appeals. The appeal was supported by Baby K's father (who was not married to her mother) and by a court-appointed guardian. However, the court ruled 2–1 that the 1986 Federal Emergency Medical Treatment and Active Labor Act (EMTALA) required the hospital to provide treatment for Baby K. The court held that, although providing assisted breathing for an anencephalic infant might not be expected to produce a medical benefit, the law, as passed by Congress, made no exceptions for situations in which the "required treatment would exceed the prevailing standard of medical care."

The appeals court's extension of the Emergency Medical Treatment Act to the Baby K case surprised most observers. The law was passed to keep private hospitals from "dumping" to public facilities patients with emergency problems but with insufficient funds or health insurance to pay for the cost of their care. (EMTALA is sometimes referred to as an "antidumping" law.) However, payment was not an issue in the Baby K case, for her mother was fully insured.

According to the mother's attorney, Ellen Flannery, the court simply applied the law in a straightforward manner. "There's no dispute that the appropriate treatment for acute respiratory distress is ventilation," she said. "The care is not physiologically futile. It will achieve the result required by the mother, and that is to stabilize the baby." The physicians in the case, she claimed, based their decision on their judgment about the quality of life such a child might have, and the law does not address such issues.

Others saw the consequences of extending the law as threatening the power of physicians, hospitals, and ethics committees to have a say in decisions about treating infants with profound birth impairments. Arthur Kohrman, head of the American Academy of Pediatrics ethics committee, was quoted as saying, "This is a profoundly important case, because it strips away the ability of physicians to act as moral agents and turns them into instruments of technology. [Anencephalic] babies are born dying, and the issue is not prolonging their death but supporting it in a humane and dignified way."

Robert Veatch, head of the Kennedy Institute for Bioethics, testifying on behalf of the mother, expressed the view that courts should not defer their judgment to that of physicians. "These are religious and philosophical judgments on which physicians have no more expertise than parents," he said.

Although the extension of EMTALA to cases of severe birth impairments raised serious concerns for pediatricians and neonatologists, courts have generally refused to apply the law to disputes over inpatient treatment. Thus, hospitals and caregivers have not generally been obliged to provide care they deem futile for patients who have already been admitted. But since the ruling in the Baby K case has never been overturned, similar disputes still sometimes arise among physicians, parents, and patients.

For Baby K, the mandated treatments only worked for so long. She died a year after the appeals court ruling, on April 5, 1995. She was two and half years old.

BRIEFING SESSION

If we could speak of nature in human terms, we would often say that it is cruel and pitiless. Nowhere does it seem more heartless than in the case of babies born with severe physical impairments and deformities. The birth of such a child transforms an occasion of expected joy into one of immense sadness. It forces the child's parents to make a momentous decision at a time when they are least prepared to reason clearly: Should they insist that everything be done to save the child's life? Or should they request that the child be allowed an easeful death?

Nor can physicians and nurses escape the moral questions that the birth of such a child may pose. Committed to saving lives, can they facilitate or hasten the death of that child, even by doing nothing? What will they say to the parents when they turn to them for advice? No one involved in the situation can escape the moral challenges that it brings.

To see more clearly the precise moral issues in such cases, we need to first consider some of the factual details that may be involved in them. We also need to discuss some key moral considerations that may be relevant to deciding how situations involving severely impaired newborns should be handled by parents, health professionals, and others.

Genetic and Congenital Impairments

The development of a fetus to the point of birth is an unimaginably complicated process, and there are many ways in which it can go wrong. Birth defects are the leading cause of infant mortality in the United States. Although some can be successfully treated, many more either are fatal or lead to a lifetime of severe disability.

Two kinds of problems are most frequently responsible for producing severe impairments in newborns:

1. *Genetic errors.* The information that is coded into DNA (the genetic material) may be in some way anomalous because of the occurrence of a mutation. Consequently, when the DNA code is "read" and its instructions followed, the child that develops will be impaired. The defective gene may have been inherited, or it may be due to a new mutation. Single-gene defects are typically inherited. For example, phenylketonuria (PKU) results when the gene that encodes the enzyme phenylalanine hydroxylase that breaks down the amino acid phenylalanine is missing or faulty. Phenylalanine is produced when protein metabolizes, and if it is not broken down, the buildup results in brain damage. Other birth defects are produced by a combination of inherited genes and mutations. Most of these defects are not well understood and occur in a sporadic (i.e., unpredictable) way.

2. *Congenital errors.* "Congenital" means "present at birth," and since genetic defects have results that are present at birth, the term is misleading. Ordinarily, however, the word is used to designate errors that result during the developmental process. The impairment, then, is not in the original coding of genes but results either from genetic damage or from the reading of the code. The "manufacture and assembly" of the materials that constitute the child's development are thus affected.

We know that many factors can influence fetal development. Radiation (such as X-rays), drugs (such as thalidomide), chemicals (such as mercury), and nutritional deficiencies (such as lack of folic acid) can all cause changes in an otherwise normal process. Also, biological disease agents, such as certain viruses or spirochetes, may intervene in development, altering the machinery of the cells, interfering with the formation of tissues, and defeating normal developmental processes. In about half the cases in which a baby is born with an impairment, however, the cause is not known.

Specific Impairments

Once an impaired child is born, caregivers are almost immediately confronted with a set of medical and moral problems. To better understand these problems, we will briefly survey some of the most common impairments found in *neonates* (newborns). Our focus will be more on the conditions themselves than on what caused them, for, as far as the moral issue is concerned, how the child came to be impaired is usually of little significance.

Down Syndrome

This is a chromosomal disorder first identified in 1866 by the English physician J. L. H. Down. Normally, humans have twenty-three pairs of chromosomes, but Down syndrome results from the presence of an extra chromosome. The condition is also called trisomy 21, for, instead of a twenty-first pair of chromosomes, the affected person has a twenty-first triple. (Less often, the syndrome is produced when the string of chromosomes gets twisted and chromosome pair number 21 sticks to number 15.)

In ways not wholly understood, the normal process of development is altered by the extra chromosome. A child with Down syndrome is born with mental disabilities and various physical abnormalities. Typically, the latter are relatively minor and include such features as a broad skull, a large tongue, and an upward tilt of the eyelids.

Down syndrome occurs in about one of every eight hundred births. The risk of a baby's being born with the condition rises with the age of the mother, although it is not known why this is so. In young women, the syndrome occurs at a rate of one in every two thousand births; in women over forty, it increases to one in one hundred, and in women over fifty, it rises to one in twelve. In 1984, researchers discovered that certain chromosomes sometimes contain an extra copy of a segment known as the *nucleolar organizing region*. This abnormality has been linked to Down syndrome, and families in which either parent has the abnormality are twenty times more likely to have an afflicted child.

There is no cure for Down syndrome— no way to compensate for the abnormality of the development process. Those with the defect generally have an IQ of about 50–80 and usually require the care and help of others. But they can learn basic tasks, establish routines, and often lead semi-independent lives. Despite their impairment, people with Down syndrome frequently take a great deal of pleasure in social life, in relationships, and in meaningful work. Sadly, the syndrome is strongly correlated with heart abnormalities and other physical problems, and as a result people with Down syndrome typically die in their twenties or thirties without intensive medical intervention. With such intervention, they can now live into their fifties and beyond. In the United States, the average life expectancy of someone with Down syndrome is fifty-six. (See the following section for an account of prenatal tests for the syndrome.)

Spina Bifida

Spina bifida is a general name for birth impairments that involve an opening in the spine. In prenatal development, the spine of the child with spina bifida fails to fuse properly, and often the open vertebrae permit the membrane covering the spinal cord to protrude through the skin. The membrane sometimes forms a bulging, thin sac that contains spinal fluid and nerve tissue. When nerve tissue is present, the condition is called *myelomeningocele*. This form of spina bifida is severe and often has an unfavorable prognosis.

Complications arising from spina bifida must often be treated surgically. The opening in the spine must be closed, and in severe cases the sac must be removed and the nerve tissue inside placed within the spinal canal. Normal skin is then grafted over the area. The danger of an infection of the meninges (meningitis) is great; thus, treatment with antibiotics is also necessary.

Furthermore, a child with spina bifida is likely to require orthopedic operations to attempt to correct the deformities of the legs and feet that occur because of muscle weakness and lack of muscular control due to nerve damage. The bones of such children are thin and brittle, and fractures are frequent.

A child born with spina bifida is almost always paralyzed to some extent, usually below the waist. Because of the nerve damage, the child will often have limited sensation in the lower part of the body. This means he will have no control over his bladder or bowels. This, along with resulting undischarged urine may result in infection of the bladder, urinary tract, and kidneys. Surgery may help with the problems of bowel and urinary incontinence.

The incidence of spina bifida is between one and ten per thousand births. Roughly two thousand babies a year are born with the disorder. For reasons that remain speculative, the spina bifida rate among African Americans is less than half that among European Americans, and among the latter the rate is inversely related to socioeconomic status. In 1994, the federal government began requiring the addition of folic acid to enriched grain products, and a 2005 study showed that, between 1995 and 2002, there was a significant decrease in the prevalence of spina bifida and anencephaly. (See the discussion that follows.) Folic acid is a B vitamin found in green vegetables, beans, and orange juice, but how it might work to provide a protective effect is unknown.

Hydrocephaly

Spina bifida is almost always accompanied by *hydrocephaly*, a term that literally means "water on the brain." When, for whatever reason, the flow of fluid through the spinal canal is blocked, the cerebrospinal fluid produced within the brain cannot escape. Pressure buildup from the fluid can cause brain damage, and if it is not released, will cause death. Although hydrocephaly is frequently the result of spina bifida, it can have several other causes and can occur late in a child's development. Treatment requires surgically inserting a thin tube, or shunt, to drain the fluid from the skull to the heart or abdomen, where it can be absorbed. The operation can save the baby's life, but physical and mental impairment is frequent. Placing the shunt

and getting it to work properly are difficult tasks that may require many operations. If hydrocephaly accompanies spina bifida, it is treated first.

Anencephaly

This term means "without brain." Anencephaly is an invariably fatal condition in which the cerebral hemispheres of the brain are completely or almost completely absent. Like spina bifida, it is a *neural tube defect* in which the fetal precursor to the skull and spine (the neural tube) fails to close completely. Although some anencephalic infants have a brain stem, the lack of a cerebrum means they are typically blind, deaf, and unresponsive. They typically die in a matter of hours or days and there is no way to treat their condition.

Esophageal Atresia

In medical terms, an atresia is the closing of a normal opening or canal. The esophagus is the muscular tube that extends from the back of the throat to the stomach. Sometimes the tube forms without an opening or so that it does not extend to the stomach. The condition must be corrected by surgery to allow the child to get food into its stomach. The chances of success in such surgery are very high.

Duodenal Atresia

The duodenum is the upper part of the small intestine. Food from the stomach empties into it. When the duodenum is closed off due to an atresia, food cannot pass through and be digested. Surgery can repair this condition and is successful in most cases.

Problems of Extreme Prematurity

A normal pregnancy lasts approximately forty weeks. The majority of infants born before twenty-five weeks of gestation typically fail to live. Almost all infants born around this stage of development have extremely low birth weights. About half of those weighing from 1 to 1.5 pounds fail to survive, and those who do have a multiplicity of physical and mental problems resulting from the fact that their bodies and brains have simply not had the time to develop adequately to cope with the demands of life outside the uterus.

The undeveloped lungs of premature infants are inefficient and prone to infections. The mechanical ventilation needed to assist their breathing may result in long-term lung damage. Extremely premature infants are also subject to cerebral hemorrhages ("brain bleeds") that may lead to seizures, blindness, deafness, mental impairments, and a variety of less noticeable disabilities. (For a discussion of extremely premature infants and the moral issues they present, see Social Context: The Dilemma of Extreme Prematurity in this chapter.)

Testing for Impairments

Genetic impairments are inherited; they are the outcome of the genetic endowment of the child. A carrier of genetic mutations can pass on the genes to his or her children. Congenital impairments are not inherited and cannot be passed on.

With proper genetic counseling, prospective parents can assess the risk that their children will be impaired by analyzing patterns of inheritance in their families. Also, some genetic diseases can be diagnosed in the embryo or fetus by identifying specific genetic anomalies. (See Chapter 3 for a discussion of screening for genetic diseases.) Some genetic conditions, such as the extra chromosome resulting in Down syndrome, can be detected by examining genetic material during fetal development. Large abnormalities in the developing fetus (such as

anencephaly) can often be detected by the use of ultrasound images.

Amniocentesis and CVS

Until recent decades, the most used and most reliable methods of prenatal diagnosis were amniocentesis and chorionic villus sampling (CVS). Both involve direct cell studies.

In amniocentesis, the amnion (the membrane surrounding the fetus) is punctured with a needle and some of the amniotic fluid is removed for examination. The procedure cannot be usefully and safely performed until fourteen to sixteen weeks into a pregnancy. The risk to the woman and the fetus from amniocentesis is relatively small, usually less than 1 percent, and the chance that the procedure will result in a miscarriage is about one in two hundred. If amniocentesis is performed eleven to twelve weeks after conception, however, there is a small increase in the probability that the child will have a deformed foot.

Chorionic villus sampling involves retrieving hair-like villi cells from the developing placenta. The advantage of the test is that it can be employed six to ten weeks after conception. Although the procedure is as safe as amniocentesis, a 1994 study by the Centers for Disease Control found that infants whose mothers had undergone CVS from 1988 to 1992 had a 0.03 percent risk of being born with missing or undeveloped fingers or toes. A later study questioned this finding and found no reason to believe that the risk of fetal damage is greater than normal.

Amniocentesis came into wide use only in the early 1960s. At first, it was restricted mostly to testing fetuses in cases in which there was a risk of Rh incompatibility. When a pregnant woman lacks a group of blood proteins called the Rhesus (or Rh) factor, and the fetus has it, the immune system of the woman may produce antibodies against the fetus. The result for the fetus may be anemia, brain damage, and even death. Early detection through amniocentesis enabled rhesus disease to be treated with anti-RhD immunoglobulin.

It was soon realized, however, that additional information about the fetus could be gained from further analysis of the amniotic fluid and the fetal cells in it. Some disorders (such as Tay-Sachs disease) can be detected by chemical analysis of the amniotic fluid, while other common genetic diseases, such as PKU, Huntington's, and muscular dystrophy, require an analysis of the genetic material. Because only males have a Y chromosome, it is impossible to examine fetal cells without also discovering the gender of the fetus.

Amniocentesis and CVS do pose slight hazards. Accordingly, neither is regarded as a routine procedure to be performed in every pregnancy. There must be some indication that the fetus is at risk from a genetic or congenital disorder. One indication is the age of the mother. Down syndrome is much more likely to occur in fetuses conceived by women over the age of thirty-five. Because the syndrome is produced by a chromosome abnormality, an examination of the chromosomes in the cells of the fetus can reveal the defect.

Triple Test

A test for Down syndrome introduced in the 1980s employs a blood sample taken from the pregnant woman. The sample is examined for the presence of three fetal proteins. About sixteen to eighteen weeks after gestation, fetuses with Down syndrome are known to produce abnormally small quantities of estriol and alpha-fetoprotein and abnormally large amounts of chorionic gonadotropin. The levels of the proteins, plus such factors as the woman's age, can be used to determine the statistical probability of a child with the syndrome. This "triple test" avoids the risks of amniocentesis and CVS, but it does result in a fairly high number of false positive Down syndrome diagnoses.

A blood test for the presence of alpha-fetoprotein can also indicate the likelihood of neural tube defects characteristic of spina bifida. Ultrasound can then be used to confirm or detect these or other developmental anomalies.

Cell-Free DNA Analysis

In recent years, researchers have developed a screening test for Down syndrome and other chromosomal anomalies that uses the trace amounts of fetal DNA that circulate in a pregnant woman's blood as early as ten weeks gestation. (These trace amounts float free of fetal cells and are thus called "cell-free.") These DNA traces are subjected to a molecular "photocopying" method known as polymerase chain reaction and then sequenced to assemble a picture of the fetus's chromosomes

A growing body of research, including a 2015 study involving 19,000 women in six different countries, suggests that cell-free DNA (cfDNA) analysis has better accuracy and a lower false positive rate than the triple test when it comes to diagnosing trisomy 21 (Down syndrome). These studies suggest that cfDNA and similar tests may become the standard means of diagnosing debilitating genetic conditions in utero, without many of the drawbacks associated with earlier screening methods.

Ethical Theories and the Problem of Birth Impairments

A great number of serious moral issues are raised by severely impaired newborns. Should they be given only ordinary care, or should special efforts be made to save their lives? Should they be given comfort care and allowed to die? Should all possible efforts be made to integrate them into family and civic life, even if this appears to increase their suffering? Who should decide what is in the interest of the child? Might acting in the interest of the child require not acting to save the child's life?

A more basic question that cuts even deeper than these concerns the status of the newborn. It is virtually the same as the question raised in Chapter 5 about the fetus: namely, Do severely impaired infants have the moral standing of persons? It might be argued that some infants are so severely impaired that they should not be considered persons in a relevant moral sense. They may be unaware of their surroundings, largely unresponsive, and incapable of basic psychological and social development. In this respect, they are worse off than most maturing fetuses.

If this view is accepted, then some major moral principles would seem not to require that we act to preserve the lives of many impaired newborns. We might have obligations to grant them consideration and treat them benevolently. But this might include euthanizing them or allow them to die out of compassion for their suffering.

One major difficulty with this view is that it is not at all clear exactly which impaired infants could legitimately be considered nonpersons. Birth defects vary widely in severity, and, unless one is prepared to tolerate infanticide generally, it is necessary to have defensible criteria for distinguishing among newborns.

By contrast, it might be claimed that the fact of membership in the human species is sufficient to deem impaired infants persons. Assuming that this is so, the question becomes, How ought we to treat a severely impaired infant person? Impaired newborns cannot express wishes, make claims, or enter into deliberations. All that is done concerning them must be done by others.

A utilitarian might decide that the social and personal cost (the suffering of the infant, the anguish of the parents, the monetary cost to the family and society) of saving the life of such an infant is greater than the social and personal benefits that can be expected for the child and the family. Accordingly, such a child might be allowed to die or be killed as painlessly as possible to end its suffering. Yet a rule utilitarian might claim, on the contrary, that the rule "Save every child where possible" would, in the long run, produce more utility than disutility.

The natural law position of Roman Catholicism is that even the most impaired newborn is a human person. Yet even this view does not require that extraordinary means be used to save the life of such a child. The suffering of the family, great expense, and the need for multiple operations would be reasons for providing only ordinary care. Ordinary care does not mean that every standard medical procedure that might help should be followed. It means only that the impaired newborn should receive care of the same type provided for a normal infant. It would be immoral to kill the child or to cause its death by withholding all care.

If the infant is a person, then Kant would regard it as possessing an inherent dignity and value. But what if the impaired infant lacks any potential to develop reason and to express an autonomous will? How, then, should we treat such an infant? Kant's principles provide no clear-cut answer. The infant does not threaten our own existence, and we have no grounds for killing him. But, it could be argued, we should still allow the child to die. We can imaginatively put ourselves in the place of the infant. Although it would be morally wrong to will our own death (which, Kant claimed, would involve a self-defeating maxim), we might express our autonomy and rationality by choosing to refuse treatment that would prolong a painful and hopeless life. If this is so, then we might act in this way on behalf of the impaired child. Indeed, it may be our duty to allow the child to die. A similar line of argument from Ross's viewpoint might lead us to decide that, although we have a prima facie duty to preserve the child's life, our actual duty is to allow him to die. As with other theoretical applications, however, much depends upon the level of impairment and suffering, and few cases are so clear-cut morally.

Some argue that this moral complexity shows that abstract debates over personhood are irrelevant and simplistic when it comes to neonatal impairments. The capabilities approach developed by Martha Nussbaum, for example, would deny that a lack of rational autonomy justifies depriving impaired infants of a chance to claim such central human capabilities such as life, bodily integrity, and social affiliation. The primary social goal would be to help impaired infants reach a threshold level of such capabilities consistent with human dignity, largely though the help of caregivers and surrogates. Nevertheless, if a child is so severely impaired as to be incapable of "some sort of active striving," such support for life and central capabilities may be futile. Thus, like Kantian moral theory, the capabilities approach might, in some circumstances, be used to justify surrogate decision-making on behalf of an impaired child that involves refusing life-saving treatment, and perhaps even food and water.

Like the capabilities approach, ethical theories rooted in disability identity politics are critical of what they see as arbitrary divisions between persons and non-persons that might allow the latter to be used or killed to suit the needs of caregivers or society. Thus many criticize the forced sterilizations of cognitively disabled children (such as that described in "The Ashley Treatment" in this chapter) as violations of consent and human dignity. Echoing their critique of "right to die" cases involving disabled adults, these theorists also question the idea

that non-impaired people can leg impose an objective standard of life "worth living" on impaired adults. (See Chapter 10 for furth sion.) They argue that such standards are just as likely to reflect societal structures set up to benefit the (temporarily) non-impaired as to further the best interests of the impaired. Thus while disability theorists have no uniform opinion about when (if ever) a severely impaired infant may be allowed to die, they are generally suspicious of claims by others (even parents) to know when an infant's life is intolerable or lacks value.

This brings us back to a basic question: Who is to make the decision about how an impaired newborn is to be treated? Traditionally, the assumption has been that this is a decision best left to the infant's parents and physicians. Because they can be assumed to have the highest concern for the infant's welfare and the most knowledge about her condition and prospects, they are the ones who should have the primary responsibility for deciding her fate. If there is reason to believe that they are not acting in a responsible manner, then the courts may step in to guarantee that the interests of the infant are served. But as we saw in Chapter 1 (see, for example Case Presentation: Faith and Medicine), such legal interventions may simply reflect a rough majority consensus about necessary and unnecessary care.

Few Americans currently advocate heroic efforts to save the lives of the infants who are most severely impaired, and hardly any advocate not treating infants with relatively simple and correctable impairments. The difficult cases are those which fall in a gray area along the moral and medical continuum. Advanced health care technologies can now preserve the lives of many infants who, in the past, would have died relatively quickly— yet frequently we still lack the power to provide those infants with a life that many would judge to be worthwhile. At the same ɪne, a failure to treat such infants does not invariably result in their deaths, and a failure to provide them with early treatment may mean that they are even more impaired than they would be otherwise.

These dilemmas are unlikely to be resolved any time soon. In the meantime, it is important to keep in mind that it is not a purely intellectual problem. The context in which particular decisions are made is one of doubt, confusion, and genuine anguish.

Envoi

In 1973, R. S. Duff and A. G. M. Campbell shocked the U.S. public by reporting that during a thirty-month period, forty-three infants at the Yale–New Haven Hospital had been permitted to die. Each of the children suffered from one or more severe birth defects. Although the staff of the hospital took no steps to end the lives of the infants, treatment was withheld from them.

Such decisions had been made for decades in hospitals throughout the world. Sometimes they were made by physicians acting alone and sometimes by physicians in consultation with families. But almost never had the situation been discussed openly and publicly.

Now there is more openness about the whole complex of moral and human problems presented by impaired newborns. There is a greater willingness to consider the possibility that saving the life of a child might not be the right act to perform—that it may even be our duty to assist the child's dying. The time of covert decisions and half-guilty conferences has, to some extent, passed. The issues are there, they are known to be there, and they must be faced.

We must also face questions about how we as a society will respond to the needs of children who are severely impaired and the associated needs of their families and caregivers. Medicine has become progressively more successful at keeping alive infants who might once have died, but as these infants grow older, they and their families are likely to face an array of medical, social, educational, and psychological problems. We have taken only small steps toward the goal of integrating impaired children and adults into our society and thus their limitations are, to some extent, shaped by our collective choices.

We have also done very little to recognize that the people who care about, and (typically) care for, impaired children need help. The constant worry of aging parents responsible for a seriously impaired adult child is captured in the question "Who will take care of her when we are dead?" This is a question that we as a society have not answered.

READINGS

Section 1: The Groningen Protocol

The Groningen Protocol: The Why and the What

James Lemuel Smith

Smith describes the problem faced by Dutch pediatrician Eduard Verhagen of dealing with infants who have a hopeless prognosis and intractable pain. Smith then presents the scheme for classifying infants with serious medical problems into three categories and the five conditions for legitimizing active infant euthanasia that make up the Groningen Protocol as developed by Verhagen and his collaborator Pieter Sauer.

Dr. Eduard Verhagen didn't start out to be an advocate for changing the law in Holland to allow active euthanasia for infants. More than anything else, it was his experience as a pediatrician forced to deal with the intractable pain of Bente Hindriks, an infant with a severe form of the invariably fatal genetic disorder called Hallopeau–Siemens syndrome that forced him to develop his ideas about infant euthanasia.

Hallopeau–Siemens is a disease that involves the blistering and peeling off of the upper layer of the skin and mucous membranes. The disorder has no effective treatment, and skin damage is accompanied by severe and unrelievable pain. Although Bente's parents asked Dr. Verhagen to terminate her life humanely to end her suffering, he was unable to do so without running the risk of being charged with homicide.

Dr. Verhagen felt that as a physician he had failed Bente and her parents. All three of them, he thought, had suffered more than was necessary, and his inability to help them remained a matter of self-reproach. As the father of three children, he knew what it was like to want to spare your child from pointless pain, but he could only imagine the horror of having to watch your child suffering such pain day after day while hoping she will die and be spared further torment. Also, Dr. Verhagen was accustomed to helping sick children, not denying them what they most needed. He helped them not only in his role as Head of Pediatrics at Holland's Groningen University Medical Center, but as a volunteer physician who had spent years providing medical care to children in underdeveloped countries.

Dr. Verhagen decided some four years after Bente's death that he had to do something to call attention to the problem presented by babies like her. His motive and his hope were that the law in the Netherlands would be eventually changed to permit infant euthanasia under certain strict conditions. Dutch law now allows euthanasia for those above the age of sixteen, but it makes no provision for younger children or infants. This leaves them, in Dr. Verhagen's view, without an option that others have, an option that, if available, could spare a certain number of them the intractable and pointless suffering that destroys the quality of their sad, brief lives.

Working toward changing the law, or at least helping pediatricians avoid being charged with a crime for an appropriate and compassionate act, Dr. Verhagen and his colleagues began to describe some of their most difficult cases to attorneys in the federal prosecutor's office in Groningen. Sometimes they even took the lawyers on medical rounds with them, giving them a sense of what it was like to be a pediatrician who has to deal with children who cannot be helped, cannot be expected to get better, and live out their lives in pain.

A Public Announcement

Although Dr. Verhagen had started his campaign to revise Dutch law around 2002, in 2005 he made public the information that he had participated in ending the lives of four infants. "All four babies had spina bifida," he said. "Not the usual type, but severely affected children where spina bifida was not the only problem. They were in constant pain."

He said that ending their suffering was worth the risk of getting charged with a crime. "In the last minutes or seconds, you see the pain relax and they fall asleep....At the end after the lethal injection, their fists are unclenched, and there is relief for everyone in the room. Finally, they get what they should have been given earlier."

Dr. Verhagen's actions and his approval of active infant euthanasia produced a flood of mail, some of it quite virulent. Much of the mail comes from Christian right groups and social conservatives in the United States. Verhagen was called "Dr. Death" and described as a "second Hitler"; comparisons to the Holocaust were common. However, he also received mail from parents from various countries telling him that they were forced to end the life of their own child when the medical profession refused to assist them.

"We know the law says you are not allowed to kill anyone against their will," Dr. Verhagen said in an interview. "We also know that death can be more humane than continued life, if it involves extreme suffering. We are facing patients and their parents who we think should be given the option of ending their [children's] lives."

Verhagen had already called for a change in the way the legal system in the Netherlands views infant euthanasia. Indeed, he expressed a wish to see such changes made throughout the world. "It's time to be honest about the unbearable suffering endured by newborns with no hope of a future," he said. "All over the world doctors end lives discreetly out of compassion, without any kind of regulation. Worldwide, the U.S. included, many deaths among newborns are based on end-of-life decisions, after physicians reached the conclusion that there was no quality of life. This is happening more and more frequently."

Dr. Verhagen made clear that in endorsing active infant euthanasia he was not talking about infants in ordinary difficulties or even those with a treatable condition that might or might not live. Rather, he had in mind infants whose continued existence was a burden to them and their families, ones who "face a life of agonizing pain."

An example, he said, "may be a child with spina bifida with a sac of brain fluid attached where the nerves are floating around. This child is barely able to breathe, and would have to undergo at least sixty operations in the course of a year to temporarily alleviate its problems. Moreover, the child would suffer such unbearable pain that it has to be constantly anesthetized. The parents watch this in tears and beg the doctor to bring an end to such suffering."

Physicians in every country face the problem that concerns Dr. Verhagen. According to one study, 73 percent of the physicians in France reported using drugs to end the life of a newborn. Some 43 percent of Dutch physicians acknowledged having performed such an act, and 2–4 percent of physicians in the United Kingdom, Italy, Spain, Germany, and Sweden said they had taken measures to terminate the life of a suffering infant. While physicians in the United States say that this happens from time to time, no survey data are available to suggest how often.

Dr. Verhagen observes that the subject of infants who suffer from unendurable pain with no prospect of improvement or long-term survival, is not one people like to be reminded of. "But it is in the interest of newborns who have to endure unbearable suffering that we draw up a nationwide protocol that allows each pediatrician to treat this delicate question with due care, knowing he followed the criteria."

Need for a Protocol

Since 1997 Dutch medical groups have asked the government to establish a board of medical, legal, and ethical experts to encourage physicians to report cases in which they decided to perform active euthanasia. Although the government has thus far failed to act, some Dutch physicians have sometimes taken steps to end the lives of infants for humane reasons.

In the March 10, 2005, issue of the *New England Journal of Medicine* Dr. Verhagen and Dr. Pieter J. J. Sauer, his colleague at Groningen, reported that a review of legal records shows that from 1997 to 2004, about three cases a year were reported to the legal authorities, and no one was prosecuted. However, the authors point out, a national survey of Dutch doctors concluded that out of about 200,000 births a year, around 15 to 20 cases of active euthanasia occurred. These figures suggest that a number of physicians are making decisions without shared guiding principles, open discussion, or oversight. In the view of Verhagen and Sauer, all cases of deliberate termination need to be reported to prevent "uncontrolled and unjustified euthanasia," and actions should be in keeping with acknowledged guidelines and open to review by a knowledgeable group.

Three Categories of Infants

In the *New England Journal of Medicine* article, Verhagen and Sauer present a set of guidelines and procedures to allow pediatricians and parents to approach the problem presented by a special class of infants made up of those with no hope of recovery who also suffer severe and continuing pain. They divide newborns and infants who might be considered candidates for end-of-life decisions into three categories:

1. *Infants with no chance of survival who are likely to die soon after birth, even if they receive the best medical and surgical care available.* Usually, these will be infants with some underlying and untreatable medical problem, such as the absence or underdevelopment of the lungs or kidneys. No matter what is done for these infants, they will not survive.

2. *Infants who are sustained by intensive care but have a bleak prognosis.* Although these infants may continue to live after being removed from intensive

care, they have a poor prognosis and a poor quality of life. Typically, these will be infants with severe brain abnormalities or severe organ damage caused by a loss of oxygen supply to fetal tissues during development.

3. *Infants who have a hopeless prognosis and experience unbearable suffering.* Even if these infants are not receiving intensive care, they have a prognosis of a poor quality of life accompanied by sustained suffering. This group includes infants with the worst forms of spina bifida (see Verhagen's description of such a case above). This group also includes infants still alive after intensive care who have a poor quality of life, continued suffering, and no hope of improvement.

When dealing with an infant in the third category, the authors say, pediatricians and medical consultants must be certain about the prognosis and discuss it with the child's parents. The physicians must also do all that they can to control the child's pain.

Even if every known pain-management step is taken, Verhagen and Sauer believe that there will be some infants whose suffering cannot be relieved and whose future holds no hope of improvement. In such cases as this, the physicians and the parents may decide that death would be a more humane prospect than the continuation of life. (Bente Hindriks, because of the ravages produced by Hallopeau–Siemens syndrome, her unrelievable pain, and her hopeless prognosis would qualify for inclusion in this category, although Verhagen and Sauer don't mention her name.) The authors estimate that only 15–20 infants a year in the Netherlands fall in the third group.

The Groningen Protocol

The Groningen Protocol consists of five medical requirements that must be fulfilled for the active euthanasia of infants to be justified:

1. The infant's diagnosis and prognosis must be certain.

2. The infant must be experiencing hopeless and unbearable suffering.

3. At least one independent physician must confirm that the first two conditions are met.

4. Both parents must give their informed consent.

5. The termination procedure must be performed in accord with the accepted medical standard.

The protocol is accompanied by a set of additional requirements that the authors describe as intended to "clarify the decision and facilitate assessment." These rules have the function of documenting particular cases of euthanasia and the grounds for them. The rules require the physician in charge to indicate what the child's medical condition was, why the decision to end its life was made, the names and qualifications of the other physicians involved, as well as the examinations they made, and their opinions about the child's condition and prognosis. The physician in charge must also describe the way in which the parents were informed and their opinions about what would be best for the child. The informed consent of the parents is required for euthanasia.

The rules also require that the physician indicate the circumstance of the child's death, who took part in the decision making, the justification for the death, when and where the procedure was carried out, what method was used (e.g., an injectable drug), and why it was chosen. A coroner must make a finding about the death, and all the information asked for in the requirements must then be reported to the office of the prosecuting attorney.

A version of the Groningen Protocol was first developed by Verhagen and Sauer in 2002. Part of the impetus behind the initial statement was the same as for the 2005 version. They wanted to transform a decision-making process that typically takes place in secret into one that is public and transparent. When the practice of infant euthanasia is standardized and brought out of the shadows, the authors believe, it becomes subject to the scrutiny of others and protects the interests of infants and their families.

Also, because infant euthanasia is still illegal in the Netherlands, the Groningen Protocol offers a way for pediatricians to provide what they consider to be appropriate help to infants and families, while also reducing the risk that they will be prosecuted for their actions. The authors admit, however, that following the protocol does not guarantee that prosecution will not occur.

Verhagen and Sauer observe that, although the Groningen Protocol suits Dutch legal and social culture, "it is unclear to what extent it would be transferable to other countries." Given the controversy in the

United States over physician-assisted suicide in adults, it seems unlikely that the Groningen Protocol will be adopted any time soon. It has at the least, however, called attention to the crucially important matter of the unrelievable suffering of doomed infants.

If the Groningen Protocol is not adopted, then what is an acceptable alternative? May we assume that the present practice of allowing children with a bleak prognosis to experience intractable pain until they die is an *unacceptable* alternative?

Section 2: The Ashley Treatment

The "Ashley Treatment"

Ashley's Mom and Dad

The young girl known only as Ashley had an apparently normal birth, but is reported to have suffered brain damage from an unknown cause. Her mental and motor faculties failed to develop, and as a result, she is completely dependent on others for her care. Although the growth of her body was proceeding along a normal developmental path, her mental and motor functions would never improve. Her parents, who identify themselves only as "Ashley's Mom and Dad," argue on their blog that the medical procedures they requested on behalf of their daughter when she was nine ("the Ashley treatment") were all intended to improve the quality of her life, and not just that of her caregivers.

With or without the treatment, the parents contend, their intention has always been to keep Ashley at home. The growth attenuation by hormone injections are designed to keep Ashley small enough to move her easily around the house and integrate her into the family's daily life; the surgery to remove her uterus and breast buds will prevent menstrual cramps and the breast discomfort of being strapped into a wheelchair. The surgeries, including a preventive appendectomy, will also spare Ashley the dangers of breast and uterine cancer and unrecognized appendicitis. The Ashley treatment, her parents argue, is in her best interest and will improve the quality of her life.

Ashley's Story

Our daughter Ashley had a normal birth, but her mental and motor faculties did not develop. Over the years, neurologists, geneticists, and other specialists conducted every known traditional and experimental test, but still could not determine a diagnosis or a cause. Doctor's call her condition "static encephalopathy of unknown etiology," which means an insult to the brain of unknown origin or cause, and one that will not improve.

Now nine years old, Ashley cannot keep her head up, roll or change her sleeping position, hold a toy, or sit up by herself, let alone walk or talk. She is tube fed and depends on her caregivers in every way. We call her our Pillow Angel since she is so sweet and stays right where we place her—usually on a pillow.

Ashley is a beautiful girl whose body is developing normally with no external deformities. . . . She is expected to live a full life and was expected to attain a normal adult height and weight. Ashley being in a stable condition is a blessing because many kids with similarly severe disabilities tend to deteriorate and not survive beyond five years of age.

Ashley is alert and aware of her environment; she startles easily. She constantly moves her arms and kicks her legs. Sometimes she seems to be watching TV intently. She loves music and often gets in celebration mode of vocalizing, kicking, and choreographing/conducting with her hands when she really likes a song (Andrea Boccelli is her favorite—we call him her boyfriend). She rarely makes eye-contact even when it is clear that she is aware of a person's presence next to her. Ashley goes to school in a classroom for special needs children, which provides her with daily bus trips, activities customized for her, and a high level of attention by her teachers and therapists.

Ashley brings a lot of love to our family and is a bonding factor in our relationship; we can't imagine life without her. She has a sweet demeanor and often smiles and expresses delight when we visit with her, we think she recognizes us but can't be sure. She has a younger healthy sister and brother. We constantly feel the desire to visit her room (her favorite place with special lights and colorful displays) or have her with us wanting to be in her aura of positive energy. We're often gathered around her holding her hand, thus sensing a powerful connection with her pure, innocent and angelic spirit. As often as we can we give her position changes and back rubs, sweet talk her, move her to social and engaging places, and manage her entertainment setting (music or TV). In return she inspires abundant love in our hearts, so effortlessly; she is such a blessing in our life!

To express how intensely we feel about providing Ashley with the best care possible, we would like to quote from a private email that we received from a loving mother with her own 6 year old Pillow Angel:

> *"In my mind, I have to be immortal because I have to always be here on Earth to take care of my precious child. Taking care of him is difficult, but it is never a burden. I am [his] eyes, ears and voice. He is my best friend, and I have dedicated my life to providing joy and comfort to him. To my last breath, everything I will ever do will be for him or because of him. I cannot adequately put into words the amount of love and devotion I have for my child. I am sure that you feel the same way about Ashley."*

The chance of Ashley having significant improvement, such as being able to change her position in bed, let alone walk, is non-existent. She has been at the same level of cognitive, mental and physical developmental ability since about three months of age. Ashley has aged and grown in size but her mental and physical abilities have remained and will remain those of an infant.

Faced with Ashley's medical reality, as her deeply loving parents, we worked with her doctors to do all we could to provide Ashley with the best possible quality of life. The result is the "Ashley Treatment."

Summary

The Ashley Treatment is the name we have given to a collection of medical procedures for the improvement of Ashley's quality of life. The treatment includes growth attenuation through high-dose estrogen therapy, hysterectomy to eliminate the menstrual cycle and associated discomfort to Ashley, and breast bud removal to avoid the development of large breasts and the associated discomfort to Ashley. We pursued this treatment after much thought, research, and discussions with doctors.

Nearly three years after we started this process, and after the treatment was published in October, 2006 by Dr. Gunther and Dr. Diekema in a medical journal that resulted in an extensive and worldwide coverage by the press and dozens of public discussion, we decided to share our thoughts and experience for two purposes: first, to help families who might bring similar benefits to their bedridden Pillow Angels; second, to address some misconceptions about the treatment and our motives for undertaking it.

A fundamental and universal misconception about the treatment is that it is intended to convenience the caregiver; rather, the central purpose is to improve Ashley's quality of life. Ashley's biggest challenges are discomfort and boredom; all other considerations in this discussion take a back seat to these central challenges. The Ashley Treatment goes right to the heart of these challenges and we strongly believe that it will mitigate them in a significant way and provide Ashley with lifelong benefits.

Unlike what most people thought, the decision to pursue the Ashley Treatment was not a difficult one. Once we understood the options, problems, and benefits, the right course was clear to us. Ashley will be a lot more physically comfortable free of menstrual cramps, free of the discomfort associated with large and fully-developed breasts, and with a smaller, lighter body that is better suited to constant lying down and is easier to be moved around.

Ashley's smaller and lighter size makes it more possible to include her in the typical family life and activities that provide her with needed comfort, closeness, security and love: meal time, car trips, touch, snuggles, etc. Typically, when awake, babies are in the same room as other family members, the sights and sounds of family life engaging the baby's attention, entertaining the baby. Likewise, Ashley has all of a baby's needs, including being entertained and engaged, and she calms at the sounds of family voices. Furthermore, given Ashley's mental age, a nine and a half year old body is more appropriate and provides her more dignity and integrity than a fully grown female body.

We call it Ashley Treatment because:

1. As far as we know Ashley is the first child to receive this treatment,

2. We wanted a name that is easy to remember and search for,

3. The name applies to a collection of procedures that together have the purpose of improving Ashley's quality of life and well-being. Growth attenuation is only one aspect of the treatment.

The Ashley Treatment

In early 2004 when Ashley was six and a half years old, we observed signs of early puberty. In a related conversation with Ashley's doctor, Ashley's Mom came upon the idea of accelerating her already precocious puberty to minimize her adult height and weight. We scheduled time with Dr. Daniel F. Gunther, Associate Professor of Pediatrics in Endocrinology at Seattle's Children's Hospital, and discussed our options. We learned that attenuating growth is feasible through high-dose estrogen therapy. This treatment was performed on teenage girls starting in the 60's and 70's, when it wasn't desirable for girls to be tall, with no negative or long-term side effects.

The fact that there is experience with administering high-dose estrogen to limit height in teenage girls gave us the peace of mind that it was safe—no surprise side effects. Furthermore, people found justification in applying this treatment for cosmetic reasons

while we were seeking a much more important purpose, as will be detailed below.

In addition to height and weight issues, we had concerns about Ashley's menstrual cycle and its associated cramps and discomfort. We also had concerns about Ashley's breasts developing and becoming a source of discomfort in her lying down position and while strapped across the chest area in her wheelchair, particularly since there is a family history of large breasts and other related issues that we discuss below. The estrogen treatment would hasten both the onset of the menstrual cycle and breast growth. Bleeding during the treatment would likely be very difficult to control.

It was obvious to us that we could significantly elevate Ashley's adult quality of life by pursuing the following three goals:

1. Limiting final height using high-dose estrogen therapy.

2. Avoiding menstruation and cramps by removing the uterus (hysterectomy).

3. Limiting growth of the breasts by removing the early breast buds.

The surgeon also performed an appendectomy during the surgery, since there is a chance of 5% of developing appendicitis in the general population, and this additional procedure presented no additional risk. If Ashley's appendix acts up, she would not be able to communicate the resulting pain. An inflamed appendix could rupture before we would know what was going on, causing significant complication.

Ashley was dealt a challenging life and the least that we can do as her loving parents and caregivers is to be diligent about maximizing her quality of life. The decision to move forward with the Ashley Treatment was not a difficult one for us as many seem to think. It was obvious to us that a reduction in Ashley's height (and therefore weight), elimination of the menstrual cycle, and avoidance of large breasts would bring significant benefits to her health and comfort. The only downside that we could think of was the surgery itself; however, the involved surgery is commonly done and is not complicated. Hysterectomy is a 1.5 hour surgery of less involvement and risk than a Fundoplication (wrapping and sewing the upper part of the stomach around the esophagus), which is commonly provided to children like Ashley to mitigate reflux and vomiting. The breast bud removal is a minor surgery with minimal risk. Furthermore, we're fortunate to have access to one of the best surgical facilities and teams at Seattle Children's Hospital. If we were in a less developed locale or country with higher risk of surgery, we would have looked at this part of the analysis differently.

Since the Ashley Treatment was new and unusual, Dr. Gunther scheduled us to present our case to the ethics committee at Seattle Children's Hospital, which we did on May 5th 2004. The committee includes about 40 individuals from different disciplines and is evenly composed of men and women. After we presented our case we waited outside while the committee deliberated the issue. The committee chairman along with Doctor Diekema, ethics consultant, conveyed the committee's decision to us, which was to entrust us with doing the right thing for Ashley. There was one legal issue that we needed to investigate related to "sterilization" of a disabled person. Upon consultation with a lawyer specializing in disability law, we found out that the law does not apply to Ashley's case due to the severity of her disability, which makes voluntary reproduction impossible. The law is intended to protect women with mild disability who might chose to become pregnant at some future point, and should have the right to do so. Furthermore, sterilization is a side effect of the Ashley Treatment and not its intent.

The combined hysterectomy, breast bud removal, and appendectomy surgery was performed without complications in July 2004. Ashley spent four days in the hospital under close supervision, and thanks to aggressive pain control her discomfort appeared minimal. In less than one month, Ashley's incisions healed and she was back to normal; it's remarkable how kids heal so much quicker than adults. Ashley's Mom had a C-section and knew first hand how Ashley would feel after surgery; thankfully, the recovery went much better than Mom anticipated.

Shortly after the surgery and recovery, we started the high-dose estrogen therapy. We completed this treatment in December 2006 after two and a half years. During this whole period, we have observed no adverse consequences.

Expenses of the surgery and of the therapy that followed, which we estimate to be about $30,000, [were] fully covered by insurance....

We hope that by now it is clear that the Ashley Treatment is about improving Ashley's quality of life and not about convenience to her caregivers. Ashley's biggest challenge is discomfort and boredom and the Ashley Treatment goes straight to the heart of this challenge. It is common for Ashley to be uncomfortable or to be bored. Even though Ashley's level of tolerance has increased along the years, she is helpless when bothered and her only recourse is to cry until someone comes to her rescue. These episodes are triggered by something as simple as sliding off the pillow, a sneeze, or a hair landing on her face and tickling/bothering her, let alone menstrual cramps, adult-level bed sores, and discomfort caused by large breasts and a constricting bra. Also, without the treatment, Ashley could not be moved as frequently or be as included in family life, and we would not experience the joy of being an intact family as often.

If people have concerns about Ashley's dignity, she will retain more dignity in a body that is healthier, more of a comfort to her, and more suited to her state of development as George Dvorsky, a member of the Board of Directors for the Institute for Ethics and Emerging Technologies, alludes to in a related article. "If the concern has something to do with the girl's dignity being violated, then I have to protest by arguing that the girl lacks the cognitive capacity to experience any sense of indignity. Nor do I believe this is somehow demeaning or undignified to humanity in general; the treatments will endow her with a body that more closely matches her cognitive state—both in terms of her physical size and bodily functioning. The estrogen treatment is not what is grotesque here. Rather, it is the prospect of having a full-grown and fertile woman endowed with the mind of a baby."

Even though caring for Ashley involves hard and continual work, she is a blessing and not a burden. She brings a lot of love to our hearts as we're sure all Pillow Angels bring their families. In the words of a mother who lost her Pillow Angel: "While I would never want her to go through the discomfort she endured during her life, I would give all I have for one more snuggle, one more gaze from her radiant eyes." If there is a prize for those who have the record of how often they are told "I Love You", we're certain that these kids would win it effortlessly. Ashley's presence in our home kindles abundant feelings of love in all members of the family. It is a joy just being with her, she brings nourishment to our souls; it is a pleasure to visit with her and sweet talk her and observe her innocent and genuine smile. Ashley sets the barometer in our home: when she is happy we're happy and when she is not we're not.

We are very fortunate that Ashley is a healthy child, outside her abnormal mental development, and is in a stable condition. We're describing our unique experience which is not universal in this regard, and most likely not even representative. We fully understand that different Pillow Angels have different problems and pose different challenges to their caregivers, and that different families have different abilities and resources to provide for their special needs children.

The decision to move forward with this treatment, unlike what most have thought, was not difficult. Ever since we researched the idea and with Ashley's doctor's confirmation that it could be done, we focused squarely on getting it done as quickly as we could to maximize the benefits. It was clear to us that the lifelong benefits to Ashley by far outweigh risk factors associated with the surgery. In contrast, the decision to insert the feeding tube into Ashley's stomach and associated surgery was a lot harder for us. Ashley's doctor suggested that we put the feeding tube in at 5 months of age because it was taking up to eight hours a day to get enough nutrition in her through a bottle. We delayed the tube insertion for years in order to spare Ashley the surgery. At five years of age we finally decided to go for the surgery, since almost every time Ashley would catch a cold she would completely refuse her bottle for days and end up dehydrated and in the emergency room.

Furthermore, we did not pursue this treatment with the intention of prolonging Ashley's care at home. We would never turn the care of Ashley over to strangers even if she had grown tall and heavy. In the extreme, even an Ashley at 300 pounds, would still be at home and we would figure out a way to take care of her.

The objection that this treatment interferes with nature is one of the most ridiculous objections of all; medicine is all about interfering with nature. Why not let cancer spread and nature takes its course. Why give antibiotics for infections? Even an act as basic as cutting hair or trimming nails is interfering with nature.

Some question how God might view this treatment. The God we know wants Ashley to have a good quality of life and wants her parents to be diligent about using every resource at their disposal (including the brains that He endowed them with) to maximize her quality of life. Knowingly allowing avoidable suffering for a helpless and disabled child can't be a good thing in the eyes of God. Furthermore, the God we know wants us to actively share our experience and learning with the rest of the world to help all Pillow Angels and other special need children in reaping the benefits of the Ashley Treatment.

We want to avoid sensationalism or philosophical debates about what we did and why we did it. We'd rather care for and enjoy Ashley than get into such endless debates. In our opinion, only parents with special-needs children are in a position to fully relate to this topic. Unless you are living the experience, you are speculating and you have no clue what it is like to be the bedridden child or their caregivers. Furthermore, in the case of the female aspects of the treatment, women are in a better position to relate to these aspects and the benefits for which they are intended....

The Ashley Treatment: Best Interests, Convenience, and Parental Decision-Making

S. Matthew Liao, Julian Savulescu, and Mark Sheehan

Liao and his coauthors argue that although growth attenuation in a severely disabled child like Ashley may be justifiable, hysterectomy and the surgical removal of breast buds are not. Small size could

From Julian Savulescu, Mark Sheehan, and S. Matthew Liao, "The Ashley Treatment: Best Interests, Convenience, and Parental Decision-Making," *Hastings Center Report* 37, no. 2 (2007): 16–20. Copyright © 2007 Hastings Center Report. All rights reserved. Reproduced by permission. (References omitted.)

be in Ashley's best interest, permitting her family to care for her at home. If the attenuation also promotes the interest of her parents, that should not count against it. Moral obligations like those of Ashley's parents do not typically require large sacrifices of health and all other interests and duties.

The benefit to Ashley of the removal of her uterus and breast buds, by contrast, is not as clear, and harms are more likely. Less invasive ways of protecting against cramps and breast discomfort might be found, and the risks of cancer and sexual abuse seem too unlikely to justify surgery. The authors also reject the argument that an immature body is more in keeping with Ashley's mental age and will give her greater dignity.

Finally, the authors encourage us to see that the right to be loved and cared for that Ashley shares with other children, disabled people, and the elderly should be recognized by society and supported by every able person by paying taxes and voting for policies that help parents and other caregivers.

The story of Ashley, a nine-year-old from Seattle, has caused a good deal of controversy since it appeared in the *Los Angeles Times* on January 3, 2007. Ashley was born with a condition called static encephalopathy, a severe brain impairment that leaves her unable to walk, talk, eat, sit up, or roll over. According to her doctors, Ashley has reached, and will remain at, the developmental level of a three-month-old.

In 2004, Ashley's parents and the doctors at Seattle's Children's Hospital devised what they called the "Ashley Treatment," which included high-dose estrogen therapy to stunt Ashley's growth, the removal of her uterus via hysterectomy to prevent menstrual discomfort, and the removal of her breast buds to limit the growth of her breasts. Ashley's parents argue that the Ashley Treatment was intended "to improve our daughter's quality of life and not to convenience her caregivers." They also "decided to share our thoughts and experience . . . to help families who might bring similar benefits to their bedridden 'Pillow Angels,' " which means that this treatment has public policy implications.

In the case of incompetent children like Ashley, parents are the custodians of the child's interests and are required to make decisions that protect or promote those interests. Doctors should also offer treatments that are in Ashley's best interests. It would be wrong to offer a treatment that was against the interests of the child but in the parents' (or others') interests. The central questions in medical ethics in relation to this case are: Were these treatments in Ashley's best interests? Do they treat her as a person with dignity and respect, and were they likely to make her life go better?

Ashley's parents argue that they sought the Ashley treatment in order to alleviate Ashley's "discomfort and boredom." Their contention that stunting Ashley's growth was done for sake of improving "our daughter's quality of life and not to convenience her caregivers" is controversial.

According to her parents, keeping Ashley small—at around seventy-five pounds and four feet, five inches tall—means that Ashley can be moved considerably more often, held in their arms, be taken "on trips more frequently," "have more exposure to activities and social gatherings," and "continue to fit in and be bathed in a standard size bathtub." All this serves Ashley's health and well-being because, so the parents argue, "the increase in Ashley's movement results in better blood circulation, GI functioning (including digestion, passing gas), stretching, and motion of her joints," which means that Ashley will be less prone to infections.

Undoubtedly, the parents are right that Ashley will benefit in the manner they have proposed if they can do all these things for her. The claim about the value of small size in a particular social circumstance is certainly not unique. Dwarves have given the same argument as a justification for preferring to have short children. They have argued that parenting dwarves is desirable for them because of their own size and because they have made modifications to their homes and their surroundings to take into account their short stature.

As a general point, it is entirely conceivable that in some natural, social, or psychological circumstances, having a normal body may be a disadvantage. In H.G. Wells' short story "The Country of the Blind," Nunez, a mountaineer in the Andes, falls and comes upon the Country of the Blind. Nunez has normal vision, but in this society of blind people, he is disadvantaged, and he eventually consents to have his eyes removed. Similarly, in a world of loud noise, being able to hear could be a disadvantage. In the case of apotemnophilia—a body dysmorphic disorder in which the patient feels incomplete possessing all four limbs—doctors justify amputation by reasoning that the patient's psychology demands it. In Ashley's case, having a normal-sized body could be a disadvantage. Stunting Ashley's growth may then be in her overall interest, given her likely natural and social circumstances.

Of course, Ashley's parents may have had other motives besides her benefit. Many critics have claimed that what her parents were really after was to make things easier or more convenient for themselves. Convenience may have been at least *part* of their motivation. Her parents could have found ways to take care of Ashley even if she had grown to her normal size of five feet, six inches. They argue that they were already near their limits when lifting Ashley; but if their own convenience was no consideration, they could have augmented their strength by hiring people to help them, or by going to the gym, or by taking steroids, and so on. We are not advocating any of these things; we are asserting only that since the parents *could* have taken these measures, part of the rationale for making Ashley smaller may have been their own convenience.

This said, acting out of the motive to convenience the caregivers or otherwise promote their interests is not necessarily wrong, for two reasons. First, motives may only form part of the justification of the treatment of children. Whether the treatment will benefit or harm them is just as important, and sometimes even more so. Imagine a parent who takes a child with appendicitis to a hospital merely hoping that the child will get admitted so that the parent can get some badly needed sleep. Does this make it wrong to perform an appendectomy? Obviously not. In such a case, the justification of the procedure depends on the interests of the child and not on the motives of the parents (though of course the two can be related).

Second, in any plausible moral theory, moral obligations should typically not be so demanding that one must make enormous sacrifices in order to fulfil them. As Judith Jarvis Thomson observes, "nobody is morally *required* to make large sacrifices, of health, of all other interests and concerns, of all other duties and commitments . . . in order to keep another person alive." Exactly where the demands of morality stop, especially in the case of parents, is not easy to say. But, arguably, if Ashley's parents have to take steroids, which may have side effects, in order to move Ashley around, or if they will have to impoverish themselves in order to hire additional caregivers, then these alternatives might just be too demanding, and Ashley's parents would not be obligated to pursue them.

Of course, someone might accept that the demands of morality have limits but still question whether stunting Ashley's growth for her caregivers' convenience is justified. Indeed, many are worried that the Ashley Treatment might represent a return to the practices of the eugenics movement and be an affront to human dignity. In particular, it has been asked whether, if it is permissible to stunt Ashley's growth to keep her small, why it is not also permissible surgically to remove her legs to keep her small. Needless to say, it is disturbing to think of a scenario in which severely disabled institutionalized children are subjected to mass surgery and growth-stunting to make the staff's work easier.

These questions raise issues concerning the ethics of body modification. Some forms of plastic surgery are performed on children: "bat ears" are sometimes corrected to prevent a child's being teased, and growth hormone or estrogen treatment is sometimes provided to children predicted to have short or tall stature. However, other forms of body modification that might be allowed in adults are not permitted in children. A Scottish surgeon, Robert Smith, amputated the healthy legs of two patients suffering from apotemnophilia. The patients had received psychiatric and psychological treatment prior to the operation, but did not respond. Both operations were carried out with private funding, and the patients said they were satisfied with the results. But this kind of surgery could not be ethically performed on healthy children because it is not plausibly in their interests, given the risks to, and the stress such an operation would impose on, their bodies. For this reason, surgically removing Ashley's legs just so she would be easier to care for would be unethical.

Giving Ashley estrogen to stunt her growth is obviously controversial but may be justifiable in this circumstance. Imagine that as a part of Ashley's condition, her body would grow to five times the size of other people. She would be enormous. In such a case, it does not seem too objectionable to arrest this kind of development through pharmacological means to allow her to be nursed and cared for, even if this is done partly for the caregivers' convenience. That is, suppose that, if her development was not arrested, providing her with decent care would eventually require twenty people. If this is right, the question is not whether development *may* be arrested, but only *when* it may be arrested.

Here it is important to point out that decisions of this kind should be made on a case by case basis, with independent ethical review, such as occurred in this case through a hospital's clinical ethics committee. In general, it is inappropriate for institutions to biologically modify their patients to make them easier to manage, though clearly many demented people are sedated for this purpose. The benefits of being cared for at home by one's family may warrant imposing some burdens on incompetent dependents to enable them to remain at home and to make it possible for care to be delivered there. When the parents' resources are limited, the state, with its greater resources, should not resort to biological modification when the patient's quality of life can be preserved through social services.

***

The removal of Ashley's uterus and her breast buds is another matter. Ashley's parents argue that a hysterectomy will allow her to avoid the menstrual cycle and the discomforts commonly associated with it, eliminate "any possibility of pregnancy," and also eliminate the possibility "of uterine cancer and other common and often painful complications that cause women later in life to undergo the procedure." We find these arguments debatable.

For starters, it is unclear how much discomfort women suffer from the menstrual cycle, and whether the level of discomfort justifies hysterectomy. Also, even if Ashley will experience some discomfort, it is unclear why less invasive methods—such as giving Ashley pain killers whenever she experiences cramps—are not sufficient. Furthermore, removing Ashley's uterus may cause her ovaries not to function normally as a result of a compromised supply of blood. This may result in Ashley's ovaries

not producing enough of the hormones that would otherwise protect her against serious common diseases such as heart disease and osteoporosis.

Regarding unwanted pregnancies, while this does occur sometimes, the parents' statement gives the impression that sexual abuse is a given to one in Ashley's situation. Also, the parents may be in danger of blaming the victim. Ashley would get pregnant only through sexual abuse, but surely action should be taken against the offenders rather than Ashley. In any case, there are less invasive ways of avoiding pregnancy, such as putting Ashley on birth control pills.

Finally, regarding the possibility of uterine cancer and other painful complications, it seems premature to undertake a preventive measure when no one knows whether the symptoms will ever manifest. Giving Ashley regular health checkups seems to be much more appropriate and less invasive.

According to Ashley's parents, surgically removing Ashley's breast buds is justified because Ashley will not be breastfeeding. In addition, their presence "would only be a source of discomfort to her" because Ashley is likely to have large breasts, and "large breasts are uncomfortable lying down with a bra and even less comfortable without a bra." Moreover, they "impede securing Ashley in her wheelchair, stander, or bath chair, where straps across her chest are needed to support her body weight." Furthermore, removing her breasts also means that she can avoid the possibility of painful fibrocystic growth and breast cancer, which runs in Ashley's family. Finally, according to the parents, large breasts "could 'sexualize' Ashley towards her caregiver, especially when they are touched while she is being moved or handled, inviting the possibility of abuse." Again, we find these arguments problematic. We shall start with the ones that have been addressed previously.

In arguing that the breasts could "sexualize" Ashley, the parents are again in danger of blaming the victim for possible abuse. Moreover, someone might sexually abuse Ashley whether she has breasts or not. The focus should be on the potential sex offenders.

The argument that breasts would make securing Ashley in her wheelchair difficult, and so on, is an argument from convenience. Like the previous argument about size, it depends on how likely the harm to Ashley would be and how great the sacrifice of coping with management would be. Unlike Ashley's height and weight, in this case, it does not seem too demanding to require the parents to look for straps that would be more suitable for a larger breast size. Even if Ashley had been allowed to grow her breasts to their full potential, surely there are disabled persons with similar breast sizes, and their caregivers have apparently been able to use straps that are suitable for them (although the situation may be different when the patient's disability is as grave as Ashley's).

The possibility of painful fibrocystic growth and breast cancer is similar to the risk of uterine cancer; here, too, undertaking a preventive measure when the symptoms have not manifested seems premature. Even in the case of familial breast cancer, such as cancer linked to the genes BRCA 1 and 2, it is still not standard medical practice to offer prophylactic mastectomy to children, even those with a permanent intellectual disability that renders them incompetent. Many would argue that screening is preferable until there is more debate on the justification of prophylactic surgery in incompetent people.

The argument that Ashley does not need her breasts because she will not breastfeed (making her breasts only a "source of discomfort") assumes that the sole function of having breasts is for breastfeeding. Allowing Ashley to develop breasts may enable her to form and complete her gender identity. It is true that gender assignment surgery has been performed on children at birth in cases of intersex conditions, but there is a growing consensus that surgery should be delayed until the child can make his or her own decision about it. Ashley will never (on the evidence provided) be able to decide for herself. But there is a difference between gender assignment and gender *elimination*. Ashley's parents argue that since Ashley has the mental state of a three-month-old, it is more fitting for her to have the body of an infant. They cite the statement of George Dvorsky, a member of the board of directors for the Institute for Ethics and Emerging Technologies, approvingly:

> *If the concern has something to do with the girl's dignity being violated, then I have to protest by arguing that the girl lacks the cognitive capacity to experience any sense of indignity. Nor do I believe this is somehow demeaning or undignified to humanity in general; the treatments will endow her with a body that more closely matches her cognitive state—both in terms of her physical size and bodily functioning. The estrogen treatment is not what is grotesque here. Rather, it is the prospect of having a full-grown and fertile woman endowed with the mind of a baby.*

This argument implies that anyone with the mind of a baby should have the body of a baby, but there's no reason to think this is true. Indeed, suppose a woman in her forties has such severe dementia that her mental state is reduced to that of a baby; to hold that she should no longer have breasts is absurd.

It is important to remember that surgical procedures like hysterectomy are not without risks. Anaesthetics are occasionally lethal, and the surgical complications can include perforation of the bowel, infection, and occasionally death. All told, drug treatment to stunt growth seems more justifiable than the surgical modifications.

* * *

Ashley's case calls to attention the fact that every able person in our society has at least a prima facie duty to provide support and assistance to those who are providing care, not just for the likes of Ashley, but also for all normal children, the elderly, and others in care. Because of their basic, biological need for love, children have a human right to be loved. Successfully discharging the duty to love children requires considerable time and resources. Possibly some parents can successfully discharge this duty using their own resources. But for many others, it can be quite difficult, owing perhaps to the demands of employment or of other family members. However, if the right of children to be loved is a human right, and if the duties that stem from such a human right are applicable to all able persons in appropriate circumstances, then all other able persons in appropriate circumstances have associated duties to help parents discharge their duties to love their children. Such help might mean supporting better child care programs or advocating flexible workplace policies that would make it easier for parents to care for their children. It might also mean paying taxes and voting for policies that would help parents discharge their duties.

This argument can be extended to the case of Ashley and others who require care, such as the elderly. Those who require care, like Ashley, have a fundamental need—and, therefore, a human right—to be cared for; and we, as members of society, have an associated duty to support policies that help their families care for them.

One of the main objections to the Ashley Treatment is that Ashley's disadvantage is socially constructed. If more resources were available for her care, then she could be nursed and cared for in a normal adult size. Those who defend the Ashley Treatment are right to respond that because these resources are not now adequately provided, Ashley's parents may be taking the only option open to them. Indeed, to deny her both the necessary social resources and medical treatment is to doubly harm her. If we as a society believe that it is undignified, as a matter of human rights, for Ashley to undergo these treatments, then we must be prepared to provide her caregivers with enough assistance and support that they would not have to resort to these means. Upholding human dignity comes with a price, and if it is what we should value as a society, then we must be prepared to pay to uphold it.

Section 3: The Status of Impaired Infants

Examination of Arguments in Favor of Withholding Ordinary Medical Care from Defective Infants

John A. Robertson

Robertson defends a conservative natural law position in criticizing two arguments in favor of withholding "necessary but ordinary" medical care from impaired infants. He rejects the claim made by Michael Tooley that infants are not persons and argues that, on the contrary, there is no nonarbitrary consideration that requires us to protect the past realization of conceptual capability but not its potential realization.

The second argument that Robertson considers is one to the effect that we have no obligation to treat impaired newborns when the cost of doing so greatly outweighs the benefits (a utilitarian argument). Robertson claims that we have no way of making such assessments. Life itself may be of sufficient worth to an impaired person to offset his or her suffering, and the suffering and cost to society are not sufficient to justify withholding care.

1. Defective Infants Are Not Persons

Children born with congenital malformations may lack human form and the possibility of ordinary, psychosocial development. In many cases mental retardation is or will be so profound, and physical incapacity so great, that the term "persons" or "humanly alive" have odd or questionable

meaning when applied to them. In these cases the infants' physical and mental defects are so severe that they will never know anything but a vegetative existence, with no discernible personality, sense of self, or capacity to interact with others. Withholding ordinary medical care in such cases, one may argue, is justified on the ground that these infants are not persons or human beings in the ordinary or legal sense of the term, and therefore do not possess the right of care that persons possess.

Central to this argument is the idea that living products of the human uterus can be classified into offspring that are persons, and those that are not.

Conception and birth by human parents does not automatically endow one with personhood and its accompanying rights. Some other characteristic or feature must be present in the organism for personhood to vest, and this the defective infant arguably lacks. Lacking that property, an organism is not a person or deserving to be treated as such.

Before considering what "morally significant features" might distinguish persons from nonpersons, and examining the relevance of such features to the case of the defective infant, we must face an initial objection to this line of inquiry. The objection questions the need for any distinction among human offspring because of

> *the monumental misuse of the concept of "humanity" in so many practices of discrimination and atrocity throughout history. Slavery, witchhunts and wars have all been justified by their perpetrators on the grounds that they held their victims to be less than fully human. The insane and criminal have for long periods been deprived of the most basic necessities for similar reasons, and been excluded from society....*
>
> *Even when entered upon with the best of intentions, and in the most guarded manner, the enterprise of basing the protection of human life upon such criteria and definitions is dangerous. To question someone's humanity or personhood is a first step to mistreatment and killing.*

Hence, according to this view, human parentage is a necessary and sufficient condition for personhood, whatever the characteristics of the offspring, because qualifying criteria inevitably lead to abuse and untold suffering to beings who are unquestionably human. Moreover, the human species is sufficiently different from other sentient species that assigning its members greater rights on birth alone is not arbitrary.

This objection is indeed powerful. The treatment accorded slaves in the United States, the Nazi denial of personal status to non-Aryans, and countless other incidents, testify that man's inhumanity to man is indeed greatest when a putative nonperson is involved. Arguably, however, a distinction based on gross physical form, profound mental incapacity, and the very existence of personality or selfhood, besides having an empirical basis in the monstrosities and mutations known to have been born to women, is a basic and fundamental one. Rather than distinguishing among the particular characteristics that persons might attain through the contingencies of race, culture, and class, it merely separates out those who lack the potential for assuming any personal characteristics beyond breathing and consciousness.

This reply narrows the issue: should such creatures be cared for, protected, or regarded as "ordinary" humans? If such treatment is not warranted, they may be treated as nonpersons. The arguments supporting care in all circumstances are based on the view that all living creatures are sacred, contain a spark of the divine, and should be so regarded. Moreover, identifying those human offspring unworthy of care is a difficult task and will inevitably take a toll on those whose humanity cannot seriously be questioned. At this point the argument becomes metaphysical or religious and immune to resolution by empirical evidence, not unlike the controversy over whether a fetus is a person. It should be noted, however, that recognizing all human offspring as persons, like recognizing the fetus to be a person, does not conclude the treatment issue.

Although this debate can be resolved only by reference to religious or moral beliefs, a procedural solution may reasonably be considered. Since reasonable people can agree that we ordinarily regard human offspring as persons, and further, that defining categories of exclusion is likely to pose special dangers of abuse, a reasonable solution is to presume that all living human offspring are persons. This rule would be subject to exception only if it can be shown beyond a reasonable doubt that certain offspring will never possess the minimal properties that reasonable persons ordinarily associate with human personality. If this burden cannot be satisfied, then the presumption of personhood obtains.

For this purpose I will address only one of the many properties proposed as a necessary condition of personhood—the capacity for having a sense of self—and consider whether its advocates present a cogent account of the nonhuman. Since other accounts may be more convincingly articulated, this discussion will neither exhaust nor conclude the issue. But it will illuminate the strengths and weaknesses of the personhood argument and enable us to evaluate its application to defective infants.

Michael Tooley has recently argued that a human offspring lacking the capacity for a sense of self lacks the rights to life or equal treatment possessed by other persons. In considering the morality of abortion and infanticide, Tooley considers "what properties a thing must possess in order to have a serious right to life," and he concludes that:

> [h]aving a right to life presupposes that one is capable of desiring to continue existing as a subject of experiences and other mental states. This in turn presupposes both that one has the concept of such a continuing entity and that one believes that one is oneself such an entity. So an entity that lacks such a consciousness of itself as a continuing subject of mental states does not have a right to life.

However, this account is at first glance too narrow, for it appears to exclude all those who do not presently have a desire "to continue existing as a subject of experiences and other mental states." The sleeping or unconscious individual, the deranged, the conditioned, and the suicidal do not have such desires, though they might have had them or could have them in the future. Accordingly, Tooley emphasizes the capability of entertaining such desires, rather than their actual existence. But it is difficult to distinguish the capability for such desires in an unconscious, conditioned, or emotionally disturbed person from the capability existing in a fetus or infant. In all cases the capability is a future one; it will arise only if certain events occur, such as normal growth and development in the case of the infant, and removal of the disability in the other cases. The infant, in fact, might realize its capability long before disabled adults recover emotional balance or consciousness.

To meet this objection, Tooley argues that the significance of the capability in question is not solely its future realization (for fetuses and infants will ordinarily realize it), but also its previous existence and exercise. He seems to say that once the conceptual capability has been realized, one's right to desire continued existence permanently vests, even though the present capability for desiring does not exist, and may be lost for substantial periods or permanently. Yet, what nonarbitrary reasons require that we protect the past realization of conceptual capability but not its potential realization in the future? As a reward for its past realization? To mark our reverence and honor for someone who has realized that state? Tooley is silent on this point.

Another difficulty is Tooley's ambiguity concerning the permanently deranged, comatose,

or conditioned. Often he phrases his argument in terms of a temporary suspension of the capability of conceptual thought. One wonders what he would say of someone permanently deranged, or with massive brain damage, or in a prolonged coma. If he seriously means that the past existence of a desire for life vests these cases with the right to life, then it is indeed difficult to distinguish the comatose or deranged from the infant profoundly retarded at birth. Neither will ever possess the conceptual capability to desire to be a continuing subject of experiences. A distinction based on reward or desert seems arbitrary, and protection of life applies equally well in both cases. Would Tooley avoid this problem by holding that the permanently comatose and deranged lose their rights after a certain point because conceptual capacity will never be regained? This would permit killing (or at least withholding of care from) the insane and comatose—doubtless an unappealing prospect. Moreover, we do not ordinarily think of the insane, and possibly the comatose, as losing personhood before their death. Although their personality or identity may be said to change, presumably for the worse, or become fragmented or minimal, we still regard them as specific persons. If a "self" in some minimal sense exists here then the profoundly retarded, who at least is conscious, also may be considered a self, albeit a minimal one. Thus, one may argue that Tooley fails to provide a convincing account of criteria distinguishing persons and nonpersons. He both excludes beings we ordinarily think of as persons—infants, deranged, conditioned, possibly the comatose—and fails to articulate criteria that convincingly distinguish the nonhuman. But, even if we were to accept Tooley's distinction that beings lacking the potential for desire and a sense of self are not persons who are owed the duty to be treated by ordinary medical means, this would not appear to be very helpful in deciding whether to treat the newborn with physical or mental defects. Few infants, it would seem, would fall into this class. First, those suffering from malformations, however gross, that do not affect mental capabilities would not fit the class of nonpersons. Second, frequently even the most severe cases of mental retardation cannot be reliably determined until a much later period; care thus could not justifiably be withheld in the neonatal period, although this principle would permit nontreatment at the time when nonpersonality is clearly established. Finally, the only group of defective newborns who would clearly qualify as nonpersons is anencephalics, who altogether lack a brain or those so severely brain-damaged that it is immediately clear that a sense of self or personality can never develop. Mongols, myelomeningoceles, and other defective infants from whom ordinary care is now routinely withheld would not qualify as nonpersons. Thus, even the most coherent and cogent criteria of humanity are only marginally helpful in the situation of the defective infant. We must therefore consider whether treatment can be withheld on grounds other than the claim that such infants are not persons.

2. No Obligation to Treat Exists When the Costs of Maintaining Life Greatly Outweigh the Benefits

If we reject the argument that defective newborns are not persons, the question remains whether circumstances exist in which the consequences of treatment as compared with nontreatment are so undesirable that the omission of care is justi-fied. As we have seen, the doctrine of necessity permits one to violate the criminal law when es-sential to prevent the occurrence of a greater evil. The circumstances, however, when the death of a nonconsenting person is a lesser evil than his con-tinuing life are narrowly circumscribed, and do not include withholding care from defective infants. Yet many parents and physicians deeply committed to the loving care of the newborn think that treating severely defective infants causes more harm than good, thereby justifying the withholding of ordinary care. In their view the suffering and diminished quality of the child's life do not justify the social and economic costs of treatment. This claim has a growing commonsense appeal, but it assumes that the utility or quality of one's life can be measured and compared with other lives, and that health resources may legitimately be allocated to produce the greatest personal utility. This argument will now be analyzed from the perspective of the defec-tive patient and others affected by his care.

a. The Quality of the Defective Infant's Life

Comparisons of relative worth among persons, or between persons and other interests, raise moral and methodological issues that make

any argument that relies on such comparisons extremely vulnerable. Thus the strongest claim for not treating the defective newborn is that treat-ment seriously harms the infant's own interests, whatever may be the effect on others. When maintaining his life involves great physical and psychosocial suffering for the patient, a reason-able person might conclude that such a life is not worth living. Presumably the patient, if fully informed and able to communicate, would agree. One then would be morally justified in withhold-ing lifesaving treatment if such action served to advance the best interests of the patient.

Congenital malformations impair development in several ways that lead to the judgment that deformed retarded infants are "a burden to themselves." One is the severe physical pain, much of it resulting from repeated surgery that defective infants will suffer. Defective children also are likely to develop other pathological features, leading to repeated fractures, dislocations, surgery, malfunctions, and other sources of pain. The shunt, for example, inserted to relieve hy-drocephaly, a common problem in defective children, often becomes clogged, necessitating frequent surgical interventions.

Pain, however, may be intermittent and manage-able with analgesics. Since many infants and adults experience great pain, and many defective infants do not, pain alone, if not totally unmanageable, does not sufficiently show that a life is so worth-less that death is preferable. More important are the psychosocial deficits resulting from the child's handicaps. Many defective children never can walk even with prosthesis, never interact with normal children, never appreciate growth, adolescence, or the fulfillment of education and employment, and seldom are even able to care for themselves. In cases of severe retardation, they may be left with a vegetative existence in a crib, incapable of choice or the most minimal responses to stimuli. Parents or others may reject them, and much of their time will be spent in hospitals, in surgery, or fighting the many illnesses that beset them. Can it be said that such a life is worth living?

There are two possible responses to the quality-of-life argument. One is to accept its premises but to question the degree of suffering in particular cases, and thus restrict the justification for death to the most extreme cases. The absence of opportunities for schooling, career, and interaction may be the fault of social attitudes and the failings of healthy persons, rather than a necessary result of congenital malformations. Psychosocial suffering occurs because healthy, normal persons reject or refuse to relate to the defective, or hurry them to poorly funded institutions. Most nonambulatory, mentally retarded persons can be trained for satisfying roles. One cannot assume that a nonproductive existence is necessarily unhappy; even social rejection and non-acceptance can be mitigated. Moreover, the psychosocial ills of the handicapped often do not differ in kind from those experienced by many persons. With training and care, growth, development, and a full range of experiences are possible for most people with physical and mental handicaps. Thus, the claim that death is a far better fate than life cannot in most cases be sustained.

This response, however, avoids meeting the quality-of-life argument on its strongest grounds. Even if many defective infants can experience growth, interaction, and most human satisfactions if nurtured, treated, and trained, some infants are so severely retarded or grossly deformed that their response to love and care, in fact their capacity to be conscious, is always minimal. Although mongoloid and nonambulatory spina bifida children may experience an existence we would hesitate to adjudge worse than death, the profoundly retarded, nonambulatory blind, deaf infant who will spend his few years in the back-ward cribs of a state institution is clearly a different matter.

To repudiate the quality-of-life argument, therefore, requires a defense of treatment in even these extreme cases. Such a defense would question the validity of any surrogate or proxy judgments of the worth or quality of life when the wishes of the person in question cannot be ascertained. The essence of the quality-of-life argument is a proxy's judgment that no reasonable person can prefer the pain, suffering, and loneliness of, for example, life in a crib at an IQ level of 20, to an immediate, painless death.

But in what sense can the proxy validly conclude that a person with different wants, needs, and interests, if able to speak, would agree that such a life were worse than death? At the start one must be skeptical of the proxy's claim to objective disinterestedness. If the proxy is also the parent or physician, as has been the case in pediatric euthanasia, the impact of treatment on the proxy's interests,

rather than solely on those of the child, may influence his assessment. But even if the proxy were truly neutral and committed only to caring for the child, the problem of egocentricity and knowing another's mind remains. Compared with the situation and life prospects of a "reasonable man," the child's potential quality of life indeed appears dim. Yet a standard based on healthy, ordinary development may be entirely inappropriate to this situation. One who has never known the pleasures of mental operation, ambulation, and social interaction surely does not suffer from their loss as much as one who has. While one who has known these capacities may prefer death to a life without them, we have no assurance that the handicapped person, with no point of comparison, would agree. Life, and life alone, whatever its limitations, might be of sufficient worth to him.

One should also be hesitant to accept proxy assessments of quality-of-life because the margin of error in such predictions may be very great. For instance, while one expert argues that by a purely clinical assessment he can accurately forecast the minimum degree of future handicap an individual will experience, such forecasting is not infallible, and risks denying care to infants whose disability might otherwise permit a reasonably acceptable quality-of-life. Thus given the problems in ascertaining another's wishes, the proxy's bias to personal or culturally relative interests, and the unreliability of predictive criteria, the quality-of-life argument is open to serious question. Its strongest appeal arises in the case of a grossly deformed, retarded, institutionalized child, or one with incessant unmanageable pain, where continued life is itself torture. But these cases are few, and cast doubt on the utility of any such judgment. Even if the judgment occasionally may be defensible, the potential danger of quality-of-life assessments may be a compelling reason for rejecting this rationale for withholding treatment.

b. The Suffering of Others

In addition to the infant's own suffering, one who argues that the harm of treatment justifies violation of the defective infant's right to life usually relies on the psychological, social, and economic costs of maintaining his existence to family and society. In their view the minimal benefit of treatment to persons incapable of full social and physical development does not justify the burdens that care of the defective infant imposes on parents, siblings, health professionals, and other patients. Matson, a noted pediatric neurosurgeon, states:

> [I]t is the doctor's and the community's responsibility to provide [custodial] care and to minimize suffering, but, at the same time, it is also their responsibility not to prolong such individual, familial, and community suffering unnecessarily, and not to carry out multiple procedures and prolonged, expensive, acute hospitalization in an infant whose chance for acceptable growth and development is negligible.

Such a frankly utilitarian argument raises problems. It assumes that because of the greatly curtailed orbit of his existence, the costs or suffering of others [are] greater than the benefit of life to the child. This judgment, however, requires a coherent way of measuring and comparing interpersonal utilities, a logical–practical problem that utilitarianism has never surmounted. But even if such comparisons could reliably show a net loss from treatment, the fact remains that the child must sacrifice his life to benefit others. If the life of one individual, however useless, may be sacrificed for the benefit of any person, however useful, or for the benefit of any number of persons, then we have acknowledged the principle that rational utility may justify any outcome. As many philosophers have demonstrated, utilitarianism can always permit the sacrifice of one life for other interests, given the appropriate arrangement of utilities on the balance sheet. In the absence of principled grounds for such a decision, the social equation involved in mandating direct, involuntary euthanasia becomes a difference of degree, not kind, and we reach the point where protection of life depends solely on social judgments of utility.

These objections may well be determinative. But if we temporarily bracket them and examine the extent to which care of the defective infant subjects others to suffering, the claim that inordinate suffering outweighs the infant's interest in life is rarely plausible. In this regard we must examine the impact of caring for defective infants on the family, health professionals, and society-at-large.

The Family. The psychological impact and crisis created by birth of a defective infant is devastating. Not only is the mother denied the normal tension release from the stresses of pregnancy, but both parents feel a crushing blow to their dignity, self-esteem, and self-confidence. In a very short time, they feel grief for the loss of the normal expected child, anger at fate, numbness, disgust, waves of helplessness, and disbelief. Most feel personal blame for the defect, or blame their spouse. Adding to the shock is fear that social position and mobility are permanently endangered. The transformation of a "joyously awaited experience into one of catastrophe and profound psychological threat" often will reactivate unresolved maturational conflicts. The chances for social pathology—divorce, somatic complaints, nervous and mental disorders—increase and hard-won adjustment patterns may be permanently damaged.

The initial reactions of guilt, grief, anger, and loss, however, cannot be the true measure of family suffering caused by care of a defective infant, because these costs are present whether or not the parents choose treatment. Rather, the question is to what degree treatment imposes psychic and other costs greater than would occur if the child were not treated. The claim that care is more costly rests largely on the view that parents and family suffer inordinately from nurturing such a child.

Indeed, if the child is treated and accepted at home, difficult and demanding adjustment must be made. Parents must learn how to care for a disabled child, confront financial and psychological uncertainty, meet the needs of other siblings, and work through their own conflicting feelings. Mothering demands are greater than with a normal child, particularly if medical care and hospitalization are frequently required. Counseling or professional support may be nonexistent or difficult to obtain. Younger siblings may react with hostility and guilt, older with shame and anger. Often the normal feedback of child growth that renders the turmoil of childrearing worthwhile develops more slowly or not at all. Family resources can be depleted (especially if medical care is needed), consumption patterns altered, or standards of living modified. Housing may have to be found closer to a hospital, and plans for further children changed. Finally, the anxieties, guilt, and grief present at birth may threaten to recur or become chronic.

Yet, although we must recognize the burdens and frustrations of raising a defective infant, it does not necessarily follow that these costs require non-treatment, or even institutionalization. Individual and group counseling can substantially alleviate anxiety, guilt, and frustration, and enable parents to cope with underlying conflicts triggered by the birth and the adaptations required. Counseling also can reduce psychological pressures on siblings, who can be taught to recognize and accept their own possibly hostile feelings and the difficult position of their parents. They may even be taught to help their parents care for the child.

The impact of increased financial costs also may vary. In families with high income or adequate health insurance, the financial costs are manageable. In others, state assistance may be available. If severe financial problems arise or pathological adjustments are likely, institutionalization, although undesirable for the child, remains an option. Finally, in many cases, the experience of living through a crisis is a deepening and enriching one, accelerating personality maturation, and giving one a new sensitivity to the needs of spouse, siblings, and others. As one parent of a defective child states: "In the last months I have come closer to people and can understand them more. I have met them more deeply. I did not know there were so many people with troubles in the world."

Thus, while social attitudes regard the handicapped child as an unmitigated disaster, in reality the problem may not be insurmountable, and often may not differ from life's other vicissitudes. Suffering there is, but seldom is it so overwhelming or so imminent that the only alternative is death of the child.

Health Professionals. Physicians and nurses also suffer when parents give birth to a defective child, although, of course, not to the degree of the parents. To the obstetrician or general practitioner the defective birth may be a blow to his professional identity. He has the difficult task of informing the parents of the defects, explaining their causes, and dealing with the parents' resulting emotional shock. Often he feels guilty for failing to produce a normal baby. In addition the parents may project anger or hostility on the physician, questioning his professional competence or seeking the services of other doctors. The physician also may feel that his expertise and training are misused when employed to maintain the life of an infant whose chances for a productive existence are so diminished. By neglecting other patients, he may feel that he is prolonging rather than alleviating suffering.

Nurses, too, suffer role strain from care of the defective newborn. Intensive-care-unit nurses may work with only one or two babies at a time. They face the daily ordeals of care—the progress and relapses—and often must deal with anxious parents who are themselves grieving or ambivalent toward the child. The situation may trigger a nurse's own ambivalence about death and mothering, in a context in which she is actively working to keep alive a child whose life prospects seem minimal.

Thus, the effects of care on physicians and nurses are not trivial, and must be intelligently confronted in medical education or in management of a pediatric unit. Yet to state them is to make clear that they can but weigh lightly in the decision of whether to treat a defective newborn. Compared with the situation of the parents, these burdens seem insignificant, are short term, and most likely do not evoke such profound emotions. In any case, these difficulties are hazards of the profession—caring for the sick and dying will always produce strain. Hence, on these grounds alone it is difficult to argue that a defective person may be denied the right to life.

Society. Care of the defective newborn also imposes societal costs, the utility of which is questioned when the infant's expected quality of life is so poor. Medical resources that can be used by infants with a better prognosis, or throughout the health-care system generally, are consumed in providing expensive surgical and intensive-care services to infants who may be severely retarded, never lead active lives, and die in a few months or years. Institutionalization imposes costs on taxpayers and reduces the resources available for those who might better benefit from it, while reducing further the quality of life experienced by the institutionalized defective.

One answer to these concerns is to question the impact of the costs of caring for defective newborns. Precise data showing the costs to taxpayers or the trade-offs with health and other expenditures do not exist. Nor would ceasing to care for the defective necessarily lead to a reallocation within the health budget that would produce net savings in suffering or life; in fact, the released resources might not be reallocated for health at all. In any case, the trade-offs within the health budget may well be small. With advances in prenatal diagnosis of genetic disorders, many deformed infants who would formerly require care will be aborted beforehand. Then, too, it is not clear that the most technical and expensive procedures always constitute the best treatment for certain malformations. When compared with the almost seven percent of the GNP now spent on health, the money in the defense budget, or tax revenues generally, the public resources required to keep defective newborns alive seem marginal, and arguably worth the commitment to life that such expenditures reinforce. Moreover, as the Supreme Court recently recognized, conservation of the taxpayer's purse does not justify serious infringement of fundamental rights. Given legal and ethical norms against sacrificing the lives of nonconsenting others, and the imprecisions in diagnosis and prediction concerning the eventual outcomes of medical care, the social-cost argument does not compel nontreatment of defective newborns.

Ethical Issues in Aiding the Death of Young Children

H. Tristram Engelhardt, Jr.

Engelhardt contends that children are not persons in the full sense. They must exist in and through their families. Thus, parents, in consultation with a physician, are the appropriate ones to decide whether to treat an impaired newborn when (1) there is not only little likelihood of a full human life but also the likelihood of suffering if the life is prolonged or (2) the cost of prolonging the life is very great.

Engelhardt further argues that it is reasonable to speak of a *duty* not to treat an impaired infant when this will only prolong a painful life or lead to a painful death. He bases his claim on the legal notion of a "wrongful life." This notion suggests that there are cases in which nonexistence would be better than existence under the conditions in which a person must live. Life can thus be seen as an injury, rather than as a gift.

Euthanasia in the pediatric age group involves a constellation of issues that are materially different from those of adult euthanasia. The difference lies in the somewhat obvious fact that infants and young children are not able to decide about their own futures and thus are not persons in the same sense that normal adults are. While adults usually decide their own fate, others decide on behalf of young children. Although one can argue that euthanasia is or should be a personal right, the sense of such an argument is obscure with respect to children. Young children do not have any personal rights, at least none that they can exercise on their own behalf with regard to the manner of their life and death. As a result, euthanasia of

From *Beneficent Euthanasia*, edited by Marvin Kohl. Buffalo, NY: Prometheus Books, 1975.

young children raises special questions concerning the standing of the rights of children, the status of parental rights, the obligations of adults to prevent the suffering of children, and the possible effects on society of allowing or expediting the death of seriously defective infants.

What I will refer to as the euthanasia of infants and young children might be termed by others infanticide, while some cases might be termed the withholding of extraordinary life-prolonging treatment. One needs a term that will encompass both death that results from active intervention and death that ensues when one simply ceases further therapy. In using such a term, one must recognize that death is often not directly but only obliquely intended. That is, one often intends only to treat no further, not actually to have death follow, even though one knows death will follow.

Finally, one must realize that deaths as the result of withholding treatment constitute a significant proportion of neonatal deaths. For example, as high as 14 percent of children in one hospital have been identified as dying after a decision was made not to treat further, the presumption being that the children would have lived longer had treatment been offered.

Even popular magazines have presented accounts of parental decisions not to pursue treatment. These decisions often involve a choice between expensive treatment with little chance of achieving a full, normal life for the child and "letting nature take its course," with the child dying as a result of its defects. As this suggests, many of these problems are products of medical progress. Such children in the past would have died. The quandaries are in a sense an embarrassment of riches; now that one *can* treat such defective children, *must* one treat them? And, if one need not treat such defective children, may one expedite their death?

I will here briefly examine some of these issues. First, I will review differences that contrast the euthanasia of adults to euthanasia of children. Second, I will review the issue of the rights of parents and the status of children. Third, I will suggest a new notion, the concept of the "injury of continued existence," and draw out some of its implications with respect to a duty to prevent suffering. Finally, I will outline some important questions that remain unanswered even if the foregoing issues can be settled. In all, I hope more to display the issues involved in a difficult question than to advance a particular set of answers to particular dilemmas.

For the purpose of this paper, I will presume that adult euthanasia can be justified by an appeal to freedom. In the face of imminent death, one is usually choosing between a more painful and more protracted dying and a less painful or less protracted dying, in circumstances where either choice makes little difference with regard to the discharge of social duties and responsibilities. In the case of suicide, we might argue that, in general, social duties (for example, the duty to support one's family) restrain one from taking one's own life. But in the face of imminent death and in the presence of the pain and deterioration of a fatal disease, such duties are usually impossible to discharge and are thus rendered moot. One can, for example, picture an extreme case of an adult with a widely disseminated carcinoma, including metastases to the brain, who because of severe pain and debilitation is no longer capable of discharging any social duties. In these and similar circumstances, euthanasia becomes the issue of the right to control one's own body, even to the point of seeking assistance in suicide. Euthanasia is, as such, the issue of assisted suicide, the universalization of a maxim that all persons should be free, *in extremis*, to decide with regard to the circumstances of their death.

Further, the choice of positive euthanasia could be defended as the more rational choice: the choice of a less painful death and the affirmation of the value of a rational life. In so choosing, one would be acting to set limits to one's life in order not to live when pain and physical and mental deterioration make further rational life impossible. The choice to end one's life can be understood as a noncontradictory willing of a smaller set of states of existence for oneself, a set that would not include a painful death. That is, adult euthanasia can be construed as an affirmation of the rationality and autonomy of the self.

The remarks above focus on the active or positive euthanasia of adults. But they hold as well concerning what is often called passive or negative euthanasia, the refusal of life-prolonging therapy. In such cases, the patient's refusal of life-prolonging therapy is seen to be a right that derives from personal freedom, or at least from a zone of privacy into which there are no good grounds for social intervention.

Again, none of these considerations applies directly to the euthanasia of young children, because they cannot participate in such decisions. Whatever else pediatric, in particular neonatal, euthanasia involves, it surely involves issues different from those of adult euthanasia. Since infants and small children cannot commit suicide, their right to assisted suicide is difficult to pose. The difference between the euthanasia of young children and that of adults resides in the difference between children and adults. The difference, in fact, raises the troublesome question of whether young children are persons, or at least whether they are persons in the sense in which adults are. Answering that question will resolve in part at least the right of others to decide whether a young child should live or die and whether he should receive life-prolonging treatment.

The Status of Children

Adults belong to themselves in the sense that they are rational and free and therefore responsible for their actions. Adults are *sui juris*. Young children, though, are neither self-possessed nor responsible. While adults exist in and for themselves, as self-directive and self-conscious beings, young children, especially newborn infants, exist for their families and those who love them. They are not, nor can they in any sense be, responsible for themselves. If being a person is to be a responsible agent, a bearer of rights and duties, children are not persons in a strict sense. They are, rather, persons in a social sense: others must act on their behalf and bear responsibility for them. They are, as it were, entities defined by their place in social roles (for example, mother–child, family–child) rather than beings that define themselves as persons, that is, in and through themselves. Young children live as persons in and through the care of those who are responsible for them, and those responsible for them exercise the children's rights on their behalf. In this sense children belong to families in ways that most adults do not. They exist in and through their family and society.

Treating young children with respect has, then, a sense different from treating adults with respect. One can respect neither a newborn infant's or very young child's wishes nor its freedom. In fact, a newborn infant or young child is more an entity that is valued highly because it will grow to be a person and because it plays a social role as if it were a person. That is, a small child is treated as if it were a person in social roles such as mother–child and family–child relationships, though strictly speaking the child is in no way capable of claiming or being responsible for the rights imputed to it. All the rights and duties of the child are exercises and "held in trust" by others for a future time and for a person yet to develop.

Medical decisions to treat or not to treat a neonate or small child often turn on the probability and cost of achieving that future status—a developed personal life. The usual practice of letting anencephalic children (who congenitally lack all or most of the brain) die can be understood as a decision based on the absence of the possibility of achieving a personal life. The practice of refusing treatment to at least some children born with meningomyelocele can be justified through a similar, but more utilitarian, calculus. In the case of anencephalic children one might argue that care for them as persons is futile since they will never be persons. In the case

of a child with meningomyelocele, one might argue that when the cost of cure would likely be very high and the probable lifestyle open to attainment very truncated, there is not a positive duty to make a large investment of money and suffering. One should note that the cost here must include not only financial costs but also the anxiety and suffering that prolonged and uncertain treatment of the child would cause the parents.

This further raises the issue of the scope of positive duties not only when there is no person present in a strict sense, but when the likelihood of a full human life is also very uncertain. Clinical and parental judgment may and should be guided by the expected life-style and the cost (in parental and societal pain and money) of its attainment. The decision about treatment, however, belongs properly to the parents because the child belongs to them in a sense that it does not belong to anyone else, even to itself. The care and raising of the child falls to the parents, and when considerable cost and little prospect of reasonable success are present, the parents may properly decide against life-prolonging treatment.

The physician's role is to present sufficient information in a usable form to the parents to aid them in making a decision. The accent is on the absence of a positive duty to treat in the presence of severe inconvenience (costs) to the parents; treatment that is very costly is not obligatory. What is suggested here is a general notion that there is never a duty to engage in extraordinary treatment and that "extraordinary" can be defined in terms of costs. This argument concerns children (1) whose future quality of life is likely to be seriously compromised and (2) whose present treatment would be very costly. The issue is that of the circumstances under which parents would not be obliged to take on severe burdens on behalf of their children or those circumstances under which society would not be so obliged. The argument should hold as well for those cases where the expected future life would surely be of normal quality, though its attainment would be extremely costly. The fact of little likelihood of success in attaining a normal life for the child makes decisions to do without treatment more plausible because the hope of success is even more remote and therefore the burden borne by parents or society becomes in that sense more extraordinary. But very high costs themselves could be a sufficient criterion, though in actual cases judgments in that regard would be very difficult when a normal life could be expected.

The decisions in these matters correctly lie in the hands of the parents, because it is primarily in terms of the family that children exist and develop—until children become persons strictly, they are persons in virtue of their social roles. As long as parents do not unjustifiably neglect the humans in those roles so that the value and purpose of that role (that is, child) stands to be eroded (thus endangering other children), society need not intervene. In short, parents may decide for or against the treatment of their severely deformed children.

However, society has a right to intervene and protect children for whom parents refuse care (including treatment) when such care does not constitute a severe burden and when it is likely that the child could be brought to a good quality of life. Obviously, "severe burden" and "good quality of life" will be difficult to define and their meanings will vary, just as it is always difficult to say when grains of sand dropped on a table constitute a heap. At most, though, society need only intervene when the grains clearly do not constitute a heap, that is, when it is clear that the burden is light and the chance of a good quality of life for the child is high. A small child's dependence on his parents is so essential that society need intervene only when the absence of intervention would lead to the role "child" being undermined. Society must value mother–child and family–child relationships and should intervene only in cases where (1) neglect is unreasonable and therefore would undermine respect and care for children, or (2) where societal intervention would prevent children from suffering unnecessary pain.

The Injury of Continued Existence

But there is another viewpoint that must be considered: that of the child or even the person that the child might become. It might be argued that the child has a right not to have its life prolonged. The idea that forcing existence on a child would be wrong is a difficult notion, which, if true, would serve to amplify the foregoing argument. Such an argument would allow the construal of the issue in terms of the perspective of the child, that is, in terms of a duty not to treat in circumstances where treatment would only prolong suffering. In particular, it would at least

give a framework for a decision to stop treatment in cases where, though the costs of treatment are not high, the child's existence would be characterized by severe pain and deprivation.

A basis for speaking of continuing existence as an injury to the child is suggested by the proposed legal concept of "wrongful life." A number of suits have been initiated in the United States and in other countries on the grounds that life or existence itself is, under certain circumstances, a tort or injury to the living person. Although thus far all such suits have ultimately failed, some have succeeded in their initial stages. Two examples may be instructive. In each case the ability to receive recompense for the injury (the tort) presupposed the existence of the individual, whose existence was itself the injury. In one case a suit was initiated on behalf of a child against his father alleging that his father's siring him out of wedlock was an injury to the child. In another case a suit on behalf of a child born of an inmate of a state mental hospital impregnated by rape in that institution was brought against the state of New York. The suit was brought on the grounds that being born with such historical antecedents was itself an injury for which recovery was due. Both cases presupposed that nonexistence would have been preferable to the conditions under which the person born was forced to live.

The suits for tort for wrongful life raise the issue not only of when it would be preferable not to have been born but also of when it would be *wrong* to cause a person to be born. This implies that someone should have judged that it would have been preferable for the child never to have had existence, never to have been in the position to judge that the particular circumstances of life were intolerable. Further, it implies that the person's existence under those circumstances should have been prevented and that, not having been prevented, life was not a gift but an injury. The concept of tort for wrongful life raises an issue concerning the responsibility for giving another person existence, namely the notion that giving life is not always necessarily a good and justifiable action. Instead, in certain circumstances, so it has been argued, one may have a duty *not* to give existence to another person. This concept involves the claim that certain qualities of life have a negative value, making life an injury, not a gift; it involves, in short, a concept of human accountability and responsibility for human life. It contrasts with the notion that life is a gift of God and thus similar to other "acts of God" (that is, events for which no man is accountable). The concept thus signals the fact that humans can now control reproduction and that where rational control is possible humans are accountable. That is, the expansion of human capabilities has resulted in an expansion of human responsibilities such that one must now decide when and under what circumstances persons will come into existence.

The concept of tort for wrongful life is transferable in part to the painfully compromised existence of children who can only have their life prolonged for a short, painful, and marginal existence. The concept suggests that allowing life to be prolonged under such circumstances would itself be an injury of the person whose painful and severely compromised existence would be made to continue. In fact, it suggests that there is a duty not to prolong life if it can be determined to have a substantial negative value for the person involved. Such issues are moot in the case of adults, who can and should decide for themselves. But small children cannot make such a choice. For them it is an issue of justifying prolonging life under circumstances of painful and compromised existence. Or, put differently, such cases indicate the need to develop social canons to allow a decent death for children for whom the only possibility is protracted, painful suffering.

I do not mean to imply that one should develop a new basis for civil damages. In the field of medicine, the need is to recognize an ethical category, a concept of wrongful continuance of existence, not a new legal right. The concept of injury for continuance of existence, the proposed analogue of the concept of tort for wrongful life, presupposes that life can be of a negative value such that the medical maxim *primum non nocere* ("first do no harm") would require not sustaining life.

The idea of responsibility for acts that sustain or prolong life is cardinal to the notion that one should not under certain circumstances further prolong the life of a child. Unlike adults, children cannot decide with regard to euthanasia (positive or negative), and if more than a utilitarian justification is sought, it must be sought in a duty not to inflict life on another person in circumstances where that life would be painful and futile. This position must rest on the facts that (1) medicine now can cause the prolongation of the life of seriously deformed children who in the past would have died young and that (2) it is not clear that life so prolonged is a good for the child. Further, the choice is made not on the basis of costs to the parents or to society but on the basis of the child's suffering and compromised existence.

The difficulty lies in determining what makes life not worth living for a child. Answers could never be clear. It seems reasonable, however, that the life of children with diseases that involve pain and no hope of survival should not be prolonged. In the case of Tay-Sachs disease (a disease marked by a progressive increase in spasticity and dementia usually leading to death at age three or four), one can hardly imagine that the terminal stages of spastic reaction to stimuli and great difficulty in swallowing are at all pleasant to the child (even insofar as it can only minimally perceive its circumstances). If such a child develops aspiration pneumonia and is treated, it can reasonably be said that to prolong its life is to inflict suffering. Other diseases give fairly clear portraits of lives not worth living: for example, Lesch-Nyhan disease, which is marked by mental retardation and compulsive self-mutilation.

The issue is more difficult in the case of children with disease for whom the prospects for normal intelligence and a fair lifestyle do exist, but where these chances are remote and their realization expensive. Children born with meningomyelocele present this dilemma. Imagine, for example, a child that falls within Lorber's fifth category (an IQ of sixty or less, sometimes blind, subject to fits, and always incontinent). Such a child has little prospect of anything approaching a normal life, and there is a good chance of its dying even with treatment. But such judgments are statistical. And if one does not treat such children, some will still survive and, as John Freeman indicates, be worse off if not treated. In such cases one is in a dilemma. If one always treats, one must justify extending the life of those who will ultimately die anyway and in the process subjecting them to the morbidity of multiple surgical procedures. How remote does the prospect of a good life have to be in order not to be worth great pain and expense? It is probably best to decide, in the absence of a positive duty to treat, on the basis of the cost and suffering to parents and society. But, as Freeman argues, the prospect of prolonged or even increased suffering raises the issue of active euthanasia.

If the child is not a person strictly, and if death is inevitable and expediting it would diminish the child's pain prior to death, then it would seem to follow that, all else being equal, a decision for active euthanasia would be permissible, even obligatory. The difficulty lies with "all else being equal," for it is doubtful that active euthanasia could be established as a practice without eroding and endangering children generally, since, as John Lorber has pointed out, children cannot speak in their own behalf. Thus although there is no argument in principle against the active euthanasia of small children, there could be an argument against such practices based on questions of prudence. To put it another way, even though one might have a duty to hasten the death of a particular child, one's duty to protect children in general could override that first duty. The issue of active euthanasia turns in the end on whether it would have social consequences that refraining would not, on whether (1) it is possible to establish procedural safeguards for limited active euthanasia and (2) whether such practices would have a significant adverse effect on the treatment of small children in general. But since these are procedural issues dependent on sociological facts, they are not open to an answer within the confines of this article. In any event, the concept of the injury of continued existence provides a basis for the justification of the passive euthanasia of small children—a practice already widespread and somewhat established in our society—beyond the mere absence of a positive duty to treat.

Conclusion

Though the lack of certainty concerning questions such as the prognosis of particular patients and the social consequence of active euthanasia of children prevents a clear answer to all the issues raised by the euthanasia of infants, it would seem that this much can be maintained: (1) Since children are not persons strictly but exist in and through their families, parents are the appropriate ones to decide whether or not to treat a deformed child when (a) there is not only little likelihood of full human life but also great likelihood of suffering if the life is prolonged, or (b) when the cost of prolonging life is very great. Such decisions must be made in consort with a physician who can accurately give estimates of cost and prognosis and who will be able to help the parents with the consequences of their decision. (2) It is reasonable to speak of a duty not to treat a small child when such treatment will only prolong a painful life or would in any event lead to a painful death. Though this does not by any means answer all the questions, it does point out an important fact— that medicine's duty is not always to prolong life doggedly but sometimes is quite the contrary.

DECISION SCENARIOS

The questions following each decision scenario are intended to prompt reflection and discussion. In deciding how to answer them, you should consider the information provided in the Social Context and Case Presentations, as well as in the Briefing Session. You should also make use of the ethical theories and principles presented in Part VI: Foundations of Bioethics, and the arguments offered in the relevant readings in this chapter.

DECISION SCENARIO 1

Wrongful Life?

Susan Roth was looking forward to being a mother. She had taken leave from her retail job three months before her baby was due so that she could spend the time getting everything ready. Her husband, David, was equally enthusiastic about becoming a father, and the couple spent many hours happily speculating about what their first child would be like.

"I hope they don't mix her up with some other baby," Ms. Roth said to her husband as she was wheeled into the delivery room.

She didn't know yet that there would be little chance of confusion. The Roth infant was born with severe anatomical deformities. Her arms and legs had failed to develop, her skull was misshapen, and her face distorted. Her large intestine emptied through her vagina, and she had no muscular control over her bladder.

When she was told about these conditions, Ms. Roth said, "We cannot let her live, for her sake and ours." On the day she left the hospital, Susan Roth took a bottle of baby formula and mixed in a lethal dose of a tranquilizer that had been procured by

David Roth. She then fed the bottle to the child who died later that evening.

Roth and her husband were charged with infanticide. During the court proceedings, the Roths admitted to the killing but said they were satisfied that they had done the right thing. "I knew I could not let my baby live like that," Ms. Roth said. "If only she had been mentally disabled, she would not have known her fate. But she had a healthy brain. She would have known. Placing her in an institution might have helped me, but it wouldn't have helped her."

The jury, after deliberating for two hours, found the Roths guilty of the charge.

1. Would the Roth baby's situation satisfy the criteria that would allow the Groningen Protocol to be followed?

2. Does the unimpaired mental capacity of her child support Roth's claim that the killing was justifiable? Might unimpaired intelligence make the "injury of continued existence" even greater, as she contends?

3. On what grounds might the killing of the Roth infant be condemned as morally wrong?

4. Could the best-interest-of-the-infant standard offer any support for the Roths' actions?

DECISION SCENARIO 2

Another Ashley?

Brookhaven, as we will call it, is a long-term care facility in the Washington metropolitan area. Most of Brookhaven's patients are in residence there for only a few months; either they succumb to their ailments or they recover sufficiently to return to their homes.

But for some patients, death is not imminent nor is recovery a possibility. They linger on at Brookhaven, day after day and year after year. Juli Meyers is such a patient, although that is not really her name.

Juli is seventeen and has been in Brookhaven for six years. Before Brookhaven, there were other institutions. In fact, Juli has spent most of her life in hospitals and special-care facilities. But Juli does not seem to be aware of any of this.

At Brookhaven, she spends her days lying in a bed surrounded with barred metal panels. The bars have been padded with foam rubber. Although most of the time Juli is curled tightly in a fetal position, she sometimes flails around wildly and makes guttural sounds. The padding keeps her from injuring herself.

Juli's body is thin and underdeveloped, with sticklike arms and legs. She is blind and deaf and has no control over her bowels and bladder. She is totally dependent on others to clean her and care for her. She can swallow the food put into her mouth, but she cannot feed herself. She makes no response to the people or events around her.

There is no hope that Juli will walk or talk, laugh or cry, or show any other signs of awareness. She suffers from one of the forms of Schilder's disease, which causes the nerve fibers that make up the central nervous system to degenerate. The cause of the degeneration is not fully known, nor is it known how to halt the process. The condition is irreversible, and Juli will never experience improvement in her health or cognition.

At birth Juli seemed perfectly normal and healthy, but at three months she began to lose her sight and hearing. She made the vocalizations typical of babies less and less frequently. By the end of her first year, she made no sounds at all and was completely blind and deaf. Also, she was losing control of her muscles, and her head lolled on her shoulders as if her neck were broken.

Juli became highly susceptible to infections, and more than once she came down with pneumonia. One time, when she was on the critical list, a specialist suggested to her mother that it would be pointless to continue treating her. Even if she recovered from the pneumonia, she would remain hopelessly impaired. Her mother, Imogen Meyers, angrily rejected the suggestion and insisted that everything possible be done to save Juli's life.

Although not wealthy, the family bore the high cost of hospitalization and treatments. Ms. Meyers devoted herself to caring for Juli at home, and the other four children in the family received little of her or their father's attention. Eventually, Ms. Meyers began to suffer from severe depression, and when Juli was eight and a half, her parents decided that she would have to be placed in an institution. Since then, Juli has changed little. No one expects her to change. Her mother visits her three times a month and brings Juli freshly laundered and ironed clothes.

1. What arguments can be offered to support Ms. Meyers's decision not to allow Juli to die?

2. Are there any grounds for supposing that Juli is being made to suffer "the injury of continued existence"?

3. Could Julie be regarded as an appropriate candidate for the "Ashley Treatment"?

4. Is it possible to justify using society's limited medical resources to keep Juli alive?

5. Evaluate the following argument: Opponents of abortion oppose spending public funds for abortion on the grounds that they (the opponents) are being forced to support murder, which is a serious moral wrong. Keeping Juli alive is a serious moral wrong. Therefore, no public funds should be used for this purpose.

DECISION SCENARIO 3

No Food, No Water?

Irene Towers had been a nurse for almost twelve years; for the last three of those years she had worked in the neonatal unit of Halifax County Hospital. It was a job she loved. Even when the infants were ill or required special medical or surgical treatment, she found the job of caring for them immensely rewarding. She knew that without her efforts many of the babies would die.

Irene Towers was on duty the night that conjoined twins were born to Corrine Couchers and brought at once to the neonatal unit. Even Irene, with all her experience, was distressed to see them. The twin boys were joined at their midsections in a way that made it impossible to separate them surgically. Because of the position of the single liver and the kidneys, not even one twin could be saved at the expense of the life of the other. Moreover, both children were severely deformed, with incompletely developed arms and legs and misshapen heads. As best as the neurologist could determine, both had suffered severe brain damage.

The father of the children was Dr. Harold Couchers, a slightly built man in his early thirties who was a specialist in internal medicine with a private practice.

Irene felt sorry for him the night the children were born. When he went into the room with the obstetrician to examine his sons, he had already been told what to expect. He showed no signs of distress as he stood over the slat-sided crib, but the corners of his mouth were drawn tight, and his face was empty of expression. Most strange for a physician, Irene thought—he merely looked at the children and did not touch them.

Later that evening, Irene saw Couchers sitting in the small conference room at the end of the hall with Dr. Cara Rosen, Corrine Couchers's obstetrician. They were talking earnestly and quietly when Irene passed the open door. Then, while she was looking over the assignment sheet at the nursing station, the two of them walked up. Dr. Rosen took a chart from the rack behind the desk and made a notation. After returning the chart, she shook hands with Couchers, and he left.

It was not until the end of her shift that Irene read the chart; Dr. Rosen's note said that the twin boys were to be given neither food nor water. At first Irene couldn't believe the order. But when she asked her supervisor, she was told that the supervisor had telephoned Dr. Rosen and that the obstetrician had confirmed the order.

Irene said nothing to the supervisor or to anyone else, but she made her own decision. She believed it was wrong to let the children die. They deserved every chance to fight for their lives, and she was going to help them the way she had helped hundreds of other babies in the unit.

For the next week and a half, Irene saw to it that the children were given water and fed the standard infant formula. She did it all herself, on her own initiative. Although some of the other nurses on the floor saw what she was doing, none of them said anything to her. One even smiled and nodded to her when she saw Irene feeding the children.

Apparently someone else also disapproved of the order to let the twins die. Thirteen days after their birth, an investigator from the state Family Welfare Agency appeared in the neonatal ward. The rumor was that her visit had been prompted by an anonymous telephone call.

Late in the afternoon of the day of that visit, the conjoined twins were made temporary wards of the agency, and the orders on the chart were changed—the twins were now to be given food and water. On the next day, the county prosecutor's office announced publicly that it would conduct an investigation of the situation and decide whether criminal charges should be brought against Dr. Couchers or members of the hospital staff.

Irene was sure that she had done the right thing. Nevertheless, she was glad to be relieved of the responsibility.

1. Is there a morally relevant distinction between not treating (and allowing to die) and not providing such minimal needs as food and water (and allowing to die)?

2. What line of ethical reasoning might support the actions taken by Irene Towers?

3. Did Towers exceed the limits of her responsibility, or did she act in a morally heroic way? Why?

DECISION SCENARIO 4

The Messenger Case

On February 8, 1984, Traci Messenger had an emergency caesarean section at the E. W. Sparrow Hospital in East Lansing, Michigan, and her son, Michael, was delivered after only twenty-five-weeks gestation—fifteen weeks premature. Michael weighed less than two pounds, was very likely to have serious brain damage, and was given a 30 to 50 percent chance of survival.

Before Traci Messenger's surgery, Michael's father, Dr. Gregory Messenger, a dermatologist on the staff of the hospital, had spoken with his wife's physicians and requested that no extraordinary measure be taken to prolong the child's life. However, after the child was born, the neonatologist, Dr. Padmoni Karna, insisted that the baby be given respiratory support and diagnostic tests.

About an hour after Michael was delivered, Dr. Messenger went into the child's room and asked the nurses to leave. He then disconnected the life-support system, setting off an alarm. The child died, and the hospital called the police. A short time later, the county prosecutor, Donald E. Martin, charged Dr. Messenger with manslaughter.

Although most states, including Michigan, allow parents to decide to withdraw life support from their ailing child, Martin said he had decided to prosecute because Dr. Messenger had not waited for the results of medical tests. "The father appeared to make a unilateral decision to end life for his infant son," Martin said.

Messenger's attorney replied that Dr. Messenger had several warnings of severe medical problems during delivery and immediately after birth. Monitoring of the baby suggested that he was not receiving sufficient oxygen and would be severely brain damaged. Blood tests at birth indicated that the baby had a 14 percent blood oxygen level, and, as a physician testified at a preliminary hearing, five minutes at a less-than-50-percent level is enough to damage the brain. "The parents made a decision when the outcome was so grim and the prognosis was so bad; they indicated 'we do not want this intervention.' I think it was incumbent on hospital personnel to honor their directive, and they didn't do that."

Dr. Karna said that she would have agreed to remove the life support, given the blood-test results, but that Dr. Messenger had acted without consulting her.

1. Would the Messenger infant have been likely to suffer "the injury of continued existence"?

2. On what grounds might one support the claim that the infant should be treated?

3. Suppose that after hearing the test results the parents and Dr. Karna disagreed as to whether the infant should be treated. Whose opinion should be decisive?

4. Would considering the "best interest" of the infant be of help in resolving a conflict between the Messengers and Dr. Karna?

DECISION SCENARIO 5

Pointless Suffering?

Ginny Rutten was born with a severe form of a genetic condition called epidermolysis bullosa. The disease causes the skin and mucous membranes to blister and tear—often down to the layer of fat and muscle. Ginny cannot drink, because the lining of her mouth is blistered and swollen, and so can take no nourishment by mouth. Areas of her skin have eroded, producing patches of raw flesh resembling third-degree burns. Because of the breakdown of her skin, she experiences almost constant pain, and the dehydration that skin breakdown produces leads to electrolyte imbalances that put her at risk of heart arrhythmia and death.

Ginny has a disease for which there is no cure and not even a treatment to prevent the blistering and peeling of her skin. In addition to enduring the pain from skin loss, children with the disease often lose their fingers and suffer from a drawing up—contracture—of their arms and legs from scarring. Most people with epidermolysis bullosa need total care their entire lives, which are likely to last only a few months or years. No case of a cure or even a lengthy remission is on record.

Ginny screams in pain for much of the time she is awake. She is sedated by a morphine drip and sleeps in brief cycles. Her physicians and the hospital ethics committee are debating whether or not to feed Ginny artificially, either by an IV drip or through a surgical opening into her stomach, and so keep her alive. Her parents ask that she not be fed or hydrated artificially, and be allowed to die.

1. How would Ginny's case be classified within the categories of the Groningen Protocol?

2. What conditions must Ginny's case meet to satisfy the requirements spelled out in the Groningen Protocol?

3. Can Ginny's case be regarded as one involving the injury of continued existence?

4. If Ginny is neurologically healthy, does this imply that she ought to be treated, even if treating her only prolongs her pain?

5. We routinely euthanize animals to protect them from pointless suffering which cannot be relieved. What are possible arguments for and against treating some impaired infants the same way?

Euthanasia and Physician-Assisted Death

CHAPTER CONTENTS

CASES AND CONTEXTS

CASE PRESENTATION
Brittany Maynard and Physician-Assisted Death

Brittany Maynard loved her life. She was twenty-nine, had been married for a year, and was starting a career as an elementary school teacher in the San Francisco Bay Area. She was an enthusiastic world traveler, teaching at orphanages in Nepal and climbing Mount Kilimanjaro. She and her husband, Dan Diaz, had recently started trying to have a child.

But on January 1, 2014, Brittany Maynard was diagnosed with terminal brain cancer. For months, she had been experiencing headaches that her doctor had diagnosed as migraines. After a severe episode over the New Year's holiday, a brain scan revealed she had a grade 2 astrocytoma tumor and Maynard was told she had about ten years to live. To try to prevent the tumor from growing, her physicians opened her skull and performed a partial resection of her left temporal lobe. But the cancer soon returned. In April, Maynard's diagnosis was changed to a grade 4 glioblastoma—the most aggressive form of brain cancer—and she was given a prognosis of six months.

Maynard's options were limited. Glioblastomas are highly invasive, and the tools her physicians had left, such as full-brain radiation, involved brutal side effects and no chance of a cure.

"After months of research, my family and I reached a heartbreaking conclusion," Maynard later wrote. "There is no treatment that would save my life and the recommended treatments would have destroyed the time I had left." Maynard investigated hospice care, but soon realized that it might do little to prevent the outcome she feared most: lingering for weeks or months, possibly in acute pain, while her family coped with her seizures, personality changes, and progressive loss of cognition, continence, and motor skills.

"Because the rest of my body is young and healthy, I am likely to physically hang on for a long time even though cancer is eating my mind," she wrote. "And my family would have to watch that."

So Maynard began to investigate a third option. In 1995, Oregon voters passed a "Death with Dignity"

ballot measure, which allows terminally ill Oregonians to self-administer a lethal dose of barbiturates, specifically prescribed by their doctors. Patients must have a prognosis of six months or less, must be mentally competent, and must make repeated requests for the prescription. Maynard wanted to be sure she had an option "to end my dying process if it becomes unbearable." So she and her family decided to uproot their lives in California and move to Oregon. She also decided to make her decision public, writing an Op-Ed for CNN and producing two videos that have been viewed over thirteen million times on YouTube.

"I've had the medication for weeks," she wrote in her Op-Ed. "I am not suicidal. If I were, I would have consumed that medication long ago. I do not want to die. But I am dying. And I want to die on my own terms."

Death with Dignity

Brittany Maynard quickly became the new face of the "aid-in-dying" movement, drawing both criticism and praise. But the movement itself is not new. Since the 1870s, Americans have debated whether health care providers should be able to help terminally ill patients hasten their deaths, a practice which critics have often called "physician-assisted suicide" and view as both immoral and socially dangerous. Proponents see it as an act of autonomy and self-preservation in the face of imminent death. They thus try to distinguish it from both suicide and the voluntary active euthanasia that has been allowed in the Netherlands for over thirty years and has been more recently legalized in Belgium, Colombia, and Luxembourg. (See Briefing Session for more on various forms of euthanasia.)

To better understand Brittany Maynard's story and the controversy around physician-assisted death (PAD), it will be useful to look more closely at the Oregon Death with

Dignity Act, which has served as the model for similar laws in Washington and Vermont.

The Law. Oregon's 1994 "Written Request for Medication to End One's Life in a Humane and Dignified Manner," or Death with Dignity Act, was the first physician-assisted death measure passed by any state. The law does not permit a physician to play an active role in ending a patient's life. The major provision of the measure is that it allows physicians to prescribe lethal drugs for terminally ill patients without risking criminal prosecution.

The law spells out a set of conditions that must be met by patients and physicians:

1. A primary care physician and a consulting physician must both agree that the patient has six months or less to live.

2. The patient must make two oral requests (at least forty-eight hours apart) for drugs to use to terminate his or her life.

3. The patient must wait at least fifteen days after the initial oral request, then make a written request to the physician.

4. If either physician thinks the patient has a mental disorder or is suffering impaired judgment from depression, they must recommend the patient for counseling.

5. The patient can terminate the request at any time during the process.

6. The physician prescribing the drugs must inform the patient of such feasible alternatives as hospice care, comfort care, and pain control.

Under the law, a physician is not permitted to assist a patient to die by any means more active than prescribing a drug that can cause death and indicating the manner in which the drug can be used.

Legal Controversy

In 1994, the Oregon law was approved by a slim margin of 52 to 48 percent of voters. Opponents of the law immediately challenged it in court. The legal battle took three years; then, in 1997, the opponents mounted an effort to have it repealed through a voter initiative. The effort failed, and the law was approved once more—this time by 60 percent of the voters.

Despite voter approval, physicians were initially uncertain about what might happen to them if they fulfilled a patient's request for a lethal prescription. Responding to pressure from conservative lawmakers, the U.S. Drug Enforcement Administration (DEA) initially threatened to impose sanctions on any physician who wrote such prescriptions. Attorney General Janet Reno overruled the DEA's threat in 1998, arguing that drug laws were intended to block illicit drug dealing and that there was no evidence that Congress ever meant for the DEA to play a role in medical practice.

In November 2001, Attorney General John Ashcroft reversed the course taken by Reno, holding that "prescribing, dispensing or administering federally controlled substances to assist suicide" is "not a legitimate medical purpose." Ashcroft's successor, Alberto Gonzales, accepted the same view. In response, Oregon filed suit against the Justice Department, and eventually the case went to the U.S. Supreme Court. In January 2006, the Court upheld the decisions of two lower courts and ruled 6–3 that the Justice Department had acted without legal authority in attempting to restrict the actions of Oregon physicians.

The ruling was made on the narrow ground that the regulation of medical practice is a state, not a federal, matter. The ruling left open the possibility that Congress could pass a law explicitly forbidding the prescribing of drugs by physicians to help patients hasten their deaths. However, because the ruling held that the regulation of medical practice is a state issue, it also opened the way for other states to pass assisted-death laws.

In March 2009, Washington became the second state to pass a "Death with Dignity" ballot initiative, with 60 percent of the vote. The law is modeled closely on the Oregon law, including the age requirement, waiting period, and certification by two physicians that the patient has no more than six months to live. In May 2013, Vermont enacted a similar law, this time through the state legislature. Courts in both Montana and New Mexico have ruled that it is not illegal for a physician to prescribe lethal medications for terminally ill patients under certain conditions, although no regulatory mechanism has been put in place in either state. Bills similar to the Vermont law have been introduced in at least seven other states.

Ethical Controversy

Objections to physician-assisted death have tended to fall into three general categories: those concerned with the professional and ethical obligations of physicians, those concerned with the risk of a "slippery slope" toward abuse, and those concerned with the preservation of life as a primary value.

Professional Obligations. Critics of PAD often point out that physicians take an oath not to knowingly harm patients and argue that widespread adoption of the practice would undermine patients' trust that their doctors are committed to saving their lives.

Defenders of PAD such as Brittany Maynard have argued that such objections are expressions of medical paternalism and that PAD is a logical extension of recognizing principles of patient autonomy and informed consent. They argue that medical emphasis on extending life without adequate concern for the quality of that life does its own kind of harm. Defenders argue that there is little moral or practical difference between PAD and the widely accepted ethical and legal rights of patients to refuse life-saving care and of physicians to administer pain-relieving drugs that may have a secondary effect that causes death (so called "indirect euthanasia.")

Both defenders and critics generally acknowledge that PAD is already practiced in the forty-five states where it is illegal, although they often disagree about the extent. Studies in the late 1990s showed that between 3 and 18 percent of physicians have honored requests to assist terminally ill patients in dying. A 1998 investigation by the *New England Journal of Medicine* found that about 6 percent of physicians had honored such requests, and a 2003 investigation found about 16 percent of requests being honored among critical care specialists. These studies have found physicians not only prescribing lethal doses of medication but also administering lethal injections. They have also found that, in general, the patients involved meet the criteria for PAD set out by the Oregon law, although many appear to have been depressed about their situations. There are also widespread reports of hospice and palliative care providers offering morphine to the families of dying patients with suggestions that they should "not worry about the dose" and "just give as much as needed."

Opponents of PAD legalization argue that it should remain an underground practice, perhaps morally appropriate (and not prosecuted) in exceptional cases, but also not officially recognized (and possibly encouraged) by law. Defenders agree that PAD should be an exception after all other avenues have been pursued, but argue it should be brought out of the shadows so it can be regulated.

Slippery Slope. Critics of PAD contend that widespread legalization of the practice would lead to abuses. They argue that it would put additional pressure on the poor and the elderly, who are already undervalued by society, to end their lives so as not to be a burden on others. Some older women who think of themselves primarily as caregivers and helpmates might be particularly subject to such pressures. There is also concern that PAD might let physicians simply bypass the difficult and expensive work of providing effective hospice and palliative care to control the suffering of terminally ill patients. In addition, disability rights groups such as "Not Dead Yet," as well as advocates for the mentally ill, have raised concerns that PAD could extend beyond those with terminal diagnoses to the depressed, the disabled, or anyone else whose life physicians could be convinced is "not worth living."

Defenders of PAD argue that the Oregon experience shows that it is possible to legalize the practice without sliding down the slippery slope. One of the requirements of the law is that all physician-assisted deaths must be tracked and reported to the police. In the past seventeen years, 1,327 Oregonians have received prescriptions under the law and 859 have died as a result of taking them. The majority of these were well-educated, well-insured, and financially secure, and 90 percent were enrolled in hospice. Over half were men. The primary reasons patients cited for taking advantage of the law appear to have mirrored those of Brittany Maynard: loss of autonomy, dignity, and the ability to participate in activities that made life enjoyable. (Far fewer were concerned with being a burden on others.) While identifying clinical depression in terminally ill patients is difficult, studies have suggested that those who take advantage of the law are no more likely to be depressed than others with terminal diagnoses. Finally, defenders point out that PAD represents less than two-tenths of 1 percent of deaths in Oregon, and that over a third of those who receive prescriptions decide not to use them.

Although many critics acknowledge that the Oregon law has not yet produced evidence of abusive practices, they point to disturbing examples from the voluntary active euthanasia programs in Holland and Belgium. Dozens of cases have been reported in those countries in which patients have sought and received euthanasia for depression, mental illness, and other non-lethal conditions. In addition, data from the 1990s found a high percentage of "nonvoluntary" euthanasia deaths, in which patients had become unconscious or incompetent and could thus not reiterate their requests to die. The number of people euthanized in both Belgium and Holland has more than doubled in the past five years, to the point that one out of thirty-five Dutch people now dies with medical assistance. Defenders of U.S. PAD laws say comparisons with these European programs are inappropriate, since in the United States PAD can only be self-administered by competent patients, and that the safeguards against abuse are much stronger.

Preservation of Life. A different group of critics argue that by hastening their own deaths, terminally ill PAD patients devalue life itself. These critics hold that there is meaning and value to be derived even from terrible suffering and that the dying process should not be cut short. Such was the perspective of Kara Tippetts, the wife of a Colorado pastor who was herself dying of cancer in 2014 and wrote an open letter to Brittany Maynard.

"You have been told a lie," Tippetts wrote to Maynard. "A horrible lie, that your dying will not be beautiful. That the suffering will be too great." Others, such as Pastor David Watson of Calvary Chapel in Staten Island, criticized Maynard on the grounds that "God determined when she would be born and God should determine when she's going to die." Vatican officials also condemned Maynard's decision to seek PAD, calling it "an absurdity" that involved "saying no to life and to everything it means."

Defenders of PAD grant that this is a perfectly legitimate perspective to have on one's own death, but it is illegitimate to try to impose it on others. Just as we no longer force terminally ill patients to stay on ventilators or dialysis machines against their will, we should not prevent them from self-administering lethal drugs to end their lives. In their view, letting someone die by removing a ventilator is no different than writing them a barbiturate prescription. Both are means by which autonomous patients can choose to hasten their deaths.

Are PAD Laws Necessary?

Some argue PAD laws such as Oregon's are not needed, precisely because society has already recognized patients' right to refuse treatment and thereby hasten death through a variety of legal decisions and mechanisms.

In 1990, the Supreme Court implicitly acknowledged a "right to die," by allowing the withdrawal of life-sustaining treatment when "clear and compelling evidence" shows that this reflects an individual's wish. (See Case Presentation: The Cruzan Case later in this chapter.) As a direct result of this decision, Congress passed the Patient Self-Determination Act, which requires hospitals to inform patients that they have the right to refuse or discontinue treatment, and can put their wishes into practice through advance directives and durable powers of attorney.

Proponents of PAD laws acknowledge that the legal right to refuse treatment, combined with hospice or palliative care, may be sufficient for many, perhaps most, terminally ill patients. But they also point out that terminally ill people who decide to let death take its course are often frustrated in carrying out their wishes. Surveys of physicians and other health care workers show that many are not aware of laws allowing them to withhold or discontinue such care as mechanical ventilation, kidney dialysis, and feeding tubes. Many believe that once a treatment has been started, it is illegal to discontinue it. Courts have repeatedly upheld the right of individuals to decide that they do not want to be fed or hydrated at a certain point in their treatment, yet in one survey 42 percent of health care workers rejected this right as an option patients could select. Finally, a number of studies have shown that patients' *advance directives* about their care—such as living wills and durable powers of attorney—are frequently disregarded by physicians, lost by institutions, or deemed too vague to guide definite actions. (For more on advance directives, see this chapter's Briefing Session.)

Despite the efforts of patients to control what happens to them at the end of their lives, they may be forced to accept care decisions made by physicians or nurses in accordance with their own values or institutional policies. Patients' wishes may also be overruled by family members who convince health care providers to disregard advance directives—sometimes with the threat of lawsuits. Thus, laws such as those in Oregon, Washington, and Vermont are viewed by many as the only way patients can be sure that they can claim autonomy and informed consent in the final days of their lives.

Public Opinion, Medical Opinion

Roughly 7 in 10 Americans say they believe that physicians should be allowed to "legally end a patient's life by some painless means," a question that has had majority support since the mid-1990s. The majority support drops to 58 percent, however, when the question is framed as whether physicians should be allowed to "assist the patient to commit suicide."

Physicians, perhaps not surprisingly, have been less enthusiastic about laws that might seem to contradict their professional obligations and underscore the limits of their ability to fight disease. A 2013 poll of *New England Journal of Medicine* readers found that 65 percent opposed PAD and official AMA policy still finds it "fundamentally incompatible with the physician's role as healer." But even medical opinion may be shifting on the topic of PAD. In the fall of 2014, during the height of the media focus on Brittany Maynard's story, a Medscape survey of seventeen

thousand U.S. physicians found that 54 percent of them supported allowing physician-assisted death, up from just 46 percent in 2010.

Envoi

Throughout the summer of 2014, Brittany Maynard's headaches grew worse and she began to experience memory problems and seizures. Nevertheless, she managed to take a last hiking trip in Alaska with her mother and visit the Grand Canyon with her husband. She volunteered for the PAD advocacy group Compassion & Choices and started a fund to try to get more laws like Oregon's passed.

But as her disease began to advance quickly and her physical and mental symptoms grew more debilitating, Maynard worried she might wait too long, become paralyzed, and lose the capacity to decide "when enough is enough."

"When people criticize me for not waiting longer, or, you know, whatever they've decided is best for me, it hurts," she said in an interview, "because really, I risk it every day."

After a particularly awful period, during which she had multiple seizures and found she couldn't remember her husband's name, she made plans to take the prescription. She died in her bedroom in Portland, Oregon, on November 1, 2014, surrounded by her family. It took roughly five minutes for her to lose consciousness and about thirty minutes for her breathing to stop.

"I made my decision based on my wishes, clinical research, choices, discussions with physicians, and logic," she wrote in one of her last blog posts. "I am not depressed or suicidal or on a 'slippery slope.' I have been in charge of this choice, gaining control of a terrifying terminal disease through the application of my own humane logic."

SOCIAL CONTEXT
When the Diagnosis Is Death

The complexity and ambiguity of the human body means that no society has ever been quite sure about how to define death. Some cultures, for example, have not considered a person

dead until three days after her heart stops beating. Others have viewed sleep and death as equivalent states of different duration, both of which involve the soul leaving the body.

Today, technological medicine can produce an "illusion of life" that can be particularly painful and confusing for family members and friends of the deceased. The person's blood may circulate, his chest may rise and fall, and her temperature may be normal. But these signs of life are illusions, created by drugs and machines.

Death as a Practical Matter

"When is someone dead?" didn't become a practical question until the rise of intensive care medicine in the 1950s and the increasing success of organ transplantation in the 1970s. People began to ask, "If a physician switches off the ventilator that is keeping a patient's body supplied with oxygen, is this homicide?" and "If a surgeon removes the heart from a breathing patient, has she killed him?"

These questions became more than academic exercises for a few surgeons who were arrested and charged with homicide in such cases, and finding answers became more urgent for personal and practical reasons. If surgeons couldn't remove organs from a body with a beating heart without fearing a trial and a prison sentence, they could no longer perform transplants.

Discussions during the 1970s and 1980s about determining criteria for death led to the development of four basic conceptions of what it means to be dead:

1. *Cardiopulmonary.* A person is dead when her heart stops beating and she is no longer breathing. This is the traditional definition of death as "the permanent cessation of breathing and blood circulation." It is akin to what people have in mind when they say, "He died twice while they were operating on him."

2. *Whole Brain.* Death is "the irreversible cessation of all brain functions."

A person is dead when his brain displays no organized electrical activity and even the brain stem, which controls basic functions such as breathing and blood pressure, is electrically silent.

3. *Higher Brain.* Death is the permanent loss of consciousness. An individual in an irreversible coma is dead, even though her brain stem continues to regulate her heartbeat and blood pressure.

4. *Personhood.* Death occurs when someone ceases to be a person. Relevant to deciding whether this has happened is information about the absence of mental activities such as reasoning, remembering, experiencing an emotion, anticipating the future, and interacting with others.

Death as a Diagnosis

The definition of death in the 1985 federal Universal Determination of Death Act is a straightforward endorsement of the first two concepts:

An individual who has sustained either (1) irreversible cessation of circulatory and respiratory functions or (2) irreversible cessation of all functions of the entire brain, including the brain stem, is dead.

This definition is embodied in the laws of all fifty states, but society's use of both concepts can cause confusion. Many people don't see how someone whose body is still working can be declared dead. But many others don't see how someone can be declared dead unless a doctor makes sure that he is brain dead. The key to eliminating such confusions is recognizing that death is a diagnosis governed by two sets of criteria. In some circumstances, cardiopulmonary criteria are appropriate, while in others, brain death criteria are. Neither set trumps the other.

A physician makes a diagnosis by confirming the hypothesis that the patient's disorder best fits into a particular category. Thus, a five-year-old girl who has a fever, light sensitivity, and a red, pustular rash has chicken pox. Symptoms and signs define the "chicken pox" category, and the data about the girl confirm the hypothesis that these criteria are met. The same is so when "death" is the diagnostic category, using the following two sets of criteria:

Cardiopulmonary. The cardiopulmonary criteria dictate that a patient is dead when his circulatory and respiratory functions have irreversibly ceased. To determine whether the data support this hypothesis, the physician examines the patient. She may feel for a pulse in the carotid or femoral artery and use a stethoscope to listen for heart and lung sounds. She may use an ophthalmoscope to see if the blood in the vessels in the retinas has broken into the stagnant segments that indicate that the blood isn't circulating. (This criterion is called the *boxcars sign*.) She may also perform an electrocardiogram to determine whether the heart is displaying any electrical activity.

Whole Brain. The diagnosis of death by means of whole-brain criteria follows a similar diagnostic procedure, but two restrictions govern the use of such criteria. First, they don't apply to anencephalic infants or children under two. Anencephalic infants are born without brain hemispheres, and because they lack even the potential for consciousness, it makes no sense to test for its loss. Also, young children develop at such different rates neurologically that clinical and imaging tests can't be used to make reliable predictions. For these groups, only cardiopulmonary criteria are appropriate for determining death.

Second, before a physician pronounces someone in a coma dead, he must rule out reversible causes. He must establish that drugs, an internal chemical imbalance (as

in diabetes), or hypothermia isn't the cause of the coma. Patients with these conditions may show clinical signs of death, yet recover consciousness. Thus, it is crucial for the examining physician to be sure that a patient hasn't consumed something that might cause a reversible coma.

Once these preliminary conditions are met, the physician examines the patient to determine whether her brain stem has suffered irreversible damage. She is removed briefly from a ventilator, at least once and often twice, to see if an increase in carbon dioxide in her blood will trigger her body to breathe. If it doesn't, then damage to the brain stem is indicated.

The physician tests other reflexes controlled by the brain stem. He strokes the back of the patient's throat to check her gag reflex, shines a light in her eyes to see if her pupils contract, touches her eyeball to test for a blink response, and sticks her with a needle to look for a pain response. He may turn her head to the side to see if her eyes move with it (also known as the *doll's eyes sign*).

Clinical observations like these are the prime data used to determine death. Often, however, an MRI or a CT scan is obtained to look for the amount and location of the brain damage, and an electroencephalogram (EEG) is employed to confirm the clinical judgment that the patient's brain has undergone irreversible structural damage. (The brain probably will show some electrical activity, because isolated groups of cells remain active, but there must be no pattern of organized activity.) These tests are most likely to be used when a patient is young or was not expected to die from her injury or disease. The physician relies on the data they produce to decide whether they support the hypothesis that the patient's brain has suffered an irreversible loss of all functions. If so, death is the diagnosis.

Acceptance

The cardiopulmonary criteria in the Uniform Determination of Death Act are traditional, but the brain-death criteria are modeled on those in the 1968 report of the Harvard Medical School's Ad Hoc Committee to Examine the Definition of Brain Death. The committee was explicit about why a definition was needed: "Our primary purpose," the report stated, "is to define irreversible coma as a new criterion for death," because the cardiopulmonary criteria "can lead to controversy in obtaining organs for transplantation." Also, the committee wanted to avoid wasting resources on patients who are unable to benefit from life-support measures and to spare their families the financial and emotional costs of supporting them.

More than 99 percent of the people who die in hospitals are still pronounced dead by traditional cardiopulmonary criteria. Those declared dead by brain-death criteria are always patients receiving intensive care. Once they are declared dead, they are taken off life support or, with the consent of their families, their organs are removed for transplantation.

The Harvard Committee was successful in both its aims. The concept of brain death has been widely accepted and has freed many families from the doubt and guilt involved in deciding to remove someone from life support. The concept also improved the success rate of transplants by allowing surgeons to use undamaged organs from bodies kept functioning by intensive care measures.

Higher Brain Function and PVS

Some would like to see society adopt the third concept and define death as the "irreversible loss of *higher* brain function." This would expand the criteria for determining death to include those in a persistent vegetative state (PVS).

Those diagnosed with PVS have damaged cerebral hemispheres, and this results in their not being aware of themselves or their surroundings. They are incapable of thinking or intentional movement, but if their brain stems are undamaged, their autonomic nervous system continues to control their reflexes.

Thus, PVS patients can breathe and excrete, their hearts beat, their muscles respond to stimuli, and they cycle through regular sleep–wake patterns. Although their eyelids may blink and their eyes move, they lack the brain capacity needed to see.

After six months to a year, PVS patients are not likely to recover even the most rudimentary form of consciousness. They aren't like patients diagnosed as "minimally conscious," who have some episodes of awareness and a small, yet real, possibility of waking up. PVS patients remain vegetative for as long as they live, which may be for decades. As we will see later in this chapter, Karen Quinlan lived for almost ten years, and Nancy Cruzan was allowed to die after seven. Terri Schiavo slipped into a coma in 1990 and died in 2005, only after a protracted legal battle by her parents to keep her husband from ordering her removed from life support. (See this chapter's Case Presentations on Quinlan, Cruzan, and Schiavo.)

PVS patients require total care. They must be fed through a surgically implanted gastric tube, hydrated with IV fluids, bathed and toileted, kept on special mattresses and turned to avoid pressure sores, given antibiotics to prevent infections, and provided with around-the-clock nursing care.

If the "irreversible loss of higher brain function" were accepted as the third legal definition of death, PVS patients could be declared dead and no longer given life-support measures, including gastric feeding and IV hydration. Such acceptance wouldn't require a court decision or even a request from the family.

Adopting this criterion would mean that as many as fifty thousand PVS patients in the United States could be removed from life support. This would result in immense savings, because it costs about one hundred thousand dollars a year to provide care for a PVS patient. The money, proponents of the higher-brain function criterion argue, could be better spent on extending the lives of those who are conscious and can play a role in the lives of their family and society.

Nevertheless, it seems unlikely that the higher brain definition will ever be widely accepted. For one thing, it lacks the precision and certainty that made the whole-brain definition uncontroversial. Given the same data from brain scans and clinical tests, doctors can disagree about when higher brain functions have been permanently lost. Studies show further that PVS can be misdiagnosed, so some patients who are capable of recovery might fall victim to a bad diagnosis. Also, the families of some PVS patients believe that no matter how long the odds, the patient may eventually emerge from the coma.

Loss of Personhood

The definition of death as the loss of personhood has widespread resonance. We understand what a friend means when she says her mother's progressive dementia has so destroyed her as a person that she might as well be dead.

We see how someone with a degenerative neurological disorder such as Alzheimer's or Huntington's may reach a stage at which he has lost so much cognitive and emotional functioning that he may no longer be thought of as a person. If we

could agree that he has lost whatever is essential to being a person, then, given the "loss of personhood" definition of death, it would be morally permissible for us to withdraw life support.

Resonant or not, the definition is not likely to gain the support necessary to be adopted as a legal criterion. Exactly what attributes are required to qualify as a person is open to dispute, and we are unlikely to get general agreement on exactly when someone has lost so many of them that he has lost his personhood. Diagnosing death might thus come to be seen as arbitrary. Worse, critics charge, it could open the door to abuse: the old, the poor, and the disabled might stop measuring up to personhood and not be given needed support.

Some people will always believe that an individual they care about, no matter how mentally and physically impaired, is the same person as before. Looking like a person and having a history as a person are seen by many as sufficient for being a person. This attitude is not likely to change.

Circle Completed

We end where we began: death can be defined as the permanent failure of heartbeat and respiration or as the permanent failure of the whole brain. These definitions, it is widely agreed, have served us well. That they are seen as objective and precise gives them a strength that the other two definitions can't match. Leaving well enough alone seems to most observers to be our best option.

We can hope that as the concept of brain death becomes more familiar, caregivers will be spared the pain and uncertainty that often accompanies unrealistic hopes for a loved-one's recovery. Whether diagnosed by cardiopulmonary criteria or whole-brain criteria, the diagnosis is the same.

CASE PRESENTATION
Karen Quinlan

At two in the morning on Tuesday, April 14, 1975, Mrs. Julie Quinlan was awakened by a telephone call. When she hung up she was crying. "Karen is very sick," Mrs. Quinlan said to her husband, Joseph. "She's unconscious, and we have to go to Newton Hospital right away."

The Quinlans thought their twenty-one-year-old daughter might have been in an automobile accident. But the doctor in the intensive care unit told them that wasn't so. Karen was in a critical comatose state of unknown cause and was being given oxygen through a mask taped over her nose and mouth. She had been brought to the hospital by two friends who had been with her at a birthday party. After a few drinks, she had started to pass out, and her friends decided she must be drunk and put her to bed. Then someone checked on her later in the evening and found that Karen wasn't breathing. Her friends gave her mouth-to-mouth resuscitation and rushed her to the nearest hospital.

Blood and urine tests showed that Karen had not consumed a dangerous amount of alcohol. They also showed the presence of 0.6 milligrams of aspirin and the tranquilizer Valium. Two milligrams would have been toxic, five lethal. Why Karen stopped breathing was mysterious. But it was during that time that part of her brain died from oxygen depletion.

After Karen had been unconscious for about a week, she was moved to St. Clare's Hospital in nearby Denville, where testing and life-support facilities were better. Dr. Robert J. Morse, a neurologist, and Dr. Arshad Javed, a pulmonary internist, became her physicians. Additional tests were made. Extensive brain damage was confirmed, and several possible causes of the coma were ruled out.

No Longer the Same

During the early days, the Quinlans were hopeful. Karen's eyes opened and closed, and her mother and her nineteen-year-old sister, Mary Ellen, thought that they detected signs that Karen recognized them. But Karen's condition began to deteriorate. Her weight gradually dropped from 120 pounds to 70 pounds. Her body began to contract into a rigid fetal position, until her five-foot-two-inch frame was bent into a shape hardly longer than three feet. She was now breathing mechanically, by means of an MA-1 respirator that pumped air through a tube in her throat. By early July, Karen's physicians and her mother, sister, and brother had come to believe it was hopeless to expect her ever to regain consciousness.

Only her father continued to believe it might be possible. But when he told Dr. Morse about some encouraging sign he had noticed, Dr. Morse said to him, "Even if God did perform a miracle so that Karen would live, her damage is so extensive she would spend the rest of her life in an institution." Mr. Quinlan then realized that Karen would never again be as he remembered her. He now agreed with Karen's sister: "Karen would never want to be kept alive on machines like this. She would hate this."

Need to Go to Court

The Quinlans' parish priest, Father Thomas Trapasso, had also assured them that the moral doctrines of the Roman Catholic Church did not require the continuation of extraordinary measures to support a hopeless life. Before making his decision, Mr. Quinlan asked the priest, "Am I playing God?" Father Thomas said, "God has made the decision that Karen is going to die. You're just agreeing with God's decision, that's all."

On July 31, after Karen had been unconscious for three and a half months, the Quinlans gave Drs. Morse and Javed their permission to take Karen off the respirator. The Quinlans signed a letter authorizing the discontinuance of extraordinary procedures and absolving the hospital from all legal liability.

"I think you have come to the right decision," Dr. Morse said to Mr. Quinlan.

But the next morning Dr. Morse called Mr. Quinlan back. "I have a moral problem about what we agreed on last night," he said. "I feel I have to consult somebody else and see how he feels about it." The next day, Dr. Morse called again. "I find I will not do it," he said. "And I've informed the administrator at the hospital that I will not do it."

The Quinlans were upset and bewildered by the change in Dr. Morse. Later they talked with the hospital attorney and were told by him that, because Karen was over twenty-one, they were no longer her legal guardians. The Quinlans would have to go to court and be appointed to guardianship. After that, the hospital might or might not remove Karen from the respirator.

Mr. Quinlan consulted attorney Paul Armstrong. Because Karen was an adult without income, Quinlan explained, Medicaid was paying the $450 a day it cost to keep her alive. The Quinlans thus had no financial motive in asking that the respirator be taken away. Mr. Quinlan said that his belief that Karen should be allowed to die rested on his conviction that it was God's will, and it was for this reason that he wanted to be appointed Karen's guardian.

Legal Arguments

Armstrong filed a plea with Judge Robert Muir of the New Jersey Superior Court on September 12, 1975. He explicitly requested that Mr. Quinlan be appointed Karen's guardian so that he would have "the express power of authorizing the discontinuance of all extraordinary means of sustaining her life."

Later, on October 20, Mr. Armstrong argued the case on three constitutional grounds. First, he claimed that there is an implicit right to privacy guaranteed by the Constitution and that this right permits individuals or others acting for them to terminate the use of extraordinary medical measures, even when death may result. This right holds, Armstrong said, unless there are compelling state interests that set it aside.

Second, Armstrong argued that the First Amendment guarantee of religious freedom extended to the Quinlan case. If the court did not allow them to act in accordance with the doctrines of their church, their religious liberty would be infringed. Finally, Armstrong appealed to the "cruel and unusual punishment" clause of the Eighth Amendment. He claimed that "for the state to require that Karen Quinlan be kept alive, against her will and the will of her family, after the dignity, beauty, promise, and meaning of earthly life have vanished, is cruel and unusual punishment."

Karen's mother, sister, and a friend testified that Karen had often talked about not wanting to be kept alive by machines. An expert witness, a neurologist, testified that Karen was in a chronic vegetative state and that it

was unlikely that she would ever regain consciousness. Doctors testifying for St. Clare's Hospital and Karen's physicians agreed with this. But, they argued, her brain still showed patterns of electrical activity, and she still had a discernible pulse. Thus, she could not be considered dead by legal or medical criteria.

On November 10, Judge Muir ruled against Joseph Quinlan. He praised Mr. Quinlan's character and concern, but he decided that Mr. Quinlan's anguish over his daughter might cloud his judgment about her welfare, so he should not be made her guardian. Furthermore, Judge Muir said, because Karen was still medically and legally alive, "the Court should not authorize termination of the respirator. To do so would be homicide and an act of euthanasia."

Appeal

Mr. Armstrong appealed the decision to the New Jersey Supreme Court. On January 26, 1976, the court convened to hear arguments, and Mr. Armstrong argued substantially as before. But this time the court's ruling was favorable to the Quinlans. The court agreed that Mr. Quinlan could assert a right of privacy on Karen's behalf and that whatever he decided for her should be accepted by society. It also set aside any criminal liability for removing the respirator, claiming that if death resulted, it would not be homicide, and that, even if it were homicide, it would not be unlawful. Finally, the court stated that if Karen's physicians believed that she would never emerge from her coma, they should consult an ethics committee to be established by St. Clare's Hospital. If the committee accepted their prognosis, then the respirator could be removed. If Karen's present physicians were then unwilling to take her off the respirator, Mr. Quinlan was free to find a physician who would.

Six weeks after the court decision, the respirator still had not been turned off. In fact, another machine, one for controlling body temperature, had been added. Mr. Quinlan met with Morse and Javed and demanded that they remove the respirator. They agreed to "wean" Karen from the machine, and soon she was breathing without mechanical assistance. Dr. Morse and St. Clare's Hospital were determined that Karen would not die while under their care. Although she was moved to a private room, it was next door to the intensive care unit.

They intended to put her back on the respirator at the first sign of breathing difficulty.

Because Karen was still alive, the Quinlans began a long search for a chronic care hospital. Twenty or more institutions turned them away, and physicians expressed great reluctance to become involved in the case. Finally, Dr. Joseph Fennelly volunteered to treat Karen, and she was moved from St. Clare's to the Morris View Nursing Home.

The End—After Ten Years

For many years, Karen Quinlan continued to breathe. She received high-nutrient feedings and regular doses of antibiotics to ward off infections. During some periods she was more active than at others, making reflexive responses to touch and sound.

On June 11, 1985, ten years after she lapsed into a coma, Karen Quinlan finally died. She was thirty-one years old.

Her father died of cancer on December 10, 1996, at the Karen Quinlan Center of Hope, a hospice Joseph and Julia Quinlan had founded with money they received from the film and book rights to their daughter's story. Up until his death, Joseph Quinlan continued to support the right of patients and their families to discontinue the use of life-sustaining technologies, but he opposed all forms of physician-assisted death.

CASE PRESENTATION

The Cruzan Case: The Supreme Court Upholds the Right to Die

In the early morning of January 11, 1983, twenty-five-year-old Nancy Cruzan was driving on a deserted county road in Missouri. The road was icy and the car skidded, then flipped over and crashed. Nancy was thrown from the driver's seat and landed face down in a ditch by the side of the road.

An ambulance arrived quickly, but not quickly enough to save her from suffering irreversible brain damage. Nancy never regained consciousness, and her physicians eventually concluded that she had entered into what is known medically as a *persistent vegetative state*, awake but unaware. The higher brain functions responsible for recognition, memory, comprehension, anticipation, and other cognitive functions had all been lost.

Her arms and legs were drawn into a fetal position, her knees against her chest, and her body stiff and contracted. Only loud sounds and painful stimuli evoked responses, but even those were no more than neurological reflexes.

"We've literally cried over Nancy's body, and we've never seen anything," her father, Joe Cruzan, said. "She has no awareness of herself."

Nancy was incapable of eating, but her body was sustained by a feeding tube surgically implanted in her stomach. She was a patient at the Missouri Rehabilitation Center, but no one expected her to be rehabilitated. She could only be kept alive.

"If only the ambulance had arrived five minutes earlier—or five minutes later," her father lamented.

The cost of Nancy Cruzan's care was $130,000 a year. The bill was paid by the state. Because she was a legal adult when her accident occurred, her family was not responsible for her medical care. Had she been under twenty-one, the Cruzans would have been responsible for her medical bills, as long as they had any financial resources to pay them.

Five Years Later

In 1988, five years after her accident, Nancy was almost thirty years old, and her physicians estimated that she might live another thirty years. She was, like some ten thousand other Americans, lost in the dark, dimensionless limbo between living and dying. Those who love them can think of them only with sadness and despair. Given a choice between lingering in this twilight world and dying, most people find it difficult to imagine anyone would choose not to die.

Hope eventually faded even for Nancy Cruzan's parents. They faced the fact she would never recover her awareness, and the time came when they wanted their daughter to die, rather than be kept alive in her hopeless condition. As Nancy's legal guardians, they asked that the feeding tube used to keep her alive be withdrawn.

Officials at the Missouri Rehabilitation Center refused, and Joe and Louise Cruzan were forced to go to court.

Lower Court Decisions

During the court hearings, the family testified that Nancy would not have wanted to be kept alive in her present condition. Her sister Christy said Nancy had told her that she never wanted to be kept alive "just as a vegetable." A friend testified that Nancy had said that if she were injured or sick she wouldn't want to continue her life, unless she could live "halfway normally." Family and friends spoke in general terms of Nancy's vigor and her sense of independence.

In July 1988, Judge Charles E. Teel of the Jasper County Circuit Court ruled that artificially prolonging the life of Nancy Cruzan violated her constitutional rights. He wrote, "There is a fundamental right expressed in our Constitution as 'the right to liberty,' which permits an individual to refuse or direct the withholding or withdrawal of artificial death-prolonging procedures when the person has no cognitive brain function."

Missouri Attorney General William Webster appealed the ruling, arguing that Teel had misread Missouri statutes. In November 1988, in a 4–3 decision, the Missouri Supreme Court overruled the decision of the lower court: Nancy Cruzan's parents would not be allowed to disconnect the feeding tube.

The court focused, in particular, on the state's "living will" statute. The law permits the withdrawing of artificial life-support systems in cases in which individuals are hopelessly ill or injured and there is "clear and convincing evidence" that this is what they would want done. The act specifically forbids the withholding of food and water. Judge Teel's reasoning in the lower court decision was that the surgically implanted tube was an invasive medical treatment and that the Missouri law permitted her parents, as guardians, to order it withdrawn.

The Missouri Supreme Court held that the evidence as to what Nancy Cruzan would have wanted did not meet the "clear and convincing" standard required by the law. Also, the evidence did not show that the implanted feeding tube was "heroically invasive" or "burdensome." In the circumstance, then, the state's interest in preserving life should override other considerations.

The court found "no principled legal basis" to permit the Cruzans "to choose the death of their ward." Thus, "in the face of the state's strongly stated policy in favor of life, we choose to err on the side of life, respecting the right of incompetent persons who may wish to live despite a severely diminished quality of life." William Colby, the Cruzans' attorney, appealed the ruling to the U.S. Supreme Court, and for the first time the Court agreed to hear a case involving "right to die" issues.

Supreme Court Decision

On June 25, 1990, the Supreme Court issued a landmark ruling. In a 5–4 decision, it rejected Colby's argument that the Court should overturn as unconstitutional the State of Missouri's stringent standard requiring "clear and convincing evidence" as to a comatose patient's wishes. The decision came as a cruel disappointment to Nancy Cruzan's parents, because it meant that they had lost their case.

Yet, for the first time in U.S. judicial history, the Court recognized a strong constitutional basis for living wills and for the designation of another person to act as a surrogate in making medical decisions on behalf of another. Unlike the decisions in *Roe v. Wade* and *Quinlan,* which relied on an implied right of privacy in the Constitution, the Court decision in *Cruzan* appealed to a Fourteenth Amendment "liberty interest." That interest involves being free to reject unwanted medical treatment. The Court found grounds for this interest in the common-law tradition, according to which, if one person even touches another without consent or legal justification, then battery is committed.

The Court regarded the latter finding as the basis for requiring that a patient give informed consent to medical treatment. The "logical corollary" of informed consent, the Court held, is that the patient also possesses the right to withhold consent. A difficulty arises, though, when a patient is in no condition to give consent. The problem becomes one of determining what the patient's wishes would be.

Justice Rehnquist, in the majority opinion, held that the Constitution permits states to decide on the standard that must be met in determining the wishes of a comatose patient. Hence, Missouri's rigorous standard that requires "clear and convincing proof" of the wishes of the patient was allowed to stand. The Court held that it was legitimate for the state to err on the side of caution, "because an erroneous decision not to terminate treatment results in the maintenance of the status quo," while an erroneous decision to end treatment "is not susceptible of correction."

Justice William Brennan dissented strongly from this line of reasoning. He pointed out that making a mistake about a comatose patient's wishes and continuing treatment also has a serious consequence. Maintaining the status quo "robs a patient of the very qualities protected by the right to avoid unwanted medical treatment."

Justice Stevens, in another dissent, argued that the Court's focus on how much weight to give previous statements by the patient missed the point. The Court should have focused on the issue of the best interest of the patient. Otherwise, the only people eligible to exercise their constitutional right to be free of unwanted medical treatment are those "who had the foresight to make an unambiguous statement of their wishes while competent."

One of the more significant aspects of the decision was that the Court made no distinction between providing nutrition and hydration and other forms of medical treatment. One argument on behalf of the state was that providing food and water was not medical treatment. However, briefs filed by medical associations made it clear that determining the nutritional formula required by a person in Nancy Cruzan's condition and regulating her feeding are medically complex procedures. The situation is more comparable to determining the contents of an intravenous drip than to giving someone food and water.

The Missouri living-will statute explicitly prohibited the withdrawal of food and water. However, the law was not directly at issue in the *Cruzan* case, because Nancy Cruzan's accident occurred before the law was passed. The Court's treatment of nutrition and hydration as just another form of medical treatment has since served as a basis for challenging the constitutionality of the Missouri law, as well as laws in other states containing a similar provision.

The Supreme Court decision placed much emphasis on the wishes of the individual in accepting or rejecting medical treatment. In doing so, it underscored the importance of living wills and other *advance directives* as a way of indicating our wishes if something should happen to render us incapable of making them known directly. In some states, though, living wills have legal force only when the individual has a terminal illness (Nancy Cruzan did not) or when the individual has been quite specific about what treatments are unwanted. Because of such limitations, some legal observers recommend that individuals also sign a *durable power of attorney*, designating someone to make medical decisions for them if they become legally incompetent. (For more on advance directives, see this chapter's Briefing Session.)

The Court's decision left undecided the question of the constitutionality of physician-assisted death or suicide. Some state courts have held that, although individuals have a right to die, they do not have a right to the assistance of others in killing themselves. Other states, such as Oregon, Washington, Vermont, and Montana, have made it legal for physicians to prescribe drugs to help patients end their lives.

A Final Court Ruling

What of Nancy Cruzan? The State of Missouri withdrew from the case, and both the family's attorney and the state-appointed guardian filed separate briefs with the Jasper County Circuit Court asking that the implanted feeding tube be removed. A hearing was held to consider both Nancy Cruzan's medical condition and evidence from family and friends about what she would wish to be done. On December 14, 1990, Judge Charles Teel ruled that there was evidence to show that her intent, "if mentally able, would be to terminate her nutrition and hydration," and he authorized the request to remove the feeding tube.

Even after the tube was removed, controversy did not end. About twenty-five protesters tried to force their way into Nancy Cruzan's hospital room to reconnect the feeding tube. "The best we can do is not cooperate with anyone trying to starve an innocent person to death," one of the protest leaders said.

Twelve days after the tube was removed, on December 26, 1990, Nancy Cruzan died. Her parents, sisters, and grandparents were at her bedside. Almost eight years had passed since the accident that destroyed her brain and made the remainder of her life a matter of debate.

"We all feel good that Nancy is free at last," her father said at her graveside.

The *Cruzan* decision, by acknowledging a "right to die" and by finding a basis for it in the Constitution, provided states with new opportunities to resolve the issues surrounding thousands of other tragic cases.

CASE PRESENTATION
Jack Kevorkian: Moral Leader or Doctor Death?

On August 5, 1993, Thomas W. Hyde, Jr., a thirty-year-old Michigan construction worker, was taken inside a battered white 1968 Volkswagen bus parked behind the apartment building in the Detroit suburb of Royal Oak, where a sixty-five-year-old retired pathologist named Jack Kevorkian lived.

Kevorkian fitted a respiratory mask over Hyde's face and connected the plastic tubing leading from the mask to a short cylinder of carbon monoxide gas. He placed a string in Hyde's hand that was attached to a paper clip crimping the plastic tubing and shutting off the flow of gas. Hyde jerked on the string, pulled loose the paper clip, then breathed in the carbon monoxide flowing into the mask. Twenty minutes later, he was dead.

Hyde suffered from amyotrophic lateral sclerosis (ALS), a degenerative and progressive neurological disorder. He was paralyzed, unable to swallow, and, without continual suction procedures, would have choked to death on his own saliva. He reported that he was in great pain and had approached Kevorkian to help him end his life.

In a videotape made on July 1, 1993, Hyde had told Kevorkian, "I want to end this. I want to die." Hyde was the twentieth person whom Jack Kevorkian had assisted in ending his own life.

Trial

After the death of Thomas Hyde, Jack Kevorkian was arrested and charged with violating a 1992 Michigan law that had been enacted specifically to stop his activities. The law applies to anyone who knows that another person intends to commit suicide and who either "provides the physical means" or "participates in a physical act" by which the suicide is carried out. However, the law explicitly excludes those administering medications or procedures that may cause death "if the intent is to relieve pain or discomfort."

On May 2, 1994, a jury found Kevorkian not guilty of the charge of assisting suicide. As one juror said, "He convinced us he was not a murderer, that he was really trying to help people out." According to another, Kevorkian had acted to relieve Hyde's pain, and that is allowed by the law.

Several jurors expressed skepticism and resentment at the attempt to legislate behavior falling within such a private sphere. "I don't feel it's our obligation to choose for someone else how much pain and suffering they can go through," one said. "That's between them and their God."

After the decision, Kevorkian reiterated his position that people have a right to decide when to end their lives. He acted, he said, to protect that right. "I want that option as I get older, and I want it unencumbered, unintimidated, free with my medical colleagues," he said. "So I did it for myself, too, just as any competent adult would want to do."

Kevorkian always insisted that he practiced physician-assisted death (PAD) only in accordance with stringent safeguards. "You act only after it is absolutely justifiable," he said. "The patient must be mentally competent, the disease incurable." He maintained that multiple physicians should determine that a candidate for assisted death was incurable and that a psychiatrist should assess the patient's mental state and determine that he or she was competent. In practice, Kevorkian did not proceed in this fashion, because other physicians refused to cooperate with him.

Critics

Critics charged that without the safeguard of a psychiatric evaluation, patients who sought out Kevorkian to help them kill themselves were likely to be suffering from depression. Hence, they couldn't be regarded as having made an informed, rational decision to end their lives.

Other critics worried that if physicians are allowed to play a role in terminating the lives of patients, that role could expand. Physicians might begin by assisting those who ask their help, but then move on to making their own decisions about who should live. Or they might even be recruited to carry out a government policy identifying those who should be "assisted" in dying. On this view, the potential for abuse is so serious that physicians should not be associated in any way with procedures intended to end the lives of patients.

Finally, some critics, though disagreeing with Kevorkian, believed he had successfully pointed out a major flaw in the U.S. health care system: the medical profession was so committed to preserving life that it failed to humanely address cases in which death is inevitable. Rather than help people kill themselves, critics said, physicians ought to concentrate on alleviating the pain of terminally-ill patients, and allow them to spend their remaining time with their families and friends.

It was in keeping with such aims that hospitals and other institutions set up hospices to provide nursing care and support for the dying and established palliative care specialties to alleviate their suffering. Despite early resistance from the medical establishment, by 2010, over 45 percent of Americans were dying in hospice. (See this chapter's Briefing Session for more on this topic.)

A Charge of Murder

In 1998, the Michigan Department of Consumer and Industry Services, the state agency responsible for licensing physicians, charged that Jack Kevorkian was practicing medicine without a license by assisting forty-two people in committing suicide. (Kevorkian said that he had actually assisted in 120 deaths.)

Although the agency had issued a cease-and-desist order, Kevorkian continued to help terminally ill people die. That same year, the Michigan legislature passed a law making assisting in suicide a crime, but Kevorkian announced that he would continue his activities despite the law.

In September 1998, Dr. Kevorkian administered a lethal injection to Thomas Youk, a fifty-two-year-old man in an advanced stage of ALS. For the first time, Kevorkian, by his own direct action, caused the death of a person, thus moving from physician-assisted death to active euthanasia.

Kevorkian videotaped the event and offered the tape to the CBS program *Sixty Minutes,* which broadcast excerpts from the tape on national television. About 15.6 million households watched the program.

Kevorkian said he had given the tape to CBS in the hope that it would lead to his arrest and become a test case for assisted death and active euthanasia.

"I want a showdown," Kevorkian told a reporter. "I want to be prosecuted for euthanasia. I am going to prove that this is not a crime, ever, regardless of what words are written on paper."

The prosecutor of Oakland County, Michigan, filed first-degree murder charges against Jack Kevorkian. He said that Dr. Kevorkian's actions clearly fit the definition of premeditated murder and that the consent of the man killed was no legal defense.

On April 13, 1999, Jack Kevorkian was found guilty of second-degree murder and sentenced to a prison term of ten to twenty-five years. "This trial was not an opportunity for a referendum," Judge Jessica Cooper said at the sentencing.

Follow-up

Kevorkian was denied parole in 2005, but in June 2007, after eight years in prison, he was paroled on the grounds of good behavior. Kevorkian had already announced that once he was free, he would not go back to assisting people in dying, but would, rather, campaign to change laws to make such practices legal. He kept this resolution, and after his parole he gave lectures on college campuses, made an unsuccessful run for Congress, and published books advancing his views. In June 2011, he died in a Michigan hospital from a blood clot associated with liver cancer and kidney problems. He was eighty-three and had remained adamant about his views up until the end.

Jack Kevorkian continues to loom large in the public consciousness. Those sympathetic to the views espoused by Kevorkian believe he did more than anyone else to force society to face an issue that it had chosen to ignore. His critics believe he made a circus of what should be a serious and deliberative discussion about end-of-life decisions.

CASE PRESENTATION
Terri Schiavo

Early in the morning of February 25, 1990, Michael Schiavo was awakened by a dull thud. Startled, he jumped out of bed and discovered his wife Terri

collapsed in the hallway. Michael knelt down and spoke to her, but she was unconscious. He called 911, but by the time the paramedics arrived and resuscitated Terri, she had suffered damage from which she would never recover.

Terri and Michael had met when she was in her second semester at Bucks County Community College in Pennsylvania. They married in 1984 and soon moved to St. Petersburg, Florida. Michael worked as a restaurant manager and Terri got a job as a clerk with an insurance company. Terri's parents, Robert and Mary Schindler, also moved to Florida to be near their daughter and son-in-law. Relations between the parents and the young couple were friendly.

After Terri collapsed at home, she was rushed to the nearest hospital and treated for an apparent heart attack. A blood assay done at the hospital showed that she was suffering from a potassium imbalance, and her doctors thought that this had probably triggered the heart attack. The potassium imbalance, some physicians later suggested, might have been the result of bulimia, the eating disorder with which she had apparently struggled since high school, when she lost fifty pounds during her senior year. The cycle of overeating, purging, and dieting characteristic of bulimia can cause changes in the blood's electrolyte levels. Such changes may in turn disrupt the electrical signals controlling the heart and produce cardiac arrest.

Diagnosis

Whatever the reason for Terri's collapse, she failed to regain consciousness. Once she was out of immediate danger, the hospital neurologists performed a series of tests and examinations: Did she respond to a simple command like "Squeeze my hand"? Did her eyes track moving objects? Did her pupils respond to light? Did she show any sign of recognizing Michael or her parents? The answers to these questions were always no.

Terri's neurological responses were distinctly abnormal, and she showed no signs of cognitive functioning. In addition, CT scans of her brain revealed that the disruption of the oxygen supply to her brain had damaged the cerebral cortex. The more primitive parts of her brain were undamaged, but the parts responsible for even the most basic forms of thinking and self-awareness had been destroyed.

The neurologists, after reviewing all the evidence, reached the conclusion that Terri Schiavo had suffered damage to her brain that was both severe and irreversible. She was diagnosed as being in a persistent vegetative state.

Persistent Vegetative State

Persistent vegetative state (PVS) is a specific diagnosis, not to be confused with brain death. People diagnosed with PVS have damaged or dysfunctional cerebral hemispheres, and this results in their not being aware of themselves or their surroundings. They are incapable of thinking and of deliberate or intentional movement. Yet when the brain stem is undamaged, as it was in Terri's case, the autonomic nervous system and a range of bodily reflexes remain intact. (See Social Context: When the Diagnosis Is Death in this chapter.)

PVS patients are still able to breathe and excrete; their hearts beat, and their muscles behave reflexively. The patients cycle through regular sleep–wake patterns, but although their eyelids may blink and their eyes move, they lack the brain capacity to see. Some PVS patients may smile or tears may run down their cheeks, but these events are reflexive and thus only accidentally connected to circumstances in which such responses might be appropriate.

If a patient's brain is injured but not substantially destroyed, the patient may remain in a vegetative state for only a short time. Such a recovery is unusual, however. After a vegetative state lasts four weeks, neurologists consider it *persistent*. In most cases of PVS, if a change for the better has not occurred after three months, it is not likely to occur at all. After six months, PVS patients virtually never recover even the most rudimentary form of consciousness. They remain vegetative as long as they live, which may be for decades. (Karen Quinlan lived almost ten years after lapsing into unconsciousness: see the Case Presentation: Karen Quinlan in this chapter.) PVS patients require complete care, including feeding through a gastric tube surgically implanted in the stomach and hydration through an IV line, for the remainder of their lives. Because they are prone to infections, they must be carefully monitored and given IV antibiotics prophylactically. They must be kept on special mattresses and moved regularly to prevent the development of *bedsores*, ulcers caused by the breakdown of the skin and underlying tissue from the constant pressure of the body's weight.

Neither Brain Dead nor Minimally Conscious

PVS patients have no higher-level brain functioning, but they are not brain dead. To be considered brain dead, a patient must be diagnosed as lacking in any detectable brain activity. This means that even the brain stem (which keeps the heart beating and the lungs functioning) must show no functional or electrical activity.

PVS patients are also not in a *minimally conscious state*. Those who fit into this diagnostic category show at least some episodes of awareness. Their eyes may track movement from time to time, though not always. They may intermittently respond to commands like "Squeeze my hand," although attempts at any further communication often fail.

Neurologists consider minimal consciousness an appropriate diagnosis when the available evidence suggests that the patient displays some glimmer of consciousness at least some of the time. Brain scans of minimally conscious patients, for example, show that their language areas respond when a loved one speaks to them. PVS patients display none of these characteristics. Also, minimally conscious patients have a much greater chance of recovering more consciousness than do PVS patients. Even so, the expectation of any recovery is low, and if it does occur, it is likely to be marginal.

Dispute over Guardianship

Michael Schiavo, as Terri's husband, became her legal guardian as soon as she was diagnosed as mentally incompetent. In 1992, he sued his wife's gynecologists for malpractice to get the money to pay for her private care. The theory behind the suit was that they had failed to detect the potassium imbalance that led to a heart attack, which, in turn, led to the loss of oxygen that caused her brain damage. (After Terri Schiavo died, an autopsy showed no evidence that she had suffered a heart attack.) Michael won the suit. He was awarded $750,000 earmarked for Terri's extended care and another $300,000 to compensate him for his loss and suffering.

In 1993, a year later, Michael and his wife's parents, Robert and Mary Schindler, had a disagreement over the care Terri was receiving. Michael later claimed that the disagreement was really over money and that the Schindlers wanted to force him to give them a share of

his $300,000 malpractice award. They filed a suit asking the court to remove Michael as Terri's guardian and appoint them in his place. The court found no reason to hold that the care Michael was providing Terri was inadequate, and the suit against him was dismissed.

Treatment Decisions: The Legal Battles

The struggle over the fate of Terri Schiavo became intricate and confusing after the falling-out between Michael and the Schindlers. The clearest way to follow the dispute is to consider events in chronological order.

1994. Four years after Terri's PVS diagnosis, Michael met with the doctors taking care of her to ask about the likelihood of her ever regaining consciousness. He learned from them that this was unlikely ever to happen. Michael then told the long-term care facility where she was a patient that he didn't want her to be resuscitated if she suffered a life-threatening event. (This is known as a *do not resuscitate,* or DNR, order.)

Relations between Michael and the Schindlers continued to deteriorate, particularly after Michael and his girlfriend Jodi Centonze had two children together. (The Schindlers had originally encouraged Michael to move on with his life, and he started a relationship with Centonze only after Terri had been in a nursing home for four years.) Supporters of the Schindlers denounced Michael as an adulterer who was not fit to act as Terri's guardian.

1998–2003. Four years after Michael had authorized the DNR order and eight years after Terri was diagnosed as being in a PVS, Michael filed a legal petition to authorize him to order the removal of her gastric tube and allow her to die. Michael argued that, even though Terri had left no written instructions, she had repeatedly expressed the view that she would not want to be kept alive under circumstances resembling her present condition. Robert and Mary Schindler opposed Michael's petition, claiming that Terri was capable of recovering consciousness.

The court found in favor of Michael, but between 1998 and 2003 the Schindlers continued to engage in legal maneuvers to block Michael's efforts to allow Terri to die. They sought support from pro-life groups and members of the religious right, urging them to appeal to elected officials for help in keeping Terri alive. In violation of a court order, they showed a videotape of Terri that convinced many viewers that she had some cognitive function.

When Terri's feeding tube was removed under court order on October 15, 2003, the Florida state legislature quickly passed "Terri's Law," allowing the governor to order the tube replaced. Governor Jeb Bush signed the order, and President George W. Bush made a public statement praising the action.

Vigils and demonstrations continued around Woodside Hospice, where Terri was a patient. Fundamentalist religious conservatives, both Catholic and Protestant, joined other groups in attaching themselves to the Schiavo case. Most had specific agendas, some connected with promoting religious values, others with promoting disability rights. Very few counterdemonstrators appeared in what was often a hostile, angry environment. Michael Schiavo was compared to Hitler and called a murderer.

Starting in 2001, the Schindlers began to file accusations of abuse against Michael. From 2001 to 2004, they made nine accusations that included neglect of hygiene, denial of dental care, poisoning, and physical harm. All were investigated by the Florida Department of Children and Families. (Agency reports released in 2005 concluded that there were no indications of any harm, abuse, or neglect.) The Schindlers also contended that Terri's condition was not the result of a heart attack. In their view, Michael tried to strangle his wife but failed to kill her. But they offered little evidence for this view, other than the fact that Michael eventually established a relationship with another woman.

2005. When Terri's Law was ruled unconstitutional by a state court, the Florida attorney general appealed the case to the Florida Supreme Court, which upheld the lower court ruling. When the Schindlers appealed the decision to the U.S. Supreme Court, the case was again refused. On March 18, 2005, the Florida Circuit Court once more ordered the gastric tube removed.

Various members of the U.S. Congress were approached by groups affiliated with the Schindlers and asked to intervene in the Florida case. Speaker of the House Tom DeLay, a Texas Republican, said that the removal of Terri's feeding tube would be "an act of medical terrorism." One of the Schindlers' spiritual advisors said, "We pray that this modern-day crucifixion will not happen."

During the ensuring days, Congress devoted much of its attention to what could be done to prevent Terri's feeding tube from being removed. Senate Majority Leader Bill Frist, Republican of Tennessee, said that Congress had to act on the bill because "These are extraordinary circumstances that center on the most fundamental of human values and virtues: the sanctity of human life." Frist, a transplant surgeon as well as a senator, had earlier claimed to be able to tell from the videotape of Terri that she was not in a persistent vegetative state. (He received much criticism from the medical community for making a diagnosis without examining the patient or the medical records.)

Republican majorities in the House and Senate passed a bill that allowed the Schindler's case against removal of the feeding tube to be heard in federal court. After President Bush signed the bill into law, the Schindlers were allowed to file a sequence of petitions and appeals to replace the tube—which had been removed, for the third time, in accordance with the Florida court's order. But the Schindler's efforts were rejected by the federal courts, and a court-appointed neurologist ruled out the possibility of a misdiagnosis. The Supreme Court refused to intervene in the case for the fourth and fifth times.

With the Schindlers and their supporters running out of options, Governor Jeb Bush threatened to send state agents to forcibly replace the gastric tube, but this move was preemptively blocked by a federal judge. Nevertheless, protesters remained outside Terri Schiavo's hospice, with some blocking the entrance and others attempting to enter and bring cups of water to her—a symbolic gesture because Schiavo could not swallow.

Death

On the morning of Thursday, March 31, 2005, just after nine o'clock, Terri Schiavo died at Woodside Hospice. Michael was at her bedside and cradled her head as she stopped breathing. At Michael's request, neither her parents nor her brother or sister was present, although all of them had paid her a last visit at the hospice. Thirteen days had passed since Terri's feeding tube had been withdrawn. The end came, as is typical in such cases, as a result of dehydration.

The acrimony toward Michael by the Schindlers and their supporters did not end with Terri's death. "After these recent years of neglect at the hands of those who were supposed to care for her, she is finally at peace with God for eternity," Terri's sister, Suzanne Vitadamo, said in a public statement. "His [Michael's] heartless cruelty continued until the very last moment," said a priest who had sided with the Schindlers.

Michael Schiavo neither appeared in public nor made any statement. His lawyer, speaking on his behalf, said that "Mr. Schiavo's overriding concern here was to provide for Terri a peaceful death with dignity. This death was not for the siblings and not for the spouse and not for the parents. This was for Terri."

Autopsy

Three months after Terri Schiavo's death, the results of her autopsy were made public. They revealed that her brain had shrunk to less than half its normal weight due to the destruction caused by a loss of oxygen. No treatment nor the passage of time could ever have restored Schiavo to even the lowest levels of awareness or motor control. Her brain had atrophied and forever lost those capacities. The autopsy showed that the original diagnosis of persistent vegetative state had been correct.

The autopsy failed to find any signs of trauma or strangulation, undercutting the assertion by the Schindlers that Michael had abused Terri and thus was responsible for her condition. Also, no evidence was found suggesting that she had been neglected or received inadequate or inappropriate care.

Envoi

Incredibly, the conflict over Terri Schiavo did not end with her death. The Schindlers attempted to have independent experts witness the autopsy, but the Pinellas County Medical Examiner refused their request. Videotapes, photographs, and tissue samples from the autopsy were made available by the agency's office, however.

The Schindlers also petitioned a court for the right to determine the disposition of their daughter's body. They said that they wanted her to be buried in Florida so that they could visit her grave. The court rejected the petition, holding that Michael Schiavo had the right to make such decisions.

Terri Schiavo's body was cremated in April 2005. Michael's lawyer announced that his plan was to bury Terri's ashes in Huntingdon Valley, Pennsylvania, where she had grown up and where the couple had met so many years earlier.

BRIEFING SESSION

Death comes to us all. Many of us hope that when it comes it will be swift and allow us to depart without prolonged suffering, our dignity intact. We also hope to spare our friends and family the emotional and financial burdens of watching us linger in a hopeless medical condition. Contemporary medical science is adept at extending our lives, but that extension can come with a profound loss of our autonomy, our well-being, and our sense of self.

Such considerations may prompt us not only to plan for death but, under some circumstances, attempt to hasten it. We may refuse certain treatments, stop eating and drinking, or take even more active steps to try to have what the ancient Greeks called "a good death" or *euthanasia*. Framed this way, the question might seem uncontroversial. Should we not be able to snip the thread of life when the weight of suffering and hopelessness grows too heavy to bear? But the answer to this question is not as easy as it may seem, for hidden within it are a number of complicated moral questions. Anyone who opposes killing (either of oneself or of others) on moral grounds might also consider it necessary to object to euthanasia. For example, if we take steps to give ourselves a good or easy death, are we committing suicide? If we assist someone else's efforts to have a good or easy death, are we committing murder?

It may be, however, that the answer to these questions is no. But if it is, then it becomes necessary to specify the conditions that distinguish euthanasia from both suicide and murder. Only then can we argue, without contradiction, that euthanasia is morally acceptable but the other two forms of killing are not. Even if we believe that suicide is morally legitimate and therefore not necessary to distinguish from self-administered euthanasia, we must still consider whether hastening or causing another person's death can be distinguished from murder. We must also consider the broader social consequences of such practices, some of which our society has already accepted and others of which it still largely prohibits.

Active and Passive Euthanasia

We have just used the term *euthanasia* in its broadest sense, to refer to any form of good or easy death. In colloquial usage, however, euthanasia is often used in the narrower sense of "mercy killing" or a direct termination of another's life to end suffering. In addition, philosophers typically divide the broader category into narrower subdivisions, to bring out a number of relevant moral distinctions.

Some philosophers, for example, recognize a distinction between "active euthanasia" and "passive euthanasia," which in turn rests on a distinction between killing and letting die. To kill someone (including oneself) is to take a definite action to end the person's life (e.g., administering a lethal injection). To allow someone to die, by contrast, is to refrain from taking steps that may be necessary to prolong that person's life—failing to give an injection of antibiotics, for example. Active euthanasia, then, is direct killing and is an act of commission. Passive euthanasia is an act of omission.

This distinction is used in most contemporary codes of medical ethics (e.g., the American Medical Association's Code of Ethics) and is also recognized in the Anglo-American tradition of law. Except in special circumstances, it is illegal to deliberately cause the death of another person. It is not, however, illegal (except in special circumstances) to allow a person to die. Clearly, one might consider active euthanasia morally wrong while recognizing passive euthanasia as morally legitimate.

Some philosophers, however, have argued that the active–passive distinction is morally irrelevant with respect to euthanasia. Both are cases of causing death, and it is the circumstances in which death is caused, not the manner of causing it, that is of moral importance. Furthermore, the active–passive distinction is not always clear-cut. If a person dies after special life-sustaining equipment has been withdrawn, is this a case of active or passive euthanasia? Is it a case of euthanasia at all?

Voluntary, Involuntary, and Nonvoluntary Euthanasia

Writers on euthanasia have also typically drawn distinctions among voluntary, involuntary, and nonvoluntary euthanasia. *Voluntary euthanasia* includes cases in which a person ends his or her own life, either directly or by refusing treatment. But it also includes cases in which a person deputizes another to act in accordance with her wishes.

Thus, someone might instruct her family not to permit the use of artificial support systems should she become unconscious, suffer from brain damage, and be unable to speak for herself. Or someone might request that he be given a lethal injection after suffering third-degree burns over most of his body, suffering uncontrollable pain, and being told he has little hope of recovery.

Assisted death or assisted suicide, in which the individual requests the direct help of someone else in ending his life, falls into the category of voluntary euthanasia. (Some may think that one or more of the earlier examples are also cases of assisted death. What counts as assisted death is both conceptually and legally unclear; proponents and critics also disagree about what to call it, with the former preferring terms such as "aid in dying" and the latter generally preferring "assisted suicide.") That the individual explicitly consents to death is a necessary feature of voluntary euthanasia.

Involuntary euthanasia consists in ending the life of someone contrary to that person's wish. The person killed not only fails to give consent but expresses the desire not to be killed. No one arguing in favor of euthanasia holds that involuntary euthanasia is justifiable. But those who oppose both voluntary and nonvoluntary euthanasia often argue that to permit either runs the risk of facilitating acts of involuntary euthanasia.

Nonvoluntary euthanasia includes those cases in which the decision about death is not made by the person who is to die. Here the person gives no specific consent or instructions, and the decision is made by family, friends, or physicians. The distinction between voluntary and nonvoluntary euthanasia is not always a clear one. Physicians sometimes assume that people are "asking" to die even when no explicit request has been made. Also, the wishes and attitudes that people express when they are not in extreme life-threatening medical situations may be too vague for us to be certain about what they would choose when they are in such situations. Is the verbal statement "I never want to

be hooked up to one of those machines" an adequate indication that someone does not want to be put on a respirator should she meet with an accident and fall into a comatose state?

If the distinctions made here are accepted as legitimate and relevant, we can distinguish eight cases in which euthanasia becomes a moral decision:

1. Self-administered euthanasia
   a. active
   b. passive

2. Other-administered euthanasia
   a. active and voluntary
   b. active and involuntary
   c. active and nonvoluntary
   d. passive and voluntary
   e. passive and involuntary
   f. passive and nonvoluntary

Even these possibilities don't exhaust the cases euthanasia presents us with. For example, notice that the voluntary–nonvoluntary distinction doesn't appear in connection with self-administered euthanasia in our scheme. Yet it might be argued that it should, for a person's decision to end his life (actively or passively) may well not be a wholly voluntary or free decision. People who are severely depressed or feel pressure not to be a financial burden on family, for example, might be thought of as not having made a voluntary choice.

Hence, one might approve of self-administered voluntary euthanasia, yet think that the nonvoluntary form is wrong, since it would not be based on a dying patient's genuine decision. The patient's autonomy might be compromised by a psychiatric disability or by undue pressure from others. Indeed, much of the contemporary debate about physician-assisted death turns on this and related issues.

Defining Death

The advent of new medical technologies, pharmaceutical agents, and modes of treatment gives physicians the ability to keep certain bodily systems functioning when others have stopped. This has raised difficult questions about how we are to define death in certain situations and what actions are thus seen as causing it. Suppose someone's heartbeat, blood pressure, respiration, and liver and kidney functions can be maintained within a normal range of values by extensive medical intervention, but the person has little or no brain function. Should we still categorize this individual as a living person, even though she is in an irreversible coma or a persistent vegetative state?

If we consider the individual to be a living person, we need to decide how she ought to be treated. Should she be allowed to die or be maintained by medical means? This is the kind of question faced by families, physicians, and the courts in the *Quinlan* and *Cruzan* cases (see the Case Presentations on Karen Quinlan and Nancy Cruzan in this chapter), and it is one faced every day in dozens of unpublicized, though no less agonizing, cases.

What if an unconscious individual lacking higher cortical functioning is no longer a living person? Could a physician who disconnected a respirator or failed to give an antibiotic be said to have killed a person? If nutrition and hydration are withheld from a brain-dead individual or if the individual is given a lethal injection, is it reasonable to say that this is a case of killing? Perhaps the person died when his brain stopped functioning above a certain level. Or perhaps he died when he lapsed into a coma.

A practical question that advances in medicine have made even more pressing is when or whether a comatose individual might be considered as a source of transplant organs. If the individual remains a living person, it would be morally wrong (at least prima facie) to kill him to obtain organs for transplant. But what if the comatose individual is not really alive? What if he is dead already and no longer a person? What if he has previously indicated that he wished to be an organ donor? Then there seem to be no reasonable grounds for objecting to removing his organs and using them to save the lives of those who need them. (See Chapter 8 for a discussion of organ donation.)

Questions like the ones just raised have prompted various attempts to formally define the concept of death. In the view of many commentators, the traditional notion of death is no longer adequate to serve as a guide for the treatment of individuals in comas or lacking higher brain function—since technological medicine can keep their basic physiological functions going for years or even decades.

Four major notions or concepts of death have emerged during the last few decades. We'll list each of them, but there is a difference between specifying a concept of death and determining how the concept might be applied in particular cases. Here we will merely sketch the concepts and relevant criteria.

1. *Traditional.* A person is dead when she is no longer breathing and her heart is not beating. Hence, death may be defined as the permanent cessation of breathing and blood flow. This notion is sometimes known as the *cardiopulmonary* or *heart–lung* criterion for death.

2. *Whole brain.* Death is regarded as the irreversible cessation of all brain functions. Essentially, this means that there is no electrical activity in the brain, and even the brain stem is not functioning. Application of the concept depends on the use of electroencephalographic or imaging data.

3. *Higher brain.* Death is considered to involve the permanent loss of consciousness. Hence, someone in an irreversible coma or persistent vegetative state would be considered dead, even though the brain stem continued to regulate breathing and heartbeat. Clinical, electroencephalographic, and imaging data are relevant to applying the concept. So, too, are statistics concerning the likelihood of the individual's regaining consciousness.

4. *Personhood.* Death occurs when an individual ceases to be a person. This may mean the loss of features that are essential to personal identity or personhood. Criteria for personal identity or for being a person are typically taken to include a complex of such activities as reasoning, remembering, feeling emotion, possessing a sense of the future, interacting with others, and so on. The criteria for applying this concept have more to do with the way an individual functions than with data about her brain.

Technology makes it necessary to take a fresh look at the traditional definition of death, but technology also provides data that have allowed for the development of new definitions. It would be pointless, for example, to talk about brain death without having some means to determine when the criteria for this concept are satisfied.

The whole-brain concept of death was proposed in the 1981 *Report of the President's Commission for the Study of Ethical Problems in Medicine* and included in the Uniform Determination of Death Act of the same year. As a consequence, most state laws employing the traditional concept of death have been modified in keeping with the whole-brain concept.

The whole-brain concept has the advantage of being relatively clear-cut in application. However, applying the concept is not without difficulty and controversy. In the view of some, the concept is too restrictive and so fails to resolve some of the original difficulties that prompted the need for a new concept. For example, both Karen Quinlan and Nancy Cruzan would have been considered alive by the whole-brain criteria. However, those who favor concepts of death based on the loss of higher brain function or the loss of personhood might argue that both cases were ones in which the affected individuals were, in the respective technical senses, dead.

Furthermore, critics charge, the whole-brain concept is not really as straightforward in its application as it might seem. Even when there appears to be a complete lack of cognitive functioning and even when basic brain-stem functions appear to have disappeared, a brain may remain electrically active to some degree. Isolated cells or groups of cells continue to be alive, and monitoring of the brain yields data that are open to conflicting interpretations.

The higher brain and personhood concepts face even greater difficulties. Each must formulate criteria that can be accepted as nonarbitrary and as sufficient grounds for deciding that an individual is dead. No one has yet solved either of these problems for either of these concepts. The fact that there can be controversy over whole-brain death indicates how much harder it is to get agreement about when higher brain functions have ceased. Also, securing agreement on criteria for determining when an organism either becomes or ceases to be a person is a conceptual difficulty far from being resolved to the satisfaction of most philosophers. (For more on this topic, see Social Context: When the Diagnosis Is Death.)

Advance Directives and Refusal of Treatment

Like many other issues in bioethics, euthanasia was traditionally discussed only in the back rooms of medicine. Many physicians privately acknowledged that allowing or helping a patient to die was sometimes the most ethical course of action, but insisted in public that medicine must exclusively focus on the preservation of life. As a result, decisions about whether to allow a patient to die were often made by physicians acting on their own authority and values, rather than honoring the autonomous wishes of their patients.

In recent decades, however, the practices of euthanasia (in the broad sense of the word) have been discussed more widely and openly. Court cases, such as *Quinlan* and *Cruzan,* both widened the scope of legally permissible actions and reinforced the principle that an individual has a right to refuse or discontinue life-sustaining medical treatment. Such cases have also made it clear that there are limits to the benefits that can be derived from medicine—that, under some conditions, individuals may be better off if everything that can be done to extend and preserve life is not done.

Many of these shifts were codified in the 1991 Patient Self-Determination Act (PSDA), sometimes referred to as the "medical Miranda warning." The act requires that hospitals, nursing homes, and other health care facilities receiving federal funding provide patients with written information about the rights of citizens under state law to refuse or discontinue treatment. These requirements, along with the full implications of the *Cruzan* case, have forced institutions to acknowledge a broader sphere of patient autonomy and informed consent. Cardiologists, for example, have acknowledged that patients have a right to refuse or discontinue the use of life-sustaining devices such as pacemakers. Hospitals and long-term care facilities have acknowledged that competent patients have a right to refuse not just artificially delivered food and fluids, but also to hasten their deaths by the practice known as

voluntarily stopping eating and drinking (VSED). These rights have been broadly endorsed by the courts and ethicists alike.

In addition, the PSDA extends the sphere of patient autonomy into the future by requiring that institutions record whether a patient has an *advance directive*. Such directives are legal documents through which individuals can provide instructions about their health care in the event that they become incapacitated or incompetent to make such decisions for themselves.

The oldest form of advance directive is a *living will*, a document describing the types of potentially life-prolonging treatments a person would want and not want if unable to make medical decisions for herself. Thus, the first living-will law, the 1977 California "Natural Death Act," allowed physicians to honor patients' signed directives to withhold or discontinue "mechanical" or "artificial" life-support under certain circumstances. Later versions of living wills have included instructions about dialysis machines, pacemakers, antibiotics, and pain control drugs—as well as about "do not resuscitate" (DNR) orders to forgo CPR and other emergency procedures if a person's heart or breathing stops while under medical care.

A key feature and limitation of living wills is that they only apply to patients who have been diagnosed with terminal illnesses or are permanently unconscious (e.g., in a persistent vegetative state). Their strength is that they allow a person to express in an explicit manner how he or she wishes to be treated in advance of incapacitation. In this way, the autonomy of the individual is recognized. Even though unconscious or comatose, a person can continue to exert control over his or her life.

Critics of living wills have pointed out that they cannot possibly cover every end-of-life situation and must therefore be interpreted by health care providers who may not understand or share a patient's values and wishes. They also note that for many patients who are never diagnosed with a "terminal condition"—such as Karen Quinlan before she was put on a respirator—a living will is irrelevant. Finally, there is substantial evidence that many living wills (and other advance directives) are often lost or ignored, and that health care professionals are often unaware of their legal responsibilities to honor them.

Such problems have led some writers to recommend that individuals employ an additional type of advance directive, known as a *durable power of attorney* for health care. In such a document, an individual can name someone to act on his behalf should he become legally incompetent. Unlike the advance directive, a durable power of attorney allows a proxy to act on behalf of the signer in novel and unanticipated health care situations. For example, the proxy may (usually) order the discontinuation of artificial feeding in accordance with the signer's wishes—a request that has often been difficult to implement through living wills. In addition, a durable power of attorney, unlike most living wills, does not require a terminal diagnosis to go into effect—only incapacity or incompetence on the part of the signer. (For this reason, it is extremely important that the proxy has detailed knowledge of the signer's wishes and values, and is willing to make decisions that honor them.)

Many states now have "combination advance directives" that involve both written instructions for specific circumstances and the naming of a health care proxy to help implement them. In addition, twenty-six states now use *POLST forms* (also known as "Physician Orders for Life-Sustaining Treatment"), which translate a detailed discussion between a doctor and a seriously ill patient into a set of concrete medical instructions for end-of-life care. POLST forms are designed to be easy to recognize and to be

binding on all providers in a community—including first responders, emergency rooms, and nursing homes.

These new forms of advance directives reflect the concerns of a rapidly aging American population that is increasingly concerned with preserving autonomy and dignity during the closing years of life. In recent years, the proportion of Americans over sixty who die with an advance directive has increased dramatically, from 47 percent in 2000 to 72 percent in 2010. But Americans are also discovering that difficult and complicated end-of-life situations cannot always be managed by specifying conditions for physicians to withhold or discontinue medical treatment. Many cancers, for example, kill slowly and horribly, causing a patient to linger in a severely compromised state for months or years—even if she refuses chemotherapy or other major interventions. Equally terrifying for many Americans is the prospect of Alzheimer's disease or other forms of dementia, which can produce years of suffering, cognitive chaos, and a total loss of the self before it has any serious impact on underlying physical health. (As the baby boomers move into their seventies and eighties, some experts have predicted a nearly 300 percent increase in the number of dementia cases by 2050.)

For some aging and ailing Americans, these concerns have prompted a new push for access to physician-assisted death (PAD)—or, as we have categorized it above, self-administered active euthanasia. The practice is currently legal in five states, with "aid-in-dying" bills introduced in dozens of other state legislatures. In its American form, PAD typically allows physicians to prescribe a lethal dose of barbiturates, which a terminally ill patient may then decide to self-administer to hasten his or her death. Advocates point to safeguards against abuse or coercion in the structure of PAD laws, including certification of a six-month prognosis by two physicians, psychological evaluations for depression or other mental illness, and a requirement for multiple requests before a prescription can be written. (For more, see Case Presentation: Brittany Maynard.)

But the experience in Oregon, Washington, and other states seems to suggest that PAD may only be acceptable for a small subset of the terminally ill population—and a third of people who obtain the prescriptions end up not using them. This may be because PAD often requires a *preemptive* decision to end one's life while one is still competent to do so, a decision that can be difficult for families and patients, especially if patients are not yet experiencing the most acute phase of a terminal illness. PAD is also not an option for patients suffering from Alzheimer's disease or other forms of dementia, since it requires a competent patient to self-administer the prescription.

This is one reason why a number of prominent bioethicists have proposed one additional variant of advance directive. This type of directive would combine the established right of competent patients to voluntarily stop eating and drinking (VSED) with the equally established right to use advance directives to refuse life-sustaining treatments. The result would be an advance directive to prevent oneself from being spoon-fed or helped to drink if certain triggering conditions are met, especially those that arise in advanced dementia. Patients who already have these *advance directives to stop eating and drinking* (ADs to SED) have specified conditions such as "cannot recognize my loved ones" or "loss of most awareness of recent experiences and events" as triggering conditions for caregivers to stop assisting patients to eat and drink or to only provide "comfort feeding" without concern for nutritional sustenance.

Advocates for this approach cite research indicating that the withdrawal of food, followed a week later by a gradual withdrawal of liquids, typically causes only mild discomfort. They also argue that existing legal precedents may mean that this type of advance directive is already legal, rooted in the concepts of bodily integrity and autonomy affirmed in the *Cruzan case*. (The Court also accepted the notion that the nutrition received by Nancy Cruzan through an implanted feeding tube was a form of medical treatment that could be withdrawn, although it did not rule on the Missouri law that forbade such withdrawal.)

For advocates, ADs to SED represent a way for demented patients to exercise some measure of control over the course of a bewildering and brutal illness that may rob their lives of meaning and selfhood long before it physically kills them. For some critics, it is precisely this fact of dementia that makes the application of advance directives problematic. For at a certain point, a demented patient may no longer be viewed as numerically identical with the person who wrote the directive and perhaps should not be subject to that person's wishes—an objection that has been called the "someone else problem." Some philosophers, such as David DeGrazia, argue that this objection rests on a mistaken notion of personhood. But some advocates of ADs to SED grant that there may be specific cases—particularly those in which a demented patient seems to find pleasure or contentment in his new state—where such an advance directive should be at least temporarily disregarded on the basis of the "someone else problem."

Death and Meaning

Increasingly common to both advocates and opponents of various forms of euthanasia is a conviction that the dying process need not rob us of the values and meaning that have shaped our lives. Although the two sides may disagree about the sources of those values and meaning, there is broad consensus that dying at home, surrounded by loved ones, with adequate pain control, should not be as difficult to achieve as technological medicine sometimes makes it. They also increasingly share a conviction that extending life for its own sake may be of limited value if it comes at a high cost to the quality of one's final weeks or months. *Well-being* is not the same thing as health and survival, as the physician and writer Atul Gawande has argued at length, and many health care professionals are coming to think that their primary concern is as much with the former as the latter.

One sign of this new consensus is that 45 percent of Americans now enroll in *hospice* programs before they die, foregoing life-sustaining treatments after a terminal prognosis in order to take advantage of the pain management and comfort care that hospice provides, often at home. The rapid growth of *palliative care* as a medical specialty also reflects an emphasis on relieving symptoms and improving quality of life, although (unlike most hospice) it does not require a six-month prognosis or the complete abandonment of disease-abating treatments. Americans are increasingly refusing a "hospital death," in which temperature, pulse, and respiration are regulated and extended by medication and machinery. Many physicians are coming to see that dying patients may derive more benefit from comfort care, counseling, and vists from family and friends than from heroic medical efforts.

Indeed, a number of studies have shown that access to hospice and substantive discussions about end-of-life options not only reduce emergency room visits and overall cost of care, but actually *increase* life expectancy. Instead of avoiding the topic of prognosis and death, many physicians are coming to recognize that respect for autonomy requires a substantive conversation about patients' end-of-life priorities and

fears and about what trade-offs they may be willing to make to achieve their goals. Insurers are increasingly willing to pay for such conversations, recognizing them as a popular way of reducing the vastly disproportionate share of health care spending in the final months of life.

All of these shifts have reshaped debate over specific euthanasia practices, as patients and physicians come to see that there are many other ways of achieving "good death" besides a lethal injection. The honest recognition that death comes to us all need not cheapen the value of life or routinize its end.

Ethical Theories and Euthanasia

Roman Catholicism explicitly rejects most forms of euthanasia as being against the natural law duty to preserve life. The religion considers active euthanasia as morally identical with either suicide or murder. This position is not so rigid as it may seem, however; the *principle of double effect* (see Part VI: Foundations of Bioethics) makes it morally acceptable to give medication for the relief of pain—even if the indirect result of the medication will be to shorten the life of the recipient. The intended result is not the death of the person but the relief of suffering. The difference in intention is thus considered to be a morally significant one. Those not accepting the principle of double effect would be likely to classify the administration of a substance that would relieve pain but also cause death as an example of active euthanasia.

Furthermore, on the Catholic view there is no moral obligation to continue treatment when a person's condition is medically hopeless. It is legitimate to allow people to die as a result of their illness or injury, even though their lives might be lengthened by the use of extraordinary means. In addition, we may legitimately make the same decisions about ourselves that we make about others who are in no condition to decide. Thus, without intending to kill ourselves, we may choose measures for the relief of pain that may secondarily hasten our end. Or we may refuse extraordinary treatment and let "nature" or "God's will" determine the outcome. (See Part VI: Foundations of Bioethics for more on the Roman Catholic position on euthanasia and extraordinary means of sustaining life.)

At first sight, utilitarianism might seem to accept euthanasia in all of its forms. Whenever suffering is great and the patient's condition holds little hope of recovery, the principle of utility might be invoked to approve the hastening of death. After all, in such a case we seem to be acting to end suffering and to bring about a state of affairs in which happiness exceeds unhappiness.

Some utilitarians may argue in this fashion, but it is not the only way in which the principle of utility could be applied to end-of-life decisions. It could be argued, for example, that since life is a necessary condition for happiness, it is wrong to take any action that eliminates the possibility of all future happiness. Furthermore, a rule utilitarian might well argue that a rule such as "The taking of a human life is permissible when suffering is intense and the condition of the person permits no legitimate hope" would be open to abuse. Consequently, in the long run the rule would actually work to increase the amount of unhappiness in the world. Obviously, it is not possible to identify a single "utilitarian" position on euthanasia. The principle of utility supplies a guide for an answer, but it is not itself an answer.

Euthanasia presents considerable difficulty for Kant's ethics. For Kant, an autonomous rational being has a duty to preserve his or her life. Thus, one cannot rightly refuse needed medical care or commit suicide.

Yet our status as autonomous rational beings also endows us with an inherent dignity. If that status is destroyed or severely compromised, as it is when people become demented or comatose, then it is not certain that we have a duty to maintain our lives under such conditions. It may be more in keeping with our freedom and dignity for us to instruct others either to end our lives or to take no steps to keep us alive should we ever be in such a state. Voluntary euthanasia may be compatible with (if not required by) Kant's ethics.

By a similar line of reasoning, it may be that nonvoluntary euthanasia might be seen as a duty that we have to others. We might argue that by ending the life of a persistently comatose person we are recognizing the dignity that person possessed in his or her previous state. It might also be argued that a permanently unconscious human being is not a person in the relevant moral sense. Thus, our ordinary duty to preserve life does not hold.

According to Ross, we have a strong prima facie obligation not to kill a person except in justifiable self-defense—unless we have an even stronger prima facie moral obligation to do something that cannot be done without killing. Since active euthanasia typically requires taking the life of an innocent person, there is a moral presumption against it. However, another of Ross's prima facie obligations is that we keep promises made to others. Accordingly, if someone who is now in an irreversible coma with no hope of recovery has left instructions that in case of such an event she wishes her life to be ended, then we are under a prima facie obligation to follow her instructions. Thus, in such a case we may be justified in overriding the presumption against taking an innocent life.

Similarly, the capabilities approach, as developed by Martha Nussbaum, sees all humans (indeed, all complexly sentient

animals) as having a presumptive entitlement to continue their lives. Nevertheless,
irreversible pain and decrepitude may reach
a point where the central capability of life is
no longer a human good and may thus be
ended by individuals themselves, or, in some
cases, a well-informed and accountable surrogate. Both the capabilities approach and
virtue ethics approach would evaluate

particular end-of-life decisions against
a range of human goods and virtues
(e.g., health and affiliation, courage and
compassion). On these approaches, there is
no single standard or right (such as utility
or autonomy) against which such decisions
can be measured, only a threshold combination of virtues or capabilities that allow for
human flourishing or human dignity.

READINGS

Section 1: The Killing–Letting-Die Distinction

Active and Passive Euthanasia

James Rachels

Rachels challenges both the use and the moral significance of the
distinction between active and passive euthanasia. He argues that
since both forms of euthanasia result in the death of a person, active
euthanasia ought to be preferred to passive. Active euthanasia is
more humane because it allows suffering to be brought to a speedy
end. Furthermore, Rachels claims, the distinction itself can be shown
to be morally irrelevant. Is there, he asks, any genuine moral difference
between drowning a child and merely watching a child drown and
doing nothing to save it?

   Finally, Rachels attempts to show that the bare fact that there
is a difference between killing and letting die doesn't make active
euthanasia wrong. Killing may be right or wrong depending on the
intentions and circumstances in which it takes place; if the intentions
and circumstances are of a certain kind, then active euthanasia can
be morally right.

   For these reasons, Rachels suggests that the approval given to the
active–passive euthanasia distinction in the Code of Ethics of the
American Medical Association is unwise. He encourages physicians to
rely upon the distinction only to the extent that they are forced to do
so by law but not to give it any significant moral weight. In particular,
they should not make use of it when writing new policies or guidelines.

The distinction between active and passive
euthanasia is thought to be crucial for medical ethics.
The idea is that it is permissible, at least in some

From *New England Journal of Medicine* 292 (1975). Copyright © 1975
by MASSACHUSETTS MEDICAL SOCIETY. Reproduced by
permission.

cases, to withhold treatment and allow a patient to
die, but it is never permissible to take any direct action designed to kill the patient. This doctrine seems
to be accepted by most doctors, and it is endorsed in
a statement adopted by the House of Delegates of the
American Medical Association on December 4, 1973:

The intentional termination of the life of one human being by another—mercy killing—is contrary to that for which the medical profession stands and is contrary to the policy of the American Medical Association.

The cessation of the employment of extraordinary means to prolong the life of the body when there is irrefutable evidence that biological death is imminent is the decision of the patient and/or his immediate family. The advice and judgment of the physician should be freely available to the patient and/or his immediate family.

However, a strong case can be made against this doctrine. In what follows I will set out some of the relevant arguments, and urge doctors to reconsider their views on this matter.

To begin with a familiar type of situation, a patient who is dying of incurable cancer of the throat is in terrible pain, which can no longer be satisfactorily alleviated. He is certain to die within a few days, even if present treatment is continued, but he does not want to go on living for those days since the pain is unbearable. So he asks the doctor for an end to it, and his family joins in the request.

Suppose the doctor agrees to withhold treatment, as the conventional doctrine says he may. The justification for his doing so is that the patient is in terrible agony, and since he is going to die anyway, it would be wrong to prolong his suffering needlessly. But now notice this. If one simply withholds treatment, it may take the patient longer to die, and so he may suffer more than he would if more direct action were taken and a lethal injection given. This fact provides strong reason for thinking that, once the initial decision not to prolong his agony has been made, active euthanasia is actually preferable to passive euthanasia, rather than the reverse. To say otherwise is to endorse the option that leads to more suffering rather than less, and is contrary to the humanitarian impulse that prompts the decision not to prolong his life in the first place.

Part of my point is that the process of being "allowed to die" can be relatively slow and painful, whereas being given a lethal injection is relatively quick and painless. Let me give a different sort of example. In the United States about one in 600 babies is born with Down's syndrome. Most of these babies are otherwise healthy—that is, with only the usual pediatric care, they will proceed to an otherwise

normal infancy. Some, however, are born with congenital defects such as intestinal obstructions that require operations if they are to live. Sometimes, the parents and the doctor will decide not to operate, and let the infant die. Anthony Shaw describes what happens then:

…When surgery is denied [the doctor] must try to keep the infant from suffering while natural forces sap the baby's life away. As a surgeon whose natural inclination is to use the scalpel to fight off death, standing by and watching a salvageable baby die is the most emotionally exhausting experience I know. It is easy at a conference, in a theoretical discussion, to decide that such infants should be allowed to die. It is altogether different to stand by in the nursery and watch as dehydration and infection wither a tiny being over hours and days. This is a terrible ordeal for me and the hospital staff—much more so than for the parents who never set foot in the nursery.[1]

I can understand why some people are opposed to all euthanasia, and insist that such infants must be allowed to live. I think I can also understand why other people favor destroying these babies quickly and painlessly. But why should anyone favor letting "dehydration and infection wither a tiny being over hours and days"? The doctrine that says that a baby may be allowed to dehydrate and wither, but may not be given an injection that would end its life without suffering, seems so patently cruel as to require no further refutation. The strong language is not intended to offend, but only to put the point in the clearest possible way.

My second argument is that the conventional doctrine leads to decisions concerning life and death made on irrelevant grounds.

Consider again the case of the infants with Down's syndrome who need operations for congenital defects unrelated to the syndrome to live. Sometimes, there is no operation, and the baby dies, but when there is no such defect, the baby lives on. Now, an operation such as that to remove an intestinal obstruction is not prohibitively difficult. The reason why such operations are not performed in these cases is, clearly, that the child has Down's syndrome and the parents and doctor judge that because of that fact it is better for the child to die.

But notice that this situation is absurd, no matter what view one takes of the lives and potentials of such babies. If the life of such an infant is worth preserving, what does it matter if it needs a simple operation? Or, if one thinks it better that such a baby should not live on, what difference does it make that it happens to have an unobstructed intestinal tract? In either case, the matter of life and death is being decided on irrelevant grounds. It is the Down's syndrome, and not the intestines, that is the issue. The matter should be decided, if at all, on that basis, and not be allowed to depend on the essentially irrelevant question of whether the intestinal tract is blocked.

What makes this situation possible, of course, is the idea that when there is an intestinal blockage, one can "let the baby die," but when there is no such defect there is nothing that can be done, for one must not "kill" it. The fact that this idea leads to such results as deciding life or death on irrelevant grounds is another good reason why the doctrine should be rejected.

One reason why so many people think that there is an important moral difference between active and passive euthanasia is that they think killing someone is morally worse than letting someone die. But is it? Is killing, in itself, worse than letting die? To investigate this issue, two cases may be considered that are exactly alike except that one involves killing whereas the other involves letting someone die. Then, it can be asked whether this difference makes any difference to the moral assessments. It is important that the cases be exactly alike, except for this one difference, since otherwise one cannot be confident that it is this difference and not some other that accounts for any variation in the assessments of the two cases. So, let us consider this pair of cases:

In the first, Smith stands to gain a large inheritance if anything should happen to his six-year-old cousin. One evening while the child is taking his bath, Smith sneaks into the bathroom and drowns the child, and then arranges things so that it will look like an accident.

In the second, Jones also stands to gain if anything should happen to his six-year-old cousin. Like Smith, Jones sneaks in planning to drown the child in his bath. However, just as he enters the bathroom Jones sees the child slip and hit his head, and fall face down in the water. Jones is delighted; he stands by, ready to push the child's head back under if it is necessary, but it is not necessary. With only a little thrashing about, the child drowns all by himself, "accidentally," as Jones watches and does nothing.

Now Smith killed the child, whereas Jones "merely" let the child die. That is the only difference between them. Did either man behave better, from a moral point of view? If the difference between killing and letting die were in itself a morally important matter, one should say that Jones's behavior was less reprehensible than Smith's. But does one really want to say that? I think not. In the first place, both men acted from the same motive, personal gain, and both had exactly the same end in view when they acted. It may be inferred from Smith's conduct that he is a bad man, although that judgment may be withdrawn or modified if certain further facts are learned about him—for example, that he is mentally deranged. But would not the very same thing be inferred about Jones from his conduct? And would not the same further considerations also be relevant to any modification of this judgment? Moreover, suppose Jones pleaded, in his own defense, "After all, I didn't do anything except just stand there and watch the child drown. I didn't kill him; I only let him die." Again, if letting die were in itself less bad than killing, this defense should have at least some weight. But it does not. Such a "defense" can only be regarded as a grotesque perversion of moral reasoning. Morally speaking, it is no defense at all.

Now, it may be pointed out, quite properly, that the cases of euthanasia with which doctors are concerned are not like this at all. They do not involve personal gain or the destruction of normal healthy children. Doctors are concerned only with cases in which the patient's life is of no further use to him, or in which the patient's life has become or will soon become a terrible burden. However, the point is the same in these cases: the bare difference between killing and letting die does not, in itself, make a moral difference. If a doctor lets a patient die, for humane reasons, he is in the same moral position as if he had given the patient a lethal injection for humane reasons. If his decision was wrong—if, for example, the patient's illness was in fact curable—the decision would be equally regrettable no matter which method was used to carry it out. And if the doctor's decision was the right one, the method used is not in itself important.

The AMA policy statement isolates the crucial issue very well; the crucial issue is "the intentional termination of the life of one human being by another." But after identifying this issue, and forbidding "mercy killing," the statement goes on to deny that the cessation of treatment is the intentional termination of a life. This is where the mistake comes in, for what is the cessation of treatment, in these circumstances, if it is not "the intentional termination of the life of one human being by another"? Of course it is exactly that, and if it were not, there would be no point to it.

Many people will find this judgment hard to accept. One reason, I think, is that it is very easy to conflate the question of whether killing is, in itself, worse than letting die, with the very different question of whether most actual cases of killing are more reprehensible than most actual cases of letting die. Most actual cases of killing are clearly terrible (think, for example, of all the murders reported in the newspapers), and one hears of such cases every day. On the other hand, one hardly ever hears of a case of letting die, except for the actions of doctors who are motivated by humanitarian reasons. So one learns to think of killing in a much worse light than of letting die. But this does not mean that there is something about killing that makes it in itself worse than letting die, for it is not the bare difference between killing and letting die that makes the difference in the cases. Rather, the other factors—the murderer's motive of personal gain, for example, contrasted with the doctor's humanitarian motivation—account for different reactions to the different cases.

I have argued that killing is not in itself any worse than letting die; if my contention is right, it follows that active euthanasia is not any worse than passive euthanasia. What arguments can be given on the other side? The most common, I believe, is the following:

"The important difference between active and passive euthanasia is that, in passive euthanasia, the doctor does not do anything to bring about the patient's death. The doctor does nothing, and the patient dies of whatever ills already afflict him. In active euthanasia, however, the doctor does something to bring about the patient's death: he kills him. The doctor who gives the patient with cancer a lethal injection has himself caused his patient's death; whereas if he merely ceases treatment, the cancer is the cause of the death."

A number of points need to be made here. The first is that it is not exactly correct to say that in passive euthanasia the doctor does nothing, for he does do one thing that is very important: he lets the patient die. "Letting someone die" is certainly different, in some respects, from other types of action—mainly in that it is a kind of action that one may perform by way of not performing certain other actions. For example, one may let a patient die by way of not giving medication, just as one may insult someone by way of not shaking his hand. But for any purpose of moral assessment, it is a type of action nonetheless. The decision to let a patient die is subject to moral appraisal in the same way that a decision to kill him would be subject to moral appraisal: it may be assessed as wise or unwise, compassionate or sadistic, right or wrong. If a doctor deliberately let a patient die who was suffering from a routinely curable illness, the doctor would certainly be to blame for what he had done, just as he would be to blame if he had needlessly killed the patient. Charges against him would then be appropriate. If so, it would be no defense at all for him to insist that he didn't "do anything." He would have done something very serious indeed, for he let his patient die.

Fixing the cause of death may be very important from a legal point of view, for it may determine whether criminal charges are brought against the doctor. But I do not think that this notion can be used to show a moral difference between active and passive euthanasia. The reason why it is considered bad to be the cause of someone's death is that death is regarded as a great evil—and so it is. However, if it has been decided that euthanasia—even passive euthanasia—is desirable in a given case, it has also been decided that in this instance death is no greater an evil than the patient's continued existence. And if this is true, the usual reason for not wanting to be the cause of someone's death simply does not apply.

Finally, doctors may think that all of this is only of academic interest—the sort of thing that philosophers may worry about but that has no practical bearing on their own work. After all, doctors must be concerned about the legal consequences of what they do, and active euthanasia is clearly forbidden by the law. But even so, doctors should also be concerned with the fact that the law is forcing upon them a moral doctrine that may well be indefensible, and has a considerable effect on their practices. Of course, most doctors are not now in the position of being coerced in this matter, for they do not regard themselves as merely going along with what the law requires. Rather, in statements such as the AMA policy statement that I have quoted, they are endorsing this doctrine as a central point of medical ethics.

In that statement, active euthanasia is condemned not merely as illegal but as "contrary to that for which the medical profession stands," whereas passive euthanasia is approved. However, the preceding considerations suggest that there is really no moral difference between the two, considered in themselves (there may be important moral differences in some cases in their *consequences*, but, as I pointed out, these differences may make active euthanasia, and not passive euthanasia, the morally preferable option). So,

whereas doctors may have to discriminate between active and passive euthanasia to satisfy the law, they should not do any more than that. In particular, they should not give the distinction any added authority and weight by writing it into official statements of medical ethics.

Note

1. A. Shaw, "Doctor, Do We Have a Choice?" *The New York Times Magazine*, January 30, 1972, p. 54.

Is Killing No Worse Than Letting Die?
Winston Nesbitt

Nesbitt rejects the claim that there is no moral difference between killing and letting die. He holds that the pair of cases offered by Rachels (see previous article) to show that there is no difference, as well as the pair offered by Michael Tooley (as described here), fail to demonstrate the claim. In both pairs, the agent is prepared to kill and fails to do so only because unexpected circumstances make it unnecessary. This feature, Nesbitt argues, makes both cases in each pair *equally* reprehensible. The examples used by Rachels and Tooley are flawed and cannot support the claim that because letting die is morally acceptable, so, too, is killing. Both, in their cases, are morally unacceptable.

Nesbitt holds, finally, that there is a moral difference between killing and letting die. Letting die is *less* reprehensible than killing, because the kind of person who would let someone die poses a lesser danger than someone who would kill.

1

I want in this paper to consider a kind of argument sometimes produced against the thesis that it is worse to kill someone (that is, to deliberately take action that results in another's death) than merely to allow someone to die (that is, deliberately to fail to take steps which were available and which would have saved another's life). Let us, for brevity's sake, refer to this as the "difference thesis" since it implies that there is a moral difference between killing and letting die.

One approach commonly taken by opponents of the difference thesis is to produce examples of cases in which an agent does not kill, but merely lets

someone die, and yet would be generally agreed to be just as morally reprehensible as if he had killed. This kind of appeal to common intuitions might seem an unsatisfactory way of approaching the issue. It has been argued that what stance one takes concerning the difference thesis will depend on the ethical theory one holds, so that we cannot decide what stance is correct independently of deciding what is the correct moral theory. I do not, however, wish to object to the approach in question on these grounds. It may be true that different moral theories dictate different stances concerning the difference thesis, so that a theoretically satisfactory defence or refutation of the thesis requires a satisfactory defence of a theory which entails its soundness or unsoundness. However, the issue of its soundness or otherwise is a vital one in the attempt to decide some pressing moral questions, and we cannot wait for a demonstration of the correct moral theory

From Winston Nesbitt, "Is Killing No Worse Than Letting Die?" *Journal of Applied Philosophy* 12, no. 1 (1995): 101–105. Copyright © 1995 Wiley-Blackwell Ltd. Reprinted by permission. (Notes omitted.)

before taking up any kind of position with regard to it. Moreover, decisions on moral questions directly affecting practice are rarely derived from ethical first principles, but are usually based at some level on common intuitions, and it is arguable that at least where the question is one of public policy, this is as it should be.

2

It might seem at first glance a simple matter to show at least that common moral intuitions favour the difference thesis. Compare, to take an example of John Ladd's, the case in which I push someone who I know cannot swim into a river, thereby killing her, with that in which I come across someone drowning and fail to rescue her, although I am able to do so, thereby letting her die. Wouldn't most of us agree that my behaviour is morally worse in the first case?

However, it would be generally agreed by those involved in the debate that nothing of importance for our issue, not even concerning common opinion, can be learned through considering such an example. As Ladd points out, without being told any more about the cases mentioned, we are inclined to assume that there are other morally relevant differences between them, because there usually would be. We assume, for example, some malicious motive in the case of killing, but perhaps only fear or indifference in the case of failing to save. James Rachels and Michael Tooley, both of whom argue against the difference thesis, make similar points, as does Raziel Abelson, in a paper defending the thesis. Tooley, for example, notes that as well as differences in motives, there are also certain other morally relevant differences between typical acts of killing and typical acts of failing to save which may make us judge them differently. Typically, saving someone requires more effort than refraining from killing someone. Again, an act of killing necessarily results in someone's death, but an act of failing to save does not—someone else may come to the rescue. Factors such as these, it is suggested, may account for our tendency to judge failure to save (i.e., letting die) less harshly than killing. Tooley concludes that if one wishes to appeal to intuitions here, "one must be careful to confine one's attention to pairs of cases that do not differ in these, or other significant respects."

Accordingly, efforts are made by opponents of the difference thesis to produce pairs of cases which do not differ in morally significant respects (other than in one being a case of killing while the other is a case of letting die or failing to save). In fact, at least the major part of the case mounted by Rachels and Tooley against the difference thesis consists of the production of such examples. It is suggested that when we compare a case of killing with one which differs from it *only* in being a case of letting die, we will agree that either agent is as culpable as the other; and this is then taken to show that any inclination we ordinarily have to think killing worse than letting die is attributable to our tending, illegitimately, to think of typical cases of killing and of letting die, which differ in other morally relevant respects. I want now to examine the kind of example usually produced in these contexts.

3

I will begin with the examples produced by James Rachels in the article mentioned earlier, which is fast becoming one of the most frequently reprinted articles in the area. Although the article has been the subject of a good deal of discussion, as far as I know the points which I will make concerning it have not been previously made. Rachels asks us to compare the following two cases. The first is that of Smith, who will gain a large inheritance should his six-year-old nephew die. With this in mind, Smith one evening sneaks into the bathroom where his nephew is taking a bath, and drowns him. The other case, that of Jones, is identical, except that as Jones is about to drown his nephew, the child slips, hits his head, and falls, face down and unconscious, into the bath-water. Jones, delighted at his good fortune, watches as his nephew drowns.

Rachels assumes that we will readily agree that Smith, who kills his nephew, is no worse, morally speaking, than Jones, who merely lets his nephew die. Do we really want to say, he asks, that either behaves better from the moral point of view than the other? It would, he suggests, be a "grotesque perversion of moral reasoning" for Jones to argue, "After all, I didn't do anything except just stand and watch the child drown. I didn't kill him; I only let him die." Yet, Rachels says, if letting die were in itself less bad than killing, this defence would carry some weight.

There is little doubt that Rachels is correct in taking it that we will agree that Smith behaves no worse in his examples than does Jones. Before we are persuaded by this that killing someone is in itself morally no worse than letting someone die, though, we need to consider the examples more closely. We concede that Jones, who merely let his nephew die, is just as reprehensible as Smith, who killed his nephew. Let us ask, however, just what is the ground of our judgement of the agent in each case. In the case of Smith, this seems to be adequately captured by saying that Smith drowned his nephew for motives of personal gain. But can we say that the grounds on which we judge Jones to be reprehensible, and just as reprehensible as Smith, are that he let his nephew drown for motives of personal gain? I suggest not—for this neglects to mention a crucial fact about Jones, namely that he was fully prepared to kill his nephew, and would have done so had it proved necessary. It would be generally accepted, I think, quite independently of the present debate, that someone who is fully prepared to perform a reprehensible action, in the expectation of certain circumstances, but does not do so because the expected circumstances do not eventuate, is just as reprehensible as someone who actually performs that action in those circumstances. Now this alone is sufficient to account for our judging Jones as harshly as Smith. He was fully prepared to do what Smith did, and would have done so if circumstances had not turned out differently from those in Smith's case. Thus, though we may agree that he is just as reprehensible as Smith, this cannot be taken as showing that his letting his nephew die is as reprehensible as Smith's killing his nephew—for we would have judged him just as harshly, given what he was prepared to do, even if he had not let his nephew die. To make this clear, suppose that we modify Jones' story along the following lines—as before, he sneaks into the bathroom while his nephew is bathing, with the intention of drowning the child in his bath. This time, however, just before he can seize the child, *he* slips and hits his head on the bath, knocking himself unconscious. By the time he regains consciousness, the child, unaware of his intentions, has called his parents, and the opportunity is gone. Here, Jones neither kills his nephew *nor* lets him die—yet I think it would be agreed that given his preparedness to kill the child for personal gain, he is as reprehensible as Smith.

The examples produced by Michael Tooley, in the book referred to earlier, suffer the same defect as those produced by Rachels. Tooley asks us to con-

sider the following pair of scenarios, as it happens also featuring Smith and Jones. In the first, Jones is about to shoot Smith when he sees that Smith will be killed by a bomb unless Jones warns him, as he easily can. Jones does not warn him, and he is killed by the bomb—i.e., Jones lets Smith die. In the other, Jones wants Smith dead, and shoots him—i.e., he kills Smith.

Tooley elsewhere produces this further example: two sons are looking forward to the death of their wealthy father, and decide independently to poison him. One puts poison in his father's whiskey, and is discovered doing so by the other, who was just about to do the same. The latter then allows his father to drink the poisoned whiskey, and refrains from giving him the antidote, which he happens to possess.

Tooley is confident that we will agree that in each pair of cases, the agent who kills is morally no worse than the one who lets die. It will be clear, however, that his examples are open to criticisms parallel to those just produced against Rachels. To take first the case where Jones is saved the trouble of killing Smith by the fortunate circumstance of a bomb's being about to explode near the latter: it is true that we judge Jones to be just as reprehensible as if he had killed Smith, but since he was fully prepared to kill him had he not been saved the trouble by the bomb, we would make the same judgement even if he had neither killed Smith nor let him die (even if, say, no bomb had been present, but Smith suffered a massive and timely heart attack). As for the example of the like-minded sons, here too the son who didn't kill was prepared to do so, and given this, would be as reprehensible as the other even if he had not let his father die (if, say, he did not happen to possess the antidote, and so was powerless to save him).

Let us try to spell out more clearly just where the examples produced by Rachels and Tooley fail. What both writers overlook is that what determines whether someone is reprehensible or not is not simply what he in fact does, but what he is prepared to do, perhaps as revealed by what he in fact does. Thus, while Rachels is correct in taking it that we will be inclined to judge Smith and Jones in his examples equally harshly, this is not surprising, since both are judged reprehensible for precisely the same reason, namely that they were fully prepared to kill for motives of personal gain. The same, of course, is true of Tooley's examples. In each example he gives of an agent who lets another die, the agent is fully prepared to kill (though in the event, he is spared the necessity). In their efforts to ensure that the members of each pair of cases they produce do not differ in any morally relevant respect (except that one is a case of killing and the other of letting die), Rachels and Tooley make them *too* similar—not only do Rachels' Smith and Jones, for example, have identical motives, but both are guilty of the same moral offence.

4

Given the foregoing account of the failings of the examples produced by Rachels and Tooley, what modifications do they require if they are to be legitimately used to gauge our attitudes towards killing and letting die, respectively? Let us again concentrate on Rachels' examples. Clearly, if his argument is to avoid the defect pointed out, we must stipulate that though Jones was prepared to let his nephew die once he saw that this would happen unless he intervened, he was not prepared to kill the child. The story will now go something like this: Jones stands to gain considerably from his nephew's death, as before, but he is not prepared to kill him for this reason. However, he happens to be on hand when his nephew slips, hits his head, and falls face down in the bath. Remembering that he will profit from the child's death, he allows him to drown. We need, however, to make a further stipulation, regarding the explanation of Jones' not being prepared to kill his nephew. It cannot be that he fears untoward consequences for himself, such as detection and punishment, or that he is too lazy to choose such an active course, or that the idea simply had not occurred to him. I think it would be common ground in the debate that if the only explanation of his not being prepared to kill his nephew was one of these kinds, he would be morally no better than Smith, who differed only in being more daring, or more energetic, whether or not fate then happened to offer him the opportunity to let his nephew die instead. In that case, we must suppose that the reason Jones is prepared to let his nephew die, but not to kill him, is a moral one—not intervening to save the child, he holds, is one thing, but actually bringing about his death is another, and altogether beyond the pale.

I suggest, then, that the case with which we must compare that of Smith is this: Jones happens to be on hand when his nephew slips, hits his head, and falls unconscious into his bath-water. It is clear to Jones that the child will drown if he does not intervene. He remembers that the child's death would be greatly to his advantage, and does not intervene. Though he is prepared to let the child die, however, and in fact does so, he would not have been prepared to kill him, because, as he might put it, wicked though he is, he draws the line at killing for gain.

I am not entirely sure what the general opinion would be here as to the relative reprehensibility of Smith and Jones. I can only report my own, which is that Smith's behaviour is indeed morally worse than that of Jones. What I do want to insist on, however, is that, for the reasons I have given, we cannot take our reactions to the examples provided by Rachels and Tooley as an indication of our intuitions concerning the relative heinousness of killing and of letting die.

So far, we have restricted ourselves to discussion of common intuitions on our question, and made no attempt to argue for any particular answer. I will conclude by pointing out that, given the fairly common view that the *raison d'etre* of morality is to make it possible for people to live together in reasonable peace and security, it is not difficult to provide a rationale for the intuition that in our modified version of Rachels' examples, Jones is less reprehensible than Smith. For it is clearly preferable to have Jones-like persons around rather than Smith-like ones. We are not threatened by the former—such a person will not save me if my life should be in danger, but in this he is no more dangerous than an incapacitated person, or for that matter, a rock or tree (in fact he may be better, for he *might* save me as long as he doesn't think he will profit from my death). Smith-like persons, however, *are* a threat—if such a person should come to believe that she will benefit sufficiently from my death, then not only must I expect no help from her if my life happens to be in danger, but I must fear positive attempts on my life. In that case, given the view mentioned of the point of morality, people prepared to behave as Smith does are clearly of greater concern from the moral point of view than those prepared only to behave as Jones does; which is to say that killing is indeed morally worse than letting die.

Section 2: The Debate over Euthanasia and Assisted Death

The Wrongfulness of Euthanasia

J. Gay-Williams

Gay-Williams defines *euthanasia* as intentionally taking the life of a person who is believed to be suffering from some illness or injury from which recovery cannot reasonably be expected. Gay-Williams rejects passive euthanasia as a *name* for actions that are usually designated by the phrase and argues that these do not constitute acts of intentional killing. He argues that active euthanasia as intentional killing goes against natural law because it violates the natural inclination to preserve life. Furthermore, both self-interest and possible practical consequences of euthanasia provide reasons for rejecting it.

My impression is that euthanasia—the idea, if not the practice—is slowly gaining acceptance within our society. Cynics might attribute this to an increasing tendency to devalue human life, but I do not believe this is the major factor. The acceptance is much more likely to be the result of unthinking sympathy and benevolence. Well-publicized, tragic stories like that of Karen Quinlan elicit from us deep feelings of compassion. We think to ourselves, "She and her family would be better off if she were dead." It is an easy step from this very human response to the view that if someone (and others) would be better off dead, then it might be all right to kill that person. Although I respect the compassion that leads to this conclusion, I believe the conclusion is wrong. I want to show that euthanasia is wrong. It is inherently wrong, but it is also wrong judged from the standpoints of self-interest and of practical effects.

Before presenting my arguments to support this claim, it would be well to define "euthanasia." An essential aspect of euthanasia is that it involves taking a human life, either one's own or that of another. Also, the person whose life is taken must be someone who is believed to be suffering from some disease or injury from which recovery cannot reasonably be expected. Finally, the action must be deliberate and intentional. Thus, euthanasia is intentionally taking the life of a presumably

hopeless person. Whether the life is one's own or that of another, the taking of it is still euthanasia.

It is important to be clear about the deliberate and intentional aspect of the killing. If a hopeless person is given an injection of the wrong drug by mistake and this causes his death, this is wrongful killing but not euthanasia. The killing cannot be the result of accident. Furthermore, if the person is given an injection of a drug that is believed to be necessary to treat his disease or better his condition and the person dies as a result, then this is neither wrongful killing nor euthanasia. The intention was to make the patient well, not kill him. Similarly, when a patient's condition is such that it is not reasonable to hope that any medical procedures or treatments will save his life, a failure to implement the procedures or treatments is not euthanasia. If the person dies, this will be as a result of his injuries or disease and not because of his failure to receive treatment.

The failure to continue treatment after it has been realized that the patient has little chance of benefiting from it has been characterized by some as "passive euthanasia." This phrase is misleading and mistaken. In such cases, the person involved is not killed (the first essential aspect of euthanasia), nor is the death of the person intended by the withholding of additional treatment (the third essential aspect of euthanasia). The aim may be to spare the person additional and unjustifiable pain, to save him from the indignities of hopeless manipulations, and to avoid increasing the financial and emotional burden on his family. When I buy a pencil it is so that I can use it to write, not to contribute to an increase in the gross national product. This may be the unintended consequence of my action, but it is not the aim of my action. So it is with failing to continue the treatment of a dying person. I intend his death no more than I intend to reduce the GNP by not using medical supplies. His is an unintended dying, and so-called "passive euthanasia" is not euthanasia at all.

1. The Argument from Nature

Every human being has a natural inclination to continue living. Our reflexes and responses fit us to fight attackers, flee wild animals, and dodge out of the way of trucks. In our daily lives we exercise the caution and care necessary to protect ourselves. Our bodies are similarly structured for survival right down to the molecular level. When we are cut, our capillaries seal shut, our blood clots, and fibrogen is produced to start the process of healing the wound. When we are invaded by bacteria, antibodies are produced to fight against the alien organisms, and their remains are swept out of the body by special cells designed for clean-up work.

Euthanasia does violence to this natural goal of survival. It is literally acting against nature because all the processes of nature are bent towards the end of bodily survival. Euthanasia defeats these subtle mechanisms in a way that, in a particular case, disease and injury might not.

It is possible, but not necessary, to make an appeal to revealed religion in this connection. Man as trustee of his body acts against God, its rightful possessor, when he takes his own life. He also violates the commandment to hold life sacred and never to take it without just and compelling cause. But since this appeal will persuade only those who are prepared to accept that religion has access to revealed truths, I shall not employ this line of argument.

It is enough, I believe, to recognize that the organization of the human body and our patterns of behavioral responses make the continuation of life a natural goal. By reason alone, then, we can recognize that euthanasia sets us against our own nature. Furthermore, in doing so, euthanasia does violence to our dignity. Our dignity comes from seeking our ends. When one of our goals is survival, and actions are taken that eliminate that goal, then our natural dignity suffers. Unlike animals, we are conscious through reason of our nature and our ends. Euthanasia involves acting as if this dual nature—inclination towards survival and awareness of this as an end—did not exist. Thus, euthanasia denies our basic human character and requires that we regard ourselves or others as something less than fully human.

2. The Argument from Self-Interest

The above arguments are, I believe, sufficient to show that euthanasia is inherently wrong. But there are reasons for considering it wrong when judged by standards other than reason. Because death is final and irreversible, euthanasia contains within it the possibility that we will work against our own interest if we practice it or allow it to be practiced on us.

Contemporary medicine has high standards of excellence and a proven record of accomplishment, but it does not possess perfect and complete knowledge. A mistaken diagnosis is possible, and so is a mistaken prognosis. Consequently, we may believe that we are dying of a disease when, as a matter of fact, we may not be. We may think that we have no hope of recovery when, as a matter of fact, our chances are quite good. In such circumstances, if euthanasia were permitted, we would die needlessly. Death is final and the chance of error too great to approve the practice of euthanasia.

Also, there is always the possibility that an experimental procedure or a hitherto untried technique will pull us through. We should at least keep this option open, but euthanasia closes it off. Furthermore, spontaneous remission does occur in many cases. For no apparent reason, a patient simply recovers when those all around him, including his physicians, expected him to die. Euthanasia would just guarantee their expectations and leave no room for the "miraculous" recoveries that frequently occur.

Finally, knowing that we can take our life at any time (or ask another to take it) might well incline us to give up too easily. The will to live is strong in all of us, but it can be weakened by pain and suffering and feelings of hopelessness. If during a bad time we allow ourselves to be killed, we never have a chance to reconsider. Recovery from a serious illness requires that we fight for it, and anything that weakens our determination by suggesting that there is an easy way out is ultimately against our own interest. Also, we may be inclined towards euthanasia because of our concern for others. If we see our sickness and suffering as an emotional and financial burden on our family, we may feel that to leave our life is to make their lives easier. The very presence of the possibility of euthanasia may keep us from surviving when we might.

3. The Argument from Practical Effects

Doctors and nurses are, for the most part, totally committed to saving lives. A life lost is, for them, almost a personal failure, an insult to their skills and knowledge. Euthanasia as a practice might well alter this. It could have a corrupting influence so that in any case that is severe doctors and nurses might not try hard enough to save the patient. They might decide that the patient would simply be "better off dead" and take the steps necessary to make that come about. This attitude could then carry over to their dealings with patients less seriously ill. The result would be an overall decline in the quality of medical care.

Finally, euthanasia as a policy is a slippery slope. A person apparently hopelessly ill may be allowed to take his own life. Then he may be permitted to deputize others to do it for him should he no longer be able to act. The judgment of others then becomes the ruling factor. Already at this point euthanasia is not personal and voluntary, for others are acting "on behalf of" the patient as they see fit. This may well incline them to act on behalf of other patients who have not authorized them to exercise their judgment. It is only a short step, then, from voluntary euthanasia (self-inflicted or authorized), to directed euthanasia administered to a patient who has given no authorization, to involuntary euthanasia conducted as part of a social policy. Recently many psychiatrists and sociologists have argued that we define as "mental illness" those forms of behavior that we disapprove of. This gives us license then to lock up those who display the behavior. The category of the "hopelessly ill" provides the possibility of even worse abuse. Embedded in a social policy, it would give society or its representatives the authority to eliminate all those who might be considered too "ill" to function normally any longer. The dangers of euthanasia are too great to all to run the risk of approving it in any form. The first slippery step may well lead to a serious and harmful fall.

I hope that I have succeeded in showing why the benevolence that inclines us to give approval of euthanasia is misplaced. Euthanasia is inherently wrong because it violates the nature and dignity of human beings. But even those who are not convinced by this must be persuaded that the potential personal and social dangers inherent in euthanasia are sufficient to forbid our approving it either as a personal practice or as a public policy.

Suffering is surely a terrible thing, and we have a clear duty to comfort those in need and to ease their suffering when we can. But suffering is also a natural part of life with values for the individual and for others that we should not overlook. We may legitimately seek for others and for ourselves an easeful death, as Arthur Dyck has pointed out. Euthanasia, however, is not just an easeful death. It is a wrongful death. Euthanasia is not just dying. It is killing.

Voluntary Euthanasia: A Utilitarian Perspective

Peter Singer

Singer asks what makes it wrong, from a nonreligious view, to kill *any* being, including a human. The utilitarian answer, which he accepts, is that killing ends the possibility that the being can experience whatever further good life holds. For a "hedonistic utilitarian" this means happiness, and for a "preference utilitarian" it means the satisfaction of preferences. Thus, when unhappiness or the frustration of preferences outweighs life's positive elements, killing is preferable to not killing.

Singer addresses only voluntary euthanasia (including assisted suicide) and accepts Mill's view that individuals are the best

From Peter Singer, "Voluntary Euthanasia: A Utilitarian Perspective," *Bioethics* 17, no. 5–6 (2003): 526–541. Copyright © 2003 Wiley-Blackwell Ltd. Reproduced by permission of the author. (Notes omitted.)

judges of their own interests and should be allowed to decide when the good things of life are outweighed by the bad, making death desirable. He argues that the right to life should be viewed as an option, not as inalienable, which would make life a duty. It is necessary to determine that candidates for voluntary euthanasia are competent to make decisions and have access to palliative care, but in some instances even depressed people may be acceptable candidates.

Finally, Singer asks whether allowing voluntary euthanasia would lead to the deaths of vulnerable individuals pressured into consenting to involuntary killing, then points to studies in the Netherlands and Oregon showing that the evidence does not support this view. He concludes that the utilitarian case for allowing patients to choose euthanasia is strong.

Utilitarianism

There is, of course, no single "utilitarian perspective" for there are several versions of utilitarianism and they differ on some aspects of euthanasia. Utilitarianism is a form of consequentialism. According to *act-utilitarianism*, the right action is the one that, of all the actions open to the agent, has consequences that are better than, or at least no worse than, any other action open to the agent. So the act-utilitarian judges the ethics of each act independently. According to *rule-utilitarianism*, the right action is the one that is in accordance with the rule that, if generally followed, would have consequences that are better than, or at least no worse than, any other rule that might be generally followed in the relevant situation. But if we are talking about changing laws to permit voluntary euthanasia, rather than about individual decisions to help someone to die, this distinction is not so relevant. Both act- and rule-utilitarians will base their judgements on whether changing the law will have better consequences than not changing it.

What consequences do we take into account? Here there are two possible views. Classical, or hedonistic, utilitarianism counts only pleasure and pain, or happiness and suffering, as intrinsically significant. Other goods are, for the hedonistic utilitarian, significant only in so far as they affect the happiness and suffering of sentient beings. That pleasure or happiness are good things and much desired, while pain and suffering are bad things that we want to avoid, is generally accepted. But are these the *only* things that are of intrinsic value? That is a more difficult claim to defend. Many people

prefer to live a life with less happiness or pleasure in it, and perhaps even more pain and suffering, if they can thereby fulfil other important preferences. For example, they may choose to strive for excellence in art, or literature, or sport, even though they know that they are unlikely to achieve it, and may experience pain and suffering in the attempt. We could simply say that these people are making a mistake, if there is an alternative future open to them that would be likely to bring them a happier life. But on what grounds can we tell another person that her considered, well-informed, reflective choice is mistaken, even when she is in possession of all the same facts as we are? The difficulty of satisfactorily answering this question is one reason why I favour preference utilitarianism, rather than hedonistic utilitarianism. The right act is the one that will, in the long run, satisfy more preferences than it will thwart, when we weigh the preferences according to their importance for the person holding them.

There is of course a lot more to be said about questions internal to utilitarianism. But that is perhaps enough to provide a basis for our next topic.

When Killing Is, and Is Not, Wrong

Undoubtedly, the major objection to voluntary euthanasia is the rule that it is always wrong to kill an innocent human being. Anyone interested in an ethics that is free of religious commitments should be ready to ask sceptical questions about this view. Rule-utilitarians will not accept this rule without being persuaded that it will have better consequences than any other rule. Act-utilitarians will need to be assured that it will have the best consequences to follow the rule in *every* instance in which it applies.

The idea that it is always wrong to kill an innocent human being gains its strongest support from religious doctrines that draw a sharp distinction between human beings and other sentient beings. Without such religious ideas, it is difficult to think of any morally relevant properties that separate human beings with severe brain damage or other major intellectual disabilities from other beings at a similar mental level. For why should the fact that a being is a member of *our* species make it worse to kill that being than it is to kill a member of another species, if the two individuals have similar intellectual abilities, or if the non-human has superior intellectual abilities?

My claim that the wrongness of killing cannot rest on mere species membership is compatible with, but need not be based on, utilitarianism. Consider, for instance, the Kantian principle that it is always wrong to use someone merely as a means, and not as an end. Who is to count as "someone" for the purposes of applying such a principle? Kant's own argument in support of this principle depends on autonomy, and our autonomy, for Kant, depends on our ability to reason. Hence, it is fallacious to treat Kant's principle as equivalent to: "Never use a human being as means to an end." It would be better to read it as: "Never use an autonomous being merely as a means."

I can think of only one non-religious reason that has any plausibility at all, as a defence of the view that the boundary of our species also marks the boundary of those whom it is wrong to kill. This is a utilitarian argument, to the effect that the species boundary is sharp and clear, and if we allow it to be transgressed, we will slide down a slippery slope to widespread and unjustified killing. I will consider slippery slope arguments against allowing voluntary euthanasia towards the end of this paper. Here it is sufficient to note that this argument effectively admits that there is no intrinsic reason against attributing similar rights to life to humans and non-humans with similar intellectual capacities, but warns against the likely consequences of doing so. For our present inquiry into the underlying reasons against killing human beings, this is enough to show that one cannot simply assume that to be human is to give one a right to life. We need to ask, not: what is wrong with killing a human being; but rather, what makes it wrong to kill any being? A consequentialist might initially answer: whatever goods life holds, killing ends them. So if happiness is

a good, as classical hedonistic utilitarians hold, then killing is bad because when one is dead one is no longer happy. Or if it is the satisfaction of preferences that is good, as modern preference utilitarians hold, then when one is dead, one's preferences can no longer be satisfied.

These answers suggest their own limits. First, if the future life of the being killed would hold more negative elements than positive ones—more unhappiness than happiness, more frustration of preferences than satisfaction of them—then we have a reason for killing, rather than against killing. Needless to say, this is highly relevant to the question of euthanasia.

At this point, however, some further questions arise that suggest the relevance of higher intellectual capacities. Among these questions are: who is to decide when a being's life contains, or is likely to contain, more positive characteristics than negative ones? And what further impact will the killing of a being have on the lives of others?

Regarding the first of these questions, the nineteenth century utilitarian John Stuart Mill argued that individuals are, ultimately, the best judges and guardians of their own interests. So, in a famous example, he said that if you see people about to cross a bridge you know to be unsafe, you may forcibly stop them in order to inform them of the risk that the bridge may collapse under them, but if they decide to continue, you must stand aside and let them cross, for only they know the importance to them of crossing, and only they know how to balance that against the possible loss of their lives. Mill's example presupposes, of course, that we are dealing with beings who are capable of taking in information, reflecting and choosing. So here is the first point on which intellectual abilities are relevant. If beings are capable of making choices, we should, other things being equal, allow them to decide whether or not their lives are worth living. If they are not capable of making such choices, then someone else must make the decision for them, if the question should arise. (Since this paper focuses on voluntary euthanasia, I shall not go into details regarding life-and-death decisions for those who are not capable of exercising a choice. But to those who think that, in the absence of choice, the decision should always be "for life," I would add that even those who are most strongly against killing rarely insist on the use of every possible means of life-support, to draw life out to the last possible minute. In allowing life to end earlier than it might, they are effectively deciding for those who are not capable of making such decisions, and against life, not for it.)

The conclusion we can draw from this is as follows: if the goods that life holds are, in general, reasons against killing, those reasons lose all their force when it is clear that those killed will not have such goods, or that the goods they have will be outweighed by bad things that will happen to them. When we apply this reasoning to the case of someone who is capable of judging the matter, and we add Mill's view that individuals are the best judges of their own interests, we can conclude that this reason against killing does not apply to a person who, with unimpaired capacities for judgement, comes to the conclusion that his or her future is so clouded that it would be better to die than to continue to live. Indeed, the reason against killing is turned into its opposite, a reason for acceding to that person's request.

Now let us consider the second question: what impact does killing a being have on the lives of other beings? The answer will range from "none" to "devastating," depending on the particular circumstances. Even in the case of beings who are unable to comprehend the concept of death, there can be a great sense of loss, when a child or a parent, for example, is killed. But putting aside such cases of close relationship, there will be a difference between beings who are capable of feeling threatened by the deaths of others in circumstances similar to their own, and those who are not. This will provide an additional reason to think it wrong—normally—to kill those who can understand when their lives are at risk, that is, beings with higher intellectual capacities.

Once again, however, the fact that killing can lead to fear and insecurity in those who learn of the risk to their own lives, is transformed into a reason in favour of permitting killing, when people are killed only on their request. For then killing poses no threat. On the contrary, the possibility of receiving expert assistance when one wants to die relieves the fear that many elderly and ill people have, of dying in unrelieved pain and distress, or in circumstances that they regard as undignified and do not wish to live through.

Thus the usual utilitarian reasons against killing are turned around in the case of killing in the circumstances that apply in the case of voluntary euthanasia. But it is not only with utilitarian reasons that this happens. It is also true of the Kantian argument that to kill autonomous beings against their will shows a failure to respect them as autonomous beings.

This is true, obviously, when they do not want to be killed; and it is equally obviously false when they have autonomously decided to hasten their death. In these circumstances, it is preventing others from assisting them in carrying out their considered desire that violates their autonomy. That Kant himself took the opposite view only shows that he was influenced more by the conventional Christian morality of his day than by a thorough-going application of his own fundamental principles.

What of an argument based on a right to life? Here everything will depend on whether the right is treated as most other rights are, that is, as an option that one can choose to exercise or to give up, or if it is seen as "inalienable," as something that cannot be given up. I suggest that all rights should be seen as options. An "inalienable right" is not a right at all, but a duty. Hence the idea of a right to life does not provide a basis for opposing voluntary euthanasia. Just as my right to give you a book I own is the flip side of my right to keep my property if I choose to retain it, so here too, the right to end one's life, or to seek assistance in doing so, is the flip side of the right to life, that is, my right not to have my life taken against my will.

Against this, it will be said that we do not allow people to sell themselves into slavery. If, in a free society, people are not allowed to give up their freedom, why should they be able to give up their lives, which of course also ends their freedom?

It is true that the denial of the right of competent adults to sell themselves, after full consideration, into slavery creates a paradox for liberal theory. Can this denial be justified? There are two possible ways of justifying it, neither of which implies a denial of voluntary euthanasia. First, we might believe that to sell oneself into slavery—irrevocably to hand over control of your life to someone else—is such a crazy thing to do that the intention to do it creates an irrebuttable presumption that the person wishing to do it is not a competent rational being. In contrast, ending one's life when one is terminally or incurably ill is not crazy at all.

A second distinction between selling yourself into slavery and committing suicide can be appreciated by considering another apparently irrational distinction in a different situation. International law recognises a duty on nations to give asylum to genuine refugees who reach the nation's territory and claim asylum. Although the recent increase in asylum seekers has strained this duty, as yet no nation has openly rejected it.

Instead, they seek to prevent refugees crossing their borders or landing on their shores. Yet since the plight of the refugees is likely to be equally desperate, whether they succeed in setting foot on the nation's territory or not, this distinction seems arbitrary and morally untenable. The most plausible explanation is that it is abhorrent to forcibly send refugees back to a country that will persecute them. Preventing them from entering is slightly less abhorrent. Similarly, a law recognising a right to sell oneself into slavery would require an equivalent of America's notorious fugitive slave law; that is, those who sold themselves into slavery, and later, regretting their decision, ran away, would have to be forced to return to their "owners." The repugnance of doing this may be enough explanation for the refusal to permit people to sell themselves into slavery. Obviously, since no one changes their mind after voluntary euthanasia has been carried out, it could not lead to the state becoming involved in any similarly repugnant enforcement procedures.

Some will think that the fact that one cannot change one's mind after voluntary euthanasia is precisely the problem: if people might make mistakes about selling themselves into slavery, then they might also make mistakes about ending their lives. That has to be admitted. If voluntary euthanasia is permitted then some people will die who, if they had not opted for euthanasia, might have come to consider the remainder of their life worthwhile. But this has to be balanced against the presumably much larger number of people who, had voluntary euthanasia not been permitted, would have remained alive, in pain or distress and wishing that they had been able to die earlier. In such matters, there is no course of action that entirely excludes the possibility of a serious mistake. But should competent patients not be able to make their own judgements and decide what risks they prefer to take?

Competence, Mental Illness and Other Grounds for Taking Life

We have seen that Mill thought that individuals are the best judges and guardians of their own interests, and that this underlies his insistence that the state should not interfere with individuals for their own good, but only to prevent them harming others. This claim is not an implication of utilitarianism, and a utilitarian might disagree with it.

But those who, whether for utilitarian or other reasons, support individual liberty, will be reluctant to interfere with individual freedom unless the case for doing so is very clear.

It is sometimes claimed that patients who are terminally ill cannot rationally or autonomously choose euthanasia, because they are liable to be depressed. The American writer Nat Hentoff, for example, has claimed that many physicians "are unable to recognize clinical depression, which, when treated successfully, removes the wish for death." Even if this statement is true, it is not an argument against legalising voluntary euthanasia, but an argument for including in any legislation authorising voluntary euthanasia, a requirement that a psychiatrist, or someone else trained in recognising clinical depression, should examine any patient requesting voluntary euthanasia and certify that the patient is not suffering from a treatable form of clinical depression. Such a proposal is perfectly practicable, and when voluntary euthanasia was briefly legalised in Australia's Northern Territory a few years ago, the law did require that someone with a psychiatric qualification must certify that the patient was mentally competent to make the decision. Whether such a provision is necessary will depend on whether Hentoff's claim about the inability of physicians to recognise this condition is true.

In any case, not all clinical depression is susceptible to treatment. This leads to a different question, whether doctors should act on requests for euthanasia from patients who wish to die because they are suffering from clinical depression that has, over many years, proven unresponsive to treatment. This issue was raised in the Netherlands in 1991, when a psychiatrist, Dr. Boudewijn Chabot, provided assistance in dying to a 50-year-old woman who was severely depressed, but suffered from no physical illness. When prosecuted, Chabot contended that the woman was suffering intolerably, and that several years of treatment had failed to alleviate her distress. He thus sought to bring the case under the then-accepted guidelines for voluntary euthanasia in the Netherlands. He was convicted, but only because no other doctor had examined the patient, as the guidelines required. The Supreme Court of the Netherlands accepted the more important claim that unbearable mental suffering could, if it was impossible to relieve by any other means, constitute a ground for acceptable voluntary euthanasia, and that a person suffering from this condition could be competent.

From a utilitarian perspective, Chabot and the Dutch courts were correct. For the hedonistic utilitarian, what matters is not whether the suffering is physical or psychological, but how bad it is, whether it can be relieved, and—so that others will not be fearful of being killed when they want to live—whether the patient has clearly expressed a desire to die. Whether preference utilitarians would reach the same conclusion would depend on whether they are concerned with the satisfaction of actual preferences, or with the satisfaction of those preferences that people would have if they were thinking rationally and in a psychologically normal state of mind. It is easy to say: "If you were not depressed, you would not want to die." But why should we base our decision on the preferences a person would have if in a psychologically normal state of mind, even when it is extremely unlikely that the person in question will ever be in a psychologically normal state of mind?

Some cases of depression are episodic. A person can be depressed at times, and at other times normal. But if, having experienced many periods of depression, she knows how bad these periods are, and knows that they are very likely to recur, she may, while in a normal state of mind, desire to die rather than go through another period of depression. That could be a rational choice and one that a preference utilitarian should accept as providing a basis for assisted suicide or voluntary euthanasia. Given this, it seems possible to be rational about one's choice to die, even when depressed. The problem for the physician lies in recognising that the choice is one that would persist, even if the person were, temporarily, not depressed, but able to see that he would again become depressed. If this can be ascertained, a preference utilitarian should not dismiss such a preference.

The application of this view is probably more frequent than we realize. The World Health Organization estimates that there are about a million suicides a year and that depression or other forms of mental illness, including substance abuse, are involved in 90% of them. Moreover, the number of suicide attempts is said to be up to 20 times greater than the number of successful suicides. The WHO and many other organisations focus on suicide prevention, and if by this is meant prevention of the causes that lead people to try to end their lives, then this focus is entirely sound. But if by "suicide prevention" is meant simply preventing people from succeeding in killing themselves, irrespective of whether it is possible to change the conditions that lead them to wish to kill themselves, then suicide prevention is not always the right thing to do. It is possible that in a significant number of cases, suicide is the only way of escaping from unbearable and unrelievable suffering due to mental illness, and is in accordance with the rational preferences of the person committing suicide.

Richard Doerflinger has argued that those who invoke autonomy in order to argue for voluntary euthanasia or physician-assisted suicide are not being entirely straightforward, because they defend the autonomy of terminally ill or incurably ill patients, but not of people who are just bored with life. A recent Dutch case raised that issue. Edward Brongersma, an 86-year-old former senator in the Dutch parliament, committed suicide with the assistance of a doctor, simply because he was elderly and tired of life. The doctor who assisted him was initially acquitted, but the Dutch Ministry of Justice appealed against the acquittal. This led to the doctor's conviction, on the grounds that what he did was outside the existing rules. Nevertheless, since the court recognised that the doctor had acted out of compassion, it did not impose any penalty. A utilitarian should not find anything wrong in the doctor's action, either because the desire to die was Brongersma's considered preference, or because no one was in a better position than Brongersma to decide whether his life contains a positive or negative balance of experiences. Of course, it is relevant that Brongersma was 86 years old, and his life was unlikely to improve. We do not have to say the same about the situation of the lovesick teenager who thinks that without the girl he loves life can never again be worth living. Such cases are more akin to a temporary mental illness, or period of delusion. Neither a preference nor a hedonistic utilitarian would justify assisting a person in that state to end his life.

The reason that the focus of debate has been on people who are terminally or incurably ill, rather than on people who are simply tired of life, may just be political. Advocates of voluntary euthanasia and physician-assisted suicide find it difficult enough to persuade legislators or the public to change the law to allow doctors to help people who are terminally or incurably ill. To broaden the conditions still further would make the task impossible, in the present climate of opinion. Moreover, where terminally or incurably ill patients who want to die are concerned, both respect for the autonomy of the patients and a more objective standard of rational decision-making point in the same direction. If permissible assistance in dying is extended beyond this group it becomes more difficult to say whether a person's choice is persistent and based on good reasons, or would change over time. From a utilitarian perspective, this is a ground for saying, not that it is necessarily wrong to help those who are not terminally or incurably ill and yet want to die, but that it is more difficult to decide when the circumstances justify such assistance. This may be a ground against changing the law to allow assistance in those cases.

Palliative Care

I return now to another of Nat Hentoff's objections to the legalisation of voluntary euthanasia and physician-assisted suicide. Hentoff thinks that many physicians are not only unable to recognise depression, but also not good at treating pain, and that sometimes good pain relief can remove the desire for euthanasia. That is also true, but most specialists in palliative care admit that there is a small number of cases in which pain cannot be adequately relieved, short of making patients unconscious and keeping them that way until death ensues a few days later. That alternative—known as "terminal sedation"—is sometimes practised. Some ethicists, even non-religious ones, do not consider it equivalent to euthanasia, despite the fact that, since terminally sedated patients are not tube-fed, death always does ensue within a few days.

From a utilitarian perspective, it is hard to see that terminal sedation offers any advantages over euthanasia. Since the unconscious patient has no experiences at all, and does not recover consciousness before dying, the hedonistic utilitarian will judge terminal sedation as identical, from the point of view of the patient, to euthanasia at the moment when the patient becomes unconscious. Nor will the preference utilitarian be able to find a difference between the two states, unless the patient has, while still conscious, a preference for one rather than the other. Since additional resources are involved in caring for the terminally sedated patient, and the family is unable to begin the grieving process until death finally takes place, it seems that, other things being equal, voluntary euthanasia is better than voluntary terminal sedation.

But to return to the issue of whether better pain relief would eliminate the desire for euthanasia, there is again an obvious solution: ensure that candidates

for euthanasia see a palliative care specialist. If every patient then ceases to ask for euthanasia, both proponents and opponents of voluntary euthanasia will be pleased. But that seems unlikely. Some patients who want euthanasia are not in pain at all. They want to die because they are weak, constantly tired, nauseous, or breathless. Or perhaps they just find the whole process of slowly wasting away undignified. These are reasonable grounds for wanting to die.

It is curious that those who argue against voluntary euthanasia on the grounds that terminally ill patients are often depressed, or have not received good palliative care, do not also argue against the right of terminally ill patients to refuse life-sustaining treatment or to receive pain relief that is liable to shorten life. Generally, they go out of their way to stress that they do not wish to interfere with the rights of patients to refuse life-sustaining treatment or to receive pain relief that is liable to shorten life. But the patients who make these decisions are also terminally ill, and are making choices that will, or may, end their lives earlier than they would have ended if the patient had chosen differently. To support the right of patients to make these decisions, but deny they should be allowed to choose physician-assisted suicide or voluntary euthanasia, is to assume that a patient can rationally refuse treatment (and that doctors ought, other things being equal, to co-operate with this decision) but that the patient cannot rationally choose voluntary euthanasia. This is implausible. There is no reason to believe that patients refusing life-sustaining treatment or receiving pain relief that will foreseeably shorten their lives, are less likely to be depressed, or clouded by medication, or receiving poor treatment for their pain, than patients who choose physician-assisted suicide or voluntary euthanasia. The question is whether a patient can rationally choose an earlier death over a later one (and whether doctors ought to co-operate with these kinds of end-of-life decisions), and that choice is made in either case. If patients can rationally opt for an earlier death by refusing life-supporting treatment or by accepting life-shortening palliative care, they must also be rational enough to opt for an earlier death by physician-assisted suicide or voluntary euthanasia.

The Slippery Slope Argument

Undoubtedly the most widely invoked secular argument against the legalisation of voluntary euthanasia is the slippery slope argument that legalising physician-assisted suicide or voluntary euthanasia will lead to vulnerable patients being pressured into consenting to physician-assisted suicide or voluntary euthanasia when they do not really want it. Or perhaps, as another version of the argument goes, they will simply be killed without their consent because they are a nuisance to their families, or because their healthcare provider wants to save money.

What evidence is there to support or oppose the slippery slope argument when applied to voluntary euthanasia? A decade ago, this argument was largely speculative. Now, however, we can draw on evidence from two jurisdictions where for several years it has been possible for doctors to practice voluntary euthanasia or physician-assisted suicide without fear of prosecution. These jurisdictions are Oregon and the Netherlands. According to Oregon officials, between 1997, when a law permitting physician-assisted suicide took effect, and 2001, 141 lethal prescriptions were issued, according to state records, and 91 patients used their prescriptions to end their lives. There are about 30,000 deaths in Oregon annually. There have been no reports of the law being used to coerce patients to commit suicide against their will, and from all the evidence that is available, this does not appear to be a situation in which the law is being abused.

Opponents of voluntary euthanasia do contend, on the other hand, that the open practice of voluntary euthanasia in the Netherlands has led to abuse. In the early days of non-prosecution of doctors who carried out voluntary euthanasia, before full legalisation, a government-initiated study known as the Remmelink Report indicated that physicians occasionally—in roughly 1000 cases a year, or about 0.8% of all deaths—terminated the lives of their patients without their consent. This was, almost invariably, when the patients were very close to death and no longer capable of giving consent. Nevertheless, the report gave some grounds for concern. What it did not, and could not, have shown, however, is that the introduction of voluntary euthanasia has *led* to abuse. To show this one would need *either* two studies of the Netherlands, made some years apart and showing an increase in unjustified killings, *or* a comparison between the Netherlands and a similar country in which doctors practising voluntary euthanasia are liable to be prosecuted.

Such studies have become available since the publication of the Remmelink report. First, there was a second Dutch survey, carried out five years after the original one. It did not show any significant increase in the amount of non-voluntary euthanasia happening in the Netherlands, and thus dispelled fears that that country was sliding down a slippery slope.

In addition, studies have been carried out in Australia and in Belgium to discover whether there was more abuse in the Netherlands than in other comparable countries where euthanasia was illegal and could not be practised openly. The Australian study used English translations of the survey questions in the Dutch studies to ask doctors about decisions involving both direct euthanasia and foregoing medical treatment (for example, withholding antibiotics or withdrawing artificial ventilation). Its findings suggest that while the rate of active voluntary euthanasia in Australia is slightly lower than that shown in the most recent Dutch study (1.8% as against 2.3%), the rate of explicit *non-voluntary* euthanasia in Australia is, at 3.5%, much higher than the Dutch rate of 0.8%. Rates of other end-of-life decisions, such as withdrawing life-support or giving pain relief that was foreseen to be life shortening, were also higher than in the Netherlands.

The Belgian study, which examined deaths in the country's northern, Flemish-speaking region, came to broadly similar conclusions. The rate of voluntary euthanasia was, at 1.3% of all deaths, again lower than in the Netherlands, but the proportion of patients given a lethal injection without having requested it was, at 3% of all deaths, similar to the Australian rate and like it, much higher than the rate in the Netherlands. The authors of the Belgian study, reflecting on their own findings and those of the Australian and Dutch study, concluded:

> *Perhaps less attention is given to the requirements of careful end-of-life practice in a society with a restrictive approach than in one with an open approach that tolerates and regulates euthanasia and PAS (Physician-Assisted Suicide).*

These two studies discredit assertions that the open practice of active voluntary euthanasia in the Netherlands had led to an increase in non-voluntary euthanasia. There is no evidence to support the claim that laws against physician-assisted suicide or voluntary euthanasia prevent harm to vulnerable people. It is equally possible that legalising physician-assisted suicide or voluntary euthanasia will bring the issue out into the open, and thus make it easier to scrutinise what is actually happening, and to prevent harm to the vulnerable. If the burden of proof lies on those who defend a law that restricts individual liberty, then in the case of laws against physician-assisted suicide or voluntary euthanasia, that burden has not been discharged.

Those who, despite the studies cited, still seek to paint the situation in the Netherlands in dark colours, now need to explain the fact that its neighbour, Belgium, has chosen to follow that country's lead. The Belgian parliament voted, by large margins in both the upper and lower houses, to allow doctors to act on a patient's request for assistance in dying. The majority of Belgium's citizens are Flemish-speaking, and Flemish is so close to Dutch that they have no difficulty in reading Dutch newspapers and books, or watching Dutch television. If voluntary euthanasia in the Netherlands really was rife with abuses, why would the country that is better placed than all others to know what goes on in the Netherlands be keen to pass a similar law?

Conclusion

The utilitarian case for allowing patients to choose euthanasia, under specified conditions and safeguards, is strong. The slippery slope argument attempts to combat this case on utilitarian grounds. The outcomes of the open practice of voluntary euthanasia in the Netherlands, and of physician-assisted suicide in Oregon, do not, however, support the idea that allowing patients to choose euthanasia or physician-assisted suicide leads to a slippery slope. Hence it seems that, on utilitarian grounds, the legalisation of voluntary euthanasia or physician-assisted suicide would be a desirable reform.

Section 3:   Competence and Advance Directives

In the Matter of Karen Quinlan, an Alleged Incompetent

Supreme Court of New Jersey

The 1976 decision of the New Jersey Supreme Court in the case of Karen Quinlan helped establish the legal precedent that a right of privacy permits a patient to decide to refuse medical treatment. The court also held that this right can be exercised by a parent or guardian when the patient herself is in no position to do so. Thus, in the opinion of the court, removal of life-sustaining equipment would not be a case of homicide (or any other kind of wrongful killing), even if the patient should die as a result.

The ruling in the *Quinlan* case has had an enormous impact on decisions about discontinuing extraordinary medical measures. However, the ruling has generally been construed rather narrowly so as to apply only to mentally incompetent patients who are brain dead, comatose, or in an irreversible coma.

Constitutional and Legal Issues

I. The Free Exercise of Religion

Simply stated, the right to religious beliefs is absolute but conduct in pursuance thereof is not

From "In the Matter of Karen Quinlan," Supreme Court of New Jersey, 70 N.J. 10, 355 A. 2d 647. (This decision was issued on March 31, 1976, delivered by Chief Justice Hughes. The following abridgment omits references and case citations.)

wholly immune from governmental restraint. So it is that, for the sake of life, courts sometimes (but not always) order blood transfusions for Jehovah's Witnesses (whose religious beliefs abhor such procedure), forbid exposure to death from handling virulent snakes or ingesting poison (interfering with deeply held religious sentiments in such regard), and protect the public health as in the case of compulsory vaccination (over the strongest of religious objections).... The Public interest is thus considered paramount, without essential dissolution of respect for religious beliefs.

We think, without further examples, that, ranged against the State's interest in the preservation of life, the impingement of religious belief, much less religious "neutrality" as here, does not reflect a constitutional question, in the circumstances at least of the case presently before the Court. Moreover, like the trial court, we do not recognize an independent parental right of religious freedom to support the relief requested.

II. Cruel and Unusual Punishment

Similarly inapplicable to the case before us is the Constitution's Eighth Amendment protection against cruel and unusual punishment which, as held by the trial court, is not relevant to situations other than the imposition of penal sanctions. Historic in nature, it stemmed from punitive excesses in the infliction of criminal penalties. We find no precedent in law which would justify its extension to the correction of social injustice or hardship, such as, for instance, in the case of poverty. The latter often condemns the poor and deprived to horrendous living conditions which could certainly be described in the abstract as "cruel and unusual punishment." Yet the constitutional base of protection from "cruel and unusual punishment" is plainly irrelevant to such societal ills which must be remedied, if at all, under other concepts of constitutional and civil right.

So it is in the case of the unfortunate Karen Quinlan. Neither the State, nor the law, but the accident of fate and nature, has inflicted upon her conditions which though in essence cruel and most unusual, yet do not amount to "punishment" in any constitutional sense.

Neither the judgment of the court below, nor the medical decision which confronted it, nor the law and equity perceptions which impelled its action, nor the whole factual base upon which it was predicated, inflicted "cruel and unusual punishment" in the constitutional sense.

III. The Right of Privacy

It is the issue of the constitutional right of privacy that has given us most concern, in the exceptional circumstances of this case. Here a loving parent, *qua* parent and raising the rights of his incompetent and profoundly damaged daughter, probably irreversibly doomed to no more than a biologically vegetative remnant of life, is before the court. He seeks authorization to abandon specialized technological procedures which can only maintain for a time a body having no potential for resumption or continuance of other than a "vegetative" existence.

We have no doubt, in these unhappy circumstances, that if Karen were herself miraculously lucid for an interval (not altering the existing prognosis of the condition to which she would soon return) and perceptive of her irreversible condition, she could effectively decide upon discontinuance of the life-support apparatus, even if it meant the prospect of natural death. To this extent we may distinguish [a case] which concerned a severely injured young woman (Delores Heston), whose life depended on surgery and blood transfusion; and who was in such extreme shock that she was unable to express an informed choice (although the Court apparently considered the case as if the patient's own religious decision to resist transfusion were at stake), but most importantly a patient apparently salvable to long life and vibrant health—a situation not at all like the present case.

We have no hesitancy in deciding, in the instant diametrically opposite case, that no external compelling interest of the State could compel Karen to endure the unendurable, only to vegetate a few measurable months with no realistic possibility of returning to any semblance of cognitive or sapient life. We perceive no thread of logic distinguishing between such a choice on Karen's part and a similar choice which, under the evidence in this case, could be made by a competent patient terminally ill, riddled by cancer and suffering great pain; such a patient would not be resuscitated or put on a respirator in the example described by Dr. Korein, and *a fortiori* would not be kept *against his will* on a respirator.

Although the Constitution does not explicitly mention a right of privacy, Supreme Court decisions have recognized that a right of personal privacy exists and that certain areas of privacy are guaranteed under the Constitution. The Court has interdicted judicial intrusion into many aspects of personal decision, sometimes basing this restraint upon the conception of a limitation of judicial interest and responsibility, such as with regard to contraception and its relationship to family life and decision.

The Court in *Griswold* found the unwritten constitutional right of privacy to exist in the penumbra of specific guarantees of the Bill of Rights "formed by emanations from those guarantees that help give them life and substance." Presumably this right is broad enough to encompass a patient's decision to decline medical treatment under certain circumstances, in much the same way as it is broad enough to encompass a woman's decision to terminate pregnancy under certain conditions.

The claimed interests of the State in this case are essentially the preservation and sanctity of human life and defense to the right of the physician to administer medical treatment according to his best judgment. In this case the doctors say that removing Karen from the respirator will conflict with their professional judgment. The plaintiff answers that Karen's present treatment serves only a maintenance function; that the respirator cannot cure or improve her condition but at best can only prolong her inevitable slow deterioration and death; and that the interests of the patient, as seen by her surrogate, the guardian, must be evaluated by the court as predominant, even in the face of an option *contra* by the present attending physicians. Plaintiff's distinction is significant. The nature of Karen's care and the realistic chances of her recovery are quite unlike those of the patients discussed in many of the cases where treatments were ordered. In many of those cases the medical procedure required (usually a transfusion) constituted a minimal bodily invasion and the chances of recovery and return to functioning life were very good. We think that the State's interest *contra* weakens and the individual's right to privacy grows as the degree of bodily invasion increases and the prognosis dims. Ultimately there comes a point at which the individual's rights overcome the State interest. It is for that reason that we believe Karen's choice, if she were competent to make it, would be vindicated by the law. Her prognosis is extremely poor—she will never resume cognitive life. And the bodily invasion is very great—she requires 24-hour intensive nursing care, antibiotics, and the assistance of a respirator, a catheter and feeding tube.

Our affirmance of Karen's independent right of choice, however, would ordinarily be based upon her competency to assert it. The sad truth, however, is that she is grossly incompetent and we cannot discern her supposed choice based on the testimony of her previous conversation with friends, where such testimony is without sufficient probative weight. Nevertheless we have concluded that

Karen's right of privacy may be asserted on her behalf by her guardian under the peculiar circumstances here present.

If a putative decision by Karen to permit this non-cognitive, vegetative existence to terminate by natural forces is regarded as a valuable incident of her right of privacy, as we believe it to be, then it should not be discarded solely on the basis that her condition prevents her conscious exercise of the choice. The only practical way to prevent destruction of the right is to permit the guardian and family of Karen to render their best judgment, subject to the qualifications hereinafter stated, as to whether she would exercise it in these circumstances. If their conclusion is in the affirmative this decision should be accepted by a society the overwhelming majority of whose members would, we think, in similar circumstances, exercise such a choice in the same way for themselves or for those closest to them. It is for this reason that we determine that Karen's right of privacy may be asserted in her behalf, in this respect, by her guardian and family under the particular circumstances presented by this record. [Sections IV (Medical Factors), V (Alleged Criminal Liability), and VI (Guardianship of the Person) omitted.]

Declaratory Relief

We thus arrive at the formulation of the declaratory relief which we have concluded is appropriate to this case. Some time has passed since Karen's physical and mental condition was described to the Court. At that time her continuing deterioration was plainly projected. Since the record has not been expanded we assume that she is now even more fragile and nearer to death than she was then. Since her present treating physicians may give reconsideration to her present posture in the light of this opinion, and since we are transferring to the plaintiff as guardian the choice of the attending physician and therefore other physicians may be in charge of the case who may take a different view from that of the present attending physicians, we herewith declare the following affirmative relief on behalf of the plaintiff. Upon the concurrence of the guardian and family of Karen, should the responsible attending physicians conclude that there is no reasonable possibility of Karen's ever emerging from her present comatose condition to a cognitive, sapient state and that the life-support apparatus now being administered to Karen should be discontinued, they shall consult with the hospital "Ethics Committee" or like body of the institution in which Karen is then hospitalized. If that consultative body agrees that there is no reasonable possibility of Karen's ever emerging from her present comatose condition to

a cognitive, sapient state, the present life-support system may be withdrawn and said action shall be without any civil or criminal liability therefore on the part of any participant, whether guardian, physician, hospital or others. We herewith specifically so hold.

Advance Directives, Dementia, and "the Someone Else Problem"

David DeGrazia

DeGrazia criticizes the premises behind the "someone else problem"— the idea that the signer of an advance directive might, through dementia or other psychological impairments, become a numerically distinct individual to whom the directive would no longer apply. He argues that this problem relies on an assumption that humans are *essentially persons*, whose identities are a function of psychological continuity. Instead, DeGrazia suggests, there are several ways that we can and do exist as nonpersons, demonstrating that personhood is a contingent and temporary part of our existence.

For example, we may (like dogs and cats), exist with an awareness of ourselves as persisting over time while no longer being persons capable of complex consciousness. We may also exist as mere subjects of experience without self-awareness, in a state of rudimentary sentience. DeGrazia argues that both these states occur at some points in the development of human beings and that near life's end they may occur again, depending on the circumstances of our death. If we are essentially persons, these other states of being would involve distinct predecessors and successors to our individual identity, a conclusion that seems absurd. Instead, DeGrazia suggests that if we are essentially anything, we are essentially *animals,* and our identity is based on living a single animal life.

This conclusion dissolves the "someone else problem" and suggests that the different states of being human are only *qualitatively* dissimilar, reflecting degrees of difference. It also implies greater continuity between ourselves and other animals. Finally, it excludes the possibility of an afterlife or "beforelife," in which persons would exist independently of their animal existence.

Advance directives are an increasingly important instrument for medical decision-making. These documents permit competent adult patients to

From David DeGrazia, "Advance Directives, Dementia, and 'the Someone Else Problem'," *Bioethics* 13, no. 5 (1999): 373–391. Copyright © 1999 Bioethics. (Notes omitted.)

provide guidance regarding their care in the event that they lose the capacity to make medical decisions. One concern about the use of advance directives is distinctively philosophical: the possibility that, in certain cases in which a patient undergoes massive psychological change, the individual who exists after such change is literally a (numerically) distinct individual from the person who completed the directive. If this is true, there is good reason to question the authority of the directive in question, since it is supposed to apply to the individual who completed it, not to someone else. This may be called 'the someone else problem'.

After briefly introducing advance directives as a basis for medical decision-making, this paper elaborates 'the someone else problem' in the context of severe dementia. The paper then reconstructs the reasoning that leads to this putative problem and exposes the important underlying assumption that we are essentially persons. An alternative view of what we are, one that regards personhood as inessential, is then considered, before several arguments are advanced in favor of that alternative view. The paper next explores implications for advance directives: 'The someone else problem' is effectively dissolved, while it is noted that a related problem (one beyond the paper's scope) may persist. A few implications beyond advance directives are also identified.

How 'The Someone Else Problem' Arises

Advance directives are widely accepted as a basis for medical decision-making on behalf of formerly competent patients, because these documents are recognized as a reasonable extension of the decision-making authority of competent patients. The latter have a right to informed consent—that is, a right to make an informed, voluntary decision as to whether to accept or refuse medical care that is offered to them. In paradigmatic cases of informed consent, the patient is competent both when authorizing medical care and when receiving it (or perhaps shortly before receiving it, as with surgery requiring general anaesthesia). Cases involving advance directives are different. A competent patient completes a directive that gives instructions that are to apply only at future times when she is incompetent. Here respect for patient autonomy is conceived of as extending from one point in time into a future in which competence is lost. (There are various more specific ways of conceptualizing the authority of advance directives, but our purposes do not require enumerating them.)

Several concerns about advance directives suggest the need to limit their authority and to recognize that sometimes they should not be honored.

One such concern is the fact that people sometimes cannot grasp in detail the circumstances in which the directive will apply, so that one's present decision regarding those circumstances is significantly uninformed. Suppose a fifty-year-old completes a directive that authorizes withholding life supports in the event that he becomes demented, a preference based on his belief that he will despise such an existence while in it. Moderately demented ten years later, he is in fact cheerful much of the time and has no desire to die. The present directive is vitiated by the fifty-year-old's limited ability to know what it is like to be demented.

Another concern about the use of advance directives involves major change in an agent's values and preferences between the time of completing the directive and the time when it applies. In principle, one may always rescind an existing directive and issue another that better expresses one's new priorities. But, in practice, people may neglect to do so due to time constraints, procrastination, forgetfulness, or laziness. Suppose an intellectual completes a directive that authorizes withholding life-supports in the event of dementia, because he regards such an existence as degrading. But soon afterward, his wife dies and in his grieving he draws comfort from religion for the first time in his life. His worldview changes significantly and he comes to cherish all human life, regardless of its intellectual quality. A few years later, he is moderately demented. His advance directive is now at odds with the value system he most recently held (or still holds, to the extent that someone in his condition can be said to have a value system).

An advance directive requires its agent to project her own values into various possible future circumstances. The concerns just described highlight two major ways in which such a projection may prove inadequate: A person's life may change, or she may change, in ways that she fails to predict or fully appreciate. The next concern, however, focusses on a much more radical kind of change.

What I call 'the someone else problem' is usually raised in connection with dementia, so a brief description of that condition will be helpful. Alzheimer's dementia is characterized by gradual onset of symptoms and ongoing cognitive decline, and it is not due to specific causes associated with certain other types of dementia. These other types include vascular dementia (which is associated with multiple infarctions involving the cortex), substance-induced persisting dementia, HIV-related dementia, and dementia due to head trauma, Parkinson's Disease, Huntington's Disease, or various other medical conditions.

What the different types of dementias have in common are these three features:

1. memory impairment;

2. one or more of the following cognitive disturbances: (a) aphasia (language disturbance); (b) apraxia (impaired ability to carry out motor activities despite intact motor function); (c) agnosia (failure to identify or recognize objects despite intact sensory function); (d) disturbed executive functioning (planning, organizing, sequencing, and abstracting); and

3. as a result of the above symptoms, significant impairment in social or occupational functioning that represents a substantial decline from a previous level of functioning.

In addition to varying by type, cases of dementia vary in degree of severity. The symptoms of early Alzheimer's, for example, can be subtle: a patient may experience mild memory loss and feel unusually disorganized at times, yet be unaware that she has a significant medical condition. Severe cases of dementia, by contrast, can be shocking for associates to behold: a patient may be unable to talk, to plan one hour into the future, or to identify loved ones.

The remainder of this paper concerns **severely** demented patients, for these individuals provoke 'the someone else problem'. This putative problem arises against the backdrop of a triad of theses concerning the nature of persons, their identity over time, and their essence. Let me elaborate.

What I will call **the Psychological View** about human persons is the conjunction of two philosophical theses (with which an important third thesis, discussed later, is sometimes associated). These two theses have their home in a long philosophical tradition that stems from Locke, derives recent inspiration from Parfit and others, and currently dominates the literature. The first thesis concerns the nature of persons. According to the Lockean tradition, persons are beings with a certain kind of conscious or psychological life. While, on this view, the capacity for consciousness (which, importantly, a person retains even while sleeping) is necessary for personhood, it is not sufficient; if it were, then

all animals who have any states of consciousness at all would qualify as persons. Persons are taken to be conscious beings of a particular sort, having such traits as rationality, self-awareness, and purposive agency. The precise details of an adequate elucidation of personhood are not required here. It will suffice for our purposes to state the first thesis in this way: **Persons are beings with the capacity for complex forms of consciousness (a capacity found, for example, in normal post-infancy human beings)**.

The second thesis stemming from the Lockean tradition concerns the (numerical) identity of persons over time. What makes me the same person as a certain youth who lived most of his teens in the 1970s? According to the present tradition, for A at one time and B at a later time to be the same person, there must be sufficient psychological continuity (exemplified by memories, intentions and their fulfillment, and enduring desires and beliefs) between them. Articulating a fully adequate statement of the relation of psychological continuity proves to be agonizingly complex. But it will suffice for purposes to state the second thesis, somewhat vaguely, as follows: **The identity of persons over time is a function of psychological continuity**.

The two theses just stated, along with the clinical facts of severe dementia, help motivate 'the someone else problem'. (The crucial third thesis, which functions as a suppressed premise in the reasoning that generates this putative problem, is discussed in the next section.) In some cases, according to one line of thought, a demented patient will have such weak psychological connections with the pre-dementia person in question that the two are literally **different persons**. If a competent patient wrote an advance directive refusing life supports in the event of severe dementia, and years later such dementia results in a different person, then the directive, if honored, would seemingly direct care for **someone else**—someone other than the earlier agent. That would be a problem because advance directives are supposed to give guidance for **one's own** medical care. But I don't think this way of posing 'the someone else problem' is optimal. For it requires a very subtle judgment about when person A has so little psychological continuity with person B as to be a distinct person, and such discriminations are difficult to make with any theoretical confidence.

A better way of posing the problem goes like this. Assume that B is so demented as **not to be a person at all**.

Indeed, let us reserve the qualifier 'severely demented' for individuals who are so demented. Given the conception of persons as beings with the capacity for certain complex forms of consciousness, and even allowing that the concept of person is somewhat vague at the boundaries, undoubtedly some demented individuals fail to meet this standard. One can draw a line (or mark out a grey area) wherever one wants. So long as one is working within the Psychological View (as opposed to defining personhood in terms of possession of a soul or a human genetic code, say), one should be prepared to identify some demented individuals as nonpersons. With respect to those demented individuals, 'the someone else problem' can be posed quite starkly. Since B is not a person at all, B is a fortiori not the same person as A. Thus, according to the present line of thought, an advance directive that was completed by A and would apply to B is problematic. For the severely demented patient is someone else—someone other than the author of the directive.

The Crucial Assumption That Personhood is Essential

Let us call A 'Granny-at-fifty' and B 'Granny-at-sixty'. The above reasoning about identity over time, which generates 'the someone else problem', may be reconstructed as follows:

1. Granny-at-fifty is a person.

2. Granny-at-sixty is not a person.

3. Therefore 3. Granny-at-sixty is numerically distinct from (specifically, a 'successor' to) Granny-at-fifty.

But the conclusion 3 does not follow. For it is an open question whether the two 'Granny-stages' might be the same individual even if not the same person. So to make the argument intelligible, we must bring to the surface a suppressed premise:

1a. Granny-at-fifty is **essentially** a person.

Presumably, this is assumed on the basis of the more general assumption that **all human persons are essentially persons**—providing the third thesis, which is sometimes associated with the Psychological View. This thesis, which we may call '**person essentialism**', does not simply mean that we (persons) find personhood very important, such that losing our personhood

would entail a life not worth living. It makes the strict essentialist claim that no human being who is a person can ever exist as a nonperson; personhood is a necessary condition for the existence of a human being who is ever a person. ('Human being' here is meant in a biological sense: a member of the homo sapiens species.)

Some philosophers who accept the two theses of the Psychological View accept person essentialism as well. Occasionally, the thesis is directly stated. But, because the issue of our essence is rarely explicitly addressed by those advancing the Psychological View, it is much more common for person essentialism to be strongly **suggested** rather than directly stated. In bioethics, a number of writers (including some philosophers) who accept the two Lockean theses also assume person essentialism in defending the higher-brain conception of death—that human death is the permanent cessation of the capacity for consciousness (which, given the first two theses, entails the loss of personhood).

Whether directly stated, indirectly suggested, or just tacitly assumed, the assumption that human persons are essentially persons is rarely, if ever, defended. Perhaps that can be explained in this way. Philosophers and others have been interested in the nature of persons and their identity over time. In the background of their reasoning was an awareness that we (those discussing the issue) are persons. So it might not have occurred to them to distinguish the question of **personal** identity over time from the question of **our** identity over time. That would make it easy to assume tacitly that we are essentially persons. In the next section, I will motivate the possibility that this essentialist thesis is false, by identifying an alternative way of understanding what we are.

An Alternative View of What We are: Personhood Inessential

If someone asked you what you are, you would be correct to answer, 'a person'. But this would not be the only possible correct answer. That is because each of us instantiates many different kinds of things, many ontological categories. And, if we are not essentially persons, then we can exist as nonpersons who instantiate one or more of these kinds. The alternative view that I sketch here makes precisely this claim. I will clarify this view by briefly describing three categories, in addition to personhood, that we instantiate.

Let us define a **self** as a **being who is self-aware** in the sense of having some awareness of itself as a being persisting over time. While it is doubtful that any person could fail to be a self, since the complex consciousness required of personhood presumably includes at least minimal self-awareness, it is clear that there can be selves who are not persons. Indeed, many nonhuman animals are such beings—normal cats and dogs, for example. I say this because there is abundantly good reason to hold that many animals have some sense of having a past and future and are not simply 'frozen in the present'. Some humans are also nonpersonal selves. In fact, Granny-at-sixty is a fairly likely candidate, for most (even severely) demented individuals probably have some sense of having a past and future. Even if their memories are terrible, any self-representing memory would suffice for selfhood. Even if they cannot plan the way normal human beings can, any future-oriented desires (say, to use the bathroom) and attempts to fulfill them (say, by looking for the bathroom) would similarly suffice.

To identify another ontological category that human persons instantiate, let us define a **subject of experiences** as a being who has (conscious) mental states, whether or not she has any self-awareness. Such a being might be able to feel pain, for example. Any conscious or sentient being would qualify. Perhaps some animals are sentient and therefore qualify as subjects of experience although they have no self-awareness at all. In the case of humans, presumably fetuses are subjects before they—or the infants they grow into—become selves. And if, by any chance, Granny-at-sixty is so cognitively destroyed as to lack even minimal self-awareness, without falling into a permanent coma or persistent vegetative state (PVS), she would nevertheless be a subject. All selves are subjects, but not vice versa.

Although there are many other ontological categories that human persons instantiate, let us consider just one more, which is familiar enough to require no definition: **animals**. All homo sapiens—including the persons, 'mere selves', and 'mere subjects' among them—are animals. And it is a reasonable conjecture that many animals, such as protozoa, are not even subjects of experience.

On the alternative view of what are, we human persons are only contingently and temporarily persons. We are animals throughout our existence. At some point after coming into being, we become subjects, then selves, and still later persons. Near the end of life, depending on our medical condition and the circumstances of our death, we may well lose personhood before we die; we may even lose selfhood and subjecthood, which will be the case if we enter a state of permanent unconsciousness before dying. We will never lose our animality during our existence, however.

This brief presentation of the alternative view of what we are should clearly demonstrate that person essentialism is eminently debatable. While I will accept the Psychological View's theses about the nature of personhood and about personal identity, I will argue against person essentialism in the next section. Because any variant of the Psychological View that accepts person essentialism takes **our** identity to be a matter of **personal** identity, in challenging person essentialism I will also be challenging the associated claim that our identity consists in psychological continuity.

A Few Good Reasons to Reject Person Essentialism and The Psychological-Continuity View of Our Identity

I believe that there are at least five good reasons to reject person essentialism and the associated thesis that our identity consists in psychological continuity. Several arguments draw from the outstanding philosophical work of Eric Olson, whose recent book, *The Human Animal*, may be the best published case against the view that our identity is a matter of psychological continuity. For reasons of space, my presentation of the arguments will be somewhat compressed.

The first reason to reject person essentialism is that **it implies the absurdity that we were never born**. If we are essentially persons, we cannot ever exist as nonpersons. But newborns are nonpersons, because they lack the complex forms of consciousness that are necessary for personhood. Thus, if we are essentially persons, then we were never born. I cannot believe this. I believe, for example, that I was born in a particular university hospital on July 20, 1962. Presumably, you have similarly confident beliefs about your own birth.

Now if you were never born, then you had a nonpersonal predecessor who was born before you, the person, took its place. The second reason to reject person essentialism is that **it leaves unexplained what happened to this predecessor**. Did it die? We are not aware of any kind of death that regularly occurs in the first two years of human life. (I assume that normal human two-year-olds easily meet the criteria of personhood.) Perhaps the predecessor merely disappeared, rather than dying. Yet it was unquestionably a human organism, if it existed at all, and organisms die. So how could it go out of existence without dying? Maybe, instead, the being that preceded you continues to exist as you, the person, live. In that case, there are **two** beings associated with your body: the person and the predecessor-cum-overlapper. This idea strikes me as too strange to take seriously. I submit that there is no satisfactory account of the relationship between you and any putative predecessor.

Because person essentialism entails that you, a particular person, can never exist as a nonperson, it also entails that PVS, permanent coma, or even severe dementia (on our stipulative definition) would end your existence, since any of these conditions would result in a nonpersonal human organism. This implies that, in such circumstances, you would have a successor, which would die whenever biological life ended. The third argument against person essentialism, then, is that in such cases **it leaves unexplained the origins of a person's successor**. In the case of Granny, was her successor conceived (or otherwise biologically brought into being), say, when she was about fifty-five? We are certainly not aware of any such event that occurs at the onset of severe dementia—or even permanent unconsciousness. Did the successor somehow come into being without being conceived (or otherwise biologically brought into being)? But any successor would clearly be a human organism, a kind of mammal, and mammals are conceived, implanted, born, and so forth. Or is it possible that the human organism that lives when the person goes out of existence was actually brought into being whenever the person was, and lived along with her, inhabiting the same human body, throughout the person's life? This hypothesis of an overlapper-cum-successor strikes me as too strange to believe. I doubt that a proponent of person essentialism can offer an

adequate account of the relationship between you, the person, and your putative organismic successor.

One undeniable fact about us human beings is that we are animals. The fourth reason to reject person essentialism is that **it implies that we are not animals, even contingently**. Consider PVS, which ends the existence of a person (assuming, for simplicity's sake, that personhood was not previously lost due to dementia). The person is gone, but a human animal continues to live—spontaneously breathing, circulating blood, metabolizing, and so on. Now if the person and the animal **can** come apart, then the person cannot **be** the animal. (A thing cannot outlast itself.) But that means that you, the person, are not the animal that would survive in PVS. But surely there is at most one animal life associated with every human life. Thus, if person essentialism is true, you are not an animal at all—a conclusion that contradicts biological fact.

A fifth and final reason to reject person essentialism is that **a much more plausible essentialist claim is that we are essentially homo sapiens, animals, or organisms (members of some biological category)**. How so? For the sake of discussion, let us focus on the claim that we are essentially animals (call this 'animal essentialism'). My contention is conditional in form: **If we are essentially anything, we are essentially animals**. I put matters this way because I am not sure we are essentially anything. Maybe we have an animal aspect and a personal aspect without either being necessary to our continued existence. Even without being sure that we are essentially anything, we may ask which of the two categories—person or animal—is a more plausible candidate for our essence, if we have one.

We have already seen that ordinary human life appears to produce many instances in which we exist as nonpersons: regularly at the beginning of life and sometimes near its end. If appearances are correct, then, we cannot be essentially persons. But there are no **known** cases in which a human being has existed in a nonanimal form. Even if it is logically possible for us to exist as spirits (as in one popular conception of an afterlife) or machines (if replacing body parts, Tinwoodsman-like, would eventually be judged to destroy our animality), it is far from clear that persistence in nonanimal form is **factually** possible—that is, consistent with the laws that govern the actual universe. The world as we know it favors animal essentialism over person essentialism.

If we are essentially animals, then we are not essentially persons, in which case we must reject the psychological-continuity view of our identity. The psychological-continuity theory is a plausible account only for persons. Then what is the criterion of identity for us animals? Something like this would seem right: Animals A and B are identical if and only if A and B share a single animal life. This implies that we come into existence at the emergence of animal life (either at conception or shortly thereafter) and we go out of existence when the animal dies.

Implications for the Use of Advance Directives

We have seen powerful reasons to reject person essentialism, and the associated claim that our identity is a matter of psychological continuity. If we are essentially animals, our identity has nothing to do with psychological continuity. If, on the other hand, a thoroughly anti-essentialist view is correct, then we are limited to saying that our identity **qua persons** consists in psychological continuity, while our identity **qua animals** consists in continuity of biological life. What are the implications for the use of advance directives?

Because the reasoning that produces 'the someone else problem' assumes person essentialism, undermining the latter thesis would seem to dissolve the 'problem'. Or, at the very least, we can say that no one has shown that the severely demented patient is someone other than the signer of the advance directive, the claim that generates the putative problem. Might there be a real problem anyway? Maybe the severely demented nonperson **is**, in some significant sense, someone else.

Let's consider the possibilities. First, if animal essentialism is true, then the identity of Granny-at-fifty and Granny-at-sixty would appear to be guaranteed: They are numerically identical, the same human animal. There would be no basis for saying that the demented nonperson is numerically distinct—literally a different individual—from the earlier agent. At the same time, one might claim that, even if the two are numerically identical,

what really matters is personhood (and personal identity), so we should **regard** Granny-at-sixty, a nonperson, as someone else. A state of dementia causing loss of personhood is so drastically different from our personal existence, one might argue, that it is appropriate to ask whether advance directives should have their usual force in the event that we enter such a state.

This is an important point. Although analytic philosophers have devoted enormous attention to the issue of what our numerical identity consists in, one might reasonably question the importance of this relation. Even if our numerical identity does not consist in psychological continuity, maybe the latter relation carries more practical importance than the former. (And we can still correctly say that our **personal** identity, our identity qua persons, consists in psychological continuity.)

This line of reasoning is, if anything, more strongly motivated if the anti-essentialist view is correct. While this view opposes any argument based on person essentialism, and blocks any unqualified claim that Granny-at-fifty and Granny-at-sixty are numerically distinct, it also blocks any unqualified claim that the two are identical. For if human persons lack an essence, we must ask 'Identical qua what?' The two 'Granny-stages' are identical qua animals, but not qua persons. And, again, one might claim that personal identity is what most matters, supporting the suggestion that we should **regard** Granny-at-sixty as someone else.

The two versions of the argument dovetail into this assertion: 'Granting that we are not essentially persons, whether or not we are essentially animals, what matters is our personal identity. So loss of personhood justifies regarding the surviving individual as effectively 'someone else', raising legitimate worries about the authority of an advance directive completed by the former person.'

This argument, of course, differs from the reasoning that motivated 'the someone else problem', which took the two 'Granny-stages' to be numerically distinct on the basis of person essentialism. This paper has focussed on the latter reasoning and exposed its flaws. But clearly the present argument is worth considering, even if an adequate reply to it would take us beyond the scope of this paper. Here I will offer just a few intuitive remarks that indicate why one might question its soundness.

One way to approach the issue is to ask whether the agent of an advance directive, who contemplates the possibility of severe dementia, would (coherently) **identify with** the surviving individual. I believe I would. I can vaguely imagine being so cognitively diminished as to be a 'mere self', with only slight self-awareness over time. I hope that my actions as a person will provide well for **my** possible existence as a mere self. That is, I care about what would happen to **me** in that situation. I also identify, though barely, with the possible future old-timer who bears my name and exists as a 'mere subject': a human who is sentient but entirely lacking in self-awareness. I have some prudential (as opposed to altruistic) concern about him—and no theoretical claims persuade me that this concern is incoherent. But I don't really identify with 'myself' in a possible future state of permanent unconsciousness, because I would not **experience** such an existence, whether or not it is in some sense 'mine' (just as states of deep sleep can be 'mine').

As far as severe dementia is concerned, there may be good reasons to doubt that personhood is all that really matters. But the remarks I have offered are tentative and undeveloped. My suspicion is that we are actually dealing with a concern that is old and familiar, a concern at home with the sorts of problems discussed above in the section introducing advance directives. That's because what we are talking about here can be understood in terms of **qualitative dissimilarity**, major change in an individual over time. Seen this way, the concern does not seem to create a radical new problem as 'the someone else problem' supposedly did.

A Few Further Implications

Does the rejection of person essentialism have interesting implications beyond the use of advance directives? How about the stronger thesis that we are essentially animals? Here I simply gesture at a few implications, since a full discussion would take us well beyond the scope of this paper.

First, the defeat of person essentialism undermines one of the most important and common motivations for the higher-brain standard of death, according to which human death is the permanent loss of the capacity for consciousness. As noted earlier, many proponents of the higher-brain approach have reasoned that our loss of personhood equals our death on the assumption that we are essentially persons. The non sequitur is now apparent.

Another consequence is more psychological than logical. We all know that human beings are animals. But we are often, it seems, in partial denial of our animality. Ordinary language generally treats nonhuman animals as fundamentally different from human beings: We speak of nonhuman animals (but not of ourselves) simply as 'animals'. Moreover, much human reflection assumes that there is a wide, unbridgeable qualitative gulf between us and the rest of the animal kingdom. Thus, one frequently hears a news clip about some scientific discovery begin with the question, 'What is it that distinguishes us from animals?' Even those who are very careful with the use of 'personhood' language—including philosophers—tend to assume that the world's creatures divide determinately and exhaustively into the classes of persons (represented by normal humans at a certain stage of development) and nonpersons, with persons enjoying exclusive or radically superior moral status. But this neat ontological division is very implausible, since most personhood-relevant properties come in degrees and the immense variety of terrestrial lifeforms exhibits more continuities than dichotomies. If these tendencies in human thought indeed exhibit denial of our animality, then acceptance of the idea that we are animals (whether or not essentially)—and not essentially persons—may help to break through this denial. And doing so may help us stop treating nonhuman animals as if they were simply objects for human use or playthings for human amusement.

If we accept the claim that we are essentially animals, there are two implications concerning our destiny. First, since animals go out of existence when they die, so do we. In other words, there is no afterlife. We cannot be essentially animals and then essentially something else—such as spirits—at a later point in time. (A thing cannot exchange its criterion of identity for a different, incompatible criterion of identity partway through its existence.) Second, if we are essentially animals, then since animals come into existence when animal life begins, so do we. That is, there is no 'beforelife'. That rules out reincarnation. If we are essentially animals, then our existence, like that of other animals, is temporary.

DECISION SCENARIOS

The questions following each decision scenario are intended to prompt reflection and discussion. In deciding how to answer them, you should consider the information provided in the Social Context and Case Presentations, as well as in the Briefing Session. You should also make use of the ethical theories and principles presented in Part VI: Foundations of Bioethics, and the arguments offered in the relevant readings in this chapter.

DECISION SCENARIO 1

Not the Same Person?

Doris Wallbach was seventy-seven years old and had been suffering from advanced dementia for three years. She could neither walk nor feed herself, could barely speak, and was incontinent of urine and stool. Although she sometimes appeared to recognize her daughter for brief moments during her weekly visits, most of Doris's existence seemed to take place in an anxious and confused "eternal present." No matter how gentle and reassuring the nursing home staff tried to be, Doris still experienced being bathed and changed as terrifying bodily violations. She spent much of each day muttering and whimpering to herself in front of the television, with a pained expression on her face. Antidepressant medication had not alleviated this condition, which looked like it might continue for many years. Apart from her dementia, Doris Wallbach was in relatively good physical health.

"It's time to let her go," said Doris's daughter Susan to Jeanne Cavanagh, the facility's new head nurse. "Her advance directive specifies that if she reached this stage of dementia you are to stop spoon-feeding her and then start cutting back on liquids a week later. Her doctor told her that sequence would involve very little discomfort."

"That may be so, but I won't have my staff withholding food and water," Cavanagh said. "As long as she still swallows when we put food in her mouth, she wants to eat. We'll withhold life-saving treatment if that's what her directive says. But we're not obligated to let her starve to death."

"But Mom told us many times that she didn't want her life prolonged if she reached this point," said Susan, who held Doris's durable power of attorney. "She cared for our father when he got Alzheimer's, so she knew how bad dementia can be."

"She's not the same person she was when she wrote that directive. It's my job to care for the person who is here now. "

1. Competent patients have a well-established legal right to voluntarily stop eating and drinking (VSED), and an equally well-established right to refuse future medical treatments through advance directives. Does it follow that they should have the right to refuse food and water through advance directives?

2. Cavanagh expresses a version of what David DeGrazia calls "the someone else problem" in one of this chapter's readings. Is it a convincing reason to disregard Wallbach's advance directive? What if Wallbach's dementia were equally severe but appeared to involve less anxiety and more moment-to-moment pleasure? Should her advance directive still be honored?

3. Cavanagh acknowledges that an advance directive may oblige her to remove life-sustaining medical interventions (such as a ventilator or pacemaker) but refuses to stop spoon-feeding Wallbach. Is she drawing a clear moral distinction between these two actions, or simply reacting to the idea of "starvation"? Would the removal of a ventilator seem equally unacceptable in many cases if we called it "suffocation"?

DECISION SCENARIO 2

The Timothy Quill Case

In March 1991, Dr. Timothy Quill published an article in the *New England Journal of Medicine* in which he described how he had prescribed barbiturates

for Patricia Diane Trumbull, a forty-five-year-old woman suffering from terminal leukemia. Trumbull was in acute and constant pain, had refused aggressive treatment that gave her only a one-in-four chance of survival, and had seen a psychologist who confirmed she was not depressed. In prescribing the medication, Dr. Quill also informed Ms. Trumbull, who had been his patient for a long time, how much of the drug would constitute a lethal dose.

Ms. Trumbull later killed herself by taking an overdose of the barbiturate, and Dr. Quill was investigated by a Rochester, New York, grand jury. Although it is illegal in New York to assist someone in committing suicide, the grand jury decided not to indict Dr. Quill on the charge.

Quill's actions were later reviewed by the three-member New York State Board for Professional Medical Conduct to consider whether he should be charged with professional misconduct. The board arrived at the unanimous decision that "no charge of misconduct was warranted."

The board, in its report, distinguished between Dr. Quill's actions and those of Dr. Jack Kevorkian. (See Case Presentation: Jack Kevorkian in this chapter.) The board pointed to Dr. Quill's long-term involvement in caring for Ms. Trumbull and contrasted it with Dr. Kevorkian's lack of any prior involvement with those whom he assisted in killing themselves.

Moreover, the board pointed out that Dr. Quill "did not directly participate in any taking of life," and this, too, made his actions different from those of Dr. Kevorkian. "One is legal and ethically appropriate, and the other, as reported, is not," the board concluded.

1. Does Quill's action fall within the scope of a physician's legitimate role?

2. Why might one view Quill's action as justifiable?

3. Was Quill's action a case of active euthanasia?

DECISION SCENARIO 3

What Would He Want?

Jeffry Box was eighty-one years old when he was brought to Memorial Hospital. His right side was paralyzed, his speech was garbled, and he had trouble understanding even the simplest questions. His only known relative was a sister four years younger, and she lived half a continent away. When a hospital social worker called to tell her about her brother's condition, she was uninterested. "I haven't seen him in fifteen years," she said. "I thought he might already be dead. Just do whatever you think best for him. I'm too old to worry about him."

Neurological tests and X-ray studies showed that Box was suffering from a brain hemorrhage caused by a ruptured blood vessel.

"Can you fix it?" asked Felicia Hollins, the resident responsible for Box's primary care.

"Sure," said Carl Oceana, the staff's only neurosurgeon. "I can repair the vessel and clean out the mess. But it won't do much good."

"You mean he'll still be paralyzed?"

"And he'll still be mentally incoherent. After the operation he'll have to be put in a nursing home, because he won't be able to see to his own needs."

"And if you don't operate?" Hollins asked.

Oceana shrugged. "He'll be dead by tomorrow. Maybe sooner, depending on how long it takes for the pressure in his skull to build up."

"What would you do?"

"I know what I would want done to me if I were the patient," said Oceana. "I'd want people to keep their knives out of my head and let me die a nice, peaceful death."

"But we don't know what he would want," Hollins said. "He's never been our patient before, and the social worker hasn't been able to find any friends who might tell us what he'd want done."

"Let's just put ourselves in his place," said Oceana. "Let's do unto others what we would want done unto us."

"That means letting Mr. Box die."

"Exactly."

1. On what grounds might one object to Oceana's view?

2. Would active euthanasia be justified in this case?

3. Would the natural law view consider Box's operation mandatory?

DECISION SCENARIO 4

The Bartling Case

When William Bartling was admitted to the Glendale Adventist Medical Center in Los Angeles, he was seventy years old and suffered from five ordinarily fatal diseases: emphysema, diffuse arteriosclerosis, coronary arteriosclerosis, an abdominal aneurysm, and inoperable lung cancer. During the performance of a biopsy to diagnose the lung cancer, Bartling's left lung collapsed. He was placed in the ICU, and a chest tube and mechanical respirator were used to assist his breathing.

Bartling complained about the pain the respirator caused him, and he repeatedly asked to have it removed. When his physician refused, he pulled out the chest tube himself. This happened so often that eventually Bartling's hands were tied to the bed to keep him from doing it. He had signed a living will in an attempt to avoid just such a situation.

Following discussions with Bartling's attorney Richard Scott, hospital administrators and physicians agreed to disconnect the respirator—but the hospital's attorney overruled their decision. He argued that since Bartling was not terminally ill, brain dead, or in a persistent vegetative state, the hospital might be open to legal action.

Scott took the case to Los Angeles Superior Court. He argued that Bartling was legally competent to make a decision about his welfare and that, although he did not want to die, he understood that disconnecting the respirator might lead to his death. The hospital's attorney took the position that Bartling was ambivalent on the question of his death. His statements "I don't want to die" and "I don't want to live on the respirator" were taken as inconsistent and

so as evidence of ambivalence. Removing the respirator, the attorney argued, would be tantamount to aiding suicide or even committing homicide.

The court refused either to allow the respirator to be removed or to order that Mr. Bartling's hands be freed. To do so, the court ruled, would be to take a positive step to end treatment, and the only precedents for doing so were in cases in which the patients were comatose, brain dead, or in a chronic vegetative state.

The case was then taken to the California Court of Appeal, which ruled as follows: "If the right of a patient to self-determination as to his own medical treatment is to have any meaning at all, it must be paramount to the interests of the patient's hospitals and doctors. The right of a competent adult patient to refuse medical treatment is a constitutionally guaranteed right which must not be abridged."

The ruling came too late for William Bartling. He died twenty-three hours before the court heard his appeal.

1. Is there any merit to the hospital's position that to remove Bartling's respirator or to free his hands would be equivalent to assisting suicide?

2. How can the reasoning in the *Quinlan* case be extended to William Bartling's case?

3. What arguments can be used to support the view that it would be morally wrong to untie Bartling's hands?

4. On what grounds might Bartling's request be honored?

DECISION SCENARIO 5

Angel of Mercy?

When two plainclothes detectives arrived at Virginia Crawford's apartment at 6:30 on a Sunday morning to arrest her for murder, she was not surprised to see them.

She cried when they insisted on putting her in handcuffs before transporting her to the jail in the

county court building. Yet she had more or less expected to be arrested eventually. For almost a month, a police investigation had been conducted at Mercy Hospital, where Crawford worked as a nurse in the intensive care unit (ICU). The entire hospital staff knew about the investigation, and Crawford herself had been questioned on three occasions by officers conducting the inquiry. At the time, her answers had seemed to be satisfactory to the police, and there was no hint that she was under suspicion. Still, she always believed that eventually they would catch up with her.

The investigation centered on the deaths of four elderly patients during a period from February 1979 to March 1980. All of the patients were in the ICU at the times of their deaths. Each had been diagnosed with a terminal illness, and the charts of all the patients indicated that they had suffered irreversible brain damage and were totally without higher brain functions.

The three women and one man were all unmarried and had no immediate family to take an interest in their welfare. All of them were being kept alive by respirators, and their deaths were caused directly by their respirators being turned off. In each instance of death, Ms. Crawford had been the person in charge of the ICU.

After securing the services of an attorney, Crawford was released on bail and a time was set for her appearance in court. Through her attorney, Marvin Washington, she made a statement to the media:

"My client has asked me to announce that she fully and freely admits that she was the one who turned off the respirators of the four patients in question at Mercy Hospital. She acted alone and without the knowledge of any other individual. She is prepared to take full responsibility for her actions."

Mr. Washington went on to say that he would request a jury trial for his client. "I am sure," he said, "that no jury will convict Ms. Crawford of murder merely for turning off the life-support systems of people who were already dead."

When asked what he meant by that, Washington explained. "These patients were no longer people," he said. "Sometime during the course of the treatment, their brains simply stopped functioning in a way that we associate with human life."

Ms. Crawford was present during the reading of her statement, and after a whispered conversation with her attorney, she spoke once for herself. "I consider what I did an act of compassion and humanity," she said. "I consider it altogether moral, and I feel no guilt about it. I did for four people what they would have wanted done if they had only been in a condition to know."

1. Does the natural law view offer grounds for removing life-support systems from people who are beyond reasonable hope of recovery? If so, what are they?

2. What arguments might lead us to condemn Virginia Crawford's actions?

3. Can arguments favoring voluntary active euthanasia be extended to justify Crawford's actions?

4. Might Crawford be right about the patients already being dead, according to some concepts of death?

Part IV

Resources

Chapter 8

Organ Transplants and Scarce Medical Resources

CHAPTER CONTENTS

CASES AND CONTEXTS

CASE PRESENTATION
Lungs for Sarah Murnaghan

By age ten, Sarah Murnaghan knew she was dying. Since birth, she had been afflicted with severe cystic fibrosis (CF), a genetic disorder that causes thick, viscous mucus to clog the lungs and digestive tract. The disease has no cure, and by the time Sarah turned ten, her lungs had been severely damaged by chronic infections. She suffered from CF-related diabetes and had to be fed intravenously. Thick secretions seeped from her lungs into her throat, causing her to choke and panic if she wasn't sedated. Her spine was breaking down due to her difficulty absorbing calcium, and her hearing in both ears had been permanently damaged by the powerful antibiotics she had been prescribed to control lung infections.

In 2011, Sarah was placed on a lung transplant waiting list with Priority Status 1. This meant that she had top priority to receive a double lung transplant from another child aged twelve or younger. But pediatric lungs are scarce, due to lower death rates among children and because intensive treatments provided to children often leave their organs unsuitable for transplant. By February 2013, when Sarah was admitted to Children's Hospital of Philadelphia for her failing lungs, she had been on the waiting list for over a year, and no organs suitable for transplant had become available.

Sarah's family, however, had focused their hopes on another type of transplant, one that is riskier and less commonly performed. Instead of transplanting whole lungs from another child, they hoped that Sarah could receive a *partial lobar transplant*, in which lungs from an adult are cut down to fit into the body of a child. Only ten such adult-to-child transplants had been performed since 1987, and they often failed or required another transplant later in life, because the resized adult lungs do not grow with the child as pediatric lungs do.

As Sarah's condition grew desperately worse in the spring of 2013, her parents assumed that she would be moved to the front of the line for a pair of adult lungs, but they soon discovered that this was not the case. The allocation system for lungs developed by the national United Network for Organ Sharing (UNOS) takes into account not only the severity of a patient's condition, but also the statistical likelihood that a given transplant will be successful. The very small number of successful adult-to-child lobar transplants meant that Sarah was effectively at the end of the line for an adult lung transplant, despite the severity of her condition.

When Sarah's parents discovered that their daughter did not have priority for adult lungs, they launched a campaign on social media that attracted attention from several members of Congress. When Health and Human Services secretary Kathleen Sebelius declined to change the policy on Murnaghan's behalf, prominent conservatives called her a "death panel bureaucrat" and Murnaghan's mother charged that she was "going to let a kid die over red tape." Finally, the family filed a lawsuit challenging the UNOS policy, and on June 5, 2013, Federal Judge Michael Baylson ordered Sebelius to grant Murnaghan a second spot in the lung transplant system, this time with a fake birthday that would effectively move her to the front of the adult line. Within a week, Sarah was in surgery to receive a double lung lobar transplant from an adult donor.

Scarcity and Science

The tragic reality of organ transplantation is that there are simply not enough organs available to meet an overwhelming need. Over one hundred thousand Americans are on waiting lists for new organs, and eighteen die each day while they are still waiting. Lungs for transplant are particularly scarce and lung transplants are particularly risky. In 2010, 1,722 adults received lung transplants, but 210 died before they could receive an organ. In 2011, 351 patients died while on the waiting list. (In addition, more than 50 percent of lung transplant recipients die within five years of the procedure, due in part to the high risk of rejection and infection.) Since it is clear that many who need lung transplants to survive will not receive them, profoundly difficult questions arise about how to allocate this scarce resource.

Before 2005, both adults and children were placed in a simple "first come, first served" line for lung transplants. But many complained about the unfairness of a system in which relatively healthy patients took priority over desperately ill ones who would die unless given priority. Others pointed out that some patients are so sick with their underlying diseases that they are unlikely to survive for long, even with a transplant. If the point of a transplant is to provide real benefit and extend life, these patients should perhaps be given second priority after other urgent cases with a better chance of post-transplant survival.

To try to accommodate these competing ethical criteria, transplant experts at UNOS adopted the *lung allocation score* (LAS) in 2006. Using years of statistical data on similar cases, the LAS factors in both estimated survival length without a transplant and estimated survival time post-transplant. Together with a person's diagnosis, body mass index, age, and systolic pressure in the pulmonary artery, these estimates are used to generate an allocation score that determines priority for a transplant. Since its implementation, the LAS has been shown to have reduced both the average waiting time and the number of annual deaths for those on lung transplant waiting lists.

But for those seeking riskier and less-established transplant procedures, such as an adult-to-child partial lobar transplant, the emphasis on statistical significance in the LAS can have serious consequences. For children ten and younger, only around four hundred lung transplants of any kind have been performed, compared to over twenty-five thousand for those twelve and older. As mentioned above, only ten procedures like the one Sarah Murnaghan received had previously been attempted. These numbers are so small that they make statistical modeling impossible, which is one of the main reasons that children under twelve are not competitive in the adult lung transplant system. Still, in the years before the Murnaghan's lawsuit, UNOS had made several shifts to compensate for the relative shortage of pediatric donor lungs. It had given children under twelve priority over adults when adolescent lungs became available and expanded the size of the geographic areas in which the sickest children would get top priority.

Nevertheless, the UNOS policy was still based on data which suggested that children under twelve would do best if given organs from donors who were also under twelve, as well as research that showed substantial differences in child and adult disease states. For John P. Roberts, the president of the OPTN, the decision to prioritize adults for the adult pool and children for the child pool was based on objective criteria and medical research. For the Murnaghan family, it amounted to age discrimination.

"It shouldn't be about their age," Sarah's mother told a reporter. "If she's the sickest person, she should qualify."

Rationing and Rescue

The Murnaghans felt vindicated by Judge Baylson's decision to give Sarah top priority for an adult lung. But critics of the decision argued that it set a bad precedent in violating the UNOS policy of dividing potential recipients into those under twelve years old and those above that age. The division is based on the clinical fact that young children who are transplanted with resized adult lungs suffer more complications and are more likely to reject the transplanted organs. The result is often the waste of lungs that could be used to extend the life of someone else.

Thus, critics charged, giving in to the understandable emotional response of wanting to save the life of a child can end up supporting a policy that fails to save as many lives as otherwise would be possible.

Others were sympathetic to Judge Baylson's perspective, even though they thought his decision was misguided. In their view, he was responding to the immediate and desperate need of the child petitioning the court, rather than considering what impact his ruling might have for others.

The tendency to want to save identifiable individuals from avoidable death, even at great cost to society or to other (unidentified) persons, is known in ethical analysis as the *rule of rescue*. Its most famous example is Jessica Lynch, a toddler in Midland, Texas, who fell into a well pipe in 1987 and whose televised plight generated so many donations that she ended up with a million-dollar trust fund. If that money had been devoted to famine relief in the developing world, some critics point out, many more lives could have been saved—indeed, the donations to the toddler's family far exceeded what was needed for her rescue.

In the case of Sarah Murnaghan, critics point out that the problem is even more concrete and acute. Since a large number of patients die every year on the lung transplant waiting list, there is a good chance that Judge Baylson saved Sarah Murnaghan's life at the expense of another patient's—most likely an adolescent with similar transplant needs. (Secretary Sebelius noted that forty other patients in Murnaghan's home state of Pennsylvania were on the "highest acuity" list for a lung transplant.) Such "tragic choices" are inevitable for any organ distribution program under conditions of scarcity, but that makes it all the more important that distribution occur in a transparent, objective, and reliable fashion.

Defenders of Baylson's decision argue that it was intended to correct an arbitrary inconsistency in UNOS policy, rather than to grant a special exception or "rescue." In their view, the question of how children fare with resized adult lungs is in a state of clinical uncertainty or *equipoise*, to which the correct response is to grant them equal consideration for transplants. Although UNOS and many transplant experts still reject the blanket inclusion of children under twelve in the adult LAS pool as medically unsound, UNOS has now created a permanent process by which individual transplant candidates under twelve can apply for inclusion in the adult LAS system. Critics say the process isn't necessary, and point to a 2014 study in the *American Journal of Transplantation* that failed to find differences in mortality or transplantation rates between children and adults as a result of the LAS rules. They argue that the science still doesn't support changing policies to encourage increased use of partial lobar transplants in young children.

Envoi

Perhaps unsurprisingly, the outcome of Sarah Murnaghan's double lung transplant provided evidence to support both sides of the debate over her case. Sarah's first transplant of lungs from an adult cadaveric donor failed immediately when the organs developed a damaging condition called primary graft dysfunction. She was hooked up to an extracorporeal membrane oxygenation (ECMO) machine, which kept her alive for three days until a second pair of adult donor lungs was located. These, it was discovered, were infected with pneumonia, which may have contributed to the challenges, including a respiratory infection and a tracheostomy, that she faced before she was discharged from the hospital three months later. She was still on a ventilator and had to use a walker for months.

But in June 2014, Sarah's tracheostomy tube was removed, and she was able to breathe on her own for the first time in three years. She began riding her bike, going out to dinner with the family, and planning to return to school in the fall. She still struggled with cystic fibrosis and required physical rehabilitation and immunosuppressant drugs, but she had not yet experienced any serious episodes of transplant rejection. In September of 2014, she turned twelve years old.

Sarah Murnaghan's apparently successful transplant should be cause for celebration on all sides. But her case still raises serious questions about how scarce transplant organs should be fairly and consistently rationed. The bigger problem is that our supply of organs for transplant is still far outstripped by the number of patients in need—a situation that continues to create difficult and often tragic choices for administrators, patients, and their families.

CASE PRESENTATION
Did Steve Jobs Buy a Liver?

Steve Jobs was the legendary cofounder of Apple, Inc., and the creative force behind such innovative technology as personal computers with a graphical interface, as well as the iPod, iPhone, and iPad. He was a major figure in the world's financial community and at the time of his death had a personal net worth estimated to be around $10 billion.

In 2004, Jobs was diagnosed with pancreatic cancer, a disease that in the United States alone kills about twenty-five thousand people a year. His doctors found, however, that Jobs had an islet-cell neuroendocrine tumor, one of the few forms of pancreatic cancer that can be treated with some success. Most forms of pancreatic cancer progress so rapidly that by the time they are diagnosed treatment is ineffective. Islet-cell tumors are slow growing, however, so treatment has a decent chance of succeeding.

In July 2004, Steve Jobs was operated on to remove the tumor. Jobs received no chemotherapy or radiation treatments, and a few months after the surgery he returned to his position at Apple. Even though Jobs was back at work, he didn't seem completely well. He lost a significant amount of weight and began suffering from digestive problems. He appeared so thin and frail that his health became a matter of financial concern, as investors began to speculate about whether Jobs would be able to continue to guide Apple and maintain its profits. As news of Jobs's operation for pancreatic cancer leaked out, some observers began to interpret his fragile appearance as evidence that he still had cancer. The most likely scenario appeared to be that the islet-cell tumor had metastasized to his liver, something that would not be unusual. Neither Jobs, his wife, nor an Apple representative would make any public comment about this possibility. In January 2009, however, Jobs announced that he would take a six-month leave for health reasons.

Liver Transplant

In June 2009, reports began to surface that Jobs, who was then fifty-four years old, had received a liver transplant two months earlier. Jobs himself refused to comment, but people who had been briefed by members of Apple's board of directors confirmed to reporters that Jobs had received a liver transplant in Tennessee. Although the name of the hospital wasn't released, it didn't take long for it to leak out that the surgery had taken place at the Methodist University Hospital Transplant Institute in Memphis. The institute, which performs about 120 liver transplants a year, eventually issued a press release, with Jobs's permission, confirming that Jobs had been a patient there. He had received a liver from a deceased donor in April 2009.

At that time, Jobs was living in the San Francisco area, which is more than two thousand miles from Memphis. Why, then, many asked, did he go to a hospital in Memphis for a liver transplant? Was it because, by going to Memphis, he was somehow able to use his wealth to manipulate the transplant system and get a donor liver he didn't deserve? Donor livers are a scarce resource. Nationwide, around sixteen thousand people are on the waiting list for a new liver, and only about five thousand of them will receive one. Some suggested that Jobs may have used his great wealth to game the organ transplant system.

Getting a Liver Transplant

A 1984 U.S. law makes it illegal to buy or sell organs, so it is highly unlikely that Jobs could have bought a liver and had it transplanted at Methodist University Hospital. Nor is the organ distribution system set up so that people can jump to the front of the line. The 127 transplant centers in the United States all follow the same set of rules for allocating organs. The rules are formulated by the United Network for Organ Sharing (UNOS), an independent agency that works under a contract with the federal government and runs the Organ Procurement and Transplantation Network (OPTN). UNOS regularly audits transplant centers to make sure that they adhere to consistent definitions and categories for determining which patients are in greater need or more likely to benefit from a transplant than other patients.

Patients on the waiting list for a liver are categorized in terms of features such as their human leukocyte antigen (HLA) profile (human leukocyte antigens are proteins on cell surfaces) as well as their overall size (a liver from a large man won't do for a small child). These categories are used to help determine who is a suitable candidate for a transplant organ.

Patients are also characterized by how sick they are. Liver transplant candidates are given a Model for End-Stage Liver Disease (MELD) score that determines where they rank on the transplant list. The score ranges from 6 to 40, and the higher the score, the sicker the patient. The higher score also means the patient ranks higher on the transplant list. (When patients have the same MELD score, the one who has been on the list longer is ranked higher.)

UNOS also maintains the waiting list for transplant organs and works with the nation's fifty-eight regional organ procurement organizations (OPOs). When an organ becomes available, an OPO consults the UNOS waiting list for a suitable recipient in the relevant geographical region. Because organs begin to deteriorate as soon as they lose their blood supply, the distance they can be transported and remain viable is limited. Thus, organs are distributed first to local candidates, then to more distant ones. This means that someone local may get a liver even though his MELD score is not as high as someone farther away.

Contrary to the belief of many, there is no national waiting list for transplants, only regional ones. Regions vary considerably in both geographical area and population size. Thus, regions like New York and Los Angles have ten to fifteen times the populations of regions like St. Louis and Memphis. This means that someone needing a transplant is more likely to get one more quickly in (say) Memphis or St. Louis than in New York, Los Angeles, or San Francisco.

The national average waiting time for a transplant liver is over a year, and in regions with dense populations, the time can be more than three years. The waiting time in the Memphis region from 2002 to 2007 was four months. Thus, someone on the waiting list and needing a liver transplant was likely to have to wait a much shorter time in the Memphis region than in the San Francisco region. Those with lower MELD scores are also more likely to get a donor liver quickly in low-population regions—and may have shorter wait times than those with substantially higher scores but who live in more densely populated

regions. More organs may be available in high-population areas, but the demand is also greater. (Indeed, the demand for livers regularly exceeds the supply.)

In this situation, money can play a significant role in who gets a transplant. A transplant organ can't be bought, but unless a patient has the means (cash or insurance) to pay for the surgery, the organ-acquisition fees, the hospital stay, and the drugs and medical care needed after the surgery, the patient will not make it to the transplant list. A liver transplant costs about $600,000, so an estimated one-third of people needing one cannot qualify on financial grounds alone. Despite the recent implementation of the Affordable Care Act, it is doubtful that this figure will change substantially. Even though many more people now have medical insurance, many policies do not cover organ transplants, and even if they do, the out-of-pocket costs can still amount to tens or even hundreds of thousands of dollars.

Multicenter Registration

If you are shopping in a supermarket and are in a hurry, you look for the fastest checkout line. Often your choice is wrong, and you find yourself wishing you were in line A instead of line B. If you have to wait in line at all, it would be ideal if you could wait in all the lines at the same time—or at least all that seem to be moving quickly.

In 2003, UNOS began requiring transplant centers to notify candidates for organ transplants that they can be evaluated and registered (be put on the waiting list) at more than one center. Also, they can transfer the waiting time built up at one center to any other center. Thus, in principle, candidates for a liver transplant can register at multiple centers and so be put on multiple regional waiting lists. This gives them a better chance of reducing their wait for an organ than if they had to wait in only one line—particularly if that line happens to be in a heavily populated region like New York or San Francisco.

Everyone is eligible to register at multiple centers, but as with so much else in life, what can be done in principle is difficult or impossible for most people to do in practice. To start with, every center typically requires that anyone who wants to register for a transplant at that center be evaluated by that center. Such a workup may cost $10,000 or more, and most insurance companies are not likely to pay for multiple evaluations. Hence, individuals who want to register with several centers must be able to pay the additional evaluation costs themselves.

In addition, even when an insurance policy covers the costs of a transplant, the insurance company typically requires that the transplant be performed at a particular transplant center. This is because the company has negotiated a price with that center, so the company will refuse to pay the full cost (or perhaps any of the cost) for a transplant carried out at another center. Thus, usually the only people who can take advantage of multicenter registrations are those who can afford to pay the full $600,000 or more for a transplant.

Transplants and Wealth

Whether Steve Jobs registered at several transplant centers has not been made public. Multicenter registration would explain, though, why someone who lives in the San Francisco area received a liver transplant at a Memphis hospital. Waiting times for specific organs at transplant centers are public information. As mentioned earlier, the national average waiting time for a donor liver was 12.3 months, but the waiting time at the Methodist University Hospital Transplant Center was 3.8 months. It would have made sense for Steve Jobs to register with the Memphis center. As Michael Poreyko, director of liver transplants at Vanderbilt University, observed, a person with access to a private jet could probably reach any transplant center in the United States during the six-hour window that a donor liver remains viable and suitable for transplant.

Steve Jobs had a net worth measured in billions. He would have had no difficulty paying for the evaluations required to get onto the waiting lists at many different transplant centers. He also would have had no trouble paying for the transplant out of his own pocket. He would have had no difficulty getting access to a private plane to deliver him to a center as soon as a donor liver became available and his MELD score qualified him to be the recipient.

None of these facts indicate that Jobs did anything wrong in getting his liver transplant. Nothing at all suggests that he cheated or pushed his way to the front of the line. What the case of Steve Jobs makes clear, however, is that the organ transplant system is structured to favor the rich. Only they can afford to pay for the multiple evaluations required to register at several transplant centers, and only they have access to private planes that can rush them to a center when an organ becomes available. Finally, only the rich can afford to pay for a transplant if their insurance won't cover the costs at a particular center.

Envoi

In the end, although Steve Jobs's story exemplifies the ways in which money can provide advantages in the organ transplant system, it also demonstrates the limits of what money can buy. Less than two years after his liver transplant with an "excellent" prognosis, Jobs was forced to take another medical leave of absence from Apple. It was later revealed that his metastatic pancreatic cancer had returned. He died at his home in Palo Alto, California, on October 5, 2011.

SOCIAL CONTEXT
Acquiring and Allocating Transplant Organs

Organ transplantation is a dramatic example of how the advanced technology of contemporary medicine can extend or improve the lives of hundreds of thousands of people. Developments in surgical techniques, improvements in organ preservation, and the advent of new immunosuppressive drugs have made organ transplantation into a standard surgical therapy.

Yet behind the wonder and drama of transplant surgery lies the troubling fact that the need for transplant organs seriously and chronically outstrips the supply. Thus, against a background of a chronic shortage, physicians, surgeons, and committees must make judgments that will offer an opportunity for some while destroying the last vestige of hope for others.

Although transplanting kidneys began as early as the 1950s, the list of organs now transplanted with a significant degree of success has been expanded over the last twenty years to include corneas, bone marrow, bone and skin, livers, lungs, pancreases, intestines, faces, and hearts. All involve special problems, but we will limit discussion to solid organs—those like the heart and liver, which are complete functional units.

More than three hundred thousand kidney transplants have been performed in the United States since 1988, and about 93 percent of these organs are still functioning one year later. (Some recipients are still alive after almost forty years.) Thomas Starzl and his team successfully transplanted the first liver in 1967, and the rate of survival after five years is now about 75 percent. Also in 1967, Christiaan Barnard transplanted a human heart, and now around 75 percent of heart recipients survive more than five years. Lung transplants are still a relatively new procedure and have a 51 percent five-year survival rate. New techniques of management and the development of drugs to suppress part of the immune response have done much to increase the success rate of transplants, but additional improvements will probably require improvements in the ability to control tissue rejection. (See the Briefing Session for more details.)

Costs

A major social and moral difficulty of transplant surgery is that it is extremely expensive. For example, in the United States, the total costs of a kidney transplant average more than $250,000, a liver transplant averages more than $550,000, and a heart transplant averages almost $1 million. The immunosuppressive drugs needed to prevent rejection of a transplanted organ cost as much as $30,000 a year, and they must be taken for the remainder of

the patient's life. Despite the high costs of transplantation, it may offer cost savings over dialysis and medical treatments.

Questions have been raised in recent years about what restrictions, if any, should be placed on access to transplants. Should society cover the costs of those who need them but cannot afford them? Medicare, Medicaid, and most, but not all, insurance companies provide organ transplant coverage and pay at least part of the continuing drug and treatment costs. The End-Stage Renal Disease Program covers kidney transplants for everyone, yet people needing any other sort of transplant who don't qualify for public programs and lack appropriate insurance must find some way of raising the money. Otherwise, hospitals are not likely to provide them with an organ. Every transplant candidate, in Starzl's phrase, must pass a "wallet biopsy" to qualify.

Despite the dramatic increase in insurance coverage resulting from the implementation of the Affordable Care Act, insurance policies that will pay for a heart, liver, lung, or any other kind of organ transplant are still expensive and involve substantial out-of-pocket costs. This means that the great majority of people are still in the position of having to pass the wallet biopsy before they qualify for the transplant waiting list.

Availability

The second major problem, after cost, is the availability of donor organs. The increase in the number of transplant operations performed during the last thirty years has produced a chronic scarcity of transplant organs. About thirty thousand people a year receive transplants at the nation's transplant centers, but about seven thousand die each year while waiting for organs. To put this in perspective, this is more than twice the number of people who died in the September 11, 2001, terrorist attack on the World Trade Center.

At any given time, more than one hundred thousand people are on the transplant waiting list in the United States. Each year, as many as fifty thousand additional people register to receive organs. For each organ transplanted, three more people sign up, and those on the waiting list die at a rate of eighteen per day.

People in need of a kidney or pancreas can rely on dialysis or insulin injections to treat their diseases, but those in need of a liver, heart, or lung have limited alternative treatments available. Artificial livers remain experimental, and left ventricular assist devices can help only some heart patients. For those waiting for livers, lungs, or hearts, the lack of a suitable transplant organ can constitute a death sentence. Given the currently limited supply of organs, we face two key questions: 1) How can the supply be increased? and 2) How are those who will actually receive organs to be selected from the pool of candidates?

Increasing Supply

An obvious answer to the first question is that the supply of organs can be increased by increasing donations. Exactly how many organs that could be used for transplant fail to be retrieved from the newly deceased. According to one estimate, there are more than thirteen thousand potential donors each year, but because the next of kin either is not asked to donate or refuses to donate, or because of the circumstances of death or the condition of the organs, only about half of potential donors become actual donors.

At a time when the need for donors is increasing, the number of organ donations in the United States is decreasing or stagnant. The number of live donors peaked in 2004 and has declined since then. Although the number of deceased donors has not declined substantially

since 2008, it has also not increased. Some way to reverse these trends is desperately needed.

Required Request and Required Response Laws

The federal Uniform Anatomical Gift Act of 1984 served as a model for state organ donation laws, and virtually all states have enacted laws to promote the increase of organ donation. Some states have "required response" laws requiring people to declare, upon renewing their driver's license, whether they wish to become organ donors, and most states make it easy for people to decide to become donors at the DMV. State laws based on the act spell out a person's right to donate all or part of her body and to designate a person or institution as a recipient. A federal law passed in 1987 mandates that organ donor cards be included with tax refund checks.

Even with the support of such laws, transplant centers have been reluctant to intrude on a family's grief by asking that a deceased patient's organs be donated. Even if a patient has signed an organ donation card, the permission of the immediate family is required, in most cases, before the organs can be removed. In 1991, a federal appeals court ruled in favor of an Ohio woman who argued that the coroner who had removed her husband's corneas during an autopsy and donated them to the Cincinnati Eye Bank had violated her property rights. Her property interest in her husband's body was found to be protected under the due process clause of the Fourteenth Amendment.

In an attempt to overcome the reluctance of physicians to request organ donations, a 1986 federal law requires that hospitals receiving Medicare or Medicaid payments identify patients who could become organ donors at death. The law also requires that hospitals discuss organ donations with the families of such patients and inform them of their legal power to authorize donations. Although this "required request" law has been in effect for more than twenty years, the law has helped facilitate only a modest (about 10 percent) increase in the supply of transplant organs.

Donation before Brain Death

The majority of deceased organ donations occur after a person has been declared brain dead, often while mechanical ventilation keeps blood and oxygen flowing to vital organs. But the acute need for transplants has also prompted physicians to use the earlier *cardiopulmonary* death criterion, in order to act on the requests of patients to remove their organs when their hearts stop beating, even though they may not yet be brain dead. (See Chapter 7 for a discussion of criteria for determining death.) Hence, a person on a ventilator wanting to be weaned off the machine may allow her organs to be used for transplant, should the withdrawal result in her death. The ventilator is removed in an operating room, and three minutes after the patient's heart has stopped beating, the transplant organs are removed. In practice, most *non-heart-beating donors* are not like the one described. They have suffered severe brain damage but are not brain dead, and permission has been obtained from their families.

Critics of the practice have raised questions about using the cessation of heartbeat as a proper criterion for death. (Perhaps the patient could be resuscitated. Is three minutes long enough to wait?) Some have also wondered if the practice doesn't put pressure on mentally competent, but seriously ill, patients to give up the struggle for their lives by volunteering to become organ donors. Similarly, critics have charged, by providing a rationalization, the practice may make it too easy for the parents or other representatives of comatose patients on life support to decide to withdraw support and end the person's life.

Organ Protection before Obtaining Consent

Another innovative but controversial approach employed by some medical centers involves injecting organ-protective drugs and preservatives into patients who die in or on the way to an emergency room. The organs are not removed from the body (although some surgical steps may be taken), but by making sure the organs have a good blood supply and so are protected from damage, physicians gain additional time to seek permission from the families. Otherwise, the organs would deteriorate and be useless for transplantation.

Critics of this practice claim that hospitals do not always determine that a patient is dead before injecting drugs with the aim of preserving the organs. Thus, physicians can cause harm to still-living patients. Others claim that the practice borders on desecration and denies dignity to individuals whose dead bodies are subjected to an invasive procedure without their prior consent.

Defenders of the practice say it gives families time to recover from the shock of learning about the death of a loved one and allows them to make a more considered decision. In this respect, the practice is more humane than asking a family for permission to take an organ from a loved one at the same time they are informed of the death. Also, since organs deteriorate rapidly, taking steps to preserve them will result in more successful transplants.

Using organs from non-heart-beating cadavers and preserving the organs of the newly dead before securing consent are both practices that aim to provide a way to offset the gap between the number of transplant organs available and the number needed by those awaiting a transplant. Although twelve thousand to twenty thousand people are declared brain dead every year, one hundred thousand are in need of transplants.

Selling Organs

Another possibility for increasing the organ supply is to permit organs to be offered for sale. Before death, an individual might arrange payment for the posthumous use of one or more of his organs. Or after his death, his survivors might sell his organs to those in need. In a variation of this proposal, donors or their families might receive tax credits, or a donor might be legally guaranteed that if a family member or friend required a transplant organ, that person would be given priority in the distribution. Under any of these plans, there would be a greater incentive to make organs available for transplant.

The public reaction to any plan for marketing organs has been strongly negative. People generally regard the prospect of individuals in need of transplants bidding against one another in an "organ auction" or offering a kidney for sale on eBay as ghoulish and morally repugnant, and this attitude typically extends to all forms of the market approach. In 1984, the National Organ Transplantation Act made the sale of organs for transplant illegal in the United States. At least twenty other countries, including Canada, Britain, and most of Europe, have similar laws.

A third possibility would be to allow living individuals to sell their non-vital organs to those in need of transplants. Taking hearts from living people would be illegal, as it would involve homicide by the surgeon who removed them. However, kidneys occur in pairs, and we already permit individuals to donate one of them—indeed, we celebrate those who do. These donors typically experience few complications or long-term health problems, especially with laproscopic

procedures. Also, surgeons can now remove a lobe of a donor's liver and transplant it into a recipient with relative safety. It is thus only a short step from the heroic act of giving away a kidney or the lobe of a liver to the commercial act of selling it.

Allowing the sale of an organ would be in keeping with the generally acknowledged principle that people ought to be free to do as they wish with their own bodies. We already permit the sale of blood, plasma, bone marrow, ova, and sperm. Also, the kidney shortage is so severe that it cannot be addressed without using kidneys from living donors. Similarly, people with end-stage liver disease have no alternative to a transplant, and the need for livers outstrips the supply. Paying kidney and liver-lobe donors for their organs would thus save lives.

The most telling disadvantage to allowing such transactions as a matter of social policy, however, is that it would disproportionately impact the poor. It is all too easy to imagine a low-income parent deciding to improve the lives and opportunities of her children by selling her kidney or liver lobe.

That the economically advantaged should thrive by literally exploiting the bodies of the poor seems morally repulsive to most people. (The 1984 Organ Transplant Act was a direct response to the operations of the International Kidney Exchange, which sold kidneys from living donors in Virginia—most of whom turned out to be indigent.) The argument that someone should be permitted to do as he wishes with his body to provide for the welfare of his family seems particularly strained when the situation involves destitute individuals facing overwhelming incentives to put their lives and health at risk.

"Everyone Makes Money, Except for the Donor"

Despite strong public sentiment against selling organs, a telephone poll conducted by the United Network for Organ Sharing and the National Kidney Foundation found that 48 percent of those interviewed favored some form of "donor compensation." Under the Transplant Act, there can be none.

The law does permit payments associated with removing, preserving, transporting, and storing human organs. As a result, a large industry has developed around organ transplants. Fifty-eight procurement organizations, operating in federally defined geographical regions, collect organs from donors and transport them to the 270 hospitals with transplant facilities.

A procurement agency may be paid as much as $100,000 for its services. This amount includes fees for ambulance trips to pick up and deliver the organ, fees to the hospital for the use of the operating room where the organ is removed, costs of tissue matching and blood testing, and overhead expenses for the agency and its personnel.

In addition, costs involved in a transplant may include fees paid to local surgeons to prepare the patient for organ removal and those paid to regional transplant specialists who may perform the actual surgery. Such fees typically amount to tens of thousands of dollars. Hospitals pay for the organs they receive, but they pass on their costs and more. According to one study, hospitals may mark up the cost of an organ by as much as 200 percent to cover costs that patients are unable to pay or that exceed the amount the government will reimburse. A donor of several organs can produce considerable income for the transplanting hospital.

Some critics of current transplant practices have pointed out that everyone except the donor makes money from donated organs. Yet matters show little sign of changing. A representative of the National Kidney Foundation proposed to a congressional committee that the law be changed to allow a relatively small amount of money (perhaps $2,000) to be given to the families

of organ donors as a contribution to burial expenses. The recommendation was not acted on, and similar proposals seem no more likely to meet with success.

Given current transplant practices, it is understandable why donor families sometimes become bitter. When Judy Sutton's daughter Susan killed herself, Ms. Sutton donated Susan's heart and liver and so helped save the lives of two people. Ms. Sutton then had to borrow the money to pay for Susan's funeral. "Susan gave life even in death," Sutton told a reporter. "It's wrong that doctors make so much money off donors. Very wrong."

Presumed Consent

A possibility widely discussed as a means of increasing the number of transplant organs is adopting a policy of "presumed consent." This involves a state or federal law that allows hospitals to presume that a recently deceased person has tacitly consented to having any needed organs removed, unless the person had indicated otherwise or unless the family objects. The burden of securing consent would be removed from physicians and hospitals, and the burden of denying consent would be imposed on individuals or their families. To withdraw consent would require positive action.

A policy of presumed consent has been adopted by several European countries. Critics of the policy point out that this has not, in general, done much to reduce the shortage of transplant organs in those countries. Although legally empowered to remove organs without a family's permission, physicians continue to be reluctant to do so. Also, if families are to be given the opportunity to deny consent, they must be notified of the death of the patient, and in many cases this involves a considerable loss of time. Thus, it is doubtful that presumed consent would do a great deal to increase the number of usable transplant organs in the United States.

Altruistic Donation

After reviewing the alternative approaches, many observers argue that the present system of organ procurement by voluntary donation for altruistic reasons is the best system. It appeals to the best in people rather than to greed and self-interest, it avoids exploiting the poor, and it is efficient. Families who donate organs can gain some satisfaction from knowing that the death of a loved one brought some benefit to others.

Living Donors

Some centers have relaxed or eliminated rules requiring that a living donor belong to the same family as the recipient. This practice allows individuals motivated by love or altruism to profoundly benefit a friend, a coworker, or a complete stranger. The importance of living donors can be appreciated by considering that if only one in every three thousand people donated a kidney, the kidney shortage would be solved. Also, recipients of a kidney from a living donor have significantly higher five- and ten-year survival rates than those who receive kidneys from deceased donors.

Kidneys, as mentioned earlier, are no longer the only organs transplanted from living donors. A healthy liver rapidly regenerates, and lobes have been transplanted with success. More recently, lung segments have been added to the list. Although the risks of liver donation procedures are higher (1 death in 500 procedures) than those of kidney donation (1 death in 1,700 procedures), studies indicate that the long-term risks of having donated a kidney or a liver lobe are comparably minimal. The rate of serious complications for living lung donors appears to be significantly higher than those of kidney or liver donors, but they still only affect 4 to 5 percent of donors.

Although the use of living donors can help reduce the chronic scarcity of some organs, the practice is not without critics. Thomas Starzl, the developer of liver transplants, refused to use living kidney donors, because too often the person in a family who "volunteers" to be a donor does so only because of the pressures of family dynamics. In effect, Starzl charges, consent cannot be genuine. Those favoring the practice argue that Starzl's criticism is not a reason to reject living donors so much as a reason to design a system of securing informed consent that will protect vulnerable individuals. When the informed consent process is reliable, they hold, living organ donation is ethically sound.

The chronic shortage of transplant organs probably cannot be relieved by any one of the proposals mentioned here. Some combination of them might substantially mitigate the shortage, but we may ultimately have to rely on advances in biotechnology to fully address the problem. If genetic engineering made it possible to breed pigs with organs that did not cause rejection by the human immune system, for example, the shortage of transplant organs could be ended. Some critics worry that the use of animal transplants, even if successful, might be dangerous. Viral sequences incorporated into pig DNA might mutate or cross over in genetic recombination and produce deadly and uncontrollable viruses. Also, some question the expanded breeding of domestic animals solely to serve human wants and needs. The long-term solution, some believe, is that a powerful stem-cell technology, in addition to tissue engineering, may one day allow us to grow replacement kidneys, hearts, and livers that are compatible with an individual's immune system, making the use of immunosuppressive drugs unnecessary. Although we can imagine, in detail, how this might be achieved, it is currently still in the realm of science fiction.

Organ Allocation

Whatever innovations the future may hold, the fact remains that at present the supply of transplant organs is limited and the demand far exceeds the supply. Thus, the key question today is, How are organs to be distributed when they become available? Currently, no national policies or procedures supply a complete answer to this question. In general, such decisions are made in accordance with policies adopted by particular regional or hospital-based transplant programs.

Typically, a transplant center employs a screening committee made up of surgeons, physicians, nurses, social workers, and a psychologist to determine whether a candidate for a transplant should be admitted to the waiting list. Medical need—whether the candidate might benefit from the transplant—is the first consideration, but it is far from the only one. A committee's decisions may also be based on the patient's general medical condition, age, and ability to pay for the operation, as well as whether he has the social support needed to assist him during recovery, shows evidence of being able to adhere to a lifetime regimen of antirejection drugs, and belong to the constituency that the center is committed to serving. Factors like race and gender are considered irrelevant, but evidence suggests that in practice an individual's "social worth" (education, occupation, accomplishments) are sometimes taken into account.

Some large transplant centers employ a scoring system that involves assigning values to a list of what the center considers relevant factors. Those with the highest score are accepted as candidates and given a priority ranking. If their medical condition worsens, they may later be moved up in the ranking. At most centers, this process is carried out in a more informal fashion.

Once a patient is admitted to a center's waiting list, the allocation rules of the federally funded United Network for Organ Sharing also apply. UNOS policies stipulate the ways in which organs are distributed. Until recently, when an organ became available within one of the nine UNOS regions of the country, the institutions in the region had first claim on it, without respect to the needs of patients in other regions. In practice, few organs ever left the region in which they were donated. UNOS now stipulates that an organ must go to a patient with the greatest need, no matter what the region, assuming the organ can be transported in good condition to the patient.

The policy creates something like a national waiting list. Proponents say that it will get more organs to the patients who need them most, while critics charge that it means that the greatest number of organs go to the largest transplant centers, because the largest number of patients in acute need are there. Eventually, then, a number of centers will have to close. Some observers view this positively, for not all centers perform enough transplants to gain the experience needed to offer patients the best outcomes possible.

Some of the factors considered by transplant centers in admitting a patient to the waiting list have been criticized as morally irrelevant. A patient's social worth and ability to pay are rejected by most critics, but opinion is divided over how much weight should be given to factors such as alcoholism, drug abuse, and poor health habits. Because of the shortage of organs, people needing transplants as a result of "lifestyle diseases" caused in part by obesity, smoking, or alcohol abuse. By contrast, others would ask only that such people demonstrate a willingness to change their behavior. At present, transplant centers have much leeway in deciding which candidates to accept.

A good example of an effort to formulate acceptable guidelines for making decisions about allocating organs is the Massachusetts Task Force on Organ Transplantation. In 1985, the group issued a unanimous report that included the following recommendations:

1. Transplant surgery should be provided "to those who can benefit most from it in terms of probability of living for a significant period of time with a reasonable prospect for rehabilitation."

2. Decisions should not be based on "social worth" criteria.

3. Age may be considered as a factor in the selection process, but only to the extent that age is relevant to life expectancy and prospects for rehabilitation. Age must not be the only factor considered.

4. If not enough organs are available for all those who might benefit from them, final selections should be made by some random process (e.g., a lottery or a first-come, first-served basis).

5. Transplants should be provided to residents of New England on the basis of need, regardless of their ability to pay, as long as this does not adversely affect health care services with a higher priority. Those who are not residents of New England should be accepted as transplant candidates only after they have demonstrated their ability to pay for the procedure.

Organ transplantation continues to face two crucial problems: the chronic shortage of organs and the inability of some people needing a transplant to pay for one. The shortage problem might eventually be solved by developments in biotechnology, but the financial problem could be solved immediately by a change in social policy. For example, why should our society be willing to fund a kidney transplant for someone without insurance or adequate financial resources, yet refuse to fund someone needing a liver or heart transplant?

CASE PRESENTATION
The Prisoner Who Needed a Heart

We'll call him Ken Duke. That's not his name, but the California Department of Corrections doesn't make public the names of prisoners under its jurisdiction.

Ken Duke was a dangerous man. Not a murderer, but a violent thief. The first California conviction that got him sent to prison was for armed robbery. After serving only part of his sentence, Duke had done enough time and behaved well enough to merit parole.

But Duke's parole didn't last long. In 1996, a mere eight months after the prison bus dropped Ken Duke off in Los Angeles, he was again arrested for armed robbery in Los Angeles County. He was convicted of the crime in March 1997 and sentenced to serve a fourteen-year term

in prison. Under California law, Duke wouldn't be eligible for a second chance at parole until 2008.

Heart Damage

Ken Duke may have lived a bad life, but he also had some bad luck. Somewhere along the line, either on the street or in prison, he became infected with a virus that severely damaged his heart. For years, he lived with the damage without too much trouble, but as time passed, Duke's heart steadily deteriorated. His heart muscle weakened, and the heart lost its pumping effectiveness. It grew in size to compensate for its loss of function, but this created other problems.

Duke was given drugs to strengthen his heartbeat, but his blood circulation still slowed. Without a steady blood flow to carry away wastes, fluid built up in his lungs, reducing their effectiveness. His feet and ankles swelled, and he became so out of breath that even slight exertions, like walking across his cell, became impossible. He had to sleep with his head and shoulders raised to be able to breathe. Ken Duke was only thirty-one years old, but he was already profoundly sick and feeble, suffering from congestive heart failure.

Unique Status

Duke was transferred from the Vacaville prison hospital in Northern California to the Stanford University Medical Center, one of the nation's leading medical facilities. His condition was assessed by the Stanford physicians assigned to care for him, and they were unanimous in their conclusion: If Ken Duke didn't get a heart transplant, he would die.

Treating Duke the way they would any other patient, the Stanford physicians listed Duke with the United Network for Organ Sharing as a candidate for a donor heart. His medical condition was so precarious that he was assigned to the category of those most urgently in need of a transplant.

At the time Ken Duke's name was entered on the UNOS waiting list, about four thousand other Americans were also waiting for a donor heart. Duke was unique, though; not only was he the only prisoner on the heart transplant list, he was the only prisoner who had ever been on the list.

The United Network for Organ Sharing, the agency responsible for framing the general rules for allocating transplant organs, explicitly refuses to distinguish between prisoners and other people, so far as qualifying for an organ is concerned. *The UNOS Ethics Committee Position Statement Regarding Convicted Criminals and Transplant Evaluation* holds that "one's status as a prisoner" should not preclude anyone "from consideration for a transplant." Whether patients, incarcerated or not, actually receive a transplant depends on their medical condition and the availability of a transplant organ. It also depends on whether they have the resources to pay for the cost of the transplant. In Duke's case, the State of California was obligated to pay for his medical care, as it is for that of all prisoners.

On January 3, 2002, Ken Duke received a heart transplant. The surgery and the hospital stay cost California about $200,000. This was not the final cost of Duke's treatment, however. He would have to remain on immunosuppressive drugs for the rest of his life, receive regular medical checkups, and most likely be hospitalized for one or more episodes of rejection. The total medical costs were estimated to be about $1 million, the same as for any other heart transplant patient.

Outcry

News of Ken Duke's transplant sparked a controversy that spread throughout the country. Why was a convicted prisoner getting a heart transplant paid for by the state, when thousands of people were in need of transplants but unable to get them because they lacked the resources to pay? Was it fair to give a lawbreaker a scarce, expensive, lifesaving resource while simultaneously denying the same resource to law-abiding but low-income and uninsured citizens? Many people were angered that Ken Duke was given what so many others desperately needed to save their lives but could not afford.

This anger was articulated by *Los Angeles Times* columnist Steve Lopez. "What is this telling people?" Lopez asked. "What's the message here to the public? You know, you had two robbery convictions, you're in jail, you get sick, you're going to the top of the line, buddy." Most people, such as his father, who has heart disease, Lopez says, will never get the kind of care represented by a medical center like Stanford.

They also won't get a heart transplant just because they need one. "I had this conversation with a woman who calls me and says, my brother needs a heart transplant, and he could not get on the list. And they said, 'Well, you're going to have to raise $150,000.' And he says, 'Well, I don't have $150,000.' They're practically having bake sales."

A Special Right?

California prison officials believed they had no choice about getting a heart transplant for Ken Duke, no matter how much it cost and no matter how angry and unhappy it made the public. Duke, in the view of the officials, seemed to have both the Constitution and court decisions interpreting it on his side.

In 1976, the U.S. Supreme Court had ruled that failing to provide prisoners with "adequate medical care" would violate the Eighth Amendment of the Constitution, which guarantees that people who are incarcerated will not be subjected to "cruel and unusual punishment." Also, in 1995 a federal district court ordered correction officials to list an inmate for a kidney transplant. The officials had originally turned down the inmate's request, but he sued the state, winning not only the right to be listed for a kidney transplant but also a $35,000 settlement.

If the California Department of Corrections had failed to provide Duke with a heart transplant, corrections officials said, he would have died, and his estate could have sued the state. The estate almost certainly would have won the suit, because it would have the court rulings interpreting the Eighth Amendment on its side.

Some consider the federal courts' interpretation of the amendment as, in effect, recognizing a right to medical care that has not been recognized for those who are not prisoners. "Inmates have a Constitutional right that you and I don't have," Steve Green, a California corrections official, told a reporter. "The right to health care."

Critics argue that the legal view that states must provide prisoners with "adequate medical care" has been too generously interpreted by corrections officials. Does "adequate" care mean that every available form of medical care that might be of value in extending the life of a prisoner must be employed? Or perhaps "adequate care" means only care that is basic and does not require the use of expensive and scarce resources. Perhaps it means only the sort of care that is available to people of modest means and no health insurance. Such individuals can afford ordinary surgery, but they typically can't afford the initial and continuing costs of a heart transplant.

Others argue that when the state deprives an individual of the freedom to make a living and thus afford expensive medical treatments, it incurs a serious obligation to provide lifesaving care. If the goal of prison is the ultimate rehabilitation and social reintegration of the prisoner, the state cannot abandon that goal by willfully letting the prisoner die.

In Ken Duke's case, however, we will never know the outcome of his reintegration into society. After an initial period of good health, he died in December 2003, almost a year after his transplant.

CASE PRESENTATION
The "God Committee": Distributing Dialysis in Seattle

In 2009, former Republican vice presidential candidate Sarah Palin warned that President Barack Obama's proposed reform of the U.S. health care system would involve the creation of "death panels" composed of "faceless bureaucrats" who would decide who lives and who dies based on their "level of productivity in society."

Palin's claim was both widely circulated and widely denounced by political fact-checking organizations on the grounds that nothing in the proposed (or actual) health care legislation resembled such a panel. (For a discussion of what health care reform did include, see Chapter 9.) But a panel very much like the one Palin envisioned did exist in Seattle in the 1960s. It was established not by government but by Swedish Hospital, a private institution, and its anonymous members were not bureaucrats

but ordinary citizens: a lawyer, a pastor, a homemaker, a businessman, a labor leader, and two physicians. Together, they were responsible for deciding who would get access to the limited number of life-saving kidney dialysis machines. Their decisions made the difference between life and death for seventeen patients.

In the absence of ethical guidance from the hospital, this "God Committee" (as it became known) soon began selecting patients for dialysis based on their perceived "social worth." This included such criteria such as sex, age, marital status, occupation, net worth, educational background, and number of children, as well as other factors such as church attendance, emotional stability, and anticipated contribution to society. When their deliberations were covered in a high-profile article in *Life* magazine, the public outcry contributed to the burgeoning bioethics movement and eventually helped secure special coverage for end-stage renal disease (ESRD) under Medicare.

Lifting a Death Sentence

In 1960, kidney failure was a largely untreatable and almost invariably fatal illness. The first dialysis machine or "artificial kidney" had been developed by the Dutch physician Willem Kolff in 1939, but for decades it could only be used for temporary, reversible kidney problems. The reason was that the machine had to be attached to both a vein and an artery as it filtered uremic toxins and excess fluids from a patient's body. This process would eventually destroy all the available blood vessels, and so patients with chronic kidney disease were typically sent home to die.

The crucial step out of this impasse was taken by a University of Washington nephrologist named Belding Scribner, who devised a U-shaped Teflon shunt that could be implanted in a patient's arm or leg. The Scribner shunt could bridge the two blood vessels for months or years at a time, allowing for multiple weekly dialysis treatments through a valve in the shunt. Suddenly, Seattle physicians could, at least in theory, offer dialysis to hundreds of ESRD patients who would otherwise die in a matter of weeks. The problem was deciding who would get access to this scarce and expensive life-saving treatment.

Scarcity and Sacrifice

When the Seattle Artificial Kidney Center opened in January 1962, it had only three dialysis machines and could treat no more than nine patients total with biweekly overnight sessions. Even with a foundation grant for $100,000, the cost per patient would be over $10,000 per year. And even with narrowed criteria of medical eligibility, there were still dozens of potential dialysis candidates for every available slot.

To try to allocate this scarce medical resource, two committees were established. The first committee, composed of kidney specialists, screened dialysis candidates to exclude patients over forty-five, children, and others they deemed too ill with other conditions or emotionally unprepared for the grueling treatment regimen. The second committee was composed of members of the general public, chosen by executives of the King County Medical Society, who would make the final selections from the pool narrowed by the physicians.

At their first meetings, the members of this laypersons committee decided they would keep their own identities a secret. (For decades, they were known only by their occupations, such as the Lawyer, Minister, Housewife, and Labor Leader.) They also decided to exclude any candidate who had not been a Washington State resident when the Scribner shunts were first tested, on the grounds they had been developed with taxpayer funds at a public university. ("This was arbitrary," one of the committee members recalled, "but we had to start somewhere!")

The net result of these initial screening procedures was to reduce the ratio of dialysis candidates to available treatment slots from roughly fifty to one to a more manageable four to one. But how to make these final decisions among the remaining candidates, decisions that were literally a matter of life and death? The committee members initially considered drawing straws for each candidate or some other method of random selection, but soon agreed on a list of criteria for "social worth" that heavily emphasized earning potential, educational achievement, number of dependents, and the other demographic and social factors described above.

"As human beings ourselves, we rejected the idea instinctively of classifying other human beings in pigeonholes, but we realized we had to narrow the field somehow," the lawyer recalled.

As reconstructed by *Life* reporter Shana Alexander, the committee's deliberations over these criteria reflect both their benevolent intentions and the weight of their responsibilities. But their exchanges also reflect the shared values of a group of people drawn from similar walks of life:

> LAWYER: The doctors have told us they will soon have two more vacancies at the Kidney Center, and they have submitted a list of five candidates for us to choose from. . . .
>
> LAWYER: Are there any preliminary ideas?
>
> BANKER: Just to get the ball rolling, why don't we start with Number One—the housewife from Walla Walla.
>
> SURGEON: This patient could not commute for the treatment from Walla Walla, so she would have to find a way to move her family to Seattle.

BANKER: Exactly my point. It says here that her husband has no funds to make such a move.

LAWYER: Then you are proposing we eliminate this candidate on the grounds that she could not possibly accept treatment if it were offered?

MINISTER: How can we compare a family situation of two children, such as this woman in Walla Walla, with a family of six children such as patient Number Four—the aircraft worker?

STATE OFFICIAL: But are we sure the aircraft worker can be rehabilitated? I note he is already too ill to work, whereas Number Two and Number Five, the chemist and the accountant, are both still able to keep going.

LABOR LEADER: I know from experience that the aircraft company where this man works will do everything possible to rehabilitate a handicapped employee....

HOUSEWIFE: If we are still looking for the men with the highest potential of service to society, I think we must consider that the chemist and the accountant have the finest educational backgrounds of all five candidates.

SURGEON: How do the rest of you feel about Number Three—the small businessman with three children? I am impressed that his doctor took special pains to mention this man is active in church work. This is an indication to me of character and moral strength.

HOUSEWIFE: Which certainly would help him conform to the demands of the treatment....

LAWYER: It would also help him to endure a lingering death....

STATE OFFICIAL: But that would seem to be placing a penalty on the very people who perhaps have the most provident....

MINISTER: And both these families have three children too.

LABOR LEADER: For the children's sake, we've got to reckon with the surviving parents opportunity to remarry, and a woman with three children has a better chance to find a new husband than a very young widow with six children.

SURGEON: How can we possibly be sure of that?....

When these and other details of the panel's deliberations became public, they were criticized as reflections of a "middle-class suburban value system" that had used "prejudices and mindless clichés" to pass fatal judgments upon fellow citizens. Later critics pointed out that almost all those granted dialysis were white, male, middle-aged, and at least moderately well-off. There also seemed to be little room for social difference or nonconformity among those selected.

"The Pacific Northwest is no place for a Henry David Thoreau with bad kidneys," David Sanders and Jesse Dukeminier wrote in a famous 1967 law review article on the Seattle committee.

Good Intentions, Tough Choices

For their part, the panel members expressed ambivalence and anguish about the power they had been granted, although they also came to believe in its necessity.

"The situation, as I see it, is life and death, complicated by limitations of money," the Banker concluded at the time. "I don't know if we're doing the right thing or not." The Labor Leader granted that education and wealth should not have played a role in the deliberations, but defended his consideration of church attendance and family size.

"I do think a man ought to have some religion, because that indicates character. And I imagine a large family would be a great help—a lot of kids help keep a man from letting down even when the going gets rough."

For many critics of the committee, these arguments seemed arbitrary. If "character" was a sound medical or moral criterion for preserving someone's life, why wouldn't synagogue or mosque attendance, or dedication to secular organizations, count as strongly? And why should children—rather than friends, partners, and other kinds of dependents—be the sole index of a person's support system and value to others? On a more fundamental level, critics argued that hospital ethics committees should simply avoid such considerations of "social worth," because they tend to reflect unexamined bias. In retrospect, this is a judgment that at least some of the Seattle committee's members came to share.

"We were never consciously aware of those biases," said John Darrah, former pastor of Magnolia Lutheran Church and one of two surviving members of the committee. "But when you look at the composition of the committee, of course we would tend in that direction."

Even at the time, the members of the "God Committee" recognized that they were making problematic judgments based on limited information. Darrah recalled trying *not* to favor church members to compensate for his own biases and arguing against a proposed exclusion of anyone with a criminal record. At the time of the *Life* profile, the committee planned to hire a private investigator, a social worker, a vocational guidance counselor, and a psychiatrist—all in service of providing more accurate assessments of "social worth."

From Social Worth to Net Worth

The Seattle "God Committee" was not unique. In the early years of kidney dialysis, dozens of similar panels were assembled across the country to try to allocate the limited number of machines among a huge pool of eligible patients. Some panels considered moral and social criteria for determining whose lives would be saved by dialysis, but many more made their selections based on a more traditional (but not necessarily more just) means of rationing: the ability to pay.

Indeed, critics pointed out that even the Seattle committee, with its foundation grant, had still expected most patients to shoulder $10,000 of their dialysis expenses each year—a sum that was equivalent at the time to $68,000. When an NBC documentary revisited the Seattle committee in 1965, it found prospective patients desperately trying to raise as much as $30,000 to save their lives—while others gave up trying to raise money and resigned themselves to death. As a result, public concern grew about this other, more basic, form of rationing dialysis access.

In Seattle, all this negative publicity prompted community leaders to raise funds to help the Artificial Kidney Center purchase more machines and expand its capacity to handle forty-seven patients at a time. The problems of financial rationing also motivated Belding Scribner to develop a smaller, portable version of the artificial kidney that could be operated by family members—at dramatically lower cost.

But even the rise of home dialysis failed to make the treatment affordable for many of the patients who needed it most—who were, as they are today, disproportionately poor and afflicted with other health problems. The ability to pay still often meant the difference between life and death, and communities continued to hold bake sales and pancake breakfasts to try to save specific individuals who would die without dialysis.

In 1972, the U.S. Congress took action, spurred by media exposés and lobbying efforts by patient advocates, which included a live dialysis session in front of the House Ways and Means Committee. In an amendment to the 1965 Medicare law that added coverage for people with permanent disabilities, Congress included a provision to cover dialysis treatment for people under sixty-five diagnosed with end-stage renal disease. (Patients also had to be eligible for Social Security benefits by virtue of their work history.) At the time, it was expected that the ESRD coverage would serve as a pilot program for a larger expansion of Medicare to include further catastrophic coverage for those under sixty-five—thus expanding the pool of those insured and compensating for increased costs.

But in the end, no such expansion occurred and ESRD coverage remains an outlier—the only disease-specific coverage in the Medicare program. Moreover, it has expanded dramatically in size and cost, from ten thousand patients and $280 million in 1974 to more than five hundred thousand patients and $26.8 billion today—8 percent of Medicare's entire budget. Critics of the program argue that it has failed to reduce the mortality rate among dialysis patients (which has remained stubbornly at 20 percent for the past twenty years) and that much of its funds are siphoned off by a booming private dialysis industry. Defenders argue that keeping hundreds of thousands of people alive is worth the costs and that it is preferable to harsh rationing techniques that decide life or death on the basis of "social worth" or the ability to pay.

Envoi

As noted at the outset, the health reform measures in the Affordable Care Act (ACA) did not return to anything like the "death panel" embodied (to some degree) by Seattle Artificial Kidney Center's infamous committee. But the problem of how to allocate scarce or expensive medical resources has not gone away. The ACA has cut the number of uninsured Americans by 35 percent, in part by expanding Medicaid and by providing tax credits that allow lower-income customers to afford coverage. But a number of factors, including high co-pays and deductibles, still effectively ration a great deal of basic health care based on ability to pay. At the same time, pandemics such as the H5N1 "avian flu" still prompt public health officials to develop triage plans for how to ration scarce medical resources such as ventilators in the event of a major outbreak (see this chapter's Decision Scenario 8 for more details).

As for the ESRD program, it was modified by Congress in 2008 to "bundle" payments for dialysis, drugs, and other treatments, and to try to achieve better

outcomes by instituting "pay-for-performance" incentives. (These changes anticipated many of the ACA's Medicare pilot programs, which aim to provide more efficient and coordinated care by bundling payments to a group of providers rather than reimbursing for individual procedures.) It remains to be seen how these changes will impact the ESRD program and what place they will occupy in the long and contentious history of allocating life-saving dialysis treatment.

CASE PRESENTATION
Transplants and Disability

Sandra Jensen was born with a defective heart, but it wasn't until she was thirty-five that it began to make her so sick that she needed a heart–lung transplant to save her life. She was young and otherwise healthy, but transplant centers at both Stanford University and the University of California, San Diego, rejected her as a candidate.

The reason the centers cited was that Sandra Jensen also had Down syndrome, and some of the transplant doctors doubted that she had sufficient intelligence to care for herself after the surgery. Like other all transplant recipients, she would have to follow a complicated daily medical regimen involving dozens of medications. If she failed to adhere to the postoperative requirements, she might die, and the organs that might have saved the life of one or two other people would be wasted.

William Bronston, a state rehabilitation administrator and friend of Jensen, became her advocate. He pointed out that she had demonstrated a high level of intellectual functioning. She was a high school graduate who worked with others with Down syndrome, and she had lived on her own for several years. She was an advocate for the disabled in California and attended the signing by President Bush of the Americans with Disabilities Act in 1990.

Thanks to a strong lobbying effort by Bronston and the threat of adverse publicity, Stanford reversed its decision. On January 23, 1996, in a five-hour operation, Jensen became the first intellectually disabled person in the United States to receive a major organ transplant.

Compliance and Discrimination

Since Jensen's transplant, patients with intellectual disabilities have made some progress in getting access to organ transplants, but data suggests that such impairments are still a major obstacle, especially in heart transplants. A 2008 survey of eighty-eight transplant centers reported that 46 percent of heart programs indicated that even mild or moderate cognitive impairment would be a contraindication to transplant eligibility. In addition, the International Society for Heart and Lung Transplantation's criteria for heart transplants states that "Mental retardation or dementia may be regarded as a relative contraindication to transplantation." Since roughly 50 percent of the 250,000 people in the United States with Down syndrome suffer from heart defects, such stances can have serious and fatal consequences for these patients.

What accounts for these policies? The most commonly cited reason is the one used by the transplant centers that initially rejected Jensen's candidacy: that intellectual impairment would undermine her compliance with medical directives and cause her transplant to fail. This stance is worthy of consideration, since noncompliance with post-transplant care is one of the leading causes of transplant failure.

But subsequent studies have found no indication of difference in medical compliance or post-transplant mortality between intellectually disabled and nondisabled transplant recipients. A 2006 literature review published in the journal *Pediatric Transplantation* found high levels of postsurgical care compliance among intellectually disabled patients, in part due to the consistent support networks on which they rely. In addition, the survival rates for these patients was comparable to those of nondisabled patients. A 2010 study published in the *American Journal of Transplantation* concluded, "Currently, there is no scientific evidence or compelling data suggesting that patients with MR [mental retardation] should not have access to organ transplantation."

Critics of continued consideration of cognitive impairment in organ transplantation point out that non-disabled children and infants are routinely approved for transplants when it cannot be assumed that they will comply with medical directions without extensive assistance. They argue that compliance is serving as a cover for judgments about the social worth of the mentally disabled, with institutions making subjective assessments of patients' quality of life rather than objectively assessing the quality of their health.

"Once you get into measuring quality of life, you are one step away from deciding between a doctor's and a janitor's lifestyle, or between a famous athlete and an obscure mother of two children," argues Len Leshin, a pediatrician specializing in Down syndrome.

Some ethicists, such as NYU's Arthur Caplan, have offered a qualified defense of discriminating against the intellectually disabled in transplant decisions, arguing in the context of age requirements that "If the potential recipient is severely intellectually impaired, or is basically almost in a coma, I do not think it makes sense to consider that child for a transplant either." Critics of this argument point out that this slippery slope

runs in both directions, and that most people would be uncomfortable with restricting heart transplants to those with unusually high IQs.

Envoi

More than a year after Sandra Jensen's transplant, she was admitted to Sutter General Hospital in San Francisco. Her problem was not compliance with her immunosuppressive drug regimen, but a severe reaction to the drugs themselves—a common problem that had caused her to be admitted to the hospital several times before. She died of complications from the drug reaction on May 25, 1997.

"Every day was always precious and lived well by her," her friend William Bronston said of Jensen, after her death.

Jensen's struggle to be accepted for a transplant continues to inspire action and calls for reform. Prompted, in part, by Jensen's story, the California Assembly passed a bill in 1996 to prohibit transplant centers from discriminating against the physically or intellectually disabled unless such disabilities are "medically significant" to the transplant. But the situation is different in many other states. In January of 2012, Children's Hospital of Philadelphia denied a kidney transplant to a three-year-old child on the grounds that she had intellectual disabilities, until the ensuing national controversy forced the hospital to reverse its decision. This and similar cases make it clear that policies on transplants for the intellectually disabled remain inconsistent and unresolved across the United States.

BRIEFING SESSION

Few of us have as much as we desire of the world's goods. Usually, this is because we don't have enough money to pay for everything we want. We have to make choices. If we wish to take a vacation in Florida, we can't afford to buy a new phone. Sometimes, even when we have the money, we can't buy some item because the supply is inadequate or nonexistent. A manufacturer, for example,

might not be turning out a new phone fast enough to meet the demand for it. Or, to take a different sort of case, we can't buy fresh figs in Minnesota in January, because they simply aren't available.

In some circumstances, we can't acquire an item because its supply is limited and our society has decided that it falls into a category of goods that require more than money to acquire. The item may then be formally rationed on the basis of social priorities.

During wartime, for example, the military is supplied with all the food it needs, and food for civilians may be rationed. Thus, even those able to pay for a pound of butter may not be permitted to buy it.

Medical goods and services include medications, care by physicians, visits to the emergency room, stays in hospitals, surgical operations, MRIs, diagnostic laboratory tests, in vitro fertilization, bone-marrow transplants, blood transfusions, genetic screening, respirators, and so on. These goods and services are not available to everyone who wants or needs them. To acquire them in our society, except in special circumstances, you must have the means of paying for them. This means having cash or adequate insurance coverage or being covered by a government program. You can't get so much as a CT scan unless you can demonstrate your ability to pay. (Under federal law, emergency services to get you medically stable must be provided by hospitals receiving federal money.)

In the case of some medical goods and services, however, the need and ability to pay are not enough. Such was the case with the first dialysis machines. That's the way it sometimes is when there is a shortage of a crucial vaccine. That's the way it always is when we have to decide who gets the next donor liver, heart, or kidney that becomes available.

These are decisions about distributing scarce resources. Most of this chapter focuses on the distribution of transplant organs. Aside from the distribution of health care itself, parceling out donated organs to people likely to die unless they receive them is the most pressing medical distribution problem in our society. The issues that arise in distributing transplant organs are not, in principle, different from those that arise in connection with any scarce commodity.

Transplant organs are of particular concern, however—not only because they can save and extend lives and so ought not be wasted, but because we currently have no way of eliminating the shortage. We can't simply crank up production, the way we can with drugs or diagnostic equipment. Nor is there an equivalent of building more hospitals or training more physicians and nurses.

Transplants, Kidneys, and Machines

The story of Robin Cook's novel *Coma* takes place in a large hospital in contemporary America. What sets the novel apart is a plot that hinges on the operations of a large-scale black market in transplant organs. For enormous fees, the criminals running the operation will supply corneas, kidneys, or hearts to those who can pay.

Cook claims that the inspiration for his novel came from an advertisement in a California newspaper. The anonymous ad offered to sell for $5,000 any organ that a reader wanted to buy. In this respect, Cook's novel seems rooted firmly in the world we know today.

Organ transplants have attracted a considerable amount of attention in the last few years. Not only are transplants dramatic, often providing last-minute reprieves from almost certain death, but the science of organ transplantation is rich with promise. We can easily imagine a future in which any injured or diseased organ can be replaced almost as easily as the parts of a car. Kidneys, hearts, lungs, livers, intestines, and pancreases are now regularly transplanted and perhaps before long the list will be extended to include ovaries, testes, spleens, gallbladders, esophagi, and stomachs. The basic problem with organ transplants, however, remains the phenomenon of tissue rejection by the immune system.

Controlling Rejection

Proteins that are alien to our bodies trigger its defense mechanisms. In the pioneering work with kidney transplantation, the proteins in the transplanted tissues were matched as carefully as possible with those of the recipient; then powerful immunosuppressive drugs were used in an effort to allow the host body to accommodate the foreign tissue. But these drugs left the body open to infections that it could normally defeat.

Use of the drug cyclosporin dramatically improved the success of organ transplants when it was first used almost three decades ago. Cyclosporin selectively inhibits only part of the immune system and leaves enough of it functional to fight off most of the infections that were once fatal to large numbers of transplant recipients. Also, although tissue matching is important, particularly for kidneys, matches do not have to be as close as before and may be dispensed with altogether.

Now over 90 percent of transplanted kidneys function after one year; in the 1970s, only about 50 percent did. Since 1970, the one-year survival rate for children with liver transplants has increased from 38 percent to more than 75 percent, and there is good reason to believe that if children survive for one year, they have a genuine chance to live a normal life. About 88 percent of heart transplant recipients now live for at least one year, a major increase over the 20 percent rate of the 1970s. (For complete statistics, see the United Network for Organ Sharing website).

Allocation and Scarcity

Because of the relatively high rate of success in organ transplants, the need for organs (kidneys in particular) is always greater than the supply. (The black-market operation in Cook's novel is thus not wholly unrealistic.) In such a situation of scarcity and need, it is frequently necessary to decide whom among the candidates for a transplant will receive an available organ.

Relatively objective considerations such as the "goodness" of tissue matching, the size of the organ, and the general medical condition of the candidates may rule out some individuals. But it may still be necessary to select recipients from the remaining pool of candidates. Who should make such choices? Should they be made by physicians? Should they be made by a committee or board? If so, who should be on the committee? Should a patient have an advocate to speak for his interest—someone to "make a case" for his receiving the transplant organ? Should the decision be made in accordance with a set of explicit criteria? If so, what criteria are appropriate? Are matters such as age, race, gender, and place of residence irrelevant? Should the character and accomplishments of the candidates be given any weight? Should people be judged by their estimated "worth to the community"? Should the fact that someone is a parent be given any weight?

What if a transplant candidate is a smoker, an alcoholic, or obese? Are these conditions to be considered "medical" or "behavioral" risk factors that may legitimately be employed to eliminate someone as a candidate for a transplant? Or are they to be treated as aspects of people's chosen "lifestyle" that cannot be used as a basis for denying them an organ needed to save their lives?

These are just some of the questions relevant to the general issue of deciding how to allocate medical goods in situations in which the available supply is surpassed by a present need. Similar questions arise in the distribution of such goods and services as hospital beds, physician consultations, nursing care, physical therapy, medications, diagnostic MRIs, chemotherapy, coronary angiography, or any of the hundreds of other resources used in delivering medical care. All resources, economists remind us, are limited, so we must always face the problem of how to distribute them. It was a shortage of machines, rather than transplant organs, that focused public attention on the issue of scarce medical resource allocation in modern America.

Kidney Machines in Seattle

The shortage occurred most dramatically in the early 1960s when the Artificial Kidney Center in Seattle, Washington, initiated an effective treatment program for people with renal diseases. Normal kidneys filter waste products from the blood that have accumulated as a result of ordinary cellular metabolism—salt, urea, creatinine, potassium, uric acid, and other substances. These waste products are sent from the kidneys to the bladder, where they are then secreted as urine. Kidney failure, which can result from any of a number of diseases, allows waste products to build up in the blood, frequently causing high blood pressure, tissue edema (swelling), muscular seizure, and even heart failure. Unremedied, the condition results in death.

When renal failure occurs, *hemodialysis* is a way of cleansing the blood of waste products by passing it through a cellophane-like tube immersed in a chemical bath. The impurities in the blood pass through the membrane and into the chemical bath by osmosis, and the purified blood is then returned to the patient's body.

At the beginning of the Seattle program, there were many more candidates for dialysis than units (dialysis machines) to accommodate them. As a response to this situation, the Kidney Center set up a committee to select patients who would receive treatment.

In effect, the committee was offering some people a much greater chance of survival than they would have without access to dialysis equipment.

As other centers and hospitals established renal units, they faced the same painful decisions that Seattle had. Almost always there were many more patients needing hemodialysis than there was equipment available to treat them. It was partly in response to this situation that Section 299-1 of Public Law 92-603 was passed by Congress in 1972. Ever since, those with end-stage renal disease who require hemodialysis or kidney transplants have been guaranteed treatment under Medicare. (See Case Presentation: The "God Committee" for more.)

Dialysis Costs and Decisions

More than five hundred thousand patients are now receiving dialysis paid for by Medicare. Present costs are per year, and the patient load is increasing by about seventy thousand per year. Dialysis saves lives, but the cost is high.

Although the average cost of each treatment session has dropped from $150 in 1973 to the current $120, many more groups of patients now have dialysis than were treated earlier. In particular, the treatment population now includes many more elderly and diabetic people than was envisioned when the dialysis program was established.

Quite apart from the cost, which is about four times higher than originally expected, dialysis continues to present moral difficulties. Resources are still finite, so although virtually everyone needing dialysis can be accommodated, physicians face the problem of deciding whether everyone should be referred. If a physician believes a patient isn't likely to gain benefits from dialysis sufficient to justify the expense or isn't likely to show up for appointments, should she recommend the patient for dialysis anyway? Not to do so may mean death for the patient in the near future, yet the social cost (measured in terms of the expense of equipment and its operation, the cost of hospital facilities, and the time of physicians, nurses, and technicians) may be immense—$100,000 or more per year for a single person.

Nor does dialysis solve all problems for patients with end-stage kidney disease. Although time spent on the machine varies, some patients spend five hours, three days a week, attached to the machine. Prolonged dialysis can produce neurological disorders, severe headaches, gastrointestinal bleeding, and bone diseases. Psychological and physical stress is always present, and severe depression is common, particularly before dialysis treatments. One study showed that 5 percent of dialysis patients take their own lives, and "passive suicide," resulting from dropping out of treatment programs, is the third most common cause of death among older dialysis patients. (The overall death rate for those on dialysis is about 20 percent per year. The worst outlook is for diabetics starting dialysis at age fifty-five or older. After one year, only 18 percent are still alive.) For these reasons, strong motivation, psychological stability, age, and a generally sound physical condition are factors considered important in deciding whether to approve a person for dialysis.

The characteristics required to make someone a "successful" dialysis patient may also be linked to socioeconomic status and education. Not only must a patient be motivated to save his life, but he also must understand the need for the dialysis, adhere to a strict diet, have the free time and resources to show up for dialysis sessions, and have a predictable schedule. As a consequence, when decisions about whether to admit a patient to dialysis are based on subjective estimates of "patient compliance," members of more privileged groups may get priority. Selection criteria that are apparently objective may actually involve hidden class or cultural biases.

Various ways of dealing with both the costs and the personal problems presented by dialysis are currently under discussion. In the view of some, increasing the number of kidney transplants would do the most to improve the lives of patients and to reduce the cost of the kidney program. (See Social Context: Acquiring and Allocating Transplant Organs for a discussion of proposals for realizing this objective.) Others have pressed for training more patients to perform home dialysis, which is substantially cheaper than dialysis performed in clinics or hospitals. However, those who are elderly, live alone, or lack adequate facilities sometimes have troubling using and maintaining the complicated equipment involved. Other things being equal, should such patients be given priority for transplants?

Microallocation vs. Macroallocation

Some critics have questioned the legitimacy of the dialysis program and pointed to it as an example of social injustice. While thousands of people have benefited from the program, why should kidney disease be treated differently from other diseases? Why should the treatment of kidney disease alone be federally funded? Why shouldn't society also pay for the treatment of those afflicted with cancer, heart diseases, or neurological disorders?

Decisions regarding transplants and dialysis affect individuals in a direct and immediate way. For example, a person either is or is not accepted into a dialysis program, sometimes with life-or-death consequences. As we will see in the next chapter, there are a number of broader social issues connected with providing and distributing medical resources. But our concern here is with decisions involving the welfare of particular people in specific situations in which demand exceeds supply. The basic question becomes, Who shall get a medical resource and who shall go without?

Any commodity or service that can be in short supply relative to the need for it raises the issue of fair and justifiable distribution. Decisions that control the supply itself—that determine, for example, what proportion of the federal budget will be spent on medical care—are generally referred to as *macroallocation* decisions. These are the large-scale decisions that do not involve individuals in a direct way. Similarly, deciding what proportion of the money budgeted for health care should be spent on dialysis is a macroallocation decision.

By contrast, *microallocation* decisions directly impact individuals. Thus, when one donor heart is available and six people in need of a transplant make a claim to it, the decision as to who gets the heart is a microallocation decision. In Chapter 9, in discussing health care distribution, we will focus more on macroallocation, but here we are concerned mostly with microallocation. (The distinction between macroallocation and microallocation is often less clear than the explanation here suggests. After all, decision-making occurs at many levels in the distribution of resources, and the terms "macro" and "micro" are relative ones.)

Earlier, in connection with transplants, we considered some of the more specific questions that have to be asked about distribution. The questions generally fall into two categories: Who shall decide? and What criteria or standards should be employed in making the allocation decision? These are questions that must be answered whenever there is scarcity relative to needs and wants.

Ethical Theories and the Allocation of Medical Resources

Discussions of the distribution of limited medical resources sometimes use the analogy of a group of people adrift in a lifeboat.

If some are sacrificed, the others will have a much better chance of surviving. But who, if anyone, should be sacrificed?

One answer to this question is that no one should be. Simply by virtue of being human, each person in the lifeboat has equal worth. Thus, any action that involved sacrificing someone for the good of the others in the boat would not be morally defensible. This tenet might suggest that the only right course of action would be simply to do nothing.

This point of view may be regarded as compatible with Kant's ethical principles. Because each individual may be considered to have inherent value, considerations such as talent, intelligence, age, social worth, and so on are morally irrelevant. Accordingly, there seem to be no grounds for distinguishing those who are to be sacrificed from those who may be saved. In the medical context, this would mean that when there are not enough goods and services to go around, then no one should receive them.

This is not a result dictated by Kant's principles, however. One might also argue that the fact that every person is equal to every other in dignity and worth does not require the sacrifice of all. A random procedure—such as drawing straws—might be used to determine who is to have an increased chance of survival. In such a case, each person is being treated as having equal value, and the person who loses might be regarded as exercising autonomy by sacrificing himself.

The maxim underlying the sacrifice would, apparently, be one that would meet the test of the categorical imperative. Any rational person might be expected to sacrifice himself in such a situation and under the conditions in which the decision was made. In the case of medical resources, a random procedure would seem to be a morally legitimate procedure.

Both the natural law view and Ross's view would seem to support a similar line of argument. Although we all have a duty, on these views, to preserve our lives, this does not mean that we do not sometimes have to risk them. Just such a risk might be involved in agreeing to abide by the outcome of a random procedure to decide who will be sacrificed and who saved.

Utilitarianism does not dictate a specific answer to the question of who, if anyone, should be saved. It does differ radically in one respect, however, from those moral views that ascribe an intrinsic value to each human life. The principle of utility might suggest that we ought to take into account the consequences of sacrificing some people rather than others. Who, for example, is more likely to make a contribution to the general welfare of the society, an accountant or a nurse? This approach opens the way to considering the "social worth" of people and makes morally relevant such characteristics as education, occupation, age, record of accomplishment, and so on.

To take such an approach would require working out a set of criteria to assign values to various properties of people. Those to be sacrificed would be those whose point total put them at the low end of the ranking. Here, then, a typical "calculus of utilities" would be relied on to solve the decision problem. The decision problem about the allocation of medical resources would follow exactly the same pattern.

This approach is not required by the principle of utility, however. Many would argue that a policy formulated along those lines would have so many harmful social consequences that some other solution would be preferable. Thus, a utilitarian might argue that a better policy would be one based on some random process. In connection with medical goods and services, a "first-come, first-served" approach might be superior. (This is a particularly logical option for rule utilitarianism.)

Rawls's principles of justice seem clearly to rule out distributing medical resources on the criterion of "social worth." Where special benefits are to be obtained, access to those benefits must be of value to all and open to all, which might suggest a lottery or some other fair procedure. At the same time, Rawls's *difference principle* permits the unequal allocation of resources to the extent that they benefit the least advantaged members of society. This might suggest privileging sicker patients, children, the poor, or others who are "worse off," based on some metric or other. Many theories of capability and identity follow Rawls in this priority, while emphasizing how medical allocation decisions must take account of potentially unequal distributions *within* the family, and as a result of gender, ethnic, and other social structures.

No ethical theory that we have considered gives a straightforward answer to the question of who shall make the selection. Where a procedure is random or first come, first served, the decision-making process requires only establishing the right kind of social arrangements to implement the policy. Only when social worth must be judged and considered as a relevant factor in decision-making does the procedure assume importance. (This is assuming that medical decisions about appropriate care—decisions that establish a class of candidates for the limited resources—have already been made.)

A utilitarian answer as to who shall make the allocation decision might be that the decision should be made by those who are in a good position to judge the likelihood of an individual's contribution to the welfare of the society as a whole. Since physicians are not uniquely qualified to make such judgments, leaving decisions to an individual physician or a committee of physicians would not be the best approach. A better one would perhaps be to rely on a committee composed of a variety of people representative of the society.

Many other moral questions connected with the allocation of scarce resources arise than have been mentioned here. We have not, for example, considered whether an individual should be allowed to make a case for receiving resources. Nor have we examined any of the problems associated with employing specific criteria for selection (such as requiring that a person be a resident of a certain community or state). We have, however, touched upon some basic issues that continue to generate intense moral discussion and debate.

READINGS

Section 1: Who Deserves Transplant Organs?

Wanted, Dead or Alive? Kidney Transplantation in Inmates Awaiting Execution

Jacob M. Appel

Appel argues that death row inmates should be allowed to be candidates for kidney transplants. Although the state has determined that the inmate does not deserve to live, it would be wrong for a medical decision to lower his quality of life while he is waiting for execution. Also, if the inmate was wrongly convicted, denying him a transplant would result in the irreversible suffering of an innocent person.

Appel also argues that the life expectancy of a death row inmate is different in kind from the "natural" one used in kidney allocation, so the inmate's life expectancy should not be considered relevant to a transplant decision. Finally, Appel points out, a kidney transplant costs less than dialysis, so the money saved could be used to meet other health care needs.

The United States Supreme Court has held since 1976 that prison inmates are entitled to the same medical treatment as the free public. In most states, this care includes major organ transplants—a matter that has produced widespread debate following California's decision in 2002 to subsidize a $1 million heart transplant for a 31-year-old convicted robber in his fourth year of a 14-year sentence, and Minnesota's provision of a $900,000 lifesaving bone-marrow transplant to an incarcerated murderer with leukemia. This controversy surrounding the cost of prisoners' health needs—both economic and social—took a

From Jacob M. Appel, "Wanted, Dead or Alive? Kidney Transplantation in Inmates Awaiting Execution," *The Journal of Clinical Ethics* 16, no. 1 (2005): 58–60. Copyright © 2005 JCE. All rights reserved. Used with permission. (Notes omitted.)

macabre turn in 2003 when Horacio Alberto Reyes-Camarena, a 47-year-old dialysis patient on Oregon's death row, formally requested a kidney transplant. Such a procedure would have been likely to save the state money in the long run, as the transplant itself would have cost between $80,000 and $120,000 with an approximately $12,000 additional annual charge for immunosuppressant drugs. Dialysis, on the other hand, costs Oregon $121,025 per patient each year. The surgery also appeared to be in Reyes-Camarena's best medical interests; studies report that a kidney transplant can decrease mortality in end-stage renal patients by up to 82 percent. However, with more than 59,000 Americans waiting for kidneys, nearly 200 of them in Oregon, the prospect of such a transplant drew considerable criticism.

A review panel ultimately rejected Reyes-Camarena's request—for undisclosed reasons. Yet with a graying and increasingly ill prison population, the question is bound to resurface: Should death row inmates be eligible for kidney transplantation? A combination of ethical and practical considerations suggests that they should be considered.

The American healthcare system still has an ambivalent attitude toward the premise that, to paraphrase George Orwell, some patients are more equal than others. In a society that is reluctant to expand overall medical expenditures, care continues to be allocated based upon a patient's ability to pay. However, the medical community has grown increasingly unwilling to allow non-economic social factors, such as the sick individual's perceived moral worth, to shape the quality of his or her care. Negative experiences with the "God committees" of the pre-Medicare era, in which lay people and physicians used criteria of "social worth" such as "level of education" and "future potential" to decide which renal patients were to receive scarce dialysis treatments and which would die, have turned many in both the medical profession and the public at-large against this sort of rationing. While some commentators argue that patients' past disease-inducing behaviors should be used to determine their eligibility for scarce medical resources, such as barring liver transplants for recovered alcoholics, far fewer argue that the general social value or moral history of patients should determine the quality or nature of their care. When it comes to healthcare, "bad people" are as equal as the rest of us.

The case of a death row inmate who requests a kidney transplant challenges these general principles in two ways. First, the criminal justice system—and not the medical community—has made a determination of social worth; according to the state, the inmate's social value is so low that he or she deserves execution. Second, although kidney transplants increase survival rates over dialysis, the decision not to transplant is not an automatic death sentence. Ignoring for a moment the ethics of capital punishment and the morality of a physician facilitating the practice— both somewhat dubious propositions—it does not follow that just because the state can take an individual's life, the medical community can lower the quality of that life in the interval prior to execution. Reducing the food rations of death row inmates, for example, would certainly be unacceptable. The state's determination of social worth only finds that the condemned

prisoner no longer deserves life—a far higher bar than a determination that he or she is no longer worthy of healthcare prior to death. Moreover, the accuracy of the state's determination is often questionable. Conservative estimates suggest that 75 percent of death sentences are overturned on appeal, and one in 15 death row prisoners is eventually exonerated of all charges. If physicians were to use the state's imprecise and fluctuating determination of social value to determine transplant eligibility, even innocent individuals of high social worth would suffer—and some would inevitably die. Alternatively, an effort by doctors to re-examine the criminal justice system's decision and to deny transplant only in cases of obvious guilt would place physicians in the awkward "social worth" evaluating role they are seeking to avoid.

A second set of objections to death row transplantation relies not upon considerations of social worth, but instead upon those of medical prognosis. Life expectancy, for instance, is considered to be a perfectly legitimate factor in allocating kidneys among free individuals. To place a kidney in an inmate who will soon die, the argument goes, is nothing more than squandering an organ. Several false premises underlie this reasoning. First, only a small fraction of death row inmates are ever actually executed. Of those who are eventually executed, the Bureau of Justice Statistics estimates that their life expectancy on death row now approaches 13 years; 13 years is also the estimated half-life of a cadaver-donor kidney transplant—meaning that half of all transplanted death row inmates would die of natural causes before their execution dates. When all of these factors are combined, the number of organs that would be "squandered" is relatively small. Second, the difference between the use of "natural" life expectancy as a factor in the allocation of kidneys and the use of the probability of execution as a factor is morally significant. The former has long been a staple of medical justice. In a system in which scarce resources must be distributed on some basis, this system affords optimal organ use without making or affirming value judgments about the lives of individuals. In contrast, the use of a prediction of life expectancy that incorporates the probability of execution inevitably subrogates "medical justice" to "social justice," and affirms value judgments about the "social worth" of individuals. Such an approach rejects the egalitarian notion that non-economic social factors should play no role in the allocation of healthcare resources.

The general public, and many in the medical community, may have a visceral objection to death row transplants. When it comes to kidneys, however, the economics should give them some solace. Since transplantation costs less than dialysis, the state can reallocate the revenue saved toward other health-care projects—presumably including many lifesaving endeavors. More lives might be saved by re-allocating these funds than would be saved by making the kidneys available to free people, especially when one remembers that kidney transplant is often a life-enhancing rather than a life-lengthening procedure. Many people do not want to hear this, of course. Much of the public would probably be willing to sacrifice healthcare resources if it meant that convicted murderers would not receive medical care. Courts have had the wisdom to think otherwise. They have not carved out exceptions for transplant cases and/or death row inmates, and no convincing reason exists for them to do so.

Alcoholics and Liver Transplantation

Carl Cohen, Martin Benjamin, and the Ethics and Social Impact Committee of the Transplant and Health Policy Center, Ann Arbor, Michigan

Cohen, Benjamin, and their associates examine the moral and medical arguments for excluding alcoholics as candidates for liver transplants and conclude that neither kind of argument justifies a categorical exclusion.

The moral argument holds that alcoholics are morally blameworthy for their condition. Thus, when resources are scarce, it is preferable to favor an equally sick non-blameworthy person over a blameworthy one. The authors maintain that if this argument were sound, it would require physicians to examine the moral character of all patients before allocating scarce resources. But this is not feasible, and such a policy could not be administered fairly by the medical profession.

The medical argument holds that because of their unhealthy addiction, alcoholics have a lower success rate with transplants. Hence, scarce organs should go to others more likely to benefit. The authors agree that the likelihood of someone's following a treatment regimen should be considered, but they maintain that the consideration must be given case by case. We permit transplants in cases where the prognosis is the same or worse, and the categorical exclusion of alcoholics is thus unfair. We cannot justify discrimination on the grounds of alleged self-abuse, "unless we are prepared to develop a detailed calculus of just deserts for health care based on good conduct."

Alcoholic cirrhosis of the liver—severe scarring due to the heavy use of alcohol—is by far the major cause of end-stage liver disease. For persons so afflicted, life may depend on receiving a new, transplanted liver. The number of alcoholics in the United States needing new livers is great, but the supply of available livers for transplantation is small. *Should those whose end-stage liver disease was caused by alcohol abuse be categorically excluded from candidacy for liver transplantation?* This question, partly medical and partly moral, must now be confronted forthrightly. Many lives are at stake.

Reasons of two kinds underlie a widespread unwillingness to transplant livers into alcoholics: First, there is a common conviction—explicit or tacit—that alcoholics are morally blameworthy, their condition the result of their own misconduct, and that such

From *JAMA* 265 (March 13, 1991): 1299–1301. Reprinted by permission. (Notes omitted.)

blameworthiness disqualifies alcoholics in unavoidable competition for organs with others equally sick but blameless. Second, there is a common belief that because of their habits, alcoholics will not exhibit satisfactory survival rates after transplantation, and that, therefore, good stewardship of a scarce lifesaving resource requires that alcoholics not be considered for liver transplantation. We examine both of these arguments.

The Moral Argument

A widespread condemnation of drunkenness and a revulsion for drunks lie at the heart of this public policy issue. Alcoholic cirrhosis—unlike other causes of end-stage liver disease—is brought on by a person's conduct, by heavy drinking. Yet if the dispute here were only about whether to treat someone who is seriously ill because of personal conduct, we would not say—as we do not in cases of other serious diseases resulting from personal conduct—that such conduct disqualifies a person from receiving desperately needed medical attention. Accident victims injured because they were not wearing seat belts are treated without hesitation; reformed smokers who become coronary bypass candidates partly because they disregarded their physicians' advice about tobacco, diet, and exercise are not turned away because of their bad habits. But new livers are a scarce resource, and transplanting a liver into an alcoholic may, therefore, result in death for a competing candidate whose liver disease was wholly beyond his or her control. Thus we seem driven, in this case unlike in others, to reflect on the weight given to the patient's personal conduct. And heavy drinking—unlike smoking, or overeating, or failing to wear a seat belt—is widely regarded as morally wrong.

Many contend that alcoholism is not a moral failing but a disease. Some authorities have recently reaffirmed this position, asserting that alcoholism is "best regarded as a chronic disease." But this claim cannot be firmly established and is far from universally believed. Whether alcoholism is indeed a disease, or a moral failing, or both, remains a disputed matter surrounded by intense controversy.

Even if it is true that alcoholics suffer from a somatic disorder, many people will argue that this disorder results in deadly liver disease only when coupled with a weakness of will—a weakness for which part of the blame must fall on the alcoholic. This consideration underlies the conviction that the alcoholic needing a transplanted liver, unlike a nonalcoholic competing for the same liver, is at least partly responsible for his or her need. Therefore, some conclude, the alcoholic's personal failing is rightly considered in deciding upon his or her entitlement to this very scarce resource.

Is this argument sound? We think it is not. Whether alcoholism is a moral failing, in whole or in part, remains uncertain. But even if we suppose that it is, it does not follow that we are justified in categorically denying liver transplants to those alcoholics suffering from end-stage cirrhosis. We could rightly preclude alcoholics from transplantation only if we assume that qualification for a new organ requires some level of moral virtue or is canceled by some level of moral vice. But there is absolutely no agreement—and there is likely to be none—about what constitutes moral virtue and vice and what rewards and penalties they deserve. The assumption that undergirds the moral argument for precluding alcoholics is thus unacceptable. Moreover, even if we could agree (which, in fact, we cannot) upon the kind of misconduct we would be looking for, the fair weighting of such a consideration would entail highly intrusive investigations into patients' moral habits—investigations universally thought repugnant. Moral evaluation is wisely and rightly excluded from all deliberations of who should be treated and how.

Indeed, we do exclude it. We do not seek to determine whether a particular transplant candidate is an abusive parent or a dutiful daughter, whether candidates cheat on their income taxes or their spouses, or whether potential recipients pay their parking tickets or routinely lie when they think it is in their best interests. We refrain from considering such judgments for several good reasons: (1) We have genuine and well-grounded doubts about comparative degrees of voluntariness and, therefore, *cannot pass judgment fairly.* (2) Even if we could assess degrees of voluntariness reliably, *we cannot know what penalties different degrees of misconduct deserve.* (3) *Judgments of this kind could not be made consistently in our medical system*—and a fundamental requirement of a fair system in allocating scarce resources is that it treat all in need of certain goods on the same standard, without unfair discrimination by group.

If alcoholics should be penalized because of their moral fault, then all others who are equally at fault in causing their own medical needs should be similarly penalized. To accomplish this, we would have to make vigorous and sustained efforts to find out whose conduct has been morally weak or sinful and to what degree. That inquiry, as a condition for medical care or for the receipt of goods in short supply, we certainly will not and should not undertake.

The unfairness of such moral judgments is compounded by other accidental factors that render moral assessment especially difficult in connection with alcoholism and liver disease. Some drinkers have a greater predisposition for alcohol abuse than others. And for some who drink to excess, the predisposition to cirrhosis is also greater; many grossly intemperate drinkers do not suffer grievously from liver disease. On the other hand, alcohol consumption that might be considered moderate for some may cause serious liver disease in others. It turns out, in fact, that the disastrous consequences of even low levels of alcohol consumption may be much more common in women than in men. Therefore, penalizing cirrhotics by denying them transplant candidacy would have the effect of holding some groups arbitrarily to a higher standard than others and would probably hold women to a higher standard of conduct than men.

Moral judgments that eliminate alcoholics from candidacy thus prove unfair and unacceptable. The alleged (but disputed) moral misconduct of alcoholics with end-stage liver disease does not justify categorically excluding them as candidates for liver transplantation.

Medical Argument

Reluctance to use available livers in treating alcoholics is due in some part to the conviction that, because alcoholics would do poorly after transplant as a result of their bad habits, good stewardship of organs in short supply requires that alcoholics be excluded from consideration.

This argument also fails, for two reasons: First, it fails because the premise—that the outcome for alcoholics will invariably be poor relative to other groups—is at least doubtful and probably false. Second, it fails because, even if the premise were true, it could serve as a good reason to exclude alcoholics only if it were an equally good reason to exclude other groups having a prognosis equally bad or worse. But equally low survival rates have not excluded other groups; fairness therefore requires that this group not be categorically excluded either.

In fact, the data regarding the post-transplant histories of alcoholics are not yet reliable. Evidence gathered in 1984 indicated that the 1-year survival rate for patients with alcoholic cirrhosis was well below the survival rate for other recipients of liver transplants, excluding those with cancer. But a 1988 report, with a larger (but still small) sample number, shows remarkably good results in alcoholics receiving transplants: 1-year survival is 73.2%—and of 35 carefully selected (and possibly nonrepresentative) alcoholics who received transplants and lived 6 months or longer, only two relapsed into alcohol abuse. Liver transplantation, it would appear, can be a very sobering experience. Whether this group continues to do as well as a comparable group of nonalcoholic liver recipients remains uncertain. But the data, although not supporting the broad inclusion of alcoholics, do suggest that medical considerations do not now justify categorically excluding alcoholics from liver transplantation.

A history of alcoholism is of great concern when considering liver transplantation, not only because of the impact of alcohol abuse upon the entire system of the recipient but also because the life of an alcoholic tends to be beset by general disorder. Returning to heavy drinking could ruin a new liver, although probably not for years. But relapse into heavy drinking would quite likely entail the inability to maintain the routine of multiple medication, daily or twice-daily, essential for immunosuppression and survival. As a class, alcoholic cirrhotics may therefore prove to have substantially lower survival rates after receiving transplants. All such matters should be weighed, of course. But none of them gives any solid reason to exclude alcoholics from consideration categorically.

Moreover, even if survival rates for alcoholics selected were much lower than normal—a supposition now in substantial doubt—what could fairly be concluded from such data? Do we exclude from transplant candidacy members of other groups known to have low survival rates? In fact we do not. Other things being equal, we may prefer not to transplant organs in short supply into patients afflicted, say, with liver cell cancer, knowing that such cancer recurs not long after a new liver is implanted. Yet in some individual cases we do it. Similarly, some transplant recipients have other malignant neoplasms or other conditions that suggest low survival probability. Such matters are weighed in selecting recipients, but they are insufficient grounds to categorically exclude an entire group. This shows that the argument for excluding alcoholics based on survival probability rates alone is simply not just.

The Arguments Distinguished

In fact, the exclusion of alcoholics from transplant candidacy probably results from an intermingling, perhaps at times a confusion, of the moral and medical arguments. But if the moral argument indeed does not apply, no combination of it with probable survival rates can make it applicable. Survival data, carefully collected and analyzed, deserve to be weighed in selecting candidates. These data do not come close to precluding alcoholics from consideration. Judgments of blameworthiness, which ought to be excluded generally, certainly should be excluded when weighing the impact of those survival rates. Some people with a strong antipathy to alcohol abuse and abusers may, without realizing it, be relying on assumed unfavorable data to support a fixed moral judgment. The arguments must be untangled. Actual results with transplanted alcoholics must be considered without regard to moral antipathies.

The upshot is inescapable: there are no good grounds at present—moral or medical—to disqualify a patient with end-stage liver disease from consideration for liver transplantation simply because of a history of heavy drinking.

Screening and Selection of Liver Transplant Candidates

In the initial evaluation of candidates for any form of transplantation, the central questions are whether patients (1) are sick enough to need a new organ and (2) enjoy a high enough probability of benefiting from this limited resource. At this stage the criteria should be noncomparative. Even the initial screening of patients must, however, be done individually and with great care.

The screening process for those suffering from alcoholic cirrhosis must be especially rigorous—not for moral reasons, but because of factors affecting survival, which are themselves influenced by a history of heavy drinking—and even more by its resumption. Responsible stewardship of scarce organs requires that the screening for candidacy take into consideration the manifold impact of heavy drinking on long-term transplant success. Cardiovascular problems brought on by alcoholism and other systematic contraindications must be looked for. Psychiatric and social evaluation is also in order, to determine whether patients understand and have come to terms with their condition and whether they have the social support essential for continuing immunosuppression and follow-up care.

Precisely which factors should be weighed in this screening process have not been firmly established. Some physicians have proposed a specified period of alcohol abstinence as an "objective" criterion for selection—but the data supporting such a criterion are far from conclusive, and the use of this criterion to exclude a prospective recipient is at present medically and morally arbitrary.

Indeed, one important consequence of overcoming the strong presumption against considering alcoholics for liver transplantation is the research opportunity it presents and the encouragement it gives to the quest for more reliable predictors of medical success. As that search continues, some defensible guidelines for case-by-case determination have been devised, based on factors associated with sustained recovery from alcoholism and other considerations related to liver transplantation success in general. Such guidelines appropriately include (1) refined diagnosis by those trained in the treatment of alcoholism, (2) acknowledgment by the patient of a serious drinking problem, (3) social and familial stability, and (4) other factors experimentally associated with long-term sobriety.

The experimental use of guidelines like these, and their gradual refinement over time, may lead to more reliable and more generally applicable predictors. But those more refined predictors will never be developed until prejudices against considering alcoholics for liver transplantation are overcome.

Patients who are sick because of alleged self-abuse ought not be grouped for discriminatory treatment—unless we are prepared to develop a detailed calculus of just deserts for health care based on good conduct. Lack of sympathy for those who bring serious disease upon themselves is understandable, but the temptation to institutionalize that emotional response must be tempered by our inability to apply such considerations justly and by our duty *not* to apply them unjustly. In the end, some patients with alcoholic cirrhosis may be judged, after careful evaluation, as good risks for a liver transplant.

Objection and Reply

Providing alcoholics with transplants may present a special "political" problem for transplant centers. The public perception of alcoholics is generally negative. The already low rate of organ donation, it may be argued, will fall even lower when it becomes known that donated organs are going to alcoholics. Financial support from legislatures may also suffer. One can imagine the effect on transplantation if the public were to learn that the liver of a teenager killed by a drunken driver had been transplanted into an alcoholic patient. If selecting even a few alcoholics as transplant candidates reduces the number of lives saved overall, might that not be good reason to preclude alcoholics categorically?

No. The fear is understandable, but excluding alcoholics cannot be rationally defended on that basis. Irresponsible conduct attributable to alcohol abuse should not be defended. No excuses should be made for the deplorable consequences of drunken behavior, from highway slaughter to familial neglect and abuse. But alcoholism must be distinguished from those consequences; not all alcoholics are morally irresponsible, vicious, or neglectful drunks. If there is a general failure to make this distinction, we must strive to overcome that failure, not pander to it.

Public confidence in medical practice in general, and in organ transplantation in particular, depends on the scientific validity and moral integrity of the policies adopted. Sound policies will prove publicly defensible. Shaping present health care policy on the basis of distorted public perceptions or prejudices will, in the long run, do more harm than good to the process and to the reputation of all concerned.

Approximately one in every 10 Americans is a heavy drinker, and approximately one family in every three has at least one member at risk for alcoholic cirrhosis. The care of alcoholics and the just treatment of them when their lives are at stake are matters a democratic policy may therefore be expected to act on with concern and reasonable judgment over the long run. The allocation of organs in short supply does present vexing moral problems: if thoughtless or shallow moralizing would cause some to respond very negatively to transplanting livers into alcoholic cirrhotics, that cannot serve as good reason to make such moralizing the measure of public policy.

We have argued that there is now no good reason, either moral or medical, to preclude alcoholics categorically from consideration for liver transplantation. We further conclude that it would therefore be unjust to implement that categorical preclusion simply because others might respond negatively if we do not.

Section 2:   Acquiring Transplant Organs

The Donor's Right to Take a Risk

Ronald Munson

Ronald Munson asks whether, given the associated risks, we should permit people to donate a liver lobe and whether, by operating on a donor for the benefit of a recipient, surgeons are violating the dictum "Do no harm." He claims that, while autonomy warrants consent, we must take measures to guarantee that consent is both informed and freely given. So far as benefit is concerned, Munson maintains, when consent is valid, living donors can be viewed as benefiting themselves, as well as the recipients of their gift.

Mike Hurewitz, a 57-year-old journalist, died at Mount Sinai Hospital in Manhattan on Sunday [January 13, 2002] after an operation to remove part of his liver for transplant. The recipient, his younger brother, is apparently doing well. The procedure

From *The New York Times*, January 19, 2002. Reprinted by permission.

of liver-lobe transplantation, hardly more than a decade old, can save lives, but it can also lead to disaster. The case of the Hurewitz brothers illustrates both. The risk of death for a donor may be as high as 1 in 100. Yet even when the magic works, when donor and recipient survive, the procedure raises troubling questions. The death of Mike Hurewitz gives those questions a sharper edge.

Given the risk and the potential for family pressure, should we permit people to become liver donors? Are physicians violating the "do no harm" rule by operating on healthy donors, causing them pain and risking their lives, yet bringing them no medical benefit?

These questions have urgency because for end-stage liver disease, we have no effective treatment other than transplantation. The lives of people in kidney failure can be extended considerably by dialysis, and those with heart failure can often be sustained by an implantable pump, but we have no machines capable of taking over the liver's functions.

The lack of an alternative results in a high demand for cadaver livers. About 19,000 people are now on the waiting list for those organs, but only 5,000 will get transplants, and about 2,000 die each year waiting for livers.

Until the advent of liver transplants from live donors, a patient who could not get a liver was doomed. Now there is hope. In this procedure, the liver segments in the donor and the recipient grow back to full size in about a month. The success of liver-segment transplantation, first used in treating children, has led surgeons to begin using adults as donors for other adults.

That the benefits of liver transplantation seem totally one-sided raises questions about whether a donor is giving informed consent. Our society recognizes the autonomy of individuals, which means letting people decide which risks they take. Most parents, given a chance to save the life of a desperately ill child, would willingly gamble their own. Some people might risk themselves for a sister, husband or close friend, while others might decide otherwise.

For consent to be legitimate, it must be both informed and freely given. A potential donor must be educated about the pain and risks, including death, that the surgery involves. Most important, potential donors must be protected from the overt and subtle pressures of friends and relatives. They must be free to say no as well as yes.

One way to ensure that the interests of prospective donors are recognized is to create a federal agency that would make certain that hospitals meet minimum standards when employing these new therapies and would monitor how hospital review boards screen potential donors. The boards also need to be able to shield potential donors from coercion. For example, in cases when an individual decides against becoming a donor, a board should simply inform the intended recipient that the potential donor is "not suitable" without further explanation.

But even when consent is valid, are doctors harming liver donors while bringing them no benefit? That might be true, but only under an overly narrow understanding. As a Massachusetts court reasoned in 1957, a teenager who donated a kidney to his twin brother was not only saving his brother's life but also promoting his own emotional well-being and health, which would be adversely affected if his brother died. When informed consent is valid, living donors can be viewed as exercising their autonomy and doctors can legitimately be viewed as helping both patient and donor.

Until we can develop machines, employ animal organs or grow new livers using stem cells, we are dependent on transplants, including living donor transplants. We must rely on the courage of people like Mike Hurewitz. They are moral heroes; they must not be made medical dupes.

The Case for Allowing Kidney Sales

Janet Radcliffe-Richards, A. S. Daar, R. D. Guttmann, R. Hoffenberg, I. Kennedy, M. Lock, R. A. Sells, N. Tilney, and the International Forum for Transplant Ethics

Radcliffe-Richards and her coauthors argue that although some may feel disgust at the idea of selling kidneys, this is not a sufficient reason to deny people a necessary treatment. The authors critically examine

Reprinted from *The Lancet* 531, no. 9120 (June 27,1998): 1950–1952, Janet Radcliffe-Richards et. al., "The Case for Allowing Kidney Sales," Copyright © 1998, with permission from Elsevier, Inc. (Notes omitted.)

the objections that kidney sales would exploit the poor, benefit the rich unfairly, undermine confidence in physicians, threaten the welfare of women and children, and lead to the sale of hearts and other vital organs. The authors hold that until stronger objections are offered, the presumption should be in favor of kidney sales as a way of resolving the current shortage.

When the practice of buying kidneys from live vendors first came to light some years ago, it aroused such horror that all professional associations denounced it and nearly all countries have now made it illegal. Such political and professional unanimity may seem to leave no room for further debate, but we nevertheless think it important to reopen the discussion.

The well-known shortage of kidneys for transplantation causes much suffering and death. Dialysis is a wretched experience for most patients, and is anyway rationed in most places and simply unavailable to the majority of patients in most developing countries. Since most potential kidney vendors will never become unpaid donors, either during life or posthumously, the prohibition of sales must be presumed to exclude kidneys that would otherwise be available. It is therefore essential to make sure that there is adequate justification for the resulting harm.

Most people will recognise in themselves the feelings of outrage and disgust that led to an outright ban on kidney sales, and such feelings typically have a force that seems to their possessors to need no further justification. Nevertheless, if we are to deny treatment to the suffering and dying we need better reasons than our own feelings of disgust.

In this paper we outline our reasons for thinking that the arguments commonly offered for prohibiting organ sales do not work, and therefore that the debate should be reopened. Here we consider only the selling of kidneys by living vendors, but our arguments have wider implications.

The commonest objection to kidney selling is expressed on behalf of the vendors: the exploited poor, who need to be protected against the greedy rich. However, the vendors are themselves anxious to sell, and see this practice as the best option open to them. The worse we think the selling of a kidney, therefore, the worse should seem the position of the vendors when that option is removed. Unless this appearance is illusory, the prohibition of sales does even more harm than first seemed, in harming vendors as well as recipients. To this argument it is replied that the vendors' apparent choice is not genuine. It is said that

they are likely to be too uneducated to understand the risks, and that this precludes informed consent. It is also claimed that, since they are coerced by their economic circumstances, their consent cannot count as genuine.

Although both these arguments appeal to the importance of autonomous choice, they are quite different. The first claim is that the vendors are not competent to make a genuine choice within a given range of options. The second, by contrast, is that poverty has so restricted the range of options that organ selling has become the best, and therefore, in effect, that the range is too small. Once this distinction is drawn, it can be seen that neither argument works as a justification of prohibition.

If our ground for concern is that the range of choices is too small, we cannot improve matters by removing the best option that poverty has left, and making the range smaller still. To do so is to make subsequent choices, by this criterion, even less autonomous. The only way to improve matters is to lessen the poverty until organ selling no longer seems the best option; and if that could be achieved, prohibition would be irrelevant because nobody would want to sell.

The other line of argument may seem more promising, since ignorance does preclude informed consent. However, the likely ignorance of the subjects is not a reason for banning altogether a procedure for which consent is required. In other contexts, the value we place on autonomy leads us to insist on information and counselling, and that is what it should suggest in the case of organ selling as well. It may be said that this approach is impracticable, because the educational level of potential vendors is too limited to make explanation feasible, or because no system could reliably counteract the misinformation of nefarious middlemen and profiteering clinics. But, even if we accepted that no possible vendor could be competent to consent, that would justify only putting the decision in the hands of competent guardians. To justify total prohibition it would also be necessary to show that organ selling must always be against the interests of potential vendors, and it is most unlikely that this would be done.

The risk involved in nephrectomy is not in itself high, and most people regard it as acceptable for living related donors. Since the procedure is, in principle, the same for vendors as for unpaid donors, any systematic difference between the worthwhileness of the risk for vendors and donors presumably lies on the other side of the calculation, in the expected benefit. Nevertheless the exchange of money cannot in itself turn an acceptable risk into an unacceptable one from the vendor's point of view. It depends entirely on what the money is wanted for.

In general, furthermore, the poorer a potential vendor, the more likely it is that the sale of a kidney will be worth whatever risk there is. If the rich are free to engage in dangerous sports for pleasure, or dangerous jobs for high pay, it is difficult to see why the poor who take the lesser risk of kidney selling for greater rewards—perhaps saving relatives' lives, or extricating themselves from poverty and debt—should be thought so misguided as to need saving from themselves.

It will be said that this does not take account of the reality of the vendors' circumstances: that risks are likely to be greater than for unpaid donors because poverty is detrimental to health, and vendors are often not given proper care. They may also be underpaid or cheated, or may waste their money through inexperience. However, once again, these arguments apply far more strongly to many other activities by which the poor try to earn money, and which we do not forbid. The best way to address such problems would be by regulation and perhaps a central purchasing system, to provide screening, counselling, reliable payment, insurance, and financial advice.

To this it will be replied that no system of screening and control could be complete, and that both vendors and recipients would always be at risk of exploitation and poor treatment. But all the evidence we have shows that there is much more scope for exploitation and abuse when a supply of desperately wanted goods is made illegal. It is, furthermore, not clear why it should be thought harder to police a legal trade than the present complete ban.

Furthermore, even if vendors and recipients would always be at risk of exploitation, that does not alter the fact that, if they choose this option, all alternatives must seem worse to them. Trying to end exploitation by prohibition is rather like ending slum dwelling by bulldozing slums: it ends the evil in that form, but only by making things worse for the victims. If we want to protect the exploited, we can do it only by removing the poverty that makes them vulnerable, or, failing that, by controlling the trade.

Another familiar objection is that it is unfair for the rich to have privileges not available to the poor. This argument, however, is irrelevant to the issue of organ selling as such. If organ selling is wrong for this reason, so are all benefits available to the rich, including all private medicine, and, for that matter, all public provision of medicine in rich countries (including transplantation of donated organs) that is unavailable in poor ones. Furthermore, all purchasing could be done by a central organisation responsible for fair distribution.

It is frequently asserted that organ donation must be altruistic to be acceptable, and that this rules out payment. However, there are two problems with this claim. First, altruism does not distinguish donors from vendors. If a father who saves his daughter's life by giving her a kidney is altruistic, it is difficult to see why his selling a kidney to pay for some other operation to save her life should be thought less so. Second, nobody believes in general that unless some useful action is altruistic it is better to forbid it altogether.

It is said that the practice would undermine confidence in the medical profession, because of the association of doctors with money-making practices. That, however, would be a reason for objecting to all private practice; and in this case the objection could easily be met by the separation of purchasing and treatment. There could, for instance, be independent trusts to fix charges and handle accounts, as well as to ensure fair play and high standards. It is alleged that allowing the trade would lessen the supply of donated cadaveric kidneys. But, although some possible donors might decide to sell instead, their organs would be available, so there would be no loss in the total. And in the meantime, many people will agree to sell who would not otherwise donate.

It is said that in parts of the world where women and children are essentially chattels there would be a danger of their being coerced into becoming vendors. This argument, however, would work as strongly against unpaid living kidney donation, and even more strongly against many far more harmful practices which do not attract calls for their prohibition. Again, regulation would provide the most reliable means of protection.

It is said that selling kidneys would set us on a slippery slope to selling vital organs such as hearts. But that argument would apply equally to the case of the unpaid kidney donation, and nobody is afraid that that will result in the donation of hearts. It is entirely feasible to have laws and professional practices that allow the giving or selling only of non-vital organs. Another objection is that allowing organ sales is impossible because it would outrage public opinion. But this claim is about western public opinion: in many potential vendor communities, organ selling is more acceptable than cadaveric donation, and this argument amounts to a claim that other people should follow western cultural preferences rather than their own. There is, anyway, evidence that the western public is far less opposed to the idea than are medical and political professionals.

It must be stressed that we are not arguing for the positive conclusion that organ sales must always be acceptable, let alone that there should be an unfettered market. Our claim is only that none of the familiar arguments against organ selling works, and this allows for the possibility that better arguments may yet be found.

Nevertheless, we claim that the burden of proof remains against the defenders of prohibition, and that, until good arguments appear, the presumption must be that the trade should be regulated rather than banned altogether. Furthermore, even when there are good objections at particular times or in particular places, that should be regarded as a reason for trying to remove the objections, rather than as an excuse for permanent prohibition.

The weakness of the familiar arguments suggests that they are attempts to justify the deep feelings of repugnance which are the real driving force of prohibition, and feelings of repugnance among the rich and healthy, no matter how strongly felt, cannot justify removing the only hope of the destitute and dying. This is why we conclude that the issue should be considered again, and with scrupulous impartiality.

Refuse to Support the Illegal Organ Trade

Kishore D. Phadke and Urmila Anandh

Phadke and Anandh observe that, although organ sales are prohibited in all countries, society in general has shifted toward regarding transplant organs as commodities that can be bought. In developing countries such as India, laws against organ sales are not enforced and the practice has popular support. The authors call for the medical profession to refuse to be a part of "this unscrupulous trade," which exploits the poor, discourages altruistic giving, commercializes the body, and undercuts human dignity.

The Issue of Altruism and Autonomy

It is argued that as altruism has failed to supply enough organs, resulting in many patients waiting for a kidney, the option of paid organ donation should be explored. Maybe the sale of body parts is a necessary social evil and hence our concerns should focus not on some philosophic imperative such as altruism, but on our collective responsibility of maximizing life-saving organ recovery.

From Kishore D. Phadke and Urmila Anandh, "Ethics of Paid Organ Donation," *Pediactric Nephrology* 17, issue 5 (May 2002): 309–311. Copyright © 2002 IPNA. With kind permission of Springer Science+Business Media. Reproduced by permission. (Notes omitted.)

However, the above argument appears at once as an easy way out with tremendous moral and ethical implications for society. By advocating financial incentives (it is difficult to fix a price), a deliberate conflict is created between altruism and self-interest, reducing freedom to make a gift. The concept that human organs are spare parts that can be bought and sold can adversely influence respect for the human body and human dignity. It puts organ sale in the same category of paid human body transactions as prostitution and slavery. When organs are "thingified," these marketing practices can lead to serious erosion of cherished values in society. This issue has been highlighted in Iran, where the selling of organs is allowed. It has been shown that in almost all instances, the donor–recipient relationship becomes pathological. Fifty-one percent of donors hated the recipients and 82% were unsatisfied with their behavior. Some sections of society may be treated as saleable commodities rather than as human beings. The medical profession compromises its deontological commitments (that all individuals have a value beyond price) by adopting a mainly utilitarian ethic (maximizing the good for the largest number). The medical profession also has a moral obligation to use its influence to change the cultural behavior of society. For example, if female feticide is the cultural behavior of society, the medical profession, instead of accepting it, should make active efforts to bring about a behavioral change in society. It should be remembered that, once a moral barrier is broken, it is difficult to contain abuses in society, even by regulation or law.

On the face of it, the act of selling an organ may seem justifiable on the principle of autonomy. However, it should be noted that human autonomy has limitations. This is because "no man is an island entire of itself; every man is a piece of the continent, a part of the main." The act of selling should be considered as arising out of narcissism—too much self-focusing rather than mere execution of autonomy.

It is usually the poor who donate and poverty is perhaps the most significant factor in making a person vulnerable to coercion.

Since the consent for kidney sale can be considered to be under coercion, it cannot be accepted as a valid consent.

Can and Should Paid Organ Donation Be Regulated?

It has been suggested that the concerns relating to malfunction of the organ trade, such as exploitation by middlemen or brokers, may be addressed organizationally through a centralized coordinated organ bank or "National Commission for Kidney Purchase—NCKP."

Rewarded gifting or compensation (tax rebates, burial grants, future medical coverage, tuition subsidies for children) to the donors has been suggested. Although paid organ donation in an ideal situation (i.e. without exploitation, with justice to everyone and transparent) may be acceptable, we have reservations as to whether the regulation and implementation of regulatory law on this subject is a possibility at all in a developing country such as India. In many developing countries, including India, a great degree of societal and governmental dysfunction exists. Rampant corruption colors almost every monetary transaction. Vigilance against wrong and unjust practices in relation to the existent laws is grossly inadequate. Sufficient legal resources, checks, controls and balances for such a system to keep it from getting on the slippery slope of commercialism do not exist. The boundaries between pure compensation and incentives for organ donation with potential for inducement, manipulation, coercion and exploitation will be difficult to define and monitor in developing countries. Only the rich who can afford to buy kidneys will derive benefits, thus violating the principle of justice. Organ donation will be practiced with a neglect of beliefs, sentiments and emotions. It will be practiced in backstreet clinics without adequate facilities for postoperative care. This practice will only enhance high morbidity and mortality among recipients who have bought living-unrelated donor kidneys. The slippery slope of commercialism is no ethical illusion but a recurrent reality in India.

Cadaver organ transplantation is in its infancy in the developing world, and legalizing paid organ donation will kill the cadaver program without any increase in the number of transplants.

Also, paid organ donation should not be looked upon as a measure of alleviating the poverty of individuals. There are 3.5 billion poor people worldwide and there are better ways to address poverty issues, which include providing fresh drinking water, adequate sewage facilities, and immunization programs.

Are the Issues Different in the Developed World?

We feel it is logical to think that universalistic ethics promoting human life and dignity transcend time, space, national boundaries and boundaries of social circumstances. The differences in expression of fundamental ethical principles merely reflect inequities in resources between first and third world countries. Complex modes of moral reasoning and considerations of ethics of rights, as well as social responsibilities, should guide the practice of modern medicine everywhere. The regulatory forces may be considered to be better developed in the developed world, making regulated sale of organs an achievable proposition. It is suggested though, that the principle of minimizing ethical risk should be pursued, wherein promotion of living-related donor programs, cadaver programs and xenotransplantation should be explored to the fullest extent before embarking on commercialization of transplantation. The business nature of organ donation and neglect of altruism will alter the attitudes of society toward medical professionals, with the development of suspicion and loss of respect. This may be considered an unhealthy trend.

Conclusions

The question of organ shortage and the problem of patients awaiting the availability of organs will continue to exist. Offering paid organ donation as a solution to this problem raises many ethical and moral issues. WHO guidelines issued in 1989 clearly state that "commercialization of human organs and tissues should be prevented, if necessary by penal sanctions. National and International measures should be adopted to prevent the utilization of organs and tissues obtained through the exploitation of the economic needs of the donor or their relatives." As of now, no regulatory body has endorsed paid organ donation. The organ trade is likely to take unfair advantage of poor people and poor countries. Paid organ donation will exploit the poor, commercialize the human body, deter altruism, and retard the progress of living-related, cadaver and animal organ donor programs. In a society that acknowledges gift giving and resource sharing, there is no place for organ marketing. "Even if it is banned, it will go on anyway" is a very inadequate reason to support it. It is high time that health professionals stop turning a blind eye, becoming accomplices to the unscrupulous and illegal organ trade. It is our plea that the medical community, ethicists, etc., address the issue in its totality before they think of legalizing the organ trade.

Section 3:   Allocation Principles in Medicine

Rationing Schemes for Organ Transplantation

George J. Annas

Annas takes a position on transplant selection that introduces a modification of the first-come, first-served principle. He reviews four approaches to rationing scarce medical resources—market, selection committee, lottery, and customary—and finds that each has disadvantages so serious as to make them all unacceptable. An acceptable approach, he suggests, is one that combines efficiency, fairness, and a respect for the value of life. Because candidates should both want a transplant and be able to derive significant benefits from one, the first phase of selection should involve a screening process that is based exclusively on medical criteria that are objective and as free as possible of judgments about social worth.

Since selection might still have to be made from this pool of candidates, it might be done by social-worth criteria or by lottery. However, social-worth criteria seem arbitrary, and a lottery would be unfair to those who are in more immediate need of a transplant—ones who might die quickly without it. After reviewing the relevant considerations, a committee operating at this stage might

From "The Prostitute, the Playboy, and the Poet: Rationing Schemes for Organ Transplantation," reprinted by permission of the author and *The American Journal of Public Health* 75, no. 2 (1985): 187–189. (Notes omitted.)

allow those in immediate need of a transplant to be moved to the head of a waiting list. To those not in immediate need, organs would be distributed in a first-come, first-served fashion. Although absolute equality is not embodied in this process, the procedure is sufficiently flexible to recognize that some may have needs that are greater (more immediate) than others.

In the public debate about the availability of heart and liver transplants, the issue of rationing on a massive scale has been credibly raised for the first time in United States medical care. In an era of scarce resources, the eventual arrival of such a discussion was, of course, inevitable. Unless we decide to ban heart and liver transplantation, or make them available to everyone, some rationing scheme must be used to choose among potential transplant candidates. The debate has existed throughout the history of medical ethics. Traditionally it has been stated as a choice between saving one of two patients, both of whom require the immediate assistance of the only available physician to survive.

National attention was focused on decisions regarding the rationing of kidney dialysis machines when they were first used on a limited basis in the late 1960s. As one commentator described the debate within the medical profession:

> Shall machines or organs go to the sickest, or to the ones with most promise of recovery; on a first-come, first-served basis; to the most 'valuable' patient (based on wealth, education, position, what?); to the one with the most dependents; to women and children first; to those who can pay; to whom? Or should lots be cast, impersonally and uncritically?

In Seattle, Washington, an anonymous screening committee was set up to pick who among competing candidates would receive the life-saving technology. One lay member of the screening committee is quoted as saying:

> The choices were hard ... I remember voting against a young woman who was a known prostitute. I found I couldn't vote for her, rather than another candidate, a young wife and mother. I also voted against a young man who, until he learned he had renal failure, had been a ne'er do-well, a real playboy. He promised he would reform his character, go back to school, and so on, if only he were selected for treatment. But I felt I'd lived

long enough to know that a person like that won't really do what he was promising at the time.

When the biases and selection criteria of the committee were made public, there was a general negative reaction against this type of arbitrary device. Two experts reacted to the "numbing accounts of how close to the surface lie the prejudices and mindless cliches that pollute the committee's deliberations," by concluding that the committee was "measuring persons in accordance with its own middle-class values." The committee process, they noted, ruled out "creative nonconformists" and made the Pacific Northwest "no place for a Henry David Thoreau with bad kidneys."

To avoid having to make such explicit, arbitrary, "social worth" determinations, the Congress, in 1972, enacted legislation that provided federal funds for virtually all kidney dialysis and kidney transplantation procedures in the United States. This decision, however, simply served to postpone the time when identical decisions will have to be made about candidates for heart and liver transplantation in a society that does not provide sufficient financial and medical resources to provide all "suitable" candidates with the operations.

There are four major approaches to rationing scarce medical resources: the market approach; the selection committee approach; the lottery approach; and the "customary" approach.

The Market Approach

The market approach would provide an organ to everyone who could pay for it with their own funds or private insurance. It puts a very high value on individual rights, and a very low value on equality and fairness. It has properly been criticized on a number of bases, including that the transplant technologies have been developed and are supported with public funds, that medical resources used for transplantation will not be available for higher priority care, and that financial success alone is an insufficient justification for demanding a medical procedure. Most telling is its complete lack of concern for fairness and equity.

A "bake sale" or charity approach that requires the less financially fortunate to make public appeals for funding is demeaning to the individuals involved, and to society as a whole. Rationing by financial ability says we do not believe in equality, but believe that a price can and should be placed on human life and that it should be paid by the individual whose life is at stake. Neither belief is tolerable in a society in which income is inequitably distributed.

The Committee Selection Process

The Seattle Selection Committee is a model of the committee process. Ethics Committees set up in some hospitals to decide whether or not certain handicapped newborn infants should be given medical care may represent another. These committees have developed because it was seen as unworkable or unwise to explicitly set forth the criteria on which selection decisions would be made. But only two results are possible, as Professor Guido Calabresi has pointed out: either a pattern of decision-making will develop or it will not. If a pattern does develop (e.g., in Seattle, the imposition of middle-class values), then it can be articulated and those decision "rules" codified and used directly, without resort to the committee. If a pattern does not develop, the committee is vulnerable to the charge that it is acting arbitrarily, or dishonestly, and therefore cannot be permitted to continue to make such important decisions.

In the end, public designation of a committee to make selection decisions on vague criteria will fail because it too closely involves the state and all members of society in explicitly preferring specific individuals over others, and in devaluing the interests those others have in living. It thus directly undermines, as surely as the market system does, society's view of equality and the value of human life.

The Lottery Approach

The lottery approach is the ultimate equalizer which puts equality ahead of every other value. This makes it extremely attractive, since all comers have an equal chance at selection regardless of race, color, creed, or financial status. On the other hand, it offends our notions of efficiency and fairness since it makes no distinctions among such things as the strength of the desires of the candidates, their potential survival, and their quality of life. In this sense it is a mindless method of trying to solve society's dilemma which is caused by its unwillingness or inability to spend enough resources to make a lottery unnecessary. By making this macro spending decision evident to all, it also undermines society's view of the pricelessness of human life. A first-come, first-served system is a type of natural lottery since referral to a transplant program is generally random in time. Nonetheless, higher income groups have quicker access to referral networks and thus have an inherent advantage over the poor in a strict first-come, first-served system.

The Customary Approach

Society has traditionally attempted to avoid explicitly recognizing that we are making a choice not to save individual lives because it is too expensive to do so. As long as such decisions are not explicitly acknowledged, they can be tolerated by society. For example, until recently there was said to be a general understanding among general practitioners in Britain that individuals over age 55 suffering from end-stage kidney disease not be referred for dialysis or transplant. In 1984, however, this unwritten practice became highly publicized, with figures that showed a rate of new cases of end-stage kidney disease treated in Britain at 40 per million (versus the U.S. figure of 80 per million) resulting in 1500–3000 "unnecessary deaths" annually. This has, predictably, led to movements to enlarge the National Health Service budget to expand dialysis services to meet this need, a more socially acceptable solution than permitting the now publicly recognized situation to continue.

In the U.S., the customary approach permits individual physicians to select their patients on the basis of medical criteria or clinical suitability. This, however, contains many hidden social worth criteria. For example, one criterion, common in the transplant literature, requires an individual to have sufficient family support for successful aftercare. This discriminates against individuals without families and those who have become alienated from their families. The criterion may be relevant, but it is hardly medical.

Similar observations can be made about medical criteria that include IQ, mental illness, criminal records, employment, indigence, alcoholism, drug addiction, or geographical location. Age is perhaps more difficult, since it may be impressionistically related to outcome. But it is not medically logical to assume that an individual who is 49 years old is necessarily a better medical candidate for a transplant than one who is 50 years old. Unless specific examination of the characteristics of older persons that make them less desirable candidates is undertaken, such a cutoff is arbitrary, and thus devalues the lives of older citizens. The same can be said of blanket exclusions of alcoholics and drug addicts.

In short, the customary approach has one great advantage for society and one great disadvantage: it gives us the illusion that we do not have to make choices; but the cost is mass deception, and when this deception is uncovered, we must deal with it either by universal entitlement or by choosing another method of patient selection.

A Combination of Approaches

A socially acceptable approach must be fair, efficient, and reflective of important social values. The most important values at stake in organ transplantation are fairness itself, equity in the sense of equality, and the value of life. To promote efficiency, it is important that no one receive a transplant unless they want one and are likely to obtain significant benefit from it in the sense of years of life at a reasonable level of functioning.

Accordingly, it is appropriate for there to be an initial screening process that is based *exclusively* on medical criteria designed to measure the probability of a successful transplant, i.e., one in which the patient survives for at least a number of years and is rehabilitated. There is room in medical criteria for social worth judgments, but there is probably no way to avoid this completely. For example, it has been noted that "in many respects social and medical criteria are inextricably intertwined" and that therefore medical criteria might "exclude the poor and disadvantaged because health and socioeconomic status are highly interdependent." Roger Evans gives an example. In the End Stage Renal Disease Program, "those of lower socioeconomic status are likely to have multiple comorbid health conditions such as diabetes, hepatitis, and hypertension" making them both less desirable candidates and more expensive to treat.

To prevent the gulf between the haves and have nots from widening, we must make every reasonable attempt to develop medical criteria that are objective and independent of social worth categories. One minimal way to approach this is to require

that medical screening be reviewed and approved by an ethics committee with significant public representation, filed with a public agency, and made readily available to the public for comment. In the event that more than one hospital in a state or region is offering a particular transplant service, it would be most fair and efficient for the individual hospitals to perform the initial medical screening themselves (based on the uniform, objective criteria), but to have all subsequent nonmedical selection done by a method approved by a single selection committee composed of representatives of all hospitals engaged in a particular transplant procedure, as well as significant representation of the public at large.

As this implies, after the medical screening is performed, there may be more acceptable candidates in the "pool" than there are organs or surgical teams to go around. Selection among waiting candidates will then be necessary. This situation occurs now in kidney transplantation, but since the organ matching is much more sophisticated than in hearts and livers (permitting much more precise matching of organ and recipient), and since dialysis permits individuals to wait almost indefinitely for an organ without risking death, the situations are not close enough to permit use of the same matching criteria. On the other hand, to the extent that organs are specifically tissue- and size-matched and fairly distributed to the best matched candidate, the organ distribution system itself will resemble a natural lottery.

When a pool of acceptable candidates is developed, a decision about who gets the next available, suitable organ must be made. We must choose between using a conscious, value-laden, social worth selection criterion (including a committee to make the actual choice), or some type of random device. In view of the unacceptability and arbitrariness of social worth criteria being applied, implicitly or explicitly, by committee, this method is neither viable nor proper. On the other hand, strict adherence to a lottery might create a situation where an individual who has only a one-in-four chance of living five years with a transplant (but who could survive another six months without one) would get an organ before an individual who could survive as long or longer, but who will die within days or hours if he or she is not immediately transplanted. Accordingly, the reasonable approach seems to be to allocate organs on a first-come, first-served basis to members of the pool but permit individuals to "jump" the queue if the second level selection committee believes they are in immediate danger of death (but still have a reasonable prospect for long-term survival with a transplant) and the person who would otherwise get the organ can survive long enough to be reasonably assured that he or she will be able to get another organ.

The first-come, first-served method of basic selection (after a medical screen) seems the preferred method because it most closely approximates the randomness of a straight lottery without the obviousness of making equity the only promoted value. Some unfairness is introduced by the fact that the more wealthy and medically astute will likely get into the pool first, and thus be ahead in line, but this advantage should decrease sharply as public awareness of the system grows. The possibility of unfairness is also inherent in permitting individuals to jump the queue, but some flexibility needs to be retained in the system to permit it to respond to reasonable contingencies.

We will have to face the fact that should the resources devoted to organ transplantation be limited (as they are now and are likely to be in the future), at some point it is likely that significant numbers of individuals will die in the pool waiting for a transplant. Three things can be done to avoid this: (1) medical criteria can be made stricter, perhaps by adding a more rigorous notion of "quality" of life to longevity and prospects for rehabilitation; (2) resources devoted to transplantation and organ procurement can be increased; or (3) individuals can be persuaded not to attempt to join the pool.

Of these three options, only the third has the promise of both conserving resources and promoting autonomy. While most persons medically eligible for a transplant would probably want one, some would not—at least if they understood all that was involved, including the need for a lifetime commitment to daily immunosuppression medications, and periodic medical monitoring for rejection symptoms. Accordingly, it makes public policy sense to publicize the risks and side effects of transplantation, and to require careful explanations of the procedure be given to prospective patients before they undergo medical screening. It is likely that by the time patients come to the transplant center they have made up their minds and would do almost anything to get the transplant. Nonetheless, if there are patients who, when confronted with all the facts, would voluntarily elect not to proceed, we enhance both their own freedom and the efficiency and cost-effectiveness of the transplantation system by screening them out as early as possible.

Conclusion

Choices among patients that seem to condemn some to death and give others an opportunity to survive will always be tragic. Society has developed a number of mechanisms to make such decisions more acceptable by camouflaging them. In an era of scarce resources and conscious cost containment, such mechanisms will become public, and they will be usable only if they are fair and efficient. If they are not so perceived, we will shift from one mechanism to another in an effort to continue the illusion that tragic choices really don't have to be made, and that we can simultaneously move toward equity of access, quality of services, and cost containment without any challenges to our values. Along with the prostitute, the playboy, and the poet, we all need to be involved in the development of an access model to extreme and expensive medical technologies with which we can live.

Who Should Get Influenza Vaccine When Not All Can?

Ezekiel J. Emanuel and Alan Wertheimer

Emanuel and Wertheimer argue against the "save the most lives" principle for allocating resources in case of an influenza pandemic, as endorsed by (among others) the National Vaccine Advisory Committee. The authors formulate a "life-cycle allocation principle" based on the notion of someone's living through all the stages of life.

From Ezekiel J. Emanuel and Alan Wertheimer, "Who Should Get Influenza Vaccine When Not All Can?" *Science* 312, no. 5775 (May 2006): 854–855. Reprinted with permission of AAAS. (Notes omitted.)

The principle, as refined, gives priority to those between early adolescence and middle age, because they have more developed interests than younger people and because they have more remaining stages to live through than older people. Like the advisory committee, the authors also assign priority status to those working on producing and distributing the vaccine, as well as to health care workers who administer the vaccine and take care of patients.

The potential threat of pandemic influenza is staggering: 1.9 million deaths, 90 million people sick, and nearly 10 million people hospitalized, with almost 1.5 million requiring intensive-care units (ICUs) in the United States. The National Vaccine Advisory Committee (NVAC) and the Advisory Committee on Immunization Policy (ACIP) have jointly recommended a prioritization scheme that places vaccine workers, health-care providers, and the ill elderly at the top, and healthy people aged 2 to 64 at the very bottom, even under embalmers. The primary goal informing the recommendation was to "decrease health impacts including severe morbidity and death"; a secondary goal was minimizing societal and economic impacts. As the NVAC and ACIP acknowledge, such important policy decisions require broad national discussion. In this spirit, we believe an alternative ethical framework should be considered.

The Inescapability of Rationing

Because of current uncertainty of its value, only "a limited amount of avian influenza A (H5N1) vaccine is being stockpiled." Furthermore, it will take at least 4 months from identification of a candidate vaccine strain until production of the very first vaccine. At present, there are few production facilities worldwide that make influenza vaccine, and only one completely in the USA. Global capacity for influenza vaccine production is just 425 million doses per annum, if all available factories would run at full capacity after the vaccine was developed. Under currently existing capabilities for manufacturing vaccine, it is likely that more than 90% of the U.S. population will not be vaccinated in the first year. Distributing the limited supply will require determining priority groups.

Who will be at highest risk? Our experience with three influenza pandemics presents a complex picture. The mortality profile of a future pandemic could be

U-shaped, as it was in the mild-to-moderate pandemics of 1957 and 1968 and interpandemic influenza seasons, in which the very young and the old are at highest risk. Or, the mortality profile could be an attenuated W shape, as it was during the devastating 1918 pandemic, in which the highest risk occurred among people between 20 and 40 years of age, while the elderly were not at high excess risk. Even during pandemics, the elderly appear to be at no higher risk than during interpandemic influenza seasons.

Clear ethical justification for vaccine priorities is essential to the acceptability of the priority ranking and any modifications during the pandemic. With limited vaccine supply, uncertainty over who will be at highest risk of infection and complications, and questions about which historic pandemic experience is most applicable, society faces a fundamental ethical dilemma: Who should get the vaccine first?

The NVAC and ACIP Priority Rankings

Many potential ethical principles for rationing health care have been proposed. "Save the most lives" is commonly used in emergencies, such as burning buildings, although "women and children first" played a role on the Titanic. "First come, first served" operates in other emergencies and in ICUs when admitted patients retain beds despite the presentation of another patient who is equally or even more sick; "Save the most quality life years" is central to cost-effectiveness rationing. "Save the worst-off" plays a role in allocating organs for transplantation. "Reciprocity"—giving priority to people willing to donate their own organs—has been proposed. "Save those most likely to fully recover" guided priorities for giving penicillin to soldiers with syphilis in World War II. Save those "instrumental in making society flourish" through economic productivity or by "contributing to the well-being of others" has been proposed by Murray and others.

The save-the-most-lives principle was invoked by NVAC and ACIP. It justifies giving top priority to workers engaged in vaccine production and distribution and health-care workers. They get higher priority not because they are intrinsically more valuable people or of greater "social worth," but because giving them first priority ensures that maximal life-saving vaccine is produced and so that health care is provided to the sick. Consequently, it values all human life equally, giving every person equal consideration in who gets priority regardless of age, disability, social class, or employment. After these groups, the save-the-most-lives principle justifies priority for those predicted to be at highest risk of hospitalization and dying. We disagree with this prioritization.

Life-Cycle Principle

The save-the-most-lives principle may be justified in some emergencies when decision urgency makes it infeasible to deliberate about priority rankings and impractical to categorize individuals into priority groups. We believe that a life-cycle allocation principle based on the idea that each person should have an opportunity to live through all the stages of life is more appropriate for a pandemic. There is great value in being able to pass through each life stage—to be a child, a young adult, and to then develop a career and family, and to grow old—and to enjoy a wide range of the opportunities during each stage. Multiple considerations and intuitions support this ethical principle. Most people endorse this principle for themselves. We would prioritize our own resources to ensure we could live past the illnesses of childhood and young adulthood and would allocate fewer resources to living ever longer once we reached old age. People strongly prefer maximizing the chance of living until a ripe old age, rather than being struck down as a young person.

Death seems more tragic when a child or young adult dies than an elderly person—not because the lives of older people are less valuable, but because the younger person has not had the opportunity to live and develop through all stages of life. Although the life-cycle principle favors some ages, it is also intrinsically egalitarian. Unlike being productive or contributing to others' well-being, every person will live to be older unless their life is cut short.

The Investment Refinement

A pure version of the life-cycle principle would grant priority to 6-month-olds over 1-year-olds who have priority over 2-year-olds, and on. An alternative, the investment refinement, emphasizes gradations within a life span. It gives priority to people between early adolescence and middle age on the basis of the amount the person invested in his or her life balanced by the amount left to live. Within this framework, 20-year-olds are valued more than 1-year-olds because the older individuals have more developed interests, hopes, and plans but have not had an opportunity to realize them. Although these groupings could be modified, they indicate ethically defensible distinctions among groups that can inform rationing priorities.

One other ethical principle relevant for priority ranking of influenza vaccine during a pandemic is public order. It focuses on the value of ensuring safety and the provision of necessities, such as food and fuel. We believe the investment refinement combined with the public-order principle (IRPOP) should be the ultimate objective of all pandemic response measures, including priority ranking for vaccines and interventions to limit the course of the pandemic, such as closing schools and confining people to homes. These two principles should inform decisions at the start of an epidemic when the shape of the risk curves for morbidity and mortality are largely uncertain.

Like the NVAC and ACIP ranking, the IRPOP ranking would give high priority to vaccine production and distribution workers, as well as health-care and public health workers with direct patient contact. However, contrary to the NVAC and ACIP prioritization for the sick elderly and infants, IRPOP emphasize[s] people between 13 and 40 years of age. The NVAC and ACIP priority ranking comports well with those groups at risk during the mild-to-moderate 1957 and 1968 pandemics. IRPOP prioritizes those age cohorts at highest risk during the devastating 1918 pandemic. Depending on patterns of flu spread, some mathematical models suggest that following IRPOP priority ranking could save the most lives overall.

Conclusions

The life-cycle ranking is meant to apply to the situation in the United States. During a global pandemic, there will be fundamental questions about sharing vaccines and other interventions with other countries. This raises fundamental issues of global rationing that are too complex to address here.

Fortunately, even though we are worried about an influenza pandemic, it is not upon us. Indeed,

the current H5N1 avian flu may never develop into a human pandemic. This gives us time both to build vaccine production capacity to minimize the need for rationing and to rationally assess policy and ethical issues about the distribution of vaccines.

DECISION SCENARIOS

The questions following each decision scenario are intended to prompt reflection and discussion. In deciding how to answer them, you should consider the information provided in the Social Context and Case Presentations, as well as in the Briefing Session. You should also make use of the ethical theories and principles presented in Part VI: Foundations of Bioethics, and the arguments offered in the relevant readings in this chapter.

DECISION SCENARIO 1

First Come, First Served?

The microsurgical team at Benton Public Hospital consisted of twenty-three people. Five were surgeons, three were anesthesiologists, three were internists, two were radiologists, and the remaining members were various sorts of nurses and technicians.

Early Tuesday afternoon on a date late in March, the members of the team were preparing Hammond Cox for surgery. Mr. Cox was a fifty-nine-year-old unmarried man who worked as a janitor in a large apartment building. While performing his duties, Cox had caught his hand in the mechanism of a commercial trash compactor. The bones of his wrist had been crushed and blood vessels severed.

The head of the team, Herbert Lagorio, believed it was possible to restore at least partial functioning to Cox's hand. Otherwise, the hand would have to be amputated.

Cox had been drunk when it happened. When the police ambulance brought him to the emergency room, he was still so drunk that a decision was made to delay surgery for almost an hour to give him a chance to burn up some of the alcohol he had consumed. As it was, administering anesthesia to Cox would incur a greater-than-average risk. Furthermore, blood tests had shown that Cox already suffered from some degree of liver damage. In both the short- and long-term, Cox was not a terribly good surgical risk.

Lagorio was already scrubbed when Carol Levine, a resident in emergency medicine, had him paged.

"This had better be important," he told her. "I've got a patient prepped and waiting."

"I know," Dr. Levine said. "But they just brought in this thirty-five-year-old female with a totally severed right hand. She's a prominent biology professor and was working late in her lab when some maniac looking for drugs came in and attacked her with a cleaver."

"What shape is the hand in?"

"Excellent. The campus cops were there within minutes, and there was ice in the lab. One of the cops had the sense to put the hand in a plastic bag and bring it with her."

"Is she in good general health?"

"It seems excellent," Dr. Levine said.

"This is a real problem."

"You can't do two cases at once?"

"No way. We need everybody we've got to do one."

"How about sending her someplace else?"

"No other hospital in the region is set up to do what has to be done."

"So what are you going to do?"

1. Does a first-come, first-served criterion require that Cox receive the surgery?

2. Can the different chances of a successful outcome in each case be used as a criterion without violating the notion that all people are of equal worth?

3. Should the fact that Cox's injury is the consequence of his own negligence be considered in determining who should get priority for surgery?

4. In your view, which patient should have the potential benefits of the surgery? Give reasons to support your view.

DECISION SCENARIO 2

Robbing the Dead?

"We haven't been able to get in touch with his wife or any family member," nurse Richard Wike told Sam Long, the emergency room's chief surgeon. "Dr. Sen has declared him dead, but we've left him on the respirator."

"Call the organ procurement people," Long said. "Tell them we've got a twenty-four-year-old head-trauma victim with usable heart, kidneys, lungs, and liver, and they should arrange for surgical teams to remove them."

"Don't we have to get the consent of at least somebody in the family?" Wike asked.

"Not anymore," Dr. Long said. "We're operating under the new policy of conscription."

1. What is organ conscription?

2. Is conscription ethically preferable to the present policy of requiring explicit consent?

3. Critics of conscription object that it involves an unjustified "taking" of organs and thus is a violation of the due process clause of the Constitution. Is conscription the moral equivalent of robbing the dead? Why or why not?

4. On what grounds might one argue that consent is not "ethically required" for using cadaveric organs?

DECISION SCENARIO 3

Taking a Chance for Love

"We think Natasha's got about a sixty percent chance of surviving if we can transplant her with a lung," Dr. Mary Wicker said. "We've got her listed with UNOS, but the chance of getting a lung in time varies from slight to none."

"Can you use my lungs?" Sara Besinny asked. "She's my only child. I'd give my life for even a ten percent chance."

"We couldn't take your whole lung," Dr. Wicker said. "That would kill you, and we can't do that. But you may be eligible to donate a segment. Segments have been used successfully at this

hospital and elsewhere. But somebody needs to talk to you about the risks and make sure you understand what donating a lung segment means."

1. Should Besinny be allowed to risk her life, if the chance that Natasha would be helped is less than fifty–fifty?

2. Should we permit people to become living donors, despite the risks?

3. Are transplant surgeons causing harm to living donors by operating on them to benefit someone else?

DECISION SCENARIO 4

Buying a Liver

"Your baby's liver is not fully developed," Dr. Robert Amatin said. "The bile duct is missing, and blood can't flow through the liver the way it's supposed to."

Clarissa Austin nodded. She had already made up her mind to do whatever she had to do to ensure that her baby was all right.

"That means the liver can't do its job and that the blood is backing up," Amatin continued. "Surgery really can't correct a problem like this."

"Can you give him a new liver?"

Amatin avoided answering the question directly. "A transplant is his best hope," he said. "If we can surgically remove the malformed liver and attach a new one, the baby has a very good chance of living."

"I'll be happy to give permission if that's what you're waiting for," Clarissa said.

"It's not that simple," Dr. Amatin said. He looked uncomfortable. "It really comes down to a matter of money."

"I don't have much money," Clarissa said. "You know I'm on Medicaid, and I don't have any insurance."

"Medicaid will pay for the surgery, but not for an organ."

"How much does a liver cost?"

"I've got a family right now that says it wants $15,000 for their baby's liver. She died this morning."

"I can't get money like that," Clarissa said.

"I can ask them to come up and talk to you. Maybe they would take less, or maybe you could work out some kind of deferred payment with them."

"What if I can't?"

Dr. Amatin shook his head. "I can't arrange for a transplant without an organ that size, and I suspect they will try to find somebody else to sell it to."

"That's not fair," Clarissa said. "Just because I haven't got the money, my baby is going to die."

1. Does the possibility of situations like the one just described demonstrate that the present policy of relying on donated organs is best?

2. Why might one object to selling organs? Do these objections apply to all kinds of organ sales—for example, to a government-regulated market with set prices as well as to a free market? If it is permissible to give away organs, why should it be thought wrong to sell them?

3. What other procurement policy, besides voluntary donation and organ sales, might be considered as a means to increase the number of transplant organs?

4. Is Clarissa Austin correct in saying that it would be unfair for her child not to have a new liver because she cannot afford to pay the asking price? If it is not unfair for Austin's child to be deprived of a luxury good because of her inability to pay, why is this allocation unfair? How is an organ different from other commodities on the market?

5. Some critics claim that organ sales will promote the *commodification* of the human body. What, if anything, is wrong with that?

DECISION SCENARIO 5

Selling a Kidney

Colin Benton, a British citizen, died of renal disease in the summer of 1988 after a kidney transplant failed. Benton's widow later revealed that the donor kidney had been obtained from a Turkish citizen who traveled to London for the surgery. The kidney donor was paid the equivalent of $4,400. When asked why he had sold the organ, the man explained that he needed the money to pay for medical treatment for his daughter. It was this case that led the British Parliament to outlaw organ sales.

1. On what grounds might one claim that it is wrong for society to allow people to sell organs?

2. Is there a moral distinction between donating a kidney out of benevolence and selling one for financial gain?

3. If a parent has no other way to raise money for surgery necessary to preserve the life of his child, is it morally permissible for him to sell a kidney? Is he blameworthy if, given the opportunity, he refuses to do so?

4. Is selling one's kidney different in any morally relevant way from selling one's labor under potentially hazardous conditions (e.g., mining coal)?

DECISION SCENARIO 6

Lifestyle Factors

Dr. Sarah Brandywine hurried into Omar Kline's inner office. Dr. Kline was transplant coordinator at Midwestern General Hospital, and he was expecting her. She had called him as soon as she realized

the dimension of the problem with her patient, Jonathan Wardell.

"So tell me about Mr. Wardell," Dr. Kline said, nodding toward the chair beside his desk.

"He's a fifty-one-year-old man who came to the hospital two days ago because he was frightened by the jaundice and ascites he developed over the course of the last week," Brandywine said. "He had been experiencing fatigue and loss of appetite several weeks prior to the jaundice. His liver is swollen and lumpy."

"Sounds like cirrhosis," Kline said. "I'm sure you did liver function tests, but what about a biopsy?"

"We did both yesterday, and I called you right after the final results. There's so much scarring that Mr. Wardell has little liver function left." She shook her head. "I want to put him on the transplant list."

"What's the cause of his disease?"

"It's alcohol induced."

"No way." Kline shook his head. "No livers for alcoholics. No ifs, ands, or buts about it."

"This is a man with two kids." Dr. Brandywine tried to keep her voice level. "One's twelve, and the other is eight. Their mother died two years ago, and their dad is all they've got left."

"Sure, the kids make it particularly sad," Kline said. "But look, thirty thousand people a year die from alcoholic cirrhosis, and we can't treat them all."

"I agree we can't, but why not treat some?" Brandywine leaned forward. "Do all alcoholics deserve an automatic refusal?"

"I'm afraid so," Kline said. "These are people who created their own problems. There are far from enough livers to go around, so it's only fair for us to focus on better candidates."

"But look, this guy's got two kids depending on him." Brandywine squeezed her hands into fists. "If I can get him into a rehab program, can we promise him the chance at a liver then? Not a guaranteed liver, but a chance at one?"

"The answer's still no." Kline paused. "I'm not saying alcoholics can't get sober, but I am saying they're bad risks. If we give a transplant to somebody whose liver was destroyed by biliary cirrhosis, we're likely to get a good long-term survival. But if we transplant somebody who's been heavily drinking for the last ten or twenty years, we're not likely to get good results. The guy may promise to stop drinking, and maybe he'll do it for a while. But chances are good that within a few years, he's going to be back in the hospital with liver failure again, and alcohol is going to be the cause."

"I admit the numbers are against me." Brandywine inhaled deeply then sighed. "There's nothing I can say to convince you?"

"We can't afford to risk wasting a liver," Kline said. "That's what I've got to convince you of." He shook his head. "I hate to think about Mr. Wardell's children, but I've also got to think about the parents with cirrhosis who aren't alcoholics."

1. State explicitly the two arguments that Kline invokes against liver transplants for alcoholics.

2. Why should so-called "lifestyle" factors be considered relevant in making transplant decisions? By the same reasoning, shouldn't we deny heart transplants to people who, through overeating or lack of exercise, have allowed themselves to become obese? Why should alcoholics be held to a higher standard than others needing transplants?

3. If you were responsible for determining whether there would be a categorical exclusion of alcoholics from receiving liver transplants, what would you decide? How would you justify that decision?

DECISION SCENARIO 7

How Many Livers Are Fair?

"Karen's rejecting the liver," Dr. Sola Beni said. "We aren't going to be able to save it, and to stay alive, she will need another liver."

"Can Karen withstand another operation?" asked Asha Singer, the hospital's patient care coordinator. "She's only five, and she seems so fragile."

"I'm not so worried about her response to the surgery as I am about getting her another liver," Beni said.

"At least she'll be at the top of the waiting list, won't she?" Singer asked. "I mean, I've looked at her numbers and she's clearly dying."

"She has already had one liver," Dr. Beni said. "The probability of success with a liver transplant decreases with each new transplant. We can get another liver for Karen only if there are no other good first-time candidates on the list for a donor liver." Beni shook his head. "Otherwise, all we can do is make her comfortable and wait for the end."

1. Should Karen's age be relevant to whether she gets another liver?

2. Is a policy of "one donor liver per patient, unless the liver will otherwise go to waste" a fair one?

3. If Karen received a second liver and her body rejected it, should she be eligible for a third liver?

4. Should Karen be at the top of the waiting list for a new liver?

DECISION SCENARIO 8

Who Gets the Ventilators?

In 2010, the government of New York State became aware of a potentially imminent public health crisis. The virus H5N1 was already spreading through the Eastern Hemisphere, and it was possible that the virus might become a genuine pandemic. Because respiration was affected, those falling seriously ill would most likely develop pneumonia and need respiratory support. They would have to be put on *ventilators*—breathing machines—or die.

In the case of a genuine pandemic, it would not be possible to manufacture and operate as many ventilators as would be needed. The number of patients requiring respiratory help might well soar into the tens of thousands. Thus, New York health officials produced a set of rules for rationing ventilators—a triage plan—in the event of a pandemic. (The basic concept of triage is that resources such as medical care, surgery, and drugs should go to those likely to receive sufficient benefit from them for recovery, rather than to those who will recover without these resources or to those who will die whether they receive them or not. Some triage plans may employ different priorities. For example, a military triage plan may direct resources to help individuals who can return to the fight, even though they might live without receiving them.)

The report *Allocation of Ventilators in a Public Health Disaster* (prepared by a New York state task force in 2007–2009) makes the preservation of life the basic criterion. Factors such as age, gender, race, education, and even the patient's underlying health status are not used to allocate ventilators.

The operative criterion is whether a patient is likely to survive if given respiratory support. Saving the greatest number of people is the aim of the plan.

The plan calls for a triage officer to make respirator decisions, not someone involved in the care of the patient. Also, patients who are not chosen are to be given the best care possible under the circumstances. Excluded from consideration are people with metastatic cancer with a poor prognosis, those suffering from severe burns or end-stage organ disease (e.g., liver failure), people who have suffered recurrent cardiac arrest, and those with neurological conditions with a high expected mortality. Patients needing dialysis are also among those excluded.

Medical personnel—doctors, nurses, respiratory therapists, X-ray technicians, and so on—are not given a preferential status under the New York plan. The view of the task force was that anyone who becomes so sick as to need respiratory support is not likely to recover quickly enough to contribute to public health efforts.

1. What besides promoting the greatest number of survivors might be the aim of a triage plan for allocating respirators?

2. "Women and children first" was a traditional directive for allocating such equipment as lifeboats. Gender-based prioritization has been largely rejected as a form of sexism and paternalism, but should other identity categories be considered in triage plans?

3. What arguments can be offered to justify using age as a cutoff point for allocating respirators?

Chapter 9

Distributing Health Care

CHAPTER CONTENTS

CASES AND CONTEXTS

CASE PRESENTATION

The Way It Was: Robert Ingram Can't Afford to Be Sick

Robert Ingram (as we will call him) was fifty-two years old and worried about his health, a result of two months of sharp, stabbing pains on the left side of his chest. When the pains came, he felt cold and sweaty, and although he tried to ignore them, he found that he had to stop what he was doing and wait until they passed.

At first, he hadn't mentioned his symptoms to his wife, Jeri. He hoped and believed that they would simply go away. Eventually, he had to tell her, after the pain hit him at home, while he was moving a broken armchair out to the trash. Jeri had seen him put the chair down and put a hand to his chest.

When he told her how long he'd been having the pains, Jeri insisted he call Lane Clinic for an appointment. At first, Robert resisted. He didn't want to miss a day's work. He operated Bob's Express, which picked up car and truck parts from the smaller supply houses and delivered them to mechanics and garages within a twenty-mile radius. He'd founded the business only a year ago, after working as a mechanic himself for almost thirty years.

He had hoped to be able to expand, but there weren't as many deliveries to make as he'd counted on. The big supply houses had their own distribution system, and he had to scramble to get business from the wrecking yards and the rebuilders.

Robert was making enough money to pay operating expenses and rent, but not much more. He owned a Chevy Silverado pickup and a ten-year-old Ford station wagon. Jeri took the phone orders from their home office, and Robert and Phil made the rounds. Robert was his own boss, which is what he and Jeri most liked about the business. He worked hard, but he didn't have to answer to anybody.

On the day of his appointment, Robert asked Phil to cover for him. He drove the Ford to the clinic so he'd be able to go directly from there to Ace Distributors and pick up a box of parts he had to deliver.

Dr. Luc Tran looked young enough to be a teenager, but he seemed to know exactly what he was doing. He moved the stethoscope over Robert's chest, listening to his heart. He had him walk across the room, then listened to it again. Tran asked about Robert's parents and grandparents. Robert told him that both grandfathers had died of heart attacks in their late fifties. One of his grandmothers was still alive, but the other had also died of a heart attack.

Then Tran asked about the chest pain itself. How long had he had it? What did it feel like? How long did it last? Did anything in particular seem to bring it on? Did he ever get it while sleeping? Did it start when he was carrying groceries or simply walking? Did the pain seem to radiate down his left arm? Did his arm feel numb? Did the last two fingers tingle?

Robert did his best to answer all the questions, but he didn't see the point to them. He was almost sorry he'd come. It was easy to believe that nothing was seriously wrong with him while he was sitting on the edge of the examining table talking to Dr. Tran. He needed to be making his deliveries. Otherwise, Phil would get hopelessly behind. Late deliveries could cost them customers.

Dr. Tran finished his examination and asked Robert to get dressed and have a seat in the chair beside the small built-in desk. Tran left the room for ten minutes or so, then returned. He took the swivel chair beside the desk.

"I'm worried that you may be on the verge of a heart attack," Tran told Robert. "You may already have had one or more small attacks."

"Wouldn't I have known it?" Robert could hardly believe what he was hearing.

"Not necessarily," Dr. Tran said. "The blood gets blocked for a moment, some tissue dies. You feel pain, and then it's over." He paused. "But what concerns me most is that your coronary arteries may be significantly blocked by plaque, and if that's so, the outcome could be devastating."

"You mean I could die."

"Exactly," Dr. Tran said. "We need to know what shape your heart's in, so I want you to have a coronary angiogram. I'm going to refer you to a cardiologist, and she may want you to have an ultrasound as well."

Seeing Robert's blank look, Tran explained what was involved in the angiogram, then talked about the images sonography could produce.

"Do you really need to take a look at my heart like that?" Robert asked. "Couldn't you just let it go at listening?"

"We need to find out if you've got some blocked coronary arteries," Dr. Tran said. "We also need to get some sense of how your valves are working and what size your heart is. Otherwise, we'd just be guessing and basing a treatment on what we *thought* was happening. Technology lets us go beyond that."

Tran leaned forward and touched Robert's knee. "Don't worry. Angiography is quite safe, really. And the ultrasound amounts to nothing at all."

"But what will they *cost*?"

Tran paused and thought for a moment.

"I'm not sure, exactly. Probably in the neighborhood of five to seven thousand dollars. Maybe more if Dr. Goode needs for you to spend the night at the hospital."

"Then it's all out of the question," Robert said. "I don't have the money."

"Your insurance should cover both procedures."

"I don't have insurance, doctor." Robert shook his head. "I run my own business, and I put all my money back into it. I can't even mortgage my house, because it's rented."

"You're not old enough to qualify for Medicare," Tran said. "Do you own some property or jewelry? Something you can sell?"

"All I own is a broken-down station wagon and part of a pickup truck. I still owe money on the truck. Maybe I could sell it for enough to pay it off and pay for those tests you want me to have."

"If the tests show what I think they might," Tran said, "you'll need coronary artery bypass surgery. That will cost in the neighborhood of thirty thousand dollars—perhaps as much as fifty, depending on complications and hospital stays."

"That's just laughable," Robert said. "No way I could raise thirty thousand. Not even if my life depended on it."

"I worry that it might," Dr. Tran said. "But selling your truck would have the advantage of qualifying you for Medicaid. In this state, if you have assets under three thousand, you qualify."

"But if I sold my truck, I'd have to go out of business," Robert said. "I wouldn't have any way to earn a living, and my wife's sickly. She can't work a regular job, because of her headaches."

"Don't you have some family you could borrow from?"

"Maybe I could borrow a thousand from Jeri's mother, but she lives on Social Security. And there's nobody else. Our friends haven't got any more money than we do."

"I don't know what to say."

"Can't you just give me some pills?"

"I don't see any alternative," Dr. Tran said. "But I'm uncomfortable doing it, because I don't know exactly what we're up against. As I told you, you could be on the verge of having a heart attack. We could help you with the right tests and, if necessary, the right sort of surgery. But as it is . . ."

"I'll just have to take my chances," Robert said, "until I'm either rich enough or poor enough to get the right treatment."

The Affordable Care Act

In March 2010, the U.S. Congress passed the Patient Protection and Affordable Care Act (ACA), which was then signed into law by President Barack Obama. The debate surrounding the legislation was both heated and partisan. Despite various attempts at arriving at a compromise on some of the provisions, when the ACA (also sometimes called "Obamacare") came to a vote, it failed to secure the support of a single Republican. Despite the lack of bipartisanship displayed in the vote, the need for a plan to reform the way health care was distributed and funded in America had long been recognized by members of both major parties.

By 2010, the United States was facing a health care crisis that had reached a critical stage. Some thirty-seven to forty-seven million people—roughly 20 percent of the population—lacked health insurance, and hundreds of thousands of people attempting to get insurance were turned down by insurers because of preexisting medical conditions (e.g., being diabetic or having been treated for cancer). Each year, hundreds of thousands of individuals and their families were plunged into despair and bankruptcy by having their insurance canceled after they fell ill with a serious and expensive disease or by discovering that they had exceeded the reimbursement limits allowed by their insurance company. (A 2005 Harvard study found that about half of all personal bankruptcies each year—about seven hundred thousand—involved unpaid medical expenses.)

At the same time, the annual cost of *uncompensated care* provided to uninsured individuals had reached $84.9 billion before the implementation of the ACA. The majority of this uncompensated care was provided in hospitals, all of which, since 1986, have been required by federal law to provide stabilizing treatment to critically ill patients, regardless of their ability to pay. (In other words, they are not allowed to let poor patients die in the parking lot or "dump" them in charity wards.) By 2011, uncompensated care had reached 6 percent of hospital operating expenses, with substantial portions of those losses

covered by federal and state taxpayers, and much of the rest passed on to insured consumers in the form of higher prices and premiums.

These dynamics were intertwined with the overall rise in the cost of medical care. Health care spending reached 17.4 percent of the nation's gross domestic product before the implementation of the ACA, far higher than that of any other developed country. Economists and politicians alike recognized the need to try to find a way to provide medical care to more citizens while also "bending the cost curve," so that the society would have the resources to meet other pressing needs.

To address these problems, the authors of the Affordable Care Act focused both on expanding health care coverage and on trying to find more efficient and less costly ways of delivering quality care. The two efforts had to go hand in hand, most experts concluded, because the price of health care had become inextricably bound up in the insurance-based payment system. In the sections that follow, we will discuss the major objectives of the ACA for different parts of the American health care system and provide a preliminary assessment of its impact in each.

Expanded Coverage

One of the central goals of health care reform was to substantially increase the percentage of Americans covered by health insurance and to address the problems of both the *uninsured* and the *underinsured*—those whose coverage leaves them financially responsible for a large percentage of their medical costs, thus aggravating the cycle of medical debt and uncompensated care. To attempt to achieve this goal, the ACA employs a number of interrelated policies and mechanisms.

Guaranteed Issue. Since 2014, the ACA has prohibited insurers from denying coverage to applicants on the grounds that they have a preexisting medical condition. Insurers are also required to charge consistent rates based on age and population averages, rather than basing premiums on individual health status.

Before the implementation of the ACA, individuals who had been treated for chronic and expensive conditions—such as Crohn's disease, colon cancer, Parkinson's disease, or rheumatoid arthritis—often found it impossible to get coverage from any insurer in their states. (Other preexisting conditions that could result in coverage denials included asthma, hepatitis, and obesity, as well as being pregnant, having had a heart attack, or being a victim of domestic violence.) If individuals with preexisting conditions were offered coverage, the premiums were often prohibitively expensive, costing thousands of dollars a month and as much as twenty thousand dollars a year. Insurers avoided covering such individuals for obvious reasons—because their medical costs were likely to be greater than average and negatively impact the company's earnings. (Most U.S. insurers are for-profit corporations that need to generate revenue for shareholders; the few that are not still face competitive pressure to cut costs.)

One result of this situation is that many people with serious conditions avoided going to the doctor, so as not to be branded as "uninsurable" as a result of diagnoses recorded in their medical charts. (See Case Presentation: The Threat of Genetic Discrimination in Chapter 3 for more on this topic.) Others found themselves trapped in jobs or marriages that they would have preferred to leave, because they feared losing the insurance coverage that came with their job or their spouse's job.

The ACA's requirement of a *guaranteed issue* of insurance, regardless of preexisting condition, thus removed a substantial barrier to coverage for many Americans and has been one of its most popular features. (Even most Republican members of Congress say they would keep this provision of the bill.) But as the authors of the ACA knew, forcing insurers to take all applicants would increase the number of sick people in their risk pools, a problem which led directly to one of the ACA's more controversial features.

Individual Mandate. A famous dilemma for any kind of insurance is known as the *free rider problem*. In health care, this typically involves healthy and young people who fail to get insurance until later in life, when they become sick or injured. These individuals then get a "free ride" on the money put into the system by those who have been paying insurance premiums all along. In health care, this is not just a problem of fairness, however. Since roughly 80 percent of care is typically spent on the sickest 20 percent of people, any insurance risk pool that contains mostly sick people will soon become financially insolvent. This problem, often called *adverse selection*, creates risk pools with insufficient numbers of healthy people to balance out sick ones, and can lead to a financial "death spiral" for any insurance system.

A primary goal in health insurance is thus to create large enough risk pools to compensate for the problems of adverse selection and free riders. For example, in Medicare, Medicaid, and other *single-payer* insurance systems, the government imposes a broad-based tax on all residents and in return guarantees them insurance when they are retired and sick, or if they are poor and sick. (Social Security insurance and the Veteran's Health Administration also work this way.) A different strategy, employed in Medicare's "Part D" prescription drug benefit, imposes higher premiums on those who wait longer to enroll in the system after they turn sixty-five.

A third strategy, employed by the Affordable Care Act and some state insurance plans, is to impose a tax penalty on those who don't get insurance or (what amounts to the same thing) to give a tax benefit to those who do. Such incentives are designed to enforce what is known as an *individual mandate* to buy into private insurance pools.

The ACA thus requires almost all Americans to carry health insurance or else pay a tax penalty. The penalty started during the 2014 tax year at 1 percent of the violator's income (or $95, whichever is higher) and climbs to a maximum of 2.5 percent (or $695 if that is higher) in 2016, to be adjusted thereafter only for cost-of-living increases. The mandate does not apply to Native Americans who receive care from the federal Indian Health Service, individuals who object to insurance on religious grounds, or those with incomes so low (under $9,350) they are not required to file a tax return.

The individual mandate was criticized by conservatives as an unconstitutional infringement on personal liberty—although, ironically, it was actually first developed by conservative economists as an alternative to single-payer tax-based insurance systems. The mandate also faced multiple legal challenges, but it was upheld by the Supreme Court in June 2012. (The Court ruled that the mandate just imposed a tax on an activity rather than compelling individuals to purchase insurance.)

Insurance Exchanges and Subsidies.

Prior to the ACA, the most common reason Americans cited for not getting medical insurance was that they could not afford the monthly premiums. This group included the large number of Americans who could not get insurance through their jobs or were self-employed and were also not covered by government programs such as Medicare. These individuals were typically middle-class and lower-middle-class workers who could not afford the high cost of individual health insurance but were not poor enough to qualify for Medicaid. (One hypothetical example is Robert Ingram, in this chapter's Case Presentation: Robert Ingram Can't Afford to Be Sick.)

Under the ACA, these individuals can purchase competitively priced policies through regulated state insurance *exchanges* or *marketplaces*. The new plans in these marketplaces must cover a standard package of "essential health benefits," have standardized cost-sharing options, and cannot base premiums on anything beyond geography, income, age, tobacco use, and level of cost-sharing. Households earning up to 400 percent of the federal poverty line (i.e., an income of about $46,000) can receive substantial tax credits to defray the cost of their insurance premiums for plans purchased through the exchanges.

A primary goal of these exchanges or marketplaces is to encourage insurance companies to compete to offer the best package of benefits at the lowest price, following a general rule of "the more you pay, the more you get. " The law requires that coverage for essential benefits be listed in a standardized format so that plans can be easily compared. Insurance plans are stratified into different levels of value—Bronze, Silver, Gold, and Platinum—based on how much of a typical person's health care expenses they cover. The most popular plans are in the Silver category and cover 70 percent of typical health care costs. Plans in a given tier vary by deductible, coinsurance, premium, and network of providers available.

Opponents of the ACA had argued that these exchanges would lead to double-digit premium increases in the individual market and drive insurers out of this sector. Since the marketplaces opened in October 2013, however, premiums have so far generally followed the pre-ACA trends and only increased 4 to 6 percent on average, while increased competition in the exchanges appears to have reduced premiums in some regions. At the same time, the trend toward increased cost-sharing in many plans has continued unabated, and many provider networks have narrowed. The insurance industry has so far done quite well in the individual market, with record increases in their stock prices in recent years.

Whether these conflicting dynamics in the individual insurance market will benefit consumers in the long run remains an open question. But for the 11.7 million Americans who had obtained insurance by the end of the second enrollment period, the chance to buy subsidized policies on the ACA exchanges appears to have considerable appeal. The subsidies, in particular, appear to have removed one of the significant barriers to getting health insurance in the United States.

Medicaid Expansion. Medicaid is a joint program of the federal and state governments designed to provide access to medical care for families and children who fall below the poverty line. It is the single largest source of public health coverage in the United States, accounting for 16 percent of total personal health spending and covering nearly 70 million Americans.

But since Medicaid is funded by matching grants to state governments, the amount of reimbursed care that Medicaid

programs provide to needy families has varied widely from state to state. In many states, Medicaid is only available to those making as little as 44 percent of the federal poverty line—or just $8,840 a year for a family of three.

Although federal laws require that poor children receive support for their medical care, similar rules have not applied to adults. Before the passage of the ACA, only about a dozen states offered care for parents who fell below the poverty line, and most excluded childless adults. Parents not eligible to receive care often did not know that their children were eligible, and the result was that the entire family did not have access to medical care.

The ACA was designed to make significant changes in the Medicaid program. The law initially made everyone under the age of sixty-five with earnings less than 138 percent of the federal poverty line eligible for subsidized medical care under the Medicaid program. For the first time, people without children are eligible for Medicaid, so long as they have incomes less than about $16,105. (A family of three had to make less than about $27,310.)

However, in June of 2012 the Supreme Court ruled that states were not required to expand their Medicaid program and could continue to offer Medicaid only to the people who would have been eligible prior to the ACA. As of March 2015, twenty-two states had declined to expand their Medicaid programs—a somewhat surprising result since the federal government pays the full cost of this expansion for the first three years and still covers 90 percent after 2020. (Four states have reversed course and opted to take advantage of these funds after initially refusing Medicaid expansion.)

The lack of Medicaid expansion in many states has left roughly 4 million uninsured adults in a "coverage gap" between traditional Medicaid and the ACA's marketplace subsidies. The majority of these individuals are working full or part time but still live below the federal poverty line. They are concentrated in southern states that have both large uninsured populations and limited Medicaid eligibility, such as Texas, Florida, and Georgia.

Nevertheless, since the implementation of the ACA, more than 10.7 million individuals have gained health coverage, largely as a result of Medicaid expansions in twenty-nine states. As such it represents the single largest source of expanded coverage under the ACA. Nevertheless, questions remain about the quality of care that Medicaid can purchase in many states. During the first two years of the ACA, the federal government increased reimbursement rates as much as 90 percent to encourage more physicians to accept Medicaid, but those rates expired at the beginning of 2015. Although a number of states have increased their funding to compensate for this reduction, many of these newly insured Americans may find it hard to find physicians willing to treat them.

Increased Competition. Before the implementation of the ACA, about a third of uninsured Americans said they couldn't afford to purchase the health coverage offered by their employers. Under the new law, if an employee has to pay 60 percent or more of the costs of the insurance plan offered by her employer or if the plan costs the employee more than 9.5 percent of her income, she may choose to go to an ACA exchange and buy her own medical coverage. There is no guarantee that the employee will be able to get a better or cheaper plan, but because the exchanges are competitive marketplaces, she has a chance of doing better. She may also be able to obtain subsidies on the exchange if her income is less than four times the federal poverty level.

These somewhat elaborate rules are designed to continue support for employer-based insurance and allow employees to keep their present plans if that is what they want. Yet the rules also introduce an element of competition to encourage employers to offer reasonably priced, good-quality insurance plans.

Results. By March 2015, some 16.4 million uninsured individuals had obtained health insurance since the ACA's coverage provisions took effect. By many estimates, the law has halved the percentage of Americans without insurance and produced the largest drop in the ranks of uninsured in over four decades. Nevertheless, the law has so far left tens of millions uninsured and underinsured. Thus its primary goal of expanded coverage remains only partially achieved.

Employment-Based Coverage

Most people in the United States get their health insurance through their employer. The ACA does little to change these *group plans*, although for some employees with inadequate group coverage, it offers a chance to use the ACA exchanges to obtain an individual plan. For the roughly 96 percent of American businesses that have less than fifty full-time employees, the act provides tax incentives to help them cover insurance for their workers. For the roughly 4 percent of employers who have more than fifty employees, the act charges them a fee if they don't insure 70 percent of them by 2015 and 95 percent of them by 2016. Since most large employers already offer coverage to their full-time employees, however, this *employer mandate* is expected to have a relatively small impact. Finally, the ACA also standardizes and regulates some aspects of employer-sponsored coverage.

No lifetime limits. As with individual policies, the ACA requires that existing group insurance plans comply with the new rule against setting lifetime limits for coverage on a set of "essential health benefits." These services include emergency services, hospitalizations, laboratory services, maternity care, mental health and substance abuse treatment, outpatient or ambulatory care, pediatric care, prescription drugs, preventive care, and rehabilitative services. "Grandfathered" plans (plans purchased before March 23, 2010) do not have to follow this (and many other) ACA rules.

Small-Business Tax Credits. To continue to support and encourage the current systems of employer-based medical coverage, the ACA has also provided tax subsidies to small businesses that offer coverage to their employees. The hope is that small businesses that offered their employees no insurance before may be inclined to introduce an employee health plan.

Medicare Coverage

Medicare is the federally funded and operated medical insurance plan for people age sixty-five or older. Unlike the ACA, which relies on the various payers in the private insurance market, Medicare is a "socialized" single-payer insurance program. It is supported by payroll deductions, and under the program, everyone enrolled is entitled to the same benefits. Medicare determines the goods and services it is willing to pay for, and within those limits, an individual's medical need, not his ability to pay, determines what he receives.

The ACA does not fundamentally change Medicare. Medicare will continue to cover the disabled and those over sixty-five. However, the law does expand several ongoing

pilot programs that explore ways to control health care costs. These programs include efforts to decrease readmission after hospital stays. Several models are being tested including specialized clinics, enhanced home care services, partnerships between hospitals and nursing homes, and home visits by doctors. Models that pay doctors on a group basis, referred to as *accountable care organizations* (ACOs), are also being used. In 2014, two hundred ACO pilot studies were underway to determine their optimal size and organization. The ACA also tries to improve quality of care by including a measure that takes away a small amount of funding from hospitals that have high readmittance rates of Medicare patients.

Independent Payment Advisory Board. Perhaps the most famously controversial feature of the ACA is an advisory panel that has no appointed members and has never met. This *Independent Payment Advisory Board* (IPAB) was designed by Congress to achieve something it had previously been unable to do: (1) create mechanisms to restrain Medicare spending that could resist partisan politics; and (2) help moderate the overall rise in health care spending. In the language of the Obama administration, the panel was introduced to help "bend down the cost curve."

The IPAB is supposed to be staffed with nonpartisan experts who will be responsible for reviewing Medicare spending. If spending exceeds the rate of growth predicted by the Congressional Budget Office, the advisory board would make recommendations to Congress about what steps should be taken to bring spending under control. Congress must then either accept the panel's recommendations and act on them or come up with its own plan to reduce spending.

But the IPAB quickly became mired in the partisan political conflict it was supposed to rise above. Despite the fact that the IPAB is explicitly prohibited from increasing cost-sharing or restricting Medicare benefits or eligibility, it was termed a "death panel" by some Republicans. Precisely because the IPAB *can't* cut such benefits, it was opposed by the American Medical Association, which worried its cuts would instead come out of provider payments.

In the end, both of these concerns have turned out to be moot, since Medicare spending has unexpectedly slowed down in recent years, growing at just 1.5 percent annually and projected to stay below the IPAB targets until 2022. President Obama has seen no need to make politically costly appointments to a board with nothing to do, so for now the IPAB remains a merely speculative controversy. But it demonstrates the difficulty of making any attempt to moderate spending in one of America's most popular social programs.

Expanded Drug Benefits. By 2020, the Affordable Care Act will alter the way in which Medicare recipients pay for prescription drugs. The system is currently structured so that someone in a Medicare drug plan must pay a $310 deductible, after which the plan will pay 75 percent of the costs of drugs until the total annual drug cost of $2,830 is reached. The recipient is then in the so-called "doughnut hole," in which there is no Medicare contribution to drug costs. Once the recipient has spent up to the amount of $4,550 (including deductible and co-payments) annually on drugs, the recipient has crossed to the other side of the dough-nut hole. He then qualifies for "catastrophic coverage" and has to pay only $2.40 for each refill of a generic drug and $6.00 (or 5 percent of the cost if higher) for a proprietary drug.

This payment scheme has been denounced as ill conceived and unfair since it appears to force the sickest people to pay the most for the drugs they need. The result has often been that people who reach the doughnut hole either stop taking their medications or take them less often, thus reducing or even eliminating the therapeutic effects of those medications.

By 2020, the ACA will close the doughnut hole by covering 75 percent of both brand name and generic drugs in the "gap" period. For the immediate future, it provides seniors with rebates on the money they have spent for prescription drugs and with discounts of 50 percent on proprietary drugs.

Free Preventive Care. Medicare is now required to provide enrollees with the same preventive care benefits that the private and small group plans offered through the ACA exchanges are required to offer. Previous fees and co-payments for vaccinations, annual checkups, and blood tests have been discontinued. The thinking behind this change is that encouraging people to monitor their health and take steps to avoid preventable diseases such as pneumonia will reduce overall costs in the long run.

High Earners Pay More. Under the ACA, people who make more than $200,000 a year have been required since 2013 to increase their payroll tax contributions to the Medicare program, from 1.45 percent to 2.35 percent. Investment income, previously exempt from payroll taxes, is taxed at a 3.8 percent rate.

Regulating Insurers

The private insurance industry continues to play a central role in the reforms introduced by the ACA. Some critics believe that this is likely to produce a health care system that falls far short of what could have been achieved by reform.

A single-payer approach, such as the Canadian system or an expanded "Medicare for all," would have been more successful in reducing the costs of care and making it available to all citizens, some argue. Because insurance companies are committed to making a profit for their shareholders, they have an incentive to deny care to patients and to avoid insuring those who are likely to suffer from costly illnesses. (Indeed, the ideal medical insurance client for a company is someone who pays premiums for decades, is never sick or injured, and then drops dead, without ever having been treated or hospitalized.) Also, the administrative costs of operating insurance plans—including the high salaries of executives, costs for reviewing treatment plans and hospitalizations, as well as marketing and billing expenses—will always be much higher than the costs in a tax-based single-payer system.

Whatever the merits of a single-payer system, a national shift to such a system did not look politically feasible in 2010, nor does it today. The ACA does take into account some of the more important limitations of a health care system in which insurance companies continue to play a major role and regulates the business practices of these companies by limiting the amount they can spend on administration and profits. Insurers are now required to spend at least 80 percent of the money they collect in premiums on paying health care costs and are required to rebate *overheads* (sales costs, administration, and profits) that exceed 20 percent. Since 2011, this *medical loss ratio* (MLR) provision has yielded more than $5 billion in rebates to consumers and substantially reduced overhead spending, according to a 2015 study.

The following provisions of the ACA were also intended to prevent companies from restricting access to care in ways that may have been good for the company's bottom line, but which had become incompatible with a widespread expansion of affordable coverage.

No Preexisting Condition Denials.
Traditionally, insurance companies were able to "cherry pick" which applicants for medical coverage they were willing to

insure. They could decide to deny insurance to someone they believed to be a bad risk because of past diagnoses. Thus, women treated for breast cancer at some point in their lives most likely would be denied policies, and so would people with chronic ailments such as rheumatoid arthritis, diabetes, or ulcerative colitis, as well as those who were HIV positive or infected with hepatitis C. Insurers could, and often did, also charge higher premiums on the basis of gender (though not race or ethnicity).

Prior to the implementation of the ACA, applications for medical insurance required applicants to supply information about their medical history and authorized the company to examine all their medical records. Applicants were also typically required to provide information about their family medical history (causes of death of parents or grandparents, diseases diagnosed in parents and siblings). Insurance companies used this information to assess the risk that an applicant would develop a serious and expensive disease. Failure to provide the information, omitting relevant facts, or lying about a medical condition or treatment could be grounds for a company to refuse to insure an applicant or for canceling the policy of someone the company had already insured. Although insurance companies can continue to seek information about an individual's medical history, they are no longer permitted to use this information as grounds for refusing coverage.

Insurers also cannot charge people with preexisting medical conditions higher premiums. Nor can they, in general, deny coverage on the basis of current health status. Thus, someone with colon cancer who has lost his job and his insurance should now be able to get health insurance coverage by buying a policy through an ACA insurance exchange. Obtaining coverage would have been nearly impossible for this individual just a few years ago.

No Cancellations for Illness. A 2009 congressional investigation found that three large insurance companies had canceled the policies of more than nineteen thousand people after they became ill. These insurance companies had routinely reviewed the policies of clients who developed medical problems that incur high costs (e.g., breast cancer) and looked for a reason to "rescind" (cancel) the policy.

The congressional investigation showed that the grounds companies used to cancel policies were often flimsy (e.g., the client had failed to mention being treated for acne as a teenager, which was considered a preexisting condition). If policyholders contested cancellations or coverage denials in court, the insurers often appeared to intentionally draw out the proceedings—forcing policyholders with limited resources to forego treatments before the cases came to trial.

To address such questionable practices, the ACA prohibits insurers from canceling policies retroactively when patients develop serious and expensive illnesses. Still, a 2015 study published in the *New England Journal of Medicine* found that many insurers were structuring their drug prices and using drug-specific deductibles in an apparent effort to discourage patients with certain diagnoses (e.g., those with HIV) from enrolling in their plans.

No Lifetime Benefits Cap. Medical care is expensive, and before the ACA, insurance policies typically placed an upper limit on the amount of money a policy would pay out for an individual patient or a family. The lifetime amount was frequently $1 million. Although this may seem like a lot of money, the costs of treatment for a serious illness requiring multiple surgeries or long-term hospitalizations can easily exceed $1 million. The care provided at a major medical center to a newborn with a serious heart defect, for example, can exceed $1 million before the child is even one year old, leaving parents with a terrible set of choices if coverage is capped. Similarly, the cumulative costs of treating a patient for a chronic incurable disease like diabetes can easily exceed the lifetime limit of an insurance policy in just a few years.

Under the old health care system, patients were frequently forced to sell off their assets—houses, cars, and even household goods—to raise money for treatment. Some couples divorced for no reason other than so that the sick spouse could qualify for Medicaid and avoid forcing the other into bankruptcy. (If, however, Medicaid could show that this was the motive behind the divorce, the agency could seize the assets of the healthy spouse.)

Once individuals had expended their resources, they might have to declare bankruptcy to escape hundreds of thousands of dollars in medical debt. David Himmelstein of Harvard Medical School has conducted nearly a decade's worth of research that has found medical bills to be a leading cause of personal bankruptcy in the United States. Himmelstein estimated that around nine hundred thousand cases of medical bankruptcy occurred in 2009, and each bankruptcy had an impact on the personal lives (children, spouse, other dependents) of an average of 2.7 people. Thus, about twenty-four million people a year in the United States suffered the consequences of not being able to pay their medical bills. Many of these individuals had insurance when they got sick, but lost it due to cancellation or exhausting their policies' resources.

The ACA is intended to make it impossible for an insurance company to refuse to pay the legitimate medical expenses of a client, no matter what the cumulative costs. The goal is to make medical bankruptcy a rare and exceptional occurrence, as it is in most other developed nations.

Preventive Care for All

One aim of the ACA is to improve outcomes and reduce health care spending by requiring insurers to cover, without any additional cost to patients, a range of services that will either prevent disease or identify it at an early stage, when it is typically more effective and less costly to treat. This includes such services as health screenings (e.g., mammograms and HIV tests) and vaccinations (such as flu shots and pneumonia vaccinations).

The congressional authors of the ACA approached insurance as a tool that could be used to help people avoid disease and stay healthy. If patients are told about personal risk factors for certain diseases, the information may allow them to change their habits to reduce the chance that they will get sick. Reducing the disease burden in the society is supposed to lead to a decrease in the overall amount we spend on medical treatment—although there is not always a clear correlation between the two.

One of the ACA's goals for preventive and primary care is to offer better coverage in *underserved areas*. Physicians tend to cluster in major urban centers and, within those areas, in more affluent neighborhoods. This tendency makes it difficult for rural or poor inner-city patients to obtain reliable access to health care and to the preventive care that is one of the ACA's primary strategies for lowering health care costs. To encourage more physicians to practice in underserved areas, from 2011 to 2015 the ACA provided a 10 percent premium to physicians who see patients in rural areas or in the inner city. This part of the ACA echoes a provision of Medicare policy, which also pays a 10 percent bonus to physicians practicing in underserved areas.

Eventually, the provision of effective preventive care should reduce the disease burden in the United States, as it has in many other developed countries. Because the cost of treatment is usually many times more than the cost of prevention, preventive services should, over time, lower the cost of health care.

Envoi

The sketch of the ACA presented here does little more than capture some of its more prominent features. Also, we have yet to see the effects of the ACA on our health care system over several decades. However, after five years of gradual implementation, some basic observations can be made.

The ACA has established universal *insurability*. No one can be denied health insurance based on their health status, and health insurers cannot refuse to cover preexisting conditions. This *guaranteed issue* allows people who formally had limited options—because they were afraid of losing their health insurance—many new opportunities, including changing jobs and starting new businesses. The ACA also imposes a *community rating* pricing system on insurance sold through the health care exchanges that prevents consumers from being charged on the basis of individual health status.

The ACA has cut the number of uninsured Americans by about half, the most substantial reduction in decades, and subsidies reducing the price of health insurance premiums have allowed millions who formerly could not afford health insurance to purchase policies through the health care exchanges.

Nevertheless, the United States continues to have tens of millions of citizens who lack health insurance, despite the ACA's mandate that everyone must have coverage. There is also controversy over the value of health insurance purchased through the ACA, with many describing these policies as *underinsurance* due to the high level of cost-sharing allocated to patients with individual plans. Although the act was specifically designed not to change the financing arrangements of employer-sponsored group insurance, there are concerns that new market dynamics are "spilling over" into group policies, forcing employees to share more costs and obtain care in narrower networks.

The largest number of people to get health insurance due to the ACA are those who obtained coverage through the expansion of Medicaid to include everyone at or below 138 percent of the federal poverty level. However, this expansion of coverage has been limited by the fact that twenty-two states have chosen not to accept federal funds to expand their Medicaid programs.

The full impact of the Affordable Care Act will only become clear over a long period of time. No one knows at this point exactly what sort of health care system we are going to have in the next five to ten years. Many can already point to flaws in the system, and even when it is fully operational, it will no doubt be easy to imagine how it can be improved. Yet even the ACA's harshest critics often acknowledge that in specific respects the system now emerging is significantly better than the system that it is replacing. Tens of millions of Americans in need of medical care now have, for the first time in decades, a reasonable chance of gaining access to it. That in itself constitutes a major step forward.

SOCIAL CONTEXT

The Health Care Crisis: The Road to Reform

A crisis exists in a social institution when factors are present that tend to destroy the institution or render it ineffective in achieving its goals. Two major factors present in the American health care system at the beginning of the twenty-first century put it in a state of crisis: the increasing cost of health care and the failure to deliver a decent minimum of health care to everyone in need of it.

In the early 2000s, these factors became hard to ignore, as the cost of care continued to spiral upward while the number of people unable to pay for care steadily grew. By 2010, it was clear to politicians, economists, the business community, and the public that the health care system needed to be changed in substantial ways to bring costs under control and to extend medical care to those lacking resources to obtain it. It was against the background sketched below that the

debates over health care reform took place in 2009 and 2010.

Cost of Health Care

In 1960, total health spending in the United States was $27 billion. In 1970 it rose to $75 billion, and by 1983 it had increased to $356 billion. Around 1994, managed care plans were widely instituted to bring down costs, but although they reduced the rate of health care inflation, they did not stop it. By 1996, health care costs had climbed to $1 trillion. By 2000, spending on health care rose to $1.3 trillion, a 7 percent increase over 1993, the year major health care reform was proposed by the Clinton administration. While the rise in health care costs has slowed substantially in recent years, Americans still spent $2.9 trillion on health care in 2013, which amounts to an average of $9,255 per person, regardless of age. Health care costs now make up about 18 percent of the nation's gross domestic product (GDP), compared to about 7 percent of GDP in 1970. Over the past forty years, health care spending has typically risen faster than the GDP has grown, sometimes at a rate of more than 10 percent a year.

Although other industrialized nations have also experienced increases in health care costs over the past half century, none of them comes close to the United States in terms of the rate of inflation or the absolute spending levels. For example (to take the most recent comparative figures), the United States spent $8,745 per person on health care in 2012, compared to $4,602 in Canada, $4,288 in France, $4,811 in Germany, and only $3,289 in Britain.

The Uninsured

Another factor that has distinguished the United States from other industrialized nations has been its very high percentage of people who lack any form of insurance coverage for medical expenses—a problem that is intertwined with the high cost of health care. Although medical spending had stopped increasing at a double-digit rate by 2005, it was still rising much more quickly than the earnings of U.S. workers, which made both insurance and out-of-pocket payment for medical care increasingly difficult for Americans to afford.

The number of people without medical insurance in 2010 was estimated to be between thirty-seven and forty-five million (as much as 16 percent of the entire population). These figures likely minimized the scope of the problem, however, because people often lose their insurance when they change jobs or become unemployed, and it often takes several months before they can enroll with a new employer's plan. At the time health care reform was being debated, analysts estimated that sixty million people were uninsured for at least some part of each year. Half of those without insurance were children or families with children. Children made up about 25 percent of the uninsured.

Until provisions of the ACA became operative in 2014, no employers were required by law to offer health insurance, and often they did so only as a fringe benefit to attract the workforce they wanted. In order to compete with foreign companies employing lower-wage workers, many U.S. companies stopped offering health insurance to their employees or reclassified them as contract workers to avoid offering such benefits. (In 2006, there were eight million fewer jobs with health insurance than in 2000.)

Even when employers offer health insurance, employees usually have to contribute to premium payments in a group plan. Workers in low-wage jobs often report that they can't afford to pay the portion of premium costs that are passed on to them. A worker making $800 a month who has to pay even $75 a month for insurance coverage is left with a substantially reduced income. Group plans may also fail to cover an employee's spouse or children, and the family may be forced to seek coverage in the individual insurance market. Since individual insurance was traditionally extremely expensive in the United States, with monthly premiums as high as $4,000 a month for some older or sicker individuals, many people joined the ranks of the uninsured despite being offered coverage by their employers.

The large percentage of Americans without insurance made for a less healthy population, as many people delayed medical care due to prohibitively high out-of-pocket expenses or to avoid being labeled "uninsurable" due to preexisting conditions. In the view of many critics, health care reform to address these issues had been long overdue. But choosing the right road to reform also required an assessment of the U.S. health care system to determine why it is so expensive and whether such expense can be justified by the quality of care.

Why Are Costs of Medical Care So High?

Economists point out that in medicine, a surplus of goods and services generally does not drive prices down. Rather, it may drive up demand. The availability of powerful drugs, laboratories, high-technology equipment, hospital beds, trauma centers, and a variety of medical services tends to increase the probability that they will be used.

Health care is different from other goods and services, such as televisions or auto repair, in that consumers rarely have the knowledge or authority to say "no." (In emergencies, they typically have no choice at all about consuming medical care.) Many economists believe that this *information asymmetry* between consumers and providers means that health care does not function as a normal market. This general problem contributes to health care inflation around the globe, and it generates a range of strategies to contain costs in different societies. Yet there are also a number of specific factors that must be considered when trying to determine why medical care is so expensive in the United States.

Drug Costs. From 1995 to 2000, the cost of drugs in the United States doubled, and from 1990 to 2000, it tripled. Starting in 1996, the cost of pharmaceuticals began rising by more than 10 percent a year, a rate of increase that has only recently dropped below double digits. In 2013, prescription drugs cost Americans more than $271 billion, which is more than six times the $40 billion that they cost in 1990.

Drug manufacturers justify high prices by citing the costs of research for producing new and effective drugs. Critics, however, point to a profusion of "me-too" drugs that are typically expensive variations on older, cheaper drugs that are equally effective. Such drugs tend to be those most aggressively advertised to physicians and consumers, despite the fact that they can cost seven or eight times as much as their generic equivalents. There are also concerns that even genuinely new drugs are being developed with too little benefit at too high a cost.

In 2012, physicians at Sloan-Kettering Cancer Center made headlines by refusing, on the grounds of its price, to prescribe Zaltrap, a colon cancer drug made by Sanofi that added only forty-two days to a patient's estimated survival—at a cost of more than $75,000. In 2011, Bristol-Myers Squibb introduced a melanoma drug that cost $38,000 a month for a three-month treatment, and Yervoy introduced a prostate-cancer drug that cost $93,000 for a course of treatment. Although cancer drugs are undoubtedly expensive to research and develop, critics argue that manufacturers inflate their R&D estimates to justify arbitrary pricing. (After Sloan-Kettering made public its refusal to carry Zaltrap, Sanofi cut the price of the drug by 50 percent.) Although it is difficult to get financial data on the development of specific drugs and devices, it is worth noting that the pharmaceutical and medical device industries are two of the five most profitable in the United States, with typical profit margins as high as 20 percent.

No Price Negotiation. One of the primary reasons that pharmaceutical and other health care costs are so high in the United States is that insurers have limited ability to negotiate prices with manufacturers and providers. Almost all other industrialized nations negotiate aggressively with providers and device and drug makers, which generally results in much lower prices than those in the United States. (For example, an MRI in France costs around $360, compared to more than $2,800 in the United States; a day in a French hospital costs, on average, just $853, compared to $4,287 in a U.S. one.) Large group insurers in the United States can exert some control over the demand for medical goods and services, but since drug makers, hospitals, laboratories, and physicians' groups typically offer different rates to different insurers, it can be difficult for any one of them to gain substantial leverage over prices or control costs.

The sole exceptions to this rule are Medicare and Medicaid, which are able to establish reimbursement rates for their tens of millions of members. One result of this is that health care prices under these plans are substantially lower than average prices under commercial plans, and the pace of Medicare inflation, for example, has been slower than that of the private sector for over forty years. (Medicare is explicitly prohibited from negotiating with pharmaceutical companies, however, as a result of a controversial provision in the 2003 Medicare Prescription Drug Benefit Law.)

Aggressive Medicine, Advanced Technology.

Americans tend to take an interventionist attitude toward dealing with disease, and many, when faced with a serious illness, choose the most aggressive approach to treatment. It usually costs more money to attack a disease than to wait to see how it responds to less aggressive options. Such early interventions are also more likely to involve hospitalizations, as well as expensive new medical tests and technologies such as MRIs, CT scans, chemotherapy, radiation, and transplants.

Many of these interventions are useful and likely give patients many more years of high-quality life. There is also a growing body of evidence, however, that Americans receive far more testing and more treatment than they actually need. A 2014 study found that 25 to 42 percent of Medicare patients had, in one year, received at least one of

twenty-six tests and treatments that major scientific and professional organizations have consistently determined to have no medical benefit. (These include performing an electrocardiogram for a simple headache, doing an MRI for low-back pain absent neurological symptoms, and implanting a coronary stent in patients with stable cardiac disease.) A 2010 Institute of Medicine Report found that wasteful testing and treatment accounted for some 30 percent of health care spending in the United States. Some of this waste is a result of *overdiagnosis* and *overtreatment*—the accurate but unnecessary diagnosis and treatment of diseases that are highly unlikely to cause problems for patients during an average life span.

Many physicians are understandably more concerned about doing too little rather than doing too much—a concern that is heightened by the high number of malpractice lawsuits in the United States. But there is also evidence that unnecessary scans and surgeries can cause real harm to patients, through increased radiation exposures, surgical errors, and other adverse events. Since America's fee-for-service payment system also rewards providers for doing more rather than less, it is easy for them to err on the side of overdiagnosis and overtreatment. A famous analysis of El Paso and McAllen, Texas—two mid-sized border cities with almost identical demographics—found 40 percent more surgery, 100 percent more bladder scopes, three times as many bypass and stent operations, and five times more home-health spending in McAllen than El Paso. As a result, McAllen had some of the highest per capita health care spending in the country—while El Paso had some of the lowest. Yet El Paso had as good or better health outcomes than McAllen. The crucial difference appeared to be that a much higher percentage of McAllen's physicians had ownership stakes in surgical, imaging, and home-health facilities, a pattern that fueled a culture of profit-maximization in that city's health care institutions, thus driving up health care costs.

Administrative and Marketing Costs.

Health care in the United States is paid for mostly by individuals through their medical insurance, and this way of paying for care involves costly overhead expenses. Each private insurer requires a large bureaucracy to assess risks, set premiums, design and advertise benefit packages, compete for customers, review claims, and decide whether to pay them.

A 2003 study by researchers from the Harvard Medical School and the Canadian Institute for Health Information found that thirty-one cents of every dollar spent on health care in the United States goes to pay administrative costs. (Later studies by the Congressional Budget Office have found a similar level of overhead expenses.) This is nearly double the amount spent by the Canadian single-payer system. In administrative costs alone, Americans spend $752 more per person than Canadians do on health care each year. (By some estimates, U.S. health care costs could be reduced by almost a third by adopting a system comparable to the Canadian one.)

As with many other expenses associated with health insurance, the amount of administrative cost may vary with the size of the risk pool. A 2010 study by the Congressional Budget Office found that in large businesses (those with over a thousand employees), health care administrative costs were 7 percent, compared to businesses with fewer than twenty-five employees, in which administrative costs were 26 percent. The lesson here, some reformers believe, is that even if a single-payer system is not adopted, insurance should be regulated by public-private agencies to lower the costs of administration, marketing, and executive compensation.

Implicit Versus Explicit Rationing.

Americans are typically unwilling to accept the explicit rationing of resources that would involve, for example, denying heart transplants to people in their seventies or mammograms to women in their thirties. Instead, Americans have generally been more comfortable with the kind of *implicit rationing* that denies or grants such expensive medical goods and services to individuals based on their ability to pay. There is little question that such attitudes about health care spending contribute substantially to the high cost of care in our society. Although the ACA does not attempt to shift such attitudes or impose a different rationing scheme, the act does aim to lower overall health care costs by stressing preventive medicine. By increasing the number of people who receive basic and preventive care, the act is likely to reduce the number of late-stage interventions that are the most expensive and least effective.

Effectiveness

The United States spends more on health care than any other country in the world. It is reasonable to ask, then, if American health care is any better than it is in other industrialized countries.

Despite the fact that U.S. per capita spending on health care is so much more than that of the other countries, the usual ways of measuring national health outcomes don't show that the United States is getting more for its money. Indeed, that it seemed to be getting less was one of the primary arguments in favor of national health reform.

Statistics collected by the World Health Organization and the CIA rank the United States thirty-forth in life expectancy (tied with Cuba and Colombia), fifty-forth in infant mortality (between Serbia and Poland), and forty-seventh in maternal mortality (between Iran and Hungary). A child in the United States is 2.5 times as likely to die by age five as a child in Singapore or Sweden, and an American woman is eleven times as likely to die in childbirth as a woman in Ireland. A 2009 Robert Wood Johnson

Foundation report cited a study showing that when nineteen developed countries were compared with respect to their success in avoiding preventable deaths among their citizens, the United States ranked in last place. Similarly, a 2013 study by the National Research Council and the Institution of Medicine found that Americans, regardless of socioeconomic status, live shorter lives and have more injuries and illnesses than people in sixteen other developed nations.

Some of America's relatively poor health outcomes appeared to be directly linked to the high cost of its health care. A 2005 study in the journal *Health Affairs,* for example, showed that Americans were far more likely to go without medical treatment than Europeans. Because of their worry about the cost, a third of Americans in the survey failed to consult a doctor when they were sick, failed to get a test recommended by their doctor, or failed to see a doctor for a follow-up visit after an initial treatment. Forty percent of those in the survey had failed to fill a prescription because of the cost.

The survey also showed that sicker adults in the other countries generally did not wait longer for essential treatment than those in the United States. (Americans typically had shorter waits for elective surgeries—e.g., hip replacements—than people in Canada or Britain, but the waits for such procedures in Germany were even shorter.) Other studies have shown that Americans typically find it more difficult to see a doctor when they need one than do people in other industrialized countries. One reason for these discrepancies seems to be that the United States spends a larger proportion of its budget on high-technology medicine (MRIs, endoscopies, etc.) than on doctors' visits and hospitalizations. Also, medical insurers have traditionally been more likely to pay for more expensive forms of intervention (e.g., foot amputations needed by diabetics) than for patient education, monitoring, and preventive care.

Need for a Change

The ACA was passed by the U.S. Congress and signed into law by President Obama in March 2010. The Obama administration emphasized two major aims of the legislation. First, the ACA is designed to extend health insurance coverage to the vast majority of Americans. Those who cannot afford market premiums receive tax subsidies to help them afford standardized plans on the insurance exchanges. Those who are too poor to pay anything toward an insurance policy are supposed to get coverage through the expansion of Medicaid, and those over age sixty-five will still be insured by the Medicare program.

Second, the ACA aims to slow the growth of health spending in the United States. The hope is that it can do so, in part, by seeing to it that more people receive preventive care. When people are able to avoid getting sick, the cost of care falls, and even when a disease is unavoidable, treating it at an early stage is less expensive than treating it at a later stage.

Most provisions of the ACA have now been implemented (primarily in 2014), but it is much too early to say whether the ACA will be successful in achieving its goals. Will it lead to an increase in life expectancy? Reduce infant and maternal mortality? Lower the overall cost of health care in the United States?

It is clear that the millions of Americans who were previously unable to afford even basic health care for themselves and their children are now able to do so. Despite many uncertainties and setbacks, the richest nation in the history of the world has made an initial commitment to ensuring that all its citizens receive a decent minimum of medical care.

BRIEFING SESSION

Some historians of medicine estimate that it was not until the middle 1930s that the intervention of a physician in the course of an illness was likely to affect its outcome in a substantial way. The change was brought about by the discovery and development of antibiotic agents such as penicillin and sulfa drugs. They made it possible, for the first time, both to control infection and to provide specific remedies for a variety of diseases. Additional advances in treatment modalities, procedures, and technology have helped establish contemporary medicine as an effective enterprise.

Before these dramatic advances occurred, there was little reason for anyone to be particularly concerned with the question of access to medical care within society. The situation in the United States has changed significantly, and over the decades, many physicians, philosophers, political theorists, and politicians have argued that everyone ought to be guaranteed at least a basic amount of medical care. In part, this view is a reflection of the increased effectiveness of contemporary medicine, but it is also due to the growing awareness of the serious difficulties faced by disadvantaged groups within society.

The previous chapter focused on one aspect of the problem of the distribution of medical resources—that of allocating limited resources among competing individuals in a particular situation. In the current chapter, we need to call attention to some of the broader social issues—issues that transcend moral decisions about particular people and raise questions about the basic aims and obligations of society.

Needs and Rights

For more than thirty years, a variety of observers (ranging from economists and religious leaders to philosophers and physicians) argued that the United States was in the midst of a health care crisis. Some of these arguments are outlined in this chapter's Social Context: The Health Care Crisis, and we need not repeat them here. But one element of the crisis that was frequently invoked was the absence of any program to provide health care for all members of society. That people should be forced to do without even basic health care for primarily financial reasons seemed to some a morally intolerable state of affairs. During the political debates over health care reform in 2009 and 2010, the failure of American society to extend needed care to all of its citizens was often cited as a reason to support the adoption of particular reforms.

The view that a society has a duty to see to the health care needs of its citizens is frequently based on the claim that everyone has a right to health care. Thus, it is often argued, society has a duty to provide that care; if it does not, then it is sanctioning a situation that is inherently wrong. To remedy the situation requires redesigning the nation's health care system and present practices, to see to it that all who need health care have access to it.

This was not, in the end, an argument that played a substantial role in persuading Congress to pass the Affordable Care Act (ACA). Making health care affordable so that millions more people might secure the health insurance needed to pay for it was one of the major arguments offered to support the legislation. (Another major argument was that extending health care to those without it would have the effect of lowering the overall cost of care to society.) Thus, an aim of the legislation was to help more people pay for basic medical care.

The legislation itself mentioned no right to care, nor does it change the basic market-based economic model: those needing medical care must find a way to pay for it. They will need either insurance or sufficient funds, and if they lack both, society will step in and help them obtain a basic level of care, in the form of Medicaid coverage or tax subsidies to obtain private insurance. Those who need more than basic care (e.g., a heart transplant) and are unable to find a way to pay for it may be denied such treatments.

Some critics of the ACA condemn it on the ground that it does not recognize a right to health care. Thus, although the act will cover basic care for more people than society previously did, it will still tolerate the large gap between those who need very expensive care and can pay for it and those who need the same care but cannot afford it. If a right to health care were recognized, some argue, the society would take responsibility for closing this gap and erasing the inequality it represents.

The language of *rights* is very slippery. To understand and evaluate arguments that involve claiming (or denying) rights to health care, it is important to understand the nature of the claim. The word *rights* is used in several distinct ways, and a failure to be clear about its use in any given case can lead to confusion.

The following distinctions are offered to help capture some of the more important sorts of things that people have in mind when they talk about rights.

Claim Rights, Legal Rights, and Statutory Rights

Suppose I own a copy of the book *Fan Mail*. If so, then I may be said to have a right to do with the book whatever I choose. Other people may be said to have a duty to recognize my right in appropriate ways. Thus, if I want to read the book, burn it, or sell it, others have a duty not to interfere with me. If I lend the book to someone, then he or she has a duty to return it.

Philosophers of law generally agree that a *claim right* to something serves as a ground for other people's duties. A claim right, then, always entails a duty or duties on the part of someone else.

Generally speaking, legal rights are claim rights. Someone has a *legal right* when someone else has a definable duty, and legal remedies are available when the duty is not performed. Either the person can be forced to perform the duty, or damages of some sort can be collected for failure to perform. If I pay someone to put a new roof on my house by a certain date, she has contracted a duty to perform the work we have agreed to. If the task is not performed, then I can turn to the legal system for enforcement or damages.

Statutory rights are claim rights that are explicitly recognized in legal statutes or laws. They impose duties on certain classes of people under specified conditions. A hospital contractor, for example, has a duty to meet certain building codes. If he fails to meet them, he is liable to legal penalties. But not all legal rights are statutory rights. Such considerations as "customary and established practices" may sometimes implicitly involve a legally enforceable claim right.

Moral Rights

A *moral right,* generally speaking, is a right that is stated in or derived from the principles of a moral theory. More specifically, to say that someone has a moral right to certain goods or a certain manner of treatment is to say that others have a moral duty to see to it that she receives what she has a right to. A moral right is a certain kind of claim right. Here, though, the source of justification for the right and for the corresponding duty lies in moral principles and not in the laws or practices of a society.

According to W. D. Ross, for example, people have a duty to treat other people benevolently. This is a duty that is not recognized by our legal system. We may, if we wish, treat others in a harsh and unsympathetic manner and, in doing so, violate no law. (See the discussion of Ross in Part VI: Foundations of Bioethics.)

Of course, many rights and duties that are based upon the principles of moral theories are also embodied in our laws. Thus, to take Ross again as an example, we have a prima facie duty not to injure or kill anyone. This duty, along with its correlative right to be free from injury or death at the hands of another, is reflected in the body of statutory law and common law that deals with bodily harm done to others and with killing.

The relationship between ethical theories and the laws of a society is complicated and controversial. The fundamental question is always the extent to which laws should reflect or be based upon an ethical theory. In a society such as ours, it does not seem proper that an ethical theory accepted by only some people should determine the laws that govern us all. It is for this reason that many object to laws regulating sexual activity, pornography, and abortion. These are considered best regarded as a part of personal morality.

At the same time, however, it seems that we must rely upon ethical theories as a basis for evaluating laws. Unless we are prepared to say that what is legal is, in itself, what is right, we must recognize the possibility of laws that are bad or unjust. But what makes a law bad? A possible answer is that a law is bad when it violates a right derived from the principles of an ethical theory. Similarly, both laws and social practices may be criticized for failing to recognize a moral right. A moral theory, then, can serve as a basis for a demand for the reform of laws and practices.

Clearly, there is no sharp line separating the moral and the legal. Indeed, virtually all of the moral theories discussed in Part VI have been used by philosophers and other thinkers as the basis for principles applying to society as a whole. Within such frameworks as utilitarianism, natural law theory, and Rawls's theory of a just society, legal and social institutions are assigned roles and functions in accordance with more general moral principles.

Political Rights

Not everyone attempts to justify claims to rights by referring such claims directly to a moral theory. Efforts are frequently made to provide justification by relying on principles or commitments that are generally acknowledged as basic to our society. (Of course, to answer how these are justified may force us to invoke moral principles.) Our society, for example, is generally seen to be committed to individual autonomy and equality, among other values. It is by reference to commitments of this sort that we often evaluate proposals and criticize practices.

From this point of view, to recognize health care as a right is to acknowledge it as a political right. This means showing that it is required by our political commitments or principles. Of course, it may also mean resolving any conflicts that may arise from other rights that seem to be demanded by our principles, too. But this is a familiar state of affairs. We are all aware that the constitutional guarantee of freedom of speech, for example, is not absolute and unconditional: it can conflict with other rights or basic commitments, and we look to the courts to provide us with guidelines to resolve the conflicts.

Health Care as a Right

With the distinctions that we have discussed in mind, let's return to the question of a general right to health care. What can those who make such a claim be asserting?

Obviously, everyone in our society is free to seek health care and, when the proper arrangements are made, to receive it. That is, health care is a service available in society, and people may avail themselves of it. At the same time, however, no physician or hospital has a duty to provide health care that is sought. The freedom to seek does not imply that others have a duty to provide what we seek.

In the United States, there is no legally recognized claim right to health care. Even if I am sick, no one has a legal duty to see to it that I receive treatment for my illness. I may request care, or I may attempt to persuade a physician that it is his or her moral duty to provide me with care. But I have no legal right to health care, and if someone refuses to provide it, I cannot seek a legal remedy. (One notable exception involves hospitals that receive federal money. They *do* have a legal duty to treat people faced with life-threatening emergencies until they are stabilized. Another involves discrimination on the basis of race, religion, national origin, or disability, which is prohibited by federal laws in most facilities that serve the general public, even those that don't receive federal funds.)

I may, of course, contract with a physician, clinic, or hospital for care, either in general or for a certain ailment. If I do this, then the other party acquires a legally enforceable duty to provide me the kind of care that we agreed upon. Contracting for health care, in this respect, is not relevantly different from contracting for a new roof on my house.

Those who assert that health care is a right cannot be regarded as making the obviously false claim that there is a legal right to care. Their claim, rather, must be interpreted as one of a moral or political sort. They might be taken as asserting something like "Everyone in our society ought to be entitled to health care, regardless of his or her financial condition."

Anyone making such a claim must be prepared to justify it by offering reasons and evidence in support of it. The ultimate source of the justification is most likely to be the principles of a moral theory. For example, Kant's principle that every person is of inherent and equal worth might be used to support the claim that every person has an equal right to medical care simply by virtue of being a person.

Justification might also be offered in terms of principles that express the aims and commitments of the society. A society that endorses justice and equality, one might argue, must be prepared to offer health care to all if it offers it to anyone.

However justification is offered, to claim that health care is a right is to go beyond merely expressing an attitude. It is to say more than something like "Everyone would like to have health care" or "Everyone needs health care."

A consequence (and aim) of the ACA is to increase the number of people who can make a claim right for health care. Those with low incomes who, before the act went into effect, would have to do without medical care because they had no insurance or money to pay for it, now have greater access to insurance. (Individuals who make less than $47,080 in 2015 can get a tax subsidy to make up the difference between the cost of a basic policy and what they can pay; those who make less than $16,105 now have access to Medicaid coverage, if they live in a state that expanded Medicaid under the ACA; and those sixty-five or older continue to have Medicare.)

Health care reform could have gone beyond the rights recognized in the ACA. It could have endorsed the notion that every citizen has a right to as much health care as is needed and available (e.g., a liver transplant) or is entitled to receive as much needed care as anyone else (including the rich). Instead, the act recognizes only a claim right to basic care, and even exercising that right requires having a way (cash, insurance, or public program) to pay for the care sought.

The language of "rights" is frequently used in a rhetorical way to encourage us to recognize the wants and needs of people—or even other organisms, such as animals and trees. This is a perfectly legitimate way of talking. But, at bottom, to urge that something be considered a right is to make a claim requiring justification in terms of some set of legal, social, or moral principles. Some of those unhappy about the ACA believe that the Obama administration passed over the opportunity to make the argument that the principles of U.S. society, as embodied in the Constitution, require that we recognize a right to health care.

Objections

Why not recognize health care for all as a right? Virtually everyone would admit that in the abstract it would be a good thing. If this is so, then why should anyone wish to oppose it? Briefly stated, arguments against a right to health care are most frequently of two kinds.

First, some argue that we live in a market economy and medical care is simply a commodity like cars, houses, or vacations on tropical islands. For people to receive medical care, it is perfectly legitimate for us to ask for them to find a way to pay for it. They may compete for jobs that offer health insurance, establish savings accounts to accumulate funds needed for medical care, pay cash for drugs and treatments, or use earnings from their jobs to buy the insurance they decide they need. If they decide to use their income to make mortgage payments on a house instead of buying an insurance policy, then they must accept the consequences. We should not, as a society, provide for the improvident at the expense of those who spend their money wisely. It violates the principles of the marketplace to give away a commodity—medical care—that should be purchased, and the market will punish the improvident.

Conservative critics of the ACA object strenuously to its requirement that (virtually) everyone in the United States purchase health insurance or pay a (modest) tax penalty. They regard this as an unwarranted intrusion of the state into the affairs of individuals. People are being required, critics say, to spend their money in ways that they have not chosen. This means that they are forced to accept restrictions on the exercise of their autonomy.

Second, some critics have pointed out that, although it is possible to admit health care to the status of a right, we must also recognize that health care is only one social good among others. Education, defense, law enforcement, housing, legal assistance, environmental protection, and so on are other goods that are also sought and needed by members of our society. It is impossible to admit all of these (and perhaps others) to the status of rights, for the society simply cannot afford to pay for them all.

Defenders of health care as a right have a number of responses to these arguments. The first line of criticism fails to recognize that it is contrary to basic moral commitments of our society to treat everything as a commodity. We do not, for example, buy and sell slaves, rent children to pedophiles, or allow transplant organs to be sold in public auctions.

Some argue that medical care, unlike golf lessons or even a painting by Degas, is not a commodity in the ordinary sense. People who do not receive health care suffer pain, lose functions like the ability to walk, and even die. Health, some argue, is a condition necessary to enjoy the goods of the world, and because medical care is often essential to preserve or restore health or (at least) relieve suffering, medical care is not an ordinary commodity that individuals can simply elect not to consume. A society committed to protecting the autonomy of individuals (or, in the language of the Declaration of Independence, promoting "life, liberty, and the pursuit of happiness") has a moral duty to see to it that its citizens receive the medical care needed to make this possible.

The second line of argument does not necessarily lead to the conclusion that we should not recognize a right to health care. It does serve to warn us that we must be careful to specify exactly what sort of right—if any—we want to support. Do we want to claim, for example, that everyone has a right to a certain minimum of health care? Or do we want to claim that everyone has a right to equal health care? Rights can have scope, and we may not be able to fulfill claims of the broadest sort.

Furthermore, this line of argument warns us that we have to make decisions about what we, as a society, are willing to pay for. Would we, for example, be willing to give up all public support for education in order to use the money for health care? Probably not. But we might be willing to reduce the level of support for education in order to increase that for health care. Whatever we decide, we have to face up to the problem of distributing our limited resources. This is an issue that is closely connected to what sort of right to health care (or, the right to what sort of health care) we are prepared to endorse.

The need for health care calls attention to fundamental issues about rights, values, and social goals. If we are to recognize a right to health care, we must be clear about exactly what this involves. Are we prepared to offer only a "decent minimum"? Does justice require that we make available to all whatever is available to any? Are we prepared to ask the wealthy to make sacrifices to satisfy the basic needs of fellow citizens?

Such questions are of more than academic interest. How they are resolved will affect us all, directly and indirectly, through the character of our society. For the first time in U.S. history, the country has made a commitment to providing basic health care to its citizens. We do not yet know all the ways that the provisions of the ACA will play out in practice. However, the act represents the country's first step toward recognizing at least a limited amount of health care as a right for all.

READINGS

Section 1: Health Care and Equal Opportunity

Autonomy, Equality and a Just Health Care System

Kai Nielsen

Kai Nielsen claims that autonomy requires a society in which equality is also a fundamental value. A society of equals is committed to an equality of conditions, so everyone is equally entitled to have basic needs met. Where the life of everyone matters equally, everyone should receive the same quality of medical treatment, regardless of the ability to pay. Hence, two- or three-tier systems are unjustified.

From Kai Nielsen "Autonomy, Equality and a Just Health Care System," *International Journal of Applied Philosophy* 4, issue 3 (Spring 1989): 39–44, DOI: 10.5840/ijap19894316. Copyright © 1989 Philosophy Documentation Center. All rights reserved. Reproduced by permission. (Notes omitted.)

To achieve equality, Nielsen argues, medicine must be taken out of the private sector. If physicians were put on salaries in a government-operated system (such as that in Britain), this would remove the profit motive and allow them to practice better medicine. The result would be "a health care system befitting an autonomy-respecting democracy committed to the democratic and egalitarian belief that the life of everyone matters equally."

I

Autonomy and equality are both fundamental values in our firmament of values, and they are frequently thought to be in conflict. Indeed the standard liberal view is that we must make difficult and often morally ambiguous trade-offs between them. I shall argue that this common view is mistaken and that autonomy cannot be widespread or secure in a society which is not egalitarian: where, that is, equality is not also a very fundamental value which has an operative role within the society. I shall further argue that, given human needs and a commitment to an autonomy respecting egalitarianism, a very different health care system would come into being than that which exists at present in the United States.

I shall first turn to a discussion of autonomy and equality and then, in terms of those conceptions, to a conception of justice. In modernizing societies of Western Europe, a perfectly just society will be a society of equals and in such societies there will be a belief held across the political spectrum in what has been called *moral* equality. That is to say, when viewed with the impartiality required by morality, the life of everyone matters and matters equally. Individuals will, of course, and rightly so, have their local attachments but they will acknowledge that justice requires that the social institutions of the society should be such that they work on the premise that the life of everyone matters and matters equally. Some privileged elite or other group cannot be given special treatment simply because they are that group. Moreover, for there to be a society of equals there must be a rough equality of condition in the society. Power must be sufficiently equally shared for it to be securely the case that no group or class or gender can dominate others through the social structures either by means of their frequently thoroughly unacknowledged latent functions or more explicitly and manifestly by institutional arrangements sanctioned by law or custom. Roughly equal material resources or power are not things

which are desirable in themselves, but they are essential instrumentalities for the very possibility of equal well-being and for as many people as possible having as thorough and as complete a control over their own lives as is compatible with this being true for everyone alike. Liberty cannot flourish without something approaching this equality of condition, and people without autonomous lives will surely live impoverished lives. These are mere commonplaces. In fine, a commitment to achieving equality of condition, far from undermining liberty and autonomy, is essential for their extensive flourishing.

If we genuinely believe in moral equality, we will want to see come into existence a world in which all people capable of self-direction have, and have as nearly as is feasible equally, control over their own lives and can, as far as the institutional arrangements for it obtaining are concerned, all live flourishing lives where their needs and desires as individuals are met as fully as possible and as fully and extensively as is compatible with that possibility being open to everyone alike. The thing is to provide institutional arrangements that are conducive to that.

People, we need to remind ourselves, plainly have different capacities and sensibilities. However, even in the extreme case of people for whom little in the way of human flourishing is possible, their needs and desires, as far as possible, should still also be satisfied in the way I have just described. Everyone in this respect at least has equal moral standing. No preference or pride of place should be given to those capable, in varying degrees, of rational self-direction. The more rational, or, for that matter, the more loveable, among us should not be given preference. No one should. Our needs should determine what is to be done.

People committed to achieving and sustaining a society of equals will seek to bring into stable existence conditions such that it would be possible for everyone, if they were personally capable of it, to enjoy an equally worthwhile and satisfying life or at least a life in which, for all of them, their needs, starting with and giving priority to their more urgent needs, were met and met as equally and as fully as possible, even where their needs are not entirely the same needs. This, at least, is the heuristic, though we might, to gain something more nearly feasible, have to scale down talk of meeting needs to providing conditions propitious for the equal satisfaction for everyone of their *basic* needs. Believers in equality want to see a world in which everyone, as far as this is possible, have equal whole life prospects. This requires an equal consideration of their needs and interests and a refusal to just override anyone's interests: to just regard anyone's interests as something which comes to naught, which can simply be set aside as expendable. Minimally, an egalitarian must believe that taking the moral point of view requires that each person's good is afforded equal consideration. Moreover, this is not just a bit of egalitarian ideology but is a deeply embedded considered judgment in modern Western culture capable of being put into wide reflective equilibrium.

II

What is a need, how do we identify needs and what are our really basic needs, needs that are presumptively universal? Do these basic needs in most circumstances at least trump our other needs and our reflective considered preferences?

Let us start this examination by asking if we can come up with a list of universal needs correctly ascribable to all human beings in all cultures. In doing this we should, as David Braybrooke has, distinguish *adventitious* and *course-of-life* needs. Moreover, it is the latter that it is essential to focus on. Adventitious needs, like the need for a really good fly rod or computer, come and go with particular projects. Course-of-life needs, such as the need for exercise, sleep or food, are such that every human being may be expected to have them all at least at some stage of life.

Still, we need to step back a bit and ask: how do we determine what is a need, course-of-life need or otherwise? We need a relational formula to spot needs. We say, where we are speaking of needs, B needs x in order to y, as in Janet needs milk or some other form of calcium in order to protect her bone structure. With course-of-life needs the relation comes out platitudinously as in "People need food and water in order to live" or "People need exercise in order to function normally or well." This, in the very identification of the need, refers to human flourishing

or to human well-being, thereby giving to understand that they are basic needs. Perhaps it is better to say instead that this is to specify in part what it is for something to be a basic need. Be that as it may, there are these basic needs we *must* have to live well. If this is really so, then, where they are things we as individuals can have without jeopardy to others, no further question arises, or can arise, about the desirability of satisfying them. They are just things that in such circumstances ought to be met in our lives if they can. The satisfying of such needs is an unequivocally good thing. The questions "Does Janet need to live?" and "Does Sven need to function well?" are at best otiose.

In this context David Braybrooke has quite properly remarked that being "essential to living or to functioning normally may be taken as a criterion for being a basic need. Questions about whether needs are genuine, or well-founded, come to an end of the line when the needs have been connected with life or health." Certainly to flourish we must have these things and in some instances they must be met at least to a certain extent even to survive. This being so, we can quite properly call them basic needs. Where these needs do not clash or the satisfying [of] them by one person does not conflict with the satisfying of the equally basic needs of another no question about justifying the meeting of them arises.

By linking the identification of needs with what we must have to function well and linking course-of-life and basic needs with what all people, or at least almost all people, must have to function well, a list of basic needs can readily be set out. I shall give such a list, though surely the list is incomplete. However, what will be added is the same sort of thing similarly identified. First there are needs connected closely to our physical functioning, namely the need for food and water, the need for excretion, for exercise, for rest (including sleep), for a life supporting relation to the environment, and the need for whatever is indispensable to preserve the body intact. Similarly there are basic needs connected with our function as social beings. We have needs for companionship, education, social acceptance and recognition, for sexual activity, freedom from harassment, freedom from domination, for some meaningful work, for recreation and relaxation and the like.

The list, as I remarked initially, is surely incomplete. But it does catch many of the basic things which are in fact necessary for us to live or to function well. Now an autonomy respecting egalitarian society with an interest in the well-being of its citizens—something moral beings could hardly be without—would (trivially) be a society of equals, and as a society of equals it would be committed to (a) *moral* equality and (b) an equality of *condition* which would, under conditions of moderate abundance, in turn expect the equality of condition to be rough and to be principally understood (cashed in) in terms of providing the conditions (as far as that is possible) for meeting the needs (including most centrally the basic needs) of everyone and meeting them equally, as far as either of these things is feasible.

III

What kind of health care system would such an autonomy respecting egalitarian society have under conditions of moderate abundance such as we find in Canada and the United States?

The following are health care needs which are also basic needs: being healthy and having conditions treated which impede one's functioning well or which adversely affect one's well-being or cause suffering. These are plainly things we need. Where societies have the economic and technical capacity to do so, as these societies plainly do, without undermining other equally urgent or more urgent needs, these health needs, as basic needs, must be met, and the right to have such medical care is a right for everyone in the society regardless of her capacity to pay. This just follows from a commitment to *moral* equality and to an equality of condition. Where we have the belief, a belief which is very basic in non-fascistic modernizing societies, that each person's good is to be given equal consideration, it is hard not to go in that way, given a plausible conception of needs and reasonable list of needs based on that conception. If there is the need for some particular regime of care and the society has the resources to meet that need, without undermining structures protecting other at least equally urgent needs, then, *ceteris paribus*, the society, if it is a decent society, must do so. The commitment to more equality—the commitment to the belief that the life of each person matters and matters equally—entails, given a few plausible empirical premises, that each person's health needs will be the object of an equal regard. Each has an equal claim, *prima facie*, to have her needs satisfied where this is possible. That does not, of course, mean that people should all be treated alike in the sense of their all getting the same thing. Not everyone needs flu shots, braces, a dialysis machine, a psychiatrist,

or a triple bypass. What should be equal is that each person's health needs should be the object of equal societal concern since each person's good should be given equal consideration. This does not mean that equal energy should be directed to Hans's rash as to Frank's cancer. Here one person's need for a cure is much greater than the other, and the greater need clearly takes precedence. Both should be met where possible, but where they both cannot then the greater need has pride of place. But what should not count in the treatment of Hans and Frank is that Hans is wealthy or prestigious or creative and Frank is not. Everyone should have their health needs met where possible. Moreover, where the need is the same, they should have (where possible), and where other at least equally urgent needs are not thereby undermined, the same quality treatment. No differentiation should be made between them on the basis of their ability to pay or on the basis of their being (one more so than the other) important people. There should, in short, where this is possible, be open and free medical treatment of the same quality and extent available to everyone in the society. And no two- or three-tier system should be allowed to obtain, and treatment should only vary (subject to the above qualification) on the basis of variable needs and unavoidable differences in different places in supply and personnel, e.g., differences between town and country. Furthermore, these latter differences should be remedied where technically and economically feasible. The underlying aim should be to meet the health care needs of everyone and meet them, in the sense explicated, equally: everybody's needs here should be met as fully as possible; different treatment is only justified where the need is different or where both needs cannot be met. Special treatment for one person rather than another is only justified where, as I remarked, both needs cannot be met or cannot as adequately be met. Constrained by ought implies can; where these circumstances obtain, priority should be given to the greater need that can feasibly be met. A moral system or a social policy, plainly, cannot be reasonably asked to do the impossible. But my account does not ask that.

To have such a health care system would, I think, involve taking medicine out of the private sector altogether including, of course, out of private entrepreneurship where the governing rationale has to be profit and where supply and demand rules the roost. Instead there must be a health care system firmly in the public sector (publicly owned and controlled) where the rationale of the system is to meet as efficiently and as fully as possible the health care needs of everyone in the society in question. The health care system should not be viewed as a business anymore than a university should be viewed as a business—compare a university and a large hospital—but as a set of institutions and practices designed to meet urgent human needs.

I do not mean that we should ignore costs of efficiency. The state-run railroad system in Switzerland, to argue by analogy, is very efficient. The state cannot, of course, ignore costs in running it. But the aim is not to make a profit. The aim is to produce the most rapid, safe, efficient and comfortable service meeting traveller's needs within the parameters of the overall socio-economic priorities of the state and the society. Moreover, since the state in question is a democracy, if its citizens do not like the policies of the government here (or elsewhere) they can replace it with a government with different priorities and policies. Indeed the option is there (probably never to be exercised) to shift the railroad into the private sector.

Governments, understandably, worry with aging populations about mounting health care costs. This is slightly ludicrous in the United States, given its military and space exploration budgets, but is also a reality in Canada and even in Iceland where there is no military or space budget at all. There should, of course, be concern about containing health costs, but this can be done effectively with a state-run system. Modern societies need systems of socialized medicine, something that obtains in almost all civilized modernizing societies. The United States and South Africa are, I believe, the only exceptions. But, as is evident from my own country (Canada), socialized health care systems often need altering, and their costs need monitoring. As a cost-cutting and as an efficiency measure that would at the same time improve health care, doctors, like university professors and government bureaucrats, should be put on salaries and they should work in medical units. They should, I hasten to add, have good salaries but salaries all the same; the last vestiges of petty entrepreneurship should be taken from the medical profession. This measure would save the state-run health care system a considerable amount of money, would improve the quality of medical care with greater cooperation and consultation resulting from economies of scale and a more extensive division of labor with larger and better equipped medical units. (There would also be less duplication of equipment.) The overall quality of care would also improve with a better balance between health care in the country and in the large cities, with doctors being systematically and rationally deployed throughout the society. In such a system doctors, no more than university professors or state bureaucrats, could not just set up a practice anywhere. They would no more be free to do this than university professors or state bureaucrats. In the altered system there would be no cultural space for it. Placing doctors on salary, though not at a piece work rate, would also result in its being the case that the financial need to see as many patients as possible as quickly as possible would be removed. This would plainly enhance the quality of medical care. It would also be the case that a different sort of person would go into the medical profession. People would go into it more frequently because they were actually interested in medicine and less frequently because this is a rather good way (though hardly the best way) of building a stock portfolio.

There should also be a rethinking of the respective roles of nurses (in all their variety), paramedics and doctors. Much more of the routine work done in medicine—taking the trout fly out of my ear for example—can be done by nurses or paramedics. Doctors, with their more extensive training, could be freed up for other more demanding tasks worthy of their expertise. This would require somewhat different training for all of these different medical personnel and a rethinking of the authority structure in the health care system. But doing this in a reasonable way would improve the teamwork in hospitals, make morale all around a lot better, improve medical treatment and save a very considerable amount of money. (It is no secret that the relations between doctors and nurses are not good.) Finally, a far greater emphasis should be placed on preventative medicine than is done now. This, if really extensively done, utilizing the considerable educational and fiscal powers of the state, would result in very considerable health care savings and a very much healthier and perhaps even happier population. (Whether with the states we actually have we are likely to get anything like that is—to understate it—questionable. I wouldn't hold my breath in the United States. Still, Finland and Sweden are very different places from the United States and South Africa.)

IV

It is moves of this *general* sort that an egalitarian and autonomy loving society under conditions of moderate scarcity should implement. (I say "general sort" for I am more likely to be wrong about some of the specifics than about the general thrust of my argument.) It would, if in place, limit the freedom of some people, including some doctors and some patients, to do what they want to do. That is obvious enough. But any society, any society at all, as long as it had norms (legal and otherwise) will limit freedom in some way. There is no living in society without some limitation on the freedom to do some things. Indeed a society without norms and thus without any limitation on freedom is a contradiction in terms. Such a mass of people wouldn't be a society. They, without norms, would just be a mass of people. (If these are "grammatical remarks," make the most of them.) In our societies I am not free to go for a spin in your car without your permission, to practice law or medicine without a license, to marry your wife while she is still your wife and the like. Many restrictions on our liberties, because they are so common, so widely accepted and thought by most of us to be so reasonable, hardly *seem* like restrictions on our liberty. But they are all the same. No doubt some members of the medical profession would feel quite reined in if the measures I propose were adopted. (These measures are not part of conventional wisdom.) But the restrictions on the freedom of the medical profession and on patients I am proposing would make for both a greater liberty all around, everything considered, and, as well, for greater well-being in the society. Sometimes we have to restrict certain liberties in order to enhance the overall system of liberty. Not speaking out of turn in parliamentary debate is a familiar example. Many people who now have a rather limited access to medical treatment would come to have it and have it in a more adequate way with such a socialized system in place. Often we have to choose between a greater or lesser liberty in a society, and, at least under conditions of abundance, the answer almost always should be "Choose the greater liberty." If we really prize human autonomy, if, that is, we want a world in which as many people as possible have as full as is possible control over their own lives, then we will be egalitarians. Our very egalitarianism will commit us to something like the health care system I described, but so will the realization that, without reasonable health on the part of the population, autonomy can hardly flourish or be very extensive. Without the kind of equitability and increased coverage in health care that goes with a properly administered socialized medicine, the number of healthy people will be far less than could otherwise feasibly be the case. With that being the case, autonomy and well-being as well will be neither as extensive nor as thorough as it could otherwise be. Autonomy, like everything else, has its material conditions. And to will the end is to will the necessary means to the end.

To take—to sum up—what since the Enlightenment has come to be seen as the moral point of view, and to take morality seriously, is to take it as axiomatic that each person's good be give[n] equal consideration. I have argued that (a) where that is accepted, and (b) where we are tolerably clear about the facts (including facts about human needs), and (c) where we live under conditions of moderate abundance, a health care system bearing at least a family resemblance to the one I have gestured at will be put in place. It is a health care system befitting an autonomy respecting democracy committed to the democratic and egalitarian belief that the life of everyone matters and matters equally.

Equal Opportunity and Health Care

Norman Daniels

Daniels argues that health care differs from ordinary commodities in such a way that its distribution should not be governed by the usual rules of buying and selling in the market economy. Because disease and disability restrict the opportunities that would otherwise be available to individuals, given their skills and talents, the distribution of health care in a just society, Daniel argues, should be governed by the principle of "fair equality of opportunity."

The normal function of the health care system, under this principle, would be to help guarantee fair equality of opportunity to those in society who have been disadvantaged by disease or disability.

A natural place to seek principles of justice for regulating health-care institutions is by examining different general theories of justice. Libertarian, utilitarian, and contractarian theories, for example, each support more general principles governing the distribution of rights, opportunities, and wealth, and these general principles may bear on the specific issue of health care. But there is a difficulty with this strategy. In order to apply such general theories to health care, we need to know what kind of a social good health care is. An analysis of this problem is not provided by general theories of justice. One way to see the problem is to ask whether health-care services, say personal medical services, should be viewed as we view other commodities in our society. Should we allow inequalities in the access to health-care services to vary with whatever economic inequalities are permissible according to more general principles of distributive justice? Or is health care "special" and not to be assimilated with other commodities, like cars or personal computers, whose distribution we allow to be governed by market exchanges among economic unequals?

Is health care special? To answer this question, we must see that not all preferences individuals have—and express, for example, in the marketplace—are of equal moral importance. When we judge the importance to society of meeting some-one's preferences we use a restricted measure of well-being. We do not simply ask, how much does the person want something? Or, how happy an individual will be if he gets it? Rather, we are concerned whether the preference is for something that affects well-being in certain fundamental or important ways (cf. Scanlon 1975). Among the kinds of preferences to which we give special weight are those that meet certain important categories of need. Among these important needs are those necessary for maintaining normal functioning for individuals, viewed as members of a natural species. Health-care needs fit this character-ization of important needs because they are things we need to prevent or cure diseases and disabilities, which are deviations from species-typical functional organization ("normal functioning" for short).

This preference suggests health care may be special in this restricted sense: Health care needs are important to meet because they affect normal functioning. But there is still a gap in our answer: Why give such moral importance to health-care needs merely because they are necessary to preserve normal functioning? Why is preserving normal functioning of special moral importance? The answer lies in the relationship between normal functioning and opportunity, but to make the relationship clear, I must introduce the notion of a normal opportunity range.

The *normal opportunity range* for a given society is the array of life plans reasonable persons in it are likely to construct for themselves. The normal range is thus dependent on key features of the society—its stage of historical development, its level of material wealth and technological development, and even important cultural facts about it. This dependency is one way in which the notion of normal opportunity range is socially relative. Facts about social organization, including the conception of justice regulating its basic institutions, will also determine how that total normal range is distributed in the population. Nevertheless, that issue of distribution aside, normal functioning provides us with one clear parameter affecting the share of the normal range open to a given individual. It is this parameter that the distribution of health care affects.

The share of the normal range open to individu-als is also determined in a fundamental way by their talents and skills. Fair equality of opportunity does not require opportunity to be equal for all persons. It requires only that it be equal for persons with similar skills and talents. Thus individual shares of the normal range will not in general be *equal,* even when they are *fair* to the individual. The general principle of fair equality of opportunity does not imply leveling indi-vidual differences. Within the general theory of justice, unequal chances of success which derive from un-equal talents may be compensated for in other ways. I can now state a fact at the heart of my approach: Impairment of normal functioning through disease and disability restricts individuals' opportunities rela-tive to that portion of the normal range their skills and talents would have made available to them were they healthy. If individuals' fair shares of the normal range are the arrays of life plans they may reasonably choose, given their talents and skills, then disease and disability shrinks their shares from what is fair.

Of course, we also know that skills and talents can be undeveloped or misdeveloped because of social conditions, for example, family background or racist educational practices. So, if we are interested in having individuals enjoy a fair share of the normal opportunity range, we will want to correct for special disadvantages here too, say through compensatory educational or job-training programs. Still, restoring normal functioning through health care has a particular and *limited* effect on an individual's shares of the normal range. It lets them enjoy that portion of the range to which a full array of skills and talents would give them access, assuming that these too are not impaired by special social disadvantages. Again, there is no presumption that we should eliminate or level individual differences: These act as a baseline constraint on the degree to which individuals enjoy the normal range. Only where differences in talents and skills are the results of disease and disability, not merely normal variation, is some effort required to correct for the effects of the "natural lottery."

One conclusion we may draw is that impairment of the normal opportunity range is a (fairly crude) measure of the relative importance of health-care needs, at least at the social or macro level. That is, it will be more important to prevent, cure, or compensate for those disease conditions which involve a greater curtailment of an individual's share of the normal opportunity range. More generally, this relationship between health-care needs and opportunity suggests that the principle that should govern the design of health-care institutions is a principle guaranteeing fair equality of opportunity.

The concept of equality of opportunity is given prominence in Rawls's (1971) theory of justice, and it has also been the subject of extensive critical discussion. I cannot here review the main issues (see Daniels 1985, Chapter 3), nor provide a full justification for the principle of fair equality of opportunity. Instead, I shall settle for a weaker, conditional claim, which suffices for my purposes. Health-care institutions should be among those governed by a principle of fair equality of opportunity, provided two conditions obtain: (1) an acceptable general theory of justice includes a principle that requires basic institutions to guarantee fair equality of opportunity, and (2) the fair equality of opportunity principle acts as a constraint on permissible economic inequalities. In what follows, for the sake of simplicity, I shall ignore these provisos. I urge the fair equality of opportunity principle as an appropriate principle to govern macro decisions about the design of our health-care system. The principle defines, from the perspective of justice, what the moral *function* of the health-care system must be—to help guarantee fair equality of opportunity. This relationship between health care and opportunity is the fundamental insight underlying my approach.

My conditional claim does not depend on the acceptability of any particular general theory of justice, such as Rawls's contractarian theory. A utilitarian theory might suffice, for example, if it were part of an ideal moral code, general compliance with which produced at least as much utility as any alternative code (cf. Brandt 1979). That utilitarian theory could then be extended to health care through the analysis provided by my account. Because Rawls's is the main general theory that has incorporated a fair equality of opportunity principle, I have elsewhere suggested in some detail (Daniels 1985, Chapter 3) how it can be extended, with minor modifications, to incorporate my approach. These details need not distract us here.

The fair equality of opportunity account has several important implications for the issue of access to health care. First, the account is compatible with, though it does not imply, a multitiered health-care system. The basic tier would include health-care services that meet health-care needs, or at least important needs, as judged by their impact on opportunity range. Other tiers might involve the use of health-care services to meet less important needs or other preferences, for example, cosmetic surgery. Second, the basic tier, which we might think of as a "decent basic minimum," is characterized in a principled way, by reference to its impact on opportunity. Third, there should be no obstacles—financial, racial, geographical— to access to the basic tier. (The account is silent about what inequalities are permissible for higher tiers within the system.) Social obligations are focused on the basic tier.

The fair equality of opportunity account also has implications for issues of resource allocation. First, I have already noted that we have a crude criterion—impact on normal opportunity range—for distinguishing the importance of different health-care needs and services. Second, preventive measures that make the distribution of risks of disease more equitable must be given prominence in a just health-care system. Third, the importance of personal medical services, despite what we spend on them, must be weighed against other forms of health care, including preventive and public health measures, personal care and other long-term-care services. A just distribution of health-care services involves weighing the impact of all of these on normal opportunity range. This point has specific implications for the importance of long-term care, but also for the introduction of new high-cost technologies, such as artificial hearts, which deliver a benefit to relatively few individuals at very great cost. We must weigh new technologies against alternatives and judge the overall impact of introducing them on fair equality of opportunity—which gives a slightly new sense to the term "opportunity cost."

This account does not give individuals a basic right to have all of their health-care needs met. Rather, there are social obligations to provide individuals only with those services that are part of the design of a system which, on the whole, protects equal opportunity. If social obligations to provide appropriate health care are not met, then individuals are definitely wronged. Injustice is done to them. Thus, even though decisions have to be made about how best to protect opportunity, these obligations nevertheless are not similar to imperfect duties of beneficence. If I could benefit from your charity, but you instead give charity to someone else, I am not wronged and you have fulfilled your duty of beneficence. But if the just design of a health-care system requires providing a service from which I could benefit, then I am wronged if I do not get it.

The case is similar to individuals who have injustice done to them because they are discriminated against in hiring or promotion practices on a job. In both cases, we can translate the specific sort of injustice done, which involves acts or policies that impair or fail to protect opportunity, into a claim about individual rights. The principle of justice guaranteeing fair equality of opportunity shows that individuals have legitimate claims or rights when their opportunity is impaired in particular ways—against a background of institutions and practices which protect equal opportunity. Health-care rights in this view are thus a species of rights to equal opportunity.

The scope and limits of these rights—the entitlements they actually carry with them—will be relative to certain facts about a given system. For example, a health-care system can protect opportunity only within the limits imposed by resource scarcity and technological development for a given society. We cannot make a direct inference from the fact that an individual has a right to health care to the conclusion that this person is entitled to some specific health-care service, even if the service would meet a health-care need. Rather, the individual is entitled to a specific service only if it is or ought to be part of a system that appropriately protects fair equality of opportunity....

Section 2:   Health Care and the Affordable Care Act

Obamacare: What the Affordable Care Act Means for Patients and Physicians

Mark A. Hall and Richard Lord

Hall and Lord argue that the Affordable Care Act is not the radical transformation of the American health care system that its opponents feared and that many of its proponents sought. It offers neither *socialized medicine* (in which government assumes responsibility for the provision of care) nor *socialized insurance* (in which government insurance pays for care). There is nothing in the act that tells physicians how to practice nor tells insurers how to ration reimbursement for care. As a regulatory reform of the existing private insurance

Reproduced from "Obamacare: What the Affordable Care Act Means for Patients and Physicians," Mark A. Hall and Richard Lord, *BMJ* 349 (2014): g5376 © 2014 with permission from BMJ Publishing Group Ltd.

market, the law cannot be expected to achieve universal coverage or substantially reduce health care costs in the United States.

Instead, Hall and Lord contend that the law's central achievement has been to eliminate policies and costs that had rendered millions of Americans *uninsurable.* By prohibiting insurers from screening applicants for preexisting conditions and requiring that they charge rates based on population averages rather than health status, the law removes barriers to coverage for millions of Americans. By providing tax subsidies and expanding Medicaid in many states, the law has also made coverage affordable for most of the population. The result, as of 2014, was that nine million previously uninsured Americans had gained health coverage, and the uninsured had dropped from 18 to 9 percent of the population. At the same time, the insurance industry has remained profitable and costs to both consumers and the government have so far been lower than expected.

Nevertheless, the law has triggered new market dynamics that have narrowed provider networks and increased cost-sharing in many policies. The unpredictable outcomes of these shifts, combined with the largely unaddressed problem of health care inflation, means that additional reforms will almost certainly be required.

Not since the civil rights era has a federal social initiative in the United States been as contentious and polarizing as the ongoing debate over the Patient Protection and Affordable Care Act of 2010 ("Affordable Care Act"). Much of the intense opposition to this law has been motivated by political partisanship or by a belief that Congress used inappropriate legislative procedures to enact the law. But much of the social and political debate focuses on health policy concerns. Will the act achieve its stated goals and avoid unintended consequences? Will it constitute a major intrusion into how medicine is practiced and reimbursed? And, if so, will that be to the detriment or benefit of patients and physicians?

Fierce and often emotional discussions of these questions often obscure a basic understanding of how the act functions. Confusion is understandable considering the law's complexity, so it is important to separate the law's core essentials from its more peripheral features. Also, many claims about the act are based on conjecture or implausible assumptions. Many patients will look to their physicians for information and guidance. Accordingly, this review begins with a description of how the act came about and what it aims to achieve. It then provides a summary of the act's major impacts on patients and physicians, based on reputable empirical studies.

Health insurance before the Affordable Care Act

The healthcare system in the US struggles more than systems in other industrialized countries with two basic aspects of healthcare finance and delivery. It spends far more per person on healthcare than any other country, yet it is the only country in the developed world that fails to provide healthcare coverage for almost all of its residents. In 2010, 50 million people (16% of the population) had no public or private health insurance coverage, at the same time that the US spent close to $3tr (£1.8tr; €2.3tr) a year on medical care. In proportion to its size, the US spends 50-100% more than peer nations, even though these other countries have healthcare coverage for almost all of their residents.

One reason that the US spends this much is that financing for healthcare is more fragmented and privatized than in other developed countries. More than half the population has private insurance, mainly sponsored by employers for their workers and families (fig 1⇓). Most private insurers are managed care companies that encourage or require people to use doctors or hospitals in contracted networks. Outside the workforce, the federal Medicare program covers people who are disabled or over 65 years and retired. Medicaid, a joint state and federal program, covers some people who are poor, but,

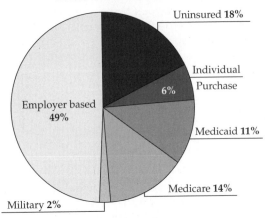

Before the Affordable Care Act

Uninsured **18%**

Individual Purchase **6%**

Medicaid **11%**

Medicare **14%**

Military **2%**

Employer based **49%**

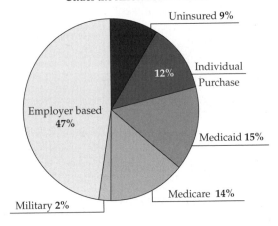

Under the Affordable Care Act

Uninsured **9%**

Individual Purchase **12%**

Medicaid **15%**

Medicare **14%**

Military **2%**

Employer based **47%**

Figure 1

conditions were excluded for one year, and insurers varied their small group rates according to age and other health risk factors.

History of the Affordable Care Act

Republicans versus Democrats

A more socialized solution for healthcare reform favored by some left wing Democrats in the US would be to expand Medicare or create something like it that, along with Medicaid, covered everyone in a "single payer" system, like that in Canada. Despite Medicare's relative popularity with US patients and its success with constraining healthcare spending, staunch opposition to anything that smacks of socialized insurance keeps Congress from even considering "Medicare for all."

Right wing (Republican) proponents would prefer a less ambitious law that uses government subsidies mainly to help only those people who are not insurable, leaving the rest of the market to function as normal. This would also allow insurers to continue medical underwriting practices that screen people for health status and exclude pre-existing conditions. Moreover, because the 20% of people with the most expensive medical needs account for about 80% of spending, uninsurable people are much more expensive than people realize and support for them is likely to be chronically underfunded. Indeed, adequate funding of the top end of the medical expense distribution would end up "socializing" a major portion of medical spending.

Middle ground

The act was designed to avoid these extremes of right and left by aiming for a middle course that preserves a private insurance market for most people, but reforms the market so that it advances rather than undermines health policy goals. Essentially, the act attempts to make the defective individual market function much more like the successful large group market for people above the poverty line. The act also expands Medicaid to cover everyone near or below the poverty line. This is the same pragmatic combination of approaches that conservative thought leaders (such as the Heritage Foundation) had previously advanced and that was successfully implemented in Massachusetts by its former governor Mitt Romney, a Republican.

in most states, before the act's expansion, it covered only those who fitted into prescribed categories, such as single parents, children, and pregnant women.

People without public coverage or group insurance at work have had difficulty obtaining individual insurance, not only because of its expense, but also because private insurers screened people for health status (a process called medical underwriting) and either declined to cover people with potentially costly medical conditions, or charged them substantially more, or excluded coverage for their existing conditions. This is why only about 6% of the US population had individual (non-group) coverage. Before reform, insurance for small employers shared characteristics with both large group and individual insurance: small group insurance was more available and offered better coverage than in the individual market, but pre-existing

How the act was passed

By using private market approaches endorsed by conservative thinkers to pursue liberal social goals, the Democrats who crafted the act hoped that it would be acceptable to a broad swathe of the political and policy spectrum. Despite this reasonable expectation, Republicans uniformly opposed it, and the political consequences of this response are stark. Massachusetts' surprising election of a Republican to fill the seat vacated by Senator Kennedy's death in 2009 left Democrats one vote short of the supermajority needed to avoid blocking techniques by the opposition. Although the Senate previously had adopted a version of the Affordable Care Act, it differed from the House version. There was now no opportunity for a reconciliation process or careful proofreading. Instead, using legislative rules that allow purely budgetary and tax measures to advance with simple majority support, the Senate adopted a patchwork of amendments that made the Affordable Care Act acceptable to the House, and President Obama signed the law into effect in 2010.

Universal insurability

Before discussing what the act covers it is helpful to clarify what it does not cover. It is not about regulating how private insurers pay providers. Also it does not achieve truly universal coverage, because it cuts the number of uninsured by only about a half (fig 1). Even after full implementation, 30 million people will still be uninsured. (About a quarter of the remaining uninsured will be eligible for Medicaid but not yet enrolled, another quarter will decline to purchase affordable private insurance, another quarter will still face unaffordable premiums, and the remaining quarter will not be US citizens or long term legal residents.)

If the act does not control costs or provide universal coverage, what does it do? The act's core and most important achievement is universal insurability. From 1 January 2014 insurers can no longer turn anyone away or refuse to cover pre-existing conditions (which is called "guaranteed issue"). In addition, insurers have to charge individuals and small groups rates that are based on population averages (which is called "community rating") rather than basing rates on individual characteristics. Guaranteed issue with community rating is an obvious boon for people who previously could not qualify, but universal insurability also benefits people who previously had good coverage. The knowledge that coverage will be available

regardless of what happens enables people to change jobs, start new businesses, leave unhappy relationships, and make other major life choices that previously depended—at least to some extent—on whether insurability might be threatened in the process.

Accomplishing the core goal of universal insurability requires more than simply regulating insurers. For this to work, people need subsidies so that they can afford insurance. And, to prevent people from simply waiting until they are sick to enroll, which would drive up insurance premiums even more, the act imposes an individual mandate in the form of a tax penalty (ranging from 1% of taxable income in 2014 to 2.5% in 2016) if people fail to enroll in insurance that is affordable. (Affordable is defined for this purpose as single coverage costing ≤8% of household income). The act also requires larger employers (those with more than 50 full time equivalent workers) to pay a tax if they decline to offer minimum essential benefits. Administrative complications delayed this employer mandate (as it is known) for a year, until 2015.

Core insurance provisions

Most of the act's core insurance provisions flow from these few fundamentals—guaranteed issue, subsidies, and individual and employer mandates. Because insurance is expensive, sliding scale premium tax subsidies are needed all the way up to four times the poverty level, which is almost $100 000 for a family of four—substantially more than the median household income. For people who cannot afford to contribute substantially to their cost of care, states can now expand Medicaid to cover everyone at or below 133% of poverty, rather than the uneven patchwork of Medicaid eligibility criteria that existed between various states.

To determine eligibility for subsidies and to facilitate choice among qualified plans, states are invited to create insurance exchanges, but if they do not, the federal government will operate one for them. Exchanges are web portals where people can shop among qualified insurers and determine their eligibility for subsidies. To qualify, insurers have to satisfy numerous criteria, to ensure that people (and the government) receive decent value for their money and that insurers compete on fair terms. Requirements include offering a standard set of "essential health benefits" that cover a comprehensive range of services.

The act also requires insurers to package their patient cost sharing mechanisms (such as deductibles and copayments) in standard ways—labeled bronze, silver, gold, and platinum—according to whether insurance, on average, pays for 60%, 70%, 80%, or 90% of the required covered benefits.

The constitution and Medicaid

Immediately after the act became law, lawsuits that challenged its constitutionality were filed. Clearly, the federal government has constitutional authority to require Medicare for all, but doing something short of that—expanding Medicaid and requiring people to buy private coverage—was attacked as exceeding congressional powers. In what is undoubtedly the health law case of the century, the Supreme Court ruled partially in both sides' favor. It held that the Medicaid expansion is permissible but only if states can opt out of the expansion and still keep their current Medicaid funding. And, it ruled that the "individual mandate" is valid, but only if it is construed simply as a tax on a personal choice to decline coverage rather than as a penalty for violating a regulatory law that prohibits being uninsured.

This ruling allowed the act to survive, just barely (by a vote of 5-4 on the individual mandate), but in a weakened form. In particular, about half of US states so far have declined to expand Medicaid.... In those states the subsidized exchanges can reach down to the poverty level but not below. This means that a high proportion of uninsured people on a low income in these states have no new options, even though people earning just a few dollars more qualify for free private coverage on the exchanges. Many states chose this upside down effect because they say they cannot afford their very small portion of the Medicaid expansion costs. Skeptics claim that politics, not state finances, are the main driver of states' decisions to refuse Medicaid expansion. They note that all of the states that refused are led by Republicans, and that they all also refused to establish insurance exchanges.

Although states struggle to balance their budgets, state finances are not a compelling reason to refuse Medicaid expansion. The federal government will pay the full costs of expansion for the first two years and 90% of the costs by 2020. This would reduce states' existing financial burden of caring for the uninsured and would pay for additional care that saves citizens' lives and relieves suffering. Moreover, Medicaid expansion would create jobs that generate more state and local tax revenue, sufficient to offset most or all of the states' small fraction of Medicaid costs.

These refusals come at a high cost for states and their citizens. Opting out of Medicaid expansion does not relieve state citizens from paying the federal taxes that fund the act in other states. Not expanding puts many US hospitals in a particularly difficult position because those that serve a higher than average share of the uninsured will continue to do so, but the act cuts federal funds to support this uncompensated care across the board, having anticipated that all states would expand. It is not surprising, therefore, that several major medical centers across the country that have announced that they are cutting jobs are in states that have not expanded Medicaid.

Misconceptions about the act

Socialized Insurance   The act's most vociferous opponents say that it socializes medicine, meaning that the government has taken over the delivery of care. However, that is a misuse of the nomenclature. The distinction between socialized medicine and socialized insurance is that, with socialized insurance, the government pays for rather than delivers care. Considering the insurance element, congressional leaders originally proposed selling government insurance on the new exchanges and allowing older people to buy into Medicare before age 65 years, but both of these "public option" ideas were stripped from the law before it was passed to garner enough votes in the Senate. Essentially what is left is a system for subsidizing and regulating the purchase of the same kind of private insurance that was already being sold in the market.

This subsidy and regulation scheme has many "social" elements, such as modified community rating, but they are not greatly more socialized than certain elements that prevailed in the market before the Affordable Care Act. The act allows individual and small group insurers to charge the oldest adults only three times more than the youngest adults. Threefold variation is less than the fivefold one that insurance actuaries would like, but a threefold variation is much more flexible than the market based form of community rating seen within large employer groups, where every worker in a group is charged exactly the same rate regardless of age.

Although the act mandates coverage of at least 60% of the actuarial value of a package of essential health benefits, the 60% level is much lower than what insurance typically covers in employer groups, and it is similar to what previously prevailed in the individual market. Similarly, the essential health benefits package is based mainly on what was the most popular insurance plan recently sold in each state's small group market. Some other important aspects of the act push the private market towards more coverage and cross subsidization than occurs in the unregulated market, but overall the act mirrors rather than displaces many aspects of existing insurance market conditions. It is always possible that Congress might adopt further reforms that are more socialized than the Affordable Care Act, but nothing in the act's structure makes this likely.

Socialized Medicine It is also not accurate to say that the act socializes medical practice or payment. It does nothing that directly alters the fundamentals of how private insurance pays healthcare providers. One reason that the act was ultimately endorsed by the American Medical Association, the American Hospital Association, and other major industry and trade groups is that it did not implement comprehensive payment reform or regulation for providers. The act contains several innovations in payment methods, described below, but most of these are demonstration or pilot projects under Medicare, which already regulates payment rates, and these innovations build on ones that were already under way before the act came into law.

Similarly, despite concern that the government would control and ration care, the act does little to directly alter prevailing standards of practice or clinical autonomy. It creates new institutions that aim to improve quality and value (administered by the Patient Centered Outcomes Research Institute and the Center for Medicare and Medicaid Innovation), but they mostly just fund research or make proposals. Some potentially influential initiatives have not even been implemented, either because of a lack of funding (National Health Care Workforce Commission) or continued political and policy opposition (Independent Payment Advisory Board). Even if established, most of these study commissions and advisory boards differ little in their fundamentals from those that have been in place for decades, such as the Agency for Healthcare Research and Quality and the Medicare Payment Advisory Commission.

Naturally, the story is more complex than this, but despite a sometimes alarming plethora of new organizations and acronyms, there is no new government authority that requires physicians to change how they practice or tells private insurers how to pay for care. Just the opposite, to assure that the act's initiatives do not compromise patient care or interfere with clinical judgment, the law contains a series of restrictive provisos that preclude "any recommendation to ration health care" (Independent Payment Advisory Board), any use of "dollars per quality adjusted life year" (Patient Centered Outcomes Research Institute), or any denial of benefits based on "age, disability, or expected length of life" (essential health benefits).

Budget Buster Another misconception is that the act puts the federal government deeper into debt. Certainly, the act is not inexpensive; it is expected to cost about $1tr of federal spending over the first decade, even though it was not fully in effect for several of those years. Nevertheless, the law is designed to cover the federal government's costs through various tax increases and spending cuts (mainly to Medicare), so it is not expected to increase federal debt for the foreseeable future according to the Congressional Budget Office (CBO), whose expertise and neutrality is not seriously questioned. Naturally, such projections often prove to be inaccurate and other government programs such as Medicare have ended up costing much more than initially forecast. However, this is not the experience so far. Because initial insurance rates were lower than expected, and about half the states have not expanded Medicaid, the CBO now projects that costs to the federal government will be about $30bn less per year than originally forecast.

Government Mandated Insurance Finally, there is merit to both sides of the debate about whether the act forces people to give up their previous insurance. The act will have little or no effect on most people who are already insured (fig 1). Eligibility for Medicare remains the same and expands for Medicaid. Large employers are not expected to, and so far are not planning to, drop coverage (although this remains speculative because of a two year reprieve for the employer mandate). However, because small employers are not subject to an employer mandate, a fair number of them (but fewer than half) are expected to drop coverage, especially if many of their employees are eligible for substantial subsidies on the exchange.

The act mandates that insurance sold to individuals and small groups (initially, groups of fewer than 50, but increasing to 100 in 2017) cover a comprehensive set of essential health benefits. Also, it caps out of pocket payments at $6350 for individuals and $12 700 for families. For those who want to avoid these mandates and keep the coverage they have, the law clearly permits continued renewal of plans that existed at the time of enactment, for as long as the insurer and the policyholder both wish to maintain coverage. This explicit statutory protection is the basis for President Obama's controversial pledge that, "if you like your insurance plan, you can keep it." This was true when the law first passed, but to remain true people had to have the same coverage that they had in 2010 and insurers had to avoid making any substantial changes to their plans. People and insurers change coverage frequently. Therefore, by the time the law's main provisions took effect in 2014, millions of people were no longer eligible to keep their coverage. Moreover, many insurers decided to cancel their existing plans because it did not make business sense to keep plans that could not be sold to new subscribers. In addition, some states decided to require these cancellations. The ensuing uproar led the Obama administration to allow insurers to keep in place coverage that they had planned or begun to cancel. However, for many insurers this continuation was not feasible or was not allowed by state regulators.

Even for cancellation deadlines that were extended, sooner or later people will have to conform to the act's benefit minimums for individuals and small groups. Whether or not these minimum benefits are good policy is, of course, subject to debate. For instance, should coverage for maternity care be required even if many policyholders simply cannot have children? And, should insurance cover "habilitative services" that go beyond merely rehabilitating patients, to include various therapies that help people cope with chronic disabilities? Although coverage of these services is more comprehensive than what prevailed previously in the individual market, this coverage is similar to the most popular plans that had been for sale in the small group market and a bit less generous than what prevails for large employer groups.

Impact on patients and consumers

For reasons just explained, the Affordable Care Act has little effect on the insurance coverage of roughly three quarters of the population (fig 1). The law's main effect is that the number of people who are uninsured will be roughly halved by moving them to Medicaid (those below the poverty line) or subsidized private insurance sold through the new government exchange. Everyone with Medicare, and most people with Medicaid or employment based insurance, will continue to receive the same kind of coverage, from the same source, at price increases that are in line with medical cost inflation. Medicare recipients will be covered for more preventive care and will see coverage for prescription drugs expand. People with large group insurance (including self funded insurers) will also have better coverage for preventive services and will no

longer be subject to lifetime or annual limits on total claims. These and other requirements undoubtedly add to the cost of insurance, but many of them have only a minor or negligible impact, in part because most private insurance already complied with the bulk of the act's requirements.

The act's primary impact is on the 18% of people who are uninsured, the 6% who have individual coverage, and the small proportion (so far) of people whose employers are dropping group coverage. These roughly 80 million people will need to decide between the following options:

- Remain as they are and pay a tax penalty (1% of income in 2014, increasing to 2.5% in 2016),unless they qualify for an exemption
- Enroll in Medicaid or with an employer plan, if eligible
- Purchase subsidized private insurance on the exchange (if their income is between 133% and 400% of the poverty line)
- Purchase full price insurance on their own.

Undocumented immigrants are not eligible for Medicaid or the exchanges. Also, in states that do not expand Medicaid, people below the poverty level have no new options because exchange subsidies are available only above the poverty line.

During the first open enrollment period (which ended in March 2014), about eight million people purchased individual insurance through the state and federal exchanges, exceeding expectations despite severe software problems. About a quarter of these enrollees were previously uninsured. Another six million uninsured people enrolled with Medicaid. This enrollment surge could cause patients in some parts of the country to face a shortage of available physicians, especially primary care physicians, but this has not yet happened, and efforts (described below) are being made to increase primary care capacity.

Effect on insurance exchanges

Most of the insurance exchanges offer a good range of choice at prevailing prices. Fears that the new law would drive insurers from the market in droves have not materialized. To the contrary, in each market segment (individual, small group, and large group), roughly 500 insurers throughout the country had at least 1000 members in 2012. Moreover, insurers' stock prices have risen substantially more than the rest of the stock market, and new insurers are entering the individual market in many states, in response to the opportunity for increased enrollment through the exchanges.

Effect on community and average rates

Similarly overstated are charges that the act has caused massive "rate shock." It is true that community rating will increase rates for younger people by 30-40%, but it will also significantly lower rates for older people. Early indicators of the market-wide effect on insurance rates are encouraging. Average rates for 2014 in the individual market (which includes the new exchanges) are almost 20% lower than the CBO initially projected, and in line with, or lower than, prevailing rates for group insurance.

It is true that these rates exceed what many people previously paid in the individual market. But insurance under the act has better coverage (sometimes better than people want). Also, insurance now covers all pre-existing conditions and allows people to undergo periods of non-coverage without worrying about their ability to requalify for coverage. Moreover, this insurance cannot be cancelled or rescinded and its premiums do not increase as steeply with age, or at all when people get sick or injured. These benefits come at a cost, which insurers require people to pay, but which the act subsidizes for most people.

Premium subsidies

The act's premium subsidies vary substantially according to income and family composition. It is therefore not easy to summarise the impact of these subsidies. However, because subsidies are available to people who earn up to four times the poverty level, most people who purchase individual insurance will be eligible for some subsidy. Among those who qualify, the subsidy averages about $5000 per family. The full net impact of these various components of insurance pricing (average rate, age rating, exchange subsidies) is not yet known but there will be more winners than losers. Still, if only a small minority of existing policyholders face increases substantially more than general medical cost trends, this will amount to a few million people who will be worse off than before.

Medical loss ratio

Another of the act's benefits for consumers is its regulation of insurers' medical loss ratio, which is the proportion of the premium spent on medical claims and quality improvement as opposed to overheads such as sales costs, administration, and profits. Requiring insurers to rebate overheads that exceed 20% in the individual and small group markets, or 15% in the large group market, has resulted so far in almost $2bn of consumer rebates. In addition, insurers reduced their overhead expenses by a similar amount after enactment of the law, and apparently in response to it.

Summary of the act's impact on patients and consumers

The act seems to have had no unwanted consequences for most patients and consumers. However, the act has had a negative effect on less than 5% of people—those who are younger, healthier, and wealthier and so had lower rates and are not eligible for substantial financial assistance. There is also legitimate concern that the initial favorable market performance may not persist. Insurers' initial pricing was based on actuarial assumptions about the unknown age and health status mix of enrollees under the new market rules. If the actual experience is substantially worse, rates for individual coverage could rise considerably, or participating insurers could decline.

Impact on physicians and hospitals

Provider capacity and patient access

The surge in enrollment is expected to place a strain on provider capacity, especially for primary care physicians. The full extent of this has not yet been seen, but various measures are under way to increase primary care capacity. The act increases funding for community health centers, and it increases payment rates under Medicare and Medicaid for primary care physicians and for team based patient centered medical homes. The act also focuses on making more use of physician extenders, such as nurse practitioners and telemedicine. More time and research are needed to know whether these measures will suffice and how best to organize and fund primary care. Without these improvements, the act's increased coverage may not achieve its full potential to increase access to care and produce a measurable improvement in population health.

Cost control

The Affordable Care Act, despite its name, is much more about the cost of insurance than the cost of healthcare. Nevertheless, key provisions of the act are designed to help "bend the cost curve" in ways that could change how physicians work together across specialties and with hospitals. Almost all of these cost control initiatives focus on Medicare. They include the Community Care Transitions Program, the Value Based Purchasing Program, and the Shared Savings Program. The major goal of these Medicare provisions is to move toward healthcare services being paid for on the basis of value rather than volume. In particular, Medicare is expected to make greater use of bundled payments for episodes of illness, which hold hospitals and physicians jointly responsible for cost and quality for an episode of care.

Pilots completed to date have had variable success and the optimal arrangements have not been clearly defined. The open structure of accountable care organizations, for example, makes it more difficult for them to coordinate and manage care. Accordingly, these organizations have not yet shown substantial savings.

The prospect of marked change in Medicare payments might make the relationship between hospitals and physicians more collaborative or contentious. Initially, at least, providers are becoming more closely aligned. Many physician groups are being bought by hospitals, converting physicians from small business owners to employees. It is too early to know whether these payment and organizational changes will enhance or erode the patient-physician interaction. Physicians may be rewarded for spending more time with patients rather than simply ordering more tests. But there is also the potential that cost or institutional constraints will make patients more wary of physicians' motivations.

The act continues existing trajectories

Medicine has been beset for decades with changes like these. Considering the Affordable Care Act's size, importance, and complexity, the tendency is to attribute almost everything that happens in healthcare delivery, especially unwelcome changes, to the act. But much of the current change was under way before the act and clearly would have continued anyway. Adoption of electronic medical records, for example, received a major bolus of funding from the bipartisan American Recovery and Reinvestment Act of 2009, and most delivery system changes directly fostered by the Affordable Care Act are focused on Medicare and not on private insurance. For private insurance, the act continues to leave payment of healthcare providers to unregulated market forces. Its most overt cost control measure is to tax employers, starting in 2018, that offer especially generous health insurance. The act has, however, put into motion market forces that are bringing about further change in the private sector, in the form of narrower networks (see below) and increased patient cost sharing.

Narrower networks

To offer the most competitively priced product on the new exchanges, many insurers have asked providers to charge substantially less than they usually charge commercial insurers by accepting reimbursement closer to Medicare levels. Providers that are unwilling are often dropped from the networks that insurers offer on the exchanges. Thus, many insurers have much narrower networks for their products sold through the exchanges than those that they sell simultaneously to groups outside the exchanges.

Narrow networks will provide a market test of the economic theory that individuals are more willing than employers to sacrifice breadth of choice among providers for lower premiums. Employers are less willing to do this when they choose a plan that covers a large number of workers, many of whom might find that their preferred physicians or hospitals are not in a narrow network. Individuals however may be willing to shop among different plans on the basis of which one has their preferred providers or they might be more willing to change physicians to save their own money.

If narrow networks persist, they might also expand beyond the government exchanges to offer lower cost options for employer groups, possibly through private exchanges. If so, providers may face increasingly tough choices about how great a discount they are willing to confer. More than just price discounting, narrow networks form the scaffolding to construct private sector accountable care organizations and other arrangements that use alternative payment methods, such as capitation and bundled payment for episodes of care. Again, outside of Medicare, these are not required by the act, but they could develop in response to the market structures and forces that the act engenders.

Increased patient cost sharing

Another important trend affecting physicians is an increase in patient cost sharing. All insurance sold to individuals and small groups must cover the same comprehensive set of essential health benefits that are commonly covered in the large group market. However, insurers can attach markedly different levels of patient cost sharing to these comprehensive benefits, through various combinations of deductibles and copayments.

Patient cost sharing has increased substantially in recent years as employers seek to keep premiums in check. The exchanges present individuals with the same trade-off between premiums and cost sharing. In response, most consumers prefer the intermediate level of cost sharing offered by the silver plan, which requires patients on average to pay for 30% of their treatment costs. This is similar to what prevailed recently among small groups but is more cost burden than is common among large groups. Next most popular are bronze plans, which average 40% patient cost sharing, similar to the cost sharing level that had been most common in the individual market.

Insurers are also experimenting with which combination of the cost sharing elements is most appealing for consumers—for example, whether patients prefer lower deductibles that apply to all sources of treatment or higher deductibles that do not apply to primary care.

As patients sort through these options, they will increasingly turn to their physicians for better information about the actual costs of care and the availability of less costly options. Physicians are not accustomed to discussing treatment costs with patients, except perhaps to pick between generic and branded drugs. We may be at the beginning of a shift in the doctor-patient relationship that requires a much more cost conscious style of patient communication and medical decision making.

Future prospects

The act's major provisions took effect only on 1 January 2014. Therefore, it is far too early to judge whether it is a shining success or utter failure. Most likely, it will be something in between, but it remains to be seen whether its advantages exceed its shortfalls and which aspects perform better or worse. Naturally, views will differ on how its performance should be measured. However, on the basis of the act's content and structure, it should not be expected to solve the major faults of US healthcare. Instead, it can be claimed to be successful if it substantially reduces the number of people who lack insurance without accelerating the increase in medical costs. The ultimate goals of universal coverage, effective cost containment, and optimal quality will have to await additional reforms.

Conclusion

Despite ideological opposition, the Affordable Care Act is not a radical transformation of health insurance or medical practice. Most Americans keep the same kind of insurance that they had before the act was passed. About half of US states have expanded Medicaid to cover all citizens near to the poverty line. People above the poverty line without job based insurance may now turn to new health insurance exchanges to buy normal private insurance, regardless of their health condition. Government subsidies make this private insurance affordable for most people, and people who decline to purchase insurance that the government deems affordable must pay a moderate penalty. Although these insurance reforms still fall short of achieving truly universal coverage, they do achieve universal "insurability," meaning that no one must worry about becoming uninsurable.

The act also contains various provisions that have some effect on medical practice, but nothing that fundamentally changes the government's relations with hospitals and physicians. Almost all of the act's payment reforms are localized to Medicare, which already regulates payment rates, and most of these innovations are being done only on a pilot basis.

The act does not directly change how private insurers pay hospitals and physicians. Nevertheless, it has set into motion market dynamics, such as narrower networks and increased patient cost sharing, which are affecting medical practice. In response, many hospitals and physicians are forming closer and larger affiliations. Further time and study are needed to learn whether these evolutionary changes will achieve their goals without harming treatment relationships.

How to Transcend Obamacare

Avik Roy

Roy argues that the "government takeover" of health care occurred not with the 2010 passage of the Affordable Care Act, but in the twentieth-century creation of Medicare, Medicaid, and the Veterans Health Administration. These single-payer government insurance programs are, in Roy's view, both financially unsustainable and immoral infringements on economic liberty. Drawing comparisons with health care systems in Switzerland and Singapore, Roy argues that the ACA's exchanges—in which individuals can buy regulated private insurance policies—are actually more market-oriented than many Republican proposals for replacing Medicare. Thus, a genuinely conservative, free-market approach to health care reform could use the exchanges as a basis for dismantling Medicare and Medicaid and transferring retirees and the poor back into the private insurance market with tax subsidies and health-savings accounts. By removing the mandate to buy insurance and other regulatory mechanisms of the ACA, conservatives could "transcend" Obamacare without having to repeal it. The result, according to Roy and his colleagues at the libertarian Manhattan Institute, would be a less expensive, more efficient, and genuinely market-based health care system.

For four and a half years, conservatives have been adamant in their desire to repeal Obamacare. The case for repeal goes something like this:

> The Affordable Care Act is the largest expansion of the entitlement state since the 1960s. It represents a tipping point—perhaps a point of no return—in the transformation of America from a free, constitutional republic into a European-style social democracy. The law represents an unprecedented intrusion of the government into our lives, far worse than anything that has come before. Furthermore, because Obamacare is our newest entitlement, it's less entrenched than older programs, and therefore represents our best opportunity to roll back Big Government.

It's an understandable—and widely held—view. And it's an accurate one, in important ways. But there are a couple of things it gets wrong about our current situation, and that's a good thing.

It turns out that repealing Obamacare is not our only hope for reversing the triumph of the entitlement state. Indeed, there may be an even better one.

Avik Roy, "How to Transcend Obamacare," *National Review Online*, August 13, 2014.

The government takeover of health care took place in 1965, not 2010

One thing you often hear conservatives say about Obamacare is that it represents "the government takeover of the U.S. health-care system." This is not precisely true. The actual government takeover of the U.S. health-care system took place in 1965, when Lyndon Johnson signed into law the bills enacting Medicare and Medicaid: the "Great Society."

Medicare and Medicaid were—and are—single-payer, government-run health-insurance programs for the elderly and the poor, respectively. Today, nearly a third of the U.S. population is on single-payer health care, thanks to Medicare and Medicaid. These programs have profoundly distorted the U.S. health-care system, in ways that make health care more expensive for everyone else. Well before anyone had heard of Barack Obama, Medicare and Medicaid had placed America on a path to bankruptcy.

Many conservatives fear that Obamacare is a "Trojan horse" for single-payer health care in the United States. But in 2013—before Obamacare went online—93 million Americans were on either Medicaid or Medicare. Another 6 million got coverage through the Veterans Health Administration, the most socialized health-care system in the U.S. That means that nearly 100 million Americans were on single-payer health care, or its facsimile, before Obamacare went into effect.

Obamacare builds on the LBJ legacy, to be sure. The law expands the scale and scope of the Medicaid program. Overall, Obamacare increases federal health-care spending by about 15 percent. But in 2012, U.S. government entities were *already* spending $4,160 on health care for every man, woman, and child in the country. That's more than all but two other countries in the entire world.

Many European economies are freer than America's

When it comes to government health-care spending, then, the U.S. is actually worse off than most of the European countries at which we wrinkle our noses. Indeed, when it comes to economic freedom, the U.S. has fallen behind many of its European competitors.

In the 2014 edition of the Heritage Foundation's Index of Economic Freedom, the U.S. ranked 12th, behind Hong Kong, Singapore, Australia, Switzerland, New Zealand, Canada, Chile, Mauritius, Ireland, Denmark, and Estonia. One of the things that's remarkable about that list is that every single country on it save Mauritius has some form of universal health care. That's not to say that all of those countries have health-care systems that are freer than America's. Canada's, especially, is the type of single-payer rationing-dependent system that makes Americans recoil. But a few of these higher-ranked countries in the Heritage survey do have health-care systems that are more market-oriented than ours. And it behooves us to learn from what they do better.

The two most notable examples are Switzerland (No. 4 on the Heritage list) and Singapore (No. 2). Neither could be called a libertarian utopia. But both have health-care systems that spend far less than ours and deliver comparable—if not higher—quality.

While nearly a third of Americans are on single-payer health care, not one Swiss citizen is. The Swiss use a system quite similar to that of Obamacare's exchanges, in which individuals can buy subsidized and regulated private insurance plans. While the Swiss system shares many of Obamacare's unattractive features—most notably its individual mandate—Switzerland's per capita government spending on health care is less than half that of the United States.

Singapore does have a single-payer system for catastrophic coverage. But all other health spending is funneled through health-savings accounts: precisely the instrument that free-market health-policy analysts have long advocated. Because Singaporeans control their own health dollars, their government spends about a fifth of what we do on health care.

We can learn two things from Switzerland and Singapore. First, that there are countries out there with freer health-care systems than our own. Second, that it is possible to have one of the freest economies in the world while also ensuring that every citizen has health insurance.

Free-market reform must tackle Medicare and Medicaid

The impressive results of Switzerland and Singapore drive home a powerful message: that health care works best when individuals have more control over their own health spending. The Left can't bring itself to believe this; there, it's an article of faith that "disinterested" government experts will make better and more cost-efficient decisions for you than you would make for yourself.

But the examples of Switzerland and Singapore also drive home the problem with focusing solely on Obamacare. If we were to spend all our capital "repealing and replacing" Obamacare, we might not have enough left to tackle the real drivers of unsustainable single-payer health care in America: Medicare and Medicaid.

One of the ironies of our partisan health-care debate is that Paul Ryan's plan to reform Medicare employs a "Medicare exchange" that is actually to the *left* of Obamacare's. The current version of the Ryan plan contains a government-run public option, unlike the Obamacare exchanges. And the Obamacare exchanges are more aggressively means-tested than the Ryan Medicare reforms. To put it another way: If we gradually migrated future retirees onto Obamacare's exchanges, the result would actually be *more* market-oriented than that of implementing the Ryan plan for Medicare.

Migrating the Medicaid population onto exchanges would also yield dividends. Exchange-based plans would give those below the poverty line access to high-quality, private insurance and phase out single-payer public-option health insurance. Over the long run, only private insurers will have the competence and the incentive to come up with innovative, cost-efficient ways to improve health outcomes for the poor.

In short, migrating future retirees and low-income Americans onto exchanges could yield substantial benefits to the quality and cost of subsidized health coverage. But there's no reason we should accept the Obamacare exchanges as they are.

Bring freedom, choice, and affordability back to insurance markets

Instead of forcing Americans to buy insurance plans that they neither need nor want—the Obamacare way—we should convert the exchanges into real marketplaces, places where people can voluntarily buy coverage that is suited to them. We can do this by repealing Obamacare's individual and employer mandates, and by rolling back the plethora of new federal regulations and tax hikes that make insurance more costly without improving its quality.

It's possible to do all this while still ensuring that Americans with preexisting conditions can obtain coverage at a reasonable price. Indeed, in a new Manhattan Institute paper entitled "Transcending Obamacare: A Patient-Centered Plan for Near-Universal Coverage and Permanent Fiscal Solvency," we estimate that this collection of reforms could increase by 12 million the number of Americans with health insurance, over and above projected Obamacare levels.

"That sounds expensive," you might say. But using a microsimulation model from the University of Minnesota—a comparable technique to the one used by the Congressional Budget Office—we project that over three decades this approach would actually reduce federal spending by $10.5 trillion, and federal revenues by $2.5 trillion, for a net deficit reduction of $8 trillion. If the Medicare portion of the deficit savings were applied to shoring up the Medicare program, it would make the Medicare trust fund *permanently solvent*. Not merely for four or six or twelve years, but forever.

How is this possible? Several reasons. First, the Manhattan Institute plan makes consumer-driven health plans, with health-savings accounts, the centerpiece of a reformed set of state-based insurance exchanges. This drives down the cost of insurance policies for a single person by approximately 17 percent. Because health insurance is cheaper—especially for young and healthy people—more people freely choose to buy it.

Second, the plan deploys the power of private competition and choice to drive costs down. The market-driven Medicare prescription-drug benefit, for all of its flaws, spent 43 percent less in 2013 than it had been

projected to in that year. Government bean-counters have a hard time understanding that harnessing market forces keeps costs much lower than in traditional government-run programs, but it does. Furthermore, the Affordable Care Act itself specifies a long-term growth rate for exchange-based subsidies that serves as an additional control against spiraling costs.

Third, the plan focuses federal subsidies on the people who truly need them: the poor and the sick. One of the main reasons American health care is so expensive is that we spend trillions of dollars subsidizing health coverage for the well-to-do. More than four-fifths of Americans receive federally subsidized health insurance; in Switzerland, only about one-fifth do. That's the difference between an entitlement leviathan (ours) and a true safety net (theirs).

We'll get gradual reforms in the near term, big dividends in the long term

A key to this approach is to make gradual reforms today that pay off down the road. The plan's deficit savings in the first decade are minimal: $29 billion from 2016 to 2025. But over time, as the plan shifts downward the growth of health-care entitlements, the rate of savings grows: $1.3 trillion in decade two, and $6.7 trillion in decade three.

While the Manhattan Institute plan is perfectly compatible with the "repeal and replace" framework favored by Republicans—you simply repeal Obamacare and replace it with the structure outlined above—the plan doesn't *require* the total repeal of Obamacare.

As a result, this approach solves a political conundrum for Republicans: how to bring our health-care entitlements under control, while avoiding the political pitfalls that would come from repealing the health-insurance plans that, according to the CBO, 36 million Americans will be on by 2017. If there's one thing that Obamacare has taught us, it's that Americans don't like it when you disrupt their health-insurance arrangements. Any reforms that conservatives seek to implement must respect that sentiment, and reflect the principles of voluntarism and incrementalism.

The good news is that we can do this. We can solve the problem that conservatives care about more than any other—that America is broke—while actually making the health-care system work *better* for everyone. The poor and the sick and the elderly will benefit from higher-quality, fiscally sustainable health coverage. And average tax-paying Americans will benefit from affordable insurance, lower long-term tax liabilities, and a consumer-driven health-care system that is centered around them rather than the bureaucracy.

In 1981, in a speech at the University of Notre Dame, Ronald Reagan said, "The years ahead are great ones for this country, for the cause of freedom and the spread of civilization. The West won't contain Communism; it will transcend Communism. It won't bother to denounce it; it will dismiss it as some bizarre chapter in human history whose last pages are even now being written."

His point was that we as Americans shouldn't spend our time hoping and waiting for Communism to fail. Instead, we should work to ensure that capitalism *succeeds*, and thereby leave the Soviet economy in the dust.

It's time for conservatives to bring Reagan's lesson to health reform. Instead of waiting for Obamacare to fail, we should instead devote ourselves to liberating the *entire* U.S. health-care system from government control. If we do that, and demonstrate the value of our economic principles with tangible results, it won't matter whether we have formally repealed Obamacare. We will have transcended it, and solved the most important policy problem of our time: that of unsustainable government spending. If we want our children and grandchildren to inherit the country we grew up in, we have no time to waste.

Some Lessons from the Affordable Care Act's First Five Years

John P. Geyman

Geyman argues that although the Affordable Care Act has effected some positive changes by reducing the ranks of the uninsured, it has failed to restrain health care spending, make insurance genuinely affordable, or improve the quality of care. These failures are largely attributable, in Geyman's view, to a for-profit insurance industry that fragments risk pools, wastes billions on marketing and bureaucratic overhead, and chronically underinsures patients in the pursuit of shareholder dividends. Geyman argues that a single-payer form of national health insurance is the only way the United States will be able to create a fiscally solvent and morally sound health care system. By eliminating the administrative waste of medical underwriting and allowing the government to negotiate drug prices down to the levels charged in European countries, a single-payer system would generate enough savings to cover the uninsured and expand benefits. Far from constituting a liberal bureaucratic solution, Geyman argues that a single-payer system should appeal to conservatives in the United States—as it does to conservatives in the rest of the developed world—for its clinical and fiscal efficiency, its intolerance for free-riding, and its simplified administrative infrastructure.

From John P. Geyman, "A Five-Year Assessment of the Affordable Care Act: Market Forces Still Trump the Common Good in U.S. Health Care," *International Journal of Health Services* 45, no. 2 (April 2015): 209–225. Copyright © 2015 by SAGE Publications, Inc. Reprinted by permission of SAGE Publications, Inc.

The ACA's track record at age five is decidedly mixed. On the one hand, it has accomplished these positive changes:

- Government-sponsored exchanges have been established in every state, whereby the uninsured can shop for coverage.

- About 8 million have done so, 57 percent of whom gained insurance for the first time.

- About 7 million have gained new Medicaid coverage.

- Parents can now keep their children on their policies until age 26.

- Some new funding has been provided for community health centers, together with some increased reimbursement for primary care physicians on a temporary basis.

Notwithstanding these gains, ongoing problems remain, some exacerbated by the ACA:

- Many employers are shifting from a defined benefit to a defined contribution system, while others are shifting employees to the exchanges or dropping coverage altogether.

- Insurers are offering policies of decreasing value and raising premiums with little restraint.

- Narrow networks are limiting choice of physicians and hospitals across the country as expanding hospital systems gain near-monopoly market shares.

- The shortage of primary care physicians limits access for millions of the newly insured, especially for those on Medicaid with its low reimbursement rates.

- There is no evidence yet that the ACA has improved quality of care.

- Administrative bureaucracy, especially on the private side, has increased exponentially.

- New profitable markets have arisen that have increased prices and costs throughout the market-based system.

- By 2019, when the ACA is fully implemented, there will still be about 36 million uninsured (including nearly 5 million in the Medicaid"coverage gap"in opt-out states), plus an unknown number who choose not to participate in the exchanges, often because of costs.

What can we learn from the ACA's experience to date? The following lessons already stand out.

1. Health care "reform" through the ACA was framed and hijacked by corporate stakeholders

Based on ideology and political forces, the architects of the ACA never questioned whether the deregulated private marketplace could bring needed reforms. More fundamental questions were not asked, such as whether health care is a right or privilege based on ability to pay, whether universal access to care is the overriding goal, or whether health care is just a commodity for sale on an open market.

The political process was commandeered by corporate money and conflicts of interest among the drafters of the legislation. Lobbyists also played a major role in guiding the more than 2,000-page bill to its final passage. By the time of its enactment, about 4,525 lobbyists, eight for every member of Congress, had been hired at a cost of $1.2 billion.

2. You can't contain health care costs by permitting for-profit health care industries to pursue their business "ethic" in a deregulated marketplace

With new markets through health care exchanges and expansion of Medicaid, together with friendly federal subsidies and no effective price controls, corporate stakeholders have thrived under the ACA. Prices and costs continue to escalate for hospitals, physicians, and drug and medical device manufacturers as increasing consolidation and market power go forward among hospital systems and providers. One venture capitalist promoting investment opportunities for private exchanges under the ACA sees the likelihood to "turn chaos into gold." In fact, health care stocks soared by almost 40 percent in 2013, the highest of any sector in the S&P 500.

3. You can't reform the delivery system without reforming the financing system

It was a naïve and ill-informed approach to think that we could cover more people at more affordable costs while retaining, even subsidizing, a largely for profit, multi-payer financing system. Insurers are gaming the new system in new ways, still trying to avoid sicker enrollees, maximize their profits, and keep their shareholders happy. UnitedHealth Group, the nation's largest insurer, has recently reported a drop in its medical-loss ratio to

79.9 percent and higher earning projections based on the increasing prevalence of high-deductible health plans and provider contracts linking reimbursement to performance.

4. The private health insurance industry does not offer enough value to be bailed out by government

The government has been more than friendly to the insurance industry through a number of perks, including longstanding tax exemptions for employer-sponsored insurance, overpayments to Medicare Advantage plans, and, with the ACA, permissive provisions including subsidized premiums through the exchanges, expansion of private and public markets, and a new "risk corridor system" protecting insurers from losses in the new marketplace. But these are some of the many reasons that the industry does not warrant a bailout by government at taxpayer expense:

- The overhead of private Medicare Advantage plans averages 19 percent versus 1.5 to 2 percent for traditional Medicare. The administrative overhead of the 1,300 private insurers in the United States is more than five times higher than that of the single-payer program in two Canadian provinces.

- We are seeing an epidemic of *underinsurance* and high levels of cost sharing, with some deductibles ranging as high as $8,000 to $10,000 per year. The actuarial value of plans through the ACA's exchanges range from 60 percent to 90 percent (with silver plans at 70% the most common), while the insurance industry is pushing for copper plans with an actuarial value of only 50 percent.

- Private insurers game the system for more profits instead of service to patients. As examples: Medicare Advantage plans have commonly claimed that enrollees are sicker than they are, thereby receiving $122.5 billion in overpayments since 2004 (35); some insurers are marketing short-term plans that last less than 12 months, evading any of the ACA's requirements.

- In the last three years, 32 executives of the country's largest for-profit health insurers have received a total of $548.4 million in cash and stock options.

- Accountability and regulation of insurance premiums remain lax and vary widely from state to state.

5. In order to achieve the most efficient health insurance coverage, we need the largest possible risk pool to spread risk and avoid adverse selection

The larger and more diverse the risk pool is, the more efficient insurance can be in having healthier people share the costs of sicker people at affordable costs for everyone. But the ACA has perpetuated and further exacerbated fragmentation of risk pools in the United States. We cannot ignore the 20-80 Rule, which states that 20 percent of the population accounts for almost 80 percent of all health care spending. Despite assurances of the ACA's supporters, there appears to be no way that it can develop a big enough risk pool to avoid adverse selection, given the motivations of private insurers and the predictable behavior of markets. This is especially true since many younger, healthier people are not signing up on the exchanges, one-third of men between the ages of 50 to 64 have chosen to remain uninsured, and at least 12 million people are expected to file for one or another kind of exemption from the individual mandate.

Why the Affordable Care Act Should Be Replaced By National Health Insurance

The ACA, based as it is on subsidized continuation of a large private insurance industry, brings us restricted choices of physicians and hospitals, and in some cases of insurers, such as in rural areas. We still fall short of universal access, are growing the ranks of the underinsured, have little cost containment, and still restrict some essential services based on ability to pay. Consumer protection from high costs of care remains elusive. A recent study by the Kaiser Family Foundation found that one in three Americans *with health insurance* still have difficulty paying their medical bills. The study identified many ways that insured people still face burdensome medical debt, including through in-network cost sharing, out-of-network costs, "inadvertent" out-of-network care, health plan coverage limits or exclusions, and unaffordable premiums.

Although just halfway through its original legislative life (2010–2019), the ACA has already set in place trends that we can assume will fail to meet its original goals—provide near-universal access, contain costs, make health care affordable, and improve its quality.

It is clear that more fundamental reform is needed, especially in financing of U.S. health care.

Economic Imperative

Given the enormous amount of money already going to inefficiency, administrative waste, and profits in today's health care system, there is plenty of money available to fund NHI and still achieve other savings. NHI will both save money and contain costs. It will provide universal coverage for all Americans, remove financial barriers to care, cover all essential health care services, provide free choice of physicians and hospitals anywhere in the country, cut costs by bulk purchasing as already takes place in the Veterans Administration system, and dramatically reduce administrative waste. It will initiate a transition process away from the business "ethic" toward a service-oriented ethic.

A classic 2013 study by Gerald Friedman, professor of economics at the University of Massachusetts, shows how this can be accomplished. He concludes that enactment of H.R. 676: The Expanded and Improved Medicare for All Act now in the U.S. Congress would save an estimated $592 billion annually by cutting administrative waste of the private health insurance industry ($476 billion) and reducing pharmaceutical prices to European levels ($116 billion). These savings would be enough to cover all 44 million uninsured and upgrade benefits for all other Americans, including dental and long-term care. Savings would also cover $51 billion in transition costs, such as retraining displaced workers and phasing out investor-owned, for-profit delivery systems over a 15-year period. About $154 billion of the savings could be applied to deficit reduction. Regressive funding sources that totaled more than $1.72 billion in 2014 would be replaced by a progressive taxation system....

The payroll tax would be the main tax for all Americans with annual incomes below $225,000, amounting to $900 for those with incomes below $60,000, $6,000 for those making $100,000, and $12,000 for those with incomes of $200,000. Most Americans would pay less for health care than they do under the ACA, and only 5 percent of Americans would pay more for insurance under NHI.

NHI would bring us public financing, with one big risk pool, coupled with a private delivery system. We could expect improvement in quality of care as investor ownership is phased out, since investor ownership has long been associated with higher costs and lower quality, whether for hospitals, health maintenance organizations, dialysis centers, nursing homes, or mental health centers.

As physicians and hospitals transition to a not-for-profit system, the profit motive disappears from the equation, allowing physicians to practice evidence-based medicine without today's perverse business incentives and administrative hassle in dealing with many payers. Business would likewise do well with NHI, being relieved of the burden of providing employer-sponsored insurance, paying less than it does now, gaining a healthier workforce, and being able to compete better in global markets with other countries that have one or another form of universal health insurance.

The Moral Case for National Health Insurance

The dominant culture in the U.S. market-based health care system, unchanged by the ACA, still treats healthcare services as commodities, just products for sale on an open market. When one among us has a major accident or serious illness threatening life and/or bankruptcy, we are brought up short in realizing how unfair, inhumane, and cruel our system can be. Too often, there is no safety net to catch us.

In sharp contrast to almost all other advanced countries around the world, health care as a human right remains controversial in the United States, especially among conservatives. Within our system, it is still a privilege based on ability to pay.

Conservatives in many other advanced countries around the world have long favored the concept of health care as a human right. Donald Light, Ph.D., a Fellow at the University of Pennsylvania's Center for Bioethics and author of *Benchmarks for Fairness for Health Care Reform*, has found that conservatives and business interests in every other industrialized country have supported universal access to necessary health care on the basis of four conservative moral principles: anti-free riding, personal integrity, equal opportunity, and just sharing. He suggests these 10 guidelines for conservatives to hold to these principles:

1. Everyone is covered, and everyone contributes in proportion to his or her income.

2. Decisions about all matters are open and publicly debated. Accountability for costs, quality and

value of providers, suppliers, and administrators is public.

3. Contributions do not discriminate by type of illness or ability to pay.

4. Coverage does not discriminate by type of illness or ability to pay.

5. Coverage responds first to medical need and suffering.

6. Nonfinancial barriers by class, language, education, and geography are to be minimized.

7. Providers are paid fairly and equitably, taking into account their local circumstances.

8. Clinical waste is minimized through public health, self-care, prevention, strong primary care, and identification of unnecessary procedures.

9. Financial waste is minimized through simplified administrative arrangements and strong bargaining for good value.

10. Choice is maximized in a common playing field where 90–95 percent of payments go toward necessary and efficient health services and only 5–10 percent to administration.

It is remarkable that these commonsense guidelines have not gained consensus within the business and corporate class in the United States as health care becomes ever more expensive, inefficient, unfair, wasteful, and beyond the reach of a growing part of the population. We seem to have a societal blind spot in failing to seriously address this problem.

Conclusion

The ACA built upon the flaws of our market-based system and, quite predictably, is failing to contain costs and provide broad access to affordable, quality health care. Corporate interests still trump the common good in U.S. health care. More fundamental reform is required based upon universal access to health care as a right. A broad-based social movement will be needed to support a larger role of responsible government in enacting NHI and protecting it from privatization. Until that happens, we can expect continued turmoil and increasing public backlash to a dysfunctional system that places profits over service. It is just a matter of time before the country will be forced to choose between discredited, deregulated markets and a more efficient single-payer system that ensures access to essential health care for all Americans.

DECISION SCENARIOS

The questions following each decision scenario are intended to prompt reflection and discussion. In deciding how to answer them, you should consider the information provided in the Social Context and Case Presentations, as well as in the Briefing Session. You should also make use of the ethical theories and principles presented in Part VI: Foundations of Bioethics, and the arguments offered in the relevant readings in this chapter.

DECISION SCENARIO 1

Free Rider

"I'd like you to come back in a week and let me have another look at you," Dr. Jane Mallory said. "I suspect you've got a form of inflammatory bowel disease, and I want to see how you do with the drugs and diet. If we can't get the disease under control, you might have to have surgery."

"I'm sorry, Doctor," Dan Hinshaw said. "I just don't have the money. I don't have health insurance and I won't be able to get it until the next enrollment period. I'll come back then."

"Technically, Mr. Hinshaw, the Affordable Care Act requires that you have insurance," Mallory objected. "If you can't afford it, you can get a subsidy to reduce your premiums."

"I know, but I figured it was cheaper to pay the tax penalty," Hinshaw said. "Even with the subsidy, insurance was going to cost me almost two thousand dollars a year and I've always been very healthy. I didn't think the government had the right to tell me what to do."

"But by waiting to get treated, you're probably going to cost yourself—and the taxpayers—even more."

1. Critics of the Affordable Care Act often object to its requirement that everyone have health insurance. What arguments can be advanced for and against this requirement?

2. Would it be reasonable to drop the insurance requirement for adults? If so, should society provide care to someone in need because he decided he didn't want to spend money on insurance? What impact might such "free riding" have on the solvency of the insurance system as a whole? (See Social Context: The Affordable Care Act for more.)

DECISION SCENARIO 2

Custodial Care

"Let me explain it to you, Mr. Faust," Dr. Charles Young said. "Although your wife is covered by Medicare, we cannot pay for the care she is receiving in the nursing home. As an Alzheimer's patient, she's getting 'custodial' care, and that is explicitly excluded from Medicare coverage. Do you have any insurance?"

"My wife and I both have coverage through my job. But the benefits office told me exactly the same thing: My policy doesn't cover long-term, chronic, or custodial care."

"I'm sorry to hear that," Young said. "That means that you'll have to pay the total cost of the care yourself."

"Where can a sales rep get that kind of money?" Faust said. "A nursing home will cost me fifty or sixty thousand dollars a year. If I sell our house and use all our savings, I could pay for a year or two, but then I wouldn't have anything to live on myself. How could I pay rent? How could I eat?"

"The only alternative is to divest yourself of your assets so you cannot be held legally responsible for paying for your wife's care. Then you and she can both get assistance under the Medicaid program."

"Then I have to literally become a pauper before I can get any help?"

"I'm sorry to say that's true."

1. Should a national health care program pay for the custodial care required by patients with Alzheimer's and similar diseases?

2. Should family members (adult children or grandchildren) be required by law to help pay the health care expenses of other family members?

3. Should people with incomes adequate to cover the cost of long-term custodial care be ineligible to participate in any federally supported long-term-care insurance plan?

DECISION SCENARIO 3

Rationing or Realism?

Khaled Jan was finishing up charts in his office at Baruch Cancer Center, when Linda Carlucci, the local rep for BioQuest, knocked twice and walked in.

"You forgot to pick up your Tralpaz mug, Khaled." Carlucci placed a stylish blue coffee mug on his desk. "We designed these so that the word *cancer* disappears when you fill it with hot water. Pretty cool, hunh?"

"BioQuest is nothing if not cool," Jan said. "But I need to tell you, Linda, that the Pharmacy Committee has decided not to list Tralpaz in the hospital's formulary."

"Why not? Are you questioning our interpretation of the research?"

"Not at all," Jan said. "We agree that a course of Tralpaz extends the median survival of a patient with advanced colorectal cancer by forty-three days."

"Then what's the problem, Khaled?"

"The problem is that a three-month course of Tralpaz costs almost $80,000. We don't feel it's right to charge patients—or the Medicare taxpayers—so much for so little benefit. Desperate patients want to believe these drugs are cures, and a lot of them end up paying tens of thousands out of pocket." He slid the coffee mug back across his desk toward Carlucci.

"Who are you to tell a dying patient that six extra weeks aren't worth eighty grand, Khaled?" Carlucci smiled and pushed the mug back a few inches toward Jan.

"Linda, we both know there are already two other drugs in the formulary that provide the same meager benefit." Jan started packing up his briefcase. "Look, I don't blame BioQuest for trying to maximize profits for shareholders—although frankly, I don't see how your profit margins could get any bigger. But the price of cancer drugs has doubled in the past decade. You guys don't feel any real market pressure because Medicare is legally obligated to pay for everything the FDA approves and can't negotiate prices. We decided we had to take a stand."

"But that's rationing, Khaled. Does the hospital want to get a reputation for that?"

"Maybe not, Linda. But BioQuest is also rationing. You just do it based on people's ability to pay."

1. Is the Pharmacy Committee's decision not to list Tralpaz a form of rationing? Are high drug prices that prevent the poor or underinsured from accessing them a form of rationing? Is either practice unethical or unnecessary?

2. A traditional, unwritten rule among American physicians is that they should never consider the cost of a drug or treatment before prescribing it, but only whether it is beneficial to their patients. Should the rule change?

3. Assuming it is possible to assign a monetary value to forty-three extra days of life, is $80,000 a fair price for it? Would it be a fair price for an extra year of life? What if the side effects are severe?

DECISION SCENARIO 4

Not the Best Option

"We can offer you a couple of options," Dr. Kenton said.

"Whatever will make the pain stay away," Bill Czahz said.

"We can do coronary artery bypass surgery. Two arteries are involved, so for you it would be a double bypass."

"This isn't something experimental?"

"No, it's a well-established procedure with a good safety record. About 80 percent who have surgery get rid of their angina."

"I don't much like the idea of being opened up, but I'd do most anything to stop those chest pains."

"The other option is that we can treat you medically. We can try you on some drugs and shift your diet, and monitor the results. People we treat this way do a bit better in terms of life expectancy than those treated surgically. That's slightly misleading, though, because those who have surgery usually have worse cases of the disease."

"What about the angina pains?" Czahz asked.

"There's the problem. Medical treatment can do something about the pains, but it's not as effective as surgery."

"So I'll take the surgery."

"Do you have any insurance other than the Basic Care policy?" Kenton asked.

"That's all I have." Czahz shrugged. "I never saw the need for more."

"Now you will." Kenton sighed. "Basic Care won't cover the cost of bypass surgery. It's an optional procedure under the HHS guidelines, and they won't kick in the extra money to pay for it."

"So I have to make up the difference myself?"

"Right," Kenton said. "You'd have to come up with about fifteen thousand in cash."

"Dr. Kenton, there's no way I can do that."

"Okay, then. I just wanted you to know what the possibilities were. We can put you on a treatment program, and I'm sure you'll do just fine."

"But what about the angina pain?"

"We'll do what we can," Kenton said.

1. Some critics of the ACA have promoted "catastrophic care for everyone" as a cheaper alternative. But such basic packages often decline to cover or charge high co-insurance for some effective but expensive treatments. (The same criticism has been leveled at some of the cheaper plans offered on the ACA exchanges.) If it is not economically feasible to guarantee the best possible care for everyone, would it be better to provide no care

to some who cannot pay, deny the best treatment to some who can pay, or offer several "tiers" of insurance, as does the ACA?

2. Is a multi-tiered health care system compatible with a single-payer system? What are the advantages and disadvantages of each approach?

DECISION SCENARIO 5

Should Women Pay Higher Premiums?

"Did everything look okay with the benefit package, Ms. Rudzautak? And may I call you Anna?" Rafael Soares flipped open Rudzautak's H.R. file and started checking the paperwork for signatures.

"Sure, Rafael," Rudzautak said. "The coverage looks good. There is just one thing…." She paused, and Soares glanced up at her over the top of his glasses. "Well, I was just talking with Azmi Lao—he's another recent hire…."

"Azmi's a great guy."

"Definitely. Anyway, we were comparing notes and it looks like we selected the exact same plan, with the same coinsurance and deductible. But I'm getting charged almost $150 dollars more per month. Perhaps there was some mistake?"

"No mistake at all Anna. In all our plans, premiums for women typically run 30 to 40 percent higher than those for men."

"I thought that was banned under Obamacare."

"It was, but our plans have been 'grandfathered' in, so they don't have to change yet." Soares closed the file and cleared his throat. "Look, Anna, the difference might seem unfair, but statistics show that women, on average, use more health care than men. You also live longer than we do, so you have more time to access care."

"But those are just averages, Rafael."

"All insurance is based on averages. Think of it this way: if I wish to drive a Lexus and eat caviar, everyone agrees that I should pay more for those luxuries than someone who is content to drive a Civic and eat hot dogs, right?"

"Sure, Rafael. But if I get breast cancer, it's not because I *wish* to use more expensive health care, it's because I *need* to use it. Health care isn't a normal commodity like cars or food. Unless I'm willing to die early, I can't just stop consuming it or choose 'discount' chemotherapy. Isn't that the whole point of trying to make sure everyone gets health insurance?"

1. Before implementation of the ACA, American women's premiums frequently exceeded men's by as much 48 percent, with the result that women paid a combined $1 billion more than men each year for the same plans. Since statistics suggest that women do, on average, use more health care than men, was such "gender rating" appropriate?

2. Does fairness demand that people likely to consume more health care be charged higher premiums? If so, should insurers be allowed to charge steeper rates or even deny coverage to people with expensive preexisting conditions such as asthma or diabetes?

3. Make a list of some ways that health care is, and is not, like other commodities. Also assess how the health care market is, and is not, like the market for other goods and services. How should such considerations influence our national health insurance policies?

Part V

Challenges

Medicine in a Pluralistic Society

CHAPTER CONTENTS

CASES AND CONTEXTS

SOCIAL CONTEXT
Women, Men, and Biomedical Research

In January of 2013, the U.S. Food and Drug Administration made an unprecedented announcement. Twenty years after its approval of the insomnia drug zolpidem (better known by its brand name Ambien), the FDA had decided to require all manufacturers of the drug to cut the recommended dose for women in half. The decision followed pharmacokinetic studies demonstrating that average blood plasma levels of zolpidem in female patients were approximately 50 percent higher than those in males, independent of body weight. Eight hours after taking the drug, women were also five times more likely than men to have plasma concentrations of zolpidem over 50 ng/mL—the level at which the drug can seriously impair daily activities such as driving. The policy shift made zolpidem the first prescription drug in the United States with differential doses for men and women, and constituted a major correction in clinical practice. But many scientists and physicians were perplexed that the problem had not been discovered years earlier.

"How did it happen that for twenty some years, women, millions of them, were essentially overdosing on Ambien?" asked Larry Cahill, a neuroscientist at the University of California–Irvine.

As Cahill and others soon pointed out, it was not so surprising that the most popular sleep medication in the country—prescribed 40 million times each year—was being incorrectly dosed for half the population. Disparities in drug reactions, along with a host of other differences between men and women, are commonly not reflected in medical research and practice. One reason is that until the early 1990s, women were systematically excluded from most clinical trials—and as a result, most drugs and treatment regimens were developed on the basis of studies conducted with male subjects alone. (Zolpidem was approved by the FDA in 1992.)

Even today, the use of male-only research cohorts in animal studies continues to be the norm in roughly 80 percent of research across a wide range of disciplines. A similar imbalance exists in the study of tissue cultures that are genetically male. Although women now make up more than half of the subjects in NIH research, they are still starkly underrepresented in the more than half of all clinical trials that are carried out by pharmaceutical companies and device manufacturers.

The vast majority of medical research still fails to analyze outcomes by sex, and the NIH awards only about 3 percent of its annual grants to research on sex differences.

Such failures to account for sex can have a negative health impact on both men and women. They can leave us in the dark about key differences in life expectancy, adverse drug reactions, disease progression, and the provision of care. At the same time, they can mask the way in which such differential outcomes may also be a result of *gender*—the socially enforced patterns of behavior, bias, and expectation that shape much of the lived experience of being a man or a woman.

But despite decades of lobbying by advocates for both men's and women's health, a 2010 Institute of Medicine Report found that "a lack of analyzing and reporting of data separately for males and females continues to limit researchers' ability to identify potentially important sex and gender differences." To better understand this situation, it will be helpful to take a step back and look at the recent history of sex- and gender-based policies in modern medicine.

History

In 1977, the FDA issued a set of guidelines that formally excluded all women "of child-bearing potential" from participating in Phase I and Phase II clinical trials. The guidelines were ostensibly rooted in concern about severe fetal anomalies that had been caused by prenatal exposure to the sedative thalidomide and the synthetic hormone DES—although neither of those public health crises involved women's participation in clinical research. At the same time, the 1977 policy simply formalized a long-standing set of practices with regard to male and female patients.

For much of modern medical history, it was taken for granted that the most effective treatments for men were also the best treatments for women. The "70 kilogram white male" was famously assumed to be the anatomical norm for the human species, and women's bodies were primarily understood through their reproductive differences from those of men. Women were thus typically regarded as a subspecialty of medicine, rather than constituting half of the data set required for any comprehensive understanding of human health.

In an era when women were largely excluded from civil society and led lives that were circumscribed (and often shortened) by unplanned pregnancies, childbirth, and caregiving, perhaps such an approach was not surprising. Such myopia was also influenced by the fact that nearly all physicians and researchers were white men.

But even after changing social norms, better contraception, and reduced maternal mortality rates allowed women a greater role in public life, the medical establishment still often viewed women's health care primarily in terms of their reproductive capacities. In the 1950s and 1960s, the specialties physicians sometimes called "bikini medicine"—obstetrics and gynecology—saw rapid growth, even as "normal" medical research was still focused on male subjects. The reasons cited for this avoidance of female research subjects were varied, but the most common arguments involved potential harm to offspring (as embodied in the 1977 FDA policy) or the notion that hormones associated with ovarian cycles would render research cohorts that included women too complicated or heterogeneous.

Women's Health

In the 1970s and 1980s, a reinvigorated women's health movement began to question the rationale for excluding women from medical research and to denounce its practical consequences. They argued that men are not free from hormonal complexity and that if menstruation really impacted research so dramatically, it was all the more reason women should be included—since otherwise physicians would end up informally experimenting on women in clinical practice. With regard to reproduction, women's health advocates found no reason to think that male sperm and testes are any more resistant to cytotoxic chemicals than female ova and ovaries, and they questioned why no one seemed concerned about the reproductive activities of male research subjects. With regard to the remote chance of a research subject becoming pregnant by accident, they argued that paternalistic concern for fetal safety did not justify second-guessing women's decision to participate in research—a choice that men were allowed to make without anyone asking about how it might affect their offspring. They also reminded researchers that pregnant women suffer from illness and receive treatments, and thus deserve to have confidence that those treatments are evidence-based.

Perhaps most persuasively, women's health advocates pointed to large, influential studies on topics such as aging, heart disease, and strokes that had not included female subjects but were nevertheless being used to guide clinical practice for both women and men. The landmark Baltimore Longitudinal Study on "Normal Human Aging," for example, included no women from 1958 until 1978—because, its deputy director claimed, the study's facilities initially had only one restroom. Similarly, a major Harvard School of Public Health study of stroke and heart attack risk involved forty-five thousand male subjects and no women, despite widespread knowledge that cardiovascular disease killed at least as many women as men. (The disease is, in fact, the leading cause of death for women, and since 1984, it has killed more women than men each year.) Other research on heart disease, such as the massive Multiple Risk Factor Intervention Trial, also studied tens of thousands of men and no women.

A tipping point came in 1982, when a groundbreaking study called the Physicians' Health Survey was met with both acclaim and ridicule. The study, led by Charles Hennekens, convincingly demonstrated that small, regular doses of aspirin could reduce the likelihood of a first heart attack by as much as 30 percent. But the scope of this important finding for preventive medicine was also called into question by the fact that all 22,071 of its research subjects were men.

"We didn't want to neglect women," Hennekens said, in the face of intense criticism, "but we couldn't study them in that population." Indeed, at the time the Physicians Health Survey had begun, only 10 percent of Hennekens's candidate subject pool—registered U.S. physicians between forty and eighty-four years old—were women.

Like much of the research mentioned above, Hennekens's study appears to be less a sexist plot to exclude women than a result of a complicated interaction between medical science and the broader cultural structures in which it operates—a type of interaction we will encounter throughout this chapter. Sometimes this interaction can be benign or positive; at other times it can profoundly mislead medical practice and distort scientific results.

Harms to Women

In the early 2000s, several multiyear studies involving thousands of subjects concluded that aspirin's heart attack prevention effect for men could *not* be reproduced in women—although it did offer women some protection against stroke. The finding was significant because daily aspirin use is associated with serious side effects, such as a substantially increased risk of gastrointestinal bleeding. But confirmation that the conclusions of the Physicians' Health Survey could not, in fact, be simply generalized to female patients turned out to be just one of many ways that the neglect of sex and gender differences in medicine can have serious consequences for patients.

A 2001 General Accounting Office review of drugs withdrawn during the late 1990s found that eight out of ten caused statistically greater health risks for women than for men. In recent decades, a large number of antibiotics, antihistamines, and cholesterol drugs have also been shown to trigger potentially fatal heart arrhythmias and other serious side effects more frequently in women than in men.

Many of these differential outcomes appear to be rooted in the fact that these drugs and treatments were not studied using female subjects—from animal studies all the way through Phase III trials. For example, in the 1980s, physicians began recommending hormone replacement therapy (HRT) to prevent heart attacks in women, even though data about its safety and efficacy were scarce. When studies were finally conducted, they showed that the hormone turned out to significantly increase a woman's risk of dying of a heart attack. In other cases, differential outcomes between men and women appear to be based on gender "typecasting"—vague cultural assumptions, for instance, that heart attacks are a "male problem" while disorders of the reproductive system are a "female problem."

Up until the 1980s, for example, heart disease research focused almost exclusively on the symptoms men typically displayed—such as crushing chest pain, shortness of breath, and pain radiating down the left arm. But since then, multiple studies have not only found that more women than men die of heart disease, but also that their symptoms were being missed or undertreated because they did not conform to this "male model." Women's heart attacks often involve shortness of breath, abdominal pain, nausea, and weakness, and research has shown that both women and their physicians have a tendency to dismiss these symptoms as psychosomatic or noncardiac in nature.

A 2008 study found that 62 percent of physicians were likely to refer men with classic heart attack symptoms to a cardiologist, but only 30 percent would make such a referral for a woman with the same symptoms. Only 13 percent would prescribe heart medication for the woman, compared to 47 percent for the man. Similarly, earlier research showed that men with heart disease symptoms were substantially more likely than women to receive a diagnostic cardiac catheterization. Even when such diagnostic procedures were performed and abnormal results appeared, women were twice as likely as men to have their symptoms attributed to psychological or noncardiac causes.

"In training, we were taught to be on the lookout for hysterical females who come to the emergency room," said Adam Splaver, a prominent Florida cardiologist, echoing the explanations of many other physicians over the years. In the 1980s, researchers found a tendency among physicians to underdiagnose or dismiss women at risk of lung cancer. Others determined that women with kidney disease severe enough to require dialysis were as much as 30 percent less likely to receive a kidney transplant than men with the same medical profile.

Many of these early findings were summed up in a 1990 report by the American Medical Association's Council on Ethical and Judicial Affairs. The council found evidence that "non-biological or non-clinical factors" as well as "social or cultural biases" were likely influencing clinical practice. (Similar patterns of underdiagnosis and undertreatment were also found with regard to nonwhite patients—a topic we will address later in this chapter.) The report concluded that "medical treatments for women are based on a male model, regardless of the fact that women may react differently to treatments than men or that some diseases manifest themselves differently in women than in men." The authors suggested that such distortions in practice and perception "may be doing a disservice to both sexes."

Harms to Men

Even though men's disease symptoms may still be taken more seriously than women's, the "male model" for research and treatment does not appear to make men healthier than women. The overall mortality rate for men is 41 percent higher than it is for women, and although the "life expectancy gap" appears to be slowly closing in the developed world, American women still live, on average, five years longer than American men. Men are also more likely than women to die from the nation's leading causes of death such as cancer, diabetes, stroke, and kidney disease. Men are more than twice as likely as women to die from accidents or HIV/AIDS, and roughly four times more likely than women to commit suicide or be murdered. They are dramatically more likely than women to have autism, inguinal hernias, and aortic aneurysms, and heart disease tends to strike them earlier in life.

Many of these differential outcomes result from behavioral differences that appear to be linked to our culture's gender norms and (possibly) to hormones such as testosterone that are more prevalent in men. Studies have shown men far more prone than women to risky and violent behaviors, which may explain why they continue to die from accidents and HIV at twice the rate women do. Men are also more likely than women to smoke, to binge drink, and to disregard long-standing dietary recommendations regarding vegetables, red meat, and cholesterol intake. Finally, men are more likely to skip regular medical exams and to delay medical care—with some studies showing a rate of preventative care visits and annual exams twice as high for women as for men. Men are also significantly less likely than women to have health insurance, in part because they are less likely to be single parents.

Although there is little evidence that such differences are the result of discrimination against men or "reverse sexism," that is no justification for ignoring the harmful impact that gender-based expectations (and perhaps biology itself) appear to have on men. The social stigmatization that men still frequently face if they appear physically vulnerable, hypochondriacal, or act "like a girl" can constitute a very serious harm if it prevents them from seeking medical care or induces them to take unnecessary risks with their health. Furthermore, the notion that reproductive health is a "women's issue"—along with the superior organization and fundraising of women's health advocates—has produced some disparities in education and research.

Major federal programs such as the Women's Health Initiative have conducted groundbreaking research on the efficacy of treatments such as calcium and vitamin D supplements, estrogen replacement therapy, and low-fat diets—overturning years of wishful thinking and anecdotal assumptions about women's health. Dozens of federally funded outreach programs aim to inform women about the risks and prevention of breast and cervical cancer. But far fewer programs conduct research on men's reproductive health, inform men about the importance of exams for testicular and prostate cancer, or specifically encourage men to improve their health through better diet and exercise.

Men's health advocates estimate that research funding for breast cancer exceeds that for prostate cancer by as much as 40 percent, despite a comparable number of prostate and breast cancer diagnoses each year. (On the other hand, breast cancer kills roughly 13,000 more Americans each year than prostate cancer does, and breast cancer typically afflicts women at a much earlier stage of life than prostate cancer does men.) Although there is considerable debate about whether men are currently over- or underrepresented in clinical research, single-sex clinical trials for women do appear to have outpaced single-sex clinical trials for men—something that should cause concern given the poor state of men's health in general.

Different, Not Opposite

Despite lingering conflicts between men's and women's health advocates over resources and research, it is clear that both groups benefit when research and treatment becomes sensitive to biological and physiological differences between men and women. Indeed, an accurate accounting of sexual differences in biomedical research seems essential to the larger societal goals of *precision* or *personalized medicine*, which aims to tailor treatments to the specific genetic and physiological disease states of individuals.

"You really can't get to personalized medicine until you at least split the population in half," notes Teresa Woodruff, a professor of obstetrics and gynecology at Northwestern University. (See Social Context: Precision Medicine in Chapter 3 for more on this topic.)

But the deeper that researchers dig into biological and physiological differences between men and women, the more complicated and unpredictable those differences often appear to be. For example, the X and Y chromosomes that (partly) influence the external characteristics we typically think of as male and female have distinctive evolutionary histories, which go on to shape the complex regulatory roles these different chromosomes play in men's and women's cells. It is sometimes suggested that men may have greater susceptibility to certain genetic diseases because the XY pairing among their chromosomes lacks the "backup system" that women have, with their XX pairing. Women also express significantly more

genes than men, since roughly 15 percent of the genes in their second X-chromosome remain activated. Increased awareness of how different cells in the same tissue can vary genetically—a phenomenon known as *mosaicism*—further complicates the picture, as two cells side by side in women's bodies may express different versions of the X chromosome. Not only does each cell in the human body have a sex involving distinctive biochemical processes, but the expression of that sex may vary from cell to cell. Still other kinds of differences between men and women are shaped by different quantities of hormones at work during different stages of prenatal development, such as the "masculinizing" androgens produced by the adrenal glands, as well as the more familiar ratios of testosterone and estrogen produced by both ovaries and testes.

Such complexity is an indication of how poorly actual human bodies fit the "male model" of traditional research, which often treated women as if they were more or less just men with "atypical" reproductive systems. It also undermines the idea that men and women are (apart from a few aspects of their reproductive systems) complementary or "opposite." Instead, men and women display intricate differences at the genetic and cellular level that elude such easy categorizations.

These extensive and complicated differences are one of the reasons why the continued reliance in many fields on male animal models and male cell cultures is particularly problematic. It also helps explain why, in recent decades, researchers have identified dozens of differences between men and women in such nonreproductive features as kidney function, gastric enzymes, and liver metabolism. They have found new physiological sex differences in the expression of autoimmune disorders, metabolic disorders, mental illnesses, hypertension, and cancer. In animal models, researchers have found that over 50 percent of the active genes in the liver, lipids, and muscles—as well as 13 percent of those in the brain—differ in expression according to sex.

As in the case of zolpidem discussed above, it is thus not surprising that studies continue to show extensive differences in men's and women's responses to a wide range of drugs, including anesthetics, antipsychotics, and antimalarials, as well as alcohol, tobacco, and cocaine. Studies have shown that women require about half as much influenza vaccine as men do to achieve the same level of immunity, although it is not clear why. Some of these differential responses appear be caused by the different percentages of lipids, on average, in men's and women's bodies. (Lipophilic drugs, which are attracted to fat cells, may thus stay in women's bodies longer than they do in men's.) But many other differences in men's and women's responses to drugs and treatments are currently unexplained, due to the overwhelming complexity of sex differences.

Sex, Gender, and Culture

Our expanding knowledge of physiological differences between men and women offers scientifically and morally compelling reasons to decisively reject the "70 kilogram white male" prototype for medical research and practice. Such knowledge makes the approach to women as biological complements or "atypical" men seem crude and primitive. But such earlier models of sexual difference—not to mention earlier biomedical models of race, ethnicity, disability, and sexuality—should prompt both humility and somber reflection. Earlier medical conceptions of women as abnormal versions of men, defined by and held hostage to their reproductive anatomy, are a reminder of how medicine may end up merely reflecting and reinforcing preexisting social hierarchies. In a similar fashion, we should recall how pseudoscientific theories of race have helped justify and reinforce institutions such as American slavery and segregation, and fueled genocidal ideologies from Nazi Germany to Rwanda. Even the criterion of sexual difference between males and females has varied with historical and technological epochs, in an effort to impose neat divisions on a spectrum of sexual differences that are considerably messier than most societies have recognized. (See Case Presentation: Intersex Care for more on this topic.)

Recalling this history does not necessarily mean that we must abandon biomedical inquiry as hopelessly ideological or relative to cultural imperatives. But it is a reminder of how difficult it can be to separate nature from culture, science from stereotype. There is a legitimate concern that medicine, in tailoring treatments to certain social categories, may end up simply reinforcing oppressive cultural structures. Much of the medical history we examine in this text—from the Tuskegee experiments to the electroshock "cures" of homosexuality to the "eugenic" sterilization of the disabled—suggests that practitioners and researchers must be careful of assuming that they have ever reached a scientific plateau free from cultural prejudice and privilege.

At the same time, it is one of the premises of this chapter and, indeed, this entire text, that bioethics can contribute to the realization of a more genuinely pluralistic and egalitarian society. One of the foundational ideas behind such a society, as elaborated by thinkers ranging from Thomas Jefferson to Martin Luther King, Jr., is that the recognition of human dignity, autonomy, and vulnerability should depend not on the accidents of birth or biology but on our commonalities as persons or citizens in a moral community. Which commonalities get to define personhood or citizenship is, of course, a matter of serious moral contention—as we have seen, for example, in our discussion of abortion, euthanasia, and animal rights. But however we come to define moral community, we need not ignore or suppress differences among us, as the "universal" white male medical model did for centuries. Instead, pluralism charges physicians and researchers to acknowledge and engage with human diversity, offering genuine respect and evidence-based care to all those who seek it.

Policing Pregnancy

In March 2009, a young mother named Samantha Burton was admitted to Tallahassee Memorial Hospital with symptoms of premature labor. Burton was, by all accounts, a typical middle-class mom. She was twenty-nine years old and twenty-five weeks pregnant with her third child. She and her husband already had two little girls, and Burton had been working two jobs to help make ends meet. Although she had smoked an occasional cigarette during her pregnancy, she had been actively trying to quit, and she was by no means a heavy smoker. Burton had also received regular prenatal care, which was part of the reason she had rushed to the hospital when she began to experience what to her seemed like contractions.

"I was desperately hoping to receive the care I needed to save my baby," Burton later recalled. At the hospital, Burton was examined by obstetrician Jana Bures-Forsthoefel, who concluded that Burton was not in premature labor, but did have a ruptured membrane and thus was at serious risk of miscarriage. Bures-Forsthoefel ordered Burton to spend the rest of her pregnancy on continuous bed rest at the hospital, and also lectured her about smoking.

Burton was alarmed, but she also found the obstetrician's manner "brusque and overbearing," and she questioned her orders. She didn't refuse bed rest, but pointed out that she had two toddlers to care for and said that she would need to rest at home with a nurse or at the house of a friend who lived near the hospital. When Bures-Forsthoefel rejected these options, Burton began to doubt she could get the care she needed at Tallahassee Memorial Hospital (TMH). Eventually, Burton expressed her intention to leave and to seek a second opinion at another hospital, and that is when her situation took a dramatic turn.

Soon after Burton expressed her wish to be discharged, Bures-Forsthoefel returned to her hospital room in the company of several TMH attorneys. They handed Burton a telephone, and she found herself in a conference-call legal hearing with Florida Circuit Court Judge John Cooper. In the hearing, Bures-Forsthoefel gave testimony as "the unborn child's attending physician" rather than Burton's obstetrician. A newly appointed special assistant state attorney (who also worked for the hospital), argued on behalf of the fetus's interests. Burton was denied legal counsel but was allowed to represent herself.

The next day, Judge Cooper ruled against Burton's requests for a second opinion and a change of hospitals, and instead he ordered her to submit to "any and all medical treatments" the TMH staff deemed necessary to "preserve the life and health of [her] unborn child." Cooper also ordered that Burton be forcibly confined to her hospital bed for the duration of her pregnancy—perhaps as much as fifteen weeks. Cooper justified these restrictions based on the doctrine of *parens patriae* (literally "parent of the country;" or the country as parent). The doctrine allows states to overrule parental decisions on behalf of the "best interest" of a child. Just three days into Burton's state-ordered confinement, however, TMH surgeons performed a caesarean section and found that Burton's fetus had already died in utero. She was allowed to leave the hospital the next day.

Court-Ordered Care

Although Samantha Burton's story is dramatic, it is less unusual than one might expect. Researchers have documented hundreds of cases during the last several decades in which pregnant women have lost their physical liberty in efforts to promote fetal interests, and more than thirty of these cases involved forced C-sections and other involuntary medical interventions.

In 1996, for example, Laura Pemberton, another Florida woman, decided to give birth vaginally after having had a previous caesarean section—a practice known as "vaginal birth after caesarean" or VBAC. Her physician believed that there was a 3 to 6 percent chance that her previous caesarean scar would rupture during a vaginal delivery, with potential risk to her fetus, and he insisted she have another caesarean. But Pemberton and her husband had spent months reviewing the medical research on VBAC and concluded that the risks of a repeated C-section were as great as, or greater than, a vaginal birth. Already in favor of natural childbirth due to their Christian faith, the couple arranged to deliver the baby at home with a midwife in attendance.

Pemberton was already in labor at full term when local hospital officials obtained a court order to force her to submit to a caesarean. State Attorney William Meggs entered Pemberton's bedroom with the court order, accompanied by paramedics and sheriff's deputies. Wearing only a bathrobe, Pemberton was taken into custody, strapped to a gurney by her wrists and ankles, and driven to the hospital, where an emergency hearing was already under way. Second Circuit Judge Phillip Padovano heard testimony while Pemberton lay on an exam table, still having contractions, with her cervix 9 centimeters dilated. As in the Burton case, Pemberton was denied legal counsel, although her fetus was granted a lawyer. Between her contractions, Pemberton testified that she had made an informed choice with regard to VBAC and that she and her fetus were in good health. Unconvinced, Judge Padovano ordered the caesarean section to go forward, and Laura Pemberton was placed under anesthesia, despite her protests and pleas that she be allowed to continue her labor.

Fortunately, both Pemberton and her baby survived the surgery, and her supporters note that she has gone on to deliver four more children vaginally (including twins) without complications. She and her husband have avoided mainstream medicine for these births, however, for fear that physicians might again call on the state to intervene.

Medical Debate

Cases such as Burton's and Pemberton's have generated significant medical, moral, and legal controversy. Supporters of such interventions argue that the providers of medical care are equally responsible for two distinct patients, the fetus and the pregnant woman. Thus, forced care is sometimes necessary to preserve the life or health of the fetus, despite the wishes of the woman. Critics of such interventions contend that, in addition to denying informed consent to pregnant women, such interventions are often based on rushed and questionable medical judgments.

For example, the relative risks of VBAC versus repeat caesarean section is the subject considerable debate in the medical literature, a debate that was ongoing at the time of Laura Pemberton's forced caesarean. Many studies indicate that the risk of uterine rupture in VBAC is less than 1 percent, and that the risk of neonatal brain damage or death is about one in two thousand. In contrast, the *maternal* death rate for caesareans is substantially higher than that associated with vaginal deliveries. Although Laura Pemberton's previous caesarean scar was longer and wider than many, which may have increased her risks of uterine rupture, many experts still doubt that the risks outweighed those associated with repeat caesarean sections.

With regard to Samantha Burton's case, no one doubts that her condition was gravely dangerous both for her and her fetus. But roughly a decade of research has failed to find clear evidence that antepartum bed rest is effective in preventing miscarriage or preterm birth. Also, bed rest has numerous side effects such as blood clots, muscle atrophy, and decreased infant birth weight, not to mention the psychosocial effects for women who are so isolated and confined. Although still often prescribed by physicians, bed rest has been rejected as a treatment by the American College of Obstetricians and Gynecologists (ACOG), until clinical trials prove it has benefits that outweigh its harms.

Medical critics of forced care argue that such clinical ambiguities recommend a policy of respecting a pregnant woman's right to refuse treatment. The Board of Trustees of the American Medical Association, for example, has concluded that physicians "should not be responsible for policing the decisions that a pregnant woman makes that affect the health of herself and her fetus, nor should they be liable for respecting an informed, competent refusal of medical care." The AMA, ACOG, and other professional associations have also argued that such interventions distort the clinical relationship, making the physician operate as "an agent of the state rather than as an independent patient counselor."

Moral Debate

Advocates of such interventions, on the other hand, argue that the state has a strong moral interest in preserving fetal life and health, which must be balanced against the rights of pregnant women. They argue that the urgency of cases such as Burton's and Pemberton's doesn't allow time for a medical committee to evaluate all the options.

"This is good people trying to do things in a right fashion to save lives, whether some people want them saved or not," said Florida state attorney Meggs, who was involved in both the Burton and Pemberton cases. "When it involves an unborn child we become the representative of the child when nobody else will represent it."

Meggs and others who view themselves as defenders of fetal interests point to child welfare laws that impose special obligations upon parents and also limit their ability to refuse treatments that may be in the best interests of their children. (For examples of such situations, see Case Presentations: Faith and Medicine, and Healing the Hmong in Chapter 1.) These advocates argue that pregnant women have special obligations to defer to physicians who conclude that their fetus's life or health is at risk, especially if they have chosen to carry a pregnancy to term.

"We've charged people who have killed a pregnant woman with two counts of murder," Meggs argues. "Why can't we try to keep the child alive?"

By contrast, moral critics of forced interventions argue that pregnancy should not undermine competent adult women's right to refuse treatment. They contend that even if we grant full personhood to the fetus, as Meggs apparently does, our common law tradition places very minimal "Samaritan" obligations on one person to help another, even when they have prior special relationships. (For a philosophical version of this argument, see the article by Judith Jarvis Thomson in Chapter 5.)

Furthermore, critics note that although society imposes some special obligations on parents, it does not force them to undergo risky medical procedures or give up their basic autonomy in order to preserve the life or health of their children. A father, for example, cannot be legally compelled to donate bone marrow to his child, even if he is the only compatible donor and the donation is necessary to preserve the child's health or life. Nor can physicians force a parent to donate blood to a child, even if it would save the child's life. (Pregnant women, by contrast, have on a number of occasions been forced to accept involuntary blood transfusions in the name of fetal interests.) To critics, it seems bizarre and immoral to place greater restrictions on the rights of *potential* mothers than we do on *actual* parents for the sake of their already-born children.

"Society does not legally require parents to undergo a risk of life, health, or bodily invasion in order to carry out

their moral obligations to provide medical care for their children," concluded the AMA Board in their rejection of forced care. "Few, if any, medical procedures meant to benefit the fetus would entail no risk to a pregnant woman's health."

Legal Debate

Not surprisingly, the moral debate over an issue that is sometimes called "maternal–fetal conflict" has also been played out in the courts. Both Samantha Burton's and Laura Pemberton's cases have generated legal rulings—with surprising and controversial results. Before we explore these decisions, however, it is necessary to step back and look at one more pivotal case, a forced caesarean section in 1987 that led to the landmark decision known as *In re A.C.* It is this case that informs much of the legal debate over the treatment of Samantha Burton and Laura Pemberton.

Angela Carder's Ordeal. In June 1987, when she was newly married and twenty-five weeks pregnant with her first child, Angela Carder was diagnosed with the metastatic recurrence of a bone cancer that had been successfully treated years before. After her diagnosis, Carder's initial plan was to pursue the same aggressive chemotherapy and radiation that had worked against her earlier cancer. But after her condition swiftly deteriorated, Carder decided, in consultation with her physicians, to pursue these measures only for palliative benefit and to extend her life. Carder and her physicians also agreed not to consider interventions on behalf of her fetus until twenty-eight weeks gestation, based on an assessment that an earlier caesarean section would only hasten Carder's death and likely kill her fetus or leave it with lifelong impairments.

Then, as so often happens in medical crises, events began to move very rapidly. Carder developed intense pain and severe breathing problems, depriving her and her fetus of adequate oxygen for several hours, until she was intubated and put on a respirator. In accordance with Carder's previously stated wishes, her husband, parents, and physicians opted to keep her comfortable with increased pain medication, even if these posed risks to the fetus. They also decided against putting her through a caesarean surgery she had already rejected for that stage of gestation.

But administrators at George Washington University Medical Center (GWUMC), where Carder was being treated, soon reached a different conclusion. The hospital was concerned about the potential legal consequences of abandoning a potentially viable fetus, especially given the Reagan administration's intense focus on pro-life issues following the "Baby Doe" cases. (See Chapter 6 for more on this topic.) The hospital called in Judge Emmett Sullivan, of the District of Columbia Superior Court, for an emergency hearing, and Sullivan appointed lawyers for both Carder and her fetus. In the hearing, Judge Sullivan accepted the assessment of a neonatologist who had not examined Carder that her fetus had a 50 to 60 percent chance of survival. (Carder's physicians testified that the fetus's chances of survival were much lower, due to its oxygen deprivation and drug exposures.) Sullivan issued a preliminary ruling in favor of a caesarean section, and Carder's physicians went to inform her of the decision.

Given the tragic complexity of the situation and her heavy sedation, it is not surprising that Angela Carder's reaction to the proposed C-section was both contradictory and hard to interpret. At first, she appeared to consent to the procedure. But when asked a second time, multiple witnesses reported that she clearly mouthed the words, "I don't want it done. I don't want it done." When this statement was reported in the hearing as further proof of Carder's refusal, the GWUMC and fetal lawyers argued that Carder's wishes should no longer be considered, since her death was imminent anyway. The only consideration should be the interests of the fetus. This argument apparently swayed Judge Sullivan, as well as a three-judge appellate court panel that rejected a last-minute appeal by Carder's lawyers. Over the objections of most of the hospital's obstetrics department, Angela Carder was wheeled into surgery and her baby, a girl, was delivered by caesarean section. As predicted by Carder's physicians, the baby's lungs were underdeveloped and she lived for roughly two hours. Angela Carder lived two more days before lapsing into a coma and dying. Her death certificate listed the caesarean surgery, along with her cancer, as a contributing cause of her death.

In re A.C.   Nearly three years after Carder's death, the full District of Columbia Court of Appeals vacated Judge Sullivan's ruling, along with that of the three-judge appeals panel. The full appeals court ruled that the "right to

bodily integrity is not extinguished simply because someone is ill, or even at death's door" and that the only relevant factor in the case should have been Angela Carder's wishes. If Carder was found competent, respect for patient autonomy should have allowed her to choose whether or not to undergo the caesarean. If she was incompetent, the hospital should have accepted "a well-founded surrogate's decision" based on Carder's past statements and values. The court rejected the appeals court's "balancing of interest" between Carder and her fetus, holding that "in virtually all cases the question of what is to be done is to be decided by the patient—the pregnant woman—on behalf of herself and the fetus." Although future technologies, for example, might produce situations "extraordinary or compelling enough to justify a massive intrusion into a person's body" represented by forced care, no such situation could be currently imagined.

Uncertain Precedents.   In the years following *In re A.C.*, the ruling became a widely cited precedent, serving as a legal bulwark for recognizing the rights of pregnant women to patient autonomy and informed consent. The settlement of a wrongful death suit against GWUMC by Carder's family also led to new hospital guidelines being adopted across the country that emphasized the autonomy of pregnant patients and the moral harm of forced interventions. As a result, many assumed that the issue of "maternal–fetal conflict" would fade away. But as the Burton and Pemberton cases demonstrate, the issues raised twenty years ago in *In re A.C.* often remain points of fierce contention, in both medical practice and jurisprudence.

In August 2010, for example, Florida's 1st District Court of Appeals rejected Judge Cooper's ruling that confined Samantha Burton to her hospital bed and forced her to undergo a caesarean and other procedures. The court of appeals ruled that Cooper had blatantly misapplied the *parens patriae* "best interest" standard, since it had been developed with regard to *born children*, whose medical care—unlike that of fetuses—has no direct impact on the privacy or autonomy rights of their mothers. Nevertheless, the Florida court found that there might be situations—if fetal viability had been established through specific evidence and the proposed intervention was narrowly tailored and relatively unintrusive—where a "compelling state interest" in fetal life could override a woman's right to informed consent.

Critics of this decision note that the idea of a "compelling state interest" in fetal life comes from the *Roe v. Wade* and *Casey* rulings, in which fetal viability marks the point at which states may restrict the right to *abortion*. (See Chapter 5 for a detailed discussion of both cases.) But, critics point out, *Roe* and *Casey* give no indication that a state's interest in fetal life would allow it to restrict women's broader rights to bodily integrity and physical liberty—the kinds of restrictions implied in confining them in hospitals or forcing them to undergo unwanted surgeries. Furthermore, critics of both the *Burton* and *In re A.C.* decisions ask, how are physicians to know when an interest in viable fetal life becomes "compelling" or "extraordinary" enough to involve the law?

One answer to that question came in a Florida district court's 1999 dismissal of Laura Pemberton's argument that her forced caesarean surgery violated her rights. Drawing on both *Roe* and *In re A.C.*, the court concluded that the 2 percent chance of uterine rupture from attempting a vaginal birth, as acknowledged by Pemberton's medical experts, constituted an "extraordinary and overwhelming" situation that justified the state's intervening to save a viable fetus—even at the expense of the mother's rights to bodily integrity and informed refusal of care.

The decision baffled many legal critics, who could not believe that even the 4 to 6 percent chance of uterine rupture claimed by the hospital's experts could justify dragging Pemberton from her home and forcing her to have surgery against her will. They pointed out that competent patients are regularly allowed to face much higher risks through refusal—or acceptance—of many other medical treatments, and that it is not unusual for parents to make such choices for their born children. But for many advocates, if the state recognizes independent legal rights for a fetus, those rights can and should frequently trump those of the women who carry them.

"Whatever the scope of Ms. Pemberton's constitutional rights in this situation," the Florida court concluded, "they clearly did not outweigh the interests of the State of Florida in preserving the life of the unborn child."

Envoi

Laura Pemberton's case, along with those of Burton and Carder, are reminders of what radically divergent perspectives Americans have come to hold on issues such as fetal life and the rights of pregnant women. These differences of perspective are shaped, in part, by America's deep polarization over the issue of abortion. That ongoing battle has often cast the maternal–fetal relationship in inherently adversarial terms and made pregnancy itself a subject of intense public scrutiny. (Much of this scrutiny has been on the consumption of legal and illegal substances by pregnant women—sometimes with questionable evidence of harm to a developing fetus. See Decision Scenario: Pregnancy and Cocaine for more on this topic.)

Disagreements over forced treatments for pregnant women, however, do not fit neatly into categories such as "pro-life" and "pro-choice." Laura Pemberton, for example, is an ardent opponent of abortion, who now sometimes shares platforms with pro-choice advocates as she speaks out against her state-mandated caesarean. (She decided not to appeal the ruling in her case.) Samantha Burton has avoided the political limelight, returning to work and parenting in Tallahassee and refusing any monetary reward from her lawsuit so as to keep the focus on the goal of ensuring that "nobody else has to go through what I went through."

What these women appear to share, along with other advocates for pregnant women, is the sense that pregnancy does not justify the abridgement of basic freedoms that are almost never taken away from competent and law-abiding adult males, even if they father children. In reclaiming pregnancy as a realm of private medical decisions, they thus argue for a moral and legal concept that is much older than abortion rights: namely, equal protection under the law.

CASE PRESENTATION

The Tuskegee Syphilis Study: Bad Blood, Bad Faith

The way the U.S. Public Health Service conducted the Tuskegee Study of Untreated Syphilis in the Negro Male constituted one of the most serious failures of medical research ethics in modern American history. It also probably did more than any other single event to promote distrust of physicians, researchers, and the entire medical establishment in the African American community.

Ironically, the Tuskegee Syphilis Study was, at least initially, the outgrowth of a program of deliberate efforts to improve the health of poor African Americans in the rural South. Its organizers were not rogue scientists with a hidden agenda, but some of the leading American figures in the evolving field of public health. The study's findings were regularly published in major medical journals and approved by many who thought of themselves as promoting the interests of African Americans. The story of Tuskegee is thus, in part, the story of how "good intentions" may help medical scientists justify profoundly troubling practices and policies.

A Modern Plague

At the turn of the twentieth century, syphilis was viewed much the way AIDS was when it first appeared in 1980s. Syphilis was a largely untreatable and often deadly disease, spread primarily by sexual contact. Women could also infect their children in utero, who were sometimes born dead or blind and diseased. The association with sex, particularly sex outside of marriage, had long made syphilis a source of shame and social disgrace. In the Victorian era, patients suffering from the brain damage caused by late-stage syphilis were often confined to mental asylums, a practice that only underscored the disease's connection with stigma and social deviance.

In 1905, however, Fritz Schaudinn and Erich Hoffmann identified the causative agent of syphilis, a small corkscrew-shaped bacterium, or *spirochete*. A year later, August Wassermann introduced a diagnostic blood test for the disease. And in 1911, Paul Ehrlich introduced salvarsan, the first targeted antisyphilitic drug (and the first chemotherapy agent), after systematically testing hundreds of chemical compounds. Although salvarsan and later arsenic compounds could not cure syphilis, they could, in many cases, halt the disease and render it noninfectious. These major scientific developments raised the hopes that syphilis and other infectious diseases might soon be eradicated, and helped spur the growth of the public health movement in Europe and the United States.

Unfortunately, this new fight against infectious diseases often came with a set of assumptions about the people who were believed to carry them. In the United

States, the association of syphilis with immorality was often combined with a eugenic "science" of racial difference, one that viewed African Americans as both hypersexual and specially prone to disease. (These assertions echoed similar claims about Jewish racial inferiority and disease susceptibility that were evolving in Europe and the United States.) The result was that U.S. public health officials often saw African Americans as uniquely susceptible to syphilis and other sexually transmitted diseases, and tended to view their incidence in poor African American communities as "natural" and inevitable. All of these dynamics helped shape the ambitious public health project that would become the infamous Tuskegee syphilis study.

Macon County, Alabama

In 1929, the U.S. Public Health Service (PHS) and the Julius Rosenwald Fund initiated a program to diagnose and treat syphilis in the African American population of Macon County, Alabama, and a number of other poor, rural communities with a high incidence of the disease. Shortly after the program began, however, the stock market crash extinguished hopes of funding the large-scale program, which was abandoned with only 1,400 individuals having received partial treatment for syphilis.

Taliaferro Clark, chief of the PHS Venereal Disease Division, was determined to salvage something from the Macon Project. He decided that even if there was no money for treatment, the service could do a six-month "study in nature" of untreated syphilis. From the beginning, Clark appears to have seen the prevalence of syphilis among poor African Americans as a natural phenomenon, rooted in what he saw as their innate promiscuity and "rather low intelligence." Instead of approaching syphilis as a tragic, but contingent, outgrowth of American rural poverty, Clark and other organizers saw it an opportunity to test out theories of racial difference. Did the disease behave the same in blacks as in whites, or did innate differences make blacks more (or less) susceptible to its ravages? Clark also saw the study as an opportunity to test the hypothesis that treatment was simply unnecessary in latent syphilis cases.

The PHS accepted Clark's proposal and, in doing so, tacitly endorsed a research program that involved deceiving research subjects about the nature of their illness. From the beginning, the study would deliberately withhold potentially effective treatments from participants while giving them the impression that they were being appropriately treated. That the subjects were all rural, impoverished, and poorly educated African American men makes it hard to avoid the conclusion that the PHS regarded these individuals as little more than experimental animals.

In 1932, PHS officials presented an observational research proposal to the Tuskegee Institute (a historically black medical institution located in Macon County), and its director, R. R. Moton, agreed to Tuskegee's participation. The institute would be paid for its assistance, and its interns and nurses would have the opportunity to work for the government, a major incentive during the height of the Depression.

With the help of Tuskegee and black churches and community leaders, the PHS researchers began to recruit subjects for the study. The initial response was poor, however, until the researchers promised participants free medical treatment, blood tests, and examinations. In rural Alabama, where few people, black or white, could afford to consult a physician, such an offer by a federal health agency constituted a valuable opportunity.

No Diagnosis, No Treatment

What the participants were not told was that they would not be given any more specific diagnosis than "bad blood" and would be "treated" only with placebos. The PHS doctors sometimes claimed that "bad blood" was the term used by rural blacks to mean syphilis. But the term was really a vague catchall category that could include anything from iron deficiency and sickle-cell disease to leukemia or syphilis. It was used to explain why people felt sluggish, tired easily, or had a low energy level. There was, however, nothing vague about the disease the researchers were studying.

In its primary stage, syphilis causes a genital, anal, or mouth ulcer. Known as a chancre, this pus-filled sore containing bacterial spirochetes usually heals within a month or two. Six to twelve weeks after infection, the disease enters its secondary stage. It is marked by skin rashes that may last for months, swollen lymph nodes, headaches, bone pain, fever, loss of appetite, and fatigue. Highly infectious sores may also develop on the skin. The secondary stage lasts for about a year; then the

disease becomes latent. During this inactive stage, which may last for many years or even a lifetime, the person may appear perfectly healthy.

About 30 percent of the time, however, people with untreated syphilis progress to the tertiary stage. One marked effect is the destruction of the tissues making up the bones, palate, nasal septum, tongue, skin, or almost any other organ in the body. Infection of the heart may lead to the destruction of the valves or the aorta, causing aneurysms that can rupture and cause immediate death. Infection of the brain can lead to general paralysis and to progressive brain damage, an outcome that caused victims to be placed in nineteenth-century mental asylums.

Despite the severity of these symptoms, none of the Tuskegee subjects diagnosed with "bad blood" were given any form of effective treatment. The vials, pills, and capsules they did receive were, in fact, nothing more than placebos, vitamins at best, and contained no ingredient active against syphilis. At the same time, painful (and potentially harmful) spinal taps to test for latent syphilis were presented to the subjects as "special treatment." A sham diagnosis was matched by a sham treatment.

Unfortunately, despite the medical counterfeiting, the subjects' syphilis was real enough to maim and kill. At the end of the six-month study period, the data showed that untreated syphilis in blacks was just as deadly as in whites. This was seen as an important finding, because it contradicted the widely held opinion that blacks tolerated syphilis better and were less harmed by it.

Study Extended

After the initial six months, Raymond A. Vonderlehr, a PHS officer, obtained permission to extend the study to collect more data. An African American nurse, Eunice Rivers, was added to the staff. She was assigned to recruit men to the study who were free of the disease and so could serve as a control group. The study came to involve 600 African American men—399 diagnosed with syphilis and 201 free of the disease.

Nurse Rivers also had the job of monitoring the study participants and making sure they showed up for annual examinations administered by the PHS physicians. She was given a government car, and some subjects came to see it as a special privilege to be driven by Rivers to the school where the exams were conducted. Because the study offered participants fifty dollars for burial expenses if they agreed to an autopsy at their death, participants spoke of themselves as belonging to "Nurse Rivers's Burial Society."

For decades, reports from the Tuskegee study were published in peer-reviewed medical journals such as the *Journal of the American Medical Association*, and from time to time PHS officers presented the study's findings to Congress. No one raised any questions about the ethics of the study or asked whether the participants had been informed that they had syphilis and weren't being treated for it. Such silence persisted despite published reports that "nearly twice as large a proportion of the syphilitic individuals as of the control group has died."

In 1938, the passage of the National Venereal Disease Control Act required the PHS to provide treatment for people suffering from syphilis or other venereal diseases, even if they couldn't afford to pay for it. Yet participants in the Tuskegee study were considered experimental subjects and exempted from the requirements of the law. Study participants who sought treatment from local clinics were turned away at the explicit request of Vonderlehr and other PHS officials, who distributed lists of participants to local physicians. At the outbreak of the Second World War, the PHS gave local draft boards a list of 256 subjects, insisting that they not be treated for syphilis by military physicians, and securing draft exemptions for at least fifty of them.

Perhaps most crucially, when penicillin—which is highly effective against the syphilis spirochete—became available in the mid-1940s, the PHS also withheld it from the study participants. Even as subjects died, went blind, or suffered brain damage, the study went on without any treatments being offered. When some did manage to obtain treatment, Vonderlehr, now head of the PHS Venereal Disease Division, wrote, "I hope that the availability of antibiotics has not interfered too much with this project."

In 1947, Nazi physicians and scientists who had taken part in vicious, senseless, and often deadly human experiments were tried for war crimes at Nuremberg. One of the outcomes of the trial was the formulation of the Nuremberg Code to govern the participation of subjects in experimentation. (See Chapter 2.) The key element of the Code is the requirement that subjects give their free and informed consent before becoming research participants—a requirement that was consistently violated by the Tuskegee study. Even after the Nuremberg Code was widely distributed, officials at the PHS failed to grasp its relevance to the research they were conducting.

Beginning of the End

In 1964, Irwin J. Schatz, a Detroit physician, wrote to PHS researcher Anne Q. Yobs that he was "utterly astounded by the fact that physicians allow patients with a potentially fatal disease to remain untreated when effective therapy is available." But Schatz received no reply. Two years later, Peter Buxtun, a social worker hired by the PHS as a venereal disease investigator, heard rumors about the Tuskegee study and, after reading the research based on it, sent a letter to the new head of the Division of Venereal Disease, William J. Brown, to express his serious moral concerns.

Buxtun received no response, but eventually he was invited to a meeting at the headquarters of the Centers for Disease Control with PHS official John Cutler. Cutler was a principal investigator in the Tuskegee study and had led an earlier study in Guatemala in which hundreds of research subjects had been deliberately infected with syphilis without their knowledge. (See Case Presentation: "The Devil's Experiment" in Chapter 11.) When Buxtun presented his concerns, Cutler verbally attacked him for questioning the study's premises.

"He was infuriated," Buxtun recalled, and said Cutler treated him like "a lunatic who needed immediate chastisement." Cutler insisted that the experiment would eventually help physicians treat black patients with syphilis—a position he would publicly defend until the end of his life.

Buxtun left the PHS voluntarily to go to law school, but he didn't forget about Tuskegee. In 1968, he wrote another letter to Brown, arguing that the study supported "the thinking of Negro militants that Negroes have long been used for 'medical experiments' and 'teaching cases' in the emergency wards of county hospitals." He said the Tuskegee subjects could hardly be regarded as volunteers and observed that whatever justifications had been offered for the experiment in 1932 were no longer relevant. He expressed hope that the subjects in the study would be given appropriate treatments.

This time, Buxtun's letter produced action—but not much. In 1969, the Centers for Disease Control convened a panel to review the Tuskegee study. With only one dissenting member, it concluded that the study should go on, based on the theory that treating the subjects with penicillin might cause them more harm than good. (More than half of patients given penicillin for syphilis suffer a temporary, but potentially severe, reaction to endotoxins released by dying spirochetes.)

Early in July 1972, Peter Buxtun finally turned over the materials he had accumulated on the Tuskegee study to Associated Press reporter Jean Heller, and on July 25, after interviewing officials in the PHS, Heller broke the story nationally.

Public anger was swift in coming. The experiment was denounced by the assistant secretary of health, education, and welfare, who launched an investigation into why study participants never received treatment. Congressional hearings were conducted, which eventually led to the 1974 Belmont Report and the establishment of institutional review boards for human subjects research. (See Chapter 2 for more.)

Most important, the Tuskegee study came to an immediate halt. During the study's forty-year history, at least twenty-eight subjects had died directly from advanced syphilitic lesions, and complications from the disease had played a role in the deaths of dozens more. Since 1972, the federal government has paid out $10 million in out-of-court settlements to the subjects, their spouses, and their children, many of whom appear to have been infected or born with syphilis during the course of the study. The last survivor of the experiment, Ernest Hendon, died in 2004.

On May 16, 1997, President Bill Clinton formally apologized to the survivors of the Tuskegee Study. "What was done cannot be undone," he said in a White House ceremony. "But we can end the silence. . . . We can look at you in the eye and finally say on behalf of the American people, what the United States government did was shameful, and I am sorry. . . . To our African American citizens, I am sorry that your federal government orchestrated a study so clearly racist."

SOCIAL CONTEXT

Race, Poverty, and Disparity: A Crisis in Public Health

"Tell me someone's race. Tell me their income. And tell me whether they smoke," said Donald Berwick, a Boston pediatrician who served on the President Clinton's Commission on Health Care Quality. "The answers to those three questions will tell me more about their longevity and health status than any other questions I could possibly ask. There's no genetic blood test that would have anything like that for predictive value."

Berwick's statement is a tragic but still accurate commentary on the stark disparities in American health care. The Census Bureau predicts that by 2043, the United States will be a "majority-minority" nation, in which no racial or ethnic group makes up more than half the population. (This is already the case for enrollment in America's public schools and will be true of America's children by 2020.) Yet European

Americans still, on average, tend to receive better health care and have better health outcomes than their non-white fellow citizens. Even as people of color in increasing numbers have become scientists and physicians, social inequalities, especially those connected with inequalities of wealth and income, are still with us, and still have a profound impact on health and longevity.

This impact is especially severe for African Americans. To a considerable extent, the black community continues to experience the effects of social prejudice and institutionalized discrimination, with a profound impact on their socioeconomic status, health status, and trust in medical institutions. According to the most recent U.S. census, the net worth of the average black household is just $6,314, compared with $110,500 for the average white household. Although African Americans no longer constitute the largest minority in the United States, they have the highest death rate of any group, and their negative health outcomes are intertwined with the high levels of poverty, segregation, and incarceration that impact many African American communities.

Of course, African Americans are not the only ethnic group with health problems. Native Americans have higher levels of diabetes, and Hispanic Americans have higher incidences of disabling or fatal strokes. Each group has distinctive health care needs, and many of these problems are associated with prejudice, negative attitudes, or flawed social policies, along with cultural and linguistic barriers. In what follows, we will limit our discussion to examining medical care and medical research issues pertaining to African Americans, but similar observations could be made with respect to other ethnic and cultural groupings.

African Americans and Health Care

The gap between the health of African Americans and other groups is evident in a host of statistical evidence. To take just a few tragic examples, the infant mortality rate among African Americans is twice that of European Americans, and black infants are nearly twice as likely to be born with low birth weight. The life expectancy gap between African and European Americans is 3.8 years, with black men and women living 4.7 and 3.3 fewer years, respectively, than their white counterparts. Black women are three times more likely than white women to die in childbirth, and 40 percent more likely to die of breast cancer, even though white women are more likely than black women to be diagnosed with the disease. African American patients have a 10 percent lower survival rate five years after a cancer diagnosis than do European Americans. They are seven times more likely to die of tuberculosis and three times more likely to die of HIV/AIDS. (By one 2010 estimate, if

African Americans constituted a separate country, they would have the sixth-highest rate of HIV/AIDS infection in the world.) Blacks are significantly more likely than whites to suffer from diabetes and obesity, and to have high cholesterol and high blood pressure—factors that likely contribute to the heart disease that makes up more than a quarter of the life expectancy gap between blacks and whites. (See Case Presentation: BiDil and Beyond for more.)

It is possible that a small portion of these health disparities result from variable genetic predispositions among different groups. Evidence suggests that African Americans have more of a genetic tendency than other groups in the United States to develop sickle-cell anemia and perhaps prostate cancer, and more black women than white women may be predisposed to develop early breast cancers that respond poorly to hormone treatments. (By contrast, African Americans appear to be less susceptible than other groups to chronic liver disease and Alzheimer's.) Yet sociopolitical categories based on skin color and external features have generally been shown to be poor predictors of underlying genetic differences, and most researchers believe that the vast majority of disparate health outcomes between African Americans and other groups is a result of social and environmental factors. (See this chapter's Briefing Session for more on the concept of race.)

Poverty and Prisons

Researchers often point to the strikingly different socioeconomic conditions between African Americans and European Americans in the United States to explain the health disparities between these groups. (Socioeconomic measures generally include income, occupation, education, and housing conditions.) Independent of race, socioeconomic status (SES) has been shown to have a profound impact on health, with studies across Westernized societies commonly demonstrating a tenfold gap between the highest and lowest rung of the SES ladder when it comes to respiratory and cardiovascular diseases, rheumatoid disorders, and a number of cancers. Studies have shown that the poorest black Americans are three times as likely to experience heart disease or stroke as the richest black Americans, and that the poorest white males in America die about a decade earlier than the richest white males.

Since African Americans are the ethnic group with the highest poverty rates in the United States and a typical white household has sixteen times the wealth of the typical black household, it should not be surprising that poverty has a dramatic and disparate impact on the two groups. Some of this impact is direct and obvious. More than a third of inner-city black children experience lead poisoning from substandard housing, for example, and impoverished African American neighborhoods are notorious for their lack of pharmacies, fresh produce, and gyms. The high-fat, high-salt food that is often the only option in poor neighborhoods (and plays a role in some traditional African American cuisine) likely accounts for some of the hypertension and diabetes that afflicts the African American community. Poverty is strongly associated with poor nutritional and health literacy, and it also directly impacts one's ability to afford medical care and health insurance. Although the uninsured rate among black adults has fallen from 25 percent to 16 percent since the implementation of the Affordable Care Act, it is still 5 percent higher than that of whites, and health outcomes still reflect decades of lack of insurance and underinsurance.

At the same time, socioeconomic status has been shown to have strong *indirect* effects on health. In a famous longitudinal study begun in 1967, Michael Marmot and other epidemiologists have followed over ten thousand British civil servants, ranging from blue-collar employees to top executives, who work at the Whitehall administrative complex in London. It is perhaps not surprising that they found much higher rates of heart disease, lung disease, gastrointestinal disease, and some cancers among the low-ranked workers (e.g., porters and office messengers) than among high-ranked ones (e.g., professionals and administrators). Even the fact that people at the lowest civil service grade were three times more likely to die of a heart attack than those at the highest grade might be assumed to result from greater risk factors such as smoking, lack of exercise, or obesity. But when the Whitehall researchers controlled for such risk factors, they found that they only accounted for a third of the health disparities between workers of low and high socioeconomic status. Nor could such disparities be attributed to differential access to health care, since the United Kingdom, unlike the United States, has universal socialized medicine.

Although there is ongoing debate about how to interpret the Whitehall results, most researchers believe that they can be attributed to the increased psychosocial stress associated with low socioeconomic status. High levels of stress hormones such as cortisol and epinephrine, along with other results of prolonged psychosocial stress, have been shown to impede tissue repair, immune system function, and even cognition. They also appear to increase the risk and severity of conditions such as type 2 diabetes, asthma, and heart disease. Although many people at the top of the socioeconomic spectrum have demanding jobs, they typically have more control, stability, and predictability in their lives—factors that animal and human studies suggest are decisive in stress-related ill health. There is also growing evidence that the mere awareness of one's socioeconomic status (being made to feel poor or like a "second-class" citizen) increases the negative physiological effects of stress.

These conclusions may help explain some of the stark health disparities between European Americans and other groups. They may also help elucidate why African Americans often rank last in health outcomes, even though Latino Americans (for example) are more likely to lack health insurance and almost as likely to live in poverty. From the slavery era to the present, African Americans have typically had the lowest social status of any group, experiencing even more discrimination and fewer civil rights protections than immigrants who came to America voluntarily and at later stages.

Today, many observers find the most acute expression of this lower status in the treatment of African Americans by the criminal justice system. Although exemplified in recent years by high-profile killings of unarmed black men by police, even more psychosocial stress is likely caused by the fact that black men are more than six times more likely than white men to be imprisoned, and almost one in three African American men will go to prison during his lifetime. While there is intense public debate about what accounts for this incarceration gap, few question its devastating community impact or that it is deeply intertwined with America's "war on drugs," which has been disproportionately waged in urban African American neighborhoods. This approach continues in many cities, despite extensive research indicating that blacks are, on average, no more (or even slightly less) likely than whites to use or sell illegal drugs.

Treatment Differences

Another, more direct explanation for disparate health outcomes among different ethnic groups is that they experience differential or discriminatory treatment in America's health care system. There is little question that traditional Western medicine centered the great majority of its efforts on understanding and treating the disorders of the white male, who was implicitly taken as the standard patient and research subject. Since the typical physician and researcher was also a male of European descent, perhaps this result is unsurprising. But even as non-whites have been admitted in increasing numbers to the ranks of physicians and researchers, there is still suggestive evidence that members of these groups experience differential treatment as patients.

In the 1990s and 2000s, a series of large studies found that African American and other non-white patients were significantly less likely than white patients to receive appropriate diagnostic tests when presenting with the same symptoms of treatable lung cancer and heart attacks. Even when diagnosed and referred to specialists, blacks were about half as likely to receive surgeries for their lung cancers and half as likely to get angioplasties and other standard surgical treatments for heart disease. Blacks with diabetes-related circulatory problems were more likely to have limbs amputated than whites with similar conditions and more likely to receive the most invasive (but least expensive) forms of hysterectomy. Studies also showed physicians less likely to prescribe analgesic pain medication to non-whites than whites with the same symptoms, particularly if pain condition was based on self-reports (e.g., a migraine).

Some of these differences may derive from poor communication between physicians and patients, as well as the wealth and insurance gaps described above. It may also be influenced by a factor we will discuss below: the mistrust of medical institutions that arose as a result of discriminatory and abusive patterns in medical research and clinical practice. Nevertheless, a substantial body of research that attempts to quantify subconscious negative associations has found that majorities of physicians have at least moderate implicit biases against African American and other non-white patients. Those who do have been shown to be less likely to prescribe aggressive clot-busting treatments to (hypothetical) non-white patients with symptoms of heart attack. Similar correlations have been found between implicit bias and less effective pain management for African American patients, and subsequent studies have shown that implicit bias is, in general, a fairly good predictor of behavior.

Such findings lead some researchers to suspect that subtle or unconscious racism may be a significant factor affecting the health care of black people. Whatever the explanation, the findings support the general view that African Americans receive, on average, less care and less sophisticated care than European Americans receive.

The Tuskegee Effect

One of the most glaring examples of the biomedical establishment's disparate treatment of African Americans is the Tuskegee study, in which hundreds of black men with syphilis were left untreated for decades so researchers from the U.S. Public Health Service could study the "natural course" of the disease. (See Case Presentation: The Tuskegee Syphilis Study, in this chapter.) But while Tuskegee represents a flagrant abuse of medical authority, it was preceded by a long-standing pattern of exploitation that began with the medical experiments that physicians conducted on slaves—typically without regard for their suffering or permanent injury—and extended into the era of segregation and beyond. (For more on this history, see Case Presentation: The Afterlife of Henrietta Lacks in Chapter 3.)

Such practices resulted in a deep distrust of the U.S. medical establishment in the African American community that likely contributes to some of today's disparate

health outcomes. Studies have shown that African Americans often seek treatment later than members of other groups and are less likely to return for follow-up evaluations. Mistrust and suspicion generated by Tuskegee and other abuses may also contribute to the low representation of African Americans in clinical trials—although nonwhites, as well as women, were generally not recruited for such trials until recent decades.

Of course, African Americans are not the only groups to have received unfair or inadequate treatment by the medical establishment. Native Americans, in particular, have suffered from substandard medical care and poor nutrition on the reservations that replaced their precolonial communities, and their health outcomes are often even worse than those of African Americans. Latino and Asian immigrants, as well as poor Americans more generally, have often had reason to view the medical establishment with suspicion, due to discriminatory or inadequate treatment. Although Medicare, Medicaid, and the more recent provisions of the ACA have mitigated some of the most egregiously substandard medical care for the poor, a large percentage of health care providers still refuse to accept Medicaid patients, and many working-class Americans still find themselves underinsured or unable to pay their out-of-pocket medical bills.

Still, there is evidence of some significant, albeit inadequate, progress in the medical care and health status of historically marginalized groups. As noted above, the percentage of African Americans who lack health insurance has fallen by over half since the beginning of 2014. From 1970 to 2013, life expectancy for blacks increased by 17 percent (compared to an 11 percent increase for whites). Although the life expectancy gap between the two groups persists, it has narrowed to its lowest recorded level, as has the gap in the overall death rate. When it comes to biomedical research, the National

Institutes of Health now requires that all NIH-supported studies include minorities and women, unless there are legitimate reasons to justify their exclusion.

Such changes in policy and statistical outcomes are important, but they are unlikely to have as much impact as shifts in the daily interactions between physicians and patients. One important change likely to improve the health of African Americans is the cultivation of greater trust in medical institutions. The Tuskegee effect will likely linger for years; to mitigate its effects, the medical establishment must make concerted efforts to earn and deserve the trust of black patients.

Treating patients with respect, taking seriously their reservations about diagnostic tests or proposed interventions, and taking the time to educate them about medical conditions and treatment options are important in securing the trust of any group of patients. If African Americans are more distrustful than other groups, it is because they have more reason to be.

CASE PRESENTATION

BiDil and Beyond: The Controversy over Race-Based Medicine

In the 1970s, a cardiologist named Jay Cohn began to experiment with potential treatments for heart failure—the incurable and often fatal deterioration of the heart's pumping capacity that afflicts more than five million Americans. Cohn focused on drugs that expand the blood vessels (vasodilators) and allow more blood to leave the heart. The premise was that an effective vasodilator, although it would not be a cure for heart failure, might mitigate the worst symptoms and extend the lives of those with the disease.

The most promising strategy involved two existing generic vasodilators, isosorbide dinitrate and hydralazine, a combination that Cohn patented and called BiDil. In the 1980s, he conducted a clinical trial of BiDil, using it to treat heart-failure patients in a veterans' hospital, and concluded that the drug lowered the death rate. But the FDA found that the reduced mortality Cohn attributed to BiDil wasn't statistically significant and refused to approve the drug.

This would have been the end of the story for most drugs, but the BiDil trial had also produced one result Cohn saw as surprising. The trial involved 630 people, and 180 of them were African Americans. When only the black participants were considered, the data showed that BiDil reduced deaths to a degree that *was* statistically significant.

Cohn developed a hypothesis to explain this difference. Exactly how BiDil works was not certain, but it was known to increase the level of nitric oxide in the body. Nitric oxide, for its part, causes smooth muscle tissue to relax. (It is this property that makes it a vasodilator.) People with heart failure are often found deficient in nitric oxide, and studies have suggested that African Americans, on average, have lower nitric oxide levels than other groups in the United States. Almost a million of the five million Americans diagnosed with heart failure are black, a disproportionate rate that constitutes a major public health crisis. Thus, if BiDil showed special effectiveness in treating heart failure in African Americans, both society and the drug's makers might have a great deal to gain.

Special Study Needed?

In 1999, the Boston-based biotech company NitroMed acquired the rights to BiDil and announced its intention to market it as a drug specifically designed for African Americans. (Cohn was by then working as a consultant to NitroMed.) Although the FDA expressed skepticism about Cohn's retrospective analysis of his earlier studies, NitroMed and Cohn were able to obtain approval for a further clinical trial, this one called A-HeFT (for African American Heart Failure Trial) and made up exclusively of African American subjects.

The decision to approve a single-race study was controversial both within and outside the FDA. Critics argued that if the goal was to establish BiDil as a drug that worked best for African Americans, then the study should include subjects from other groups, to serve as a comparison and control. They pointed out that neither of the generic drugs in BiDil had been designed with a specific ethnic group in mind, nor was the drug *pharmacogenomic*—designed to target any specific genetic variant. (See Case Presentation: The Promise of Precision Medicine in Chapter 3.) These critics concluded that the race-specific presentation of BiDil was primarily rooted in a "niche-marketing" strategy and an effort to extend the patent on BiDil—which had been set to expire in 2007.

For its part, the company anticipated that testing a drug using exclusively African American subjects might cause a controversy. NitroMed officials met with representatives of the Congressional Black Caucus and the NAACP, arguing for the potential benefit of BiDil to the African American community, and ultimately securing their support. NitroMed also enlisted the Association of Black Cardiologists for help in recruiting patients for the trial.

The A-HeFT study ultimately enrolled 1,050 African American patients with heart failure. The results, announced in early 2005, showed that BiDil not only significantly reduced hospitalizations and treatment costs, but also reduced the number of expected deaths by 43 percent. Impressed by this outcome, the researchers stopped the trial early and the American Heart Association called BiDil one of the year's most significant developments in cardiac care. On June 23, 2005, the FDA approved BiDil as the first drug intended to treat disease in a specific racial category. The drug's patent was extended to 2020 and NitroMed made an initial public offering of its stock the next month.

Drugs and Disparities

Although the A-HeFT trial was applauded for its success in reducing mortality and hospitalizations, many continued to question whether the approval of BiDil as a race-specific drug was justified. Critics pointed out that many European Americans, Asian Americans, and Latinos also show deficiencies in nitric oxide and argued that the drug should not have been limited to African American patients. Others questioned why a trial that included only African Americans was not taken to reflect the drug response of humans

generally, while drugs approved on the basis of all-white research cohorts are commonly prescribed to everyone and not marketed as "white drugs."

Perhaps the most serious critique of BiDil and other race-based drugs involves the deep disparities between African Americans and other groups, especially European Americans, when it comes to health outcomes. These disparities are intertwined with the long and painful history of slavery, institutionalized racism, and poverty that has shaped the African American experience. Critics charge that drugs like BiDil revive discredited notions of innate racial difference and are thus likely to produce complacency about the social and environmental factors involved in America's stark racial health divide. (For more, see Social Context: Race, Poverty, and Disparity.)

Race as Genetic Proxy

As we saw in Chapter 3, genetic information has the power to heal and to hurt. Assertions of genetic inferiority, for example, have been major components of racism and anti-Semitism. African Americans in particular, given their experience of slavery and discrimination, have strong reasons to be suspicious of any effort to single them out as a group associated with disease.

Most researchers acknowledge that social categories of race are, at best, a poor proxy for genetic health differences. External factors such as skin color and hair texture tell us relatively little about an individual's genetic ancestry, which is often influenced by centuries of migration and reproduction across cultural and geographic divides. (For more on various concepts of race, see this chapter's Briefing Session.)

Defenders of BiDil and other race-specific treatments claim that they are merely a way station on the road to personalized *precision medicine*. Once we identify the genetic and epigenetic factors that make drugs such as BiDil effective, they argue, the use of race as a crude "biomarker" for certain genetic predispositions will no longer be necessary. Indeed, they suggest that this process will further undermine and complicate traditional (and discredited) notions of discreet racial categories.

There is some evidence that this prediction is already being realized in biomedical research. In 2011, for example, researchers identified how two genetic mutations associated with sickle-cell disease provide a defense against malaria, confirming a long-standing hypothesis that these mutations were an adaptive response to malarial environments. These genetic adaptations of the hemoglobin protein appear in many different regions (including parts of Europe and India) that have a high incidence of malaria, and thus vary independently of skin color, facial features, or other traditional determinants of race. Such findings are significant, because the 14 percent incidence of the sickle-cell mutation among African Americans was, for decades, taken as a sign that sickle cell was a "black" illness and used as a basis for employment and other forms of discrimination. (See the Briefing Session in Chapter 3.)

The 2005 discovery of a variant gene associated with heart attacks is another example of how genetic research may tend to complicate, rather than confirm, traditional notions of racial difference. The variant, a haplotype called HapK that spans the leukotriene A4 hydrolase gene, appears at a rate of about 27 percent among self-identified European Americans and 6 percent among self-identified African Americans, and in both groups it is associated with increased risk of heart attack. Evidence suggests, however, that because most people of African ancestry have only been introduced to the variant in recent centuries, they have fewer genetic adaptations to compensate for its effects on the heart. (It is believed that HapK heightens inflammatory responses to infectious disease—a response that can also damage the heart.) This may explain why having HapK is associated with a dramatic increase in heart attack risk for African Americans (250%) and only a modest increase for European Americans (16%).

Like the contemporary genetic understanding of sickle-cell disease, this explanation of the HapK variant moves past traditional categories of race to present a complex picture of the interactions between genes and the environment, influenced by periods of isolation and interaction among people in different geographic regions. The findings support neither the traditional view that certain diseases go with geographically defined races nor—as the researchers pointed out—with the "mixing" of those races. (There was no evidence of increased heart attack risk among "mixed race" individuals who lacked the HapK variant.) Such results suggest how precision medicine may be able to transcend divisive racial categories in favor of more neutral and detailed accounts of genetic ancestry.

Questions remain, however, as to how such information should be used by clinicians and drug makers, who do not yet have the ability to sequence the genome of every patient. For example, should studies of drugs developed to mitigate the effects of HapK focus exclusively or disproportionately on African American patients? Supporters of this type of approach, such as Jay Cohn, contend that it is "always best to study a drug in a highly responsive group" rather than testing it in large (and multiethnic) research cohorts. Critics, such as the genetic epidemiologist Charles Rotimi, argue that such single-group studies are likely to miss the ways in which deleterious environmental factors might contribute to results such as the increased heart attack rate among African American carriers of HapK. Such trials also fail to tell us about the potential effectiveness of such drugs in other groups—for example, the European and Asian Americans who actually have the HapK mutation in much greater numbers.

Envoi

In 2009, NitroMed announced that it was suspending its marketing efforts for BiDil and was open to buyout offers for the drug. Sales for BiDil were poor, which some observers attributed to reluctance by physicians to prescribe a race-targeted drug. Others pointed to the high cost of BiDil, which could amount to $2,800 a year per patient, as well as to a disproportionately high level of adverse reaction reports. Defenders of BiDil consider it a "scientific tragedy" that more African Americans did not embrace a drug that constitutes, in their view, the best available treatment for heart failure in the black community. They consider it equally tragic that progress has been slow on dozens of other race- and ethnicity-focused drugs announced by manufacturers in the early 2000s.

Yet even defenders typically acknowledge that race-specific treatments may be eclipsed by the rise of genuinely personalized precision medicine. When clinicians and researchers gain access to rapid genetic sequencing that allows them to tailor treatments to needs of individuals, race will likely remain relevant to medicine only as a social and political category.

CASE PRESENTATION

The Bouvia Precedent: Patient Autonomy or Disability Discrimination?

On September 3, 1983, Elizabeth Bouvia was admitted, at her own request, to Riverside General Hospital in Riverside, California. She sought admission on the grounds that she was suicidal. Bouvia was twenty-six years old and had lived with severe cerebral palsy for her entire life. She was almost completely quadriplegic, although she had the partial use of one arm. She could speak clearly and could chew her food, but required assistance with eating and many other tasks. In addition to her paralysis, Bouvia suffered intense pain from degenerative arthritis.

Despite the severity of her impairments, Bouvia had earned a bachelor's degree in social work, traveled through Europe with her mother, gotten married, and lived independently with the assistance of a state-financed home attendant. Then, in the early 1980s, Bouvia's situation became more difficult. She grew alienated from her parents, she suffered a miscarriage, she and her husband separated, and she lost the state grant that paid for her transportation needs. The special program for disabled students that was helping her pursue a master's degree at San Diego State University was discontinued. Bouvia came to believe that her only options were life in a convalescent home or an intolerable struggle with her disabilities.

After her admission, Bouvia told the hospital staff that she wished to starve herself to death. She asked to be provided with hygienic care and painkilling medicines but no food. The hospital's chief of psychiatry, Donald Fischer, told Bouvia that if she did not eat, he would have her declared mentally incompetent and a danger to herself. She could then be force-fed. Bouvia responded by calling local newspapers and asking for legal assistance. She told reporters that she could no longer endure the "mental struggle" of being "trapped in a useless body."

"It's not that I don't have the will to live," Bouvia told reporters. "But it's too much of a struggle to live within the system or to depend on someone in the system. In reality, my disability is going to keep me from doing the living I want to do."

These arguments made sense to Richard Scott, a founder of the Hemlock Society and a prominent "right to die" attorney associated with the Southern California American Civil Liberties Union, who asked to represent Bouvia after he read about her case in the papers. For Scott, Bouvia was "a tragically developmentally disabled person" who had "come to realize she is completely unemployable," and had thus made a rational choice to die.

For members of the growing disability rights movement, however, such arguments seemed bizarre. Many had impairments equivalent to Bouvia's and many were gainfully employed—including Ed Roberts, a quadriplegic recipient of a MacArthur "Genius" grant who was then director of California's state rehabilitation system. They saw no reason that Bouvia, like many other quadriplegics with cerebral palsy, couldn't live a long and happy life. In their view, her wish to die was not a direct result of her impairments but instead the result of a "disabling environment" that had failed to provide the accommodations that could give her life purpose and meaning. They interpreted her public statements as a cry for help, and offered to meet with her to discuss how she might obtain better services and community support.

Bouvia refused these offers, however, stating, "I am fully aware of the resources available to me....I choose not to use them." She retained Scott to help her secure a court order to prevent the hospital from either discharging or force-feeding her. At the court hearing, Bouvia testified that she found it "humiliating" and "disgusting" to be dependent on others for "every personal need," and concluded, "I am choosing this course of action due to my physical limitation and disability."

On behalf of his client, Scott argued that Bouvia's decision to refuse nourishment was "exactly medically and morally analogous to the patient deciding to forgo further kidney dialysis," knowingly accepting death as the consequence. Although he framed the matter as one of patient autonomy, Scott also presented Bouvia's wish as a logical, perhaps even inevitable, consequence of her impairments.

Judge John H. Hews rejected Scott's arguments. He expressed the view that Ms. Bouvia was a competent, rational, and sincere person whose decision was based on her physical condition and not upon her recent misfortunes. Nevertheless, allowing her to starve to death in the hospital would "have a profound effect" on the staff, other patients, and other disabled people. Bouvia was not terminally ill and might expect to live another fifteen to twenty years or more. Accordingly, Hews held that "the established ethics of the medical profession clearly outweigh and overcome her own rights of self-determination" and "force-feeding, however invasive, would be administered for the purpose of saving the life of an otherwise nonterminal patient and should be permitted." In effect, Hews concluded that Bouvia had a right to commit suicide, but she did not have the right to have others assist her. When Bouvia later refused to eat, Hews authorized the hospital to feed her against her will, a ruling the California Supreme Court subsequently let stand.

In February 1986, however, Elizabeth Bouvia prevailed in a different court case. She won an injunction to stop High Desert Hospital of Lancaster, California, where she had become a patient, from using a nasogastric tube to feed her against her wishes. Her victory represented a shift in the legal landscape, a process that would culminate in the *Cruzan* decision, with its affirmation of competent patients' rights to refuse treatment—including food and water. (See Case Presentation: The Cruzan Case in Chapter 7.)

But even as the courts inched closer to recognizing a "right to die," Elizabeth Bouvia began to express ambivalence about her own death. After checking out of the hospital and attempting to starve herself in a Mexican motel room, she concluded "I want to get better," and began eating again. In 1987, she again attempted to end her life through starvation, but found that the side effects of taking pain medication without food were too severe.

All the factors that go into any individual's conclusion that life is no longer worth living are complicated and difficult for strangers to assess. There is little doubt that the burden that Elizabeth Bouvia bears in terms of pain and impairment are heavier than most, with a profound impact on her quality of life. Still, many disability rights proponents see in Bouvia's ambivalence about death a confirmation that her choice was neither inevitable nor logical. In their view, her case exemplified the ways in which different circumstances may impact the quality and perceived value of disabled people's lives. Bouvia, for her part, said she appreciated the concern of the disabled community but expressed her belief that "all people, whether or not disabled, should be free to determine their own future—personally, privately and individually."

With regard to individual privacy, Elizabeth Bouvia appears to have achieved her aims. As of this writing, she has been out of the public eye for more than a decade, although she is generally assumed to still be alive. (Her attorney, Richard Scott, committed suicide in 1992.) Nevertheless, Bouvia's original plan to die and Judge Hews's decision that "the established ethics of the medical profession" outweighed her right to self-determination have continued to inform bioethical debate about both disability rights and physician-assisted death.

Although a deep concern with patient autonomy prompted many in the early bioethics movement to support Bouvia's request to die, some prominent bioethicists have, in recent years, come to question their earlier positions. With regard to Bouvia's and similar cases, some have joined disability scholars in looking first to the social causes of poor life quality among the severely disabled. Before championing a right die, they argue, bioethicists should first work to ensure that that such individuals receive the services and accommodations that might help them live less difficult and more satisfying lives.

CASE PRESENTATION
Lee Larson and Cochlear Implants

Christian and Kyron Larson were born deaf, but for the first few years of the brothers' lives, almost no one around them saw this as a disadvantage. Their deaf mother, Lee Larson, was raising them in a close-knit community of other deaf people in a small town outside of Grand Rapids, Michigan. (Their father, who was also deaf, was separated from their mother and lived in California.) The boys' first words were in American Sign

Language (ASL), and the language was the family's primary mode of communication. Like many other deaf people, Lee Larson saw being deaf as a source of self-esteem, and took pride in passing on the linguistic and cultural heritage of Deaf society to her sons.

In 2001, however, Christian and Kyron were enrolled in an elementary school that offered only oral–aural instruction for the deaf, since there was no space left in the school district's ASL-based program. Overwhelmed by an environment without signing, Kyron and Christian—who were then two and three years old, respectively—struggled to communicate with staff and peers. As a result, school officials urged that Lee Larson agree to cochlear implant surgeries for the boys, to prevent them from falling behind in school.

The Implant Dilemma

Contrary to popular perception, cochlear implants do not "restore" normal hearing to deaf people. Instead, the implants transform oral speech and other sounds into electrical impulses that stimulate surviving auditory nerve fibers—impulses that many deaf people can learn to interpret, to varying degrees. The implants, which are surgically embedded within the skull, have the best chance of altering communication capacity when employed early and combined with a "total immersion" oral–aural environment at home (i.e., no ASL). Even with this environment, children born deaf do not typically reach a level of oral–aural communication that is comparable to that of a hearing person. Many report being trapped in a kind of "limbo" between the hearing and Deaf worlds, fully proficient in neither. There is also a risk of serious side effects from cochlear implant procedure, which involves drilling a hole in the skull. Possible adverse events include facial nerve injuries, meningitis, and cerebrospinal fluid leakage, although their incidence has decreased over the past decade. Considering these factors, and after consulting with several friends who regretted getting cochlear implants, Larson decided against early implantation for Christian and Kyron.

"I want them to grow up with strong self-esteem, not trying to be somebody they are not," she later said. "I want them part of the Deaf culture." The boys' father shared this view, and school officials reluctantly accepted the decision.

But then the Larson family's story took a dramatic turn. Lee Larson went out of town to visit friends in Ohio, and she left the boys in the care of a trusted deaf friend—a woman with several other disabilities. Already in conflict with Larson over cochlear implants, school officials filed a legal negligence complaint against her for leaving the boys with the woman. A state court eventually ruled that Larson was negligent—citing evidence that the friend may have physically abused the boys—and placed Larson's children in temporary foster care. It mandated that Larson take parenting classes toward the goal of family reunification and appointed a special *guardian ad litem* for the boys. It was the guardian, an attorney named Joseph Tevlin, who then took a highly unusual step.

The Trial

After consulting with school officials and the boys' new foster parents (who were neither deaf nor proficient in ASL), Tevlin filed a motion for the state court to order that the Larson boys immediately undergo cochlear implant surgery. Even though Lee Larson retained her parental rights, Tevlin argued that implants were necessary for the boys to "realize their full potential in life" and that swift action had to be taken while they were young. The Michigan Family Independence Agency, which oversees the state's foster care system, disagreed with Tevlin's request and advised the court that legal parents retain the right to make decisions about elective surgeries, whether or not a child is in foster care. Nevertheless, the state prosecutor joined Tevlin in arguing that Larson's earlier decision against cochlear implants was a form of medical neglect and the boys' continued lack of implants constituted a medical emergency. Judge Kathleen Feeney agreed to a trial to consider the motion and ordered the Larson boys to be physically evaluated for implant surgery.

The Larson case soon attracted the attention of the national media and the disability rights and Deaf communities. In a court packed with activists and reporters, Tevlin argued that a lack of implants would cost the boys career and educational opportunities. He was joined by a state expert who testified that the implants were necessary for the language-processing areas of the boys' brains to develop fully.

For Larson's side, experts countered that it was access to language itself, not spoken language, that was necessary for normal brain development. They presented evidence that ASL is a legitimate natural language, with its own complex grammar, syntax, art, and culture. (Approximately one million Americans use ASL as their primary language.) There was no research evidence, they argued, that implants would benefit the Larson boys in language acquisition or improve their schoolwork.

On the fourth day of the trial, Lee Larson took the stand. In a voice choked with emotion, she said (and signed) that she should be the one make the decision.

"They are my flesh and blood. I am deaf. God made them deaf. I do not want them to have implants. It is not safe." When asked by the prosecutor how the boys would get along in the wider world without implants, Larson responded, "Look at me. I am deaf. I am in the hearing world and the deaf world. . . . I get along."

Medical Model, Social Model

As the legal scholar Alicia Ouellette has pointed out, the Larson case exemplifies a conflict between two competing models of disability. Tevlin's and the prosecutor's arguments were rooted in a *medical model*, in which the disadvantages of deafness are the natural result of an individual's physical defects. The only way to remove the disadvantage, on this view, is to try to modify the defective trait and bring individuals closer to normal (i.e., average) human functioning. To deprive the Larson boys of an opportunity to pursue such functioning, was, from Tevlin and the prosecutor's perspective, an act of neglect. (The boys could always pursue greater ASL literacy later, they suggested.)

By contrast, Lee Larson's arguments were rooted in a *social* or *cultural model* of disability. From this perspective, the disadvantages of a given trait (e.g., deafness) are shaped as much by a "disabling" social environment as by physical impairments. Indeed, under alternative social circumstances, the "defective" trait may actually be an advantage. In this regard, disability studies scholars often point to the example of Martha's Vineyard, an island off the coast of Massachusetts on which hereditary deafness used to be so common that almost all residents, hearing and deaf, knew how to

use sign language. Under these circumstances, deaf children tended to outperform hearing children in school, and deaf residents had equal success in work and social life. (See this chapter's Decision Scenario: Martha's Vineyard for more.)

Based on the cultural model, deafness is often viewed as just one form of difference in a pluralistic society. Forcing parents to accept cochlear implants for their deaf children is, on this view, like forcing Amish parents to make their children computer-literate, on the grounds that raising them with traditional Amish limitations on technology would harm their subsequent ability to join the broader society. (See Case Presentation: Faith and Medicine in Chapter 1 as well as Dena Davis's article in Chapter 3, for further discussion.)

Envoi

The two sides in the Larson case had sharply different concerns about potential harm. Tevlin and the prosecutor feared that the boys would be harmed by not getting implants soon enough to successfully participate in hearing society. In addition to their concerns about the potential side effects of implants, Larson and her allies feared that the boys would be harmed by forcing them to stop using the primary language they shared with their mother and the wider Deaf culture.

In the end, however, the case turned less on questions of harm than of parental rights. Judge Feeney said of the Larson boys that she had "no doubt it would be in their best interest to have implants," but ruled that getting implants did not qualify as an emergency measure. Thus, as long as parental rights had not been terminated, the state could not overrule Larson's determination of her children's best interests.

Lee Larson and the disability rights proponents who filled the courtroom were elated by the decision (although disturbed by Feeney's conclusions about the children's "best interest"). Since Larson had, by all accounts, been doing well in her parenting classes, she was expected to regain custody of Kyron and Christian after Feeney's decision a few months later. But for reasons that remain unclear in the public record, this did not occur. Lee Larson eventually lost custody of the boys and moved to Ohio. The Larson boys were adopted and both received cochlear implants.

CASE PRESENTATION
Intersex Care: Beyond Shame and Surgery

As a teenager, Pidgeon Pagonis had a recurring dream of lying in a hospital bed as it glided through the corridors of an institution.

"All I could do was see upwards, which was fluorescent lights zooming by, and then I looked down and I saw rolls of toilet paper soaked in blood between my legs. I always thought it was a nightmare," Pagonis recalled.

It turned out to be a nightmare rooted in painful realities. By the age of twelve, Pagonis had undergone three surgical procedures that were shrouded in secrecy and shame, and which no adult would fully explain. The surgeries left Pagonis with genital scar tissue, pain, and deadened sexual sensation. Yet only one of the procedures was performed for a medical reason (and this was speculative and prophylactic). Indeed, the explicit purpose of the surgeries was cosmetic, an attempt to "normalize" parts of Pagonis's anatomy that physicians considered too aberrant to be left as they were.

Pidgeon Pagonis was one of millions of babies around the world who are born *intersex*, with genitals, internal anatomy, and/or chromosomes that don't fit neatly into typical designations of male and female. Such variations are often called *differences of sex development* (DSD), an umbrella term that encompasses both recognized genetic conditions and *idiopathic* variations that have no clear medical cause. Many people with DSDs are perfectly healthy, and those who are not usually require treatment that has nothing to do with their sex or gender identity. Nevertheless, since the 1950s, tens of thousands of intersex children have been subjected to "normalizing" surgeries, hormonal treatments, and other procedures that physicians and parents have deemed necessary for social adjustment. For many patients, however, the result of such efforts is an arbitrary sex assignment that leaves them physically and emotionally scarred, with reduced sexual function and a deep sense of shame. Such was the case for Pagonis, who was born in 1986 and was originally named Jennifer.

As a result of a condition called partial androgen insensitivity syndrome (PAIS), Jennifer Pagonis was born with XY chromosomes and undescended testes, along with a partial vagina and other external features that were closer to those of a typical female. Nevertheless, surgeons judged Pagonis's clitoris to be "half a centimeter too long" and removed it when Pagonis was three. They also removed the internal testes, on the grounds they might become cancerous. Physicians instructed Jennifer's parents to raise their child as a girl and to never mention her XY chromosomes or other intersex features. They also took further surgical steps to "feminize" Pagonis's anatomy—despite evidence that as many as 50 percent of PAIS patients end up not accepting the gender given to them as children.

"When I was 11, the surgeons at the local Children's Hospital decided their work wasn't finished," Pagonis recalled. The result was a vaginoplasty, a surgical attempt to create a vaginal canal for the sole purpose of sexual penetration.

"Their…goal was to make sure I could have 'normal sex with my husband.' " But years after the surgery, Pagonis still found that intercourse with men was almost always intensely painful, not to mention sexually unsatisfying. "I still don't think my high school boyfriend knows I didn't have a clitoris," Pagonis recalled.

In college, Pagonis learned about PAIS, obtained medical records of being born with XY chromosomes, and embarked on a new life with a new name. Now twenty-nine, Pidgeon does not identify as either male or female, prefers the gender-neutral pronoun *they*, and has flourished in a close-knit Chicago community of intersex, transgender, and genderqueer activists. Pagonis does not blame their parents for approving the surgeries, but is dismayed that some surgeons still carry out such "normalization" procedures on intersex children, despite growing consensus among pediatric organizations that such childhood surgeries are unnecessary and harmful.

"We deserve to have the chance to experience life, love, and the pursuit of happiness with our original beautiful bodies intact," Pagonis testified in 2013, at a forum on intersex rights held by the Organization of American States (OAS).

Surgery and Secrecy

That intersex rights is now a matter of concern for international organizations like the OAS can be directly attributed to the work of activists and educators such as Bo Laurent. When Laurent was born in 1956, her physicians were so alarmed by her "mixed" anatomy that they kept her mother sedated for nearly three days while they tried to decide on a course of action. Baffled by genitals that combined a vagina with a phallus that they could not clearly categorize as a penis or a clitoris, the physicians eventually decided Laurent should be raised as a boy—with the understanding that the child's troubling anatomy should be kept secret. But when Laurent was one, physicians discovered that she also had a uterus and internal *ovotestes* (which combine both ovarian and testicular tissue) and decided to reverse their original gender assignment. Concerned primarily with how these genitals might be perceived by others rather than how they might later feel to Laurent herself, the surgeons completely removed the phallus so she could be reintroduced to the world as an "acceptable" girl.

"They performed a clitorectomy and they told my parents to move to another town and not tell anyone where they went and never tell me what happened," Laurent recalled. "All those things were so traumatizing, frightening and pain-producing for my parents that it made it hard for them to relate normally to me." Her parents later told her that her surgeries had been performed to relieve stomachaches.

It was only after Laurent became a sexually active lesbian that she realized that her "normalizing" surgeries had robbed her of a clitoris and the ability to have an orgasm, and only after years of struggle and isolation that she finally located other intersex people. Together they formed the Intersex Society of North America (ISNA) in 1993 and began to challenge standards of care that relied on surgery and secrecy.

Most of those standards had been developed in the early 1950s by a Johns Hopkins psychologist named John Money, in collaboration with the pioneering pediatric endocrinologist Lawson Wilkins. Money and Wilkins abandoned traditional attempts to categorize "hermaphrodites" and "pseudo-hermaphrodites" according to various criteria of "true" sex, and instead focused on a treatment approach that became known as "optimum gender of rearing." As one of the first psychologists to develop a social theory of gender (he coined the term "gender identity"), Money was deeply committed to the idea that children are born psychosexually neutral and that gender is socially constructed during the first years of a child's life. To this end, he successfully promoted a treatment protocol for intersex patients that was based on gender plasticity: any child could be made into a "real" boy or girl just by altering the appearance of their bodies and convincing caregivers and peers to reinforce this sex assignment. The result was an emphasis on early surgical and hormonal treatments, to create the "standard" sexual features that were seen as the key to psychosocial health.

Money's theoretical emphasis on the social construction of gender was applauded by some feminists, who had good reasons to reject oppressive notions of women's and men's "natural" roles. But in practice, the "optimum gender of rearing" approach was often highly paternalistic and tradition-bound. Since gender was assumed to be entirely malleable, the physicians whom Money trained often ignored the early tendencies and preferences of intersex children, and frequently managed the treatment process without obtaining fully informed consent from parents, much less patients. Decisions about sex assignments were often made based on arbitrary measurements and surgical convenience: genetic (XY) boys whose penises were judged to be too small were castrated, then given vaginoplasties and hormone treatments; genetic (XX) girls whose clitorises were judged too large were given clitorectomies or clitoroplasties. In general, the "success" of these procedures was evaluated against a traditional and lopsided view of heterosexual intercourse. (A successful vaginoplasty, for example, was defined by its ability to accommodate an average-sized penis, rather than its capacity for erotic sensation or self-lubrication.)

Finally, even as the "optimum gender of rearing" approach became the standard of intersex care around the developed world, it turned out that the science behind it was meager, and sometimes even fraudulent. There were no long-term studies that proved that "normalized" intersex children had any better psychological or social outcomes than those who were left intact, and huge numbers of former patients were "lost to follow-up." It also turned out that Money had, for decades, knowingly published misleading accounts of his primary "success story."

After a urologist accidentally burned off most of seven-month-old David Reimer's penis in an attempt at cauterized circumcision, Money persuaded his parents to have his testes removed and to raise him as a girl, with the eventual goal of vaginoplasty and full transition. But despite Money's published reports that Reimer had been successfully transformed into an "active little girl," it was later revealed that Reimer had resisted the sex assignment from early on, only reluctantly taking estrogen pills and refusing a vaginoplasty. At age fourteen, Reimer had his estrogen-created breasts removed and took testosterone injections, and later had other surgeries to transition back to a male. He eventually married, but struggled with depression and financial instability, and committed suicide in 2004.

Although Reimer was not born intersex, his case is often taken to exemplify the broader ethical problems with performing cosmetic "normalizing" procedures on nonconsenting infants. The problem is not so much that physicians get their gender assignments "wrong" (although some patients, such as Reimer, experience a clear conflict between assigned sex and internal gender identity). In fact, evidence suggests that most intersex people keep the (sometimes arbitrary) social gender assignments they receive as children and that their gender identities, like many other people's, can be complicated and malleable to some degree. The problem, as most intersex activists see it, is that such gender assignments typically start with irreversible cosmetic surgeries that have lasting consequences for the sexuality, fertility, and self-image of nonconsenting minors.

"I don't know one intersex individual who is happy with the treatment they have received from the physicians," said Howard Devore, a clinical psychologist who identifies as intersex. "One's sexual feeling, ability to feel like they can couple with another human being, is literally destroyed by some doctor's idea of how genitals are supposed to look."

Binaries and Beyond

Roughly one in every two thousand children is born with a difference of sexual development that prompts consultation with a sex differentiation specialist, although firm numbers are hard to come by. (Some estimates are as low as one in 4,500, while others are higher, with some biologists estimating that 1.7 percent of the population deviates, to some degree, from standard definitions of male and female.) DSD is an umbrella term for a wide range of variations, some of which are associated with identifiable genetic conditions such as PAIS or congenital adrenal hyperplasia, while others are idiopathic. Some intersex people have external features that appear to be typically male or female, but have atypical chromosome patterns, hormone ratios, or internal sex organs. Others have external features that seem to fall somewhere between the usual sex types. There is no simple rule for distinguishing a clitoris from a penis or scrotal from labial tissue, and many intersex people have combinations or blends of these structures. (This is not particularly surprising, since male and female genitals develop from the same fetal tissue.)

When all these variations are taken into account, many biologists argue that sex differences start to look more like a *spectrum* than a *binary* system composed of two neatly opposite poles. Although the vast majority of people fall into two main clusters, nature does not draw a clear line between male and female. (That is something humans impose on nature.) Similarly, *gender*—the social and individual experience of sex differences—also clearly involves a spectrum of masculine and feminine behaviors and social norms, with considerable variation among individuals and cultures. As we have seen throughout this text, both nature and nurture are often intertwined and considerably more complicated than the categories humans devise to make sense of our lives.

Given this complexity, it should not be surprising that some intersex individuals, like Pidgeon Pagonis, ultimately resist the idea of a fixed or "true" gender identity that medical assignment simply reversed. For some other people with DSDs, the feeling that their underlying identity contradicts a previous medical and social sex assignment is more central. It should be noted, however, that this is distinct from the sense of painful contradiction that some transgender people feel with regard to their natal sex and gender assignment (although the two experiences occasionally overlap). In schematic terms, *intersex* people have anatomies that don't fit neatly into the categories of binary sex, whereas *transgender* people have an internal experience of gender identity that (to varying degrees) does not match their birth anatomy and gender assignment. Thus trans people often struggle to obtain sex reassignment procedures as adults, while intersex people often wish they had been spared sex-assignment procedures as children. (See this chapter's Briefing Session and Case Presentation: The *DSM* and Sexual Minorities for more.) As mentioned above, evidence suggests that most intersex people do not actually reject the gender assignments given to them as children or wish to live beyond gender binaries. But they typically resent being subjected to cosmetic surgeries before the age of consent, as well as growing up with a sense of shame and secrecy about having anatomy that had to be medically "fixed."

With regard to surgeries and other early medical interventions, the position of intersex advocates such as Bo Laurent and ISNA has been consistent for over two decades. They believe that intersex children should be given a preliminary "best guess" social gender assignment, along with therapy and social support, but that medically unnecessary surgeries and hormones should be reserved for adults or adolescents who choose such treatment themselves. They argue that performing cosmetic genital surgeries on infants is akin to the widely condemned practice of *female genital cutting* or *female genital mutilation* (FGM), and often has similar results. (See Case Presentation: Cutting and Culture in Chapter 11.)

Defenders of cosmetic "normalizing" procedures argue that leaving newborns with "ambiguous" genitalia sets them up for social ostracism and psychological harm, and they point out that other infant cosmetic procedures are performed for harelips and birthmarks. At root, their argument is that we cannot expect society to alter its traditional categories of sexual anatomy and that children with DSDs will do best if they are instead altered to meet them. Intersex advocates argue that such social expectations are mostly about such things as hair and clothes, not genitals. As for psychosocial harm, they point out that similar arguments were made for attempts to "cure" or closet LGBT people, and that the impact of the gay rights and feminist movements shows that society can change its attitudes about such topics.

There is some evidence such arguments have already had an impact on the medical community. In 2006, the journal *Pediatrics* released a consensus statement on intersex care signed by fifty international medical experts, as well as some patients' advocates, including Bo Laurent. The statement echoes ISNA's recommendation for a quick, preliminary gender assignment and instructs physicians to discourage cosmetic surgical interventions. It notes that there is no scientific evidence that such interventions improve psychosocial outcomes. The statement is nonbinding, however, and there is evidence that many physicians still present surgery as a first-line option. Other physicians are pursuing a controversial (and potentially dangerous) off-label treatment of pregnant women with dexamethasone steroids, to try to prevent the intersex results of the genetic condition known as congenital adrenal hyperplasia (CAH).

Nevertheless, there is evidence that many societies are becoming less concerned with binary sex and gender determinations as a precondition to acknowledging someone as a person. It is significant that sex no longer determines whom one can marry in the United States, Ireland, and many other countries. It is also striking that Australia, New Zealand, Nepal, and Germany have introduced "X" or blank box options on some forms of government identification, as an alternative to "M" or "F." Although such designations are likely most useful for transgender and other people who challenge social gender categories—rather than the majority of intersex people who accept them—these changes seem to reflect a growing acceptance of diverse identities when it comes to sex and gender. It is still hard to imagine a society where the first question people ask about a newborn is not, "Is it a boy or a girl?" But perhaps these shifts have already made the answer less important.

SOCIAL CONTEXT

The *DSM* and Sexual Minorities

The *Diagnostic and Statistical Manual of Mental Disorders* (*DSM*) is commonly called the "bible" of psychiatry. But the

DSM also serves as a canonical book of mental health for insurers, government agencies, and the U.S. legal, correctional, and educational systems—not to mention the rest of the medical profession. Written by committees of the American Psychiatric Association (APA), the *DSM* originated in efforts to make the field more consistent and objective by defining each diagnosis using lists of symptoms and quantitative thresholds.

But in the years since its first edition in 1952, the *DSM* has also been repeatedly criticized, even by some of its former authors, for being arbitrary, inconsistent, or shaped by cultural and financial biases. Critics have presented evidence that even psychiatrists trained in *DSM* criteria frequently give the same patient contradictory diagnoses or find disorders in objectively healthy individuals. Critics also point to a more than 200 percent increase in identified diagnoses since the first edition and argue that the *DSM* reflects a "medicalization of normalcy" or "disease mongering" by a profession with deep financial ties to the industry that develops drugs to treat mental disorders.

Much of this controversy is rooted in the profound political, social, and economic impact of where we draw the line between mental health and mental illness. Nowhere is this impact more apparent than in the *DSM*'s history of variable, and even contradictory, approaches to the mental health of *sexual minorities*—individuals whose sexuality, gender identity, or sex differs markedly from that of the majority group in society. The *DSM*'s shift away from viewing homosexuality and transgender identities as pathological has been widely praised, for example, as lesbian, gay, bisexual, and transgender (LGBT) people have gained greater acceptance and recognition in society at large. But these shifts have also undermined the *DSM*'s authority as an objective arbiter of the line between sickness and health.

Medicalizing Homosexuality

The *DSM*'s original 1952 listing of homosexuality as a "sociopathic personality disturbance" was unsurprising for its time, but it was not inevitable. Indeed, many ancient societies and even early Christian Europe appear to have largely tolerated or accepted homosexuality as part of the normal range of human behaviors. But in the late Middle Ages, a broad condemnation of all non-procreative sexual acts began to take root in the Catholic Church, driven, in part, by the rise of natural law philosophers such as Thomas Aquinas. (See Chapter 12 for more on Aquinas's philosophy.)

The Church's hostility to homosexuality (and other non-procreative sex) soon spread to secular institutions, which imposed harsh criminal sanctions on a broad class of consensual heterosexual and homosexual acts that fell under the heading of "sodomy," making some of them punishable by death. These and similar laws spread throughout Europe and to the American colonies. When, in the late nineteenth and early twentieth centuries, physicians began to take an interest in homosexuality, even as an illness, they often saw themselves as agents of social progress, because medicalizing sexual minorities seemed more beneficent than categorizing them as sinful or criminal. Indeed, some who were seen as medical authorities on homosexuality, such as Havelock Ellis and Sigmund Freud, came to believe that it could be a natural and healthy variation on normal human development. Freud famously wrote to a concerned American mother that homosexuality, while no advantage, was "nothing to be ashamed of, no vice, no degradation; it cannot be classified as an illness."

But toward the middle of the twentieth century, the pendulum began to swing in the other direction. In Europe, gay men and (to a lesser extent) lesbians were some of the first targets of Nazi eugenic and extermination policies, and tens of thousands were sent to their deaths in concentration camps. (There they were forced to wear an identifying pink triangle, the equivalent of the Jewish yellow star.) In the United States, American psychiatrists and psychologists developed theories of homosexuality as a pathology caused by "close-binding" mothers or other familial dynamics. To "cure" their condition, gays and lesbians were involuntarily committed to psychiatric facilities and forced to undergo electroshock therapy, chemical and surgical castration, clitoridectomies, and sometimes even lobotomies. Physicians also devised a treatment regimen termed "aversion therapy," which subjected patients to repeated electrical shocks (frequently to the genitals) as they viewed homoerotic images.

The pathological status of homosexuality in psychiatry and medicine was mirrored by widespread social persecution of lesbian, gay, and bisexual (LGB) individuals. Even a rumor of homosexuality was enough to get one fired, discharged from the military, socially ostracized, and subjected to severe and sometimes deadly violence. Courts tended to excuse attacks on homosexuals, and police raids on gay and lesbian bars and social clubs were pervasive. In this atmosphere of intimidation and fear, the biomedical study of LGB populations was almost exclusively performed on prisoners and people already under psychiatric care, and it generally involved little rigorous empirical testing. In what is now considered a classic example of *selection bias* in research, these studies tended to confirm psychologists' cultural assumptions that nonheterosexual desire was associated with psychological problems. All of these factors contributed to the *DSM*'s 1952 listing of homosexuality.

De-Medicalizing Homosexuality

But even as social and medical discrimination against LGB people increased, some researchers began to take a closer look at the evidence. Between 1948 and 1953, the pioneering sexologist Alfred Kinsey published the results of two massive studies of human sexual behavior, which found that as many as 37 percent of men and 13 percent of women reported reaching orgasm with a same-sex partner, and that as much as 10 percent of the population was predominantly or exclusively homosexual. (See Briefing Session for an analysis of Kinsey's studies.) Anthropological research demonstrated that LGB individuals existed in nearly all cultures, and zoologists found that homosexuality was common in nonhuman species.

In 1957, the psychologist Evelyn Hooker confronted the selection bias issue head-on by refusing to limit her research on gay men to psychiatric patients or prisoners. Instead, she worked to assemble a research cohort with equal numbers of gay and straight men, all of whom were functioning normally in society. She then administered standard psychological measurements of mental health and adjustment to the men and asked prominent experts on these tests to evaluate them without knowledge of the subjects' sexual orientation. Not only could the experts not distinguish the homosexuals from the heterosexuals, but they rated them the same on their level of mental health and social adjustment. Hooker's findings have since been replicated in dozens of studies and systematic reviews, using a variety of psychological tests on both women and men.

The publication of the second edition of the *DSM* in 1968 coincided with the rise of the modern gay rights movement—often taken to have begun when a crowd of gay, lesbian, and transgender New Yorkers fought back against a police raid on a popular Greenwich Village bar called the Stonewall Inn. Drawing inspiration from the feminist and African American civil rights movements, gay rights advocates soon came to believe that the definition of their identities by the medical establishment had played a significant role in their oppression.

By 1968, homosexuality was no longer categorized as "sociopathic" in the *DSM*, but it was still listed as a form of "sexual deviance," which led gay activists to confront APA members at their annual meetings. They also persuaded some gay and lesbian APA members to testify about the burdens of having to hide their identities in order to practice. (John Fryer, a prominent professor of medicine and psychiatry, testified in disguise as "Dr. H. Anonymous" at a 1972 APA panel discussion.)

After meeting with gay activists and conducting their own research review, Dr. Robert Spitzer and the rest of the APA Nomenclature Task Force concluded in 1973 that the weight of the evidence indicated that homosexuality was not, in itself, an illness and should thus be eliminated from the *DSM*. This conclusion was affirmed by the APA Board of Trustees, which took the unusual step of opening the decision to the entire APA membership. To the surprise of those who still saw homosexuality as a pathology, the referendum to delist homosexuality was approved by the entire membership by a vote of 58 percent. The decision was accompanied by an official APA position statement supporting civil rights protections for homosexual persons.

The APA's landmark 1973 decision was a major step toward advancing the civil rights of LGB individuals, including the right to marry, which was ultimately affirmed by the U.S. Supreme Court in 2015. The decision also prompted other major mental health organizations to officially declare that homosexuality is not a mental disorder. But it did not entirely eliminate homosexuality from the *DSM*. As a compromise with the APA's more conservative members, *DSM* editions through 1987 included a diagnostic category called "ego-dystonic homosexuality,"

which referred to the subjective distress that some LGB people might feel about their sexual orientation. Critics pointed out that there was no equivalent category for distress heterosexuals might feel about their own desires, and argued that the real root of "ego-dystonic homosexuality" was the widespread social prejudice against LGB populations. (It was thus akin to diagnosing African Americans with a mental illness if they were distressed by racism.)

These arguments eventually proved decisive, with the APA's removal of the diagnosis in 1987, but not before it had fostered a new generation of "conversion" therapies, many modeled on the "aversion" therapies of the 1950s. Although efforts to "cure" homosexuality have been banned in a number of states and officially condemned by the APA as causing psychological harm and increased suicide risk (especially in teens), such practices continue in some states, despite substantial evidence that changing sexual orientation through "treatment" is most likely impossible.

The *DSM* and Transgender Identities

At the same time that the APA was eliminating homosexuality as a listed diagnosis in the 1980s, it was introducing what would become an equally controversial diagnosis called "gender identity disorder" (GID) with regard to some members of the transgender community. The term *transgender* encompasses a wide range of identities, but it most commonly refers to a profound ongoing experience of having a gender that does not "match" the gender one was assigned at birth. It is typically contrasted with the term *cisgender*, which refers to people who do experience such a match. Transgender people may be heterosexual, bisexual, or homosexual, since sexuality is different from *gender*— the set of behaviors, norms, and social roles associated with being a man or a woman.

Some trans people identify with one traditional gender assignment or another, while others experience their gender identity as lying somewhere between or beyond these categories. (For more on these topics, see this chapter's Briefing Session.)

As with LGB individuals, there is little evidence that trans people have any greater propensity to mental illness than the general population, but they tend to face even more acute stigma and discrimination. To be sure, gender roles, clothes, and behaviors are highly variable across epochs and cultures, and the often arbitrary nature of these divisions means that everyone is *gender nonconforming* to some degree. But as transgender people soon discover, there are often sharp limits to how much gender nonconformity society will tolerate, particularly for those still perceived as male. Although many traditional cultures—such as those in Samoa, Albania, Hawaii, Thailand, and parts of India—do have formal roles for "third" or alternatively gendered individuals, mainstream U.S. culture does not currently provide much room for such variety. As a result, trans adults and children are frequently subject to bullying, ridicule, employment discrimination, and violence. It is estimated that over half of transgender youth will have made at least one suicide attempt by the time they are twenty, and their attempts to socially transition are often blocked by dress codes and other institutional policies enforcing gender norms.

Not surprisingly, living in a social role and (frequently) a body that doesn't match one's interior gender identity can be acutely distressing and psychologically harmful for some (but not all) transgender individuals. Cisgender people sometimes try to think their way into this experience by imagining what it would be like to be forced to live one's life in drag, but the more relevant thought experiment is probably to imagine how it would feel to be forced to physically transition to the other sex. This experience of internal dissonance is, in fact, a primary reason that some transgender people seek gender reassignment surgeries or hormonal treatments, and is sometimes described as "being a man trapped in a woman's body" or vice versa.

Defenders of the *DSM*'s category of "gender identity disorder" viewed it as a well-intentioned effort to recognize the psychological intensity and emotional burden of living with a "strong and persistent cross-gender identification," as *DSM-IV* put it. For some transgender people, the GID diagnosis also provided the primary means of obtaining insurance coverage for gender reassignment surgeries and other treatments. But critics argued that GID was used as a broad brush that simplified and stigmatized transgender experience, implying that transgender people were diseased, not just different. Critics also suggested that the transgender "mental disorder" might be partially caused by living in a society with limited tolerance for gender ambiguity.

As a result of decades of lobbying within and outside the APA, the 2013 *DSM-V* changed GID to *gender dysphoria*, and specified that being transgender or gender nonconforming "is not, in itself, a mental disorder." Instead, gender dysphoria is explicitly defined as a temporary condition that is typically treatable through social and/or physical gender transition, along with counseling and other forms of psychological support. The stated objective is to assist those individuals who need help with transition and psychological distress, while not stigmatizing those who are happy with their lives.

Still, the new diagnosis demonstrates how politically and ethically fraught any medical concept can be, especially when it involves a politically charged category such as gender. Take the example of gender-nonconforming or transgender children—genetic boys and girls who have a deep identification with the other gender and insist on dressing and acting accordingly, despite the frequently high social costs.

On the one hand, many gender traditionalists have used the gender dysphoria category to argue for "normative" therapies that punish or otherwise discourage boys from wearing dresses or girls from cutting their hair short and engaging in rough and tumble sports. On the other hand, some transgender activists have used gender dysphoria to argue that such children should be helped with early social transition to the other gender, in anticipation of full hormonal and surgical treatment when they are older. A third group, one which includes many parents, argue that what such children really need is just time and social space free from bullying, ridicule, and the rigid enforcement of gender norms. If gender-nonconforming children wish later to fully transition from one gender to another, they can do so, but the immediate problem is an intolerant social environment. Such debates are a reminder that medical categories, especially those of mental health, involve questions of both individual well-being and competing visions of a just society.

Problems of Living

The history of discarded psychiatric diagnoses with roots in social prejudice—including such terms as drapetomania, neurosis, hysteria, and premenstrual dysphoria—has long provided fodder for broader critiques of psychology and psychiatry. In the 1950s and 1960s, an *anti-psychiatry* movement arose, led by thinkers such as the psychiatrist Thomas Szasz, the historian Michel Foucault, and the sociologist Erving Goffman, which argued that mental illness was a metaphor and a means of social control. Szasz, in particular, suggested that the *DSM*'s categories should be broken up into

either neurological conditions or "problems of living" that involve nonconformity and social conflict. (See Szasz's essay later in this chapter.) The force of such arguments was blunted, to some degree, by the rise of "functional" diagnosis in medicine and psychiatry, which explicitly acknowledged that disease may have both physical and psychosocial origins. They were also undermined by the decline of psychoanalysis and other psychodynamic theories, and stronger evidence of a physiological basis for conditions such as schizophrenia and bipolar disorder.

Nevertheless, there are indications that the *DSM*, with its origins in the psychoanalytic era, may be losing some of its authority in American life and science. In May 2013, two weeks before the publication of *DSM-V*, the National Institute of Mental Health (NIMH) withdrew its support for the manual, based, in part, on the lack of specifically cited research evidence for its diagnostic categories.

"Unlike our definitions of ischemic heart disease, lymphoma, or AIDS, the *DSM* diagnoses are based on a consensus about clusters of clinical symptoms, not any objective laboratory measure," wrote NIMH's director Thomas Insel. This landmark decision was accompanied by a stinging critique of *DSM-V* by Allen Francis, former chair of the *DSM-IV* task force. Francis called the new manual a "bonanza for drug companies" that would lead to "massive over-diagnosis and harmful over-medication." Particularly egregious, in Francis's view, were new diagnoses such as "Disruptive Mood Dysregulation Disorder," which he argued would medicalize (and medicate) childhood temper tantrums, "Minor Neurocognitive Disorder," which would do the same for the minor memory lapses of old age, and new diagnostic criteria for "Major Depressive Disorder" that would include grief after the death of a loved one. He also suggested that the manual would fuel overprescription of antidepressants and antianxiety medications by obscuring "the already fuzzy boundary between generalized anxiety disorder and the worries of everyday life.

Meanwhile, concern continues to grow about the potential harms of socially biased therapeutic categories and techniques. In April 2015, the White House called for a nationwide ban on "conversion" therapies, following the suicide of seventeen-year-old Leelah Alcorn, a transgender teen from Ohio. Born as Joshua, Alcorn had experienced a strong cross-gender identification since the age of four and had been enrolled in years of conversion therapy by her parents. In her suicide note posted to Tumblr, Alcorn wrote, "The only way I will rest in peace is if one day transgender people aren't treated the way I was, they're treated like humans, with valid feelings and human rights. Gender needs to be taught about in schools, the earlier the better." She also noted the alarmingly high rate of suicide among gay and transgender teens and condemned psychiatric efforts to change her identity as biased and abusive.

"My death needs to mean something," Alcorn concluded. "Fix society. Please."

BRIEFING SESSION

"We hold these truths to be self-evident, that all men are created equal, that they are endowed by their Creator with certain unalienable Rights, that among these are Life, Liberty and the pursuit of Happiness." So begins the preamble to the American Declaration of Independence.

Despite the moral flaws of its authors (Thomas Jefferson and others owned slaves), the words of the Declaration have inspired over two centuries of reforms, revolutions, and movements for social justice around the world. In endorsing the proposition that "all men are created equal," the Declaration rejected the inherited hierarchies of political power and caste embodied in institutions such as the British aristocracy and monarchy. The revolutionary claim to equality refused to respect arbitrary divisions between "highborn" and "lowborn" citizens and the assumptions about "natural" superiority and inferiority on which they were based. Drawing on the natural rights philosophies of John Locke and others, the founders argued for a more expansive view of the qualities and capacities that human beings share, as the foundation for moral and political community.

Determining the criteria for such community has, however, been the subject of long-standing debate and even civil war. The early interpretation of "all men are created equal" notoriously failed to grant citizenship and equal moral status to African slaves, women, Native Americans, and other non-Europeans. Social and political restrictions in the new nation also severely limited the rights and civic participation of sexual minorities and the disabled.

Even when we recognize that conclusions about superiority, inferiority, and human value cannot be derived from categories listed above, however, it is still abundantly clear that *individuals* are born unequal. They have different physical capacities and features, different intellectual and emotional strengths, and they inherit radically different opportunities and socioeconomic resources—often based on social categories like the ones just mentioned. Whatever the founders meant by equality, it does not seem to describe an existing state of affairs. So what does this standard mean, and to whom does it apply?

Starting in the nineteenth century, Americans began to develop a conception of equality as an ever-evolving social and political ideal, rooted in the notion that all members of society are of equal worth and should have equal moral standing. In 1857, a senatorial candidate named Abraham Lincoln rejected the "obvious untruth" that at the time of the revolution Americans "were then actually enjoying that equality" or were about to achieve it. Instead, he argued, equality was meant to serve as

> *a standard maxim for free society, which should be familiar to all, and revered by all; constantly looked to, constantly labored for, and even though never perfectly attained, constantly approximated, and thereby constantly spreading and deepening its influence, and augmenting the happiness and value of life to all people of all colors everywhere.*

This idea of equality as an evolving ideal of moral and political standing was explicitly invoked by Martin Luther King, Jr., and other leaders of the African American civil rights movement. In 1963, King stood on the steps of the Lincoln Memorial and argued that "when the architects of our great republic wrote the magnificent words of the Constitution and the Declaration of Independence, they were signing a promissory note to which every American was to fall heir." Honoring that promissory note, in King's view, meant not only rejecting the formal and informal structures of systematic racial injustice, but also the pseudoscience of race that had been used to justify slavery, Jim Crow, and other racist institutions. Just as the founding fathers had denied the legitimacy of "superior" bloodlines, the civil rights and anticolonial movements of the twentieth century challenged taxonomies of race that had deemed non-Europeans inferior and subhuman.

In a similar fashion, the feminist movement rejected pseudoscientific accounts of women's bodies and intellectual capacities that were used to deny them the right to vote and to occupy positions of political and economic power. Later waves of feminism went on to challenge patterns of gender discrimination, reproductive restrictions, and sexual violence as limiting women's ability to participate fully in public life. At the same time, nonheterosexual and gender atypical Americans began to reject biomedical accounts of their desires and identities as pathological or "unnatural," along with the discrimination and violence that kept them in the closet. Like earlier liberation movements, they drew on the ideal of American equality to claim basic rights to marry, start families, and participate in civil society—claims that were broadly affirmed in a 2015 Supreme Court decision. In a similar fashion, disability rights activists began to question why public life and the built environment were structured around one set of physical abilities that even "able-bodied" Americans only exercised for part of their lives. They argued that there was nothing natural or inevitable about existing barriers to their full participation in civil society, only a set of discriminatory social choices.

In these and many other movements for social change, we can identify several related themes. First, there is a rejection of social hierarchies based on supposedly natural or biological difference and an argument that much of that difference has been *socially constructed* or structured. (Similar arguments were advanced by the founders against the "natural" hierarchies of monarchy and aristocracy.) Second, there is an embrace of equality as an evolving and expanding "maxim for free society," to use Lincoln's formulation. On this view of equality, social and political participation should not be limited by morally arbitrary differences among persons; rather, diversity should be taken as a foundation of democratic society.

Such a view of society is often called *pluralistic*, in that it embraces diverse (plural) ways of being and living, as well as different religious and philosophical conceptions of a good life. Pluralism assumes these differing *comprehensive views* are likely come into conflict and, indeed, pluralistic forms of *justice* generally seek to identify fair terms of societal interaction to which the adherents of these conflicting views could all agree.

Nevertheless, there is plenty of room for sharp bioethical disagreement in a pluralistic society, as represented throughout this text. Some of the conflict involves persons who, for various reasons, may not be able to fully exercise or express their autonomous interests—such as young children or the severely mentally ill. (See Chapter 1 for examples of such situations.) Conflicts also arise over the definition of personhood itself, with regard to the beginning and end of human life and with regard to nonhuman animals. (Chapters 2, 5, 6, and 7 address these issues.) As we have seen, many of these conflicts involve *moral continua* in which it may be difficult to draw sharp moral lines and where ethical positions may shift across a particular continuum. (Many people, for example, are more comfortable granting serious moral consideration to eight-month-old fetuses or

chimpanzees than they are to two-day-old embryos or tadpoles.)

All of these conflicts involve our struggle to locate the borders of the moral community defined by the ideal of equality. Perhaps that struggle is, as Lincoln and King suggested, always unfinished. Not only are the borders of moral community contentious and blurred, but even within that community the ideal of equality remains elusive, "constantly labored for...though never perfectly attained."

In the discussion that follows, we do not presume to advance the cause of equality in a pluralistic society or argue for its expansion in any particular direction. Instead, we will explore some key bioethical distinctions around race, sex, gender, and disability that help make sense of the pluralistic society we already have. These conceptual distinctions have played an important role both in the identity-based social movements discussed above and in their sometimes fraught encounters with the institutions of biomedical science.

Concepts of Race and Ethnicity

In 1851, the prominent Louisiana physician Samuel Cartwright published a paper in the *New Orleans Medical and Surgical Journal* describing a mental disorder called "drapetomania," which was then thought to be afflicting African slaves. The primary diagnostic symptom of this disorder was an "addiction" to "absconding from service," which was believed to be caused by an imbalance in the blood or humors. (The disease was seen as closely related to "dysaesthesia aethiopis," an affliction diagnosed in freed slaves, with symptoms such as skin lesions, lethargy, and malingering.) Cartwright, who was considered a leading expert on the "diseases and peculiarities of the negro race,"

recommended prophylactic treatments for drapetomania that included whipping and the removal of both big toes to prevent those afflicted from acting on their urge to escape their owners. These "treatments" were likely to return slaves to the "submissive state which was intended for them to occupy."

To contemporary readers, Cartwright's paper is often seen as a classic case of pseudoscientific medicine tailored to a sociopolitical power structure. But at the time, Cartwright's ideas were widely distributed and taken seriously by the southern medical establishment and beyond. They were part of a large body of medical literature that attempted to use craniometry, hematology, evolutionary theory, and eugenics to justify race-based social and political structures before and after the Civil War. Such theories helped rationalize physicians' use of slaves to test new drugs and surgical procedures (often without anesthesia), and later abusive experiments on nonwhites in mental hospitals and in clinical research. (See Case Presentation: The Afterlife of Henrietta Lacks in Chapter 2 and Case Presentation: The Tuskegee Syphilis Study in this chapter.) These pseudoscientific ideas were also embodied in such policies as the widespread segregation of black and white blood supplies by the Red Cross, the U.S. military, and many hospitals up through the 1950s and 1960s.

Convenient biological theories of race have not, of course, been limited to the United States or a focus on African Americans. Decades before the Holocaust, for example, medical scientists in Europe and beyond developed elaborate theories of Jewish racial characteristics that included sloped skulls, flat feet, hooked noses, and male menstruation, as well as psychological "symptoms" such as avarice, nymphomania, and laziness. The medical establishments of colonial powers endorsed detailed taxonomies of physiological and psychological racial differences that helped bolster colonial rule over subject populations in Asia, Africa, and Latin America.

Given this history, it should not be surprising that there is considerable controversy about which, if any, concepts of race should be employed in medical practice and research. Although scientific theories of discreet genetic races were largely discredited in the 1970s, some researchers and clinicians still argue that social categories of race can be used as effective "proxies" for genetic patterns of geographic ancestry and migration. Others argue that race is only useful in biomedical science as a way of tracking and mitigating the health effects of social and political categories. To explore these disagreements, it will be useful to distinguish among several different conceptions of race that have been employed in biomedical science.

Traditional Concepts of Race

Traditional or "folk" conceptions of race played a significant role in mainstream biology up until the rise of detailed genetic analysis in the 1970s. Traditional notions of race took surface traits such as skin color, hair texture, and facial features, and assumed they correlated to a host of underlying genetic and physiological differences, including disease susceptibility, character traits, intelligence, and so on. Such groupings were often based on arbitrary continental divisions and achieved biomedical respectability in the nineteenth century with explicit (and typically colonial) hierarchies of inferiority and superiority among categories such as the "Caucasoid," "Mongoloid," "Negroid," and "Australoid" races.

In 1972, however, the Harvard biologist Richard Lewontin dealt a serious blow to traditional categories of race when he demonstrated that 85 percent of all human genetic variation occurred *within* such geographic categories, compared to 15 percent among them. This finding was the opposite of what one would expect to find if races had serious biological significance. Another blow came when the Human Genome Project (HGP) revealed that both kinds of variation observed by Lewontin accounted for just 0.1 percent of human genetic material. The discovery that humans are 99.9 percent genetically identical undermined traditional racism's assumption of separate evolutionary trajectories and suggested, as the geneticist Spencer Wells puts it, "We are all descendants of people who lived in Africa recently." Further research has indicated that surface features such as skin color or hair texture are poor surrogates for the complicated histories of ancestral migration and environmental adaptation that produce genetic diversity. In addition, these features vary independently of each other and do not correspond to any cluster of genes or heritable traits. As a result of such evidence, almost all biologists have abandoned the traditional conception of race, agreeing with the HGP's director Craig Venter, that "race has no genetic or scientific basis."

Race as Proxy

Even though scientists generally view races as sociocultural constructs, some still argue that these constructs can be used as *proxies* for more precise genetic subgroups within or across traditionally defined races. Some argue, for example, that because people who lived in the same geographic region were more likely to have reproduced and shared genetic material with the people around them, we can expect to find clusters of homogenous genetic traits among people whose ancestors came from the same geographic region, and perhaps even among people whose ancestors came from the same continent.

A related version of this view, more common in biomedical settings, argues from the relative incidence of certain disease states in a given population to the use of race as a proxy medical concept. Thus, the higher-than-average incidence of the Tay-Sachs and BRCA1/2 gene mutations among people with Ashkenazi Jewish ancestry might argue for a revival of the (largely abandoned) concept of a Jewish biological race. Similarly, the higher-than-average incidence of sickle-cell disease among people whose ancestors hail from sub-Saharan Africa might argue that medicine treat all self-identified African Americans as belonging to the same biological race. Proponents argue that similar correlations between sociocultural race categories and conditions such as cystic fibrosis, lactose intolerance, heart disease, and hypertension mean that these categories can be used as effective proxies for underlying genetic realities.

Critics raise objections to both versions of the "race as proxy" position. First, they contend that continental race categories are much too broad to capture the complicated cultural, regional, and migratory factors that shape reproduction and genetic ancestry. For example, the sociocultural concept of the Caucasian or white race includes the descendants of dozens of different peoples in Europe who lived in a wide range of environments, mingled with some of their neighbors (and not with others), and experienced complicated histories of migration, famine, and disease. (This category also includes the descendants of groups, such as Ashkenazi Jews, who frequently had less genetic exchange with their neighbors due to factors such as racism and religion.) Critics point to similar geographic and cultural complexity in the genetic histories of Africa, Asia, and other regions.

With regard to the medical use of race as proxy, critics also argue that rapid medical assessments based on perceived or self-identified race are likely to misdiagnose and mistreat many patients. For example, the rate of sickle-cell anemia is seven times higher among some subgroups in Asia than it is among some subgroups in Africa, despite the common assumption that sickle-cell is an African or African American condition. Although people of European ancestry have higher-than-average rates of cystic fibrosis, the condition is far more common in northwestern Europe than other parts of the region. Furthermore, due to complex histories of immigration or colonization, many people who are lumped into the same racial category (such as "black") may come from radically different ancestral groups. Such categories are thus no substitute for a careful interview about symptoms, environment, and family history.

As for the use of race as a proxy in biomedical research, critics raise several methodological concerns. Analyzing a given research cohort by traditional race categories may allow researchers to find some clusters of similar genetic variations. But it may simultaneously prevent them from seeing other clusters that cross these (largely arbitrary) geographic divisions. Given what is known about the distribution of genetic variations in the human population, such race-crossing clusters of genetic homogeneity should be expected.

Finally, attributing racial health disparities to underlying genetic differences may cause researchers to overlook the ways in which such disparities are created by social, environmental, and political conditions. For example, the fact that African Americans have, on average, much higher rates of hypertension than European Americans was for decades assumed to result from innate differences. Then epidemiologist Richard Cooper conducted large comparative studies demonstrating that hypertension rates in West Africans were comparable to or significantly lower than that of U.S. whites, while Germans (for example) had much higher rates than Americans in general. The results suggested that the racial gap in the United States is likely the result of environmental factors (such as stress, diet, and living conditions) rather than genetics. Similarly, a 2015 systematic review of genetic research on heart disease disparities published in the *American Journal of Epidemiology* found "little or no" evidence that the gap between populations of African and European ancestry was caused by genetic factors. This finding is of critical importance, since black men and women still have twice the risk of dying from heart disease compared with white men and women. (See Case Presentation: BiDil and Beyond and Social Context: Race, Poverty, and Disparity.)

Race as Construct

Despite criticisms of the traditional and proxy views of race, few scientists advocate the abandonment of racial terminology in research and clinical practice. This is, in

part, because categories of race still appear to have such a profound impact on people's lives and health, especially African Americans. To take only a few well-known statistics, self-identified African American men live, on average, about five years less than self-identified white men, and black women four years less than white women. African American cancer patients are 10 percent less likely than white ones to be alive five years after diagnosis, and African American women are 40 percent more likely than white women to die of breast cancer, despite being slightly less likely than white women to get the disease. African Americans are significantly more likely than whites to lack health insurance, to suffer from diabetes and obesity, and to be homicide victims. In addition to experiencing higher-than-average incarceration, crime, and poverty rates, African American neighborhoods are typically characterized by an abundance of low-quality fast food and a striking dearth of pharmacies, gyms, and fresh produce. Like nonwhite communities more generally, such neighborhoods also have disproportionately high levels of toxic air pollution, industrial pollution, and toxic waste storage facilities.

Given these and other factors, it is easy to see how social and political race categories might dramatically impact average health outcomes. In order to monitor and attempt to mitigate disparities associated with racial categories, it may, therefore, be necessary for physicians to employ such categories, even if they share the U.S. Institute of Medicine's conclusion that race is ultimately "a construct of human variability based on perceived differences." This pragmatic use of race as a social construct is what the anthropologist Michael Montoya calls *descriptive* rather than *attributive*, in the sense that it pragmatically reports on the results of racial categorizations rather than attributing essential qualities or traits to a given population. Such usage is based on either *self-ascribed* or *other-ascribed* racial categories, with the understanding that these labels may be arbitrary or even contradictory for the same person.

Indeed, one of the troubles with the use of race as a socially constructed category is that racial designations are so variable. As late as the 1940s, some southern states still legally enforced slavery-era "one drop of blood" policies, which designated anyone with any degree of African ancestry as black and thus ineligible to marry a white person. This sense that African parentage still "trumps" other designations when it comes to social and political perception has prompted some people with European–African ancestry (such as President Barack Obama) to self-identify as African American rather than, say, Irish American. At the same time, genomic databases indicate that over six million self-identified European Americans have between 1 and 28 percent African ancestry, while self-identified African Americans have, on average, 24 percent European ancestry. (It is notable that Obama's only genetic connection to African slaves is through his white mother.) Self-identified Latinos have, on average, 65 percent European ancestry, 18 percent Native American ancestry, and 6 percent African ancestry, which further testifies to the complex history of colonialism, slavery, and sex (both voluntary and coerced) across racial categories in the Americas.

In light of this complexity, some critics argue that physicians and other professionals who deal with the general public should eschew even the descriptive use of racial categories, in anticipation of a genuinely "color-blind" society. (Such anticipation has also motivated rollbacks of affirmative action and voting-rights laws, on the premise that America will soon enter a "postracial" age.) Unfortunately, there is substantial evidence that physicians—like police officers, real estate agents, and loan officers—still "see" race and often act on race-based perceptions even when they think of themselves as "color-blind." Efforts to verify, quantify, and correct such bias suggest that descriptive categories of race may be necessary for the foreseeable future, even as we question the groupings they claim to denote.

One final reason for making use of socially constructed conceptions of race is that "color-blind" approaches may mask the ways in which dominant racial groups tend to become the implicit standard for what is normal, valuable, and admirable. In the United States, cultural and other characteristics of European Americans have often been taken as a "nonracial" norm—against which other groups stand out as exotically "ethnic." This dynamic is well illustrated by the lack of expectation that whites in general disavow the actions of white criminals (such as Oklahoma City bomber Timothy McVeigh), while members of other groups are generally expected to publicly condemn the actions of "their" criminals. (Korean Americans, for example, were expected to disavow Cho Seung-Hui, who committed a 2008 mass shooting at Virginia Tech.) The sense that nonwhite and immigrant groups must somehow "prove themselves" is often paired with a tendency to forget about the socioeconomic privileges and support systems that often come with belonging to society's historically dominant group. In medicine, such amnesia can lead to clinical bias, paternalism, and a lack of empathy for patients. For these and other reasons, attempting to understand how "whiteness" operates as an ethno-racial category can be a useful step toward creating a more genuinely pluralistic society.

Concepts of Sex, Gender, and Sexuality

Just as the unequal treatment of African Americans and other nonwhites has often been rooted in biomedical concepts of race and ethnicity, biological and medical conceptions of sex, gender, and sexuality have often been used to limit opportunities for women and sexual minorities. For centuries, women's intelligence, rationality, and employability, as well as their sexual and reproductive autonomy, were devalued and dismissed by naturalistic accounts of their biological limitations. Although such misogyny was by no means limited to Western culture, the rise of scientific medicine in the West provided new grounds for denying women political and economic rights, frequently based on dubious accounts of their reproductive and hormonal systems. (Diagnoses such as "hysteria" were infamously sex-specific and based on pseudoscientific claims about the uterus or *hyster*.) Similarly, the historical stigmatization and persecution of LGBT and other sexual minority populations received new impetus from distorted medical conceptions of gender and sexuality. (See Social Context: Women, Men, and Biomedical Research and The *DSM* and Sexual Minorities for more.) This history calls for careful attention to our concepts of sex, gender, and sexuality.

Concepts of Sex

In popular culture, sex and gender are sometimes used interchangeably, but most scholars draw a distinction between these terms. In many disciplines, *sex* is used to refer to a set of genetic, anatomical, and physiological characteristics whereas *gender* refers to a set of behaviors, norms, and social roles (such as masculinity or femininity), as well as the internal experience of these roles (a *gender identity*).

It is too simple, however, to say that sex is a result of biological nature and gender of socially constructed nurture. In real life, it can be difficult to disentangle sex from gender and gender from sex. For one thing, there is significant evidence that different levels of hormones such as testosterone and estrogen have a significant impact on prenatal brain development, which likely plays at least some role in social and individual gender differences across different cultures. Physiological sex features go far beyond reproductive anatomy and may play a more significant role in our bodies and behaviors than we realize. At the same time, almost everyone's experience of having a sex is mediated, from birth onward, by an elaborate and often coercive set of cultural expectations, conventions, and norms that vary depending on whether we are perceived as male or female.

Nor is the division between male and female as simple and straightforward as many people assume. Just as our definitions of life and death have changed with our culture and our science (see Case Presentation: When the Diagnosis Is Death in Chapter 7), so have our definitions of sex difference. In different eras, physicians have relied on different criteria such as external anatomy (genitals), internal anatomy (ovaries or undescended testicles), and chromosomes (XX or XY), among other markers, to divide males from females. Although for most people these markers line up in one direction or another, millions of babies around the world are born with *differences of sex development* (DSD), which means their bodies do not fit neatly into typical definitions of male and female. When we factor in the different chromosomal, hormonal, and anatomical variations on the two main groupings of male and female, sex may actually look more like a spectrum than a binary. (See Case Presentation: Intersex Care.)

Concepts of Gender

It is perhaps more obvious that *gender* constitutes a spectrum rather than a binary. There is clearly a wide variety of "masculine" and "feminine" behaviors, tastes, personalities, activities, and interests that are prevalent to varying degrees among all human beings—in part because categorizing such traits by gender is highly variable and subjective. It is also clear that what is considered acceptable masculine and feminine dress, behavior, occupation, etc., changes (often radically) over time, frequently in response to broad societal shifts and social movements. In many eras, it would have been unthinkable for gender roles to include women wearing pants and serving in the military or men working as models, nurses, or primary caregivers (to take a few random examples).

Nevertheless, societies often draw and redraw lines (some sharp, some blurry) between ways of acting and living that are seen as *gender conforming* and others that are *gender nonconforming*. Some degree of gender nonconformity has often been tolerated or even approved, as seen in the female "tomboy" role accepted in Anglo-American culture, as well as in various formal roles for "third gender" individuals in the traditional cultures of (for example) Samoa, Thailand, India, Bangladesh, Albania, and among Native Americans. Other kinds of gender nonconformity, however, have typically been met with social stigma, bullying, discrimination, and violence.

It is thus both significant and remarkable that some individuals in almost every human society go beyond gender nonconformity and instead refuse the gender identities assigned to them at birth, despite the high social costs and very real physical dangers that often accompany such refusals. The term *transgender* encompasses a broad range of experiences and identities, but it is most generally defined in terms of nonidentification with the gender one was assigned at birth. It is contrasted with the term *cisgender*, which typically refers to a "match" between one's internal identity and one's natal gender assignment. (*Cis* is a Latin prefix that means "on the same side as.") Transgender people may be straight, gay, or bisexual, since sexual attraction is different from (albeit often related to) gender. Some trans people identify with one traditional gender category and change their names, preferred pronouns, and clothes to better match it. Others feel their gender identity lies somewhere along a spectrum between male and female or refuse gender categories (and gendered pronouns) altogether.

In 2013, the American Psychiatric Association (APA) abandoned the diagnostic term "gender identity disorder," which critics charged had been used to stigmatize transgender individuals. The APA's new term, *gender dysphoria*, is defined to make clear that being transgender or gender nonconforming "is not, in itself, a mental disorder." Instead, it is framed in terms of the distress associated with a mismatch between one's gender identity and one's socially assigned gender, a temporary condition typically treatable through psychological therapy and social transition, as well as (in some cases) physical sex reassignment. (See Social Context: The DSM and Sexual Minorities.) Similarly, there are signs of increased tolerance for transgender identities in popular culture, as seen in the coverage of such figures as Caitlyn Jenner and Laverne Cox.

Despite such changes, transgender people remain one of the most stigmatized groups in contemporary America and are frequently subject to employment discrimination and violence. There are also ongoing debates about when and if children should be allowed to socially transition to the other gender and at what, if any, point adolescents should begin physical sex transition. As with many other bioethical issues in this chapter, such debates often revolve around whether existing social norms should be at least partially accepted in defining what is healthy or "natural," or whether such norms should be rejected as arbitrary and unjust.

Concepts of Sexual Orientation

In recent decades, no social movement has done more to question the justice and legitimacy of existing social norms than the civil rights struggle of lesbian, gay, and bisexual (LGB) individuals. This movement is often aligned with the struggle for social and political recognition by transgender, genderqueer, and intersex individuals (as discussed above) and so is often referred to as the *LGBT* or *LGBTQI* rights movement. However one refers to these related movements, it is clear that they have helped change the assumptions that the heterosexual majority makes about sexuality, gender, and social norms. The twenty-eight years between the full delisting of homosexuality as a psychological disorder in the *DSM* and the nationwide legalization of same-sex marriage in 2015 have involved some significant shifts in how non-heterosexual people are perceived and treated.

As with feminism and the African American civil rights movement, many of these shifts have revolved around biomedical conceptions of what is considered healthy or natural. Just as the landmark 1967 *Loving v. Virginia* decision rejected "antimiscegenation" statutes that outlawed interracial marriage as unnatural and dysgenic, the *Obergefell v. Hodges* decision concluded that the traditional restriction of marriage to heterosexuals could not be grounded in biology or morality.

There appears to be growing consensus in America and most other developed nations that sexual orientation, like race and gender, is not a legitimate basis for discrimination or the denial of basic human rights. Nevertheless, there is still considerable confusion and disagreement about what sexual orientation actually is. To the extent that sexual orientation is increasingly viewed as a morally neutral category, such debates have less political urgency than they once did. But the following concepts of sexual orientation are still relevant to biomedical ethics and to the provision of inclusive and appropriate care to LGB populations.

Innate Sexual Orientation. There is evidence that sexual orientation has a genetic component, although most scientists believe there is no such thing as a single "straight gene" or a "gay gene." Nevertheless, many different studies over several decades have found associations between homosexuality and a range of different genetic variations, including a landmark study of gay siblings in 2014. Other studies suggest that differences in prenatal hormones, brain development, and even birth order may play some role in sexual orientation, along with social and environmental factors.

Compelling evidence for innate sexual orientation also comes from the animal world, which features widespread homosexual behavior, and even exclusive homosexuality. Some animal bisexuality and homosexuality has been linked to specific genetic variations, and some evolutionary biologists believe such variations may be the result of adaptive advantages for family groups. (The idea is that enhanced "male-loving" or "female-loving" genes are passed on to both male and female offspring, producing increased heterosexual desire in some offspring and homosexual desires in their opposite-sex siblings.)

Conceptions of innate homosexuality correspond to the consistent reports of most gay men and many lesbians that they were "born that way," and knew from a young age that their experiences of love and desire were different from those of heterosexual children. Innate conceptions have also constituted one line of argument for LGB rights, often with the assumption that sex, race, and sexual orientation are all fixed categories derived from nature. Critics of this argument question both the "naturalness" of race and sex and the assumption that nature provides any reliable guide to moral legitimacy. If there is no sound moral argument against nonheterosexual acts or relationships, then why must they be defended as something that LGB people "cannot help"? After all, there are many "changeable" identities involving religion, disability, and pregnancy (for example) that are still viewed as deserving of social accommodation and civil rights protections.

Sexual Orientation as Spectrum. Between 1948 and 1953, the pioneering sexologist Alfred Kinsey published two groundbreaking reports on sexuality, based on interviews with over ten thousand American men and women between the ages of twenty and thirty-five. Kinsey famously found that 37 percent of the men and 13 percent of the women reported achieving orgasm with at least one same-sex partner. By contrast, he found rates of exclusive or predominant homosexuality for both men and women of 10 percent or somewhat lower. Although Kinsey's volunteer study cohort was later criticized for insufficient randomness, subsequent research has continued to find many degrees of bisexuality between exclusively gay and exclusively straight. (Kinsey used a 0–6 scale, with 3 representing equally balanced bisexuality.)

Although there is very little support for the notion that sexual orientation is a "choice," there is evidence that it may shift over the course of a lifetime, particularly for women. This, combined with evidence that social and environmental factors play at least some role in the development of sexual orientation, may argue against conceptions of sexual orientation as neatly and immutably divided among heterosexual, homosexual, and bisexual. If the legal acceptance of same-sex relationships and marriages is ultimately accompanied by reduced stigmatization of non-heterosexual identities more generally, we may also find that these competing conceptions of sexual orientation simply matter less than they do today.

Concepts of Disability

Between 1907 and 1963, over sixty thousand Americans were forcibly sterilized in accordance with eugenics laws that had been enacted in more than thirty states. The focus of these sterilizations were the so-called "socially inadequate," a category that included "feebleminded," "deformed," epileptic, and mentally ill individuals, as well as the deaf and the blind, according to the model eugenics law that formed a basis for most of the state laws. Upheld by the U.S. Supreme Court in 1927, these laws were repeatedly cited by Adolf Hitler as inspiration for his larger program of forced sterilization in Nazi Germany. Although notoriously variable in application (often targeting single and African American mothers with no disabilities), the primary focus of these American eugenic efforts were the disabled.

These involuntary sterilizations were widely supported by American physicians and the general public, and they continued in some states through the 1970s. Though widely condemned today, they were typical of an era that often viewed people with disabilities (especially mental or developmental disabilities) as less than fully human. Such individuals were frequently confined to state institutions and had few opportunities for employment or participation in public life. It was not uncommon for their families to shun them or deny their very existence, out of shame or fear of being associated with "the defective."

This situation only began to change in the 1970s and 1980s, with the rise of the modern disability rights movement. Joining forces across different forms of disability, activists fought for better access to transportation and public facilities, lobbied against workplace discrimination, and challenged institutionalization with new models for independent living. Some of these objectives were advanced with the 1990 Americans with Disabilities Act (ADA), which established accessibility standards for public facilities and transportation, required that large employers provide"reasonable accommodations" for disabled workers, and prohibited disability-based employment discrimination against otherwise qualified candidates. Nevertheless, more than twenty years after the passage of the ADA, only about 20 percent of the disabled population is employed, compared to 64 percent of people without a disability. It is estimated that about half the people who live below the poverty line in America have one or more disabilities.

During this same period, however, people with disabilities have achieved new visibility in public life. Consider, for example, Stephen Hawking, the renowned theoretical physicist with extensive paralysis from the motor neuron disease ALS, who uses a computerized device to communicate and an electric wheelchair to move. Or consider Temple Grandin, the prominent animal scientist and author with sensory processing impairments and other cognitive anomalies as a result of her autism. Just a few decades ago, it is likely that these and other prominent figures would have been confined to institutions, sequestered by their families, or forced to conceal their disabilities—as President Franklin Delano Roosevelt concealed his polio-related disabilities throughout his political career.

Still, many disability rights advocates argue that we are a long way from achieving a society that genuinely accepts physical and neurocognitive diversity. Organizing society around the largely temporary status of being "able-bodied" represents both an error and a grave injustice, they contend. Such perspectives challenge traditional conceptions of what disability actually is, and are the subject of intense debate both within and beyond the field of bioethics. As we consider some of these competing concepts, it will be helpful to keep in mind how the social status of disability has and has not changed. It is an indication of how much the perceived value of disabled people's lives—both in their own eyes and the eyes of others—may change in relation to social and technological conditions.

Medical Concepts of Disability

Medical conceptions of disability are generally premised on the idea that there is a universal standard of functioning for a human being. If an individual's physical or mental functioning falls persistently below that standard, she is disabled, and medicine's sole responsibility is try to bring her as close as possible to the normal level of functioning. On this view, disabilities are objective, nonrelative, and natural. They are located in the bodies of the disabled and that is where they should be addressed.

To revisit the example of Stephen Hawking, most medical concepts of disability would frame Hawking's disability in terms of the way his motor neuron disease prevents him from walking, feeding himself without assistance, or forming verbal speech with his mouth and tongue. The goal of treatment would be to bring Hawking's functioning as close as possible to the normal model of walking, self-feeding, and speaking so as to facilitate his integration into the society around him.

Social Concepts of Disability

Many social concepts of disability, by contrast, reject the idea of a universal standard of human functioning. They suggest there is nothing natural or inevitable about our society's expectations for walking, eating, and speaking, and so forth, and it is those expectations that create handicaps for certain individuals. In developed nations, for example, we typically expect people to be able to walk for short distances unassisted, but do not consider them disabled if they cannot walk ten miles without an assistive device (e.g., a car or a bus). Nor do we consider children disabled before they can feed themselves, and we often see the later loss of such ability as a natural function of old age, rather than as disability per se. Similarly, in a society like ours, where computer-assisted communication has become standard for the majority, someone who relies on it, instead of verbal speech, is much less disabled than he would be in a society that relies on telephones and face-to-face interactions.

Social models of disability often draw distinctions among *impairments*, *disabilities*, and *handicaps*. On this view, an *impairment* refers to atypical or abnormal features of one's body or brain, such as a weakened leg or facial muscles. *Disability* refers to specific incapacities or limitations caused by these impairments, such as an inability to walk or form words with one's mouth. *Handicap*, by contrast, refers to the social disadvantages that one faces as a result of one's impairments and disabilities. It is this last category that varies most dramatically from society to society and is typically the primary focus of social models of disability.

Although physicians tend to assume that it is the severity of one's impairments or disabilities that has the biggest impact on one's quality of life, many studies suggest that handicaps are actually most decisive. The degree to which society provides accommodations to allow disabled people to participate in civil society and access social goods may often be more important than the degree to which their disability is "fixed" by medicine. As we have seen earlier in this chapter and this text, a lack of social accommodation and support may also play a decisive role in whether a disabled person considers her life worth living, and may inform discussions about physician-assisted death and prenatal

genetic screening. (See Case Presentation: Elizabeth Bouvia and Chapters 7 and 3 for more on these topics.)

Disability as Difference

An extension of the social model of disability rejects the idea that the differences in body and brain function typically associated with disabilities actually represent drawbacks or limitations. Thus, many in the Deaf community argue that their communication in American Sign Language (ASL) forms the basis of a distinctive culture that is as legitimate, enriching, and rewarding as the hearing culture around them. Some reject medical interventions to mitigate deafness (such as cochlear implants), as concessions to hearing society that would only distance them from their language and community. (See Case Presentation: Lee Larson and Cochlear Implants.)

Similar arguments have been advanced about the auditory and braille-based culture developed by the blind, as well as the distinctive kinds of movement and interaction that develop in communities of people who use wheelchairs. People with autism such as Temple Grandin have demonstrated that powerful intellectual abilities and sensitivities can arise from having a brain that is wired differently from the non-autistic people she calls "yakety-yaks." One can easily imagine an argument that the slow and deliberate form of communication created by Hawking's computer-assisted speech constitutes an advantage over those who can express themselves more rapidly—and sometimes thoughtlessly.

Critics of the disability-as-difference position do not deny that disabilities are often associated with valuable alternate capacities and vibrant social communities. But they question whether a disability can itself be seen to constitute a culture, rather than a shared limitation. Thus, they reject some efforts to perpetuate disability-based cultures, such as prenatal selection for disabled children or public campaigns against cochlear implants. (See Dena Davis's essay in Chapter 3.) Defenders of the disability-as-difference view argue that racial minorities also experience limited opportunities due to devalued physical features, but few suggest they should be medically "fixed" to ease integration into the majority group.

Nature and Norms

The Declaration of Independence famously derives equal moral standing from "the Laws of Nature and of Nature's God," a phrase that has been the subject of intense debate for almost 250 years. For many of those who take a natural law or theological view of ethics, the laws of nature are *teleological* ("goal-directed") and as such provide ethical guidance about the character of a just society and the boundaries of ethical pluralism. Such views tend to generate sharp disagreement over what is, in fact, "natural," and indeed we have seen that many of our contemporary debates over race, sex, gender, sexuality, and disability turn on this very question.

There is ample evidence from the nonhuman animal world, for example, that homosexuality and cross-gender behaviors can be quite "natural," yet there is still considerable disagreement among natural-law and religious thinkers about whether or not they are morally acceptable. (The Catholic Church, for example, condemns such behaviors.) Similar debates about the potentially "unnatural" (and thus immoral) status of interracial marriage and reproduction by people with disabilities also divided thinkers who saw nature as a guide to moral conduct. Some natural law theorists have seen such differences as morally irrelevant features of natural human diversity, while others have

seen them as having moral significance that generates specific duties and prohibitions. Identifying the goals of nature (or nature's God) is thus a notoriously tricky and controversial business, subject to many varieties of interpretation.

By contrast, many other ethicists believe that nature is neither teleological nor a good evaluative standard for societal norms. Devastating diseases (such as cancer) may be thoroughly "natural" and beneficial treatments (such as radiation therapy) seem comparatively "unnatural." Many conclude that labeling something "unnatural" is no guide to whether or not is it morally wrong. For these thinkers, biomedical ethics in a diverse society must be established on the basis of some other standard than nature.

There is not space here for a detailed examination of how Kantian, Rawlsian, utilitarian, and other theories might approach the identity categories discussed in this chapter. But it is worth noting that these theories tend to abstract from our natural, embodied differences and attempt to derive moral standing from a neutral standard such as utility or autonomy. Such approaches tend to be friendly to pluralistic and egalitarian societies, because they imply that there are many different sources of utility and many different ways of exercising autonomy, even when constrained by the categorical imperative or the basic structure of a just society. These theories tend to argue that the morally arbitrary differences among citizens or patients, such as race or gender, should not stand in the way of their equal treatment by society and its medical institutions, and this neutrality allows for an ongoing expansion of moral community. (Kant famously condemned homosexuality and other forms of non-procreative sex, for example, but many contemporary Kantians believe his philosophy is compatible with these forms of sexuality so long as they involve respect for partners as ends in themselves.)

Still, for many contemporary theorists, classical criteria of equal standing miss something important about our moral lives with others, particularly when we are sick, vulnerable, or in need of medical care. From infancy to old age, such states occupy a substantial portion of everyone's life, and suggest that moral community must be rooted in something broader than a capacity for rational autonomy or the pursuit of utility in the public arena. Instead, theories of care, capability, and virtue argue that our ethics and our bioethics must embrace a broader notion of human dignity and equal respect, one that takes into account relationships of dependency and caregiving and the domestic sphere in which they often take place. On the capabilities view, for example, a just society is one that promotes central capabilities such as bodily integrity, life planning, social affiliations, and political participation for all its members, both disabled and (temporarily) non-disabled alike. It also calls for these standards of justice to apply to the "personal" sphere of unpaid domestic caregiving, where gender norms often limit human capabilities and asymmetrical relationships cannot be easily reduced to competing claims for autonomy. The "capability failures" often associated with disability, ethnicity, or sex and gender roles must not be taken as natural or inevitable, on this view, but must be evaluated as part of society's— and medicine's—overall success in promoting human dignity and flourishing.

READINGS

Section 1: Gender, Research, and Medicine

The Woman Question in Medicine

Hilde Lindemann

Lindemann points to the ways in which medicine has been shaped by *androcentrism*—a tendency to approach men as the paradigmatic model of the human species and to approach women as physically and mentally defective departures from the norm. She argues that androcentrism persists in the long-term results of excluding women from clinical trials, in the failure to report research outcomes by sex, and in pay and other disparities between male and female physicians.

Furthermore, Lindemann suggests that a tendency to value women primarily as caregivers or mothers distorts the practice and profession of medicine. When eight times as many female as male physicians end up practicing part time, few question its roots in unequal divisions of domestic labor. When false information circulates about dangers to fetuses posed by everyday substances, medicine tends to err on the side of policing pregnant women's behavior, rather than considering their health for its own sake. Such practices spring less from individual sexist beliefs than from unexamined social structures, Lindemann argues. They can only be changed by acknowledging gender as a larger system, one that resembles and overlaps with social hierarchies based on race, class, and disability.

It has been about forty years since the women's movement added its voices to the U.S. culture wars, demanding an end to the long history of social practices and institutions that favor men's interests, preoccupations, and concerns over women's and place women in positions of subservience to men. Since then, women have invaded many strongholds that had previously been reserved for men only. According to the U.S. Department of Labor, women now make up almost 47 percent of the paid labor force, and 40 percent of them work in managerial positions. On average, they earn 80 percent of what men do, and in the sixteen-to-twenty-four age bracket, they earn 93 percent of what young men earn. So it seems a fitting time to see whether they are doing as well in their encounters with medicine. In this paper, I'll take a look first at the history of physicians' attitudes toward women, and then at three contemporary areas of medicine in particular: health research relevant to women, health policies, and women's success at working their way into the medical profession. Because the picture that emerges is somewhat less than rosy, I'll end with a few ideas for how bioethicists might want to think about the current state of affairs.

That Was Then

First, a little history. Physicians are taught to note physiological differences between men and women, but, like everyone else, they don't always fully appreciate the degree to which the differences between women and men are not facts of nature but constructions of society. Because our culture is persistently focused on men, it seems normal and natural to many of us that man should be the measure—the unstated point of reference—for what is paradigmatic of human beings. Woman is then defined in terms of her departure from that standard. The history of this idea goes back at least as far as Aristotle, who defines woman as a "deformed man."

In bodily terms, woman's difference from man is most evident in her reproductive organs, so these have become associated with her identity in a way that a man's have not. In the mid-1800s, for example, the German physician Rudolph Virchow wrote, "Woman is a pair of ovaries with a human being attached, whereas man is a human being furnished with a pair of testes." Another physician writing at about the same time explained, "It is as if the Almighty in creating the female sex had taken a uterus and built up a woman around it."

Woman's reproductive difference from man has been taken as a defining characteristic, but it has also marked her as *abnormal*. Where man is the norm, woman is not merely different, but deviant. The Victorian anthropologist James Allen treated woman as a kind of stunted man, noting that "physically, mentally, and morally, woman is a kind of adult child. . . . Man is the head of creation." And in medical circles in the nineteenth and early twentieth century, the thought that female functions were inherently pathological was advanced as a physiological fact. As the president of the American Gynecology Society stated in 1900:

> *Many a young life is battered and forever crippled on the breakers of puberty; if it crosses these unharmed and is not dashed to pieces on the rock of childbirth, it may still ground on the ever-recurring shallows of menstruation, and lastly upon the final bar of the menopause ere protection is found in the unruffled waters of the harbor beyond reach of sexual storms.*

Nor has the idea of woman's abnormality been confined only to her reproductive system. Women's physical deviance from the male standard has long been thought to imply mental deviance as well. Aristotle, you will remember, said that "the deliberative element in women lacks authority," and Kant observed that "a woman is embarrassed little that she does not possess high insights; that she is timid, and not fit for serious employment, and so forth; she is beautiful and captivates, and that is enough."

The acceptance by the medical profession of Darwinian evolutionary theory opened a large debate in the Victorian era concerning woman's supposed lack of rationality. One such theory was that because men's brains weighed 10 percent more than women's brains on average, feminine irrationality could be chalked up to the "missing five ounces" of gray matter. This theory, however, ran afoul of "the elephant problem"—namely, that elephants, whose brains weigh more than men's, ought to be considerably smarter than humans of either sex. The difficulty this posed prompted a shift to the idea that the *ratio* of brain to body size is what determines intellect, but unfortunately for scientists, the ratio was discovered to be higher in women than in men.

The theory was abandoned.

The debate over the intellectual capacity of women's brains was not ended, however. In 1873, Dr. Edward Clarke, a professor of medicine at Harvard, published *Sex in Education; or, A Fair Chance for the Girls*, which went through seventeen editions over the next few years. Clarke surveyed the best medical thinking regarding women and after scholarly reflection concluded that the mental exertion required for higher education sapped a woman's body of its vital forces to such an extent that her uterus would atrophy. Putting a woman's brain to masculine use would thus make her an asexual monster. This was something of a double-bind, though, for cleverness and daring were considered to be the traits that allowed a species to evolve, which meant that males were to be the innovators who could best adapt to harsh environments, while women were merely to reproduce whatever hereditary material they were given. So, in theory, at any rate, as men continued to ascend the evolutionary ladder, women would continue to devolve, growing frailer and less intelligent with every generation.

The devolution of women meant that they were obviously not fit to train as physicians. The trouble, according to one Victorian doctor, was that their menstrual cycles directly interfered with their brain function:

> One shudders to think [he wrote] of the conclusions arrived at by female bacteriologists or histologists, at the period when their entire system, both physical and mental, is, so to speak, "unstrung," to say nothing of the terrible mistakes which a lady surgeon might make under similar conditions.

A number of women did, of course, become physicians in that era. In 1847, after vainly seeking admission to eleven medical schools, Elizabeth Blackwell was allowed to attend Geneva Medical College in upstate New York and, graduating first in her class, in 1849 became the first woman physician in the United States. However, hospitals and dispensaries uniformly refused to extend her practice privileges. She was even refused lodging and office space when she tried to set up a private practice. Nevertheless, she persevered, and in 1857 she opened the New York Infirmary for Women and Children in the slums of New York City.

The first African American woman doctor was Rebecca Lee Crumpler, who received her degree from the New England Female Medical College in 1864. Except for a brief interval when she doctored newly freed slaves in Richmond, Virginia, Crumpler practiced medicine in Boston, also specializing in the care of women, children, and the poor. By the end of the nineteenth century, the ranks of women physicians had swelled to over seven thousand. As Mary Putnam Jacobi, another pioneering physician, wrote in 1891, "It is perfectly evident from the records, that the opposition to women physicians has rarely been based upon any sincere conviction that women could not be instructed in medicine, but upon an intense dislike to the idea that they should be so capable."

How About Now?

The twentieth century brought a number of improvements in the status of women—including, in 1920, the right to vote—and the gradual acceptance of middle-class women in the workplace (poor women, of course, have always worked for pay). But the persistent assumption that man's body is the norm and woman's body is abnormal means that women have been chronically excluded from human subjects research. The infamous Tuskegee experiment, begun in 1932 to observe the natural progress of syphilis in African Americans, enrolled 399 men but no women (which shows you that exclusion isn't always a bad thing). The Baltimore Longitudinal Study, begun on men in 1958 to investigate the physiology of aging, by 1984 still had no data on women. The Physician's Health Study, begun in 1981 to investigate whether aspirin could decrease the risk of heart disease, enrolled 22,000 men but no women. The possible impact of caffeine on heart disease was studied in 45,589 male research subjects beginning in 1986; no female subjects were included. And my favorite pilot study, conducted at Rockefeller University in 1989 to investigate how obesity affects breast and uterine cancer, enrolled only men.

The General Accounting Office reported in 1992 that only half of new drugs were then being analyzed by gender for safety, and under half were analyzed for efficacy. A careful 1994 Institute of Medicine study, spearheaded by Ruth Faden, was unable to demonstrate conclusively that women have systematically been barred from research, but because so many protocols failed to specify the gender ratios of their research populations, it was not possible to know for certain what difference, if any, gender might have made in those trials. Thus, throughout the twentieth century, women's bodies were viewed fundamentally as analogs to the male norm, when of course they are not. Undeniable differences were then viewed as pathological departures, and because the departures were assumed to be mistakes in the real design, they did not need to be studied: science was concerned only with the real design.

Sex disparities have been widely documented for a variety of disorders: "in autoimmune diseases such as rheumatoid arthritis, lupus and multiple sclerosis; in some psychological disorders, including major depressive disorder, schizophrenia, autism, eating disorders and attention deficit hyperactivity disorder; and in chronic fatigue syndrome, asthma and several types of cancer." For that reason, in 1993 Congress passed the NIH Revitalization Act, requiring the National Institutes of Health to insure that phase III clinical trials would be "designed and carried out in a manner sufficient to provide for a valid analysis of whether the variables being studied in the trial affect females or members of minority groups, as the case may be, differently than other subjects in the trial."

A prominent epidemiologist objected to the Revitalization Act on the ground that, "while the path to disease may be different for men and women, the treatment usually works equally well for both." But that is just false. The lack of knowledge about sex disparities means that women have been subjected to potentially life-threatening delays before being correctly diagnosed and forced to accept treatments that do not function properly for them. As the authors of a recent study point out, "This has been demonstrated in the field of cardiology, where the numbers of women dying of heart infarction at a young age significantly dropped after two decades of research and the dissemination of essential information about gender differences in clinical presentation, symptoms, diagnostic and therapeutic approaches."

Despite the NIH's congressional mandate, an analysis of findings from randomized, controlled trials published in nine high-impact medical journals in 2004 showed that "eighty-seven percent of the studies did not report any outcomes by sex or include sex as a covariate in modeling." A 2010 survey of research incorporating a gender analysis in nine medical sub-specialties concludes that, while published studies incorporating sex and gender in the research design have increased markedly since the 1990s, "a striking underrepresentation of research about gender differences in management characterizes all disciplines but cardiology": most subfields hover around 10 percent, compared to cardiology's 22 percent. The authors of the September 2010 IOM report, *Women's Health: Progress, Pitfalls, and Promise*, likewise note that "a lack of analysis and reporting of data separately for males and females continues to limit researchers' ability to identify potentially important sex and gender differences."

One possible reason for this continued lack of understanding may be that women themselves are not well positioned to conduct clinical research: in 2008, only 23 percent of all funded grants went to women investigators. Matters are even worse when it comes to leadership roles in setting research agendas. A key position of power and influence is that of principal investigator of a large center grant. But consider the Clinical and Translational Science Award program emanating from the NIH— one of the largest center grants in research history. CTSA PIs wield tremendous clout in determining what kinds of research will be pursued, yet only three of the initial twenty-four CTSAs went to women. Equally disturbing is the discrepancy in salaries offered by NIH Institutional Mentored Scientist Development Awards. Those that build research capacities in women's health—an area that attracts women—are considerably lower than awards to researchers in oncology, aging, drug abuse, and clinical research. It should come as no surprise, then, that currently only 28.5 percent of NIH Institutes are headed by women.

The comparative lack of good data on women's health is only compounded by the unreliable data that women—especially pregnant women—receive from their doctors and other well-wishers. Most of the master narratives about pregnancy currently circulating widely in the United States depict the good pregnant woman as vigilantly guarding her bodily purity so as to provide an unsullied environment for her growing fetus. They (and the people who act on them) tell her to refrain from ingesting alcoholic beverages. They tell her to discontinue the use of antidepressants,

Chapter 10 Medicine in a Pluralistic Society 789

antihistamines, and asthma medications. They tell her to quit drinking coffee. They tell her to

> avoid an array of foods from soft cheese to sushi, to sleep in a specified position (currently, avoiding stomach and back, with left side preferred to right), to avoid paint (including those with low volatile compounds), to avoid changing the cat litter, not to sit in the bathtub longer than ten minutes, not to sample the cookie dough, to avoid loud music, and even to keep a laptop computer several inches from [her] pregnant bell[y], "just in case."

Insofar as master narratives guide behavior, they are essential for human social life; without them, we would not know what we are supposed to do. But because they work on us subliminally, at a visceral rather than a rational level, they tend to be evidence-resistant. For example, there are simply no data to show that moderate consumption of alcohol while pregnant is harmful to the fetus, and the rest of the forbidden substances and activities in the list above likewise carry no evidence of harm—indeed, some of them actually carry evidence of safety. Yet because pregnant women's behavior is policed by others acting on the basis of these narratives and the women themselves frequently internalize them, they are likely to find that *even if they know the countervailing evidence*, they cannot bring themselves to put into their bodies anything they wouldn't feed their babies-to-be.

Whereas for clinical trials the woman question was one of exclusion, when it comes to pregnancy, the question is one of intense and unrelenting pressure to perform. But notice that the focus is not really on the women—it's on what's best for the growing fetus. Pregnant women do not get praised when they do all the things they are supposed to do to guard their fetuses' well-being—they just get demerits if they fail to do any of them. The reasons for this are complex; certainly one difficulty has been that the interconnectedness of fetus and gestating woman is something our moral theories are particularly ill equipped to capture, with the result that the fetus tends to take center stage and the woman tends to become the incubator or maternal background. This makes it easier to value the woman primarily for the work she does in bringing the fetus to term, harder to value her for her own sake.

There's a long history, of course, of physicians giving pregnant women advice about what to eat, what to think, how much exercise to take, and what kind

of environment to surround themselves with, not to mention how to care for the baby once the pregnancy is over. What's worth noticing about this history, though, is how the advice goes in and out of fashion, depending less on medical evidence than on social attitudes toward women at any particular point in time. Possibly today's physicians are immune to these attitudes where their women patients are concerned, but there isn't really any reason to think so.

Discriminatory Health Policies. At the moment, health care insurance is rife with policies and practices that are unfair to women. Only six percent of women aged eighteen to sixty-four are able to purchase insurance outside the workplace, usually because they are discriminated against both when they apply for coverage and when their premiums are calculated. In most states, it's legal for companies selling individual health policies to engage in "gender rating"—that is, to charge women more than men for the same coverage, even for policies that exclude pregnancy and childbirth care. And these policies do often exclude maternity coverage, or charge much more for it; only fourteen states require policies in the individual market to cover maternity care. Insurers also apply gender rating to group coverage, but laws against sex discrimination in the workplace prevent employers from passing along higher costs to their employees based on sex. As a result, smaller or midsize businesses that employ mostly women either cannot afford to insure their workers at all, or they have to offer plans with very high deductibles.

Some insurance companies also use the "preexisting condition" clause in their policies to deny coverage to women who have had a prior caesarean section. And as if that isn't bad enough, eight states and the District of Columbia permit them to deny coverage to women who have been victims of domestic violence. From a business point of view, this makes good sense: both surgical birth and beatings are predictors of higher costs to the company. From a human perspective, though, it amounts to kicking women when they're already down.

The recently passed health insurance reform bill, slated for implementation in 2014, would do away with many of these abuses. Gender rating would no longer be allowed, individual policies would have to offer maternity care, and neither prior C-sections nor having been the target of domestic assault would count as reasons to deny women coverage. However, the reform bill does not address the fundamental problem, which is that health insurance is tied to paid work. As women over thirty disproportionately work in low-paying jobs with no benefits and tend disproportionately either to cut back on their paying jobs or drop out of the workforce to care for their children and ill or elderly family members, tying insurance to paid work makes what is already an unfair division of gendered labor even more unfair.

Women in Medicine. In 2004, the Association of American Medical Colleges reported that for the first time in history, women made up the majority of medical school applicants. By 2005, 49 percent of medical school students and 42 percent of residents were women. Today, a robust 70 percent of ob-gyns are women, as are roughly half of pediatricians and psychiatrists. This shows substantial progress, but it by no means indicates that women have finally reached parity in medicine. In general surgery, only one-fourth of residents are women. In urology, it's about 12 percent; in neurosurgery, 10 percent; in orthopedic surgery, 9 percent. And women physicians continue to earn less than their male colleagues—an estimated 25 to 35 percent less, depending on the specialty.

Part of the reason for the discrepancy in pay is that most women physicians are primary care doctors, but women doctors also work fewer hours than men. About a third of women pediatricians work part time, for example, compared to only 4 percent of men. A preference for work flexibility and fewer hours is widely attributed to a "lifestyle choice," but we might want to think about the extent to which such choices are socially shaped. That the brunt of the responsibility for child care and care of the chronically ill continues to fall heavily on women, and that cutting back on paid work and seeking job flexibility might be a rational way to discharge that responsibility, calls into question how free a lifestyle choice such part-time work really is.

It's worth pointing out, though, that even full-time women doctors see fewer patients than their male counterparts—an average of 87 patients per week compared to men's 102— and this might also affect how much they are paid. A 2002 analysis in the *Journal of the American Medical Association* accounts for the lower patient ratio by explaining that women doctors typically spend more time talking with and counseling

patients than men doctors do, which raises interesting questions about whether that makes a difference in their respective patients' health outcomes. There may be reason to think so: a study published in *BMJ* in 2007 found that the United States' average patient-physician time (thirty minutes a year for adults) was about half New Zealand's and a third of Australia's, and linked this to our relatively poor health outcomes when compared to other developed countries. A study of the impact of the physician's gender on patient care might well show similar results.

Women's advancement to leadership positions in academic medicine has been unduly slow. Only 17 percent of tenured professors, 16 percent of full professors, 10 percent of department chairs, and 11 percent of deans in U.S. medical schools are women. Women faculty do more of the tasks that have been called "institutional housekeeping," consistently earn less than men with comparable productivity, and, if they have children, have less secretarial support and fewer institutional research dollars than male faculty or faculty women without children. According to a study published in the *Annals of Internal Medicine* in 2000, rates of reported gender-based discrimination in medical schools ranged from 47 percent for the youngest faculty to 70 percent for the oldest. Of the women faculty who had been sexually harassed, 80 percent perceived gender bias in their institution, which might have been expected, but equally disturbing is that 61 percent of women who had *not* been harassed also thought the academic environment was sexist.

Nor is the gender disadvantage in leadership confined to medical schools. Not only are a mere six out of twenty-one NIH Institutes headed by women, but the editorial boards of the *Journal of the American Medical Association,* the *New England Journal of Medicine,* and the *Annals of Internal Medicine* consist of 6 percent, 19 percent, and 19 percent women, respectively. The AMA Board of Trustees consists of four women and seventeen men. The AAMC has never, in all its 130-year history, had a woman president.

Five Closing Points

How are we to make sense of this jumble of facts about the history of doctors' opinions of women, clinical research on women, health care insurance for women, and women in medicine? The picture that emerges is disturbing—just the sort of thing, one might think, that calls out for bioethical analysis. Bioethicists are meant, after all, to engage in critique, perhaps especially where health care practices and institutions forcibly exclude or problematically include half the adult population. For the most part, however, we have been remarkably slow to criticize medicine's shortcomings regarding women. It's only feminist bioethicists—a tiny subset of the field—who, for the last twenty years or so, have been raising the woman question, but they have not gotten much of a hearing from their nonfeminist colleagues. That, I think, is a serious problem for bioethics.

So what might a feminist bioethicist do with these data? Well, this one would like to draw them together by means of five closing points.

1. The androcentrism that has been so glaring in the history of medicine has not entirely gone away. Androcentrism is the view that man is the paradigmatic human being, the most basic and obvious example of the species, and it is still quite visible in the areas I have examined. You can see it particularly well in how researchers still don't seem to feel the need to report outcomes of clinical trials by sex, and in how drug doses are keyed to masculine bodies.

2. By the logic of androcentrism, if man is the measure of human being, then woman must be inferior. If women were just different, then men would be as different from women as women are from men, but they aren't—they're more important. So then women are less important. You can see this in the low levels of funding for women's health, and in the pay gap between men and women physicians.

3. Women are not valued socially for themselves alone, but for something else: their fetuses, for example, or the care they give to their families and friends. The list of things that pregnant women are expected to do or to refrain from doing, at a considerable cost to themselves, is only one of many signs of this kind of indifference. It's evident, too, in what would otherwise be an amazing coincidence—namely, that one-third of women doctors, but only 4 percent of their male colleagues, just happen to choose to practice part time, presumably the better to serve their families.

4. Let me be clear. Doctors do not believe that men are paradigmatic human beings, and they also do not think women are inferior. But the data plainly indicate that androcentrism and poor treatment of women persist. The reason is not that men sit around figuring out how to perpetuate the oppression of women. Rather, it's that gender is a *system*. It's the result of social practices and institutions that work together quite impersonally to favor the interests of men over women. Here, health insurance coverage is a good example. Insurers clearly don't mean anything personal by excluding contraception from their health care plans—it's just that the plans are biased in favor of men, and the insurance companies profit from this.

5. If you want to find out about women, you have to ask them—it's no use counting on men to do the necessary research because, by and large, they seem to be indifferent to the woman question. That's apparent in the lack of data on women in clinical trials and the lack of women in leadership roles in clinical research just compounds the problem. This point was brought home to me clearly in my research for this paper: if you scan the list of citations you will see that with a single glaring exception, every study I could find on the status of women in medicine was conducted by women.

Finally, just as sexism is not confined to medicine alone, but is found in every part of our society, so, too, abusive power relations are not confined to women alone—there are many other forms of oppression. The generalizations derived from the snapshot of women I've offered here might apply equally well to other social groups who are on the lower rungs of hierarchies of power. If so, then a feminist bioethics has theoretical resources to offer a bioethics for those other groups.

Take disability bioethics. (1) The equivalent, for disabled people, to androcentrism is the strong social bias toward people with normal bodies and abilities. (2) The logic of ableism, like that of androcentrism, is that disabled people are inferior. But, (3) whereas women are socially valued for services they can provide, disabled people do not seem to be socially valued for much of anything, so here is an important difference between gender and disability. Nonetheless, (4) as with sexism, the bias is not personal—it is systemic, shored up by many practices and institutional arrangements that favor the able-bodied. And finally, (5) if you want to find out about disabled people, you have to ask them, not wait for able-bodied people to do the research.

It's not that all oppressions are the same—they aren't. Or that abusive power systems aside from gender don't each already have their own theorists—they do. And, of course, oppressions overlap because people frequently belong to several oppressed groups at the same time. But if feminist bioethicists have theoretical resources to contribute to disability bioethics, elder bioethics, queer bioethics, a bioethics of race, or a bioethics of poverty, then it's also true that they have much to learn from the theorists of these other oppressions. To date, they have almost never done so.

In bioethics, the best and most interesting work is often interdisciplinary. What makes feminist bioethics feminist is its primary focus on gender. But because women come in various races, classes, degrees of poverty, degrees of disability, and degrees of queerness, we feminist bioethicists could address the woman question in medicine and bioethics considerably more fully if we joined forces with the colleagues who theorize these other imbalances of power. Everyone—doctors, other health care professionals, bioethicists, patients, and society as a whole—might benefit from the result.

The Rights of "Unborn Children" and the Value of Pregnant Women

Howard Minkoff and Lynn M. Paltrow

Minkoff and Paltrow argue that legislation expanding the definition of "child" to include fetuses has adverse effects for pregnant women. Laws criminalizing the death or injury of a fetus during the commission of a crime have been used against women and establish a parity between the life of a fetus and the life of a pregnant woman. This suggests a need to balance the rights of the two if they ever conflict and, potentially, to subordinate the rights of the woman to the rights of the fetus.

The move to establish parity, the authors argue, grants rights to the unborn denied to born individuals. For example, no born person can be forced to have surgery to benefit someone else. Similarly, laws requiring women intending to terminate a pregnancy to listen to a monologue about fetal pain confer on midterm fetuses rights denied to born humans of any age. This happens, the authors claim, at the expense of autonomy, informed consent, and justice.

A quarter century after the "International Year of the Child," we now seem to be in the era of the "Unborn Child." Partly this is because of medical advances: highly refined imaging techniques have made the fetus more visually accessible to parents. In good measure, however, the new era is a product of political shifts. In 2004, President Bush signed into law the Unborn Victims of Violence Act, which makes it a separate federal offense to bring about the death or bodily injury of a "child in utero" while committing certain crimes, and recognizes everything from a zygote to a fetus as an independent "victim" with legal rights distinct from the woman who has been harmed. In 2002, the Department of

From Howard Minkoff and Lynn M. Paltrow, "The Rights of 'Unborn Children' and the Value of Pregnant Women," *Hastings Center Report* 36, no. 2 (2006): 26–28. Copyright © 2006 Hastings Center Report. All rights reserved. Reproduced by permission.

Health and Human Services adopted new regulations expanding the definition of "child" in the State Children's Health Insurance Program "so that a State may elect to make individuals in the period between conception and birth eligible for coverage." Finally, Senator Brownback and thirty-one cosponsors have proposed the Unborn Child Pain Awareness Act, a scientifically dubious piece of legislation that would require physicians performing the exceedingly rare abortions after twenty weeks to inform pregnant women of "the option of choosing to have anesthesia or other pain-reducing drug or drugs administered directly to the pain-capable unborn child."

The legislative focus on the unborn is aimed at women who choose abortion, but it may also have adverse consequences for women who choose not to have an abortion, and it challenges a central tenet of human rights—namely, that no person can be required to submit to state enforced surgery for the benefit of another.

The historical context of fetal rights legislation should make the most fervent proponents of fetal rights—pregnant women—wary. Often, in the past, expansions of fetal rights have been purchased through the diminution of pregnant women's rights. The fetal "right" to protection from environmental toxins cost pregnant women the right to good jobs: for nearly ten years before the U.S. Supreme Court ruled against such polices in 1991, companies used "fetal protection" policies as a basis for prohibiting fertile women from taking high-paying blue collar jobs that might expose them to lead. The fetal "right" to health and life has cost women their bodily integrity (women have been forced to undergo cesarean sections or blood transfusion), their liberty (women have been imprisoned for risking harm to a fetus through alcohol or drug use), and in some cases their lives (a court-ordered cesarean section probably accelerated the death in 1987 of Angela Carder, who had a recurrence [sic] of bone cancer that had metastasized to her lung). The fetal "right" not to be exposed to pharmaceutical agents has cost pregnant women their right to participate in drug trials that held out their only hope of cure from lethal illnesses. The vehicle for these infringements on pregnant women's rights has been third parties assertions that they, rather than the mother, have the authority to speak for the fetus in securing these newly defined rights. For example, employers have argued for the right to speak for the fetus in determining when a work environment is inappropriate for the fetus. In mandating cesarean section, the courts have apparently concluded that the judiciary is better positioned to speak for the fetus and that a competent but dying mother's wishes to refuse surgery are no longer worthy of consideration. Most recently, a state's attorney has taken up the cudgel for the fetus by charging a woman with murder for her refusal to consent to a cesarean section.

It is within the context of these attempts to wrest the right to speak for the fetus from mothers that legislation that will expand the rights of the fetus—such as the Unborn Victims of Violence Act—must be considered. The act makes the injury or death of a fetus during commission of a crime a federal offense, the punishment for which "is the same as the punishment...for that conduct had that injury or death occurred to the unborn child's mother." As written, the

law appears unambiguously to immunize pregnant women against legal jeopardy should any act of theirs result in fetal harm: "Nothing in this section shall be construed to permit the prosecution...of any woman with respect to her unborn child." But similar statutory guarantees proffered in the past have not been decisive. In 1970 the California Legislature created the crime of "fetal murder" and specifically excluded the conduct of the pregnant woman herself, but women who suffered stillbirths were nevertheless prosecuted under the statute. The prosecutor explained that "The fetal murder law was never intended to protect pregnant women from assault by third parties which results in death of the fetus. The purpose was to protect the unborn child from murder."

In Missouri cases, a woman who admitted to smoking marijuana once while pregnant and a pregnant woman who tested positive for cocaine were charged with criminal child endangerment on the basis of a statute that declares the rights of the unborn—yet also includes an explicit exception for the pregnant woman herself in language strikingly similar to that used in the Unborn Victims Act ("nothing in this section shall be interpreted as creating a cause of action against a woman for indirectly harming her unborn child by failing to properly care for herself"). The state argued that this language did not preclude prosecution of the pregnant women because "the pregnant woman is not in a different position than a third-party who injures the unborn child" and because her drug use "'directly' endangered the unborn child."

Even if the historical record did not contain these examples of a legislative bait and switch, the principles codified by the new federal statute would be worrisome. When laws create parity between harming pregnant women and harming members "of the species Homo sapiens" of any gestational age (as the Unborn Victims of Violence Act specifies), they establish symmetry between the rights of pregnant women and those of fetuses. In so doing, they suggest a need to balance rights when those rights appear to conflict with each other, and potentially to subordinate the rights of the women to those of the fetus. But to take this stance is not merely to elevate the rights of the unborn to parity with those of born individuals. It is in fact to grant them rights previously denied to born individuals: courts have allowed forced surgery to benefit the unborn, but have precluded forced surgery to benefit born persons. In 1978 Robert McFall sought a court order to force his cousin David Shimp, the only known compatible donor, to submit to a transplant. The court declined, explaining: "For our law to compel the Defendant to submit to an intrusion of his body would change every concept and principle upon which our society is founded. To do so would defeat the sanctity of the individual and would impose a rule which would know no limits."

The Unborn Child Pain Awareness Act is yet another example of a law focused on the fetus that devalues pregnant women and children and sets the stage for further erosion of their human rights. It mandates that prior to elective terminations, physicians deliver a precisely worded, though scientifically questionable, monologue that details the purported pain felt by the fetus and allows for fetal pain management. In so doing, it introduces two damaging concepts. First, it makes women and abortion providers a unique class, excluded from the standard medical model in which counseling is provided by a physician who uses professional judgment to determine what a reasonable individual would need in order to make an informed choice about a procedure. Instead, legislators' judgment is substituted for a physician's determination of the appropriate content of counseling.

Second, it elevates the rights of the midtrimester fetus beyond those of term fetuses, as well as those of its born siblings. Congress has never mandated that mothers be told that there may be fetal pain associated with fetal scalp electrodes or forceps deliveries. Nor have doctors been compelled to speak to the pain that accompanies circumcision or, for that matter, numerous medical conditions for which people are prevented from receiving adequate palliative care. Indeed, there is no federal law scripting counseling about the pain that could accompany any procedure to any child, or indeed any person, after birth. Society has generally relied on professionals to exercise medical judgment in crafting the content of counseling, and on medical societies to [ensure] that counseling evolves as science progresses.

While support for fetal rights laws is now *de rigueur* among politicians, there is apparently no similar mandate to address the social issues that truly threaten pregnant women and victimize their fetuses. Although states increasingly are seeking ways to arrest and punish women who won't undergo recommended surgery or who are unable to find drug rehabilitation programs that properly treat pregnant women and families, no means have been found to guarantee paid maternity leave or to proffer more

than quite limited employment protections from discrimination for women when they are pregnant. Many of our nation's tax and social security policies, rather than bolstering women's social standing, help to ensure mothers' economic vulnerability. Hence, the opposition to the Unborn Victims of Violence Act from some activists must be recognized as the logical consequence of years of having mothers beatified in words and vilified in deeds.

These arguments should not be misconstrued as evidence of a "maternal–fetal" conflict. Unless stripped of their rights, pregnant women will continue to be the most powerful advocates for the wellbeing of unborn children. Clashes between the rights of mothers and their fetuses are used as Trojan horses by those who would undermine the protections written into law by *Roe*. Proponents of the right-to-life agenda recognize that when fetal rights expand, the right to abortion will inevitably contract. Furthermore, the responsibilities of physicians in this environment are clear and are grounded in the principles of professionalism— primacy of patient welfare, patient autonomy, and social justice. Those principles require that patients' needs be placed before any "societal pressures" and that "patients' decisions about their care must be paramount." These words are bright line guideposts for clinicians who may at times feel caught in a balancing act. Whether the counterclaim to a pregnant woman's right to autonomy is a societal demand for drug test results obtained in labor, an administrator's request to get a court order to supersede an informed woman's choice, or a colleague's plea to consider fetal interests more forcefully, these principles remind us that no other concern should dilute physicians' commitment to the pregnant woman.

The argument that women should not lose their civil and human rights upon becoming pregnant is predicated neither on the denial of the concept that an obstetrician has two patients, nor on the acceptance of any set position in the insoluble debate as to when life begins. The courts have provided direction for those dealing with the competing interests of two patients, even if one were to concede that the fetus in this regard is vested with rights equal to that of a born person. A physician who had both Robert McFall (potential marrow recipient) and David Shimp (potential donor) as patients may well have shared the judge's belief that Shimp's refusal to donate his marrow, and thereby to condemn McFall to death, was "morally reprehensible." But the clinician would ultimately have to be guided by the judge's decision to vouchsafe David Shimp's sanctity as an individual. Pregnancy does not diminish that sanctity or elevate the rights of the fetus beyond that of Robert McFall or any other born person. Thus, while the obstetrician's commitment to his "other" patient (the fetus) should be unstinting, it should be so only to a limit set by those, to quote Justice [Blackmun] "who conceive, bear, support, and raise them." To do otherwise would be to recruit the medical community into complicity with those who would erode the rights of women in the misguided belief that one can champion the health of children by devaluing the rights of their mothers.

Section 2:   Race, Research, and Medicine

The Dangers of Difference: The Legacy of the Tuskegee Syphilis Study

Patricia A. King

King argues that recognizing racial differences in medicine poses a dilemma. Even when the intention is to help a stigmatized group, the result may be to cause harm. She proposes that research always begin with the presumption that, with respect to disease, blacks and whites are biologically identical. While the presumption may be shown to be wrong in the course of the study, it acknowledges that, historically speaking, more harm has come from imputing racial differences than from ignoring them.

It has been sixty years since the beginning of the Tuskegee syphilis experiment and twenty years since its existence was disclosed to the American public. The social and ethical issues that the experiment poses for medicine, particularly for medicine's relationship with African Americans, are still not broadly understood, appreciated, or even remembered. Yet a significant aspect of the Tuskegee experiment's legacy is that in a racist society that incorporates beliefs about the inherent inferiority of African Americans in contrast with the superior status of whites, any attention to the question of differences that may exist is likely to be pursued in a manner that burdens rather than benefits African Americans.

The Tuskegee experiment, which involved approximately 400 males with late-stage, untreated syphilis and approximately 200 controls free of the disease, is by any measure one of the dark pages in the history of American medicine. In this study of the natural course of untreated syphilis, the participants did not give informed consent. Stunningly, when penicillin was subsequently developed as a treatment for syphilis, measures were taken to keep the diseased participants from receiving it.

Obviously, the experiment provides a basis for the exploration of many ethical and social issues in medicine, including professional ethics, the limitations of informed consent as a means of protecting research subjects, and the motives and methods used to justify the exploitation of persons who live in conditions of severe economic and social disadvantage. At bottom, however, the Tuskegee experiment is different from other incidents of abuse in clinical research because all the participants were black males. The racism that played a central role in this tragedy continues to infect even our current well-intentioned efforts to reverse the decline in health status of African Americans....

The Dilemma of Difference

In the context of widespread belief in the racial inferiority of blacks that surrounded the Tuskegee experiment, it should not come as a surprise that the experiment exploited its subjects. Recognizing and

From Patricia A. King, "The Dangers of Difference: The Legacy of the Tuskegee Syphilis Study," *Hastings Center Report* 22, no. 6 (1992): 35–38. Reprinted by permission of the author and publisher. Copyright © 1992 The Hastings Center. (Notes omitted.)

taking account of racial differences that have historically been utilized to burden and exploit African Americans poses a dilemma. Even in circumstances where the goal of a scientific study is to benefit a stigmatized group or person, such well-intentioned efforts may nevertheless cause harm. If the racial difference is ignored and all groups or persons are treated similarly, unintended harm may result from the failure to recognize racially correlated factors. Conversely, if differences among groups or persons are recognized and attempts are made to respond to past injustices or special burdens, the effort is likely to reinforce existing negative stereotypes that contributed to the emphasis on racial differences in the first place.

This dilemma about difference is particularly worrisome in medicine. Because medicine is pragmatic, it will recognize racial differences if doing so will promote health goals. As a consequence, potential harms that might result from attention to racial differences tend to be overlooked, minimized, or viewed as problems beyond the purview of medicine.

The question of whether (and how) to take account of racial differences has recently been raised in the context of the current AIDS epidemic. The participation of African Americans in clinical AIDS trials has been disproportionately small in comparison to the numbers of African Americans who have been infected with the human immunodeficiency virus. Because of the possibility that African Americans may respond differently to drugs being developed and tested to combat AIDS, those concerned about the care and treatment of AIDS in the African American community have called for greater participation by African Americans in these trials. Ironically, efforts to address the problem of underrepresentation must cope with the enduring legacy of the Tuskegee experiment—the legacy of suspicion and skepticism toward medicine and its practitioners among African Americans.

In view of the suspicion Tuskegee so justifiably engenders, calls for increased participation by African Americans in clinical trials are worrisome. The question of whether to tolerate racially differentiated AIDS research testing of new or innovative therapies, as well as the question of what norms should govern participation by African Americans in clinical research, needs careful and thoughtful attention. A generic examination of the treatment of racial differences in medicine is beyond the scope of this article. However,

I will describe briefly what has occurred since disclosure of the Tuskegee experiment to point out the dangers I find lurking in our current policies.

Inclusion and Exclusion

In part because of public outrage concerning the Tuskegee experiment, comprehensive regulations governing federal research using human subjects were revised and subsequently adopted by most federal agencies. An institutional review board (IRB) must approve clinical research involving human subjects, and IRB approval is made contingent on review of protocols for adequate protection of human subjects in accordance with federal criteria. These criteria require, among other things, that an IRB ensure that subject selection is "equitable." The regulations further provide that

> [i]n making this assessment the IRB should take into account the purposes of the research and the setting in which the research will be conducted, and should be particularly cognizant of the special problems of research involving vulnerable populations, such as women, mentally disabled persons, or economically or educationally disadvantaged persons.

The language of the regulation makes clear that the concern prompting its adoption was the protection of vulnerable groups from exploitation. The obverse problem—that too much protection might promote the exclusion or underrepresentation of vulnerable groups, including African Americans—was not at issue. However, underinclusion can raise as much of a problem of equity as exploitation.

A 1990 General Accounting Office study first documented the extent to which minorities and women were underrepresented in federally funded research. In response, in December 1990 the National Institutes of Health, together with the Alcohol, Drug Abuse and Mental Health Administration, directed that minorities and women be included in study populations,

> so that research findings can be of benefit to all persons at risk of the disease, disorder or condition under study; special emphasis should be placed on the need for inclusion of minorities and women in studies of diseases, disorders and conditions that disproportionately affect them.

If minorities are not included, a clear and compelling rationale must be submitted.

The new policy clearly attempts to avoid the perils of overprotection, but it raises new concerns. The policy must be clarified and refined if it is to meet the intended goal of ensuring that research findings are of benefit to all. There are at least three reasons for favoring increased representation of African Americans in clinical trials. The first is that there may be biological differences between blacks and whites that might affect the applicability of experimental findings to blacks, but these differences will not be noticed if blacks are not included in sufficient numbers to allow the detection of statistically significant racial differences. The second reason is that race is a reliable index for social conditions such as poor health and nutrition, lack of adequate access to health care, and economic and social disadvantage that might adversely affect potential benefits of new interventions and procedures. If there is indeed a correlation between minority status and these factors, then African Americans and all others with these characteristics will benefit from new information generated by the research. The third reason is that the burdens and benefits of research should be spread across the population regardless of racial or ethnic status....

The third justification carries with it the obvious danger that the special needs or problems generated as a result of economic or social conditions associated with minority status may be overlooked and that, as a result, African Americans and other minorities will be further disadvantaged. The other two justifications are problematic and deserve closer examination. They each assume that there are either biological, social, economic, or cultural differences between blacks and whites....

The Way Out of the Dilemma

Understanding how, or indeed whether, race correlates with disease is a very complicated problem. Race itself is a confusing concept with both biological and social connotations. Some doubt whether race has biological significance at all. Even if race is a biological fiction, however, its social significance remains.

In the wake of Tuskegee and, in more recent times, the stigma and discrimination that resulted from screening for sickle-cell trait (a genetic condition that occurs with greater frequency among African Americans), researchers have been reluctant to explore associations between race and disease. There is increasing recognition, however, of evidence of heightened resistance or vulnerability to disease along racial lines. Indeed, sickle-cell anemia itself substantiates the view that biological differences may exist. Nonetheless, separating myth from reality in determining the cause of disease and poor health status is not easy. Great caution should be exercised in attempting to validate biological differences in susceptibility to disease in light of this society's past experience with biological differences. Moreover, using race as an index for other conditions that might influence health and well-being is also dangerous. Such practices could emphasize social and economic differences that might also lead to stigma and discrimination.

If all the reasons for increasing minority participation in clinical research are flawed, how then can we promote improvement in health status of African Americans and other minorities through participation in clinical research, while simultaneously minimizing the harms that might flow from such participation? Is it possible to work our way out of this dilemma?

An appropriate strategy should have as its starting point the defeasible presumption that blacks and whites are biologically the same with respect to disease and treatment. Presumptions can be overturned of course, and the strategy should recognize the possibility that biological differences in some contexts are possible. But the presumption of equality acknowledges that historically the greatest harm has come from the willingness to impute biological differences rather than the willingness to overlook them. For some, allowing the presumption to be in any way defeasible is troubling. Yet I do not believe that fear should lead us to ignore the possibility of biologically differentiated responses to disease and treatment, especially when the goal is to achieve medical benefit.

It is well to note at this point the caution sounded by Hans Jonas. He wrote, "Of the new experimentation with man, medical is surely the most legitimate; psychological, the most dubious; biological (still to come), the most dangerous." Clearly, priority should be given to exploring the possible social, cultural, and environmental determinants of disease before targeting the study of hypotheses that involve biological differences between blacks and whites. For example, rather than trying to determine whether blacks and whites respond differently to AZT, attention should first be directed to learning whether response to AZT is influenced by social, cultural, or environmental conditions. Only at the point where possible biological differences emerge should hypotheses that explore racial differences be considered.

A finding that blacks and whites are different in some critical aspect need not inevitably lead to increased discrimination or stigma for blacks. If there indeed had been a difference in the effects of untreated syphilis between blacks and whites such information might have been used to promote the health status of blacks. But the Tuskegee experiment stands as a reminder that such favorable outcomes rarely if ever occur. More often, either racist assumptions and stereotypes creep into the study's design, or findings broken down by race become convenient tools to support policies and behavior that further disadvantage those already vulnerable.

What's Wrong with Race-Based Medicine?
Dorothy E. Roberts

Roberts examines the development of the heart disease drug BiDil, and concludes that its approval as a "race-specific" pharmaceutical was both scientifically flawed and ethically dubious. She notes that BiDil's component drugs were developed for cardiac patients regardless of race and not aimed at any supposed African American genotype. Since the drug's second, dramatically successful trial involved only self-identified African Americans, there is no basis for concluding that it works better for them than any other group. Roberts argues that the drug should thus have received FDA approval without regard to race—as she suggests it would have been if the subjects had all been white.

Instead, Roberts suggests that BiDil's "niche marketing" campaign distorts scientific results and reinforces discredited biological concepts of race. Roberts points to a range of studies indicating that social and environmental factors rather than genetics are the most likely explanation for racial disparities in health. She argues that the popularity of biological explanations for such disparities reflects a familiar refusal to address social problems such as poverty, limited access to health care, and mass incarceration that afflict African American communities.

I. INTRODUCTION

In June 2005, the Food and Drug Administration (FDA) announced a historic decision: it approved the first pharmaceutical indicated for a specific race. BiDil, a combination drug that relaxes the blood vessels, was authorized to treat heart failure in self-identified black patients. BiDil had been tested in the African-American Heart Failure Trial (A-HeFT) launched in 2001. A-HeFT enrolled 1,050 subjects suffering from advanced heart failure,

From Dorothy E. Roberts, "What's Wrong with Race-Based Medicine?: Genes, Drugs, and Health Disparities," *Minnesota Journal of Law, Science & Technology* 12, no 1 (2011): 1–21. (Notes omitted.)

all self-identified African Americans. A-HeFT showed that BiDil worked; in fact, it worked so spectacularly that the trial was stopped ahead of schedule. BiDil increased survival by an astonishing 43 percent. Hospitalizations were reduced by 39 percent. It was a momentous accomplishment for Jay Cohn, the University of Minnesota cardiologist who invented BiDil and had pioneered vasodilators as an important treatment for heart failure.

Given evidence of BiDil's efficacy, but little evidence that race mattered to its efficacy, the FDA should have made one of two decisions: reject the request for race-specific approval or approve BiDil for all heart failure patients, regardless of race. Instead, the FDA put race at the center of its decision, sparking controversy and paving the way for a new generation of racial medicines.

No one is complaining that BiDil is available to people who will benefit from it. The problem is that BiDil was made available on the basis of race. Its racial label elicited three types of criticism: scientific, commercial, and political. I will discuss the first two controversies en route to what I consider the main problem with race-based medicine, its political implications. By claiming that race, a political grouping, is important to the marketing of drugs and that race-based drugs can reduce health disparities, which are caused primarily by social inequality, those who promote racialized medicine have made it a political issue. Yet, having made these political claims, these very advocates answer criticism by saying that we must put aside social justice concerns in order to improve minority health. This article explains why marketing pharmaceuticals on the basis of race is more likely to worsen racial inequities than cure them.

II. RACE-SPECIFIC MEDICINE IS SCIENTIFICALLY FLAWED

What does it mean for a pharmaceutical to be race-specific? A drug that is labeled for use by a particular race sounds like it has been developed based on scientific evidence that its ingredients work for one group and not for others because of some underlying biological difference. But there is no such drug or scientific evidence supporting it. BiDil is a case in point. It does not contain new ingredients. It was not designed only for black people. Nor was it developed to target any particular genotype that only black people supposedly have or are more likely to have. Instead, it combined into a single pill two generic drugs that had been prescribed to patients regardless of race for over a decade. In fact, Dr. Cohn originally intended to market it to patients of any race who could benefit from it. There is not even scientific proof that BiDil works differently in black people because the clinical trial that tested BiDil enrolled only "self-identified" African Americans. There is no basis for a comparative statement if only one group has been tested.

Its maker, NitroMed, asked the FDA to authorize BiDil as a race-specific drug on grounds that its clinical trial involving only African American patients showed a dramatic reduction in their heart failure deaths. In other words, the company argued that, because BiDil was tested only on blacks, the FDA should label it as a drug for blacks only. As Jane Kramer, NitroMed's vice president of corporate affairs, would later explain, "That doesn't mean that it works in all African Americans and it doesn't mean that it doesn't work in other patients. It just means that we know it clearly works in African Americans."

This kind of logic had never resulted in a racial indication before. In the past, the FDA has had no problem generalizing clinical trials involving white people to approve drugs for everyone. That is because it believes that white bodies function like human bodies. However with BiDil, a clinical trial involving all African Americans could only serve as proof of how the drug works in blacks. By approving BiDil only for use in black patients, the FDA emphasized the supposed distinctive, and substandard, quality of black bodies. It sent the message that black people cannot represent all of humanity as well as white people can.

Why did BiDil work especially well in black patients? NitroMed had no scientific evidence to answer this question, but it speculated that the mechanism had to do with biological difference. In a March 2001 press release, NitroMed explained that BiDil works especially well for African Americans because "observed racial disparities in mortality and therapeutic response rates in black patients may be due in part to ethnic differences in the underlying pathophysiology of heart failure." NitroMed sought FDA approval based on pure speculation that race was a good enough proxy for some underlying genetic or pathophysiological difference without conducting any investigation whatsoever to test this claim. The researchers who reported BiDil's effectiveness for African American heart patients recognized this flaw and simply promised to correct it at some future time.

The FDA expounded the race-as-proxy theory in a January 2007 article in *Annals of Internal Medicine* explaining its approval of BiDil. "We hope that further research elucidates the genetic or other factors that predict the usefulness of hydralazine hydrochloride-isosorbide dinitrate," the author wrote. "Until then, we are pleased that one defined group has access to a dramatically life-prolonging therapy." In other words, a racially-defined group could serve as a temporary substitute for the yet undiscovered genetic or other factor that identifies who will benefit from BiDil.

The issue crystallized during the FDA hearing on BiDil in a debate between two Advisory Committee members. Vivian Ota Wang from the National Institutes of Health's National Human Genome Research Institute challenged the use of race in the A-HeFT trial as a proxy for an underlying biological trait that explained how BiDil worked. "There is a presumption here that somehow this self-identified social identifier is somewhat equivalent or representative of a biological process, and I am not sure it really is," Ota Wang pointed out. "We need to really carefully look at the issue of self-identified racial categories because if the assumption is that these population differences are biological, the self-identified population is a social and political construct." The Committee Chair, Cleveland Clinic cardiologist Steven Nissen, dismissed Ota Wang's concerns. "We are using self-identified race as a surrogate for genomic-based medicine and I don't think that is unreasonable." Nissen said. "I wish we had the genetic markers . . . to decide who is going to respond to what drug but, in the absence of that, we have to use the best available evidence, . . . and that evidence was used in this trial and it worked." Later, Dr. Nissen more bluntly reiterated, "We're using self-identified race as a surrogate for genetic markers." Nissen dismissed the worry that this rationale for approving a race-specific drug would reinforce a genetic definition of race by asserting, "Drugs aren't racist; people are."

Not only was the racial indication scientifically flawed, but race became a reason for lowering the FDA's scientific standards. In 1989, Dr. Cohn obtained a patent on a "method of reducing mortality associated with congestive heart failure." The patent made no mention of race. In 1996, the company he licensed the rights to submitted a New Drug Application for BiDil to the FDA. Like Cohn's patent application, this application for marketing approval did not mention race. Its evidence of the drug's efficacy consisted of a retrospective analysis of clinical trials Cohn conducted in the 1980s. The FDA Advisory Committee that reviewed the application was not convinced. The issue was not BiDil's effectiveness; it was the FDA's statistical standards. The Advisory Committee found that the reanalysis of old data, which were not collected to test a new drug for FDA approval, failed to meet the narrow criteria for statistical significance. Another prob-

lem was that BiDil would be prescribed as an adjunct to standard ACE inhibitor and beta blocker therapies, therapies that were not combined with the BiDil ingredients in the earlier trials. Consequently, the FDA denied approval in 1997.

During the 2004 FDA hearing on Cohn's application to market BiDil as a race-specific drug, the question of statistical standards was raised again. Ota Wang and Nissen also differed on the standards the FDA should use to evaluate BiDil. Nissen took the position that the remarkable improvement in health experienced by the A-HeFT patients on BiDil should outweigh concerns about the statistical strength of trial data. "I have to approve a drug when I think there's evidence you can reduce mortality by 43 percent," he said, "As a clinician, I find the evidence more than adequate to vote for approval." Comparing heart failure among African Americans to an "orphan disease," Nissen argued that "you make some adjustments sometimes because you want to encourage trials in special populations and diseases which are of public health importance which we have few therapies for." In other words, to Nissen, heart failure suffered by African Americans was a special type of illness that warranted exceptions to the rules, as in the case of rare medical conditions.

Ota Wang objected to the "notion that for some types of research, for some types of communities or populations we can actually lower the bar in terms of scientific integrity that we are using to evaluate the research." In response, Nissen reiterated the orphan disease analogy. "So, if you are developing a drug for a disease and there are not many people that have it, you get some points for doing that." he said. "I am arguing that it is not unreasonable public policy to make some adjustment for that." Statistical weaknesses in the data that ordinarily posed problems for FDA approval were overlooked because BiDil was a drug for black people. Apparently, Dr. Nissen was not referring to heart failure in general, a common ailment that is far from an "orphan" disease, but to black people's heart failure. The very issues about statistical data that led the FDA to deny approval for BiDil when it was for the general population were now overlooked because BiDil had become a race-specific drug.

Perhaps the overwhelming evidence from the A-HeFT trial that BiDil was beneficial for many patients was a compelling reason to discount the statistical concerns and make it widely available on the market. The stunning trial results gave the FDA grounds to approve the drug without insisting on its statistical rules or further investigation of why BiDil worked so well, but what the A-HeFT trial did not do was give the FDA grounds to base its decision on race. We should be concerned that the FDA's acceptance of race-specific drugs will turn into a rationale for "lowering the bar" of the scientific standards the agency usually applies in evaluating new drugs.

III. RACE-SPECIFIC MEDICINE IS COMMERCIALLY MOTIVATED

A second problem with racial indications for pharmaceuticals is that they are guided by the market and not by science. Race is becoming a niche market that gives pharmaceutical companies an opportunity to extract new profits from existing drugs. Again, BiDil provides an illustration.

Recall that the FDA denied Cohn's original application to market BiDil without regard to race. With his original race-neutral patent due to expire in less than 10 years, Cohn needed a strategy for salvaging his pharmaceutical venture. Cohn's second chance came from reconceiving BiDil as a race-specific drug. It was only after the FDA rejection that Cohn turned BiDil—the exact same drug that he had patented without regard to race—into a therapy for African Americans. Cohn submitted a new patent for BiDil with a critical difference from the original one. The new patent added the key language: the "present invention provides methods for treating and preventing mortality associated with heart failure *in an African American patient.*" The new patent, issued in 2000, lasts until 2020, buying thirteen more years of intellectual property control over the drug.

NitroMed's success at using race to gain FDA and patent approval, as well as support from influential political players, signaled the potential profitability of race-specific drugs. Legal scholar Jonathan Kahn argues that BiDil's racial labeling gave the pharmaceutical industry "a new model of how to exploit race in the marketplace by literally capitalizing on the racial identity of minority populations," providing "a cheaper, more efficient way to gain the US Food and Drug Administration's approval for drugs." Supporting his view is evidence of the growing use of race as a genetic category to obtain patent protection. Using the U.S. Patent Office database, Kahn reviewed gene-related patent applications filed between 1976 and 2005 that employed racial or ethnic categories.

Kahn discovered a five-fold increase in racial patents during that period. Race was not mentioned in any application filed in 1976–1997. From 1976–2005 twelve gene-related patents were issued using race or ethnicity, and from 2001–2005 sixty-five gene-related patents applications were filed using race or ethnicity.

Using racial categories to patent an invention and to carve out a racially-defined market for it is nothing new. There is a long history, dating back to the 1800s, of patenting all sorts of products that involve race: chemicals to straighten kinky hair, creams to lighten dark skin, and toys that celebrate or mock people of color. For example, a patent from 1940 for an arcade game featured a figure of a "negro stealing a chicken" as a target. "As soon as the target is initially moved, with the negro moving toward the hen house, a successful hit will cause him to reverse his direction of movement and leave the hen house," the inventor explained. The Civil Rights Movement ushered in patents for dolls, games, and teaching materials that celebrated diversity, ethnic holidays, and civil rights leaders. A more recent patent filed in 2006 for a device that quickly removes natural or synthetic braids that have been attached to human hair claims to benefit African Americans because they "genetically have hair that resists the formation of longer lengths."

Race and ethnic heritage are used by patent applicants in a variety of ways, some more harmful than others. The problem with recent gene-related patents is that they treat race as a biological category. Treating racial identity as a component of a genetic commodity further solidifies the view that race is biological. "The patent process takes race as a social category and recodes it as 'natural,'" Kahn writes. The growing number of biomedical studies and patents that rely on race suggests that biotech companies are poised to launch a new generation of racial pharmaceuticals.

It would be naïve to believe that, given our market-driven system, biomedical research can proceed without private funding and without converting discoveries into marketable products. But it is equally naïve to ignore the influence of pharmaceutical money on the way biomedical research is conducted. The A-HeFT researchers surely were motivated by a desire to alleviate the suffering of black heart failure patients, but their ties to the pharmaceutical industry helped to steer their path to a cure.

My quarrel with the commercial aspects of BiDil's development is not that the people involved made money. Congress has ensured that profit is the central incentive for the pharmaceutical industry to research and market medications. In his commentary on my lecture, Jay Cohn conceded that "there's a commercial benefit to this—of course. How else do drugs get developed in this country except on the basis of commercial potential? So if you want to criticize that, you can criticize the entire economic strategy in America and maybe Dorothy would like to do that." It is one thing for biomedical researchers and pharmaceutical companies to profit from scientific innovation; it is quite another for the profit motive to steer the science that is being innovated. Commercial interests induce pharmaceutical companies to exaggerate or invent the therapeutic importance of race. NitroMed did not make money from a drug that was developed to treat heart failure in black patients. It made money by converting a drug for heart failure into a drug for African Americans based on unscientific claims about racial difference.

IV. RACE-BASED MEDICINE IS POLITICALLY DANGEROUS

Despite these criticisms, is it not a good thing that BiDil is on the market? Supporters of race-specific drugs counter the scientific and commercial challenges I discuss by arguing that these drugs are critical to advancing health in two very important ways: they are a step toward developing personalized medicine, and they are immediately addressing health disparities based on race.

I argue that it is precisely these two claims that make race-based medicine not only scientifically flawed but politically dangerous. By reinforcing a biological definition of race and cure for health disparities that are false, race-based medicine supports a new biopolitics of race that threatens to make health and other social inequalities even worse.

For the last decade, genetic scientists have promised to soon develop personalized medicines that will enable doctors to predict, diagnose, and treat illnesses according to each patient's own unique genome. Researchers in the field of pharmacogenomics, which studies the genetic origins of disease and differential responses to medications, are trying to develop "tailored" drugs that are safer and more effective than conventional medicines. But a decade after completion of the Human Genome Project, researchers have failed to discover the genes that cause common diseases, which were predicted to enable

the development of gene-targeted medicines. "There is absolutely no question that for the whole hope of personalized medicine, the news has been as bleak as could be," summed up molecular biologist David Goldstein, director of Duke University's Center for Human Genome Variation, in September 2008. Despite statistically linking hundreds of common variants to various diseases, scientists discovered that they account for only a tiny fraction of the genetic risk. Instead, most common diseases are caused by a host of rare genetic variants that evade detection by genome-wide association studies.

Despite the lack of genetic data—or perhaps because of it—race has become the magic fix to bridge the gap between the promise and disappointment of personalized medicine. Pharmocogenomic researchers treat race as a crucial first step to producing designer drugs because, they argue, race can serve as a proxy for individual genetic difference. Until science is able to match therapies to each individual's unique genotype, race functions as a handy surrogate.

The FDA's press release announcing its approval of BiDil stated that the decision "represent[ed] a step toward the promise of personalized medicine." But what did BiDil have to do with personalized medicine? It was not a drug designed for black people at all, let alone one tailored to match some race-based genetic difference. It was developed to treat heart failure regardless of race and regardless of genetics. Yet despite having nothing to do with pharmacogenomics, "the step toward personalized medicine" claim became one of the leading rationales for race-based medicine. In *FDA Week*, Michael Warner, a former regulatory affairs specialist for the Biotechnology Industry Organization, falsely asserted that "BiDil is the first time, the highest profile time, the model of 'let's identify a target population and let's develop a drug for that population' has been pursued."

A second basis for defending race-based pharmaceuticals is the claim that their health benefits outweigh their power to reinforce race as a biological category. Prominent African American scientists, doctors, and advocates endorsed BiDil to redress past discrimination against African Americans in medical treatment and access to health care. Ever since their enslavement in the United States, African Americans have been victims of both medical abuse, such as the infamous syphilis study in Tuskegee, Alabama, and medical neglect. BiDil supporters argued that a race-specific drug fulfilled a longstanding demand that science attend to the particular needs of African Americans whom historically had been excluded from good medical care and clinical trials while suffering disproportionately from heart disease. Representative Donna Christenson implored the FDA to approve BiDil as a remedy for medical wrongs against African Americans "for whom treatment has been denied and deferred for 400 years."

Many used the health disparities as a reason to ignore the scientific flaws in race-based medicine. Gary Puckrein, executive director of the National Minority Health Month Foundation, has championed BiDil as an important response to high rates of heart disease among African Americans. Although he acknowledged "[c]oncern about the medical and scientific validity of the concept of race," he dismissed such concern as "under present circumstances, impractical." Similarly, Keith Ferdinand, chief science officer of the Association of Black Cardiologists, wrote that "race lacks any true biologic definition," but BiDil is a "life-saving drug" that addresses "evidence of racial and ethnic differences in cardiac care in the United States which may significantly affect health outcomes." In other words, these BiDil advocates argue that the urgency of addressing the African American health crisis with race-specific drugs overrides objections that race is a social and not a genetic grouping....

These activists and researchers with ties to the pharmaceutical industry try to stifle criticism of racial medicine by portraying objections as roadblocks to African Americans' access to lifesaving treatment. They imply that objecting to race-specific medicine is tantamount to denying black patients the medicine they need. Behind this argument is the false assumption that it is impossible to develop drugs that benefit blacks without classifying people by race.

It is unfair to accuse people who oppose racial labeling of trying to keep lifesaving drugs from dying patients. No critic of race-specific medicine seeks to deny lifesaving drugs to African American people. We never argued that BiDil should be withheld from the market. Just the opposite is true: we argued that if it were to be marketed, it should be made more widely available—without regard to race. We simply see no justification for marketing medicines according to race and worry about their potential to divert attention away from more significant social reasons for

health disparities. Studying and eliminating the social determinants of health inequities is a far more promising course than searching for race-specific genetic differences.

Portraying BiDil as a solution to a racial gap in mortality implies the gap stems from racial differences in disease and drug response. Adding a genetic explanation for this difference attributes health disparities to flaws inside black people's bodies rather than to flaws in the society they live in. It supports the increasingly popular but misguided view that the tiny percentage of genetic difference among human beings is distributed by race and that this difference creates inequities in health.

In his commentary on my lecture, Dr. Cohn objected that I raised "concerns that all of us have about inequality of healthcare that BiDil was never developed to address." Although Cohn belatedly protests the insertion of health disparities into the debate about BiDil, it was BiDil advocates who first relied on the mortality gap between blacks and whites to gain support for the drug and who painted BiDil as a response to centuries of discrimination against African Americans. As Susan Reverby has observed, the "shadow of Tuskegee" hung over the FDA hearing and put pressure on the advisory committee to approve BiDil as a therapy for black people.

While listening to African American advocates for race-specific medicine, the FDA Advisory Committee ignored the evidence presented by Dr. Charles Rotimi, a researcher at Howard University's Human Genome Center, that showed high rates of hypertension among blacks stemming from environmental rather than genetic causes. To Dr. Rotimi, it made no sense to conclude that blacks are "selectively acquiring bad genes" for the numerous conditions marked by racial gaps in mortality. It is implausible that one race of people evolved to have a genetic predisposition to heart failure, hypertension, infant mortality, diabetes, and asthma. There is no evolutionary theory that can explain why African ancestry would be genetically prone to practically every major common illness. "There must be something in our social environment that drives people toward poor health, and only by addressing that can we reduce health disparity," Dr. Rotimi concluded.

Many scientific studies that show that racially unequal health outcomes stem from unequal social conditions support Dr. Rotimi's views. Some, like a study of racial gaps in breast cancer mortality in Chicago, show that the geographical concentration and historical changes in racial health disparities could not possibly stem from genetic difference. White women in Chicago are slightly more likely than black women to get breast cancer. Black women are twice as likely to die from it. That is a startling statistic by itself. But what is equally shocking is that Chicago's black and white breast cancer mortality rates were identical in 1980. The astounding gap emerged over the course of the next twenty-five years. The most likely explanation is that black women did not have access to the technologies and therapies that lowered white women's cancer mortality rate. Moreover, the disparity in breast cancer mortality in New York City is only fifteen percent, making the racial gap in Chicago ten times greater than in New York—a disparity unexplained by genetic difference.

Dr. Richard Cooper's global comparison of hypertension similarly refutes a genetic explanation for race-based health inequities. His study revealed that blacks in Nigeria and Jamaica have rates of hypertension similar to that of whites in the United States and much lower than that of African Americans. Perhaps Nigerians and African Americans are genetically prone to high blood pressure, but there is something in the environment that is causing elevated rates in this country. But that is just the point: if our goal is eliminating the gap between white and black hypertension in the United States, our focus should be on the social causes of the gap. Continuing to hunt for a genetic component of racial differences only distracts us from the more relevant issue of identifying and tackling the preventable causes of hypertension, which have a similar impact regardless of race. This approach would help everyone who lives in conditions that cause high rates of hypertension....

Researchers still do not know why blacks get and die from heart failure at a much earlier age than whites. But if I were a scientist, I would start looking at the effects of young black men's seventy-five per cent chance of being incarcerated in some cities. Heart disease researchers should be more interested in the fact that black men are seven times more likely than whites to be imprisoned in this country than the less significant genetic differences many are so fixated on.

Attributing health inequities to genetic difference is part of a broader trend, what I call a new biopolitics of race, that is focusing on race at the molecular level while discounting its impact on society. At the other end of the political spectrum from the African American advocates I quoted earlier, are conservatives who claim that racial differences are real at the genetic level and also charge their critics with relying on political ideology rather than science. They argue that race is a natural category that became politicized only in the last few decades because of post-civil rights identity politics. This ignores the real origins of racial classifications that accommodated European, and later American, imperialism and slavery—the quintessential example of using science to achieve political ends. Conservatives point to racial medicine as scientific confirmation of racial differences that liberals have denied in order to be politically correct.

Sally Satel, a fellow at the American Enterprise Institute, has long defended the use of race in medical practice in response to biological differences between members of different racial groups. At a 2004 American Enterprise Institute Symposium entitled, *Race, Medicine, and Public Policy*, she concluded, "It is evident that disease is not colorblind, and therefore doctors should not be either." Not surprisingly, Satel supports race-specific pharmaceuticals. "Social race is the phenomenon constructionists have in mind.... Biological race, however, is what BiDil's developers are concerned with—that is, race as ancestry."

According to this view, racial differences are real at the molecular level and merely constructed in society; therefore, doctors and researchers cannot be colorblind, but social policy should be. Genomic science, these conservatives argue, now gives people license to act on biological differences between races to better understand their health and identities. In this ingenious twist of political logic, those who criticize racial medicine because of its social impact are seen as interfering with health on the basis of racial ideology.

A renewed trust in inherent racial differences provides a convenient but false explanation for persistent inequities despite the end of de jure discrimination. It is also the perfect complement to social policies that implement the claim that racism has ceased to be the cause of African Americans' unequal status. Race consciousness in social programs like affirmative action is under assault at the very moment that race consciousness in medicine is ascending. As Chief Justice Roberts stated in one of several recent Supreme Court decisions chiseling away at government's use of race to address institutionalized inequality, "The way to stop discrimination on the basis of race is to stop discriminating on the basis of race."

There is a long history of using a biological definition of race to make social inequities seem natural—the result of inherent difference instead of societal injustice. As Evelynn Hammonds has noted, "[T]he appeal of a story that links race to medical and scientific progress is in the way in which it naturalizes the social order in a racially stratified society such as ours."

While the racial gap in life expectancy widens, owing largely to the government's failure to address structural inequities, the poor health of African Americans opens new markets for pharmaceutical companies. The claim that race-based biotechnologies will shrink the gap based on genetic difference is a powerful way to deflect concerns about their unjust social impact and the social inequality that actually drives poor minority health. We should be against an approach that promotes individual health through technological cures as a way of ignoring larger social inequities. This view sets up a false dichotomy between health and social justice: it treats health and justice as opposing values, weighs them against each other, and declares health the winner. It hides the social factors that determine health not only for individuals but for the entire nation. Letting health trump social justice does not really improve the welfare of most people; it supports the interests of big business and the most privileged members of society.

The promotion of race-based medicine misrepresents the relationship between genes, drugs, and health disparities. Of course, pharmaceuticals can help improve sick people's health and effective pharmaceuticals should be available to people who would benefit from them. But health inequities are not caused by genes and cannot be eliminated with drugs. Promoting race-based medicine with the myth that poor minority health is caused by genetic difference will only widen the gap, diverting us from the real solution. It makes no sense to put aside social justice concerns in order to improve minority health. A more just society would be a healthier one.

Bioethics: The Need for a Dialogue with African Americans

Annette Dula

Dula argues for the importance of expanding bioethics to include the perspectives of nonwhite ethnic and cultural groups. While she focuses on African Americans, her argument is also designed to apply to Hispanics, Native Americans, Asians, and other groups with neglected or marginalized health care needs.

The African American perspective, according to Dula, has been shaped by systematic medical neglect (a problem mostly ignored by bioethics) and by an emphasis on action and social justice in the work of black philosophers. Reviewing the history of the birth control movement and the Tuskegee experiment, Dula identifies a need for specifically African American perspectives on health care. The entrance of blacks into professional psychology and the "white women's movement" illustrate how such perspectives can change social perceptions of a group, weaken stereotypes, and promote justice. Dula concludes by calling for a broader bioethics community that explores and articulates "the perspectives of African Americans and other poor and underserved peoples."

Reprinted from "*It Just Ain't Fair*": *The Ethics of Health Care for African Americans*, edited by Annette Dula and Sara Goering. Westport, CT: Praeger, 1994, 12–20. Copyright © 1994 by Annette Dula and Sara Goering. Reprinted by permission. (Notes omitted.)

Introduction

...I intend to show that the articulation and development of professional bioethics perspectives by minority academics are necessary to expand the narrow margins of debate. Without representation by every sector of society, the powerful and powerless alike, the discipline of bioethics is missing the opportunity to be enriched by the inclusion of a broader range of perspectives. Although I use African-American perspectives as an example, these points apply to other racial and ethnic groups— Hispanics, Native Americans, and Asians—who have suffered similar health care experiences.

In the first section of this chapter, I suggest that an African-American perspective on bioethics has two bases: (1) our health and medical experiences and (2) our tradition of black activist philosophy. In the second section, through examples, I show that an unequal power relationship has led to unethical medical behavior toward blacks, especially regarding reproductive issues. In the third section, I argue that developing a professional perspective not only gives voice to the concerns of those not in the power circle but also enriches the entire field of bioethics.

Medical and Health Experiences

The health of people and the quality of health care they receive reflect their status in society. It should come as little surprise, then, that the health experiences of African Americans differ vastly from those of white people. These differences are well documented. Compared to whites, more than twice as many black babies are born with low birthweight and over twice as many die before their first birthday. Fifty percent more blacks than whites are likely to regard themselves as being in fair or poor health. Blacks are included in fewer trials of new drugs—an inequity of particular importance for AIDS patients, who are disproportionately black and Hispanic. The mortality rate for heart disease in black males is twice that for white males; research has shown that blacks tend to receive less aggressive treatment for this condition. More blacks die from cancer, which, unlike the situation in whites, is likely to be systemic by the time it is detected. African Americans live five fewer years than do whites. Indeed, if blacks had the same death rate as whites, 59,000 black deaths a year would not occur. Colin McCord and Harold P. Freeman, who reported that black

men in Harlem are less likely to reach the age of 65 than are men in Bangladesh, conclude that the mortality rates of inner cities with largely black populations "justify special consideration analogous to that given to natural-disaster areas."

These health disparities are the result of at least three forces: institutional racism, economic inequality, and attitudinal barriers to access. Institutional racism has roots in the historically unequal power relations between blacks and the medical profession, and between blacks and the larger society. It has worked effectively to keep blacks out of the profession, even though a large percentage of those who manage to enter medicine return to practice in minority communities—where the need for medical professionals is greatest. Today, institutional racism in health care is manifested in the way African Americans and poor people are treated. They experience long waits, are unable to shop for services, and often receive poor quality and discontinuous health care. Moreover, many government programs do not target African Americans as a group. As a result, benefits to racially defined populations are diffused. There is hope: Healthy People 2000 complemented by the Clinton health care proposal can go a long way to reducing these problems.

Black philosopher W. E. B. Du Bois summed up the economic plight of African Americans: "To be poor is hard, but to be a poor race in a land of dollars is the very bottom of hardships." Poor people are more likely to have poor health, and a disproportionate number of poor people are black. African Americans tend to have lower paying jobs and fewer income-producing sources such as investments. Indeed, whites on average accumulate eleven times more wealth than do blacks. Less money also leads to substandard housing—housing that may contain unacceptable levels of lead paint, asbestos insulation, or other environmental hazards. Thus, both inadequate employment and subpar housing available to poor African Americans present health problems that wealthier people are able to avoid. In addition, going to the doctor may entail finding and paying for a babysitter and transportation, and taking time off from work at the risk of being fired, all of which the poor cannot afford.

Attitudinal barriers—perceived racism, different cultural perspectives on health and sickness, and beliefs about the health care system—are a third force that brings unequal health care. Seeking medical help may not have the same priority for poor people as it has for middle-class people. One study in the *Journal of the American Medical Association* revealed that, compared to whites, blacks are less likely to be satisfied with how their physicians treat them, more dissatisfied with their hospital care, and more likely to believe that their hospital stay was too short. In addition, many blacks, like people of other racial and ethnic groups, use home remedies and adhere to traditional theories of illness and healing that lie outside of the mainstream medical model. Institutional racism, economic inequality, and attitudinal barriers, then, contribute to inadequate access to health care for poor and minority peoples. These factors must be seen as bioethical concerns. Bioethics cannot be exclusively medical or even ethical. Rather, it must also deal with beliefs, values, cultural traditions, and the economic, political, and social order. A number of medical sociologists have severely criticized bioethicists for ignoring cultural and societal particularities that limit access to health care.

This inattention to cultural and societal aspects of health care may be attributed in part to the mainstream Western philosophy on which the field of bioethics is built. For example, renowned academic bioethicists such as Robert Veatch, Tom Beauchamp, and Alasdair MacIntyre rely on the philosophical works of Rawls, Kant, and Aristotle. In addition, until recently the mainstream Western philosophic method has been presented primarily as a thinking enterprise, rarely advocating change or societal transformation. Thus, for the most part, Western philosophers have either gingerly approached or neglected altogether to comment on such social injustices as slavery, poverty, racism, sexism, and classism. As pointed out in *Black Issues in Higher Education*, until recently mainstream philosophy was seen as above questions of history and culture.

Black Activist Philosophy

The second bias for an African-American perspective on bioethics is black activist philosophy. Black philosophy differs from mainstream philosophy in its emphasis on action and social justice. African-American philosophers view the world through a cultural and societal context of being an unequal partner. Many black philosophers believe that academic philosophy devoid of societal context is a luxury that black scholars can ill afford. Moreover, African-American philosophers have

purposely elected to use philosophy as a tool not only for naming, defining, and analyzing social situations but also for recommending, advocating, and sometimes harassing for political and social empowerment—a stance contrary to mainstream philosophic methods. Even though all bioethicists would do well to examine the thinking of such philosophers as Alain Locke, Lucius Outlaw, Anita Allen, Leonard Harris, W. E. B. Du Bois, Bernard Boxill, Angela Davis, Cornel West, William Banner, and Jorge Garcia, references to the work of these African Americans are rarely seen in the bioethics literature.

Although the professionalization of bioethics has frequently bypassed African-American voices, there are a few notable exceptions. Mark Siegler, director of the Center for Clinical Medical Ethics at the University of Chicago, included three African-American fellows in the 1990–91 medical ethics training program; Edmund Pellegrino of the Kennedy Institute for Advanced Ethics co-sponsored three national conferences on African-American perspectives on bioethics; and Howard Brody at Michigan State University is attempting to diversify his medical ethics program. In addition, a number of current publications offer important information for bioethicists. For example, the National Research Council's *A Common Destiny: Blacks and American Society* provides a comprehensive analysis of the status of black Americans, including discussions on health, education, employment, and economic factors, as does the National Urban League's annual *The State of Black America;* Marlene Gerber Fried's *From Abortion to Reproductive Freedom* presents many ideas of women of color concerning abortion; and several journals (e.g., *Ethnicity and Disease,* published by the Loyola University School of Medicine, and *The Journal of Health Care for the Poor and Underserved*) call particular attention to the health experiences of poor and underserved people. Finally, literature and narrative as forms of presenting African-American perspectives on bioethics are now being explored.

Clearly, bioethics and African-American philosophy overlap. Both are concerned with distributive justice and fairness, with autonomy and paternalism in unequal relationships, and with both individual and societal ills. African-American philosophy, therefore, may have much to offer bioethics in general and African-American bioethics in particular.

Mainstream Issues Relevant to African Americans

A shocking history of medical abuse against unprotected people is also grounds for African-American perspectives in bioethics. In particular, reproductive rights issues—questions of family planning, sterilization, and genetic screening—are of special interest to black women.

A critical examination of the U.S. birth control movement reveals fundamental differences in perspectives, experiences, and interests between the white women who founded the movement and African-American women who were affected by it. Within each of three phases, the goals of the movement implicitly or explicitly served to exploit and subordinate African-American as well as poor white women.

The middle of the nineteenth century marked the beginning of the first phase of the birth control movement, characterized by the rallying cry "Voluntary Motherhood!" Advocates of voluntary motherhood asserted that women ought to say "no" to their husbands' sexual demands as a means of limiting the number of their children. The irony, of course, was that, while early white feminists were refusing their husbands' sexual demands, most black women did not have the same right to say "no" to these and other white women's husbands. Indeed, African-American women were exploited as breeding wenches in order to produce stocks of enslaved people for plantation owners. August Meier and Elliott Rudwick comment on slave-rearing as a major source of profit for nearly all slaveholding farmers and planters: "Though most Southern whites were scarcely likely to admit it, the rearing of slaves for profit was a common practice. [A] slave woman's proved or anticipated fecundity was an important factor in determining her market value; fertile females were often referred to as 'good breeders.' "

The second phase of the birth control movement gave rise to the actual phrase "birth control," coined by Margaret Sanger in 1915. Initially, this stage of the movement led to the recognition that reproductive rights and political rights were intertwined; birth control would give white women the freedom to pursue new opportunities made possible by the vote. This freedom allowed white women to go to work while black women cared for their children and did their housework.

This second stage coincided with the eugenics movement, which advocated improvement of the human race through selective breeding. When the white birth rate began to decline, eugenists chastised middle-class white women for contributing to the suicide of the white race: "Continued limitation of offspring in the white race simply invites the black, brown, and yellow races to finish work already begun by birth control, and reduce the whites to a subject race preserved merely for the sake of its skill."

Eugenists proposed a twofold approach for curbing "race suicide": imposing moral obligations on middle-class white women to have large families and on poor immigrant women and black women to restrict the size of theirs. For the second group, geneticists advocated birth control. The women's movement adopted the ideals of the eugenists regarding poor, immigrant, and minority women, and it even surpassed the rhetoric of the eugenists. Margaret Sanger described the relationship between the two groups: "The eugenists wanted to shift the birth-control emphasis from less children for the poor to more children for the rich. We went back of that [*sic*] and sought first to stop the multiplication of the unfit." Thus, while black women have historically practiced birth control, they learned to distrust the birth control movement as espoused by white feminists—a distrust that continues to the present day.

The third stage of the birth control movement began in 1942 with the establishment of the Planned Parenthood Federation of America. Although Planned Parenthood made valuable contributions to the independence, self-esteem, and aspirations of many women, it accepted existing power relations, continuing the eugenic tradition by defining undesirable "stock" by class or income level. Many blacks were suspicious of Planned Parenthood; men, particularly, viewed its policies as designed to weaken the black community politically or to wipe it out genetically. From the beginning of this century, both public and private institutions attempted to control the breeding of those deemed "undesirable." The first sterilization law was passed in Indiana in 1907, setting the stage for not only eugenic, but also punitive sterilization of criminals, the feebleminded, rapists, robbers, chicken thieves, drunkards, and drug addicts. By 1931 thirty states had passed sterilization laws, allowing more than 12,145 sterilizations. By the end of 1958, the sterilization total had risen to 60,926. In the 1950s several states attempted to extend sterilization laws to include compulsory sterilization of mothers of "illegitimate" children. As of 1991, sterilization laws were still in force in twenty-two states. They are seldom enforced, and where they have been, their eugenic significance has been negligible.

Numerous federal and state measures perpetuated a focus on poor women and women of color. Throughout the United States in the 1960s, the federal government began subsidizing family planning clinics designed to reduce the number of people on welfare by checking the transmission of poverty from generation to generation. The number of family planning clinics in a given geographical area was proportional to the number of black and Hispanic residents. In Puerto Rico, a massive federal birth control campaign introduced in 1937 was so successful that by the 1950s, the demand for sterilization exceeded facilities, and by 1965, one-third of the women in Puerto Rico had been sterilized.

In 1972 Los Angeles County Hospital, a hospital catering to large numbers of women of color, reported a sevenfold rise in hysterectomies. Between 1973 and 1976, almost 3,500 Native American women were sterilized at one Indian Health Service hospital in Oklahoma. In 1973 two black sisters from Montgomery, Alabama, 12-year-old Mary Alice Relf and 14-year-old Minnie Lee Relf, were reported to have been surgically sterilized without their parents' consent. An investigation revealed that in the same town, eleven other young girls of about the same age as the Relf sisters had also been sterilized; ten of them were black. During the early 1970s in Aiken, South Carolina, of thirty-four Medicaid-funded deliveries, eighteen included sterilizations, and all eighteen involved young black women. In 1972 Carl Schultz, director of the Department of Health, Education, and Welfare's Population Affairs Office, acknowledged that the government had funded between 100,000 and 200,000 sterilizations. These policies aroused black suspicions that family planning efforts were inspired by racist and eugenist motives.

The first phase of the birth control movement, then, completely ignored black women's sexual subjugation to white masters. In the second phase, the movement adopted the racist policies of the eugenics movement. The third stage saw a number of government-supported coercive measures to contain the population of poor people and people of color. While blacks perceive birth control per se as beneficial, blacks have historically objected to birth control as a

method of dealing with poverty. Rather, most blacks believe that poverty can be remedied only by creating meaningful jobs, raising the minimum wage so that a worker can support a family, providing health care to working and nonworking people through their jobs or through universal coverage, instituting a high-quality day care system for low- or no-income people, and improving educational opportunities.

Informed Consent

Informed consent is one of the key ethical issues in bioethics. In an unequal patient–provider relationship, informed consent may not be possible. The weaker partner may consent because he or she is powerless, poor, or does not understand the implications of consent. And when members of subordinate groups are not awarded full respect as persons, those in positions of power then consider it unnecessary to obtain consent. The infamous Tuskegee experiment is a classic example. Starting in 1932, over 400 poor and uneducated syphilitic black men in Alabama were unwitting subjects in a Public Health Service experiment, condoned by the surgeon general, to study the course of untreated syphilis. Physicians told the men that they were going to receive special treatment, concealing the fact that the medical procedures were diagnostic rather than therapeutic. Although the effects of untreated syphilis were already known by 1936, the experiment continued for forty years. In 1969 a committee appointed by the Public Health Service to review the Tuskegee study decided to continue it. The Tuskegee experiment did not come to widespread public attention until 1972, when the *Washington Star* documented this breach of medical ethics. As a result, the experiment was halted. Unfortunately, however, the legacy of the experiment lingers on, as several chapters in this volume illustrate.

It may be tempting to assume that such medical abuses are part of the distant past. However, there is evidence that violations of informed consent persist. Of 52,000 Maryland women screened annually for sickle cell anemia between 1978 and 1980, 25 percent were screened without their consent, thus denying these women the benefit of prescreening education or follow-up counseling, or the opportunity to decline screening. A national survey conducted in 1986 found that 81 percent of women subjected to court-ordered obstetrical interventions

(Caesarean section, hospital detention, or intra-uterine transfusion) were black, Hispanic, or Asian; nearly half were unmarried; one-fourth did not speak English; and none were private patients. When in 1981, a Texas legislator asked his constituency whether they favored sterilization of women on welfare, a majority of the respondents said that welfare benefits should be tied to sterilizations.

How a Professional Perspective Makes a Difference

Thus far, I have shown some grounds for African-American perspectives on bioethics, based on black activist philosophy and the unequal health status of African Americans. I have also argued that a history of medical abuse and neglect toward people in an unequal power relationship commands our attention to African-American perspectives on bioethics issues. In this final section, I will argue that a professional perspective can voice the concerns of those not in the power circle. Two examples—black psychology and the white women's movement—illustrate that professional perspectives can make a difference in changing society's perceptions and, ultimately, policies regarding a particular population.

Black Psychology

Until recently, mainstream psychology judged blacks as genetically and mentally inferior, incapable of abstract reasoning, culturally deprived, passive, ugly, lazy, childishly happy, dishonest, and emotionally immature or disturbed. Mainstream psychology owned these definitions and viewed African Americans through a deficit–deficiency model—a model it had constructed to explain African-American behavior. When blacks entered the profession of psychology, they challenged that deficit model by presenting an African-American perspective that addressed the dominant group's assessments and changed, to a certain extent, the way society views blacks. Real consequences of black psychologists' efforts to encourage self-definition, consciousness, and self-worth have been felt across many areas: professional training, intelligence and ability testing, criminal justice, and family counseling. Black psychologists have presented their findings before professional conferences, legislative hearings, and policy-making task forces. For example,

black psychologists are responsible for the ban in California on using standardized intelligence tests as a criterion for placing black and other minority students in classes for the mentally retarded. The Association of Black Psychologists publishes the *Journal of Black Psychology,* and black psychologists contribute to a variety of other professional journals. As a result of these and other efforts, most respected psychologists no longer advocate the deficit–deficiency model.

The Women's Movement

The women's movement is another example of a subordinated group defining its own perspectives. The perspectives of white women have historically been defined largely by white men; white women's voices, like black voices, have traditionally been ignored or trivialized. A mere twenty years ago, the question, "Should there be a woman's perspective on health?" was emotionally debated. Although the question is still asked, a respected discipline of women's studies has emerged, with several journals devoted to women's health. Women in increasing numbers have been drawn to the field of applied ethics, specifically to bioethics, and they debate issues such as maternal and child health, rights of women versus rights of the fetus, unnecessary hysterectomies and Caesareans, the doctor–patient relationship, and the absence of women in clinical trials of new drugs. Unfortunately, however, the mainstream women's movement is largely the domain of white women. This, of course, does not mean that black women have not been activists for women's rights; on the contrary, African-American women historically have been deeply involved in fighting both racism and sexism, believing that the two are inseparable. Many black women distrust the movement, criticizing it as racist and self-serving, concerned only with white middle-class women's issues. Black feminists working within the abortion rights movement and with the National Black Women's Health Project, an Atlanta-based self-help and health advocacy organization, are raising their voices to identify issues relevant to African-American women and men in general, and reproductive and health issues in particular. Like black psychologists, these black feminists are articulating a perspective that is effectively promoting pluralism.

Conclusion

The disturbing health inequities between blacks and whites—differences in infant mortality, average life span, chronic illnesses, and aggressiveness of treatment—suggest that minority access to health care should be recognized and accepted as a *bona fide* concern of bioethics. Opening the debate can only enrich this new field, thereby avoiding the moral difficulties of exclusion. Surely the serious and underaddressed health concerns of a large and increasing segment of our society are an ethical issue that is at least as important as such esoteric, high-visibility issues as the morality of gestational surrogacy. The front page of the August 5, 1991, *New York Times* headlined an article, "When Grandmother Is Mother, Until Birth." Although interesting and worthy of ethical comment, such sensational headlines undermine the moral seriousness of a situation in which over 37 million poor people do not have access to health care.

There is a basis for developing African-American perspectives on bioethics, and I have presented examples of medical abuse and neglect that suggest particular issues for consideration. Valuable as our advocacy has been, our perspectives have not gained full prominence in bioethics debates. Thus, it is necessary to form a community of scholars to conduct research on the contributions as well as the limitations of perspectives of African-American and other poor and underserved peoples in this important field.

Section 3:   Bioethics and Sexual Minorities

Legal and Ethical Concerns about Sexual Orientation Change Efforts

Tia Powell and Edward Stein

Powell and Stein note the long and often brutal history of medical interventions aimed at changing the sexual orientation of lesbian, gay, and bisexual individuals. Although they condemn self-styled "therapists" who seek to change LGB orientations as both harmful and unprofessional, they question the premises behind laws outlawing their efforts. Insofar as such laws depend on the premise that LGB orientations must be innate, immutable, or unrelated to affirmative choice in order to be accepted as legitimate and healthy, they do a disservice to LGB experiences and rights.

Powell and Stein point to evidence that sexual orientation is likely a product of both genetics and environment, and that for many LGB people, especially women, sexual orientation may shift over time. Although there is considerable evidence that sexual orientation is not a matter of choice, they note that acting on and publicly affirming same-sex desires *are* choices—ones that are essential to any nontrivial concept of LGB rights. A more forthright and inclusive stance would insist that there is no medical or moral reason to object to same-sex desires, "whether inborn, changeable, or chosen," and that any efforts to "treat" such desires is thus illegitimate and unethical. Given

From Tia Powell and Edward Stein, "Legal and Ethical Concerns about Sexual Orientation Change Efforts," LGBT Bioethics: Visibility, Disparities, and Dialogue, special report, *Hastings Center Report* 44, no. 5 (2014): S32–S39. Copyright © 2014 Hastings Center Report. All rights reserved. Reproduced by permission. (Most notes omitted.)

widespread agreement with this view among professional societies, insurers, and courts, they conclude that fringe practitioners who claim they can and should change sexual orientation will have fewer and fewer opportunities to do harm.

The United States has recently made significant and positive civil rights gains for lesbian, gay, and bisexual people,[1] including expanded recognition of marriages between people of the same sex. Among the central tropes that have emerged in the struggle for the rights of LGB people are that they are "born that way," that sexual orientations cannot change, and that one's sexual orientation is not affected by choice. Writer Andrew Sullivan put it this way:

> [H]omosexuality is an essentially involuntary condition that can neither be denied nor permanently repressed. . . . [S]o long as homosexual adults as citizens insist on the involuntary nature of their condition, it becomes politically impossible to deny or ignore the fact of homosexuality. . . . [The strategy for obtaining LGB rights is to] seek full public equality for those who, through no fault of their own, happen to be homosexual.

This idea of linking LGB rights to empirical claims about sexual orientations has become so central that casting doubt on these claims is, in many circles, tantamount to opposing LGB rights. Nonetheless, claims about innateness, immutability, and lack of choice about sexual orientation should not be the primary basis for LGB rights.

In this essay, we take a critical look at laws that ban certain attempts to change sexual orientations. In 2012, California passed a law that prohibits "a mental health provider" from "engag[ing] in sexual orientation change efforts with a patient under 18." Although the two federal district courts that considered constitutional challenges to this law reached opposite results, the federal appellate court that heard the consolidated appeal upheld the constitutionality of the California law. In 2013, New Jersey passed a law virtually identical to California's, which was also upheld in federal court. As of this writing, legislatures in the District of Columbia, Florida, Hawaii, Illinois, Massachusetts, Minnesota, New York, Ohio, Pennsylvania, and Washington are considering very similar laws, while Maryland, Virginia, and Wisconsin considered and withdrew or rejected such laws. By contrast, the Texas Republican Party, at its state convention this year, included in its party platform support for "the

legitimacy and efficacy of counseling, which offers reparative therapy and treatment for those patients seeking healing and wholeness from their homosexual lifestyle" and, for this reason, declared that "no laws or executive orders shall be imposed to limit or restrict access to this type of therapy."

We strongly reject attempts to change sexual orientations. Such practices reflect bias against sexual minorities and are harmful to recipients. Nonetheless, we question what seem to be presumptions undergirding laws banning sexual orientation change efforts, namely that sexual orientation is always innate and immutable and does not reflect choices. We suggest that such presumptions about sexual orientations are not only weak starting points for laws like California's and New Jersey's but also, more generally, that immutability, innateness, and lack of choice are poor arguments for the rights of LGB people. In sum, such claims about the nature and origins of sexual orientation are neither good science nor good politics and are not an appropriate foundation for prohibiting sexual orientation change efforts or for LGB rights generally. Instead, support for LGB rights should be grounded in an intellectually rigorous and appropriately humble approach to science and the limits of scientific knowledge. Arguments for LGB rights should be grounded within the context of justice, fairness, equality, and human rights.

Sexual Orientation Change Efforts

For centuries, including for much of the twentieth century, LGB people were subject to various forms of medical intervention, including surgeries such as castration, removal of the clitoris and ovaries, and lobotomy; electroconvulsive treatment (commonly referred to as electroshock therapy); hormone therapy; and wrenching psychoanalysis. Much changed, however, starting in 1973, the year that homosexuality was eliminated from the American Psychiatric Association's *Diagnostic and Statistical Manual of Mental Disorders* (*DSM*), the authoritative catalogue of mental illnesses used in the United States and throughout much of the world. Since 1973, all major professional associations in mental health care have produced position statements documenting that same-sex sexual orientation is not a mental or physical illness and explicitly opposing efforts to change orientation. These statements are both influenced by and shape social attitudes and public opinion toward LGB people and help remove stigma toward people with same-sex attractions. These position statements also have additional practical effects: for example, health insurance will not cover treatments for something that is not an illness nor support techniques rejected by mainstream therapeutic groups.

As more mental health organizations rejected the view of homosexuality as a disorder, researchers and practitioners who still wished to engage in invasive interventions to "treat" LGB people faced significant hurdles. Mainstream institutions that conduct and oversee human subjects research would not approve research aimed at eradicating same-sex orientation, even for voluntary adult research participants, since there was no accepted benefit to offset the risks. Thus, there could be no approved research to study the efficacy of invasive interventions. Performing these treatments in the clinical context also became more difficult, since invasive interventions typically require a medical or mental health degree, a license, and malpractice insurance. Since these radical attempts to change orientation fall outside of best practice standards delineated by professional societies, licensed practitioners risk losing the ability to work if they engage in practices so far from the mainstream.

As a result, interventions that at least appear less damaging—for example, talk therapy, cognitive-behavioral therapy, and prayer—have taken center stage. However, a substantial body of research and numerous patient accounts indicate that such methods can cause significant psychological damage. Attempted and completed suicide, substance abuse, depression, anxiety, and a range of other symptoms have been attributed to therapies that attempt to change sexual orientations. Though most current attempts to change sexual orientations focus on nonphysical modalities like those mentioned above, a few practitioners also still try to change orientation through aversive therapies such as administration of electric shocks and nausea-inducing medications. We will refer to all such attempts as "sexual orientation change efforts," or "SOCE," though these interventions may be referred to by proponents by other names, including "reparative therapy" or "conversion therapy."

Disturbed by reports of harms caused by attempts to change sexual orientations and inspired by the desire to protect LGB people and advance LGB rights, various state legislatures have introduced laws addressing such practices. In 2012, California became the first state to pass such a law. The California law sets out various findings of fact, including (1) "[b]eing lesbian, gay, or bisexual is not a disease, disorder, illness, deficiency, or shortcoming"; (2) "[m]inors who experience family rejection based on their sexual orientation face especially serious health risks; and (3) "California has a compelling interest in protecting the physical and psychological well-being of minors . . . and . . . protecting [them] against exposure to serious harms caused by sexual orientation change efforts." The law also quotes reports from eleven professional organizations in support of these findings. The law prohibits "a mental health provider [from] engag[ing] in sexual orientation change efforts with a patient under 18 years of age" and says that engaging in such efforts is "unprofessional conduct and shall subject a mental health provider to discipline by the [relevant] licensing entity."

The law defines the prohibited practices as follows:

"Sexual orientation change efforts" means any practices by mental health providers that seek to change an individual's sexual orientation. This includes efforts to change behaviors or gender expressions, or to eliminate or reduce sexual or romantic attractions or feelings toward individuals of the same sex.

"Sexual orientation change efforts" does not include psychotherapies that: (A) provide acceptance, support, and understanding of clients or the facilitation of clients' coping, social support, and identity exploration and development, including sexual orientation-neutral interventions to prevent or address unlawful conduct or unsafe sexual practices; and (B) do not seek to change sexual orientation.

The New Jersey law is virtually identical to the California law except that it explicitly excludes "counseling for a person seeking to transition from one gender to another" from the definition of sexual orientation change efforts. The laws proposed by other states are, for the most part, substantively similar to the California and New Jersey laws, although some omit the lengthy findings of fact.

The Texas Republican party plank supporting sexual orientation change efforts was a reaction to these laws and proposed laws.

The rationale for these laws is that the prohibited practices (a) attempt to cure that which is not a disease and (b) are ineffective in attaining this stated goal and yet (c) cause harm to the very people these practices are allegedly supposed to help. These points are correct, but they do not alone justify the laws. Not every harmful and ineffective procedure a doctor or mental health professional might perform is subject to direct legal stricture. (For example, so-called rebirthing therapy—whereby a practitioner attempts to reenact the birthing process through physical techniques involving restraints designed to create emergence from an artificial "womb"—a practice that is risky and completely lacking in any scientific or therapeutic basis, has been banned by only two U.S. jurisdictions.) More importantly, support for the laws stems in part from the belief that sexual orientation is innate, immutable, and not chosen and, also, that these empirical claims have desirable legal and ethical implications.

Consider two quotations from supporters of these laws. In an interview about the New Jersey law before Governor Chris Christie signed it, Troy Stevenson, the head of a state LGBT organization that lobbied for the law said,

> [Therapy to change sexual orientations] is an abuse of the term therapy and it is abuse in no uncertain terms. Any attempt to take an immutable and fundamental aspect of a person's character and change it to suit someone else's will is selfish and often soul destroying for the victim. The [New Jersey] legislation . . . will save lives; it will protect our youth; and it is vital that the Governor sign [it] as soon as possible."

A lobbyist for the National Center for Lesbian Rights, an LGBT rights organization that supported the California law, summarized part of the argument made to Governor Jerry Brown for signing it:

> [T]he California Legislature, the California Supreme Court, the Federal District Court and the Ninth Circuit in upholding the Federal District Court decision in Perry[] have all found sexual orientation to be an immutable characteristic. If it is immutable, then the state shouldn't be licensing individuals who are saying

> they can change this immutable characteristic and who take money from the public to engage in this discredited practice.

Plainly, empirical claims about the immutability of sexual orientations played a role in the support of laws prohibiting sexual orientation change efforts.

These laws and proposed laws have various limitations. First, they fail to prohibit persons who are not licensed mental health care professionals from engaging in sexual orientation change efforts, thus excluding from regulation clergy and other unlicensed individuals who engage in these practices, and they fail to prohibit attempts to change the sexual orientations of people over the age of eighteen. Second, one might plausibly argue that the California law undermines the autonomy of minors by not allowing them to make certain decisions about their own mental health treatment, as they are generally allowed to do. Third, the laws may be unnecessary because state licensing bodies can already sanction (including by revoking licenses) those who engage in inappropriate treatment practices. Similarly, malpractice actions punish practitioners who use unsafe or ineffective treatment modalities rejected by their professional peers, and a first-of-its-kind consumer fraud lawsuit brought in New Jersey has a similar goal.

Innateness, Immutability, and Choice

We find these forms of existing regulation, coupled with educational efforts within medicine and the larger society, of greater likely efficacy and efficiency than state-by-state bans. We want to focus, however, on the linkage between these laws and claims that sexual orientation is innate, immutable, and unassociated with choice. These linkages oversimplify important issues and are dangerous to LGB rights.

Innateness. Are LGB people "born that way"— that is, are sexual orientations the result of genetic or other factors present at birth, or are they shaped by factors emerging after birth, particularly from the environment? This question is based on false premises. First, it is impossible to discern whether a trait is present at birth when it consists in thoughts and feelings that an infant cannot demonstrate. Second, insofar as the idea that LGB people are "born that way" makes a claim about a genetic basis for sexual orientation, it falls short because human traits are rarely the result of only genes or the environment. Rather, complex human traits generally result from interactions between genes and the environment. Genetic factors affect seemingly environmental traits (for example, what a person's major will be in college), and environmental factors contribute to the expression of genetic traits (for example, skin color). Traits can be placed on a continuum associated with the extent to which they are constrained by genetic factors—genetic factors more tightly constrain one's blood type than one's college major. Properly understood, whether sexual orientation is innate is a question about where sexual orientation fits on the continuum between blood type and college major. While many scientists conducting research on sexual orientation and the majority of people in the United States think that sexual orientation is innate, we think this is far from proven. For instance, among gay men who have an identical twin, between fifty and eighty percent of the twin brothers are not gay. Plainly, both biological and environmental factors shape the development of sexual orientations—in heterosexual as well as in gay people. Could genes play a role in forming gay or heterosexual sexual orientation? Yes. Is there a "gay gene" that alone determines orientation? No, and it is a misrepresentation of existing research to make such a claim.

Could sexual orientation be in some way predetermined but not visible at birth, by a combination of genetic and uterine environmental factors? Certainly other traits arise in this way, such that they will unfold with development but are not seen in newborns. Eye color is one example, for a child may be born with brown eyes that shift to blue over the first few months. Though intriguing as a hypothesis, current research data fall far short of proving such a claim, particularly if it is applied to all persons. As we will discuss later, there is evidence that sexual orientation is somewhat fluid for some members of the population, undermining the notion that orientation is always firmly predetermined at birth and simply awaiting the right developmental moment for expression.

Immutability. Some advocates for LGB rights focus on immutability in light of the Equal Protection Clause of the Fourteenth Amendment of the U.S. Constitution. Supreme Court jurisprudence has interpreted the Fourteenth Amendment's requirement of "equal protection" to require heightened scrutiny of laws that make use of suspect classifications like

race, ethnicity, national origin, and illegitimacy. In seeking to define those classifications that warrant heightened scrutiny, the Supreme Court has sometimes focused on "obvious, immutable, or distinguishing characteristics." There is, however, considerable legal debate about the importance of immutability in supporting rights for various minority groups, and the Supreme Court has not mentioned immutability in its recent equal protection or its recent LGB rights cases. We find several objections to linking LGB rights to immutability.

First, true immutability is a problematic legal criterion, for there are very few human traits that are legally salient and yet cannot be changed. For example, established medical procedures make sex change possible, but surely the mutability of gender does not change the legal standard that should be applied to laws that might discriminate on the basis of gender.

Second, some equate being "born that way" with immutability, but there is no necessary connection between a characteristic's being innate and its being immutable. Hair color is clearly a genetic trait yet one that changes radically across the lifespan (even without chemical intervention); a person can have blond hair in early childhood, dark hair in adulthood, and gray hair in old age. Further, immutability does not require innateness. Having an antibody in one's bloodstream might be something that can't be changed once the antibody has developed, but it is not innate. By analogy, sexual orientation does not need to be innate in order to be immutable, and it can be innate without being immutable. Thus, while current research suggests that genetic and other biological factors likely play a role in the development of sexual orientations, this does not tell us that orientations are unchangeable.

Immutability and Alternative Models for Sexual Orientation Development. A growing body of research suggests that the development of sexual orientation can follow different trajectories for different people. In the standard account of same-sex sexual orientation development, a person has childhood experiences of same-sex attractions, matched by a growing realization of difference from others, followed by an emerging capacity to integrate a positive gay identity. Research supporting this model is generally based upon querying adults about childhood recollections. Such a research model is inherently problematic in that it relies on the adult's current understanding of past events rather than on the real-time process of development, which may be quite different. An additional problem is that current research suggests that this model is applicable to more men than women.

Indeed, emerging evidence collected over some decades indicates significant differences between men and women in the development of sexual orientation. In an important book, Lisa Diamond summarizes the work of other scholars and presents new findings through her longitudinal studies of sexual minority women. She finds that women's orientation corresponds more to a range of sexual attractions rather than a discrete category, with most respondents in her sample showing at least some degree of a mixture of same-sex and different-sex attraction. The degree of fluidity in attractions to same-sex or different-sex partners differs between individuals and within one individual over time. Diamond further finds that one's identity as gay or straight is not a perfect predictor of the ability to form a sexual attraction to a person in the unexpected category. Women who identify as lesbian can be attracted to men; women who identify exclusively as heterosexual may develop, even in later life, a sexual attraction within the context of an intimate same-sex relationship.

One of the strong ethical insights that emerges from the work of Diamond is that women with variable degrees of same-sex and different-sex attractions have been led to believe that they are rare, anomalous, psychologically immature, and unstable based on their fluctuating sexual attractions. Diamond argues that, while women with fluctuating degrees of same- and other-sex attractions do not fit the "standard account" of the development of sexual orientation, their trajectory is normal, not uncommon, and consistent with psychological and sexual maturity. Indeed, Diamond finds that a mixture of sexual attraction to same-and other-sex partners is the norm in her longitudinal study of sexual minority women. Insisting on immutability in same-sex orientation both inside and outside the LGB community undermines the sense of self-acceptance and normalcy for women whose experience does not follow this standard account. In contrast, we support a strategy for enhancing LGB rights that will not exclude or marginalize those whose sexual orientation is fluid. This point is crucial to our reservations about the wisdom and ethical implications of linking immutability to support for LGB rights.

By analogy, it is helpful to compare Diamond's work, and the controversy surrounding it, to the work of Carol Gilligan in the 1970s on sex differences in the development of moral choice. Gilligan found that in the standard model of moral development, a model derived from research involving men and boys, women tended to fall lower on the developmental scale. Gilligan proposed an alternative model for moral development based on research involving women, placing greater emphasis on relationships and responsibilities and less on abstract principles. Gilligan's work played a role in the process of addressing sex discrimination in research by pointing out that it was scientifically unsound to exclude women from research on the grounds that they would "muddy" the data and then make the claim that the results of such research could simply be applied to women, who would then be found wanting in their ability to attain standards based exclusively on men.

Diamond notes a similar process in her work on sexual orientations and women. Far from seeing women with fluid sexual orientations as "muddying" the data, Diamond insists that the experiences of these women *are* the data—that this diversity is key to understanding the complexity of sexual orientations in women and in people generally. Indeed, views on fluidity in orientation have the potential to shift the understanding of changes in male sexual orientation, particularly for men who have had heterosexual relationships in one period of their lives and then move toward same-sex relationships. Current practice often encourages such men to view early other-sex relationships as false steps on the road to maturity. While this may be true for some, for others, sexual orientation may have shifted in a manner similar to that described by Diamond in her study of women.

Choice. Whether sexual orientation is the result of choice is a distinct question from whether it is immutable or innate. Although issues involving sexual orientation and choice are complicated, the evidence is strong that people's conscious choices do not play a strong role in the development of sexual orientations. Though Diamond has documented incidents of shifting sexual orientation, her research subjects view this change as outside their deliberate control and not as a matter of choice. As one young woman stated, regarding her gradual diminution of same-sex attractions: "I mean straight culture—yuck, bad! I never really wanted to be heterosexual but I don't have much choice in the matter."

We concur, therefore, with the widespread view that attraction to same or other-sex partners is not a matter of conscious choice. However, even if sexual orientation is not chosen, most of what is legally and ethically relevant about being an LGB person *is* the result of conscious choice. Actually engaging in sexual acts with a person of the same sex, publicly or privately identifying as an LGB person, and marrying a person of the same sex and raising children together are *choices*. In other words, an LGB person could decide to be celibate, closeted, single, and childless. Support for LGB rights is precisely support to make these *choices* and to do so without fear of discrimination or violence. The right simply to have same-sex attractions, without the right to act on these desires or to express the related identities, would be an empty right indeed. By analogy, the right of a free expression of religion is among the most central in U.S. law, and this is a right based on choice. We reject the argument that a right cannot be vigorously protected if it reflects a choice. Thus we retreat from arguments in support of LGB rights that insist on lack of choice. To the contrary, it is the right to make choices that reflect the legal equality of those with a same-sex orientation that is under attack, and it is the right to make such choices that we support.

Accepting Change

We unequivocally reject efforts to eradicate, reduce, or disguise same-sex attraction. We wish, however, to remove the stigma attached to sexual minorities who experience shifts in sexual attraction, and note that this stigma can arise from those who oppose LGB rights as well as from those who support them. An insistence on immutability reiterates an oppressive script, in which the lived experiences of some sexual minorities are denied by others, in part for political purposes. The efforts of a majority to deny the experience of sexual desires and attractions of some members of a minority, as well as the identities associated with them, is not an acceptable path to justice. The careful and respectful study of the development of sexual orientations across the spectrum of human experience, and the acknowledgement that scientific knowledge on this topic is far from complete, are better foundations for supporting LGB rights and respect for LGB persons

than linking rights to claims about etiology based on uncertain scientific foundations.

The key aim of laws banning sexual orientation change efforts is to prevent a practice that shores up prejudice and undermines a stable and positive identity for LGB individuals. We strongly believe that sexual orientation change efforts ought to be abandoned, but—like LGB advocates in Maryland who withdrew the proposed law in the state's legislature—we doubt that laws banning sexual orientation change efforts provide the best route to promoting LGB rights and the social situation for LGB people. Ineffective and harmful treatments disappear over time and in response to a range of existing mechanisms, including changing societal views, research documenting harm and measuring efficacy or lack thereof, guidance documents from professional societies, insurance coverage, and malpractice and other kinds of lawsuits—such as the recent consumer fraud suit brought in New Jersey. We believe all these mechanisms currently operate to decrease the attempts to change sexual orientations.

To the extent that laws against sexual orientation change efforts are supported on the basis of the belief that sexual orientations are immutable, they actually contribute to a distorted view of sexual orientation. We urge supporters of LGB rights not to cleave to unproven scientific tenets regarding immutability as a basis for rights. Rather, thoughtful and respectful analysis of the development of crucial aspects of human identity, including the development of the full variety of sexual orientations, is a better route toward understanding and civil rights. We are unlikely to promote human flourishing for minorities by denying key aspects of their experience. Indeed, such an approach mirrors the worst aspects of prejudice.

We support a legal strategy that moves away from claims that orientation is innate, immutable, and unrelated to choice. These claims are not only based on shaky science, but they also do not promote freedom and equality for all members of the LGB community. For some people, claims about immutability in sexual orientation create yet another oppressive mold they fail to fit. Instead, we favor efforts that support LGB rights that include encouraging people to maintain key aspects of their identity, rather than hiding distinguishing characteristics in deference to the prejudice of the majority. Our laws and jurisprudence do not push women and racial and ethnic minorities to hide or simplify their identities. The same should be true for sexual minorities. Attraction to people of the same sex, whether inborn, changeable, or chosen, does not reflect disease or defect and should not serve as the basis of discrimination. Within the context of health care, we must work to eradicate practices that indicate otherwise, not only regarding efforts to change orientation but also including more subtle aspects of medical culture that undermine the dignity of the LGBT community. Similarly, within the law, efforts must support the rights of LGBT people to work, love, parent, and live in equality.

Note

1. We do not in this paper address the broader group of sexual minorities, including transgender persons. Our arguments focus specifically on sexual orientation rather than gender identity, so we limit our discussion to lesbians, gays, and bisexuals, represented by the "LGB" acronym. We are fully supportive of transgender rights, but this paper does not consider the arguments for such rights, although we do think that there are also problems with making arguments for transgender rights that appeal to innateness, lack of choice, and immutability, especially since some transgender persons seek to adapt and change some aspects of the self (typically, parts of their bodies) to align them with other aspects of self (their gender identities).

Sex Beyond the Karyotype

Alice Dreger

How does one know if one is a man or a woman? The question has profound consequences for our lives, but Dreger argues it is actually difficult to answer. The most common response—chromosomal karyotype determines sex—is complicated by the fact that some people have thoroughly "female" phenotypes (observable traits) yet turn out to have XY karyotypes, while others have thoroughly "male" phenotypes and XX karyotypes, with many variations in between. Indeed, most of us don't actually know our genetic karyotypes but operate as men and women anyway. Other common answers—that genitals or internal organs or brain development determine sex—are complicated by a spectrum of natural variations on the two main themes of anatomical difference, with no clear place to draw the line. "People like their social categories neat," Dreger writes. "Nature is a slob."

Since most public acts (including marriages) occur without any verification of biological sex, Dreger considers the idea that social roles determine sex. But this answer is also too simple, due to the persistence of sex differences across cultures and the resistance of some gender identities (e.g., transgender ones) to intense social training. Ultimately, gender identity is the result of complicated interactions between biology and environment, and there is no single decisive criterion of sex difference. Dreger concludes that we should structure our social systems based on values like justice and fairness, rather than pretending that nature can draw the lines for us.

When I teach a course on concepts of sex, I often begin by asking students to write down answers to two questions:

From "Sex Beyond the Karyotype" by Alice Dreger © Alice Dreger, "Sex Beyond the Karyotype," in *Controversies in Science and Technology 2: From Chromosomes to the Cosmos*, edited by Daniel Lee Kleinman and Jo Handelsman. New Rochelle, NY: Mary Ann Liebert, Inc, 2007.

1. *Do you think you're a man or a woman?*

2. *What makes you think that?*

These two questions were inspired long ago by my own seventh grade "health" class. The teacher was the indomitable Mr. Beijer, a man who never failed simultaneously to embarrass and amuse us. When we came to the first day of the sex education unit, we found ourselves voluntarily divided into girls on one side of the room and boys on the other—as if we thought talking about sex could get you pregnant. Mr. Beijer stood before us for a few minutes, silently observing with raised eyebrows the gender territorialism, all the while making us even more nervous. Then he asked:

"How can you tell if someone is a boy or a girl?"

We giggled and blushed, and no one answered. So he repeated:

"How can you tell if someone is a boy or a girl?"

More giggles.

Finally one nerdy guy stuck his hand up and answered confidently: "By the genes." We all breathed a sigh of relief. Until . . .

"That's right!" answered Mr. Beijer. "You pull those jeans down!"

My own students tend to answer my questions along these same two lines. They either think that they are men or women because of their genes—or more generally their "sex chromosomes" (I'll explain shortly why that term is in scare-quotes)—or because of their genitals. Less often, they point to some aspect of physiology: "I menstruate, so I must be a woman." Or they point to a vague sense of gender identity: "I seem to feel like other men feel, so I must be a man." Occasionally someone makes a reference to sexual orientation. A few years before the "Age of Will and Grace," one student answered, "I know I'm a man because I'm sexually attracted to women." Another student put me in stitches by responding: "Well, I know I'm a man because my boyfriend is gay."

So what's the right answer? How do you know if you're a man or a woman? Or, put a bit differently, what makes someone a man or a woman? Does being male make you a man? Does being a woman make you female? For that matter, what makes a person male or female?

Who Cares?

First, a metaquestion: Why does all this matter? Well, for a lot of reasons. For one, as Mr. Beijer would want me to remind you, knowing whether you're male or female (or somewhere in between) can give you important clues about your body, like whether you can get pregnant, whether you're at risk for cervical or prostate cancer, whether frequently riding a bicycle with a racing seat might make you infertile (watch out, guys!). At a psychological level, whether you think of yourself as a man

or a woman affects your sense of self, including your sense of how you fit in the world. This is partly because your social status as a man or woman matters very much. To use just a few examples, you can't be perceived as a mother if you're not perceived as female, and mothers and fathers tend to hold different kinds of places in cultural folklore and sentimentality. Men are frequently discouraged from becoming elementary school teachers or day-care providers because people more readily associate sexual abuse of young children with men, even though the vast majority of men are not sexual predators and some women are. If you're a woman, you're significantly less likely than a man to become a member of Congress, a top executive, or a physicist, and significantly more likely to be raped. People who think of themselves as straight aren't going to be sexually interested in you if you appear to be of the same gender as them; same goes for people who think of themselves as gay if you appear to be of the "opposite" gender.

Children in our culture (and indeed in every culture) are taught what it means to be members of their genders. In the United States, many boys are actively discouraged from crying, i.e., they're taught to suppress emotions that might make them appear weak, and many girls are actively taught to attend quickly to the needs of others. Boys are also frequently taught that they're supposed to be attracted to (and partner with) girls, and vice versa. For example, our local community center sometimes holds "mother-son" or "father-daughter" dances, but never mother-daughter or father-son dances because, as I was once told by a horrified neighbor to whom I suggested the idea, "that would be gay."

Similarly, legally your gender or sex identity matters a lot. In the United States, only men are allowed to marry women and vice versa. I couldn't have married my husband if the state of Indiana had believed he was female or I was male. A few states now allow civil unions, but even those are restricted by gender, because they are restricted to men partnering with men, and women with women. There's a federal law that prohibits genital cutting done on girls for cultural reasons—a practice sometimes called "female circumcision" or "female genital mutilation"—but a parent can easily and legally have a boy's foreskin cut off for cultural reasons. (It's known as "routine neonatal male circumcision.") Title IX was specifically designed to protect girls and women from discrimination in athletics programs, because historically they have been discriminated against. Only men can be drafted into the military, even though many women now serve in combat zones. In short, your sex and gender identities matter a lot.

Do Your "Sex Chromosomes" Make You a Man or a Woman?

So, given how much your gender identity matters, what makes you a man or a woman? Many people assume that what makes you a man is having XY chromosomes and what makes you a woman is having XX chromosomes. This is because they think XY will turn an embryo into a male, and XX will turn an embryo into a female. The truth is that most people don't know their karyotypes, but they assume they know what "sex chromosomes" they have in their cells. But guess what? You could be a man with an XX karyotype or a woman with XY without knowing it.

All embryos start off basically the same—with "protogonads" that might eventually become ovaries or testes (or ovotestes, i.e., organs with both testicular and ovarian tissue), and with the first rudiments of genital organs. In most cases, whether the fetus has a Y chromosome will determine whether it becomes male or female. The region of the Y chromosome that initiates male-typical development is called *SRY*. But here's the kicker—the first of several: *SRY* can be translocated (moved over) to an X chromosome. As a consequence, an embryo may have an XX combination with the *SRY* gene, and in this instance it will develop along a male-typical pathway. The man who ultimately results from this development will have male genitalia, testes, and undergo a male puberty. He may never find out he's XX because he's pretty much like men who are XY. Meanwhile, an XY combination with a non-functioning *SRY* results in an embryo developing along the female-typical path. The woman with this genetic background will develop as female. She may never find out she's XY because she is pretty much like women who are XX.

So, wait, you say; maybe then a functioning *SRY* makes you male, and the lack of a functioning *SRY* makes you female? Well, a functioning *SRY* gene is a necessary but not a sufficient condition to developing as a typical male. That's because *many* genes besides those located on the "sex chromosomes" contribute to sex development, including *WT-1* on chromosome 11,

SOX9 on 17, and *SF-1* on 9. That's why "sex chromosome" is a misnomer for the X and Y; there are many genes on the other chromosomes that make important contributions to sex development, and there are genes on the X chromosome that code for traits having nothing to do with sex.

SRY certainly is important. In the first trimester of prenatal life, *SRY* causes the undifferentiated protogonads to morph into testes, and the testes start making the "masculinizing" hormones that contribute to other parts of the body (genitals, brain, etc.) becoming male-typical. That's why a person with an XXY karyotype (a variation called Klinefelter syndrome) will develop mostly along a male-typical pathway—because he has an operational *SRY*. A person with one X and no Y in her karyotype (Turner syndrome) or XXX (Triple X syndrome) will develop mostly along a female-typical pathway—because she has no *SRY*. What happens to folks with mosaic karyotypes—where some cells may have XX and others XY, for example—depends on the particulars of their situation. There are even some people with three different kinds of karyotypes in their cells—in other words, each cell has one of three different "sex chromosome" combinations.

Now, there are also some women, like my friend Jane Goto, who have a functioning *SRY* gene (on a Y chromosome) but develop much more female-typical than male-typical. Jane and other women like her have a condition called complete androgen insensitivity syndrome (CAIS). As the name implies, they lack the receptors that would ordinarily respond to androgens ("masculinizing" hormones), so although they have testes, prenatally their genitalia form as female-typical—so typical that CAIS is often not diagnosed until the teen years or sometimes even later. At puberty a CAIS girl's body naturally changes to look like a typical woman's, with rounded breasts, hips, female-typical fat and muscle patterns, etc. This happens because the excess testosterone produced by their testes gets converted to estrogen through a process called aromatization. (The same process makes some men who take too many steroids end up with female-typical breasts and shrunken testicles.) Because the girl has no ovaries or uterus, she does not menstruate, even though it is clear she is undergoing a feminizing puberty. A gynecologist puts a speculum in the girl's vagina and discovers it is shorter than average and ends in a pouch, without a cervix or uterus; a karyotype confirms that she has XY chromosomes.

In terms of their bodily conformation and genitals, CAIS women look like other women, except that they never get hairy in the pubic region, armpits, or on their arms and legs like most girls and women, because that kind of body hair requires androgen-sensitivity. (Most other women make some testosterone in their ovaries and androgens in their adrenal glands, so they get relatively hairy after puberty. This is presumably why I'm hairier than Jane unless I shave.) CAIS women have female self-identities, are raised as girls, frequently marry men, and often adopt children because, like many other women, they wish to be mothers.

Then Maybe Your Internal Anatomy is What Makes You Male or Female?

But aren't CAIS women really men inside women's bodies? I don't think it makes any sense to think of them that way. Yes, they have testes, but remember that they're having none of the obvious responses to androgens ("masculinizing" hormones). And it doesn't really make sense to assign people a sex or gender identity based simply on what gonads they do or don't have. People have tried, though. I trace the history of this in *Hermaphrodites and the medical invention of sex* (1998). Would a man like Lance Armstrong who gets testicular cancer and has his testicles removed no longer be a man? Would your mother or adult daughter no longer be a woman if her ovaries were removed for some medical reason? Did my friend Cheryl Chase magically go from *not* being a girl to *being* a girl when doctors removed the testicular portions of her ovotestes when she was a child?

Well, then beyond the gonads—maybe CAIS girls and women have "masculine" brains? Not by the usual scientific meanings of that. In prenatal life, several small regions of the brain differentiate according to sex. So far as we know, this happens because, although in prenatal life both typical females and typical males have their brains exposed to androgens, typical females are exposed to fewer androgens than typical males, because the body of an average female fetus makes fewer androgens than the body of an average male fetus. Now, as a result of having the *SRY* gene, fetuses with CAIS have the male-typical hormone mix coursing about them prenatally, *but* remember that they don't have androgen receptors, so those "masculinizing" hormones seem to have

no effect on their brains. In other words, if you lined up in a spectrum the "masculinization" of the prenatal brains from androgen exposure, and you put the most "feminine" (least androgenized) on the left and most "masculine" (most androgenized) on the right, the order would go like this: CAIS women (like Jane); sex-typical women (like me, so far as I know); sex-typical men (like my husband, so far as he and I know). Because CAIS girls are identified and raised as girls, it is safe to assume that whatever sex differentiation happens in their brains because of gender-based nurture probably happens in the female-typical way.

Okay, so here's another sex development variation to consider: Some men have male-typical external anatomy, male-typical prenatal brain development, and ovaries. This can happen when an individual has XX chromosomes (with no *SRY* translocation) and an extreme form of virilizing congenital adrenal hyperplasia (CAH). The lack of the *SRY* gene means the protogonads morph into ovaries. So you would expect female-typical development to cascade from there. But the adrenal glands in these fetuses are in overdrive, making lots of androgens. As a consequence, the genitals and the brain get masculinized, enough so that a few of these children are not identified as having ovaries until they are adults. Relatively late diagnosis is rarer nowadays because of widespread screening for CAH in newborns. They're raised as boys with no one being the wiser. I got a call a few years back from a nineteen-year-old man who had just discovered he had ovaries and a uterus, XX chromosomes, and virilizing CAH. Let's call him Matthew. Matthew had learned he needed medical treatment for the metabolic dangers of his CAH (it can be quite dangerous), but beyond that, had some good questions about his identity: "How do I tell my parents and my girlfriend? And should I become a woman, and get the equivalent of sex-change surgery—get my male genitals changed to female, and change my endocrine system to be more like that of a female?" I suggested he tell his loved-ones soon and carefully, with the help of a counselor. As for his last question— should he become a woman?—I asked him, "Did you ever think of yourself as a woman before?" He said no, he had always been a boy and a man. "So why," I asked him, "would you let your ovaries tell you who you are? I don't let my ovaries tell me who I am." He said his doctor had told him that he might be fertile as a female, if he underwent surgery and medical management, but I asked him, "Do you want to be a mother?" "No," he said, "I've always wanted to be a father." I gently suggested to him he would have to think long and hard about this, and maybe he would have to consider grieving the loss of his fertility as a man and having his ovaries removed. He would need absolutely no surgery to convince anyone he was a man; he was a man.

So Maybe Your Genitals Are What Make You a Man or a Woman?

When your gender gets identified by someone else during a prenatal sonogram, just after birth, or at the showers of your local gym, it is usually because of your genitals. But genitals don't actually come in just two flavors (so to speak). The clitoris and the penis are homologues; that means that they develop from the same protoorgan in prenatal life, and so, as it turns out, you can have pretty much every variation between a classic penis and a classic clitoris. The same is true for the labia majora and the scrotum, which are also homologues. And on and on with homologous sex organs. Now, you can say, "Well, those people are the exceptions," but as it turns out, it is really hard to figure out who exactly "those people" are. What I mean by that is this: How small does a penis have to be before it counts as something other than a penis? How big does a clitoris have to be?

Because sex development is complicated—as I'm sure you've gathered by now!—some people seem to be born with sex-atypical genitals (sex-atypical when compared to their karyotypes) but sex-typical internal anatomies and brain development So, you can have a man like Hale Hawbecker who is male-typical except for being born with a very small penis. Hale tells his story in *Intersex in the age of ethics* (1999). You can also have women with CAH who are born with large clitorises but seem to be female-typical in terms of internal anatomy and brain development. And again, beyond these congenital variations, I'd ask the after-birth-change question: if a boy lost his penis in an accident, would he no longer be a male or a boy? Genitals seem like a very odd way to define for sure a person's sex or gender identity.

To sum up where we've been so far: 1. most people don't know their karyotypes, yet they seem to think of themselves and function as males/men or females/women anyway; in other words, although we may act like karyotypes are the basis for our social

gender system, in practice they're not; 2. because *SRY* can be translocated or nonfunctional, you can be an XX male/man or an XY female/woman; 3. because more than the "sex chromosomes" are needed for sex development, you can't just look at a karyotype and guess a phenotype; 4. you can't just look at a person's gonadal status and guess the rest of his or her body type or gender identity, and it doesn't seem to make any sense to say that a person is the sex his or her gonads are, regardless of everything else going on; 5. ditto with genitals; 6. prenatal brain development involves some "sex differentiation" but that differentiation is not simply a result of one's karyotype, and brain development doesn't always match gonad or genital type.

So Are Social Roles What Make You a Man or a Woman?

Keep in mind that, for thousands of years, people knew very little about gonads and nothing about genes or chromosomes, yet they managed to have gender identities. That's in part because, in the past, as now, in practice how you are treated in terms of your gender (and many other things, for that matter, like race and age and ability) is based on rough assumptions about your apparent biology. In the case of gender, these are rough assumptions that we consciously or more often unconsciously apply to people because they look like boys or men, girls or women.

Because researchers have figured out that a person's social role and self identity and biology are not the same things, they use the terms "gender identity" to talk about a person's self identity and/or social identity, and "sex" to talk about a person's biology. A person's gender usually starts with the announcement "It's a boy!" or "It's a girl!" (an announcement based on perceived sex, in a prenatal sonogram or at birth), and the establishment of your gender happens again and again throughout your life when people refer to you as a boy/man or a girl/woman, or treat you as a boy/man or a girl/woman, simply because of how they perceive the clothed you. For example, a person assigns you a gender identity by using the masculine (he) or feminine (she) pronoun to talk about you, or by inviting you to play in a women's soccer league, or by walking or talking or flirting or working with you in gender-specific ways. A man is regendered when he is identified as a "male nurse," and a woman undergraduate is regendered when she is labeled a "coed." Many (if not all) social encounters involve implicit or explicit gender attribution.

In practice, gender identity also gets implied or reinforced in encounters understood to be "homosexual" or "heterosexual." That's because what "homosexual" means is that same-gendered people are connecting in some sexual way, and what "heterosexual" means is that the same is happening for "opposite"-gendered people. In this sense, my student was right when he said he knew he was a man because his boyfriend is gay. Think also about the way genders get established when a woman driver tries to flirt her way out of a traffic ticket from a male cop—she's appealing as a woman to his presumed straight masculinity.

Sometimes someone ascribes the wrong gender to you. This can happen now and then by accident, when you are misidentified in a quick encounter, or it can happen all the time if you're in the situation where the gender you were assigned when you were a child isn't the one you feel. Max Beck was born with "ambiguous genitalia." As was the practice then, doctors recommended that his parents raise him as a girl, which they did, naming their child Judy. The doctors removed Judy's testes and surgically altered her genitals to make them look more like a girl's. To make a complicated life story too short, Judy ultimately became a lesbian, falling in love and partnering with another lesbian woman named Tamara, before figuring out that she really felt like a man. Max changed his name and his legal gender and so was able to marry Tamara. (In this sense, I think my student was wrong when he said "I know I'm a man because my boyfriend is gay." I think Tamara is still a woman even though her lover is now a man.)

Only a small percentage of people who are transgender—i.e., who do not feel themselves to be the gender they were assigned as children—seem to have some intersex condition like Max does. Most appear to be born with male-typical or female-typical bodies but feel so wrong in their social gender identities they are willing to undergo much personal struggle to achieve a social gender identity that matches their sense of self.

In this way, many people who are transgender express the same thing as my student who said this: "I think I'm a man because I seem to feel like other men feel." What does that mean? Well, Lisa Lees expressed it to my sex class this way: When I was socially identified as a man, and people related to me as a man, I always felt like there was something wrong in that interaction. When I became socially identifiable as a woman, the interactions felt right; I felt like who they were seeing was who I was seeing in myself.

So Does Biology Not Matter At All?

Hmm, not so fast. If biology didn't matter at all to most people's gender identities, then it wouldn't make sense that every culture in the world maintains some gender role expectations for boys/men versus girls/women, would it? By the way, some cultures have more than two sets of roles, but all have at least two based on male-typical and female-typical. It also wouldn't make sense that, all over the world, *on average* young girls tend to be more interested in role-playing of supportive social relationships (like pretending to be a mother or the cook for the family) and *on average* young boys tend to be more interested in playing with objects that they can manipulate (like blocks, balls, and trucks).

When I started doing work on sex development variations, like a lot of other feminists I believed that boys and girls were different because they were *taught* to be different. I thought gender identity was all a result of nurture. But that no longer makes sense to me, in part because of cross-cultural studies, but also because I've met and learned of enough people (like Max Beck and, for that matter, Lisa Lees) who, in spite of intense gender training, ended up with a very different gender identity than the ones they were taught.

Sometimes gender warriors talk about wanting to get rid of gender altogether, but I really doubt that is ever going to happen. I think most people—for complex reasons of nature and nurture—feel some kind of gender. It's important not to forget that, even while naive beliefs about gender are sometimes used to oppress people, gender is also frequently pleasurable for people. Three women chatting in a bathroom are often enjoying their genders. A dad playing ball with his son is often enjoying his gender. A woman having sex with a man as a woman having sex with a man is enjoying her gender. The idea of getting rid of gender strikes me as not only naive, but pretty oppressive, too.

What Now?

I think, given all this, we can come to at least five conclusions about sex and gender identity in humans: 1. We tend to act like biology is the basis for our social gender distinctions, but in fact in day-to-day interactions, it is your social presentation that matters. (The state of Indiana did not require me and my husband to submit evidence of our karyotypes, gonadal types, or even genitals to get hitched. They just made me get a rubella titer.) 2. It is safe to assume that nature (biology) and nurture (environment) contribute to every individual's experience of sex and gender identity. 3. It is equally safe to assume that, for any given individual, you're not going to be able to predict with certainty by looking at her or him what a karyotype will show, what organs she or he has got inside, or what gender identity she or he will end up with. 4. You can, in practice, try to divide people into two sexes by picking some biological marker and deciding that's what really, really, *really* matters. So you can decide to use possession or lack of a Y chromosome, or possession or lack of an operative *SRY* gene, or gonadal tissue type, or phallus size, or whatever you want. But you're always going to find someone who, by this system, ends up in a category that doesn't seem to make sense because it doesn't line up with the rest of what you have in mind when you say "male" or "female" or "man" or "woman." People tend to like their social categories neat. Nature is a slob. Any attempt to divide people neatly into two sex types is ultimately a social action, not a scientific (or natural) one, and it should be recognized as such. 5. Just because something is natural doesn't mean it is good. Just because boys around the world tend to play with weapons more than girls doesn't mean only men should get drafted; just because girls on average may be more attentive to the needs of others than boys doesn't mean men shouldn't be allowed and expected to cook and clean for their families; just because there are lots more types of sex than two doesn't mean we have to have hundreds of gender types in our culture. We should not try to line up our social systems with what (we assume) is happening in the natural world, but should, rather, base our social systems on a developed sense of justice and fairness. Knowing more and more about the nature of sex doesn't tell us what to do about men, women, and other people. It just helps us begin to think about what to do.

Section 4: Bioethics and Disability

Who Is Disabled? Defining Disability

Susan Wendell

Wendell considers the United Nations and other definitions that distinguish *impairments* (loss of average physical structures and functions) from *disabilities* (loss of ability to perform normal activities) from *handicaps* (barriers to societal participation conditioned by one's physical, social, and cultural environment). She commends such definitions for their recognition that disabled people's limitations may be the unnecessary result of societal choices rather than their own physical or mental traits. Wendell points out, however, that the thresholds for impairments and disabilities are also relative to what is "normal" for a given society, and should be evaluated in light of both prevailing conditions and social justice.

Wendell argues that disability is inherently contextual—a claim she underscores with regard to both the elderly and the deaf. The disabilities of the elderly demonstrate how, for most people, being healthy

Republished with permission of Taylor and Francis Group LLC Books, from "Who Is Disabled? Defining Disability," Susan Wendell, in *The Rejected Body: Feminist Philosophical Reflections on Disability*. New York: Routledge, 1996, 11–32; permission conveyed through Copyright Clearance Center, Inc. (Notes omitted.)

and nondisabled is only a temporary condition. Deaf culture demonstrates that when the disabled can control their own environments, their capacities often no longer seem diminished, but may instead produce valuable and rewarding structures of shared human life.

The question of how we should define disability is not merely the beginning of an analytic exercise. We encounter the problem of definition as soon as we take an interest in disability. For example, how many people have disabilities? Estimates of the incidence of disability worldwide and within countries vary greatly among the estimators, because not only methods of gathering information about disabilities, but also understandings of what constitutes disability, vary greatly among those gathering the information. Questions of definition arise in countless practical situations, influence social policies, and determine outcomes that profoundly affect the lives of people with disabilities.

Definitions of disability officially accepted by government bureaucracies and social service agencies determine people's legal and practical entitlement to many forms of assistance, where assistance is available. This may include economic help for such purposes as: education, training, and retraining; obtaining equipment, such as wheelchairs for basic mobility or computers for basic communication; modifying a home or a vehicle to enable a person with a disability to use it; hiring assistants to help with bodily maintenance and household tasks; even obtaining medical supplies such as medications and bandages. For people with disabilities who are unemployed, it includes the basic support to buy food and shelter. It also includes eligibility for accessible housing and special forms of transportation, and even for such seemingly minor (but actually major) means of access as a disabled parking sticker.

Socially accepted definitions of disability determine the recognition of disability by friends, family members, and co-workers. Recognition of a person's disability by the people s/he is closest to is important not only for receiving their help and understanding when it is needed, but for receiving the acknowledgement and confirmation of her/his reality, so essential for keeping a person socially and psychologically anchored in a community. It is not uncommon for friends and even family members to desert a person who has debilitating symptoms that remain undiagnosed. They may insist that the ill person is faking, or mentally ill and unwilling to get appropriate treatment. People whose disability is unrecognized are frequently pressured to keep up a pretense of normality, to continue to work as if nothing were wrong, and/or to undergo unnecessary psychiatric treatment.

Definitions of disability are important to those who are organizing people with disabilities for political purposes, for example, to press for fuller recognition of their rights, for increased accessibility to public places, or for better opportunities to work. There have been struggles within political groups of people with disabilities, especially in recent years, to include more categories of people. For example, people with AIDS and with debilitating chronic illnesses like ME fought within disability groups for the recognition that they too are disabled, share similar needs and struggles, and suffer similar forms of insult, discrimination, distrust, and exclusion.

Definitions of disability affect people's self-identity. Recognizing yourself as disabled and identifying with other people who are disabled and learning about their experiences can all contribute to understanding and interpreting your own experiences, and to knowing that you are not alone with problems that you may have believed were unique to you. But being identified as disabled also carries a significant stigma in most societies and usually forces the person so identified to deal with stereotypes and unrealistic attitudes and expectations that are projected on to her/him as a member of this stigmatized group.

A careful effort to define disability can clarify our conceptions of disability and reveal misconceptions and false stereotypes. For example, for many people the paradigmatic disabled person is a young, healthy, paraplegic man who has been injured in an accident but continues to be athletic, or a young, healthy, professionally successful blind woman who has 'overcome' her handicap with education. In fact, arthritis, rheumatism, heart and respiratory disease, stroke, Parkinsonism, hypertension, and epilepsy are major causes of disability in Canada, the United States, and Great Britain, and many people with disabilities in these countries are also ill and/or old (Health and Welfare Canada and Statistics Canada 1981; Statistics Canada 1986 and 1991; Pope and Tarlov 1991; LaPlante 1991; Bury 1978).

The United Nations Definitions

The United Nations definition of disability (UN 1983: I.c. 6–7) is widely used and tends to be favoured by disability activists and other advocates of greater opportunities for people with disabilities (Wright 1983, 10–12; Fine and Asch 1988, 5–6). It offers the following definitions of and distinctions among impairment, disability, and handicap:

> "Impairment: *Any loss or abnormality of psychological, physiological, or anatomical structure or function.* Disability: *Any restriction or lack (resulting from an impairment) of ability to perform an activity in the manner or within the range considered normal for a human being.* Handicap: *A disadvantage for a given individual, resulting from an impairment or disability, that limits or prevents the fulfillment of a role that is normal, depending on age, sex, social and cultural factors, for that individual."*
>
> *Handicap is therefore a function of the relationship between disabled persons and their environment. It occurs when they encounter cultural, physical or social barriers which prevent their access to the various systems of society that are available to other citizens. Thus, handicap is the loss or limitation of opportunities to take part in the life of the community on an equal level with others. (UN 1983: I.c. 6–7)*

There are two things I like about the UN definitions. First, they are general enough to include many conditions that are not always recognized by the general public as disabling, for example, debilitating chronic illnesses, such as Crohn's disease, which limit people's activities but do not necessarily cause any immediately observable disability. I shall return to this aspect of the definitions later in this chapter. Second, the definition of *handicap* explicitly recognizes the possibility that the primary causes of a disabled person's inability to do certain things may be social; they may be lack of opportunities, lack of accessibility, lack of services, poverty or discrimination, and they often are. It is this latter aspect of the definitions that makes them appealing to advocates for people with disabilities.

Nevertheless, there are several criticisms I have of the UN definitions that may throw some light on the nature of disability and the problems associated with denning it. First, the definitions of "impairment" and "disability" seem to imply that there is some universal, biologically or medically describable standard of structure, function, and human physical ability. As we shall see, there would be important advantages to employing some universal standards, should we be able to agree on them. Yet surely what are "normal" structure, function, and ability to perform an activity all depend to some degree on the society in which the standards of normality are generated. For example, I, who can walk about half a mile several times a week but not more, am not significantly disabled with respect to walking in my society, where most people are not expected to walk further than that in the course of their daily activities. But in some societies, in Eastern Africa for example, where women normally walk several miles twice a day to obtain water for the household, I would be much more severely disabled. It is not just that I would be considered more disabled in those societies but that I would in fact need constant assistance to carry on the most basic life activities. What is normal ability in urban Western Canada is neither normal nor adequate ability in rural Kenya.

Failure to recognize that standards of structure, function, and ability are socially relative could be dangerous to people with disabilities. If the standards employed are generated by people in highly industrialized societies, many people in less industrialized societies and in rural areas where there are fewer technological resources will be considered non-disabled when they are in fact in need of special assistance to survive and participate in life where they are.

On the other hand, definitions of impairment and disability could be relativized too much to some societies. If most people in a particular society are chronically undernourished, that society's standards of "normal" functioning might become so low as to mask the widespread disability among its citizens that starvation is causing. Another particularly disturbing example is the genital mutilation of girls. In societies where the majority of people approves of the practice and the vast majority of girls has been mutilated, the girl who has a clitoris (and other external sexual organs, depending on the form of mutilation practiced) is considered abnormal. Yet because genital mutilation often causes' severe in-fections, shock, hemorrhage, and chronic physical and mental health problems, in addition to reducing or destroying some women's capacities for sexual pleasure, I cannot believe that the rest of the world should accept uncritically those societies' stand-ards of normal structure and function for women. To do so seems a betrayal of the girls and women whose lives, health, and sexuality are endangered by mutilation.

Iris Marion Young's statement that "women in sexist society are physically handicapped," and her arguments in support of it present another strong challenge to the idea that culturally relative standards of physical structure, function, and abil-ity should be accepted. Young argues that lack of opportunities and encouragement to develop bodily abilities, rigid standards of feminine bodily com-portment, and constant objectification and threat of invasion of their bodies combine to deprive most women in sexist societies of their full physical potential. In these societies, a "normal" woman is expected to lack strength, skills, and the range of movement that "normal" men are expected to possess and that she might have developed had she grown up in a less sexist society. If we accept these standards uncritically, we will tend to overlook the ways that those societies create physical disadvan-tages for women.

Thus there seem to be problems both in denying the social and cultural relativity of impairment and disability (as used in the UN definitions) and in accepting it. The UN definitions seem to recognize the relativity of standards of ability while attempt-ing to universalize them by using the phrase "in the manner or within the range considered normal for a human being." Unfortunately, that does not amount to a practical recognition of the relativity of disability. A woman in Kenya who can walk only as much as I can will still not be considered disabled with respect to walking, because her ability falls within the worldwide *range* considered normal. Nor does it universalize standards enough to create the basis for criticizing societies whose standards of health and good functioning fall too low for some or all of their members. The standards of such soci-eties could still be seen to fall, by definition, in the "range considered normal for a human being.". . . .

In addition, the UN definitions suggest that we can be disabled, but not handicapped, by the

normal process of aging, since although we may lose some ability, we are not "handicapped" unless we cannot fulfill roles that are normal *for our age*. Yet the fates of old people and of people with disabilities tend to be linked in a society because aging is disa-bling. A society that provides few resources to allow disabled people to participate in its activities will be likely to marginalize all people with disabilities, in-cluding the old, and to define the appropriate roles of old people as very limited, thus disadvantaging them. I think the UN should recognize that old people can be handicapped unnecessarily by their societies, but its definitions seem to prevent that recognition.

Realizing that aging is disabling helps non-disabled people to see that people with disabilities are not 'Other,' that they are really themselves at a later time. Unless we die suddenly, we are all disabled eventually. Most of us will live part of our lives with bodies that hurt, that move with difficulty or not at all, that deprive us of activities we once took for granted, or that others take for granted—bodies that make daily life a physical struggle. We need understandings of disability and handicap that do not support a paradigm of humanity as young and healthy. Encouraging everyone to acknowledge, accommodate, and identify with a wide range of physical conditions is ultimately the road to self-acceptance as well as the road to increasing the opportunities of those who are disabled now.

Ron Amundson objects to Norman Daniels's classifying the disabled with the group Daniels calls the "frail elderly," that is, those who, according to Daniels, are experiencing a normal reduction in bio-medical functioning associated with aging. Amundson says of this: "To the extent that frailty and opportunity reduction is a natural consequence of aging, classi-fying disability with age-frailty again falsely depicts handicaps as a natural and expected part of human existence" (Amundson 1992, 115).

I appreciate Amundson's concern that grouping the "frail elderly" together with nonelderly people with disabilities will lead most people to assume that the opportunities of the latter are reduced by nature and not by the failures of society. But I prefer challenging the underlying assumption about what is natural to pressing the distinction between the two groups. It is not obvious to me that the reduction of opportunities experienced by the elderly are any more attributable to nature than the reduction of opportunities experienced by nonelderly people with disabilities. True, there may be many physical feats they will never accomplish again, but this is also true of nonelderly people with disabilities, and it does not imply for either group that their opportunities to do other things must be diminished. In fact, many elderly people who used to take too many limitations on their activities for granted now take advantage of improvements in accessibility, such as ramps and lowered curbs, that were made with nonelderly people with disabilities in mind. I imagine that if we did not construct our environment to fit a *young* adult, non-disabled, male paradigm of humanity, many obstacles to nonelderly people with disabilities would not exist.

When disability is carefully distinguished from the expected frailties of old age, we lose the main benefit of the insight that aging is disabling. That insight enables non-disabled people to realize that they are temporarily non-disabled, and that in turn enables them to see that it is in their own direct interest to structure society so that people with disabilities have good opportunities to participate in every aspect of social life. Therefore, I do not think that for most social and political purposes it is a good idea to make distinctions among disabilities according to whether they were brought on by aging. It is partly for this reason, and partly because it does not relativize handicaps to sex roles, that I prefer Amundson's less qualified definition of "handicap" to the UN definition.

How Should Disability Be Defined?

I am not going to recommend specific definitions that I would like to see adopted by the United Nations. The definitions they use have to serve specific political purposes of the World Health Organization and other agencies, and they have to be arrived at by a complex process of political compromise, of which I know virtually nothing. My purpose in criticizing the UN definitions is to bring to light issues that may be glossed over or missed altogether if we accept them too readily and try to apply them in all contexts.

Nevertheless, I think that on the basis of the discussion so far, I can summarize some characteristics that good definitions, for both educational and practical purposes, should have: Good defini-

tions of impairment and disability should recognize that normal (i.e., unimpaired) physical structure and function, as well as normal (i.e., non-disabled) ability to perform activities, depend to some extent on the physical, social, and cultural environment in which a person is living, and are influenced by such factors as what activities are necessary to survival in an environment and what abilities a culture considers most essential to a participant. However, they should also take into account the possibility that some members of a society may have a vested interest in defining 'normal' structure, function, and ability for other members in ways that disadvantage those other members and/or mask ill treatment of them. Thus it is important before accepting a society's standards of normality to compare them to those of other societies; if they are lower than, or markedly different from, many others, or if they are different for different groups (e.g., sexes, races, classes, or castes), the possibility that disability is more widespread in that society than its standards would recognize should be carefully examined.

In addition, some terms, such as *handicap*, may be useful to refer specifically to any loss of opportunities to participate in major aspects of the life of a society that results from the interaction of a disability with the physical, social, and cultural environment of the person who has it. The fact that a society does not consider an opportunity necessary or appropriate for a person belonging to some particular group (e.g., age, sex, class) may be irrelevant to whether the person is handicapped, since it is not unusual for a society to handicap large groups of its own people. On the other hand, not every loss of opportunity is a handicap, despite the fact that one often hears or reads the observation that everyone is disabled or handicapped in some way (for example, see Murphy 1990, 66). I will not go into detail here about how much loss of opportunity constitutes a handicap but will discuss this as an aspect of the social creation of disability in the next chapter.

In general usage, the distinction between "disability" and "handicap" is not usually maintained. Introducing it does have an educational function, reminding people that many of the obstacles faced by people with disabilities are not necessary consequences of their physical conditions. On the other hand, it also tends to create the mistaken impression that disability is purely biological and handicap is social, when in fact both are products of biological and social factors.

Some Politics of Disability Identity

Whether to identify oneself as disabled can be a contentious political issue. For example, there is a lively debate among the Deaf about whether to include themselves in disability rights groups, since many Deaf people do not consider themselves disabled. Because the Deaf have sign language and a rich culture separate from hearing people, it is very clear that the Deaf are not disabled in all *contexts*. As Roger J. Carver puts it:

> *Indeed, as one enters into the world of the Deaf, disability as a factor in their lives ceases to exist. A hearing person unfamiliar with the language and customs of the Deaf community will instantly find himself handicapped in such a context, arising from his disability in the area of communication. In the same vein, a Deaf person will feel the same way when he [sic] is among speaking hearing persons. This handicap is no different from that incurred by visiting a foreign country in which a different language is spoken. It explains in large part why the Deaf do not feel at home among other disabled persons; they do not share the same communications system. Put "wheelies" together into a group; they are still confronted by the reality of their disability. The same is true for the blind or even the hard of hearing. (Carver 1992)*

From medical and rehabilitative practitioners' point of view (which is also the point of view of most hearing people), a deaf child is disabled by her inability to hear, and so the child becomes the focus of efforts to 'normalize' her as far as possible within the hearing community. But from another, equally valid point of view, the same child is handicapped by hearing people's (often including her parents') ignorance of Sign. In a Deaf, signing community, she is already normal, assuming that she has signing ability appropriate for her age. The validity of this second point of view is weakened or even forsaken when the Deaf identify themselves as people with disabilities and join disability rights groups to work for their own welfare.

On the other hand, since most medical and rehabilitative authorities, as well as the hearing majority,

consider the Deaf disabled, the Deaf must often identify themselves as people with disabilities in order to obtain the equipment and services they need. Carver says, "In the eyes of the Hearing, our technical devices are medical devices or 'assistive living aids;' in the eyes of the Deaf, they are mundane, everyday instruments in much the same way the Hearing regard their telephones, TV sets, alarm clocks, and doorbells" (Carver 1992).

Moreover, since the Deaf are widely regarded as disabled, they are treated in some of the same ways as (other) people with disabilities, and therefore they have some common causes with (other) people with disabilities, including the goal of being accepted as different rather than rejected as defective (Vlug 1992). For this reason, some of the Deaf identify themselves as people with disabilities and/or want to work within organizations of people with disabilities.

Many of the same things Carver says about the Deaf are true of most people with disabilities: We are disabled in some, but not all, contexts; the disability in a given situation is often created by the inability or unwillingness of others to adapt themselves or the environment to the physical or psychological reality of the person designated as 'disabled'; and people with disabilities often regard the accommodations they make to their physical conditions as ordinary living arrangements and their lives as ordinary lives, despite their medicalization by professionals and most people's insistence that they are unusually helpless or dependent. These facts are more obvious in the case of the Deaf, because the contexts in which the Deaf are not disabled are more readily available, more total, and more public than for most people with disabilities. Thus Carver says that other people with disabilities are still confronted with their disabilities when they are in each other's company; but that is not entirely true. It is true that people who use wheelchairs still have the same difficulty walking when they are in the exclusive company of other people who use wheelchairs, but walking is out of the question for the whole group, and so it is not an issue or an obstacle to participating fully in the group's activities. Disability is contextual for everyone, not only for the Deaf.

Widespread perceptions that people with disabilities are similar in very significant ways create the category, "people with disabilities." Thus it is various aspects of their treatment by their societies that people with disabilities are most likely to have in common; these will often be aspects of social oppression. In North America, they include: verbal, medical, and physical abuse; neglect of the most basic educational needs; sexual abuse and exploitation; enforced poverty; harassment by public and private sector bureaucracies; job discrimination; segregation in schools, housing, and workshops; inaccessibility of buildings, transportation, and other public facilities; social isolation due to prejudice and ignorant fear; erasure as a sexual being; and many more subtle manifestations of disability-phobia, experienced as daily stress and wounds to self-esteem. As in every oppressed group, not everyone will have experienced all aspects of the oppression, but the pattern of oppression produces overlapping patterns of experience among group members. This overlap, combined with the awareness that many things happened to them because they are identified *by others* as members of the group, can motivate people of diverse experiences to work together for their common welfare, to identify themselves willingly as members of the group, and to redefine for themselves what being one of the group means.

The Myth of Mental Illness

Thomas S. Szasz

Szasz argues that what we call "mental illness" is no more than a misleading metaphor. The concept of illness implies deviation from a norm or standard. For physical illness, the norm is physiological; but for mental illness, Szasz claims, the norm is socially determined. The social norm is then taken as having the same status as the physiological norm, which thus tends to identify nonconformity with mental illness. The result is both a denial of individual autonomy and a failure to deal with the genuine issues at the root of human conflict. The real problems we should be dealing with, Szasz argues, are the "problems of living" that people face in society. Once we abandon the "myth of mental illness," we can focus our attention on the genuine ethical and social issues.

My aim in this essay is to raise the question "Is there such a thing as mental illness?" and to argue that there is not. Since the notion of mental illness is extremely widely used nowadays, inquiry into the ways in which this term is employed would seem to be especially indicated. Mental illness, of course, is not literally a "thing"—or physical object—and hence it can "exist" only in the same sort of way in which other theoretical concepts exist. Yet, familiar theories are in the habit of posing, sooner of later—at least to those who come to believe in them—as "objective truths" (or "facts"). During certain historical periods, explanatory conceptions such as deities, witches, and microorganisms appeared not only as theories but as self-evident *causes* of a vast number of events. I submit that today mental illness is widely regarded in a somewhat similar fashion, that is, as the cause of innumerable diverse

From Thomas S. Szasz, "The Myth of Mental Illness", 1960. Text in the Public Domain. Originally published in *The American Psychologist* 15, no. 2 (February 1960): 113–118. (References omitted.)

happenings, As an antidote to the complacent use of the notion of mental illness—whether as a self-evident phenomenon, theory, or cause—let us ask this question: What is meant when it is asserted that someone is mentally ill?

In what follows I shall describe briefly the main uses to which the concept of mental illness has been put. I shall argue that this notion has outlived whatever usefulness it might have had and that it now functions merely as a convenient myth.

Mental Illness as a Sign of Brain Disease

The notion of mental illness derives its main support from such phenomena as syphilis of the brain or delirious conditions—intoxications, for instance—in which persons are known to manifest various peculiarities or disorders of thinking and behavior. Correctly speaking, however, these are diseases of the brain, not of the mind. According to one school of thought, *all* so-called mental illness is of this type. The assumption is made that some neurological defect, perhaps a very subtle one, will ultimately be found for all the disorders of thinking and behavior. Many contemporary psychiatrists, physicians, and other scientists hold this view. This position implies that people *cannot* have troubles—expressed in what are *now called* "mental illnesses"—because of differences in personal needs, opinions, social aspiration, values, and so on. *All problems in living* are attributed to physicochemical processes which in due time will be discovered by medical research.

"Mental illnesses" are thus regarded as basically no different than all other diseases (that is, of the body). The only difference, in this view, between mental and bodily diseases is that the former, affecting the brain, manifest themselves by means of mental symptoms, whereas the latter, affecting other organ systems (for example, the skin, liver, etc.), manifest themselves by means of symptoms referable to those parts of the body. This view rests on and expresses what are, in my opinion, two fundamental errors.

In the first place, what central nervous system symptoms would correspond to a skin eruption or a fracture? It would *not* be some emotion or complex bit of behavior. Rather, it would be blindness or a paralysis of some part of the body. The crux of the matter is that a disease of the brain, analogous to a disease of the skin or bone, is a neurological defect, and not a problem in living. For example, a *defect* in a person's visual field may be satisfactorily explained by correlating it with certain definite lesions in the nervous system. On the other hand, a persons *belief*—whether this be a belief in Christianity, in Communism, or in the idea that his internal organs are "rotting" and that his body is, in fact, already "dead"—cannot be explained by a defect or disease of the nervous system. Explanations of this sort of occurrence—assuming that one is interested in the belief itself and does not regard it simply as a "symptom" or expression of something else that is *more interesting*—must be sought along different lines.

The second error in regarding complex psychosocial behavior, consisting of communication about ourselves and the world about us, as mere symptoms of neurological functioning is *epistemological*. In other words, it is an error pertaining not to any mistakes in observation or reasoning, as such, but rather to the way in which we organize and express our knowledge. In the present case, the error lies in making a symmetrical dualism between mental and physical (or bodily) symptoms, a dualism which is merely a habit of speech and to which no known observation can be found to correspond. Let us see if this is so. In medical practice, when we speak of physical disturbances, we mean either signs (for example, a fever) or symptoms (for example, pain). We speak of mental symptoms, on the other hand, when we refer to a patients *communication about himself, others, and the world about him*. He might state that he is Napoleon or that he is being persecuted by the Communists. These would be considered mental symptoms *only* if the observer believed that the patient was *not* Napoleon or that he was *not* being persecuted by the Communists. This makes it apparent that the statement that "X is a mental symptom" involves rendering a judgment. The judgment entails, moreover, a covert comparison or matching of the patient's ideas, concepts, or beliefs with those of the observer and the society in which they live. The notion of mental symptom is therefore inextricably tied to the *social* (including *ethical*) con*tex*t in which it is made in much the same way as the notion of bodily symptom is tied to an *anatomical* and *genetic context* (Szasz, 1957a, 1957b).

To sum up what has been said thus far: I have *tried* to show that for those who regard mental symptoms as signs of brain disease, the concept of mental illness is unnecessary and misleading. For what they mean is that people so labeled suffer from diseases of the brain; and, if that is what they mean, it would seem better for the sake of clarity to say that and not something else.

Mental Illness as a Name for Problems in Living

The term "mental illness" is widely used to describe something which is very different than a disease of the brain. Many people today take it for granted that living is an arduous process. Its hardship for modern man, moreover, derives not so much from a struggle for biological survival as from the stresses and strains inherent in the social intercourse of complex human personalities. In this context, the notion of mental illness is used to identify or describe some feature of an individual's so-called personality. Mental illness—as a deformity of the personality, so to speak—is then regarded as the *cause* of the human disharmony. It is implicit in this view that social intercourse between people is regarded as something *inherently harmonious*, its disturbance being due solely to the presence of "mental illness" in many people. This is obviously fallacious reasoning, for it makes the abstraction "mental illness" into a *cause*, even though this abstraction was created in the first place to serve only as a shorthand expression for certain types of human behavior. It now becomes necessary to ask: "What kinds of behavior are regarded as indicative of mental illness, and by whom?"

The concept of illness, whether bodily or mental, implies *deviation from some clearly defined norm*. In the case of physical illness, the norm is the structural and functional integrity of the human body. Thus, although the desirability of physical health, as such, is an ethical value, what health *is* can be stated in anatomical and physiological terms. What is the norm deviation from which is regarded as mental illness? This question cannot be easily answered. But whatever this norm might be, we can be certain of only one thing: namely, that it is a norm that must be stated in terms of *psychosocial, ethical,* and *legal* concepts. For example, notions such as "excessive repression" or "acting out an unconscious impulse" illustrate the use of psychological concepts for judging (so-called) mental health and illness. The idea that chronic hostility, vengefulness, or divorce are indicative of mental illness would be illustrations of the use of ethical norms (that is, the desirability of love, kindness, and a stable marriage relationship). Finally, the widespread psychiatric opinion that only a mentally ill person would commit homicide illustates the use of a legal concept as a norm of mental health. The norm from which deviation is measured whenever one speaks of a mental illness is a *psychosocial and ethical one*. Yet, the remedy is sought in terms of *medical* measures which—it is hoped and assumed—are free from wide differences of ethical value. The definition of the disorder and the terms in which its remedy are sought are therefore at serious odds with one another. The practical significance of this covert conflict between the alleged nature of the defect and the remedy can hardly be exaggerated.

Having identified the norms used to measure deviations in cases of mental illness, we will now turn to the question: "Who defines the norms and hence the deviation?" Two basic answers may be offered: (a) It may be the person himself (that is, the patient) who decides that he deviates from a norm. For example, an artist may believe that he suffers from a work inhibition; and he may implement this conclusion by seeking help *for* himself from a psychotherapist, (b) It may be someone other than the patient who decides that the latter is deviant (for example, relatives, physicians, legal authorities, society generally, etc.). In such a case a psychiatrist may be hired by others to do something *to* the patient in order to correct the deviation.

These considerations underscore the importance of asking the question "Whose agent is the psychiatrist?" and of giving a candid answer to it (Szasz, 1956, 1958). The psychiatrist (psychologist or nonmedical psychotherapist), it now develops, may be the agent of the patient, of the relatives, of the school, of the military services, of a business organization, of a court of law, and so forth. In speaking of the psychiatrist as the agent of these persons or organizations, it is not implied that his values concerning norms, or his ideas and, aims concerning the proper nature of remedial action, need to coincide exactly with those of his employer. For example, a patient in individual psychotherapy may believe that his salvation lies in a new marriage; his psychotherapist need not share this hypothesis. As the patient's agent, however, he must abstain from bringing social or legal force to bear on the patient which would prevent him from putting his beliefs into action. If his *contract* is with the patient, the psychiatrist (psychotherapist) may disagree with him or stop his treatment; but he cannot engage others to obstruct the patient's aspirations. Similarly, if a psychiatrist is engaged by a court to determine the sanity of a criminal, he need not fully share the legal authorities' values and intentions in regard to the criminal and the means available for dealing with him. But the psychiatrist is expressly barred from stating, for example, that it is not the criminal who is "insane" but the men who wrote the law on the basis of which the very actions that are being judged are regarded as "criminal." Such an opinion could be voiced, of course, but not in a courtroom, and not by a psychiatrist who makes it his practice to assist the court in performing its daily work.

To recapitulate: In actual contemporary social usage, the finding of a mental illness is made by establishing a deviance in behavior from certain psychosocial, ethical, or legal norms. The judgment may be made, as in medicine, by the patient, the physician (psychiatrist), or others. Remedial action, finally, tends to be sought in a therapeutic—or covertly medical—framework, thus creating a situation in which *psychosocial, ethical,* and/or *legal deviation* are claimed to be correctible by (so-called) *medical action*. Since medical action is designed to correct only medical deviation, it seems logically absurd to expect that it will help solve problems whose very existence had been defined and established on nonmedical grounds. I think that these considerations may be fruitfully applied to the present use of tranquilizers and, more generally, to what might be expected of drugs of whatever type in regard to the amelioration or solution of problems in human living.

The Role of Ethics in Psychiatry

Anything that people *do*—in contrast to things that *happen* to them (Peters, 1958)—takes place in, a context of value. In this broad sense, no human activity is devoid of ethical implications. When the values underlying certain activities are widely shared, those who participate in their pursuit may lose sight of them altogether. The discipline of medicine, both as a pure science (for example, research) and as a technology (for example, therapy), contains many ethical considerations and judgments. Unfortunately, these are often denied, minimized, or merely kept out of focus; for the ideal of the medical profession as well as of the people whom it serves seems to be having a system of medicine (allegedly) free of ethical value. This sentimental notion is expressed by such things as the doctor's willingness to treat and help patients irrespective of their religious or political beliefs, whether they are rich or poor, etc. While there may be some grounds for this belief—albeit it is a view that is not impressively true even in these regards—the fact remains that ethical considerations encompass a vast range of human affairs. By making the practice of medicine neutral in regard to some specific issues of value need not, and cannot, mean that it can be kept free from all such values. The practice of medicine is intimately tied to ethics; and the first thing that we must do, it seems to me, is to try to make this clear and explicit. I shall let this matter rest here, for it does not concern us specifically in this essay. Lest there by any vagueness, however, about how or where ethics and medicine meet, let me remind the reader of such issues as birth control, abortion, suicide, and euthanasia as only a few of the major areas of current ethicomedical controversy.

Psychiatry, I submit, is very much more intimately tied to problems of ethics than is medicine. I use the word "psychiatry" here to refer to that contemporary discipline which is concerned with *problems in living* (and not with diseases of the brain, which are problems for neurology). Problems in human relations can be analyzed, interpreted, and given meaning only within given social and ethical contexts. Accordingly, it *does* make a difference—arguments to the contrary notwithstanding—what the psychiatrist's socioethical orientations happen to be; for these will influence his ideas on what is wrong with the patient, what deserves comment or interpretation, in what possible directions change might be desirable, and so forth. Even in medicine proper, these factors play a role, as for instance, in the divergent orientations which physicians, depending on their religious affiliations, have toward such things as birth control and therapeutic abortion. Can anyone really believe that a psychotherapist's ideas concerning religious belief, slavery, or other similar issues play no role in his practical work? If they do make a difference, what are we to infer from it? Does it not seem reasonable that we ought to have different psychiatric therapies—each expressly recognized for the ethical positions which they embody—for, say, Catholics and Jews, religious persons and agnostics, democrats and communists, white supremacists and Negroes, and so on? Indeed, if we look at how psychiatry is actually practiced today (especially in the United States), we find that people do seek psychiatric help in accordance with their social status and ethical beliefs (Hollingshead & Redlich, 1958). This should really not surprise us more than being told that practicing Catholics rarely frequent birth control clinics.

The foregoing position which holds that contemporary psychotherapists deal with problems in living, rather than with mental illnesses and their cures, stands in opposition to a currently prevalent claim, according to which mental illness is just as "real" and "objective" as bodily illness. This is a confusing claim since it is never known exactly what is meant by such words as "real" and "objective." I suspect, however, that what is intended by the proponents of this view is to create the idea in the popular mind that mental illness is some sort of disease entity, like an infection or a malignancy. If this were true, one could *catch* or *get* a "mental illness," one might *have* or *harbor* it, one might *transmit* it to others, and finally one could get *rid* of it. In my opinion, there is not a shred of evidence to support this idea. To the contrary, all the evidence is the other way and supports the view that what people now call mental illnesses are for the most part *communications* expressing unacceptable ideas, often framed, moreover, in an unusual idiom. The scope of this essay allows me to do no more than mention this alternative theoretical approach to this problem (Szasz, 1957c).

This is not the place to consider in detail the similarities and differences between bodily and mental illnesses. It shall suffice for us here to emphasize only one important difference between them: namely, that whereas bodily disease refers to public, physicochemical occurrences, the notion of mental illness is used to codify relatively more private, sociopsychological happenings of which the observer (diagnostician) forms a part. In other words, the psychiatrist does not stand *apart* from what he observes, but is, in Harry Stack Sullivan's apt words, a "participant observer." This means that he is *committed* to some picture of what he considers reality—and to what he thinks society considers reality—and he observes and judges the patient's behavior in the light of these considerations. This touches on our earlier observation that the notion of mental symptom itself implies a comparison between observer and observed, psychiatrist and patient. This is so obvious that I may be charged with belaboring trivialities. Let me therefore say once more that my aim in presenting this argument was expressly to criticize and counter a prevailing contemporary tendency to deny the moral aspects of psychiatry (and psychotherapy) and to substitute for them allegedly valuefree medical considerations. Psychotherapy, for example, is being widely practiced as though it entailed nothing other than restoring the patient from a state of mental sickness to one of mental health. While it is generally accepted that mental illness has something to do with man's social (or interpersonal) relations, it is paradoxically maintained that problems of values (that is, of ethics) do not arise in this process.[1] Yet, in one sense, much of psychotherapy may revolve around nothing other than the elucidation and weighing of goals and values—many of which may be mutually contradictory—and the means whereby they might best be harmonized, realized, or relinquished.

The diversity of human values and the methods by means of which they may be realized is so vast, and many of them remain so unacknowledged, that they cannot fail but lead to conflicts in human relations. Indeed, to say that human relations at all levels—from mother to child, through husband and wife, to nation and nation—are fraught with stress, strain, and disharmony is, once again, making the obvious explicit. Yet, what may be obvious may be also poorly understood.

This I think is the case here. For it seems to me that — at least in our scientific theories of behavior—we have failed to *accept* the simple fact that human relations are inherently fraught with difficulties and that to make them even relatively harmonious requires much patience and hard work. I submit that the idea of mental illness is now being put to work to obscure certain difficulties which at present may be inherent—not that they need be unmodifiable—in the social intercourse of persons. If this is true, the concept functions as a disguise; for instead of calling attention to conflicting human needs, aspirations, and values, the notion of mental illness provides an amoral and impersonal "thing" (an "illness") as an explanation for *problems in living* (Szasz, 1959). We may recall in this connection that not so long ago it was devils and witches who were held responsible for men's problems in social living. The belief in mental illness, as something other than man's trouble in getting along with his fellow man, is the proper heir to the belief in demonology and witchcraft. Mental illness exists or is "real" in exactly the same sense in which witches existed or were "real."

Choice, Responsibility, and Psychiatry

While I have argued that mental illnesses do not exist, I obviously did not imply that the social and psychological occurrences to which this label is currently being attached also do not exist. Like the personal and social troubles which people had in the Middle Ages, they are real enough. It is the labels we give them that concerns us and, having labeled them, what we do about them. While I cannot go into the ramified implications of this problem here, it is worth noting that a demonologic conception of problems in living gave rise to therapy along theological lines. Today, a belief in mental illness implies—nay, requires—therapy along medical or psychotherapeutic lines.

What is implied in the line of thought set forth here is something quite different. I do not intend to offer a new conception of "psychiatric illness" nor a new form of "therapy." My aim is more modest and yet also more ambitious. It is to suggest that the phenomena now called mental illnesses be looked at afresh and more simply, that they be removed from the category of illnesses, and that they be regarded as the expressions of man's struggle with the problem of *how* he should live. The last mentioned problem is obviously a vast one, its enormity reflecting not only man's inability to cope with his environment, but even more his increasing self-reflectiveness.

By problems in living, then, I refer to that truly explosive chain reaction which began with man's fall from divine grace by partaking of the fruit of the tree of knowledge. Man's awareness of himself and of the world about him seems to be a steadily expanding one, bringing in its wake an ever larger *burden of understanding* (an expression borrowed from Susanne Langer, 1953). *This burden*, then, *is to be expected and must not be misinterpreted*. Our only *rational* means for lightening it is *more understanding,* and appropriate *action* based on such understanding. The main alternative lies in acting as though the burden were not what in fact we perceive it to be and taking refuge in an outmoded theological view of man. In the latter view, man does not fashion his life and much of his world about him, but merely lives out his fate in a world created by superior beings. This may logically lead to pleading nonresponsibility in the face of seemingly unfathomable problems and difficulties. Yet, if man fails to take increasing responsibility for his actions, individually as well as collectively, it seems unlikely that some higher power or being would assume this task and carry this burden for him. Moreover, this seems hardly the proper time in human history for obscuring the issue of man's responsibility for his actions by hiding it behind the skirt of an all-explaining conception of mental illness.

Conclusions

I have tried to show that the notion of mental illness has outlived whatever usefulness it might have had and that it now functions merely as a convenient myth. As such, it is a true heir to religious myths in general, and to the belief in witchcraft in particular; the role of all these belief-systems was to act as *social tranquilizers*, thus encouraging the hope that mastery of certain specific problems may be achieved by means of substitutive (symbolic-magical) operations. The notion of mental illness thus serves mainly to obscure the everyday fact that life for most people is a continuous struggle, not for biological survival, but for a "place in the sun," "peace of mind," or some other human value. For man aware of himself and of the world about him, once the needs for preserving the body (and perhaps the race) are more or less satisfied, the problem arises as to what he should

do with himself. Sustained adherence to the myth of mental illness allows people to avoid facing this problem, believing that mental health, conceived as the absence of mental illness, automatically insures the making of right and safe choices in one's conduct of life. But the facts are all the other way. It is the making of good choices in life that others regard, retrospectively, as good mental health!

The myth of mental illness encourages us, moreover, to believe in its logical corollary: that social intercourse would be harmonious, satisfying, and the secure basis of a "good life" were it not for the disrupting influences of mental illness or "psychopathology." The potentiality for universal human happiness, in this form at least, seems to me but another example of the I-wish-it-were-true type of fantasy. I do not believe that human happiness or well-being on a hitherto unimaginably large scale, and not just for a select few, is possible. This goal could be achieved, however, only at the cost of many men, and not just a few being willing and able to tackle their personal, social, and ethical conflicts. This means having the courage and integrity to forego waging battles on false fronts, finding solutions for substitute problems—for instance, fighting the battle of stomach acid and chronic fatigue instead of facing up to a marital conflict.

Our adversaries are not demons, witches, fate, or mental illness. We have no enemy whom we can fight, exorcise, or dispel by "cure." What we do have are *problems in living*—whether these be biological, economic, political, or sociopsychological. In this essay I was concerned only with problems belonging in the last mentioned category, and within this group mainly with those pertaining to moral values. The field to which modern psychiatry addresses itself is vast, and I made no effort to encompass it all. My argument was limited to the proposition that mental illness is a myth, whose function it is to disguise and thus render more palatable the bitter pill of moral conflicts in human relations.

Note

1. Freud went so far as to say that: "I consider ethics to be taken for granted. Actually I have never done a mean thing" (Jones, 1957, p. 247). This surely is a strange thing to say for someone who has studied man as a social being as closely as did Freud. I mention it here to show how the notion of "illness" (in the case of psychoanalysis, "psychopathology," or "mental illness") was used by Freud—and by most of his followers—as a means for classifying certain forms of human behavior as falling within the scope of medicine, and hence (by *fiat*) outside that of ethics!

DECISION SCENARIOS

The questions following each decision scenario are intended to prompt reflection and discussion. In deciding how to answer them, you should consider the information provided in the Social Context and Case Presentations, as well as in the Briefing Session. You should also make use of the ethical theories and principles presented in Part VI: Foundations of Bioethics, and the arguments offered in the relevant readings in this chapter.

DECISION SCENARIO 1

Gender and Clinical Trials

"The next drug is an antibody-based HIV treatment," Clark Skolnick said, clicking to a new slide in his presentation. "We call it acytotropa, and we think it can be used long term. We've done safety testing and Phase I trials, and we're partnering with Gay Men's Health Crisis to recruit a cohort for large-scale clinical testing."

"Are they going to include women in the cohort?" asked Marta Jiménez, looking up from her laptop:

"We've asked them not to. We don't want the liability risk of some subjects becoming pregnant. We don't know what the drug might do to a fetus."

"But women make up a quarter of the HIV-positive population."

"Look, we know that women, including plenty of pregnant women, get HIV, and that most of them get it through heterosexual sex." Skolnick grimaced and closed down his PowerPoint. "If we were really targeting at-risk groups we'd actively recruit more straight people, IV-drug users, the incarcerated, and so on. But this trial has to come in under budget, and since it's privately funded we're under no obligation to cast a wider net."

"But how will you know that the drug will work for women?" Jiménez said.

"We'll extrapolate from the male subjects. If problems do come up when the drug goes on the market, we can always adjust the dosage for women then."

"So you'll be essentially conducting an uncontrolled post-market trial?"

"It wouldn't be the first time."

1. Is pregnancy risk a sufficient reason to exclude women from clinical trials? Should female subjects be required to show proof of reliable birth control? Should male subjects face similar requirements to avoid genetic harm to potential offspring?

2. Should HIV drug trials make an effort to recruit at-risk populations?

3. Should drugs marketed to the general public be tested on all subpopulations that might respond differently to them? Should this be required by law?

DECISION SCENARIO 2

Racism and Patient Autonomy

In the fall of 2013, Tonya Battle was a registered nurse in the neonatal intensive care unit at Hurley Medical Center in Flint, Michigan, where she had worked for twenty-five years. Battle was at an infant's bedside when an unfamiliar man walked into the NICU and reached for the child.

"Hi, I'm Tonya and I'm taking care of your baby. Can I see your band?" Battle recalled asking the man, referring to the identification band issued to parents.

"I need to see your supervisor," the man replied. Battle directed him to her charge nurse, who returned a few moments later and told Battle she would no longer be caring for the baby. The charge nurse said the man had demanded that no African American nurses care for his child and had rolled up his sleeve to reveal a swastika tattoo.

"I just was really dumbfounded," Battle said. "I couldn't believe that's why he was so angry." Battle was even more dumbfounded when a note appeared on the baby's medical chart that read, "Please, no African-American nurses to care for... baby per dad's request." Although the note was later removed, no African American nurses were assigned to the child for over a month, according to lawsuits filed by Battle and three other black nurses. In February 2014, Hurley settled Battle's lawsuit for $200,000.

1. The American Medical Association's 2001 code of ethics prohibits physicians from refusing to treat patients based on race, gender, or sexual orientation. But studies suggest that patients' requests for different providers based on racial and other prejudices are common and frequently honored. How might honoring such requests be justified in the service of a good therapeutic bond?

2. Defenders of accommodating patient prejudices argue that doing otherwise is akin to a firefighter assessing the moral worth of a homeowner before putting out a fire. They argue that respect for patient autonomy requires granting patients the care they request, no matter how repugnant their views. Might there be other reasons to refuse such requests, including their potential to create a "hostile work environment"?

3. A patient's belief that some providers are evil wizards or androids would likely not be accommodated in most hospitals, and would likely prompt a psychiatric evaluation. Does accommodating racist beliefs, rather than treating them as psychiatric issues, grant them undue legitimacy?

DECISION SCENARIO 3

Pregnancy and Cocaine

In 1999, a South Carolina woman named Regina McKnight delivered a stillborn baby girl she had planned to name Mercedes. Although evidence later suggested that the sole cause of the stillbirth was likely a severe infection of the amniotic fluid and umbilical cord, McKnight was arrested for homicide by child abuse after she tested positive for cocaine use. After fifteen minutes of deliberation, a jury found her guilty and she was sentenced to twelve years in prison.

In 2008, the South Carolina Supreme Court unanimously overturned McKnight's conviction, concluding that the state had relied on "outdated" evidence to support the conclusion that her cocaine use had caused the stillbirth. An adequate defense, the Court concluded, should have introduced "recent studies showing that cocaine is no more harmful to a fetus than nicotine use, poor nutrition, lack of prenatal care, or other conditions commonly associated with the urban poor." To avoid being retried, McKnight pleaded guilty to manslaughter and was released, having already served eight years of her original sentence.

1. Although cocaine use during pregnancy has been linked to low birth weight and premature birth, research shows that it typically has fewer long-term risks for a fetus than alcohol use, and instead poses risks comparable to those associated with cigarette smoking and poor prenatal nutrition. Should these last two behaviors also be grounds for "fetal child abuse" charges, if a miscarriage or stillbirth occurs?

2. Eighteen states treat substance abuse during pregnancy as child abuse, and some use it as grounds for civil commitment of pregnant women. (See Chapter 1 for more.) Despite evidence that alcohol has significantly worse effects on fetal development, prosecutors in these states have tended to focus on pregnant cocaine users, especially African American women such as Regina McKnight. Does the illegality of cocaine use justify this differential treatment? Or should such prosecutions, if they are justified at all, be based on the relative risk of harm to the fetus?

3. Research suggests that smoking, drinking, drug use, and toxic exposures can damage men's sperm and increase the likelihood of birth defects in their offspring. If society aims to prevent harms to the unborn, should these behaviors be legally regulated for men who are attempting or planning to have children?

DECISION SCENARIO 4

Gender Dysphoria?

"You're in perfect health, Kai. I wish all my patients took such good care of themselves." Amy Okoro clicked out of Kai Selden's chart. "Unless there's anything else, I probably won't see you before next year's physical."

"There is actually something, Dr. Okoro." Kai Selden slipped on his jacket and began straightening his tie in the mirror. "I've finally decided that I'm ready to try hormone treatments. I still don't know about surgery, but I've lived as a man long enough to know I'm ready to take the next step."

"I know you've considered physical transition for years and researched potential side effects," Okoro said. "So I'd be happy to prescribe an initial course of hormones. There is just one thing." Okoro sat down again and opened her laptop. "For any chance of insurance coverage, I'll need to refer you to a psychiatrist who can give you a diagnosis of 'gender dysphoria.' It's just a formality, but the cost difference can be huge."

"I thought you might say that." Selden sighed. "Don't get me wrong, I'm grateful that my insurance might cover this. But I'm a pretty happy person. I have an amazing wife and a job I love. The only thing I feel 'dysphoric' about is when teenagers threaten me on the subway or when waiters question my right to use the men's room."

"I understand your frustration," said Okoro. "But the latest *DSM* also makes it clear that being transgender isn't a mental illness."

"I know. I just wish I didn't have to be diagnosed with one to pay for hormones. I think it's society that is sick, not me."

1. The American Psychiatric Association has explicitly stated that being transgender is a social difference rather than a disease. Should there still be a diagnostic category associated with it in the *DSM*?

2. In contrast to famous examples such as Caitlyn Jenner and Laverne Cox, most transgender people who seek physical transition struggle to cover the costs. Even if being transgender is no longer deemed an illness, should society provide transitional support for those who don't fit easily into its current categories of sex and gender?

3. Assess Kai Selden's claim that the real sickness lies in society's rigid gender norms. Is it possible to separate definitions of illness from social values?

DECISION SCENARIO 5

Neurodiversity?

"Has Korvin received any treatment since his autism spectrum diagnosis?" Dr. Colin Lafram gazed through a one-way mirror into the room where seven-year-old Korvin Car was showing a therapist a map of the Tokyo subway system.

"No, and I don't believe he needs it," said Korvin's father, Szafir Car. "Autism is a valuable part of human diversity. Why do you doctors insist on trying to make him 'normal,' if he's happy the way he is?"

"Maybe 'normal' isn't the goal," said Lafram. "But we would like Korvin to see a behavioral therapist for his communication and social delays. We could also treat his anxiety attacks with antidepressants."

"He only gets anxious when other kids pick on him for being different," Car said. "Listen, Korvin knows more about public transportation than most experts in the field, and he notices patterns and details in the world that would never occur to you or me. Why insist that he's 'delayed' just because he doesn't make eye contact when he talks?"

"I respect your opinion, Mr. Car. You're right that Korvin will probably always be different from

other children, and in many ways that is a gift. But without treatment, he could fall behind and have serious difficulties relating to his peers and teachers." Lafram turned to face Car. "What if we approach therapy as a way to supplement, rather than replace, Korvin's current interests and social style? We won't try to 'normalize' him, just broaden his range."

"Maybe. I'll need to think it over."

1. Neurological diversity advocates like Car contend that dyslexia, ADHD, and autism provide as many gifts as impairments. Evaluate this argument. Can it be extended to the more severe forms of autism and other cognitive disabilities?

2. The prominent writer and animal scientist Temple Grandin argues that individuals on the autistic spectrum can make uniquely valuable social contributions because their brains are "wired differently." But she also says that her own autism would have prevented her from engaging with the world, if not for the intervention of speech therapy and drugs. Does Grandin's perspective reflect a medical or social model of disability, or something in between? (See this chapter's Briefing Session for more.)

DECISION SCENARIO **6**

Race-Based Medicine?

"The idea of a drug for a specific race isn't just racist, it's absurd," Chao Zhou said. "We all belong to the human race, and we've been exchanging genes for millennia. It's the dominant group in a society that introduces racial distinctions so that it can exert social control over the 'inferior' races."

"Wait a minute, Chao," Mona Solarin said. "Sure, race is a social and political construct. But people with ancestors from the same regions often share specific clusters of genes." She smiled. "No doubt we all came from Africa thousands of years ago, but my grandfather left the continent just forty years ago."

"Yeah, but you've also got a Latino grandparent," Chao said. "That's my point."

"No, it's not," Mona said. "It's mine. Way more of my ancestors came from sub-Saharan Africa than from Latin America. That puts me at higher risk, on average, for sickle-cell disease than Asians or whites, because there is more malaria in Africa." She held up a finger before Zhou could respond. "For the same reason, it's not absurd to think that some drugs might be more likely to benefit me more than they would people from other groups."

1. Suppose a clinical trial for the (imaginary) drug Colesta shows it to be significantly more effective in lowering cholesterol in self-identified Chinese Americans than in any other segment of the population—although all sub-groups receive some benefit. Also, Colesta seems more effective for Chinese Americans than any other cholesterol-lowering drug. Is there any good reason, besides "niche marketing," to limit Colesta prescriptions to Chinese Americans?

2. Making the same assumptions, would it be morally legitimate to deny everyone, including Chinese Americans, access to Colesta on the grounds that race has no biological legitimacy and it is socially harmful to foster such divisions?

Chapter 11

The Challenge of Global Bioethics

CHAPTER CONTENTS

CASES AND CONTEXTS

"The Devil's Experiment": STD Research in Guatemala

Her name was Berta. She was a patient at the National Psychiatric Hospital in Guatemala City, Guatemala. In February 1948, researchers injected her with syphilis spirochetes to study the course of the disease. After a month, they noted that Berta had developed red bumps on her left arm near the injection site, as well as lesions on her arms and legs. After a few more weeks, her skin began to sag and atrophy. Three months after her exposure, the researchers decided to treat the syphilis they had caused, but by that time it was too late. Berta was in the process of dying, for reasons the researchers did not record.

Instead, they decided to study the effect of additional infections on Berta's ailing body. On August 23, they took gonorrhea-infected pus from another research subject and injected it into Berta's eyes, urethra, and rectum. They also reinfected her with syphilis. Several days later, they noted that Berta's eyes had filled with gonorrheal pus and that she was bleeding from her urethra. On August 27, the researchers made note of Berta's death.

Reading the record of Berta's final months, it would be easy to assume that hers was an isolated case involving rogue scientists in the employ of a lawless dictatorship. But, in fact, Berta was one of 1,308 Guatemalan research subjects who were, without their knowledge or consent, deliberately infected with syphilis, gonorrhea, and other sexually transmitted diseases (STDs), as part of a large study funded by the U.S. National Institute of Health. The study, which involved Guatemalan soldiers, prisoners, sex workers, psychiatric patients, and orphans, was carried out by researchers from the U.S. Public Health Service from 1945 to 1956, with the full backing of U.S. health officials, including the surgeon general. The ostensible goal of the research was to determine the effectiveness of the topical agent orvus-mapharsen, as well as penicillin, in preventing or treating STD infections. Nevertheless, records show

that only about half of those deliberately infected received any treatment, and eighty-three of the research subjects had died by the study's conclusion. No effort was made to obtain informed consent from participants, but the study's director, John C. Cutler, was convinced that this approach was justified by the larger benefits to public health—a conviction he maintained a decade later in his work as a lead investigator for the Tuskegee Syphilis Study. (See Case Presentation: Bad Blood, Bad Faith in Chapter 10.) Even as the original treatment-focused goals of the Guatemala studies fell away, Cutler argued that the policy of deliberate infections was justified by "the opportunity offered here to study syphilis from the standpoint of pure science."

Prisoners and Precedents

In 1943, the United States was in desperate need of a better scientific understanding of STDs. With hundreds of thousands of American troops overseas, the National Research Council estimated that each year they were contracting 350,000 new cases of gonorrhea, many of them the result of men patronizing sex workers. The military cost of these infections was the estimated equivalent of losing two full armored divisions every year, and the financial cost of treating them over $34 million. The military and financial costs of other STDs, such as syphilis, had also been a primary focus of the U.S. surgeon general, Thomas Parran.

Under these circumstances, prophylactic and other treatments for STDs became a top priority for the U.S. government, especially in its Public Health Service (PHS), Committee on Medical Research (CMR), and Office of Scientific Research and Development (OSRD). Working with academic researchers, the leaders of these organizations developed a plan to study prophylactic STD treatments on prisoners at the U.S. Penitentiary in Terre Haute, Indiana.

The experiments would involve the deliberate infection of incarcerated volunteers, but only, health officials emphasized, "after the risks have been fully explained and after signed statements have been obtained." In other words, the volunteers had to give what we now think of as informed consent—although cash stipends and letters of commendation for parole may have compromised it. (See Social Context: Prisoners as Test Subjects? in Chapter 2.)

The Terre Haute study was led by high-ranking PHS officials, including John F. Mahoney and his subordinate John Cutler, who was just twenty-eight years old. Mahoney and Cutler soon encountered serious challenges in their project at Terre Haute. The main problem was that none of their techniques for exposing prisoners to STDs was sufficiently effective or reliable to test prophylactic treatments. In particular, none was as effective as "the natural method of infection—sexual intercourse," the researchers noted.

By 1944, the Terre Haute research had to be abandoned, but its failure set the stage for the research that many of the same U.S. health officials would initiate three years later in Guatemala. In particular, it motivated researchers such as Cutler to focus on alternative methods of infecting subjects with gonorrhea, syphilis, and chancroid (another genital infection). This would come to include spinal injections, genital abrasions, and the use of Guatemalan sex workers to inoculate research subjects—all controversial methods that likely contributed to the secrecy surrounding the later study. This secrecy also contributed to the abandonment of a key element of the Terre Haute study: the informed consent of research subjects.

The "Natural Method"

In 1946, the surgeon general and the National Research Council approved an initial grant for a "Guatemala study dealing with the experimental transmission of syphilis to human volunteers." The study was to be led by Cutler, with a staff of surgeons, serologists, and bacteriologists from the PHS, and it was based in a specially constructed new Venereal Disease Research Laboratory in the heart of Guatemala City.

Like the Terre Haute study, the Guatemalan research was originally supposed to test improved diagnostic and prophylactic techniques for STDs, and Cutler presented it as such to Guatemalan officials. But like the earlier research, it soon became focused on the basic problem of reliably achieving STD infections.

Some of the first experiments that Cutler directed in Guatemala City involved efforts to use the "natural method" to infect research subjects. Cutler's team exposed female sex workers to powerful strains of gonorrhea or syphilis, then paid them to have sex with prisoners or low-ranking soldiers. The study's records show that some of these sex workers were as young as sixteen and that some were instructed to have sex with as many as eight soldiers in just over an hour.

According to the Presidential Bioethics Commission that studied the Guatemalan experiments, few to none of the exposed sex workers, prisoners, or soldiers knew they were being intentionally infected with STDs. Indeed, the record shows that top U.S. health officials were well aware that the original plan for informed "volunteer groups" had been quickly abandoned by Cutler's team. Senior PHS and NIH officials such as Richard Arnold, Cassius Van Slyke, John Heller, and John Mahoney visited Guatemala to observe the intentional exposure experiments and advised Cutler about how many clients the sex workers should see per day to maximize transmission rates. But none of the study's funders or supervisors appear to have questioned the subject's lack of informed consent. Indeed, Cutler reported telling Guatemalan patients and officials that "the treatment is a new one utilizing serum followed by penicillin," while acknowledging in the same letter that this was "double talk" designed to conceal the policy of deliberate STD infection.

Nevertheless, the U.S. officials were fully aware that the experiments could sound ethical alarm bells, and they often discussed the need for secrecy. Cutler wrote that "it was deemed advisable, from the point of view of public and personnel relations, to work so as few people as possible know the experimental procedure." Surgeon General Parran endorsed the project and was regularly briefed on "all the arrangements," but also noted the potential for scandal, joking to the PHS official who kept him updated, "You know, we couldn't do such an experiment in this country."

Artificial Inoculation

Despite the support of top U.S. health officials, Cutler and his colleagues soon encountered problems. Their primary challenge was that even with the "natural" method of exposure, gonorrhea and syphilis infection rates were still too low for effective study of prophylactic treatments. So they began to devise alternative methods of artificial inoculation, in an effort to raise infection rates. These included the introduction of syphilis spirochetes through intravenous injections, as well as through punctures at the base of the skull—a procedure which left one subject paralyzed and several others with bacterial meningitis. They also began to abrade and scarify subjects' genitals before coating them with emulsions containing syphilis or gonorrhea, or inserting toothpicks soaked in such emulsions deep into subjects' urethras. The team also expanded their research pool to psychiatric patients such as Berta, after Cutler grew frustrated by "Indians" in the prison system whom he deemed too "uneducated and superstitious" to fully cooperate.

With all these vulnerable populations, Cutler's team "told patients little to nothing and used no consent forms," according to the Presidential Bioethics Commission. Although Cutler obtained informal permission from institutional directors and commanding officers, it appears that these agreements were usually about serum-based "treatments" or vaccinations, rather than about the practice of intentional exposure. The study's records show that only about half of those intentionally infected were followed or offered treatment for the STDs to which the researchers had exposed them.

Take, for example, the experience of Federico Ramos. In 1948, Ramos was a low-ranking soldier in the Guatemalan army and was ordered to report to a clinic run by U.S. physicians. At the clinic, the physicians gave him an unidentified injection and had him return for several more over the next few months. Soon afterward, Ramos began to experience episodes of pain and bleeding with urination, among other symptoms. It was not until two decades later, however, that he was finally diagnosed with syphilis and gonorrhea and received treatment. In the meantime, he had returned to his remote village and infected his wife, who passed on the diseases to the couple's children. Ramos and his family blame the United States for their decades of STD symptoms.

"My father didn't know how to read and they treated him like an animal," said Ramos's son Benjamin. "This was the devil's experiment."

Ethically Impossible

In 1947, the ruling in the Nazi doctors' trial at Nuremberg put a spotlight on nonconsensual medical research with the potential to cause suffering and lasting harm. That spring, a prominent *New York Times* health reporter, unaware of the Guatemalan experiments, dismissed the idea that anyone would "shoot living syphilis germs into human bodies" as "ethically impossible."

These developments alarmed Cutler, who wrote his colleagues about the increased need to limit information about the Guatemalan research to those "who can be trusted not to talk." Cutler's supervisor Richard Arnold raised particular concern about the nonconsensual character of Cutler's "experiment with the insane people" and suggested that in subsequent reports there was "no reason to say where the work was done and the type of volunteer." In February 1948, Surgeon General Parran was replaced, and Cutler was advised by his superiors to "get our ducks in line" and to start winding down the research. By the time Cutler left Guatemala by the end of that year, the study had reached few of its original objectives and was buried by the PHS. The final reports on the study were labeled "SECRET-CONFIDENTIAL" and edited to remove the researchers' names.

Despite the failure of the Guatemala project, John Cutler went on to flourish in the field of public health, becoming assistant surgeon general in 1958 and holding prestigious appointments at the University of Pittsburgh for the better part of three decades. His career was tarnished only by the revelation of his prominent role in the Tuskegee syphilis study during the 1960s, work he continued to defend up until his death in 2003. By contrast, Cutler hid evidence of the Guatemala STD study, and when he did cite data from it in published papers, he pretended it had come from other studies.

A Cautionary Tale

In 2005, the Wellesley College historian Susan Reverby was researching a book on Tuskegee when she discovered evidence of the Guatemala STD studies in Cutler's and Parran's papers. The public revelation of the study's methods led to an international outcry and a formal apology by President Obama to Guatemala's President Álvaro Colom. Many prominent bioethicists compared the U.S. researchers' actions to those of the Nazi physicians and argued they were significantly worse than the abuses of Tuskegee study. (In the latter case, researchers withheld treatment from hundreds of African American men who already had syphilis, but they did not deliberately infect them with the disease.)

In 2011, a special Presidential Commission for the Study of Bioethical Issues published a landmark report, based on 125,000 documents associated with the Guatemala research as well as a fact-finding trip to the region. The commission concluded that the experiments involved "unconscionable basic violations of ethics, even as judged against the researchers' own recognition of the requirements of the medical ethics of the day." It called the events in Guatemala a "cautionary tale of how the quest for scientific knowledge without regard to relevant ethical standards can blind researchers to the humanity of the people they enlist into research."

Despite the Presidential Commission's detailed review of the extant documents, many questions remain about the Guatemala STD studies. For example, due to omissions in the records the researchers left behind, it remains unclear how many of the eighty-three subject deaths that occurred during the study may have been caused by the deliberate inoculation policy, and how many by preexisting illnesses, such as tuberculosis. There are also conflicting reports about whether or not children from the national orphanage were deliberately exposed to STDs—although it is well established that these orphans (some as young as nine) were used in serological experiments conducted by the researchers to develop better diagnostic tools for STDs.

Contextual Ethics

Perhaps the most persistent questions about the experiments are those regarding the motivations and beliefs of the U.S. health officials and researchers.

For although there is extensive evidence that they knew their actions might violate evolving ethical norms in the United States, there is also evidence that they believed that they were making important and beneficent contributions to human health in Guatemala and beyond.

Cutler and his colleagues did help the Guatemalan military establish its own STD treatment program, and they provided free medical care to 140 Guatemalans with malaria, tuberculosis (TB), and preexisting STDs who would otherwise not have been treated. Indeed, Cutler believed his intentional STD exposure methods were "worthwhile and justified" on the grounds that "we now have given them a program of care for venereal disease, which they have lacked in the past."

A fundamental assumption of this perspective, one shared by Cutler and his superiors, is that bioethical standards that apply in the United States need not apply in places like Guatemala, so long as benefit is being provided. This issue remains relevant today, as an increasing share of U.S. biomedical research takes place abroad, often in countries with high rates of poverty and disease. (A 2010 study by the U.S. Department of Health and Human Services found that 80 percent of new drug applications relied on clinical trial data from other countries.) In recent years, questions have arisen about whether trial subjects in developing nations are providing fully informed consent and whether they are being exposed to risks that would not be taken in the developed world. In some controversial cases, destitute research subjects have been given placebos or experimental drugs that would not have been allowed in studies conducted in richer countries. (See Case Presentation: Clinical Trials in the Developing World.)

For their part, many Guatemalans see the STD studies as just one part of their nation's long and painful history with the United States. They point out that in the 1940s, Guatemala was the quintessential "banana republic," with much of its land and government effectively controlled by a single U.S. company, United Fruit. In 1954, the CIA deposed Guatemala's democratically elected president when he threatened the company's interests, and the country was run by a series of U.S.-backed military dictatorships for the next forty years. Human rights groups estimate those governments murdered more than two hundred thousand of their political opponents and engaged in ethnic cleansing of Mayans and other indigenous groups. In light of this history, many Guatemalans view the STD experiments as simply one more example of U.S. hemispheric imperialism and racism. They tend to see the "good intentions" of Cutler and others in the context of America's Cold War objectives.

Envoi

A month after the Presidential Commission for the Study of Bioethical Issues released its report in 2011, the Guatemalan government issued its own report on the STD research. The Guatemalan Presidential Commission found evidence of explicit and conscious racism in the Cutler teams' approach to indigenous research subjects and called the experiments "a crime against humanity" rooted in Guatemala's subordinate position vis-à-vis the United States. The report called for reparation and compensation for the survivors of the experiments, a request the United States has so far not honored. Nevertheless, in the wake of the report, the U.S. Department of Health and Human Services announced a $1.8 million grant to improve treatment and prevention of HIV and other STDs in Guatemala, and to improve human subjects protections there.

In April 2015, nearly 800 Guatemalan plaintiffs filed a billion-dollar lawsuit against Johns Hopkins University and the Rockefeller Foundation, both of which employed many of the officials who approved and implemented the Guatemala experiments. The suit alleges that both institutions had "substantial influence" over the design and implementation of the research, something that the defendants deny.

No matter how these disputes between the two countries are resolved, it is clear that the Guatemala STD studies will cast a long shadow in discussions of bioethics and international relations. Like the Tuskegee experiments (and, indeed, the Nuremberg trials), they demonstrate how scientific zeal and a belief in one's good intentions are insufficient for the ethical practice of medical research.

CASE PRESENTATION
Clinical Trials in the Developing World

In 1995, the National Institutes of Health and the Centers for Disease Control and Prevention initiated a series of clinical trials in developing countries with the aim of reducing HIV transmission from pregnant women to their fetuses or newborn babies. The studies involved 12,211 women in five African countries, Thailand, and the Dominican Republic.

From the start, the trials generated fierce controversy and serious ethical debate. At issue, among other questions, was whether human subjects protections and standards of care required in richer countries had to be employed in poorer countries, where such protections and such care were generally not available.

Regimen 076

When it came to preventing HIV transmission during pregnancy and birth, the "gold standard" had already been established by the early 1990s. The results of clinical trials conducted in the United States and reported in 1994 showed that if pregnant women testing positive for HIV followed a treatment regimen using the drug zidovudine (ZDV, previously called AZT), the risk of the virus being transmitted to their children was reduced by almost two-thirds. The chance of untreated HIV-positive women passing on the virus is about 25 percent, but when the women were treated with ZDV, the transmission rate dropped to around 8 percent. By employing ZDV and other anti-retroviral treatment regimens, many developed nations have been able to reduce the number of babies born with HIV to less than fifty a year.

The ZDV protocol requires women to take the drug during the last twelve weeks of their pregnancy, then receive an intravenous dose of it during delivery. The newborns are given the drug for the first six weeks of their lives. Because the federal study establishing the effectiveness of this treatment was assigned the number 076, the treatment is referred to as the 076 regimen.

A Thousand HIV-Positive Babies a Day

UNICEF estimates that in the world as a whole, about one thousand HIV-positive babies are born every day. Most of them are born in countries whose citizens are too poor to afford the high-priced treatments that could lower this number substantially. In the 1990s, the 076 regimen cost about $1,000, putting it out of the reach of most people in the developing world.

Aside from the expense of the drug, other factors stood in the way of using the 076 regimen in underdeveloped countries. Many of these countries lacked a sufficient number of hospitals and the equipment needed to administer ZDV intravenously during delivery. Also, most mothers in non-industrialized countries breast-feed their babies, and though generally the practice is beneficial to the infant, the HIV virus can be transmitted through breast milk. Yet feeding infants prepared formula not only often goes against custom, but costs more than most women can afford.

Against this backdrop, representatives of the World Health Organization (WHO), the United Nations, the National Institutes of Health (NIH), and the Centers for Disease Control and Prevention (CDC) met in Geneva in 1994 to design clinical trials to determine whether any short-term regimen using oral doses of ZDV could be effective in reducing the maternal–fetal transmission ("vertical transmission") of the HIV virus. A short-term course of oral medication would be both cheaper and easier to administer than the standard regimen used in richer countries.

How Should Effectiveness Be Judged?

Having decided to test short-term ZDV regimens, the trial organizers in Geneva faced a second question. What comparison group should be used to judge the effectiveness of the experimental regimens? One possibility would be to compare them to 076. In the developed world, most trials compare experimental treatments to the current standard of care, which in richer countries was 076. This option was rejected by the Geneva group, however. In their view, administering 076 to women who might benefit from it in the countries involved was not a realistic prospect, due to financial and logistical factors.

Alternatively, the experimental treatments might be compared to the current standard of care in the countries where the trials would be conducted. But the difficulty

with this approach was that this standard treatment was frequently nonexistent in these countries. In many, if not most, cases, HIV-positive pregnant women received no care at all. Thus, the Geneva group ultimately decided that results of the clinical trials involving different doses of zidovudine could best be judged by comparing them with the results obtained by administering a substance with no known therapeutic value—that is, with a *placebo*.

Tests involving placebos in the United States have become rare when a potentially lethal or disabling disease is involved. The principle is generally accepted that patients deserve to receive treatments that represent the accepted standard of medical care for their condition. Experimental treatments must show promise of being superior in at least some respects to the standard of care, or there is no justification for employing them. (The idea that there should be genuine uncertainty about whether the experimental or standard treatment is better is often called *clinical equipoise,* discussed in greater detail in Chapter 2.) Based on these ethical considerations, the results of a test of an experimental treatment are generally compared with the results of the standard treatment, at least in publicly funded research.

The Geneva group, however, took the standard of care for preventing vertical HIV transmission to be that for the countries in which the test would be conducted, not the standard of care in North America or Western Europe. Because HIV-positive pregnant women in those countries would typically receive no treatment, the planners reasoned that women receiving placebos would be no worse off than otherwise. Indeed, because even those in the placebo group would be provided with free general health care, they would gain benefits they wouldn't ordinarily receive.

Use of Placebos Challenged

The decision to give placebos to about half the women in the ZDV study was controversial from the beginning. Marc Lallemant, an NIH-sponsored investigator working in Thailand, refused to administer them to his patients. CDC researchers in the Ivory Coast wrote to the agency's headquarters to report that their African collaborators did not feel comfortable giving patients placebos. Critics estimated that because of the deliberate withholding of a known and effective treatment, more than one thousand babies would become HIV positive who might have escaped infection.

"We have turned our backs on these mothers and their babies," said Peter Lurie of Public Citizen, the consumer rights organization. The group also wrote to the secretary of health and human services, Donna Shalala, and demanded that the clinical trial be redesigned to eliminate placebos. Instead, the group argued, a short course of ZDV should be compared with the 076 regimen, despite the higher cost this would entail. Because ZDV is known to be effective against HIV and in reducing vertical transmission of the virus, all women in the trial would at least be receiving doses of a drug appropriate as a treatment for their disease.

The head of the CDC's AIDS program, Helene Gayle, defended the clinical trial as it was designed. "This was done with a lot of discussion from the international community, following international codes of ethics," she said. "Part of doing ethical trials is that you are answering questions that are relevant for those countries."

Some physicians and officials in the countries involved also rejected the ethical questions being raised about the trials. Viewing the objections as a form of condescension, they saw them as suggesting that Africans were unable to decide what was in their best interest. "One has the impression that foreigners think that once white people arrive here they can impose what they want and we just accept it in ignorance," said Dr. Toussaint Sibailly of the Ivory Coast. "If that was once the case, those days are long past."

This view was supported by AIDS researchers Joseph Saba and Arthur Ammann. They suggested that yielding to critics and giving every pregnant woman some level of treatment with an effective drug would require extending the studies several more years. But with more than one thousand children a day becoming HIV infected, they suggested that such a delay was unacceptable. "Americans should not impose their standard of care on developing countries," they claimed.

Another Tuskegee?

In contrast to the defenders of the ZDV trials, Marcia Angell, executive editor of the *New England Journal of Medicine*, denounced the study in an editorial that compared it to the Tuskegee syphilis experiments. "Only when there is no known effective treatment is it ethical to compare a potential new treatment with a placebo," she wrote, adding in an interview that "Some of the same arguments that were made

in favor of the Tuskegee study many years ago are emerging in a new form in the [ZDV] studies in the third world."

Indeed, many of the investigators in the infamous Tuskegee syphilis study rationalized withholding effective treatment from their research subjects based on the assumption that poor African Americans in rural Alabama would be unlikely to receive such treatment even if they were not enrolled in the trial. Thus, the investigators argued, the fringe benefits of participating in the Tuskegee study made them better off than they would have been otherwise. (This assumption is questionable, however, since many of the Tuskegee subjects did obtain some treatment outside the study. See Case Presentation: The Tuskegee Syphilis Study in Chapter 10.)

At the same time, the Tuskegee researchers never told the participants that they were experimental subjects who might receive no relevant treatment for their disease. In this respect, at least, the ZDV clinical trials can be distinguished from the Tuskegee study, since the design of the ZDV trials required that participants be informed of their diagnosis and consent to treatment. Even given the requirement of informed consent, however, some observers questioned whether impoverished research subjects in underdeveloped countries had sufficient medical and technological knowledge to provide legitimate consent to a trial involving placebos.

Is Informed Consent Genuine?

Subsequent interviews with subjects in the ZDV trials indicated that some had agreed to participate with an inadequate understanding of the trial and its potential risks. After interviewing study participants in Abidjan, Ivory Coast, reporter Howard W. French concluded that "despite repeated explanations by project case workers, the understanding of these mostly poor and scantily educated subjects does not match the complexity of the ethical and scientific issues involved."

Even the informed consent of subjects who were better off and better educated was called into question. A thirty-one-year-old mother with a law degree, whom French interviewed, said that the researchers had not made it clear to her that ZDV was already known to be effective in controlling the transmission of HIV from mother to infant. How would she feel if she learned she had been in the placebo group? "I would say it was an injustice for sure," she told French.

Other participants appeared to see little problem with the use of placebos. "People are trying to help us," another mother in the study said. "And if a bunch of people have to die first, I am ready to risk my life too, so that other women and their babies survive. If I got the placebo, that will hurt for sure. But there is no evil involved."

An End to Placebos

On February 18, 1998, the Centers for Disease Control and Prevention announced that placebos would no longer be used in the ZDV clinical trials. The use was not discontinued for moral reasons, but because data showed that the use of about $80 worth of ZDV administered in the last four weeks of pregnancy could reduce transmission of the HIV virus by about 50 percent.

The decision was based on a study of 393 women in Thailand, some of whom received placebos. "We are very pleased," Philip Nieburg said. "The controversy was unfortunate, but we feel the placebo-controlled trial that we did was very necessary."

Sidney Wolfe, director of Public Citizen's Health Research Group, argued that the trial was unnecessary, because data supporting the outcome were already known from the trials of the 076 regimen. "This is inexcusable, sloppy research," he said. "They have wasted a large number of lives and a huge amount of money."

The Trovan Trial and Beyond

The elimination of placebos in the ZDV research was not the end of controversies surrounding informed consent and standards of care used in developing-world clinical trials. For example, in 2009, the pharmaceutical giant Pfizer agreed to pay $75 million to settle civil and criminal charges that it had illegally tested an experimental antibiotic on children during a 1996 meningitis outbreak in Nigeria. Subsequent investigations found that the antibiotic, trovafloxacin (sold as Trovan®), had not previously been tested on children and that Pfizer had not obtained permission from parents to treat their children with an experimental drug. (It was also determined that the company's certificate of approval from a hospital ethics board had been forged.)

The Pfizer trial compared trovafloxacin with the current standard of care for meningitis, ceftriaxone, but critics later charged that patients had been given insufficient doses of ceftriaxone, to improve the chances of a positive Trovan result. Pfizer argued that the eleven children who

died during the study (five on trovafloxacin and six on ceftriaxone) had all succumbed to the meningitis epidemic, which ultimately killed more than 15,000 Africans. Nevertheless, Trovan was later discontinued in the United States due to FDA concerns about its potential to cause acute (and sometimes fatal) liver damage. Many of the Nigerian children also showed signs of arthritis and tendon problems, which are associated with the entire class of powerful antibiotics (fluoroquinolones) to which trovafloxacin belongs. (See Decision Scenario: The Trovan Trial at the end of this chapter.)

Like the ZDV trial organizers, Pfizer representatives argued that subjects in the Trovan study were better off than the average patient. (The meningitis epidemic killed 10 percent of those infected in Nigeria, while only 5 percent of the trovafloxacin patients died.) Critics charged that the trial had exposed patients to unnecessary risks without their informed consent, especially given the fact that the aid group Doctors Without Borders was dispensing another standard-of-care meningitis treatment in the same hospital. Questions remain about whether experimental research is ever appropriate in the catastrophic medical crises that are still far too common in the developing world.

Envoi

At the end of 2014, there were 2.6 million children living with HIV, roughly 90 percent of them in sub-Saharan Africa. While the world has seen a 58 percent reduction in the number of new HIV infections among children, roughly 1000 are still born with the virus each day. Although the pharmaceutical industry has been persuaded, under pressure from governments and advocacy groups, to lower the price of antiretroviral drugs such as ZDV in the developing world, many pregnant HIV-positive women still cannot afford the three or more drug combination therapy that has become the standard of care for preventing transmission. As a result, many forego antiretroviral treatment and instead rely on cheaper drugs, such as oral doses of nevirapine (Viramune), which has been shown to cut a baby's risk of HIV infection by as much as 25 percent. Unfortunately, the drug has also been shown to increase the mother's risk of developing drug-resistant strains of the HIV virus, if used on its own.

Should pregnant women be given a drug that may help protect their newborns, but only at the cost of their own health and safety? Should the standard of care for serious diseases such as HIV be determined by international or local practice? Is it ever permissible to lower research standards in a medical crisis, on the grounds that subjects are still better off than they would otherwise be? Such questions are likely to continue to generate controversy and ethical debate, especially given the stark disparities in public health and medical care around the world.

SOCIAL CONTEXT
Pandemic: AIDS Worldwide

An infectious disease reaches pandemic proportions when it spreads to a far-reaching geographical area. HIV/AIDS originated in Africa, but it first made its presence known as an epidemic disease with dozens, then hundreds, then thousands of cases in the United States, starting in the 1970s and 1980s.

The HIV virus has now spread worldwide, and AIDS, the immunodeficiency condition that it causes, has become one of the largest and most feared killers in the history of infectious epidemic diseases. The number of people infected with the virus and the number who go on to die from AIDS are staggeringly large. The problems of prevention, treatment, and management that HIV/AIDS presents to the world community are as complex and difficult to cope with as the disease itself.

The number of people who have died from AIDS-related causes since the epidemic began in the late 1970s is estimated at thirty-nine million. This figure could be more or less, but whether or not it is accurate is, in an important way, irrelevant. When a disease is responsible for the deaths of millions of people every year, with over five thousand new cases each day, the world is faced with a health crisis that demands a collective response.

Scope of the Disease

The most recent estimates from the United Nations indicate that, throughout the world, over a million people a year die from AIDS and the opportunistic infections and tumors that accompany it. About two million people become newly infected with HIV, and thirty-seven million people are living with the infection. More than two and a half million children are infected with HIV, and each year one hundred and fifty thousand of them die from the disease. About a quarter million new HIV cases each year are among children.

The picture that emerges from these bare statistics is of a world burdened by an infectious disease that is both unrelenting and deadly. In many societies, people become infected at a faster rate than they die, so the disease burden continues to grow. About 95 percent of the new infections occur in the developing world, two-thirds of them in sub-Saharan Africa. These are the regions least equipped to deal with the disease, and the impact AIDS has on human lives goes beyond the suffering of individuals. The disease strikes people in their most productive years, destroying health and life, devastating the economy, and leaving behind orphaned children who add to society's burdens.

AIDS orphans

Worldwide, an estimated eighteen million children have been orphaned as a result of AIDS. About fifteen million of them are in sub-Saharan Africa, in hard-hit countries like Zambia and Botswana, where more than 10 percent of children under seventeen are estimated to have lost one or both parents to AIDS. The loss of parents is a personal tragedy for children, but it also threatens

Global HIV/AIDS

Category	Estimate
People living with HIV/AIDS	36.9 million
Adults living with HIV/AIDS	34.3 million
Women living with HIV/AIDS	17.4 million
Children living with HIV/AIDS	2.6 million
People newly infected with HIV each year	2.0 million
Children newly infected with HIV each year	0.22 million
Annual AIDS deaths	1.2 million
Child AIDS deaths	0.15 million

More than 39 million people have died of AIDS since the epidemic started.

Sub-Saharan Africa has over 15 million AIDS orphans.

At the end of 2012, women accounted for 52 percent of all adults living with HIV in low- and middle-income countries.

the stability and the future of societies. Households are destroyed, and children are often separated from siblings and sent to live with relatives or in institutions. AIDS orphans are frequently forced to drop out of school to try to support themselves or their families.

In poorer countries, even intact families frequently find it difficult to feed and care for children. Although many families once might have taken in the orphaned children of relatives or neighbors, the great increase in the number of AIDS orphans has made it impossible for many to uphold traditional practices. Neither families nor governments can provide AIDS orphans with the care and opportunities they need, and the social stigma associated with HIV often compounds the problem.

Sub-Saharan Africa: Region of Disaster

The size of the HIV/AIDS pandemic is daunting and vast. To better understand its impact, we will narrow our focus, for the moment, to the part of the African continent that lies below the Sahara Desert, one of the eight regions of the world studied by UNAIDS (the Joint United Nations Programme on HIV/AIDS). The bare statistics for sub-Saharan Africa are in some ways more dramatic than any narrative discussion of the epidemic. (Statistics for the other regions are available at the UNAIDS website.)

The countries in this vast region contain only 13 percent of the world's population, yet nearly 70 percent of people infected with HIV live there. More than twenty-five million people in the population (over 5 percent) are HIV positive, and in 2012 there were an estimated 1.6 million new HIV infections. About 1.2 million people in Africa died from AIDS that year. Of the roughly thirty-seven million people in the world infected with HIV, twenty-three million are in sub-Saharan Africa.

South Africa, with 6.8 million cases, has the highest number of HIV/AIDS infections of any single country. At least 18 percent of the adult population is infected and an estimated 410,000 children under fifteen are living with HIV. AIDS orphans in South Africa number 2.5 million and account for half of all orphans in the country.

Women are particularly vulnerable to HIV in South Africa, and in sub-Saharan Africa more generally. (Sixty percent of those infected in the region are women.) The HIV prevalence among young South African women aged twenty to twenty-four is 17.4 percent, more than three times higher than that of men in the same age bracket (5.1 percent). In the twenty-five to twenty-nine age bracket, the rate of HIV infection among women is double that of men.

Some of this gender disparity is due to physiological factors. In the unprotected heterosexual sex responsible for most HIV transmission, women are estimated to be four times more vulnerable to infection than men. But the disparity is also shaped by power imbalances between men and women that make it difficult for women to refuse sex, to guarantee that their partners are monogamous, or to ensure that they use condoms. Multiple studies in sub-Saharan Africa have shown that women who have experienced violence at the hands of intimate partners are significantly more likely to be infected with HIV as those who have not.

Unfortunately, the South African government's response to the HIV epidemic has not always been effective or evidence-based. In an October 1999 speech to Parliament, President Thabo Mbeki said that AIDS drugs posed "a danger to health" and expressed doubts about whether HIV infection was the cause of the disease. He later suggested that AIDS was a way for the vested interests represented by Western governments, drug companies, and scientists to seek money and power, while advancing racist stereotypes about sexually promiscuous Africans. Such conspiratorial views are, without question, shaped by the very real abuses of the colonial and white apartheid eras, but they can also do serious harm when granted legitimacy by public figures. (Mbeki's health minister subsequently recommended that citizens prevent AIDS by consuming lemon juice, beets, and herbal medicines.)

Although Mbeki's successor, Jacob Zuma, has thoroughly rejected his predecessor's views on the HIV virus and emphasized the crucial role of antiretroviral (ARV) drugs in treating the disease, much damage had been done. A 2008 Harvard study estimated that South Africa could have prevented thirty-five thousand deaths during Mbeki's administration, had it provided sufficient levels of ARV drugs to people with AIDS and to HIV-positive pregnant women to prevent them from transmitting the virus to their children. Nevertheless, South Africa now has the largest HIV treatment program in the world, with more than 3.1 million people on ARV therapy. This program is almost entirely funded by domestic sources and has helped

South Africa achieve a 58 percent decline in AIDS-related deaths over the past five years.

Some Progress, Much Hope

Since the mid-1990s, countries in North America and Western Europe have successfully used combinations of antiretroviral (ARV) drugs to prevent HIV infection from developing into AIDS, thereby allowing HIV-positive individuals to lead long and relatively healthy lives. At the same time, these countries have been able to extend the lives of people with AIDS through intensive treatment of associated disorders and infections.

These treatment strategies have become a model for the rest of the world. But adopting this model in underdeveloped countries has faced many obstacles, ranging from the costs of ARV drugs to the lack of health care networks to diagnose and monitor patients. Much has been achieved in recent years to overcome these obstacles. In July 2015, the UNAIDS announced that fifteen million people, most of them in the developing world, are now on antiretroviral medication. This represents a twenty-two-fold increase from the year 2000, and now covers 40 percent of all people living with HIV. Much of this change is a result of sustained activism, patient advocacy, and political pressure that prompted the pharmaceutical industry to lower the prices of ARV treatments in the developing world. Prices have fallen from around $10,000 a year per person in 2000 to about $100 a year in 2014, at least for first-line drugs. (Second-line treatments are still prohibitively expensive for most people in low- and middle-income countries.)

This expanded access to treatment has been matched by progress on other fronts. Since 2000, new HIV infections have fallen by 35 percent globally and AIDS-related deaths have fallen by 41 percent. It has been estimated that the global response to HIV has prevented

30 million HIV infections and 7.8 million AIDS-related deaths during the same period. The number of pregnant HIV-positive women with access to ARV therapy has increased to 73 percent and new HIV infections among children have fallen by 58 percent.

Most of the progress has been made possible by an increase in the amount of money available to pay for HIV drugs and other interventions. In 1996, total global spending on HIV/AIDS was $300 million; by 2014, it had risen to roughly $22 billion. More than half (57 percent) of the $187 billion that has been invested in AIDS relief since 2000 has come from the domestic budgets of the countries most affected. But international aid programs have also been pivotal in building the momentum and infrastructure necessary to sustain effective HIV interventions. Since 2002, the Global Fund to Fight AIDS, Tuberculosis, and Malaria, for example, has disbursed more than $15.7 billion in more than 151 countries.

The U.S. government began funding the struggle against the AIDS pandemic in 1986, and in 2003 President George W. Bush initiated the President's Emergency Plan for AIDS Relief (PEPFAR). Since its founding, the PEPFAR program has committed over $65 billion to HIV/AIDS programs, to the Global Fund, and to bilateral tuberculosis initiatives. President Obama has since expanded PEPFAR, so that its funding, combined with private donors such as the Bill and Melinda Gates Foundation, make the United States the largest international contributor to HIV/AIDS relief in the world.

Money Well Spent?

Not all experts in global health policy believe that spending so much money on HIV/AIDS is the best strategy. It is not that they think the money is wasted or that millions of individuals don't benefit from treatment and prevention programs. Rather, they believe that the focus on HIV/AIDS has led the international community to ignore a range of health-related problems in developing countries that, if addressed, would produce greater reductions in mortality and morbidity.

Daniel Halperin, for example, points out that millions of African children and adults die of malnutrition, pneumonia, diarrhea, and many other common poverty-related conditions. Diarrhea, for example, is simple to treat, and most of the deaths it causes could be easily prevented. One-fifth of all global deaths from diarrhea occur in Congo, Ethiopia, and Nigeria. These three countries have relatively low levels of HIV infection, yet they receive hundreds of millions of dollars a year to support AIDS programs—money that might be better spent combatting conditions that cause childhood diarrhea.

Halperin's observations can be extended to other countries and circumstances. The majority of those in the underdeveloped world lack clean drinking water, yet contaminated water is the source of many infections. Money spent on sewage systems and clean water might make a bigger impact on the health of the population than a similar amount spent on HIV/AIDS. Further, the money from the Global Fund and other agencies sometimes exceeds the amount that can be put to use in a given country. Yet the funds cannot be used for any other purpose.

Given these circumstances, Halperin asks, "With 10 million children and a half million mothers in developing countries dying annually of largely preventable conditions, should we multiply AIDS spending, while giving out a pittance for initiatives like safe-water projects?"

The Promise of Prevention

An ounce of prevention is worth more than a pound of cure, and the most effective and definitive solutions to the HIV/AIDS pandemic still lie in efforts to stop the virus from spreading. Although traditional education measures that encourage condom use, abstinence, and monogamy have helped create double-digit decreases in new HIV infections, only slightly more than half (54 percent) of HIV-positive people know they have the virus. They help generate the unacceptably high number of new HIV infections each year—roughly 2 million in 2014.

The failure to bring HIV/AIDS under control has convinced many that the most effective means of curtailing the spread of the virus is likely to involve preventing the virus from causing infection after exposure. The ideal method for achieving this would be a safe, cheap, and effective vaccine, like those that brought smallpox, mumps, measles, whooping cough, and tetanus under control. Although promising steps have been taken toward developing a vaccine in recent years, none has yet emerged that is reliable and safe.

Another hope still unrealized is the development of a microbicide gel or cream that would kill HIV on contact. While limited as a preventive measure, it might at least reduce HIV infection in women, who suffer the majority of new HIV infections in the developing world. This approach would have the additional advantage of preventing the vertical spread of HIV: fewer babies would be born infected because their mothers are HIV-positive.

Perhaps the most promising option for stopping the spread of HIV is a worldwide program of intensive testing and treatment.

In 2008, epidemiological researchers developed a mathematical model to predict what would happen if most adults and adolescents were tested every year for HIV and if those who tested positive were immediately treated with anti-retroviral drugs. The model predicted that the rate of HIV transmission could be reduced to such a low level that AIDS would virtually disappear within a decade. The reason is that those infected would, due to early treatment, carry such a low level of the virus that the chance of their passing it on to others would be significantly reduced. This phenomenon has likely already contributed to the significant drop in new HIV infections since 2000, but the large number (46 percent) of HIV-positive individuals who don't know their status suggests it may be difficult (and expensive) to achieve greater gains.

Regardless of which strategies are employed in the coming decades, two basic conclusions are accepted by most experts in public health. The first is that HIV/AIDS is a global catastrophe that continues to produce mass suffering and lost human potential around the world, especially in low- and medium-income nations. The second is that the richer nations, out of self-interest if not out of altruism or a sense of justice, must continue to invest the money and human capital that might finally bring the pandemic under control.

CASE PRESENTATION
Cutting and Culture

Like many other American teens, Leyla grew up connected to two radically different worlds. There was the Midwestern United States where she was born and raised, with its shopping malls, video games, and fast food. But there was also rural Somalia, with its camel herds and mud-walled houses, the place where her parents had grown up and where her extended family still lived.

Leyla was thrilled when her parents told her she would be travelling with them back to Somalia over her school vacation, and would finally meet her grandparents.

"Even though I'm one of four girls, I was the one they picked to go. I felt like I really was the lucky one," she recalled.

But soon after Leyla arrived in Somalia, she discovered another purpose of the visit. Her mother took her to a remote village and told her she was going to be "cut"—that her clitoris would be removed as part of a traditional practice opponents call *female genital mutilation* (FGM) and others call *female genital cutting* (FGC). Although she was terrified of what was about to happen to her, Leyla felt she had no choice but to cooperate when she was taken to the cutter's house.

"They had to hold me down," Leyla recalled. "There was no anaesthetic, no gloves, no pain medication after, no nurse to take care of you. It was the most painful thing I have experienced. They cut you like they are cutting paper. It's like you die."

Left bleeding in a side room with a wad of cotton in her underwear, Leyla struggled to reconcile what had just happened to her with the world she had grown up in.

"I felt like I was dreaming and that at some point I'd wake up. I felt so violated. Why didn't they just let me decide when I got older instead of ambushing me in the middle of nowhere?"

A Global Practice

Nearly a decade later, Leyla is still struggling with the physical and psychological effects of her ordeal. Although her experience is atypical for an American woman, it is strikingly common for women who live in some parts of Africa, the Middle East, and Asia.

The World Health Organization (WHO) estimates that as many as 30 million girls and women undergo FGM/C every year, most between infancy and age fifteen, and some 100 to 140 million are already living with its effects. In seven countries, including Egypt, Mali, and Guinea, more than 85 percent of women have undergone the procedure, and in Somalia, 98 percent have. The practice has also followed patterns of immigration, with the result that as many as five hundred thousand women in the United States have had or are at risk of having FGM/C, many through so-called "vacation cuttings" like Leyla's. Nevertheless, in the countries where it is practiced, as well as in the West, FGM/C has rarely been discussed in public, in part because understanding what it entails requires a frank discussion of female sexual anatomy.

The WHO has identified four types of FGM/C, although there are local variations among these categories. *Type I*, also called *clitoridectomy*, involves the total or partial removal of the clitoris, along with the clitoral hood. *Type II*, also called *excision*, typically involves clitoridectomy along with removal of the labia minora and/or the labia majora. Types I and II likely represent the majority of FGM/C, although there are strong regional differences in prevalence.

In Somalia as in several other North African countries, over 90 percent of FGM/C is *Type III*, also known as *infibulation*. Type III FGM/C involves the narrowing of the vaginal orifice by cutting and stitching together the labia, along with the removal of part or all of the other external genitalia. Practitioners often refer to this procedure as "sealing" girls, and indeed the catgut or wild-thorn stiches they put in generally leave only a pencil-sized hole to allow for urination and menstruation. Following infibulation, girls' legs are often bound together for ten days until the remaining vulvar tissue fuses together in a smooth surface, which is taken to be more attractively virginal than natural female anatomy. Upon marriage, these women must be "reopened" for sex, and men thus sometimes take a knife to their wedding nights.

Medical Risks

For most Westerners, not to mention many men and women from the societies where the practice is most prevalent, the details of FGM/C are deeply disturbing. They point out that female cutting almost always involves the infliction of excruciating pain on children. (This is true even in the small but growing number of cases where anesthesia is used in the initial procedure.) For this reason, FGM/C is often defined as a form of torture by international organizations as well as by several national constitutions, including Somalia's—although that war-torn country has yet to pass any specific laws against the practice.

The health risks of FGM/C have been well established by researchers around the world. It is not uncommon for girls to bleed to death during the procedure or to die of sepsis or tetanus shortly thereafter. Infibulation comes with particularly severe risks for women, including recurrent infections from backed-up urine and menses. All forms of FGM/C increase the risk of urinary incontinence, abscesses, HIV-transmission, and pain with sex, with many of these problems caused or aggravated by scar tissue. Reduced or deadened sexual sensation is a primary side effect—and often the primary objective—of FGM/C.

The practice also significantly increases childbirth complications. Studies have shown that women who have undergone some forms of FGM/C are 70 percent more likely to hemorrhage after giving birth and twice as likely to die in childbirth. Type III FGM/C has been shown to increase infant mortality by as much as 55 percent, often due to a neonate's head being crushed by scar tissue in the vaginal canal. No study has shown a medical benefit to FGM/C.

Cultural Imperialism?

Given this body of research, many Westerners view FGM/C as a backward and barbaric remnant of a tribal past, unrelated to modern medicine. But such assumptions ignore both the history of similar practices in the West and the increasing numbers of health care professionals who perform FGM/C around the world. According to estimates by the United Nations Population Fund, one out of five girls who undergo FGM/C are now cut by a trained medical professional, a proportion that appears to be on the rise. In Egypt, where roughly 90 percent of women have undergone some form of FGM/C, three out of four procedures now involve medical professionals.

Many of these practitioners claim that the health risks of FGM/C are exaggerated by critics and point to the continued popularity of male circumcision in the West and beyond as proof that cosmetic genital surgery can be legitimately performed on nonconsenting children. They argue that "female circumcision" is an equally acceptable expression of culture and religion and that Westerners who criticize it are thus engaging in hypocrisy and cultural imperialism. Proponents of the practice also typically make their own biomedical claims to justify it.

"One, it will stabilize her libido," said Lukman Hakim, chairman of a social service organization in Indonesia that performs hundreds of Type I cuttings every year. "Two, it will make a woman look more beautiful in the eyes of her husband. And three, it will balance her psychology." This mixed emphasis on female chastity, cultural standards of beauty or hygiene, and mental health benefits is common among FGM/C proponents and practitioners.

"This tradition is for keeping our girls chaste, for lowering the sex drive of our daughters," a Somali cutter named Maryan Hirsi Ibrahim told *New York Times* columnist Nicholas Kristof. "This is our culture."

Although such arguments may ring hollow to contemporary Western ears, they bear striking similarity to those that have been put forward for related practices in Western societies. As recently as the 1950s, clitoridectomies were still being performed in Europe and the United States to treat perceived pathologies such as hysteria, nymphomania, melancholia, homosexuality, and masturbation, as well as for diagnoses that are still part of clinical practice, such as epilepsy and schizophrenia. (In the West, however, cutting was not typically deemed necessary for "healthy" women.) Many defenders of FGM/C also point to the increasing popularity of breast augmentation and labial reduction surgeries as evidence that the West still believes that women's bodies must be "fixed" to make them socially acceptable. Although most of these nontherapeutic procedures are sought out by consenting adults, some involve younger patients, and defenders often argue that children in both sets of societies are eager to have such procedures performed. (See Case Presentation: Intersex Care in Chapter 10 for more on childhood cosmetic surgeries in the West.)

It is clear that nontherapeutic genital cutting is almost always bound up with cultural conceptions of gender, sexuality, and physical beauty. But with the exception of Judaism, there is little evidence that either male or female circumcision has a religious origin. Although FGM/C is more common among Muslim societies, there is no Islamic scriptural source for it and the practice predates both Christianity and Islam almost everywhere it is prevalent.

Finally, although both male circumcision and FGM/C appear to be primarily cultural in origin, comparison of the two practices often seems metaphorical and misleading. As many critics have pointed out, Types I and II FGM/C are generally more comparable to the removal of the entire penis and/or testes rather than just the foreskin. Although most male circumcisions are not performed for therapeutic reasons, the practice has been shown to have therapeutic benefits, with some studies showing a 60 percent reduction in HIV infection among circumcised men. No such benefits and significant harm has been shown to result from FGM/C. Although both practices raise questions about cosmetic surgeries on nonconsenting minors, FGM/C typically involves older children, less or no anesthesia, and more extensive damage to tissue with concentrated nerve endings. As described by Hibo

Wardere, an anti-FGM/C activist who was cut at age six in Somalia, the procedure involves "being engulfed in pain from head to toe—like fireworks going off everywhere and you don't know how to stop them. I prayed to God to just take me then and there."

Gender and Power

Unlike male circumcision, FGM/C is almost always defended in terms of the need for society to restrain the sexuality of those who are cut. (Clitoridectomies in the West were often framed in similar terms.)

"From a young age you were told girls who weren't cut were promiscuous," said Ayshah, a woman from Somalia who underwent FGM/C when she was five years old. "They were dirty, nobody wanted to marry them, they were ugly." Indeed, the most common defenses of the practice claim that it will ensure marital fidelity, preserve female virginity before marriage, and eliminate "masculine" traits in girls. These views are often shared by both men and women (who make up the majority of cutters), and some women, such as Ayshah, recall being eager to be cut—in part because of the gifts, sweets, and praise that typically follow the procedure.

It is clear, however, that FGM/C is almost always accompanied by deeply rooted structural inequalities between men and women. In societies where women are not allowed to work outside the home and cannot own or inherit land, girls are frequently viewed as an economic burden until they can elicit a dowry through marriage. In many societies in Africa and the Middle East, FGM/C is a rite of passage that marks the end of a girl's formal schooling and her eligibility for marriage—often to an older, financially secure man. Indeed, many critics suggest that FGM/C can only be discussed in the context of the seven hundred million women alive today who were forced into marriage as children. Furthermore, they suggest it reflects the same global devaluation of girls and women that produces lopsided sex-selection practices, neglect of girls' health, and more than 100 million females who are "missing" (relative to statistical norms) in Asia and Africa, because they failed to survive gestation, birth, or childhood. (See the Chapter 10 Briefing Session for more on this topic.) FGM/C is also strongly associated with patterns of sexual violence against women, "honor killings" of rape victims, and the global sex trafficking and forced prostitution that currently involves over four million women and girls.

Of course, these phenomena are hardly limited to societies or cultures that practice FGM/C, and many industrialized nations, including the United States, continue to struggle with disturbingly high levels of sexual violence, gender disparity, and human trafficking. Indeed, the persistence and global scale of gender-based inequality is so daunting that practices such as FGM/C can sometimes seem inevitable or unchangeable.

But the history of the twentieth century suggests that deeply entrenched cultural practices regarding gender may change with surprising speed. For ten centuries, generations of Chinese women had their feet systematically bound and broken to conform to an ideal of feminine beauty. But around the turn of the twentieth century, the practice fell out of favor and had almost completely disappeared in the span of a few decades. In the West, demands that women wear corsets or bonnets and not wear pants—cultural practices that were in place for generations—gave way as women gained greater social and financial autonomy. Medically unnecessary clitoridectomies and hysterectomies were also curtailed as women gained access to the medical profession and became active in patients' rights movements.

It is worth noting that none of these changes was accomplished through legal means, and some critics argue that prohibitions on FGM/C are counterproductive, driving the practice underground in a spirit of resistance to foreign norms. As long as the perceived social advantages of FGM/C remain as a necessary precondition to marriages and dowries, it will continue, they contend. Others argue that the lasting physical and psychological harm of FGM/C preclude any toleration of one of the world's most pervasive abuses of human rights. In line with such arguments, Nigeria banned FGM/C in May 2015, making it the twenty-third African nation to do so. (The practice has been illegal in the United States since 1996, but "vacation cuttings" such as Leyla's were not included in the law until 2012.)

One of the most successful campaigns against FGM/C has been led by the human rights group Tostan, which has focused on medical education campaigns in African villages. As a result, thousands of such villages have taken pledges to replace FGM/C with rituals involving "circumcision with words." Such rituals are designed to ensure that girls who have not been cut will still be marriageable and will not face ostracism or abuse. Still, groups like Tostan are competing with the "medicalization" of FGM/C by health professionals, who can earn extra money by performing the procedures and making unsubstantiated claims about their medical benefit. Thus, in Africa as in the rest of the world, medicine often serves as the stage for fierce debates over gender, power, and identity.

Leyla, for her part, emphasizes the potential benefits of a broad-based educational campaign in the United States and beyond, to educate physicians about how to treat FGM/C and to teach families about its risks.

"There needs to be more warning, more information. There needs to be a place where people can get help. My mother thought she was fulfilling her motherly duties," Leyla told a reporter from *The Guardian*. "That's why I'm telling my story. If I can stop this happening to just one more girl then it will have been worth it."

BRIEFING SESSION

In June of 2015, a commission of more than forty leading physicians, epidemiologists, and climatologists, organized by the *Lancet* medical journal, warned that climate change constituted a "medical emergency" that threatened to erase fifty years of progress in global public health. Based on sharp increases in heat stress, drought, flooding, violent storms, vector-borne diseases, population displacement, and food insecurity, "[c]limate change is the biggest global health threat of the 21st century," the commission concluded. In a separate report, the World Health Organization estimated that by 2030, at least 250,000 deaths a year will be directly attributable to climate change.

The serious health effects of our planet's changing climate have been on the horizon for nearly a century. In 1917, the inventor Alexander Graham Bell noted that the industrial revolution was contributing to "a sort of greenhouse effect," in which the earth's radiant heat was trapped by pollutants in the atmosphere. The continued burning of coal and oil, he claimed, was likely to produce a net result in which "the greenhouse becomes a sort of hot-house," raising average global temperatures and wreaking havoc on human societies.

Bell's warning has been followed by almost a century of dramatic temperature increase, violent shifts in regional climates, and the melting of the polar ice caps. Since comprehensive record keeping began in 1880, the Earth's average global temperature has risen 0.8 degrees Celsius, and NASA predicts that at current emissions rates, it will have risen between 2°C and 6°C by the end of the twenty-first century. Even a 2°C increase has not been seen on Earth for 125,000 years, and the speed of the current temperature increase is over twenty times faster than any past warming pattern after ice ages. Thirteen of the fifteen hottest years on record have occurred since 2000, with 2014 eclipsing both 2005 and 2010 for the warmest global average.

Climate change is already having a significant impact on human health, with unprecedented heat, drought, and extreme weather patterns killing thousands every year, and rising sea levels threatening the coastal living conditions of nearly half the world's population. Regional climate shifts are already increasing the range of diseases borne by vectors such as mosquitos and snails, and studies suggest that climate change will expose at least an additional two billion people to malaria and dengue fever before the end of the century. Many other changes, such as the impact on viral and bacterial mutations, are only beginning to be understood.

Destructive dynamics such as climate change do not respect national boundaries. As the 2014 Ebola outbreak and the 2010 H1N1 swine flu pandemic made clear, effective action for any single nation's public health is often intertwined with global health. The interdependence of national economies and cultures is paralleled by increasing interdependence of their populations' health status, a pattern that is mirrored by the global scope of our environmental problems and the moral complexity of addressing them. There is more consensus about the *anthropogenic* ("human generated") nature of climate change than practically any other issue in science. But collective action on both climate change and global public health remain elusive.

Many of the disagreements over these global health issues involve questions of fairness and disparity. For example, the annual amount of money spent on health care per person in Bangladesh is $32. By contrast, the amount of money spent on health care per person in the United States is $9,146. Bangladesh emits 0.3 percent of the world's greenhouse gases, but in the three-foot sea level rise that climate scientists expect to occur by 2100, Bangladesh will lose 17 percent of its land—displacing eighteen million people and severely impacting their health and livelihoods.

How global health care and other disparities developed and who is responsible for addressing them are, of course, hotly contested questions. Some foreign-policy realists and libertarians argue that moral responsibility does not extend beyond national borders and the promotion of fair trade agreements. Others argue that our bioethical responsibilities are *cosmopolitan*—meaning that they stretch beyond the ties of kinship or shared citizenship (although cosmopolitans typically acknowledge that such ties do have special claims on us).

A related set of questions concerns the extent to which bioethical principles and judgments are *relative* to local customs and cultures, and the extent to which diverse cultures may be able to agree on some moral universals. It might be fairly easy to achieve an overlapping international consensus about the immorality of Nazi- or Tuskegee-style

medical experiments, for example, but much harder to find consensus on a woman's right to make medical decisions for herself independent of a male family member. Nontherapeutic surgery on children's genitals and other body parts is another example of an issue that divides the world's diverse societies. (See Case Presentation: Cutting and Culture.) Trying to identify a set of basic moral commitments or principles that might bridge some of these disagreements is a particularly urgent problem in bioethics and has prompted critical reflection on traditional notions of autonomy and informed consent associated with medical ethics in the West.

There is little question that "globalization" is an ancient phenomenon, and that most of the world's cultures are, in fact, the results of millennia of trade and social interchange among different regions and peoples, blurring any neat division between East and West, North and South. But the speed of international travel, trade, and communications is accelerating these interchanges, while shared problems, from climate change to HIV, make moral consensus and collective action all the more important. The scale and complexity of these global biomedical issues, however, make it difficult to provide a comprehensive account of them in an introductory text. In this chapter, we instead opt to discuss a few representative problems that we believe will continue to pose ethical and practical challenges for decades to come. Although this chapter, like the rest of this book, is firmly rooted in the North American perspectives of its authors, we hope that it also suggests the broader range of voices that must be involved in any genuinely global discussion of bioethics.

Duty and Disparity

Imagine, for the moment, that you are a successful dermatologist, walking back from lunch near your office in a prosperous North American suburb. On your walk, you pass a wading pool in a local park and notice some splashing at the far end. Coming closer, you see that a toddler is drowning in the pool, which can't be more than three feet deep. There is no one else in the park and it is clear that if you don't intervene to save the child, she will die. In order to do so, however, you will have to wade in and ruin an expensive pair of Italian shoes. Furthermore, in five minutes you are scheduled to excise a patient's facial mole—a procedure that, while potentially therapeutic, you know is being performed mostly for cosmetic reasons.

Should you wade in and save the child, even though it will ruin your shoes and cause you to miss the procedure? Nearly everyone presented with this scenario says yes, that you should obviously make these minor sacrifices in order to save the child's life. In fact, most people say that under these circumstances you have a moral *duty* to save the child from drowning.

But in practice, some philosophers argue, most of us make the opposite choice. They point out that in poor countries over seventeen thousand children under five die each day from highly preventable illnesses such as pneumonia, dysentery, and malaria. Due to global communications and more effective aid distribution networks, privileged people in rich countries have the power to intervene decisively to save the lives of children who are literally dying before our eyes. Instead, many of us devote our extra money to luxury goods and our time to recreation and lucrative careers. If saving the life of the drowning child in front of us is truly an ethical duty, how can our failure to intervene in these other situations be justified?

The scenario above is based on a famous thought experiment developed by the bioethicist Peter Singer, whose work on animal research appears in Chapter 2. Singer used the drowning child scenario to argue that we have a moral obligation to prevent very bad outcomes by making less-bad sacrifices, and called for privileged people to give a significant percentage of their incomes to international aid organizations that have proven effectiveness in saving lives.

One need not endorse Singer's general principle, however—and many bioethicists have not—to see the challenge that such scenarios pose for global bioethics in general and for medical ethics in particular. Physicians are generally seen to take on special ethical responsibilities of beneficence and nonmaleficence (that is, to promote good and avoid causing harm) with regard to the sick and suffering. In crises, they are expected to follow the principle of *triage*—prioritizing patients based on the severity of their conditions. More generally, polls show that the overwhelming majority of physicians choose to study medicine out of a desire to help people and make a difference. The drowning child scenario raises serious questions about whether biomedical treatment and research is being properly directed toward the most urgent suffering and sickness, and about whether "making a difference" can be justifiably limited to one's own community or nation.

There is little doubt that global afflictions such as HIV, malaria, tuberculosis, dysentery, cholera, schistosomiasis, and yellow fever constitute the majority of the world's disease burden and are causally associated with grinding poverty. These diseases prey on the 1.1 billion people who lack access to safe drinking water, the 2.6 billion who lack basic sanitation, and 800 million who are malnourished. Yet the vast majority of health care resources are still devoted to "First-World problems" such as cancer, hypertension, and heart disease, largely due to financial and political incentives. At the same time, medical specialties such as cardiology, dermatology, and urology continue to grow and pull down the highest salaries, while shortages of infectious disease and family medicine specialists reflect their place at the bottom of the physician pay scale.

Defenders of this status quo argue that patients are, in effect, voting with their dollars, and that the higher salaries for urologists, for example, reflect their greater value to society. On this view, suffering and sickness in other societies might be an occasion for optional private charity, but it does not engender professional or moral obligations. Critics argue that biomedical markets are a particularly poor guide to social value. Prescribing antibiotics to people with dysentery will never be a revenue-generating enterprise, nor will treating destitute HIV patients with antiretroviral medications. But both interventions have enormous potential to alleviate suffering.

Others argue that we have a moral obligation to address global health disparities because we are materially involved in the medical conditions of foreigners. They contend that international financial institutions such as the World Bank and International Monetary Fund are structured to favor wealthy countries. Poor nations are, in part, poor because of the colonial and postcolonial theft of their natural resources and the long-standing suppression of human rights and human potential. On this view, the obligation to alleviate poverty-driven illness abroad is less like rescuing a drowning child than assisting a child one has hit with one's car.

Globalized Clinical Trials?

Issues of equity also arise with regard to the design and implementation of clinical trials. Health care disparities are so steep between poor and rich countries that many desperately ill people in the former effectively receive no treatment at all while most people in the latter receive high-quality (but expensive) treatment. Some researchers have argued that because many expensive treatments are not widely available in poor countries, trials in those countries need not provide standard-of-care treatments to control groups—as is generally required by the Declaration of

Helsinki and other codes of medical research ethics. In a number of controversial studies in the 1990s, for example, researchers gave placebos to poor HIV-positive pregnant women, because their impoverished societies' "standard" treatment for avoiding maternal–fetal HIV transmission was typically no treatment at all. (See Social Context: Clinical Trials in the Developing World.)

Defenders of such trials argue that they made some subjects better off and no subjects worse off than they would otherwise have been. They also claim that if the results are used to benefit the broader population, then it is clearly better that such trials occur rather than not occur. But critics suggest that the real question is not whether such studies should occur or not, but why offering First-World standards of care in Third-World research contexts is deemed "unrealistic" or "unfeasible" in the first place. If such current best treatments are, in fact, medically and scientifically inappropriate for destitute patients in poor countries, then lower-standard studies may be justified. (This position is similar to that adopted in the most recent version of the Declaration of Helsinki, which is reprinted in Chapter 2.) But if the decision has been influenced by financial considerations (either in denying poor people expensive treatments or in selecting a poor country as a cheaper place to conduct research), then subjects are being exploited. Critics argue that ethical research must not blindly accept and perpetuate immoral health care disparities between rich and poor nations. Defenders argue that such disparities are the responsibility of government and aid organizations, and that biomedical research is ill suited to address such problems.

Relativism and Pluralism

A persistent challenge for any global approach to bioethics is that different societies and cultures appear to disagree over specific biomedical practices and policies, and their members often cite different or even incompatible values to justify these positions. Some societies prohibit abortion, homosexuality, and birth control, while others legalize euthanasia, recreational drug use, and prostitution. Some societies tolerate female genital cutting, while others restrict both male and female circumcision to varying degrees. Approaches to informed consent and patient autonomy vary widely across societies, with some cultures in Asia and Africa, for example, emphasizing a more collective approach to medical decision-making that involves family or community groups.

In the Anglo-American tradition, bioethics developed with an emphasis on the application of universally binding ethical principles such as nonmaleficence and informed consent, with much of the debate revolving around the scope of their application. While this analytic approach, sometimes known as *principalism,* is both efficient and powerful, it has often failed to engage directly with biomedical concepts from non-Western cultures. When such issues do arise, they have often been framed as a conflict between cultural relativism and objectivism. *Cultural relativism* is the view that there are no universally objective principles or values beyond the beliefs and customs of specific cultures, and thus there can be no basis for cross-cultural criticism or debate. By contrast, ethical *objectivism* holds that there are a set of universal and objective values and principles that have application everywhere.

As many critics have argued, however, the choice between these two positions can be artificial and misleading. Cultural relativism in ethics, critics argue, is a notoriously ambiguous and possibly self-contradictory view that few people actually hold. The cultural relativist's most basic claim—that cultures have no right to judge and should therefore tolerate each other—is itself the type of cross-cultural

evaluation that relativism forbids. Indeed, cultural relativism appears to have no ethical grounds for criticizing aggressive intolerance between or within cultures. So long as a culture's dominant or majority view endorses slavery or involuntary euthanasia, for example, the relativist must consider such practices "right for them" in that culture. Also, critics say, there are notorious problems assessing the boundaries of any given culture and formulating its views, and most cultures (and individuals) are in fact *multicultural,* shaped by many different subcultural and foreign influences.

These long-recognized problems with relativism do not, however, require that we endorse a view of ethics as consisting of a set of universally objective "moral facts" or principles that can be applied everywhere without regard to cultural difference. As many ethical theorists have pointed out, our everyday use of moral language mostly involves the practice of persuasion and dialogue, rather than the application of universal concepts and principles. We use the language of values and principles primarily to try to persuade others and to shape their thoughts, emotions, and actions—not to make objective statements about the world. Based on this perspective, other approaches to the problem of moral diversity have been developed that avoid the extreme versions of both objectivism and relativism.

Some of these approaches seek to identify a rough set of overlapping human norms and values that are shared across cultures but expressed differently in different societies. Finding such overlap in global bioethics involves careful attention to the specific cultural and religious values that shape disputed practices or policies. Take the expectation in some Asian and African cultures that competent patients may delegate their informed consent to family members or community leaders. Rather than simply imposing 'Western' principles of truth-telling and patient autonomy on these situations, an alternative approach would take seriously the collectivist values that may underlie such delegations of responsibility. Recognizing the importance of familial and communal affiliation to patients' well-being may challenge us to expand traditional conceptions of patient autonomy, while also being mindful of the risks of cultural coercion and undue influence. (Michelle Gold's article in Chapter 1 provides an example of this type of moral reflection.) The premise of such cross-cultural exchange is that there is enough overlap in the moral vocabularies of different societies to engage in meaningful bioethical dialogue. Although this process is unlikely to resolve all sources of disagreement, the goal is to identify some basic values that are central to human flourishing and human dignity, even as societies have come to express them in substantially different ways.

A key feature of many newer approaches to developing a global bioethics is that they are explicitly *pluralistic*. They assume that different people and cultures will have different conceptions of the good and that their biomedical practices will be shaped by different views on health, morality, and religion. For example, unlike utilitarian or most Kantian approaches to moral judgment, which reduce complex situations to a single metric of value (e.g., the promotion of utility or application of the categorical imperative), pluralism avoids commitment to a single comprehensive view. Instead, pluralistic approaches seek to find overlapping consensus on some basic principles and policies that different groups can endorse even though they hold radically different comprehensive views. According to John Rawls, such approaches are "political" in that they seek moral agreement for pragmatic purposes, rather than to abolish religious and philosophical disagreements.

A pluralistic approach to evaluating the moral legitimacy of female genital cutting, for example, could not simply rely on the notion, associated with contemporary Western ethics, that individuals are autonomous (self-determining) and so it is wrong to perform surgery on them without their consent. Relying on such a notion would run counter to the idea in many traditional societies that individuals are not, in themselves, fully autonomous, but gain status as a person only as part of a society or in relationship to divinity. The pluralistic approach might instead endorse a broader human capability, such as the ability to secure one's bodily integrity, to challenge practices such as genital cutting.

As such, this view might be endorsed both by those who value bodily integrity as a way of honoring God's creation and those who value it based on Kant's conception of autonomous control over one's own body. Such overlapping consensus may not incorporate all viewpoints or convince all supporters of FGM/C, but pluralists argue that it usefully allows room for local variations on broadly shared conceptions of human dignity and human rights.

It is worth noting that some of the most successful campaigns against FGM/C appear to have employed strongly pluralistic approaches to the issue. The Senegal-based organization Tostan has successfully brokered hundreds of intervillage agreements in Africa to replace FGM/C with a "circumcision by words"— a ceremony that preserves marriageability and a cultural rite of passage for girls who receive it. Drawing on local community values, such educational campaigns seek to align diverse religious and cultural perspectives around a pragmatic shift in biomedical practice. (See Case Presentation: Cutting and Culture.)

Pluralistic approaches to bioethics are rooted in the view that moral community—both within and among societies—admits of multiple conceptions of the good. In this, they follow the work of W. D. Ross and other theorists going back to Aristotle who see social goods as varied and incommensurable. The difficulty for all such views is that they provide little guidance when we face conflicts among recognized values and the duties they engender. Critics argue that they provide insufficient moral clarity to resolve the tragic biomedical choices posed by such phenomena as HIV, global health disparities, and climate change. Defenders of a pluralistic approach to bioethics argue that it provides the only appropriate and effective framework through which the world's diverse peoples can take collective action to address the urgent problems we face.

READINGS

Section 1: Global Health and Distributive Justice

The Distribution of Biomedical Research Resources and International Justice

David B. Resnik

Resnik cites research showing that only 10 percent of the world's biomedical research funding is devoted to the problems that cause 90 percent of the world's disease burden, most of it shouldered by the developing world. Resnik attributes this disparity to two main causes: (1) research on diseases that afflict the developing world (such as malaria and TB) is not viewed as financially rewarding by corporations; (2) such research is not viewed as politically reward- ing by governments, in part because it is not promoted by advocacy groups as cancer and heart disease research is.

Nevertheless, the 90/10 divide is profoundly unjust, Resnik claims. He argues for a cosmopolitan version of distributive justice, in which we are not excused from obligations to the least advantaged just because they happen to live in a different nation. In order to address this injustice, Resnik calls for (1) advocacy groups to lobby corpora- tions and governments for developing-world diseases as they do for developed-world ones; and (2) a UN-administered trust to help fund and patent biomedical R&D for the 90 percent.

The distribution of resources for research and development (R&D) in biomedicine has a direct impact on the progress of the health sciences and the distribution of health. Money spent on biomedical

From David B. Resnik, "The Distribution of Biomedical Research Resources and International Justice," *Developing World Bioethics* 4, no. 1 (2004). ISSN 1471-8731 (print); 1471–8847 (online). Copy- right © 2004 Blackwell Publishing Ltd. (Most references omitted.)

R&D can have a positive impact on disease and disability, longevity, infant mortality, and other measures of the health of a population. Differences in research funding can also be a factor in racial and ethnic health disparities. For many years there have been racial and ethnic disparities in health in the United States (US). While many different factors, such as poverty, discrimination, and educational at- tainment contribute to these disparities, inadequate research on health problems unique to racial and ethnic minorities also plays a role. In an attempt to address racial and ethnic differences in cancer incidence, mortality and treatment, the National Cancer Institute has developed a programme to fund research on problems uniquely affecting minority and medically under-served groups.

If one compares the developed and the developing world, one also finds great disparities in many different health indicators, such as life expectancy, infant mortality, disability, and quality of life. Once again, many different factors, such as poverty, overpopulation, famine, education, culture and religion, and political and military turmoil, are responsible for these disparities. However, there is little doubt that the global distribution of biomedical research resources plays some role in the health gap between rich and poor countries and that closing this gap would probably have a positive impact on the health of developing nations. According to some estimates, less than 10% of the world's biomedical R&D funds are dedicated to addressing problems that are responsible for 90% of the world's burden of disease.[1] Multinational corporations and government agencies of the developed world spend billions of dollars each year on R&D pertaining to diseases that are of great concern to populations in developed societies, such as cancer, heart disease, diabetes, obesity, and hypertension, while they allocate far less money to research on diseases that are of special concern to the developing world, such as malaria, tuberculosis, yellow fever, and dysentery. (Hereinafter, this paper will refer to this funding disparity as the 90/10 divide.)

This paper will explain why the 90/10 divide exists and what should be done about it. It will argue that the divide exists because: 1) multinational pharmaceutical and biotechnology companies do not regard R&D investments on the health problems of developing nations to be economically lucrative; and 2) government biomedical research agencies face little political pressure to allocate funds for the problems of developing nations. This paper will argue that the 90/10 divide is unjust, and that developed nations have a moral obligation to address these disparities related to biomedical research funding. To facilitate this effort, developed countries should establish a trust fund dedicated to research on the health problems of developing nations similar to the Global AIDS Fund.

UNDERSTANDING THE 90/10 DIVIDE

To understand the causes of the 90/10 divide, one must explore the economic and political factors that affect R&D funding. First, most of the funding for biomedical R&D is provided by developed nations. From 1981–1995, 12 nations from the developed world—Australia, Canada, Denmark, France, Germany, Italy, Japan, the Netherlands, Sweden, Switzerland, the US, and the United Kingdom (UK) sponsored 80% of all the R&D in the world, with the US by far the leading sponsor of R&D. In 1995, the US spent almost as much on basic research ($41 billion) as ten of the other top countries combined, excluding Japan. For most countries in the developed world, the government is the main sponsor of R&D, although the contributions of private sources of funding, i.e. corporations or foundations, have been increasing over the last decade. In the US, UK, Japan, Sweden, and Switzerland, private funding sources outspent public funding sources by at least a 1.8 to 1 ratio.

In the US, there are four main sponsors of R&D: private industry, which sponsors approximately 60% of R&D; government agencies (35%); colleges and universities (3%); and private foundations (2%). Private corporations are by far the leading sponsors of biomedical R&D in the US. In 2001, pharmaceutical and biotechnology companies located in the US spent $45.6 billion on R&D, and 70% of the clinical trials in the US were sponsored by private industry. From 1998–2003, the NIH budget nearly doubled from $15 billion to $27.3 billion.

Private foundations in the US spent no more than $2 billion on biomedical R&D in 2001. While this amount appears small compared to the billions spent by private companies or government agencies, it is a very significant and growing source of funding, especially for R&D that addresses the problems of the developing world. Indeed, most private foundations that sponsor biomedical R&D seek to distinguish themselves from government and industry sponsors by attempting to bridge the gaps in R&D funding. Private foundations have historically been able to sponsor research that was economically risky or politically unpopular. A good example of this strategy is the Bill and Melinda Gates Foundation, which has focused on addressing global health disparities. Since its establishment in 2000, the Foundation has raised a $24 billion endowment and has spent approximately $3 billion on global health grants, including $500 million on AIDS research and prevention, $100 billion on tuberculosis research and prevention, and $750 million on vaccine research. Another significant private foundation in the US is the Howard Hughes Medical Institute, which spent just over $600 million on biomedical research in 2001. The largest private foundation for biomedical research in the UK, the Wellcome Trust, spent about $600 million on research in 2001.

Since most of the world's R&D is sponsored by developed nations, to understand the 90/10 divide one must explore how private companies and government agencies in the developed world allocate their R&D funds. In examining the methods that private firms use to make R&D allocation decisions, one must bear in mind that private firms are in business to make a profit, and that they do this by selling or licensing drugs, biologics, and medical devices. R&D on a new drug or biologic is very expensive. According to industry estimates, it takes an average of 10–12 years and $800 million to develop a new product and bring it to the market. To protect their R&D investments, companies apply for patent protection over their products. During the term of the patent, which usually lasts 20 years, the company will have exclusive rights to make, use, or commercialise its invention. Once the patent expires, the company will still have exclusive rights over the trademarked name that designates its invention, but other companies can make, use, or commercialise the invention under a non-trademarked (generic) name. Thus, a private company will usually have about 8–10 years to recoup its R&D investment while the product is still under patent. Although pharmaceutical companies tend to have high profit margins (10% or greater), R&D funding in biomedicine is a risky business. About 1/3 of new drugs are profitable, and even less become drug 'blockbusters', such as Viagra or Prozac. Companies must also frequently withdraw profitable drugs from the market, due to safety concerns or litigation.

Given these economic facts, it is easy to see why companies decide to set R&D priorities based on factors that affect the profitability of a new product, such as the size of the potential market, consumer demand, the scope of intellectual property protection, the expected time from the laboratory to the market, and liability costs. Very few private companies are interested in spending money on developing vaccines for diseases that afflict the developing world, since consumer demand for these drugs is weak and intellectual property protection is uncertain. Unless private companies can expect a good return on their investment, they will probably not invest much money in R&D related to the problems of the developing world. They may, however, decide to allocate some R&D funds to the problems of the developing world if they regard that decision as a donation to a worthy cause justified by a sense of social responsibility.

To understand how government funding agencies make biomedical R&D allocation decisions, one must bear in mind that government agencies are accountable to politicians and the general public. The NIH, for example, is part of the executive branch of the federal government. The President of the United States, through the Director of the Department of Health and Human Services (DHHS), has direct oversight authority over the NIH. Since Congress allocates government funds to the DHHS and NIH, it also oversees the NIH. Although scientific review panels determine which research proposals are funded, public opinion helps to shape the NIH's funding priorities. The NIH consults with members of Congress and the Executive branch, biomedical researchers, physicians, other federal agencies, such as the Food and Drug Administration, and patient advocacy groups to set its funding priorities. Disease advocacy groups have played an increasingly visible and influential role in setting funding priorities at the NIH ever since AIDS activists began to organise themselves in the 1990s. The NIH now spends more money on research on HIV/AIDS than on research on any other disease.

Most of the research sponsored by the NIH has a great deal of significance for the developing world. Patients in developing nations benefit from NIH-sponsored research on HIV/AIDS, cancer, heart disease, alcoholism and drug abuse, and prenatal care. However, the NIH sets aside relatively little money to study problems unique to the developing world. The NIH has only one institute or centre devoted to international research. The Fogarty International Center allocates about $45 million per year on grants to improve global health. While this is not a trivial amount of money, it represents less than 0.5% of the NIH's total budget.

The NIH spends very little money on the health problems of the developing world because there is very little political pressure in the US to sponsor research on these problems. Americans want more research on cancer, heart disease, diabetes, hypertension, depression, obesity, and other diseases that have a significant impact on America's disease burden. US citizens, to put it bluntly, would rather spend their tax dollars on the health problems of their own country than on the health problems of a poor country in Africa, South America, or Asia. Perhaps developing nations need their own disease advocacy group to put political pressure on the NIH. Although the discussion so far has focused on the economic and political conditions in the US, similar conditions also exist in other developed nations.

We have thus arrived at the root causes of the 90/10 divide: the divide exists because biomedical research on the health problems of the developing world is neither financially lucrative nor politically popular. While some private foundations spend a great deal of money on the health problems of the developing world, their contribution is not enough to help close the gap.

THE 90/10 DIVIDE AND INTERNATIONAL JUSTICE

Is the 90/10 divide unjust or unfair? To answer this question, one must provide an account of international justice, since disparities in the distribution of research resources between rich and poor countries concern justice between and among different nations. Although there is not sufficient space in this paper to provide an in-depth analysis of international justice, it will be useful to survey the different views and describe an approach that may apply to the 90/10 divide.

A traditional notion of justice, found in Plato's *Republic*, conceives of justice as a relationship among different people within a nation or state. A just state, according to Plato, is rationally ordered. Other theorists, such as Hobbes, Locke, and Rousseau have followed this national approach to justice. The basic problem of international justice is to show how there can be justice among nations. Sceptics claim international justice is impossible because: 1) states are not moral agents; 2) moral agreement is impossible among states; and 3) there are no agreed upon legal systems that can enforce international law. A sceptic would argue that there is nothing unfair or unjust about the 90/10 divide, since there are no principles of international justice. The distribution of R&D resources may be a problem of justice within a particular nation, but it is not a problem of justice among nations.

I believe justice among nations is possible. First, even though states lack some of the characteristics of moral agency, such as consciousness or free will, they can act as political agents. States can make collective decisions and take collective action. Second, moral agreement among states, while very difficult, is not impossible. Most of the nations of the world accept the premise that nations should respect each other's sovereignty and avoid military aggression except in self-defence. Third, although there continue to be many problems with agreeing upon international laws and procedures, the nations of the world are working toward forms of dispute resolution, such as the United Nations, the World Trade Organization, and the International Court of Justice.

If international justice is possible, then what is the best account of international justice? Realists treat nations as having independent moral status and regard international justice as a relationship between and among nations. According to realists, geographically sovereign states are politically autonomous agents. The duties and rights of sovereign states are similar to the duties and rights of moral agents. Sovereign nations have the right to make their own laws, govern their own people, defend their territory, promote their own interests, and enter agreements with other sovereign nations. States also have duties to respect the rights of other states.

Critics of the realist approach include sceptics, who reject the notion of international justice, as well as cosmopolitans, who accept the idea of international justice but reject realism. According to the cosmopolitan view, international justice is a relationship among people who happen to live in different states, not a relationship between different states. Political legitimacy derives from the rights and interests of the people who are governed. Control over a territory (geographical sovereignty) is not the same as political sovereignty. Sometimes states are morally justified in violating another state's territorial integrity in order to overthrow or reform an oppressive government. While states play a key role in the implementation of international justice, they have no *sui generis* moral standing.

Since cosmopolitanism avoids the difficulties of realism, but also rejects scepticism, this paper will adopt a cosmopolitan approach to international justice. International justice depends on the relationships between people, not governments. What are some of the principles of international justice? To answer this question, it will be useful to apply three basic approaches to national justice to the international realm.

A libertarian approach to international justice would mirror the libertarian approach to national justice. The libertarian would argue that the rules and principles of justice among politically legitimate nations should respect national rights and sovereignty. A nation, like an autonomous person, has rights to life, liberty, and property, which are limited only by the requirement that the nation not interfere with the rights of another nation. A nation should engage in ethical business practices in its dealings with other nations: it should honour its agreements with other nations, negotiate in good faith, and refrain from fraud, deception, or manipulation. However, a nation has no positive, moral duties to benefit other nations. A nation is free to acquire as much wealth as it can by honest means. The purpose of systems of international laws is to protect the rights of sovereign states, not to redistribute wealth among rich and poor nations.

A libertarian would not view that 90/10 divide as unjust or unfair. Sovereign states are free to make funding decisions based on their interests and goals, provided that they do not violate the rights of other sovereign states or the rights of citizens within sovereign states. The gap in the distribution of research resources between rich and poor nations is as fair as the income gap between rich and poor citizens within the same nation. The morally relevant issue is not that the gap exists but how it has arisen. If the 90/10 divide is the result of a fair process that respects rights, then it is just.

There is not sufficient space in this paper to provide a thorough critique of libertarian philosophy. The main problem with the libertarian view is that it does not give adequate consideration to the plight of the least advantaged members of society. Libertarians have no qualms about huge differences in income, education and health among different people of the same nation or of different nations. Since I believe that a just nation (or community of nations) must have policies that promote the interests of their least advantaged members, I will reject the libertarian approach to international justice and consider other approaches.

A utilitarian approach to international justice would hold that principles of justice should promote the greatest balance of benefits/burdens for all people in the world. Utilitarians tend to favour health policies that maximise social goods at a relatively low cost, such as sanitation, immunisations, birth control, and programmes to fight famine, poverty, and ignorance. If one assumes that reduction in the burden of disease increases utility, then a utilitarian would favour allocation policies that are most effective at reducing the world's overall disease burden. A utilitarian would probably regard the 90/10 divide as unjust because it would produce more net utility to shift some of the world's biomedical research resources from the problems of the developed world to those of the developing world.

One problem with the utilitarian approach to justice, according to many critics, is that justice always depends on empirical facts about connections between means and ends. Utilitarianism makes no special provisions for the least advantaged members of society, because justice is always a function of whatever rules or policies happen to maximise overall utility. Thus, a utilitarian account of justice should be supplemented by some non-utilitarian principles of justice that make special provisions for the least advantaged members of society.

Egalitarians favour rules and policies that promote the interests of the least advantaged members of society, and an egalitarian would probably regard the 90/10 divide as unjust. Egalitarian theories hold that equality is the defining feature of a just society. Of course, egalitarians hold different views about the nature of equality or how to best secure it. This paper will briefly consider how John Rawls' influential theory would apply to the 90/10 divide.

Rawls' theory is very complex, and he revised and reinterpreted his views several times. Readers are probably familiar with his approach to national justice, which he developed in *A Theory of Justice* and revised in *Political Liberalism*. Readers are probably less familiar with Rawls' theory of international justice, which he developed in *The Law of Peoples*. For the sake of brevity, this paper will not discuss Rawls' theory of international justice, but it will consider how his theory of national justice would apply to the 90/10 divide.

Rawls defends two principles of justice. The first principle requires that all members of society have the same scheme of basic rights and liberties; the second, also known as the difference principle, permits social and economic inequalities in society, provided that the inequalities do not interfere with fair equality of opportunity and they benefit the least advantaged members of society. Rawls also argues that the first principle takes precedence over the second, and that fair equality of opportunity takes precedence over allowing for social and economic inequalities that benefit the least advantaged members of society.

Rawls' difference principle addresses the distribution of primary goods in a just society. Primary goods—those things that any rational person would want—include 'rights and liberties, powers and opportunities, income and wealth.' The first principle of justice requires that all rights and liberties in society be distributed equally, but the second principle permits other primary goods to be distributed unequally, provided that there is fair equality of opportunity in society and the least advantaged members benefit from the unequal distribution. Although Rawls does not include health as a primary good, one might argue that health promotes fair equality of opportunity.

If we view the equality principle and the difference principle as applying internationally, then the 90/10 divide would be unjust if it: 1) interfered with the basic scheme of rights and liberties, 2) undermined equality of opportunity, or 3) did not benefit the least advantaged members of society. While it seems unlikely that the 90/10 divide interferes with basic rights and liberties, one could easily infer that the 90/10 divide undermines equality of opportunity or does not benefit the least advantaged members of the world. The 90/10 is unjust because it contributes to international health disparities, and these disparities have a substantial impact on the welfare of the world's least advantaged people.

To summarise, from a utilitarian and an egalitarian perspective, the 90/10 divide is unjust. How should individuals and societies respond to this inequity? The remainder of the paper will address this question.

POLITICAL AND ECONOMIC BARRIERS TO CLOSING THE 90/10 DIVIDE

As noted earlier, private foundations are already pulling their weight when it comes to addressing the 90/10 divide. Although these foundations deserve high praise for their extraordinary efforts to address the health problems of the developing world, their efforts are no substitute for commitments from governments or private corporations. However, there are some political and economic barriers to increasing funding from the government and private industry.

The main barriers to increasing government funding for R&D on the health problems of the developing world are political. First, R&D on problems that have their main impact on the developing world do not have as much popular support as R&D on problems that have their main impact on the developed world. Second, even research that has popular appeal will not obtain government support if no advocacy group lobbies the government for money. Perhaps the developing world needs its own interest group to lobby governments for biomedical R&D funding.

How could an advocacy group convince citizens from developed nations that they should spend their tax dollars on R&D on the health problems of the developing world? First, one could make the moral argument that developed nations have a moral duty, as a matter of international justice, to fund R&D on the health problems of the developing world. However, this argument will not convince people who are sceptical about international justice or who take a libertarian approach to justice. Second, one might make the pragmatic argument that the health problems of the developing world will eventually affect the developed world. In the era of global travel and commerce, diseases in one part of the world can rapidly affect another. HIV/AIDS spread from Africa to the rest of the world. Severe, Acute Respiratory Distress Syndrome (SARS) spread quickly from China to Toronto.

How can one convince pharmaceutical and biotechnology companies that they should invest their money in conducting R&D related to the health problems of the developing world? First, one could make a moral argument that private corporations have a social responsibility to help promote access to medications that are desperately needed in the developing world. Companies can fulfil their social responsibilities through research and development, price reductions for the developing world (also known as stratified marketing or equity pricing schemes), and drug give-aways. However, this argument may not be very convincing to most companies. Even companies that endorse social responsibility may prefer to discharge their duties through charitable causes in the developed world, which can provide more public recognition than charitable causes in the developing world.

Second, one could make the pragmatic argument that private corporations can profit financially from investing money on R&D that addresses the health problems of the developing world. However, there are problems with this strategy as well. As we saw earlier, private companies make their R&D decisions based on factors that affect profit potential. Most of these factors do not favour investment of R&D funds in health problems that affect the developing world. Although the developing world represents a potentially enormous market, consumers in the developing world do not have enough money to buy medications priced at even nominal levels. Developing nations cannot afford patented medicines and can barely afford unpatented ones. Furthermore, intellectual property protection is uncertain in the developing world. The most significant intellectual property treaty, Trade Related Aspects of Intellectual Properties (TRIPs), which has been signed by members of the World Trade Organization (WTO), allows nations to take various measures, including compulsory licensing and parallel importing from signatory countries, to deal with national emergencies. Several years ago, Pfizer, Merck, Glaxo and other pharmaceutical companies brought litigation to stop developing nations from exercising their rights under the TRIPs agreement. Although these companies eventually dropped the litigation, due to international political pressure, intellectual property rights in the developing world remain contentious. Prior to signing the TRIPs agreement, many developing nations did not honour pharmaceutical patents. In order to encourage developing nations to sign the agreement, developed nations made several concessions to developing nations, such as a phase-in period and provisions to deal with national emergencies. As countries renegotiate the TRIPs agreement, these issues will certainly resurface. One might argue that developing nations should honour intellectual property treaties in order to encourage pharmaceutical companies to make R&D investments in the health problems of the developing world. Conversely, one might argue that this is a high price to pay for medications that benefit the developing world, and that it would be wiser to encourage government investment in R&D for the developing world, rather than rely on pharmaceutical companies to take responsibility for developing new medications.

Given the political and economic obstacles to closing the 90/10 divide, it would be wise to rely on neither the public nor the private sector to take care of the problem. Those who are concerned about the divide should form advocacy groups to encourage governments from developed nations and pharmaceutical and biotechnology companies to increase the amount of money they spend on R&D on the health problems of the developing world. To facilitate, encourage, and organise investment of R&D funds and lighten the burden faced by any single nation or company, the UN should establish a trust fund to hold and distribute money contributed by governments or private firms from developed nations similar to the Global AIDS Fund. The trust fund could sponsor R&D, including basic research and clinical trials, on the health problems of the developing world. To prevent private firms from gaining exclusive control of its products, the fund could also acquire patents on the medications developed through the fund, and it could issue non-exclusive licenses to developing nations to manufacture and distribute medications. To keep the cost of drugs low, the fund would not charge a fee for licensing. Pharmaceutical companies could also contribute money to the fund as a gesture of their social responsibility to the developing world, with the understanding that they would have no patent rights over medications developed from the fund. They could still sponsor their own R&D related to the health problems of the developing world and continue to pursue the intellectual property rights accordingly, but there would be an intellectual property-free zone of important medications, biologics, and medical devices developed through the trust fund. Private charities could also contribute to the fund. As the world's largest investor in biomedical R&D, the US should set the pace for this trust fund. Large pharmaceutical companies, such as Pfizer, Merck and Glaxo, could also serve as pacesetters for this fund. Although charities and corporations would be able to contribute to the fund, it would not be wise to rely too heavily on private sources of funding. Most of the money for the fund would probably need to come from governments of the developed world.

Note

1. S. Benatar. Avoiding Exploitation in Clinical Research. Cambridge *Quarterly of Healthcare Ethics* 2000; 9: 562–565. 'Burden of Disease' is a measurement of several different factors related to the impact of a disease on individuals and society including the incidence of the disease, mortality rate, the degree of disability caused by the disease, the impact of the disease on life expectancy, economic and social aspects of the disease, and public health considerations. See: Institute of Medicine. 1998. *Scientific Opportunities and Public Needs: Improving Health Priority Setting and Public Input at the National Institutes of Health.* Washington, DC. National Academy Press.

Global Environmental Change and Health: Impacts and Inequalities

A. J. McMichael, S. Friel, A. Nyong, and C. Corvalan

Michael et al. present evidence that human-generated climate change and environmental destruction pose a grave threat to human health, particularly to vulnerable populations in the developing world. These differential outcomes are caused not only by regional differences in climate change severity, but also by "unequal access to environmental fundamentals." Privatization of these public goods aggravates the problem, they argue, as do industrialization and modernization policies that improve the health of some at the expense of others who depend on the environment for subsistence.

The authors argue that health care professionals have special responsibilities and capacities to mitigate the health impacts of environmental devastation. One means is through preventive actions—to try to reduce their societies' carbon emissions, for example. Another is through helping vulnerable groups adapt and survive in spite of the earth's weakened "life support systems."

Human actions are changing many of the world's natural environmental systems, including the climate system. These systems are intrinsic to life processes and fundamental to human health, and their disruption and depletion make it more difficult to tackle health inequalities. Indeed, we will not achieve the UN millennium development health goals if environmental destruction continues. Health professionals have a vital contributory role in preventing and reducing the health effects of global environmental change.

Problems of focus

In 2000 the United Nations set out eight development goals to improve the lives of the world's disadvantaged populations. The goals seek reductions in poverty, illiteracy, sex inequality, malnutrition, child deaths, maternal mortality, and major infections as well creation of environmental stability and a global partnership for development. One problem of this itemisation of goals is that it separates environmental considerations from health considerations. Poverty cannot be eliminated while environmental degradation exacerbates

From "Global Environmental Change and Health: Impacts, Inequalities, and the Health Sector," by A. J. McMichael and colleagues, *BMJ* 336 (January 26, 2008) © BMJ. (References and some figures omitted.)

malnutrition, disease, and injury. Food supplies need continuing soil fertility, climatic stability, freshwater supplies, and ecological support (such as pollination). Infectious diseases cannot be stabilised in circumstances of climatic instability, refugee flows, and impoverishment.

The seventh millennium development goal also takes a limited view of environmental sustainability, focusing primarily on traditional localised physical, chemical, and microbial hazards. Those hazards, which are associated with industrialisation, urbanisation, and agriculture in lower income countries, remain important as they impinge most on poor and vulnerable communities. Exposure to indoor air pollution, for example, varies substantially between rich and poor in urban and rural populations. And the World Health Organization estimates that a quarter of the global burden of disease, including over one third of childhood burden, is due to modifiable factors in air, water, soil, and food. This estimated environment related burden is much greater in low income than high income countries overall (25% versus 17% of deaths—and widening further to a twofold difference in percentages between the highest and lowest risk countries). Heavy metals and chemical residues contaminate local foods, urban air pollution causes premature deaths, and waterborne enteric pathogens kill two million children annually.

These relatively localised environmental health hazards, though, are mostly remediable. Meanwhile, a larger scale, less remediable, and potentially irreversible category of environmental health hazard is emerging. Human pressures on the natural environment, reflecting global population growth and intensified economic activities, are now so great that many of the world's biophysical and ecological systems are being impaired. Examples of these global environmental changes include climate change, freshwater shortages, loss of biodiversity (with consequent changes to functioning of ecosystems), and exhaustion of fisheries. These changes are unprecedented in scale, and the resultant risks to population health need urgent response by health professionals and the health sector at large.

Who will be affected

The health effects of global environmental change will vary between countries. Loss of healthy life years in low income African countries, for example, is predicted to be 500 times that in Europe. The fourth assessment report of the Intergovernmental Panel on Climate Change concluded that adverse health effects are much more likely in low income countries and vulnerable subpopulations. These disparities may well increase in coming decades, not only because of regional differences in the intensity of environmental changes (such as water shortages and soil erosion), but also because of exacerbations of differentials in economic conditions, levels of social and human capital, political power, and local environmental dependency.

These differential health risks also reflect the wider issue of access to global and local "public goods." Most of the world's arable land has now been privatised; stocks of wild species (fish, animals, and wild plants) are declining as population pressures and commercial activities intensify; and freshwater is increasingly becoming subject to market pricing. Social policies should therefore pay particular attention to the health inequalities that flow from unequal access to environmental fundamentals.

Availability of safe drinking water illustrates the point about access to what, historically, was common property: 1.1 billion people lack safe drinking water, and 2.6 billion lack basic sanitation. Beyond diarrhoeal disease, water related health risks also arise from chemical contamination—such as arsenic as a cause of skin pigmentation, hyperkeratosis, cardiovascular disease, neuropathy, and cancer.

Role of social conditions

The relation of environmental impoverishment to health risks and inequalities is complex. Environmental degradation impairs health, while health deficits (for example, malnutrition or depletion of the workforce from AIDS) can amplify environmental mismanagement. This causes inequalities in both health endangering exposures and health outcomes.

India provides a good example of the complexity of these relations. The country's average life expectancy is relatively low but is expected to improve with industrialisation and modernisation. Industrialisation is contributing to the rapid increase of coal burning in India, and the resultant addition to global emissions and climate change amplifies health risks worldwide. These health risks will affect the world's most vulnerable populations.

The risks to population health from environmental change have far reaching implications for prevention strategies (fig 1). Global changes result in loss of natural resources. Resolution of these risks therefore requires a different approach from that used for the more familiar challenges presented by time limited and reversible local environmental contamination.

Climate change and health

Human induced global climate change is now an acknowledged reality. We have taken a long time to recognise the resultant health risks, current and future, and their unequal effects around the world, but the topic is now attracting much attention. Risks to health will arise by direct and indirect pathways and will reflect changes in both average climate conditions and in climatic variability. The main risks are:

- Effects of heat waves and other extreme events (cyclones, floods, storms, wildfires)

- Changes in patterns of infectious disease

- Effects on food yields

- Effects on freshwater supplies

- Impaired functioning of ecosystems (for example, wetlands as water filters)

- Displacement of vulnerable populations (for example, low lying island and coastal populations)

- Loss of livelihoods.

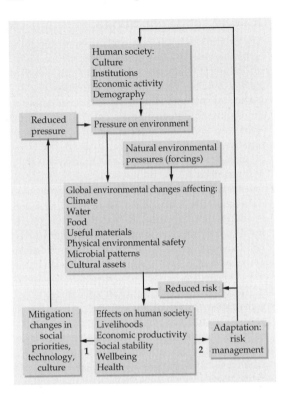

Fig 1 | Relations between human induced global environmental changes affect health and social policy responses. True primary prevention (path 1) reduces or eliminates the human pressures on environment. A more defensive type of prevention is attained through adaptive interventions to lessen risk (path 2), particularly in vulnerable communities

Extreme weather events, infection, and malnutrition will have the greatest health effects in poor and vulnerable populations (box 1). In sub-Saharan Africa over 110 million people currently live in regions prone to malaria epidemics. Climate change could add 20-70 million to this figure by the 2080s (assuming no population increase, and including forecast malaria reductions in West Africa from drying). Any such increase would exacerbate poverty and make it harder to achieve and sustain health improvements.

Some links between climate change and human health are complex. For example, the predicted drying in sub-Saharan Africa could increase the incidence of HIV infection, as impoverished rural farming families move to cities where conditions foster sex work and unsafe sex.

BOX 1 AFRICA AND CLIMATE CHANGE

Africa is very vulnerable to climate change because of other environmental and social stresses. The economy depends critically on agriculture, which accounts for two thirds of the workforce and up to half of household incomes and food.

- Climate models predict regional increases in mean temperatures of several degrees centigrade by 2100, a decline in summer rainfall in southern and northern Africa and some increase in west and east Africa. Drying, plus the demands of population growth and economic development, will exacerbate regional water scarcity

- Falls in crop yields due to 1-2°C warming by 2050 would add an estimated 12 million additional Africans to the 200 million currently undernourished

- Extreme events such as flooding . . . will affect food availability by damaging roads, storage, and markets—floods in 2000 in Mozambique damaged about 10% of farmland and 90% of irrigation, displaced two million people, and affected up to 1.5 million livelihoods (mostly in poor rural areas)

- Livestock viral diseases such as east coast fever, foot and mouth disease, blue tongue virus, Rift valley fever are climate sensitive. Regional increases in temperature and rainfall could affect tsetse fly habitat and hence trypanosomiasis in livestock

- Climate change and agricultural downturn in Africa may force populations to move, generating conflicts over territory. Pastoralists forced to search for grazing land because of wells drying up may partly explain the Darfur crisis in Sudan

Roles for doctors and other health professionals

The spectrum of potential strategies to reduce health risks is wide, commensurate with the diversity of threats to health posed by climate change and other global environmental changes.

Local policies and actions, both to mitigate environmental change at source and to adapt to existing and unavoidable risks to health, will often need support from health attuned policies at provincial, national, and international levels. For example, community programmes to mosquito-proof houses will need to be reinforced by improvements in the national surveillance of infectious diseases and in outbreak warning systems.

Doctors and other health professionals have particular knowledge, opportunity, and, often, political leverage that can help ensure—through advocacy or direct participation—that preventive actions are taken. Actions include promoting public understanding, monitoring and reporting the health effects of environmental change, and proposing and advocating local adaptive responses.

Various websites list and discuss actions for doctors to take, both individually and collectively. For example, the US Centers for Disease Control and Prevention lists 11 functions for the public health system and practitioners for responding to climate change. And Doctors for the Environment Australia has run a successful, continuing, national campaign of patient education by distributing posters and pamphlets for use in doctors' waiting rooms.

Adaptive strategies to lessen health risks

Many local actions can be taken to reduce the vulnerability of communities and populations. These will vary considerably between different regions of the world, and in relation to prevailing socioeconomic conditions and available resources. During Australia's...prolonged drought (2001–7), some rural health doctors reported that fostering and supporting communal activities (community choirs, social gatherings, financial advisory networks, etc) increased local resilience against depression associated with loss of livelihood.

Climate change and other large scale environmental changes are unlikely to cause entirely new diseases (although they may contribute to the emergence of new strains of viruses and other microbes that can infect humans). Rather, they will alter the incidence, range, and seasonality of many existing health disorders. Hence, existing healthcare and public health systems should provide an appropriate starting point for adaptive strategies to lessen health effects.

Preventive action

Although adaptive strategies will minimise the effects of climate change, the greater public health preventive challenge lies in stopping the process of climate change. This requires bold and far sighted policy decisions at national and international levels, entailing much greater emissions cuts than were being proposed a decade ago.

Scientists have concluded that we need to prevent atmospheric carbon dioxide concentrations exceeding 450–500 ppm to avoid the serious, perhaps irreversible, damage to many natural systems and ecological processes that a global average temperature increase of 2-3°C would cause. This requires early radical action as today's concentrations are approaching 390 ppm (compared with 280 ppm before industrialisation). Health professionals, acting through citizens' or professional organisations, have both the opportunity and responsibility to contribute to resolving this momentous issue. Improving awareness of the problem is the first step. Since 1993, doctors from 14 countries (including six low income countries) have had a central role in the Intergovernmental Panel on Climate Change's assessment of the health effects of climate change. We should also add this topic, including its relevance to health professional activity, to the medical curriculum.

The health sector, meanwhile, must minimise greenhouse gas emissions from its own infrastructure, especially hospitals. Health researchers should act to minimise greenhouse gas emissions from their own studies.

Conclusion

The Stern report, in 2006, highlighted the potentially great damage to the world's economic system from unconstrained climate change. The greater risk, however, is to the vitality and health of all species, including humans, if current trends continue to weaken the earth's life support systems. The health professions have a crucial role in promoting public understanding of this fundamental association and health protecting responses to it.

Section 2: Clinical Trials in the Developing World

Human Rights and Maternal–Fetal HIV Transmission Prevention Trials in Africa

George J. Annas and Michael A. Grodin

Annas and Grodin argue that unless a therapy that is being tested in a poverty-stricken country will actually be made available to those who need it in that country, research subjects are likely being exploited. The mere possibility that the therapy will be feasible for use in the impoverished country is not enough to justify the testing. Nor is the fact that scientists from the host country are involved. Even when the testing is justified, research subjects must not be drawn from the most vulnerable groups and informed consent of participants is required.

Introduction

Since the adoption of the Universal Declaration of Human Rights by the United [Nations] General Assembly in 1948, the countries of the world have agreed that all humans have dignity and rights. In 1998, the 50th anniversary of the Universal Declaration of Human Rights, the Declaration's aspirations have yet to be realized, and poverty, racism, and sexism continue to conspire to frustrate the worldwide human rights movement. The human rights and public health issues of maternal–fetal human immunodeficiency virus (HIV) transmission prevention trials in Africa, Asia, and the Caribbean are not unique to acquired immunodeficiency syndrome (AIDS) or to those countries. Open discussion of these issues provides an opportunity to move the real human rights agenda forward. This is why Global Lawyers and Physicians (GLP), a transnational organization dedicated to promoting and protecting the health-related provisions of the Universal Declaration of Human Rights, joined with Ralph Nader's Public Citizen organization to challenge the conduct of a series of AIDS clinical trials in these developing countries.

The Clinical Trials

In 1994, the first effective intervention to reduce the perinatal transmission of HIV was developed in the United States in AIDS Clinical Trials Group

From *American Journal of Public Health* 88, no. 4 (April 1998): 560–563. With permission from the American Public Health Association. (References omitted.)

(ACTG) Study 076. In that trial, use of zidovudine administered orally to HIV-positive pregnant women as early as the second trimester of pregnancy, intravenously during labor, and orally to their newborns for 6 weeks reduced the incidence of HIV infection by two thirds (from about 25% to about 8%). Six months after stopping the study, the US Public Health Service recommended the ACTG 076 regimen as the standard of care in the United States. In June 1994, the World Health Organization (WHO) convened a meeting in Geneva at which it was concluded (in an unpublished report) that the 076 regime was not feasible in the developing world. At least 16 randomized clinical trials (15 using placebos as controls) were subsequently approved for conduct in developing countries, primarily in Africa. These trials involve more than 17,000 pregnant women. Nine of the studies, most of them comparing shorter courses of zidovudine, vitamin A, or HIV immunoglobulin with placebo, are funded by the Centers for Disease Control and Prevention (CDC) or the National Institutes of Health (NIH).

Most of the public discussion about these trials has centered on the use of the placebos. The question of placebo use is a central one in determining how a study should be conducted. But we believe the more important issue these trials raise is the question of whether they should be done at all. Specifically, when is medical research ethically justified in developing countries that do not have adequate health services (or on US populations that have no access to basic health care)? This question is especially pertinent since February 1998 when, on the basis of a Thailand study that demonstrated that a short course of zidovudine reduced HIV transmission by 50%, CDC, NIH, and the United Nations Program on AIDS (UNAIDS) officials announced that they would recommend that the use of placebo be halted in all mother-to-fetus transmission studies.

Research on Impoverished Populations

The central issue involved in doing research with impoverished populations is exploitation. Harold Varmus, speaking for NIH, and David Satcher, speaking for CDC, both seem to realize this. They wrote in the *New England Journal of Medicine* last year that "trials that make use of impoverished populations to test drugs for use solely in developed countries violate our most basic understanding of ethical behavior." However, instead of trying to demonstrate how the study interventions, such as a shorter course of zidovudine (AZT), could actually be delivered to the populations of the countries in the studies, they assert that the studies can be justified because they will provide information that the host country can use to "make a sound judgment about the appropriateness and financial feasibility of providing the intervention." However, what these countries require is not good intentions, but a real plan to deliver the intervention, should it be proven beneficial.

Unless the interventions being tested will actually be made available to the impoverished populations that are being used as research subjects, developed countries are simply exploiting them in order to quickly use the knowledge gained from the clinical trials for the developed countries' own benefit. If the research reveals regimens of equal efficacy at less cost, these regimens will surely be implemented in the developed world. If the research reveals the regimens to be less efficacious, these results will be added to the scientific literature, and the developed world will not conduct those studies. Ethics and basic human rights principles require not a thin promise, but a real plan as to how the intervention will actually be delivered. Actual delivery is also, of course, required to support even the utilitarian justification for the trials, which is to find a simple, inexpensive, and feasible intervention in as short a time frame as possible because so many people are dying of AIDS. No justification is supportable unless the intervention is actually made widely available to the relevant populations.

Neither NIH nor CDC (nor the host countries) has a plan that would make the interventions they are studying available in Africa, where more than two thirds of the people in the world reside who are infected with HIV. As an example, Varmus and Satcher point out that the wholesale cost of zidovudine in the 076 protocol is estimated to be in excess of $800 per mother and infant and that this amount is far greater than what most developing countries can pay for standard care. The CDC estimates the cost of the "short course" zidovudine regimens being investigated to be roughly $50 per person. The cost of merely screening for HIV disease, a precondition for any course of therapy, is approximately $10, and all pregnant women must be screened to find the cases to treat. These costs must be compared with the total per capita health care expenditures of the countries where this research is being conducted. Given this fact, African countries involved in the clinical trials (or some other funder) must make realistic assurances that if a research regimen proves effective in reducing mother-to-fetus transmission of HIV, resources will be made available so that the HIV-positive pregnant women in their countries will receive this regimen.

However, the mere assertion that the intervention will be feasible for use in the developing countries is simply not good enough, given our experience and knowledge of what happens in Africa now. For example, we already know that effectively treating sexually transmitted diseases such as syphilis, gonorrhea, and chancroid with the simple and effective treatments that are now available can drastically lower the incidence of HIV infection. Yet, these inexpensive and effective treatments are not delivered to poor Africans. For example, a recent study showed that improving the treatment of sexually transmitted diseases in rural Tanzania could reduce HIV infections by 40%. Nonetheless, this relatively inexpensive and effective intervention is not delivered. Vaccines against devastating diseases have also been developed with sub-Saharan African populations as test subjects.

Cultural Relativism or Universal Human Rights?

In their article in the *New England Journal of Medicine*, Varmus and Satcher sought to bolster their ethical position by quoting the chair of the

AIDS Research Committee of the Uganda Cancer Institute, who wrote a letter to Dr. Varmus:

> *These are Ugandan studies conducted by Ugandan investigators on Ugandans. . . . It is not NIH conducting the studies in Uganda, but Ugandans conducting their study on their people for the good of their people.*

Two points are especially striking about Varmus' and Satcher's using this justification. First, their justification is simply not accurate. If NIH and CDC were not involved in these studies, these agencies would not have to justify them; indeed, the studies would not have been undertaken. These US agencies *are* involved—these trials are not just Ugandans doing research on other Ugandans. Second, and more importantly, the use of this quotation implies support for an outdated and dangerous view of cultural relativism.

Even if it were true that the studies in question were done by Ugandans on Ugandans, this would not mean that the United States or the international community could conclude that they should not be criticized. (This rationale did not inhibit criticism of apartheid in South Africa, genocide in Rwanda, or torture and murder in the Congo.) Human Rights Watch, referring to repression in Central Africa, said in its December 1997 review of the year on the issue of human rights that the slogan "African solutions to African problems" is now used as a "thin cover" for abusing citizens. That observation can be applicable to experimentation on citizens as well.

The other major justification both NIH and CDC use for the trials is the consensus reached at the June 1994 meeting of researchers at WHO. Of the many analogies that have been drawn between the HIV transmission prevention trials and the US Public Health Service's Tuskegee syphilis study, perhaps most striking is their reliance on professional consensus instead of ethical principle to justify research on poor, black populations. As historian James Jones wrote in his book *Bad Blood*, which was written about the Tuskegee experiment: "The consensus was that the experiment was worth doing, and in a profession whose members did not have a well-developed system of normative ethics, consensus formed the functional equivalent of moral sanction."

Neither researcher consensus nor host country agreement is ethically sufficient justification for choosing a research population. As the National Research Council's committee on Human Genome Diversity

properly put it, in the context of international research on human subjects, "[s]ensitivity to the specific practices and beliefs of a community cannot be used as a justification for violating universal human rights." Justice and equity questions are also important to the ability of individual research subjects to give informed consent.

Informed Consent

Research subjects should not be drawn from populations who are especially vulnerable (e.g., the poor, children, or mentally impaired persons) unless the population is the only group in which the research can be conducted and the group itself will derive benefits from the research. Even when these conditions are met, informed consent must also be obtained. In most settings in Africa, voluntary, informed consent will be problematic and difficult, and it may even preclude ethical research. This is because, in the absence of health care, virtually any offer of medical assistance (even in the guise of research) will be accepted as "better than nothing" and research will almost inevitably be confused with treatment, making informed consent difficult.

Interviews with women subjects of the placebo-controlled trial in the Ivory Coast support this conclusion. For example, one subject, Cecile Guede, a 23-year-old HIV-infected mother participating in a US-financed trial, told the *New York Times*, "They gave me a bunch of pills to take, and told me how to take them. Some were for malaria, some were for fevers, and some were supposed to be for the virus. I knew that there were different kinds, but I figured that if one of them didn't work against AIDS, then one of the others would." The *Times* reporter who wrote the front-page story, Howard W. French, said, "For Ms Guede, the reason to enroll in the study last year was clear: it offered her and her infant free health care and a hope to shield her baby from deadly infection. . . . [T]he prospect of help as she brought her baby into the world made taking part in the experiment all but irresistible."

Persons can make a gift of themselves by volunteering for research. However, it is extremely unlikely that poor African women would knowingly volunteer to participate in research that offered no benefit to their communities (because the intervention would not be made available) and that would only serve to enrich the multinational drug companies and the developed world. Thus, a good ethical working rule is that researchers should presume that valid consent cannot be obtained from impoverished populations in the absence of a realistic plan to deliver the intervention to the population. Informed consent, by itself, can protect many subjects of research in developed countries, but its protective power is much more compromised in impoverished populations who are being offered what looks like medical care that is otherwise unavailable to them.

The International Community and the AIDS Pandemic

If the goal of the clinical trials is to reduce the spread of HIV infection in developing countries, what strategy should public health adopt to achieve this end? It is not obvious that the answer is to conduct clinical trials of short-term zidovudine treatment. In the developed world, for example, HIV-infected women are advised not to breast-feed their infants because 8% to 18% of them will be infected with HIV from breast milk. However, in much of the developing world, including in most African countries, WHO continues to recommend breast-feeding because the lack of clean water still makes formula-feeding more dangerous. As long as this recommendation stays in effect, and is followed, even universal use of the ACTG 076 regimen, which would lower the overall newborn infection rate by about 16%, would only likely serve to reduce the incidence of HIV infection in infants by about the same amount that it is increased by breast-feeding (8% to 18%). A more effective public health intervention to improve the health of women and their children may be to put more efforts into providing clean water and sanitation. This will help not only to deal with HIV, but also to alleviate many other problems, including diarrheal diseases.

President Jacques Chirac of France was on target in his December 1997 speech to the 10th International Conference on Sexually Transmitted Disease and AIDS in Africa, which was held in the Ivory Coast. President Chirac proposed creating an international "therapy support fund" that is primarily funded by European countries (the former colonial powers in Africa). Although he put emphasis on the new drugs available for AIDS treatments, it would be more useful to consider the public health priorities of the countries themselves, for example, prevention, especially in areas such as sanitation, water supply, nutrition, education, and the delivery of simple and effective vaccines and medical treatments for sexually transmitted diseases.

Conclusion

Actual delivery of health care requires more than just paying lip service to the principles of the Universal Declaration of Human Rights; it requires a real commitment to human rights and a willingness on the part of the developed countries to take economic, social, and cultural rights as seriously as political and civil rights.

We're Trying to Help Our Sickest People, Not Exploit Them

Danstan Bagenda and Philippa Musoke-Mudido

Bagenda and Musoke-Mudido respond to critics of clinical trials in Africa involving comparisons of new therapies with placebos in preventing the transmission of HIV from mothers to their infants. The authors argue that such factors as cost, nutrition, social practices, culture, and environmental circumstances make it inappropriate to compare testing in developed countries with testing in Africa. They insist that the women enrolled in the HIV trials received intensive education counseling in their local languages, which explained potential risks and chances of getting a placebo. The authors express skepticism about those who claim to speak on behalf of Africa, yet have never worked with its people.

Every day, like the beat of a drum heard throughout Africa, 1,000 more infants here are infected with HIV, the virus that causes AIDS. At Old Mulago Hospital, we are trying to educate people about AIDS, as well as study new therapies to prevent the disease's rampant spread. Recently, some of these studies have been attacked, with comparisons made to the notorious Tuskegee experiment in which black men in the United States were denied treatment for syphilis. Tuskegee? Is this really what is happening here in our mother–child clinic?

Our country lies in the heart of Africa, along the Great Rift Valley and Lake Victoria. It is one of those hardest hit by the AIDS epidemic. A few years ago, visitors here in the capital were greeted by the macabre sight of empty coffins for sale—piled in pyramids from adult to baby size—along the main road. These grim reminders have since been removed by city authorities, but the AIDS epidemic is omnipresent. In this city of 1 million, about one out of every six adults is infected with HIV. Hospitals and clinics like ours, which provide free medical care and therefore serve the poorest communities, are stretched beyond their resources.

At the Mulago Hospital, where more than 20,000 women deliver each year, we are trying to find effective therapies to stop transmission of HIV from pregnant women to their babies. About one in five babies becomes infected with HIV during pregnancy and delivery. If the mother breast-feeds her baby, there is an additional 15- to 25-percent chance that the baby will later become infected. There is no available treatment for the disease in Uganda. After careful consideration among researchers from developing and developed countries, the World Health Organization (WHO) recommended in 1994 that the best way to find safe and effective treatment for sufferers in countries in the developing world is to conduct studies in which new treatments, better tailored to the local population, are compared with placebos (inactive pills).

Women who enroll in our studies undergo intensive education and individual counseling. They are given a comprehensive consent form, written in the local language, which they are encouraged to take home and discuss with their families. It describes the potential risks of participating in the study and their chances of receiving a placebo. Only when they and their counselors are satisfied that all questions have been answered are they asked to sign the form. Our careful attention to these measures has consistently met the standards of national and international ethical review committees.

Results from a clinical trial in the United States and France, known as the ACTG 076 protocol, showed as long ago as 1994 that if a mother takes zidovudine (AZT) daily from the middle of her pregnancy until delivery, receives intravenous AZT during delivery, gives her infant oral AZT for the first six weeks of life and does not breast-feed, the transmission of HIV from mother to child can be reduced by two-thirds. The ACTG 076 protocol immediately became the recommended therapy in the United States. But it is not possible to simply transplant this protocol to Uganda for three main reasons: At a cost of between $800 and $1,000 per person, it is far too expensive; it requires treatment to begin in the middle of a pregnancy; and it means mothers must abstain from breast-feeding.

Some critics in the United States have asserted that we should compare new therapies with the ACTG 076 protocol rather than with a placebo. But in Uganda, the government health expenditure is $3 per person per year, and the average citizen makes less than $1 per day. We think it is unethical to impose expensive treatment protocols that could never be used here. The situations are not parallel. In America, for instance, antibiotics are often overprescribed; but here in Uganda we have difficulty even obtaining many needed antibiotics—to treat common complaints like ear infections. It is also naive to assume that what works for Americans will work for the rest of the world. Differences in nutrition, economics, societal norms and culture, and the frequency of tropical diseases make such extrapolations dangerously ethnocentric and wrong.

Many pregnant women here never show up for prenatal care and, of those who do, 70 percent make their first visit after the 30th week of pregnancy—too late for the U.S. treatment protocol. Should we make a study available only to the minority of women who come early for care and tell the others, sorry, you came too late? We need to find treatments that will reach the most women possible—ones that can be given late in pregnancy or during labor.

There is also a huge gap between the United States and Uganda in breast-feeding practices. Should we apply the ACTG 076 protocol and tell women in the clinic not to breast-feed and instead give their babies infant formula? Access to clean water is a formidable challenge here, and we still remember the shocking epidemics of infant diarrhea and mortality in the early 1970s, when multinational companies shamelessly marketed formula in Africa. Despite the known risks of transmitting HIV through breast milk, the Ugandan Ministry of Health, UNICEF and WHO still encourage African women to breast-feed as the nutritional benefits outweigh the risks of HIV transmission.

There are other factors we need to take into account. Every day, we treat both mothers and infants for malaria and iron deficiency. Both diseases contribute to anemia, which is also a major side effect of AZT. We are worried that AZT will exacerbate anemia in women and infants here. If we are to find out whether the new treatments are safe, the best way is to compare them with a placebo. How could we evaluate the safety of a new treatment if we compared it with the treatment used in America— one that has its own side effects? Could we really tell Ugandans that we had evaluated a new therapy for side effects using the best possible methods?

The AIDS epidemic has touched all our lives. Each of the 90 staff members in the mother–child health clinic has lost a family member, a loved one or a close friend. There is no dividing line between patients with HIV and those of us who care for them. A few years ago, we all chipped in money when a staff member needed to pay for the burial of a loved one, but recently we realized that we were all giving and receiving the same.

The ethical issues in our studies are complicated, but they have been given careful thought by the local community, ethicists, physicians and activists. Those who can speak with credibility for AIDS patients in Africa are those who live among and know the people here or have some basic cross-cultural sensitivity. We are suspicious of those who claim to speak for our people, yet have never worked with them. Callous accusations may help sell newspapers and journals, but they demean the people here and the horrible tragedy that we live daily.

In the next several months, we expect to see results from our study and others like it in Ivory Coast, South Africa, Tanzania and Thailand. We hope they will help bring appropriate and safe therapies to the people of the developing world. That hope is the driving force that brings us back to our work in the clinic after each of the all-too-frequent burials.

Section 3: Health, Culture, and Globalization

Redirecting the Female Circumcision Debate

Angela Wasunna

Wasunna examines the moral and practical implications of Western legal bans on *female genital mutilation* (FGM), also known as *female genital cutting* or *circumcision* (FGC). She argues that although FGM/C is a medically unacceptable practice, efforts to outlaw it in countries that practice both male circumcision and adult cosmetic surgeries are both misguided and hypocritical. Male circumcision is generally less harmful than FGM/C, Wasunna acknowledges, but argues that both are performed for cosmetic, rather than

From "Towards Redirecting the Female Circumcision Debate: Legal, Ethical and Cultural Considerations," *McGill Journal of Medicine* 5, no. 2 (2000): 104–110. Copyright © 2000 by MJM. (References omitted.)

therapeutic, reasons. She also points to other nontherapeutic procedures routinely performed on Western women, such as breast
implants, face-lifts, and liposuction, and questions why cultural pressures are not seen to undermine informed consent for such procedures, as it often is for FGM/C.

Justifications for FGM/C on religious, psychosexual, and hygienic
grounds have been discredited, Wasunna notes, but explains its persistence due to asymmetrical gender structures, resistance to Western
influence after colonialism, and the financial incentives of its often
elderly practitioners. The ingrained traditions and taboos around
FGM/C should thus be approached through rigorous, culturally sensitive education campaigns, rather than legal bans—which Wasunna
believes only drive the practice underground.

The World Health Organization reports that
between 100 and 137 million women, mostly
in Africa, have undergone some form of female
circumcision (also referred to as female genital
mutilation). Female circumcision is practiced in
more than twenty African countries as well as
in Oman, South Yemen, and the United Arab
Emirates. Moslem populations of Indonesia and
Malaysia also practice circumcision. Despite
regional variation in its prevalence, female
circumcision is more accurately considered an
ethnic practice with no direct relation to political
or geographical boundaries; for example, in Kenya,
the Meru practice excision, whereas the Luo do
not; in Nigeria, the Yoruba, Ibo and Hausa practice
excision but the Nupes of Fulani do not.

This paper is an attempt to redirect the debate
against female circumcision. The paper questions
the legality of enacting criminal sanctions against
female circumcision in western nations, while
permitting other similar practices. To this end, the
paper examines the historical and cultural context
of the practice and, further, draws parallels between
this procedure, male circumcision, and other forms
of surgery. The paper investigates some international
legislative responses to female circumcision. The
paper further explores the "double-standard"
application of laws in western countries that have a
high immigrant presence, in the context of female
circumcision, and concludes by examining what
direction the law should take in this debate. The
position of the author is that although female
circumcision is a medically unacceptable practice,
the use of criminal law in western countries is
nevertheless hypocritical and redundant. The most

effective way to end female circumcision in its entirety
is through aggressive education and the creation of
alternatives for communities affected by the practice.

ORIGINS OF FEMALE CIRCUMCISION

The origins of female circumcision are obscure
but the practice most likely dates back thousands
of years. Herodotus reported that female circumcision took place in ancient Egypt during the
fifth century B.C. and there is also evidence that
early Romans and Arabs had adopted the practice. At some uncertain point in history, excision
practices became associated with the obsessive
preoccupation with virginity and chastity that
still characterizes many African and Arab cultures
today; this combination resulted in the more
radical practice of infibulation (for description
of procedures, see Box 1).

Giorgis has suggested that the origin of female
circumcision can be traced to the patriarchal family
system, in which a woman could have only one
husband while a man could have several wives.
Along with other elaborate formal and informal
sanctions, strong patriarchal systems fostered female
circumcision, therein restricting women's sexuality for
the preservation of the male's lineage.

Another explanation is offered by the Egyptian
pharaonic belief in the bisexuality of the gods:

> *Now, just as certain gods are believed to be
> bisexual, so every person is believed to be endowed
> with the masculine and feminine "souls".
> These souls reveal their respective physiological
> characteristics in and through the procreative
> organs. Thus, the feminine soul of the man is in the*

BOX 1 THE PROCEDURES

At the physical level, female circumcision cannot be equated to male circumcision since the former generally involves far more extensive and permanent damage to the sexual organs and frequently has significant effects on the health of the individuals subjected to it (see text). This is part of the reason why female circumcision is abhorred, unlike male circumcision where the debate centers on stress to the infant, with relatively few people decrying its long-term effects.

Types of Female Circumcision

Mild *Sunna*	Pricking, slitting, or removal of the prepuce of the clitoris causing relatively little if any damage. "*Sunna*" is an Arabic word meaning "tradition".
Modified *Sunna*	Partial or total excision of the body of the clitoris.
Clitoridectomy / Excision	Removal of part or all of the clitoris and part or all of the labia minora. The vaginal opening is often occluded by the extensive scar tissue that results from the procedure.
Infibulation / Pharaonic circumcision	Consists of clitoridectomy and the excision of the labia minora and the inner layers of the labia majora. The raw edges are subsequently sewn together with catgut or made to adhere to each other by means of thorns. This causes the remaining skin of the labia majora to form a bridge of scar tissue over the vaginal opening. A small sliver of wood or straw inserted into the vagina prevents complete occlusion and thereby leaves a passage for urine and menstrual flow.
Introcusion	Enlargement of the vaginal opening by tearing it downward.
Intermediate	Modified version of pharaonic circumcision consisting of removal of the clitoris and part of the labia minora but leaving the labia majora intact. Suturing with catgut then narrows the introitus.
Recircumcision or refibulation	Performed on women who have given birth, or who are widowed or divorced to simulate a virginal vagina. The procedure is called "*adla*" (tightening) and is most frequently performed on women who have had previous pharaonic or intermediate circumcisions. The edges of the scar are pared and sewn together, or the loose tissue is stitched. Refibulation is sometimes referred to as "*Adlat El Rujal*" meaning men's circumcision as it is designed to create greater sexual pleasure for the man.

Traditional practitioners of female circumcision vary among different ethnic groups. Apart from midwives, barbers may perform the procedure, as is the case in Egypt and Northern Nigeria. In Northern Zaire the traditional circumciser is a male priest. Instruments used include razor blades, scissors, knives, thorns and pieces of glass. Antiseptic and anesthetics are not usually used although medicinal herbs would be used to assist the healing process or to help clot the blood.

prepuce, whereas the masculine soul of the woman is situated in the clitoris. This means that as the young boy grows up and is finally admitted into the masculine society, he has to shed his feminine properties. This is accomplished by the removal of the prepuce, the feminine portion of his original sexual state. The same is true with a young girl, who upon entering the feminine society is delivered from her masculine properties by having her clitoris or her clitoris and her labia excised. Only thus circumcised can the girl claim to be fully a woman and thus capable of the sexual life.

Excision and infibulation are by no means unique to Africa, and have at some time in history been practiced and are indeed still practiced in several parts of the world. Female clitoral excision was practiced in the English-speaking world during the 19th century. One reason that has been provided for its practice in the West is denoted in the following passage:

> *Isac Baker Brown (1812–1873) was considered one of the ablest and most innovative gynecological surgeons in England. ... Dr. Brown was seeking a surgical solution to cure the vexing mental disorders of women. According to the doctor, the main culprit was masturbation. The treatment was clitoridectomy.*

American physicians not only adopted clitoridectomy, but they also extended the scope of the operation to include oophorectomy (i.e. removal of the ovaries). Lesbian practices, suspected lesbian inclinations, and an aversion to men were all treated by clitoral excision, as were hyper-sexuality, hysteria and nervousness. Until 1905, labia were infibulated in the United States to prevent masturbation and this type of surgery was reportedly performed in mental hospitals as late as 1935.

Historically then, female circumcision has not been an exclusively Arab/African phenomenon. But why did the practice take root and survive in certain societies and not in others?

WHY FEMALE CIRCUMCISION CONTINUES TODAY

What are the forces that drive people in the 20th Century, in this age of technological advancement and knowledge, to still succumb to this practice? The most common response is tradition. Considering the question more carefully, the main reasons for the continuation of female circumcision may be loosely classified into four categories: 1) psychosexual, 2) religious, 3) sociological, as well as 4) hygienic and aesthetic reasons.

Psychosexual Factors

A common belief in countries where female circumcision is prevalent is that the clitoris is an aggressive organ, threatening the male organ and even endangering the baby during delivery. Alternatively, because the focus of sexual desire is recognized to be the clitoris, many cultures believe that excision is necessary to protect the woman

against her over-sexed nature, saving her from temptation, suspicion and disgrace while preserving her chastity. These beliefs must be understood in the context of societies where virginity (for a woman) is an absolute pre-requisite for marriage and where an extramarital relationship provokes the most severe penalties. In addition, in both Sudan and Egypt, female circumcision is believed to increase male sexual pleasure during intercourse.

Religious Factors

As alluded to above, female circumcision is a practice that transcends cultural, religious, and political boundaries though it is clearly more common today within certain groups. The custom of female circumcision does not appear to have originated in Islam, but has been accepted by it. It is believed that clitoridectomy was an original African institution adopted by Islam at the conquest of Egypt in 742 A.D. Though it is worth noting that female circumcision is not practiced in most Islamic countries and, in fact, it is not in accordance with the Koran.

Sociological Factors

Female circumcision is viewed by many as a way of socializing female fertility and forming an initiation rite of development into adulthood. In many parts of Africa, elaborate ceremonies surround the practice. The event is filled with symbolic song, dance and chants intended to teach the young girl her duties and desirable characteristics as wife and mother.

Hygiene and Aesthetics

In some societies, the clitoris is considered unpleasant to both sight and touch and it is a sign of maturity when a woman's "ugly genitalia" have been removed. Certain societies believe that female circumcision maintains good mental and physical health in a woman. Though once shared by western physicians, belief in the health benefits of clitoridectomy have been dispelled (see above). On the contrary, there are in fact significant medical complications (see below).

Having examined the four main factors why female circumcision continues to thrive in certain societies, it is still not clear why the custom has persisted given that many of these factors have either disappeared or are now given little or no credibility. What then are the possible explanations for the continued existence of female circumcision?

Historically women have been persuaded to see their sexual impulses in terms of what suits men. This suggestion must be considered in the context of the total economic and social structure of the societies concerned. For example, marriage has traditionally been, and continues to be, the only secure future for a woman in certain communities of Africa, the Middle East, and Asia. In many of these societies, failing to excise one's daughter is to practically ensure her ruination, since no one would marry an uncircumcised woman. It is still believed that the more severe the procedure, the less the risk that the girl will disgrace her family.

Second, female circumcision is arguably an irreplaceable source of revenue for the operators who are mostly older women. Only a very limited number of roles are open to women living in rural areas of Africa, thus, to put an end to this practice would invariably put an end to an otherwise profitable, centuries old business.

Third, older women themselves perpetrate the practice with much zeal having themselves previously undergone the same suffering. Senior women possess a deep conviction that in upholding and enforcing tradition, they hold together the fabric of a society that must, at whatever costs, be defended against external threats.

Fourth, since genital mutilations are not generally visible, health education programs have not been directed towards this practice. The scarcity of data showing the distress and physical damage of this practice makes it difficult to convince people of the urgency in dealing with the issue. Furthermore, the private nature of the practice and the taboo surrounding talk of genitals and sexuality discourages open discussion about female circumcision.

Fifth, because of the destructive effects of colonialism in Africa, western efforts on the part of missionaries or colonial administrators to eliminate female circumcision have been largely unsuccessful. Fears of a weakening of traditional customs as well as of the ill effects of western influences seem to be at the root of the resistance to change.

FEMALE CIRCUMCISION, MALE CIRCUMCISION, AND OTHER NON-THERAPEUTIC PRACTICES

The debate as to the similarities and differences between female and male circumcision has been ongoing for some time now, and it is valuable in reconsidering how we view each of these practices.

The major difference between female and male circumcision is the degree of mutilation. The extent of female circumcision is variable (see Box 1) but, nonetheless, the procedure is usually more risky, more painful, takes longer to heal, and has greater permanent repercussions than male circumcision. The immediate complications of female circumcision include hemorrhage, infection, and urinary retention, which if left untreated can be fatal. Long-term complications are also common especially for women who have been infibulated. Blocking of the urethral or vaginal opening by scar tissue can lead to a build up of urine and menstrual blood, which in turn can cause chronic pelvic and urinary tract infections. Female circumcision can also cause obstetric complications and may increase sexual transmission of the human immunodeficiency virus. Furthermore, it has profound effects on sexuality and intercourse.

Male circumcision is usually seen to be less harmful, but advocates against it claim that this procedure can also have long-term effects including meatal stenosis (constricted urinary opening), recurrent urethritis, progressive loss of sensitivity from keratinization, tight or painful erections from excessive skin loss, and various degrees of sexual dysfunction. In addition, psychological dysfunction such as feelings of parental violation, mutilation, betrayal or low self-esteem from a lack of natural wholeness have been reported, though this is can also be true for female circumcision.

Despite differences in the extent of their harmful effects, neither female nor male circumcision have clear therapeutic benefits. Claims have been made that male circumcision decreases the risk of penile cancer, cervical cancer (in sexual partners), urinary tract infection, and sexual transmitted diseases while improving overall hygiene. Even if these claims were true (and there is conflicting evidence suggesting they are not), the risk reduction is most likely trivial compared to that achieved by using condoms or maintaining good foreskin hygiene, meaning that routine neonatal circumcision should not necessarily be the norm.

While most would agree that female circumcision is driven by social conformity, few stop to consider whether the same pressures may be at work in the case of male circumcision. At least in certain parts of the world (particularly North America), parents are under pressure from society to have their sons circumcised. It is not clear whether their decision is made with proper understanding and appreciation of the procedure. It is clear that cultural, social and historical perspectives around infant circumcision influence physicians and parents; this amounts to indirect coercion. If the same social forces are at work in the case of both female and male circumcision, why then is one practice more socially acceptable than the other?

Female circumcision is by no means the only practice conducted on women for non-therapeutic purposes. Take for instance those practices that have arisen out of the western world's obsession with physical appearance, namely, breast implants, liposuction, stomach stapling, collagen lip implants, face freezing techniques, face-lifts, rib-removal and other forms of cosmetic surgery. The driving force behind all of these practices is social pressure or, stated more aggressively, social oppression.

From an ethical and legal point of view, any move to apply criminal sanctions to female circumcision must be met with similar actions to apply criminal sanctions to male circumcision and other "unnecessary" surgical procedures because these practices are based on the same underlying principles.

THE MEDICAL PROFESSION'S OPPOSITION TO FEMALE CIRCUMCISION

A number of reasons have been cited to explain the medical profession's opposition to female circumcision. One reason is that physicians should not perform unnecessary procedures even when requested to do so. This stems from the Hippocratic Oath's credo of first do no harm. However, if this is the view of the medical profession, then practices such as cosmetic surgery for purely aesthetic purposes, as described above, should similarly be condemned by the medical profession and should also be prohibited by law.

Another reason offered for the medical profession's opposition to female circumcision is that this practice is nothing more than mutilation which is never permitted in the name of medicine. Yet, where does this statement then place male circumcision, a practice that arguably has no medical value and could also be classified as mutilation? Moreover, unnecessary cosmetic surgery could be considered mutilation. In fact, it has been argued that the majority of episiotomies are unnecessary and could be considered another form of female genital mutilation.

A further reason that has been offered is that consent to the practice of female circumcision can never be given freely because of social pressures. Once again, however, if we subscribe to this reasoning, we would have to condemn other practices such as breast implants since many women who undergo these procedures are usually doing so as a result of inappropriate societal influence that pushes them to look a certain way. It has also been argued that consent for male circumcision by parents is neither properly informed nor purely voluntary. In short, the singling out of female circumcision from other similar procedures cannot be justified.

INTERNATIONAL RESPONSE AND ACTION

Female circumcision raises a number of human rights issues including the rights of women, the rights of children, the right to good health and the right to development. Because female circumcision transcends geopolitical borders, it has become an international issue.

The United Nations have been playing a leading role in formulating and coordinating actions against female circumcision. For instance, in 1984, the Inter-African Committee (IAC) on Traditional Practices Affecting the Health of Women and Children was formed by delegates to a conference held in Dakar, Senegal. The IAC believes in a soft approach to the abolition of female circumcision and, in addition to the support of the World Health Organization (WHO) and the United Nations Children's Fund (UNICEF), has gained the support of some of the African ruling elite. Its national chapters in Africa conduct information campaigns in Africa showing the harmful effects of traditional practices. Despite the fact that many nations have ratified conventions that lay down international standards in relation to female circumcision, the lack of political will to enforce these conventions has meant that these standards are seldom upheld (see below).

In the African context, most anti-circumcision laws were passed by the colonial powers, which looked down upon the indigenous cultures with contempt. These laws were blanket laws aimed at criminalizing a host of customary or cultural practices perceived by the imperialists as "barbaric". Today these laws have proved to be ineffective and serve as "dead letter laws" with no precise parameters for application. Most African nations have been independent for several decades now and it is necessary to re-assess the relationship between Governments and their people on this question. Furthermore, in the post-independence era, only a few African countries have specific legislation against female circumcision; these include Sudan, Egypt, the Ivory Coast, and Burkina Faso.

So long as a majority of the population in practicing nations continue to believe that female circumcision is a perfectly legitimate practice and serves the common good, legal sanctions that incriminate practitioners and families may be counterproductive. Indeed, criminal sanctions and regulations are effective only once a substantial body of public opinion has been raised against the practice. Education is fundamental in changing public opinion, as well as in offering reasonable alternatives to female circumcision that still accomplish some of its social functions. In Kenya, for example, a ceremony similar to a "circumcision ritual" has been set up in which twenty five mother-daughter pairs take part in a six day ceremony during which the girls are taught the importance of womanhood and the responsibilities it carries with it. The girls are considered women at the end of the six days, not because of any physical circumcision, but because of the "secret" knowledge they attain. The ceremony is known as *Ntanira na Mugambo* which literally means "circumcision through words."

In western countries, especially those with large immigrant populations, the issue has gained legislative recognition and action. Countries such as Canada, the United States the United Kingdom, Sweden, Switzerland, Australia and France have criminalized the practice. In Canada, female genital "mutilation" is condoned only where it can be proved to be of benefit to the physical health of the person, or where it will restore the person's reproductive functions or sexual appearance. Further, to be valid, the person must be at least eighteen years of age and there must be no resulting bodily harm.

Interestingly, the implication of this law is that interventions of this nature must only take place for therapeutic purposes. If we were to apply this law to male circumcision (which, in the present wording, it clearly does not), then male circumcision might also be outlawed for being non-therapeutic in nature.

THE ROLE OF LAW

Is the use of criminal law appropriate in solving the male and female circumcision debate? Would the threat of criminal sanctions necessarily restrain the practice of female circumcision or even male circumcision in light of the social realities and cultural diversities? Can such action be interpreted as a tool for change in social behavior?

According the great jurist Roscoe Pound, "Enforcement of law is not a problem in homogenous societies where the formal law merely codifies widely shared and observed practices." Therefore, when a society is not homogeneous and a subset of citizens supports a certain behavior, the simple act of criminalizing that behavior may not necessarily result in a reduction of its practice. Moreover, in some instances, legal enforcement has actually led to the exacerbation of the original problem. A good example is abortion where, despite its prohibition in certain jurisdictions, the practice did not wither away but instead persisted, albeit underground, causing women to undergo this procedure in unhygienic conditions where the risks associated with the procedure were increased manifoldly.

Given the differences in attitudes towards female circumcision, it is unlikely that a purely legal solution to the problem of female circumcision, such as a prohibition on its practice, will bring this practice to a halt. Instead, a great deal of work needs to be done in educating the public as well as the affected populations that circumcision is a practice that has outlived its purpose. Rigorous, culture-sensitive campaigns are needed if the attitude of the populations practicing circumcision is to be changed.

Multicultural countries such as the US and Canada should emulate what Governments in some African countries are doing. They should launch public education campaigns among affected immigrant populations in their countries. It is only once the target populations appreciate that female circumcision is harmful that there will be sufficient justification in laying criminal sanctions against the practice. The justification will in fact be the strong consensus among the affected populations that the practice is indeed harmful. Using the law may be a political, emotional and even a moral response on the part of western governments, however, in reality it does nothing more than to increase hostility and defiance among the people who currently practice female circumcision. We must keep this in mind at all times, and only use the force of criminal law as a last resort and with the utmost caution.

Global Bioethics: Utopia or Reality?

Sirkku K. Hellsten

Hellsten criticizes the traditional "top-down" application of universal moral principles in bioethics, arguing that such an approach is particularly inappropriate to non-Western cultures and contexts. An individualistic emphasis on autonomy as a universal value, for example, tends to disregard alternative conceptions of human dignity at work in more collectivist societies. It may also prove inadequate when confronted with the interpersonal implications of genetic testing or the power dynamics at play in biomedical conceptions of illness and health.

Hellsten takes FGM/C as one example of a biomedical "health" practice that actually operates to enforce social hierarchies and power structures—and points to related "biopolitical" practices in the West. She argues that such practices should be evaluated not just in terms of *universal* values (such as autonomy), but also in terms of *local* values (such as solidarity), both of which FGM/C fails to promote. Such an approach would reflect a bioethics rooted in neither relativism nor moral absolutism, but a more humble *particularism*—which attends to both local and global values.

Medical ethics first appeared as a recognizable academic discipline in the 19th century, as a professional ethic that developed as the medical profession was refined and distinct roles and duties of doctors and nurses, in relation to their patients, were formalized. Since this time, medical ethics has grown in prominence and is a compulsory part of studies in medicine in many countries. Medical ethics has been concerned primarily with prescribing the ethics of the doctor-patient relationship and, thus, the key issues have been the duty to maintain patient confidentiality and the need to gain fully informed consent. The primary methodology of early medical ethics was 'principlism', which is still well established in the West—although it is widely criticized, particularly by academics. Principlism is the application of a small set of principles, to any ethical dilemma, to determine the right or best course of action. Principlism became a popular methodology in medical ethics in the 1960s and 1970s in the USA and a version of principlism was endorsed by the United States (US) National

Commission for the Protection of Human Subjects of Biomedical and Behavioral Research in the *Belmont Report* (1979). This report identified three 'basic ethical principles' of biomedical and behavioral research, namely: respect for persons; beneficence; and justice. In the same year, Beauchamp and Childress published *Principles of Biomedical Ethics*—now in its fifth edition and the most widely known text on medical ethics— defining four, somewhat similar principles: autonomy; non-maleficence; beneficence; and justice. These four principles became the four principles of medical ethics and applying them became *the* standard (in fact one could almost say the 'official') methodology of medical ethics. Thus, medical ethics, as taught to practitioners, essentially consists of learning how to apply these principles, augmented by an understanding of the legal framework and consequences of such decisions.

One reason why principlism has been so successful in medical ethics is its simplicity: it appears to provide applicable solutions for hard-pressed medical practitioners and members of ethics committees. It presented 'frameworks of general guidelines that condensed morality to its central elements and gave people from diverse fields an easily grasped set of moral standards.' It also

From Sirkku K. Hellsten "Global Bioethics: Utopia or Reality?," *Developing World Bioethics* 8, no. 2 (2008): 70–81. Copyright © 2008 Blackwell Publishing Ltd. (Most references omitted.)

provides and coincides with the traditional codes of conduct in the medical profession that seem to have some applicability throughout time and in different environments. However, while the principles of non-maleficence, beneficence and justice at least appear to have applicability at various times and in various environments, principlism is often criticized for disregarding morally relevant perspectives and approaches, for not being sensitive to different cultural, economic and social contexts, and for ignoring information that makes the applicability of these principles doubtful. In addition, the plausibility of the principle of autonomy is particularly questioned by bioethicists and physicians from non-Western cultures and even by some Western medical practitioners working in utterly different cultural and economic contexts, such as many parts of the Third World. For example, in traditionally more collectivist cultures, the starting point for health care and medical treatment is not the individual, the patient himself or herself, but rather the close environment and in particular the family. In many Asian countries, such as Japan, China, the Philippines, and Indonesia, as well in various parts of Africa, people do not practice self-determination in the same explicit fashion required by the principles of individualist, Western medical ethics. The decision-making is rather based on the values of social responsibility, solidarity, and egalitarianism in a sense that the family as a whole, or even the community, is expected to take part in making decisions with, and sometimes on behalf of, the patient. The ideals of social responsibility and solidarity are central because, on the one hand, the family and community have special obligations to take care of the sick, not only in terms of material aid, but also in helping the patient to make difficult decisions in order to make everything work smoothly in the best interest of the patient and thus save him or her further anxiety and trouble. On the other hand, the wider good of the community, and social harmony in a sense of consensus, must also be included in the decision-making process.

Thus, cultural values and different concepts of justice may create conflict in applying particular principles and medical guidelines across the globe. Even other concepts central to bioethics, such as health, disease and sickness tend to be social and cultural constructs. Their meaning may vary from one time to another, and from one place to another,

according to different worldviews, belief systems and values. However, in the Western context, and in medical ethics, it is commonly accepted that modern medicine is based upon scientific descriptions of the human body. This implies that there is a universal or universalistic knowledge of health—that there is an accepted approach that applies to health problems the world over—because 'objective' science cannot vary from one country to another, during a given time period at least.

Roy Brauman, the former director of Doctors Without Borders (until 1994), has given illuminating examples of the thorny ethical dilemmas that the health care professional may face in an international or widely multicultural environment. These dilemmas are related to a conflict between the promotion of the best possible medical cure available, while simultaneously considering the overall well-being of the patient in relation to his or her cultural beliefs and environment. Brauman's first example comes from the war in Mogadishu, Somalia where international medical experts were trying to help the casualties of war but found that the decisions they made, based on Western medical knowledge and technical diagnosis, would lead to conflicts that might cause more suffering and harm to the patient. For instance, in cases in which the only solution to save a victims life would call for an amputation (because of massive infections that could not be treated properly locally), many wounded young people would refuse to be amputated. They preferred to die with the entire body than to live with a visible mutation. This caused ethical dilemmas for the surgeons and other international medical team members and, in fact, was a violation of their whole *raison d'etre*, for their being there, in the first place. If a doctor cannot amputate to save lives in a war situation, his or her role as a healer is seriously diminished. The lives of some of the doctors were actually threatened because they were trying to convince the wounded that it was in their best interest to be amputated. From the point of view of Somali people, however, their best interest was not to be amputated; instead it was *not* to remain alive at any cost. The principles of autonomy, benevolence and non-maleficence were challenged by the local concepts of human dignity and well-being, and by the cultural interpretations of health and injury.

Another example shows the problems of applying the promotion of the principle of justice globally, or across cultural borders, in a situation of scarcity. In Uganda, the northeastern region of Karamoja was suffering from a famine that affected about 50,000 people but the food aid sent there was not sufficient. International medical aid workers witnessed a terrible struggle for survival in the area and established feeding stations according to the traditional approach which allocated food to the most malnourished—which were usually children under five, as well as pregnant women. However, the food was locally taken away from these original target populations to be given to the elders of the villages. The moral value that the Western medical professionals give to children and pregnant women—based not only on the fact that children and women are usually the most vulnerable, but also that children are innocent and that they are the future—was challenged by the local customs and values. In these communities, the elders were of supreme importance, not only because of local values of social coherence, social authority, and decent social standards, but also due to their wisdom that keeps the community alive. After all, as logically explained by the locals, children are a renewable natural resource, while the elderly cannot be replaced.

All in all, principlism can be seen very much as a product of its history and, therefore, part of the Western individualist context, privileging individuals over communities and taking a very specific view of justice—one that essentially deals with individuals' rights, rather than underlying structural issues or the impact of wider socio-political factors. Feminists, as well as non-Western bioethicists, have criticized the dominance of principlism by pointing out the problems of the universal application of its Western, individualist, and positivist assumptions. Thus, while principlism has remained the prominent approach to medical ethics—particularly within the medical and scientific communities—presently there have been alternative methods of medical ethics, and new approaches to bioethics, that can bring wider and more inclusive approaches to ethical issues in a global context.

FROM MEDICAL ETHICS TO BIOETHICS—INTERDEPENDENCY OF SCIENCE, MEDICINE AND HEALTH CARE

In addition to the difficulties in applying particular principles as universal guidelines across borders, there are other issues that have contributed to the expansion of the scope of ethics in medical science, and health care in general, leading to a wider study of bioethics. The area of study of bioethics is not concerned merely with issues of medical practice (although these issues do form part of the area of study), but also with wider issues of medical and scientific practice, advancement and capability in the socio-political context. In addition to a widening of the field of medical ethics, bioethics also includes perspectives and critiques that are very different from the traditional Western medical ethics.

The wider discipline of bioethics was a response to dramatic advances in science and technology, and public reaction to such developments. Thus, in a way, bioethics has developed alongside medical ethics as a complementary, and often overlapping, area of inquiry, rather than a separate approach. Bioethics is characterised by those issues that stretch beyond the medical sphere, particularly issues which are controversial in the public arena: new types of ethical dilemma that traditional sources of moral authority failed to deal with, and that, therefore, needed to be addressed by a new type of discipline. For instance, the new genetic and biotechnologies create possibilities that were once unimaginable and that our past moral frameworks, or traditional ethics (such as traditional medical ethics), are unable to address. Genetics raises questions that challenge traditional medical ethics in two main ways: first, genetics further threatens traditional core concepts and principles, such as those of consent and confidentiality; and second, it raises more fundamental questions about meaning and identity, which are also outside the remit of traditional medical ethics.

While some new ethical dilemmas brought up by genetics fall within the remit of traditional medical ethics, such as the use of genetic technologies in health care, others have a much wider social and ethical scope, such as the acquisition and use of genetic material, and genetic knowledge in general, that affect the global power relations between rich and poor countries.

One of the reasons why new genetics challenge individualistic principlism is that genetic material reveals information not just about the individual but also about consanguineous relations and continues to be potentially identifying when compared with database information, thereby challenging the traditional mainstays of medical ethics—those of informed consent and confidentiality upheld by autonomy and beneficence.

According to current medical practice, confidentiality is owed to the individual patient, irrespective of whether this information impacts on others (and potentially other patients of the healthcare professional). Such potential conflicts of interest and duty mean that a debate is necessary as to whether confidentiality is owed to the individual alone, and whether this duty should continue to trump all other potential ethical responsibilities of the practitioner. In a similar manner, informed consent, often the 'gold standard' of good (medical and research) ethical practice, is inadequate in the genetic arena if it is intended to protect autonomy and guarantee confidentiality. Such questions are far from academic when not only family members but also other third parties, such as insurance companies and employers, have an interest in knowing the genetic status of individuals.

Genetics also raises issues that are outside the traditional scope of medical ethics, which tend to protect not only Western values but also other Western (political and economic) interests. For example, the discussion above regarding the potentiality of genetics to identify consanguineous relations and the wider ethnic group (particularly if its members are genetically homogenous, such as certain indigenous populations) raises questions about the possibility of group rights and group consent.

These questions simply cannot be adequately addressed from the Western individualist perspective of traditional medical ethics. Moreover, and perhaps more fundamentally, genetics influences our understandings of human being identity and meaning of human value in a wider perspective. There is the increasing global fear that the mapping of the human genome will allow for individual genetic blueprints and comprehensive testing, providing information about each individual's future health and lifespan, as well as the vulnerabilities of particular genetic groups. Such assumptions have led to theories of genetic determinism and reductionism, which are presented as a threat to notions of human dignity and individual identity, as well as having potential practical consequences of discrimination and the creation of a genetic under-class locally and globally.

BIOPOLITICS AND THE SUPREME POWER OF 'OBJECTIVE SCIENCE'

Genetics offers humans a chance to manipulate and design life and explain the previously inexplicable (e.g. behaviour, emotion, sexuality). Other developments of science and technology, such as reproductive and life-saving or prolonging technologies that expand medical capabilities, have led to a need to reconsider and analyze the meaning of such concepts as 'health', 'illness' and 'normality', as well as 'identity', 'humanity' and 'life', within Western medical science and health care practice. As Michel Foucault pointed out, even before the latest advancements in genetic and biotechnology, in a Western society there is a tendency for 'biopolitics'. With the term 'biopolitics', Foucault refers to the social power relations that define the concepts of 'health' and 'sickness', or 'normality' and 'abnormality', with regard to the opinions of the experts, the majority, or those in positions of authority and power in general. Fou-cault's analysis is useful when we think about how political and legal decision-making tends to go hand in hand with medicalization and geneticization of our societies, whether we think about the health issues locally or globally.

'Biopolitics' works both in global and local levels. Various practices that are justified in the name of 'health' and 'normality'—according to the given expectations—further enforce the existing unbalanced power relations. For example, such health threatening practices as genital mutilations, which are in one culture considered important for one's 'holistic well-being', are actually there to enforce certain social hierarchies and power structures. Simultaneously, at the global level, these very same practices may in other cultures be seen as dangerous and harmful; rearranging the local and global hierarchies based on who has the final say in medical science and expertise in what is 'the right kind of health', what is the 'best desirable and attainable health' and what is 'holistic well-being'.

For global bioethical reflection, it would be important to go back to the evaluation of both facts and values involved in the debates on bioethical issues across the globe. If we take female genital mutilation as our example case here, it is evident that we need a wider perspective to the cultural arguments for the prevalence of the practice. Often we can find a contradiction between local values presented to support this practice and the actual reasons for the maintenance of the practice itself. When we critically reflect on the fact and value relationship in relation to not only what we are thought to consider as universal bioethical values (individual autonomy and rights) but also to various local values (such as solidarity and egalitarianism in Africa, for example), we can easily see that practices such as genital mutilations do not promote either universal or local values.

Globally speaking (whether we talk about female or male genital mutilations), these traditions have themselves often been quite universally/globally practiced—in one form or another. Many traditions, that the Western individualists may now consider as 'non-Western', primitive ways of life of yet 'uncivilized' cultures, may also have been practiced (or still exist) in slightly different forms within Western culture, though they are supported by a different justification. Genital mutilations in the West, for example, have been based on medical rather than traditional rationalizations. All in all, throughout time, various forms of genital mutilations in different parts of the world have been defended by a variety of justifications (varying from religion to science, from tradition to 'fashion'). In international debates, this tends to mix values and facts together and the different parties in any disputes tend to confuse what is really agreed—or not agreed—on shared or local values, or (f)actual practices claimed to realize these values.

Setting different traditions in a normative context: that is, in the framework of what should, and what should not, be accepted, can often be an example of 'biopolitics', in which those with apparently more 'objective' scientific knowledge give guidelines to those more 'primitive and ignorant'. This intentional 'confusion' between values and facts can enforce biased global power relations. By appealing to 'the only one right view, of objective science' that is also related to medical and technological development, rich developed countries maintain their position as the model for ideal development and are able to retain political and economic control over developing countries. Many political and economic interests can be disguised in the name of science and development in national and international policy making, as well as in medical law. In other words, 'biopolitics' uses what it presents as factual knowledge about human health and turns it into normative ideals of 'health' and 'normality'. The criteria are set by what is considered as objective facts produced by objective scientific knowledge. The social

(and individual) goals of 'being healthy' or 'living a normal life' gain a double status: they are not considered only as scientific biological facts but they are also turned into social norms that we impose on ourselves, and on others.

Therefore, in 'biopolitics', global and local social injustices can often be based on apparently scientific explanations while, in fact, we are using science and technology to justify our deep-rooted prejudices and to support other political and economic interests. However, since science and technology, for their part, are also always one way or another socially constructed, their development is based on the particular values and goals of the people working on different stages of their development. Thus, the results of science and their interpretations are far from being objective but are also culturally situated and socially and politically constructed. For instance, it is interesting to remember that while the human genome project is now defended by appealing to its benefits for medicine and, through that, to our well-being and health, sequencing DNA was originally started as a military project in order to find out how the atomic bomb affected its victims.

Bioethical analysis needs to be able to move far beyond the individual concerns of traditional medical ethics and the focus on the doctor-patient relationship and be set in a wider socio-political context. It must analyse existing power relations and potential consequences of set guidelines, principles and laws. It also needs to address deep philosophical, social and religious questions of meaning and identity in relation to the 'biopolitical' classification of people, traditions and other health related phenomena. This means that while the four principles of medical ethics can still be used as general guidelines, they must be understood in a much broader way, and their interpretations and applicability in different contexts should be further debated and reconsidered.

GLOBALIZATION OF THE STUDY OF BIOETHICS OR GLOBALIZATION OF BIOETHICAL PRINCIPLES AND NORMS?

The expansion of bioethics has further developed into what has come to be called 'global bioethics'.

It is evident that the distinction between these fields of study is blurred and their existence as independent disciplines can be questioned. Many of the issues discussed with regard to genetics, infectious diseases, use of body parts, etc., are clearly global issues—issues that cannot be resolved within one area of sovereignty or one nation state—as evidenced by the growing body of international agreements, guidelines and codes that address these global bioethical dilemmas. Bioethical decisions made in one jurisdiction affect decisions and practices of other jurisdictions. No longer can effective policy-making regarding bioethical issues take place in isolation without consideration of the practices of other jurisdictions. It is this interrelatedness of all countries and peoples that has called for a study of 'global bioethics', and such study has to be related to the 'biopolitical' issues of global justice.

If the distinction is to be made, we could state that *global bioethics* attempts to address bioethical issues in the global context, taking into account many factors—economic, social, political, religious, and cultural—and adopting various ethical methodologies in its quest for global solutions. Examples of bioethical issues, which cannot be addressed effectively in isolation, are many, as are examples of decisions and practices endorsed by one nation state that have affected those well outside the borders of that state. For instance, in the case of genetics there are global components particularly in connection with property rights. There is the question of whether genetic material is personal property, common property, intellectual property, or a part of a person or an extension of a person—or of peoples. Not only scientific or medical factors but also economic realities and markets play a central role in defining the nature of genetic material and the guidelines to the acquisition, access, and use of genetic information. Sometimes whole groups are treated as property and sources for research, and vulnerable populations without any real economic or legal bargaining power may lose their right to their own genetic heritage. In light of such developments the need for global action on these matters is undeniable and becomes increasingly important as the new genetics, stem cell technologies and other advances lend commercial importance and value to the tissues and genomes of populations in developing countries. In global 'bioethics', the very issue of property rights—and the concept of property itself—could be globally challenged from the point of view of different cultural views.

The issues of new genetics are important for global bioethics, since they bring up the issue of global justice and the applicability of universal principles in the form of international guidelines and ethical standards for medical practice and scientific research. Thus, another important, partly related, issue in global bioethics is international research ethics: particularly in connection with research that is done by First World researchers and firms in Third World countries. What standards are the researchers to follow and how can they make sure that the required 'informed consent' is really informed and assented. What if the local customs call for collective or communal rather than individual consent? How much information should the research objects obtain on the research and its methodology; how much can they actually understand if they are not well educated?

The inconsistency of the existing rules and regulations across the world is also evident when we consider the effects of patenting regimes on developing countries, 'medical trafficking' of goods, services and people (as well as human material in general), and 'reproductive tourism', which for instance includes patients travelling to different countries to benefit from procedures forbidden in their home country, such as German couples travelling to Belgium for pre-implantation genetic diagnosis (PGD), individuals travelling to the Netherlands for euthanasia, or Irish women travelling to the United Kingdom for abortions. In new genetics this also contains the trafficking of body parts and materials sold by the poor to 'medical merchants' for the benefit of the affluent—essentially reducing some human beings to spare parts for others. Particular concern is yet again in the relationship between the rich and the poor; the vulnerability and victimization of the less affluent (whether we talk about individuals, groups of people, or countries) is inevitable.

What all these above-mentioned issues have in common, in terms of global bioethics, is the recognition of the global context, particularly the economic disequilibrium and the potential for exploitation of those already most vulnerable and disadvantaged—the use of 'biopolitics' to maintain existing power relations between nations. Thus, concern about economic power and vulnerability should be the central concern of global bioethics for justice. Here, justice can not be defined merely as individual and rights-based but also in terms of community and groups. It has to take into account the economic, social and political context and different understandings of the meaning of health, well-being, quality of life, and identity in relation to one's self worth. The issues of justice and the problems of inequality have to be present in the globally practiced study of bioethics, particularly when we pay attention to local priorities. Therefore, the most pressing ethical dilemmas in genetics in the West and, in general, the use of new medical and biotechnology, may be low on the list of ethical priorities in poor, developing countries.

Placing global justice at the heart of global bioethics helps us to acknowledge that particular issues in bioethics, which are important in some parts of the world, may not have the same priority elsewhere. For instance, issues that are at the heart of Western bioethics, like reproductive technologies, genetic therapy and cloning may seem less urgent to large parts of the developing world, and in general in poorer countries where even contraception and the most basic healthcare are scarce and high-tech medical and health care procedures virtually nonexistent. In fact, from the point of view of the poor countries, the debates on euthanasia, gene therapy or cloning often appear to have little relevance to 'global bioethics' unless directly related to the distributive justice of medical resources across the world. Only countries with an abundance of resources have the luxury of debating the ethical issues related to the use of the latest medical advancement and biotechnology. In developing countries, the debates tangled around 'low-tech issues' concerning doctor-patient relationships and codes of ethics and basic health vs holistic well-being continue to be of fundamental importance.

Therefore, the most pressing controversies may be different in different places: key issues in the West may include abortion, euthanasia, access to reproductive technologies and the rightness of PGD, whereas the most urgent issues in developing countries are access to basic healthcare, preventing and treating curable (but often still fatal) diseases such as malaria, cholera and diarrhoea, and fighting the endemic spread of HIV/AIDS. Particularly in relation to HIV/AIDS, within the Western ethical approach there appear to be built-in double standards that focus on prevention in poor countries and access to treatment in affluent countries. These standards are based on

economic rationalizations rather than on any plausible moral argument that could be related to the highly promoted values of autonomy, equality and justice. However, while global priorities appear different, the 'global biopolitics' is the main shared problem.

The issue of global eugenics is not unrelated either. Indeed, from the perspective of global 'biopolitics' and global bioethics, the issues are linked in questions such as: whether or not it is justified to help families in rich countries to have children that are as genetically healthy as medical technology can produce (or 'designer babies') instead of redeploying the resources to build basic healthcare in the developing world; or, whether it is justified to devote vast economic and social resources to fertility treatments and other artificially assisted pregnancies by using ever-increasing forms of assisted reproductive technologies, while at the same time encouraging poor countries to follow strict population control programmes.

Thus, not only is global bioethics defined by the global scope of its inquiry, but also by its methodology, which reflects the understanding of the same concepts in a different context. Non-Western studies in bioethics have brought 'global bioethics' a perspective that approaches the ethical issues from a non-individualist perspective. Looking at the ethical dilemmas from different perspectives helps to widen the conceptual analysis and set reflective argumentation in a more inclusive new context.

Other constituent areas of study in global bioethics are issues such as ownership (particularly of genetic materials and information), patents for new drugs, local means of traditional healing, the use of genetically modified organisms, testing and trial of new drugs or new biotechnology, global pharmaceutical markets, and so on. All in all, a large part of the world's diseases could easily be prevented or treated with a more equal distribution of resources and a more open understanding of the interdepen-dency of different issues involved in health problems across the world. One of the central goals of global bioethics should therefore be the revelation of global 'biopolitics' and the building of global 'biodemocracy'.

GLOBALIZING BIOETHICAL NORMS

When the study of bioethics is globalized it tends to be comparative rather than normative, taking a critical approach to any universal principles that could be accepted or applied cross-culturally or trans-culturally. Thus, it appears that bioethics in different parts of the world and in different cultures is descriptive. However, it has inherent prescriptive elements that can lead either to radical cultural relativism—or to more modest cultural particularism. While a relativist view would claim that there are no universal principles in bioethics, a particularistic view might agree on the possibility of finding some shared principles but would question whether they can be applied globally due to different social contexts and interpretation of values involved.

In the Western context there is still a tendency to interpret the 'global' of global bioethics as 'universal', not in a descriptive but in a normative sense, and, thus, to invoke universalistic philosophy. Such philosophy is clearly founded on Western individualist assumptions. Normative universalism in ethics has been criticised for not being global but essentially a Western export, and thus a form of cultural imperialism. Clearly there are examples of this tendency in some areas of global bioethics: for example, research ethics, when concerned with research in the Third World. Researchers and ethicists may recognise that the request for informed consent is a Western and individualist notion. Nevertheless, they attempt to find ways to make it acceptable and comprehensible to the more collectivistic cultures they work in (for example by seeking additional communal consent), as a rule. Thus, the notion of individual informed consent as a necessary guarantor of ethical research prevails, despite the fact that it does not fit in all cultural contexts.

Not only do researchers and ethics committees fail to question whether individual informed consent is relevant in a particular research context, but they also continue to focus on informed consent as the key ethical issue for research in the developing world, rather than, for instance, access to healthcare, inducement to participate, or trial aftercare, all of which could arguably be claimed to be more important issues.

The biggest challenge to 'global bioethics' is in defining its normative stand in relation to the universalism-relativism debate. One of the central features of global bioethics has been to recognise the importance of the particular, and the danger inherent in universalism as a form of Western cultural imperialism. This strong criticism of universalism appears to take global bioethics towards ethical relativism. On the other hand, global bioethics, in practice, does set an absolutist claim for global justice in relation to local injustices and inequalities.

CONCLUSIONS

Do we need 'global bioethics'; if so, can it show us any normative guidelines in the issues of medical and bioethics across the globe? First, there is an evident need to expand the study of bioethics internationally to cover various cultures and economic and social contexts in order to bring out the globally burning issues in bioethics in order to get a grasp of the cultural issues involved in the understanding of various values as the basis for international ethical and legal agreements. Second, particularistic analysis of local problems and their relation to global issues and, particularly, to globalized markets can reject the extreme cultural relativist position that holds that any form of global ethic, global ethics, or even ethical discussion is prohibitive because of the impossibility of stepping outside the moral framework of one's own cultural community. Third, caution towards exportation and importation of Western, or any other, cultural values as if they were universal as such is important. The values and cultural practices have to be separated in the issues of ethical values as the basis for international standards and guidelines. Thus, I endorse, both descriptively and normatively, a 'global bioethics not a global bioethic', a global bioethics that recognises the importance of the local while thinking globally. While finding a consensus on the normative guidelines for international bioethics might not be in sight, looking for global and local ethical solutions is essential. It may help different countries, cultures and people to better understand each other and each other's problems, beliefs and underlying reasons for cultural value conflicts. It is as important for the current study of 'global bioethics' to make distinctions as to its areas of study and to set its own goals in order to avoid the prevalent confusion between facts and values, 'global bioethics' is needed to turn the biased 'biopolitics' into global 'biodemocracy'.

DECISION SCENARIOS

The questions following each decision scenario are intended to prompt reflection and discussion. In deciding how to answer them, you should consider the information provided in the Social Context and Case Presentations, as well as in the Briefing Session. You should also make use of the ethical theories and principles presented in Part VI: Foundations of Bioethics, and the arguments offered in the relevant readings in this chapter.

DECISION SCENARIO 1

Global Crises, Individual Responsibilities?

"So, Danny, I heard you chose a specialty." Sohel Rana and Danny Salgado were crossing the quad together after grand rounds.

"Yeah, I finally sent off residency applications today," Danny said. "Guess I'll end up a urologist like my dad. Probably the least I can do 'cause he's paying my tuition." Danny shrugged. "You're doing the family medicine residency at UCLA, right?"

"Yes, it will come in handy when I go back to Pakistan to practice."

"Dude, I don't get it," Danny said, with a sigh. "I know there's a primary care shortage and all, but that family medicine rotation we did was *rough*. Plus the pay is probably crap, right? I mean, no offense, but couldn't you do better?"

"Guess it depends on what you mean by better." Sohel smiled. "Sure, I know urologists and orthopedic surgeons can do a lot of good. But in the village where I'm from, most people don't live long enough to worry about their prostate and no one can afford a joint replacement. The average life expectancy in Pakistan is just sixty-six years old."

"So what are you saying, Sohel? Should we all become GPs and infectious disease specialists and practice in the Third World?"

"No, but I do think we should stop devoting the majority of research and practice funds to 'First World' conditions like cancer and cardiovascular disease, when the vast majority of death and suffering is caused by conditions such as malaria, tuberculosis, and dysentery. We triage in local emergencies, why not in global ones?"

"I don't see why we're supposed to make medical sacrifices to help poor people on the other side of the world. It's not like we made them poor."

"Some people would argue that Western colonialism did. Or that you've at least benefited from their poverty." Sohel stopped and turned to face Danny. "Listen, what I'm saying is actually very simple. I watched two of my baby sisters die of amoebic dysentery. Their deaths were completely preventable. That's why I decided to become a doctor. What about you?"

"I'm sorry, Sohel. We're obviously just coming from different worlds here…"

"No need to apologize, but you're wrong about different worlds. You're a good guy, Danny. If one of my sisters were dying right in front of you, I'm sure you'd do everything you could to save her, right?"

"Of course."

"My point is that thousands of children like her *are* right in front of you, because technology and travel have made the world smaller. People in rich countries, especially physicians, could save the lives of millions of poor people with minimal sacrifice, but in general, they choose to look away and 'do better' for themselves."

1. It has been estimated that less than 10 percent of biomedical research funds are devoted to problems that cause 90 percent of the world's disease burden. Are such global disparities a violation of medical or social ethics? The legitimate outcome of a global market in health care? What, if any, changes should be made to address these disparities?

2. As professionals charged with saving lives and alleviating suffering, do physicians have special responsibilities with regard to preventable disease and death in the developing world? Would they have such responsibilities if the death and suffering were taking place ten feet away from them? Do technology, travel, and money effectively make global health crises local emergencies?

DECISION SCENARIO **2**

The Trovan Trial

In 1996, Nigeria was hit with a meningitis outbreak that ultimately killed more than 15,000 people, most of them children. The pharmaceutical giant Pfizer approached the outbreak not only as an opportunity to help patients, but also to test its experimental fluoroquinolone antibiotic, Trovan® (trovafloxacin), which was about to be reviewed by the FDA. At the height of the epidemic, a Pfizer team chartered a jet to Kano, Nigeria, and quickly set up a clinical trial in the city's overcrowded infectious disease hospital. They selected one hundred children to receive trovafloxacin and another hundred to receive ceftriaxone, an established treatment. After just two weeks, the Pfizer team left Kano, citing the survival of all but five of the trovafloxacin subjects as evidence of the drug's effectiveness and "blockbuster" potential.

In 1997, however, the FDA found numerous discrepancies in the Kano trial records, prompting Pfizer to withdraw its application for similar use of Trovan in American children. In 1999, hundreds of liver-damage cases (six of them fatal) among U.S. trovafloxacin patients prompted the FDA to severely limit use of the drug, even for adults. Meanwhile, a Nigerian government panel filed criminal and civil charges against Pfizer, after concluding that the company had failed to obtain informed consent for experimental treatment from parents in Kano and had given the control group dangerously low doses of ceftriaxone. (Six children died in the ceftriaxone cohort.) A *Washington Post* investigation later found that the Trovan trial's certificate of approval from the hospital had been forged and backdated. Critics also faulted the company for failing to track subjects after two weeks, and said it had ignored reports of paralysis, arthritis, joint problems, and other side effects in the trovafloxacin cohort. (In the United States, similar adverse reactions have prompted the FDA to ban several other fluoroquinolone antibiotics or give them "black box" warning labels.)

In 2001 Pfizer withdrew Trovan from the market. In 2009 it agreed to settle the Nigerian civil and criminal cases, paying more than $75 million to affected families and to sponsor local public health programs.

1. In defending the medical benefits of the Trovan trial, Pfizer representatives pointed to the 10 percent overall death rate for those afflicted by the Nigerian meningitis epidemic and the 5 percent death rate among the trovafloxacin subjects. By what standard should benefit be judged in poor and underdeveloped nations? Is an increased survival rate sufficient, even if it comes with debilitating side effects?

2. The aid group Doctors Without Borders was offering another established meningitis treatment in the same Kano infectious disease hospital—a fact that lawsuits claimed had been withheld from the Trovan trial subjects. Should experimental trials ever be conducted during medical crises such as the Nigerian epidemic? What if banning trials in such situations meant that far fewer patients would receive treatment?

DECISION SCENARIO **3**

Circumcision or Mutilation?

"Female circumcision is no different from male circumcision, as practiced in the West," said Khatra Ibrahim, during a WHO forum on women's health. "Both are nontherapeutic expressions of culture, and no culture has a right to judge another's practices."

"I have to disagree with you on both fact and the principle," said Quibilah Wallace, a delegate from the United States. "Male circumcision may be a Western cultural tradition, but it can reduce HIV transmission by as much as 60 percent, which is why millions of African men have opted for the procedure as adults." Wallace adjusted her hijab and took a sip of water. "As for cultural practices, what about slavery? Are you saying that other societies had no right to judge America when it enslaved my great-great-grandparents?"

"All I know is that no Westerner had a right to stop me from embracing my Somali culture and making myself clean, as I chose to do several years ago," Ibrahim said. "How would you American women like it if Africans tried to stop you from getting breast implants or labial reductions?"

"That's different. Just because I believe in moral dialogue across cultures doesn't mean I believe outsiders should intervene to restrict the choices of consenting adults. But most FGM is performed on girls who can't legally consent to a procedure that will have lifelong effects on their sexuality and their health."

1. Can cross-cultural judgments, or even coercive interventions, be morally justified? Is the appropriate response to such practices as genital cutting relativist, objectivist, or perhaps something in between? (See this chapter's Briefing Session.)

2. How might female genital cutting in Africa, Asia, and the Middle East be seen to resemble Western practices such as male circumcision, breast implants, and labial reduction surgery? How is it different?

3. Some argue that adult women who opt to undergo genital cutting (such as Ibrahim) or choose to wear a headscarf (such as Wallace) can't really consent to such practices, due to cultural or religious pressure. Is this argument persuasive? Can the same case be made with regard to Western beauty standards that prompt many women to alter their bodies, sometimes at considerable risk to their health?

DECISION SCENARIO 4

Debts and Disparities

"Thank you, Ambassador Shafiq, for joining us today," said Germaine Guidry, special representative for the U.S. Office of Global Health Diplomacy. "I'm pleased to announce that the United States, Britain, and other G-14 nations are prepared to offer Bangladesh over twenty billion dollars in low-interest loans to mitigate the current flooding and malaria epidemic in the Ganges–Brahmaputra–Meghna Delta."

"Ambassador Guidry, much as we appreciate your offer, I need to remind you that my government has determined that the U.S., the U.K., and other G-14 nations already owe Bangladesh far more than twenty billion," Ahmed Shafiq said, leaning forward over the microphone. "Climatologists have demonstrated that the flooding of nearly 20 percent of our country and the associated malaria outbreak are a direct result of climate change.

Since Bangladesh is responsible for less than 0.05 percent of greenhouse gas emissions, we insist that those nations, such as the United States, which are responsible for roughly 20 percent of emissions, compensate countries harmed by their ongoing extravagance. We therefore view your twenty billion as a debt to be collected and not as a loan."

1. How should the health costs associated with climate change be distributed? Should those nations who have contributed more to the problem pay more to cover negative health consequences?

2. Average health spending per person in the United States is over 285 times greater than the amount spent on the average Bangladeshi. Is this inequality an injustice in itself or does it require redress only if it is the result of colonial exploitation or the degradation of shared global resources?

DECISION SCENARIO 5

ABCs

"In Uganda, we use the ABC approach to fight HIV," Kenneth Musoke said, as he guided his visitor around the Mburo Field Hospital. "*A* is for abstinence, *B* is 'be faithful,' and *C* is use a condom. The approach is all about personal responsibility."

"With respect, Dr. Musoke, I have to disagree with you," said Kebeh Lamine, a visiting official from UN-AIDS. "The ABC campaign is a good start, but it will also take social and economic change if we're going to end the HIV epidemic here." Lamine gestured to the long line of women standing outside in brightly colored *gomesi*, waiting to sign up for antiretroviral treatment. "How can a woman abstain if local culture says she has no right to refuse sex with her HIV-positive husband? How can she take personal responsibility if she has no social or economic power to demand that her partner be faithful or use condoms?"

"You have been listening to too many Westerners at the UN, my dear." Musoke smiled and patted Lamine on the shoulder. "We have to fight HIV our own way, whether cultural imperialists like it or not."

"There is nothing Western about basic human rights, Dr. Musoke. Those rights formed the basis of our independence struggles *against* imperialism. Not to mention our campaign against Western

companies who price-gouge for antiretroviral drugs." Lamine snapped her briefcase shut and extended a hand to Musoke. "Rest assured, we can make African culture more just without necessarily making it Western."

1. Can epidemics such as HIV be defeated through individual choices alone, or do they require broader changes in culture and society, as Lamine suggests?

2. Is there anything inherently "Western" about principles such as autonomy or equality? Can versions of these principles also be found in traditional and non-Western cultures?

3. What are the strengths and weaknesses of the ABC program, as described by Dr. Musoke?

DECISION SCENARIO 6

Tuskegee in the Congo?

"It's a moral outrage to conduct a placebo-controlled trial of Exhiv in countries like the Congo," Dr. Sally Andrews said. "We already know that the standard dose of Exhiv is effective against HIV, so to enroll people who may get a placebo is denying them established treatment for their disease."

"Worse than that," said Jamal Brenner, a representative from Care International, "It deceives subjects into thinking they're getting treated when they aren't. The investigators should be comparing Exhiv with triple antiretroviral therapy or some other effective treatment. The Congo study uses the same rationale as the Tuskegee experiments."

Charlene Stein, a liaison from Exhiv's manufacturer, shook her head. "You can't compare what's standard in the United States with practices in the developing world. Many patients in the Congo who are HIV positive get *no* sort of treatment whatsoever,

so the Congo study offers participants at least a fifty–fifty chance of being treated. Every volunteer has gone through a long and informative consent procedure. They all know they might get a placebo. If Exhiv acts the ways the investigators think it will, we will be able to provide an effective drug to millions of HIV-positive people who would otherwise go untreated."

"But you're sacrificing the lives of some individuals to benefit others," Andrews objected. "Don't you see how wrong that is?"

1. Explain what arguments might be used to support Stein's position.

2. On what grounds might the Congo study be considered exploitation?

3. How might a utilitarian respond to Andrews's final objection? Granted Kant's notion that individuals possess inherent worth, would such a response be decisive?

Part VI

Foundations of Bioethics

Chapter 12

Ethical Theories, Moral Principles, and Medical Decisions

CHAPTER CONTENTS

"He's stopped breathing, Doctor," the nurse said. She sounded calm and deliberate. By the time Dr. Sarah Cunningham had reached Matteo Sabatini's bedside, the nurse was already providing cardiopulmonary resuscitation. But Sabatini still had the purplish blue color of cyanosis, caused by a lack of oxygen in his blood.

Sarah Cunningham knew that if Sabatini was to survive, he would have to be given oxygen fast and placed on a respirator. But should she order this done?

Matteo Sabatini was an old man, almost ninety. So far as anyone knew, he was alone in the world. His health was poor. He had congestive heart disease and was dying slowly and painfully from intestinal cancer. Wouldn't it be a kindness to Sabatini to allow him this quick and painless death? Why condemn him to lingering on for a few extra hours or weeks?

The decision that Sarah Cunningham faces is a moral one. She has to decide whether she should order the medical procedures that might prolong Sabatini's life or not order them and accept the consequence that he will almost surely die within minutes.

This kind of case rivets our attention because of its immediacy and drama. But there are many other situations that arise in the context of medical practice and research that require moral decisions. Some are equal in drama to the problem facing Dr. Cunningham, while others are not so dramatic but are of at least equal seriousness. There are far too many to catalogue, but consider this sample: Should physicians ever lie to their patients? Should parents be able to allow their children to be used as experimental subjects? Should people suffering from genetic diseases get access to assisted reproduction? Should women's access to abortion be restricted in certain cases? Should children with serious birth defects be allowed to die? Do terminally ill people have a right to physician-assisted death? Does everyone have a right to medical care?

Such questions are likely to strike some of us as overly abstract or academic. This attitude often changes, however, when we find ourselves in a position to make or influence biomedical decisions that impact specific individuals. It changes, too, when we find ourselves on the receiving end of such decisions.

But whether we view these problems abstractly or concretely, they generate the same question: Are there any rules, standards, or principles that we can use as guides when we are faced with moral decisions? If there are, then Dr. Cunningham need not be wholly unprepared to decide whether she should order steps taken to save Matteo Sabatini's life. Nor need we be unprepared to decide issues like those discussed above.

The branch of philosophy concerned with principles that allow us to make decisions about what is right and wrong is called *ethics* or *moral philosophy. Bioethics* is specifically concerned with moral principles and decisions in the context of medical practice, policy, and research. Bioethics has a specialized focus but remains a part of the discipline of ethics. Thus, if we are to answer our question as to whether there are any rules or principles to use when making moral decisions in the medical context, we must turn to general ethical theories and to a consideration of moral principles that have been proposed to hold in all contexts of human action.

In the first section, we will discuss five major ethical theories that have been put forward by philosophers. Each of these theories represents an attempt to supply basic principles we can rely on in making moral decisions. We'll consider these theories and examine how they might be applied to moral issues in the medical context. We will discuss the reasons that have been offered to persuade us to accept each theory, but we will also point out some of the difficulties each theory presents.

In the second section, we will examine and illustrate several moral principles that are of special relevance to biomedical research and practice. These principles are frequently appealed to in discussions of practical ethical problems and are sufficiently uncontroversial to be endorsed in a general way by any of the ethical theories mentioned in the first section. (The application of these principles independent of traditional moral theories is sometimes called *principlism*.)

In the third and final section, we will consider approaches to ethical theory that are not identified with a specific set of foundational principles. These include the capabilities approach, virtue ethics, care ethics, and various identity-based theories. We will consider how these theories may be used in making moral decisions, but we will also call attention to some of the criticisms urged against them.

The three sections are not dependent on one another, and it is possible to profit from one without reading the others. (The price for this independence is a small amount of repetition.) Nevertheless, reading all three sections is recommended. Readers will find it easier to follow and evaluate many of the book's Briefing Sessions, as well as Social Context and Case Presentations, if they have at least some familiarity with these various approaches to ethical theory and moral principles.

BASIC ETHICAL THEORIES

Ethical theories attempt to articulate and justify principles that can be employed as guides for moral decision-making and as standards for the evaluation of actions and policies. In effect, such theories attempt to define what it means to act morally, and in doing so, they stipulate in a general fashion our duties or obligations.

Ethical theories also offer a means to explain and justify actions. If our actions are guided by a particular theory, then we can explain them by demonstrating that the principles of the theory required us to act as we did. In such cases, the explanation also constitutes a justification. (In some cases, we may justify our actions by showing that the theory *permitted* our actions—that is, didn't require them, but didn't rule them out as wrong.)

Advocates of a particular ethical theory present what they consider to be good reasons and relevant evidence in its support. Frequently, their aim is to show that the theory is one that any reasonable individual would find persuasive or would endorse as correct. Accordingly, appeals to faith, ideology, or other comprehensive views of the world are not considered to be either necessary or legitimate to justify the theory. Rational persuasion alone is regarded as the basis of justification.

In this section, we will briefly consider four general ethical theories and one theory of justice that has an essential ethical component. In each case, we will begin by examining the basic principles of the theory and the grounds offered for its acceptance. We will then explore some possible applications of the theory that arise within the medical context. Finally, we will mention some of the practical consequences and conceptual difficulties that raise questions about the theory's adequacy or correctness.

Utilitarianism

The ethical theory known as utilitarianism was given its most influential formulation in the nineteenth century by the British philosophers Jeremy Bentham (1748–1832) and John Stuart Mill (1806–1873). Bentham and Mill did not produce identical theories, but both of their versions have become known as "classical utilitarianism." Subsequent elaborations and qualifications of utilitarianism usually draw on the formulations of Bentham and Mill, so their theories are worth careful examination.

The Principle of Utility

The foundation of utilitarianism is a single apparently simple principle. Mill calls it the "principle of utility" and states it this way: *Actions are right in proportion as they tend to promote happiness, wrong as they tend to produce the reverse of happiness.*

The principle focuses attention on the *consequences* of actions, rather than on some feature of the actions themselves. The *utility* or "usefulness" of an action is determined by the extent to which it produces happiness. Thus, no action is *in itself* right or wrong. Nor is an action right or wrong by virtue of the actor's hopes, intentions, or past actions. Consequences alone are important. Breaking a promise, lying, causing pain, or even killing a person may, under certain circumstances, be the right action to take. Under other circumstances, the action might be wrong.

We need not think of the principle as applying to just one action that we are considering. It supplies the basis for a kind of cost–benefit analysis to employ in a situation in which several lines of action are possible. Using the principle, we are supposed to consider the possible results of each action. Then we are to choose the one that produces the most benefit (happiness) at the least cost (unhappiness). The action we take may produce some unhappiness, but it is a balance of happiness over unhappiness that the principle tells us to seek.

Suppose, for example, that a patient in a large hospital is near death: she is in a coma, an EEG shows only minimal brain function, and a respirator is required to keep her breathing. Another patient has just been brought to the hospital from the scene of an automobile accident. His kidneys have been severely damaged, and he is in need of an immediate transplant. There is a good tissue match with the first patient's kidneys. Is it right to hasten her death by removing one of them for transplant?

If we view this scenario in isolation, the principle of utility would likely prompt us to view the removal of the kidney as justified. The woman is on the brink of death, with little-to-no chance of recovery, while the man has a good chance of surviving if he receives the kidney. It is true that the woman's life is threatened even more by the surgery. It may in fact kill her. But, on balance, the kidney transplant seems likely to produce more happiness than unhappiness. In fact, it seems better than the alternative of doing nothing. For in that case, both patients are likely to die.

The principle of utility is also called the "greatest happiness principle" by Bentham and Mill. The reason for this name is clear when the principle is stated as follows: *Those actions are right which produce the greatest happiness for the greatest number of people.* This alternative formulation makes it obvious that, in deciding how to act, it is not just my happiness or the happiness of a particular person or group that must be considered. According to utilitarianism, every person is to count just as much as any other person. That is, when we are considering how we should act, everyone's interest must be considered. The right action, then, will be the one that produces the most happiness for the largest number of people.

Mill is particularly anxious that utilitarianism not be construed as a sophisticated justification for crude self-interest. He stresses that, in making a moral decision, we must look at the situation objectively. We must, he says, be a "benevolent spectator" and then act in a way that will bring about the best results for all concerned. This view is summarized in a famous passage:

> The happiness which forms the utilitarian standard of what is right in conduct is not the agent's own happiness, but that of all concerned. As between his own happiness and that of others, utilitarianism requires him to be as strictly impartial as a disinterested and benevolent spectator. In the golden rule of Jesus of Nazareth, we read the complete spirit of the ethics of utility. To do as you would be done by, and to love your neighbor as yourself, constitute the ideal perfection of utilitarian morality.

The key concept in both formulations of the principle of utility is "happiness." Bentham simply identifies happiness with pleasure—pleasure of any kind. The aim of ethics, then, is to increase the amount of pleasure in the world to the greatest possible extent. In furtherance of this aim, Bentham recommends the use of a "calculus of pleasure and pain," in which characteristics of pleasure such as intensity, duration, and number of people affected are measured and assigned numerical values. To determine which of several possible actions is the right one, we need only determine which one receives the highest numerical score. Unfortunately, Bentham does not tell us what units to use or how to make the measurements.

Mill also identifies happiness with pleasure, but he differs from Bentham in a major respect. Unlike Bentham, he insists that some pleasures are "higher" than others. Thus, pleasures of the intellect are superior to, say, purely sensual pleasures. This difference in the concept of pleasure can become significant in a medical context. For example, Mill's view might assign reduced value to the life of a dementia patient with severely diminished cognition, but who still gets intense pleasure from eating ice cream. The loss of "higher pleasures," such as reading or meaningful conversation with loved ones, cannot be compensated by any quantity of pleasure derived from ice cream. (For Bentham, by contrast, pleasure is pleasure, no matter what the source.)

Both Mill and Bentham regard happiness as an intrinsic good. That is, it is something good in itself or for its own sake. Actions, by contrast, are good only to the extent to which they tend to promote happiness. Therefore, they are only *instrumentally* good. Since utilitarianism determines the rightness of actions in terms of their tendency to promote the greatest happiness for the greatest number, it is considered to be a *teleological* ethical theory. (*Teleological* comes from the Greek word *telos*, which means "end" or "goal.") A teleological ethical theory judges the rightness of an action in terms of an external goal or purpose—"general happiness" or utility for utilitarianism. However, utilitarianism is also a *consequentialist* theory, for the outcomes or consequences of actions are the only considerations relevant to determining their moral rightness. Not all teleological theories are consequentialist.

Some more recent formulations of utilitarianism have rejected the notion that happiness, no matter how defined, is the sole intrinsic good that actions or policies must promote. Critics of the classical view have argued that the list of things we recognize as valuable in themselves should be increased to include ones such as knowledge, beauty, love, friendship, liberty, and health. According to this *pluralistic* view, in applying the principle of utility we must consider the entire range of intrinsic goods that an action is likely to promote. Thus, the right action is the one that can be expected to produce the greatest sum of intrinsic goods. In most of the discussion that follows, we will speak of the greatest happiness or benefit, but it is easy enough to see how the same points can be made from a pluralistic perspective.

Act and Rule Utilitarianism

Utilitarians generally accept the principle of utility as the standard for determining the rightness of actions. But they divide into two major groups over how to apply the principle.

Act utilitarianism holds that the principle should be applied to particular acts in particular circumstances. *Rule utilitarianism* maintains that the principle should be used to test rules, which can in turn be used to decide the rightness of particular acts. Let us consider each of these views and see how it works in practice.

Act utilitarianism holds that an act is right if, and only if, no other act could have been performed that would produce a higher utility. Suppose an infant is born with severe impairments. The child has an open spine, severe brain damage, and dysfunctional kidneys. What should be done? (We will leave open the question of who should decide.)

The act utilitarian holds that we must attempt to determine the consequences of the various actions that are open to us. We should consider, for example, these possibilities: (1) Give the child only the ordinary treatment that would be given to a healthy infant; (2) give the child special treatment for his problems; (3) give the child no treatment—allow him to die; (4) actively end the child's life in a painless way.

According to act utilitarianism, we must explore the potential results of each possibility. We must realize, for example, that when such a child is given only ordinary treatment, he will be worse off, if he survives, than if he had received special treatment. Also, an impaired child allowed to die may suffer more pain for a longer period of time than one killed by a lethal injection. Furthermore, a child treated aggressively will have to undergo numerous surgical procedures of limited effectiveness. We must also consider the child's family and assess the emotional and financial effects that each of the possible actions will have on them. Then, too, we must take into account such matters as the "quality of life" of a child with severe brain damage and multiple impairments, the effect on physicians and nurses in killing or allowing the child to die, and the financial costs to society in providing long-term care.

After these considerations, we should then choose the action that has the greatest utility. We should act in the way that will produce the most benefit for all concerned. Which of the possibilities we select will depend on the precise features of the situation: how impaired the child is, how good his chances are for living a tolerable life, the values and financial status of the family, and so on. The great strength of act utilitarianism is that it invites us to approach each case as unique. In another case with different circumstances, we might, without inconsistency, choose another of the possible actions.

Act utilitarianism shows a sensitivity to specific cases, but it is not free from difficulties. Some philosophers have pointed out that there is no way that we can be sure that we have chosen the right action. We are sure to be ignorant of much relevant information. Besides, we can't predict with much confidence what the results of our actions will be. There is no way to be sure, for example, that even a severely impaired infant will not recover sufficiently to live a better life than we predict.

The act utilitarian can reply that acting morally doesn't require omniscience. We must only make a reasonable effort to obtain relevant information, which we can use to determine the likely consequences of our actions. Acting morally doesn't require anything more than this.

Another objection to act utilitarianism is more serious. According to the doctrine, I am obligated to keep a promise only if keeping it will produce more utility than some other action. If some other action will produce the same utility, then keeping the promise is permissible but not obligatory. Suppose a surgeon promises a patient that only she will perform an operation, then allows a well-qualified resident to perform part of it. Suppose all goes well and the patient never discovers that the promise was not kept. The outcome for the patient is exactly the same as if the surgeon had kept the promise. From the point of view of act utilitarianism, there is nothing wrong with the surgeon's failure to keep it. Yet critics charge that there is something wrong—that, in making the promise, the surgeon took on an obligation. Act utilitarianism is unable to account for obligations incurred by such actions as promising and pledging, critics say, for such actions involve something other than consequences.

A third objection to act utilitarianism arises in situations in which nearly everyone must follow the same rules in order to achieve a high level of utility, but even greater utility can be achieved if a few people disregard the rules. Consider the relationship between physicians and the Medicaid insurance program. The program pays physicians for services provided to patients with very low incomes. The program would collapse if most physicians were not honest in billing Medicaid for their services. Not only would many poor people suffer, but many physicians would lose a source of income.

Suppose a particular physician believes that the requirements to qualify for Medicaid are too restrictive and that many who urgently need medical care are denied coverage. As an act utilitarian, she reasons that it is right for her to apply for funding under Medicaid to open a free clinic. She intends to bill for services she does not provide, then use that money to treat those not covered by Medicaid. Her claims will be small compared to the entire Medicaid budget, so it is unlikely that anyone who qualifies for Medicaid will go without treatment.

Since she will tell no one what she is doing, others are not likely to be influenced by her example and make false claims for similar or less altruistic purposes. The money she is paid will bring substantial benefit to those in need of health care. Thus, she concludes, by violating the rules of the program, her actions will produce greater utility than would be produced by following the rules.

The physician's action would be morally right, according to many act utilitarians. Yet, critics say, we expect an action that is morally right to be one that is right for everyone in similar circumstances. If every physician in the Medicaid program acted in this way, however, the program would be destroyed and thus produce no utility at all. Furthermore, according to critics, the physician's action produces unfairness. Although it is true that the patients she treats at her free clinic gain a benefit they would not otherwise have, similar patients elsewhere must go without treatment. The Medicaid policy, whatever its flaws, is at least prima facie fair in providing benefits to all who meet its requirements. Once again, according to critics, more seems to be involved in judging the moral worth of an action than can be accounted for by act utilitarianism.

In connection with such objections, some critics have gone so far as to claim that it is impossible to see how a society in which everyone was an act utilitarian could function. We could not count on promises being kept nor take for granted that people were telling us the truth. Social policies would be no more than general guides to action, and we could never be sure that people would regard themselves as obligated to adhere to the provisions of those policies. The critics are not necessarily right, of course, and defenders of act utilitarianism have made substantial efforts to answer such criticisms. Some have denied that the theory has those implications; others have argued that some of our common moral perceptions should give way to more rational standards. For example, concerning euthanasia, Carl Wellman writes,

> Try as I may, I honestly cannot discover great hidden disutilities in the act of killing an elderly person suffering greatly from an incurable illness, provided that certain safeguards like a written medical opinion by at least two doctors and a request by the patient are preserved. In this case I cannot find any way to reconcile my theory with my moral judgment. What I do in this case is to hold fast to act-utilitarianism and distrust my moral sense. I claim that my condemnation of such acts is an irrational disapproval, a condemnation that will change upon further reasoning about the act.... That I feel wrongness is clear, but I cannot state to myself any rational justification for my feeling. Hence, I discount this particular judgment as irrational.

Rule utilitarianism maintains that an action is right if it conforms to a rule of conduct that, according to the principle of utility, will produce at least as much utility as any other rule applicable to the situation. A rule like "Provide only ordinary care for severely brain-damaged newborns with multiple impairments" would, if established, allow us to decide about the course of action to follow in situations like the one described above.

The rule utilitarian is concerned with assessing the utility not of individual actions but of particular rules. In practice, then, we do not have to go through the calculations involved in determining in each case whether a specific action will increase utility. All that we have to establish is that following a certain rule will, in general, result in a situation in which utility is maximized. Once rules are established, they can be relied on to determine whether a particular action is right.

The basic idea behind rule utilitarianism is that having a set of rules that are consistently observed produces the greatest social utility. Having everyone follow the same rule in each case of the same kind yields more utility for everyone in the long run. An act utilitarian can agree that having rules may produce more social utility than not having them. But the act utilitarian insists that the rules be regarded as no more than rough guides to action, as "rules of thumb." Thus, for act utilitarianism it is perfectly legitimate to violate a rule if doing so will maximize utility in that instance. By contrast, the rule utilitarian holds that rules must be followed, even though following them may produce less net utility (more unhappiness than happiness) in a particular case.

Rule utilitarianism can endorse rules such as "Keep your promises." Thus, unlike act utilitarianism, it can account for the general sense that, in making promises, we are placing ourselves under an obligation that cannot be set aside for the sake of increasing utility. If "Keep your promises" is accepted as a rule, then the surgeon who fails to perform all of an operation herself when she has promised her patient she would do so has not done the right thing, even if the patient never learns the truth.

Rule utilitarians recognize that circumstances can arise in which it would be disastrous to follow a general rule, even when it is true that, *in general*, greater happiness would result from following the rule all the time. Clearly, we should not keep a promise to meet someone for lunch when we have to choose between keeping the promise and rushing a heart-attack victim to the hospital. It is consistent with the theory to formulate rules that include appropriate escape clauses. For example, "Keep your promises, unless breaking them is required to save a life" and "Keep your promises, unless keeping them would lead to a disastrous result unforeseen at the time the promise was made" are rules that a rule utilitarian might regard as likely to produce greater utility than "Always keep your promises no matter what the consequences may be." What a rule utilitarian cannot endorse is a rule like "Keep your promises, except when breaking a promise would produce more utility."

This would cause the rule utilitarian's position to collapse back into act utilitarianism.

Of course, rule utilitarians are not committed to endorsing general rules only. It is compatible with the view to offer quite specific rules, and in fact there is no constraint on how specific a rule may be. A rule utilitarian might, for example, establish a rule such as, "If an infant is born with an open spine, severe brain damage, and dysfunctional kidneys, then the infant should receive no life-sustaining treatment."

The possibility of formulating a large number of rules and establishing them separately opens this basic version of rule utilitarianism to two objections. First, some rules are likely to conflict when they are applied to the same case and basic rule utilitarianism offers no way to resolve such conflicts. What should a physician do when faced both with a rule like that above and with another that directs him to "Provide life-sustaining care to all who require it"? Rules that pass the test of promoting utility when considered individually may express contradictory demands. A further objection to basic rule utilitarianism is that establishing rules to cover many different circumstances and situations results in such an abundance of rules that employing them to make moral decisions becomes difficult, if not impossible.

Partly due to such difficulties, some rule utilitarians have instead tried to establish the utility of a fixed set of rules or an entire moral code. The set can include rules for resolving potential conflicts, and an effort can be made to keep the rules few and simple to minimize the practical difficulty of employing them. Once again, as with basic rule utilitarianism, the principle of utility is employed to determine which set of rules, out of the various sets considered, ought to be accepted.

In this more sophisticated form, rule utilitarianism can be characterized as the theory that an action is right when it conforms to a set of rules that has been determined to produce at least as much overall utility as any other set. It is possible to accept as constraints certain social and economic institutions, such as private property and a market economy, and then argue for the set of rules that will yield the most utility under those conditions. However, it is also possible to argue for a different set of rules that would lead to the greatest possible utility, quite apart from those social forms. Indeed, such a set might be defended in an effort to bring about changes in present society that are needed to increase the overall level of utility. Utilitarianism, whether act or rule, need not be limited to individual moral obligation. It is also a social and political theory.

We have already seen that rule utilitarianism, unlike act utilitarianism, makes possible the sort of obligation we associate with making promises. But how might rule utilitarianism deal with the case of the physician who files false Medicaid claims to raise funds to operate a free clinic? An obvious answer, although certainly not the only one possible, is that any set of rules likely to be adopted by a rule utilitarian will contain at least one rule making fraud morally wrong. Without a rule forbidding fraud, no social program that requires the cooperation of its participants is likely to achieve its aim. Such a rule protects the program from miscalculations of utility that individuals may make for self-serving reasons, keeps the program focused on its goals, and prevents it from becoming fragmented. Even if a few individuals commit fraud, the rule against it is crucial in discouraging a large majority from committing it. Otherwise, as we pointed out earlier, such a program would collapse. By requiring that the program operate as it was designed, rule utilitarianism also preserves prima facie fairness, because only those who qualify receive benefits.

The most telling objection to rule utilitarianism, according to some critics, is that it is inconsistent. The justification for a set of moral rules is that the rules maximize utility. If rules are to maximize utility, then it seems obvious that they may require that an act produce more utility than any other possible act in a particular situation. Otherwise, the maximum amount of utility would not result. But if the rules satisfy this demand, then they will justify exactly the same actions as act utilitarianism. Thus, the rules will deem it permissible to sometimes break promises, make fraudulent claims, and so on. When rule utilitarianism moves to block these possibilities by requiring that rules produce only the most utility overall, it becomes inconsistent: the set of rules is said to maximize utility, but the rules will require actions that do not maximize utility. Thus, rule utilitarianism seems both to accept and reject the principle of utility as the ultimate moral standard.

Preference Utilitarianism

Some critics have questioned the wisdom of using happiness or any other intrinsic value (e.g., knowledge or health) as a criterion of the rightness of an action. The notion of an intrinsic value, they have argued, is too imprecise to be used as a practical guide. Furthermore, it is not at all clear that people share the same values, and even if they do, they are not committed to them to the same degree. One person may value knowledge more than health, whereas someone else may value physical pleasure over knowledge or health. As a result, there can be no clear-cut procedure for determining what action is likely to produce the best outcome for an individual or group.

The effort to develop clear-cut procedures for determining the best action or policy has led some thinkers to replace considerations of intrinsic value with considerations of actual preferences. What someone wants, desires, or prefers can be determined, in principle, in an objective way by consulting the person directly. In addition, people are often able to do more than merely express a preference.

Sometimes they can rank their preferences from that which is most desired to that which is least desired.

Such a ranking is of special importance in situations involving risk, for individuals can be asked to decide how much risk they are willing to take to try to realize a given preference. A young woman with a hip injury who is otherwise in good health may be willing to accept the risk of surgery to increase her chances of being restored to many years of active life. By contrast, an elderly woman in frail health may prefer to avoid surgery and accept the limitations that the injury imposes on her physical activities. For the elderly patient, not only are the risks of surgery greater because of her poor health, but even if the surgery is successful, she will have fewer years to benefit from it.

Alternatively, the older woman may place such a premium on physical activity that she is willing to take the risk of surgery to improve her chances of securing even a few more years of it. Only she can say what is important to her and how willing she is to take the risk required to secure it.

These considerations about personal preferences can also be raised with regard to social preferences. Statistical information about what people desire and what they are willing to forego to see their desires satisfied becomes relevant to institutional and legislative deliberations about what policies to adopt. For example, a crucial question facing our own society is whether we are willing to provide everyone with at least a basic minimum of health care, even if this requires harming the private insurance industry or reducing spending on other social goods.

Employing the satisfaction of preferences as a criterion for the moral value of an action or policy makes it possible to incorporate determinate data into our ethical deliberations. The life expectancy of infants with specific impairments at birth can be estimated on a statistical basis; surgical procedures can be associated with a certain success rate and a certain mortality rate. Similarly, a particular social policy has a certain financial cost, and if implemented, the policy is likely to mean the loss of other possible benefits and opportunities.

Ideally, information of this kind should allow a preference utilitarian to calculate the best course of action for an individual or group. The best action will be the one that best combines the satisfaction of preferences with other conditions (e.g., financial costs and risks) that are at least minimally acceptable. To use the jargon of the theorists, the best action is the one that maximizes the preference utilities of the person or group.

A utilitarianism that employs preferences has the advantage of suggesting more explicit methods of analysis and decision-making than the classical formulation. It also has the potential for being more sensitive to the expressed desires of individuals. However, preference utilitarianism is not free from specific difficulties.

Perhaps most obvious is the problem posed by preferences that we would generally regard as unacceptable. What are we to say about those who prefer mass murder, child abuse, or torturing animals? A second problem involves *adaptive preferences*, or the way people's preferences are often shaped (and limited) by the social conditions currently available to them. These problems suggest that subjective preferences cannot be treated equally or taken at face value, and we must have a way to distinguish acceptable from unacceptable ones. Whether this can be done by relying on the principle of utility alone is doubtful. In the view of some commentators, some other moral principle (or principles) is needed.

Difficulties with Utilitarianism

Classical utilitarianism is open to a variety of objections. Here we will concentrate on only one, however, for it seems to reveal a major flaw in the structure of the entire theory. This serious objection is that the principle of utility appears to justify the imposition of great suffering on a few people for the benefit of many people.

Certain kinds of human experimentation forcefully illustrate this possibility. Suppose an investigator is concerned with acquiring a better understanding of human brain functions. She could learn a great deal by systematically destroying the brain of one person and carefully noting the results. Such a study would offer many more opportunities for increasing medical knowledge than traditional studies that focus on animals or human subjects with accidental brain damage. We may suppose that the investigator chooses a subject without education or training, without family or friends, who cannot be regarded as making a significant contribution to society. The subject will die from the experiment, but it is not unreasonable to suppose that the knowledge of the human brain gained from the experiment will improve the lives of many more people.

The principle of utility seems to make such experiments legitimate because the outcome is a greater quantity of good than harm. One or a few have suffered immensely, but the many will profit to an extent that far outweighs that suffering.

Clearly, what is missing from such scenarios is the concept of *justice*. It cannot be right to increase the general happiness at the expense of one person or group. There must be some way of distributing happiness and unhappiness and avoiding exploitation. Mill acknowledged that utilitarianism needed a principle of justice, but many contemporary philosophers do not believe that such a principle can be derived from the principle of utility. In their opinion, utilitarianism as an ethical theory suffers severely from this defect. Yet some philosophers, while acknowledging the defect, have still held that utilitarianism is the best substantive moral theory available.

Kant's Ethics

For utilitarianism, the rightness of an action depends upon its consequences. In stark contrast to this view is the ethical theory formulated by the German philosopher Immanuel Kant (1724–1804). For Kant, the consequences of an action are morally irrelevant. Rather, an action is right when it accords with a rule satisfying a broader principle that he calls the *categorical imperative*. Since this is the basic principle of Kant's ethics, we will begin our discussion with it.

The Categorical Imperative

If I decide to have an abortion and act on my decision, it is possible to view my action as involving a rule. I can be thought of as endorsing a rule to the effect that "Whenever I am in circumstances like these, then I will have an abortion." Kant calls such a rule a *maxim*. In his view, all reasoned and considered actions can be regarded as involving maxims.

The maxims in such cases are personal or subjective, but they can be thought of as candidates for moral rules. If they pass the test imposed by the categorical imperative, then we can say that the actions they approve are right. Furthermore, in passing the test, these maxims cease to be merely personal and subjective. They gain the status of objective rules of morality that hold for everyone.

Kant formulates the categorical imperative in this way: *Act only on that maxim which you can will to be a universal law.* Kant calls the principle *categorical* to distinguish it from *hypothetical* imperatives. The latter tell us what to do if we want to bring about certain consequences—such as happiness. A categorical imperative prescribes what we ought to do without reference to any consequences. The principle is an "imperative" because it is a command.

The test imposed on maxims by the categorical imperative is one of generalization

or *universalizability*. The central idea of the test is that a moral maxim is one that can be generalized to apply to all cases of the same kind. That is, it could be adopted as a maxim by everyone who is in a similar situation, and thus willed as a universal law. For a maxim to satisfy the categorical imperative, it is not necessary that we be willing in some psychological sense to see it universally adopted. Rather, the test is one that requires us to avoid inconsistency or logical conflict in what we will as a universal law.

Suppose, for example, that I am a physician and I tell a patient that he has a serious illness, although I know that he doesn't. This may be to my immediate advantage, for the treatment and the supposed cure will increase my income and reputation. The maxim of my action might be phrased as, "Whenever it is to my advantage, I may lie to healthy patients and tell them that they have serious illnesses."

Now suppose that I try to generalize my maxim. In doing so, I will discover that I am willing the existence of a universal practice with contradictory properties. If "Whenever it is to my advantage, I may lie to healthy patients and tell them that they have serious illnesses" is made a universal law, then trust in the diagnostic pronouncements of physicians will soon be destroyed. But my scheme depends on my patients' trusting me and accepting the truth of my lying diagnosis.

It is as if I were saying, "Let there be a rule of truth telling such that people can assume that physicians are telling them the truth, but let there also be a rule that physicians may lie to their patients when it is in the interest of the physician to do so." In willing both rules, I am willing something contradictory. Thus, I can will my action in an exceptional case, but I can't will that my action be universal without generating a logical conflict.

Kant claims that such considerations show that it is always wrong to lie. Lying produces a contradiction in what we will. On one hand, we will that people believe what we say—that they accept our assurances and promises. On the other hand, we will that people be free to give false assurances and make false promises. Lying thus produces a self-defeating situation, for, when the maxim involved is generalized, the very framework required for lying collapses.

Similarly, consider the egoist who seeks only his self-interest and so makes "Never show mercy or compassion for others" the maxim of his actions. When universalized, this maxim results in the same kind of self-defeating situation that lying does. Since the egoist will sometimes find himself in need of mercy and compassion, if he wills the maxim of his action to be a universal law, then he will be depriving himself of something that is in his self-interest. Thus, in willing the abolition of mercy and compassion out of self-interest, he creates a logical contradiction in what he wills.

Another Formulation

According to Kant, there is only one categorical imperative, but it can be stated in three different ways. Each version is intended to reveal a different aspect of the principle. The second formulation, the only other we will consider, can be stated in this way: *Always act so as to treat humanity, either in yourself or in others, always as an end and never only as a means.*

This version illustrates Kant's notion that every rational creature has worth in itself. This worth is not conferred by being born into a society with a certain political structure, nor even by belonging to a certain biological species. The worth is inherent in the mere possession of rationality. Rational creatures possess what Kant calls an "autonomous, self-legislating will." That is, they are able to consider the consequences of their actions, make rules for themselves, and direct their actions by those self-imposed rules. Thus, rationality confers upon everyone intrinsic worth and dignity.

This formulation of the categorical imperative rules out some of the standards of "social worth" that have been used to determine who should receive certain medical resources (such as kidney dialysis) when the demand is greater than the supply. Standards that make a person's education, accomplishments, or social position relevant seem contrary to this version of the categorical imperative. They violate the basic notion that each person has an inherent worth equal to that of any other person. Unlike dogs or horses, people cannot be judged on "show points."

For Kant, all of morality has its ultimate source in rationality. The categorical imperative, in any formulation, is an expression of rationality, and it is the principle that would be followed in practice by any purely rational being. Moral rules are not mere arbitrary conventions or subjective standards. They are objective truths that have their source in the rational nature of human beings.

Duty

Utilitarianism identifies the good with happiness or pleasure and makes the production of happiness the supreme principle of morality. But for Kant, happiness is at best a conditional or qualified good. In his view, there is only one thing that can be said to be good in itself: a good will.

Will is what directs our actions and guides our conduct. But what makes a will a "good will"? Kant's answer is that a will becomes good when it acts purely for the sake of duty.

We act for the sake of duty (or from duty) when we act on maxims that satisfy the categorical imperative. This means, then, that it is the motive force behind our actions—the character of our will—that determines their moral character. Morality does not rest on results—such as the production of happiness—but neither does it rest on the feelings, impulses, or inclinations that may prompt us to act. An action is right, for Kant, only when it is done for the sake of duty.

Suppose that I decide to donate one of my kidneys for a transplant. If the only consideration behind my action is the hope of approval or praise, or even a compassionate aversion to another's suffering, then, although I have done the right thing, my action has no inner moral worth. I may have acted *in accordance with duty* (done the same thing duty would have required), but I did not act *from duty.*

This view of duty and its connection with morality captures attitudes we frequently express. Consider a nurse who gives special care to a severely ill patient. Suppose we learned that the nurse was providing such extraordinary care only because he hoped that the patient or her family would reward him with a special bonus. Knowing this, we would be unlikely to view the nurse's actions as morally laudable. We might even think the nurse was being greedy or cynical, and say that he was doing the right thing for the wrong reasons.

Kant distinguishes between two types of duties: perfect and imperfect. (The distinction corresponds to the two ways in which maxims can be self-defeating when tested by the categorical imperative.) A *perfect duty* is one we must always observe; an *imperfect duty* is one that we must observe only on some occasions. I have a perfect duty not to injure another person, but I have only an imperfect duty to show love and compassion. I must sometimes show it, but when I show it and which people I select to receive it are entirely up to me.

My duties determine what others can legitimately claim from me as a right. Some rights can be claimed as perfect rights, while others cannot. Everyone can demand of me that I do him or her no injury. But no one can tell me that I must make him or her the recipient of my love and compassion. In deciding how to discharge my imperfect duties, I am free to follow my emotions and inclinations.

For utilitarianism, an action is right when it produces something that is intrinsically valuable (happiness). Because actions are judged by their contributions to achieving a goal, utilitarianism is a teleological theory. By contrast, Kant's ethics holds that an action has features in itself that make it right or dutiful. These features are distinct from the action's consequences. Such a theory is called *deontological*, a term derived from the Greek word for "duty" or "obligation."

Kant's Ethics in the Medical Context

Four features of Kant's ethics are of particular importance in dealing with issues in medical treatment and research:

1. No matter what the consequences may be, it is always wrong to lie.

2. We must always treat people (including ourselves) as ends and not as means only.

3. An action is right when it satisfies the categorical imperative.

4. Perfect duties give a basis for claims that certain rights should be recognized.

We can present here only two brief examples of how these features can be instrumental in resolving biomedical issues, but each suggests a broader set of related moral problems.

Our first application of Kant's ethics has bearing on medical research. The task of medical investigators would be easier if they did not have to inform patients that they were research subjects. Patients could then become subjects without even knowing it, and more often than not would face negligible risks. Even though no overt lying would be involved, Kantian principles would reject this procedure as wrong. For it would require treating people as a means only and not as ends in themselves.

Likewise, it would be wrong for an investigator to claim that a treatment is being offered for therapeutic purposes when it is really being offered as part of an experiment. Lying is always wrong, according to Kantian ethics. Nor could the researcher justify this deception by telling herself that the study is of such importance that it is legitimate to lie to the patient. On Kant's principles, good results never make an action morally right. Thus, a patient must give voluntary and informed consent to become a subject of medical experimentation. Otherwise, the patient is being deprived of autonomy and treated instrumentally, as a means only.

Just as Kant's principles place restrictions on researchers, they also place limits on the actions of potential research subjects. We may volunteer to be subjects because we expect the research to bring us direct benefit. Similarly, we may volunteer because we view participation in research as an occasion for fulfilling an imperfect duty to improve overall human welfare. But we also have a duty to treat ourselves as ends and so act to preserve our dignity and value as bearers of rational humanity. Therefore, it would be wrong for us to volunteer for an experiment that risked our lives or cognitive capacities without first satisfying ourselves that the experiment was legitimate and necessary.

Our second application of Kant's ethics in a medical context bears on the relationship between patients and caregivers. A physician, for example, has only an imperfect duty to accept me as a patient. She has a duty to make use of her skills and talents to treat the sick, but I cannot legitimately insist on being the beneficiary. How she discharges her duty is her decision.

If, however, I am accepted as a patient, then I can make some legitimate claims. I can demand that nothing be done to cause me pointless harm, because it is never right to injure a person. Furthermore, I can demand that I never be lied to or deceived. Suppose,

for example, I am given a placebo (a harmless but inactive substance) and told that it is a powerful and effective medication. Or suppose that a biopsy shows that I have an inoperable form of cancer, but my physician tells me, "There's nothing seriously wrong with you." In both cases, the physician may suppose that she is deceiving me "for my own good": the placebo may be psychologically effective and make me feel better, and the lie about cancer may save me from useless worry. Yet, by being deceived, I am being denied the dignity inherent in my status as a rational being. Lying is wrong in general, and in such cases it also deprives me of my autonomy, of my power to make decisions and form my own opinions. As a result, such deception dehumanizes me.

As an autonomous rational being, a person is entitled to control over his or her own body. This means that medical procedures can be performed on me only with my permission. It would be wrong even if the interventions were needed "for my own good." I may voluntarily put myself under the care of a physician and submit to her recommendations, but the decision belongs to me alone.

In exercising control over my body, however, I also have a duty to myself. Suppose, for example, that I refuse to allow surgery to be performed on me, although I have reason to believe it necessary to preserve my life. Since I have a duty to preserve my life, as does every person, my refusal is morally unjustifiable. Even here, however, it is not legitimate for others to *force* me to "do my duty." In fact, in Kantian ethics it is impossible to force another to do his or her duty because it is not the action, but the maxim involved, that determines whether or not one's duty has been done.

It is obvious even from these brief examples that Kantian ethics is a fruitful source of principles and concepts for analyzing moral issues in medical research and practice. The absolute requirements imposed by the categorical imperative can be a source of strength and even of comfort. By contrast, utilitarianism requires us to weigh alternative courses of action by anticipating their consequences and deciding whether our choice can be justified by the expected results. Kant's ethics saves us from this kind of doubt and indecision: we know we must never lie, no matter what good may come of it. Furthermore, the most severe defect of utilitarianism—the lack of a principle of justice—is provided by Kant's categorical imperative. When every person is to be treated as an end and never as only a means, the possibility of legitimately exploiting some for the benefit of others is wholly eliminated.

Difficulties with Kantian Ethics

Kant's ethical theory is complex and controversial. It has problems of a theoretical sort that manifest themselves in practice and may lead us to doubt whether the absolute rules determined by the categorical imperative can always provide a straightforward solution to our moral difficulties. We will limit ourselves to discussing just three of these theoretical problems.

First, Kant's principles may seem to prompt us to resolve conflicts among duties in ways that seem intuitively wrong. I have a duty to keep my promises, for example, and I also have a duty to help those in need. Suppose, then, that I am a physician and I have promised a colleague to attend a staff conference. Right before the conference starts, I am talking with a patient who lapses into an insulin coma. If I get involved in treating the patient, I'll have to break my promise to attend the conference. What should I do?

The answer is obvious: I should treat the patient. Our moral intuition tells us this. But for Kant, keeping promises is a perfect duty, while helping others is an imperfect one. This suggests that according to Kantian principles, I should abandon my patient and rush off to keep my appointment.

Something is apparently wrong with a view that holds that a promise should never be broken—even when the promise concerns a relatively trivial matter and the consequences of keeping it are disastrous.

Another problem with the categorical imperative arises because we are free to choose how to formulate a maxim for testing. In all likelihood, none of us could approve a maxim such as "Lie when it is convenient for you." But what about "Lie when telling the truth is likely to cause harm to another"? This seems like a much better candidate for a universal law. Now consider the maxim "Whenever a physician has good reason to believe that a patient's life will be seriously threatened if she is told the truth about her condition, then the physician should lie." This seems like an even stronger candidate for a universal law.

Yet these three maxims could apply to the same medical situation. Since Kant does not tell us how to formulate our maxims, it is clear that many actions that at first seem to fail the categorical imperative test will apparently pass it if we describe the situation in sufficient detail. In other words, it is possible to will that everyone act just as we are inclined to act whenever they find themselves in *exactly* this kind of situation. But this leaves unsettled the broader moral questions raised by the situation—e.g., whether it is ever permissible to lie. The categorical imperative, then, does not seem to solve our moral problems quite so neatly as it first appears to.

A final problem arises from Kant's notion that we have duties to rational beings or persons. Ordinarily, we have little difficulty with this commitment to persons, yet there are circumstances, particularly in the medical context, in which serious problems arise. Consider, for example, a fetus at various stages of development. Is the fetus at any stage to be considered a rational being? The way this question is answered can make all the difference in deciding about the rightness or wrongness of abortion.

A similar difficulty is present when considering how to treat an infant with serious birth impairments. Is it our duty to care for this infant and do all we can to see that she lives? If the infant is not a person, then perhaps we do not owe her the sort of treatment it would be our duty to provide a similarly afflicted adult. For many critics, such cases suggest that the notion of a person as an autonomous rational being is both arbitrary and too restrictive. It begs important moral questions.

Another difficulty connected with Kant's concept of a rational person is the notion of an "autonomous self-regulating will." Under what conditions can we assume that an individual possesses such a will? Does a child or a mentally impaired person? What about someone in prison? Without such a will, in Kant's view, such an individual cannot legitimately consent to be the subject of an experiment or even give permission for necessary medical treatment. This notion of the will requires considerable development before Kant's principles can be relied on to resolve ethical questions in medicine.

The difficulties that we have discussed require serious consideration. This does not mean, of course, that they cannot be resolved or that, because of them, Kant's theory is worthless. As with utilitarianism, there are many philosophers who believe the theory is the best available, despite its shortcomings. That it captures many of our intuitive beliefs about what is right (not to lie, to treat people with dignity, to act benevolently) and supplies us with a test for determining our duties (the categorical imperative) recommend it as a powerful and compelling ethical theory.

Ross's Ethics

The Scottish philosopher W. D. Ross (1877–1971) presents an ethical theory in his book *The Right and the Good* that can be seen as an attempt to combine aspects of utilitarianism and aspects of Kantianism. Ross rejects the utilitarian notion that an action is made right by its consequences alone, but he is also troubled by Kant's absolute rules. Not only do such rules fail to show sensitivity to the complexities of actual situations, but they sometimes conflict with one another. Like Kant, Ross is a deontologist, but with an important difference: Ross believes that it is necessary to consider consequences in making a moral choice, even though he believes that it is not the results of an action taken alone that make it right.

Moral Properties and Rules

For Ross, there is an unbridgeable distinction between moral and nonmoral properties. There are only two moral properties—rightness and goodness—and these cannot be replaced by, or explained in terms of, other properties. Thus, to say that an action is right is not at all the same as saying that it causes pleasure or increases happiness, as utilitarianism claims.

Ross does not deny, however, that there is a connection between moral properties and nonmoral ones. What he denies is the possibility of establishing an identity between them. Thus, it may be right to relieve someone's suffering, but right is not identical with relieving suffering. (More precisely, the rightness of the action is not identical with the action's being a case of relieving suffering.)

Ross also grants that we must often establish many nonmoral facts about a situation before we can legitimately make a moral judgment. If I see a physician administering an injection, I cannot say whether she is acting rightly without determining what she is injecting, why she is doing it, how it will impact the patient's condition, and so on. Thus, rightness is a property that depends partly on the nonmoral properties that characterize a situation. I cannot determine whether the physician is doing the right thing or the wrong thing until I determine what the non-moral properties are.

Ross believes that there are cases in which we have no genuine doubt about whether the property of rightness or goodness is present. The world abounds with examples of cruelty, lying, and selfishness, and in these cases we are immediately aware of the absence of rightness or goodness. The world also abounds with examples of compassion, candor, and generosity in which rightness and goodness are clearly present. Ross claims that our experience with such cases puts us in a position to recognize rightness and goodness with the same degree of certainty as when we grasp the mathematical truth that a triangle has three angles.

Furthermore, according to Ross, our experience of many individual cases allows us to recognize the validity of a general statement like "It is wrong to cause needless pain." We apprehend such rules in much the same way that we come to recognize the letter *A* after having seen it written or printed in a variety of handwritings or typefaces.

Thus, our moral intuitions can supply us with moral rules of a general kind. But Ross argues that these rules cannot be absolute. They can serve only as guides to assist us in deciding what we should do. Ultimately, in any particular case we must rely not only on the rules but also on reason and our understanding of the situation.

Thus, even with rules, we may not recognize what the right thing to do is in a given situation. We intuitively grasp, Ross suggests, that there is always a right thing to do, but what it is may be far from obvious. In fact, doubt about what is the right way of acting may arise just because we have rules to guide us. We become aware of the fact that there are several possible courses of action, and all of them may seem to be right.

Consider the problem of whether to lie to a terminally ill patient about his condition.

Let us suppose that, if we lie to him, we can avoid causing him at least some useless anguish. But then aren't we violating his trust in us to act morally and to speak the truth?

In such cases, we seem to have a conflict in our duties. It is because of such familiar kinds of conflicts that Ross rejects the possibility of discovering absolute, invariant moral rules such as "Always tell the truth" and "Always eliminate needless suffering." In cases like the one above, we cannot hold that both rules are absolute without contradicting ourselves. Ross says that we have to recognize that every rule has exceptions and must in some situations be overridden.

Actual Duties and Prima Facie Duties

If rules such as "Always tell the truth" cannot be absolute, then what status can they have? When our rules come into conflict in particular situations, how are we to decide which rule applies? Ross answers this question by making use of a distinction between what is actually right and what is *prima facie* right. Since we have a duty to do what is right, this distinction can be expressed as one between *actual duty* and *prima facie duty*.

An actual duty is simply what my real duty is in a situation. It is the action that, out of the various possibilities, I ought to perform. Frequently, however, I may not know what my actual duty is. In fact, for Ross, the whole problem of ethics might be said to be the problem of knowing what my actual duty is in any given situation.

Prima facie literally means "at first sight," but Ross uses the phrase to mean something like "other things being equal." Accordingly, a prima facie duty is one that dictates what I should do when other relevant factors in a situation are not considered. If I promised to meet you for lunch, then I have a prima facie duty to meet you. But suppose I am a physician, and just as I am about to leave for our appointment, the patient I am with suffers cardiac arrest. In such circumstances, according to Ross's view, I should break my promise and render aid to the patient. My prima facie duty to keep my promise is not absolute. It constitutes a moral reason for meeting you, but there is also a moral reason for not meeting you. I also have a prima facie duty to aid my patient, and this is a reason that outweighs the first one. Thus, aiding the patient is both a prima facie duty and, in this situation, my actual duty.

The notion of a prima facie duty permits Ross to offer a set of moral rules stated in such a way that they are both universal and free from exceptions. For Ross, for example, lying is always wrong, but it is wrong prima facie. It may be that in a particular situation my actual duty requires that I lie. Even though what I have done is prima facie wrong, it is the morally right thing to do if some other prima facie duty that requires lying in this case is more stringent than the prima facie duty to tell the truth. (Perhaps only by lying am I able to prevent a delusional patient from committing suicide.) I must be able to explain and justify my failure to tell the truth, and it is of course possible that I may not be able to do so. It may be that I was confused and misunderstood the situation or failed to consider other alternatives. I may have been wrong to believe that my actual duty required me to lie. However, even if I was correct in my belief, that I lied is still prima facie wrong. It is this fact (and for Ross it is a fact) that requires me to explain and justify my action.

We have considered only a few simple examples of prima facie duties, but Ross is more thorough and systematic than our examples might suggest. He offers a list of duties that he considers binding on all moral agents. Here they are in summary form:

1. *Duties of fidelity*: telling the truth, keeping actual and implicit promises, and not representing fiction as history.

2. *Duties of reparation*: righting the wrongs we have done to others.

3. *Duties of gratitude*: recognizing the services others have done for us.

4. *Duties of justice*: preventing a distribution of pleasure or happiness that is not in keeping with the merits of the people involved.

5. *Duties of beneficence*: helping to better the condition of other beings with respect to virtue, intelligence, or pleasure.

6. *Duties of self-improvement*: bettering ourselves with respect to virtue or intelligence.

7. *Duties of nonmaleficence*: avoiding or preventing injury to others.

Ross doesn't claim that this is a complete list of the prima facie duties. However, he does believe that the duties on the list are all ones that we acknowledge and are willing to accept as legitimate and binding without argument. He believes that if we simply reflect on these prima facie duties, we will see that they may be truly asserted. As he puts the matter:

> I . . . am claiming that we know them to be true. To me it seems as self-evident as anything could be, that to make a promise, for instance, is to create a moral claim on us in someone else. Many readers will perhaps say that they do not know this to be true. If so I certainly cannot prove it to them. I can only ask them to reflect again, in the hope that they will ultimately agree that they also know it to be true.

Notice that Ross explicitly rejects the possibility of providing us with reasons or arguments to convince us to accept his list of prima facie duties. We are merely invited to reflect on certain kinds of cases, such as those involving promises. Ross is convinced that this reflection will bring us to accept his claim that these are true duties. Ross, like other intuitionists, tries to get us to agree with his moral perceptions in much the same way as we might try to get people to agree with us about our color perceptions. We might, for example, show a paint sample to a friend and say, "Don't you think that looks blue? It does to me. Think about it for a minute."

We introduced the distinction between actual and prima facie duties to deal with those situations in which duties seem to conflict. The problem, as we can now state it, is this: What are we to do in a situation in which we recognize more than one prima facie duty and it is not possible for us to act in a way that will fulfill all of them? We know, of course, that we should act in a way that satisfies our actual duty. But that is just our problem. What, after all, is our actual duty when our prima facie duties are in conflict?

Ross offers us two principles to deal with cases of conflicting duty. The first principle is designed to handle situations in which just two prima facie duties are in conflict: *That act is one's duty which is in accord with the more stringent prima facie obligation.* The second principle is intended to deal with cases in which several prima facie duties are in conflict: *That act is one's duty which has the greatest balance of prima facie rightness over prima facie wrongness.*

Unfortunately, both these principles present problems in application. Ross does not tell us how we are to determine when an obligation is "more stringent" than another. Nor does he give us a rule for determining the "balance" of prima facie rightness over wrongness. Ultimately, according to Ross, we must simply rely upon our perceptions of the situation. There is no automatic or mechanical procedure that can be followed. If we learn the facts in the case, consider the consequences of our possible actions, and reflect on our prima facie duties, we should be able to arrive at a conclusion as to the best course of action—in Ross's view, something that we as moral agents can and must do.

Perhaps there is no direct way to answer the following abstract question: Is the duty not to lie to a patient more stringent than the duty not to cause needless suffering? So much depends on the character and condition of the individual patient that an abstract determination of our duty based on balance or stringency would be useless. However, knowing the patient and the broader circumstances, we should be able to perceive what the right course of action is.

Ross further believes that there are many situations in which there are no particular difficulties about resolving the conflict between prima facie duties. For example, most of us would agree that if we can save someone from serious injury by lying, then we have more of an obligation to prevent the injury than we do to tell the truth.

Ross's Ethics in the Medical Context

Ross's moral rules are not absolute in the sense that Kant's are; consequently, as with utilitarianism, it is not possible to say what someone's duty would be in an actual concrete situation. We can discuss, however, the general advantages that Ross's theory brings to medical–moral issues. We will mention only two for illustration.

First and most important is Ross's list of prima facie duties. The list of duties can serve an important function in the moral education of physicians, researchers, and other medical personnel. The list encourages each person who is responsible for patient care to reflect on the prima facie obligations that the person has toward patients and to set aside one of those obligations only when morally certain that another obligation takes precedence.

The specific duties imposed in a prima facie way are numerous and can be expressed in terms relevant to the medical context: do not injure patients; do not distribute scarce resources in a way that fails to recognize individual worth; do not lie to patients; show patients kindness and understanding; educate patients in ways useful to them; do not hold out false hopes to patients; and so on.

Second, like utilitarianism, Ross's ethics encourages us to show sensitivity to the unique features of situations before acting. Like Kant's ethics, however, Ross's also insists that we look at the world from a particular moral perspective. In arriving at decisions about what is right, we must learn the facts of the case and explore the possible consequences of our actions. Ultimately, however, our actions must be guided by what is right, rather than by what is useful or what will produce happiness.

Since, for Ross, actions are not always justified in terms of their results, we cannot say unequivocally, "It is right to trick this person into becoming a research subject because the experiment will benefit thousands." Yet, we also cannot say that it is always wrong to trick a person into participating. An action is right or wrong regardless of what we think about it, but in a particular case circumstances might justify a researcher in allowing some other duty to take precedence over the duty of fidelity.

Fundamentally, then, Ross's ethics offers us the possibility of gaining the advantages of utilitarianism while recognizing the moral force of duties that the principle of utility fails to acknowledge. Ross's ethics accommodates not only our intuition that certain actions should be performed just because they are right but also our inclination to pay attention to the results of actions and not just the motives behind them.

Difficulties with Ross's Moral Rules

The advantages Ross's ethics offers over both utilitarianism and Kantianism are offset by some serious difficulties. To begin with, it seems false that we all intuitively grasp the same principles. We are well aware that people's beliefs about what is right and about what their duties are typically result from the kind of education and experiences that they have had. The ability to perceive what is good or right does not appear to be universally shared. Ross does say that the principles are the convictions of "the moral consciousness of the best people." In any ordinary sense of "best," there is reason to say that such people don't always agree on moral principles. If "best" means "morally best," then Ross's claim starts to seem circular: the best people are those who acknowledge the same prima facie obligations, and those who recognize the same prima facie obligations are the best people.

Some have objected that Ross's list of prima facie duties seems incomplete. For example, Ross does not explicitly say that we have a prima facie obligation not to steal, but most people would hold that if we have any prima facie duties at all, the duty not to steal must surely be counted among them. Of course, stealing might be covered by some other obligation—the duty of fidelity, perhaps, since stealing may violate a trust. Nevertheless, for a theory based on intuition, the omission of such widely recognized duties makes Ross's list seem peculiarly incomplete.

Further, some critics have questioned whether there is even a prima facie obligation to uphold some of the duties Ross lists. Suppose that I promise to lie about a friend's physical condition so that she can continue to collect insurance payments. Some would say that I have no obligation at all to keep such an unwise promise. In such a case, there would be no conflict of duties, because I don't have even a prima facie duty to keep such a promise.

Finally, Ross's theory, some have charged, seems to be false to the facts of moral disagreements. When we disagree with someone about an ethical matter, we consider reasons for and against some position. Sometimes the discussion results in agreement. But, according to Ross's view, this should not be possible. Although we may discuss circumstances and consequences and agree about the prima facie duties involved, ultimately I arrive at my judgment about the duty that is more stringent or has the greatest degree of prima facie rightness, and you arrive at yours. At this point, it seems, there can be no further discussion, even if the two judgments are incompatible. At this point, a choice between the two judgments becomes arbitrary.

Few contemporary philosophers are willing to endorse Ross's ethical theory without substantial qualification. The need for a special kind of moral perception (or intuition) marks the theory as unacceptable for many. Yet others acknowledge that the theory has great value in illuminating such aspects of our moral experience as reaching decisions when we feel the pull of conflicting obligations. Furthermore, at least some acknowledge Ross's prima facie duties as constituting an adequate set of moral principles.

Rawls's Theory of Justice

In 1971, the Harvard philosopher John Rawls (1921–2002) published *A Theory of Justice*, a work that has been described as the twentieth century's most important contribution to moral and political philosophy. Over forty years later, the implications of Rawls's landmark text continue to generate intense debate in fields as diverse as law, economics, political science, and medicine.

One commentator, R. P. Wolfe, argues that Rawls attempts to develop a theory that combines the strengths of utilitarianism with those of Kantian and Rossian deontology, while avoiding the weaknesses of each view. As we have seen, utilitarianism claims that happiness is the primary good and offers a direct procedure for answering ethical questions. But it is hampered by its lack of a principle of justice. Kant and Ross make rightness a fundamental moral criterion

and emphasize the essential dignity of human beings. Yet neither provides a workable method for solving problems of social morality. Clearly, Rawls's theory of justice promises much if it can succeed in integrating the strengths of utilitarian and deontological ethics.

The Original Position and the Principles of Justice

For Rawls, the central task of government is to preserve and promote the liberty and welfare of individuals. Given this task, principles of justice are needed to serve as standards for the design and ongoing evaluation of social institutions and practices. They provide a way of resolving conflicts among competing claims and a means of protecting legitimate interests. In a sense, the principles of justice constitute a blueprint for the development of a just society.

But how are we to formulate principles of justice? To answer this question, Rawls makes use of a hypothetical device he calls *the original position*. We are asked to imagine a group of people much like those who make up our own society. These people display the ordinary range of intelligence, talents, ambitions, convictions, and social and economic advantages and disadvantages. They include both sexes and members of various ethnic, cultural, and religious groups.

Now, we are asked to suppose that this group is placed behind what Rawls calls a *veil of ignorance*. This means that each person is made ignorant of his or her sex, race, social position, economic condition, talents, skills, and so on. The distribution of such characteristics is "arbitrary from a moral point of view," Rawls argues, and knowledge of them could bias the selection of just principles. We are also asked to assume that these individuals are capable of cooperating with one another, that they adhere to standards of rational decision-making, and that they have a sense of justice and a will to adhere to the principles they adopt. Finally, we are to assume that they all desire what Rawls calls *primary goods*: the rights, opportunities, powers, wealth, income, resources and so on that are both worth possessing in themselves and necessary to securing the more specific goods an individual may want.

Rawls argues that the principles of justice chosen by such a group will be just if the conditions under which they are selected and the procedures for agreeing on them are *fair*. The original position, with its veil of ignorance, presents a situation in which alternative notions of justice can be discussed freely by all. Since the ignorance of the participants means that individuals cannot seek advantage for themselves by choosing principles that favor their own circumstances, the eventual choices of the participants will be fair. Since the participants are assumed to be rational, they will be persuaded by the same reasons and arguments. These features of the original position lead Rawls to characterize his view as *justice as fairness*.

We might first assume that some people in the original position would gamble and promote principles that would introduce gross inequalities in their society. For example, some might argue for slavery. If these people should turn out to be masters after the veil of ignorance is stripped away, they will have much to gain. If they turn out to be slaves, then they will have much to lose. However, since the veil of ignorance keeps individuals from knowing their actual positions in society, it would not be rational for them to endorse a principle that might condemn them to a miserable life at the bottom of the social order. The risks are simply too great.

Given the uncertainties of the original situation, there is a better strategy that these rational people would choose. In the economic discipline known as game theory, this strategy is called the *maximin*, or "maximizing the minimum." When we choose in uncertain situations, the maximin strategy directs us to select, from all the alternatives, the one whose worst possible outcome is better than the worst possible outcome of the other alternatives. (If you don't know whether you're going to be a slave, you shouldn't approve a set of principles that permits slavery when you have other options.)

Acting in accordance with this strategy, people in the original position would, Rawls argues, agree on the following two principles of justice:

1. Each person is to have an equal right to the most extensive total system of equal basic liberties compatible with a similar system of liberty for all.

2. Social and economic inequalities are to be arranged so that they are both (a) to the greatest benefit of the least advantaged ... and (b) attached to offices and positions open to all under conditions of fair equality of opportunity.

For Rawls, these two principles are taken to govern the distribution of all social goods: liberty, property, wealth, and social privilege. The first principle has priority. It guarantees a system of equal liberty for all. Furthermore, because of its priority, it explicitly prohibits the bartering away of liberty for social or economic benefits. (For example, a society cannot withhold the right to vote from its members on the grounds that voting rights damage the economy.)

The second principle governs the distribution of social goods other than liberty. Although society could organize itself in a way that would eliminate differences in wealth and abolish the advantages that attach to different social positions, Rawls argues that those in the original position would not choose this form of egalitarianism. Instead, they would opt for the second principle of justice, in accordance with the maximin strategy. This means that, in a just society, differences in wealth and social position can be tolerated only when they can be shown to benefit everyone and to benefit, in particular, those who have the fewest advantages. A just society is not one in which everyone is equal, but one in which inequalities can be demonstrated as legitimate.

Furthermore, there must be genuine equality of opportunity for acquiring access to the greatest social benefits. Merely *formal* equal opportunities to compete for socioeconomic privileges are not genuinely *fair* if patterns of discrimination or inherited advantage make for an uneven playing field. Thus, for example, those who face barriers to entering medical schools because of present or past discrimination, could, on this ground, claim a right to compensatory assistance to help them qualify. (Of course, in a society grounded in Rawls's ideal theory, the structure of social institutions would already eliminate much discrimination and inherited advantage.)

Rawls argues that these two principles are required to establish a just society. Furthermore, in distributing liberty and social goods, the principles guarantee the worth and self-respect of the individual. People are free to pursue their own conception of the good and to fashion their own lives. Ultimately, the only constraints placed on them as members of society are those expressed in the principles of justice.

Yet Rawls also acknowledges that those in the original position would recognize that we have duties both to ourselves and to others. They would, for example, take measures to protect their interests if they should meet with disabling accidents, become mentally disturbed, or require emergency surgery. Thus, Rawls approves a form of paternalism: others should act for us when we are unable to act for ourselves. When our preferences are known to them, those acting for us should attempt to implement our wishes. Otherwise, they should act for us as they would act for themselves if they were viewing our situation from the standpoint of the original position. Paternalism is thus a duty

to ourselves that would be recognized by those in the original position.

Rawls is also aware of the need for principles that bind and guide individuals as moral decision-makers. He claims that those in the original position would reach agreement on principles for such notions as fairness in our dealings with others, fidelity, respect for persons, and beneficence. From these principles, we incur some of our obligations to one another.

But, Rawls claims, there are also *natural duties* that would be recognized by those in the original position. Among those Rawls mentions are (1) the duty of justice—supporting and complying with just institutions; (2) the duty of helping others in need or jeopardy; (3) the duty not to harm or injure others; and (4) the duty to keep our promises. For the most part, these are duties that hold between or among people. They are only some of the duties that would be offered by those in the original position as unconditional duties.

Notice that Rawls endorses many of the same personal obligations that Ross offers as prima facie duties. Rawls, however, recognizes that the problem of conflicting duties was left unsolved by Ross and so argues for a ranking of duties from highest to lowest priority. Rawls believes that a full system of principles worked out from the original position would include rules for such a ranking. Rawls's primary concern in *A Theory of Justice*, however, is with justice in social institutions, and so he does not attempt to establish any rules for ranking duties.

Rawls's Theory of Justice in the Medical Context

Since Rawls's preliminary account of natural duties overlaps substantially with Ross's prima facie duties, we can take many duties, such as beneficence and fidelity, to apply, prima facie, to medical–moral situations in Rawls's just society.

Rawls also endorses the legitimacy of paternalism, although he does not attempt to specify detailed principles to justify individual cases. He does tell us that we should consider the preferences of others when they are known to us and when we are in a situation in which we must act for them because they are unable to act for themselves. For example, suppose we know that a person believes in the efficacy of electroconvulsive therapy ("shock treatments," or ECT) for the treatment of severe depression. If that person should become so depressed as to be unable to reach a decision about his own treatment, then we might, according to Rawls's paternalism, be justified in seeing to it that he received ECT.

To take a related case, suppose you are a surgeon performing a routine appendectomy on a patient whose advance directive says she does not want any invasive or disabling procedures performed on her that will not extend her life more than six months. Suppose, in course of the operation, you discover that that she has a form of metastatic colon cancer that could be temporarily abated (but not cured) by a colostomy procedure. If, in your best judgment, the colostomy would not extend her life more than six months, you have a duty to refrain from performing it, even if you are convinced that inaction will hasten her death. The procedure is clearly contrary to her own conception of the good, which Rawls's concept of paternalism is designed to protect.

The most important question for our exploration of Rawls's theory is how the two principles of justice might apply to the social institutions and practices of medical care and research. Most obviously, Rawls's principles repair utilitarianism's flaw with respect to the social benefits of medical exploitation. It would never be right, in Rawls's view, to exploit one group of people or even one person for the benefit of others. Thus, experiments in which people are forced to be subjects or are tricked into participating are ruled out. They involve a violation of basic liberties of individuals and of the absolute respect for persons that the principles of justice require.

A person has a right to decide what risks she is willing to take with her own life and health. Thus, voluntary consent is required before someone can legitimately become a research subject. However, society might decide to reward research volunteers with money, honors, or social privileges to encourage participation in research. Provided that the overall structure of society already conforms to the two principles of justice, this is a perfectly legitimate practice, so long as it brings benefits (ideally) to everyone and the rewards of participation are open to all.

Regarding the allocation of social resources in the training of medical personnel (physicians, nurses, therapists, and so on), one may conclude that such investments are justified insofar as they work to the advantage of the worst off in society. Public money may be spent in the form of scholarships and institutional grants to educate individuals who may then derive great social and economic benefits from their education. But, for Rawls, the inequality that is produced is not necessarily unjust if it conforms to the second "difference principle" of justice. Society can invest its resources in this way if it brings benefits to those most in need of them.

One implication of Rawls's theory seems to be that everyone is entitled to health care. First, it could be argued that health is among the *primary goods* that Rawls's principles are designed to protect and promote. After all, without health, an individual is hardly in a position to pursue other, more specific goods, and those in the original position might be imagined to be aware of this fact and to endorse only those principles of justice that would require providing at least basic health care to all members of society. In Chapter 9, Norman Daniels argues that categorizing health as a primary good is the most reasonable position to take if Rawls's principles are to be used as a basis for evaluating our current health policies and practices. Furthermore, it could be argued that the inequalities of the health care system can be justified only if those in most need can benefit from them. Given the extreme inequality that still characterizes the U.S. system, Rawls's principles seem to call for a reform that would use taxes or some other mechanism to provide health care to those who are unable to pay.

However, it is important to point out that it is not at all obvious what kind of health care system follows from Rawls's position. For one thing, it is not clear that Rawls's principles are intended to be directly applied to our society as it is. Our society includes among its members people with severe disabilities and people with fatal and chronic diseases. If Rawls's principles are to be crafted by and for those with normal physical and psychological abilities and needs, as he sometimes suggests, then it is not immediately clear that the difference principle, for example, should be directly and fully applied to those with severe impairments and fatal illnesses. Otherwise, the principles of justice might require that we devote a vastly disproportionate share of social resources to making only marginal improvements in the lives of the severely ill and disabled. Deferring consideration of such individuals to a later stage of justice, however—as Rawls sometimes suggests we should—raises questions about whether his just society is sufficiently inclusive and representative. (We will return to this question in our discussion of capabilities theory below.)

It seems reasonable to hold that Rawls's principles, particularly the second, can be used to limit access to certain kinds of health care. In general, individuals may spend their money in any way they wish to pursue their notions of what is good. Thus, if someone wants cosmetic surgery to change the shape of his chin and has the money to pay

a surgeon, then he may have it done. But if medical facilities or personnel should become overburdened and unable to provide needed care for the most seriously afflicted, then the society might be justified in heavily taxing or regulating cosmetic surgery. By doing this, it would then increase the net access to essential health care for all members of society. The desires of the rich for cosmetic surgery would not be permitted to take priority over the needs of the poor for basic health care.

Difficulties with Rawls's Theory

Rawls's theory is still the subject of intense philosophical and political discussion. The debate is often highly technical, and a wide variety of objections have been raised to the theory. At present, however, there are still no decisive objections that would be acknowledged as legitimate by all critics. Rather than attempt to summarize the debate, we will simply point to two aspects of Rawls's theory that have been acknowledged as difficulties.

One criticism concerns the original position and its veil of ignorance. Rawls does not permit those in the original position to know anything of their own purposes, plans, or interests—of their conception of the good. They do not know whether they prefer tennis to Tennyson, pleasures of mind over pleasures of the body, religious piety or scientific skepticism. They are allowed to consider only those goods—self-respect, wealth, social position—which Rawls puts before them. Thus, critics have said, Rawls has excluded morally relevant knowledge. It may be difficult to see how people could agree on principles to regulate their lives when they are so ignorant of their basic desires and purposes. Rawls seems to have biased the original position in his favor, and this calls into question his claim that the original position is a fair and reasonable way of arriving at principles of justice.

A related criticism questions how Rawls's just society could achieve stability over time, given the diverse religious, philosophical, and cultural conceptions of the good its citizens hold. Rawls later acknowledged that he sidestepped this problem in *A Theory of Justice* with the stipulation that all citizens in a well-ordered society endorse the principles of justice. But contemporary societies are characterized by a "reasonable pluralism" of incompatible comprehensive doctrines, and it is not immediately clear that they would all embrace justice as fairness over time. In his second major work, *Political Liberalism*, Rawls attempts to answer this criticism by recasting justice as fairness as a *political* (rather than philosophical) ideal of social cooperation that could form the basis of *overlapping consensus* among people with incompatible religious and secular views. Not derived from any particular comprehensive viewpoint, this political ideal is rooted in freestanding normative claims for civility and the exercise of public reason. Civic conduct is to be rooted in the *criterion of reciprocity*: the sincere and reasonable belief that the terms of social cooperation could reasonably be accepted by others as free and equal citizens, free from coercion or manipulation.

Whether this strategy ensures the stability of a just society characterized by reasonable pluralism is still a matter of considerable debate, as we will see in our discussion of the capabilities approach later in this chapter.

Natural Law Ethics and Moral Theology

The general view that the rightness of actions is something determined by nature itself, rather than by the laws and customs of societies or the preferences of individuals, is called *natural law theory*. Moral principles are thus regarded as objective truths that can be discovered in the nature of things by reason and reflection. The basic idea of the theory was expressed succinctly by the Roman philosopher Cicero (103–43 B.C.E.):

"Law is the highest reason, implanted in Nature, which commands what ought to be done and forbids the opposite. This reason, when firmly fixed and fully developed in the human mind, is Law." The natural law theory originated in classical Greek and Roman philosophy and has strongly influenced the development of moral and political theories. Indeed, all the ethical theories we have discussed are indebted, to some degree, to the natural law tradition. The reliance upon reason as a means of establishing ethical principles and the emphasis on the natural abilities and inclinations of human nature are just two of the threads that are woven into the theories that we have discussed.

Purposes, Reason, and the Moral Law as Interpreted by Roman Catholicism

The natural law theory of Roman Catholicism was given its most influential formulation in the thirteenth century by St. Thomas Aquinas (1225–1274 C.E.). Contemporary versions of the theory are mostly elaborations and interpretations of Aquinas's basic statement. Thus, an understanding of Aquinas's views is important for grasping the philosophical principles that underlie the Roman Catholic position on such issues as abortion, contraception, and assisted reproduction.

Aquinas was writing at a time when the texts of Aristotle (384–322 B.C.E.) were first becoming widely available in the West, and Aquinas's philosophy incorporates many of Aristotle's principles. A fundamental notion he borrows from Aristotle is the view that the universe is organized in a *teleological* way. That is, the universe is structured in such a way that each thing in it has a goal or purpose (*telos*). Thus, when conditions are right, a tadpole will develop into a frog. In its growth and change, the tadpole is following "the law of its nature." It is achieving its goal.

Humans have a material nature, just as tadpoles do, and in their own growth and development they, too, conform to a natural law. But Aquinas also claims that humans possess a trait that no other creature does: reason. Thus, the full development of human potentialities—the fulfillment of human purpose—requires that we follow the direction of the law of reason, as well as the laws of material human nature.

The development of reason is one of our ends as human beings, but we also rely upon reason to determine what our ends are and how we can achieve them. It is this function of reason that leads Aquinas to identify reason as the source of the moral law. Reason is practical in its operation, for it directs our actions so that we can bring about certain results. In giving us directions, reason imposes an obligation on us, the obligation to bring about the results that it specifies. But Aquinas says that reason cannot arbitrarily set goals for us. Reason directs us toward our good as the goal of our actions, and that good is discoverable within our nature. Thus, reason recognizes the basic principle "Good is to be done and evil avoided."

Nevertheless, this principle is purely formal, or empty of content. To make it a practical principle, we must consider what the human good is. According to Aquinas, the human good is that which is suitable or proper to human nature. It is what is "built into" human nature, much in the way that a frog is already "built into" a tadpole. Thus, the good is that to which we are directed by our natural inclinations as both physical and rational creatures.

Like other creatures, we have a natural inclination to preserve our lives; consequently, reason imposes on us an obligation to care for our health, not to kill ourselves, and not to put ourselves in positions in which we might be killed. We realize through reason that others have a rational nature like ours, and we see that we are bound to treat them with the same dignity and respect that we accord ourselves. Furthermore, when we see

that humans require a society to make their full development possible, we realize that we have an obligation to support laws and practices that make society possible.

For example, since we have a natural inclination to propagate our species (viewed as a "natural" good), reason places on us an obligation not to thwart or pervert that inclination. As a consequence, to fulfill this obligation within society, reason supports the institution of marriage for the purposes of raising children.

Reason also finds in our nature grounds for procedural principles. For example, because everyone has an inclination to preserve his life and well-being, no one should be forced to testify against himself. Similarly, because all individuals are self-interested, no one should be permitted to be a judge in her own case.

Physical inclinations, under the direction of reason, point us toward our natural good. But, according to Aquinas, reason itself can also be a source of inclinations. For example, Aquinas says that reason is the source of our natural inclination to seek the truth, particularly the truth about the existence and nature of God.

From the few examples we have considered, it should be clear how Aquinas believes it is possible to discover natural goods in human nature. Relying upon these as goals or purposes to be achieved, reason will then work out the practical way of achieving them. Thus, through the subtle application of reason, it should be possible to establish a body of moral principles and rules. These are the doctrines of natural law.

Because natural law is founded on human nature, which is regarded as unchangeable, Aquinas regards natural law itself as unchangeable. Moreover, it is seen as the same for all people, at all times, and in all societies. Even those without knowledge of God can, through the operation of reason, recognize their natural obligations.

For Aquinas and for Roman Catholicism, this view of natural law is just one aspect of a broader theological framework. The teleological organization of the universe is attributed to the planning of a creator: goals or purposes are ordained by God. Furthermore, although natural law is discoverable in the universe, its ultimate source is divine wisdom and God's eternal law. Everyone who is rational is capable of grasping natural law. But because passions and irrational inclinations may corrupt human nature and because some people lack the abilities or time to work out the demands of natural law, God also chose to reveal our duties to us in explicit ways. The major source of this revelation is taken to be the Christian scriptures.

Natural law, scriptural revelation, the established interpretation of the scriptures, and the Church's traditions and teachings are regarded in Roman Catholicism as the sources of moral ideals and principles. By guiding one's life by them, one can develop the rational and moral part of one's nature and move toward the goal of achieving the sort of perfection that is suitable for humans.

This general moral–theological point of view is also the source of particular Roman Catholic doctrines and principles that have special relevance to medicine. We will consider here just two of the most important principles.

The Principle of Double Effect. A particular kind of moral conflict arises when the performance of an action will produce both good and bad effects. On the basis of the good effect, it seems it is our duty to perform the action; but on the basis of the bad effect, it seems to be our duty not to perform it.

Let's assume that the death of a fetus is in itself a bad effect and consider a case like the following: A woman who is three months pregnant is found to have uterine cancer. If the woman's life is to be saved, her uterus must be removed at once. But if the uterus is removed, then the life of the fetus will be terminated. Should the operation be performed?

The principle of double effect is intended to help in the resolution of these kinds of conflicts. The principle holds that such an action should be performed only if the intention is to bring about the good effect and the bad effect will be an unintended or indirect consequence. More specifically, four conditions must be satisfied:

1. The action itself must be morally indifferent or morally good.

2. The bad effect must not be the means by which the good effect is achieved.

3. The motive must be the achievement of the good effect only.

4. The good effect must be at least equivalent in importance to the bad effect.

Are these conditions satisfied in the case mentioned above? The operation itself, if this is considered to be the action, is at least morally indifferent. That is, in itself it is neither good nor bad. That takes care of the first condition. If the woman's life is to be saved, it will not be *by means of* killing the fetus. It will be by means of removing her cancerous uterus. Thus, the second condition is met. The goal of the surgeon, we may suppose, is not the death of the fetus but saving the life of the woman. If so, then the third condition is satisfied. Finally, since two lives are at stake, the good effect (saving the life of the woman) is at least equal to the bad effect (the death of the fetus). The fourth condition is thus met. Under ordinary circumstances, then, these conditions would be considered satisfied, and such an operation would be morally justified according to the principle of double effect. This principle has a wide range of applications in medical ethics. It bears on such topics as sterilization, organ transplants, euthanasia, and the use of extraordinary measures to maintain life.

The Principle of Totality. The principle of totality can be expressed in this way: an individual has a right to dispose of his or her organs or to destroy their capacity to function only to the extent that the general well-being of the whole body demands it. Thus, it is clear that we have a natural obligation to preserve our lives, but, according to the Roman Catholic view, we also have a duty to preserve the integrity of our bodies. This duty is based on the belief that each of our organs was designed by God to play a role in maintaining the functional integrity of our bodies—that each has a place in the divine plan. Since we are taken to be the custodians of our bodies, not their owners, it is our duty to care for them in trust.

The principle of totality has implications for a great number of medical procedures. Strictly speaking, cosmetic surgery is morally right only when it is required to maintain or ensure the normal functioning of the rest of the body. More important, procedures that are typically employed for contraceptive purposes—vasectomies and tubal ligations—are ruled out. Such procedures are seen to involve "mutilation" and the destruction of the only proper function of reproductive organs.

As an ethical theory, natural law theory is sometimes described as teleological. In endorsing the principle "Good is to be done and evil avoided," the theory identifies a goal with respect to which the rightness of an action is to be judged. As the principle of double effect illustrates, the intention of the individual who acts is crucial to determining whether the goal should be sought. In a sense, the intention of the action—what the individual wills—defines the action. Thus, euthanizing a terminally ill patient and controlling the patient's pain at the risk of killing him are not necessarily the same actions, even when their external features are indistinguishable. Unlike utilitarianism, which is also a teleological theory, natural law theory is not consequentialist: the outcome of an action is not the sole feature to consider in determining the action's moral character.

Applications of Roman Catholic Moral–Theological Viewpoints in the Medical Context

Roman Catholic ethicists and theologians have developed an influential body of medical–moral doctrine, from which we will consider just four topics.

First, the principle of double effect and the principle of totality have definite implications for the conduct of biomedical research. Since we hold our bodies in trust, we are responsible for assessing the risks of participating in such research. Thus, we need to be fully informed of the nature of the experiment and the risks that it poses for subjects. If, after obtaining this knowledge, we decide to participate, our informed consent must be given freely and not as the result of deception or coercion.

Because human experimentation carries with it the possibility of injury and death, along with potential benefits, the principle of double effect and its four conditions can be applied. If scientific evidence indicates that a sick person may benefit from participating in a particular experiment, then her participation is morally justifiable in spite of associated risks. If, however, the evidence indicates that the chances of helping that person are slight and that she may die or be gravely injured, then participation is probably not justifiable. In general, the likelihood of a person's benefiting from the experiment must exceed the danger of that person's suffering greater losses.

A person who is incurably ill may volunteer to be an experimental subject, even though she cannot reasonably expect personal gain in the form of improved health. The good that is hoped for is good for others, in the form of increased medical knowledge. Even here, however, there are constraints imposed by the principle of double effect. There must be no likelihood that the experiment will seriously injure anyone, and the probable value of the knowledge expected to result must balance the risk run by the patient. Not even the incurably ill can be made subjects of trivial experiments.

The good sought by healthy volunteers is also the good of others. The same restrictions mentioned in connection with the incurably ill apply to research on healthy subjects. In addition, the principle of totality places constraints on what a person may volunteer to do with his or her body. No healthy person may submit to an experiment that involves a high probability of serious injury, impaired health, mutilation, or death.

A second medical topic that has been addressed by Roman Catholic ethicists is whether "ordinary" or "extraordinary" measures are to be taken in the preservation of human life. While it is believed that natural and divine law impose on us a moral obligation to preserve our lives, Catholic moralists have interpreted this obligation as requiring that we employ only ordinary means. In medical professions, the phrase "ordinary means" is typically used to refer to procedures that are standard or widely accepted, in contrast to untried or experimental procedures. But from the standpoint of Catholic medical ethics, "ordinary" applies to "all medicines, treatments, and operations which offer a reasonable hope of benefit for the patient and which can be obtained and used without excessive expense, pain, or other inconvenience." Thus, by contrast, extraordinary means are those which offer the patient no reasonable hope of benefit or whose use causes serious hardship for the patient or others.

Medical measures that would save the life of a patient but subject him to years of pain or severe physical or mental impairment are considered extraordinary. A patient or his family are under no obligation to choose such measures, and physicians are under a positive obligation not to advocate for them.

A third medical topic commonly addressed by Catholic ethicists is euthanasia. In official Roman Catholic doctrine, euthanasia in any form is considered immoral. It is presumed to be a direct violation of God's dominion over creation and the human obligation to preserve life. The Ethical Directives for Catholic Hospitals is explicit on the matter of taking a life:

> The direct killing of any innocent person, even at his own request, is always morally wrong. Any procedure whose sole immediate effect is the death of a human being is a direct killing.... Euthanasia ("mercy killing") in all its forms is forbidden.... The failure to supply the ordinary means of preserving life is equivalent to euthanasia.

According to this view, it is wrong to allow even infants suffering from severe physical and mental impairments to die. If their lives can be sustained by ordinary means, there is an obligation to do so. It is also wrong to facilitate the deaths of the terminally ill, either by taking steps to bring about their deaths or by failing to take steps to maintain their lives by ordinary means.

It is never permissible to hasten the death of a person as a direct intention. It is, however, permissible to administer drugs that alleviate pain. The principle of double effect suggests that giving such drugs is a morally justifiable action even though the drugs may indirectly hasten the death of a person.

Finally, perhaps the most prominent and controversial feature of Catholic medical ethics is its position on abortion. According to the Roman Catholic view, from the moment of conception, the embryo (later, the fetus) is considered to be a person with all the rights of a person. For this reason, direct abortion at any stage of pregnancy is regarded as morally wrong. Abortion is "direct" when it results from a procedure "whose sole immediate effect is the termination of pregnancy." This means that what is generally referred to as therapeutic abortion, in which an abortion is performed to safeguard the life or health of the woman, is considered wrong. For example, a woman with serious heart disease who becomes pregnant cannot morally justify an abortion on the grounds that the pregnancy is a serious threat to her life. Even when the ultimate aim is to save the life of the woman, direct abortion is viewed as a moral wrong.

We have already seen, however, that the principle of double effect permits the performance of an action that may result in the death of a fetus if the action satisfies the four criteria for applying the principle. Thus, *indirect* abortion can be considered morally permissible. That is, the abortion must be the outcome of some action (for example, treatment of uterine cancer) that is performed for the direct and total purpose of treating a pathological condition affecting the pregnant woman. The end sought in direct abortion is the termination of the pregnancy, but the end sought in indirect abortion is the preservation of the woman's life.

Difficulties with Natural Law Ethics and Moral Theology

Our discussion has centered on the natural law theory of ethics as it has been interpreted in Roman Catholic theology. Thus, there are two possible types of difficulties: those associated with natural law ethics in its own right and those associated with its incorporation into theology. The theological difficulties go beyond the scope of our discussion here. We will restrict ourselves to considering difficulties that arise with natural law theory as formulated by Aquinas. Since it is this formulation that has been used in Roman Catholic moral theology, we shall be identifying difficulties that impact it as well, albeit indirectly.

A fundamental problem for Aquinas's natural law theory is rooted in the assumption, borrowed from Aristotle, that the universe is organized in a teleological fashion. (This is the assumption that every kind of thing has a goal or purpose.) This assumption is essential to Aquinas's ethical theory, for he identifies the good of a thing with its natural mode of operation. Without this

assumption, we are faced with the great diversity and moral indifference of nature. Inclinations, even when widely shared by humans, are no more than inclinations. There are no grounds for considering them "goods," and they have no moral status. The universe is bereft of the natural values that were to form the basis of our ethical obligations.

There are, in fact, many reasons to reject the teleological premise. Physics surrendered the notion of a teleological organization in the universe as early as the seventeenth century: the rejection of Aristotle's physics also entailed the rejection of Aristotle's teleological view of the world. For a time, this left biology as the last major source of arguments in favor of teleology. But contemporary evolutionary theory shows that the apparently purposive character of evolutionary change can be accounted for by the operation of natural selection on random mutations over millions of years. Also, the development and growth of organisms can be explained by the presence of genetic information that controls these processes. The tadpole develops into a frog because evolution has produced a genetic program that directs a sequence of complicated chemical changes. Thus, no adequate grounds seem to exist for asserting that the teleological organization of nature is anything more than apparent.

Science and "reason alone" do not support teleology. It can be endorsed only if one is willing to assume that any apparent teleological organization is the product of a divine plan. Yet, because all apparent teleology can be explained in nonteleological ways, this assumption seems neither necessary nor legitimate.

Without its foundation of teleology, Aquinas's theory of natural law ethics seems to collapse. This is not to say, of course, that some other natural law theory—one not requiring the assumption of teleology—might not be persuasively defended.

MAJOR MORAL PRINCIPLES

Making moral decisions is always a difficult and demanding task. Abstract discussions of morality never quite capture the feelings of uncertainty and self-doubt we often experience when called upon to decide what ought to be done or to judge whether someone did the right thing. There are no mechanical processes or algorithms we can apply in a situation of moral doubt. There are no computer programs to supply us with the proper decision when given the relevant data.

In a very real sense, we are on our own when it comes to making ethical decisions. This does not mean that we are without resources and must make arbitrary or naive decisions. When we have the luxury of time, when the need to make a decision is not pressing, we may attempt to work out an answer to a moral question by relying upon a general ethical theory, such as those discussed earlier or those addressed in this chapter's final section. However, in ordinary life we rarely have the opportunity or time to engage in an elaborate process of reasoning and analysis.

One approach to this problem, sometimes called *principlism*, is to apply freestanding moral principles that have been derived from and justified by various moral theories. A principle such as "Avoid causing needless harm" can serve as a more direct guide to action and decision-making than, say, Kant's categorical imperative. It can help establish a set of moral obligations for medical practitioners to use their knowledge and skills to protect patients from injury. For example, they should not expose a patient to the needless risk of a diagnostic test that does not promise to yield useful information.

In this section, we will present and illustrate five moral principles. All are of special relevance to decisions regarding medical care and research. These principles have their limitations and they are in no sense complete. Moral issues arise, even in the context of medicine, for which they can supply no direct guidance. In other situations, the principles themselves may come into conflict and point toward incompatible solutions. (How can we both avoid causing harm and allow a terminally ill patient to die?) The principles themselves indicate no means of resolving such conflicts, for, even if grouped together, they do not constitute a coherent moral theory. To resolve conflicts, it may be necessary to employ a more comprehensive moral theory, of the kind addressed in the preceding and following sections.

It is fair to say, however, that each of the five basic moral theories we have discussed endorses the legitimacy of these principles. Not all of these theories would formulate them in the same way, and not all would grant them the same moral weight. Nevertheless, each theory would accept them as expressing appropriate guidelines for moral decision-making.

Indeed, the best way to think about the principles is as guidelines. They are in no way rules that can be applied automatically. Rather, they express standards to be consulted in attempting to arrive at a justified decision. As such, they provide a basis for evaluating actions or policies as well as for making individual moral decisions.

The principles help guarantee that our decisions are the result of genuine moral inquiry and not of our whims or prejudices. By attempting to apply these principles, we are more likely to reach decisions that are reasoned, consistent, and applicable to similar cases.

The Principle of Nonmaleficence

"Above all, do no harm" is perhaps the most famous and most quoted of all moral maxims in medicine. It captures in a succinct way what is widely considered to be the overriding duty of anyone responsible for patient care. We believe that, in treating a patient, physicians and others should not by carelessness, malice, inadvertence, or avoidable ignorance do anything that will cause injury to the patient.

The maxim is one expression of what is sometimes called in ethics the *principle of nonmaleficence*. The principle can be formulated in various ways, but here is one relatively uncontroversial way of stating it: *We ought to act in ways that do not cause needless harm or injury to others*. Stated in a positive fashion, the principle tells us that we have a duty to avoid maleficence—that is, to avoid harming or injuring other people.

In the most obvious cases, we violate the principle of nonmaleficence when we intentionally do something we know will cause someone harm. For example, suppose that, during the course of an operation, a surgeon deliberately severs a muscle, knowing that, by doing so, she will cripple the patient. Then the surgeon is guilty of maleficence and is morally (as well as legally) blameworthy for her action.

The principle may also be violated when no malice or intention to do harm is involved. A nurse who carelessly administers the wrong medication and causes a patient to suffer irreversible brain damage may have had no intention of causing the patient any injury. However, the nurse is negligent in his actions and fails to exercise due care in discharging his responsibilities. His actions result in an avoidable injury to his patient. Hence, he fails to meet his obligation of nonmaleficence.

The duty imposed by the principle of nonmaleficence is not a demand to accomplish the impossible. We cannot reasonably expect perfection in the practice of medicine. The results of treatments are often unpredictable and may cause more harm than good. Our knowledge of diseases is only partial and decisions about diagnosis and therapy typically involve judgment calls with no guarantee of success. Consequently, we recognize that we cannot hold health professionals accountable for every instance of death and injury involving patients under their care.

Nevertheless, we can demand that physicians and others live up to reasonable standards of professional responsibility. In their conduct as practitioners, we can expect them to be cautious and diligent, patient and thoughtful. We can expect them to pay attention to what they are doing and to deliberate about whether a particular procedure should be performed. In addition, we can expect them to possess the knowledge and skills relevant to the proper fulfillment of their duties.

These criteria and others like them make up the standards of performance that define what we have a right to expect from physicians and other health professionals. In the language of the law, these are the standards of "due care," and it is by reference to them that we evaluate the medical care given to patients. Failure to meet the standards opens practitioners (physicians, nurses, dentists, therapists) to the charge of moral or legal maleficence.

In our society, we have attempted to guarantee that at least some due-care standards are met by relying upon such measures as degree programs, licensing laws, certifying boards, and hospital credentials committees. Such an approach offers a way of ensuring that physicians and others have acquired at least a minimum level of knowledge, skill, and experience before assuming the responsibilities attached to their roles.

This approach is also designed to foster such virtues as diligence, prudence, and caution, but there is of course no way of guaranteeing that physicians will exhibit those virtues in particular cases. Haste, carelessness, and inattention are always possible, as is the potential that a patient will suffer injury as a result.

The standards of due care are connected in some respects with such factual matters as the current state of medical knowledge and training, and the immediate circumstances in which a physician provides care. For example, in the 1920s, it was not at all unusual for general practitioners to perform relatively complicated surgeries, particularly in rural areas. In performing such surgeries, these physicians were acting in a reasonable and expected fashion and could not legitimately be charged with violating the principle of nonmaleficence.

Over the past century, however, changes in medical practice have altered our beliefs about what is reasonable and expected. Today, a general practitioner who performs surgery without special training and board certification may be legitimately criticized for maleficence. The standards of due care in surgery are now higher and more exacting than they once were, and the general practitioner who undertakes to perform most forms of surgery causes her patients to undergo an unusual and unnecessary risk.

This hypothetical case also illustrates the point that no actual harm or injury need occur for someone to have violated the principle of nonmaleficence. The general practitioner performing surgery may not cause any injury to her patients, but she exposes them to a possibility of harm that is greater than it needs to be. It is in this respect that she is not exercising due care in her treatment and so can be charged with maleficence. She has subjected her patients to *unnecessary risk*—risk greater than they would take in the hands of a trained surgeon.

It is important to stress that the principle of nonmaleficence does not require that a physician subject a patient to no risks at all. Virtually every form of diagnostic testing and medical treatment involves some degree of risk to the patient, and to provide medical care at all, a physician must often act in ways that involve the risk of permanent injury. For example, a physician who takes a thorough medical history, performs a physical examination, and then treats a patient's bacterial infection with a safe and well-established antibiotic cannot be held morally responsible if the patient suffers a severe drug reaction. That such a thing might happen is a possibility that cannot be foreseen in an individual case.

Similarly, a serious medical problem may justify subjecting a patient to serious risk, (assuming the patient provides informed consent). A life-threatening condition, such as an occluded right coronary artery, may warrant coronary-bypass surgery with all its attendant dangers.

In effect, the principle of nonmaleficence tells us to avoid needless risk and, when risk is an inevitable aspect of an appropriate test or treatment, to minimize the risk as much as is reasonably possible. A physician who orders a lumbar puncture for a patient who complains of occasional headaches is acting inappropriately, given the nature of the complaint, and is subjecting his patient to needless risk. By contrast, a physician who orders such a test after examining a patient with severe and recurring headaches, a fever, pain and stiffness in his neck, and additional symptoms of meningitis is acting appropriately. The risk to the patient from the lumbar puncture is the same in both cases, but the risk is warranted in the second case and not in the first. A failure to act with due care violates the principle of nonmaleficence, even if no harm results, whereas acting with due care does not violate the principle, even if harm does result.

The Principle of Beneficence

"As to diseases, make a habit of two things—to help or at least to do no harm." This directive, from the Hippocratic writings of ancient Greece, stresses that the physician has two duties. The second ("at least to do no harm") we discussed in connection with the principle of nonmaleficence. The first ("to help") we will consider here in connection with the principle of beneficence.

Like the previous principle, the principle of beneficence can be stated in various ways. Here is one formulation: *We should act in ways that promote the welfare of other people.* That is, we should help other people when we are able to do so.

Some philosophers have expressed doubt that we have an actual duty to help others. We certainly have a duty not to harm other people, but it has seemed to some that there are no grounds for saying that we have a duty to promote their welfare. We would deserve praise if we did, but we would not deserve blame if we did not. From this point of view, being beneficent is beyond the scope of duty.

We need not consider whether this view is correct in general. For our purposes, it is enough to realize that the nature of the relationship between a physician and a patient does impose the duty of acting in the patient's welfare. That is, the duty of beneficence is inherent in the role of physician. A physician who was not acting for the sake of the patient's good would, in a very real sense, not be acting as a physician.

That we recognize the principle of beneficence as a duty appropriate to the physician's role is seen most clearly in cases in which the physician is also a researcher and her patient is also an experimental subject. In such instances, there is a possibility of a role conflict, for the researcher's aim of acquiring knowledge is not always compatible with the physician's aim of helping the patient. (See Chapter 1 for a discussion of this problem.)

The duty required by the principle of beneficence is inherent in the role not only of physicians but of all health professionals. Nurses, therapists, clinical psychologists, social workers, and others accept the duty of promoting the welfare of their patients or clients as an appropriate part of their responsibilities. We trust nurses and other health professionals to act in our best interests; it is this expectation that makes them part of what we call "the helping professions."

The extent to which beneficence is required as a duty for physicians and others is a more difficult problem. In practice, we recognize limits on what can be expected even from those who have chosen to make a career of helping others. We do not expect physicians to sacrifice completely their self-interest and welfare on behalf of their patients. We do not think their duty demands that they be thoroughly selfless. If some are, we may praise them as secular saints or moral heroes, but that is because their actions exceed the demands of duty. At the same time, we would have little good to say of a physician who always put his interest above that of his patients, who never made a personal sacrifice to promote their interests.

Just as there are standards of due care that implicitly define what we consider to be right conduct in protecting patients from harm, so there seem to be implicit standards of beneficence. We obviously expect physicians to help patients by providing them with appropriate treatment. More than this, we expect physicians to be prepared to make *reasonable* sacrifices for the sake of their patients. Even in an age of "health care teams," a single physician assumes responsibility for a particular patient when that patient is hospitalized or treated for a serious illness. It is this physician who is expected to make the crucial medical decisions, and we expect her to realize that discharging her responsibility may involve an interruption of private plans and activities. A surgeon who is informed that her postoperative patient has started to bleed can be expected to cancel her plan to attend a concert. Doing so is a reasonable duty imposed by the principle of beneficence. If she fails to discharge the duty, then, in the absence of mitigating circumstances, she will become the object of legitimate disapproval from her patient and her medical colleagues.

It would be very difficult to spell out exactly what duties are required by the principle of beneficence. Even if we limit ourselves to the medical context, there are so many ways of promoting someone's welfare and so many different circumstances to consider that it would be virtually impossible to provide anything like a catalogue of appropriate actions. However, such a catalogue is hardly necessary. Most people can distinguish between reasonable and unreasonable expectations in common medical scenarios, and it is this sense that we rely on in making judgments about whether physicians and others are fulfilling the duty of beneficence in their actions.

The principles of nonmaleficence and beneficence also impose broader social duties. In the most general terms, we look to society to take measures to promote the health and safety of citizens. The great advances made in public health during the nineteenth century were made because many societies recognized a responsibility to attempt to prevent the spread of disease. Water treatment plants, immunization programs, and quarantine restrictions all reflect, to varying degrees, a recognition of society's duty of nonmaleficence.

Although it has done so to a lesser extent than most other industrialized democracies, the United States has also recognized duties of beneficence and nonmaleficence in connection with the distribution of health care and health insurance. The Medicaid insurance program for the poor and the Medicare insurance program for the elderly are major efforts to address at least some of the health needs of a large segment of the population. The Affordable Care Act is a broad-based effort to extend insurance coverage to tens of millions of Americans who could not previously afford it and did not qualify for Medicaid or Medicare. Prenatal programs for pregnant women and public clinics are among the other investments societies have made to promote the health of citizens.

Less obvious than programs that provide direct medical care are those that support medical research and basic science. Directly or indirectly, many of these programs make a substantive contribution to meeting society's health care needs. Much basic research is relevant to acquiring an understanding of the processes involved in both health and disease, and much medical research is specifically aimed at developing effective diagnostic and therapeutic measures.

In principle, social beneficence has no limits, but in practice it must. Social resources, like tax revenues, are finite, and each society must decide how they are to be spent. Housing and food for the poor, education, defense, the arts, and the humanities are just some of the areas demanding support in the name of social beneficence. Medical care is one among many claimants, and we must decide as a society what proportion of our social resources we want to commit to it. Are we prepared to guarantee to all a high level of medical care or are citizens entitled to only minimal "catastrophic" care? Should opportunities for longer and healthier lives currently available to some (the rich or well insured) be made available to all (the poor and uninsured)? Just how beneficent we are obligated to be—and can afford to be—in health care distribution is still a matter of intense debate. (See Chapter 9 for more.)

The Principle of Utility

The principle of utility can be formulated as follows: *We should act in such a way as to bring about the greatest benefit and the least harm.* As we discussed earlier, this principle is the foundation of the moral theory of utilitarianism. However, the principle need not be regarded as unique to utilitarianism. It can be thought of as one moral principle among others that present us with a prima facie duty; as such, it need not always take precedence over others. In particular, we should question whether it is ever justified to deprive someone of important rights on the grounds that in doing so we could bring benefit to many others.

We need not repeat the discussion of the principle of utility presented earlier, but it may be useful to consider here how that principle relates to the principles of nonmaleficence and beneficence. When we consider the problem of distributing social resources, it becomes clear that acting in accordance with the principles of nonmaleficence and beneficence usually involves trade-offs. To use our earlier example, as a society we are concerned with providing for the health care needs of our citizens. To accomplish this end, we may support various programs—Medicare, Medicaid, legislation such as the ACA, hospital-building programs, medical research, and so on.

However, there are limits to what we can do. Medical care is not the only focus of social concern. We are interested in protecting people from harm and in promoting their interests, but there are many forms of harm and many kinds of interest to be promoted. With finite resources at our disposal, the more money we spend on health care, the less we can spend on education, housing, law enforcement, non-medical science, the humanities, and so on. Furthermore, at a certain level of funding, health care spending only produces marginal improvements in health.

The aim of social planning is to balance the competing needs of the society. Taken alone, the principles of nonmaleficence and beneficence are of no help in resolving conflicts among social needs. Here the principle of utility can serve to establish and rank such

needs and to help determine the extent to which it is possible to satisfy a given social need in comparison with others. In effect, the principle imposes a duty on us all to use our collective resources to do as much good as possible. That is, we must do the most good *overall*, even when this means we are not able to meet all needs in a particular area.

The application of the principle of utility is not limited to large-scale social issues, such as how to divide our resources among medical care, defense, education, and so on. We may also rely on the principle when we are deliberating about the choice of alternative means of accomplishing an aim. For example, our society might decide to institute a mandatory screening program to detect phenylketonuria (PKU) in infants but decide against a program to detect Tay-Sachs, another serious genetic condition. PKU can often be treated successfully if discovered early enough, whereas early detection of Tay-Sachs makes little or no difference in the outcome of the disease. Furthermore, PKU is widely distributed in the population, whereas Tay-Sachs is mostly limited to patients of Ashkenazi Jewish ancestry. Health officials might decide that additional money spent on screening for Tay-Sachs would not be justified by the results. The money could do more good, and produce more benefits, were it spent some other way.

The principle of utility is also relevant to making decisions about the diagnosis and treatment of individuals. For example, as we mentioned earlier, no diagnostic test can be justified if the risk of harm it imposes on the patient is greater than the value of the information likely to be gained. Invasive procedures are associated with a certain rate of injury and death (morbidity and mortality). It would make no sense to subject a patient to a kidney biopsy if the findings were not likely to affect the course of treatment or if the risk from the biopsy were greater than the risk from the suspected disease. Medical policy analysts already employ the formal tools of decision theory to assist physicians in determining whether a particular mode of diagnosis, therapy, or surgery can be justified in individual cases. Underlying such analysis is the principle of utility, which directs us to act in a way that will bring about the greatest benefit and the least harm.

Principles of Distributive Justice

We expect (and can demand) to be treated justly in our dealings with other people and with institutions. If our insurance policy covers up to thirty days of hospitalization, then we expect a claim against the policy for that amount of time to be honored. If we arrive in an emergency room with a broken arm before the arrival of someone else with an injury of equal severity, we expect to be attended to before that person.

We do not always expect that being treated justly will work to our direct advantage. We should recognize that we have an obligation to pay our fair share of taxes, even if we do not directly benefit from all the roads, sanitation, scientific research, law enforcement, and other services government provides. If a profusely bleeding person arrives in the emergency room after we do, we recognize that she is in need of immediate treatment and should be attended to before we are.

Justice has at least two major aspects. Seeing to it that people receive that to which they are entitled, that their rights are recognized and protected, falls under the general heading of *noncomparative justice*. By contrast, *comparative justice* is concerned with the application of laws and rules and with the distribution of burdens and benefits.

The concern of comparative justice that is most significant to the medical context is *distributive justice*. As the name suggests, distributive justice concerns the distribution of such social benefits and burdens as medical services, tax credits, welfare payments, public offices, and military service. In general, the distribution of income and wealth has been a primary focus of distributive justice analysis. In medical ethics, the focus has been the distribution of health care and health insurance. Are all in the society entitled to receive health care benefits, whether or not they can afford to pay for them? If so, then is everyone entitled to the same amount of health care? (See Chapter 9 for a discussion of these issues.)

Philosophical theories of justice attempt to resolve questions of distributive justice by providing a detailed account of the features of individuals and society that will justify our making distinctions in the ways we distribute benefits and burdens. If some people are to be rich and others poor, if some are to have greater opportunities or powers or privileges than others, then there must be some rational and moral basis for such distinctions. We look to theories of justice to provide us with such a basis. (This is, for example, a primary objective of Rawls's "justice as fairness.")

Theories of justice differ significantly, but at the core of all of them is the basic principle that "Similar cases ought to be treated in similar ways." The principle expresses the notion that justice involves fair treatment. For example, it is manifestly unfair to award different grades to two people who give the same answers on a multiple-choice exam. If two cases are the same, then it is arbitrary or irrational to treat them differently. To justify different treatment, we would have to show that the cases are also dissimilar in some relevant respect.

This fairness principle is known as the *formal* principle of justice. It is called formal because, like a sentence with blanks, it must be filled in with information. Specifically, we must be told what factors or features are to be considered *relevant* in deciding whether two cases are similar. If two cases differ in relevant respects, we may be justified in treating them differently. We may do so without being either irrational or arbitrary.

Theories of distributive justice present us with *substantive* (or *material*) principles of justice. The theories present us with arguments to show why certain features or factors should be considered relevant in deciding whether cases are similar. The substantive principles can then be referred to in determining whether particular laws, practices, or public policies can be considered just. Further, the substantive principles can be employed as guidelines for framing laws and policies and for developing a just society.

Arguments in favor of particular theories of justice are too lengthy to present here. However, it will be useful to consider briefly four substantive principles that have been advanced by various theorists. To a considerable extent, differences among these principles help explain ongoing disagreements in our society about how such social goods as income, education, and health care should be distributed. Although the principles themselves direct the distribution of burdens (taxation, public service, and so on) as well as benefits, we will focus here on benefits. The basic question answered by each principle is "Who is entitled to what proportion of society's goods?"

The Principle of Equality

According to the principle of equality, all benefits and burdens are to be distributed equally. Everyone is entitled to the same sized slice of the pie, and everyone must bear an equal share of the social burdens. The principle, strictly interpreted, requires a thoroughgoing egalitarianism: everyone is to be treated equally in the distribution of social goods.

The principle of equality has a great deal of intuitive plausibility for societies that are not too far above the margin of production. When there is enough to go around but not much more, then it is manifestly unfair for some to have more than they need and for others to have less than they need. When a society is more affluent, however, debate often arises about questions of *desert*—who, if anyone, deserves or merits a larger share of social goods.

One of the strongest arguments for the principle of equality is that many, perhaps most, claims to a larger share of social goods appear to be rooted in *luck* rather than desert. If I am born into an affluent family and receive a first-class education, can I really be said to *deserve* the socioeconomic advantages that come with my good fortune? For that matter, if I am born with a high IQ or unusual physical strengths or talents, have I really done anything to *deserve* the advantages derived from my good luck in the "natural lottery"? Even the ability to make a sustained effort under adverse conditions, some social scientists have found, is strongly influenced by upbringing and other forms of natural and social luck. If these inherited advantages and disadvantages are, as John Rawls argues, "arbitrary from a moral point of view," then perhaps the principle of equality is the only just way of distributing society's benefits and burdens.

Although Rawls's theory remains an egalitarian one, he does not, as we have seen, ultimately endorse the principle of equality. Instead, his second principle of justice claims that unequal distributions of social benefits can be just, provided that the resulting inequality will work out to *everyone's* advantage. (This means ensuring that inequalities benefit those who are worst off in society.)

The Principle of Need

The principle of need is an extension of the egalitarian principle of equal distribution. If goods are parceled out according to individual need, those who have greater needs will receive a greater share. However, the outcome will be one of equality. Since the basic needs of everyone will be met, everyone will end up at the same level. The treatment of individuals will be equal, in this respect, even though the proportion of goods they receive will not be.

What is to count as a need is a significant question that cannot be answered by a principle of distribution alone. Obviously, basic biological needs (food, clothing, shelter) must be included, but what about other needs, such as access to health care or police protection or social and religious affiliation? One way of analyzing needs is Rawls's concept of primary goods: the resources, rights, opportunities, and powers that allow a person to participate as a full member of a society and to pursue his own conception of a good life. Another account of needs is provided by the capabilities approach (see below), which proposes a minimal set of freedoms and entitlements that allow a person to lead a life of human dignity.

What constitutes a "basic" or "central" need is, of course, a matter of considerable controversy. The difficulty of resolving the question of needs is seen in the fact that even in our affluent society—the richest in the history of the world—we are still debating the question of whether health care should be available to all.

The Principle of Contribution

According to the principle of contribution, people should get back that proportion of social goods that is the result of their productive labor. If two people work to grow potatoes and the first works twice as long or twice as hard as the second, then the first should be entitled to twice as large a share of the harvest.

The difficulty with this principle in an industrialized, capitalistic society is that contributions to production can take forms other than time and labor. Some people risk their money in investments needed to make production possible, and others contribute crucial ideas or inventions. How are comparisons to be made? Furthermore, in highly industrialized societies it is the functioning of the entire system, rather than the work of any particular individual, that creates the goods to be distributed. A single individual's claim on the outcome of the whole system may be very small.

Nonetheless, it is individuals who make the system work, so a plausible argument can be made that individuals should benefit from their contributions. If it is true that it is the system of social organization itself that is most responsible for creating the goods, then this is an argument for supporting the system through taxation and other means. If individual contributions count for relatively little (although for something), there may be few substantive grounds for attempting to distinguish among them in distributing social benefits.

The Principle of Effort

According to the principle of effort, the degree of effort made by an individual should determine the proportion of social goods received by that individual. Thus, the administrative assistant who works just as hard as the CEO of a company should receive the same share of goods as the CEO. Those who exert less effort will receive proportionally less than those who work harder.

The advantage of the principle is that it captures one sense of what is fair—that those who do their best should be similarly rewarded, while those who do less than their best should be less well rewarded. The principle assumes that people have equal opportunities to do their best and that if they do not, it is their own fault.

One difficulty with this assumption, as discussed above, is that societies rarely provide individuals with genuinely equal opportunities. Individuals are born with different socioeconomic advantages and disadvantages, more or less effective parents, and are subject to different cultural and social expectations and prejudices. Even if these differences could somehow be equalized, individuals are still subject to the "natural lottery" discussed above, which, in addition to unevenly distributing talents, abilities, and disabilities, may also impact a person's willingness (or even capacity) to exert herself under adverse conditions. The principle of effort is also hampered by the difficulty of measuring or comparing effort or "doing one's best" for different people under different social and individual circumstances.

Such difficulties do not necessarily disqualify the principle of effort, or any of the other principles just discussed, from playing a role in our moral deliberations. Each principle has its shortcomings, but this does not mean that adjustments cannot be made to correct the weaknesses. A complete theory of justice need not be limited in the number of principles that it accepts, and it is doubtful that any theory can be shown to be both fair and plausible if it restricts itself to only one principle. Although theories vary in their application and elaboration, they can be grouped according to which principles they emphasize. For example, Marxist theories select need as basic, whereas libertarian theories stress personal contribution as the grounds for distribution. Utilitarian theories employ that combination of principles which promises to maximize both private and public interests.

Joel Feinberg, to whom the preceding discussion is indebted, is an example of a theorist who advocates for a combination of principles. Feinberg sees the principle of equality based on needs as the basic determination of distributive justice. After basic needs have been satisfied, the principles of contribution and effort should be given the most weight. According to Feinberg, when there is economic abundance, the claim to "minimally decent conditions" can reasonably be made for every person in the society. To have one's basic needs satisfied under such conditions amounts to a fundamental right. However, when everyone's basic needs are taken care of and society produces a surplus of goods, considerations of contribution and effort become relevant. Those who contribute most to the increase in goods or those who work the hardest to produce it can legitimately lay claim to a greater share.

The principles of justice we have discussed may seem at first to be intolerably abstract and thus irrelevant to the practical business of society. However, it is important to recognize that almost any criticism of a society's status quo laws and practices must draw on abstract arguments and principles. The claim that society is failing to meet the basic needs of all of its citizens and that this is unfair or unjust is a powerful charge. It can be a call to action in the service of justice. If the claim can be substantiated, it has more than rhetorical power. It imposes upon us all an obligation to eliminate the source of the injustice.

Similarly, in framing laws and formulating policies, we expect those who occupy positions of power and influence to make their decisions in accordance with principles. Prominent among these must be principles of justice. It may be impossible in the conduct of daily business to apply any principle directly or exclusively, for we can hardly remake our society overnight. Yet if we are committed to a just society, then the principles of justice can at least serve as guidelines for political, social, and economic decision-making. They can serve to remind us that it is not always fair for the race to go to the swift, especially if the runners have different starting places.

The Principle of Autonomy

The principle of autonomy can be stated as follows: *Rational individuals should be permitted to be self-determining*. According to this formulation, we act autonomously when our actions are the result of our own choices and decisions. Thus, autonomy and self-determination are equivalent.

Autonomy is associated with the status we ascribe to rational beings as persons in the morally relevant sense. This status is rooted in the notion that persons are by their very nature uniquely qualified to decide what is in their own best interest. They are, to use Kant's terms, ends in themselves, not means to some other ends. As such, they have an inherent worth, and it is the duty of others to respect that worth and avoid treating them as though they were just ordinary parts of the world to be manipulated according to the will of someone else. A recognition of autonomy is a recognition of that inherent worth, and a violation of autonomy is a violation of our concept of what it is to be a person. To deny someone autonomy is to treat that individual as something less than a person.

This view of autonomy and its centrality to moral personhood is shared by several major ethical theories. At the core of each theory is a concept of the rational individual as a moral agent who, along with other moral agents, possesses an unconditional worth. Moral responsibility itself is based on the assumption that such agents are free to determine their own actions and pursue their own aims.

Autonomy is significant not only because it is a condition for moral responsibility, but because it is through the exercise of autonomy that individuals shape their lives. We might not approve of what other people do with their lives. It is sad to see talent wasted and opportunities for personal development rejected. Nevertheless, as we sometimes say, "It's his life." We recognize that people are entitled to attempt to make their lives what they want them to be and that it would be wrong for us to take control of their lives and dictate their actions, even if we could. We recognize that a person must follow her own freely chosen path.

Simply put, to act autonomously is to decide for oneself what to do. Of course, decisions are never made outside of a context, and the world and the people in it exert influence, impose constraints, and restrict opportunities. It is useful to call attention to three interrelated aspects of

autonomy in order to get a better understanding of the ways in which autonomy can be exercised, denied, and limited. We will look at autonomy in the contexts of actions, options, and decision-making.

Autonomy and Actions

Consider the following situations: A police officer shoves a demonstrator off the sidewalk during an abortion protest. An attendant in a psychiatric ward warns a patient to stay in bed or be strapped down. A corrections officer warns a prison inmate that if he does not donate blood he will not be allowed out of his cell to eat dinner. A state law requires that anyone admitted to a hospital be screened for HIV.

In each of these situations, actual force, the threat of force, or potential penalties are employed to direct the actions of an individual toward some end. All involve some form of coercion, and the coercion is used to restrict the freedom of individuals to act as they might choose. Under such circumstances, the individual ceases to be the agent who initiates the action as a result of his or her choice. The individual's initiative is set aside, wholly or partially, in favor of someone else's or society's aims.

Autonomy is violated in such cases even if the individual intends to act in the way that is imposed or demanded. Perhaps the prison inmate would have donated blood anyway, and surely many patients would have wanted to be screened for HIV anyway. However, the use of coercion makes the wishes or intentions of the individual partly or totally irrelevant to whether the act is performed.

Autonomy as the initiation of action through one's own intervention and choice can clearly be restricted to a greater or lesser degree. Someone who is physically forced to become a subject in a medical experiment, as in a Nazi concentration camp, is almost entirely deprived of autonomy. The same is true of someone manipulated into becoming a research subject without knowing it. In the infamous Tuskegee syphilis study, participants were led to believe they were receiving appropriate medical treatment when in fact such treatment was being actively withheld to study the effects of their disease. The situation is somewhat different for someone who agrees to become a research subject in order to receive needed medical care. Such a person is acting under strong coercion, but the loss of autonomy is less severe. It is at least possible to refuse to participate in the research, even if the cost of doing so may be extremely high.

In situations more typical than these, autonomy may be compromised rather than denied. For example, someone who is poor, medically unsophisticated, or simply has a passive disposition may find it very difficult to preserve his power of self-determination when he becomes a patient in a hospital. Medical authority, represented by physicians and the hospital staff, may prove so daunting that he does not feel free to exercise his autonomy. In such a case, even though no one may be deliberately attempting to infringe on the patient's autonomy, social and psychological factors may constitute a force so coercive that the patient feels he has no choice but to follow the recommendations of his caregivers.

Autonomy and Options

Autonomy involves more than mere freedom from duress in making decisions. There must be genuine options to choose among. A forced option is no option at all, and someone who is in the position of having to take what he can get does not exercise genuine self-determination or freedom of choice.

In our society, economic and social conditions frequently limit the options available in medical care. As a rule, the poor simply do not have the same medical options available to them as the rich. Someone well-insured or financially well-off who might be helped by a heart transplant or a second-line cancer drug can decide whether or not to try these interventions. Such options are not generally available to someone who is uninsured or underinsured and struggling to make ends meet.

Similarly, a woman who depends on Medicaid and lives in a state in which Medicaid funds cannot be used to pay for abortions may simply not have the option of having an abortion. Her choice is not a genuine one, for she lacks the means to act otherwise. The situation is quite different for a wealthy woman faced with the same question. She may decide against having an abortion, but whatever she decides, the choice is real. She is autonomous in a way that the poor woman is not.

Those who believe that one of the goals of our society is to promote and protect the autonomy of individuals have frequently argued that we must do more to offer all individuals the same range of health care options. If we do not, they have suggested, then our society will continue to become more stratified and unequal, with reduced social mobility and genuine autonomy for those on the bottom strata. Since health is clearly a social good that gives the healthy greater opportunities and options, those who are rich will have greater freedom of action than those who are poor.

Autonomy and Decision-Making

More is involved in decision-making than merely saying yes or no. In particular, relevant information is an essential condition for genuine decision-making. We are exercising our autonomy in the fullest sense only when we are making *informed* decisions.

It is pointless to have options if we are not aware of them; we can hardly be said to be directing the course of our lives if our decisions must be made in ignorance of information that is available and relevant to our choices. This is part of why lying and other forms of deception are so destructive to autonomy. If someone with a progressive and ordinarily fatal disease is not told about it by her physician, then she is in no position to decide how to shape what remains of her life. The lack of a crucial piece of information—that she is dying—is likely to lead her to make decisions different from the ones she would make were she in possession of that information.

Information is a key to protecting and preserving autonomy in most medical situations. A patient who is not informed of alternative forms of treatment and their associated risks is denied the opportunity to make his own wishes and values count for something in his own life. For example, someone with heart disease who is not informed of the relative merits of pharmaceutical treatments and lifestyle changes—but is told only that he is a candidate for coronary-artery bypass surgery—is in no position to decide what risks he wishes to take and what ordeals he is prepared to undergo. A physician who does not supply the patient with the information he needs is restricting his autonomy. The principle of autonomy requires *informed* consent, for consent alone does not involve genuine self-determination.

Making decisions "for the good" of others (paternalism), without consulting their wishes, deprives them of their status as autonomous agents. For example, some people at the final stages of a terminal illness might prefer to be allowed to die without heroic interventions, while others might prefer to sustain their lives for as long as medical skill and technology make possible. If physicians or family members assume responsibility for such a decision, without regard for the patient's explicit or implicit wishes, then no matter what the motive, they are denying to the patient the power of self-determination.

Because autonomy is so thoroughly bound up with informed consent and decision-making, special problems arise in the case of those unable to give consent and make decisions. Patients who are under anesthesia, comatose, severely brain damaged, psychotic, or seriously mentally impaired may be incapable

of making decisions on their own behalf. The nature of their condition has already deprived them of their autonomy. Of course, this does not mean that they have no status as moral persons or that they have no interests. But, to varying degrees, it usually falls to others to see that their interests are served.

The situation is similar for those, such as infants and young children, who are incapable of understanding medical decisions. Any consent that is given must be given by others. But what are the limits of consent that can legitimately be given for some other person? Consenting to needed medical care seems legitimate, but what about rejecting needed medical care? What about consenting to becoming a subject in a research program? These questions are as crucial as they are difficult to resolve.

Restrictions on Autonomy

Autonomy is not an absolute or unconditional value. We would regard it as absurd for someone to claim that she was justified in committing a murder because she was only exercising her power of self-determination. Such a defense would be morally ludicrous. We do, however, value autonomy and recognize a general duty to respect it and even to promote its exercise. We typically demand compelling reasons to justify restricting the power of individuals to make their own choices and direct their own lives.

We will briefly examine four principles that are frequently appealed to in justifying restrictions on autonomy. These principles are typically addressed in the context of social and legal theory, for it is through laws and penalties that a society most directly regulates the conduct of its citizens. However, the principles can also be appealed to in justifying the policies and practices of institutions (such as hospitals) and the actions of individuals that affect other people.

Appealing to a principle can provide, at best, only a prima facie justification for restricting autonomy. Even if the principle can be used to justify a particular restriction of freedom, we may still value the lost freedom more than what is gained by restricting it. Furthermore, the principles themselves are frequently the subjects of controversy, and, with the exception of the harm principle, it is doubtful that any of the principles would be consistently endorsed by philosophers and legal theorists.

The Harm Principle. According to the harm principle, we may restrict the freedom of people to act if the restriction is necessary to prevent harm to others. In the most obvious case, we may take action to prevent violent acts such as robbery, assault, rape, or murder. We may act to protect someone who is at apparent risk of harm from the actions of someone else. The risk of harm need not be the result of an intention to harm. Thus, we might take steps to see that a surgeon whose skills and judgment have been impaired by drug use is not permitted to operate. The risk that he poses to his patients warrants the effort to keep him from acting as he wishes.

The harm principle may also be used to justify laws that exert coercive force and so restrict freedom of action. Laws against homicide and assault are clear examples, but the principle extends to the regulation of institutions and practices. People may be robbed at the point of a pen, as well as at the point of a knife, and the harm produced by fraud may be as great as that produced by outright theft. Careless or deceptive medical practitioners may cause direct harm to their patients, and laws that regulate the standards of medical practice restrict the freedom of practitioners for the protection of patients.

The Principle of Paternalism. In its weak version, the principle of paternalism is no more than the harm principle applied to the individual himself. According to the principle, we are justified in restricting someone's freedom to act if doing so is necessary to prevent him from harming himself. Thus, we

might force an alcoholic into a treatment program and justify our action by claiming that we did so to prevent him from continuing to harm himself through drinking.

In its strong version, the principle of paternalism justifies restricting someone's autonomy if by doing so we can benefit her. In such a case, our concern is not only with preventing the person from harming herself, but also with promoting her good in a positive way. The principle might be appealed to even in cases in which our actions go against the person's known wishes. For example, a physician might decide to treat a patient with a placebo (an inactive drug), even if she has asked to be told the truth about her medical condition and her therapy. He might attempt to justify his action by claiming that if the patient knew she was receiving a placebo, then the placebo would be less likely to be effective. Since taking the placebo while believing that it is an active drug makes her feel better, the physician may claim that by deceiving her he is doing something to help her.

Paternalism may be expressed in laws and public policies, as well as in private actions. Some have suggested that criminal drug laws constitute a prime example of governmental paternalism. By making certain drugs illegal and inaccessible and by placing other drugs under the control of physicians, the laws aim to protect people from themselves. Self-medication is virtually eliminated, and the recreational use of some (but not other) drugs is prohibited. The price for such laws is a restriction on individual autonomy. Some have argued that the price is too high and that the most the government should do is educate the public about the consequences of using certain drugs.

The Principle of Legal Moralism. The principle of legal moralism holds that a legitimate function of the law is to enforce morality by outlawing actions or practices that are considered immoral. Hence, legal restrictions placed on autonomy are justified by the presumption that the prohibited actions are immoral and so ought not to be performed.

To a considerable extent, laws express the values of a society and the society's judgments about what is morally right. In our society, homicide and theft are recognized as crimes, and those who commit them are guilty of legal, as well as moral, wrongdoing. Society attempts to prevent such crimes and to punish offenders.

The degree to which the law should embody moral judgments is hard to determine. It is particularly difficult to answer in a pluralistic society like ours, in which there may be sharp differences of opinion about the moral legitimacy of some actions. As recently as the mid-twentieth century, for example, materials considered obscene could not be freely purchased, information on contraceptives could not be freely distributed, birth control could not be legally prescribed in many states, and the conditions of divorce were generally stringent and punitive. Even now, all fifty states prohibit polygamous marriages and prostitution is illegal in all states except parts of Nevada. One foundation for such laws is the belief that the practices proscribed are morally wrong.

The ongoing debate over abortion reflects, in some of its aspects, a conflict between those who favor strong legal moralism and those who oppose it. Many who consider abortion morally wrong would also like to see it made illegal once more. Others, even though they may disapprove of abortion, believe that it is a private moral matter and that attempts to regulate it by law are unwarranted intrusions of state power.

The Welfare Principle.   The welfare principle holds that it is justifiable to restrict individual autonomy if doing so will provide benefits to others. Those who endorse this principle do not generally present it as requiring major sacrifices of our autonomy or welfare in order to benefit others. Rather an ideal application of the principle would be the case in which we give up only a little autonomy to bring about a great deal of benefit to others.

For example, transplant organs are in short supply because their availability depends mostly on their being freely donated. The situation could be dramatically changed by a law requiring that organs from the recently deceased be harvested and made available for transplant. Such a law would end the present system of voluntary donation, and in doing so it would restrict our freedom to decide what is to be done with our bodies after death. However, it could be argued that the benefit others might gain from such a law easily outweighs the comparatively modest restriction of autonomy that it would involve.

The four principles we have just discussed are not the only ones that offer grounds for abridging the autonomy of individuals, but they are the most relevant to medical policy and decision-making. It is important to keep in mind that merely appealing to a principle is not enough to warrant restrictions of autonomy. A principle points in the direction of an argument, but it is no substitute for one. The high value we place on autonomy gives its preservation a high priority, and compelling considerations are required to justify compromising it. In the view of some philosophers who endorse the position taken by Mill, only the harm principle can serve as grounds for legitimately restricting autonomy. Other theorists find persuasive reasons to do so based on other principles.

BEYOND PRINCIPLISM

Most of traditional Western ethics is based on the assumption that ethical beliefs are best represented by a set of rules or abstract principles. Kant's categorical imperative, Mill's principle of utility, and Ross's list of prima facie duties attempt to supply guides for moral action and decision-making that apply in all circumstances.

Moral decisions thus typically involve bringing a case under a rule, similar to the way that courts apply statutory laws to cases brought before them. Much ethical debate, like much legal debate, concerns whether an abstract rule does or does not apply in a concrete case.

In recent decades, however, some ethical theorists have turned away from the principle-governed, legalistic approach to ethics in favor of various alternative approaches. Some of these theorists have emphasized the importance of character as the source of moral action, whereas others have stressed the central role of shared concerns and the crucial importance of social practices and institutions in shaping our moral lives.

We will present here some brief sketches of ethical approaches that (according to their proponents) cannot be reduced to sets of abstract principles. Although moral theorists debate such questions as whether the virtue of being a truthful person (a character trait) isn't ultimately derived from the duty to tell the truth (a principle), we will steer clear of these issues. Rather, as with theories based on principles, we will restrict ourselves to a general statement of each alternative approach, indicate how it might be applied in a medical context, and then discuss some of the difficulties it faces as a moral theory.

The four theories discussed here have been presented by their proponents in a variety of versions, some of them quite elaborate and philosophically sophisticated. Here, however, we will be presenting only sketches.

The Capabilities Approach

One recurrent criticism of principle-based ethical theories is that they fail to adequately address human diversity and the profound impact that personal and social differences may have on individual lives. For example, we have seen how the principle of utility appears to tolerate exploitation or even slavery, provided that the unhappiness of a subordinate minority is outweighed by the happiness of the dominant group. Even the more nuanced versions of the utilitarianism, such as those based on individuals' expressed desires, face the problem of *adaptive preferences*. As demonstrated by economists such as Amartya Sen, people in subordinate roles typically learn to stop wanting social goods that have been put out of their reach. Thus, for a variety of reasons, principles that reduce questions of morality and justice to a single subjective standard (e.g., satisfactions or preferences) may end up reinforcing an unjust status quo.

At the same time, principles that evaluate morality and justice using a uniform objective standard (such as a fair share of

material resources) have their own difficulties handling interpersonal differences. As Sen famously observed in his critique of John Rawls's account of *primary goods* (which uses wealth and income for interpersonal rankings), a poor person with a serious disability will need a considerably larger share of resources to achieve the same level of well-being as an equally poor person who has no significant impairments. To take another example, pregnant women and children require considerably more protein to achieve the same level of health and well-being as other members of society.

It should be noted that many of these differences are not just individual, but *social*, and may thus require structural change and not just material compensation. A society whose culture devalues female offspring may not only have to spend disproportionately more on girls' health and education, but also may also need to actively promote cultural change, if it is to grant women full citizenship. Similarly, a society with a built environment exclusively designed for "normal" adult citizens who can (at least temporarily) climb stairs and stand upright may need to provide such accommodations as ramps, lifts, and accessible bathrooms if it seeks to promote the genuine well-being of citizens who use wheelchairs. By pursuing a homogenous, abstract standard of social good, critics charge, traditional theories often fail to account for the substantively different opportunities that people have (or don't have) in their lives.

As a corrective to such theories, economists such as Sen and philosophers such as Martha Nussbaum have developed the *capabilities approach* to social justice and interpersonal comparisons of well-being. When evaluating social policies and practices, this approach recommends that we ask, *What is each person actually able to do and to be?* In other words, just societies and individuals should focus on the set of substantial freedoms or opportunities that each person, viewed as an end in herself, can actually choose to exercise. Rather than reducing these substantial freedoms or *capabilities* to an abstract scale of value (such as utility, wealth, or per-capita gross national product), justice entitles individuals to a core set of qualitatively distinct *central capabilities* that are, according to Nussbaum's version of the approach, implicit in our basic understanding of human dignity.

With this emphasis on respect for the freedom and dignity of every individual viewed as an end in himself, the capabilities approach has many affinities with the deontological ethics of Kant, Ross, and Rawls. But Nussbaum and Sen question deontology's tendency to rely on "automatic" decision procedures—based, for example, on the categorical imperative or the original position—to determine the right action, policy, or principles. Instead, like consequentialists, they argue that policies and practices should be evaluated in the light of their *outcomes*: whether they actually help people achieve the minimum threshold of capabilities that they have good reason to value.

The capabilities approach also rejects the assumption, present in both Kant's and Rawls's account of social cooperation, that it must be pursued by and for the *mutual advantage* of free and equal parties with a high level of rational autonomy. Nussbaum notes that such views not only exclude cognitively impaired people from the entitlements of justice and personhood, but also fails to reflect the large portion of most "normal" people's lifespans that is spent in states of dependency, vulnerability, and asymmetrical relationships. These states constitute an important part of our human dignity and rationality, not something to be contrasted with it—a point that will also be emphasized by proponents of care ethics (see below). The result is a broader conception of human agency, rooted in "active striving," and an account of social cooperation that incorporates benevolent and altruistic motives, not just the pursuit of mutual advantage.

Central Capabilities

If the capabilities approach relies neither on mechanical decision procedures nor on applying abstract principles to cases, then how is it to guide moral decision-making and just policy-making? Nussbaum proposes that the justice of societies and policies be evaluated on the basis of ten central capabilities. Beneath a specified minimal threshold of each of these central capabilities, she argues, individuals are unable to lead lives worthy of their human dignity and cannot achieve genuine human functioning:

1) *Life.* Being able to live a normal human lifespan; 2) *Bodily health.* Being able to achieve good health, most fundamentally on the basis of adequate nutrition and shelter; 3) *Bodily integrity.* Being able to move safely in one's environment, free from violence or sexual assault, and exercising reasonable control over one's reproductive and sexual life; 4) Being able to use one's *senses, imagination, thought, and reason*, especially as facilitated by literacy,

numeracy, and freedom of expression and worship; 5) *Emotions*. Being able to form the range of attachments and relationships crucial for human development; 6) *Practical reason*. Being able to plan and pursue a life in accordance with one's own conception of the good; 7) *Affiliation*. Being able to engage in social interactions consistent with both self-respect and solidarity, enjoying freedom of assembly and freedom from systematic discrimination; 8) *Other species*. Being able to live as part of the natural world of plants and animals; 9) Being able to enjoy *leisure time and play*; 10) Being able to exercise reasonable *control over one's material and political environment*, through equal basic political rights, property rights, employment opportunities, and freedom from unwarranted search and seizure.

We do not have space to summarize Nussbaum's arguments for each of these central capabilities, but a few points are needed to complete our sketch. First, these capabilities are plural and *incommensurable* sources of value—a just society cannot compensate a lack of basic voting rights with better health care. Second, the capabilities are presented as freestanding political goals that could form the basis of an overlapping consensus in a pluralistic society. In keeping with Rawls's idea of *political liberalism* (see above), Nussbaum does not argue for the capabilities on the basis of any particular comprehensive view of religion, philosophy, or human psychology. To explain why leisure and play should receive special protection in a just society, for example, she seeks to demonstrate, on an empirical and intuitive basis, how those deprived of leisure (e.g., who must work multiple jobs or who have a "double day" of both formal employment and unpaid caregiving) are ultimately unable to access the set of capabilities that constitute a full and dignified human life.

Finally, it is important to distinguish capabilities (what agents can be and do) from realized *functionings* (their actual beings and doings). Sen and Nussbaum argue that just policies should generally promote only the former and not the latter, in keeping with their emphasis on human agency and reasonable pluralism.

The Capabilities Approach in the Medical Context

From its origins in the work of Amartya Sen and the United Nation's *Human Development Index*, the capabilities approach has taken health and healthcare as a primary focus. This is partly because health can be a profoundly "fertile" capability (facilitating many other substantive freedoms) or a profoundly "corrosive" one (eliminating other capabilities). Drawing heavily on Rawls's theory of justice, the approach is also especially concerned with the long-term health effects of poverty, particularly on an international scale. Minimally decent societies and policies should try to prevent "morally arbitrary" factors, such as being born to a mother with no health insurance and poor prenatal nutrition, from condemning individuals to a life that falls below basic capability levels.

But health policies must also look beyond mere *means*, such as distribution of resources, to examine how individual and social differences limit what people can actually do and be. A person afflicted by intestinal parasites has limited capability to convert a fair share of food into healthy human functioning. Similarly, achieving a just social minimum in a culture that tolerates widespread economic discrimination or sexual violence against girls and women may require special efforts to help them reach a basic level of health and related capabilities. Pursuing the central capability thresholds may require similar efforts by physicians and policy-makers to support the health of groups that are despised or marginalized on the basis of religion, ethnicity, caste, sexuality, or other factors.

Such obligations are particularly demanding when it comes to people with serious physical and mental impairments. Rather than treating the disabled as if they belonged to a different species, we are to promote all ten central capabilities implied by their worth and dignity as members of the human species. This moral claim applies to all degrees of physical and mental disability, with the exception of those in anencephalic and permanent vegetative states (who are judged incapable of the "active striving" necessary for genuine human functioning). Thus, a just society will likely direct resources not just to accessible public accommodations, but also to new avenues of social and political participation for the disabled. This requirement derives, in part, from the recognition that all members of society experience extended states of impairment and dependency that should not, insofar as possible, prevent them from achieving central human capabilities.

Of course, the approach would not force the disabled (or anyone else) to achieve actual *functionings* such as voting or literacy or cultural expression, but only work to provide them with substantive freedom to pursue these varied dimensions of human life. On similar grounds, the capabilities approach would also reject mandatory lifesaving interventions (such as blood transfusions) for those who refuse them (such as Jehovah's Witnesses). In Sen and Nussbaum's view, there is a significant moral difference between policies that promote health and those that promote *health capabilities*—only the latter is an appropriate goal for a just and pluralistic society.

Difficulties with the Capabilities Approach

Like some other pluralistic approaches to value (such as that of W. D. Ross, discussed above), the capabilities approach has been criticized for relying on "intuitionistic balancing" when it comes to competing ends. Without a uniform standard to evaluate the right or the good, how are we to choose among compet-

ing capabilities, or, for that matter, competing claims to the human dignity that those capabilities are said to embody? (The conflicts of moral standing frequently invoked in the abortion debate would seem to exemplify these competing claims.) Thus, critics charge, capabilities provide insufficient guidance for biomedical and other moral decisions.

Defenders of the approach point out that traditional ethical theories also tend to rely on intuition when it comes to first principles (such as utility or autonomy) and the design of decision procedures (such as Rawls's original position). They argue that the capabilities approach involves no "balancing," since justice requires that a minimal threshold of all ten central capabilities be met. Proponents such as Nussbaum have also provided an account of abortion that, while granting a fetus's possession of human dignity, argues that its capabilities are primarily potential and dependent. Thus, its claim to moral standing must, for a large set of cases, be trumped by protection of the pregnant woman's central capabilities. (Its claims may, however, allow for restrictions on abortions for some dubious reasons, such as sex-selection, and limits on how late in pregnancy abortions may be performed, with exceptions for women's life and health.)

Despite such applications, neither Sen nor Nussbaum claim that their account of capability is a full-fledged ethical theory but rather a framework for comparative quality-of-life assessment and a "partial" account of social justice. Although influential in development economics and in some constitutional law debates, the capabilities approach is just a few decades old. It remains to be seen if it will retain its appeal as it is applied to an increasing number of problems in bioethics, public policy, and beyond.

Virtue Ethics

Every culture is populated by real and fictional figures who represent the sort of people we may seek to become. Some figures are seen as perfect, while others are people who, despite their flaws, demonstrate *character* in confronting life's problems and struggles. To name only a few historically important figures, consider Moses, Gautama Buddha, Socrates, Confucius, Jesus, Marcus Aurelius, Augustine, Voltaire, Harriet Tubman, Abraham Lincoln, Karl Marx, Susan B. Anthony, Florence Nightingale, Anne Frank, Mohandas Gandhi, Martin Luther King, Jr., Mother Teresa, and Nelson Mandela. It would be easy to make an even longer list of fictional characters who evoke our admiration and make us feel that we would be better people if we could be more like them.

Virtue ethics is ethics based on character. Its fundamental idea is that a person who has acquired the proper set of dispositions will do what is right when faced with a situation involving a moral choice. The virtuous person is both the basic concept and the goal of virtue ethics. The virtuous person is one who does right, because she is just that sort of person. Right actions flow out of character, and the virtuous person has a disposition to do the right thing. Rules need not be consulted, calculations need not be performed, abstract duties need not be considered.

On this view, people become virtuous in the same way they become good swimmers. Practice, personal effort, and reflection, as well as upbringing and education, all play a role. As with swimming, some people may be more naturally inclined to become virtuous than others. Those who are naturally patient, reflective, and slow to anger may find it easier than those who are impatient, impulsive, and short-tempered.

Families and social institutions—such as schools, clubs, and athletic teams, as well as religious institutions—play a role in shaping our moral character. They tell us how we should behave when we lose a school election or win a soccer game. They teach us what we should do when we have a

chance to take money without anyone's finding out, when we witness a case of discrimination or harassment, or when we ourselves are treated unfairly.

Quite apart from explicit teachings or doctrines, the lives of historical figures such as Jesus, Mohammed, and Buddha have served as examples of what it is possible for a person to become. Perhaps no one can achieve the level of moral perfection such people represent, but they offer us models for fashioning ourselves and handling everyday moral questions.

When a Christian asks, "What would Jesus do?" it is not typically a call for divine intervention. Rather, it is an occasion for reflection, for trying to imagine what someone living a life like Jesus's would do. We try to improve our character by becoming more like those who are admirable. Hence, in addition to education and social influences, we must engage in self-criticism and make deliberate efforts to improve.

The Virtues

Like the capabilities approach, virtue ethics provides a plural account of values, and both have roots in the Greek philosopher Aristotle's account of the varied dimensions of human flourishing. *Virtue* is a translation of the ancient Greek word *arete*, which can be loosely translated as "excellence." (Virtue ethics is also called *aretaic ethics*.) The excellent tennis player demonstrates in playing tennis that she possesses characteristics needed to play the game well. Similarly, the virtuous person demonstrates through living that she possesses the appropriate range of excellences.

Virtues have traditionally been categorized as either moral or nonmoral:

Moral virtues: *benevolence, compassion, honesty, charity, sincerity, sympathy, respect, consideration, kindness, thoughtfulness, loyalty, fairness, and so on.*

Nonmoral virtues: *rationality (or intelligence), tenacity, capability, patience, prudence, skillfulness, staunchness, shrewdness, proficiency, and so on.*

The distinction between moral and nonmoral virtues is far from clear, but the rough idea is that those in one set are associated with living a good (moral) life, whereas those in the other are associated with practical aspects of living. A thief can be patient (a nonmoral virtue), but not fully honest (a moral one). By contrast, an honest person may lack patience. How to classify *courage* presents a problem. A courageous thief may be more successful than a cowardly one, but a benevolent person lacking the courage to put his views into practice will be ineffective.

Virtue Ethics in the Medical Context

Consider the hypothetical example of Dr. Charles Holmes, an orthopedic surgeon who has chosen his specialty because the money is good and the hours reasonable. He treats the patients and then he goes home. Holmes has technical expertise, but he lacks compassion for his patients and is not interested in their values or hopes for their lives. He shows no tact in dealing with patients' fears and questions, and barely acknowledges that they are people.

Dr. Holmes is far removed from our notion of what a physician as a compassionate healer should be. In treating his patients as broken machines, he may help them in important ways, but his skills as a physician are deficient. Holmes, we might say, lacks the disposition necessary to be an excellent or even a good physician.

From at least the time of the ancient Greeks, the Western tradition in medicine has expected physicians to be virtuous, and more recently that expectation has expanded to include nurses, medical technicians, and all who care for patients. Medical history includes many accounts of caregivers whose actions make them moral examples. During the Black Death (bubonic plague) pandemic in fourteenth-century Europe, scores of physicians tended to their patients, even though they risked infection themselves. The British nurse Florence Nightingale, braving harsh conditions and the threat of death, helped care for troops during the Crimean War and helped establish nursing as a profession. In recent years, African and Western medical professionals have taken considerable risks to combat the Ebola epidemic in West Africa, and dozens have been infected with the deadly virus while caring for patients.

Virtue ethics calls attention to medicine at its moral (and practical) best. Courage, loyalty, integrity, compassion, and benevolence, along with determination and intelligence, are virtues associated with physicians and others who provide what we consider the right sort of care for their patients. Virtue ethics, with its emphasis on character and behavioral dispositions, comes closer to capturing our notion of the ideal health professional than do rule-based accounts of moral decision-making such as Kant's ethics or utilitarianism.

Difficulties with Virtue Ethics

A fundamental difficulty with virtue ethics is that it provides us with no explicit guidance in deciding how to act in particular circumstances. Suppose someone is terminally ill, in great pain, and asking for assistance in dying. Should we agree to help? We may ask, "What would Jesus do?" and the answer may be "I don't know." Medicine constantly faces the problem of deciding what specific actions ought to be taken, but virtue ethics is about character and dispositions. Even a perfectly benevolent person (one disposed to act benevolently) may not know how to distribute organs that are in short supply. Further, virtue ethics does not supply any clear way to resolve moral conflicts. What if one gynecologist thinks it wrong to abort a fetus at twenty-three weeks gestation, but another does not? How can they go about resolving their dispute using the concept of virtue? The answer is not clear.

Also, virtues, like duties, can be incompatible when put into action. If I am a transplant coordinator and try to show gratitude to my pastor by allowing her to jump to the top of the waiting list for a liver, this action will conflict with my commitment to fairness. But if virtues are not ranked, how do I decide whether to prioritize gratitude or fairness? Surely we don't think it would be right for me to put my pastor at the head of the list, but on what grounds can virtue ethics say that it would be wrong?

Care Ethics

With their emphasis on abstraction, philosophers sometimes seem to forget that our moral life typically takes place in the context of ongoing relationships of mutual understanding, concern, and obligations to specific individuals. That such relationships involve nuanced moral responsibilities that cannot be captured by abstract principles is a conviction that helps motivate *care ethics* as a theoretical approach to interpersonal morality. Care ethics is not, however, a unified doctrine that can be captured in a set of formal statements. It is perhaps best characterized as a family of beliefs about the way values should be manifested in character, behavior, and social practices. It is unified by a set of shared concerns and commitments, as well as by its critique of traditional Anglo-American approaches to philosophical ethics.

Much of the early philosophical work in care ethics grew out of the feminist movement and psychologist Carol Gilligan's research on gender differences in moral development. Gilligan's work is, in part, a response to that of her academic mentor, Lawrence Kohlberg, who had concluded that women were "less developed" in their moral reasoning than men, because they

appeared less adept at applying universal principles to particular cases. Gilligan rejects Kohlberg's hierarchical account of moral development and instead argues for an alternative, but equally legitimate, *style* of moral reasoning that she finds to be more common in women than men.

Gilligan famously reinterprets a classic case from Kohlberg's research, in which a girl and a boy were asked whether a (fictional) man named Heinz should steal an overpriced drug he cannot afford, in order to save the life of his ailing wife. Gilligan takes the girl's answer—that Heinz should not steal the drug, lest he go to prison and leave his wife in an even worse situation—to exemplify an ethical style focused on the specific interests of multiple people in communicative relationships over time. She takes the boy's conclusion—that Heinz *should* steal the drug because the right to life takes priority over property rights—to represent the individualistic and mechanical application of principles more characteristic of men and male-dominated academic philosophy.

Based on Kohlberg's and her own subsequent studies, Gilligan argues that women are more likely to view ethical dilemmas in terms of a network of ongoing relationships, in which compromise, creativity, and communication are necessary to resolve conflicts in a way that minimizes harm and respects everyone's interests. By contrast, Gilligan argues that men are more likely to try to resolve moral conflicts by applying abstract rules, even if that means ignoring the specific characteristics and needs of some of the people involved in the situation.

Gilligan characterizes the more typically female response to situations of moral conflict as expressing an *ethic of care* and the more typically male response as expressing an *ethic of justice*. She emphasizes, however, that there isn't a consistent correlation between these types of response and gender. According to Gilligan, ideal moral agents should employ both approaches to ethical decision-making, even if there is currently a gender-based asymmetry in their use. The question of whether care ethics is a specifically *feminine* mode of reasoning, however, has been a source of ongoing debate as care ethics has evolved. So has the question of whether it constitutes an outgrowth or a particular strand of *feminist ethics* (which will be discussed in the next section).

Some philosophers have reserved the term *feminist* for approaches that also examine care and caregiving in the context of gender-based power imbalances and divisions of labor between men and women. *Feminist ethics*, on this view, is primarily concerned with the symbolic and empirical structures of gender and how such structures might be changed to achieve full social and political equality for women and men. *Care ethics* need not have such explicit feminist concerns, although it may share the same general aims and point of view.

Even so, many feminists see this terminological distinction as less important than the need to make sure that women's perspectives and concerns are represented within ethics. According to them, the ethical tradition has concentrated on the development of sweeping abstract theories that fail to acknowledge the importance of values more typically prized by women; as a result, philosophers have traditionally assigned those values little or no role in moral decision-making or the moral life. Care ethics is seen as a means of enriching philosophical ethics with moral insights derived from interdependent caregiving relationships, nuanced communication skills, and reasoning from particular cases.

Values, Not Principles

Ethical theories as diverse as utilitarianism and Kantian ethics have in common a reliance upon abstract principles, both as an expression of the theory and as a means of resolving moral conflicts. Thus, to decide whether an action is morally legitimate, we can appeal, for example, to the principle of utility or to the categorical imperative. Moral theories can be viewed as providing a decision procedure for arriving at morally justified conclusions in particular cases: to justify an action, bring it under a rule.

Care ethics questions whether it is appropriate to rely on abstract rules or principles where certain kinds of relationships are concerned. Should we perform a utilitarian calculation before giving a friend a ride to the hospital? Should parents consult the categorical imperative before deciding whether to immunize their children against polio? Of course not. Relationships such as friendship and parenthood require that we give of ourselves and provide appropriate assistance and care. These demands are bound up with the trust, vulnerability, and commitment that characterizes ongoing relationships. Other interpersonal roles—being a spouse, aunt, uncle, grandparent, pastor, nurse, physician, teacher, or therapist—involve other complex relational requirements. To treat people in such relationships as if they were simply unconnected autonomous agents, bound only by abstract moral rules, seems both inappropriate and bizarre.

Care ethics rejects outright the idea that abstract principles can capture everything relevant to making moral decisions. It reflects a deep skepticism that our moral lives with others can be subsumed "under a rule" or shown to be an "instance" of a general principle. This does not mean, however, that care ethics views our relational duties as merely intuitive, subjective, or a natural outgrowth of love. Indeed, care ethics, like feminist ethics more generally, is highly critical of the notion that caregiving duties (i.e., those of mothers) are natural, blindly emotional, or beyond rational scrutiny. Instead, care ethics insists that we derive our moral duties from a sophisticated understanding of the specific relational context in which a moral problem has arisen. This requires a deep and detailed understanding of the people involved and their interests and feelings. Only then is it possible to resolve the problem in a way that is sensitive to everyone's needs.

In evaluating such situations, we must use critical intelligence to grasp relationships and details about the people, the circumstances, and the moral problem. But equally important, we must use *empathy* to understand the concerns and feelings of the people involved. We must identify with those in need or conflict, see what is at stake from their point of view, and ascertain their worries and concerns. We must also bring to the situation of moral conflict or doubt such traditional "women's values" as caring, consideration, compassion, understanding, generosity, humility, and a willingness to assume responsibility.

These are the very values we must rely on to resolve moral conflicts and address the needs of the people involved. Such a process must go beyond determining who is in the wrong or being treated unfairly. Rather, the point is to find a way out of the conflict that takes into account the concerns and feelings of those involved.

According to care ethics, the traditional ethical model of a disinterested, detached, and dispassionate judge reviewing the objective facts in a case and then issuing an impartial decision about the moral acceptability of an action is both inappropriate and inadequate. It excludes the very values that are most relevant to moral situations and most important to the people who are involved. Moral decisions should not be impartial, in an abstract and bloodless way; rather, they should show partiality to *everyone* involved.

Like virtue ethics, care ethics emphasizes the development of an appropriate character. As a society, we should make an effort, by teaching and example, to develop individuals, both male and female, who respond ap-propriately to moral situations. They should be people who recognize the importance of personal relationships, respect individuals, and accept responsibility. If they have acquired the proper character and interpersonal skills, they will bring to bear the values (described above) that we associate with caring for and about people.

Care Ethics in the Medical Context

Suppose the parents of a severely impaired newborn boy are told by the child's physicians that his treatment ought to be discontinued and he should be given only "comfort care" and allowed to die. The parents' initial response is to reject the recommendation and insist that everything possible be done to preserve the life of their child. How might such a conflict be resolved by the approach advocated by care ethics?

The parties to the conflict must discuss their positions freely and openly. (We need not assume that only two positions are involved.) The physicians must explain in detail the baby's medical condition, discuss the therapy they may be able to offer, and be forthcoming about its limitations. If they believe the child will die in a few hours or days, no matter what they do, they must be both candid and sensitive about this expectation. They might gently point out that the only possible intervention involves extensive and painful surgery, that it is almost certain to be unsuccessful, and that it will make demands on the resources of the hospital, the society, and the parents themselves.

For their part, the parents might talk about their hopes for their son and their willingness to love and nurture a child with severe physical and mental impairments. They might discuss the guilt they would feel about giving up the struggle and allowing the child to die. They might discuss their experiences with other children or talk about the difficulties they had conceiving the baby who is now not expected to live.

No particular outcome can be predicted from such a discussion. We might imagine education taking place and compromises developing. We might imagine the physicians coming to a greater appreciation of what the child means to the parents and why they are so reluctant to allow him to die. The parents, for their part, might come to understand that the physicians are concerned for their family and are also frustrated and saddened by their inability to help the child get better. Such an exchange might involve adjustments on the part of all participants. The parents might come to realize that their child is almost certain to die no matter what is done. The physicians might realize that they can make the death easier for the parents to bear by allowing them to hold the child and spend time with him.

Other moral conflicts or questions might be approached in a similar fashion. How should family members and physicians handle a terminally ill patient's request for assistance in dying? How should health providers approach the second-trimester abortion request of a pregnant woman with bipolar disorder who lives below the poverty line? Care ethics insists that we not abstract from the details of these cases and retreat to universal principles. Instead, the complexities of the people and relationships involved are essential moral data. This is particularly true, care ethicists suggest, when the relationships involved are *embodied* and *dependent*, involving intimate caregiving duties, familial bonds, and, in pregnancy, shared bodily space and merged human existence.

Medicine, nursing, and related disciplines have traditionally been associated with the values of caring. We have expected practitioners to manifest, in their character and conduct, such qualities as concern, compassion, sympathy, kindness, and a willingness to take responsibility and to help patients in their charge. In this respect, care ethics is asking us to recognize a traditional approach to biomedical practice. However, care ethics also reassures us that this approach is legitimate, even though no abstract principles are involved. Further, it demonstrates how we may rely on those same values and dispositions when we are faced with moral conflicts in medicine.

Difficulties with Care Ethics

A frequent criticism of care ethics is that Gilligan's empirical claims about the different moral reasoning styles of women and men are not confirmed by more recent data. Without taking a stand on this question, we can observe that these empirical claims are not crucial to care ethics. It is enough for the theorist to demonstrate the importance of the values that belong to the ethic of care—by demonstrating their pivotal role in the moral life of individuals and society, and how they can be employed as guides to resolve cases of moral doubt and conflict.

Other critics have argued that although care ethics usefully claims moral values and practices often ignored or unappreciated in traditional ethics, it does not constitute a separate, full-fledged theory, such as utilitarianism or Ross's intuitionism. Some have suggested, for example, that the principle of beneficence ("Act so as to promote the good of others") can be construed as implying a duty to care. Some care ethicists have endorsed the use of such a principle, while others have insisted that the care ethic remains distinct from the traditional enterprise of philosophical ethics.

A more important criticism may be that, like virtue ethics, which also typically rejects principles as necessary to moral reasoning, care ethics provides us with no clear procedure for resolving moral conflicts. We may approach such conflicts with all the values implicit in a care ethic and still not know how to make a decision. When a number of people are in need of the same kidney for transplant, how should we decide who gets the organ? Should we, in the manner suggested by care ethics, have a discussion with them all, listen to their needs and concerns, and then make a decision? It seems unlikely that such a group could reach a consensus, particularly in the short time allowed under such circumstances. If we make a choice among these individuals' conflicting needs and values, some will claim that they have been treated unfairly, no matter how nuanced our understanding of their specific circumstances. Such cases suggest that an abstract principle of justice may, at least in some situations, yield more satisfactory results than the values of care ethics.

These objections might be answered satisfactorily by care ethicists. Even so, they are prima facie shortcomings that require serious responses.

Feminist Ethics and Critical Theories of Identity

Over the past half century, a variety of theories have been developed to explore the ethical implications of political and social categories such as gender, race, sexuality, and disability. Academic disciplines such as critical race theory, queer theory, and disability studies have focused not just on personal identity, but also on how it is shaped and positioned in social and political life. This approach was largely pioneered by work in feminist ethics, which will be our primary focus here—in part because feminist thought has had the most sustained influence on contemporary academic philosophy.

From the perspective of feminism and other identity-based theories, the "principlism" of traditional Anglo-American ethics is compromised by the facts of the social world. The unequal distribution of political and social power and the inequalities attached to the accidents of birth, race, gender, and sexual identity mean that even such basic principles as autonomy may be restricted or distorted in their application. Indeed, as we have seen in our earlier discussion of the capabilities approach, universal principles and uniform metrics of well-being can sometimes mask profound disparities among different groups and individuals.

For example, when the burdens of child-rearing (not to mention gestation) fall exclusively or disproportionately on women, a principle of reproductive autonomy will mean something very different for women than it does for men. Similarly, universal principles of bodily integrity, consent, and freedom of association may provide few protections for women or LGBT individuals if society tolerates widespread patterns of sexual violence and harassment against them. Classical liberal principles of civil rights and economic freedom may elude people of color if they become subtly but indelibly associated with criminality or deviance in the eyes of police officers and loan officers.

The ideal of an autonomous ethical subject, applying universal principles and operating outside of social power relations, is, according to most of these theories, little more than a self-serving fiction. It is only plausible, they argue, if one enjoys the social privileges that come with such attributes as financial security, whiteness, masculinity, heterosexuality, or the absence of disability. Genuine social equality is necessary for the exercise of autonomy, and such equality does not exist under present social conditions. People constrained by discrimination, dependence on others, or disproportionate caregiving responsibilities are not equal to those who are free of such burdens, and thus lack their autonomy. Evidence of such disparities may be dramatic and concrete—exemplified by the number of women in the U.S. Congress, the percentage of women who have experienced sexual assault, or the percentage of African American men who will be incarcerated during their lifetimes. It may also be subtle—exemplified by the ways in which what is socially acceptable or healthy comes to be associated with European culture or heterosexuality. Both types of evidence are marshaled by critical theories of identity to argue for an alternative approach to ethical deliberation.

Identity-focused theorists insist that ethics should first address unjust social arrangements, practices, and institutions, rather than debate abstract principles. As this approach first developed in feminist ethics, it has often been concerned with uncovering and eliminating the sources of inequality. Feminist theorists have critiqued institutions and social practices that undermine women's agency in the workplace, the family, and in sexual and reproductive relationships. As Susan Sherwin puts the point, feminist ethics cannot be satisfied just by calculating increases in happiness and invoking moral principles. Rather, it must also ask *whose* happiness is increased and how the principles affect different individuals in social and cultural hierarchies. In the final analysis, she writes, "Positive moral value attaches to actions or principles that help relieve oppression, and negative value attaches to those that fail to reduce oppression or actually help to strengthen it."

In practice, ethical theories of identity have often focused on the way cultural *structures*, such as those that sustain gender or race or heterosexuality, come to reinforce hierarchies of power and privilege, and may distort the perceptions of people in both dominant and subordinate groups. Critical race theory, for example, examines how the "color-blind" assumptions of social policies and academic theories often mask pervasive patterns of institutional racism and white privilege. At the same time, queer theory has analyzed how the enforcement

of "compulsory" heterosexuality grants extensive privileges to straight, gender-conforming couples while stigmatizing others as deviant or unnatural. Drawing on (European) continental philosophy, these ethical approaches are often conceived as *critical* or *deconstructive*, which often means that they focus on the morally arbitrary, self-contradictory, or internally incoherent aspects of such concepts as "whiteness," "disability," "deviance," or "femininity."

Not surprisingly, this critical strategy sometimes comes into conflict with earlier approaches to interpersonal morality, such as care ethics. Some feminist scholars, for example, find Gilligan's version of care ethics too reliant on "essentialist" or stereotypical notions of women as emotion-driven, self-effacing, or focused on parochial domestic concerns. They argue that this ignores the unequal division of caregiving labor and other power imbalances that have limited women's participation in public life. At worst, they claim care ethics risks valorizing oppressive social structures, such as those that have historically confined women to the lower "helping" ranks of medicine and education, and burdened them with a "double day" of formal employment and domestic caregiving. Caring has a legitimate place in feminist ethics, they argue, but it must be seen as a disposition desirable for all people across divisions of gender, class, race, sexuality, and disability.

Critical Theories of Identity in a Medical Context

Since identity-based theories of ethics encompass a wide range of political movements and intellectual commitments, it would be difficult to provide a unified account of their approaches to medical research and practice. Nevertheless, we can at least describe some of the recurrent themes and strategies of their work in biomedical ethics and highlight a few representative issues.

First, in keeping with the critical and deconstructive approach described above, identity-based approaches often scrutinize biomedical concepts, ranging from controversial diagnoses such as "premenstrual dysphoric disorder" and "gender dysphoria" to more general notions like health, disability, and race. They are particularly concerned with the ways in which such concepts have positioned the members of subordinate groups as aberrant, diseased, or deficient in relation to an arbitrary model of the healthy human body (often explicitly defined as male, white, non-disabled, etc.). The Briefing Session in Chapter 10 considers a number of these concepts and their relationship to social and political power structures.

Second, identity-based theories have advanced a range of arguments on specific biomedical policy issues such as race-based medicine, cochlear implants, assisted reproduction, and abortion. Feminist philosophers, for example, have argued that without reliable access to contraception and abortion, women effectively become "fetal containers," who lack the autonomy that men take for granted in their familial, economic, and sexual lives. At the same time, feminist scholars have explored the overlapping identities and embodied experiences involved in pregnancy, and argued against the adversarial model employed in many discussions of "maternal–fetal conflict."

Third, feminist and other identity-based theories have proposed specific strategies for the evaluation and care of patients. Many of these involve attention to the "intersecting" roles of different social categories and experiences in a patient's life. Consider, for example, a widowed seventy-two-year-old Latina patient with leukemia and difficulty walking who says she may refuse a second course of chemotherapy and sign up for hospice. An identity-based approach to this woman's

situation might encourage providers and others involved in her care to consider the following sorts of questions: (1) Does the woman believe she is not entitled to further treatment based on traditional gender norms regarding female self-sacrifice and other-focused caregiving? (2) Have the woman's providers offered her the same aggressive treatment options that they would offer comparable patients of European ancestry? (Some studies suggest that physicians, on average, offer less aggressive interventions to nonwhite patients.) (3) Does the woman lack assistive resources (e.g., a motorized scooter, home health aide, or accessible transportation) that might allow her to maintain social relationships and participate in public life, despite her physical impairments? (4) As a widow, does the woman believe she has no valuable function left in life, beyond heterosexual marriage or maternal caregiving? Does she feel like a burden to her adult children and useless to the broader society?

In sum, providers and others are encouraged to view the woman's decision to discontinue treatment as potentially involving many other factors beyond patient autonomy and informed consent. They are asked to examine how a variety of social and cultural factors might be influencing her decision and making it less than free.

Difficulties with Identity-Based Ethical Theories

The multiplicity of viewpoints and conceptual strategies involved in each of the identity-based theories discussed above has led some critics to charge that none provides the relatively unified set of moral concepts offered by theories such as utilitarianism or Kantian ethics. Some identity-focused ethicists have responded by insisting that moral knowledge is not essentially theoretical and denying that the proper role of ethics is to provide us with "automatic" decision procedures for action. Rather, ethics is about people, and it has the aim of facilitating their mutual understanding and accommodating the differences among them. Only by engaging in constructive critique and exchange across difference can individuals resolve conflicts and find solutions to their problems.

One difficulty with this view of ethics is that while it has many strengths for analyzing injustice at the level of policy, culture, and social practice, it can seem ill-equipped to confront cases of individual wrongdoing. Suppose someone who is HIV positive claims that he has no responsibility to warn sexual partners of his HIV status or to practice safe sex. "That's their problem and their risk," he says. It is not immediately clear on what grounds an identity-based theory might criticize his position, assuming it is not rooted in prejudice or privilege. It is also not clear how such theories might offer support for the man's position. If we decide that asking for "grounds" is simply the wrong approach, then what is the right approach to resolve the problem of someone's acting in ways that will endanger others needlessly?

A second difficulty of this view of ethics is that it seems to open identity-based approaches to the charge of cultural relativism. If ethics is (in Margaret Urban Walker's phrase) a "socially embodied" practice involving critique and dialogue *within* cultural structures, on what basis can it make moral assessments from *outside* a particular culture? As discussed in Chapter 11, practices such as slavery, child marriage, and genital cutting may be rooted in elaborate, culturally specific justifications. Without recourse to some universal principles, it is not clear how outsiders can support reformers in other cultures against those who wish to perpetuate socially oppressive practices. As with virtue ethics and care ethics, a commitment to doing without principles or rules doesn't seem to offer a way of assessing actions, policies, and practices from the outside.

To be sure, many feminist and other identity-focused theorists acknowledge a role for universal moral concepts, so long as they are not employed to simply ignore or bypass the impact of social power structures. There are, for example, many feminist philosophers whose critiques of misogynistic behavior or patriarchal culture is rooted in a neo-Kantian, contemporary utilitarian, or another "hybrid" approach. Others, such as Martha Nussbaum, offer universal concepts (e.g., the central capabilities discussed above), which are designed to advance feminist and other identity-based concerns, while allowing for different interpretations and applications in different cultures. In the development of contemporary philosophy, as in everyday life, ethical deliberation often involves a dynamic interplay between the universal and the particular.

RETROSPECT

The two major tasks of this chapter have been to introduce readers to a range of influential ethical theories and to discuss a number of widely accepted moral principles. One aim in performing these tasks was to make it easier to follow the arguments and discussions in the first eleven chapters of this book.

Another, and ultimately more serious, aim has been to call attention to ethical approaches that readers may wish to consider adopting in their own moral deliberations. In this regard, the problems raised in the Social Context and Case Presentations may be taken as opportunities to test competing theories and principles. You may find that some of the theories that we have discussed here are inadequate to handle complex biomedical issues, although they may seem satisfactory in simpler and more familiar cases. Or you may discover that some commonly accepted moral principles produce contradictory results or conclusions that are difficult to accept. Other theories or principles may appear to give definite and persuasive answers to medical–moral problems, but you may find that they rest on unacceptable premises. Such a dialectical process of claims and criticism is slow and frustrating. Yet it offers the best hope of settling on theories and principles that we can accept with confidence and employ without misgivings.

During the last half century, considerable effort has been devoted to the moral problems of medical practice and research. Without question, bioethics has made genuine progress in analyzing a number of pivotal issues and securing agreement about how they should be handled. Nevertheless, a large number of moral issues in medicine

remain unsettled or even unexplored. In the absence of moral consensus on these issues, we continue to face the urgent demands of everyday medical decision-making.

Under these circumstances, we cannot attempt to resolve all doubts about moral principles and only then apply them to biomedical problems. The dialectical process must be made practical. We must formulate and test theories at the same time as we try to answer urgent moral questions. We must do our best to discover the principles of aerodynamics while staying aloft.

To a considerable extent, that is the continuing ambition of this book. Medical research and practice is an area in which there are still many more legitimate ethical questions than satisfactory answers. But the growth of the bioethics movement has helped ensure that the answers that we do have are better supported and better reasoned than those available a half century ago.